UNDER NORTHERN EYES

Caribbean and Latin American Studies

Jack W. Hopkins, general editor

UNDER NORTHERN EYES:
LATIN AMERICAN STUDIES AND US
HEGEMONY IN THE AMERICAS 1898-1990

Mark T. Berger

with a foreword by Jack W. Hopkins

Indiana University Press
Bloomington and Indianapolis

The paper used in this publication meets the minimum requirements of
American National Standard for Information Sciences--Permanence of
Paper for Printed Library Materials, ANSI Z39.48-1984.

Manufactured in the United States of America

Library of Congress Cataloging-in-Publication Data

Berger, Mark T., 1955-
    Under Northern eyes: Latin American studies and U.S. hegemony in
the Americas, 1898-1990 / Mark T. Berger.
        p.   cm. -- (Caribbean and Latin American studies)
    Includes bibliographical references and index.
    ISBN 0-253-31172-1 (alk. paper)
    1. Latin America--Relations--United States. 2. United States--
Relations--Latin America. 3. United States--Foreign
relations--20th century. 4. Latin America--Study and teaching--
United States. 5. Learning and scholarship--Political Aspects--
United States. 6. Latin America--Historiography. 7. Latin
Americanists--United States--Attitudes. I. Title. II. Series.
F1418.B418 1995
980'.007'073--dc20   94-44645

1 2 3 4 5 00 99 98 97 96 95

To the memory of Perle Berger, who knew both the power of knowledge and the pleasure of a good book

It is only natural that they insist on measuring us with the yardstick that they use for themselves forgetting that the ravages of life are not the same for all, and that the quest of our own identity is just as arduous and bloody for us as it was for them. The interpretation of our reality through patterns not our own serves only to make us ever more unknown, ever less free, ever more solitary.

Gabriel García Márquez

Contents

Contents

Preface

This book was finished in a political and intellectual climate dramatically different from the one that attended its inception in 1987. The end of the Cold War and the waning of the revolutions in Central America not only provide the chronological cut-off point for this work, but the context in which the first draft was written. This study is an attempt to clarify the connection between Latin American studies in North America and US hegemony in Latin America, with a particular focus on the Central American crisis of the 1980s. It is not about Latin America, but about the way in which professional discourses on Latin America have contributed throughout the twentieth century to US efforts to control and manage events in the Americas. It offers no solutions as such to the difficult circumstances in which a majority of Latin Americans find themselves. However, it may shed some light on the resilience of US hegemony and the staying power of the grossly inequitable politico-economic order and social formations in the region. At the same time, over the course of this project, I have become more convinced than ever that the primary dynamics of historical and political change grow out of factors which are specific to a particular area or region, and broader international processes, such as the projection of US power in Latin America, are important, even crucial at certain junctures, but secondary to any overall understanding of the historical trajectories and political transitions of the various social formations in Central and South America and around the world. Although US hegemony and a powerful Latin American studies profession provide part of the broader context in which political and social change in Latin America takes place, and Latin American ideas about history and politcs are articulated, US power and North American knowledge is not capable of determining the course of all intellectual and cultural processes or political challenges, even in Central America. I hope and fully expect that the rural and urban poor of Central America, and the Americas (North and South) will gain the power to pursue their own paths to development and write their own histories.

In the leadup to the publication of this book I had originally planned to include an epilogue "Latin America and Latin American Studies in the 1990s". However, to cover the developments in scholarship on Latin America since 1990 would have required at least one more substantive chapter and made the book unduly long. Such an attempt would have to include the growing significance of the study of the comparative political economy and comparative history of Latin America and East Asia, which emerged in the late 1970s, but has blossomed in the context of the end of the Cold War and the growing recognition that the rise of East Asia represents a turning point in world history with dramatic implications for the Americas.[1] I would have also liked to address the increasingly important debates within anthropology and their impact on the wider study of Latin America.[2] Linked to this is the growing interest in post-structuralism and the various debates about post-colonialism, nationalism, and the politics of identity.[3] There are also important new developments in the study of the labour movement and political change.[4] And a growing literature seeks to put the revolutionary and reformist struggles of the past few decades in perspective.[5] More generally, the theory and practice of progressive politics and the new social movements has become an increasingly important focus.[6] These are just a few trends which I find the most interesting. At the same time, although new and innovative approaches to the study of Latin America continue to emerge, the overall argument about the North American study of Latin America between 1898 and 1990 made in this book still has considerable relevance in the last decade of the twentieth century.

Acknowledgements

This book would never have been completed without the support of my parents Theodore Macdonald Berger and Margery Helen Berger. It would be impossible to fully acknowledge their contribution to my studies and my work. This is also true of my brothers Paul Berger and Bruce Berger, and my sister Heather (Berger) Haberstock. I also owe a long standing debt to my uncle and aunt Thomas Berger and Beverly Berger, and my cousins David Berger and Erin Berger, whose support during my years as an undergraduate and graduate student at the University of British Columbia, went well beyond that expected of members of a modern extended family. My grandmothers, Perle Berger and Ina Dunsmore, have been sources of support and inspiration over the years.

At a time when I was trying to find my feet in a new country Therese Sands and Jean Sands and the rest of their family were supportive and generous. As were numerous other Australian friends. The friendship and influence of many people involved in Latin American solidarity work in Australia has also been appreciated and I thank them all. A number of friends in Sydney helped me along and influenced me more than they might realize. In particular I thank Vanita Seth, Sebastian Job, Peter Colley, Jasper Goss and John Tate.

The research for part of this book was conducted while I was a recipient of a scholarship from the Faculty of Arts at the University of New South Wales. The scholarship and the support of the Dean of the Faculty of Arts, John Milfull, are fully appreciated. The staff of the Library at the University of New South Wales, were always helpful. This book is based on a wide range of secondary sources and in this regard the Inter-Library Loans office was especially generous with its assistance.

This book began as a PhD thesis in the School of History, at the University of New South Wales. The School provided an atmosphere in which history and ideas were the subject of keen debate and I enjoyed the support and intellectual stimulation provided by staff members and my fellow postgraduates inside and outside of the School. Of the latter, Nick Doumanis and Milan Voykovic made my years at UNSW particularly memorable. I also owe an important intellectual debt to Max Harcourt whose prodigious memory and penetrating analysis made every conversation an event. Ian Tyrrell, illuminated many problems to which I addressed myself over the years. Mike Pearson has also stimulated my thinking and supported my work. In a university system that rests on a combination of clientelism (if not feudalism) and economic rationalism, he and Robert Lee (Head of Humanities at the University of Western Sydney) looked out for my teaching-career in an exemplary fashion. Richard Cashman, also of the School of History at the University of New South Wales, generously allowed me to use his computer and his house at a key period in the writing of this manuscript. For that I am very grateful. The ready assistance provided by the School secretaries, Libby Nugent, Jenny Granger and Cynthia Payone was very much appreciated.

What follows was completed while I was working as a history/politics lecturer in the School of Social and Economic Development (SSED) at the University of the South Pacific. A number of my colleagues in SSED made my time there memorable, and stimulated my thinking about the issues raised in this book and other related matters. My many conversations with the late Simione Duratalo and his own efforts to write about social and political change in Fiji in a way which privileged historical specificity over global trends contributed to the development of my ideas. Doug Borer and Sitiveni Ratuva kept me on my toes, while the members of the Department of History/Politics, Vanessa Griffen, Tarcisius Kabutaulaka, Premjeet Singh, Claire Slatter, and Urmilla Prakash, all made the department a congenial place to work. The head of the Department of History/Politics, Doug Munro, was always very supportive of my research. By the time the finishing touches were being made to the final manuscript I had taken up a position in the School of Humanities at Murdoch University in Perth, Western Australia. The lively atmosphere of the School and my various new colleagues have made it all the easier to start a new job and finish the book.

This study has also benefited from the support, encouragement and critical comments of Jim Levy of the School of Spanish and Latin American Studies (University of New South Wales). He also generously gave me the use of his office and library for a number of months while he was overseas. Peter Ross, of the School of Spanish and Latin American Studies also read and commented on virtually all of what follows in an earlier form.

David McCreery (Georgia State University) and Jack Hopkins (Indiana University) also read this work in draft and made very useful comments. Barry Carr (La Trobe University), Morris Morley (Macquarie University) and Jorge Nef (University of Guelph) all read an earlier version from beginning to end and made a multitude of invaluable criticisms.

John Gallman of Indiana University Press also helped this project along, while Jeff Ankrom, of Indiana University Press, did an amazingly thorough job of copy-editing the final mauscript, while the last minute assistance of Penelope Claringbull and Gerard Greenfield made sure that the manuscript emerged as quickly as possible.

Roger Bell (School of History University of New South Wales), provided the constructive criticism and sage advice which ensured that what started as a half-baked idea in 1987 became a PhD thesis and then a book.

My greatest intellectual and personal debt is the one I owe to Catherine Waldby whose influence and support defies measurement.

It is customary, and in this case not an exaggeration, to say that any insights which this work might contain can be traced to the advice, assistance and support of the people I have mentioned, and to many others who have shaped my ideas and work. Any shortcomings are the sole responsibility of the author.

Mark T. Berger, June 1995

Foreword

Mark Berger, in **Under Northern Eyes**, offers us a sweeping examination of North American historiography on Latin America in the context of the emergence of the United States as a regional and global power. In this very ambitious study, he has critically examined virtually the entire academic output on Central America over a hundred-year period. In a remarkable linking of various academic traditions, Professor Berger has also produced a valuable research tool with an encyclopedic bibliography that should serve scholarship well.

With unprecedented scope, Berger relates the historiography on Latin America to the continuities and changes in US foreign policy. He is particularly concerned with elucidating the relationship between US dominance in Central America and the North American study of that region. That relationship is considerably more complex than has been commonly recognized; thus Berger makes it central to his examination.

The major organizing concept of the study is the notion of 'discourse'. This serves as a means to investigate the political and historical circumstances which have shaped the social sciences and the interpretations flowing from them. Such factors, even if they are not determinants of knowledge, at least influence it in powerful ways. Sometimes, as Berger observes, "what is often most significant about a discourse is the 'silences' and the 'histories' that go unnoticed".

The reader should interpret historiography broadly, for this is a work that examines an extraordinarily vast literature. Some of Berger's interpretations and conclusions will be controversial, and these are likely to spark an extended debate among scholars and practitioners.

However, Professor Berger convincingly demonstrates how the dominant North American academic discourse played an important role in the development and maintenance of US hegemony in Central America in particular. He shows how the early writings served to legitimate US policies, sometimes by focusing on Pan Americanism, or emphasizing the harmony of interests between North and South, or even by reference to the 'civilizing mission'. And that same mission lived again in the form of modernization theory during the Kennedy years. In turn, the rise of a conservative academic discourse during the Reagan administration produced a challenge to the dominant liberal discourse, basing its arguments on the superiority of North American civilization, anticommunism, and the need to project US power.

Professor Berger has produced a major work that is likely to occupy an important place in the literature on Latin America and inter-American relations.

Jack W. Hopkins
Professor of Public and Environmental Affairs
Indiana University

UNDER NORTHERN EYES

Introduction

UNDERSTANDING LATIN AMERICA

Since the 1960s a number of writers have sought to deal with the relationship between the North American historical and social science professions and the hegemonic position of the US in the post-1945 international political and economic order.[1] At the same time studies which critically examine the historical origins of North American social science have begun to appear.[2] The rise and transformation of the political science profession has been evaluated.[3] And there are now books which analyze the evolution of the North American historical profession and its output.[4] There have also been some studies which take the historiography of US diplomacy as their object.[5] Over the past two decades a great deal of work has scrutinized the rise of development theory after World War II, and much of it deals, at least indirectly, with the relationship between the study of development and the US-dominated liberal world order.[6] The emergence of area studies has attracted some critical attention.[7] There are a growing number of important works which focus specifically on the history and politics of development theory in relation to Latin America.[8] And a large number of articles look at Latin American studies and the historiography of inter-American relations.[9]

Despite the growing amount of work which situates Latin American theories of development in their wider political and historical context and the proliferation of articles on the study of Latin America there has been no attempt to deal comprehensively and critically with the rise of Latin American studies in the context of the US rise to hemispheric and global predominance.[10] At the same time, most of the studies that seek to deal, even tangentially, with the relationship between US power in, and the generation of North American knowledge about, Latin America remain committed to either a radical (marxist or marxist-derived) or a liberal teleology. Their conceptions of history are linear and, while the dynamics are understood differently, radical and liberal work is written in relation to an ideal historical narrative which reads 'history' as a progression towards democratic industrialism. Radical analyses of the power-knowledge relationship still tend to see US power as unitary and view knowledge as an unproblematic ideological function of the dominant national and international capitalist elites. Meanwhile, many liberal analyses make only a limited effort to conceptualize power relations and, in some cases, continue to imply that knowledge exists outside of its object.

US Power and North American Knowledge

This study seeks to go beyond radical and liberal teleologies by making the relationship between power and knowledge central to the examination of the North American study of Latin America. Building on imperial state theory, recent international relations theory derived from Gramsci, and discourse analysis, it attempts to locate the North American understanding of Latin America within the context of the emergence and transformation of Latin American studies specifically and the historical and social science professions more generally.[11] It also attempts to relate the emergence and growth of Latin American studies to the continuities and changes in US foreign policy in Latin America and the rest of the so-called Third World.[12] The production of North American knowledge about Latin America is examined in the context of the universities, research centers, the various branches of the US government, and the numerous national and international organizations and philanthropic foundations which provide the institutional setting for the dominant professional discourses on Latin America. Despite the view that there is, or ought to be, a distinction between academic activity and the conduct of US foreign policy, the growth of Latin American studies specifically, and area studies and the social sciences more generally, has been intimately connected to US expansion in Latin America and the rest of the world.[13] It will be emphasized here that Latin American studies, as a set of professional discourses and practices which emerged in North America during the first half of the twentieth century, has facilitated the creation and maintenance of the institutions, organizations, inter-state relations, and politico-economic structures that reinforce and underpin the US hegemonic position in the Americas.

The vicissitudes of the professional discourses on Latin America will be examined with a particular concern to elucidate the relationship between US dominance in Central America and the North American study of Central America.[14] This focus is a result of the events of the late 1970s and 1980s: the revolutionary ferment in Central America, particularly Guatemala, El Salvador and Nicaragua, and the reactionary upsurge in the region and in North America which was part of the wider revival of the Cold War.[15] The events of the 1979 to 1990 period highlighted the complexity of the relationship between the conduct of US foreign policy and the work of Latin American specialists. In the 1980s influential sections of the Latin American studies profession adopted an overtly critical position in relation to Reagan's policy of military reconquest in Central America. The 1980s saw an outpouring of literature which directly or indirectly challenged US foreign policy in the region and often offered detailed policy alternatives. While the Central American debate became central to the direction of North American work on Latin America as a whole, Latin American specialists also engaged, to an unprecedented degree, in a wide range of lobbying and activism (there was also a countering effort by conservatives and powerful conservative discourses emerged, or underwent a revival, to reinforce the Reagan agenda). The events of the 1970s and 1980s suggest a complicated relationship between the work of Latin American studies specialists and US foreign policy. And this study flows directly from a desire to gain a theoretical and an historical perspective on the connection between US power in and North American knowledge of Latin America.

Theories of Imperialism and the Rise of Pax Americana

Analytical approaches to power and knowledge which involve the concepts of genealogy and discourse have been far more influential in literary criticism, cultural studies, anthropology and social history than in the disciplines which are the main focus of this study--history and political science.[16] The view taken here is that an attempt to synthesize an historical political economy approach with elements borrowed from critical theory, or post-structuralism, can not only help to clarify the connection between US foreign policy and the social sciences, but can also make a contribution to a major debate which has been a preoccupation of historians (especially diplomatic historians) and political scientists (especially international relations specialists) in North America. This is the debate about how to conceptualize European, US and Japanese economic and politico-military power in the nineteenth and twentieth centuries. This debate flows from the growing number of theories of imperialism and theories of international relations which stretch back at least to Hobson and Lenin's studies of imperialism which appeared in the early years of the twentieth century.[17] By linking a focus on discourse and the power-knowledge relationship to the imperialism debate we can reconceptualize US foreign policy. Such an approach moves beyond the preoccupation with the connection between politico-strategic (diplomatic and bureaucratic) factors and economic or commercial (national and transnational capital) interests and structures.[18]

Until at least the early 1970s most North American historians and political scientists regarded imperialism as the formal acquisition of colonies. For many years the term was used interchangeably with colonialism. However, while most writers continue to define colonialism as the formal establishment of colonies, the term imperialism, following its introduction into marxist theory by Lenin (who was influenced by Hobson's work), has gradually been adopted by marxists and a growing number of liberals to cover both the formal and informal control and exploitation of weaker peoples by powerful industrial nation-states.[19] At the same time, this broadening of the definition of imperialism has continued to raise problems for those North Americans who are unwilling to conceptualize the activity of the US government and US-based transnational companies as imperialism. Instead, they have preferred to talk in terms of spheres of influence and interdependence.[20] From the point of view of many US citizens, formal US imperialism in the early years of the twentieth century was distinct from and more benign than the activities of its European and Japanese counterparts, while the notion of informal imperialism, particularly as it is used by marxists, is regarded as a misleading way to conceptualize indirect US politico-military and economic influence before and after 1945.[21]

In the years between 1898 and the onset of the Cold War, North American politicians from Theodore Roosevelt to Harry Truman, along with journalists and historians, often represented the US as the historical inheritor of the mantle of the classic empire-civilizations, particularly the Roman and British empires. An overwhelmingly positive interpretation of Pax Romana and Pax Britannica, which emphasized empire-civilization rather than imperialism, underpinned the US rise to dominance before 1945 and the liberal internationalism of the Cold War.[22] According to this view, at the beginning of the century the US embarked on a civilizing mission to help modernize a number of 'backward' countries in the circum-Caribbean and Central America, as well as Southeast Asia. The dominant interpretation for many years was that US imperialism was a short-lived experiment which ended in Latin America with the Good Neighbor Policy in 1933, and in the Philippines with independence in 1946.[23] In the years after 1945 the conventional wisdom held that after World War II, the US had rid itself of its remaining formal imperial commitments and certainly did not practice informal imperialism. It was widely believed in North America that with the Second World War the US had taken up its historical mission as a global civilization, and that the subsequent Cold War expansionism brought prosperity, freedom, and security for all in its wake--Pax Americana.

After World War II the North American commitment to a US civilizing mission was strengthened by US economic expansion and by its rise to political and military predominance in international affairs. The US emerged as the most important actor in the post-1945 global political economy. During the first twenty years of the Cold War, most North American historians and political scientists assumed that the US had a global mission and needed to play a leading role in the emerging Third World for reasons that rested on but transcended US national security concerns and economic interests. In this situation, government officials, academics and journalists continued to avoid the term imperialism, and were reluctant to see the US as an imperial power. Although the language of North American diplomacy in the post-1945 era was often anti-imperial, US foreign policy was not. US support for decolonization and independence in Africa, Asia and Oceania was often circumscribed by its support for its European allies and by its own expanding economic and national security interests.[24] Between 1946 and 1954, for example, the US backed the French effort to retain control of Vietnam.[25] At the end of the 1950s, the view that US foreign policy as a whole was imperial found one of its most famous advocates in William Appleman Williams, whose work heralded the rise of New Left diplomatic history.[26] But it was not until the end of the 1960s that Williams's approach gained any purchase.[27] Ironically, in the context of the debate in the late 1980s over perceived US decline, the use of the term imperialism appeared to become more acceptable.[28]

Despite the partial absorption of imperialism into both academic parlance and the popular lexicon, there is still considerable debate about the dynamics and structure of US imperialism. For example, although the North American political scientist Tony Smith embraced the term 'imperialism' in the 1980s, he explicitly sought to distinguish his approach from marxist theories of imperialism. Smith treated political and economic factors as independent variables. In his view, US imperialism, as well as earlier European imperialism, could be seen as "the effective domination by a relatively strong state over a weaker people whom it does not control as it does its home population, or as the effort to secure such domination". He argued that the relationship is imperial in political terms when a "weaker people" is unable to control or determine what it perceives as its "fundamental domestic or foreign concerns for fear of foreign reprisals that it believes itself unable to successfully counter". In socio-economic terms, imperialism "exists" for Smith "when the local division of labor and the corresponding class relations of the weaker people can be demonstrated to have originated or to be sustained by external forces to such a degree that, failing these foreign connections, the local socio-economic structure could not survive".[29] Ultimately, however, Smith assumed that politico-strategic factors could be separated from economic factors. In an article in the mid-1980s he argued that the "essence" of US imperialism in the post-1945 era was "anti-communism", and this was for "reasons" which "would seem to be essentially political".[30] Despite revisions, and the greater acceptance of the term 'imperialism' in North America, as evidenced by Smith's work, the dominant approach to US foreign policy, after World War II particularly, still emphasizes the primacy of political factors.[31] The interpretations of US Cold War expansion offered by many

North American specialists, not to mention the popular versions, continue to rest on a revised, but still exceedingly positive, vision of Pax Americana (this appeared to reach new heights in the Reagan years, although it probably became even more pronounced with the end of the Cold War).[32] And, as will be argued below, with particular reference to US relations with Latin America, the relatively positive interpretation of US global expansion generated by the dominant historical and social science discourses, despite their often critical engagement with US foreign policy, contributes to the overall strength and legitimacy of US hegemony.

In contrast to the approach articulated by most liberal and conservative scholars, this study rests on the assumption that economic factors are both historically and currently central to the formulation and practice of US foreign policy. Of particular relevance to any discussion of economics and US foreign policy in Latin America is the theory of the imperial state which has been developed by Latin American specialists Morris Morley and James Petras. They have challenged the bureaucratic politics model as well as other liberal theories which treat politics as an independent variable in relation to economic expansion and capital accumulation.[33] They have also questioned the usefulness of work which emphasizes transnational capital's independence from the state.[34] Imperial state theory provides a major point of departure in any effort to clarify US relations with Latin America. And, despite its shortcomings, imperial state theory is an important aspect of the conception of US hegemony on which this study relies. The theory of the imperial state focuses on "the interface between permanent (economic) and short-term (non-economic) objectives". Morley and Petras argue that the theory of the imperial state can serve as a core concept to provide a more comprehensive explanation of US imperialism in particular instances and over the longer term. National security considerations, politico-strategic interests, ideological factors and bureaucratic conflict often have a direct impact on US foreign policy in Latin America and around the world. However, they can only be understood in terms of the way in which they mesh with the "underlying long-term economic concerns" (such as trade relations, investment and access to strategic raw materials) of the US imperial state. They also emphasize the way in which the socio-economic order in the Americas is becoming increasingly "internationalized".[35] From this perspective, at the center of confrontations which are framed in national security and ideological terms, such as the Central American crisis of the 1980s, the overall objective of the US imperial state is the maintenance of an inter-American and world systems which support the interests of an increasingly well integrated international capitalist class.

Although their primary focus is the post-1945 period, Petras and Morley extend their analysis back to the 1890s. They argue that since that time the expansion of US capital overseas has always been facilitated by the US imperial state. In his important and detailed study of US-Cuban relations Morley notes that by the end of the nineteenth century the US had begun to supplant the British as the dominant power in the Americas and was emerging as a "globally competitive imperial power". Up to the 1930s the US imperial state attempted to maintain and expand its global economic reach by emphasizing an 'Open Door' policy with regard to North American overseas trade and investment. US economic influence was particularly strong in Latin America in this period. World War II, argued Morley, brought fundamental changes to international capitalism, particularly the decline of a number of Washington's major rivals, such as Britain and France. The Bretton

Woods agreement of 1944 which initiated the establishment of the International Monetary Fund (IMF) to curtail foreign exchange difficulties and the International Bank for Reconstruction and Development (World Bank) to dispense loans aimed at encouraging private foreign investment around the world--was the cornerstone of US international economic predominance after 1945.[36]

While transnational corporations have been key actors in the post-1945 capitalist expansion and accumulation process, the US imperial state has been central to the generation of the global economic, military and political context underpinning international trade and foreign investment. This flowed from widespread consensus in top North American military and civilian circles in the late 1940s. All agreed that the US had a long-range interest in the maintenance and expansion of its access to markets and raw materials, and that the US had a crucial stake in the liberal capitalist reconstruction of as much of Europe and Asia as possible. In this situation, Washington policy-makers concluded that the existing governmental and military structures were insufficient, and existing agencies had their tasks expanded, while a number of new government agencies were created. The US imperial state, as it blossomed after 1945, has been defined by Morley as all those government organizations "charged with promoting and protecting the expansion of capital across state boundaries by the multinational corporate community". Since the 1950s the National Security Council, and sometimes the State Department, have been at the top of a growing "web of interrelated, yet functionally specific agencies", the activities of which are aimed at "world-wide US capital accumulation and reproduction".[37]

By the 1950s, in pursuit of national security objectives in Latin America, Africa, Asia and the Middle East, the US imperial state supported a growing number of anti-communist governments. These governments, many of them dictatorships such as the Somoza dynasty in Nicaragua, could be relied upon to cooperate with the US and provide "active" and "unequivocal support" for US regional and international objectives. At the same time, many of these anti-communist states, such as Cuba, opened their borders wide to foreign investment, and North American manufacturers were provided "full access" to their economies. An important, even key, variable affecting the US president and his executive's attitude towards a particular regime was the role it was willing to allocate to private capital, especially North American capital. The support of Latin American, Asian and then African regimes for US regional and international objectives has generally been "measured against the provision of conditions within their own country for capital accumulation and expansion". The repressive methods of many of these governments have been evaluated by US officials mainly with reference to their effect on the interests of capital. The economic stakes have not always been as direct as they were in the case of Cuba, for example. But, behind confrontations which are framed in strategic terms, such as in Central America in the 1980s, Washington's overall objective has been the maintenance of an international system which supports the accumulation and expansion of capital. The US continues to function as an imperial state by relying on collaborator states which are linked to the US by economic and military treaties and arrangements. These collaborative linkages are maintained by the continued benefits from the relationship which flow to the local elites. The strength of the US imperial state in a country can be measured by the degree to which it has become enmeshed in the social structure of the client state, established "durable linkages" with crucial institutional and governmental elements, as well as its ability to do what Morley has described as "sustain" the "collaborating classes".[38]

The long term importance of economic factors and their fundamental linkage to politico-strategic factors, as articulated by imperial state theory, is central to any understanding of US foreign policy. While this study builds on imperial state theory to conceptualize the US position in the international political and economic order, the term 'hegemony' will be used to characterize US foreign policy in Latin America and many parts of Africa, the Middle East, Asia and Oceania. The concept of hegemony has gained considerable currency in international relations theory in recent years. As a general term, implying an international position of leadership and dominance, which rests on a mixture of consent and coercion it is now widely used. It has also been given a more specific and detailed meaning by international relations theorists using the work of Antonio Gramsci.[39] This latter approach to hegemony will be used in this study, along with imperial state theory, to represent US dominance in Latin America and around the world.

An emphasis on the imperial state, the linkages between politico-strategic and economic factors and the internationalization (or globalization) of class structure in the Americas can be meshed with the conception of US hegemony in international affairs, first articulated by Robert Cox, and later taken up by Stephen Gill. Cox and Gill emphasize that US hegemony does not simply flow from Washington's ability to manage global politics and the world economy, but is based on a notion of an international "civil society", which is articulated by the hegemonic power in the context of an international economic order based on linkages between social classes across national boundaries. In his 1990 study of US hegemony and the Trilateral Commission, Gill argued that "hegemony would be fully achieved when the major institutions and forms of organizations--economic, social and political--as well as the key values of the dominant state become models for emulation in other subordinate states". Gill emphasized that the hegemony of bourgeois liberalism in the West rests on a generally "consensual order" and the political process and political conflict remains more or less rooted in the "acceptance of the agenda and key ideas of the bourgeoisie". This entails a functioning parliamentary democratic system and the minimal reliance on "illegitimate force". According to this model "the patterns of emulation are most likely in the core or most developed states, rather than in the less-developed periphery". International hegemony can be defined as a political economic and social system, which is articulated in "universal norms, institutions and mechanisms" and establishes "general rules for the behaviour of states, and for those forces of civil society that act across national boundaries--rules which support the dominant mode of production".[40]

Cox and Gill's conceptualization of the US as a hegemonic power in the international system is compatible with the idea, as articulated by imperial state theorists, that capital expansion and capital accumulation remain the core interests of the US imperial state. Their approaches also point to the importance of an array of agencies, organizations and strategies which have emerged to protect those interests. The idea of the imperial state, and the view of US hegemony offered by Cox and Gill, provide important theoretical positions from which to discuss US predominance in Latin America and elsewhere. In particular they point to the importance of long-term US goals which transcend individuals, particular types of regimes, and specific foreign policy crises. And they also highlight the inter-connectedness of politics and economics in the inter-American and international system and the internationalization of class structure in the western hemisphere. Following this approach, the US can be seen as having emerged as the hegemonic power in Central America and the Caribbean by the 1920s.[41] Washington moved subsequently to expand and consolidate its hegemony in Latin America and Asia, and emerged after 1945 as the hegemonic power at the center of the international capitalist system. The US entered a crisis of hegemony at the end of the 1960s, which resulted in the gradual and uneven restructuring of US hegemony during the 1970s and 1980s. The main objective of hegemonic restructuring was to ensure that the US imperial state retained a position of relative dominance. The changes were also made to facilitate the continued existence of economic and political structures complementary to transnational capitalism. By the 1970s the US had declined economically relative to the rising economic power of Japan and Germany, in particular, but also in relation to the economic and political assertiveness of states in Asia, the Middle East and Latin America. However, the US continues as the militarily and 'ideologically' hegemonic power, and the major economic power, in an international system in which the other major international and regional powers continue to rely on US military protection. And, at least in the short term, the end of the Cold War has further enhanced US hegemony.

Latin American Studies and the Pursuit of Truth

At the same time, this conception of US hegemony flows from marxist discourses which, despite their strengths, are still structured by assumptions about objectivity and emphasize the centrality of historical materialism in understanding their objects of study. Most radical work remains premised on a radical teleology, continues to conceptualize power in centralized terms, seeing it as embedded in class relations and state structures. In particular, the marxist approaches to the relationship between power and knowledge continue to link historians and political scientists in ideological terms to a particular politico-economic class or interest.[42] To complement an approach to US hegemony based on the interplay of politico-military power and long-term economic interests and the expansion of an international civil society rooted in political and economic liberalism, a notion of discourse, which draws on the work of Michel Foucault and Edward Said, is used as a major organizing concept.[43] The use of discourse can be seen as part of an effort to interrogate the political and historical circumstances which have shaped the social sciences as a whole. Foucault's work is a direct challenge to the 'truth effects' of the social sciences, and his historical methodology--which he has characterized as genealogy--attempts to subvert the teleology of liberal and marxist historical methodology. This book will point to the way in which, despite revisions, liberal historiography and social science has linked past events to the fulfilment of the western idea of progress and the rise of the liberal democratic nation-state. It will also emphasize how marxist historiography, although it has become increasingly sophisticated, has continued to rely on the unfolding of class struggle and the eventual attainment of socialism as an organizing metaphor. The representations of history as liberal or radical (marxist) teleology can be seen as attempts to systematize the past and enlist it in the defense of the established or the anticipated order. A genealogical approach attempts to disrupt the appearance of steady development. It is not concerned to uncover the truth of a real past event, but rather to demonstrate that all history and social science is interpretation. History and social science discourses have been constituted around the pursuit of truth. However, the interpretations they generate are located in a context of power relations, which precludes arrival at the truth outside of the language, categories and assumptions of their discourses.

The concept of discourse facilitates the questioning of the view that history and the social sciences generally and Latin American studies more specifically are driven by the objective pursuit of truth. The use of discourse points to the historical and political determinants of knowledge. This approach problematizes the central ideas on which historical and social science disciplines rest and calls for a reconceptualization of their main objects of study. In this situation, the assumptions which have moulded the historical and social science disciplines and discourses and their objects of study, such as 'Latin America', are no longer regarded as truths beyond scrutiny, or as objects of study which exist outside of the various disciplines. The Latin American studies discourses and their objects become effects of the very emergence and expansion of US power. Those ideas most central to any discourse usually remain unexamined. What is often most significant about a discourse is the silences and the histories that go unmentioned.

Social science discourses and disciplines are also shaped more specifically by the institutional context from which they emerge. The emergence of professional historical and social science discourses can be located in the context of the 'search for order' in late nineteenth century North America, which spawned a culture of professionalism in North American universities. This culture of professionalism was linked to the constitution of a particular discipline as relatively autonomous via the postulation of the "incommensurability" of its knowledge with other forms of knowledge. In effect, an emergent discipline "established" its exclusive claim to "a specific bit of the universe". The object of the knowledge was considered to delimit the field of the discipline itself. This professionalization process was related to the institutionalization of particular disciplines, such as diplomatic history, international relations and political science, insofar as professional competence was defined as self-contained and isolated from other disciplines.[44] For example, diplomatic history was constituted as an object of study and became a relatively discrete discipline in the wake of World War I, by which time the US position as a overseas power had reached a stature that made the continuation and expansion of US diplomacy an imperative. This was followed by the gradual emergence of 'Latin American studies' as a increasingly discrete specialization located in particular professional disciplines, as US hegemony in Latin America was consolidated. The activity of professional diplomatic historians or that of specialists in Latin American history, rested upon their object. And this object was defined for him or her by institutionalized disciplinary boundaries and by US diplomacy and US hegemony in Latin America.

The professional historical and social science discourses, more generally, are made up of a whole range of discursive practices across a number of disciplines which can be found in a variety of institutional settings. From this perspective 'Latin America' is the product of particular discourses and not an independent pre-given object about which specialists make discoveries. Furthermore it must be emphasized that all knowledge about a specific object has particular effects on the object it sets out to know and understand. The discourses are central to bringing their object into being. Also, like any other specialized discipline, or set of disciplines, the rationality and plausibility of 'Latin American studies' is crucially dependent on assumptions located outside the discipline in parallel disciplines and in broader, shared social, political and cultural assumptions. What this book seeks to explore is how and why the objects of the historical and social science discourses generally, and professional Latin American studies discourses more specifically, have been constructed and how specific constructions are linked to foreign policy practices and the management of US hegemony.

'Discourse', in the context of Foucault and Said's work then, is not just a synonym for 'language'. It takes on a much more particular meaning in relation to the languages of professional expertise, especially the languages of the social sciences. Discourses, in practice, demarcate what can be said, at the same time as they provide the metaphors, analogies, concepts, and models with which practitioners can make new assertions. Individual discourses, or sets of discourses, are not examined to determine if they are true. They are examined in order to elucidate how they produce, and rely on, truth effects, make claims to epistemological validity, and construct meanings and extend and consolidate their legitimacy and the legitimacy of institutional structures to which the discourses are linked. As already mentioned the concept of discourse is different from the radical conception of ideology in a number of ways. Ideology, as it is often used by marxists and radicals, flows from a historical materialist approach and refers to the distortion of knowledge to advance the interests of a national or international ruling class, or a segment of that ruling class which monopolizes state, and imperial state, power.[45] The concept of discourse does not propose an exterior real, or the possibility of a form of knowledge that is outside of power relations. While ideology is usually used by radicals in a way which implies that ideology is operating to deflect attention from a true political or socio-economic situation, such as the oppression and exploitation of the people of Latin America by the region's political and socio-economic elites and their international allies, discourse analysis emphasizes that discourses work to create reality insofar as they the constitute their objects as they talk about them.

From this perspective, Latin American studies in North America, as an array of professional disciplines, is seen as neither progressing towards scientific truth nor as conspiring with political and socio-economic power structures to exploit the majority of the population of Latin America. History and the social sciences generally, and Latin American studies more specifically, cannot be understood at the level of intention. At the same time history and the social sciences are discourses and practices which actively work to construct the institutions and apparatuses that taken together help constitute, manage and contain the object of study, such as 'Latin America'. Following this it can be argued that the North American historical and social science professions facilitate the creation and maintenance of the national and international organizations, institutions, inter-state relations and politico-economic structures that sustain and extend US hegemony in Latin America and around the world. Furthermore history and social science disciplines derive their power and authority from their linkages to these organizations, institutions and political structures.

The dominant North American historical and social science discourses facilitate the construction of the norms that are translated into ideal policy and behaviour goals on the part of individual and national actors in the international politico-economic arena. Latin American studies discourses fulfil a normative function in the case of relations inside and between nations operating in the inter-American system over which the US exercises hegemony. At the same time, there is a gap between Latin American studies and the management of US hegemony. There is both relative independence and interdependence with regard to their particular objects and interests. Furthermore, while power is located in the Latin American studies discourses, it is not monolithic. Power is always exercised in relation to a resistance, although there is always an imbalance between the forces of domination and resistance. Neither power nor resistance should be essentialized, and power is not simply the possession of one group or class over another, nor is it inherent in the state or some other national or international apparatus. Power also lies in those assumptions which are legitimated by the language, categories and rhetoric of the discourses, and in the images which the discourses generate. Whenever North American radicals and Latin American revolutionaries have challenged US hegemony they have had to erect "reverse" discourses which adopt the language and categories of the discourses they seeks to unseat. The radicals and revolutionaries have to challenge the dominant discourses on their opponents' terms.[46]

Ultimately, the relationship between power and knowledge, as mapped out by writers working with the concept of discourse, provides a conceptual framework that illuminates the profound linkages between the North American historical and social science discourses and the hegemonic position and aspirations of the US imperial state. At the same time, it should be emphasized that the linkages between the social sciences and US hegemony are not being represented here as causal but as complementary and interconnected. This approach emphasizes a more diffuse conception of power, allowing historians and social scientists to be seen as neither subordinate to Washington nor independent from Washington (this often includes radicals). They are positioned in a broad and complex web of institutions, organizations and structures linked together by a set of discourses, which, even when they are oppositional, can still have a complementary relationship to the maintenance of US hegemony.

Throughout this study, an effort is made to deal with the dominant discourses on Latin America in relation to the linkages between Latin American studies and US foreign policy. However, there will be a somewhat more detailed focus on a number of individual North American academics who are generally regarded as the major figures in their field in a particular era, or can be held up as representative of the professional discourses in some way. This could lead to the charge that there is too much focus on the "great men of historiography".[47] But what will be emphasized about certain academics and their work is not their singularity, or their greatness, but the way in which they reflect particular discourses. Nor will this study focus on the writers in a biographical fashion. Ultimately, this study is historiographical, in the broadest sense of the term, and it is concerned to locate the North American work on Latin America generally, and on Central America more specifically, within the wider continuities and changes which characterize both the dominant professional historical and social science discourses, and US imperial state policy. The focus is on authors only insofar as this helps to locate their texts.[48]

It is assumed that work produced by an historian or a social scientist has a significance outside the author's intentions and that ascertaining the author's motives is not particularly relevant to the wider role of the text. Efforts which focus on identifying an author's intentions have often been a way of challenging a given reading of a text. This allows an author, or a commentator, to adopt a position which denies the validity of an interpretation with which they do not agree, and privileges an interpretation which claims to know what the author really intended. Any reading, or interpretation, of an author's work can be challenged by arguing that the reader has not understood the author's real motives, thus avoiding the question of the text's wider significance, which has less to do with the author's intentions and more to do with the political and social context and power relations within which it was written and received. Texts which deal with history, political science and development can be best understood in terms of the historical continuities and transformations occurring in the period in which they were written, and it is presumed that the reason an author writes a particular text flows not from the intrinsic qualities of the author but from the discourses in which the author is located. The historiography can be regarded as a reflection and a product of the discourses from which it emerges.

Although the assumptions which have guided the dominant North American historical and social science discourses have been challenged over the years, it will be argued here that the dominant discourses are liberal. Since the end of the eighteenth century liberalism, has been an overarching element of political, economic and intellectual life in North America. And since the turn of the century, at a time when history and the social sciences as a series of professional disciplines were beginning to emerge, liberalism has evolved as a dominant force in international political and economic discourses reinforcing and informing US hegemony world-wide. The pervasive commitment to individualism, gradual political and social change, representative government, free trade, and the sanctity of private property as universal values has had, and continues to have, a profound impact on the thinking of the vast majority of North American historians and social scientists. As Louis Hartz has argued, North American liberalism's particular character was a result of the timing of its departure as a Lockean liberal fragment from the class and national conflict of Europe.[49] Liberalism's remarkable influence in North America flowed from the way the liberal fragment was cut off from the European dialectic and the feudal and other political forces with which it had been in conflict. In North America liberal ideas about individual freedom and about political, social and economic arrangements were made 'universal' to a degree which had not been possible in Europe. This resulted in the emergence of an overwhelmingly dominant, but feral, liberalism which undermined and rejected the political, economic, social and intellectual significance of conflict in North America. This is apparent in the structure of North American universities (not to mention national political institutions) which "delegitimize conflict, in the name of pluralism". As a result critical theories that flow out of an understanding of power and/or knowledge based on conflict, and emphasize power relations, are "disarmed" by the academy. Although "scholarship and research may investigate conflict" they cannot "as such partake of it". The institution stands as the arbiter of controversy, "but never its object".[50]

The disarming character of the universities and the academic profession was readily apparent during the 1960s when dependency theory rose to a position of prominence within and beyond the Latin American studies profession. By the 1970s, liberal approaches on the one hand and radical dependency perspectives on the other were often represented as equal competitors in the debate over how to characterize North-South relations in the Americas.[51] For example, Steven W. Hughes and Kenneth J. Mijenski argued in 1980 that despite the numerous "approaches" being used to study inter-American relations, the entire field continued to be "dominated" by liberal development theory and dependency theory. At the same time, they anticipated the emergence of a new paradigm which synthesized the liberal and radical positions.[52] In the mid-1980s Thomas Bossert suggested that a major trend in social science theory generally, and Latin American studies more specifically, was "the tendency toward convergence between Marxist and non-Marxist approaches".[53] Writing in 1990 Alvin Y. So also argued that a process of "convergence" was underway.[54] In a recent issue of the **Journal of American History** which included articles on dependency theory, world-system theory, bureaucratic politics and national security, Thomas G. Paterson spoke of "sometimes competing" and "sometimes complementary" ways of "understanding" US foreign relations.[55] These articles were subsequently incorporated into a book which clearly rests on the assumption that the various approaches are equal theoretical competitors.[56] The widespread view, reflected in these and other works, that radical dependency approaches to inter-American relations (and international relations and social science as a whole) compete on equal terms with liberal approaches reflects the continuing predominance of liberal discourses and structures within and beyond the Latin American studies profession.

As Hartz has argued, the United States of America developed as a "kind of national embodiment of the concept of the bourgeoisie" at the same time as the concept itself was "rarely used" in North American political and historical thought.[57] And the view that political, social and economic conflict within the nation was illegitimate has been extended to, and continues to shape, the North American understanding of Latin America, Africa, the Middle East, Asia and Oceania. This has happened despite the power of Anglo-Saxonism and social darwinism in the late nineteenth and early twentieth century. Nor is the centrality of liberalism to the dominant political, economic and academic discourses necessarily at odds with the continued presence of doctrines premised on racial conflict and assumptions about racial and cultural inferiority (not to mention evidence of considerable political and social conflict within the US historically and currently). What is striking is that despite the racism and the social, class and ethnic conflict, it has long been a dominant assumption in North America that there is, or can be, relative political and social harmony. It is assumed that within the borders of the nation all citizens have an equal opportunity to improve their material and personal circumstances. Liberal notions about equality and relative harmony have been extended to the international arena and US policy-makers often approach foreign affairs from the point of view that there need not be significant conflict between the interests and ideals of US foreign policy. It has also been assumed that there does not have to be a major conflict between US interests and the interests and aspirations of the governments and people in Latin America and in what became known as the Third World. Central to this, and part of the dominant historical and social science discourses by the 1920s, were the embryonic liberal assumptions about political and economic development which were secularized and codified as modernization theory after World War II.[58]

North American academic interest in, and the very idea of, the Third World expanded dramatically after 1945. The imperatives of the Cold War meshed with a long-standing missionary paternalism which continued to perceive the people of Latin America, Asia, Africa and Oceania as being in need of guidance, education and reform. After World War II the North American history and social science profession took developing nations in the Third World as one of its central objects and located them on a line which assumed their need, their desire and their ability, within the existing liberal international political and economic order, to advance towards western political democracy and capitalist industrial development. Although the dominant liberal discourses have undergone many changes since World War II, they continue to be shaped by a modified version of modernization theory and a set of liberal assumptions that flow from a conception of history as a linear progression from a condition of political and economic underdevelopment and tradition to a state of liberal democratic industrialism and modernity. An idealized vision of the rise of industrial democracy and the consolidation of the nation-state in Western Europe and North America is the normative model against which the North American (and Western European) historical and social science profession has written the history of Latin America and the rest of the world. The dominant academic discourses confirm this truth at the same time as they are crucially dependent on it for their very intelligibility.

North American analysis of development and underdevelopment in Latin America and the Third World flows out of the unequal power relations between North and South, and explanations for underdevelopment continue to justify rather than explain. As Arturo Escobar has argued, "to represent the Third World as 'underdeveloped' is less a statement about 'facts' than the setting up of a regime of truth through which the Third World is inevitably known, intervened on, and managed".[59] An examination of the North American study of Latin America will show how the region and its history has been created and understood primarily in terms of the failure of the southern republics to become idealized versions of the western industrial democracies. While recognizing that the political balance of power and socio-economic configuration within particular nations in Latin America is central to any understanding of both how development and history are deployed and why the majority of the population continues to live in poverty, it will be argued that the North American understanding of Latin America serves to reinforce existing inter-American power relations and contributes to the North American management of Latin America.

The Creation of Latin America and Pan Americanism

Although some of the core assumptions which shape the professional historical and social science discourses relate to Africa, Asia, the Middle East and Oceania as well as Latin America, there are certain assumptions which are specific to the North American understanding of Latin America. These flow from the proximity of Latin America to the US, and relate to the long-standing tension between the idea of the Americas (North and South) as a historical unity and the ongoing representation of Latin America as an undifferentiated other in relation to North America.[60] North and South America have been represented as having a shared history, a shared heritage, and a shared commitment to democratic values. This has been linked to a tendency on the part of North American historians and social scientists and US policy-makers to project North American ideas about a common past and a common future on the region as a whole. At the broadest level there has been an equally powerful tendency to homogenize Latin America and objectify it as essentially different from, and in negative opposition to, North America. The US was represented as progressive, virtuous, democratic and developed. Latin America was represented as corrupt, immoral, undemocratic and underdeveloped. As we will see, the idealization of Latin America and the negative representation of Latin America have both served to bolster US hegemony in the region.

The origin of the term 'Latin America' highlights the important relationship between knowledge and power and points to the tendency in North America to perceive the region in a unitary way. The term 'Latin America' first appeared in France in the mid-nineteenth century as part of an effort by Napoleon III to underline the Latin heritage which the former Spanish colonies in the New World shared with France, and thus to legitimate French imperialism in the hemisphere. Although the Portuguese and the Spaniards did not use the term 'Latin America', European conquerors and colonists still thought of the area in a unitary fashion. The Americas (North and South) were 'discovered' as part of the quest for a more direct route to Asia. To the first Europeans it was a strange and alien New World. From the outset the New World and its history were invented. In the early years South America in particular was represented as a continent in which long-standing European legends about Amazon women, lost kingdoms, cities of gold and paradise on earth might be realized. This mythologization of Latin America as an exotic land of fantasy has continued in literature and film, and can be found in the current exotic images used to attract North American tourists or to sell coffee. The counterpart of this image of Latin America as an exotic other is the negative representation of Latin America as an unchanging and stagnant land, inhabited by uncivilized natives and ruled by barbaric despots. The tendency of US foreign policy to treat the region as a whole has also been important in the continued representation of Latin America as unitary and homogeneous. For example, the US promulgation of the Monroe Doctrine in 1823, Washington's encouragement of the formation of the Organization of American States over a century later, the Alliance for Progress in the 1960s, and President Bush's 'Enterprise for the Americas Initiative' in 1990, have all generated the image of a relatively homogeneous Latin America in need of protection, guidance and leadership from the US. The machinations of the European imperial powers, and the long-standing hegemonic aspirations of North America, help to explain why Latin America has come to be regarded as a homogeneous political, economic, social and cultural unit.[61]

Many of the concepts used to organize the academic study of the region have also facilitated reductionism and a process of unitary analysis. In recent years the development and independence of the US have been juxtaposed to the underdevelopment and dependence of Latin America. In an earlier era, North Americans conceived of the history of North America as dynamic and progressive, and this was contrasted with a history of Latin America based on the Black Legend.[62] The Black Legend ultimately postulated an essential Latin America whose problems stemmed from a basic imported, cultural flaw. Throughout the nineteenth century and beyond, North Americans perceived themselves as culturally and racially superior to Latin Americans, and there was understood to be little historical connection between North and South. According to this view, since its very foundation, the US had been a society of industrious and mainly Protestant settlers which evolved into a prospering democracy, while Latin American history took a very different path. Beginning with blood-thirsty and gold-hungry conquistadores, the history of Latin America was represented as three centuries of corrupt rule by decadent Iberian imperialism and the Roman Catholic church, which in turn spawned a multitude of stagnant and despotic personal dictatorships.[63]

From the time of Latin American independence in the 1820s to the early decades of the twentieth century this negative interpretation predominated.[64] However, with the First International Conference of American States in 1890, the establishment of the International Bureau of the American Republics and the appearance of Pan Americanism, a more positive image of an America (North and South), with a common history and a common destiny, very gradually began to emerge in North America in the twentieth century.[65] Since World War I some version of Pan Americanism has increasingly challenged, but certainly not displaced, more traditional representations of Latin America as a negative other. For example, the religious divide, which influenced earlier North American attitudes, has continued to be a factor in North American perceptions of Latin America. Hispanic America, since the days of Columbus, has been part of the Roman Catholic tradition, while Protestantism has been the dominant religious tradition in English North America since its foundation. This has helped to shape the attitude of generations of North American historians and political scientists who wrote and write about the region. North Americans have often looked across this religious gulf and explained the perceived shortcomings of the region in terms of the Catholic tradition, and explained their perceived superiority in terms of their Protestantism.[66]

Since the emergence of the professional study of Latin America, assumptions about Pan Americanism--and its variations: the Western Hemisphere idea, common history and common destiny and the special relationship--have helped to fashion the professional discourses on Latin America. Pan Americanism is as important as liberal developmentalism in locating North American efforts to understand Latin America. And it is clear that Pan Americanism had become central to the dominant professional discourses on Latin America by the early 1940s. After 1945, Pan Americanism meshed with modernization theory. Indeed, Pan Americanism and a revised version of modernization theory continue to structure the dominant professional discourses on Latin America. Pan Americanism has been and remains an important rhetorical device to be used by US policy-makers to justify whatever policy they happen to be pursuing at the time; however, the power of political rhetoric should not be underestimated. And of particular significance to the whole issue of Pan Americanism is the way in which Pan American ideals and aspirations have been conflated with the ideals and aspirations of the US imperial state.

The presumption that US interests are Pan American interests is symbolized by the way in which 'America' has become synonymous with 'the US'.

The influential Uruguayan novelist and historian Eduardo Galeano noted in the 1970s that Latin Americans "have even lost the right to call ourselves Americans, although the Haitians and the Cubans appeared in history as new people a century before the **Mayflower** pilgrims settled on the Plymouth coast. For the world today, America is just the United States; the region we inhabit is a sub-America, a second-class America of nebulous identity".[67] Over the years the conflation of the US with America has been perpetuated and defended by North Americans. In 1943 Samuel Flagg Bemis insisted that the "historical evolution of the proper adjective American has made it, without arrogation, synonymous, at least in the English-speaking world, with the less euphonious adjective United States". He saw no reason not to use the word "American" to refer to citizens of the US and on occasion in its "hemispheric sense".[68] In the early 1970s the quasi-New Left historian Robert Seidel attempted to protect himself from criticism for using 'America' to refer to the US by insisting that "it should be clearly understood that the author uses 'America' solely as an easy and conventionally used shorthand reference for the United States, but that he explicitly denies the right of North Americans to appropriate the term in the way that has antagonized Americans of all nations of the Western hemisphere".[69] More recently the North American journalist Jonathan Kwitny has also defended the use of 'America' to mean 'the US'. In his book, **Endless Enemies: The United States and the Making of An Unfriendly World**, he stated that he had wanted to "respect the sensitivity of many Latin Americans" regarding the use of the term 'American' and when he initially began writing his book he sought to use 'US' instead of 'America' or 'American'; however, he found that there were numerous instances when "only American" would suffice, and other situations where the use of the term "American" generated "added feeling or variety", and "if Latin Americans want to object they will need to come up with a graceful alternative". After noting that Fidel Castro used the term 'North American' (*norteamericano*), Kwitny dismissed it as an alternative because it was "hardly fair to Canada, Mexico and smaller countries".[70] However, Kwitny's opposition to the use of 'North America' and 'North American' appears to have as much to do with a desire not to adopt a term that would put him in agreement with Fidel Castro as it does with a concern for the "sensitivity" of Canadians and Mexicans. The use of the term *norteamericano* to refer to citizens of the US is not confined to Castro or Cuba, and it enjoys wide currency in Latin America, including Mexico.[71]

The approach to the issue of 'America' by North American historian Lester D. Langley is particularly significant for the way it highlights what is currently at stake. He has argued that Latin Americans do not resent the appropriation of the word 'America', but what they resent is the "differing images" which "America" and the "United States" represent: "America 'says one thing' but the United States 'does another'". He differentiated between the US, which is a "political entity", and "America" which is a "place". According to Langley the US "is **in** the Americas, but America is **of** the Americas". For Langley, 'America', is an idea and an 'American', whom he still defines as a citizen of the US, is someone "who believes that the promise of America can be fulfilled in the United States": that is the US can one day achieve the ideals which have come to be associated with the word 'America'.[72] Langley's commitment to the realization of "the promise of America" and his effort to distinguish between America as an idea and the US as a political entity serves to reinforce the way in which the US has manipulated 'America' and infused it with a meaning which, because of the United States's privileged position in the region, allows it to define 'America' and equate the values and aspirations of the US with the Americas. The historical appropriation of the words 'America' and 'American' by the US symbolizes and reinforces the way in which the US has presumed to speak for and lay claim to common values with the rest of the hemisphere. Of course, while the assumptions about a common history, common values, a special relationship, or a shared heritage (or at least common bonds because all Americans inhabit the Americas) are central to North American discourses on Latin America, the character of the common bonds and the shared heritage are interpreted by the hegemonic power--the United States of America. The fiction of hemispheric solidarity is shored up by constant and powerful rhetoric about partnership against external, un-American threats and about shared goals of freedom and democracy. Continued US dominance is bolstered by Pan Americanism and a vision of a unitary America. As a conscious attempt to rectify the appropriation of America, this study will use the term 'North America'.[73]

   At the same time, in a strict cartographical sense, Mexico is in North America; however, its economic relationship to the US puts it in a subordinate position. Except for its elite, Mexico is not part of the privileged community centered on North America, which includes much of Canada as well as the US, and in cultural and political terms, despite the profound US influence, Mexico is clearly part of Hispanic or Latin America. The use of 'North America' also raises questions about the relationship between Canada and the US generally and between Latin American studies in the two countries more specifically. It nonetheless can be argued that Canada (with the possible exception of Quebec) is culturally integrated with the US in many ways, and its economy is even more enmeshed in the US economy than Mexico's or any of the economies of Central America. Of course the terms of such integration are far more favorable for Canadians than for most Mexicans or Central Americans. Politically Canada also has strong ties to Washington, but in its approach to Latin America and other regions, the Canadian government has often declined to follow Washington's lead. Canada's tepid support for the war in Vietnam (at the same time as it gave shelter to large numbers of draft dodgers and provided employment for not a few radical US academics during the war) and its continuing refusal to respect US attempts to isolate Cuba reflect a relative independence with regard to both policy towards and the study of Latin America, as well as the so-called Third World more generally. As Jorge Nef has argued, despite the way Latin American studies (and area studies) in Canada in its "embryonic phase" tended to emulate the US liberal developmental approach, by the 1970s Canadian Latin American studies was following a trajectory which was relatively distinct from US-based Latin American studies despite the strong links between their respective university systems and their geographical proximity. The dominant Latin American studies discourses in Canada by the early 1980s were distinct from their US counterparts as a result of the historic importance of, and greater sympathy with, economic nationalism in Canadian academic and public life, the critical perspective of the small but significant number of academic refugees from the US who arrived during the Vietnam era, and the effect of a significant number of Latin American academics who entered Canada as political refugees. Although many radical Latin American academics also went to the US, the size of Latin American studies in the US curtailed their influence at the same time as it appears that conservative Latin

American academics gravitated towards the US while radicals opted for Canada.[74] Given these qualifications, 'North America' is understood here as a political, socio-economic and cultural term that refers primarily to the US (although it encompasses Canada to a greater or lesser degree) and is the counterpoint to 'Latin America'. While it may not be possible to see Latin American studies in Canada as completely integrated with Latin American studies in the US, there is a significant, and possibly increasing, amount of incorporation, as there is throughout the Americas.[75]

Latin American Studies and the Americas

Latin America became an object of US foreign policy in the nineteenth century, and during the first two decades of the twentieth century the US gradually assumed a dominant position in the Caribbean and Central America. Since that time, US policy-makers in Washington who dealt with Latin America have continued to see the US as a beacon of democracy and progress. They have continued to universalize the liberal values of the nation-state they represent. From 1898 to 1990 the makers of US foreign policy approached US relations with Latin America in a fashion which assumed the US had an almost divine right to expand and maintain its position of dominance. Although US policy-makers usually formulated decisions based on pragmatic considerations, policy was conceived and carried out in the context of the social and political background and assumptions that policy-makers shared with the country's national and international capitalist elite.[76] US imperial state policy related to Latin America has also continued to be articulated against the background of a commitment to a liberal teleology which understands 'history' as the rise of nations to liberal democracy and industrial capitalism. US policy-makers remain committed to the belief that North American political and economic development is the standard against which the history of the rest of the world must be measured. Combined with this is the current and historical view that US interests are not, or need not be, in significant conflict with Latin American interests. At the same time, Washington's policy prescriptions and practice have been reinforced by the majority of Latin American specialists in North America who have written about Latin America in a fashion which, despite a sometimes critical angle, complements US hegemony.

The professional study of Latin America is embedded in a long tradition of viewing Latin America through North American eyes. And it will be argued here that because of this tradition, which has rested on powerful liberal ideas and been cloaked in assertions of 'objectivity' and a commitment to scientific and rational discourses, most Latin American studies specialists are, like US policy-makers, estranged from Latin America. At the heart of the estrangement lies the profound linkage between knowledge and power. For example, the instability and turmoil in much of Central America currently and historically flows from a number of internal and external factors; however, it can also be attributed in part to the direct and indirect intervention of Washington over the years, and to the impact of North American and transnational capitalism on the region.[77] Furthermore the recurring crises can be linked to the type of knowledge produced by the dominant professional discourses, which seeks to 'understand' and objectify Central America and the Americas as a whole in a fashion which continues to complement US hegemony and a liberal international order. The profound linkage between the professional discourses on Latin America and US hegemony was laid down at the beginning, and the existence of Latin American studies flows directly from US expansion into Latin America. Latin American studies has remained within rather than outside the power relations in which it originated. Without postulating a deterministic relationship between Latin American studies specialists and US imperial state policy, the dominant professional discourses on Latin America can be seen to have played an important role in the expansion and maintenance of US hegemony in Latin America.

The crucial connection between Latin American studies, US hegemony in Latin America and the liberalism of the dominant professional discourses on Latin America will be elucidated by examining the history of Latin American studies and the North American understanding of Latin America over the past century, with a particular focus on Central America. Chapter 1 looks at the emergence of professional discourses on Latin America and their close relationship to US hegemony up to World War II. The expansion of Latin American studies after 1945 and its complementary connection to US foreign policy prior to 1968 is the subject of Chapter 2. In the period 1968 to 1979, covered in Chapter 3, the dominant professional discourses on Latin America gradually achieved a position of relative independence, although certainly not autonomy, in relation to US foreign policy. This change was a result of the unprecedented size of Latin American studies by the late 1960s and coincided with the US crisis of hegemony and the undermining of the Cold War consensus which had guided US foreign policy since the late 1940s. By the 1970s liberal discourses had appeared that were shaped by a greater awareness of their relationship to US foreign policy in Latin America. Chapter 4 charts the resurgence and brief ascendancy of conservative discourses which challenged the dominant liberal discourses. This chapter focuses on the centrality of the Central American crisis to both US foreign policy and to Latin American studies after 1979 and on how the conservative discourses which supported the Cold War revivalism of the Reagan administration were partially absorbed back into the dominant liberal discourses by the mid-1980s. The final chapter will focus on the resurgence of the dominant liberal discourses on Latin America and their important relationship to the shift of US foreign policy away from Cold War conservatism towards a liberal managerial approach which nevertheless retained elements of the conservatism of the early 1980s. Despite the changes and the challenges, a key feature of the dominant professional discourses on Latin America has continued to be their fundamentally liberal character. This has been readily apparent in the historiography on Central America specifically and Latin America as a whole. Furthermore, regardless of their greater relative autonomy since the 1960s, the professional discourses on Latin America remain closely connected to the practice of US foreign policy. The history of the emergence and vicissitudes of Latin American studies as a whole points to its fundamental connection with US hegemony and the profoundly liberal character of the professional discourses and structures in which the study of Latin America remains situated. The image of an equal contest between liberal and radical theory since the 1960s is linked to the more general representation of liberal capitalist democracy competing in the ideological marketplace on equal terms with Soviet socialism and other varieties of socialist political economy--in the wider context of the Cold War struggle between evenly matched politico-military and economic competitors. This image was particularly apparent with the 'collapse of communism' at the end of the 1980s, insofar as most explanations for the demise of the Soviet Union's empire emphasized (admittedly important) internal shortcomings without analyzing the unequal power relations between the US and the USSR which were of critical importance in shaping the outcome of the Cold War. Although, in the short term, liberalism has emerged victorious from the Cold War, this was never an equal contest. At the same time, regardless of important historical advantages, liberalism has had to make concessions in both a conservative and, to a lesser extent, a radical direction.[78] Still, despite the important changes in the global liberal politico-economic order over the past two decades, in the case of the Americas, if not the world-system, the 1960s to 1990 can be seen as a period which overall witnessed the reinvigoration of liberalism.[79] Of course, it cannot be denied that the liberal triumphalism which attended the immediate end of the Cold War has begun to fray at the edges.[80] Nevertheless the term 'liberalism' can still be used to characterize the dominant set of ideas which has historically and is currently being deployed in support of US hegemony in the inter-American system.

The theoretical and political changes that have taken place since the 1960s within the Latin American studies profession, along with the breakdown and eventual restoration of the wider US foreign policy consensus to which Latin American studies is linked, occurred in the context of power relations that worked to domesticate both conservative and radical theory and politics to historically liberal structures and discourses. These power relations ensured that even when the lack of political and theoretical consensus has appeared to be particularly acute, such as the late 1960s or the early 1980s, the institutional power relations and the dominant professional and policy discourses which work to maintain the inter-American system provided the context for the domestication of theoretical and political dissent and the reinvention of liberalism. Even with the changes that began in the 1960s, Latin American studies remains rooted in the liberal discourses and structures of the North American university system and the national political and foreign policy process. Regardless of its greater relative autonomy since the 1960s, as reflected in the rise of dependency theory, the Latin American studies profession has remained closely connected to the practice of US foreign policy in Latin America. And despite the considerable influence of dependency theory on Latin American studies and the widespread opposition in the 1980s to Reagan's policy in Central America within the Latin American studies profession, US hegemony continues to be complemented by liberal intellectual practices common to a wide range of Latin American specialists based at universities, research centers and other institutions linked to the US government and the various agencies of US hegemony. At the center of this book is the argument that throughout the twentieth century the liberal professional discourses on Latin America have made an important contribution to the diffuse character and resilience of US hegemony in the Americas. In particular, the dominant professional discourses on Latin America have been central to US efforts to manage Latin America, setting limits on the ability of North American specialists to understand Latin America.

Part I

US Hegemony and the Rise of Latin American Studies 1898-1968

Chapter 1

CIVILIZING THE SOUTH 1898-1945

*"A careful and conscientious appraisal of United States imperialism shows, I am convinced, that it was never deep-rooted in the character of the people, that it was essentially a protective imperialism, designed to protect, first the security of the Continental Republic, next the security of the entire New World, against intervention by the imperialist powers of the Old World. It was, if you will, an imperialism against imperialism. It did not last long and it was not really bad....Although national and continental (in the hemispheric sense of the word) security is the real watchword of the Latin American policy of the United States today, there is more to it than that....It has received a missionary impulse to save peoples not only from political tyranny, but also from political instability, from ignorance, from disease, from poverty, all of which the Latin American countries have possessed in varying measure....Today it has inspired the Good Neighbor of the North, working loyally within the diplomatic framework of Pan American collaboration, to fortify the political independence and territorial integrity of the nations of the New World by increasing their economic and sociological **well-being** in order to further a **general advance in civilization."***

Samuel Flagg Bemis, **The Latin American Policy of the United States: An Historical Interpretation** [New York: Harcourt, Brace and World, 1943]. pp. 385-386, 390-391. (Bemis's italics).

Between the late nineteenth century and the 1920s the US emerged as the main imperial power in the circum-Caribbean. Many countries in the region saw their economies and political institutions subordinated to the North American economy and the US government. This occurred in the wider context of the US emergence as a great power by 1898 and its rise to hemispheric and then global predominance by the end of World War II. Closely associated with the US rise to dominance in Latin America was the emergence of professional academic discourses on Latin America. Between 1898 and 1945, US diplomatic history and Latin American history emerged as distinct professional specializations. And throughout the first four decades of the twentieth century, historians dominated the professional study of Latin America. In this period the connection between the practice of US foreign policy in Latin America and the professional discourses on Latin America was even closer than in later years. The growing historiography legitimated the US rise to predominance in the circum-Caribbean and beyond, and when criticisms of US policy were made they were mild and instrumental in character. Apart from taking up positions at North American universities, many of the diplomatic historians and Latin American history specialists who came of age around World War I went on to spend at least part of their career working with the State Department, other branches of the US government or the growing number of privately funded organizations and foundations. The US retreat from direct military control in the circum-Caribbean and the rise of the Good Neighbor Policy, followed by the Second World War, provided the context in which the professional discourses on Latin America completed a shift from what can be described as Anglo-Saxonism to liberal assumptions about the superiority of North American political and economic institutions and arrangements (and their relevance as models for Latin America). By the 1930s the professional North American study of Latin America rested clearly on the view that the region would eventually progress along North American lines. The professional discourses and US foreign policy were moulded by notions about a special civilizing role for the US, an approach which was increasingly complemented by Pan American ideas about the 'common history' and 'common destiny' of the Americas.

Manifest Destiny and Dollar Diplomacy 1898-1920s

The history of the United States of America, like that of all imperial powers in the modern era, has been not only a saga of politico-military and economic expansion, but also a history of racial and cultural assertion. The first settlers arrived in North America committed to the redemption of the Old World. They articulated a mission to build a 'New World', and the notion of some sort of mission continued to inform the history of settlement and expansion. By the time of the American Revolution and the founding of the republic, many North Americans believed that the US was destined to dominate and even encompass Mexico, Central America and the Caribbean. In the last decades of the eighteenth century, George Washington conceived of the US as a 'rising empire' with a divine right to extend in whatever direction its destiny might dictate. Thomas Jefferson, Secretary of State from 1789 to 1793, and later President, foresaw Central America eventually filling up with settlers from North America. He imagined that a similar fate was in store for South America. After the War of 1812, the inevitable expansion of the US into Latin America continued as a powerful theme in North American politics and foreign policy.[1]

This was reflected in the Monroe Doctrine of 1823, which directed the European imperial powers to respect the recently achieved independence of the republics of Latin America. European respect for the Monroe Doctrine was minimal at first, and throughout the nineteenth century US relations with Central and South America were peripheral to expansion and consolidation in North America. By the 1820s, however, US diplomatic representatives first began to turn up in Central America. Following the region's independence from Spain Washington now perceived the Central American isthmus as a potentially important commercial link between the east and west coast of North America and also as a source of minerals and agricultural products.[2] In the early 1840s, for example, John Lloyd Stephens, whose books about Central America and the Yucatan were the point of departure for western archaeology's study of the ancient Maya, was despatched to Central America on a "Special Confidential Mission" by the US president. Stephens was under instructions to locate a Central American government with which Washington could enter into commercial and diplomatic relations.[3]

At the same time as Stephens's exploration of the war-torn isthmus was proving to be an archaeological success and a diplomatic and commercial failure, the idea of Manifest Destiny began to appear in North America, infusing debates about US expansion with a more virulently racist nationalism than a half-century earlier. This potent amalgam of Anglo-Saxon racism, republicanism, and ideas about 'freedom of religion' and 'democracy' envisioned the expansion of US institutions and values throughout the hemisphere. It also anticipated the regeneration of 'backward people'. Before and during the war with Mexico (1846-1848), Manifest Destiny was enlisted by the administration of James Polk, which eventually annexed thirty percent of Mexico. And throughout the period up to the US Civil War there was considerable talk in North America of expanding further southward until the US reached Central America and beyond.[4]

In 1848, when the British annexed part of the eastern coast of Nicaragua, President Polk, who was thoroughly hostile to the British, attempted to unite the five republics of Central America under US leadership against British imperialism. Throughout the nineteenth century, Britain was the major external political and economic force in Central and South America. British commercial and naval power had facilitated Latin American independence from Spain at the beginning of the nineteenth century, and British commerce and British diplomacy had moved quickly to fill the gap left by the Spanish retreat. The larger aim of Polk's 1848 effort failed. But Washington did initially emerge from the exercise with a treaty of friendship with Honduras and an agreement with Nicaragua which gave the US control over a future canal route. In return the US agreed to support Nicaraguan sovereignty and independence. However, these treaties were never formally ratified by the US Senate, and in 1850, by which time Polk's administration had been replaced by a less bellicose government, London and Washington resolved some of their differences and signed a treaty in which they agreed to cooperate in the building of a canal in the region. Britain retained its control over eastern Nicaragua, but it acknowledged the US as an emerging force in Central America.

Although Manifest Destiny and formal territorial expansion southward did not undergo a revival in the US until the end of the nineteenth century, in the 1850s Central America and the circum-Caribbean were 'discovered' by North American adventurers who sought to re-introduce slavery, acquire private fortunes and practice their own version of Manifest Destiny. In the late 1850s William Walker ruled Nicaragua and even received the diplomatic blessing of Washington. Walker's major mistake was to take on Cornelius Vanderbilt, whose steamship company used Nicaragua as a way-station on its route to California. Vanderbilt financed Central American and British efforts to eliminate Walker, who was eventually executed in Honduras in September 1860, although not before he had found time to write about his Central American exploits.[5] The US Civil War ended North American interest in incorporating some of the republics into the Union as slave states.[6]

By the late 1860s the US had emerged as an industrial power in embryo, and by the last decade of the century it had become a leading industrial and later financial power. Prior to the late nineteenth century, the Monroe Doctrine had been a relatively hollow assertion in the face of British commercial and naval power, particularly in South America. However, by the end of the century, Great Britain had acknowledged the United States' growing influence in Central America and the Caribbean, and ideas about Manifest Destiny bolstered the US emergence as a world industrial-military power. In the decade after the war with Spain in 1898, the US carved out a colony in the Philippines, annexed Puerto Rico, as well as establishing protectorates and semi-protectorates in Cuba, Santo Domingo (the Dominican Republic), Haiti, Honduras and Nicaragua. These developments, along with the setting up of the Canal Zone in Panama and the articulation of the 'Open Door' policy towards China, delineate a turning point in the history of US expansion, and represent the definitive emergence of the US as an overseas imperial power.

By the beginning of the twentieth century, US-based companies were active in many parts of Latin America. For example, in Central America by the 1890s US companies were engaged in the establishment and expansion of banana and coffee growing, railroad construction and the mining of gold and silver. British financial influence continued to be significant in Latin America generally and Central America more specifically. However, while the British invested in government utilities and bonds, North American capital created the export industries and their infrastructure, on which Central America's trade and economic existence depended by the second decade of the twentieth century. In Central America and elsewhere, the beginning of the twentieth century ushered in the era of dollar diplomacy, as North American commercial and financial interests, with Washington's diplomatic and military assistance and support, guided and shaped the economies of the circum-Caribbean until they had become integrated, in a subordinate and dependent fashion, into the North American economy. By the 1920s over fifty percent of Central America's foreign commercial activity was with the US. North American investment in Central America prior to the First World War has been estimated at less than thirty million dollars, at a time when British investment amounted to over 188 million dollars. By the end of the 1920s North American investment had reached over 227 million dollars in contrast to a British figure of under 132 million dollars.[7] The 1920s was the decade in which the export-led economic model (which rested on bananas and coffee) was consolidated in Central America, although its origins stretched back to the second half of the nineteenth century.[8]

After 1920 the regimes of Central America, and the socio-economic elite which they represented, reaped considerable benefits from cooperating with Washington. In exchange for providing political and economic stability and protecting US interests, the governments of Central America could rely on the US to provide a large portion of their supply of food, much of the market for their coffee, beef and bananas, as well as the majority of their bank loans and military needs. The Central American and Caribbean elites were aware, by the 1920s, that their way of life was dependent on North America. They were also aware that Washington was able and willing to support its hegemonic position with armed intervention.[9] For Latin America as a whole, North American investment increased from 320 million dollars in 1898 to 1.7 billion dollars by the outbreak of World War I, while British investment totalled 3.7 billion with over half of this figure flowing to Brazil and Argentina. However, during the First World War, the value of North American investment flowing into Latin America rose by 50%, while the war permanently undermined the European position in the Americas. The value of US exports to Latin America as a whole trebled between 1914 and 1929. At the same time, the US became the principal buyer of the region's tropical foodstuffs and minerals, with over 30% of all Latin American exports going to North America by 1929.[10]

The Rise of 'Latin American Studies' 1898-1920s

The US emergence as an economic and politico-military power in Latin America was central to the constitution of 'Latin America' as an object of study and the rise of 'Latin American studies' as a series of professional discourses. At the same time, the emergence of professional discourses on Latin America was an uneven process, and before the end of World War I its institutional context remained limited. This was reflected in its acute dependence on the US government in this period.[11] The weakness of the profession and its dependence on the government resulted in a limited and uncritical output. Until 1918 the small quantity of work on Latin American (and Central American) history and politics written by North Americans tended towards nationalistic apologia and provincial travel writing.[12] Prior to 1918, similar shortcomings could be found in the small number of books and articles by North Americans which focused specifically on inter-American diplomatic relations.[13] The nascent field of inter-American diplomatic history generated a body of work which was characterized by open support for US expansion in Latin America and rested on racist and nationalistic assumptions about the region and its people.[14] In the period stretching from the establishment of the American Historical Association in 1884 to the emergence of the **Hispanic American Historical Review** in 1918 (an important event in the constitution of professional discourses on Latin America), North American historians writing about Latin America were few in number, although their output did serve to legitimate US expansion southward. Despite their weakness, an identifiable group of professionals committed to the study of Latin America was emerging, and they gained in power as the US position of dominance in the circum-Caribbean and beyond was consolidated.

The work of John H. Latané, professor of American history at Johns Hopkins University in the early twentieth century, was informed by the ideas of the emerging professional discourses on Latin America. In 1900 he published **The Diplomatic Relations of the United States and Spanish America.** This book was later revised and enlarged, although neither the revision nor the enlargement was extensive, and the general interpretative thrust, when it was republished in 1920 as **The United States and Latin America**, remained unchanged. In the 1920 edition Latané argued that because of US policy the Central American republics had been "freer from wars and revolutions for a longer period than at any other time" in their collective history. He argued further that as long as "certain" Central American and Caribbean republics continued in their situation of "weakness and backwardness", Washington had no choice but to "continue to protect them" from the European powers and "supervise their affairs". As long as the US was called upon to follow this policy it would, he noted, have "to rest under the suspicion of having imperialistic designs on its weaker neighbors". It was this "suspicion" which, in his view, had to be "overcome before we can fully realize the ideal of Pan Americanism".[15]

The legitimation of US expansion embodied in Latané's work was reflected in the work of diplomatic historians as a whole. North American diplomatic historians generally took the view that the war with Spain, which had stimulated interest in diplomatic history, had converted the people of North America to an expansionist policy. Virtually all diplomatic historians regarded this conversion in a positive light. They wrote in support, and even celebration, of the conquest of the Philippines, the Open Door Policy in China, and the construction and control of the Panama Canal, as well as intervention in the Caribbean and Central America. Although the emergence of diplomatic history as a distinct subdiscipline of the historical profession began following the war with Spain and was driven forward by the subsequent expansion into the circum-Caribbean and the Philippines, it was not really consolidated as a discipline until the end of World War I. Prior to the First World War, most North American historians were still preoccupied with the national history of the United States and their own country's historical origins in Europe. It was US involvement in the First World War which really served to generate widespread interest in US foreign relations among professional historians in North America. By the 1920s the number of diplomatic historians had grown and, although most of them focused on US relations with Europe and the British Empire, the history of US relations with Latin America received greater attention than in the past. Some of the most celebrated works of diplomatic history in the 1920s and 1930s focused on US relations with Latin America.[16]

Before World War I, the still-limited historiography on US relations with Latin America, like all diplomatic history, rested on Anglo-Saxonist assumptions about North American civilization as the highest form of civilization in history. By the beginning of the twentieth century North American attitudes toward other nations and their inhabitants were based on a clearly defined "racial hierarchy".[17] The ideas about racial and cultural superiority current in North America were embedded in the work of the North American historical profession. North American historians focused on institutional history and saw the history of the United States as a tale of the rise to "freedom", stability and national consolidation. It was often also represented as the history of the triumph of the Anglo-Saxon race. Since the middle of the nineteenth century Anglo-Saxonism, which articulated the view that Anglo-Saxons were possessed of special virtues and responsibilities, had been gaining influence in North America as a whole. As scientific racialism became increasingly influential within the emergent social science and historical professions at the end of the nineteenth century Anglo-Saxonism gained further in power. Very few historians disagreed with Anglo-Saxonism, and the vast majority tacitly or wholeheartedly accepted it. Although North American historians in an earlier period had also been racist, many of the professional historians writing in the late nineteenth century, and the early decades of the twentieth century, were far more systematic in their racism than their predecessors. This was primarily because they came to intellectual maturity at a time when 'scientific' and biological racism was at its height.[18]

By the end of World War I the rise of liberal internationalism in the US had begun to erode the more extreme forms of Anglo-Saxon racism and to contribute to the gradual emergence of Pan Americanism, while the war itself had stimulated the consolidation of diplomatic history as a subdiscipline of the North American historical profession. The 1914-1918 war also provided the impetus for the emergence of the discipline of international relations. After the war, new organizations, such as the Council on Foreign Relations, sought to link social science research and education to the furthering of international understanding and the development of an 'internationalist' US foreign policy. But, apart from some attention to the circum-Caribbean, Latin America remained marginal to the discipline of international relations, and the study of US-Latin American relations was left to diplomatic historians until at least 1945. However, the internationalism driving the emergence of international relations in North America could be found in the work of some of the more prominent diplomatic historians who specialized in Latin America such as Dexter Perkins and Arthur P. Whitaker, whose writing often explicitly sought to relate the 'lessons of history' to current problems.[19] In the study of Latin America as a whole, diplomatic historians were particularly well represented. For example, William Spence Robertson and J. Fred Rippy, who were the two most frequent contributors to the **Hispanic American Historical Review** in the first three decades after its founding in 1918, were well known for their work on the diplomatic history of Latin America and on other aspects of Latin American history.[20]

The centrality of diplomatic history to the study of Latin America in the pre-1945 era was also evidenced by almost thirty percent of the **Hispanic American Historical Review**'s space being given over to articles on diplomatic history between 1918 and 1948 (in the same period only six percent of its pages were devoted to Central American topics of any kind).[21] Apart from diplomatic history, the **Hispanic American Historical Review** concentrated on colonial history for at least the first twenty years of its existence. However, like the growth of diplomatic history, which was a product of the United States' emergence as a world power, the interest in the colonial history of Latin America flowed from US expansion into the Spanish borderlands, particularly Texas, California and Florida. A focus on colonial history may also have been a result of the lingering impact of the romanticism of the nineteenth century associated with the work of writers such as William H. Prescott and their emphasis on the exoticism of Spanish imperialism, yet it was primarily the shared events on the northern periphery of the Spanish empire that sparked North American interest in Latin American colonial history.[22] This was apparent in the early work of Arthur P. Whitaker, who was Professor of History at the University of Pennsylvania and a major figure among Latin American specialists and diplomatic historians before and after 1945. A graduate of Harvard, Whitaker wrote a number of important diplomatic histories in the inter-war years. His first two books focused on the Spanish frontier in North America and US expansion into former Spanish territory. His third book looked at the US and Latin American independence.[23] Between World War I and World War II the historians who dominated 'Latin American studies' generally confined their research to diplomatic and colonial history. And political scientists, like international relations specialists, did not turn southward until the Cold War.[24]

The dominance of historians in 'Latin American studies' prior to 1945 was reflected in the way the **Hispanic American Historical Review** emerged as the main professional journal on Latin America. Also apparent in many of the contributions to the journal was the close relationship between the dominant professional discourses and US foreign policy. The journal's appearance pointed to the complementary position it occupied in relation to US hegemony in Latin America and to the rise of Pan Americanism. It also made apparent the way in which the emerging professional discourses on Latin America gained their authority from their association with the US government. The founders of the **Hispanic American Historical Review** had been greatly encouraged by the support given to their project by President Wilson and his Secretary of State. A letter from the US President adorned the front page of the first issue, highlighting the journal's liberal internationalist commitment to Pan American understanding. Charles Chapman, the first editor, argued that President Wilson's letter, on its own, was sufficient "to justify the appearance of the (journal) and to entitle it to the encouragement and support of high-minded Americans". The Secretary of State anticipated that the journal "would be of great benefit, both to the scholars of this country and to those of Latin America", and that "it would also serve the purpose for which all of us have been striving both in the past, and, particularly, in the present, namely the foundation of (a) closer relationship between all of the Americas". President Wilson hoped that the journal would "lead to very important results both for scholarship and for the increase of cordial feelings throughout the Americas".[25]

The establishment of the **Hispanic American Historical Review** had also been encouraged by the American Historical Association. And the emergence of professional discourses on Latin America dominated by historians has to be seen not only in terms of US expansion in Latin America, but in the broader context of the rise of the North American historical profession as a whole. Although historians of Latin America were partially isolated from wider trends in the social sciences for geographical and social reasons, they did not operate outside the emergence of the North American historical profession. The North American historians who led the drive towards professionalization in history generally relied on European models, especially the prestigious German historical tradition. In the late nineteenth and early twentieth century North American historians enshrined 'objectivity' as central to their profession and, at a time when a scientific approach was the distinguishing characteristic of all that was modern, the concept of scientific method was also incorporated.[26] The "second wave" of professional historians in North America, who came to prominence in the years after World War I assumed that "induction from observed facts" and a skeptical attitude towards "preformed generalizations" was "the highroad to science".[27]

At the same time, the pace of professionalization was slow. The emergence of an institutional structure made up of professional associations, regular journals, training standards, the formal transmission of academic skills, and a system of accreditation, which gave authority to the professional discourses was a gradual and uneven process. For example, the instruction given to prospective North American historians in the US or Germany at the turn of the century was not particularly rigorous. Also, up to World War I, the majority of the members of the American Historical Association were amateur historians and in the eyes of professional historians themselves, many of the most significant contributions to the historiography, up to at least 1919, were written by affluent amateur historians.[28] The slow rate at which professionalization occurred was also apparent in the size, professional character and general cohesion of the American Political Science Association (APSA) in the period prior to 1919, following its emergence as an offshoot from the American Historical Association at the turn of the century. At the beginning of the twentieth century there were fewer than one hundred full-time political science instructors in the United States, and in 1903 they came together to form the APSA. Following the APSA's first annual meeting in New Orleans in 1904 the membership of the Association rose to 214, and by the eve of World War I the Association had 1,500 members.[29] Although the **Hispanic American Historical Review** was set up in 1918 it was not until the late 1920s that the first professional association for Latin American historians, the Conference on Latin American History, was established.[30]

Furthermore, the private research organizations and the philanthropic foundations, which provided an important institutional context for the professional discourses on Latin America, emerged only around World War I. The Carnegie Endowment for International Peace first appeared in 1910; the Hoover Institution on War, Revolution and Peace was set up on the campus of Stanford University in 1919. The Twentieth Century Fund appeared in New York in 1919, while the Brookings Institution in Washington began in 1916, but was constituted in its current form only in 1927.[31] The Council on Foreign Relations was first set up in New York in 1918; however, it got off to a slow start and did not emerge as an active force until after its merger, in 1921, with the US branch of the Institute of International Affairs, which had been founded in Paris in 1919.[32] The Rockefeller Foundation, which entered the picture in 1913, following the consolidation of a number of philanthropic initiatives which had been set up by the famous millionaire over the previous decade, did not shift from its initial concern with scientific and medical research to a wider concern with international understanding until the 1920s. But already in 1919 the president of the Foundation was emphasizing that its program in international medicine was linked to a broader need to stimulate "a constant exchange of knowledge and suggestion among the many countries of the world", and by 1933 "the improvement of international understanding through cultural interchange" was a central goal of the Foundation. A famous source of Latin American fellowships, the John Simon Guggenheim Foundation, was also set up around the same time.[33] By the end of the 1920s the philanthropic foundations had established an institutional framework for international cultural relations which, although it was still relatively fragile, complemented both US foreign policy and the consolidation of 'Latin American studies'.

The most important foundation in the case of Latin America was the Carnegie Endowment for International Peace. It emerged from World War I committed to international understanding and the need to harness the research and teaching of historians and social scientists to the education of the public about international relations. The Carnegie Endowment hoped that a more internationally aware public would encourage Washington policy-makers in an internationalist direction. For example, in 1923 the director of the Carnegie Endowment's Division of Intercourse and Education emphasized the need for the development of an international outlook "which looks upon the several nations of the civilized world as cooperating equals in promoting the progress of civilization, in developing commerce and industry and in diffusing science and education throughout the world".[34] The same sentiment had stimulated Carnegie himself earlier to donate the money for the construction of the building which housed the Central American Court of Justice, which was established under Washington's auspices in 1907 (despite its involvement, Washington ignored important decisions made by the Court, and within a decade it had become an irrelevant institution). The money for the construction of the Pan American Union building was also supplied by Carnegie, and at the building's dedication he emphasized his belief that international conflict could be reduced by greater understanding between people and nations. Although many of the individuals who ran the Carnegie Endowment were pragmatic men from the Eastern financial and legal establishment, the Endowment's trustees as a group were optimistic about the prospects for international peace and committed to the view that the expansion of Western civilization brought progress and prosperity.[35] The emergence, after World War I, of organizations such as the Carnegie Endowment ensured that the 1920s would be a turning point in the consolidation of professional discourses on Latin America.

Professionalization shifted historians, and social scientists generally, from the status of 'independent' amateurs to paid scholars dependent on foundation grants, on government and on pay-cheques from the rapidly growing tertiary system. Increasingly, having the time and the research facilities to write history and the opportunity to teach history were dependent on gaining a position at a university or college. In the years after World War II, the decision to employ an academic was usually made by his (or very occasionally her) prospective colleagues; however, this was not the case in the early twentieth century. University and college presidents, with the assistance of the institutions' trustees, were, with some exceptions, in charge of hiring and firing, and they kept a close watch on academics prior to and following their appointment to a teaching position. Most universities relied on private funds, and their wealthy donors were often trustees. These well-heeled philanthropists exercised broad control over what constituted an acceptable approach to teaching and research not only because they held positions on the boards of trustees and had the ear of obedient administrators, but because they also often gave bonuses to preferred academics. As a result the general notion of "academic freedom" was "narrowly defined" and "fitfully observed". Professors were expected to conform and be 'moderate' in their interpretations. In practice it was possible to get rid of non-conformist academics on the basis that they had trespassed against the "norms of scientific objectivity", without even addressing the issue of "academic freedom".[36]

Nowhere was conformity greater than among historians of Latin America. They were subject to all the constraints associated with the organization and administration of the universities. They were also limited by the language, categories, methodology and assumptions of their professional discourses. Many of them also spent at least part of their career in government service, or working with private foundations and research organizations. Richard Morse has argued that in the years after World War I 'Latin American studies' emerged in North America as "a faintly ridiculous tail to a politico-commercial kite".[37] This is not surprising given that a key aspect of the very constitution of the professional discourses on Latin America was the development of strong links between academics, the State Department and private foundations. A Latin American specialist who exemplified the close relationship between the academy, the government and private foundations in this formative period was Leo S. Rowe, Professor of Political Science at the University of Pennsylvania. Rowe was well connected in government circles and was very sympathetic with US policy in Latin America. He served as President of the American Academy of Political and Social Science for almost thirty years (1902 to 1930), and as the Director General of the Pan-American Union from 1920 until 1946. (The Pan American Union was the secretariat of the Union of American Republics, which was set up in 1910. The Union of American Republics was the direct organizational successor to the International Union of American Republics which was founded at the first Pan American Conference in 1889, and the direct organizational predecessor to the Organization of American States, which was founded in 1948.) Although he was a political scientist, he obtained undergraduate degrees in philosophy and law, and he began his career at a time when the distinction between history and political science was less clearly defined than it later became. Rowe exercised considerable influence on the North American understanding of Latin America. Apart from acting as supervisor and mentor for Dana Munro, Rowe also inspired other prominent historians of Latin America, such as Herbert Eugene Bolton and Isaac Joslin Cox.[38]

Rowe's most well known book was **The United States and Porto Rico**, which grew out of his work for the US government in Puerto Rico at the beginning of the century. He characterized US expansion into the circum-Caribbean as "inevitable", and the countries there as "natural economic dependencies" of the United States. The bulk of his book was given over to an examination of the United States' administrative experience in Puerto Rico. He argued that the US could learn from the European colonial powers in order to deal more effectively with its growing collection of dependencies. At the same time, he argued that the North American embrace had the potential to provide the region with a level of "prosperity" which it had not known since the mid-1800s. He emphasized that the recent lessons of US administration in the Caribbean pointed to the "necessity" for "greater elasticity"; and if, in its "contact with foreign civilizations", the US demonstrated "a harsh, unbending spirit", the "feeling of distrust" which was apparent during the Spanish-American War would obstruct the "fulfillment" of the United States' "mission" in the Americas. He argued that the "real significance of the extension" of US influence into the Caribbean was not "territorial aggrandizement" but the "adaptation" of US "political ideas and standards" which the expansion required.[39] Rowe's work, like the work of other Latin American specialists, posed questions in terms that reflected the imperatives of US expansion. His career and his approach pointed to the emergence of Pan Americanism and to the way in which the dominant professional discourses on Latin America fulfilled an important legitimating function as the US gained increasing power in the Caribbean and Central America.

Backwardness and Progress in the Circum-Caribbean 1920-1933

By the end of World War I the US had established the framework to exercise relatively undisputed control in the circum-Caribbean. In the late nineteenth and early twentieth century the British and the French legitimated their domination of Africa and Asia in terms of the white man's burden and a *mission civilisatrice*, which flowed from a powerful mixture of assumptions about their racial and technological superiority.[40] In the years between 1898 and the early 1930s North Americans also justified the US right to intervene in Central America and the Caribbean in racial supremacist terms. They also usually assumed that the 'superiority' of the US conferred on it a special role in Latin America as a whole (an assumption which stretched back to the Monroe Doctrine of 1823). The main assumptions underpinning US foreign policy and structuring the dominant professional discourses on Latin America between the 1890s and 1920s were based on the eighteenth and nineteenth century justifications for continental expansion and the more or less genocidal policies inherited from the Indian frontier experience, as well as the strategic, commercial and moral imperatives articulated by military and naval thinkers, and businessmen and social reformers.[41] At the same time, after 1898 many prominent historians and politicians built on the idea that the US was the culmination of the rise of Western civilization, stretching back at least to the Roman empire, and manifested more recently in the British 'mpire-civilization' of the nineteenth century.[42] As a result North Americans insisted that they were the standard-bearers of civilization and were bringing progress and stability to the circum-Caribbean. Accordingly the region's economic improvement and political stabilization would benefit both North Americans and the inhabitants of Central America and the Caribbean. However, economic and political progress would, of course, occur at a different rate, and the US would remain for a considerable time (and in the view of some, always) at a higher level of "civilization" and political and economic "maturity".[43]

The direct military character of US intervention until the early 1930s meant that despite the emergence of reformist and liberal internationalist ideas, US hegemony and the dominant discourses on Latin America continued to rest on earlier justifications for US expansion. In this period reform Darwinism eventually won its battle with the more deterministic varieties of social Darwinism and introduced the idea of "bettering" the inhabitants of Latin America by reforming the social and political order. At the same time a large number of North Americans were unwilling to discard earlier ideas about the biological inferiority of most Latin Americans, notions which had flourished during the suzerainty of Anglo-Saxon racism. Many North Americans continued to hold the view that the 'backward' and decadent 'nature' of Central America and the Caribbean was irredeemable.[44] Under these circumstances, even as progressive and liberal reformist ideas entered the foreign policy discourses, liberal reformers continued to support the exercise of force to tame the "lesser breeds", when people or governments of the region opposed changes that were perceived to be in their own best interests. US military intervention in the region between 1898 and the 1920s was founded on an older Anglo-Saxon racism and on modern economic imperatives, and this was reflected in the dominant professional discourses on Latin America.[45]

The centrality of Anglo-Saxonism, ideas about a US mission, the growing importance of Pan Americanism, and the rise of liberal ideas about political and economic progress between World War I and World War II, was apparent in the work and career of Dana Gardner Munro. He was the most important North American to write specifically about Central America and the Caribbean in the years before 1945.[46] His work reflected the way in which Anglo-Saxonism was gradually overlaid by Pan Americanism. Munro's career and work also pointed to the profession's high degree of dependence on the government and the legitimating role that the professional discourses played in relation to the expansion of US hegemony. Munro did postgraduate work at the University of Munich in 1912 and 1913, before returning to the US to begin work on his PhD at the University of Pennsylvania under Leo Rowe's supervision. With Rowe's help the twenty-two year old Munro secured the financial assistance of the Carnegie Endowment for International Peace, which was developing a particular interest in Latin America as part of its overall desire to improve international understanding. In 1914 he headed off to Central America, where he remained, except for a brief return to the US, until 1916.[47]

For his trip to Central America in 1914 Munro took documentation which accredited him as a representative of the Carnegie Endowment and the American Academy of Political and Social Science. His initial project had been to collect material for a study of the causes of "revolutions" in Central America. He later narrowed this to a comparative study of Nicaragua and Costa Rica.[48] However, the book which emerged was a more general survey of the region. At the same time Munro still devoted attention to the original focus of his research, the causes of the revolutions and civil wars, which he characterized as the major factor in the region's modern history. **The Five Republics of Central America: Their Political and Economic Development and Their Relations With the United States** was published in 1918.[49] It is regarded as an "exception" to the "general trend" in North American work on the region up to the post-World War I period.[50] Even today, Munro's work is regarded with considerable reverence by many scholars. One recent observer described the 1918 book as a piece of "serious historical scholarship", and it is still regarded by many historians as "a standard work".[51] Writing in 1983, Ralph Lee Woodward, in his foreword to Munro's **A Student in Central America**, characterized his first book as a "classic reference work" which "remains today one of the best sources for information and insight on early twentieth century Central America".[52] The respect which Munro's first book and his later work are still accorded demonstrates the continuity of the dominant professional discourses on Latin America, and the authority which diplomats and State Department employees are still accorded by the profession.[53]

Munro's first book rested firmly on the view that there was no basic conflict of interest between US foreign policy goals and Central American interests. It reflected prevailing notions about objectivity and scientific history, as well as the gradual shift in North American understanding of historical development embodied in the rise of Pan Americanism. Munro traced the causes of Central America's lack of progress to historical-cultural and racial factors. He emphasized that the cultural legacy of Spanish colonialism prevented the ruling elite in the post-independence period from achieving any significant "advance in civilization". Munro's book reflected greater optimism than many about the likelihood that Central America would "eventually" establish "stable" political systems. While he represented the historical roots of Central American "backwardness" in a way which assumed North American superiority, unlike many North Americans at this time, he argued that Central Americans were capable of achieving a level of "civilization" more or less equivalent to that of the United States. He emphasized that the people of Central America were "not inherently unfit for self-government". He argued that North Americans themselves had once lived in the "disorderly conditions" which

existed in the "most turbulent parts" of Central America, and even today the people
of the US were not "unfamiliar" with many of the "worst evils" which afflicted
politics in Central America.[54] His approach was certainly not as racist as the
outlook of many US government officials and naval and military personnel who
dealt with Central America and the Caribbean, who continued to see race as a
permanent obstacle to political and economic progress.[55]

Munro's optimism about the ability of Central Americans to 'advance'
politically and economically depended on, and was reinforced by, his optimism
about the extremely positive role he assumed the US could play in the region. He
argued that of all the internal and external factors shaping developments in the next
twenty or thirty years, US foreign policy would probably be the most important in
directing the "course" of events in Central America. Munro's perspective, like the
dominant discourses on Latin America, was founded on the idea that the US had a
divine right to assert and maintain its hegemony in the region. Munro subscribed
to a US civilizing mission in the circum-Caribbean and beyond. He insisted that
the "political stability" and "prosperity" of Central America was the main motive
behind US policy in the region. Although he argued that it was "inevitable" that
the US exercise a "decided influence" on Central America, the "ultimate purpose" of
US foreign policy was to help the Central American republics "to attain a position
where they can manage their own affairs without outside interference". He also
argued that the beneficial "influence" of North American "civilization", which was
already growing, "could be greatly increased if the missionary educational enterprise
which has been so successful in the Orient could be turned in some measure to
these countries at our own doors". In his view the setting up of agricultural and
engineering institutes, as well as other institutes for higher education, by US based
"philanthropic" organizations could be the most important single "factor" in
advancing political and economic "conditions" in Central America. He argued that
there was "no form of assistance" which would better serve to reassure the
inhabitants of the region "of the friendly intentions of their great neighbor".[56]

After serving in the Army Air Service in 1917-1918 Munro was employed
briefly as lecturer at Georgetown University. A year after the publication of his
book, he went to work for the State Department's Foreign Trade Adviser's office as
a regional economist responsible for Mexico and Central America. In 1921 he
joined the Latin American Division of the State Department, working in
Washington until 1925, spending the last two years as Assistant Division Chief.
From 1925 to 1927 he was US secretary of legation in Panama and was then
posted to Nicaragua at the height of the second US intervention, serving as US
secretary there until 1929.[57] In 1925 the US had made a 'premature' withdrawal
from Nicaragua, after Washington decided that a decade of occupation had brought
sufficient political order for the Marines to leave. However, fighting between
political factions soon broke out, and in 1926, after Mexico gave support to the
political faction opposed to the pro-US grouping, President sent the Marines back
to Nicaragua. The Coolidge administration had earlier expressed concern about what
it perceived as the "Bolshevist" tendencies in the Mexican Revolution, and the US
return to Nicaragua was justified in terms of protecting the republic from the
blandishments of Russian Bolshevism which were seen as being transmitted into
the country by Mexico. The second intervention brought criticism from some
politicians in the US who thought that Coolidge's fears were unwarranted. This

group felt that a policy which rested on anti-bolshevism would undermine Washington's status and power in the eyes of Latin Americans and actually encourage the 'bolsheviks'.[58]

Although there was a growing debate about the efficacy of Washington's policy in the circum-Caribbean, by the second half of the 1920s the professional discourses as a whole continued to register support for Washington's interventions. For example, from 1925 to 1927 the Council on Foreign Relations (which published the journal **Foreign Affairs**) ran a study group on Caribbean Affairs, which evolved into a committee on Latin America as a whole. (A development which was clearly linked to the expansion of US hegemony beyond the confines of the circum-Caribbean.) From 1927 until 1933 this committee was led by William R. Shepherd, a professor of history at Columbia, a founding member of the Council on Foreign Relations, and a co-founder of the **Hispanic American Historical Review**.[59] Throughout the 1920s and 1930s the Council's Latin American committee provided an institutional focus for the dominant discourses on Latin America. The Council's Latin American committee legitimated US hegemony in the region, emphasizing that because the economies of the western hemisphere were so interdependent, Washington needed to exercise powerful political leadership. In the 1920-1933 period the Council's relatively unequivocal support for US policy was disrupted, in the case of Central America, on only one occasion. In an address to the Council's Central American Study Group in April 1926, Ernest Gruening, one-time progressive journalist for the **Nation** and later an Alaskan senator, articulated a highly critical perspective on US military intervention in Nicaragua. Gruening's critique had little effect. The legitimating role of the Council's Latin American committee was reflected in the Study Group's report on the situation in Central America, which was issued in December 1926 and supported the State Department's view that the need for Washington to intervene militarily in the region would gradually dissipate.[60]

Further evidence of academics' strong support for US policy in the circum-Caribbean and of their close relationship with the State Department, as well as with North American companies, was apparent in 1927 when the Academy of American Political and Social Science devoted a significant part of their bi-monthly journal to US-Central American relations. The overall tone was sympathetic and more concerned with policy implementation than criticism. Of the seven articles one was by George T. Weitzel, a former US minister to Nicaragua, another was by the President of the United Fruit Company, Victor M. Cutter, and a third was by H. W. Dodds, who had drafted and helped implement the new Nicaraguan election law in the early 1920s. Sandwiched between these representatives of the US government and the United Fruit Company were the Latin American historians William R. Shepherd of Columbia University and C. H. Haring of Harvard, while articles by Whiting Williams of the Boston-based Foreign Policy Association and Wallace Thompson were also included.[61]

The **Hispanic American Historical Review** also provided a focus of institutional support for US policy in the circum-Caribbean in the late 1920s. For example, in 1928 Charles Chapman leapt to Washington's defense in a review of Leland Jenks's book on US relations with Cuba and Melvin Knight's book on US relations with the Dominican Republic. In the pages of the **Hispanic American Historical Review** Chapman called into question Jenks's commitment to "objective scholarship", while Knight was criticized both for his youth and his inability or unwillingness to "take a calm, judicious, well-balanced view of a situation", and both writers' patriotism was deemed to be suspect.[62] Although Chapman, the veritable father of the **Hispanic American Historical Review**, never worked for the State Department in the way academics like Dana Munro did, his close relationship with Washington was beyond dispute.[63] Chapman's hostile review of Jenks and Knight was in marked contrast to the favorable review by Alfred Hasbrouck, in the previous issue of the **Hispanic American Historical Review**, of a book on US relations with Nicaragua by Henry Stimson.[64]

Henry L. Stimson was one of the most famous figures in US relations with Nicaragua in the 1920s and early 1930s. Unlike Munro, whose career trajectory became an increasingly academic one, Stimson rose to the very top of the State Department. After serving as President Coolidge's special representative in Nicaragua in 1927, he went on to be Governor-General of the Philippines in 1928 and 1929 and then to oversee the US withdrawal from Nicaragua as Secretary of State from 1929 to 1933. Stimson, who died in 1950, contributed articles to **Foreign Affairs** and other journals.[65] He also wrote on US policy in Nicaragua after his mission there. His book, **American Policy in Nicaragua**, legitimated US policy in the region. This work, like Munro's first book (on which Stimson relied) reflected optimistic support for US leadership in the region, and an emphasis on the exceptional role of the US in foreign affairs. Stimson argued that US-Nicaraguan relations, as well as US-Latin American relations more generally, had to "proceed on the strict assumption" of the Latin American republics' "continued existence as independent nations". He asserted that for a hundred years the US had been the "scrupulous protector of their independence, not only against Europe but sometimes even against themselves". According to Stimson this was "particularly true" with regard to Central America. He dismissed all charges of the US having "imperialistic designs" on Nicaragua or any other country in the region, arguing that the United States' "influence" had "uniformly" been "used for peace".[66] Stimson's career and work pointed to the close relationship between the government and the professional discourses. His racist paternalism, articulated as a complementary combination of strategic imperatives and idealism, reflected the continuity and the change in US foreign policy and in the professional study of Latin America. By the 1920s the Anglo-Saxonism which shaped US foreign policy and the dominant professional discourses was partially overlaid by Pan Americanism.

Stimson's 1927 book was preoccupied with politics and policy, particularly the positive impact of US-sponsored elections. He did not deal with economic factors; however, he did make a short defence of US fiscal policy in Nicaragua, which he characterized as "highly successful".[67] A far more detailed analysis of Washington's economic reforms and US control of Nicaragua's treasury and customs house was provided by Roscoe R. Hill, who spent eight years in Nicaragua as a member of the Nicaraguan High Commission. Like Munro, Hill had divided his time between academic work and direct employment with the US government in Central America.[68] Hill's book on Nicaragua, completed as a thesis under the supervision of William R. Shepherd, reflected the importance to the professional discourses of 'objectivity' and the idea that facts speak for themselves.

In his view both the "contributions made and the errors committed by those involved" could be discovered "from a statement of the facts". Overall his book generated the impression that a range of positive benefits had flowed from the US intervention in Nicaraguan fiscal affairs.[69] **Fiscal Intervention in Nicaragua** was a self-consciously empirical monograph with clear boundaries avoiding broader themes or questions, certain in the objectivity and science of its own methodology. Hill's approach was similar to an earlier study by Isaac Joslin Cox.[70] Like Dana Munro, Cox received his PhD from the University of Pennsylvania, where he had studied with Leo S. Rowe. Cox's 1927 book on US-Nicaraguan relations characterized the US occupation of Nicaragua as an era in which the strategically important Central American republic experienced "considerable economic improvement and development". He concluded that the setting up of a constabulary and Washington's supervision of the electoral process were "successfully under way", and that the US was in "a more responsible position" than it had ever been.[71]

The journalist Harold Norman Denny visited Nicaragua as a correspondent for **The New York Times** in the mid-1920s. He subsequently produced a book based on his visit.[72] J. Fred Rippy characterized Denny's book as "perhaps the best account" of US intervention in Nicaragua from 1909 to 1928.[73] However, the radical journalist Carleton Beals was less sympathetic when he described **Dollars for Bullets** as a "pseudo-liberal book" which endeavored to "exonerate" the "actions" of the US in Nicaragua. Beals conceded that Denny was an "unusually brilliant reporter", but he claimed that Denny himself had "confided" to Beals that because of his access to US naval and military transport and "other courtesies", he had decided against filing any reports from Nicaragua which were not "official".[74] Denny's work was influenced by the central ideas of the dominant professional discourses on Latin America. He emphasized that US-Nicaraguan relations could be understood only against the background of Washington's "basic international and strategic principles" and Central American history. He insisted that his project was to "present the story objectively, with a minimum of interpretation, permitting the facts as far as possible to interpret themselves". He assured the reader that by and large the "story reflects credit upon" the US government. However, "in dealing with incidents which might put the State Department in an unfavorable light" he "excluded accusations by biased parties, except where necessary to give every side its say". Even in those instances he drew his information from State Department publications, "official" US sources, people "friendly" towards the United States' Nicaraguan policy and "facts" he had obtained personally. To further illustrate Denny's perspective and its relationship to the dominant professional discourses it should be noted that he praised Munro's 1918 book as "comprehensive", and "important", and "unbiased".[75]

US relations with Nicaragua and Central America also attracted the attention of the international relations specialist Raymond Leslie Buell. From 1927 to 1933, the period covering the second US occupation of Nicaragua, Buell was research director of the Foreign Policy Association, acting as the Foreign Policy Association's representative at the Pan American Conference in Havana in 1928.[76] The Foreign Policy Association, along with the Carnegie Endowment for International Peace and the Council on Foreign Relations, was a major focus of North American 'internationalism' after World War I.[77] In 1930 Buell published a short book on Central America which reflected the gradual shift from Anglo-Saxonism to Pan American liberalism. He attacked the view that Central America was a "semi-savage" and "corrupt" land in a state of permanent "revolution", at the same time as he attributed the lack of progress in Central America to climate, culture and even race. However, his racism was cultural rather than biological and in his view Central America's lack of the "industrial and scientific qualities" that had gone into the making of "the civilization of the United States", could be overcome by "economic development" and "popular education". In particular he argued that it was "possible for industrially backward countries", such as those in Central America, to obtain the necessary "outside expert aid, without impairing political independence".[78] Buell's work pointed to the rise of Pan Americanism and foreshadowed the emergence of the Good Neighbor Policy. He argued that the "chief obstacle to understanding" between Washington and Latin America was the US "anti-revolution policy", which had embroiled the US in the region's "internal affairs". He concluded by emphasizing that despite the existence of Central American criticism of US policy there was "surprisingly little real anti-American feeling". He attributed this in part to President Hoover's recent "good-will tour" and to the appointment of qualified career diplomats. However, in his view the "improvement" of US-Central American relations would flow less from "new personalities" and more from "the application of new principles", such as the revision of the US nonrecognition policy.[79]

In 1929 the newly elected President Hoover and Secretary of State Stimson decided that they could start reining in the second US occupation of Nicaragua. Troop numbers were reduced as part of their wider effort to alter the direction of US policy in the circum-Caribbean and Latin America. The direct US military presence in Nicaragua was ended by January 1933, and Somoza's national guard moved to fill the space vacated by Washington and the Marine Corps. The second intervention in Nicaragua had contributed to a re-evaluation of US foreign policy in the region culminating in the Good Neighbor Policy. By the late 1920s the European 'threat' to the hemisphere had faded and North American companies clearly dominated the economic life of the region. By 1929 the US was the single largest export market for Guatemala, Honduras and Nicaragua, while US imports into Central America had risen dramatically, making the US the number one source of Central American imports, with Britain, Germany and France far behind. In Central America, US direct investments had reached the $251 million mark by 1929, more than twice what they had been in 1919. (In Latin America as a whole, direct US investments rose from $1.5 billion in 1924 to $3.5 billion in 1929, while British investment remained more or less unchanged and German and French investment declined.) By the early 1930s the State Department perceived the existence of more significant 'problems' in Europe and Asia. As a result, at a time when both a direct US military presence and the Depression were leading to more social and political disorder and growing anti-American sentiment, the national guards (which in Nicaragua and elsewhere were the direct creation of the United States) and the local constabularies were seen as ready to assume the role of maintaining order. By 1933, the US had reached a position from which it assumed it could pursue foreign policy objectives in the circum-Caribbean by using economic, political and diplomatic influence rather than by relying on direct military intervention.[80]

A number of 'Latin American studies' specialists, whose work focused on Central America or the circum-Caribbean more generally, had emerged between 1920 and 1933 as part of the rise of the professional discourses on Latin America. However, Munro remained one of the most influential specialists on the region. Following his assignment to Nicaragua (1927-1929) he became chief of the State Department's Latin America Division (1929-1930), a post that had been held a decade earlier by his supervisor and mentor Leo Rowe. By the early 1930s Munro had been posted to Haiti as US minister (1930-1932). In 1932 he left the State Department's Foreign Service to take up the position of Professor of Latin American History and Affairs at Princeton, and in 1935 he visited Latin America as Carnegie Foundation Visiting Professor. However, despite his entry into the academy he maintained his connection with the State Department, for which he continued to act as a special adviser on occasion. Following his return to academic life, Munro produced an article on Nicaragua for **Foreign Affairs**. In it he argued that, although the issue of whether or not US intervention in the republic had been "justifiable or wrong" was a "question which could not be discussed adequately without a comprehensive examination of the fundamental bases" of US foreign policy, there "was no doubt" that the "intervention" had been "beneficial" for Nicaragua. The return of the Marines in 1926 had ended "a civil war which threatened to plunge the country into the depths of anarchy" and between 1927 and 1933 "substantial progress was made towards establishing the bases of a lasting peace." Munro said that while the "future" lay "with the Nicaraguans themselves", there was "much to discourage undue optimism". Nevertheless, he took "encouragement" from the ability, by 1933, of the Nicaraguan politicians and generals, who had "plunged" Nicaragua into "a destructive civil war" in 1926, "to cooperate loyally in a program to establish permanent peace". The "new spirit evident in the relations between the two parties" made Munro "hopeful for Nicaragua's future".[81]

This was followed a year later by a book on US relations with the Caribbean, in which Munro argued that Washington's "main objective" was "the elimination of the disorderly conditions which have prevented the economic development" of the region and to prevent foreign intervention. He was also convinced that, in the case of Central America, the region's "disorderly conditions" had "unquestionably improved" since the Washington Conference of 1907. In his view a number of the republics had made "distinct progress toward the development of political institutions based on constitutional methods". He felt that it would still be "several years" before the inhabitants of Central America could enjoy "permanently stable political institutions"; however, "the progress which has already been made toward this end has been sufficient materially to affect the basic factors governing" US foreign policy in Central America. Writing in 1934, Munro apparently felt that Central America had 'progressed' enough to make the Good Neighbor Policy possible and necessary.[82]

By the early 1930s, a number of other prominent historians and Latin American specialists took the view that US interventions in Nicaragua and elsewhere in the region had not had a sufficiently positive impact to make up for the 'anti-American' sentiment which had resulted.[83] As a result, they greeted the Good Neighbor Policy with even more approval than did Munro. While the Good Neighbor Policy was often articulated in vague terms, it centered on 'non-intervention' and a new US commitment to approach the region from what it was argued was a more considerate position, one that respected Latin American 'interests' and 'aspirations'.[84] Not surprisingly, however, overall support for the Good Neighbor Policy flowed from a range of expectations and somewhat different understandings of the history of US intervention in the region. This was a result of the continuing tension within the dominant professional discourses on Latin America between an emerging liberal internationalism and a more traditional isolationism, and between the rising Pan Americanism and the earlier Anglo-Saxonism. Liberal internationalists, such as Dexter Perkins and J. Fred Rippy, highlighted the Good Neighbor Policy's "cooperative aspects". However, they remained convinced that past interventions, despite the negative response south of the border, had in some instances been necessary to safeguard US security and US 'interests', and they envisioned future situations in which the negative results which might flow from "necessary interventions" would be ameliorated by the cooperation of a number of Latin American republics in multi-lateral interventions. Although Samuel Flagg Bemis (whose work will be discussed below), saw the US occupation of Nicaragua and the Caribbean republics as overwhelming positive for all concerned, he hoped for more US "restraint" in the case of unilateral intervention and he regarded the idea of cooperative intervention unfavorably. Bemis, and others, did not advocate restraint because of any profound concern for Latin American sentiment. In their view, Washington was now sufficiently powerful in the region to keep the Europeans out and tolerate a degree of "disorder" on the periphery. At the same time, from their perspective Latin America was "maturing" to a stage where there would be a qualitative and quantitative reduction in instability south of the border, in part because of the positive impact of the US over the preceding thirty years.[85]

The growing support of the dominant professional discourses on Latin America for a shift in US policy, along with the decision in Washington that US goals in the circum-Caribbean could be better served by diplomatic and economic intervention, had clearly helped precipitate the Good Neighbor Policy. However, the shift away from military intervention to 'non-intervention' and 'cooperation', was also a result of Latin American opposition and even a partial result of more searching criticism in North America. These critics included a number of radicals influenced by progressivism and marxism. Between 1920 and 1933 radical discourses on Latin America emerged. However, they lacked the institutional and organizational context, and the governmental backing, which was so important in giving the dominant professional discourses on Latin America their power and authority. In absolute terms the radical professional discourses on Latin America gained only limited purchase in relation to the dominant professional and foreign policy discourses in this period. However, the shift in US policy and the trend towards Pan Americanism was a partial response to the rise of radical theories of 'economic imperialism'. In the 1930s progressive and radical ideas were partially incorporated into the dominant professional discourses on Latin America on terms laid down by the dominant discourses.

One of the most important early North American radicals, whose career reflected the rise and fall of radicalism between the 1920s and 1945, was the journalist Carleton Beals. His work flowed from North American populism and progressivism, as well as marxism.[86] Beals, like many other radicals from the US and elsewhere, spent a considerable amount of time in Mexico in the 1920s. Beals was soon identified by US military intelligence as a "Bolshevik leader", even though his attitude towards the Communists in Mexico was hardly one of approval, and he had a strong antipathy towards orthodox marxism.[87] Apart from his journalistic pieces, which appeared in the **New Republic, Current History, The Nation** and **The Progressive,** Beals also produced a number of books on Mexico.[88] By the mid-1920s, along with Ernest Gruening and Frank Tannenbaum, he had emerged as a North American expert on Mexico. Beals and Tannenbaum's work in particular reflected the emergence of radical discourses on Latin America, which rested on a conflict model of social change, a structural approach and an emphasis on the economic forces driving US expansion.[89] At a time when the North American understanding of Latin America was the preserve of liberal diplomatic and colonial historians and of officials of the US government, a radical perspective on political and social change in Latin America lacked influence and authority. To the disappointment of Washington, Beals's interest in Mexico gradually expanded to include the rest of Latin America. And he continued to write sympathetically about revolutionary and labor movements, land reform and economic nationalism.

By the end of the 1920s Beals had turned his attention to Nicaragua, and one of the high points of his career was his interview with Sandino in February 1928. His visit to Nicaragua and Central America was later recounted in his book **Banana Gold**, in which he analyzed the region's history and articulated a highly critical perspective on US foreign policy in Central America and US intervention in Nicaragua. He relied on the concept of 'economic imperialism' to characterize US activity in the region and questioned the often-professed altruism of the United States' motives. Beals's conception of imperialism was based on the radical theories of imperialism which flowed from Hobson and Lenin. Highly critical of US commercial and financial interests, he accorded them a central position in his analysis. Beals concluded that US foreign policy in Central America was "dominated by ignorance, opportunism" and "self interest--usually the last". Furthermore, the "self interest" was not, in his view, "always national self interest, but the self-interest of special concessionaires, banking houses, large corporations, and even the self-interest of diplomatic representatives, promoting private deals". He argued that following the years of US "paternal tutelage" Nicaragua "had become the most backward and miserable of all Central American Republics".[90] Despite his anti-imperialism and his criticism of the racism inherent in US expansion, Beals's analysis, like the dominant discourses which he challenged, still relied on deterministic national and racial categories. For example, Beals characterized "dignity among southern peoples" as merely a "protective coloring", which sounded a "false note". In his view the "deeper qualities " were a "fierceness" and "brooding" which alternated with "abandon, rhythm" and "passion".[91]

In contrast to Beals's writings the work on US imperialism in Latin America by Scott Nearing reflected a more orthodox marxism. However, like Beals, Nearing's perspective had its origins in both marxism and in North American radical populism and progressivism. Nearing completed a bachelor's degree in economics in 1905, and a PhD in 1909 at the University of Pennsylvania, where he worked as an economics instructor from 1906 to 1914. In 1914 the University of Pennsylvania promoted him to assistant professor of economics. From this point on, Nearing's career trajectory exemplified how both academic institutions and the dominant professional discourses worked to exclude radicals and radical approaches. In July 1915, Nearing was informed by the Board of Trustees that he would not be rehired. This was despite the widespread respect for Nearing among the faculty and his popularity with the students. The American Association of University Professors branded Nearing's dismissal as "an infringement of academic freedom" and considerable public debate attended the issue; however, he did not get his job back. He went on to teach at the University of Toledo for two years until he was fired from that post for his opposition to US involvement in World War I.[92] Nearing joined the CPUSA in 1927, only to be expelled in 1930, after he went ahead with the publication of **The Twilight of Empire**. It had been rejected by the CPUSA's official publishing house because Nearing's approach to imperialism as a phenomenon which stretched back to antiquity contradicted Lenin's characterization of imperialism as a post-1870 development.[93] Apart from **The Twilight of Empire**, Nearing wrote other books on imperialism over the years.[94] His most influential book was the one he wrote in the mid-1920s with Joseph Freeman, who was a member of the CPUSA for many years.[95]

Their book, **Dollar Diplomacy: A Study in American Imperialism**, examined US foreign policy and expansion world-wide, but included a chapter on the Caribbean. Despite the view of the CPUSA that Nearing's work represented an unacceptable deviation from Lenin's theory of imperialism, Nearing and Freeman articulated a relatively conventional marxist theory of imperialism. They argued that by the eve of World War I "economic interest" had driven the major European "business groups" to expand their activities into "one or more of the undeveloped continents--Africa, Asia, Australia, the Americas". These European economic interests had been followed and supported by the naval and military might of the European powers. This development, in their view, corresponded to a particular "stage in the development of economic surplus". Imperialism represented "the rise of the trading class to power" and it was "a phase through which society passes at a certain stage in its economic development".[96] This approach relied on economic determinism and envisioned the inevitable passage of all human history through set stages. In contrast to Beals, and even to much of the liberal scholarship, Nearing and Freeman gave only limited attention to the countries that were being incorporated into the US empire, and the specific character of the impact of the US on Latin America was not subject to more than the most cursory discussion.[97]

Similar problems can be found in the work of the progressive historian Harry Elmer Barnes, who was the general editor of Nearing and Freeman's book, and a former student of Charles Beard. Barnes was a passionate advocate of progressivism and "social scientific" history.[98] **Dollar Diplomacy** was part of a series of studies on US imperialism, edited by Barnes and sponsored by the Fund for Public Service, that included Leland Jenks's book on Cuba and Melvin Knight's book on the Dominican Republic (Santo Domingo), both of which, as we have seen, were roundly criticized' in the pages of the **Hispanic American Historical Review**. The series also included J. Fred Rippy's book on Colombia, as well as a number of other books which looked mainly at US conomic imperialism in Latin America.[99] Each volume in the series opened with virtually the same editor's introduction by Barnes, a classic statement of economic determinism which represented the history of imperialism as the mechanical movement through a series of historical stages.[100] At the same time, although they were not as famous as **Dollar Diplomacy**, many of the radical works on US imperialism in Latin America which appeared in this period, including most of the studies which were published under the editorship of Barnes, actually took a less deterministic approach to economic imperialism than Nearing and Freeman, or that adopted by Barnes himself.[101] Jenks's book, for example, has been characterized recently by Jerald Combs as a "more subtle and accurate assessment of US imperialism in the Caribbean" than the work of Nearing, Freeman and Barnes.[102]

Despite the differences between the various writers, the early radicals emphasized the importance of economic forces and adopted a perspective that was anti-elitist and sympathetic to the peasants and workers of Latin America. At another level, however, they shared the rational, scientific and eurocentric assumptions which shaped the dominant professional discourses. Radical and marxist work in this period was the product of a series of discourses, beginning with Marx himself, which were based on a "universalizing narrative" about the rational progression of world history and which can be seen as an inverted version of the history of European and North American expansion. Regardless of its anti-capitalism, marxism has produced a eurocentric historical knowledge that acts in complicity with the very "system" which it has set itself in opposition against.[103] Although the radical studies of US economic imperialism in Latin America, which began to appear by the late 1920s, challenged the representation of US hegemony as a civilizing mission, the radicals articulated their own civilizing mission. At the same time, the overall importance of the progressive and/or radical discourses between 1920 and 1933 and beyond should not be overestimated. After 1945 some North American historians represented the entire first half of the twentieth century as an era in which progressive history, as exemplified by the work of Charles Beard, rose to considerable influence and even predominance in North American historiography.[104] However, historians writing in the Cold War era tended to overstate the scale of the progressive influence between World War I and World War II.[105] Progressivism and radical discourses on Latin America were most influential in the 1930s. At the height of the New Deal and the Good Neighbor Policy some progressive ideas were partially incorporated into US foreign policy and into the dominant professional discourses on Latin America in a fashion which defused their more radical political implications.

The Good Neighbor and 'Greater America' 1933-1945

The rise of the US to a position of hemispheric and then global power in the decade after the Good Neighbor Policy flowed from and ensured a shift in US policy beyond the circum-Caribbean. The Pan Americanism of US foreign policy was consolidated in this period, and academics and policy-makers increasingly took a broader view of the region. At the same time, as a result of Washington's growing involvement outside the Americas, North American historians, political scientists and international relations specialists increasingly viewed Latin America from a global perspective. There was limited direct interest in Central America and the circum-Caribbean in the 1930s and 1940s. Much of what was written in this period dealt with the region in the context of the looming war in Europe, or as part of Latin America as a whole. By the mid-1930s, this was reinforced by the view, articulated by the Council on Foreign Relations for example, that the Latin American economies, particularly in the larger republics such as Mexico and Brazil, represented a possible solution to the Depression in the US. One theme of the Council on Foreign Relations' Latin American study panel in the 1930s was the need for the lowering of tariffs and the general revision of discriminatory trade policies. Many members of the Council were also concerned about the danger of the Latin American countries defaulting on North American loans and the poor future for subsequent loans and investments. [106] By the end of the 1930s some of these recommendations were reflected in US policy in Latin America.

It was in the 1930s that 'Latin American studies' was consolidated as an institutional force and as a series of professional discourses. Although the **Hispanic American Historical Review** was founded in 1918, and the first professional association for historians of Latin America, the Conference on Latin American History, appeared at the end of the 1920s, the "coming of age of Latin American history" is usually traced to the mid-1930s. The production of professional aids, such as the **Handbook of Latin American Studies** which began in 1936, intensified in this period.[107] While North America's growing coterie of Latin Americanists devoted their attention to the history of the colonial period and the nineteenth century, as well as producing economic studies and some general diplomatic history, the number of professional Latin American specialists was still small. The professional discourse continued to be characterized by a high degree of dependence on the government, a situation which only increased in the late 1930s and 1940s. Although Latin America as a whole had clearly emerged as an object of US foreign policy and as an object of professional study, Washington's growing interest outside the hemisphere, and the dependent character of the emergent 'Latin American studies' profession, ensured that the scope and power of the dominant professional discourses remained limited. By the late 1930s, the dominant professional discourses on Latin America were increasingly shaped by the imperatives of the looming war in Europe and Asia. An emphasis on hemispheric solidarity in the face of Nazi Germany and Imperial Japan was of central concern to Latin American specialists.

The US focused its attention elsewhere in the 1930s and 1940s not because Latin America was no longer important, but because US policy-makers perceived Washington's position in Latin America as stable, while the situation in Europe and Asia, as well as domestic problems, were seen as far more in need of attention. By the 1920s the European powers no longer represented a significant threat, and the North American economic position in Latin America was stronger than ever. Although Roosevelt's approach to the circum-Caribbean retreated from direct military intervention, it built on earlier US policy and consolidated US dominance in the region. The 1930s saw the emergence of a number of 'stable' dictatorships in the circum-Caribbean and in Latin America as a whole, many of which were dependent on Washington. In Central America, for example, Jorge Ubico, the godson of Justo Ruffino Barrios (who had been supreme ruler of Guatemala from 1871-1885), ruled his country from 1931-1944, while the ruthless General Maximiliano Hernandez Martinez established his dictatorship over El Salvador in 1931 and, like Ubico, remained in power until 1944. In 1932 Tiburcio Carias Andino emerged as dictator of Honduras, staying in office until 1948. In

Nicaragua Anastasio Somoza had disposed of the rebel nationalist leader Augusto Sandino by 1934 and, from his position as head of the National Guard, went on to rule the entire country until his assassination in 1956, when his sons took over.

Roosevelt's Good Neighbor Policy initially tolerated, and then welcomed, the emergence of dictatorships in the circum-Caribbean and Latin America. Dictators protected US economic interests and private property. They brought political stability and order without the cost and political problems associated with the direct military intervention of the previous decades. The New Deal expanded Washington's political influence in Latin America because the US government increasingly replaced the private North American banks as a supplier of loans. (This approach had first been advocated by William Jennings Bryan and then by Dana Munro, during his tenure as head of the Latin America desk at the State Department in the 1920s. They had emphasized that more direct control by Washington over loans to southern governments would offset the regimes' dependence on North American banks.) Roosevelt established the Export-Import Bank in 1934 to loan money to the US export industry to facilitate overseas sales. By the end of the 1930s the Export-Import Bank was funding projects throughout Latin America. In Nicaragua, for example, the conditions attached to such loans included the stipulation that the largest Nicaraguan project be run by a North American engineer, that Washington have access to project and project-related records, that Washington was to approve certain expenditures and that US materials were used in construction. Of particular importance was the requirement that the Nicaraguans encourage those small industrial and agricultural businesses which complemented, rather than competed with, North American-based operations. The US also negotiated reciprocal trade treaties with the Central American republics which, although not terribly significant economically, had important political implications. The countries increased their imports from the US, becoming more dependent on US agricultural products in particular, in exchange for political recognition and support.[108] By the end of the 1930s Washington had also set up new structures linking the US military with its Latin American counterparts, providing forums in which military men from North and South could exchange ideas. By the outbreak of World War II, the US had almost completely superseded Britain and France as Latin America's main source of military equipment and officer training and advice. When the US entered the war in December 1941, almost all of Latin America lined up publicly behind Washington.[109] The changes in the relationship between the US and Latin America during the 1930s and the 1940s reflected a broad trend in which the North American economy experienced an extended period of "state-mediated expansion", while Washington policy-makers increasingly pursued national security as a global project.[110]

The changes in the practice of US foreign policy in Latin America between the early 1920s and the early 1940s flowed from a number of different sources but were clearly linked to a shift from Anglo-Saxonism to Pan Americanism. The emergence of the Good Neighbor Policy represented the growing power of Pan Americanism and coincided with the rise of an ever more optimistic assessment of the ability of the US to guide the countries of Latin America toward economic prosperity and even political democracy. Of course, this process was uneven. In the 1930s, under the influence of the post-World War I isolationism of the 1920s and the "anti-business isolationism" which continued to be strong right

up until US entry into World War II, the North American public and many
politicians continued to display limited interest in Latin America and foreign affairs
generally. The early years of the New Deal also reinforced this situation, insofar as
the promoters of the New Deal argued that international problems should be
neglected until a powerful and smoothly operating welfare state was in place to deal
with the debilitated North American economy. However, as the 1930s progressed
the internationalism of New Deal reformism became increasingly apparent.
Washington embarked on efforts to stimulate 'free trade' via government-initiated
tariff reciprocity and then on programs of government-sponsored and financed
economic expansion, particularly in Latin America, where the Depression had
undermined US trading and financial interests. After 1933 Washington sought to
gain credibility by contrasting the non-intervention and economic development
orientation of the Good Neighbor Policy with the earlier politico-military
interventionism. A central goal articulated by the proponents of the Good Neighbor
Policy was to substitute the outdated policy of "punishing" the United States'
southern neighbors for "uncivilized behavior", with a Pan American policy which
emphasized a program of hemispheric political and economic integration,
modernization and stabilization under US leadership.[111]

Following the proclamation of the Good Neighbor Policy in 1933,
Washington sought increasingly to establish a system of inter-American relations
based on cooperation within which, in theory, the US would both honor the
'independence' of the southern republics and enter into consultation and negotiations
regarding issues of inter-American and international concern. There were an
increasing number of inter-American conferences as the 1930s progressed, and
Washington laid out conference agendas, often dominated discussion and took the
lead in the implementation of any decisions which flowed from the inter-American
conferences. Although Pan Americanism after 1933 was relatively benevolent in
contrast to German and Japanese expansion in this period, or the situation in the
British and French empires, the Pan American system served primarily as a means
by which the US could maintain its hegemony in the western hemisphere. Despite
the stated anti-interventionism of the Good Neighbor Policy, the US, operating
within a structure of Pan American cooperation, was even more interventionist
than previously. But US 'intervention' was carried out by ambassadors, foreign-
service officers, economic and military advisers backed up by economic assistance
and private capital, instead of the Marines and gunboats of the past. For example,
in August 1940, the government created the Office for the Coordination of
Commercial and Cultural Relations Between the American Republics (its name
was soon changed to Office of the Coordinator of Inter-American Affairs [CIAA])
and the first director was Nelson A. Rockefeller. The CIAA served to channel US
economic and cultural influence throughout the hemisphere to counter Axis
propaganda and economic incursions and, as we will see in Chapter 2, became a
major employer of Latin American specialists during World War II.[112]

One of the goals of the Good Neighbor Policy after 1933, which was
eventually taken up by the Office of the Coordinator of Inter-American Affairs in
1940, was to generate an environment of appreciation and respect for Hispanic
American culture. However, in practice, especially by the time the CIAA appeared,
this had less to do with the appreciation of Hispanic culture and more to do with
using cultural relations as a conduit for the transmission of North American

influence. For the first time, under Roosevelt, the State Department explicitly pursued international cultural understanding as a component in its foreign policy agenda. The initial stimulus for this is thought to have come from Laurence Duggan, who was chief of the State Department's Division of the American Republics in the 1930s, and had previously worked as an assistant director of the Institute of International Education (IIE). The IIE had been set up in 1919 at the initiative of a number of prominent cultural and international relations philanthropists. Laurence Duggan's father, Stephen Duggan, a professor of Government at City College in New York, was the organization's first director. In the 1920s private support for the 'free' movement of ideas, from the emerging cultural-relations network based on foundations like the Carnegie Endowment and the Rockefeller Foundation, complemented US foreign policy, which emphasized an Open Door economic system and a minimum of 'state' intervention. However, the international climate of 1930s, characterized by the nationalist and statist approaches of Germany, the Soviet Union, Italy and Japan, threatened the private and independent approach to international cultural relations which had emerged in North America after World War I. At this juncture Assistant Secretary of State Sumner Welles, at Duggan's suggestion, began to articulate a government policy on cultural relations. In 1935, Welles characterized cultural relations as "but another aspect of the policy of the good neighbor", emphasizing that the US desired "political relations free of suspicion and misunderstanding, economic relations conducive to a healthy international trade and cultural relations leading to a wider appreciation of the culture and civilization of other peoples". Welles emphasized that the "breaking of barriers" in the cultural sphere was as important as in the political and the economic spheres.[113]

The grandiose rhetoric was followed by a relatively modest US-funded exchange program. (Still, in contrast to earlier government efforts, it was significant.) Samuel Guy Inman, a member of numerous Pan American organizations and an unstinting proponent of cultural ties in the Americas, was employed to guide the program, which saw the exchange of one professor and two students in 1937. By 1938, neither Inman nor Duggan was particularly happy with the program, which they had hoped would be a catalyzing agent encouraging universities to, in Duggan's words, "assume their proper responsibilities with respect to educational interchange".[114] More government support was not forthcoming until information was received that extra-hemispheric powers, such as Germany, were offering the governments of Latin America technical advisers, and academics as well as student exchanges. This caused the basis for the cultural program to shift from "idealistic rhetoric" to the "language of national interest". In May 1938 the State Department set up the Division of Cultural Relations, but Welles continued to emphasis that the majority of US cultural-relations work was still expected to be done by private universities and philanthropic organizations. Although much of the rhetoric surrounding the emergence of the Division's new cultural programs (which centered on international education via lectures, courses on foreign relations, seminars, radio broadcasts) was couched in universal terms, the programs themselves were carried out mainly in the western hemisphere. They were shaped by a growing US concern for hemispheric solidarity in the face of the threat of war in Europe and Asia. At the same time, the Division's first director explained that the concentration of cultural-relations programs on the area defined by the Good Neighbor Policy was not a result of regional interests or external pressures. In his view, the cultural element in the Good Neighbor policy provided a model for the establishment of the rule of law, liberal economic relations and cultural understanding which could be applied globally. The establishment of the Division of Cultural Relations and its initial programs can be seen as the eventual inclusion of the government in, and the general refinement of, a system of international intellectual and cultural exchange which had been initiated by the private philanthropic foundations, following the foundation of the Carnegie Endowment for International Peace in 1910.[115]

Despite the government's view that North American universities were not doing enough to facilitate international understanding and cultural exchange, by the late 1920s some university-based Latin American specialists were increasingly predicting that Latin America was headed in a direction both similar and complementary to the US. They also emphasized the similarities rather than the differences between the histories and cultures of North America and Hispanic America. This interpretation, which became known as the 'Greater America' thesis and meshed with the growing strength of Pan Americanism, allowed North Americans, both specialists and non-specialists, to think they 'understood' Latin America and that the US could guide the region towards its common future.[116] A good popular example of this trend was a book by Wallace Thompson which emphasized that the "culture" of North America and Latin America originated in Europe and that they possessed a common pioneer experience. He talked of the inevitability of greater economic integration between the US and Latin America, and what was characterized as the growing political convergence of North and South. Thompson argued that although the republics of Central and South America remained politically and economically "backward", in contrast to the US, a number of the states in the region were already advancing slowly but surely "toward true democracy", and would ultimately embrace a style of government like the government of the United States. However, in his view the "real bond" between North and South was economic, and the US and Latin America were "moving with firmer tread through the channels of our common interests in commerce, in culture and our continental destiny".[117]

The most influential proponent of the 'Greater America' thesis was University of California (Berkeley) historian Herbert Eugene Bolton. The ground work for Bolton's idea of a 'Greater America' had been laid in the 1920s, during which time the most overt Anglo-Saxonist interpretations of Latin America came under siege. Bolton was a founder of the **Hispanic American Historical Review** and a major historian of the Spanish frontier in North America.[118] In 1932 he gave a now-famous address to the American Historical Association, in which he argued that the history of the Americas should be studied as a comprehensive whole rather than as two or more discrete units. The main themes of his "Epic of Greater America" were those aspects of the history of the Americas which, he argued, all Americans had in common. These characteristics included the hemisphere's common colonial origins, the ongoing transplantation of culture from Europe, the exploitation and marginalization of the indigenous peoples, the plundering of the natural resources, the emergence of, and competition between, new nations, and what was believed to be a shared and ongoing struggle for political stability and economic progress.[119]

Bolton's 1932 address to the American Historical Association symbolized the shift in the professional discourses on Latin America from Anglo-Saxonism to Pan Americanism. Bolton's call for Pan American history was favorably received in many quarters, and what became known as the 'Bolton Theory' stimulated considerable discussion and debate. But interest in the unitary and/or comparative study of the history of the Americas implied by Bolton's article faded after 1945.[120] The failure of Bolton's 'Epic of Greater America' to generate much scholarly research was a result of the continued strength of the conventional demarcation between the study of US history and the study of Latin American history. At the same time, Bolton focused primarily on the colonial history of the Americas. And as the independence era in North American and Latin American history gained importance for US historians, Bolton's significance faded.[121] Furthermore, in the context of Latin America's continued position as an object of US foreign policy, the entire edifice of post-1945 Latin American studies in North America rested more than ever on an implicit comparison between North and South.

As has been emphasized, the inter-American system which emerged after 1933 did not operate in the egalitarian fashion which the rhetoric of Pan Americanism proclaimed. The new-found regard for Latin American history and culture and the various cultural exchange programs were generally self-serving and ethnocentric. At the same time, some proponents of 'Greater America', such as the missionary Samuel Guy Inman, an indefatigable Pan Americanist who emphasized cultural understanding as the key to better hemispheric relations, remained optimistic and continued to assert that cultural understanding, even unity, was attainable in the Americas.[122] The theme of a 'common history' survived in the rhetoric and the work of government employees such as Duggan.[123] And while explicitly comparative and/or unitary studies of the Americas have never been significant, the general Pan American sentiment embodied in the notion of a 'Greater America' was certainly reflected in the work of many North American specialists who wrote about Latin America. 'Greater America' meshed with the Good Neighbor Policy and the growing desire on the part of the US to develop a hemispheric security structure. And the idea of a 'common history', with revisions, has continued to inform the work of many North American historians and Latin American specialists. As we will see some version of Pan Americanism remains central to the dominant North American discourses on Latin America.[124]

Although Bolton's 'theory' had a limited effect on the production of a unitary and/or explicitly comparative history of the Americas, he himself played an important role in the teaching, researching and writing of Latin American history. He has been characterized by Robert McCaughey as the "effective founder" of 'Latin American studies' in North America. In 1920, by which time Bolton was chairman of the History Department at Berkeley, a post he held for twenty years, he established an undergraduate history course entitled "History of the Americas", which remained a standard course in the department until 1945 and was often taken by as many as a thousand students a year. Bolton also attracted large numbers of graduate students. Over the course of his thirty-three years at Berkeley, he supervised 350 master's degrees and 105 doctorates.[125] Bolton was not regarded, even by some of his contemporaries, as a particularly gifted writer. But he produced a number of books, and wrote numerous articles for scholarly and popular journals.[126] He was a narrative historian. His work has been compared unfavorably to the work of Clarence H. Haring of Harvard, who produced few books and articles but is generally regarded as more rigorous and sophisticated than Bolton.[127] Nevertheless, of Bolton's 105 PhD students fifty-four did their work in Latin American history and over forty of them pursued academic careers. At least ten of these rose to the position of full-professor and a number of them, such as J. Fred Rippy, who was Professor of History at the University of Chicago for many years, are generally acknowledged as major historians of Latin America. Apart from Rippy, Bolton's most famous students included prominent Latin Americanists such as Charles E. Chapman, who remained at Berkeley and as we have seen was a prominent Cuba specialist and a major figure in the **Hispanic American Historical Review**, Woodrow W. Borah, who went to Princeton, John Tate Lanning, who went to Duke University, Irving A. Leonard, who began teaching at Michigan, and J. Lloyd Mecham and Charles Wilson Hackett, who took up posts at the University of Texas, as well as numerous others, such as Lawrence F. Hill (Ohio State University), Jeffrey Johnson (Stanford University), George P. Hammond (University of New Mexico) and Alfred Barnaby Thomas (University of Oklahoma and the University of Alabama), who fanned out across North America in the years after World War I.[128]

Under Bolton's guidance, in a period when most North American universities were still unprepared to commit significant resources or time to Latin America as a field of inquiry, Berkeley, between the 1920s and 1945, emerged as a major North American nexus for 'Latin American studies'. However, Bolton was perceived as a "mass producer" of PhDs, and many of his students found it hard to get academic jobs, particularly at the important eastern and northern universities. Although J. Fred Rippy taught at the University of Chicago for many years and gained work for the Council on Foreign Relations, while other former students rose to the top of the historical profession, this may have been despite their connection to Bolton and their specialization in Latin America, rather than because of it. Throughout this period many historians of Latin America were geographically and even socially isolated from the 'mainstream' of the North American historical profession. They occupied a subordinate position in relation to diplomatic historians and historians of Europe, as well as historians of North America itself. Although Bolton's contribution to the historical profession was acknowledged with his election to the post of president of the American Historical Association in the early 1930s, the study of Latin America remained relatively marginal to the institutionalization of the North American historical profession between 1898 and 1945. When Berkeley re-emerged as a major national center for Latin American research in the 1960s, at a time when academics were swamped with funding and grants, its pre-1945 reputation went unmentioned by Latin American specialists, who perceived Bolton as something of an "embarrassment".[129]

Of more long-term importance than Bolton's Berkeley was the previously mentioned Office of the Coordinator of Inter-American Affairs (CIAA), which was set up in 1940 and quickly became an important institutional focus for Latin American specialists. As we will see in Chapter 2, unlike Berkeley the CIAA had considerable direct significance for the development of 'Latin American studies' in the immediate post-1945 era. Its director, Nelson Rockefeller, was concerned about the fascist threat to the region. In 1940 he set the tone for the new approach to Latin America when he argued that "intellectual imperialism, the imperialism of ideas, was at the moment just as serious a threat to the security and defense of the hemisphere as the possibility of a military invasion".[130] The dynamic CIAA, which was explicitly regional in outlook, soon overshadowed the State Department's Division of Cultural Relations. By 1941 they had begun to work together in a Joint Committee on Cultural Relations, in which the State Department still more or less set policy, while the CIAA delivered the funds, which went to private organizations with the operational capability to carry out the various programs. By the end of 1941 hundreds of seminars on inter-American relations had been held across North America , while Pan Americanism was propagated in the school system using poster-making and essay-writing competitions. A whole range of organizations were enlisted to form links with similar organizations in Latin America and promote Pan Americanism. In this situation the mobilization of academics around a Pan American agenda was more successful than in the past. In the 1930s the Committee on Latin American Studies of the American Council of Learned Societies had made a limited effort to encourage research on Latin America with little success. At the end of the 1930s the more influential Social Science Research Council took up the cry, and in 1940 a Joint Committee on Latin American Studies was set up, with the University of Chicago anthropologist Robert Redfield, famous for his work on the Maya of the Yucatan and an influential figure in anthropology, as chairman.[131] The Joint Committee, which included the National Research Council after 1942, quite explicitly set out, in the words of a report produced by the geographer Preston James, "to focus the attention of North American social scientists on Latin American problems of pressing international concern, especially on those questions which are important in the formulation of American public policy".[132] The Committee advised the government and sought to develop 'Latin American studies' in North America and improve relations with Latin American academics. Throughout World War II the Committee's stature grew as government increasingly overshadowed the philanthropic foundations and lavished funds on Latin American research as part of the war effort.[133]

Hemispheric Security and the Advance of Civilization 1933-1945

Apart from growth of government-inspired Pan American programs and research in the 1930s and 1940s, and the work on colonial history (especially the Spanish borderlands) by historians such as Bolton, what North American research interest there was in Latin America appeared in the form of economic studies and diplomatic history.[134] As the world drifted toward war, this work was increasingly shaped by the view that Latin America needed to be incorporated into a US-led hemispheric defense system. One historian who whose work clearly reflected this theme by the late 1930s was J. Fred Rippy.[135] Rippy represented a major link between Latin American history, diplomatic history and economic history. He rose to prominence as a professor of history at the University of Chicago and, following a period as managing editor, he served as an advisory editor to the **Hispanic American Historical Review** until 1955, contributing numerous articles to the journal, most of which focused on economic themes.[136] He wrote a large number of books on Latin America over the course of his academic career, most of which dealt with some aspect of US-Latin American relations or economic history.[137] By the 1930s, his approach to diplomatic history, although clearly influenced by Pan American imperatives, tended to focus more on economic issues and was somewhat more sympathetic to the concept of 'economic imperialism' than many other diplomatic historians and Latin American specialists. In many ways his work encapsulated the way the radical critique of dollar diplomacy was brought, in a containing fashion, into the dominant professional discourses in the 1930s.

In 1935 the Council on Foreign Relations Latin American Committee decided to formally review the Good Neighbor Policy's first two years, and they hired Rippy to serve as a rapporteur and write a book, which they hoped would focus on altering North American "perceptions" of Latin Americans. Although Rippy had indicated his support for the Good Neighbor Policy before he was hired, many members of the group established to aid him in his research were hostile to the Good Neighbor Policy. There was concern that the project's terms of reference implied that the US had not been a 'good neighbor' prior to 1933. Rippy also came under considerable fire during the study group's discussion for his harsh criticism of US bankers who, in his view, had extended too many loans to the Latin Americans during the 1920s.[138] While his criticism of the bankers reflected the influence of progressivism by the 1930s, and economic factors were often given greater emphasis by writers such as Rippy, the primacy of politico-strategic considerations and idealistic motives was still asserted. This was apparent in his book on US relations with the circum-Caribbean, which reinforced the move towards a US-dominated hemispheric security system. In **The Caribbean Danger Zone** he emphasized the interplay between economic and strategic motives, and he was not uncomfortable with the term 'dollar diplomacy'. He sought to give it a wider definition than it had been given by both its proponents and many of its critics. He noted that dollar diplomacy was usually portrayed as the use of Washington's "influence" to "protect and promote the investments" of US citizens in China and Nicaragua under President Taft. In Rippy's view this was a narrow interpretation which failed to "take account of the fact that economic urges have always been a factor in the foreign relations of the United States as well as of all nations". He argued that of all the forces driving US foreign policy "none has been more constant or on the whole more decisive than the profit motive". At the same time he retreated from a radical economic interpretation, when he added that, in the broadest sense, dollar diplomacy was motivated by "strategy" and "benevolence" as well as "financial advantage", and "the profit motive was often supported by the strategy motive". He argued that it was "natural" for North American companies to receive governmental assistance "whenever they were powerful enough to influence local and national politics" in the United States.[139]

He argued further that after 1898 the "primary significance of everything" Washington "acquired" was "strategic". Rippy insisted that Central America and the Caribbean, which had been for many years "the most vital area" in Washington's "defense strategy", remained the "supreme danger zone" in the hemisphere. Rippy insisted that for the US the Caribbean basin was of such crucial strategic significance that the region's "domination by a strong aggressive power" could never be tolerated. He also argued that although US policy in the area had "departed more widely than elsewhere from ideal standards of international morality", the North American "conscience" had "always revealed itself" with "open and vigorous criticism". He emphasized that throughout history the "more prosperous and powerful nations" tended to articulate some sort of "civilizing mission" in tandem with "aggressive tendencies". He asserted that the "differences between various dynamic and prosperous nations" was primarily "a matter of intensity and method". Ultimately, adopting an exceptionalist interpretation, Rippy insisted that "because of its fundamental ideals of liberty, popular sovereignty, and equality of individual opportunity, it has been difficult for the United States to follow the path of imperialism without pangs of conscience". Writing in 1940 he asserted that "never have the people of the United States had a more profound respect for the rights, aspirations and sensitivities of their neighbors in the Caribbean region and elsewhere in Latin America". Rippy concluded that the Good Neighbor policy represented "a happy ending". At the same time he emphasized that the military withdrawal, and the renunciation of the protectorates, did not mean the rejection of the US need to intervene "to the extent deemed necessary to prevent" the region's "domination by an aggressive non-American power".[140] His work also reflected the continuing racism of the dominant discourses. He asserted that the "mixed and primitive inhabitants" of the region "tend to depress the level of culture wherever they constitute a large segment of the population, just as they depress the cultural level in some parts of the US". However, he said their low "level of culture" was because, "in their progress toward a higher plane of living", the inhabitants of the region "got a late start and encountered the handicaps of war, slavery, serfdom and other forms of exploitation as well as oppressive heat and debilitating disease". He concluded that there was no reason why "their ultimate capacity under equally favorable conditions" would not be "approximately equivalent to that of other human groups".[141]

With the steady drift toward war, other Latin American specialists followed in Rippy's path and served the war effort by writing about US-Latin American relations in a way which legitimated the US drive for hemispheric security. A book which emerged on the eve of the United States' entry into the Second World War was Wilfrid Hardy Callcott's **The Caribbean Policy of the United States 1890-1920**, which was still regarded as "useful" by Ralph Lee Woodward in the 1980s.[142] An historian of Mexico, Callcott turned to diplomatic history in the late 1930s. Like earlier writers such as Albert Bushnell Hart and Leo Rowe, Callcott characterized US expansion into Central America and the Caribbean in the period 1890-1920 as "inevitable", given the region's strategic and economic importance, the "rebirth of national pride" in the United States and the "renewed energies" which flowed from the "rapidly growing economic system".[143] By the 1930s, the professional discourses, as reflected in the work of Rippy and Calcott, were still structured by Anglo-Saxonism and ideas about a US 'mission', but they increasingly centered on Pan Americanism and a proto-liberal development theory. North American specialists on Latin America were more willing to perceive Latin Americans as capable of achieving a level of political and economic progress and development similar to that of the US, under the tutelage of a benevolent and superior North America. At the same time, the dominant professional discourses on Latin America, like US foreign policy in this era, were based on the assumption that there was no significant contradiction between US interests and the goals and aspirations of the people of Latin America.

This amalgam of Anglo-Saxon racism and an emergent Pan American liberal developmentalism was reflected in Samuel Flagg Bemis's famous historical synthesis on inter-American relations, which appeared in 1943. Bemis and Rippy demarcated the interpretive boundaries of the 'Latin American studies' profession between World War I and World War II. The continued existence of the Anglo-Saxonist racism of an earlier era was particularly apparent in Bemis's work. But the work of both authors reflected the growing power of Pan Americanism by the 1940s. Rippy's work gave some emphasis to economic forces in US foreign policy and articulated a liberal internationalist position. Bemis's work represented a defensive politico-strategic interpretation of US foreign policy and was unilateralist and even isolationist. Bemis's 1943 book, which was much broader in scope than Rippy's monograph, was quite possibly the most influential single book on inter-American history until the 1960s.[144] It came relatively late in Bemis's career and is also regarded as the "most controversial" book he ever wrote; however, despite its rather ponderous style, it was widely read and highly regarded.[145] Writing in the late 1980s, Lester D. Langley argued that Bemis had "brilliantly assessed" Washington's foreign policy in Latin America, and his book remained "the essential starting point". Langley took the view that Bemis's "classic account" was "unsurpassed for its sustained defense" of Washington's foreign policy and had "yet to be satisfactorily answered".[146]

During the first half of the twentieth century, Samuel Flagg Bemis was one of the most influential North American diplomatic historians writing about US diplomacy in Latin America and elsewhere.[147] Born in rural Massachusetts in 1891, Bemis began graduate work at Harvard on the eve of the First World War and eventually took up a professorship in history at Yale, where he remained until his retirement at the beginning of the 1960s.[148] In the inter-war years Bemis leaned towards isolationism. By the mid 1930s he was heartened by the "liquidation of imperialism" and perceived the emergence of a new neutralism.[149] While most North American historians of Latin America were supporters of Roosevelt's New Deal and the Good Neighbor policy in Latin America, Bemis, despite his generally positive view towards the Good Neighbor Policy, and the "liquidation of imperialism", was critical of Roosevelt's New Deal. In a 1934 letter to William E. Dodd of the University of Chicago, Bemis warned that the US stood "powerless and on the verge of collapse for want of a strong national government". He insisted that what was needed was a "benevolent dictator".[150] He was also a devoted anti-communist, and in 1938 he warned that the Mexican government's nationalization of its oil industry was the result of a "Communist conspiracy" directed at the United States.[151] With the outbreak of war in Europe, Bemis began to advocate an isolationist policy for the United States. At a 1939 meeting with officials from the State Department, Bemis asserted that history had demonstrated that where the US had "stuck" to its "continental position" it had "made no serious mistake in diplomacy"; however, where it had "departed from that in pursuit of imitative imperialism" it had made its "first serious mistakes". He advised that the US strengthen its position in the Western Hemisphere. He resigned from the Institute of Pacific Relations in 1939 because he said it was "pushing toward indirect intervention in the present Sino-Japanese War". In 1940 he insisted that the US could do nothing more for Europe, and Washington should concentrate all its energy on ensuring that "our continent and its outlying citadels" were "as invulnerable as possible". He was convinced that a war between the US and Japan was not in either nation's interests, but by early 1941 he no longer thought it could be avoided. Once war broke out Bemis did not criticize the government.[152]

Bemis's **The Latin American Policy of the United States** was written against this background. In it he emphasized politico-strategic, military and security motives, as well as a missionary impulse, as causes of US expansion in the late nineteenth and twentieth centuries, while generally downplaying economic, commercial and financial considerations. Bemis also emphasized that at the end of the nineteenth century "there blossomed forth an ideology based on Darwinism, a new and evangelical Manifest Destiny overseas for a chosen race, the 'Anglo-Saxon race'". Bemis criticized the social darwinism and Christian chauvinism of the "new imperialism" as an "imitation of British policy" which ultimately "misled the exuberant apostles of the New Manifest Destiny into areas of the globe beyond the real interests of the United States". Although Bemis derided Anglo-Saxonism and racism generally, his own work, like the professional discourses on Latin America before 1945, was still shaped by ideas about the superiority of Anglo-Saxon race and North American ideas and institutions. While Bemis argued that the conquest of the Philippines was a mistake, he asserted that the interests of the US were vitally concerned in Hawaii and the circum-Caribbean.[153]

In Bemis's interpretation, the US drive for empire in the circum-Caribbean and beyond was defensive. He argued that regardless of the "mistakes" made at the beginning of the twentieth century by "a youthful power in the name of those false gods, world power and imperialism, the sound core of American imperialism was essentially protective, conceived to defend the continental homeland". According to Bemis, this was substantiated by the 1930s, when the US "largely sloughed off that dominion over alien peoples that is the badge of imperialism", while continuing to control those outposts that were important to the defense of the continent even though this, at times, necessitated "a certain minimum control over foreign folk". The overarching interpretation that emerged from Bemis's book was that, in the context of the major changes to the global political and naval order at the end of the nineteenth century, the US motives for a number of interventions in the Caribbean and Central America were essentially defensive. A concern for continental security was represented as the central and natural factor in US expansion, especially in Central America. According to Bemis, these interventions resulted in "a short-lived benevolent imperialism" or "protective imperialism"--"an imperialism against imperialism" which "did not last long" and "was not really bad. This was the central feature of Bemis's interpretation of imperialism. His work represented US foreign policy and US imperialism as fundamentally different from European imperialism. For Bemis, the exceptional character of US foreign policy was rooted in the democratic outlook of the North American public. Writing at the height of World War II, Bemis argued that the "liquidation" of the "ill-fitting imperialism", and the rise of the Good Neighbor Policy, was "just in time" to ensure hemispheric solidarity when the German and Japanese threat appeared on the horizon.[154]

The idea that US imperialism after 1898 was a short-lived experiment was not an interpretation that was confined to Bemis's work. For example, Bemis's friend and contemporary Julius Pratt also argued along the same lines.[155] Not only did Bemis, like Pratt, see US imperialism as short-lived, he did not approve of the term 'dollar diplomacy'. For example, US intervention in Nicaragua was not, argued Bemis, "designed to profit private interests", but to "support" US foreign policy. Furthermore, insisted Bemis, the US interventions in Nicaragua and elsewhere were also motivated by "a certain characteristic missionary impulse" to aid the Nicaraguans and the inhabitants of the other countries in which the US intervened "by stabilizing their governments and economies."[156] Bemis was adamant that it was "unjust" to trace US intervention in Nicaragua to the "controlling power of private vested interests over the United States government". He argued that, despite the mistakes, there was no doubt that, behind the intervention "was an honest intent, at least, to stabilize and strengthen" the political situation in Central America, by replacing Zelaya's self-aggrandizing dictatorship with a "truly representative and independent government" and also "to further a union of all the Central American states on the foundation of the Washington conventions." Bemis argued that the main motive behind Washington's promotion of a "regional peace structure" was the politico-strategic protection of the Panama Canal, which would soon be finished, and to contain the possible development of an alternative canal route which was not under US control.[157] Bemis also interpreted the more general US impact on Nicaragua throughout this period as beneficial, and expressed the view that a more intensive occupation would have been of even greater benefit to Nicaragua.[158]

In keeping with Bemis's emphasis on defensive, politico-strategic and security motives, his discussion of economics was aimed at challenging what he characterized as the "myths" of "dollar diplomacy" and "economic imperialism". His refutation of both "myths" was based on a slippery notion of the connection between political sovereignty and economic control. He argued that Washington's "interventions" had been "part of a 'large' strategy of continental security", and "Wall Street had very little if anything to do with it except by invitation of the Government". He emphasized that the US bank loans allowed the republics to make good on their debts, after which "the protectorates received back their complete independence". Bemis argued that "economic imperialism" was "the use of power" by a foreign state "against the will of a foreign people", and direct investments in Latin America by US nationals could not, he concluded, be characterized as "economic imperialism". He lamented that US "direct investments" in the region (which in 1939 amounted to $2,963,000,000 dollars--43% of all US direct investment overseas) had been used to attribute "a **colonial** status" to some Latin American republics, similar to European colonies in Asia. Unfortunately, argued Bemis, "such assertions completely ignore the very obvious fact that the latter colonies are under British and Dutch sovereignties, which control the economy of the countries, whilst Latin American countries are under their own sovereignty to which their economy is subjected". Bemis argued that, although "there were some rare instances" in which sovereignty was violated in the past, "generally speaking", the US did not attempt to "control" the economy except to regulate the loans and "to prevent them from increasing to an amount beyond the country's reasonable capacity to pay, and to preserve service on the refunded loans". And these interventions were all "liquidated" by the 1930s. Bemis was convinced that "any dispassionate study" of US economic relations with Latin America, "shows that" the "exploitation" was "the other way around". In his view the southern republics had "exploited the (private) capital of the United States".[159]

Bemis's analysis of 'dollar diplomacy' and 'economic imperialism' indicated the way in which the dominant professional discourses on Latin America constituted its objects of study in a way that placed them outside the power relations that underpinned inter-American relations. In Nicaragua, for example, the United States exerted substantial political and economic influence, regardless of its formal recognition of the "sovereignty" of the government. Also in the period Bemis was writing about, the United Fruit Company exerted substantial influence on the governments of Guatemala, Honduras and Costa Rica, where its operations were most substantial. Despite his explicit discussion of dollar diplomacy and economic imperialism, Bemis managed to ignore the United Fruit Company. It was not referred to once, although his book dealt with Central America and the Caribbean at length. The exclusion of the United Fruit Company from his analysis was in keeping with his general perspective that 'dollar diplomacy' and 'economic imperialism' were misleading terms, and with his conviction that private economic interests did not influence US policy in any meaningful way. Prior to 1945, the task of directly defending the United Fruit Company was left to writers of more popular studies, such as Frederick Adams, Samuel Crowthers and Charles Morrow Wilson.[160] Wilson's work lacked the methodological rigor of the professional historians but paralleled their preoccupation in the late 1930s and early 1940s with generating hemispheric solidarity. His work also clearly reflected the idea of a US 'mission' in the region and the rise of Pan Americanism. An early version of liberal development theory, which would become central to the dominant discourses on Latin America after 1945, was also apparent. Wilson was a journalist and corporate consultant rather than an historian, but he attained a position as a Latin American 'expert' because of his experience in the region. In the early 1940s he emphasized the common interests and the 'common history' shared by the United States and Central America and the mutual benefits of 'modernization' under US leadership.[161]

Although Wilson's work reflected a more popular style, and he placed greater emphasis than some other writers did on the role of 'free-enterprise' in Latin American progress, the similarities between his work and Bemis's work, and Wilson's relationship with the United Fruit Company, locate both writers in the dominant professional discourses on Latin America. Like Wilson, Bemis emphasized the need for US initiative in the economic sphere, although he emphasized government rather than private initiative. Bemis talked about "the new dollar diplomacy", which developed in the late 1930s and began to deal increasingly with the southern republics' "foreign debts" as part of an "inter-governmental relationship" with Washington. Bemis explained the emergence of the "new dollar diplomacy" (which he infused with a positive meaning, in contrast to his earlier distaste for the use of the term 'dollar diplomacy') as a response on the part of the US to the failure of "private capital" to take an "interest in exporting itself in the old sense", which had led the republics of Central and South America to apply directly to the US government. The US government, via the Export-Import Bank and the Treasury's Stabilization Fund, both set up in 1934, and the Federal Loan Agency, founded in 1939, increasingly channeled public funds to the republics of Latin America. Bemis uncritically quoted the Assistant Secretary of State for Inter-American Affairs, Adolf A. Berle Jr., to explain the motives behind the "new dollar diplomacy". According to Berle, and this was a view which Bemis supported, Washington sought "opportunities for sound development which might add to the general safety, security, and well-being of the Western Hemisphere". Berle claimed that Washington's "new dollar diplomacy" in Latin America aimed at nothing less than "*a general advance in civilization*", a turn of phrase which Bemis liked so much he repeated two pages later, and again in his conclusion. For Bemis the "new dollar diplomacy" was an "expression of the American mission"; however, the "basic motive", in his view, was still the unchanging "political objective" of US foreign policy in Latin America: the "security of the Continental Republic". This security had now "come to be considered inseparable from 'the general safety, security, *and well-being* of the Western Hemisphere", and which in Bemis's view contributed to "the *general advance of civilization*".[162]

Bemis clearly subscribed to a US 'mission' to bring about this "advance of civilization", and he assumed that the US was more civilized than Latin America. And although his book bore evidence of the emerging Pan Americanism and even the more secular ideas about economic and political development, his effort to put the economic and political advance of the Americas in a climatological context pointed to the continuity of Anglo-Saxonist assumptions about race. His analysis, which was explicitly based on the early twentieth century climatological and racial ideas of Ellsworth Huntington, and called into question the likelihood that Latin America would ever progress economically and politically. His assumptions about race were ultimately based on a conflation of climatological and biological racism. He was not altogether convinced that "white civilization" could survive in, or belonged in, the tropics. He argued that unlike much of South and Central America, the "heart" of North America was one of the "choicest areas of the globe for the habitation and sustenance of civilization". According to Bemis, North America was "endowed with a climatological optimum for man, so necessary for the best of human health, physical and mental energy, and social progress". One of Latin America's "great natural handicaps" was that it had "no share at all of the climatological optimum".[163]

Without equivocation, he asserted that it was: "a scientific fact of political, economic, and social geography, that the areas of best and second-best climatic energy coincide geographically with the more impressive evidences of human civilization, such as maximum wheat yield, maximum of professional occupations, maximum of industrial production, greatest number of schools and colleges, of automobiles and of telephones per capita, maximum of railway networks, and best human health. All these imply social progress and political stability. There are striking exceptions to this index, such as some of the fine arts; but on the whole we cannot escape the conclusion that favorable climate is a necessary basis of modern civilization". Bemis concluded that "if the lowland tropics" were clearly inhospitable to "white populations", a view which "the best scientific opinion" supported, then "civilization" might "develop" in the "vast tropical low regions" of Central and South America, if it developed at all, "on some other than a pure Caucasian basis". In Latin America prior to the Spanish conquest, Bemis said, the "most advanced culture" was confined to "the tropical highlands and to occasional fertile river valleys in the tempered western coast". In these "more hospitable regions", which extended into present-day Bolivia, Ecuador and Colombia, and included the central plateau of Mexico, "it was neither too hot for vigorous enterprise nor too cold to live without artificial warmth." Furthermore, asserted Bemis, "tropical lowlands" not only represented "a barrier to white civilization", but it was "at least an open question whether today any advancing civilization, white, yellow, red, or brown, can develop or even endure in the unmitigated heat of the tropics; none has done so yet".[164]

Bemis's work perpetuated the idea that the tropics have been jinxed with a "primordial curse". Apart from its environmental determinism, and its significance primarily as a post-facto North American and Western European rationale, this assumption is in direct contradiction to the historical existence of the so-called "great civilizations" of ancient history, centered on the Indus Valley, Mesopotamia and Egypt, as well as the Mayan civilization, all of which are overlooked by Bemis. All of these 'civilizations' prospered in primarily tropical areas.[165] Bemis's views on race and North American expansion in the tropics were linked to wider assumptions about race and civilization which structured the European colonial discourses on Asia and Africa between the second half of the nineteenth century and the middle of the twentieth century. More specifically he also reflected earlier influential commentators on US foreign policy at the turn of the century, such as anti-imperialist Carl Shurz and pro-imperialist Theodore Roosevelt. They argued, in order to both attack and support US imperial expansion, that white people who lived in the tropics were gradually corrupted by it and/or that democracy did not develop in the tropics.[166] Bemis measured the history of Latin America against a nationalistic interpretation of the political and economic progress of the US. Latin America's failure to achieve the level of civilization of the US was ultimately traced to racial and meteorological handicaps. Although this view was increasingly submerged by Pan Americanism and liberal economic and social-scientific notions about development, earlier ideas about North American superiority remained embedded in the professional discourses and legitimated the US hegemonic position.

The shift from Anglo-Saxonism to Pan Americanism occurred in the context of the partial incorporation of progressive and/or radical ideas into the dominant professional discourses on Latin America. At the same time, some radicals and progressives continued to challenge the dominant discourses and US foreign policy. For example, in the 1930s Charles Beard criticized Washington's role in the expansion of private North American investment and trade, and pointed to dollar diplomacy in Nicaragua as a clear instance in which public interest had been subordinated to private interests. In sharp contrast to Bemis's image of US imperialism as a short-lived aberration in which economic factors played little or no role, Beard's approach pointed to broad imperial tendencies in US foreign policy and gave economic forces far more consideration.[167] Beard's work increasingly found in US foreign policy the source of the failure of the North American promise. By the mid-1930s Beard's approach to US diplomatic history was both revisionist and isolationist, and he increasingly represented the history of US foreign policy as "tragedy". While he remained located in the radical discourses, he moved increasingly towards an interpretation of the domestic history of the US as "virtuous" and "democratic", while the US tradition in foreign policy was portrayed as "corrupt" and "anti-democratic".[168]

Although Beard shared Bemis's isolationism in the 1930s, their work pointed to the rival character of the radical and liberal/conservative discourses. Beard was a progressive, and at the core of his growing isolationism and revisionism in the inter-war years was his ongoing commitment to progressive domestic reform.

As long as he was convinced that a sustained or expanded US role in foreign affairs would further his goal of a "collectivist democracy" or "worker's republic" in North America, he remained internationalist in his outlook; however, once he became convinced that his life-long goal was hampered by Washington's foreign obligations he shifted towards isolationism. The Depression and the rise of Nazism strengthened his isolationism. In two books which appeared in 1934, he made explicit his view that war was the inevitable result of international rivalry fuelled by a scramble for markets. In his view overseas commerce was advantageous to a minority in North America at the expense of the majority and was not crucial to the republic's economy. As a result the US "national interest" was best served if Washington curbed its support for foreign commerce, kept out of military and diplomatic problems in Europe and Asia, devoted its energies to resolving the United States' domestic problems and stood as a model to other countries.[169] The radical discourses lacked the institutional authority of the dominant professional discourses, and with the onset of World War II they were completely marginalized. As we will see radical professional discourses did not return to a position of even relative influence until the end of the 1960s.

Conclusion: Civilizing The South 1898-1945

Between the Spanish-American War and the Second World War a number of US diplomatic historians who wrote about Latin America could be found in the commanding heights of the North American historical profession. They spoke with authority as influential representatives of the dominant professional discourses on Latin America. Along with the diplomatic historians, Latin American history specialists monopolized the study of Latin America from the appearance of the **Hispanic American Historical Review** in 1918 until World War II. The professional historians relied on US power for their authority. In this period the relationship between the vast majority of Latin American specialists and the makers of US foreign policy was characterized by shared ideas about Latin America. They assumed that there were considerable overall benefits for Latin America associated with its growing political and economic linkages to the United States. In the years between 1898 and the early 1920s North American historians justified the US right to intervene in the circum-Caribbean in racial supremacist terms. They also assumed that US superiority conferred on it a special role in Latin America as a whole. Despite the emergence by the 1890s of Pan Americanism as a set of ideas about hemispheric cooperation and the organization and infrastructure to go with it, Pan Americanism was hardly reflected in US policy in the circum-Caribbean until the 1930s.

While the changes wrought by World War I eventually ushered in a new phase of US expansion in the circum-Caribbean, a time when the US ostensibly turned more attention to the uplift of Latin American society, US foreign policy continued to be more concerned with punishment than with cooperation and development. By the end of the 1930s, however, the various ideas associated with Pan Americanism had risen to predominance, and Latin American specialists and US policy-makers began to articulate an early version of liberal development theory, which became a key feature of US foreign policy in the years after 1945. This was connected to the reliance of North American historians on an idealized version of North American history as a model by which progress and the "advance of civilization" in Latin America was interpreted. Throughout the period from 1898 to 1945, despite the growing importance of Pan Americanism to the study of Latin America and to the practice of US foreign policy, and despite the growing strength of more secular ideas about historical development, the emerging 'Latin American studies' profession continued to be shaped by racist and nationalistic attitudes about a US civilizing mission. And this trend continued into the Cold War era as the US civilizing mission in Latin America became an anti-communist modernizing mission. And despite important changes, Latin American studies in the Cold War era continued to reflect its origins in the first half of the century, when a racial pride in the perceived superiority of the North American historical model had been predominant.

Chapter 2

MODERNIZATION AND DEVELOPMENT 1945-1968

"Our greatest challenge in Latin America since World War II has been that of mobilizing a hemisphere front against the threats posed by international Communism. The United States has been single-minded in this purpose; all else has been subordinated to this objective....It is ironic to record that after 150 years of relations with Latin America the area is still the 'soft under-belly' of hemisphere defense and a prime security concern of the United States. Since the winning of their independence most of the Latin-American nations have seemingly made little progress demonstrating that degree of political maturity essential for the realization of genuine democratic government. It is still a vast area of great instability, poverty, illiteracy, and frustration. In fact, the weakness of the Latin-American portion of the hemisphere to external threats seems to be greater today than ever before....Though temporary set backs may occur, there can be little doubt that the challenge will be met both in the United States and in Latin America, for the habit and the value of mutual cooperation has become a part of the way of life of the Americas."

J. Lloyd Mecham, **A Survey of United States-Latin American Relations** [Boston: Houghton Mifflin, 1965]. pp. 466-467.

The US emerged from the Second World War as the dominant global power driven forward by anti-communist globalism and a commitment to the construction of an open world economy within which US investors and manufacturers would play a central role.[1] Connected to this was the dramatic growth of the professional discourses on the developing or Third World. North American social science as a whole grew dramatically in scope and authority with the US rise to global hegemony. At the same time, the Cold War was the context for the emergence of a more interdisciplinary and methodologically sophisticated social science. After 1945 the dominant professional discourses on Latin America were profoundly shaped by what became known as modernization theory. As we have seen in the case of the historiography prior to 1945, Latin American specialists used an idealized version of North American and Western European history as the model by which they measured the history of Latin America. This approach was systematized between 1945 and 1968 around a concern with modernization and development. In the Cold War era the US civilizing mission in Latin America became an anti-communist modernizing mission. At the same time, the professional discourses on Latin America, like US foreign policy, continued to be shaped by Pan Americanism. And North American historiography continued to reflect liberal ideas about the complementarity of US ideals and US interests and about the existence of a relative harmony of interest between US goals and Latin American aspirations.

The Discovery of the Developing World 1945-1959

After 1945, as the wartime alliance between the US and the Soviet Union evaporated, the Truman government sought to represent the US as a beacon of liberty and democracy which was morally bound to enter into a struggle against evil itself. Fresh from the crusade against fascism, North American resources and support were redirected into another righteous cause--the crusade against international communism. US expansion was invigorated with the articulation of the Truman Doctrine in 1947. US Cold War expansionism was first directed at those areas which were believed to be open to direct military assault by the Soviet Union and its allies. The initial focus of US attention was Western Europe, Greece, Turkey and East Asia, particularly the Korean Peninsula. However, as the line of containment in Europe, and then in East Asia, was established, the focus of US concern moved towards the emerging Third World. The earlier missionary paternalism, which had accompanied US commercial and colonial expansion into the Caribbean and across the Pacific, meshed with the growing belief in the need for US assistance to the developing world to defend fledgling post-colonial democracies in Asia, and the more established republics of Latin America, from international communism.[2] Beginning with the establishment of the Organization of American States in 1948, the republics of Latin America were increasingly enlisted into Washington's Cold War project. After 1945 US policy in Latin America rested on the belief that common geography, as well as a common history and a common destiny, meant that the republics of Latin America shared with the US a commitment to democracy and the anti-communist crusade. At the same time, the orientation of US foreign policy after 1945 towards Latin America was an uneven process which remained rooted in a global approach to the containment of the Soviet Union. And the elimination of an external 'threat' to the Americas in 1945, and the decline of the New Deal, meant that numerous agencies and programs, such as Nelson Rockefeller's Office of Inter-American Affairs, which had been instrumental in extending US hegemony over the region in the 1930s and early 1940s, had their activities curtailed. The relative importance of Latin America to US globalism after 1945 is reflected in the fact that between 1945 and 1955 Latin America as a whole only received 3% of all non-military US aid distributed, while Western Europe received 65%, the Asia-Pacific almost 20%, with South Korea receiving more than all the countries of Latin America put together.[3]

The United States' strategy towards what became known as the developing world after 1945 built on the experience of the US in Europe in the late 1940s. The 1947 effort to keep Greece and Turkey from falling to international communism had relied on both military and economic aid. And after the apparent success of the economic component of the containment strategy on the eastern fringe of Europe, the Marshall Plan to facilitate the rebuilding of Western Europe got underway in 1948.[4] The US anti-communist crusade was further strengthened in early 1949 by Truman's Point Four program, which hoped to provide technical aid to the developing world in order to facilitate scientific and industrial development. Support for this type of anti-communist expansionism and this version of the US global mission was not always unanimous in North America. Domestic considerations and a desire for balanced budgets meant that many legislators sought to curb government-guided efforts to modernize the poorer countries of the world. When the Republicans, under Eisenhower, replaced the Truman administration in 1953, they attempted to resuscitate private, rather than state-directed, capitalist expansion. The Eisenhower administration initially tried to restrain the funding of development programs, and although it still retained all the various government aid agencies that had appeared under the impetus of the Truman Doctrine and the Marshall Plan, it replaced aid grants with loans. In the case of Latin America the Republican administration did not subscribe to the view, associated with the Good Neighbor Policy, that the expansion of US influence in the Americas was dependent on the steady flow of public money into the region's economic development. However, the Republicans, under Eisenhower, did support the related strategic view that it was essential that military aid be used to protect the republics of Latin America from international communism.[5]

Although US military aid to Latin America was not immediately emphasized by Washington after 1945, the US military had retained control of most of the Latin American bases which it had set up during the Second World War (the US base in northeast Brazil was given up shortly after World War II). At the outset there was considerable debate within the US administration, particularly between the State Department and the Pentagon, about the character and degree of US military ties, training and arms transfers to the governments of Latin America. At the same time, prior to 1948 the US Congress was unwilling to pass the legislation required to fortify the inter-American security system. But the emergence of the Cold War in Europe and the growing concern about communist operations in some of the Latin American republics such as Chile reversed the State Department's earlier opposition and altered the balance in Congress to favour the expansion and strengthening of US military ties with the republics to the south.[6] In this situation the US military sought to expand its training programs for Central and South American military officers. And it attempted to standardize Latin American military equipment according to US specifications. The growing, but still uneven, dependence of Latin American armed forces on the US was sanctified by the Rio Pact of 1948.[7]

More initiatives followed in the 1950s. In 1953 the Republican administration threw its weight behind the military component of the Latin American development program initiated by Truman. The US had entered into mutual defence agreements with a dozen southern republics and despatched US military missions to every country except Mexico by the end of the 1950s. While Latin America had received very little military aid during the Truman era, during the Eisenhower administration almost $400 million worth of military aid flowed southward, most of it going to Brazil, Colombia, Chile and Peru.[8] At the same time, the line between military and economic aid was increasingly blurred, as Latin American armed forces grew in size and became more dependent on expensive weaponry. Throughout the 1950s Latin American governments were besieged by growing domestic economic expectations and demands for political democracy.

They increasingly put pressure on the US to introduce a program of economic assistance similar to the Marshall Plan in Europe, while the growing US military aid to authoritarian governments in the region provoked criticism in both North and South America. At the same time, the fear that international communism was about to establish a beachhead in Guatemala in the mid-1950s served to eliminate the Republican administration's distinction between economic and military aid. Following the overthrow of the Arbenz government in 1954, the new regime had economic development funds lavished upon it by the US.[9]

The Guatemalan episode was an exception as far as the degree of attention received from Washington was concerned. Although many observers talk of US neglect in this period, it needs to be emphasized that the US always perceived that it had important interests in the region, but the apparent relative lack of threats to those interests allowed for its attention to focus elsewhere much of the time. Thus, despite the post-World War II expansion of US capital into Latin America and the increased military and political links, Central (and even South) America rarely attracted sustained US concern before the Cuban revolution. Nor did more than a small percentage of the growing number of North American area-studies specialists turn their attention to Latin America.[10] Up to the end of the 1950s Europe, Asia and the Middle East occupied Washington's attention far more than Central and South America, and this was reflected in the failure of Latin American studies to grow as dramatically as other area-studies programs in the 1950s. In the case of Central America, for example, the US government emphasized its special political relationship with the region; however, in practise, it gave Central America a very "low priority" in terms of economic aid. By the 1950s the countries of Central America were even more tightly integrated into a one or two crop export economy, controlled by the local oligarchy and foreign capital, and subordinate to the US economy. The US reinforced the increasing economic integration by continuing to tighten its military relationship with the isthmus. Washington continued to try and maintain its hegemony in Central America and the rest of the region by relying on dictators, military and economic aid, private investment and the Central Intelligence Agency. But the hostile reception accorded Richard Nixon, particularly in Venezuela in 1958, along with the initiative of Senator John F. Kennedy to push for a new US policy in the region and the Cuban revolution in 1959, all contributed to a reorientation of the Eisenhower administration's policy at the very end of the decade.[11] The shift in US foreign policy ostensibly towards the economic development of the southern republics through a major program of loans and grants was symbolized by Eisenhower's establishment of the Inter-American Development Bank in 1959, and the Kennedy administration's far more ambitious Alliance for Progress, which was launched in 1961. The Cuban revolution and Washington's rediscovery of Latin America stimulated the dramatic expansion of Latin American studies in North America over the next decade. At the same time, the resurgence of US interest in Latin America at the end of the 1950s, which was also linked with a push by US capital into the region, was focused less on Central America and more on Latin America as a whole, and was part of the consolidation of the broader turn in Washington to the communist challenge in the so-called Third World.

The Rise of Area Studies 1945-1959

In the years after World War II the dominant North American social science discourses were tightly linked to Washington's global anti-communist crusade. The imperatives of the Cold War were readily apparent in the emergence of area studies after 1945. Despite the continuity in the ideas shaping the social science profession, before and after 1945, the institutional and political changes ushered in by World War II and the subsequent Cold War served to change the professional discourses in important ways. As we have seen the 1920s saw the emergence of professional area-studies specialists generally (although the term itself was not used), and the professionalization of diplomatic history and Latin American history more specifically. However, between the wars, the growth of Latin American studies and area studies as a whole was slow. It was only with World War II that area studies entered a period of steady growth and disciplinary diversification. Beginning in the early 1940s area-studies specialists were mobilized in the crusade against fascism, and then against Soviet totalitarianism.[12] The North American area-studies specialists, writing in the post-1945 era, readily transposed the lessons of appeasement and the Nazi threat in Europe to the rest of the world, drawing the line against international communism around the globe. The Second World War brought a large number of area studies academics into direct contact with the government, reinforced the long-term linkages between the area-studies discourses and Washington, and precipitated a wave of institutional growth and expansion which continued under the impact of the Cold War.

Historians, political scientists and international-relations specialists established closer links with the US government during World War II and the subsequent Cold War than virtually any other academic disciplines except physics. The linkages evolved in a number of ways, and although not all historians and political scientists participated, the upper echelons of the historical and political-science profession were extremely well represented. A number took up full-time posts with government agencies, while others did so part-time or irregularly, while many others consciously allowed World War II and later Cold War imperatives to influence their work. Some historians, such as Samuel Eliot Morison, worked as official historians during the war and then continued in that position after 1945. The most well-known posting for historians, and the most significant for the development of area studies after World War II, was in intelligence research and analysis in the Office of Strategic Services (OSS), the forerunner of the Central Intelligence Agency (CIA). Many North American historians were recruited after 1942 by the leading North American diplomatic historian, William Langer of Harvard, who was in charge of the OSS's research and analysis branch.[13]

In terms of scale, work for the OSS represented the greatest direct involvement of historians (as well as political scientists and international-relations specialists) with the makers of US foreign policy in the history of the North American historical and social science profession. Government service during World War II reinforced the centrality of 'objectivity' to the professional historical and social science discourses. From the 1940s until the 1960s the dichotomy between the Free World and Totalitarianism, and the objectivity of such a distinction, structured the professional academic discourses, and sanctified the objectivity of any academic work carried on as part of the war against totalitarianism. It was not axiomatic that service with the government led to an uncritical attitude towards post-1945 US foreign policy. However, for most historians, and particularly diplomatic historians as well as area-studies academics generally, war-time work for the government led to an important shift in their ability to identify with Washington policy-makers. For example, after 1945, the main contribution by North American diplomatic historians to the Cold War was their wholesale representation of recent history in a manner which legitimated US global hegemony. As Peter Novick has argued, they portrayed the war against the Nazis, and then the Soviet Union, as "successive stages in one continuous and unavoidable struggle of the Free World against expansionist totalitarians". In the post-1945 era diplomatic historians produced textbooks and monographs which underpinned an anti-communist foreign policy and emphasized Washington's global mission. Although formal US imperialism from 1898 to 1933, particularly the conquest of the Philippines and the actions of Theodore Roosevelt, had sometimes been subject to criticism before 1945, in the Cold War era diplomatic historians were even more restrained in their analysis, in order to strengthen the image of Washington's global responsibility and combat any lingering isolationism in North America.[14]

Despite, or because of, diplomatic history's wholesale identification with a Pax Americana, the discipline entered a period of marked decline in the 1950s. By the beginning of the 1960s, in contrast to the period from 1920 to 1945, no diplomatic historian occupied anything but an honorary leadership position in the North American historical profession as a whole. Of course, in overall terms there were at least as many diplomatic historians in the US after World War II as before, and perhaps more. The main reason for diplomatic history's relative decline was that US globalism and the Cold War had stimulated the steady emergence of new fields of study in historical sub-disciplines or elsewhere in the social sciences.[15] The disciplinary range of area studies grew dramatically as a new generation of academics entered new historical and social science fields that had developed with the expansion and diversification of the social sciences after World War II. In particular there was a dramatic expansion after 1945 in the number of area-studies specialists who wrote about the countries of the so-called developing world or Third World. In the 1950s large amounts of money from government and private foundations became available with the intention of enhancing the North American understanding of the developing areas. Apart from those individuals who entered a growing array of disciplines and area-studies programs by the 1940s, a number of younger area-studies specialists with a background in diplomatic history or international relations were drawn into working directly for the Central Intelligence Agency, the RAND corporation, or the research sections that emerged at the Pentagon and the State Department in the wake of World War II.[16] They often joined older colleagues who had entered government service during World War II and never returned to academic life. The expansion of the diplomatic service also attracted a number of individuals with an academic background or an interest in diplomatic history.[17]

The number of historians, political scientists and international-relations specialists who worked for the government, particularly the OSS, and then went on to dominate the North American academic professions in the Cold War era is quite remarkable. Seven of the post-1945 presidents of the American Historical Association spent a period with the OSS during the war. The exiled members of the Frankfurt School, Franz Neumann, Otto Kirchheimer and Herbert Marcuse, all worked for the research and analysis branch at the OSS during World War II. Other academics who worked for the OSS and then established major reputations after World War II included the radical economists Paul Baran and Paul Sweezy, and the influential sociologists Barrington Moore, Jr., and Edward Shils.[18] European history specialists were particularly well represented. Crane Brinton, Gordon Craig, Felix Gilbert, Hajo Holborn, Leonard Krieger and Carl E. Schorske all worked for the OSS. The historian, Arthur M. Schlesinger Jr., who was an important advisor to John F. Kennedy, also served with the OSS, along with the well-known practitioner of global history L. S. Stavrianos. Economic historian Walt Whitman Rostow and political scientist Evron Kirkpatrick both worked for the OSS. While Rostow went on to be a major governmental advisor, Kirkpatrick, who rose to the presidency of the American Political Science Association, maintained strong links with the OSS's successor organization, the CIA. John K. Fairbank, professor of history at Harvard and the veritable founder of modern Chinese studies, was also employed by the OSS, as was W. Norman Brown, who is credited with founding and guiding South Asian studies in North America after the Second World War.[19] Shortly after World War II, Fairbank and W. Norman Brown both wrote influential historical surveys in the American Foreign Policy Library series about US relations with their particular area of specialization.[20]

One of the few, if not the only, Latin Americanist to work for the OSS was Donald M. Dozer, who later became professor of history at the University of California (Santa Barbara).[21] The lack of Latin American specialists in the OSS was followed by a relative decline in academic interest in Latin America in the 1950s. This decline is reflected in the number of PhDs on Latin American topics, in relation to South Asia, East Asia and the Middle East, as well as Russia and Eastern Europe, all of which increased. In 1951 Latin America was still the single most studied area in terms of PhDs; however, by the end of the 1950s it had fallen in relative terms to third place, after Russia, Eastern Europe and South Asia, and also in absolute terms from thirty percent to eighteen percent of area studies PhDs.[22] Robin Winks has argued that the lack of Latin American specialists in the OSS was the cause of the relative neglect of Latin America in the 1950s by North American area-studies specialists. In his view, because the former OSS academics were at the center of the rapid expansion of the graduate-level area-studies programs after 1945, and because they were especially oriented towards European and East Asian area studies, other area-studies programs, particularly Latin American studies, boasted fewer academics, were poorly funded and had fewer students.[23] However, Wink's explanation for the relative weakness of Latin American studies overlooks the reasons why Latin American specialists were under-represented in the OSS in the first place. The OSS was strongest in its study of Europe, the Middle East and Asia up to 1945 because that was where the war was being fought. If World War II had been fought in Latin America the OSS would have presumably recruited more Latin Americanists. Furthermore, Europe and East Asia were the major arenas of US policy in the early Cold War. Latin America's proximity to the US, and Washington's successful and relatively unchallenged inclusion of almost the entire region into the US hegemonic sphere by the 1940s, were crucial in explaining the weakness of Latin American studies in the 1950s. These factors, combined with Latin America's distance from the focus of conflict in World War II, resulted in the relative marginality of Latin American studies until the 1960s. It was not because Latin Americanists were under-represented in the OSS that Latin American studies failed to grow after the war. Latin American studies remained weak, relative to other area-studies programs, as a consequence of Latin America's position in relation to the US. This was already reflected, prior to 1945, by the location of Latin American studies on the margins of the historical and social science professions.

Although the OSS did not spawn a dynamic cohort of Latin American specialists with the prestige of the OSS graduates who went on to study Europe and Asia, World War II was a crucial period for Latin American studies. A number of Latin American experts who emerged from World War II at the top of their profession, or would rise to the top by the early 1960s, entered the Cold War era with even stronger direct links to the State Department and the government generally than many of the country's Latin American specialists before 1939. After 1940 a number of prominent Latin American specialists worked for the State Department or the Office of the Co-ordinator of Inter-American Affairs. Arthur P. Whitaker, who was professor of history at the University of Pennsylvania, a major figure among Latin American specialists and diplomatic historians before and after 1945, served as Latin American unit head at the Department of State during the war years and went on to serve on Kennedy's Latin American Task Force (the brain trust behind the Alliance for Progress) in the early 1960s.[24] Robert J. Alexander (who will be discussed below) held a number of government posts during the Second World War, including a turn with the Office of the Co-ordinator of Inter-American Affairs, and also went on to serve on President Kennedy's Task Force on Latin America. Political scientist Bryce Wood served as senior administrative assistant at the Department of State in 1942-43 before going on to serve as assistant director of the Division of Social Sciences at the Rockefeller Foundation, and then as the full-time Staff and Executive Associate of the Social Science Research Council in New York from 1950 until the early 1970s.[25] The historian Harold Peterson, who produced an important study of US relations with Argentina in the 1960s, worked in US Military Intelligence during World War II and went on to become Professor of History at State University College, Buffalo, New York.[26] The less well known Latin American historian Edward O. Guerrant worked in the Office of the Co-ordinator of Inter-American Affairs and the Department of State from 1944 to 1946.[27] According to the influential historian Lewis Hanke, by 1944 the majority of Latin American specialists were involved in some way with the war effort.[28] For Latin Americanists the Second World War had led to many of them spending greater amounts of time in Latin America. They served as cultural officers for the Office of the Co-Ordinator of Inter-American Affairs, or as political and economic analysts for the State Department, or as special assistants of some description, enhancing their links to both the region and to the US government. This also meant greater contact across disciplines and with their counterparts in Latin America, a development that was reinforced by the first significant "influx" of Latin American-born scholars into the United States.[29]

After 1945, the unprecedented institutional expansion of area-studies programs precipitated by the Cold War meant that by the early 1950s there were 29 area-studies programs on US campuses. Significantly, much of the initial funding came from private foundations such as the Carnegie Corporation and the Rockefeller Foundation. By the early 1960s there were over 100 language and area-studies programs in existence.[30] Although area studies emerged after 1945 as a less overtly ethnocentric series of discourses in contrast to the pre-World War II social science and humanities discourses, the cultural relativism of area specialists was often "specious". The language and area-studies programs emphasized language and culture as the key to understanding the various areas of the world with which they were concerned. They did this within the context of the view that they were according the various cultures the same degree of respect. They studiously avoided power relations and the dynamics of subordination and domination which were characteristic of the cultures they subject to scrutiny. The work in the 1950s of W. Norman Brown, the OSS graduate and guiding light of South Asian studies, is a good example of this approach.[31]

This perspective was also apparent in the work of the University of Chicago anthropologist and Latin American specialist Robert Redfield. He was an important area-studies figure, serving as chairman of the Joint Committee on Latin American Studies, which was set up in 1940 under the auspices of the American Council of Learned Societies and the Social Science Research Council, with direct links to the Office of the Coordinator of Inter-American Affairs under Nelson Rockefeller.[32] His work on the Maya exerted considerable influence on anthropology before and after the Second World War.[33] What has been called the Redfield tradition in anthropology emphasized culture, a folk-urban dichotomy, and focused on the local community and generally supported a tradition-modernity dichotomy and a liberal teleology. This emphasis meshed with the wider area-studies approach and with modernization theory as it emerged after World War II and continued to dominate the study of Latin America until the end of the 1960s.[34] The emphasis on culture as the key to Latin America was also apparent in work such as John Crow's **The Epic of Latin America** and **This New World: The Civilization of Latin America** by William L. Schurz, both of which appeared after 1945.[35]

The emphasis on culture and modernization which accompanied the rise of area studies reinforced the deeply rooted hostility to marxism in the United States. While marxism had enjoyed a relatively limited purchase even in the progressive climate of the 1920s and 1930s, it was completely "excluded" from North American area-studies and social-science discourses during the first two decades of the Cold War. However, historical materialism was not simply denounced. Alternatives were generated to fill the vacuum which marxism might have entered by default. The dominant professional discourses established certain parameters about acceptable terminology, categories, theory and methodology.[36] Some area-studies academics were clearly aware that their role was to articulate a theoretical alternative to marxism. For example, in the early 1980s a former member of the original Social Science Research Council Committee asserted that "the purpose" of the SSRC Committee, set up after World War II, "was to formulate a non-Communist theory of change and thus to provide a non-Marxian alternative for the developing nations".[37] The anti-marxism of this era facilitated the transformation and systematization of some of the central assumptions which had structured the dominant social-science and history discourses since their emergence in the early twentieth century. Following World War II the idea that the modernization of the Third World was essential--and that the transference of North American values and institutions, as they were idealized in the minds of many North Americans, was the solution to development problems around the globe--was central to the dominant professional discourses.[38]

Modernizing the Third World 1945-1959

Modernization theory was undoubtedly the most significant trend in area studies after World War II. Although various revised versions of modernization theory continue to mould the thinking of area-studies specialists, classic modernization theory reached the peak of its popularity in the late 1950s and early 1960s. After 1945 it was widely assumed in US government and area-studies circles that the poverty of the underdeveloped nations facilitated the spread of international communism.[39] It was also assumed that modernization would bring an end to poverty and undercut the possibility of communist revolution. The belief that the North American and Western European model of development and modernization was the ideal to which developing regions should aspire, and that they could develop with the political and economic guidance of North America and Western Europe, permeated the work of North American historians, political scientists, international-relations specialists as well as policy-makers in this period.[40] Throughout the 1950s and 1960s modernization theory was central to US Cold War expansion.

Modernization theory has its roots in the industrial revolution and the bourgeois ascendancy in late eighteenth- and early nineteenth-century Europe. Industrialization and the rise of bourgeois democracy have come to be enshrined in Western Europe and North America as the two central historical events in modern world history.[41] They formed the historical basis for assumptions which encouraged nineteenth- and early twentieth-century Western Europeans and North Americans to measure the historical development of the rest of the world, against the alleged superiority of the industrial-democratic West. After 1945 ideas about North American and Western European superiority were given new life and cast in new language, but the foundation on which they were constructed dated back to the nineteenth century.[42] Although it was more systematic, modernization theory still reflected continuity with the British Empire's 'white man's burden', the French *mission civilisatrice*, and the racist paternalism of the pre-1945 US imperial state in the Caribbean, Asia and the Pacific. Like these earlier approaches, modernization theory was committed to a period of tutelage which would end with the colonial society emerging as civilized and independent. Modernization theory still focused on the need for cultural transformation in order for the developing world to achieve modernity. History was regarded as linear, and the dominant area-studies discourses were organized around a perceived dichotomy between modern societies and their traditional forerunners. Modernization theory assumed that change in one area of a society produced consequent changes throughout the society. It emphasized the totality of change and saw modernization as a process (often called 'diffusion') which spread throughout a society, affecting economics, the type of government, social structure, values, religion and family structure. Modernization theorists viewed underdevelopment as the result of internal shortcomings specific to the underdeveloped societies in question. Their underdevelopment was seen as a result of their pre-colonial rather than their colonial history. The failure to develop was attributed variously to feudal elites concerned with retaining their position of power in traditional agrarian socio-economic structures and to cultural shortcomings, such as primordial religious loyalties and tribal obligations.[43]

Walt Whitman Rostow's book **The Stages of Economic Growth: A Non-Communist Manifesto** is widely regarded as the classic statement of modernization theory for the 1950s and early 1960s.[44] Rostow is an economist and an economic historian who served in the research and analysis branch of the OSS during World War II.[45] He went on to be a close advisor to President Kennedy, and President Johnson during the Vietnam War and currently holds a professorship at the University of Texas. Rostow both advocated and symbolized the shift in US foreign policy in the late 1950s away from containing the Soviet Union with direct military force, at a time when the Soviet Union was believed to have begun developing atomic weaponry, and towards taking the initiative in the Third World via infusions of economic and military aid as part of ambitious nation-building and counter-insurgency strategy.[46] In **The Stages of Economic Growth**, which first appeared in 1960, he argued that Britain's industrial development in the late eighteenth and nineteenth century could still serve as a model for the developing world. His stages of growth and take-off approach ignored the unequal and constraining relations that developed between Britain and non-industrial countries and the hierarchical character of contemporary international society, while also overlooking the numerous historical changes that distinguished eighteenth- and nineteenth-century Britain from developing countries of the twentieth century.

While Rostow's work may be the most important articulation of Cold War development economics, the work of Gabriel Almond represented the most influential example of modernization theory produced by a political scientist. Almond, who went straight from the University of Chicago's post-graduate program to take up a position as head of the Enemy Section with the Office of War Information in Washington, emerged as one the most influential North American political scientists of his generation and a major figure in the behavioral revolution in the social sciences, sponsored by the Ford Foundation in the 1950s.[47] Almond, who was a member of the Social Science and Research Council, co-edited with James S. Coleman a major work of modernization theory entitled **The Politics of Developing Areas**, which was first published in 1960. Despite all its shortcomings it at least advocated breaking with a narrow focus on a particular area in favour of a broadly comparative inter-disciplinary approach to the study of political development.[48] Almond and Coleman's book was preoccupied with comparing developments inside various nations while, in classic area-studies fashion, it ignored both internal power relations and the character of relations between nation-states. This is apparent in the chapter on Latin America, by George I. Blanksten, which focused on tradition and culture in relation to internal constraints on economic development and political democratization.[49] Modernization theory ultimately approached Latin America and other developing areas in terms of their ability, or inability, to develop along the lines laid down by an idealized image of the rise of the nation-state in Western Europe and North America.

In the 1950s and early 1960s modernization theorists argued that economic growth and urbanization in Latin America would stimulate the necessary social and cultural change that would lead to more 'developed' economies and more democratic politics. Early modernization theory perceived a direct causal link between economic growth, social change and democratization. It also assigned particular importance to an emerging middle class, or middle sector, which it expected would fulfil both a restraining and a progressive function.[50] This emphasis on the middle sectors was apparent in John Johnson's **Political Change in Latin America: The Emergence of the Middle Sectors**. His work represented one of the most influential applications of modernization theory to Latin America in the 1950s.[51] Modernization theory was particularly influential in political science; however, at a time when an inter-disciplinary approach to the study of developing areas was gaining influence, its impact transcended disciplinary boundaries. It structured the professional discourses as a whole, and its influence was clearly reflected in most of the North American work on the Third World. The dominant area-studies discourses substituted a US modernizing mission for the earlier US civilizing mission. However, the modernization process, like the civilizing process before it, still meant westernization. And the progress of Latin America, Asia, the Middle East, Africa and Oceania was still measured in terms of the values and institutions of the industrialized countries. Cold War development theory also clearly envisioned that the benefits of modernization, like the benefits of civilization, were to be transferred to the rest of the world under the tutelage of the United States.

Meeting the Communist Threat in Central America 1945-1959

Despite the limited interest in Latin America relative to other parts of the world, the presumption that the US had a legitimate tutelary role to play in the region after 1945 was readily apparent. After World War II the decline in interest in Latin America was a result of the perception that Latin America was relatively stable. Washington policy-makers and area-studies specialists clearly regarded the Western Hemisphere as part of the US 'sphere of influence'. As a result, if they thought that US interests were threatened, they did not hesitate to act or counsel action. Following the rise to power of the MNR in Bolivia in 1952, the US was concerned about its radical agenda, particularly land reform and the nationalization of the tin mines, and Washington initially cut off economic aid and then waited six weeks to recognize the new government. However, by the following year the Eisenhower administration had renewed the flow of aid and sought to use the resulting leverage to facilitate a moderation of the MNR's policies (significantly, although the tin mines were nationalized they were almost all locally owned and US investors had limited interests in the country).[52] Central America, particularly Guatemala, also provided a focus for US concern in the mid-1950s and resulted in an outcome very different from that in Bolivia. By the early 1950s the Council on Foreign Relations' study group on Latin America, under the chairmanship of Spruille Braden, the controversial and zealously anti-communist former diplomat, was warning all who would listen of the dangers of communist subversion in Guatemala. In 1953 the chairman of the United Fruit Company spoke to the group, at which time he emphasized the importance of acting swiftly to "eliminate" the Arbenz government.[53] In the same year Braden sounded the alarm in **Syllabus on the Communist Threat to the Americas**.[54] And there were a number of other academics, such as Robert J. Alexander, who were willing to turn their attention explicitly to the study of the communist threat in Latin America and around the world.[55] Alexander, whose politics grew out of the socialist anti-communism of the inter-war period, specialized in the study of the labor movement in Latin America. He was a student of Frank Tannenbaum and visited Latin America for the first time in 1946-1947, when he spent six months in Chile gathering material for his doctorate. Alexander's half year in Chile coincided with a rash of strikes and labor unrest in the context of considerable tension between the US and the Chilean government of Gabriel Gonzalez Videla over the latter's inclusion of members of the Chilean Communist Party in his cabinet. In the 1950s and early 1960s Alexander worked in Latin America for the AFL-CIO and the American Institute for Free Labor Development (AIFLD).[56] Beginning with his influential book on communism in Latin America in 1957 and his study of the Bolivian Revolution in 1958, he has produced a large number of works on the labor movement and the Left in Latin America.[57] As we will see, he was also a major figure behind the Alliance for Progress in the 1960s. As with Alexander's work in the 1950s, most of the studies produced on Guatemala were completely preoccupied with the perceived communist control of the Guatemalan government and the communist threat to the region.[58]

A good example of how Washington's concern about the communist threat framed the approach of US-based Latin American specialists was the request to the State Department by Ambassador Peurifoy, in the wake of Arbenz's overthrow, to send two researchers to Guatemala to assess the extent of 'communist infiltration'. One of these researchers was Richard N. Adams, who was a professor of anthropology and Assistant Director of the Institute of Latin American Studies at the University of Texas by the 1960s. Adams used the pseudonym Stokes Newbold because he also worked for the World Health Organization, and WHO was worried about having its name connected with his activities. Adams (Newbold) conducted interviews with about 250 people who had been arrested and incarcerated after Arbenz was ousted. He came to the conclusion that although many of the prisoners had been participants in the land-reform programs they knew little or nothing about communism. Although Adams's approach clearly reflected the dominance of Cold War imperatives, his failure to come to conclusions that supported Washington's vision of a widespread communist conspiracy in Guatemala failed to impress the State Department or the CIA.[59]

In 1959, however, a book by Ronald M. Schneider, took an approach which was more complementary of the US effort to demonstrate a connection between Moscow and the Arbenz government. And this book went on to be regarded for many years as the best study of Guatemala between 1944 and 1954.[60] **Communism in Guatemala: 1944-1954** was produced under the auspices of the Foreign Policy Research Institute at the University of Pennsylvania, which emerged as a major center for the study of international communism after 1945. Schneider's book was based on the 50,000 or so documents seized, with CIA encouragement, by the Guatemalan National Committee for Defense against Communism, from the Communist Party of Guatemala offices after the 1954 coup.[61] Schneider's book included a foreword by Arthur P. Whitaker, under whose supervision the study had been prepared. Robert J. Alexander, Dana Munro and Gabriel Almond all provided advice on the manuscript. Schneider represented the 1944-1954 period as a failed communist attempt to capture popular support and power. He warned that although the overthrow of the Arbenz government was "a severe blow to the immediate aims and aspirations of the Guatemalan Communists" it should not be seen as "the permanent removal of a Communist threat". Schneider concluded that "the Communist have carefully studied their failures and worked assiduously to correct their shortcomings" and "if the non-Communist politicians who are competing for leadership in Guatemala today do not show an equal ability to profit from the lessons of the Arbenz era, Communism may someday regain a position of influence in that troubled Republic".[62] Schneider's book supported the view that Guatemala had been on the verge of a communist takeover which was in danger of spreading to the rest of Central America and beyond. His work also reflected the central assumptions of modernization theory, particularly the need to undercut communist support through economic and political development along North American lines.

Another North American political scientist whose work also articulated these concerns was John D. Martz.[63] Although his focus was initially on Central America, it has shifted further south since the 1950s. However, he has maintained an interest in US foreign policy in the region as a whole.[64] Like many prominent North Americans, Martz's discovered Central America in the mid-1950s because of a concern that international communism was on the march. In 1956 he contributed to the growing number of works which assigned the communist threat a determining role in the recent history of Guatemala and Latin America more generally.[65] Of more lasting importance than his 'study of subversion' was the publication in 1959 of **Central America: The Crisis and the Challenge**.[66] Given the limited number of books available, Martz's study was widely used in the 1960s. Even in the mid-1960s it was still regarded as a "key work" on Central America.[67] At the outset Martz argued that it had been a "reasonable" assumption in 1945 that Central America "might", in time, "lift itself from its antiquated existence" to occupy a place at the side of the "older members of the global community". However, what actually occurred, according to Martz, was a slow descent into crisis. Martz traced this decline to the "extraordinary lack of maturity" of Central American nations, arguing that there would be no real "progress" in the region "without first a modicum of stable, relatively mature government". Martz concluded that the rural population was dominated by the landowners and that this situation, and the traditions on which it was based, had to be "conquered" in order for "economic development" to take place and for "political maturity" to appear. The main cause of the region's inequitable social order, as well as its political immaturity and its "failure" to "develop", was found by Martz in the "Spanish political heritage". And following independence from Spain no foundation for "democratic government" existed, and all social and political experience had been of "an authoritarian nature".[68] At the same time, his approach was sympathetic towards the region's dictators insofar as they brought order out of chaos, while acting as a bulwark against communism. He argued that "under the retarded circumstances of Central American life, dictatorship--if competently administered and genuinely concerned with national progress--has an important role to play". Martz argued that the "hunger for democracy and representative government can only be treated when physical hunger itself is curbed". Under these circumstances, he asserted, "there is a place for absolutist government". For example, in his view, Nicaragua, in economic terms, was "the soundest country" in Central America after two decades of Somoza family rule.[69]

Although his work was critical of Washington's neglect of the region, Martz was adamant that the overall impact of the US on Central America had been positive. He expressed consternation that, despite their political independence, the southern republics had blamed many of the region's problems on the United States. He concluded that the current "ill will" towards the US was one of "the burdens of international power". Ignoring earlier US interventions, Martz argued that, prior to the 1950s, the United States had "never been confronted" by this situation and "it has not rested easily under the burden", since an essential North American "characteristic is that of open, candid friendship, a belief in the inherent goodness of one's fellow, his intentions, philosophies and actions". In Martz's view the complaints about "yankee imperialism", which focused on the United Fruit Company, were usually based on "the assumption that all foreign enterprise" was "inherently and wickedly avaricious". Although, said Martz, there were certainly cases of "unfair practices", there were also "positive contributions". For example, the profits generated by the operations of large foreign companies would "inevitably funnel back in part to the host nation", and it was only "the nature of the government" which determined whether this was "converted into public works or official graft", while the salaries received by local employees of foreign firms also benefited the local economy. For Martz, as with modernization theory, private foreign capital was the answer to Central America's problems, and only with "foreign enterprise backed by unbound capital" could regional development come about.[70] This perspective was also indistinguishable from Washington's view in the 1950s, which had been emphasized repeatedly since the end of World War II. For example, in the words of Secretary of State Marshall in 1948, a "dominant theme" of US foreign policy was the "role which private capital might play in the economic development of Latin America".[71]

The importance of private enterprise to modernization and development can also be found in other studies of the period, such as the 1958 work by Stacy May and Galo Plaza. They confined their study of the United Fruit Company to a discussion of the Company's managerial operations and its social and economic impact on Central America, and they concluded that the United Fruit Company's "contributions" to "the local economies have been outstandingly" to the "advantage" of the Central American republics. Furthermore, although UFCO's "returns have been sufficient to keep it in operation and finance a considerable expansion, they have not matched the earnings of the average company of its size engaged primarily in domestic business".[72] May and Plaza's study was followed by other work which also approached the relationship between the United Fruit Company and economic development in the region from the perspective of modernization theory. There was, for example, Richard A. Labarge's tightly focused study of UFCO in Guatemala which was published in 1960.[73]

These studies of the United Fruit Company, like Martz's work, focused on what they regarded as the relative commonality rather than conflict of interest between US economic expansion and US foreign policy on the one hand, and the governments and people of Central America on the other. Martz, in particular, invoked Pan Americanism at the same time as he conflated Pan American values with North American values. He argued that the only basis for stable relations lay in "the recognition of equality and complete fulfillment of the democratic ideals of the philosophers of the American Revolution". He then quoted John Moors Cabot, a long-time employee of the State Department in Latin America and a former Assistant Secretary of State for Inter-American Affairs, who hoped "that history in our Americas shall record that here man learned to cooperate, to progress in peace and understanding, to contribute our American share to the advancement of our western civilization and our Christian religion. We owe that to the splendor of our Pan American ideals". Martz added that "we owe as much to the highest principles upon which the United States has grown to international stature".[74] Despite his emphasis on a shared heritage and a common future, Martz still tended to represent obstacles to "political maturity", democratization and economic development, as cultural. His work relied repeatedly on negative images of Central Americans as irrational, volatile and "incendiary", in implicit contrast to North Americans.[75] This patronizing emphasis on Latin American irrationality was also apparent in his approach to the Guatemalan episode. In Martz's view, the events of 1954 had resulted in "a maze of misunderstandings" which had led to a reduction in "awareness of the common bonds and interests shared through recent history". He complained that Latin Americans "read with almost naive credence the outrageously inaccurate books of ex-President Arévalo and ex-Foreign Minister Toriello", and accepted them "almost adoringly despite the men's deep personal involvement". At the same time, they rejected books on the communist threat to Guatemala and the rest of the region by Daniel James and himself, books "which recognized grievances on both sides". He argued that the acceptance of the views of Arévalo and Toriello "stir up ill will and contribute nothing toward hemispheric harmony". He argued that it was not "tiny Guatemala" which endangered the US and that the reason for Washington's "concern" was the spread of "communist underground activities" in Central America, "taking advantage of the natural political instability".[76]

   Martz's book, which was one of the most influential studies of Central America in the early 1960s, pointed to the way the Cold War moulded the dominant professional discourses on Latin America.[77] Virtually everything produced on Latin America in the 1950s was profoundly shaped by the imperatives of the Cold War. However, in contrast to Martz, some North American writers who were still part of the dominant professional discourses, sought to put more critical distance between themselves and US foreign policy. In 1951, Samuel Guy Inman wrote sympathetically about the reformist experiment in Guatemala.[78] Another important exception was a short book on Guatemala by Kalman Silvert. He was a political scientist who studied under Arthur P. Whitaker at the University of Pennsylvania, where he gained both his undergraduate and graduate degrees, receiving a PhD in 1948. For over a decade he was Professor of Government at Tulane University and Dartmouth College, as well as Staff Associate to the Director of Studies of the American Universities Field Staff. He was also the first president of the Latin American Studies Association in the mid-1960s.[79] Unlike Martz and others, Silvert questioned both the charge that the Guatemalan government was communist, and the less extreme charge that there was a communist conspiracy to take over the government. He argued that the land reform, labor organization and economic planning instituted by the Guatemalan government after 1944, had also been adopted earlier in Mexico, which had in turn "been able to witness the gradual but relentless shrinking of its organized Communist Party over the last fifteen years". El Salvador "also adopted most of the measures which Guatemala has seen fit to pass, but under the banner of a frankly conservative government". He concluded that "Guatemalan official leftism" was "not necessary to the situation, but convenient".[80] Another North American political scientist who did not frame the "Guatemalan Affair" in entirely Cold War terms was Philip B. Taylor Jr.[81] Nonetheless, Martz and Schneider's work was more representative of this period. And despite Silvert and Taylor's more nuanced approaches, all their work measured the development of Latin America against a North American model and assumed that there was no real need for conflict between US and Latin American interests, or between US ideals and security needs.

The Twilight of Diplomatic History 1959-1968

The Guatemalan episode precipitated more general North American interest in Latin America. And this interest was further stimulated when the years 1955 to 1959 saw the overthrow of a number of Latin American dictators, culminating in the ouster of Fulgencio Batista in Cuba.[82] Combined with the wave of anti-US sentiment which appeared to have gripped the hemisphere and was symbolized by the hostile response to vice-president Nixon's tour in 1958, Batista's fall caused Washington policy-makers to turn their gaze southward.[83] But it was the radicalization of the Cuban Revolution, and the subsequent growth of rural insurgencies and urban unrest throughout the region, which set off alarms in Washington. The rise of Fidel Castro gave birth to the Alliance for Progress, stimulated a renewed US commitment to greater direct and indirect military involvement, and sparked the dramatic expansion of Latin American studies. After 1959 North American efforts to 'understand' the region were redoubled. However, the decline of diplomatic history and the movement of political scientists and international-relations specialists into Latin America studies ensured that, although a whole new array of work on inter-American relations appeared, the production of general historical works on inter-American relations was limited.[84] Two exceptions to the lack of an historical synthesis were the fifth and sixth editions of **Latin America and the United States** by Graham H. Stuart (the sixth edition was co-authored by James L. Tigner). These were somewhat revised versions of a book which had first appeared in 1922. And its continued importance pointed to the weakness of the historiography of inter-American diplomacy in this period[85] In the 1960s the study of US relations with particular countries and regions in Latin America certainly increased.[86] But even at the end of the 1960s, Bemis's 1943 book was still regarded as a "useful" basic history of US diplomacy in Latin America.[87]

While diplomatic history, particularly as it related to Latin America, had entered a twilight era by the 1960s, a period in which it was increasingly overshadowed by political science and international relations, the older diplomatic historians such as Bemis continued to write. Their work still rested on the methodological approach of the pre-1945 era at the same time as it demonstrated how diplomatic history was particularly susceptible to the Cold War. In post-1945 editions of his **A Diplomatic History of the United States**, which was first published in 1936, Bemis eliminated all criticisms of US intervention beyond the western hemisphere. Previously he had argued that the security of the United States and the rest of the hemisphere did not necessarily require extra-hemispheric intervention, but after 1945 he asserted that the USSR sought "world conquest", and he praised Secretary of State John Foster Dulles for his hard-line stance.[88] Immediately after the war he also voiced his support for clandestine activity against the USSR and the transformation of the OSS into the CIA for that purpose.[89] In his 1961 presidential address to the American Historical Association, Bemis criticized Franklin D. Roosevelt for his "misjudgment of the nature and forces of Soviet policy" and he also criticized Truman and Eisenhower, and their policy of containment, which "by its very nature yield(s) the initiative to the revolutionary aggressor".[90]

Like Bemis's later writings, Dexter Perkins's work after 1945 was also rooted in traditional methodology and the logic of the Cold War. Between World War I and World War II, Perkins, who also served as president of the American Historical Association, had produced a number of works of diplomatic history which related directly to Latin America. In the 1960s he continued to write about US-Latin American relations. However, his major monographs were all published before 1945.[91] In the 1950s and early 1960s, his work rested on a Cold War-style commitment to North American exceptionalism and liberal internationalism. He can be located with the influential consensus 'school' of North American historiography which included Daniel Boorstin and Louis Hartz and dominated the writing of US history in the early Cold War era.[92] In his general historical study of US relations with the circum-Caribbean, which appeared in 1947, and then with minimal revisions in 1966, he argued that while, "in the world in which we live...force was the ultimate arbiter", it was "not true that nations act without regard to other considerations than those of pure power". He was adamant that "in particular, democratic nations, and perhaps most of all the English-speaking democracies, are powerfully affected by what they conceive to be moral considerations and by a desire to produce a world society better than that of the past" and "nowhere" had this been better demonstrated than in the policy of the United States towards the numerous small states that are its neighbors".[93] Perkins continued to be committed to 'objectivity' and perceived the writing of history as "a pure and disinterested search for truth".[94] In his autobiography Perkins blamed the Cold War "largely" on the Soviet Union.[95] In the 1960s Perkins argued that if North Americans "create a better and better society through the medium of the democratic process" and "use the vast wealth we create for the benefit of the mass of men", they could "be very sure that this fact will have an impact on other countries, not least on those of Latin America".[96] Like modernization theory, he emphasized the growth of the middle class as crucial to the economic and political development of the region. He argued that financial stability had a positive impact on the "political climate" and facilitated the "growth of that middle class" which underpins "democratic government".[97]

Of greater impact than Perkin's work by the 1960s were two books by J. Lloyd Mecham (published in 1961 and 1965), in which the influence of modernization theory was readily apparent.[98] Mecham spent most of his life working on Latin American history, turning to diplomatic history only at the end of his career.[99] By the late 1950s, his interest had turned to inter-American relations. Mecham's books of the 1960s were influential, in part, because there was a limited number of general historical works on inter-American relations available until the end of the 1960s. In 1971 the prominent Latin Americanist Federico Gil characterized Mecham's 1965 study as "probably the most thorough text on the subject".[100] First and foremost, Mecham was preoccupied with national security and the communist threat, and like Bemis and his colleague at the University of Texas, Wilfrid Hardy Callcott, he perceived US foreign policy in the region as historically consistent in its pursuit of national security. His approach to inter-American relations reflected what would later be characterized by Abraham Lowenthal as the "hegemonic presumption".[101] Mecham's work also made clear the way in which the concerns and preoccupations of Washington policy makers were central to the professional academic discourses on Latin America. For example, in line with the US government sources and the anti-communist secondary accounts on which he relied, Mecham devoted particular attention to Guatemala in the first half of that decade and to Cuba at the end of the 1950s. His work emphasized a monolithic communist conspiracy exploiting unrest in Latin America. Mecham's 1961 book, **The United States and Inter-American Security, 1889-1960**, included a lengthy chapter on "the deadly threat of aggressive, imperialistic Soviet Communism". He argued that since 1945, or even earlier, the Inter-American Security system had been "perfected and strengthened with this potential aggressor in view". However, lamented Mecham, there was also the danger of the "insidious and subversive undermining" of Central and South American governments "by the agents of international communism without the firing of a shot".[102] Mecham was particularly concerned to emphasize that communists in Latin America had to "follow the twisting Moscow line" and, while tactics changed, their "strategy" was "always in line with the Comintern strategy of world domination".[103]

In the case of Guatemala, Mecham argued that communism did not become a problem until the revolution of 1944 "provided the Communists with a unique opportunity which they cleverly exploited". And, especially under Arbenz (1951-1954) "the Communists made such rapid gains in influence as to arouse the most serious apprehension of the United States and other members of the hemisphere community".[104] The communist "setback in Guatemala", according to Mecham, actually drove Moscow to increase its Latin American activities, and as a result the "Communist conspiracy became an even greater danger" to the region. He argued that "masquerading as supernationalists" Latin American communists "penetrate behind the scenes" to "exploit" the "latent anti-United States attitude" and generate "disunity" in the hemisphere. In his view this was demonstrated by developments in Cuba at the beginning of the 1960s, which he characterized as "threatening in the extreme".[105]

A Cold War version of Pan Americanism was central to Mecham's writing. He argued that because the republics of the hemisphere "were born in popular revolt against a foreign sovereign" there existed throughout the Americas "a consciousness of community of origin". Because the republics of the south had, at least in theory, adopted US-"influenced" constitutions there was, he asserted, "a sense of community of political institutions and objectives". At the same time they "possessed a common tradition of belonging to the 'New World'" and "they shared the Western Hemisphere idea". He argued that, although the Latin Americans (in implicit contrast to North Americans) were slow to develop "permanent, stable, and truly popular, representative, republican governments", they, and the US, had never stopped "striving toward the same objective". He insisted that North Americans and Latin Americans were all "motivated by deep underlying spiritual forces" which he characterized as a "desire" for democracy, peace, independence, and improved social, economic and educational standards. Because of this commonality of purpose and shared heritage, he concluded that it was "natural" for the nations of the hemisphere to enter into "a security arrangement" founded on "the oft-declared principles of inter-American solidarity" which were now "part of the basic law of the continent".[106]

He enlisted Pan Americanism to legitimate a US modernizing mission in Latin America. In order to meet the communist challenge in Latin America Mecham exhorted the US to provide "both economic and democratic support". Washington, he said, could not "expect" the Latin Americans to give "priority to the dangers of Communist aggression until after they have been freed of native dictatorship and misrule and after they have been assisted to higher standards of living". At the same time, Mecham argued that "the problem of democracy as contrasted with dictatorship, and its relation to the threat of international Communism, is not so simple as it appears". Using the popular dichotomy between communism and dictatorship (totalitarianism and authoritarianism) which structured the conservative discourses in the 1980s, he insisted that "Latin liberals" were "sublimely heedless of the sad fact that democracy is no immediate practical alternative and cannot be until certain democratic requirements are met by their respective nations". Mecham also argued that the Latin American "masses" were "just emerging from a feudal past and lack the bases of democracy", including "experience in self government, deep respect for the law, a literate electorate, organized political parties, and respect for civil rights". Under these circumstances "the first objective should be to give all aid possible, economic and moral, to create the conditions of effective democracy, but it should never be forgotten" cautioned Mecham "that democracy develops from within".[107]

Along with the explicitly Cold War character of his work, Mecham also relied on the traditional descriptive methodology associated with diplomatic history before 1945. He looked at US diplomacy in Latin America in terms of government-to-government relations, using published government records and diplomatic correspondence, as well as secondary sources. As already noted, Mecham's books were influential, but they lacked the dedication to archival exploration, and the more authoritative voice of diplomatic historians like Arthur Whitaker whose more specialized work continued to be respected in this era.[108] But even diplomatic historians such as Whitaker saw their position in Latin American studies decline between 1945 and 1968. Latin American specialists with an area studies, political science or international relations background dominated Latin America studies by the 1960s. By this time the inter-disciplinary character and greater methodological sophistication was apparent in the work of area specialists, political scientists, anthropologists, and even historians of Latin America's colonial period.[109] An important work which pointed to the disciplinary shift in Latin American studies after 1945 was a study of the Good Neighbor Policy by the political scientist Bryce Wood.[110] Although his study was still a work of liberal diplomatic history and can still be located in the professional Cold War discourses, it broke with traditional methodology and went beyond the reductionist anti-communism associated with writers such as Mecham. Wood's book is still regarded as a key work. For example, in a review of the historiography in 1985, John J. Johnson emphasized its continued methodological importance.[111]

Published in 1961, **The Making of the Good Neighbor Policy** traced the US retreat from direct military intervention after 1933 to the growing opposition to US 'imperialism' and to the frustrating experience had by Henry Stimson, and others, on the ground in Nicaragua in the late 1920s. In Wood's view the Good Neighbor Policy evolved out of the experience of the Coolidge and Hoover administrations to emerge as policy under Roosevelt.[112] Despite its methodological and analytical advancement in relation to the diplomatic history of the inter-war years and the first decade and a half of the Cold War, Wood's study, like the wider professional discourses, continued to rest on the idea that there was relative harmony between the interests and ideals of the United States, and between US and Latin American interests. Another assumption on which Wood's book, and the professional discourses, relied was that US policy makers had the ability to define and pursue something as ineffable as the 'national interest'. Wood argued that there was a US 'national interest' in Latin America, which was "different from and superior to the private interest of any sector of American enterprise or of business enterprise as a whole". And, in his view, this was the very essence of the Good Neighbor Policy. He argued further that this and other goals of the Good Neighbor Policy had been achieved by end of the 1930s, and "by renouncing domination the United States had won a sympathy that accorded it wartime leadership acknowledged by nearly all the Latin American states". He concluded that "in its time" the Good Neighbor Policy "provided a promising demonstration of the desire of Americans to strive in good will to forget an often bitter past and, with mutual respect, to find amicable ways both to adjust differences of interest and to unite in furthering common aims".[113] Despite its greater sophistication Wood's work still clearly exhibited the influence of Cold War Pan Americanism and worked to legitimate the US modernizing mission in Latin America.

Latin American Studies and the Golden Age of Modernization Theory 1959-1968

The decline of traditional diplomatic history and the rise of political scientists such as Bryce Wood to a position of dominance in Latin American studies coincided with the dramatic overall expansion of Latin American studies in the 1960s. While Latin American studies 'took-off' in the 1960s, it had already begun to expand in the 1950s as a result of the improved institutional context for area studies generally after 1945. In the 1940s and early 1950s, although the government provided the encouragement, the initial funding for area studies came from philanthropic sources. However, Washington eventually became more directly involved, justifying the funding of area studies on the grounds of national defense.[114] In the late 1950s the National Defence Education Act (NDEA) and Public Law 480, among other things, targeted various institutions and libraries around the country to receive funds for the development of foreign-language programs and as repositories for large quantities of primary and secondary source material. The 1958 NDEA was a more or less direct response to the 'communist threat' and the realization on the part of the US government that there were vast areas of the world about which they were ignorant. The NDEA money, along with grants from private foundations and the resource material acquired with PL480, was central to the maintenance and expansion of area studies in the United States.[115] While the Sputnik crisis, which stimulated the NDEA, can be regarded as a watershed for area studies as a whole, the Cuban Revolution of 1959 was the major turning point in the rise of Latin American studies more specifically. Much of the growth in area studies in the 1950s by-passed Latin American studies and it was not until the beginning of the 1960s that Latin American studies was institutionalized nation-wide. As Richard Fagen has argued, "it took a hot wind from the South to fan the flames, and large infusions of cash from the US government and private foundations to fuel the conflagration". The meteoric rise of Latin American studies occurred at a time when the North American study of political, economic and social development in Latin America, Asia, Africa and Oceania was, as we have seen, completely under the influence of modernization theory.[116]

The growing concern in North America in the early 1960s, that the Cuban 'contagion' would spread to the rest of the hemisphere, caused a dramatic shift in US policy and stimulated what Jules Benjamin has described as "the full flowering of liberal developmentalism" in the form of the Alliance for Progress.[117] At the outset Latin American studies acted as a direct complement to the Alliance for Progress. For example, in 1960, in his capacity as 'chairman' of a Council on Foreign Relations' Discussion Group on Latin America and US policy, Lyman Bryson wrote that "(a)s regards Latin America the policy of the United States has been largely improvised and there is still time to ignore the past and found a lasting policy on knowledge acquired by the modern methods of social science".[118] The Alliance for Progress symbolized the US commitment to resist any and all change in Latin America that was contrary to the Cold War development model and threatened US interests. This was similar, in some ways, to the view that had driven Washington policy-makers in the era of the Good Neighbor Policy. And some of the individuals who had designed and carried out Roosevelt's Good Neighbor Policy were prominent in the Kennedy administration, particularly Adolf A. Berle, who had served as Ambassador to Brazil and as Assistant Secretary of State for Inter-American Affairs in the 1930s and 1940s. Berle was put in charge of Kennedy's Task Force on Latin America. Kennedy insiders Walt Whitman Rostow and Arthur M. Schlesinger, Jr., also influenced the Alliance for Progress, as did a number of other prominent liberal developmentalists, such as Seymour Martin Lipset, Cyril E. Black and Max Millikan, as well as liberal economists John Kenneth Galbraith and Robert Heilbroner.[119] Lincoln Gordon, Professor of Economics at Harvard University, who had been associated with the Marshall Plan in the late 1940s and early 1950s and who went on to be US ambassador to Brazil from 1961 to 1966 and then Assistant Secretary of State for Inter-American Affairs in 1966 and 1967, also took up a post on Kennedy's Task Force on Latin America. Gordon shifted back to the academy when he became President of Johns Hopkins University (1967-1971) and then Professor of Political Economy at Johns Hopkins School of Advanced International Studies from 1971.[120] The Task Force included

Latin American specialists Robert J. Alexander and Arthur Preston Whitaker. And Puerto Rican politicians and technocrats Teodoro Moscoso (who later became the US Agency for International Development's deputy for Latin America) and Arturo Morales Carrion were also brought into the Task Force. Apart from the Marshall Plan, Operation Pan America, introduced by President Kubitschek of Brazil, and the incipient shift in the final year of the Eisenhower administration to a greater emphasis on economic aid and public investment in development, the Task Force's proposals owed an important debt to 'Operation Bootstrap', which was initiated in Puerto Rico in the 1940s in an effort to reform the rural social order and increase capital investment. Without a doubt the Task Force Report of January 4, 1961, was a key source of US policy towards Latin America in the Kennedy era.[121] Berle and his colleagues reported to the President that the communist threat to the region was similar to, but more menacing than, the Nazi 'threat' of the 1930s and 1940s, and therefore required an even more ambitious initiative. On top of the increased economic assistance, Berle also recommended a "psychological offensive" which could serve, in his words, to channel "the vast, powerful, disparate American intellectual effort so that it reaches Latin America and Latin Americans at all levels, giving effective support to the United States social-economic-political system".[122]

The Kennedy administration built on the state-led reformism and Pan Americanism of the Good Neighbor era to breathe new life into Republican-style Cold War globalism, and confidently embarked on a policy of economic and political development in Latin America and beyond. Although by the end of the decade the overall relationship between Latin American studies and the US government had deteriorated somewhat, at the outset the support of Latin American studies specialists, was enthusiastic, and extended well beyond the handful of Latin American experts directly associated with the Alliance. For example, in 1961, J. Lloyd Mecham's work was supportive, and his outlook was clearly grounded in the basic assumptions of modernization theory and the Alliance. He argued that "forces tending to ameliorate Latin-American poverty are under way and they are gaining momentum". He noted that Mexico's economic growth rate since World War II, "has been substantially higher" than that of the countries of Western Europe and the US itself. In this situation he concluded that--since "it is the belief of most economists studying problems of development that Mexico is not isolated, but is rather the prototype of a continent which has 'achieved takeoff into sustained growth'"--it may not be "too much to hope that the satisfaction deriving from a sense of real achievement in Latin America may begin shortly to neutralize the invidious elements in the Latin feeling of economic insecurity".[123] In the early 1960s, even Frank Tannenbaum offered qualified support for the Alliance for Progress, although he did not think the Alliance went far enough. He laid out some specific recommendations to do with economic aid and the issue of expropriation. And Tannenbaum questioned what he saw as an optimistic time frame. He also expressed reservations about whether all the political and economic changes envisioned by the Alliance could occur peacefully, given the region's social structure.[124]

At the center of the Alliance for Progress was a decade-long program of land and economic reform which was going to cost 100 billion dollars and aimed at bringing about an annual growth rate of at least 2.5 percent. It also sought to achieve greater productivity in the agricultural sector, eradicate illiteracy, stimulate trade diversification, generate improvements in housing and bring about improved income distribution in the region. The Alliance for Progress was a failure. Its central unstated goal was the protection of North American investments in Latin America at the same time as many of the Alliance's reforms endangered those investments. Trade diversification threatened the US-based transnationals' monopoly in primary agricultural products and mineral extraction. Any significant land reform also threatened the interests of the still largely land-based ruling elites in Latin America. This contradiction was apparent in the way that Kennedy's reformist rhetoric went hand in hand with Washington's ever-deepening commitment to military and police aid and counterinsurgency to quash peasant-based rebellions in the region. From the very beginning, US-based transnationals and the landed oligarchies attempted to preserve the status quo and prevent any meaningful change. There were sixteen military coups within eight years of the launch of the Alliance for Progress. By the late 1960s, high rates of economic growth in many Latin American countries had been achieved. However, high growth rates had served primarily to increase social inequality, while the middle class moved to side with the ruling political and socio-economic elite as politics, instead of evolving towards democracy, moved ever further towards authoritarianism and military dictatorship. Already by the time of Kennedy's assassination, the reformist element in the Alliance had been sidelined in favour of a more straightforward approach of military and economic aid to any regime which was committed to the status quo.[125]

Washington's emphasis on the military as a means of controlling political change had given rise to greater scholarly interest in the role of the local armed forces in achieving that goal. As a result, the role of military establishments in Third World politics rapidly emerged as a focus of research. Long before the 1960s, Washington had of course supported military dictatorships in its pursuit of international order, and in some cases it had facilitated in their very creation, as in Nicaragua; however, the rationale for such a policy had never been particularly sophisticated. Yet, the explicit US modernizing mission, embodied by the Alliance for Progress and the Kennedy administration generally, provided the nexus for and even demanded the creation of a much more sophisticated justification for the support of militarism in Latin America, Asia and Africa. Some of Kennedy's advisors, such as Delesseps S. Morrison, his ambassador to the OAS and generally regarded as a conservative as far as policy debates within the administration were concerned, had argued from the outset that democracy was not achievable in Latin America. He had advocated early on that the US should support the military establishments in the region because they represented the only effective barrier to the spread of communism.[126] At the same time, by the end of the 1950s the Rand Corporation had begun seriously studying the role of the military in Latin America, Asia and Africa. This work projected an image of the military as both a stabilizing factor in the face of disorder, and the only force in society which had the administrative and technical skills to facilitate modernization. Increasingly, military officers in Latin America, Asia and Africa were represented as the vanguard of secular modernization and industrialization. Military modernization theory soon became a major sub-discipline of North American area studies, as influential members of the Kennedy administration, such as Walt Whitman Rostow, emphasized the need to cultivate members of the Third World officer class.[127] Policy-oriented academics, such as Lucian Pye, Edward Shils, and Samuel Huntington put forward a view of military elites as the key to both order and development. Pye and Shils both contributed essays to the 1962 publication by John J. Johnson entitled **The Role of the Military in Underdeveloped Countries**.[128] By mid-1962, the National Security Council was articulating a policy on "internal defense", which emphasized that "a change brought about through force by non-communist elements may be preferable to prolonged deterioration of governmental effectiveness". The National Security Council document foresaw situations in which it would be in the United States' "interest" to turn "the local military and police" into "advocates of democracy and agents for carrying forward the developmental process". This approach shaped the policy of the Kennedy and the Johnson administrations towards Latin America and the rest of the world.[129]

In the case of Latin America, operating somewhat beyond the inner circle inhabited by policy-academics, such as Rostow and Huntington, was the work of historian Edwin Lieuwen. At the beginning of the 1960s, Edwin Lieuwen's **Arms and Politics in Latin America**, which appeared under the auspices of the Council on Foreign Relations, examined the history and political significance of the armed forces in Latin America in relation to US policy, especially its military aspect. This book was followed by a book on modern militarism in Latin America, and then two others which dealt more conventionally with US foreign policy and national security in Latin America. Lieuwen stimulated a number of young historians, many of whom had started as his graduate students, to take Latin American military establishments as a focus of study.[130] Richard Millett, who published an important book in the late 1970s on Somoza's national guard, was originally one of Lieuwen's PhD students.

The shift towards military modernization theory resulted from the failure of the Alliance for Progress and the escalating war in Vietnam. Classic modernization theory had assumed that economic development would lead to political democracy and stability. By the second half of the 1960s, some area-studies specialists located within the dominant professional discourses, such as Simon G. Hanson, were pointing out that Kennedy-style modernization and development had actually served to widen the gulf between the rich and the poor and exacerbate political instability in Latin America.[131] An incident which contributed to the disillusionment of many Latin American studies specialists with modernization theory and with the Alliance for Progress, although not with liberalism, was the Project Camelot Affair. Project Camelot, which highlighted the close links between the professional study of Latin America and US foreign policy in Latin America, had been set up in 1964 by the US Army's Special Operations Research Office (SORO). Scheduled to cost 44 million dollars and take three to four years, it represented the largest single social science project ever funded by government, and was to be administered through The American University in Washington. The project, which included both US and foreign academics, sought to develop a social science model which could determine the likelihood of revolution and instability, and advise what could be done to maintain order and stability. The project specifically targeted Latin America, and those countries singled out included Guatemala and El Salvador. Project Camelot sought to develop both a means by which political and social change could be "anticipated" and a guide to "controlling" it. Following the public exposure of the Project in Chile, it was cancelled. Project Camelot was brought to an end primarily because Washington did not want to alienate the government of Chile and other Latin American governments. Just as important was the fact that the project had originated with the Department of Defense and was perceived by the State Department as trespassing on its territory. The US government distanced itself from Project Camelot and issued new guidelines regarding foreign area research. However, the State Department and the Department of Defense continued to fund research projects which pursued the same objectives as Camelot, including the study of the role of the military in political and social turmoil, the parameters of social and cultural change, counter-insurgency, civic action and political stability.[132] These concerns were readily apparent in work such as Willard F. Barber and C. Neale Ronning's **Internal Security and Military Power: Counterinsurgency and Civic Action in Latin America**.[133] In a wider sense, although the cancellation of Project Camelot had important long-term repercussions for Latin American studies, its rise and fall had only a limited impact on the professional area-studies discourses generally in this period. The fit between US policy and North American social science remained tight. For example, works, such as Huntington's **Political Order in Changing Societies** exercised a great deal of influence in the late 1960s and into the 1970s, and pointed to the continued importance of Washington's concern with political order for many area-studies specialists.[134] Huntington's politics-of-order approach, which will be discussed in Chapter 3, also pointed to the revision, rather than the rejection, of modernization theory.

The revision of modernization theory was readily apparent by the late 1960s. While most of the prominent Latin American specialists still defended US policy generally, and the Alliance for Progress specifically, the optimism of the early 1960s had faded somewhat. But the goals were not challenged, and any criticisms that were made focused on questions of implementation. William D. Rogers, a former Deputy US Coordinator of the Alliance and a former Assistant Secretary of State for Inter-American Affairs, argued that the US had responded to the social and economic needs of the region, despite having fallen short of its goals.[135] In 1967, Robert N. Burr argued that the deteriorating relations between North and South could be improved by bolstering existing organizations, such as the Organization of American States (OAS), and existing programs, such as the Alliance for Progress.[136] In a second, revised edition of **Today's Latin America**, which was originally written at the beginning of the 1960s, Robert Alexander deflected criticism of the Alliance by tracing its failure to the death of President Kennedy, following which the "climate of inter-American relations had changed". According to Alexander, Johnson lacked Kennedy's "sympathetic understanding of the crisis facing Latin America". Alexander warned that, despite the pressing problems in Vietnam and the apparent containment of Cuba, the US could not allow itself "the luxury of ignorance" about the economic and political "problems" of the southern republics. He argued that in the years after World War II Washington supported dictators and ignored the need for "the evolution of a democratic type of society and political life in these countries", while failing to "understand the deep-seated drives for social revolution" in the region. According to

Alexander, President Kennedy's Alliance for Progress had changed this situation, and he felt that if the US returned to the attitudes and actions towards Latin America which were a hallmark of the Kennedy years, then greater unity and understanding between North and South would again prevail. He concluded by making a ritual appeal to a 'common history' and a 'common destiny'. Alexander foresaw the possibility of "the unity of the Americas" increasing in the years ahead. He argued that "if Latin America's traditional belief in democracy begins to conform to a greater degree than in the past to the facts of the region's politics, most of the nations of the hemisphere will truly share a common political ideology and have common ideals to defend". Also, he perceived "economic trends" in Latin America and the US which suggested that the "mixed economies" of North and South would "become more alike".[137] Writing in 1968 Alexander, even more than other writers, defended the Alliance for Progress and modernization theory in a way which located all their problems at the level of execution, rather than scrutinizing the liberal assumptions on which they rested.

The decline of Washington's interest in Latin America, lamented by Alexander, did not translate directly into a decline for Latin American studies. The expansion sparked by the Cuban revolution and the Alliance for Progress continued throughout the 1960s. The incredible influx of public funds and foundation money, particularly the Ford Foundation's International Training and Research Program, meant that the 1960s were a period of economic abundance for Latin American studies. Latin American research in the 1960s underwent both a quantitative and a qualitative change. As we have seen, quantitatively, between 1951 and 1960 the number of PhDs awarded in Latin American studies declined, from 30% of all area studies to 18%, while the number of PhD students had also fallen off. However, after 1960 the numbers began to increase in relative and absolute terms, and by 1966 the number of PhD students addressing Latin American topics had increased, while their number as a percentage of all foreign-area PhDs in North America had levelled out. By the 1970s the number of PhD students undertaking Latin American topics in any one year had doubled, compared to the mid-1960s, and work on Latin America represented over 20% of all PhD work done in area studies in North America.[138]

Another indication of the expansion in Latin American studies in the 1960s was that between 1949 and 1958 the number of courses on some aspect of Latin America being offered at North American colleges remained constant; however, by 1969 the figure had doubled with history and literature, followed by political science, being the three main disciplines in which the courses were taught. In 1968 there were over 200 institutions of higher education in North America which belonged to the Consortium of Latin American Studies Programs, about half of which had full scale Latin American studies departments and programs.[139] Also indicative of growth in the 1960s was the increase in the number of Latin American historians in North America, which grew from 389 in 1965 to 566 in 1970.[140] As part of the dramatic overall growth in Latin American studies after 1959, even the relatively marginalized study of Central America expanded. For example, the number of PhD candidates studying topics which related to social change and economic development in Central America increased dramatically over the course of the 1960s. Political science and economics were particularly well represented in this expansion, as were geography and anthropology, and to a lesser extent history. Guatemala attracted the most attention. Between 1960 and 1974 there were 140 PhDs granted in North America on social change and/or economic development in Central America. Over 40 were on Guatemala (9 were degrees in anthropology), while 32 PhD students focused on Costa Rica. Only 5 dissertations over the whole period were on some aspect of US-Central American relations.[141]

As Latin American studies grew, new publications--such as the **Journal of Interamerican Studies**, which was established by the School of Inter-American Studies at the University of Florida (Gainesville) in January 1959 with the financial assistance of the Pan American Foundation--began to appear. The **Latin American Research Review** was established in 1965, to provide an outlet for the increased volume of North American research on Latin America. The first issue of the **Latin American Research Review** proclaimed that its goal was "to achieve greater and more systematic communication of research among individuals and institutions concerned with the study of Latin America".[142] In 1966 the Latin American Studies Association (LASA) was formed, with the assistance of the Ford Foundation's International Training and Research Program, to help link the growing number of Latin American specialists and further promote Latin American studies.[143] While the expansion of area studies in the late 1950s and early 1960s provided the context for the emergence of LASA, according to Kalman Silvert, the organization's first president, the Project Camelot scandal and the ethical debate it generated were the immediate and direct stimulus for the formation of the Latin American Studies Association.[144] Although the dramatic expansion of area studies generally, and Latin American studies more specifically, had tapered-off by the late 1960s, it would be inappropriate to speak of decline. The year 1967 has been characterized as a turning point for the language and area-studies programs. In that year the Ford Foundation ended its huge International Training and Research Program, which had been set up in 1953, while federal money was also curtailed. The costs of maintaining such programs were often picked up by the universities; however, most programs stopped growing and some did begin to shrink.[145]

Nevertheless, new standards of scholarship were laid down in the 1960s, and the range of new approaches and the inter-disciplinary character of Latin American studies as a whole were in marked contrast to the professional discourses on Latin America of the pre-1959 era. For example, the early 1960s saw a number of historical works on Central America that clearly suggested the growing methodological sophistication of Latin American studies, although they were firmly located within the Cold War liberalism of the professional discourses. The books produced by North American historians such as Thomas Karnes and Franklin D. Parker were serious works of historical scholarship.[146] These books were a qualitative improvement over books on Central America by writers such as John Martz, which had been written against the backdrop of the Guatemalan Affair. For example, Mario Rodriguez, who also produced an early historical synthesis on Central America, explicitly rejected what he called the "conspiracy" approach to events in Guatemala in the 1950s, which he attributed to writers such as Martz and Alexander. Rodriguez was a graduate of the University of California (Berkeley) who went on to become Professor of History at the University of Arizona by the mid-1960s. His 1965 book was a general history of Central America which ended with the 1950s. Rodriguez dedicated his book to the "memory of John Fitzgerald

Kennedy". In his view the Alliance for Progress had lost its way after Kennedy's death, as US policy-makers again began to emphasize the "military solution" and shifted towards the "acceptance of military regimes throughout the region", on the presumption that they "will hold the fort against the Communist invasion". He argued that this policy would "inevitably frustrate and undermine" Washington's "natural allies" in the region-"the moderate democratic elements". He insisted that "it would be wiser and more profitable for" the US "to get the Alliance for Progress back on the road which President Kennedy intended. In the long run, and despite many serious obstacles, it would cost us less and at the same time undermine the extremists throughout Latin America".[147] Rodriguez's book pointed to the continuing force of modernization theory. Like other Latin Americanists who criticized the Alliance for Progress, in the second half of the 1960s he argued that the failure of the Alliance lay in its execution rather than its conception.[148]

The continuity of liberal assumptions was dramatically apparent in a major study by Dana Munro in the mid-1960s which addressed US relations with Central America. In **Intervention and Dollar Diplomacy in the Caribbean 1900-1921** and a subsequent volume, which relied on the traditional methodology of diplomatic history, he continued to stress that US foreign policy in the region was concerned primarily with removing the "conditions" which threatened the independence of the Central American and Caribbean republics. Munro also emphasized US concern with improving economic conditions, which would in turn facilitate political stability. Although he drew attention to the possible role of private US investment, Munro emphasized that private investment had exercised no significant influence on the formulation and execution of US foreign policy.[149] He argued that the State Department "took an active part in the negotiation of loans to several Caribbean governments because it thought that the loans would forward its own policy objectives" and in every case the US government's involvement "secured better terms for the borrowing government than it could otherwise have obtained". Reducing it to a question of individual intention on the part of State Department employees, Munro assured the reader that he himself "participated in the discussions about many of these loans", and he could "testify that the people in the State Department showed no interest at all in the idea that the loans would be profitable to American bankers".[150] By focusing on US intentions, and establishing their honorable character, Munro's work was able to deflect criticism away from their effect, and disregard the broader economic context in which US expansion into the circum-Caribbean occurred. At the same time, Munro argued that Washington was concerned with "the development of democratic institutions", and "we certainly tried to encourage the holding of free elections wherever it seemed practicable to do so". According to Munro, thanks to the "efforts" of the US, Honduras and Nicaragua had "democratically elected governments" by 1933, while in Guatemala there was a government which "apparently had popular support". Munro argued that although some of the republics had "made progress toward more stable government", many had not, and the "problems" with which Washington continued to be faced in the Caribbean and Central America were "often much like those with which the State Department had to deal in the first three decades of the century".[151]

Less committed to traditional methodology were the first books in what would, after 1979, turn into a deluge of political and historical studies of Nicaragua and its relations with the United States. One of the first books of this type was a short descriptive study by Marvin Goldwert on the constabularies which the US had set up in both Nicaragua and the Dominican Republic in the period prior to the Good Neighbor Policy.[152] An important book by Neill Macauley, published in 1967, was basically a military history of the second US intervention and occupation of the country in the late 1920s and early 1930s.[153] Macauley's study had been preceded by a few earlier works which also focused on the Marines in Nicaragua; however, **The Sandino Affair** was far more detailed.[154] He represented the events in Nicaragua in the 1920s as an early model of both insurgency and counter-insurgency warfare. Important themes of his work were that Sandino was one of the first practitioners of modern guerrilla warfare, while Nicaragua in the 1920s was a testing ground for US counter-insurgency tactics. Macauley tended towards a romanticized portrayal of both the US Marines and Sandino's guerrillas. He described both the guerrillas and the Marines using the same adjectives, such as "gallant" and "brave".[155] Despite his romantic portrayal of the insurgents and counter insurgents, Macauley's analysis of the broader dynamics of US intervention put less emphasis on US idealism than earlier writers. He emphasized politico-strategic factors and power politics, without ignoring economic considerations. Macauley quoted Bryce Wood with approval when he argued that after the mid-1920s "the immediate protection of American and other foreign property in Nicaragua was no longer of first importance" to Washington. Following the renewed intervention of late 1926, Washington's policy in Nicaragua "was based fundamentally on the assertion of the supremacy of the power of the US in Central America".[156]

A year after Macauley's military history of US relations with Nicaragua appeared, a broader work on the same period, written by William Kamman, was published.[157] The interpretative position taken in Kamman's book was generally sympathetic to the US government, and it centered on the US rather than on Nicaragua. Kamman stated at the outset that the purpose of the book was "to analyze what happened" in order to help ensure "that it will not repeat itself elsewhere in American foreign relations". He also responded to pre-1945 radical perspectives on US-Nicaraguan relations and proposed to "examine" the "argument" that the United States was an "imperialist nation" which sought to "exploit" its southern neighbors, particularly Central America and the Caribbean via "dollar diplomacy"--a phrase Kamman regarded as "unfortunate". Throughout the book, he spoke in terms of "our relations" and "our policy", and while he expressed sympathy with the Marines he tended to dismiss the guerrillas as "bandits". He commiserated that the "situation" in Nicaragua was a "thankless task" and the "most unpleasant job went to the Marines".[158] Kamman's book was representative of an established approach to US foreign policy which set out to understand previous crises out of a desire to generate a foreign policy which would better serve US interests. As we will see, this approach became increasingly systematized in the 1970s.

Kamman's analysis of the basis for US policy in Nicaragua between 1925 and 1933 was shaped by longstanding assumptions about the legitimate national security concerns of the US, assumptions which were central to the professional discourses on Latin America. He argued that the basis for US policy in the region had not changed substantially since the 1820s. Since the nineteenth century the

State Department had been aware of, and concerned about, the "commercial importance, for present and future generations, of Nicaragua's San Juan River and Lake Nicaragua". At the same time, a "concern" about the "independence" of the southern republics and the desire that none of the European powers should jeopardize Washington's "hegemony in the New World", were other major factors. A final "central consideration" was the Panama Canal. The Canal has been so crucial in US policy, noted Kamman, that writers such as Bemis have suggested that the United States' Caribbean policy be named the "Panama Policy". Under this policy those countries in the region where "political and economic problems often led to fear for the safety of lives and property or fear that some non-American state might intervene, most often felt the heavy hand of the US". According to Kamman, it was not until the 1920s that Washington began to review its policy of intervention, and although Washington did not discard its interventionist policy until 1933, the "ground work for good neighborliness" was set down in this period.[159]

The general result of the US occupation of Nicaragua, as well as its control of Haiti, Cuba and the Dominican Republic, was considered by Kamman to have been "unsatisfactory in resolving many problems". At the same time he took the view that the US had brought "a measure of peace and stability" to the countries concerned. In particular, the occupation of Nicaragua generated immediate problems for the US, while the longer-term result of the US intervention in Nicaragua, in the form of the rise and consolidation of the Somoza dictatorship, was, according to Kamman, "equally troublesome" for the US. Kamman's approach to the impact of the US occupation on Nicaragua was also preoccupied with the problems it generated for Washington rather than its impact on Nicaragua. Between 1912 and 1924, the country, according to Kamman, "gradually became orderly", at the same time as Washington "encouraged such peace everywhere" in Central America. However, Kamman lamented that following a dozen years of US occupation there was a minimum of actual "change" in Nicaragua, and it remained "a country unprepared for democracy" and possessed of a "penchant for revolution". In this situation the US-sponsored "free elections" of 1924 were, in Kamman's view, doomed to failure. In a classic liberal formulation, he argued that the US government and the government of Nicaragua "thwarted one another and produced a sort of mutual defeat".[160] Kamman characterized the "mood" in the wake of the promulgation of the Good Neighbor Policy and the 1933 withdrawal from Nicaragua, as a mixture of "relief" and "apprehension". He said that the United States was happy to be rid of the "unrewarding business" and that "full sovereignty satisfied the Nicaraguans". He argued that, although after 1933 the Nicaraguan government turned to the State Department at a number of junctures, Washington was adamant that it had to address its "problems" in its "own way" and by its "own efforts". Kamman noted that this had been the situation, "at least outwardly", right up to the late 1960s; however, he did not explain the significance of his use of the term "outwardly".[161] Although Kamman adopted a position in relation to US foreign policy which was more critical than the stance of writers of an earlier era, his study was clearly within the dominant Cold War professional discourses on Latin America. A more critical perspective associated with the rise of New Left diplomatic historiography and dependency theory did not play a significant role in the North American understanding of Latin America until the 1970s. And even then the liberal professional discourses remained predominant.

Conclusion: Modernization and Development 1945-1968

After 1945 Latin American studies was transformed into a much more inter-disciplinary movement, and the work of historians was increasingly overshadowed by political scientists and international-relations specialists. At the same time, much of the work by Latin American specialists between 1945 and 1968 continued to reflect the assumptions which had been central to the professional discourses in the earlier period, when historians had predominated. The longstanding ideas about the relative harmony of US and Latin American interests gained strength after 1945, while some sort of commitment to Pan Americanism, in the context of the imperatives of the Cold War, also continued to inform the work of Latin Americanists. Between 1945 and 1968 the dominant professional discourses on Latin America rested on a conception of historical change which represented history as the success or failure of a nation's rise to democratic industrialism. It was assumed that the US had the ability and the right to guide developing nations to this goal. Thus modernization theory was at the very center of the North American understanding of Latin America in this era. However, despite its emphasis on a modernizing mission rather than the earlier civilizing mission, this shift was partial. Cold War development theory continued to be fashioned by a cultural or even a racial pride in the perceived superiority of the North American historical model. And this was obvious in the early 1960s, when the Kennedy administration and its advisers embarked on a mission to save the hemisphere from the communist threat. Washington policy-makers and Latin American specialists were driven by the concern that disorder and poverty made the region an easy target for communist subversion, and they sought to carry democracy and economic prosperity to Latin America. However, during the 1960s, revolutionary and reactionary challenges in Latin America increased. And liberal development theorists were increasingly concerned with the management of social change and the politics of order, as evidenced by the emergence of military modernization theory. By the end of the 1960s, as Washington sought to manage the numerous challenges to its far-flung empire, particularly in Vietnam, US foreign policy towards Latin America entered a decade of relative neglect. However, the growth in area studies inspired by the Cold War generated such momentum that Latin American studies had consolidated its position within the North American tertiary system by the end of the 1960s. With the post-1968 crisis of hegemony, this institutional strength provided an important context for the political changes in, and theoretical diversification of, Latin American studies in the 1970s. And as we will see it also helped make it possible for the dominant professional discourses to achieve greater relative autonomy, although certainly not independence from the practice of US foreign policy.

Part II

The US Hegemonic Crisis and the Transformation of Latin American Studies 1968-1990

Chapter 3

THE LIMITS OF POWER 1968-1979

"(T)he United States has long been its own worst enemy in Latin America. Latin American governments tend not to appeal to extrahemispheric powers for assistance, especially military assistance without good reason. Too often that reason has been an effort to maintain their independence in the face of US pressures....If the United States, given its immense economic and political power, cannot achieve its goals through negotiation, then it probably would be unwise to try to achieve them by the use of force. Force is almost by definition the worst way to resolve conflicting interests because an imposed settlement is inherently unstable in the long term....If the relaxation of international tensions persists, the presidency and the Congress will have one of their best opportunities in recent history to reexamine and reformulate US policies so that the United States is better able than in the past to come to terms with revolutionary change in Latin America in accordance with broader conceptions of the national interest."

Cole Blasier, **The Hovering Giant: US Responses to Revolutionary Change in Latin America** [Pittsburgh: University of Pittsburgh Press, 1976]. pp. 272-275.

        By 1968 the US foreign policy consensus based on containment was breaking down and the US imperial state was at the center of a wider hegemonic crisis.[1] The US mission to modernize the world along liberal capitalist lines was increasingly challenged by revolution and economic nationalism in Latin America, the Middle East, Asia and Africa, and in North America by a concern with the limits of power.[2] The crisis of US hegemony was directly connected to the crisis of the social sciences which resulted in the dramatic political and methodological diversification of the professional social science and area-studies discourses.[3] By the late 1960s, a growing number of radical Latin American specialists were arguing that North American social science generally and Latin American studies specifically were theoretically bankrupt.[4] Distinct radical professional discourses on Latin America (as well as the Middle East, Asia and Africa) emerged to challenge the dominant liberal professional discourses. At the center of the rise of the new radical discourses on Latin America was dependency theory.[5] Also apparent was the strengthening, by the end of the 1970s, of a conservative position within and outside the dominant professional discourses, which emerged as relatively distinct conservative discourses.[6] The political and methodological consensus within and beyond Latin American studies was perceived to have disappeared by the late 1970s. For example, in 1978, the Harvard Latin American specialist Jorge I. Domínguez lamented that the "state" of the professional literature on inter-American relations was "not well", and "for the purposes of facilitating the study of national public or private policies toward international affairs", the "degree of scholarly consensus" was "grossly insufficient".[7] However, despite the radical challenges and the political turmoil of the 1968 to 1979 era, the liberal discourses maintained their position of dominance within and outside the Latin American studies profession.

As with accommodation generally, it was the partial incorporation of radical approaches which contained the radical challenge and was integral to the revitalization and continued dominance of the liberal discourses in the 1970s.[8] The diffusion of radical ideas into the dominant professional discourses was part of the wider reinvention of liberalism in this period. As we have seen, the failure of the Alliance for Progress, the debacle of Project Camelot, and dissatisfaction with the war in Southeast Asia encouraged many liberal Latin Americanists to re-examine their theoretical perspectives and re-evaluate the relationship of their profession to US foreign policy.[9] However, their growing doubts about the likelihood of the US shaping the world in its own image did not result in the abandonment of liberalism. In the 1970s, liberals revised modernization theory to give it a more critical edge. They also began to adopt elements of dependency analysis, as well as other methodological approaches, such as corporatism and bureaucratic-authoritarianism and the bureaucratic politics approach. Furthermore, the liberal discourses were increasingly influenced by an emphasis on the North-South rather than the East-West axis. Nevertheless, unlike the radical reliance on a conflict model of inter-American relations, the dominant professional discourses continued to rest on the view that there was no fundamental conflict of interest between US objectives in Latin America and the aspirations of the people who lived there. And while most radicals advocated revolutionary change, or at least radical reform, the liberals continued to be optimistic about the possibility of improving North-South relations without having to make major structural changes. They acknowledged the existence of problems; however, the problems were perceived as soluble within the existing inter-American framework.

Also central to the dominant liberal discourses by the 1970s was a preoccupation with the lessons of history and a concern to pass these lessons on to Washington policy-makers.[10] This flowed from the crisis of hegemony, an increased involvement on the part of Latin American specialists in foreign-policy issues and the desire of area-studies specialists to apply their professional knowledge to problems in US foreign policy and ensure that past mistakes were not repeated. Many liberal academics were avowed reformists by the 1970s, but their growing concern with human rights, and an often explicit desire to lend their expertise to the formulation of a more benevolent foreign policy, was a quixotic project.[11] At the level of policy advice, academics have had to strike a balance between what they think and what policy-makers want to hear.[12] Liberals are limited by the dominant professional and foreign-policy discourses. The language, the categories and the questions generated by the discourses are linked to the wider university, governmental and corporate context that has ensured Latin American specialists' complementary relationship with the practice of US foreign policy. While post-Vietnam liberals were more critical of US foreign policy than their predecessors, the work of those who have explicitly sought to influence policy, as well as the work of those whose involvement is more indirect, has continued to contribute to the legitimacy and resilience of US hegemony.

The Nixon Doctrine: Problems of Empire 1968-1979

It was not until the second half of the 1970s that some of the lessons drawn by North American liberals were at least partially apparent in the practice of US foreign policy. The approach to foreign policy articulated by the Nixon administration was a relatively conservative reaction to Washington's problems of empire in the so-called Third World. In 1969, Richard Nixon entered the White House promising that his administration would find an 'honorable solution' to the war in Southeast Asia. However, the incoming administration did not attempt to redefine US objectives. The Vietnam War encouraged the Republican administration to make a conservative reassessment of Washington's means, not of its goals. During his first year in office Nixon established the basic approach which would continue as US policy until the second half of the 1970s. The Nixon Doctrine began as a relatively spontaneous assertion about a new US role in Asia. Nixon emphasized that the US would seek to avoid direct intervention to contain revolution and increasingly move to assist its allies with military and economic aid. The Nixon Doctrine was explicitly aimed at avoiding another Vietnam; however, it did little to alter a deeply rooted Cold War outlook, neither did it serve to curtail covert interventions in Chile and elsewhere in Latin America. It also amplified the traditional US policy of supporting loyal dictatorships, permitting the continuation of all the factors which had historically undermined the stability of Washington's empire. Furthermore, despite their desire to reduce the direct US commitment to maintaining Washington's global hegemony, Nixon and Kissinger's growing preoccupation with US credibility served to counter any absolute decrease in US intervention. Their concern to reassure allies, particularly in the Middle East, that Washington could still be relied upon led to the Nixon administration's aggressive support of the military dictatorship in Pakistan in the war with India in 1971. Then, in early October 1973, when Egypt and Syria attacked Israel, the US assigned considerable symbolism to the success of Israeli arms. A compromise resolution of the United Nations averted a Soviet-US confrontation, and in December the protagonists in the Middle East began peace talks. But the wide definition which Nixon and Kissinger attached to credibility precluded the reduction of US confrontations in the Third World, even if the role of US ground troops was curtailed.[13]

By the early 1970s, circumstances in Latin America as a whole, as well as Asia, the Middle East and Africa, also pointed towards greater US involvement rather than less. In response to the growing socio-economic crisis, revolutions and national liberation movements were more widespread than a decade earlier, when the US had begun escalating its commitment to South Vietnam. In Latin America in particular, radical and marxist political parties, and guerrilla movements, still threatened the stability of numerous US client regimes. In response to insurgencies in countries such as Guatemala, the US relied more than ever on covert warfare (which was relatively inexpensive and politically uninhibited) as well as on continued and growing aid to client regimes. As Congress increasingly sought to circumscribe US foreign policy before and after Watergate, the CIA's role in furthering US policy increased. US objectives in the Third World in the Nixon years were a continuation of the anti-communist goals of previous administrations. At the same time, the anti-communist continuity was also apparent in Nixon's idea that the Vietnam War could be won as much by a diplomatic deal with Soviet Union, and later China, as it could on the battlefield. This led the administration to continue to expect that the solutions to US problems of empire lay along the East-West axis.[14] At the beginning of the 1970s, Nixon and Kissinger perceived no need for a large number of allies in Latin America, the Middle East, Asia and Africa. From their perspective, Third World regimes and/or revolutions were incapable of threatening US interests, unless they were backed by a major power, as had allegedly happened in Vietnam.[15]

In Latin America more specifically, the Nixon administration was unwilling to come to grips with the region's history, preferring the further indirect militarization of US policy in the region. In 1969 Nixon sent Nelson A. Rockefeller to Latin America to meet with heads of state and then give a complete report accompanied by recommendations. Rockefeller had, of course, been involved with the region since the 1930s, serving as head of the Office of the Co-ordinator of Inter-American Affairs in the 1940s. Rockefeller was a potent symbol of US imperialism, and all four of his visits to the region in 1969 were attended with danger signals for the US. He tried unsuccessfully to visit Peru, where the reformist military government had recently nationalized a US-based oil company. His visit to Honduras ended with an anti-US riot, and Chile and Venezuela cancelled his visits. Although Rockefeller expressed some sympathy for the Latin American view that relations with the US were unequal, and he predicted that the region was "moving rapidly into a period of revolution", his recommendations embodied a military solution rather than even the most moderate changes to the structure of economic and political relations. Reflecting the shift from the early optimism of the Alliance for Progress to military modernization theory, Rockefeller argued that "without some framework for order, no progress can be achieved", and in Latin America the military was "the essential force for constructive social change". To this end, he advised that Washington should increase its military assistance to the region.[16] The Rockefeller Report was central to the shift from the Cold War liberalism of the Kennedy and Johnson era and its apparent emphasis on economic aid, the middle sectors and democratization, to military modernization with its concern with order as the key to development and progress. The Rockefeller Report clearly sanctioned military regimes and contributed to the legitimacy of the authoritarian and technocratic regimes in Brazil and elsewhere in the 1970s.[17]

At the end of 1969, Nixon launched his new policy for Latin America, under the title "Action for Progress in the Americas", which lined up with Rockefeller's recommendations and also drew on the *Consensus of Viña del Mar*, which was a result of a meeting in Chile in May 1969 between representatives of most Latin American governments.[18] Apart from some economic concessions (which had been asked for in the *Consensus of Viña del Mar*) the major thrust was the president's emphasis on taking a realistic approach to inter-American relations. This has generally been interpreted to mean that Washington was willing to deal with military governments regardless of how autocratic and repressive they were. Nixon's Latin American policy meshed with the overall concern of the Nixon Doctrine to support particular client regimes as regional policemen. The Shah of Iran was singled out in the Middle East, and the de facto military governments of Central America (which was every government except that of Costa Rica), particularly the Somoza dynasty, benefitted from this policy, as did the military regimes of South America. In the 1970s the armies of Central and South America expanded, along with a number of other military establishments around the world, as arm sales emerged as the backbone of Nixon's policy. Direct US assistance continued, and generous credit was extended to facilitate the purchase of armaments (in 1972 alone, for example, Guatemala purchased $6.5 million worth of military hardware, most of it on credit). The Central American armies continued to participate in the civic action programs which had been set up by the Alliance for Progress. These programs, which involved the use of troops in the construction of roads and schools, were aimed at improving the army's image. However, civic action tended to militarize society further and to aggravate economic inequality by giving civilian jobs to soldiers at a time of increasing unemployment and by giving high-ranking military officers even more say in social and economic planning. These programs also further linked the United States with the Central American military establishments at the local level.[19] Also, unlike the early years of the Alliance for Progress, Nixon's Action for Progress emphasized trade rather than economic aid, and contained even fewer reformist initiatives.

In contrast to the Kennedy and Johnson years, the Nixon administration sought to have a lower profile in Latin America; however, the hemisphere was too unstable in the late 1960s and early 1970s for Washington to turn its attention away from the region for too long. The emergence of a reformist military government in Peru, which initially appeared to threaten important US economic interests, drew Washington's attention southward in early 1969; however, in the long run the new regime's nationalist rhetoric was not matched by its policy. It had presented the International Petroleum Company (IPC), a subsidiary of Standard Oil, with an almost $700 million bill for back taxes. At the same time, the new government began to rely increasingly on massive private borrowing, which eventually led to a reliance on the IMF and the World Bank. By 1974 the government had agreed to compensate IPC, and US direct investment began to grow. By the late 1970s Peru was under the influence of the IMF and private banks, as far as economic policy and planning were concerned, while the military returned power to civilian governments in 1978. Far more important than Peru was the major US intervention in Chile to help General Pinochet in the overthrow of the Allende government in 1973. Allende had come to power in Chile via the democratic process, but the nationalist-marxist character of his political platform was perceived as a threat to US hegemony in the hemisphere. One of the first acts of the Allende government was to finish the nationalization of the foreign copper companies, which had begun under the less radical Frei government. Washington responded to this situation by blocking almost all US aid to Chile, preventing new loans, increasing US links with the military and expanding CIA operations in the country. In 1973 Nixon and Kissinger ensured that Allende was ousted by a military which had been well supplied for many years by the United States, while the military regime in Brazil was also shifted closer to US policy in the early 1970s, no doubt in part because of lavish US military assistance.[20] Pinochet introduced one of the most repressive regimes in Latin America. And, although the transition to democracy in Chile began in the late 1980s, Pinochet still remains head of the armed forces. In the 1970s, rather than address the broad political and economic causes of its problems of empire, the US sought to maintain its hegemony by relying on Latin America militarists. In the late 1970s the Carter administration's attempt to reverse Washington's close links with military dictators, inherited from Nixon and his predecessors, drew the US deeper into the region.

The Rise and Fall of Dependency Theory 1968-1979

It was the increasing militarism of US foreign policy by the late 1960s, and the failure of the Alliance for Progress, which provided the context for a leftward and southward shift in Latin America studies in North America. While modernization theory originated in the centers of post-war power and spread in a relatively homogeneous fashion around the globe, the reactions to modernization theory often flowed, at least in part, from more regionally specific experiences. This was readily apparent in the Latin American response to modernization theory, elements of which were imported into North America in the 1960s. A decade after Washington had tried unsuccessfully to prevent Cuba from becoming a foothold for international communism in the Western Hemisphere, a radical dependency perspective, which drew political inspiration from the Cuban revolution, had gained a foothold in Latin American studies. The emergence and growing power of dependency theory represented a direct challenge to the dominant liberal discourses on Latin America; however, by the mid-1970s dependency theory had met its demise as the radical work on Latin America was accommodated by the liberal institutional structures of the North American university system, by the dominant professional discourses and by changing political circumstances. Dependency theory, as it came to be understood in North America in the 1960s, developed out of the North American marxism of Paul Sweezy and Paul Baran and Latin American historico-structuralism, which was initially associated with Raul Prebisch and the United Nations' Economic Commission for Latin America (Comisión Economica para América Latina or CEPAL).

At the end of the 1940s Sweezy, along with Leo Huberman, had founded the radical journal **Monthly Review**. They had hoped for the expansion of the New Deal after World War II into some type of state socialism, along with greater democratic participation in North America and an international détente. Sweezy and Huberman's attempts to facilitate the revival of a domestic socialism in the late 1940s was spectacularly unsuccessful, and their critique of North American political economy lacked the authority and power of the celebratory assessments which flowed from the dominant Cold War discourses. However, in its analysis of the newly emergent Third World the journal exceeded the editors' initial expectations. **Monthly Review**'s early strength was its analysis of the expansion of US military and economic power in Latin America, the Middle East, Asia and Africa and the linkages it made between US imperialism and the "permanent war economy". At the same time, radical disillusionment with the Soviet Union had been overcome by the emergence of socialist China after 1949. This undermined doubts among North American and Western European radicals about the possibility of revolutions in Asia, Africa and Latin America. In this situation the New York based journal pushed beyond its initial project of facilitating a working-class renaissance, or at least a more democratic liberalism in North America, to generating an awareness about US imperialism and the 'wretched of the earth'.[21] Despite **Monthly Review**'s links with the universities in the 1950s it ultimately operated outside them. Its ability to articulate a marxist perspective in this period had a direct and inverse relationship to its location at the very margins of tertiary-based social science and area studies.[22]

Sweezy and Baran collaborated for many years, and it is difficult to treat their work separately. The landmark study of imperialism to emerge from the **Monthly Review** nexus was the 1957 publication of Paul Baran's **The Political Economy of Growth**.[23] In his now-classic study, Baran argued that the expansion of monopoly capitalism and the world market meant an increasingly dependent "backwardness" for the Third World. There was nothing inherent to Third World economies that led to this "backwardness"; however, once they were incorporated into the world economic order, revolution was the only way they could escape. Baran's analysis pointed to the continued importance of a comprador class, the disruption of internal markets, and the elimination of Third World industries that were potential competitors.[24] The work of Baran and Sweezy was completely at odds with modernization theory's emphasis on the infusion of North American and Western European capital as the key to self-sustaining growth in the Third World. They argued that US investment actually ensured that the Third World remained underdeveloped. Significantly, they also departed from orthodox marxism, which saw capitalism as necessary for the establishment of the preconditions for social revolution in the Third World. They reversed this idea and represented capitalism, as it emerged in the Third World, as the major obstacle to development. From their perspective, it was because thorough-going capitalist development had not occurred, and would not occur, that socialist revolution became necessary. In essays and editorials in **Monthly Review** during the 1950s and into the 1960s, Sweezy and Baran (who died in 1964), sought to articulate a global perspective on imperialism and revolution.[25] The work of Baran and Sweezy (and Harry Magdoff) provided one of the very few North American expositions of neo-marxism as it related to imperialism and underdevelopment in the Third World.[26] And after 1959 the number of articles in **Monthly Review,** and the number of books published by the Monthly Review Press on Latin America, especially on Cuba, grew steadily.[27]

While Sweezy and Baran were laying some of the intellectual groundwork for the rise of dependency theory, events in Latin America by the 1950s had stimulated a revisionist trend among Latin American economists. Raul Prebisch, head of the United Nations sponsored Comisión Economica para América Latina (CEPAL), developed a relatively conservative version of dependency theory, in the context of the shift to an import-substitution industrialization policy in Latin America.[28] Beginning as Director of Research for CEPAL in Chile in 1949, by the 1960s Prebisch was in charge of the United Nations Conference on Trade and Development (created at his instigation in 1964), a position from which he sought to encourage preferential tariffs for the exports of late-industrializing countries. However, by the early 1960s many Latin American economists had become disillusioned with the import-substitution strategy and increasingly pointed to the historically specific features of Latin America's economies, which they felt undermined the effective application of liberal economic theory to the region. They focused on land-ownership patterns, the position of foreign investment, and the linkages which flowed from an export economy. As a result, a number of influential Latin American economists were gradually drawn towards an approach to development which was far more historical than liberal development economics. At the beginning of the 1960s, a major center for the emerging historico-structuralist approach was Santiago de Chile, where there was a number of research institutions, as well as the regional CEPAL headquarters, involved in the study of Latin American development. Chile appeared to be a particularly good example of the socio-economic crisis which developed when the limits of the import-substitution strategy were reached. By the end of the 1960s the Chilean electorate had voted in a marxist government dedicated to the radical reform of the country's social and economic structures. Events in Chile attracted social scientists from around the world. And in the political cauldron of the 1960s a new approach found its way northward.[29]

André Gunder Frank, an economist who was educated at the University of Chicago, emerged in the second half of the 1960s as one of the main conduits for the entry of dependency theory into North America. A sort of Chicago boy in reverse, he first arrived in Latin America in the early 1960s, eventually taking up a position at the University of Chile from 1968 until the overthrow of the Allende government in 1973. By the early 1960s, Frank was an avowed socialist and an enthusiastic supporter of the Cuban revolution.[30] Frank was influenced by Baran's work and by the historico-structuralism of the CEPAL theorists; however, his approach differed in many ways from the work of earlier historico-structuralists such as Prebisch. It was also less historically grounded than the perspective of Fernando Henrique Cardoso (who went on to be Brazilian Finance Minister and is now President of Brazil) and Enzo Falleto's **Dependencia y desarrollo en América Latina**, which was written in Chile in the mid-1960s. This book, and Frank's **Capitalism and Underdevelopment in Latin America: Historical Studies of Chile and Brazil** are regarded as the leading statements of dependency theory at the end of the 1960s.[31] In **Capitalism and Underdevelopment in Latin America**, which was published in 1967 and included many of his earlier essays from **Monthly Review** and elsewhere, Frank outlined the concept of "the development of underdevelopment" and articulated a model of historical development which directly linked underdevelopment, and economic stagnation in the periphery, to the extraction of an economic surplus by the metropolitan powers. Following Baran, Frank made a dramatic break with classical marxism, asserting that "it is capitalism, both world and national, which produced underdevelopment in the past and which still generates underdevelopment in the present".[32] In a subsequent collection of essays, published in 1969, Frank argued that "Latin America suffers from a *colonial* underdevelopment, which makes its people economically, politically and culturally dependent, not so much on themselves or on each other as on a foreign metropolitan power". He emphasized that current "underdevelopment" was "in large part the historical product of past and continuing economic and other relations between the satellite underdeveloped and the now developed metropolitan countries. Furthermore these relations are an essential part of the structure and development of the capitalist system on a world scale as a whole".[33] As was clear in Frank's work, which became representative of the most pervasive dependency approach, dependency theory emerged in the late 1960s in a way which departed dramatically from Latin American historico-structuralism. The historico-structuralists were much more concerned with the analysis of internal historical structures, rather than adopting a deterministic focus on external factors.[34] This difference pointed to dependency theory's commitment to revolution in contrast to the moderate reformist agenda associated with historico-structuralism.

Although dependency theory flowed particularly out of the Latin American experience and had an especially significant impact in North America on the professional study of Latin America, the dramatic changes of the 1960s ensured that dependency theory--and radical ideas generally--increasingly informed the study of, and the politics in, many parts of Asia, the Middle East and Africa as well. Though not all area studies were equally affected, the crisis of the 1960s and early 1970s appears to have been most pronounced in parts of Asian studies and African studies, along with Latin American studies.[35] Although the Indian writer and activist Dadabhai Naoroji is credited with producing a particularly early reformist version of dependency theory, beginning in the 1870s, dependency ideas generated limited interest among Indian intellectuals because of India's size and the fact that more traditional forms of marxism had deep roots among the country's intelligentsia. In North America the centrality of language and culture to the area-studies programs which focused on South Asia and the relative resilience of anti-marxism and revised modernization theory, along with the liberal structures of the North American university system, acted to prevent dependency and radical ideas from making serious inroads. Obviously this was the case with China and the study of China in North America to an even greater degree.[36] Dependency theory and radical ideas may have had more impact on the study of Southeast Asia by the late 1960s because of the Vietnam War, but no significant and specifically Southeast Asian variant of dependency and radical theory can be said to have emerged in the late 1960s or 1970s.[37]

The often violent, and in some cases protracted, process of decolonization and the growing array of problems confronting the new nationalist regimes in much of Africa, which was increasingly overlaid by Cold War rivalry, ensured that the certitudes of modernization theory which had informed African studies in the 1950s and early 1960s were challenged both within Africa and within the African studies profession.[38] For example, the work of Walter Rodney linked the rise of the dependency debate in the Caribbean and Latin America to nationalist and radical debates in Africa. At the same time it contributed to the popularization of an overdetermined dependency model in North America and Western Europe.[39] The relatively weak institutional condition of the historical and social science professions in much of Africa and the growing political significance of neo-colonialism facilitated the spread of dependency theory in Africa and within African studies (by the 1970s dependency theory had also gained some purchase in Oceania and in the study of the South Pacific).[40] Nevertheless dependency theory as it emerged by the 1960s spoke particularly to the Latin American experience and although it soon gained a global purchase, often being integrated with radical perspectives flowing out of other regions on the one hand, and other area-studies programs on the other, it remained strongest within Latin American studies.

At the forefront of the emerging dependency approach in Latin American studies in North America by the late 1960s and early 1970s were radical political scientists and sociologists, such as James D. Cockcroft and Dale L. Johnson of Rutgers University, Susanne Jonas Bodenheimer of the University of California (Berkeley), James Petras at the State University of New York (Binghamton), and Ronald Chilcote and Joel Edelstein at the University of California (Riverside), who had become prominent marxist exponents of dependency analysis in North America and supporters of revolution in Latin America. They subscribed to an explicit conflict model of US-Latin American relations. Under the influence of the dependency approach, they also tended to regard external forces as a determining factor in the internal development of social structures and in ideological, political and cultural change. In contrast to the dominant professional discourse on Latin America, foreign investment and foreign aid were represented in negative terms, and the radicals held that efforts at internal improvement would be undermined by the center, as long as the periphery's dependent situation was maintained. Many North American radicals, following Frank and the revolutionary upsurge perceived to be sweeping many parts of Latin America, Asia and Africa, represented revolution as the only way the periphery could break with the structures of dependency.[41]

By the 1970s advocates of a dependency approach (of a particularly radical character) had emerged as an identifiable nexus within Latin America studies. Apart from **Monthly Review**, radical Latin American specialists were also linked to the North American Congress on Latin America (NACLA). This small research institute, which is now based in New York, was founded at Berkeley in late 1966 as a direct response to the US invasion of the Dominican Republic. NACLA's explicit aim was to draw greater attention to US military and economic involvement in Latin America. Early staff members included Roger Burbach, Patricia Flynn and Michael T. Klare. NACLA, through its bi-monthly **Latin America and Empire Report** (which later became **Report on the Americas**) and other publications, sought to develop as an alternative to the 'mainstream' media and facilitate the growth of a movement aimed explicitly at challenging US foreign policy.[42] In 1974 the journal **Latin American Perspectives: A Journal on Capitalism and Socialism** was initiated, under the managing editorship of Chilcote. Cockcroft, Johnson and Petras were all participating or co-ordinating editors, as were Susanne Jonas and Joel Edelstein.[43] The journal also had a number of prominent Latin American academics on its editorial board, including Fernando Henrique Cardoso, who had co-authored **Dependencia y desarrollo en América Latina**, as well as John Saxe Fernandez (Universidad Nacional Autonoma de Mexico) and Rodolfo Stavenhagen (Colegio de México), all of whose work had begun to appear in English in Britain and North America.[44]

The work of early dependency theorists writing about Latin America was certainly not homogeneous. However, their writing did reflect a number of shared assumptions, which can be taken as central to classic dependency theory and contrasted with classic modernization theory. Latin America was represented by modernization theorists as a place where a 'feudal aristocracy' had transplanted and replicated itself, remaining predominant into the post-1945 era. From the modernization perspective, this landed 'aristocracy' sought to impede the development of capitalism and the rise of a progressive national bourgeoisie. In contrast, dependency theorists argued that Spain and Portugal conquered Latin America in order to incorporate it within a new system of capitalist production, not to reproduce the European feudal cycle. A ruling class evolved which had no interest in developing the domestic market and national industry because its main source of income lay in export trade. Second, modernization theory argued that the economic development and expansion of Europe and North America led to the diffusion of capital and technology to the urban areas of Latin America, particularly after the 1820s, which then gradually spread to the rural area, breaking down feudalism. Dependency analysis countered that the market system imposed on Latin America created underdevelopment rather than development and the poverty of the countryside was reinforced by its subordination to the city and the international market. Third, modernization theory saw the bourgeoisie as a progressive force and argued that it would promote development through the diffusion of capital, innovations and an enterprising spirit into the 'backward areas', and lead the drive for social reforms and political democracy. Dependency theory argued that the diffusion of capital resulted in the stagnation of the rural areas and that the bourgeoisie, which was dominated by the imperial powers and subordinated to agrarian landowning interests, had no particular democratic urge and would support stable authoritarian governments. Fourth, while modernization theory saw the diffusion of capital and modern values into the 'backward areas' as the key to development, dependency theory took the view that development could be brought about only with the revolutionary overthrow of capitalism and imperialism.[45]

In the early 1970s, under the influence of dependency theory, North American radical analysis was deterministic and pugnacious.[46] This was, in part, because the theoretical debates around dependency theory were linked to the debates over political strategy in Latin America. André Gunder Frank has noted that his work between 1968 and 1973 was written "in an attempt to defend a hopefully still revolutionary position against reformism".[47] The highly politicized character of the debate was dramatically apparent in the case of **Latin American Perspectives**, which was an important forum for the dependency debate after 1974.[48] At the same time, despite the theoretical and political minefield of the late 1960s and 1970s, the North American radicals who embraced dependency theory were successful in applying the dependency perspective to their overall analysis of US foreign policy and its relationship to foreign capital and the continued subordination and dependence of Latin America.[49] The scope of dependency theory by the early 1970s could be seen in the work of James Petras, who emerged as a particularly prolific radical in this period. Petras gained a PhD in Political Science from the University of California (Berkeley) in the 1960s. He did field work in Chile during the Frei years and worked as an associate professor of political science and research associate at the Institute of Public Administration at Pennsylvania State University, before going on to the sociology department at the State University of New York (Binghampton), where he has been for over two decades. Petras approached US-Latin American relations from a perspective which synthesized the marxism of the New York **Monthly Review** school, and dependency theory as it had developed by the end of the 1960s. In **Latin America: Reform or Revolution?**, which appeared in 1968, Petras and co-editor Maurice Zeitlin emphasized the importance of class analysis and macro-economic structures. The essays in their book all assigned priority to class structure and the role of foreign investment, as well as the unequal structure of Latin American relations with the US. They emphasized the importance of a conflict model in analyzing Latin American history and political economy, and they explicitly rejected the assumption that US interests were in harmony with Latin America's economic and social development.[50] Petras's work reflected the emergence and expansion of radical professional discourses on Latin America, informed by both dependency theory and marxism.[51]

In methodological and political terms, the work of Petras and other radicals, represented a dramatic departure from the dominant liberal area-studies discourses. But in geographical terms, they continued to follow Washington's lead, often focusing on those countries, such as Cuba, that represented the most dramatic challenge to US hegemony. The political transformation in Chile in the 1960s, which Frank and a number of others had witnessed first-hand, also drew considerable attention. For example, Petras, who had been in Chile in this period, produced a number of books and articles on Chilean politics and history.[52] With the relative decline of revolutionary fortunes in Latin America by the end of the 1960s, Cuba's position as a political and economic model for the region shifted to the radical reformist experiment in Chile. The Brazilian miracle, which was represented by liberals and 'conservatives' as a successful development model for Latin America and beyond, also attracted critical radical interest.[53] Although the 1973 overthrow of the Allende government by a military coup in which the US played an explicit role, undermined the Chilean road to socialism, it served to maintain radical attention on Chile. Petras, along with his PhD student Morris Morley, with whom he went on to form a productive collaborative relationship, wrote a book documenting Washington's involvement in the coup.[54] For both radicals, and for their liberal counterparts, Cuba, Chile and Peru, as well as the larger countries of Mexico, Brazil, Argentina and Venezuela, proved to be of more concern than Central America, for example, until the late 1970s.[55]

The one Central American exception to this trend was Guatemala.[56] Although interest in Guatemala was an outgrowth of the expansion of Latin American studies after 1959, it clearly reflected the way revolution and US intervention ensured North American attention. For example, Milton Jamail, a North American radical who made an important contribution to the debate on Central America in the 1980s, completed a thesis on Guatemala at the University of Arizona in the early 1970s, looking at Guatemalan politics between 1944 and 1972.[57] One of the most prominent North American radicals in this period was Susanne Jonas Bodenheimer, who had a sustained interest in Central America, particularly Guatemala. She had close links with **Latin American Perspectives**, was a PhD student in the Department of Political Science, and a fellow at the Center for Latin American Studies at the University of California (Berkeley) in the late 1960s and early 1970s, as well as a staff member of the North American Congress on Latin America.[58] Jonas Bodenheimer produced an important critique of Latin American Studies and, as an alternative to the dominant professional discourses on Latin America, she emphasized the need for a dependency perspective informed by marxism.[59] She also mapped out a dependency perspective in K. T. Fann and Donald C. Hodges' **Readings in US Imperialism**. Despite its appearance in 1971, at the height of the Vietnam war, Fann and Hodges argued that Latin America was the most important sphere of US involvement and economic penetration, which was why their book contained more selections on Latin America than on Asia.[60] Despite their insistence on the importance of Latin America, neither Guatemala nor Central America as a whole received any significant attention. It was left to Jonas (she had stopped using the name Bodenheimer by 1974) to produce the first detailed study of Guatemala informed by dependency theory.

In her 1974 contribution to Chilcote and Edelstein's **Latin America: The Struggle with Dependency and Beyond**, Jonas argued that the underdevelopment of modern Guatemala began with the Spanish conquest. She emphasized that the "evolution of dependent capitalism since the sixteenth century set the stage for contemporary US imperialism in Guatemala". In her view, US imperialism and capitalist underdevelopment were more blatant in Guatemala and Central America generally than in the rest of Latin America.[61] Pointing to the mid-1950s, for example, Jonas argued that the US facilitated the overthrow of Arbenz in 1954 because, in the context of post-1945 US economic expansion, North American capital "could not afford to rely on an unpredictable national bourgeoisie".[62] The overthrow of the Arbenz government was followed by the "intensification of Guatemalan dependency". She argued that Guatemala's "entire 'development' strategy" after 1954 originated in the US, and the "cornerstone of the entire policy has been that foreign (US) private investment is the key to economic growth". Because the Guatemalan 'state' had avoided any substantive reforms, it became "more rather than less subservient to the Guatemalan and international bourgeoisie". The "distortion" of bourgeois democratic structures, said Jonas, has been reinforced by the "militarization" of the political process, including direct military government. She predicted the ultimate failure of the "Counter-Revolution", arguing that the unstable situation in Guatemala could be altered only by a "break with 450 years of dependent capitalism and a socialist transformation of the existing order, based on the needs and the will of the Guatemalan people".[63] Jonas's approach reflected the **Latin American Perspectives** synthesis of dependency theory with marxism's emphasis on historical materialism and class struggle. Her work was representative of the deterministic theoretical framework which underpinned the radical discourses in this period. Radicals saw Latin American history as driven by the actions and policies flowing from the metropole, at the same time as they anticipated the inevitable unfolding of class struggle and the triumph of the working class and socialism following the seizure of state power in the periphery.

By the second half of the 1970s, the ascendancy of a marxist dependency synthesis, as it was articulated by Jonas and others, had peaked. Dependency theory's demise can be traced to its failure as revolutionary prophecy and the end of the US war in Southeast Asia. The rise of the Newly Industrializing Countries in Latin America (Mexico and Brazil), and East Asia (South Korea and Taiwan), and the rise of OPEC, also helped to undermine the subordinate image of Third World nations, and contributed to the fading of radical dependency theory's luster. By the late 1970s, the North American and Western European emphasis on the corruption and authoritarianism of many Third World governments helped to shift the burden of explanation for underdevelopment back onto the elites and states of Latin America, Asia and Africa. Another important factor behind the fall of dependency theory was that by the mid-1970s the radical challenge had been partially contained by the political and theoretical incorporation of important elements of the dependency approach into the dominant liberal discourses. The demise of radical dependency theory was followed by the emergence of a number of new radical theoretical approaches. These approaches deserve mention, in part, because their very existence points to the relative diversity and autonomy achieved by the Latin American studies profession in contrast to the early years. They are also important to the wider concerns of this study because the growing number of new radical approaches continued to interact with and influence the liberal historiography and contributed to the ongoing diffusion of radical ideas into the dominant liberal discourses in the late 1970s and 1980s. Building on Petras and Morley's categorization we can distinguish between four post-dependency development theories: the state and class approach (with which Morley and Petras identify), the modes of production approach, world-system theory and neo-dependency theory.[64]

By the second half of the 1970s a marxist state and class approach had begun to emerge as a direct challenge to dependency theory. This approach linked historical materialism to the insights of the dependency debate, but placed its major emphasis on state and class structures in the periphery. Writers in this tradition often accepted dependency theory's overall critique of classical marxism: that the potential for independent capitalist development is constrained by a dependent economic position in the international economic order. At the same time, this tradition also brought together revisionist arguments which emphasized the relative potential for dependent and/or autonomous capitalist development, emphasizing that politics in Latin America (as well as Asia, the Middle East, Africa and Oceania) still enjoyed a certain degree of freedom from external pressures. They emphasized the need for more detailed class analysis and focused on local social structures, particularly the historical character of class and state formation, and the concerns and ambitions of different social groups. Building on the growing sophistication of marxist approaches to the capitalist state, as reflected in the work of Ralph Miliband and Nicos Poulantzas, many writers in this tradition emphasize the colonial and post-colonial state as the location in which the local ruling classes may initially have taken form, and through which they seek to consolidate their economic and socio-political dominance. This approach was also concerned to determine to what degree the post-colonial state reflects the interests of international capital and/or local concerns.[65] The emergent emphasis on state and class was an avowedly marxist rejection of the trajectory that dependency theory had taken by the mid-1970s. It came particularly (although not exclusively) out of a British and/or Western European context on the one hand, and an Asian, African and Latin American context on the other hand. It gained limited ground in North

America, while much of the important work in this tradition focused on Africa and Asia rather than Latin America.[66]

Also building on debates within marxism (particularly British and French marxism), the modes of production approach rose to prominence in the late 1960s and early 1970s.[67] The modes of production approach represented, among other things, a thorough response to dependency theory and later world-system theory's privileging of the market over relations of production. For example, in a well-known debate, Ernesto Laclau, an Argentine political scientist exiled in Britain, challenged Frank's sweeping characterization of Latin America as capitalist simply because it was part of a world capitalist economy.[68] This approach emphasized that some pre-capitalist modes of production in the periphery have proved highly resilient to the expansion of capitalism and have not disappeared as anticipated. The problem of underdevelopment in Latin America and beyond was seen as the result of a more protracted transition because the processes of modernization and urban industrialization in the periphery are dependent for a long time on pre-capitalist modes of production in the countryside which have articulated with an externally imposed capitalist mode of production. Although the modes of production approach was important in shifting the burden of explanation for underdevelopment back towards internal class structures and social formations on the periphery, many of its proponents tended to factor external forces out of their analysis, while they conflated the capitalist mode of production in the industrialized countries with capitalism in Latin America (as well as Asia, Africa and Oceania).[69] In part, because of its marxist origins, the modes of production approach did not gain widespread purchase in Latin American studies in North America.[70] Nevertheless, by the end of the 1970s it was shaping the work of a growing number of historians studying Latin America.[71] In particular the modes of production approach had meshed with and informed a shift in anthropology away from community studies to a theoretically sophisticated regional approach.[72] At the same time, the relatively weak purchase of the state and class approach and the modes of production approach within and outside of Latin American studies in North America is clearly reflected in the way, for example, a recent book-length analysis of theories of development by a North American based academic frames the entire debate from World War II to 1990 as a dialogue between three schools: modernization theory, dependency theory and world-system theory.[73]

In North America the theoretical eclipse of classic dependency theory (inside and outside of Latin American studies) cannot be understood without reference to the world-system theory of Immanuel Wallerstein.[74] By the 1970s, Wallerstein's world-system theory had emerged as the most important single trend in radical social science in North America. Wallerstein was influenced by dependency theory and by the work of Fernand Braudel and the Annales school.[75] As Paul Buhle has suggested, Wallerstein's first major book on world-system theory, which appeared in 1974, has quite possibly been "the most influential single book of the post-New Left era".[76] In the 1950s Wallerstein was a graduate student in sociology at Columbia University, and although his early work reflected his background in liberal sociology, by the end of 1960s he had emerged as a radical sociologist and African specialist. By 1968 he was Associate Professor of Sociology at Columbia University, where he had begun to develop his ideas about the modern world-system. The student unrest at Columbia and across the US in the late 1960s, gained his sympathy, and he produced a book which was supportive of student demands. Following a period at the Stanford Center for Advanced Study in the Behavioral Sciences and at McGill University in Montreal, he and Terence Hopkins set up the Fernand Braudel Center for the Study of Economies, Historical Systems and Civilizations at the State University of New York (Binghamton) and the journal **Review** in 1975, by which time Wallerstein's first volume in the major exposition of his world-system theory appeared.[77] By the time he published **The Modern World-System: Capitalist Agriculture and the Origins of the European World-Economy in the Sixteenth Century** he had made the transition from his liberal social science background of the 1950s and early 1960s to the view that social change in the modern world could be understood only within the framework of the historical evolution of the modern world-system as a whole. By the end of the 1970s, although he had published a second volume as well as numerous articles, his central ideas displayed considerable continuity.[78]

Wallerstein's project rests on the assumption that the modern world-system has an historical significance as a totality. At the core of his argument is the notion that a particular country's internal development can be understood only with reference to the position it occupies in the modern world-system as a whole. From his perspective the world economy is a singular entity, yet within it there are a number of political entities. World-system theorists trace the historical development of capitalism by focusing on the emergence and functioning of an international market comprising three levels, the periphery, semi-periphery and the core, and attempt to chart the trajectories of nation-states as a function of the logic of the emergence and expansion of this global capitalist economy. Inequality emerges and is maintained as a systemic characteristic because different regions within the world-system produce commodities for exchange using different labor control systems. The economic stagnation of the periphery, and the continued and even expanding gap between it and the core of the world-economy, flows from the privileged position held by core nations because of the historical terms under which they initially entered the world-economy.[79] Not surprisingly, Wallerstein's synthesis has prompted considerable debate.[80] And although he has highlighted the heuristic character of world-system theory, the emphasis on international economic relations has left world-system theorists open to charges of economic determinism. Their model has been understood to imply that the history of classes and nation-states are driven by the world capitalist system itself. Actors rarely appear to act in the system, but are acted on by it. Furthermore, despite its concern to take on a perspective which transcends the focus on the nation-state (which is conceptually central to liberal development theory and liberal historiography) world-system theory still uses the nation-state as a basic unit of analysis. The conception of power used by world-system theorists sees power located in the structure of the international economy itself, particularly in the upper levels of the international order, in contrast to a more orthodox marxist conception of power as flowing from a class relationship. As a result world-system theory tends to represent change as a function of elite decision-making, or of the system itself, rather than holding out class struggles or nation-state interactions and initiatives as the agent of political change.[81] Ultimately, the world-system model tends towards the standardization of historically particular relationships and socio-economic structures. Marxist critics of world-system theory, such as Petras and Morley, have argued that "the world economy is not homogeneous but a reality of uneven economic development, tensions and forces between competing social systems anchored in different social relations of production". They take the view that, in contrast to world-system theory, "global changes are manifested by way of national class agencies and state structures", while the "proliferation of new centers of economic power and networks" challenges "simplistic trichotomous schemas".[82]

World-system theory has attempted to go beyond the perceived shortcomings of liberal and marxist approaches. But, in many ways, it has simply synthesized them, and world-system theory remains located in the rationalist and eurocentric discourses out of which contemporary liberalism and marxism emerged. World-system theory, like dependency theory, continues to represent historical development as occurring in stages. Historically, the dominant liberal area studies discourses, which continue to be based on ideas about the superiority of North American and West European institutions and values, have been only marginally interested in differences within traditional cultures. The radical discourses have also been shaped by assumptions about the superiority of North American and Western European categories and concepts, although their hostility to tradition has been formulated in different terms. Ultimately, world-system theory has extended the marxist and the liberal social science and humanities tradition which continues to find the key to the history of the periphery in its relationship to an expanding world-system centered on North America and Western Europe. This problem is only partially resolved by the work of a number of writers influenced by world-system theory, including Daniel Chirot and L. S. Stavrianos, who began to apply Wallerstein's theory to their work on a whole range of geographical and historical cases by the second half of the 1970s.[83]

Particularly significant in this regard is the work of the North American anthropologist Eric Wolf. He rose to prominence in the 1950s with his work on southern Mexico and Guatemala. In the 1960s he spearheaded anthropology's discovery of history as part of the wider effort to bring the peasantry into history and challenge the eurocentric elitism and liberal developmentalism of the dominant professional discourses.[84] At the end of the 1970s he lamented that the 'periphery' had become as normative and negating a concept as 'traditional society', and he sought to build on and synthesize Wallerstein, Frank and the modes of production approach. He set out to write history in a way which would allow "both the people who claim history as their own and the people to whom history has been denied" to "emerge as participants in the same historical trajectory". Like the world-system approach, on which he builds, Wolf assumes that "the world of humankind" is "a totality of interconnected processes", and that those approaches which "disassemble this totality" and "then fail to reassemble it falsify reality".[85] This, however, leads to his articulation of a system which still draws its inspiration, and its logic, from the liberal and marxist discourses which continue to write the people on the periphery out of history. In the case of Latin America, the modes of production critique of Wallerstein advanced by Wolf has been taken further and explicated most forcefully by writers, such as Steve Stern, who have sought to emphasize the specific over the systemic. This has resulted in an important attempt to emphasize both historical particularity and global political economy. Building on some of the insights of world-system theory, Stern has sought to develop a much more nuanced understanding of historical change on the so-called periphery. From Stern's perspective the central dynamics of Latin American history since the colonial era have been the various approaches and popular resistance strategies of the inhabitants, the interests of mercantile and political elites whose "centers of gravity" were in the Americas, and then the world-system.[86]

By the second half of the 1970s, world-system theory and dependency theory, as well as other radical approaches were clearly influencing the work of more liberal Latin American specialists.[87] A growing number of scholars sought to draw loosely on the marxist and dependency traditions, as in the case of bureaucratic-authoritarianism. At the same time they continued to eschew a sustained radical analysis, even as they conceptualized the US role in the region in terms of politico-military hegemony and economic dependency. The neo-dependency approach, for example, clearly demonstrates the way in which dependency theory had been domesticated by the dominant liberal discourses by the 1970s. Like dependency theory, the neo-dependency approach saw developments in the periphery as driven by the actions and policies which flowed from the metropole; neo-dependency theorists were preoccupied with the center, or with national capitalism on the periphery, as the main focus of any initiative for economic development and political change. This conclusion reflected the decline of dependency theory's revolutionary political agenda at the same time as its methodology and many of its insights were built upon.[88] It was readily apparent by the second half of the 1970s that some of the categories and assumptions associated with classic dependency theory had emerged to shape the dominant professional discourses on Latin America. For example, Richard Fagen, who was president of the Latin American Studies Association in the mid-1970s, argued that, despite its shortcomings, the "issues" to which dependency theory directed Latin American specialists "warrant our most serious attention". In his view, if dependency theory left "no other long term legacy in US Latin American studies beyond recasting the manner in which we think about" the role of the US in relation to Latin American underdevelopment, then "it will not have lived--or died--in vain".[89] A year later Jorge I. Domínguez emphasized the utility of "unorthodox dependency perspectives" for research on inter-American relations.[90] A key work in the new dependency studies was Fernando Henrique Cardoso's work on "Associated

Dependent Development".[91] And a particularly good example of dependency revisionism, or neo-dependency theory, was a book on Brazil by Peter Evans which appeared in 1979 and built on Cardoso's conceptualization. Evans' study, **Dependent Development: The Alliance of Multinational, State and Local Capital in Brazil,** has been characterized as "the most important contribution to the 'new wave'" of dependency writing in the second half of the 1970s. Evans represented late-industrialization in Brazil as a strategy of successful "dependent development", in which the increasing involvement of transnational capital in the Brazilian import-substitution industrialization process had to be understood as part of a "triple alliance" between foreign companies, state elites and local companies.[92]

It was clear by the end of the 1970s that dependency theory and world-system theory, which were characterized collectively as a "new paradigm" by one prominent Latin American specialist, were being domesticated by the dominant liberal discourses on Latin America.[93] Joseph Tulchin, who was editor of the **Latin American Research Review** from the mid-1970s to the early 1980s, argued that, at the broadest level, the 1970s saw the "gradual absorption into the mainstream" of marxist concepts, as well as the related structuralist approaches of dependency theory and world-systems theory, which had meshed with entrenched empirical and functional methodology. Throughout the 1970s the role of Latin Americans in framing the North American research agenda, which had begun in the 1960s with the rise of dependency theory and the corporatist approach, continued, as concepts like bureaucratic-authoritarianism percolated northward. At the same time, the radical challenge and the liberal revision, in the context of the inter-disciplinary character of Latin American studies, was part of an increasing and often critical focus by Latin American specialists on foreign policy.[94] However, it must be emphasized that all these changes were taking place on liberal terms. Although the dominant professional discourses on Latin America were asserting a greater degree of autonomy, relative to the US imperial state, the continued overall liberal character of the Latin American studies profession, and the liberal pluralism of its institutional and organizational context, ensured that Latin American studies as a whole maintained a complementary relationship to US hegemony.

Not surprisingly, marxist Latin American specialists were critical of the use to which dependency theory was being put by the second half of the 1970s. In 1978, Ronald Chilcote defended marxist dependency theory against the proliferation of new approaches. (Significantly he did so in the pages of the **Latin American Research Review**.) He distinguished explicitly between the emergence of a bourgeois approach to dependency (new wave, or neo-dependency) on the one hand, and the evolution of a marxist approach to dependency theory, on the other hand.[95] He argued that bourgeois dependency theory was concerned with national capitalist development in "the context of international imperialism", as a possible means of ending dependency, while marxist dependency theory, which emphasized the centrality of historical materialism and class struggle, focused on the "destruction of the capitalist system", as the way to bring about an end to dependency. While bourgeois dependency theory, according to Chilcote, saw classes as becoming "autonomous" via the national development process, and focused its analysis on the national bourgeoisie, marxist dependency theory was explicitly "conflictual" and perceived the proletariat as the "essential class". Bourgeois dependency theorists, according to Chilcote's formulation, represented the state as being able to serve the nation in the "struggle" against dependency, while marxist dependency theorists conceived of the state as a means through which the "ruling class" was able to protect capitalism and the nation's dependency. Bourgeois dependency theorists tended to define imperialism as political and military expansion on the part of dominant nations, while marxist dependency theorists defined imperialism as directly linked to the monopoly stage of capitalism. Chilcote noted that in order to counter the view, associated with orthodox marxism, that socialism was unattainable "without a profound capitalist expansion led by the national bourgeoisie", marxist dependency theorists must clarify their conception of historical materialism, class struggle and imperialism. Chilcote returned to Marx to do this, and then concluded that marxist dependency theory's "search for theory" needed to begin with Lenin's view that imperialism was capitalism in its monopoly phase.[96] In the context of the general trend towards the domestication of dependency theory, Chilcote and a dwindling group of radical Latin American specialists continued to articulate a marxist dependency perspective. However, as we will see, radical Latin Americanists enjoyed a resurgence in the first part of the 1980s.

Domesticating New Left Historiography 1968-1979

The trend towards domestication which was apparent in dependency theory was part of the wider accommodation of the New Left, and was even more pronounced in the case of New Left diplomatic history. The rise and demise of New Left diplomatic history is a particularly good example of the way in which the dominant professional discourses have contained radical perspectives since the 1960s. The organized and activist New Left was at its peak in 1968 and declined dramatically within a year or two thereafter.[97] At the same time, New Left diplomatic historians, whose work had remained marginal until the end of the 1960s, rose to positions of professional prominence, as their approach was incorporated into the dominant professional discourses. New Left diplomatic history originated in the 1950s at the University of Wisconsin (Madison), where a number of historians who taught at, or were graduates of, Wisconsin's history department, defended the application of a progressive paradigm to their area of historical specialization. Their purchase was limited, however, and the Wisconsin academic Fred Harvey Harrington was probably the single major North American diplomatic historian to teach diplomatic history from a progressive point of view in the 1950s.[98] Two early students of the history of US-Latin American relations, who reflected Harrington's approach, were Robert Freeman Smith and David Healy. In their first books in the early 1960s, both of which were on US relations with

Cuba, a reflection of the interest which the Cuban revolution had stimulated, the former students of Harrington drew attention to the role of economic interests in US Cuban policy; however, unlike more radical interpretations, they represented political factors, and even racism, as more important in explaining the history of US intervention in Cuba. Smith, in particular, expressed support for the policy of containing the Soviet Union. He also emphasized the need for the US to push for social and economic reform throughout Latin America as the best way to avoid further threats to US economic interests. From his perspective, reform would undermine calls for revolution and help to halt the spread of communism.[99]

Of far greater influence, and characterized by more of a departure from the dominant liberal discourses than the work of Harrington and his followers, was the work of William Appleman Williams. He was a Madison graduate who took up a post there in 1957. In the 1960s Williams emerged at the center of New Left diplomatic history. Compared to Harrington's views, Williams's approach put more emphasis on economics, and represented imperialism as more closely linked to both capitalism and to the history of the US as a nation. **The Tragedy of American Diplomacy**, which first appeared in 1959, stands as a key work for an entire generation of diplomatic historians.[100] Initially ignored and then attacked, it gradually rose to the status of a classic. Although Williams produced a number of other important works over the course of his career, none rivaled the influence of **The Tragedy of American Diplomacy**.[101] Williams's work was shaped by the concept of "the imperialism of free trade", developed by British imperial historians Ronald Robinson and John Gallagher in the early 1950s.[102] It can also been traced to the theories of imperialism articulated by Hobson and Lenin. His overall thesis was that the US had been an imperialist power from its very inception as a republic. Prior to the Civil War, this expansion had manifested itself in territorial expansion in continental North America. By the 1890s, however, US expansion was increasingly driven by the pursuit of overseas markets. By the end of the nineteenth century the advancement of commerce was the overarching goal of US foreign policy, and in some instances, such as Hawaii and the Philippines, this had resulted in formal imperialism; however, informal empire allowed the US to gain economic and political control of another country, without administrative responsibilities, and was the preferred option. Williams argued that the informal imperialism encapsulated in the Open Door Policy towards China at the turn of the century became the cornerstone of twentieth-century US foreign policy. The Open Door policy, which encouraged all nations trading in China to subscribe to equality of commercial opportunity, flowed from North American confidence that their economy was more powerful and more efficient than any other nations. As a result, under circumstances of free trade, the US would rise to pre-eminence in world markets. According to Williams, it was Open Door diplomacy and the pursuit of free markets which drove US foreign policy in Asia and Latin America by the beginning of the twentieth century. And after 1945 Washington redoubled its efforts to establish its influence in a way that would provide the US with the benefits of colonialism without the drawbacks.[103]

Beginning in the early 1960s Williams's students and other young diplomatic historians produced a growing number of revisionist works informed and influenced by the approach to US diplomatic history mapped out in **The Tragedy of American Diplomacy**. In the first half of the 1960s, however, Latin America was given more attention by the **Monthly Review** radicals than by New Left diplomatic historians. At this time, New Left diplomatic historians focused on the roots of the US empire, the Cold War and US economic policy generally, or economic policy in Asia more specifically.[104] Walter LaFeber, a former student of Williams, gradually gained a considerable academic reputation following the 1963 publication of **The New Empire: An Interpretation of American Expansion 1860-1898**, which expanded on William Appleman Williams's approach. Challenging the established view, **The New Empire** represented the US war with Spain and the overseas imperialism which followed, along with the earlier continental expansion, as part of a continuum rooted in the imperatives of a capitalist society. LaFeber portrayed the first US steps towards overseas empire as part of a well-thought-out plan, an interpretation which stood in sharp contradiction to the predominant view that the US had "stumbled" into empire.[105] LaFeber's book won the Albert J. Beveridge Award and served to shift the debate over the emergence of the US empire in the late nineteenth century in the direction of economic imperatives. In the early 1970s a session at the convention of the Organization of American Historians was devoted to LaFeber's book, and over half of the diplomatic historians surveyed at this event claimed to have been at least "moderately" influenced by it.[106]

In the mid-1960s Latin America made an indirect appearance in a book by Lloyd C. Gardner, another student of Williams. Gardner challenged earlier interpretations of the Good Neighbor Policy, which had portrayed it as a retreat from imperialism, and represented it as a model of Open Door imperialism. Gardner, a prolific diplomatic historian who served as president of the Society for Historians of American Foreign Relations at the end of the 1980s, argued in the early 1960s that under the Good Neighbor Policy the US relied on its growing economic leverage to exercise hegemony over the southern governments, while in the post-1945 period it continued to intervene if developments endangered US economic interests or its client regimes in the region.[107] In 1964 David Horowitz wrote an important essay on the Alliance for Progress. He has often been grouped with the New Left diplomatic historians, particularly by their critics. However, unlike most New Left diplomatic historians, he was primarily a journalist-activist and has few academic credentials. In a parody of the deradicalization process, Horowitz shifted from the role of campus radical (at the London School of Economics, the University of California, and Columbia University, as well as editor of **Ramparts**, in the 1960s) to public supporter of the Reagan administration in the 1980s. In the 1960s he wrote about US foreign policy from a marxist perspective, and unlike other New Left diplomatic historians was unequivocal in locating the roots of US expansionism in the economic imperatives of the capitalist system. He emphasized that the Alliance for Progress sought to "develop Latin America *through* the influx of private capital and utilize public funds only in areas which were not directly profitable, or where the risks for private enterprise were too great". He argued that the primary goal of the Alliance was that of "heading off the social revolution in Latin America". Washington sought to protect "the basic property structure", especially "the stake of US private capital on the continent", by encouraging the minimum of reform necessary. He warned that the US "faced a considerable and ever growing task in holding back the nationalism of Latin American bourgeoisie, while at the same time coaxing them to accept 'safety-valve' reforms, in restraining the more reactionary of the powerful army leaders, while at the same time depending on them for 'stability' and in maintaining this triple alliance against the revolutionary populism of the Latin American masses". Horowitz argued that, in Latin America and the rest of the "underdeveloped world", the central concern of US policy since 1945 was "'containment' in an anti-revolutionary sense".[108]

Although New Left diplomatic historians did not subject Latin America, apart from Cuba, to much scrutiny in the 1960s, this had changed somewhat by the end of the decade. For example, in 1971, the work of David Green, a former student of LaFeber, combined the Wisconsin school approach with insights from dependency theory. In his examination of the rise and fall of the Good Neighbor Policy he also took up the containment theme pursued earlier by Horowitz. Green noted that by the end of the 1930s Roosevelt sought to complement Washington's commitment to non-intervention with "other more positive measures" intended to assist the governments of Latin America to "develop their economies and raise their standards of living". He argued that, despite the rhetoric of the Good Neighbor years, many people in Latin America after 1945 had begun to "realize" that "the Good Neighbor Policy *had never been intended* to end Latin America's economic dependence upon the United States" (Green's italics). The Good Neighbor Policy was primarily aimed at mitigating "some of the more politically abrasive features of the dependency relationship, in order to undercut militant nationalist resentment against the United States in Latin America". The situation by the end of World War II was one in which the incoming Truman administration's "overall strategy" in Latin America revolved around the use of its "leverage" to construct "a tightly knit, well-controlled system in the Western Hemisphere". The approach adopted by the US immediately after 1945, said Green, rested on the assumption that political order in Latin America "was a prerequisite for 'healthy' economic development under United States supervision". However, it was apparent by the second half of the 1950s that the "economic dependency" which the US had encouraged was actually "undermining political stability". In Green's view, the Alliance for Progress, which saw political order as flowing from economic development, was a return to, and a "modernized version" of, the Good Neighbor Policy. And like its predecessors, the Alliance began as a reaction to "revolutionary nationalism". He argued that as US support for "anti-nationalist military and political activity" in Latin America grew in the 1960s (in the form of US military, CIA or civilian advisers, or US military aid and economic and technical assistance for counter-insurgency and "stabilization" programs) it became apparent that the Alliance for Progress was still operating on the assumptions which had underpinned US policy in the region a generation before. The Good Neighbor Policy, which had emphasized "a closed hemisphere in an Open World", had in Green's view "led naturally to a policy of containment of Latin America".[109]

Green's work, like all New Left diplomatic historiography, saw a basic relationship between North American economic expansion and US foreign policy. At the same time, as the above discussion has suggested, there was nothing unitary about New Left diplomatic history at the end of the 1960s.[110] Furthermore, although Williams's thesis was perceived as radical, it was often asserted in relatively moderate fashion. Despite their kinship with Lenin's theory of imperialism, the North American New Left historians tended to reflect the view that the US could redeem itself by mild reforms which would produce a more humanitarian foreign policy.[111] Some observers have argued that at the center of New Left diplomatic history's approach there is an "ambiguity" which has never been confronted. In their view Williams's overall theoretical framework skirts the question of the basic source of US expansion. At various times the Williams' school represented US expansion as flowing either from a mistaken belief on the part of US officials that domestic economic and political exigencies necessitated expansion, or from the needs of economic and political institutions, or that capitalism had produced a widespread 'belief' in North America that domestic prosperity necessitated continued economic expansion. Richard Melanson has argued that this "ambiguity" also meant that the New Left diplomatic historians produced few policy recommendations. Although they wanted the US to engage in "a non-expansionistic diplomacy", it was unclear from their analysis whether US economic institutions needed to be "radically transformed", or if it was sufficient to rely on political leaders who did not subscribe to the 'mistaken' belief in the necessity of expansion. Or did the North American psyche need to be purged of the expansionist impulse?[112] This ambiguity was readily apparent in Williams's **Empire as a Way of Life**, which appeared on the eve of the Reagan era and included a call for the renunciation of empire, and an appeal to individual morality.[113]

As with Williams's work, much of the New Left diplomatic history which appeared in the 1970s saw the history of the periphery as determined by decisions at the center. Furthermore, New Left diplomatic historians' ambivalence about the sources of US imperialism was mirrored in their generally ambivalent attitude towards the emerging revolutionary challenges in Latin America, Asia and Africa. Although they were clearly dissatisfied with the traditional scholarship of their discipline, New Left diplomatic history had become part of the dominant liberal profession by the 1970s.[114] The domestication of New Left diplomatic historiography was facilitated by its overall ambivalence towards marxism and revolution. The incorporation process was also aided by the founding of The Society for Historians of American Foreign Relations (in 1967), which provided the specific professional context for the accommodation of the New Left approach and its advocates, at the same time as the wider institutional structures ensured that radicals and radical perspectives were contained. SHAFR was chartered in 1972 and eventually began producing the journal **Diplomatic History**, the first volume of which appeared in 1976-1977. **Diplomatic History** is *the* journal of the North American liberal diplomatic history establishment.[115] The journal provided a forum in which New Left revisionism was brought back into the mainstream of diplomatic history, at the same time as the mainstream was transformed in a way which reinvigorated liberalism.[116] By the end of the 1970s some of the most influential diplomatic historians in North America, such as Lloyd Gardner and Walter LaFeber, were former New Left diplomatic historians.[117] LaFeber's writing and his career (he has been Professor of History at Cornell University for many years) symbolized the way New Left historians, particularly the Williams school, entered the dominant professional discourses in the 1970s.[118] (LaFeber's work on Central America will be discussed in Chapter 4.)

The domestication of New Left diplomatic history was well underway by the time the US withdrew from Vietnam. However, the work of at least one New Left diplomatic historian, a scholar who came to prominence in the ferment of the Vietnam era, continued to be located in the radical professional discourses. Unlike most New Left diplomatic historians, Gabriel Kolko was working within a marxist, although avowedly independent, framework. While he can be characterized as a New Left diplomatic historian, his work owes more to the marxist tradition articulated by Baran and Sweezy than it does to the Williams school.[119] His work reflected the assumption that the imperatives of capitalism drove Washington to seek out new markets, new fields for investment and new sources of raw materials.[120] Kolko gained his PhD from Harvard at the beginning of the 1960s, and by the end of the decade he had produced an important revisionist study of US policy in the final years of World War II, and another one on the origins of modern US foreign policy.[121] In the 1970s he continued to produce radical history, and in the 1980s his books, which had become less deterministic, focused explicitly on US policy in Latin America, Asia and Africa.[122] Kolko, who has been a research professor at York University in Toronto for many years, was active in the anti-war movement. From his own perspective, since the late 1960s he has "defined a critical, independent position on world affairs". He argued that it is "impossible, undesirable and dangerous for the United States, the USSR, or any state to seek to guide the development of another nation or region". Kolko took the view that there was "no tension between (his) partisanship and a commitment to as objective and as informed an assessment of reality as possible".[123] Kolko's work in the 1968 to 1979 period continued to flow from radical (marxist) ideas about rationality and objectivity and a radical teleology that assumed the eventual triumph of socialism.

Kolko represented the very small marxist strand of New Left diplomatic history, which continued to be excluded from the dominant liberal discourses as they evolved in the 1970s.[124] The anarchist strain in the New Left critique of US foreign policy is best exemplified by the work of Noam Chomsky, Professor of Linguistics at the Massachusetts Institute of Technology. He was an early critic of the war in Vietnam, and since the late 1960s he has provided a steady flow of books and articles criticizing US foreign policy in Southeast Asia, the Middle East and the rest of the Third World. His work focused not just on US foreign policy, but on the collaborative relationship between North American academics and US Cold War expansion.[125] Chomsky's critique of Cold War liberalism successfully exposed the dubious character of the liberal claim to objectivity; however, since his rise to prominence in the late 1960s, Chomsky has continued to represent his own position as objective and rational.[126] Chomsky has also been criticized by marxists and by liberals for grounding his perspective on ethical assumptions, and there is a resonance between Chomsky's work and William Appleman Williams's call for the US to seek redemption through the renunciation of empire.[127]

Chomsky's and Kolko's work was a direct response to the war in Vietnam. And by the end of the 1960s Vietnam was the major stimulus for most critiques of US imperialism articulated by the New Left and radical area studies.[128] After 1968, the war in Vietnam also provided the context in which these critiques were increasingly well received.[129] A well-known book that clearly manifested the impact of Vietnam was **War Without End: American Planning for the Next Vietnams**, by Michael T. Klare, with a foreword by Gabriel Kolko.[130] Klare emerged as a prominent critic of US foreign policy in the 1970s. As already mentioned, he was a staff member at NACLA in the late 1960s and 1970s, during which time he wrote **War Without End**. It extended the critique of the war in Vietnam to Latin America and emphasized the linkages between US policy in Asia and the western hemisphere. This book and his later work were representative of a new concern to expose US involvement in counter-guerrilla wars, in the context of the broader links between US hegemony and counter-insurgency in the Third World.[131] In later years Klare was also involved with the Institute for Policy Studies (IPS), which was the institutional force behind many of these works.[132]

The Institute for Policy Studies, which was closely identified with the New Left, had been set up in Washington in the early 1960s by Marcus G. Raskin and Richard J. Barnet, who met while they were both working for the Kennedy administration. They were initially drawn together by their concern to counter what they saw as an increasingly militaristic trend in US foreign policy. They both resigned from the Kennedy administration and set about establishing an independent institute to formulate and publicize policy alternatives. The Institute for Policy Studies was established in October 1963. Barnet and Raskin pursued what they have described as "existential pragmatism". Throughout the second half of the 1960s and the 1970s, IPS and its publications played an important role in the civil rights movement and the growing opposition to the war in Vietnam. For example, in 1965 Raskin collaborated with Bernard B. Fall to edit and produce **The Viet-Nam Reader**. This became a basic text for the anti-war teach-ins which swept North American campuses in the late 1960s.[133] As the IPS grew, the work of its members continued to manifest an interest in the linkages between US foreign policy, Cold War expansionism and the international political and economic order. In 1968 Barnet produced an important critique of US intervention in the Third

World. Written at the height of the war in Vietnam, this book pointed to radical liberalism rather than marxism as the driving force behind the IPS and much of the New Left. In contrast to marxists and/or dependency theorists, Barnet took the view that the solution to problems of development in Latin America and beyond was "for the community of nations and for the United States...to attempt the creation of a world environment in which revolution is unnecessary".[134] Throughout the 1970s, Barnet and other academics associated with IPS continued to write about US foreign policy and the political economy of international relations. And Latin America and the Third World generally figured in their analyses.[135] Because much of the work coming out of the IPS nexus reflected a liberal revision of dependency theory and was aimed at influencing the policy process in North America and Western Europe, it tended to locate the dynamics of political and social change in the decisions and actions emanating from Washington and the other major capitals of the world.

Like New Left diplomatic history, the work of the IPS was easily incorporated into the dominant liberal discourses in the 1970s. This was particularly apparent in IPS work on the Americas. By 1970, the IPS had a limited, but growing, focus on Latin America. It provided Paul Cowan with a fellowship in the late 1960s which contributed to his publication of **The Making of an Un-American: A Dialogue With Experience** in 1970.[136] This book, conceived of by the author as a radical version of **The Ugly American**, was a personal critique of the Peace Corps, US AID, the State Department and the conduct of US foreign policy in Latin America, by a young North American who had served with the Peace Corps in Ecuador. Cowan's critique was reformist, and his principle concern was how North American ethnocentrism and elitism were at odds with the stated goals of US AID and the Peace Corps. IPS also supported a book on Chile by David Morris. Following the overthrow of Allende in 1973, his ambassador to the United States, Orlando Letelier, became director of the Transnational Institute at IPS headquarters in Washington. IPS captured the spotlight, under tragic circumstances, when Letelier and another IPS researcher, Ronni Moffitt, were assassinated at the direction of the Chilean secret police.[137] By the second half of the 1970s IPS members had links with the Democratic Party, and IPS was being perceived by some observers as a Democratic Party think tank. In the mid-1970s the IPS organized a group of Latin American specialists, which included Robert Pastor (who went on to serve on the National Security Council in the Carter administration), to produce a policy paper on Latin America.[138] This paper was later regarded by conservative critics of the Carter administration as having influenced the administration's policy in a direction consonant with the aims and objectives of the New Left. Although IPS academics have acted as consultants to the government and played a role in the foreign-policy process, the level of influence exercised by the IPS on US foreign policy can be debated.[139] It should be emphasized that despite IPS's incorporation into the dominant liberal structures and discourses in the 1970s, a liberal academic-policy nexus that had far more influence on the Carter administration's foreign policy was the Trilateral Commission. By the mid-1970s Carter, Brzezinski, Sol Linowitz and most other Carter administration foreign-policy officials were members of the Commission. In the late 1970s Carter's foreign policy, at least initially, focused on North-South rather than East-West relations and was connected to the ongoing revision of classic modernization theory, which had begun to lose some of its purchase by the mid-1960s.

Revising Modernization Theory 1968-1979

Classic modernization theory served as a complement to US foreign policy into the 1960s. US foreign policy and the dominant professional area-studies discourses in the 1950s and 1960s rested on the assumption that aid and technical assistance would lead to the economic development and political modernization of Latin America, Asia and Africa, and to the containment of communism. However, despite the flow of economic aid in the 1950s and 1960s, the gap between the rich and the poor grew and revolution spread. This provided the context for the meteoric rise of dependency theory, but following the initial shock of the theoretical and methodological crisis of the 1960s, dependency theory and the New Left approach were incorporated into the dominant liberal professional discourses. Liberal area-studies specialists borrowed from the emerging radical discourses, as well as adapting hitherto neglected theoretical models facilitating the reinvigoration of liberalism. As we have seen, an early result of the decline of classic modernization theory was the rise of military modernization theory and the emergence of a politics of order approach.[140] As US foreign policy was shifting from its ostensibly liberal reformist phase to a more conservative counter-revolutionary stance, the politics of order rather than democratization became the key issue for the dominant area-studies discourses.[141] Samuel Huntington was the most prominent exponent of the shift from classic modernization theory to the politics of order. He was a leading representative of the group of North American academics who were characterized as the New Mandarins by their dissenting colleagues in the 1960s.[142]

In 1968 Huntington produced **Political Order in Changing Societies**, one of the most influential books ever to appear on modernization in Latin America, Africa and Asia. A survey of over half of the US academics teaching courses on Latin American politics in 1973 found that 44% of them regarded Huntington's book as the most useful. In another survey of development courses generally, almost 60% of the academics surveyed regarded it as the "most important in the field".[143] Huntington held up political order as the ultimate goal of any society. He sought "to probe the conditions under which societies undergoing rapid and disruptive social and economic change may in some measure realize this goal". Huntington's major concern was with predicting what might or might not be necessary to ensure continued social order and political stability. He argued that contrary to earlier expectations the instability in Latin America and the rest of the Third World, since World War II, was primarily the result of "rapid social change and the rapid mobilization of new groups into politics coupled with the slow development of political institutions". He argued that the main political "problem" in the Third World was "the lag in the development of political institutions behind social and economic change". Furthermore, US foreign policy since 1945 had, in his view, missed this point, because Washington had focused on the "economic gap" and ignored the "political gap". He emphasized that the political gap had been ignored because of the assumption in North America that political stability flowed from "social reform" stimulated by "economic development". However, argued Huntington, economic development and political stability were actually relatively autonomous objectives.[144]

The entrenched view, that there was a connection between underdevelopment and instability, was attacked by Huntington as spurious. In his view it was the attempt to modernize, rather than "the absence of modernity", which resulted in political instability. He asserted that "poor countries" were "unstable" because they were attempting to develop and a "purely traditional society would be ignorant, poor and stable". According to Huntington, instability had to be understood primarily as a result of the "gap between aspirations and expectations", which flowed from the dramatic expansion of "aspirations" in the initial stages of "modernization". At the same time "a similar gap with similar results may be produced by the decline in expectations" and "revolutions often occur when a period of sustained economic growth is followed by a sharp economic downturn". Huntington sought to correct what he saw as an erroneous understanding of power. In his view North Americans saw power as finite, while communists emphasized "the 'collective' or expansible aspect of power". He argued that modern political systems were different from traditional systems because of "the amount of power in the system, not in its distribution", and in both systems power "may be concentrated or dispersed", but there was greater political participation in modern than in traditional systems. From his perspective the "traditional polity" was "suffering from the absence of power", and the "problem" was "not to seize power but to make power, to mobilize groups into politics and to organize their participation in politics", and this was "precisely" the approach communists took to "political change".[145]

There was a direct connection between Huntington's conclusions in **Political Order in Changing Societies**, his work for the US government in the late 1960s, and the war in Vietnam. He was associated with the United States Agency for International Development's (USAID) South East Asian Advisory Group as chairman of its Council on Vietnamese Studies from 1966 to 1969, and he spent time in South Vietnam in 1967 on behalf of the US State Department. In 1968, the year after his visit to Southeast Asia, he wrote an article that explained the Vietnamese Communist success in South Vietnam as a result of their "ability to impose authority in rural areas where authority was lacking". In his view--and this was a major theme of his book--the Communists' appeal in Vietnam did not stem from material poverty, but from "political deprivation", that is, the lack of an "effective structure of authority". In Huntington's estimation, the rural areas could not be retaken from the Communists (a view also articulated by Henry Kissinger as early as 1966, before he became Nixon's Secretary of State); however, in the three years between 1965 and 1968 approximately three million Vietnamese had fled to the urban areas, especially Saigon, where they came under RVN authority and herein lay, for Huntington, the key to combating wars of national liberation. The solution, according to Huntington, was to adopt a policy of "forced-draft urbanization" and "modernization", which quickly shifts the Third World nation in question beyond the stage where a rural-based revolution has any chance of building up enough support to capture national political power.[146]

Huntington was a co-founder and editor of the new journal **Foreign Policy**, published by the Carnegie Endowment for International Peace, which first appeared in 1970, and was a major forum for the revision of Cold War liberalism.[147] The journal had been initially sponsored by Huntington, and a number of younger members of the Council on Foreign Relations, including Stanley Hoffmann, James C. Thomson and Richard Falk, as well as David Halberstam, as a challenge to **Foreign Affairs**.[148] In the 1970s Huntington went on to develop close links with the Trilateral Commission, which was founded in 1973. He was on the Trilateral Task Force on the Governability of Democracies and authored the section on the US in the well-known Task Force report **The Crisis of Democracy**. Huntington served as the Coordinator of National Security on the National Security Council during the Carter administration, a post he resigned from in August 1978 in order to become the Director of the Center for International Affairs at Harvard.[149] Throughout the 1970s Huntington and his work clearly reflected the managerial approach to development.[150] For example, in 1974 he played a modest advisory role in Brazil, where the military regime sought to manage a process of "decompression" or liberalization of the political system at the same time as power was transferred to an acceptable configuration of civilian politicians who would not undercut the military or its political base.[151] A managerial approach was also readily apparent in his 1976 study of political participation, which among other things continued to challenge the view that there was some sort of causal connection between social and economic development and political democracy and stability.[152] But, despite his links with the Trilateral Commission, Huntington can also be positioned in the conservative discourses as they emerged at the end of the 1970s. As we will see, by the early 1980s, his work complemented the relatively brief ascendancy of Reaganism which drew less on the relatively liberal aspects of the managerial approach and more on the most conservative aspects of conservative development theory.

By the 1970s the work of a number of political scientists and historians who can be characterized as conservative development theorists was part of the trend away from economic development, social reform and democracy, towards an emphasis on the important stabilizing role of the military and political order, as exemplified in Huntington's writings. When conservatives discussed development they usually argued that historical change was not simply about the transition from tradition to modernity, but the modernizing and adapting of tradition, and that all modern societies were a mixture of traditional and modern. By the late 1960s what was of increasing concern to Washington was not change but order, and conservative development theorists looked for, and found, a possible source of stability in traditional political and social institutions, and a strong state. Their work displayed far less optimism about democratization and the potential for global economic prosperity than had been displayed by modernization theory of the 1950s and 1960s. Political development was increasingly approached in terms of the central role of the state, and stability was the main theme.[153]

Growing out of this relatively conservative approach, a growing number of Latin American specialists found an explanation for the failure of modernization theory and the Alliance for Progress: the North American misunderstanding of the political process in Latin America. They argued that the Alliance for Progress had failed partly because it was founded on a flawed political model that postulated that Latin America's traditional oligarchy was undergoing replacement through a process similar to the idealized representation of the political process in North America. This approach had envisioned political compromises and struggles between various sectors of a society whose differing interests were ultimately reconcilable. As we have seen, North American analysts usually assumed that the so-called middle sectors would be the major factor in the region's politics in the 1960s. It was also assumed that these middle sectors enthusiastically supported the objectives of the Alliance for Progress. By the end of the 1960s, faith in the middle sectors had disappeared.[154] Modernization theory had focused on change and conservative development theory focused on continuity. At the same time, a majority of Latin Americanists continued to regard economic and social change in liberal terms as an "evolutionary process"; however, they increasingly emphasized that this occurred in the context of existing political and economic structures and institutions. There was a growing tendency to underline the viability, resiliency and "naturalness" of traditional social and economic structures, in contrast to the disruptive effects of revolutionary change.[155] An influential example of this approach was **Political and Economic Change in Latin America: The Governing of Restless Nations,** by Charles W. Anderson. According to a survey made in the early to mid-1970s, this was regarded by Latin Americanists as the most important book on development and Latin American politics. Out of all the US academics teaching courses on Latin American politics, 52% responded to the survey, and 40% of the respondents ranked Anderson's book as the most significant.[156]

The rejection of classic modernization theory which was central to Anderson's book was also apparent in the work of those Latin Americanists who were more strident in their emphasis on the continuity of Iberian cultural and political traditions in Latin America. The Iberian heritage was regarded as the key to the persistence of authoritarianism and to the region's continued social and economic inequality. They argued that the "non-democratic" character of Latin American politics flowed from a southern European and Roman Catholic politico-social tradition which emphasized the importance of order, harmony and the minimalization of conflict.[157] This view was not new. It had been articulated by Claudio Véliz and Richard Morse in the early 1960s. But it was given greater coherence in the 1970s by Véliz and by scholars such as Howard Wiarda. It came to be known generally as the corporatist approach or the new corporatism, insofar as one version argued that the events of the late 1960s and early 1970s reflected a rediscovery of Latin America's corporatist roots after a century-long liberal hiatus.[158] As with dependency theory, most North American students of Latin America drew on, rather than embraced, a corporatist approach.[159] There was also evidence of efforts to synthesize or build on both dependency and corporatist approaches.[160] Overall corporatism and conservative development theory were probably less influential in Latin American studies than in other geographical sectors of area studies in North America. Liberal managerial approaches, along with a domesticated dependency approach were the most influential, while the concept of bureaucratic-authoritarianism also appeared in the 1970s, as part of a concern to explain the spread of authoritarian regimes in Latin America. It had emerged in a critical fashion from the corporatist perspective, modernization theory, dependency theory and marxism. Bureaucratic-authoritarianism--which was initially developed by the Argentinian exile Guillermo O'Donnell to explain the rise of military rule in Argentina--argued that increasing levels of industrialization rather than leading to democracy and economic equality, paralleled and even led to the disintegration of democracy and greater social and economic inequality.[161] By the 1970s, the influence of the bureaucratic-authoritarian model was significant, and the debate it had stimulated reflected the diversity which characterized Latin American studies after 1968. In the 1980s, as Latin American specialists sought increasingly to explain the apparent return to democracy, bureaucratic-authoritarianism grew increasingly important as a conceptual point of departure. At the same time (as we will see in the next chapters) the corporatist approach and conservative development theory enjoyed a resurgence in the early 1980s as part of a distinct conservative counterpoint to the liberal managerial approach and its relatively optimistic revision of classic modernization theory.

Managing the Latin American Revolution 1968-1979

By the 1970s the liberal managerial approach to revolution had become a central trend in the dominant discourses on Latin America. The influence of liberal managerialism on US imperial state policy during the Nixon years remained marginal; however, the policy towards Nicaragua, for example, followed by the Carter administration in its first two years meshed with, and may have been influenced by, the growing emphasis by Latin American studies professionals on managing the revolution in Latin America. Liberal managerialism articulated greater optimism than, but built on, Huntington's politics of order approach and conservative development theory. It also incorporated radical elements. This perspective was apparent in George C. Lodge's **Engines of Change: United States Interests and Revolution in Latin America**, which was first published in 1970.[162] In the 1950s Lodge worked for the US Department of Labor and served as Assistant Secretary of Labor for International Affairs in the late 1950s and early 1960s. He was a longtime member of the Council on Foreign Relations, and he took up the post of professor of business administration at Harvard Business School in 1963. Like Huntington, by the 1970s he was also connected with the Trilateral Commission, and he served on the Commission's Trilateral Task Force on Industrial Relations.[163] Lodge acknowledged that Huntington had been an important influence on his work, and that **Political Order in Changing Societies** was, to a great degree, "the intellectual bedrock" for **Engines of Change**. Unlike Huntington, however, Lodge's approach was more optimistic and related back to the modernization theory of the early 1960s, particularly the Alliance for Progress, in a less critical fashion. Lodge's book was an explicit call for a reassessment of US policy in Latin America and an effort to come to grips with the basic contradiction in US policy between a "commitment to change and commitment to stability". He argued that it was time for a "new formulation of interests and purpose--a new ideology--to replace that of anti-communism, which has lost both its validity and its utility".[164] According to Lodge the US had to realize that revolution in Latin America and the Third World was inevitable; however, in his view Washington still remained capable of influencing the revolution's direction, if it simply recognized the tension between stability and change within US policy. Like Huntington, Lodge emphasized that there was no direct connection between economic development and stability and democratization, arguing that a failure to recognize this was behind much of the US failure in South Vietnam and Latin America. According to Lodge the significance of communism was not its "ideology", which in his view had "become progressively obscure and unattractive", but that it represented an important guide to "power seizure, organization and control".[165]

Writing in 1970, Lodge articulated a liberal position which ran counter to the conservatism of US policy under Nixon and Ford, but would emerge at least partially in the Carter administration. At the level of broad strategy he emphasized that it was in the US "interest" to curb its support for the "status quo", at the same time as contacts with "revolutionary groups" were entered into and expanded, particularly those groups which "are most consistent with our other moral, political and economic interests" and "are moving in a direction consistent with our larger interests". It was also in the US "interest" to curb its direct and indirect military presence and open "avenues of communication" between the US and the Soviet Union, and particularly with Cuba, because "in the long run, in spite of Castro's vitriol, it seems inevitable that the mutuality of interests between Cuba and the United States will--or should--far outweigh the conflicts of interest".[166] Although Lodge argued that the Alliance for Progress had "failed", he assumed that its goals were sound and that a new mix of policies and US adaptation to changes in the region could still realize the Alliance's objectives. He did not perceive a fundamental contradiction between US interests in Latin America and the lofty aims of the Alliance for Progress. In his view, the main problem with the Alliance had been the North American idea that given the right techniques and resources a Latin American government, which "tends to be the creature of oligarchic power-holders", would "as a matter of nature" make the changes necessary to "enhance the public good". Despite his pessimism about the reformist role of the 'state', he continued to pin his hopes on "revolutionary reformers" such as Frei (in Chile) and Betancourt (in Venezuela), and even what he called "technically oriented 'modernists'" such as Anastasio Somoza of Nicaragua. He called for a "new foreign assistance policy" which "should be directed at the fulfillment of the radical changes envisaged by the Alliance for Progress". While he recommended that the US, along with the World Bank and the Inter-American Development Bank, should continue to work through the Inter-American Committee of the Alliance for Progress to maintain many existing programs, he also called for "a second and quite distinct system of assistance programs to find and fuel the critical combinations of engines of change so as to make the revolution as effective, as peaceful and as useful as possible".[167]

Like the work of George Lodge, other liberal studies which had emerged by the early 1970s, such as books by Herbert May, Robert Alexander, Harvey Perloff, Jerome Levinson, Juan de Onis and Federico Gil, were all based on the ideas which had guided the Alliance for Progress.[168] Although they did not argue that the Alliance had been a success, their work was premised on the overall compatibility between the interests of the governments and people of Latin America, and the interests of the government and people of the United States. This work also continued to rest on the belief that there was an identifiable US national interest in Latin America which could be separated from the more specific interests of North American business and that Washington had the capacity to both define and pursue this national interest.[169] From their perspective the earlier problems that had developed between Latin America and Washington had grown out of the shortcomings of previous policies, such as gunboat diplomacy, dollar diplomacy, the transitory conflation of private interests with the national interest, and Washington's lack of attention to the region. And all of these problems were believed either to have been overcome or at least surmountable. Inter-American problems were also explained in terms of a "persistent misunderstanding" between North and South caused and compounded by different cultural backgrounds and a shortage of information.[170] Although by the early 1970s liberal area-studies specialists differed with regard to particular aspects of the failure of the Alliance for Progress, they all distinguished between the benevolence of US motives and their unhappy results. The lack of success flowed from problems at the level of implementation. For example Harvey Perloff characterized the Alliance as a "truly magnificent concept" which was "carried out in a half-hearted way with a weak, underfinanced, and poorly designed mechanism".[171]

An approach which clearly pointed to both the important continuities and the changes in the analysis of the Alliance for Progress can be found in the work of Martin C. Needler. A graduate of Harvard, by the end of the 1960s Needler was the director of the Division of Inter-American Affairs and Professor of Political Science at the University of New Mexico. In the revised edition of **The United States and the Latin American Revolution**, which appeared in 1977, he argued that the Alliance for Progress was a "failure" only in the context of the "exaggerated hopes" surrounding the launch of the Alliance. In his view, social and economic change were a slow process, and the "strong cues" which the Alliance for Progress delivered were largely "responsible" for significantly "reorienting" the policies of most Latin American governments. He argued that "most" North Americans and "most" Latin Americans shared the same "values" and that the "long term" US "national interests and aspirations" could be "brought into harmony with the interests of the peoples of Latin America" if the US overcame its "narrow preoccupation with the private interests of individual economic groupings", its "shibboleths about national security" and the "ideological fixations" of the previous era. This done, North Americans would be "able to perceive the revolutionary forces at work in Latin America today" and realize that "intelligent policies for the promotion of political, as well as economic, developments can work with these forces and not against them, to produce results that are consonant with US national interests".[172] Needler's work made clear the changes to the dominant liberal professional discourses in this period. By the 1970s liberals increasingly emphasized the profound socio-economic forces at work in Latin America and the danger involved in US failure to recognize their existence. The liberal discourses emphasized diplomatic and reformist solutions, and increasingly represented conflict in Latin America in terms of the North-South axis rather than the Cold War axis. The emphasis was on managing the international political and economic order and responding to challenges from Latin America, and elsewhere in the Third World, by reform, negotiation and diplomacy.

As part of their effort to both explain the crisis of US hegemony and revise modernization theory, some liberal area-studies specialists had begun to use the bureaucratic-politics model to understand US foreign policy in Latin America and elsewhere. The bureaucratic-politics approach, which was based on earlier administrative behavior theories, argued that foreign policy flowed from the interaction, factional rivalry and individual competition between, and within, the various agencies of government attempting to retain and expand their influence. It did not, in practice, necessarily reflect the "purposeful calculation of national interests". This approach to the history of foreign policy, and contemporary inter-American relations, emphasized the wide range of influences acting on the individuals and the government departments involved in the making and execution of foreign policy, and the unforeseen and complex results. In the 1970s the bureaucratic-politics approach emerged as the theoretical centerpiece for the John F. Kennedy School of Government at Harvard. And Graham T. Allison, the author of **Essence of Decision: Explaining the Cuban Missile Crisis** (1971), the "classic statement" of the bureaucratic-politics model, became the School of Government's dean. By the end of the 1970s bureaucratic politics was regarded as one of the most influential international-relations and political-science models in North America and internationally.[173]

A major proponent of the bureaucratic-politics model in the early 1970s was Latin American specialist Abraham F. Lowenthal. In a well-known article which first appeared in the **Latin American Research Review** in 1973, he concluded that the liberal perspective, based on the modernization paradigm, and the radical perspective, based on dependency theory, both provided an "inadequate" explanation of the character of inter-American relations and the dynamics of US foreign policy in Latin America. As an alternative he argued for the relevance of the bureaucratic politics model. Lowenthal's analysis focused on the failure of the Alliance for Progress. Although the liberal approach, as it was constituted by the late 1960s, was markedly different from the radical approach, Lowenthal found them similar in important ways. Both perspectives interpreted the Alliance for Progress as if it were "a coherent policy, or set of policies" emanating from a "central apparatus". Liberals started from the view that US foreign policy was "derived from stated purposes", such as the intersection of "ideals" and "security" concerns, and they generally acknowledged that policy was also shaped in part by domestic economic and political "interests", while radicals down-played or dismissed the importance of "ideals", "security" and political "interests" and emphasized economic "interests". However, liberals and radicals both portrayed Washington as identifying "interests", outlining "goals", making "decisions" and acting according to "identifiable aims". Liberals also shared with radicals the "tendency to present analysis and explanation with a strong overlay of evaluation, even exhortation", and this was "probably" due to their reliance on the "concept and language of 'purpose' and their assumption of a unitary, rational actor who can be educated or blamed". Lowenthal lamented that virtually every article or book written on the Alliance for Progress up to the mid-1970s ended with a call to US officials to revive the Alliance's "principles" and "establish them as a guide for US actions", or with "a condemnation of the officials for exploiting Latin America and for their hypocrisy in announcing a 'policy' so different from their real intentions".[174] In Lowenthal's view, the resolution to this impasse was to be found in the bureaucratic-politics perspective. In the early 1970s, apart from Allison and Lowenthal's work, there was still only a limited effort to apply the bureaucratic-politics model to the study of inter-American relations.[175] However, its influence grew as the 1970s progressed.

One of the most important attempts to mesh the insights of a bureaucratic-politics approach with an explicitly managerial approach to revolution was the work of Cole Blasier. By the mid-1970s, the prominent Latin American specialist was applying the bureaucratic-politics model--and related approaches which emphasized domestic politics, extra-governmental actors, and transnational politics--to the history of inter-American relations. His work also moved well beyond traditional diplomatic history, attempting to link a history of international relations with domestic developments in all the countries concerned.[176] Blasier is a former foreign-service officer with the State Department, having served in Moscow, Belgrade and Bonn. He spent time as a resident scholar at the Institute of Latin America in Moscow, was responsible for the establishment of the Soviet-US Latin American studies exchange program in the late 1970s, which was operated by the Latin American Studies Association, and served as chair of the LASA Task Force on Scholarly Relations with the Soviet Union from 1980 to 1986.[177] In 1986-1987 he was president of the Latin American Studies Association, and he went on to be Chief of the Hispanic Division at the Library of Congress from 1988 to 1993. He founded the Center for Latin American Studies at the University of Pittsburgh in the mid-1960s, and served as the Center's Director for many years. He was based in the Department of Political Science at the University of Pittsburgh until he moved to the Library of Congress in the late 1980s. Blasier has published a number of books and articles, and his work clearly locates him in the dominant liberal professional discourse as it emerged in the 1970s.[178] In his best-known and most influential book, **The Hovering Giant: US Responses to Revolutionary Change in Latin America**, first published in 1976, he set out to extract lessons from history in order to avoid repeating policy mistakes. Although he did not incorporate any policy recommendations in his analysis, he did indicate his explicit support for the recommendations made by the Linowitz Commission in the mid-1970s, which Blasier characterized as an "enlightened approach" to the reconciliation of "conflicting interests" between the US and the republics of Latin America.[179]

The Hovering Giant is a landmark in the study of inter-American relations. It was the first attempt to deal systematically with Washington's reaction to revolutionary change in Latin America in the twentieth century. Blasier focused on four countries (Mexico, Guatemala, Cuba and Bolivia) and two major themes: the "revolutionary seizures" of North American investments (and Washington's "responses") and the effect of the United States' "global strategies" on Washington's policy towards Latin America. Blasier argued that the negotiated resolution of hemispheric conflicts had proven to be "more viable" than resolution by force; however, "successful compromises" have to be based on greater knowledge about the other side than has been the case historically. He admitted, however, that "knowledge of the past" did not ensure the resolution of "problems", although it might "help", and he was confident that, although policy-makers have often been "ignorant" of, and even hide, the "facts", they could not do so "forever".[180] Blasier argued that US policy was particularly concerned with revolutions in Latin America in the twentieth century because the nation's "vested interests" in the region were more substantial than elsewhere, and because Washington viewed the region as "vital" to US "strategic interests".[181] He characterized the twentieth century as a period in which the US had "dominated" Central America and the Caribbean from the beginning, while its links with the rest of the hemisphere grew dramatically after 1945, and the zenith of its influence was reached in the mid-1960s. He moved well beyond a discussion of diplomatic relations and emphasized that following World War II, North American "investment" very quickly moved to encompass not only the "extractive industries" and public utilities, where they had been traditionally based, but the manufacturing sector as well, becoming the most "dynamic" factor in the economic life of a number of southern republics. US imports and exports in Latin America have also historically been more considerable than US trade with the rest of the Third World, while the US has also acted as the major external source of Latin American finance capital, economic assistance and advice, as well as military aid and assistance. Blasier also noted that in Latin America the US has operated "a vast network of clandestine intelligence operations", much of the influence and activity of which remains relatively obscure. He pointed to the hierarchy of the Catholic Church in the United States, and the various Protestant missions in Latin America, as also having exercised considerable "influence", while North American foundations and the US media have also had their influence and impact. Blasier used the term "dependency" to characterize the relationship between the US and the Central and South American republics. He argued that "dependency has been the inevitable result of disparities in economic and political power" and the "often deeply felt, dependence on the United States became a major concern of revolutionary movements in Latin America".[182] He used the term 'dependency' in a way which drew on dependency theory but did not advocate classic dependency theory's political agenda.

With regard to his central concern, Blasier emphasized the continuity in both the southern "actions" and the United States's "reactions" between 1910 and the overthrow of Allende in the early 1970s.[183] While the southern revolutionaries had repeatedly sought increased control of their nations' economics, politics and foreign policy, as well as expanding the political participation of the urban and agrarian work force, the US had "consistently" sought to defend North American investments and expressed apprehension about the new governments' relations with "rivals" of Washington. During the Cold War North American "fears" that communism was "contagious" took on a new "intensity", which, argued Blasier, transcended the "fear" of Moscow as simply a military and nuclear threat. In his view, the overwhelming influence which anti-communism gained on the North American public after World War II, went well beyond a conflict of values and interest between Washington and Moscow. Moscow's policies and its ideology also represented a "direct challenge" to, or at least "offended", the majority of "vested interests" in the United States, which further strengthened the anti-communist 'consensus'. Blasier argued that the North American "fear of communism" affected the "judgement" of political leaders, governments officials and the general public, and impinged dramatically on the US government's ability to evaluate political changes in the southern republics "objectively". The full "extent" of this "fear" was "demonstrated", said Blasier, by Washington's actions in Guatemala in the 1950s, Cuba in the early 1960s, and in the Dominican Republic in the mid-1960s, which Blasier characterized as the climax of North American "anticommunism" in the hemisphere.[184]

Although Blasier emphasized the importance of national political and psychological determinants of US policy, he regarded strategic considerations as the most important force driving US policy in Latin America. At the same time he emphasized that strategic factors had to be analyzed in the context of bureaucratic politics. He argued that "fairly sharp distinctions may be drawn between the authority and policy outputs of top-level officials--the president and the secretary of state--on the one hand and low-level officials--those in the Department of State and ambassadors--on the other". While the "top-level officials" were involved in all situations where decisions were regarded as strategic, the majority of the "nonstrategic decisions" were handled at the departmental or the ambassadorial level. He said that the "official responses decided at lower levels tended to be in accord with US private interests or at least not blatantly opposed to them" (the US ambassador to Guatemala had "close corporate ties" and was favorable disposed towards "business as a matter of principle"). Furthermore, a "duty" of State Department officials and diplomats on foreign posting was and is, noted Blasier, to safeguard and expand private North American "interests". Other branches of the US government, such as the Treasury Department, the US military and after 1945 the Central Intelligence Agency, also occupied significant positions in the "decision-making process", and from Blasier's perspective the "intragovernmental bargaining" between these various branches "constituted the essence of the decision-making process inside the government". Blasier also argued that the bureaucratic-politics model can be applied to the regional and global level. While the Western Hemisphere falls entirely inside Washington's "sphere of influence", the US is not able to "control" every nation, but it does possess far more "influence" than any other nation-state in the region or outside it. He characterized Washington's "response" to the revolution in Guatemala, and later in Cuba, as, at least in part, "reflex reactions" seeking to "maintain informal political dominion" and "US political primacy within its sphere of influence". At the same time, the "maintenance of primacy" was important not only in regional terms, but "was perceived as "essential" to the United States' "global security", and Blasier emphasized that it was impossible to make a clear demarcation between the regional and global factors which shaped US response.[185]

While North American policy-makers and Latin revolutionaries change strategies and tactics, Blasier concluded that there were recurring "underlying problems" and "behavior patterns". Despite US fears, "revolutionary governments" in the region had "historically" not been able to rely on the "effective support" of the Soviet Union. Moscow's strong links with Cuba were an exception. Although he was not optimistic about a "reorientation" in US foreign policy towards Latin America, he did recommend that Washington "face up to realities", arguing that "suppression" had been viable only in the short term. He recommended that the US should attempt to use "the great weight of governmental power" to facilitate "negotiated settlements" between investors and revolutionaries. Blasier also suggested that Washington make an effort to curb the "negative impact" that US global policies have on inter-American relations, as when suspicion and rivalry with the USSR led to a "mistaken" assessment of the situation in Guatemala. Blasier argued that US foreign policy towards Guatemala in the mid-1950s, and towards Cuba later, had "contributed" to the emergence of guerrilla insurgencies in the region after 1960. He argued that the US "sponsored counterinsurgency programs" that had resulted in short-term gains "at immense long-term political and other costs". In Blasier's view "an imposed settlement is inherently unstable in the long term", and one of the lessons of history was that it is "both good policy and good morals" for Washington to avoid using "military or paramilitary forces against its Latin American neighbors, most of whom are largely weak and defenceless".[186]

Blasier's work pointed to the way in which the events of the 1960s had led to the transformation of the dominant liberal area-studies discourses. The book reflected an analysis of US foreign policy which was more nuanced than the approach which had characterized North American diplomatic history and the study of inter-American relations prior to the 1960s. It demonstrated the explicit concern with policy and the far more inter-disciplinary approach to Latin American history which had emerged by the 1970s. The overarching lesson of history which Blasier and others articulated by the mid-1970s was the need for Washington to adapt to regional and international changes, and that negotiation and diplomacy were actually more effective than direct or indirect military intervention. Blasier's work bore the hallmarks of the liberal concern to discard the discredited anti-communist modernizing mission in favor of an approach which recognized the limits of US power, and the increased economic and political influence of many governments in Latin America. At the same time his work reflected the continued survival of the assumption that Latin American interests and the interests of the United States could be harmonized, and that greater understanding on both sides, and some attention to the lessons of history, could lead away from conflict and towards greater prosperity for all concerned. His work meshed with the overall liberal managerial project, with its emphasis on a liberal development model and the reform and restructuring of the international system in a way which best protected US hegemony and the privileged position of the political and economic elites of the industrial democracies.

The shift in the 1970s from the East-West conflict and the containment of communism to North-South relations, the management of revolution and the moderate reform of global economic relations was clearly reflected in changes at the Council on Foreign Relations. In 1974 the Council on Foreign Relations set up the 1980s Project, initially under the supervision of Richard Ullman. Like the Trilateral Commission, the 1980s Project, which was explicitly directed at overcoming a Cold War foreign-policy paradigm, sought to bring together diplomats and academics from Japan, Europe, the United States, and even Latin America. Between 1977 and 1982, the 1980s Project sponsored twenty books. Like Trilateralist publications, they all emphasized that "interdependence" had now become more important than East-West conflict.[187] Latin American specialists were well represented in the 1980s Project. In his contribution Richard Fagen prescribed the "demilitarization of foreign policy", called for closer "public control" of "intelligence operations", and for a "substantial decoupling of business and corporate interests from the conduct of foreign policy". Mexico specialist and economist Roger D. Hansen, who served as an advisor to the National Security Council during the Carter years, emphasized a reformist strategy aimed at changing US aid and trade policy in such a way as to ensure that the basic needs of the Third World poor were met. Lincoln Gordon, Professor of Political Economy at Johns

Hopkins University and former Alliance for Progress adviser and ambassador to Brazil under Kennedy, advocated a much milder reformist agenda than the one outlined by Hansen. Jorge I. Domínguez and Bryce Wood also contributed to a 1980s Project study which sought to address Washington's neglect of human-rights abuses by governments friendly to the United States. Collectively the 1980s Project sought to chart a new course beyond the Cold War liberalism of the 1945-1968 period, and it focused far more on economic and social issues than on political and military ones. At least some of these views were reflected in the policies adopted by the Carter administration in its first year or two.[188] The Carter administration eventually shifted back to a conventional Cold War policy, but for a year or two in the late 1970s US foreign policy towards the revolutionary upsurge in Central America, particularly Nicaragua, appeared to reflect the liberal managerial approach to revolution which had become influential within the Latin American studies profession.

Central America Rediscovered 1968-1979

Prior to the late 1970s US policy-makers had demonstrated limited and episodic interest in Central America. At the same time changes were underway in the region which would turn it into a key concern of US foreign policy for much of the 1980s and a crucial focus of the Latin American studies profession. During his presidency Richard Nixon was predisposed towards ignoring Central America, while the isthmus itself appeared to be relatively quiescent. The military regime in Guatemala had reduced the guerrillas to a few isolated groups in the countryside. In El Salvador the rise of the moderate Christian Democrats gave the appearance that the country was moving towards an effective political system. The armed forces were maintaining stability in Honduras, and the life expectancy of the Somoza family in Nicaragua was being measured in generations. And Costa Rica was held up as a model to the other Central American republics. There was little concern in Washington in the late 1960s and early 1970s about a Soviet, or even a Cuban, threat to Central America. Throughout the sixties the Cubans and the Soviets had vigorously disagreed about what policy should be followed in Latin America. Following the Missile Crisis in 1962, and Khrushchev's replacement by Brezhnev in 1964, Moscow increasingly urged the Latin American Communist Parties to adopt a gradual approach to social change, at least until the proletariat became larger. This approach encouraged many Latin American revolutionaries to break with Moscow in the 1960s. The Soviet Union turned a blind eye to US intervention in the Dominican Republic in the mid-1960s, and Washington gave Moscow a free hand in its own backyard, making little or no objection to the Soviet invasion of Czechoslovakia in 1968. Throughout most of the 1960s Cuba took a far more revolutionary stance than the Soviet Union; however, in Central America at least, the Communist parties were small and closely tied to Moscow. Cuba gave some encouragement to those insurgent groups in Nicaragua and Guatemala which had split from the traditional communist movement, but following the death of Che Guevara in Bolivia, and the virtual elimination of the guerrilla groups in Colombia, Venezuela and Guatemala by the end of the 1960s, rural insurgency and Cuban militancy were curtailed. In mid-1969, in a less than prophetic analysis, Charles A. Meyer, the US Assistant Secretary of State for Inter-American Affairs, assured Congress that rural "communist insurgencies" in Central America (and further South) were "currently at a relatively low ebb" and "a significant increase in insurgency movements" was not anticipated in the near future.[189]

The relative stability of US hegemony in Central America was achieved at a price, and by the end of Nixon's presidency the substantial US military arms sales, as part of the Nixon Doctrine, were putting a particular strain on the budgets of the small countries of Central America. The onset of the oil crisis in 1973 sparked an economic recession in the US and was compounded by the collapse of the Nixon presidency itself in 1974 and the beginning of a period of relatively indecisive leadership under Gerald Ford and Jimmy Carter. The deepening economic and political crisis at the center during the mid-1970s coincided with a move towards a more revolutionary period in Central America. The dramatic rise in petroleum prices took their toll in Central America, aggravating economies already overburdened by growing military expenses and debts that dated to Alliance for Progress programs in the early 1960s. By the second half of the 1970s Central America had been badly shaken by the spread of inflation world wide, the oil crisis and the natural disasters which ravaged Guatemala, Nicaragua and Honduras between 1972 and 1976. Prior to the 1950s, apart from a decade of reformist government in Guatemala (1944-1954), the majority of the Central American population had been excluded from politics, and as a result had been regarded as irrelevant by policy-makers in Washington. However, the steady flow of foreign investment had contributed to the creation of a significant urban working class, while the expansion of the export-agriculture system had produced a growing landless peasantry. The urban labor force, the peasantry and the region's small middle class were particularly affected by the economic crisis which began to engulf the region after 1973. The revolutions that had appeared to challenge the Central American status quo in the late 1970s developed out of the social and economic crises that had emerged by 1973. During much of the 1970s Washington was absorbed by economic and leadership problems, along with instability in other provinces of its empire, and when it finally rediscovered Central America it was unable to stop the emergence of a revolutionary government in Nicaragua.[190]

Unlike Washington, the ruling regimes in Central America were much quicker to see the danger signals in the crisis which emerged after 1973. They sought to alleviate any threats to stability without actually restructuring the socio-economic and political order. The Central American oligarchies tried to expand beyond the North American market, on which they were heavily reliant, and to enter into new commercial arrangements with Europe, Japan and some of the South American countries. Following OPEC's lead the governments of Guatemala, Costa Rica, Honduras and Nicaragua, along with Panama, Ecuador and Colombia, attempted to set up the Union of Banana Exporting Countries (UPEB). The UPEB wanted to begin by collecting a one dollar export tax on every forty pounds of bananas, the price of which had not risen significantly in two decades. However, standard Fruit, United Brands and Del Monte Corporation (by the mid-1970s the banana exporting business was the biggest fruit operation in the world and it was completely dominated by these three US-based transnational corporations) were uninterested in dealing with the cartel, preferring to continue trading directly with the region's small-scale banana-growers. Ecuador quickly left the cartel, agreeing to the banana companies terms, while the Costa Rican government, responding to threats by Standard Fruit that it would withdraw completely from Costa Rica, agreed to reduce the tax to 25 cents instead of the original one dollar. Honduras soon followed suit, and it was discovered later, following the investigation of the suicide of United Brands' president in early 1975, that the fruit company had given the president of Honduras a bribe of $1.25 million, and a promise of a subsequent $1.25 million, if Honduras continued to keep the tax low. Although, these revelations led to the resignation of the Honduran president, and Costa Rica vowed to raise the tax, Ecuador, Guatemala and Nicaragua refused to support Costa Rica, and the cartel collapsed. Despite the efforts to go beyond the region's traditional dependence on the North American market, the 1970s was notable for the deepening of economic dependence in some areas. During the 1970s at least half of Central America's exports went to North America. This included the traditional bananas and coffee, as well as manufactured goods from the countries' nascent industrial sectors. In 1970, El Salvador's manufactured exports to the US were valued at $1 million, but by 1976 this figure stood at $67 million. The rise was substantial, although not as dramatic for the other countries in the region. For example, Guatemala's manufactured exports to the US market rose from $1.7 million in 1970 to $9.4 million in 1976. At the same time, Central American manufacturers remained heavily dependent on imported inputs, and this exposed local manufacturers to pressure from world-wide inflation. By the late 1970s, although industrialization was seen by many as a way out of Central America's growing economic and political problems, it also appeared to bring continued dependence on the United States.[191]

In the United States, meanwhile, the newly elected Carter administration was preoccupied with the North American economy and the restoration of the reputation of the presidency, following the ignominious reign of Richard Nixon. Superficially, Central America appeared stable, and Carter's overall foreign policy had no particular focus on Central America. Carter's views on foreign policy had been shaped by his experience as a member of the Trilateral Commission, which was founded in 1973 by prominent North American, European and Japanese academics, politicians and corporate heads. One of the co-founders and first directors of the Trilateral Commission, Zbigniew Brzezinski, became Carter's National Security Advisor in 1977. Carter's Secretary of State, Cyrus Vance, was also a member of the Trilateral Commission, as were virtually all the administration's major "foreign policy decision makers". According to Brzezinski, the Trilateral

Commission's overall approach to international relations rested on the assumption that US relations with Japan and Western Europe represented the "strategic hard core for both global stability and progress".[192] The major goal of the Trilateral Commission was to develop a cohesive and semi-permanent alliance which embraced the world's major capitalist-industrial democracies, in order to better promote stability and protect their interests. The Trilateral Commission was devoted to the maintenance and strengthening of the liberal international economic order.[193] In the context of the wider shift in the 1970s towards greater influence on the part of Third World governments at the United Nations--and in related organizations, such as the International Labour Organization (ILO), the United Nations Conference on Trade and Development (UNCTAD) and the United Nations Development Program (UNDP), along with the call for a New International Economic Order (NIEO)--the Trilateral Commission substituted an East-West view of international relations, for a North-South emphasis. It advocated accommodation, mild reform and selective intervention (rather than confrontation) with Latin America, Africa and Asia, seeking a limited amount of reform in order to maintain long-term stability. By the end of the 1970s the Brandt Commission and its **North-South** report had also emerged as a major initiative and a key document by which the elites of the industrial nation-states attempted to manage Latin America and the Third World.[194]

Against the background of the emergence of the Trilateral Commission, a growing emphasis on North-South relations, and the transformation of the dominant professional discourses in North America, Carter's policy towards Latin America specifically was initially shaped by the policy prescriptions of the Commission on United States-Latin American Relations, headed by Sol Linowitz, another member of the Trilateral Commission. Linowitz, a former ambassador to the Organization of American States and onetime chairman of Xerox Corporation, served as Carter's chief negotiator for the Panama Canal Treaty.[195] And despite Carter's global agenda, the Panama Treaty and the growing political upsurge in Central America soon brought the region into Washington's line of vision. In the case of Nicaragua, which emerged as the focus of Washington's concern, Carter and his advisors sought to manage the end of the Somoza regime by encouraging a limited amount of reform in order to maintain long-term stability, and were convinced that violent revolution would only spread if the US continued to support dictators like Somoza. At the outset the Carter administration took the view that the Sandinistas represented the symptom rather than the cause of the problem. The view from the White House was that the rather distant threat which the FSLN was believed to embody could best be eliminated if Nicaragua's political system was allowed to open gradually. By the second year of Carter's presidency--with a year and a half left until Somoza's overthrow in July 1979--it was becoming clear that Washington's minimal effort to influence events by reprimanding Somoza, and cutting back on support and aid, was not enough. An increasing number of Nicaraguans , and Latin Americans, moved to support the Sandinistas in their effort to dislodge the despised dictator. By late 1978 the US had decided to expand its involvement to prevent the FSLN from achieving power; however, within six months the US had acknowledged that its attempt to encourage a "third force" had failed.[196]

The failure of US policy in Nicaragua in the late 1970s pointed to the wider inability of the Carter administration to articulate a consistent policy towards the Third World generally. This 'failure' flowed from the contradiction in Carter's policy between his commitment to improving human rights and reducing the gap between rich and poor, and doing so with a minimum of structural change. Right from the start Carter's attempt to inject morality into foreign policy came up against strategic considerations and the continuity and inertia of the US foreign-policy bureaucracy. Career desk officers in the State Department were often able to soften reports of human-rights abuses about countries for which they were responsible, while it was immediately apparent that countries such as China, with poor human-rights records, had to be treated carefully, given their strategic importance. However, Latin America--especially Central America, where four of the five republics were run by the military--was subject to a frontal assault by Carter's human-rights crusade. The region had far less strategic significance than Iran or China, both of which bordered on the Soviet Union. And Latin American desk officers had less power than other regional desks in the State Department. The military regimes of Central and South America became showcases in Carter's new human-rights policy. In 1977, Guatemala and El Salvador, along with Argentina, Uruguay and Brazil, all came under scrutiny, but before the US could show its disapproval by cutting off military aid, all five regimes rejected further US military aid, and began buying weapons from Israel and Western Europe. Carter's isolation of the military regimes in Central and South America challenged their legitimacy and helped drive the military to aim their repression and terror at ever more moderate political groups, while the increased political polarization and the spread of revolution led to ever more repression. This cycle was dramatically apparent in Guatemala, El Salvador and Nicaragua during the Carter years. Like Kennedy and the Alliance for Progress, Carter had attempted to change the established order in Central America while avoiding revolution. And when Carter, like Kennedy before him, realized that evolutionary change would not flow from his policy, he shifted the policy.[197]

Despite the liberal and trilateralist orientation of most of the top foreign-policy makers in the Carter administration, important divisions had emerged at the outset. And in a wider sense, these divisions within the Carter administration flowed from the divisions in Congress, and among the country's political and foreign-policy elite and area-studies specialists, which had haunted the foreign policy process since Washington's failure in Vietnam in the 1960s.[198] And these divisions inside and outside the Carter administration worsened as Central America emerged as a major focus of US foreign policy in the Third World. Apart from the revolution in Nicaragua in July 1979, North American eyes had already been drawn southward by the lengthy domestic political struggle which surrounded the Panama Canal treaties between 1976 and 1978, and the ouster of El Salvador's military dictatorship in October 1979 (the sense of crisis more generally was stimulated by the revolution in Iran in January 1979, the Iranian seizure of US hostages in November 1979, and by the Soviet invasion of Afghanistan in December 1979). The debate in Washington over Central American policy--as a focus for the wider debate over the US role in Latin America, the Middle East, Asia and Africa--began right after the FSLN entered Managua and lasted for almost ten years. Within a decade, more books and articles by North American-based Latin American studies specialists appeared on Central America than had been produced in the entire 1898-1979 period. At the end of the 1970s the relatively small group of Latin American specialists, who were already focused on the region, were joined by a veritable army of academics, as a growing revolutionary upsurge challenged US hegemony in Central America and brought the isthmus to the center of the Latin American studies profession as a whole.

Because Central America had remained at the margins during the expansion of Latin American studies, most North American research on Central America prior to 1979, like Washington's relations with Central America, remained subordinate to wider concerns in Latin American studies as a whole, and to wider events in Latin America. Nevertheless, by the early 1970s a growing number of historians and political scientists, located in the dominant professional discourses, had produced important national (or regional) historical and political studies on Central America, reflecting the changes that had transformed Latin American studies as a whole before 1979. In order to help locate the dramatic growth of literature on Central America after 1979, which will be discussed in detail in the next two chapters, the more gradual expansion of the North American study of Central America between 1968 and 1979 will be reviewed here. Apart from Murdo MacLeod's study of the colonial era and a revised edition of Thomas Karnes's study of the national period, there were historical studies of particular countries, a growing interest in particular historical events, as well as research on the evolution of political movements and parties in the region, such as Thomas Walker's study of the Christian Democrats in Nicaragua.[199] In the mid-1970s Ralph Lee Woodward, Professor of Latin American History at Tulane University, produced a general history which synthesized the growing monographic research on the region and soon became a standard work.[200] Woodward's **Central America: A Nation Divided** reflected a multi-causal approach and an inter-disciplinary methodology which had discarded some of the assumptions associated with modernization theory. At the same time he still interpreted Central American history from a position that sought to understand the region in terms of why it had failed to modernize, holding up the rise and consolidation of the liberal industrial nation-states of North America and Western Europe as the model against which Central American history was made intelligible.

Significantly, North American research on US relations with the circum-Caribbean grew more rapidly in the 1970s than research on other topics. As we have seen, apart from refocusing attention on Latin American history and politics and inter-American relations as a whole, the Cuban revolution and the subsequent reorientation of US policy in a more interventionist direction had also stimulated research on earlier US interventions in Central America and the circum-Caribbean. By the early 1970s, these studies were more sophisticated than the earlier diplomatic history, which had focused on government-to-government relations and adopted a descriptive and liberal-empirical approach. Methodological improvements were facilitated by the passage of time, the inter-disciplinary character of post-1945 Latin American studies, and greater access to research and archival material.[201] The analytical framework had broadened as some diplomatic historians began incorporating ideas derived from dependency theory and New Left diplomatic history. Of course, most of the general studies of US relations with Central America (and the Caribbean), including those produced by New Left historians or influenced by dependency theory, remained centered on Washington's motives and actions. But even work by foreign-policy consultants and former diplomats reflected the decline of Cold War liberalism.[202] Some of the most important works of diplomatic history which reflected these changes in US relations with the circum-Caribbean were written by Lester Langley.[203]

Apart from Langley's work, much of the diplomatic history which began to appear in the 1970s focused on specific topics, countries or themes. US-Cuban relations continued to attract a great deal of attention, and by the end of the 1970s there was probably no facet of US hegemony in the Caribbean and Central America more thoroughly researched. There was an early general study by Lester Langley, while the work of Louis A. Pérez and Jules Benjamin clearly reflected the incorporation of dependency analysis into the dominant liberal discourses in the 1970s.[204] As with the rest of the circum-Caribbean, those Central American countries whose history had been most closely linked with the US came under greater scrutiny from diplomatic historians in the 1970s. For example, Richard Millet's book on the US role in the creation of the Nicaraguan National Guard was published in 1977.[205] It appeared at the very time the death throes of the Somoza dynasty were beginning to attract attention in the Washington. Millet, who wrote on Central America throughout the 1980s in support of a liberal understanding of the crisis and a liberal policy agenda, is now Professor of History at Southern Illinois University.[206] In the early 1960s, he studied with Edwin Lieuwen at the University of New Mexico, and while he was researching his book he received support and advice from Dana Gardner Munro. Millet's interpretation of US motives for intervention was characterized by considerable continuity with earlier North American interpretations. He emphasized that US motives were determined primarily by the perception of developments in Nicaragua itself, in the context of US interest in the republic as a possible canal route, along with ideas about international financial responsibility. Although he pointed to a concern about the security of US economic interests, there is little specific discussion of the role or significance of North American business in the country and in the making of US Nicaraguan policy.[207]

Of far greater significance was the way Millet's assessment of the US impact on Nicaragua diverged from earlier accounts. Millet argued that the overall result of US interference in the country from 1909 until 1933 had been negative. He argued that, despite its excesses, the Zelaya administration in Nicaragua in the first decade of the twentieth century "brought about a more radical change toward the modernization of Nicaragua" than any other government of Nicaragua, and the increased US pressure which led to Zelaya's resignation and ushered in over two decades of almost continuous US occupation, had "tended to retard the progress initiated by Zelaya". Millet argued further that "the major share" of the "responsibility" for Anastasio Somoza's eventual "seizure of power" lay with Washington. He emphasized that "in its drive to ensure political and financial stability" the US had "insisted upon the creation of the Guardia", which eventually served as Somoza's power base. In his view the US did not understand that the "traditional army in Nicaragua had developed in response to local conditions", and that "any attempt to create an honest nonpolitical military force without changing the nation's basic social and economic situation was probably impossible". Millet concluded that the "attempt to impose an American solution on a Nicaraguan problem had destroyed, not promoted, democratic government". In Millet's view this was "the real heritage" of the US occupation. He emphasized that by the mid-1970s Nicaragua was "a nation occupied by its own army", and the US had "helped create one of the most totally corrupt military establishments in the world". He was not optimistic about change and predicted that even with the end of the Somoza dynasty the National Guard "would play a critical role in determining the new order of power".[208]

In the 1970s, apart from Nicaragua, the Central American country which attracted the most North American attention was Guatemala.[209] An important work of liberal diplomatic history was Richard Immerman's study of US-Guatemalan relations. It represents a particularly good example of how New Left historiography and dependency theory were incorporated into the liberal discourses during the 1970s.[210] Immerman asserted that he began his research in 1973 to "expose the perfidy of the CIA". However, when his book (based on his 1978 PhD dissertation) was published, he had meshed a detailed evaluation of US foreign policy under Truman and Eisenhower to a socio-economic and political history of Guatemala. Immerman argued that the overthrow of Arbenz was not just a covert operation to protect the United Fruit Company's investments. He represented the US intervention in Guatemala in 1954 as a "critical event in the Cold War". The central theme on which his study turned was that the main "basis" for US-Guatemalan "conflict" was the inability of the US government and the North American public to "understand" the Guatemalans in an era of "Cold War tension".[211] Immerman argued that, although Latin America's strategic significance to the US after 1945 was commonly underlined, its "economic value" was not. He emphasized that, during the early Cold War years, Latin America was as important a market for US commercial exports as Europe, while US private investment in the region was greater than anywhere else apart from Canada. Despite Latin America's apparent economic importance, "the conventional view" was that Truman and later Eisenhower ignored their southern "neighbors". Immerman argued that Truman and

Eisenhower were actually both interested in the region. If they appeared to "lose interest", it was because they both adopted a Cold War policy, which emphasized "global" rather than "regional" strategy. Because US policy "reflected the overarching objective of containing communism", and because most southern republics did not represent a "threat" to US predominance, Latin America was given "less attention" and "fewer resources" than Europe and East Asia. Central to Immerman's approach, as in Blasier's work, was the view that, although the growing perception in North America in the early 1950s of a 'communist threat' to Central America was "greatly exaggerated", the "exaggerations and misperceptions did not result from lunatic paranoia". In order to "understand" why so many North Americans "misinterpreted the Guatemalan situation" he emphasized that throughout the 1950s "practically" everyone in North America "firmly believed that a Soviet-master minded international conspiracy threatened the Free World and that the Communist agents were almost impossible to identify". As Immerman pointed out, the "logic" of the "Cold War ethos" was widely accepted, and academics such as Robert Alexander, "who worked informally with the government in its campaign against Guatemala", argued that Guatemala represented "an interesting case study of how a Communist party, starting with nothing, can in a short period of time rise to a position of great influence in the public life and government of a nation".[212]

The CIA intervention, which was the focus of Immerman's book, was represented as "crucial" to the overthrow of the Guatemalan government in 1954. He argued that without US involvement Arbenz "undoubtedly would have survived". In his view the consequences of the US overthrow of Arbenz continued to hang over US policy. Writing at the beginning of the Reagan era his work reflected the liberal theme of 'our own worst enemy' when he argued that the "current dilemma" confronting the US was of its "own making". The Arbenz government had sought to "break the stranglehold of his country's underdevelopment" and in their effort to prevent what they saw as a communist takeover the "Cold Warriors wedded their fate to that stranglehold" and "they returned to power the very elements of society that had created the conditions that the 1944 revolution tried to eradicate". He noted that Guatemala "today resembles an occupied country", but "if the events in Nicaragua, and perhaps El Salvador, are any indication, strong-arm tactics can no longer control revolutionary change in Central America". While the reformist government of the 1940s and early 1950s had attempted to bring an end to "injustice through moderate reforms" the 1954 "coup" by the CIA "made moderation impossible".[213] **The CIA in Guatemala** demonstrated the way in which ideas from the radical discourses were incorporated into the dominant liberal discourses in the 1970s. Immerman's emphasis on the inevitability of revolution in the face of US unwillingness to tolerate reform, as well as his ambivalence towards revolutionary change, reflected the intersection of New Left radicalism and liberalism. The conclusion articulated here, which can be found in the work of Richard Barnet a decade earlier, was that revolution was only inevitable because of the wrong policies of the US. From this point of view moderate reforms are both possible and sufficient. This perspective found its classic statement in Walter LaFeber's **Inevitable Revolutions: The United States in Central America**, which was written in the first two years of the Reagan administration, and will be discussed in the next chapter.

Another diplomatic historian whose work demonstrated both renewed interest in Central America and the diversity of the dominant liberal discourses in the 1970s was Whitney Perkins of Brown University. Perkins had made an effort, twenty years earlier, to break from exceptionalist interpretations of formal US imperialism and approach the history of US foreign policy in the context of Western European imperial history. At the same time, his approach continued to emphasize politico-strategic considerations and was distinct from the largely unread New Left diplomatic history of the early 1960s, which also sought to locate US imperialism in the wider context of European imperial expansion.[214] Perkins foreshadowed the growing acceptance of the term imperialism by North American liberals, such as Tony Smith by the end of the 1970s.[215] But, while Smith's book drew on New Left diplomatic history and dependency theory, Perkins's approach continued to draw explicitly on liberal historiography of British imperialism. Although he was willing to discuss US imperialism in the same context as British imperialism, Perkins interpreted the dynamics of US imperialism prior to 1945 in a way which paralleled the work of the liberal historians of the British empire, such as D. K. Fieldhouse, who represented European imperial expansion as driven by instability on the periphery.[216] Perkins's analysis also emphasized that there was an independent relationship between political and economic factors in imperial expansion. He drew explicitly on the work of Ronald Robinson and John Gallagher, the main English-speaking European advocates of an approach to modern imperialism which emphasized the primacy of political considerations. Perkins relied in particular on their work on collaborating elites.[217] Perkins argued that in the early years of the twentieth century the "virtual collapse of government in several Caribbean countries coincided with a surge of strength and confidence and a naive sense of mission in the United States". He insisted that Washington's "avowed objective" in Nicaragua (as in Cuba, Haiti and the Dominican Republic) was "to promote practices and institutions of self-government that would remove both impetus and opportunity for continuing intervention". This lofty objective gave credibility to the view that "intervention would be liberating", and as a result of its "liberal political values", the US was "particularly affected by the political incapacity that makes alien rule unstable". He argued that, regardless of its economic and military "preponderance", the US "could not impose compliant political behavior", and that US policy was only able to "succeed" by adapting to the local political situation. He argued that in Nicaragua, and elsewhere, the original cause for intervention "included strategic and economic concerns"; however, "the complexities of involvement set up a dynamic of induced demand and improvised response that tended to supersede broader considerations". The "expansion" of US involvement flowed primarily from "protracted processes of political inter-action that produced the outcomes that they did because of the extreme incapacity of indigenous government to resist imposition". At no stage, according to Perkins, did US intervention "represent planned expansion". Nor did it "signify the evaporation of constraining forces and concerns in the politics and values of the United States".[218]

     Perkins's work provided a theoretical face-lift for Dana Munro's work on the same period.[219] Using an approach borrowed from liberal British historians, Perkins updated diplomatic history, as it had been practiced by Munro and others, without doing any serious damage to the assumptions on which the earlier work had rested. Perkins's work is firmly located in the dominant liberal discourses of the 1970s. Perkins articulated an image of US relations with Latin America which emphasized the limits of power. In particular, he pointed to the local constraints on US objectives and the constraints built into inter-state and inter-cultural relations. He drew attention to the way in which the US was drawn into collaborative relationships which served to aggravate rather than alleviate the local political conflict it had set out to stabilize. He also pointed to the importance of nationalism. Perkins characterized Sandino as "an authentic representative of national sentiment". And in 1981 he voiced the hope that in the wake of the 1979 revolution the "transition to a new relationship" between the US and Managua "would be quicker and smoother than has been the case with Cuba".[220] However, the incoming Reagan administration's historical understanding of the Central American crisis proved to be completely at odds with the work of historians such as Perkins.[221]

Conclusion: The Limits of Power 1968-1979

As we have seen, the Nixon-Kissinger years were characterized by a conservative militarism which was connected to the shift by modernization theorists towards an emphasis on the politics of order. This was followed by the Carter administration's rejection of a Cold War approach in favor of an emphasis on North-South conflict and a managerial approach to revolution in Latin America. Reinvigorated liberal professional discourses on Latin America intersected with the managerial foreign policy of the early Carter years. Although the dominant discourses had achieved a position of greater autonomy in relation to the practice of US foreign policy, they still legitimated Washington's position in the region. And the ongoing complementarity between the dominant discourses and US hegemony, along with the continued centrality of liberal assumptions to the professional discourses, was reflected in the historiography. As we have seen in this chapter, even radical Latin American specialists could find themselves and their work in a position which was more complementary to, than subverting of, US hegemony. The dominant professional discourses on Latin America, which accommodated and contained radical approaches in the 1970s, operated as an important constituent element in the diffuse character of US hegemony in Latin America. This became even more apparent when the relative complementarity between these discourses and the practice of US foreign policy under Carter deteriorated in relation to the crisis in Central America after 1979. As we will see in the next chapter, most liberal Latin

Americanists quickly adopted an explicitly oppositional stance towards the Reagan administration, at the same time as their overall relationship to the practice of US foreign policy in Latin America remained complementary.

Chapter 4

THE NEW COLD WAR 1979-1984

"In Latin America, the rise and fall of democratic regimes also coincided with the rise and fall of American influence. In the second and third decades of this century, American intervention in Nicaragua, Haiti, and the Dominican Republic produced the freest elections and the most open political competition in the history of those countries....Direct intervention by the American government in Central America and the Caribbean came to at least a temporary end in the early 1930s. Without exception, the result was a shift in the direction of more dictatorial regimes. It had taken American power to impose even the most modest aspects of democracy in these societies....Under the Alliance for Progress, American power was to be used to promote and sustain democratic government and greater social equity in the rest of the Western Hemisphere. This high point in the exercise of United States power in Latin America coincided with the high point of democracy in Latin America....All in all, the decline in the role of the United States in Latin America in the late 1960s and early 1970s coincided with the spread of authoritarian regimes in that area. With this decline went a decline in standards of democratic morality and human rights which the United States could attempt to apply to the governments of the region....The promotion of liberty abroad thus requires the expansion of American power; the operation of liberty at home involves the limitation of American power."

Samuel P. Huntington, **The Dilemma of American Ideals and Institutions in Foreign Policy** [Washington: American Enterprise Institute, 1981]. pp. 6-7, 9, 13.

By 1979 clearly identifiable conservative discourses had emerged to challenge the dominant liberal discourses. During the 1970s and early 1980s, conservatives articulated a particular understanding of the US crisis of hegemony. The conservative revival emphasized the superiority of North American civilization. Conservatives looked with excessive approval on the values which they believed were at the core of the US constitution and North American institutions. From their perspective North American, and Western, civilization was in the midst of a crisis of leadership. They were convinced that the continued existence of democracy and liberty in North America and Western Europe required the vigorous projection and expansion of US power around the globe. Conservatives sought to revitalize North American will and resuscitate the domino theory. They pointed to the need for a new anti-communist crusade, while a Moscow-inspired communist threat was unrelentingly emphasized as the cause of the unrest in Central America and around the world. And it was against this background, as Jimmy Carter scrambled to influence the outcome in Nicaragua, that the divisions within his administration and within the US political and foreign policy elite came to a head.[1] Against the wider backdrop of the ouster of the Shah of Iran in January 1979, the Iranian seizure of US hostages in November 1979 and the Soviet invasion of Afghanistan in December 1979, Central America emerged as a crucial focus for the Cold War revivalism which carried Ronald Reagan into the White House at the beginning of 1981.

At the outset, the Reagan administration attempted to set Central America up as a test case of Washington's intention to stop the spread of communism in the Americas, reassert the US position as a major military power, and revitalize its leadership of the global struggle against the Soviet Union (between 1981 and 1988 Ronald Reagan made more speeches on Nicaragua than on any other country except the USSR). North American radicals also saw Central America as a test case for revolution in Latin America, Asia and Africa. For example, Roger Burbach argued that a US defeat in Central America, would give the "revolutionary forces" throughout Latin America "new momentum". From his perspective such a development would be the "most serious" setback for US imperialism since Vietnam.[2] Neither the Central American revolutions nor the US-backed oligarchic reaction triumphed in the first half of the 1980s. However, the revolutions held out against the increased US military and economic aid to the governments of El Salvador and Guatemala (to a lesser degree) and to the contras. In North America, the main battle was the one conducted between the Reagan administration and the US Congress. The Central American debate was at the center of the wider foreign policy debate about the US role in the world, which stretched back to Washington's failure in Vietnam.[3] This battle was joined by an unprecedented number of Latin American specialists. The crisis in Central America emerged as a key focus of concern for the Latin American studies profession and a major theme in the historiography. In the early 1980s, Reagan's conservative revivalism generated a broad alliance between liberals and radicals opposed to the New Cold War in Central America and reinforced the common ground between the radical and the liberal understanding of the crisis. And by the end of Reagan's first term, the conservatives' effort to build a consensus around an aggressive anti-communist foreign policy in Central America and beyond had been unsuccessful.

The Conservative Revival and the Lessons of Vietnam 1979-1981

The conservative revival, which swept Reagan into the White House in 1981, originated in the 1970s as a response to the domestic and international turmoil of the 1960s.[4] The centrality of anti-communism to the conservative revival and to Cold War liberalism points to a degree of continuity between the conservative discourses of the 1980s and the Cold War discourses of the 1950s and early 1960s. But, while the conservative emphasis on order meshed with the preoccupation with stability which characterized the earlier Cold War discourses, the conservatism of the early 1980s rejected the optimistic belief in the US's ability to modernize and democratize the world embodied in classic modernization theory.[5] In the early 1980s conservatives tended to espouse the most pessimistic form of conservative development theory and the politics-of-order approach which saw order and stability, not as results of but as preconditions for the most gradual democratization and economic development. Nevertheless, modernization theory and the conservative revival rested on the diffusionist idea that North American economic expansion was a positive factor in facilitating social change. And both perspectives also held that economic growth was inherently good because it eliminated the possibility of social upheaval and undermined any need for policies aimed at the redistribution of wealth.

Although the conservative revival emphasized the positive impact of the projection of US power and North American values, unlike Cold War liberalism and modernization theory, conservative explanations for underdevelopment were often based more explicitly on biological determinism and racist ideas about natural order.[6] While the initial commitment of 1980s conservatism to the regeneration of 'backward' peoples was minimal, with the growing transition to democracy and the end of the Cold War, some conservatives adopted a more optimistic view on political and economic development. In the late 1970s and early 1980s the conservative revival was also linked to the free-market counter-revolution in development economics, which emphasized supply-side economics and recommended that Third World governments follow the North American and West European lead and privatize public companies, as well as curb the regulation of prices and wages and economic activity generally.[7] Despite the decline in the influence of conservatism on foreign policy by the mid-1980s, liberal free-market economics remained central to the resurgent liberal discourses, having been purged of some of the ideas and the unilateral international economic policies associated with the first Reagan administration. By the end of the 1980s, the centrality of a more 'reasonable' economic liberalism, to both US foreign policy and the liberal area-studies discourses, was readily apparent in the case of Central America and beyond.

The rediscovery of Central America at the beginning of the 1980s came, as we have seen, at a time when Latin American studies (particularly political scientists and international relations specialists) had been moving toward even greater involvement in policy debates for at least a decade. Of course, the very existence of Latin American studies flowed from US hegemony in Latin America, and Latin American specialists had always been implicitly, if not explicitly, involved in the analysis and formulation of US foreign policy. What was different by the 1980s was the unprecedented way in which the Reagan administration's policy in Central America so quickly alienated large numbers of liberal specialists. The often critical position adopted in relation to US foreign policy after 1968 by many Latin American studies specialists, who by the end of the 1970s were identified by conservatives as having been particularly corrupted by the New Left, was transformed into outright opposition, as Reagan's reconquest of Central America began to take its toll.[8] The events of the late 1970s brought the region to North American attention in an unprecedented fashion. And with the further militarization of US policy there was a growing concern at the center of the liberal and radical professional discourses on Latin America that the US was headed toward another Vietnam in Central America.

By the time Saigon fell in 1975, liberal and radical historians had already begun to focus on the origins of US involvement in Vietnam, why the US lost, and how another Vietnam could be avoided.[9] The history of the war in Vietnam had also attracted the attention of conservatives. In the late 1970s they began rewriting the history of Washington's unsuccessful military intervention in Vietnam, in an effort to regain support for direct US military intervention around the world.[10] Prior to his election Reagan characterized the US war in Vietnam as "a noble cause".[11] By the early 1980s, the revisionism of the "we could have won" school was increasingly linked to the Reagan administration's effort to undermine the Vietnam Syndrome and generate domestic support for a possible direct military intervention in Central America.[12] A well-known voice of the conservative renaissance contributing to the Vietnam historiography and to the debate on Central America was Norman Podhoretz (his son-in-law, Elliot Abrams, was also a conservative ideologue, who served as Assistant Secretary of State for Inter-American Affairs in the later years of the Reagan administration). Podhoretz, the long time editor-in-chief of **Commentary**, had espoused radical views in the early 1960s; however, he emerged at the center of the conservative movement by the late 1970s.[13] In early 1981, his book **The Present Danger** received the official endorsement of the newly elected President, while Podhoretz himself gained a position on the United States Information Agency's board of directors. In early 1982, Podhoretz published **Why We Were in Vietnam**, a month after Reagan himself had launched into a potted history of the war at a White House press conference.[14] In **The Present Danger** Podhoretz argued that since 1945 US foreign policy had been characterized by a "loss of clarity". He perceived a trend towards "the Finlandization of America". From his perspective the US failure in Vietnam and the overall retreat of US power stemmed from a "culture of appeasement", a "national mood of self doubt and self disgust", which undermined the US war effort.[15] Podhoretz was convinced that the US had lost the will to "contain", not to mention "roll-back", communism.[16] He also attached considerable blame to the anti-war movement, citing among its faults a failure to realize the importance of the "distinction between authoritarianism and totalitarianism". Podhoretz's analysis of the Vietnam war relied heavily on Guenter Lewy's **America in Vietnam**, and situated Kissinger and Nixon's interpretation of the war as authoritative.[17]

Nixon symbolizes the continuity between the Cold War of the 1950s and the conservatives of the 1980s. He built his early political career on anti-communism and vaulted to public prominence in the late 1940s as a member of the House Un-American Activities Committee (HUAC), in particular because of his role in the Alger Hiss espionage case. During the 1950s Nixon served as Eisenhower's vice-president. His vice-presidential visit to Latin America in 1958, particularly the stoning of his motorcade in Caracas and his hostile reception in Lima, is often regarded as a turning point in US-Latin American relations.[18] As vice-president, Nixon led the hard-line group in the Eisenhower administration, which pushed for a tougher attitude towards the nascent Cuban revolution, in order to deter other revolutionaries in the region.[19] Nixon sought the presidency for the Republicans in 1960, losing to John F. Kennedy. Of course, he was eventually elected president in 1968, on the basis of his commitment to an honorable solution in Vietnam. The last US combat troops were not withdrawn from South Vietnam until days before Nixon was inaugurated for his second term of office in early 1973. By the time the Saigon regime collapsed, in April 1975, the Watergate crisis had already driven Nixon to resign. However, despite Watergate and his involvement in the final years of the war, by the early 1980s Nixon (who died in 1994) had emerged, in the context of the conservative revival, as a respected elder statesman.[20] After his departure from the presidency he wrote a number of books on foreign policy, some of which, like **The Real War** and **No More Vietnams**, became nation-wide bestsellers.[21]

In **No More Vietnams** Nixon insisted that the United States actually won the war, but after 1973 everything the US had accomplished in a dozen years was lost "in a spasm of congressional irresponsibility" (although it was not published until 1985, this book reflected the mood of the early 1980s and made explicit the link between Vietnam and US policy in Central America). Nixon argued that between 1973 and 1975 Congress, by prohibiting the use of US military power in Vietnam and by reducing military aid to the South, initiated "a total retreat from our commitments to the South Vietnamese people". According to Nixon, the US "defeat" in Southeast Asia "was only a temporary setback after a series of victories". With Central America clearly on his mind, he argued that in Vietnam, the US "tried and failed in a just cause", and while the phrase "no more Vietnams" has often been used to mean that "we will not try again", it "should mean that we will not fail again". He argued that in the second half of the 1970s, at a time when "rhetoric about the limits of power and the promise of creative diplomacy" dominated the foreign policy debate, "dominoes fell one by one". Writing in 1985, he insisted that the challenge in Central America, as in Vietnam, was "totalitarian communist aggression". Nixon was adamant that in order to remain "effective" in international affairs, the United States sometimes had to support "authoritarian governments" even if they had poor human rights records, because they at least served to prevent the emergence of "totalitarian regimes that would deny all human rights". He concluded that although Washington's "international losing streak" was cut short by Reagan's election to the White House, "the ghost of Vietnam" continued to hang over the debate on military assistance to El Salvador and the contras, and the US still had to cleanse itself of the "paralyzing sickness" of the "Vietnam syndrome". Nixon invoked both national interest and humanitarianism. He insisted that because of the "enormous strategic" and "economic stakes" the US had to be interested in Latin America and the rest of the world, while "it would be the height of immorality to stand by and allow millions of people to suffer the fate of the people of Vietnam and other Third World countries that have had repressive totalitarian regimes imposed upon them".[22]

The unrelenting commitment to the Cold War, the continuing belief in the ability of military power to solve Washington's problems of empire and the authoritarian-totalitarian distinction were central to conservative revisionism. More specifically, as was apparent in Nixon's work, the conservative historiography on the Vietnam years was concerned with re-writing history so that North Americans would again support direct military intervention around the world. However, conservatives re-fought the war and won, by ignoring Vietnam's history and focusing on the way in which the US carried out the war militarily. They placed the burden of explanation on the anti-war movement and its role in undermining the nation's will and preventing the government from bringing the full brunt of the US military machine to bear long enough and hard enough to win. By turning the anti-war movement into a scapegoat the conservatives, many of whom were major protagonists in the war, shifted attention away from the failed policies of the US government and the national security apparatus. They focused on defects in military strategy and a failure of will in the United States; however, the war was not just a military defeat. The US lost the Vietnam war (1965-1975) because it was unable, from the outset, to establish a favorable economic, political and ideological context in Vietnam which was essential for a military victory. The US was unable to articulate a feasible limited-war doctrine and generate the technical capacity to carry it out. More broadly, the US lost because of the limits which exist on any US effort to project power. In the case of Vietnam, Washington laid down political and military objectives that were well beyond these limits.[23]

At the end of the 1970s, when they began writing directly about US-Central American relations, the conservatives adopted the same analytical perspective, and the same political objectives, as could be found in their analysis of Vietnam. While Central America emerged as a crucial focus for the conservative critique of US foreign policy, the American Enterprise Institute (AEI) appeared as a major institutional force behind the conservative assault. The AEI was founded in 1943 and for many years had been relatively marginal. In the 1970s it attracted greater corporate support and its reputation grew when former president Ford, as well as other members of his administration, spent time as resident fellows. From the mid-1970s the AEI gained influence by establishing a dialogue with, and supporting the research of, influential politicians and academics.[24] Robert A Nisbet became an adjunct scholar at AEI, while historian Gertrude Himmelfarb has served on the AEI council of academic advisers for many years. Evron M. Kirkpatrick, who had recently retired as executive director of the American Political Science Association, emerged in the early 1980s as editor of the **American Enterprise Institute Foreign Policy and Defense Review**. Samuel P. Huntington was also an adjunct scholar at AEI. In the 1970s Irving Kristol became a resident scholar at AEI, bringing greater attention to the Institute. By reaching out to influential academics the AEI, whose well funded publications were made widely available, sought to achieve a position of authority in political and foreign policy debates. The AEI played an important role in the conservative shift in domestic and foreign policy debates in North America. By the end of the 1970s AEI was a major source of policy prescription and advise for the Reagan administration. In 1981, thirty-four of the new administration's staff came from the American Enterprise Institute[25]

One of these new staff members was AEI resident fellow Jeane Kirkpatrick, who had emerged as perhaps the most well-known conservative critic of US policy in Central America.[26] Professor of Political Science at Georgetown University in Washington and a resident scholar at the American Enterprise Institute in the late 1970s, Kirkpatrick has a background in Latin American studies. Her PhD dissertation, which was published in 1971, was on politics in Argentina under Peron.[27] At the beginning of the 1970s, Kirkpatrick, Podhoretz and other nascent conservatives, formed the Coalition for a Democratic Majority, which emerged as a right-wing splinter group opposed to George McGovern's successful nomination as Democratic presidential candidate in 1972. Kirkpatrick and Podhoretz, along with Johnson's former Under-Secretary of State Eugene Rostow and long time Cold Warriors, such as Paul Nitze, also became influential members of the reconstituted Committee on the Present Danger (CPDII). The original Committee on the Present Danger emerged in the late 1940s and was disbanded in 1953, by which time "containment militarism" was the central idea in US foreign policy and national security thinking. From its inception in 1976, CPDII sought to re-establish a "militarized" containment doctrine as the cornerstone of US foreign policy. By the late 1970s, Kirkpatrick, like Podhoretz, was concerned that the "dominant culture" in the US had become "a culture of appeasement". In her view this was dangerous because the Soviet Union has historically "been consistently uninhibited in the use of force" domestically and internationally.[28]

Kirkpatrick's views on foreign policy, as articulated in the conservative journal **Commentary**, soon attracted the attention of the future president, Ronald Reagan. By the late 1970s **Commentary**, under the editorship of Norman Podhoretz, had become the Committee on the Present Danger II's key journal, and a steady assault on the Carter administration specifically, and the dominant liberal discourses more generally, was launched from its pages.[29] Kirkpatrick became a member of Reagan's foreign policy advisory group during his presidential campaign in 1980, and from 1981 until her departure from the administration in April 1985, Kirkpatrick served as US Ambassador to the United Nations. Her departure, at the beginning of Reagan's second term, points to a decline in conservative influence by the mid-1980s. Nevertheless, the policy position she developed at the end of the 1970s clearly underpinned Reagan's foreign policy at the outset of his administration, and Kirkpatrick, more than any other individual, was perceived as the author of Reagan's foreign policy in Central America in the early 1980s.[30]

Her most famous article was "Dictatorships and Double Standards", which graced the pages of **Commentary** in 1979.[31] It was a partisan attack on the Carter administration and its "loss" of Iran and Nicaragua, also addressing wider issues of US foreign policy and world history. It represents the most well-known conservative interpretation of the recent history of US foreign policy generally, and US-Central American relations more specifically, up to 1979.[32] Kirkpatrick argued that in the case of Nicaragua and Iran, in particular, the Carter administration was not only unsuccessful in bringing about its desired outcome but "actively collaborated" in the replacement of "moderate autocrats" who were "friendly" to the US by "less friendly autocrats of extremist persuasion".[33] The article's central argument was that the US was justified in its continued propping up of Somoza (like other dictators) not just because of his loyalty to the United States, or because he was better for US interests, but because he was also better for Nicaraguans. This argument was based on a crude distinction between traditional and modern rulers and between authoritarian and totalitarian regimes. According to Kirkpatrick, Somoza (and the Shah of Iran) were, in crucial ways, "traditional rulers" of "semitraditional societies". What made Somoza traditional, as far as Kirkpatrick was concerned, was that although he sought to modernize Nicaraguan agriculture he did not attempt to "reform" the country on the basis of an "abstract idea of social justice or political virtue", nor did he attempt to change "significantly" the traditional structures of status and power in the country.[34] She argued that, although a "truly bestial ruler" can rise to the top of both an authoritarian and totalitarian political structure, there were important "systemic differences between traditional and revolutionary autocracies" insofar as "traditional autocrats" only "tolerate social inequities, brutality and poverty", while "revolutionary autocracies" actually "create them". She argued that "traditional autocrats" were preferable because, although they supported traditional structures which ensured the affluence of the minority and the poverty of the majority, they did "not disturb the habitual rhythms of work and leisure, habitual places of residence, habitual patterns of family and personal relations".[35]

And, she concluded, the history of the twentieth century suggested there was little hope that "radical totalitarian regimes will transform themselves".[36]

The failure of the Carter administration in Nicaragua and elsewhere was ultimately attributed, by Kirkpatrick, to his administration's "new approach" to foreign policy. She argued that the "new approach" (which was based on the idea that the Cold War had ended and North-South problems demanded top priority) flowed from a philosophy of history, and a theory of social change, which assumed that all societies would modernize, ending in the emergence of a world community of developed, autonomous nations.[37] According to Kirkpatrick the major problem was that the modernization theory, on which the Carter administration based its view of the world, was deterministic and created the impression that developments were "manifestations of deep historical forces" which were beyond anyone's control and that the most any government could do was to act as "a 'midwife' to history", assisting political, social and economic change towards its inevitable destination.[38] This view was also flawed, according to her, by its overly "optimistic" belief in "progress", and because it viewed history and the foreign policy of the United States as possessing "moral ends". She was also distressed because it was cosmopolitan, insofar as it tried to see the world from the point of view of the "modernizing nation" and "the 'end' of history", rather than from the point of view of US intentions and interests.[39]

Conservatives such as Kirkpatrick repeatedly emphasized the need to learn the lessons of history, at the same time as they enlisted history in support of their policies in a fashion that, if nothing else, served to highlight how history is a 'fictional' enterprise.[40] The historical understanding of US foreign policy in Central America which Kirkpatrick generated was aimed explicitly at reinforcing a conservative agenda. Her interpretation of US foreign policy rested on the view that any foreign policy in the post-1945 era that was not avowedly anti-communist did not properly understand the security needs of the United States. Although she was critical of modernization theory and rejected its unilinear view of history, her work still rested on a liberal teleology. Her understanding of development was linked to conservative development theory, which despite its differences with modernization theory, still held that in the long run the rest of the world could "modernize" and "democratize" along North American and Western European lines, although political order and stability were a more important goal than 'democracy'. Her retention of certain aspects of modernization theory was also apparent in her desire to see pre-1979 Nicaragua and the rest of Central America, as well as much of the rest of the world as traditional. As more than one of Kirkpatrick's critics has pointed out, authoritarian regimes in Central America and elsewhere did not work to maintain traditional society. The military dictators of Guatemala, the oligarchy in El Salvador and the Somoza dynasty of Nicaragua had all worked to destroy many of the region's traditional structures. They alienated important traditional sectors of society such as the Catholic Church, and they drove the region's relatively conservative professional elite into alliances with radicals.[41] Ultimately returning to the liberal teleology she had criticized, Kirkpatrick still charted a western path to democracy for Third World dictatorships, although she cautioned that "decades, if not centuries, are normally required for people to acquire the necessary disciplines and habits".[42]

The conservative understanding of Central America, as reflected in Kirkpatrick's writings, was also apparent in Samuel Huntington's work by the end of the 1970s. In the early 1980s, Huntington, still Professor of Government at Harvard, became an adjunct scholar at the American Enterprise Institute (by the end of the 1980s he was on AEI's Council of Academic Advisors), which provided partial support for his research for **American Politics: The Promise of Disharmony** (also published in abbreviated form by AEI). Huntington's institutional position, and his publications in the early 1980s, point to the way in which the liberal and conservative discourses intersected and the way in which conservative organizations, like the American Enterprise Institute, had successfully generated linkages with authoritative academics and more liberal university structures (of course, the conservative drive for ascendancy ultimately involved a certain amount of incorporation into the liberal discourses). Writing on the eve of Reagan's presidency, Huntington emphasized the less repressive character, and greater likelihood of democratization, of rightist authoritarian dictatorships in contrast to communist totalitarian dictatorships. He dismissed the idea that the US was a repressive overseas power, a notion which had emerged in the 1960s, as a "myth". Huntington represented the US as the "most democratic country in the world". He found a "significant correlation" between "the rise and fall of American power in the world and the rise and fall of liberty and democracy in the world". For example, in Huntington's estimation, the major result of direct US intervention in the circum-Caribbean in the 1920s and early 1930s was the "freest elections" and the "most open political competition" in the region's history. He argued that, when direct US intervention came to an end in the 1930s, the "shift in the direction of more dictatorial regimes" was evidence that when US "intervention ended democracy ended". The same connection was made between the Alliance for Progress and a perceived trend to democracy in Latin America in the early 1960s. He concluded that the "decline" of US influence in Latin America by the late 1960s "coincided with the spread of authoritarian regimes". His work assumed that "the future of liberty in the world" was "intimately linked to the future of American power". However, while liberty overseas required an increase in US power, the promotion of "liberty" in North America was represented as flowing from the limitation of US power. Huntington was explicit in his opposition to the view that there was a "contradiction" between US power and self-interest on the one hand, and liberty and morality on the other. From his perspective the contradiction was "between enhancing liberty at home by curbing the power of the American government and enhancing liberty abroad by expanding that power".[43]

The Reconquest of Central America 1981-1984

Reagan arrived in the White House articulating a world view which was supported by the work of conservatives such as Kirkpatrick and Huntington, and was uncluttered by the relative complexity that had afflicted the Carter administration's approach to foreign affairs. As far as Reagan and his advisers were concerned, the US crisis of empire was a result of Soviet expansionism. US military might was the solution.[44] In his election campaign Reagan had decried the "Marxist Sandinista takeover of Nicaragua and the Marxist attempts to destabilize El Salvador, Guatemala and Honduras".[45] While Carter had sought to manage and then eventually to contain revolutions in Nicaragua and elsewhere, Reagan sought to develop a more aggressive approach which looked for "targets of opportunity"--

where US backing of a guerrilla insurgency might lead to the ouster of a "Marxist" regime.[46] This eventually became known as the Reagan Doctrine. Upon entering office in 1981 the Reagan administration immediately launched a project, using indirect and direct pressure, aimed at the destabilization and eventual overthrow of the Nicaraguan government. In the case of El Salvador it rapidly increased military aid, and in the case of Guatemala it reinstated and expanded the military aid which had been cut off by Carter. Central America was the object of more US military aid between 1980 and 1983 than in the entire 1950 to 1980 period. Economic aid, particularly to El Salvador, was rapidly increased, and the administration's Caribbean Basin Initiative (CBI), which was passed by Congress in 1983, proposed to reinvigorate the region via the introduction of free-market principles, private investment and a further 350 million dollars in US aid.[47]

In El Salvador the FMLN's final offensive had collapsed just as Reagan became president, and the new administration immediately set out to gain the military initiative. The administration hoped that a hard line might lead to a rapid victory and help to exorcise the ghost of Vietnam.[48] Washington quickly moved to back the Salvadoran military, but the attempt to gain the upper hand on the guerrillas soon stalled as it became apparent that the Salvadoran army, despite its larger size, its US training and aid, was not up to the task. Internationally the Reagan approach was already under attack, and as early as March 1981 the administration admitted that domestic support for Reagan's policy was weak. The 1981 "White Paper on El Salvador", which was an attempt to reverse this trend, was also less than successful. While the war continued to go badly, the guerrillas' offer of negotiations was rejected, without any effort to determine if there was any common ground. US policy was simply to intensify the war. In 1980 US military aid to El Salvador was 6 million dollars. This figure jumped to 35.5 million dollars in 1981 and 82 million dollars in 1982, while economic aid trebled from 58.5 million in 1980 to 189 million in 1982. El Salvador had emerged as the recipient of more US aid than any other country in Latin America by the middle of Reagan's first term; however, all this aid paled in contrast to the 1.5 billion dollars in flight capital that was transferred to North American and Swiss banks in this period.[49]

As a quick military victory remained out of reach, the Reagan administration began to pin its hopes on the 1982 El Salvadoran election. In March elections were held in much of El Salvador. Despite the US support for the governing Christian Democrats, led by José Napoleon Duarte, the right wing coalition, led by Roberto D'Aubuisson and the ARENA party, gained a majority of seats in the constituent assembly. D'Aubuisson's victory was a defeat for Reagan, who had hoped to establish the credibility of the "moderate" Duarte. Washington proceeded to collide with the D'Aubuisson government, which was not interested in even the pretense of reform. The land reform program, instigated by the US during the Duarte era, came to a complete halt following the election. In early 1983 the rebels were again on the offensive, and by May 1983 the center of power in the military had shifted from moderates, linked to the US, to officers of clearly right wing persuasion.[50] Meanwhile, in early 1983 Jeane Kirkpatrick visited El Salvador bestowing admiration on the D'Aubuisson government and predicting that the guerrillas were not about to win "anything". She returned to Washington to encourage Reagan to further increase military aid to counter the forward movement of the guerrillas, who were predicting military victory within a year. She also set about snuffing out the so-called two track policy of Assistant Secretary of State for Inter-American Affairs Thomas Enders. At his instigation the State Department had begun to look into the possibility of opening up negotiations with the guerrillas while the war continued. Kirkpatrick succeeded in getting Enders fired by May 1983. She returned US policy in El Salvador to its roll-back trajectory, as a steady flow of US military aid and advisors fueled the blood bath in El Salvador. At the same time, the administration sought to appease North American and international opinion by moving forward presidential elections in El Salvador, originally scheduled for March 1984, to late 1983.[51]

Reagan's preoccupation, however, was with Nicaragua, and by 1983 it had become a veritable obsession. The US warned of dire consequences if the Sandinistas did not stop aiding the FMLN in El Salvador. In late 1983 the Reagan administration increased the pressure when it conceded that the contras were not actually trying to cut off arms to El Salvador, as had been originally argued, and asked Congress for aid for the contras to pursue two goals. First to encourage the Sandinistas to begin negotiating with the other countries in the region and second to encourage Managua and its allies to stop supplying weapons, training, advice, "command and control facilities", and safe haven to El Salvadoran insurgents. This change in Washington's justification for supporting the contras heralded both its ever growing commitment to the counter-revolution and its conviction that the only means of preventing the Nicaraguan government from aiding other Central American revolutionaries was to bring it down. Washington simultaneously increased its military assistance to, and operations in, the countries neighboring Nicaragua, setting up a number of air fields in Honduras that could be used to support the contras or for a direct US attack on Nicaragua. The US also held major naval exercises off Nicaragua's Pacific and Caribbean coast, while some Reagan officials even spoke candidly about a US military victory in Central America. Certainly, from the Sandinstas' perspective, their fears of a US invasion appeared all too well founded: the "imperialists were on their doorstep" and the US intervention in Grenada in October 1983 only made US threats all the more credible.[52]

The Sandinistas' distrust of the Reagan administration was reinforced by the governments of Mexico, Panama, Colombia and Venezuela. In 1983, these alleged beneficiaries of Washington's efforts to prevent the spread of communism launched an attempt to curb US policy and bring an end to the military conflict. The Contadora group, as they were known, drew up an outline of objectives which they managed to get all five governments in Central America to agree to in principle in January 1984. The signatories agreed to try and reduce the size of military forces, end outside support to both sides in the various conflicts, and initiate programs of "national reconciliation" which included the development and improvement of electoral infrastructure and the scheduling of elections. Washington paid lip service to the Contadora initiative, but the Reagan administration did not make any effort to change the direction of its policy. It continued to pump military advisors into El Salvador and conduct CIA activities against the Sandinistas, while preparing for the largest US military maneuvers ever carried out in the region, centered on the huge US military presence which had been built up in Honduras.[53]

At the same time, the White House encountered opposition at the Pentagon, which had not forgotten Korea and Vietnam, or the smaller and more recent debacle in Lebanon in late 1983, in which over 250 troops were killed. The US generals were unwilling to become involved in a war in Central America, unless there was widespread governmental and public support. However, the Pentagon was not united. And in contrast to most generals, support for a conservative interventionist policy continued to come from General Paul Gorman, who was in charge of the US Southern Command and the top US Army officer in Central America. Gorman spearheaded the militarization of the region, attempting to establish a Central American military force under his control and turn Honduras into a major US military base. Even more supportive were those government officials who had built their careers on anti-communism. Apart from Jeane Kirkpatrick, there was William Casey, Director of the CIA, much of the National Security Council and important Defense Department policy-makers such as Fred Iklé, the hard-line Under-Secretary of Defense, and Nestor Sánchez, the Deputy Assistant Secretary of Defense for Inter-American Affairs. Sánchez was a seasoned Cold Warrior, whose career began with the CIA and later took him to the Pentagon. He had been involved with the overthrow of Arbenz, serving as deputy chief of station in Guatemala in 1954. Sánchez rose to the position of CIA director of operations for Latin America before becoming the Deputy Assistant Secretary of Defense for Inter-American Affairs under Reagan. He was Iklé's main advisor on Central America.[54] In late 1983 Sánchez contributed an article to **Foreign Policy** in which he emphasized the need for the administration's hard-line in Central America, especially El Salvador. He reiterated the Reagan administration's view that El Salvador was "the prime target of communist expansion today". From his perspective, if they came to power the "communist grip" on El Salvador "would be as total and as permanent as it is wherever they have gotten a foot in the door". He insisted that, although other countries were also threatened, and "as long as Nicaragua persists in subverting its neighbors the threat to Central America will be acute", the "immediate testing ground" for the US was El Salvador.[55]

Despite the increasing opposition which conservatives such as Sánchez sought to overcome, it was the opposition in Congress which was the focus of the Reagan administration's concern and the immediate obstacle to a conservative policy of reconquest in Central America. Following D'Aubuisson's ARENA party's election to the Assembly in El Salvador in 1982, and its efforts to curtail the 1980 land reform program, the US Senate Foreign Relations Committee voted to freeze US aid to El Salvador at the level approved for 1981. The Reagan administration insisted that Congressional aid cuts were facilitating the war's stalemate. At the beginning of 1983 the Reagan administration went on the offensive in Washington. Reagan led an attempt to extract 110 million dollars in additional military assistance from Congress. In March Reagan gave a speech which focused exclusively on El Salvador and in April, in his address to a joint session of Congress, he insisted that "the national security of all the Americas" was "at stake in Central America". He argued that "if we cannot defend ourselves there, we cannot expect to prevail elsewhere. Our credibility would collapse, our alliances would crumble, and the safety of our homeland would be put in jeopardy". Reagan's appeal failed to convince Congress, and important senators who had supported the administration, began to publicly question the efficacy of US military aid to the current government of El Salvador and called for negotiations between the guerrillas and San Salvador. Congress proceeded to cut aid to El Salvador by as much as 50%, and by the end of 1983 the level of military aid was lower than the year before. At the same time

Congress made the disbursement of 30% of the military aid dependent on the arrest, trial, and verdict on those responsible for the 1980 killing of four North American church women.[56]

It was the growing failure of the Reagan administration to generate support in Congress which led to the establishment of the National Bipartisan Commission on Central America. Established in July 1983, the same month in which Congress voted against contra aid, the Commission was instigated by Jeane Kirkpatrick's growing concern, following her visit to El Salvador in early 1983, that the situation in El Salvador was dire and greater military and economic aid was needed. The idea for a Presidential Commission apparently originated with Senator Henry Jackson, who hoped that it would serve to generate some sort of consensus, inside and outside Congress, on US foreign policy in Central America. At another level the Commission, which did not report its findings until January 1984, was a way for the administration to try and buy some breathing room, while improving its image with Congress. The Commission was launched with considerable fanfare at the same time as the White House emphasized its support for the transition to democracy in Latin America and continued to emphasize the idea that Nicaragua was a source of weapons and support for the guerrillas in El Salvador.[57] The Bipartisan Commission was a more elaborate attempt than the State Department's publication in early 1981 of **Communist Interference in El Salvador**, also known as the "White Paper on El Salvador", to build a political and historiographical consensus around an interpretation of the crisis which placed the main burden of explanation on international communism.

In August 1983 Henry Kissinger was appointed to head the Bipartisan Commission on Central America. Like Nixon, for whom he served as Secretary of State, Kissinger has an established reputation as a foreign policy expert which stretched back to the beginning of the Cold War.[58] After World War II Kissinger spent many years working in government. He is well connected in the US establishment and has a respectable academic career as an historian and international relations specialist.[59] He was Professor of Government at Harvard from 1959 to 1969 and is a member of the Council on Foreign Relations and the author of a number of books, including a 1957 best-seller on foreign policy and nuclear weapons.[60] Throughout his career Kissinger never indicated any interest in Latin America or the Third World. His approach to the Vietnam war flowed from an understanding of international relations which assigned internal developments in Vietnam a bare minimum of importance. His attitude toward Latin America was demonstrated in a well-known exchange with the Chilean Foreign Minister, Gabriel Valdes, in Washington in June 1969. Over lunch Kissinger is reported to have said to Valdes that "you come here speaking of Latin America, but this is not important. Nothing important can come from the South. History has never been produced in the South. The axis of history starts in Moscow, goes to Bonn, crosses over to Washington, and then goes to Tokyo. What happens in the South is of no importance".[61] This comment was made at a time when Kissinger and Nixon had switched the focus of US policy in Vietnam from containing communism to credibility. Although Kissinger emphasized the preservation of US prestige rather than the domino theory to legitimate the prolonged US withdrawal from Vietnam, he was willing, at least publicly, to continue to apply a version of the domino theory to Latin America. In 1970 Kissinger told a group of US journalists that "an

Allende take-over in Chile" would result in "massive problems for us, and for democratic forces in Latin America, and indeed to the whole Western Hemisphere".[62] The choice of Kissinger to chair the Commission on Central America was symbolic of the Reagan administration's concern with building a new consensus around an East-West understanding of the crisis. Kissinger represented the continuity between the earlier Cold War policy and the New Cold War policy of the 1980s.

The Kissinger Commission on Central America submitted its **Report** to President Reagan in January 1984. The **Report** made it explicitly clear that its major aim was to gain bi-partisan support in the Senate and Congress, and from the North American public, for the view that the United States' "vital interests" were endangered by Third World revolution, something Kissinger had repeatedly emphasized in the Nixon years.[63] It was greeted with praise by conservative Latin American specialists, such as Howard Wiarda, a lead consultant to the Commission, who characterized it as a "sophisticated analysis of the complex multicausality of the Central American upheaval".[64] At the same time, the centrality of the Central American debate to the professional discourses on Latin America in the 1980s, and the involvement of a large number of Latin American specialists with the Kissinger Commission, enshrined the **Report** as a major contribution to the conservative historiography. However, unlike most conservative publications the **Report** was crafted to appease differing views on the crisis in Central America. As noted by William LeoGrande, who testified before the Commission and emerged as a prominent critic of the Reagan administration, the **Report** was actually two documents in one. There was a liberal reformist document, which recommended improvements in human rights and social, political and economic reform, and there was a conservative document, which emphasized both the importance of US military aid to stop the spread of communism, and the need to encourage private sector development. The more liberal tendencies in the **Report** were in conflict with its interventionist logic and its imposition of a perspective on the crisis in Central America which assigned a central role to the East-West conflict.[65]

The **Report** made a Pan American appeal to common goals, arguing that the primary reason for US interest in the crisis was that Central America was a "near neighbor", and, as a result, "it critically involves our own security interests". Furthermore, in an attempt to mesh realism with altruism, the **Report** claimed that "what happens on our doorstep calls to our conscience". The **Report** invoked "history, contiguity, consanguinity", arguing that "when our neighbors are in trouble, we cannot close our eyes and still be true to ourselves". Such altruism was nevertheless realistic, in the **Report**'s view. The US could "make a difference", particularly because the countries of Central America were "small" and "near". While the US had a "national interest" in supporting "democratic institutions" throughout the hemisphere, it also had a "humanitarian interest" in "alleviating misery" and assisting Central Americans to address their social and economic problems. A central theme of the **Report** was that although the moral and strategic interests of the US were often seen to clash, they coincided in the case of Central America.[66] US objectives in Central America were perceived to be based on "cooperation, not hegemony or domination; partnership, not confrontation; a decent life for all, not exploitation". The Kissinger Commission emphasized that "despite our different origins", the US shared both a "hemisphere" and a "history" with

Central America. The Commission represented the Monroe Doctrine, the Good Neighbor Policy and the Alliance for Progress as "successful" for everyone. The **Report** further argued that while North and Latin America "followed different paths of national development, the nations of the Western Hemisphere have been moved from the beginning of their histories by a common devotion to freedom from foreign domination, sovereign equality, and the right of people to determine the forms and methods of their own governance". The **Report** also insisted that the US and Central America had common economic interests. It emphasized that 62% of US private investment in the Third World was in Latin America and that the region was a major trading partner of the US.[67]

It is no doubt partly because initial attempts by the Reagan government to blame the Central American crisis on the Soviet Union and Cuba were not readily accepted in the United States that the **Report** began with a twenty-five page "historical overview". This section was strongly influenced by the submission of Latin American specialist Howard Wiarda, who was top Latin Americanist at the American Enterprise Institute throughout the 1980s.[68] The **Report** emphasized that Central America's history as part of the Spanish Empire had been a hindrance to the region's economic and political development. Following Wiarda the **Report** made a direct link between the degree to which the various countries felt the impact of Spanish rule and the likelihood of democratic development after independence. It was noted that political independence was not accompanied by any significant economic or social revolution, and the tradition of authoritarian government, a centralized state and a "tolerance of corruption" continued. In the second half of the nineteenth century, "some order was brought out of the chaos" by the rise of Liberal parties in many republics; however, the main characteristic of this change was the landed elite's reconsolidation of its power under the protective wing of autocratic dictators. The period 1890 to 1930 was characterized as the "heyday of oligarchic rule" by both the **Report** and Wiarda. In these years a coffee boom transformed the region and a "commercial import/export class" emerged and allied itself with the landed elite. The **Report** argued that by the late 1920s a "dual agricultural system" made up of large and economically dominant plantations exporting bananas, coffee and sugar, and small plots devoted to subsistence agriculture, was in place and this system "reinforced the social divisions inherited from the colonial period". The "export-oriented growth" caused some "modernization" and a rise in urban living standards; however, the region's middle classes were still fragile. The Depression undermined Central America's export market precipitating an increase in "instability", which seriously challenged the oligarchic order. In Guatemala, Honduras, El Salvador and Nicaragua, new dictators emerged who continued to rule using "strong-arm methods", with the support of the middle classes. According to the Commission, these new autocrats supported a degree of "economic development" and "social modernization" and, for a time, even "enjoyed" a modicum of popular support.[69]

Continuing to rely heavily on Wiarda's analysis, the **Report** identified two major political traditions, and one minor one in Central America. The first tradition was the long-established authoritarianism, which stretched back to the colonial era. The second one was the "democratic tradition" which could be found in the various republics' constitutions, but was of only "marginal importance in practice". (The **Report** identified socialism as the "third strain" which emerged in the 1930s.) According to the Commission the "democratic tradition" did appear occasionally, such as in Guatemala in 1944 and El Salvador in 1972, "but it lacked the practical roots democracy has had in the United States and elsewhere in the West". Costa Rica, since 1948, was regarded as the only country where the "democratic" tradition had emerged. In the other countries of Central America "efforts were made to combine or reconcile the traditional and liberal orientations, and at times even to hint at the socialist one". Although these regimes were certainly not democratic, "the trend seemed to favor the growth of centrist political forces and to be leading toward greater pluralism and more representative political orders". This overall trend was reversed, argued the **Report**, in the 1970s. While the military in Honduras supported "moderate reform" and readied the republic for a "return to democracy", El Salvador, Guatemala and Nicaragua entered into an era of "closed political systems, repression and intransigence". According to the **Report** all three countries "went through a roughly parallel process in which a trend toward more open, pluralistic, and democratic societies gave way to oppression and polarization, precipitating the crisis which has now spread throughout Central America".[70]

The **Report** implied that Central America's long-standing socio-economic inequities were exacerbated by dramatic economic changes, that political movements advocating moderate reform were quashed, and that the initiative increasingly moved to radical exponents of revolution. This is the historical context for virtually every revolution in the twentieth century. However, the history of the emergence of the various Central American revolutionary movements was ignored by the Commission. No mention was made of the growing disillusionment with the reformist parties, which were increasingly frequent victims of death squads and the security forces. Nor did the burgeoning and increasingly militant mass-based urban organizations, or the radicalization of the Catholic Church, get a mention. Following twenty-five pages of historical background, in which the development of indigenous revolutionary and opposition movements is decidedly absent, the **Report** turned to Cuba, and its "efforts to export revolution to Central America". This can be seen as an explicit attempt to blame the Central American revolutions on Cuba, and undermine the legitimacy of the revolutionary movements. The Commission avoided mentioning that throughout the 1970s, when the guerrilla movements in El Salvador, Nicaragua and Guatemala emerged as major political alternatives, Cuba was not involved in Central America, and did not become involved until 1978.[71]

Not only did the **Report** interpret the history of Central America in a way which undermined the credentials of the revolutionary movements, it also glossed over the US role. And even when it directly addressed the history and current status of US relations with Central America, it continued to avoid introducing the US as a factor in the crisis. Apart from anything else, this meant a failure on the part of the Commission to address the profound nationalism which was central to the crisis and crucial in tracing the emergence and success of the revolutionary movements.[72] The Commission argued that US foreign policy by the early years of the twentieth century "focused primarily on promoting the stability and solvency of local governments so as to keep other nations out".[73] The **Report** also recognized that the economic impact of the US was important in forming negative Central American perceptions of the US. But according to the Kissinger Commission the history of "economic imperialism" and US political and military intervention was just "one side" of US-Central American relations. The **Report** argued that there was also a "history of cooperation", and Washington had "made extensive positive efforts to advance Central American development". In particular the Alliance for Progress was interpreted as a "bold and unprecedented effort", on the part of the United States, to promote basic political, social, economic, and land-related reforms. According to the **Report** US aid "was a critical factor in the surge of Central American development which began in the 1960s". The **Report** argued that the "essence" of the Alliance for Progress was that it was a "compact" between the US and the governments of Central and South America, based on the three objectives of "political democratization", "structural change" and "economic growth". However, it was only in the area of "economic growth" that "significant progress" occurred, while "structural change" and political democratization" have been "much more difficult to achieve".[74]

The positive representation of the Alliance for Progress was particularly important insofar as the Commission went on to propose the establishment of a Central American Development Organization (CADO) based on the "historic model" of the Inter-American Committee for the Alliance for Progress.[75] Despite its reference to structural problems, the **Report**'s economic and social aid policy recommendations did not address any of the structural problems which arguably represent an overwhelming obstacle to the mildly reformist project it envisioned. The recommendations were also at odds with the **Report**'s military proposals. As LeoGrande has noted, however, the Commission's emphasis on economic and human development and democracy was primarily symbolic and they were "invoked and manipulated in order to rationalize a preordained set of recommendations".[76] Development and democracy were discussed in a way which presented them as one side in a freedom-totalitarianism dichotomy. They were what emerged when totalitarianism was kept at bay. And in order to keep totalitarianism at bay, a military policy was crucial. In order to justify a military policy, the **Report** provided a history of the region which assigned a determining role to the external forces assisting the Central American insurgencies. The Commission argued that, while they had local roots, the insurgencies in Central America "depend on external support", "develop their own momentum, independent of the conditions on which they feed". Furthermore, regardless of their indigenous origins, "if they win, will create a totalitarian regime in the image of their sponsors' ideology and their own". Kissinger and his colleagues took the view that it was "outside intervention" which gave "the conflict its present character" and "once an insurgency is fully under way, and once the lines of external support are in place, it has a momentum" and "reforms alone cannot stop" a "totalitarian outcome".[77]

The Kissinger **Report** revolved around the idea that internal change was legitimate, while change that was externally inspired was not. As a history of Central America and as a prescription for US policy, the Kissinger Commission's **Report** was always hostage to its intention to spark a new consensus in Congress, and to resurrect a broader consensus around the Reagan administration's anti-communist crusade in Central America and around the world. The **Report** was contradictory, if not schizophrenic. Although it acknowledged local elements in the revolutionary movements it insisted that only the revolution's political, social and economic pre-conditions were indigenous, while the direction of the revolutionary movements were ultimately determined by Cuba and the Soviet Union.[78] Despite its historical and even multi-causal approach, the **Report** was explicit in assigning a determining role to the external 'communist threat'. The **Report** argued that the threat of "a further Marxist-Leninist advance in Central America leading to progressive deterioration and a further projection of Soviet and Cuban power in the region required us to defend against security threats near our borders". In the **Report's** view it was not just continental security which was at stake but US "credibility worldwide". The "triumph of hostile forces in what the Soviets call the 'strategic rear' of the United States would be read as a sign of US impotence".[79] This was a conservative call to the defence of the West and to the remasculinization of the US after its defeat in Vietnam.

The Kissinger **Report**, which became public in January 1984, failed to reconcile the divergent understandings of the crisis in Central America, or the differing policy prescriptions. Despite its attempts to generate a new consensus, Washington's policy impasse appeared destined to continue as Reagan entered the final year of his first term of office. The inconclusive Salvadoran elections in March 1984 also failed to resolve the divergent views in Washington when they led to a run off between Roberto D'Aubuisson (ARENA) and José Napoleon Duarte (Christian Democrats). Congress remained opposed to approving new aid to El Salvador if there was any chance that D'Aubuisson would become president. The Reagan administration threw its weight behind Duarte, even providing some funding via the CIA. When Duarte emerged as president in May 1984, the Reagan administration's El Salvadoran policy entered a new phase. The administration could point to Duarte's election as proof that democracy was developing in El Salvador, while Duarte himself could be represented as a moderate who would push ahead with reforms, the improvement of human rights and the investigation of death squad activity. In mid-May Congress unconditionally approved a major aid program for El Salvador, in part a result of Duarte's personal appeals to individual members of Congress. Following a number of trips to Washington by Duarte in the middle of 1984, support for Duarte's reform program grew, debate about El Salvador "evaporated" and Congress's willingness to approve additional military aid for El Salvador reached new heights. The relative consensus on El Salvador, which was in place by the second half of 1984, grew steadily and was set to survive as long as Duarte and electoral politics continued.[80]

While the Kissinger Commission **Report** may have eventually helped to strengthen the emerging bipartisan agreement on US support for the government of El Salvador, it was unable to generate support for aiding the contras in the wake of the international outcry over the mining of Nicaragua's harbors. Reagan made a major public effort, such as his nation-wide television address on 9 May 1984, to gain Congressional support for contra aid by conjuring up images of "a Communist Central America".[81] But Reagan's powers of persuasion did not have the desired effect. Congress opposed what was increasingly perceived as the real goal of Reagan's policy in Nicaragua: the overthrow of the Sandinistas. And it also opposed the administration's method: proxy war. It had supported the administration initially because Congress believed the contras were being used to intercept arms on the way to El Salvador. But the increasing border skirmishes and the public declarations of the contras themselves had completely contradicted this claim by 1984. Congress was willing to support governments, such as the Duarte government in El Salvador, in a counter-insurgency war but it drew the line at attempting to roll-back revolutions that had already attained state power. In April the Senate and the House condemned the mining of Nicaraguan harbors and in May the House rejected a 21 million dollar supplementary aid package. This led to the complete cut off of aid to the contras in October 1984, at the same time as stories about a CIA-contra assassination manual began to appear in the media. This was followed by further restrictions on the level of subsequent administration requests for contra aid.[82] This only encouraged the administration's Cold Warriors to pursue an ever more subterranean approach to the reconquest of Central America, the full extent of which would not begin to become public until 1987.

Following the Kissinger Commission's **Report**, more Latin American studies specialists joined the debate, and ever more articles, books, and edited collections on US policy in Central America began to appear. American Enterprise Institute fellow and Kissinger Commission consultant Mark Falcoff, along with Robert Royal, produced a large edited collection that, despite its wide range, had a policy orientation in favor of US intervention to contain a communist threat.[83] A group of Rand consultants who had briefed the Kissinger Commission in late 1983 published a revised version of their submission, which was also generally supportive of US intervention, and an East-West understanding of the crisis.[84] Although a 1984 study first prepared for the Office of the Assistant Secretary of Defense by Margaret Daly Hayes, a consultant to the Kissinger Commission, was somewhat more nuanced it also reinforced an overall East-West reading of the crisis. She argued that "the presence in Cuba of a hostile Marxist-Leninist government poses the most serious political problem for the United States in the hemisphere".[85] In 1984, the American Enterprise Institute published **The Crisis in Latin America**, which contained articles by Mark Falcoff and Howard Wiarda, and Wiarda's **In Search of Policy**, which included one of his submissions to the Kissinger Commission.[86] As we have seen, many of Wiarda's interpretations were incorporated directly into the Commission's **Report**. The commonality between Wiarda's approach and the Kissinger Commission is particularly evident in **Rift and Revolution: The Central American Imbroglio** which was edited by Wiarda and also appeared in 1984.[87] What is most significant about **Rift and Revolution** is the way in which it reinforced the general perspective of the Kissinger **Report**. The ultimate effect was very similar to that of the Kissinger **Report** itself. Like the Commission's work, **Rift and Revolution** sought to provide an overview of Central American history. It discussed the colonial past, the hispanic legacy and the failed attempts at Central American union; however, the key variable was that the current crisis was being exploited and aggravated by the Soviet Union and Cuba, and a weak US policy was in danger of losing the region completely.[88] Unlike the Kissinger **Report**, Wiarda's collection addressed the rise of indigenous revolutionary movements; however, the approach taken was preoccupied with assessing the likely success of a direct US military confrontation with the revolutionary movements.[89]

Human Rights' and 'Inevitable Revolutions' 1979-1984

Although Reagan's militant anti-communism continued to be defended inside and outside the administration, Washington's militarization of the Central

American conflict, and the disregard for the Contadora initiative at the end of 1983, ensured that North American opposition to the New Cold War in Central America also increased. Significantly, Congress was uncooperative, particularly the House of Representatives, which was controlled by the Democrats, but even the more moderate Republicans in the Senate were unsupportive. North American church groups, particularly Roman Catholics with regional connections, expressed grave doubts about the president's approach and articulated a growing concern about 'human rights' in Central America. During the first three years of the Reagan administration, the opposition on the part of North American academics, particularly the nation's large number of Latin American specialists, also solidified. The Latin American Studies Association emerged as a focus of opposition, at the same time as a number of liberals and radicals formed various organizational alliances in opposition to the conservative ascendancy. The rise of Reagan and an increasingly interventionist foreign policy in Central America created a relative commonality between radical and liberal Latin American studies specialists by the late 1970s. At the same time, the political alliance and theoretical commonality continued to be on liberal terms.

The character of the radical and liberal alliance and the emerging Latin American studies opposition at the beginning of the 1980s can be highlighted by contrasting the overall stance of the Latin American Studies Association (LASA) with the opposition to the Vietnam War in the late 1960s as it emerged within the Association for Asian Studies (the Association for Asian Studies was the major organization for professional Asian specialists by the 1970s, while the Latin American Studies Association was the major umbrella organization for professionals concerned with Latin America by the 1980s). The difference between the two cases is dramatic. The tepid response of the majority of Asian studies specialists to the war in Vietnam and the failure of the organization as a whole to mobilize in opposition to the war on the one hand, and the critical outpouring of the majority of Latin American studies specialists to Reagan's reconquest of Central America along with a growing number of LASA wide initiatives on the other hand, highlighted the political and theoretical shift which had occurred in the intervening period. In the Vietnam era, the Association for Asian Studies, which boasted a membership of almost 5,000 academics in 1970, adopted a relatively detached majority stance on the war in Southeast Asia. Theodore De Bary's presidential address to the Association for Asian Studies at the end of the 1960s called for a position on the war that was "nonpolitical but not unconcerned".[90] The active academic opposition to the war was left to the much smaller Committee of Concerned Asian Scholars, which broke from the Association for Asian Studies in the late 1960s.[91] Unlike the Association for Asian Studies, which originated in the 1940s, the Latin American Studies Association was founded in the turmoil of the 1960s at the very time when Vietnam and developments in Latin America had drawn attention to the complicity of the North American university system with US politico-military and economic expansion.[92] As already mentioned, according to the Latin American Studies Association's first president, Kalman Silvert, the scandal of Project Camelot in the mid-1960s was a direct stimulus for the establishment of LASA in 1965. Many of its members moved quickly to self-consciously engagé positions. And from the outset, said Silvert, LASA, which is now the biggest Latin American studies organization in the world and is a central organizational framework within which the dominant liberal discourses on Latin America are produced, was concerned with "the ethics of the academic-governmental relationship", as well as other questions of scholarly ethics.[93]

The concern with professional ethics eventually led to LASA's formulation, and adoption in 1980, of "a set of ethical guidelines". The guidelines emphasized that Latin Americanists in North America should seek not only "to understand our world and to make the great struggles and achievements of civilization more comprehensible to others" but also "as beneficiaries of a heritage of democratic ideals" they ought to "advocate the blessings of liberty for all peoples". At the same time, the Committee that drew up the guidelines argued that it was not laying out a "general code of ethics for the members of LASA" and that it "assumed that all members" of the organization already subscribed to "the professional principles of scholarship in general". Although "our responsibility ultimately is to ourselves", Latin Americanists also had "a responsibility to each other and to the integrity of our profession". It was emphasized that "the reputation, credibility, and effectiveness of American social scientists have been damaged by the few who have engaged in covert collaboration with intelligence agencies or who have acted unwisely in relation to autocratic host-country regimes". The guidelines argued that, "given the severity of abuses in the recent past", LASA "should take advantage of the current official interest in human rights to make known to our government and society, and to the governments and peoples of Latin America, the principles on which we stand". The Committee's list of five specific guidelines underlined the need to avoid any connection with "covert operations and covert sponsorship", the need to "guard against distortion of our own work and against the suppression by any public or private entity of information that should be in the public domain". They argued that any participation in international exchanges, or projects funded by the US government, or any other government or organization, must be done so without the scholars' "own freedom of expression and of association" being "impaired". The guidelines pointed to the need to "strengthen independent scholars, centers of research, and educational institutions", while the identity of "collaborators and sources of information" in Latin America, if they are in a situation "where there is any danger of reprisal by host governments", need to "remain anonymous unless they choose to assume the risk of being identified". Finally, the guidelines asserted that "honesty--not neutrality" was "the guiding principle of scholarship", and as a result scholars should "raise" their "voices against abuses of human rights throughout the Americas".[94]

Apart from the 1980 ethics statement by the Latin American Studies Association, many of its members were also sympathetic to the Carter administration's initial rejection of a Cold War approach to Latin America, and its apparent emphasis on human rights.[95] These overall trends ensured that LASA members would quickly find themselves at odds with the Reagan administration. In many ways this trajectory had already been prepared by Carter's drift back to a Cold War policy after 1979. The determination of the Reagan administration to further militarize US policy in Central America, and its attempt to represent the history of the region in a way that assigned a determining role to the East-West conflict, was challenged from the outset by Latin American specialists inside and outside the Latin American Studies Association. A number of edited works quickly appeared, including, for example, a volume based on a conference held at the Woodrow

Wilson International Center for Scholars in Washington in April 1981. This early crisis-reader was edited by Richard E. Feinberg, a Latin American specialist, who had been a member of the Carter administration and is now serving as Latin American expert on the National Security Council in the Clinton administration. Despite the presence of articles by Margaret Daly Hayes and Jiri Valenta, the overall tone was critical.[96] An early collection edited by John Martz and H. Michael Erisman, although it also contained an essay by Valenta which was sympathetic to the Reagan administration's East-West understanding of history, reflected an emerging liberal critique.[97] This was followed by the appearance of another, more critical volume on the Central American crisis, which grew out of a conference held by the Project on United States-Mexico relations. This book was edited by Richard R. Fagen and Olga Pellicer and included contributions by William LeoGrande and Piero Gleijeses.[98]

Thomas W. Walker, an active member of the Latin American Studies Association, and a professor of political science at Ohio University who was former director of Ohio University's Latin American Studies Program, quickly published a sympathetic study of Nicaragua.[99] The influential Central American specialist John A Booth, of the Department of Political Science at the University of North Texas, also produced a book which provided a favorable interpretation of the Nicaraguan revolution.[100] In 1982 Walker served on the national Central American Task Force of the United Presbyterian Church's Council on Church and Society. By the mid-1980s Booth was involved in reporting on elections and human rights in Guatemala for the International Human Rights Law Group.[101] Both Booth and Walker were actively involved in the LASA Task Force on Scholarly Relations with Nicaragua (Walker was the founding co-chair in 1983-1984) and LASA's annual research seminar in Nicaragua. They also served as members of the LASA delegation to observe the Nicaraguan elections in 1984 and 1990.[102]

Another Latin American specialist with close links to LASA who was firmly located in the liberal professional discourses, and who moved quickly to adopt a critical position with regard to Reagan's policy in Central America, was Cuban-born Enrique A Baloyra, Professor of Political Science at the University of North Carolina (he later moved to the Graduate School of International Studies at the University of Miami). Baloyra had worked as a consultant for the State Department during the final years of the Carter administration. His 1982 book on El Salvador was based, in part, on the report that Federico Gil, Lars Schoultz and he submitted to the Department of State in 1981. In **El Salvador in Transition** he attempted to "dispel" what he regarded as a major "fantasy" that many North Americans had about US relations with El Salvador, and about US relations with other client nations in Latin America and around the world. The "fantasy" was the persistent assumption that because of the US position as a "superpower" and the substantial resources at its disposal, it was able to "dictate the outcome of a crisis like that in El Salvador".[103]. Baloyra remained relatively critical of US policy throughout the Reagan years.[104] His application of the concept of reactionary despotism to Central America will be discussed in Chapter 5.[105]

From the outset, radicals were extremely hostile to the New Cold War in Central America. The North American Congress on Latin America was quick to provide critical coverage on Central America.[106] And **Latin American Perspectives** also began to devote more attention to the region. In early 1979 it published key FSLN documents and interviews with Daniel Ortega, Jaime Wheelock Roman and Henry Ruiz.[107] The first of many radical crisis readers appeared in 1981, entitled **El Salvador: Central America in the New Cold War**, which included articles, readings and documents by a number of El Salvadorans and a diverse group of North American academics and journalists.[108] This reader symbolized the radical and liberal alliance of the early 1980s, as did the new journals **Democracy** and **World Policy Journal**, which included important critical articles by Eldon Kenworthy, associate professor of government at Cornell University.[109] Both journals were clearly a response to the reactionary resurgence of the late 1970s. Marxists, such as James Petras and Morris Morley, also turned their attention to Central America.[110] Susanne Jonas and Marlene Dixon, of the Institute for the Study of Labor and Economic Crisis in San Francisco, also joined the radical challenge to Reagan's New Cold War in Central America.[111] There were also a growing number of books on specific Central American countries, especially Nicaragua. North American radicals were often explicitly sympathetic with the Sandinistas and with the revolutionary movements in El Salvador and Guatemala. Their understanding of the history of the region pointed to the conclusion that revolution was inevitable.[112] As these examples suggest, in the first four years of the Reagan presidency the expanding crisis encouraged a growing number of radicals to focus on countering the Cold War understanding of Central American history emanating from the Reagan administration and its supporters. They argued that the political and social unrest, the economic crisis, and the revolutionary upsurge had its roots in the colonial past, the highly stratified socio-economic structure, the isthmus's subordinate position in the international economy and in its more recent unequal relations with the US. They focused on the important role played by foreign investment and US companies, as well as US politico-military hegemony, in supporting the status quo and helping to foment the crisis, and countered the administration's emphasis on national security by arguing that what was under threat was the traditional US domination of the region. Their understanding of the history of the region pointed to the conclusion that revolution was inevitable.

This theme, and the growing alliance between radicals and liberals brought on by the Reagan administration's anti-communist crusade, was readily apparent in one of the first book-length historical critiques of US foreign policy in Central America, written by former New Left diplomatic historian Walter LaFeber. His work, and his overall position by the late 1970s, also reflected the way the alliance emerged on terms that reinforced the far more powerful liberal structures and discourses of the historical and social science professions. LaFeber, a professor of history at Cornell University, is one of North America's most influential diplomatic historians. And as we have already seen, his own career trajectory illuminated the way the profession and the university system work to contain radical challenges. By the late 1970s, he had turned his attention to Latin America, producing an important volume on the Panama Canal in 1978.[113] This was eventually followed by a companion volume on Central America. In his book **Inevitable Revolutions**, as in his study of Panama, LaFeber sought to go "beyond" traditional diplomatic history and attempt an analysis of the overall "impact" of US policy on both "the peoples and institutions of Central America".[114]

Inevitable Revolutions adopted an explicit dependency framework, dramatically highlighting the way an evolving synthesis of the Williams' school and dependency theory had been incorporated into the liberal professional discourses. LaFeber emphasized the way dependency had "stunted" the economic growth of Central America by making the region's economies depend on a small number of export crops or minerals that went as raw material to the industrialized countries. He also emphasized that the dependency relationship distorted regional politics because the crucial export sector of the economy was under the control of either foreign capital or of members of the local elite who were dependent on outside support. He countered the North American assumption that free trade and investment would bring stability and prosperity to Central America, advancing the dependency argument that foreign trade and investment were crucial to "misshaping" Central America's "history until revolution appears to be the only instrument that can break the hammerlock held by the local oligarchy and foreign capitalists". However, LaFeber argued that the "economic aspects" of dependency theory did not represent a "sufficient" explanation of how the US had "gained" such a prominent position in Central America. His interpretation emphasized the importance of US political and military power. He distinguished between the greater use of military and political power in the circum-Caribbean in contrast to South America, where direct US military intervention had been far less common. His work placed "considerable responsibility" with the US for the "revolutions" that were sweeping the region by the late 1970s. He argued that "no region in the world is more tightly integrated into the United States economic and security system than Central America" (LaFeber overlooked Canada). He concluded that the cause of the current crisis in Central America lay "in the history of how the class-ridden remains of the Spanish empire turned into the revolutionary ridden parts of the North American system".[115] LaFeber clearly articulated the view that the crisis in Central America flowed from Washington's historical intransigence, making revolution inevitable. Although he did not venture any direct policy prescriptions in his book, in a 1982 article in The Atlantic Monthly in which the overall interpretation to be found in Inevitable Revolutions was mapped out, he offered some general policy advice to Washington. He took the view that revolutions in Guatemala, El Salvador and Nicaragua "can no longer be prevented", and "if they are contained, the reprieve will be only temporary unless their causes--the gross inequities that have long been accepted as natural in these societies--are removed". LaFeber argued that the US "would be wise to step aside and allow the revolutions to work themselves out, with the single proviso that no Soviet-controlled bases or military personnel be allowed in Central America". He was adamant that "even with its power, the United states cannot roll back the Central American revolutions", but "with luck, and an understanding of the past, it can, however, help bring order out of those revolutions".[116]

LaFeber, along with other Latin American specialists, had been quick to respond to Reagan's reconquest of Central America after 1981; however, by the end of Reagan's first term in office, the initial broadsides and general policy advice was being followed by increasingly organized efforts to oppose Washington's unilateral military policy. By 1983-1984 there was a growing range of academic and popular literature and an increasingly detailed range of alternative policy proposals. Regardless of the radical tone of much of this literature, the dominant assumptions, language and categories which framed the overall challenge to the conservative discourses, as exemplified by LaFeber's work, came from the liberal professional discourses on Latin America. And by 1984, in the wake of the Kissinger **Report**, the growing number of studies which flowed from the liberal professional discourses sought more than ever to restore historical legitimacy to the revolutionary and reformist struggles in Central America, and implicitly or explicitly offered alternative policy recommendations. The policy alternatives put forward emphasized diplomatic, multi-lateral, political and economic approaches to the crisis, while underscoring the need for treating the countries of Central America as historically distinct. They also called for a reassessment of US interests in the region and the changing nature of the US position in the world. This trend was reflected by books such as the volume edited by Steve C. Ropp and James A. Morris, which was published in 1984. The contributors were all closely linked to the Latin American Studies Association. This book quite explicitly sought to ground its critique of US policy on a country-by-country history of the region.[117] Other books by liberal Latin American specialists with close connections to the Latin American Studies Association (which sought to challenge Reagan's foreign policy and engage in debate with academics more sympathetic to the Reagan administration) also began to appear by 1984.[118] The liberal critique of the Reagan administration was characterized by some as the "new realism". This approach was reflected in **From Gunboats to Diplomacy: New US Policies for Latin America**, edited by Richard Newfarmer, who was in the economics department at the University of Notre Dame for many years. By the early 1980s Newfarmer was a senior fellow at the Overseas Development Council in Washington. He has also worked as a consultant to USAID and the Senate Foreign Relations Committee, and by the second half of the 1980s he was working as an economist, specializing in Latin America and the Caribbean, for the World Bank. He served on the executive council of the Latin American Studies Association in 1989.[119]

By the end of Reagan's first term, the opposition to the New Cold War on the part of many of the Latin American Studies Association's members had coalesced into Association-wide initiatives. LASA's Task Force on Scholarly Relations with Nicaragua was set up in 1983, with Thomas W. Walker as a founding co-chair (1983-1984). At the end of 1984, the Latin American Studies Association sent a delegation, led by Wayne Cornelius, to observe the November elections in Nicaragua, producing a report that was sympathetic towards the Sandinistas, and completely at odds with the Reagan administration's efforts to undermine the elections. Washington dismissed the elections as a "Soviet style sham"; however, the LASA delegation came to the conclusion that "the range of options available to the Nicaraguan voter on most issues was broad" and "it would have been broader if the US government had not succeeded in persuading or pressuring key opposition leaders to boycott or withdraw from the elections".[120] LASA's report on the elections, which was widely circulated, resulted in criticism from the Reagan administration and its supporters, and also stimulated debate and criticism from more radical LASA opponents of Reagan's policy.[121] The Reagan administration did not respond kindly to LASA's criticisms. By 1986, there were a number of independent incidents in which US citizens, including members of the Latin American Studies Association, returning from Central America, had address books, research material, personal journals and draft articles seized and photocopied by US Customs. For example, Thomas W. Walker had a number of items in his possession photocopied by Customs officials while he was returning as a member of the November 1984 LASA Nicaraguan elections observation team. In 1985 and 1986, Michael E. Conroy, who was associate professor of economics and associate director of the Institute for Latin American Studies at the University of Texas (Austin) and then chair of the LASA Task Force on Scholarly Relations with Nicaragua, was twice subject to harassment by US Customs. Conroy, who was also a member of the National Executive Board of Policy Alternatives for the Caribbean and Central America (PACCA), had his notes, papers, books and newspapers examined.[122] A law-suit was brought against US Customs on behalf of LASA members and others, and the final verdict found against the Customs Service.[123]

Apart from the Latin American Studies Association, another focus of the growing challenge to Reagan's policy was Policy Alternatives for the Caribbean and Central America (PACCA), a coalition of liberal and radical academics and journalists set up in early 1982. Although it had links to LASA and overlapping membership, it operated outside the framework of the Latin American Studies Association. PACCA described itself as a "national network of scholars dedicated to the formulation of an alternative vision of political, economic, and social policy toward the region". As of 1984, the PACCA executive board included Roger Burbach from the Center for the Study of the Americas, Joseph Collins of the Institute for Food and Development Policy, Carmen Diana Deere of the University of Massachusetts, Xabier Gorostiaga of the Regional Office for Economic and Social Research in Managua, Saul Landau of the Institute for Policy Studies, and prominent Latin American specialists such as Richard R. Fagen of Stanford University and William LeoGrande of American University in Washington, while Nora Hamilton of the University of Southern California, Robert Armstrong of the North American Congress on Latin America, Kenneth E. Sharpe of Swarthmore College, and Michael Conroy of the University of Texas joined an expanded national executive in later years.

PACCA demonstrated the way in which Reagan's policy generated a relatively common reaction from radicals and liberals. For example, the work of PACCA executive board member Roger Burbach, who had worked for the Centro de Estudios Socio-Economicos in Chile from 1971 until the overthrow of Allende in 1973 and was director of the Center for the Study of the Americas in Berkeley, was firmly located in the radical discourses. His writing on inter-American relations reflected an approach which placed the burden of explanation on economic dependency and US politico-military domination at the same time as it emphasized the need for structural change and revolution. Burbach and the Center for the Study of the Americas had links with **Monthly Review**, and the North American Congress on Latin America (NACLA). In 1984, Burbach and Patricia Flynn edited and contributed to a collection of articles which reflected a dependency approach and interpreted revolution as inevitable, although they were not optimistic about the short-term outcome.[124] An emphasis on the need for, if not the inevitability of, revolution was even more apparent in a later book which Burbach co-authored with Orlando Nuñez, the Director of the Center for the Study of Agrarian Reform in Managua. They argued that the failure of marxism "to sink deep roots in the Americas" flowed not from the Western Hemisphere's "inherent 'unreceptiveness'" to marxism, nor was it because there had not been any "serious political organizing" on the part of marxists, but from marxism's failure "to develop a theoretical or strategic approach that responds to the specific conditions in the Americas". From an explicitly marxist position, they sought to build on the success and the lessons of the Nicaraguan revolution and theorize a strategy of liberation for North, Central and South America by revitalizing marxism as a theoretical and political project in the light of the appearance of new social forces and by internationalizing class struggle. While workers and peasants were still seen as the "'motor' of the revolutionary process", they argued that a strategy of social change had to seek a much broader political alliance which encompassed the new "third social force"--the new social movements--and they anticipated the emergence in the 1990s of a "democratic and internationalist" New Left in the Americas.[125]

Although Burbach's interest in forging a new strategy for social change and revolution which encompassed all of the Americas was apparent in some PACCA publications, its formal policy proposals and the overall perspective it generated were much milder and clearly located in the liberal discourses. In 1984, in the wake of the Kissinger **Report**, PACCA published its first major statement, entitled **Changing Course: Blueprint for Peace in Central America and the Caribbean**.[126] **Changing Course** was aimed at further activating opposition in Congress, trade unions, church groups, student groups as well as other community-based groups. In particular, the document sought to challenge the Kissinger Commission's representation of Central America as an East-West problem. PACCA located the origins of the crisis in the region's history of socio-economic stratification and political repression. It also pointed to US policy, particularly in the post-1945 era, when the Central American oligarchies "learned to shout 'communism' at the merest whisper of reform, thereby linking their own survival to US national security". Placing much of the blame for the escalation of the conflict since the 1970s, and particularly since 1981, at Washington's door, PACCA laid out a number of proposals to facilitate the movement "back from the brink of war". These recommendations included ending support for the contras, ending the Nicaraguan economic blockade, withdrawing the growing US military presence from Honduras, and the beginning of bilateral negotiations with Nicaragua. In the case of El Salvador, PACCA encouraged a move towards a political solution, the suspension of military aid, and the linking of economic aid to the government's willingness to negotiate with the guerrillas and the "elimination of state terrorism from the security forces and death squads", as well as the setting up of an interim government. They further recommended that Washington seek to generate the broadest possible range of international support for a negotiated end to the civil war and that the US "take the lead in assembling a consortium of donor nations to provide reconstruction assistance to a new transitional government". They recommended that the US government suspend all economic and military aid to Guatemala until the government in Guatemala City "demonstrates its commitment to basic human rights", supports Mexican efforts to deal with the "refugee problem" and specifically acknowledges the "threat to indigenous populations and culture in Guatemala". The PACCA proposal argued that long-term stability flowed from development, but development could not occur during wartime. They argued that when the war had been stopped, "US policies of aid, trade and investment should follow guidelines designed to encourage development and social justice". PACCA laid out a mix of liberal reformist recommendations on aid, investment and trade which stressed the need to "improve the lives of the poor", and the need to encourage those governments in the region who sought to do so.[127]

PACCA policy proposals did little more than try and encourage US foreign policy back to a liberal trajectory which was closer to the "humane and democratic alternative" to US policy which PACCA espoused. PACCA argued that US foreign policy ought to be grounded in the "principles" which the United States "seeks to further in the world". These principles, which were laid out at the beginning of many of PACCA's subsequent publications, included: respect for self-determination, respect for human rights, non-intervention, collective self-defense, peaceful settlement of disputes, and "support for democratic development and concern for democratic values". It was argued that "adherence to these principles" was "critical to working out practical programs for regional peace and development".[128] PACCA's desire to influence the policy process and generate an alternative to Reagan's military reconquest of Central America was immediately constrained by the language, categories and assumptions of the liberal discourses on foreign policy and Latin America, something the conservatives were also up against.[129] Ultimately the organization remained committed to the possibility of harmonizing US and Central American interests and goals. Like the liberal discourses, PACCA's overall approach rested on the idea that human rights and justice were compatible with, or could be made compatible with, US foreign-policy goals, and that moderate reforms flowing from domestic initiatives could change the course of US foreign policy. **Changing Course** turned the Kissinger **Report** on its head. While the Kissinger **Report** ostensibly argued that a military solution would result in the stability necessary to pursue social and economic development, PACCA rejected a military solution to the Central American crisis, arguing that military withdrawal and a negotiated settlement, followed by social and economic development aimed particularly at the impoverished majority would be the best way to realize the longer-term US goal of stability in the region. At the same time, **Changing Course** rested on the assumption that the North American values of democracy and freedom could be reflected in US foreign policy. It accepted the US hegemonic role in the region, and then sought to make that role benevolent by injecting North American principles into foreign policy, producing a revised liberal internationalism which was cognizant of international power relations but continued to subscribe to a liberal understanding of the role the US could play in Latin America.

By 1984, there were also growing number of studies by liberal journalists and journalistic books by liberal academics. These studies included James Chace's **Endless War: How We Got Involved in Central America--And What Can Be Done**.[130] He was a prominent liberal who had articulated a limits-of-power position in the 1970s, which was not far removed from the work of Richard Barnet.[131] Chace served as managing editor of **Foreign Affairs** for many years and taught at Yale, Georgetown and Columbia Universities (he was Director of Programs for International Affairs and the Media at Columbia). In the 1980s a number of his articles on Central America were published in the **New York Review of Books**. Although highly critical of Reagan's anti-communist policy, Chace was relatively optimistic about the possibility of a liberal managerial foreign policy resolving the crisis and harmonizing the interests of the US and Central America.[132] Some North American journalists, such as Raymond Bonner, offered a more pessimistic prognosis. Bonner spent three years in the US Marine Corps, including a one-year tour of duty in Vietnam. In the late 1970s, he started working as a journalist for the **Washington Post** and **Newsweek** in South America. In late 1980 Bonner was sent to El Salvador by the **New York Times**. His coverage of the war, which contradicted Washington's emphasis on the external roots of the conflict, soon came under criticism from the US Embassy in El Salvador. In mid-1982, at the encouragement of the US government, Bonner was recalled to New York. Bonner's **Weakness and Deceit: US Policy in El Salvador**, first published in 1984, was a thorough and well-documented critique of Reagan's policy in El Salvador. He emphasized that the "roots of the revolution" were to be found in the "bitter poverty and extreme repression, enforced by a tradition of ironclad military rule". He concluded that, although "it might be easier to adopt a policy by ignoring or distorting history", it was "almost certainly doomed to failure".[133] Most books by North American journalists which had appeared by the mid-1980s were critical of US foreign policy but were firmly located in the liberal discourses of professional journalism and supported general policy prescriptions of a mildly reformist character. These books flowed from a commitment to the importance of first-hand experience, common sense and the facts, and complemented the wider liberal opposition to the New Cold War articulated by the dominant professional discourses on Latin America.[134]

Conclusion: The New Cold War 1979-1984

At the end of the 1970s, North American conservatives sought to revive the global anti-communist struggle and launched a policy of reconquest in Central America. The authoritarian military officers and reactionary ruling elites of Central America found willing allies in the political and academic conservatives of the Reagan era. However, the conservative attempt to return to a golden age, in which the US stood as a beacon of liberty against an international communist movement centered on Moscow, had foundered by the end of Reagan's first term. In North America in the early 1980s, conservative policy came up against the continued power of the Vietnam Syndrome. In particular, Reagan's policy of reconquest was challenged by Congress in the context of increasingly broad domestic opposition, which included a wide range of professional Latin American specialists. Washington's New Cold War in Central America brought radical and liberal Latin American specialists together in an alliance. The Central American crisis had a profound impact on the dominant professional discourses on Latin America. Much of the radical and liberal work produced in this period articulated a direct or indirect challenge to the Reagan administration's policy in the region, and to the understanding of history offered by the conservative discourses. The Reagan administration failed to gain the support it wanted for its policy of Cold War revivalism, and by the mid-1980s the liberal professional discourses on Latin America had undergone a resurgence in the face of the still powerful but increasingly compromised conservatism. The relative decline of the New Cold War highlighted the continuing dominance of the liberal professional discourses and pointed to the way the alliance between radicals and liberals had been forged on liberal terms. By the end of 1984 it was apparent that the Reagan administration's rhetoric had not been matched by its actions.[135] However, Washington continued to rely on low-intensity conflict, indirect military aid and economic leverage, in an effort to ensure that the political and economic structure of client regimes in Central America and around the world complemented US hegemony. And Reagan's covert support for the contras ensured that a compromised conservative policy on Central America survived into the second half of the 1980s.

Chapter 5

THE TRIUMPH OF DEMOCRACY 1985-1990

"In recent years, US policies toward Latin America have been interventionist politically, often protectionist in economic terms, increasingly restrictive of immigration, patronizing in style, and unilateral in implementation. These policies have been grounded in insecurity and ultimately aimed at preserving dominance. The time has come to adopt a different stance-one that is built on confidence and trust, on what Latin Americans call **confianza***. The United States should recognize and accept Latin America's many changes instead of ignoring or resisting them. It should regard Latin America's nations neither as automatic allies nor as mere counters in a global contest, but rather as potential partners for confronting shared problems. The United States should take the first steps toward improving inter-American relations by announcing that it will actively seek a secure peace with Nicaragua and will concentrate more attention on helping to restore economic growth and strengthening democracy in the Americas.... Washington can no longer presume, command, or coerce the cooperation of Latin America, but it can help to build Hemispheric collaboration in the mutual interest of all in the Americas. If Washington can abandon the habits of dominance, the United States and Latin America can turn from conflict toward partnership."*

Abraham F. Lowenthal, **Partners in Conflict: The United States and Latin America** [Baltimore: Johns Hopkins University Press, 1987]. pp. 199-200.

Washington's overall approach to foreign policy shifted during Reagan's second term. The articulation of a policy of unequivocal support for dictators, associated with the early 1980s, gave way to a policy of supporting elections and encouraging the emergence of democratic regimes. In the context of the concern to safeguard long-term US interests, the Reagan administration moved to take advantage of the transition to democracy, especially Latin America, while continuing to rely on counterinsurgency and proxy warfare.[1] In the wake of the annual summit meetings between Washington and Moscow after 1985, the trend away from conservative anti-communism was strengthened. This trajectory was complemented by the resurgence of the dominant liberal professional discourses on Latin America as the crisis in Central America continued to shape Latin American studies in important ways in this period. Between 1985 and 1988 a managerial approach, emphasized by the liberal critics of Reagan's foreign policy, was partially re-incorporated into US foreign policy in the context of the uneven appearance of a new consensus. In Central America this shift was reflected in the gradual movement away from low-intensity conflict, and military spending towards "market counterinsurgency", which still relied on military force but increasingly sought to contain Central America by the imposition of a neo-liberal economic model.[2] However, despite the trend towards a more pragmatic approach to foreign policy by the second half of the 1980s, US policy still reflected a preference for military solutions to problems of empire. Reagan's foreign policy continued to rest on the belief that the challenge to US hegemony in the region flowed from the meddling of international communism and that US prestige world-wide was at stake in Central America. Despite the overall trend toward a new consensus on US foreign policy, the emergence of a new consensus on Central America, particularly Nicaragua, was not consolidated until the Nicaraguan elections of February 1990. The elections ended a decade of Sandinista rule and facilitated Central America's return to relative obscurity as far as Washington was concerned.

The Reagan Doctrine: Conservatism Compromised 1985-1988

US policy toward Nicaragua and Central America was the last refuge of the conservatives in the post-1985 era. Reagan's preoccupation with Nicaragua was central to the emergence of what became known as the Reagan Doctrine. Following his landslide election victory at the end of 1984, Reagan redoubled his efforts to topple the government of Nicaragua. Nothing was going to deter the actor-president's desire to support the Nicaraguan "freedom fighters", whom he likened to the founding fathers of the United States. The core of the Reagan Doctrine was best articulated by the President himself in the February 1985 State of the Union speech, in which he argued that the US "must not break faith with those who are risking their lives on every continent from Afghanistan to Nicaragua to defy Soviet-supported aggression and secure rights which have been ours from birth.... Support for freedom fighters is self-defense". Reagan insisted that Washington should continue to back the contras until the Sandinistas "say uncle".[3] Reagan's speeches were complemented by the public utterances of other administration officials, and a wave of letters, pamphlets and radio broadcasts aimed at influencing Congress and the general public. Former IPS fellow Cynthia Arnson, who worked for a Democratic member of Congress throughout the 1980s, has argued that April 1985 was virtually the first time when the amount of conservative pro-contra material reaching members of Congress was greater than the quantity of letters, books and pamphlets opposed to Reagan's policy. This propaganda offensive coincided with a formal request, on Reagan's part, for more funding. Although strong opposition to the contras continued, the majority of the members of Congress did not challenge the accuracy of the Reagan administration's claims about the Sandinistas' military build-up in Nicaragua or their role in the war in El Salvador. While Congress did not immediately move to support the contras at the time of the April 1985 request, the new consensus was starting to emerge, and a crucial vote on $14 million in humanitarian aid was defeated in the House of Representatives by only two votes. Further Congressional support for the contras was gained in May when the administration pointed to Daniel Ortega's recent trip to Moscow as proof of Nicaragua's totalitarian credentials.[4]

In June 1985 the administration continued its propaganda offensive. The administration sought in particular to exploit the fear in the southern states of the US that the country could be swamped with refugees from a communist Central America if a hard line was not taken. There was also a considerable amount of red baiting in Congress. In mid-June Congress voted 248-184 in favor of providing $27 million dollars in humanitarian aid to the contras. Twenty-one of the twenty-six Democrats who moved to support the administration between April and June came from states on the Mexican border or from other southern states. And it would be overstating the success of this vote to say that a solid consensus on Reagan's Nicaragua policy was achieved. Many members supported Reagan because they feared the political costs of opposing him, not because they were at all enthusiastic about the policy. The Congressional consensus was achieved by appealing to anti-communism and to the domestic political dangers of being perceived as "soft on communism". The administration's relative success continued into 1986, when Congress also approved military aid to the contras. But the embryonic new consensus remained fragile, and much of the aid that was approved by Congress was delayed by the Senate until October 1986.[5]

While many members of Congress continued to question Reagan's approach to Nicaragua, more enthusiastic support for his proxy war specifically, and his interpretation of Central American history more generally, could still be found among conservative Latin American studies specialists and foreign-policy analysts. For example, former radicals such as Robert S. Leiken shifted into the conservative camp in the second half of the 1980s. Leiken was a senior associate at the Carnegie Endowment for International Peace in Washington and rose to national prominence following the publication of his article "Sins of the Sandinistas" in **The New Republic**. He published a number of subsequent articles highly critical of the Sandinistas, as well as a long two-part article in the **New York Review of Books** praising Arturo Cruz, Sr., the former Nicaraguan ambassador to Washington, who had joined the Nicaraguan opposition. Leiken, along with another former radical, Bruce Cameron, became Cruz's principal advisers and worked closely with PRODEMCA (Friends of the Democratic Center in Central America), an organization which had been set up to help generate greater popular support for the Reagan administration's policies in Central America. Leiken also edited two crisis readers which contained a range of articles but overall tended towards the legitimation of the Reagan administration's understanding of the crisis and a militarized anti-communist policy in Central America.[6] Other radicals who wrote about Latin America and whose political and theoretical position had shifted dramatically by the second half of the 1980s included David Horowitz, Ronald Radosh, Barry Rubin and Joshua Muravchik.[7] For five years in the late

1960s and early 1970s, Muravchik was the national chairman of the Young People's Socialist League, which had been the youth wing of the Socialist Party. By the late 1970s, however, he was serving as the executive director of the Coalition for a Democratic Majority. And by the 1980s he was a resident scholar at the American Enterprise Institute. Muravchik's work clearly reflected a conservative understanding of history. For example, he asserted that the US was "arguably the freest country on earth, the most socially egalitarian, and the most generous and peaceful great power in history". In his view, "whatever reforms America may need today--and its success is the product of constant experiment and change--the highest imperative is not the radical transformation of America, but the preservation and perfection of its values and the extension of its liberating model to as much of the rest of the world as possible".[8]

Although, Reagan's foreign policy continued to be complemented by an influential range of conservatives, many of them had actually become disillusioned with the Reagan administration by the second half of the 1980s. In early 1982, Norman Podhoretz was already criticizing what he perceived as a lack of "overall strategy". He lamented the administration's apparent unwillingness to "move quickly and decisively" in strengthening Washington's "position in the Caribbean and the Persian Gulf", or to react with forcefulness to developments in Central and South America.[9] Apart from Podhoretz, other prominent conservatives, such as Richard Perle, had become disillusioned by the end of Reagan's first term, while Alexander Haig left the administration in 1982. By the beginning of Reagan's second term, Kirkpatrick's influence on foreign policy had declined, and in April 1985 she also left. In early 1986 she argued that "Ronald Reagan resembles Jimmy Carter more than anyone conceived possible".[10] By 1986, her own approach to US foreign policy had been modified by the rise of Gorbachev and she adopted a position which was based on a narrower definition of US national interests and US capabilities. Following developments in Eastern Europe and the Soviet Union at the end of the 1980s, she openly reversed her earlier view that totalitarian regimes could not democratize, and she voiced support for Gorbachev.[11]

A book by Michael Ledeen in the mid-1980s was one of the most comprehensive efforts to articulate the dissatisfaction conservatives felt in the face of the White House's inability to pursue a foreign policy unfettered by moderates in Congress, as well as the sustained criticism of a hostile phalanx of prominent Latin American specialists and a skeptical public. Ledeen, a trained historian, gravitated into the counter-establishment in the 1970s. In 1976 he became the first executive editor of the new journal **Washington Quarterly**.[12] The journal was published by the Center for Strategic and International Studies (CSIS) at Georgetown University in Washington, which was one of the first of the growing number of conservative think tanks to emerge in the United States. Located only six blocks from the White House, CSIS was set up in 1962 as a "direct offshoot" of the American Enterprise Institute, and until the mid-1980s was linked to Georgetown University. CSIS quickly rose to prominence when Henry Kissinger became a fellow along with other important foreign-policy intellectuals, such as

Zbigniew Brzezinski.[13] Alexander Haig was also at CSIS at the end of the 1970s. And in 1981, when Haig became Reagan's first Secretary of State, Ledeen served as Haig's 'special adviser'. When Haig resigned his post in mid-1982, Ledeen also departed from the State Department.[14] Ledeen subsequently served as a consultant to the Undersecretary of State for Political Affairs and to the Secretary of Defense, as well as being a Senior Fellow at CSIS. Ledeen has important contacts with a number of high-ranking Israelis and was involved in the Iran-Contra affair.[15] By the end of the 1980s he was a resident scholar at the American Enterprise Institute.

In **Grave New World**, published at the beginning of 1985, Ledeen argued that the North American foreign-policy elite had failed to provide the United States with continuity and leadership in foreign affairs. Ledeen represented the world as being in the midst of an East-West crisis characterized on either side by "striking indecision". According to Ledeen, the earlier struggle between opposing "strategic designs" and conflicting "political cultures" had been replaced by a situation in which the Communist Bloc and the West were floundering to articulate coherent foreign policies. He argued that, while Soviet hegemony had been battered by China and Poland, the fall of the Shah had turned Iran into a destabilizing force at the same time as another type of "radical anti-Americanism" was spreading "just south" of the US. In his view the United States appeared "baffled" by the "challenge" it faced in Central America. Although Ledeen interpreted the crisis in the Soviet Union as structural, the crisis in North America was represented as flowing from the policy elite's inability to define "clearly" and "resolutely" pursue the "national interest". The solution, from Ledeen's perspective, was the creation of a policy elite that was "better informed about the world" and "prepared to fight for our vital interests". Ultimately, however, foreign policy, in his view, "must come from the top--above all, from the White House--and if the vision at the top is flawed, policy will suffer accordingly". Ledeen concluded that the "national interest" dictated "that policy-makers be qualified and they have effective power to design and conduct policy". Ledeen saw bipartisanship as essential to "effective" foreign policy as well. He emphasized that the "lack" of bipartisanship made it "more difficult" for the government to articulate and carry out foreign policy. And echoing the conservative interpretation of Vietnam, he argued that this also provided "our adversaries" with a chance to achieve on Capitol Hill what they could not "gain in their own direct efforts in the international arena".[16]

Apart from Congress, Ledeen pointed an accusatory finger at North American universities, which were, in his view, "producing fewer really well-educated generalists from whom our best foreign policy minds are traditionally drawn". He argued that since the 1970s there was a dwindling of support for the "serious study of foreign areas", while the quality of the work produced was "generally low", and the outlook of the various area experts was "abstract and divorced from reality". According to Ledeen, Latin American studies in particular was "unusually low in quality". He traced the cause of this situation to the "conceptual model used to 'explain' the history and sociology" of the region, which he characterized as "a sort of pidgin Marxism copied from nineteenth-century

Europe and transposed willy-nilly onto Latin America". From his perspective, this had "quite understandably distorted the picture, with unfortunate results for scholarship and more serious drawbacks for policy".[17] Similar concerns were raised in 1985 by Irving Louis Horowitz, who lamented "a broad policy dissensus within the field of Latin American studies", which he attributed to the widespread influence of marxism and anti-Americanism on the profession. From his perspective, anti-Americanism was a sort of psychosocial disorder which had infected Latin American studies as a result of its prolonged exposure to its object, Latin America, and more particularly because of its links to a "narrow stratum of the intelligentsia" in Latin America.[18] An almost identical assessment of Latin American studies was made by Mark Falcoff, an AEI fellow, Senate Foreign Relations Committee staff member, and lead consultant to the Kissinger Commission. Writing in the pages of the US Information Agency's **Problems of Communism**, Falcoff attacked Thomas Walker and John Booth's books on Nicaragua. Although their work certainly represented a form of 'engagé liberalism', Falcoff represented them as "examples of the kind of 'committed' scholarship that characterizes so much of Latin American studies in the United States today, in which vulgar Marxism is combined with Latin American nationalism in irregular (and sometimes inconsistent) amounts".[19] The conservative hostility towards a Latin American studies profession which had gone both marxist and native was articulated in an even more visceral way by both Accuracy in Academia and by the President of the US himself. Accuracy in Academia was set up in 1985 to identify those academics who were passing on "incorrect information", which threatened the "nation's heritage or national security".[20] And, in early 1986, Ronald Reagan publicly attacked E. Bradford Burns of UCLA as a propagandist for the government of Nicaragua. At a press luncheon Reagan asserted that the prominent historian was "dispersing disinformation" about US policy in Central America.[21]

A particularly detailed attack on the approach of liberal and radical Latin American specialists was provided in 1985 by Howard Wiarda. In the 1980s, Wiarda was a lead consultant to the Kissinger Commission, and as we have seen he was a significant figure in the debate about US policy in Central America. His work aspired to a balance and reasonableness, which often served to obscure its overall conservative interpretive and policy position. Wiarda's work, like that of the American Enterprise Institute (where he served as director of the Center for Hemispheric Affairs from 1981 to 1987), played an important supporting role in relation to the conservatism of US foreign policy in the 1980s. In 1985 Wiarda criticized the ethnocentrism of earlier US foreign policy in the Third World and of North American social science and development theory.[22] His preoccupation was the failure of North America and Western Europe to understand and appreciate the cultural differences in the rest of the world. But, despite his critique of North American social science generally, his particular target was the liberal and radical discourses on the Third World as they emerged in the 1970s. Wiarda argued that, because of the "strong social-democratic bias" on which much North American and Western European development writing rested, North American specialists have ignored, or neglected, the elitist, authoritarian and Catholic aspects of traditional Latin American society.[23] Ironically, only a dozen years earlier, Irving Louis Horowitz had lamented the continued preoccupation on the part of North American and Western European academics with elites in Latin American history and politics.[24] But despite a long history of elite-centered academic research, which gave way to a focus on the peasantry and the urban poor only in the late 1960s and 1970s, Wiarda insisted that, because North American social scientists "do not like elite-structured societies", they have avoided studying elites, while producing a substantial literature on peasants and the labour movement. He argued further that because social science generally favored "democratic" and "civilian" forms of government, and regarded coups as "aberrations" and "dysfunctional", Western social science overlooked the "normality, regularity, workability, often legal-constitutional basis" of coups, as well as "their functional similarity to elections, and the fact (that) the former may not be more comic opera than the latter". He took the view that the North American "antimilitary bias" acted to prevent "us from seeing these events neutrally and scientifically".[25] In particular, in his view, North Americans and West Europeans had failed to appreciate the "strength and workability" of a number of "traditional institutions". He proposed that social scientists reexamine the "truths" they held to be "self-evident", and take a "new and stronger dose of cultural relativism".[26] However, like the liberal and radical discourses which he criticized, his own conservative position and his policy proposals were ethnocentric. Furthermore, he relied on politico-cultural reductionism and continued to assume that there was no significant conflict between US and Latin American interests.

While Wiarda was attacking Washington's liberal and radical critics, the Reagan administration continued to battle Congress to gain support for its war on Nicaragua. By June 1986 Reagan had worn down Congressional opposition and a $100 million package, including $70 million in military aid to the contras, was approved by the House of Representatives; however, an array of delay tactics were used in the Senate which prevented the military aid from moving south until the end of October 1986. By that time the administration's subterranean option, under the direction of Oliver North, was regularly carrying out the delivery of supplies and military equipment to the contras based in Honduras and Costa Rica. Congressional committees had also begun to ask questions about possible administration involvement in covert aid to the contras, a line of inquiry that was stimulated by the Sandinistas' downing of a contra supply plane and the capture of one of its North American crew members. An important player in the efforts to provide assistance to the contras (initially through lawful means and then by soliciting funds from other countries, using a legal loophole, following Congress's rejection of aid to the contras in mid-1986), was the conservative ideologue Elliot Abrams, who had become Assistant Secretary for Inter-American Affairs in the middle of 1985. Abrams, who ruled out negotiations with the Sandinistas, appeared in front of congressional committees and repeatedly denied any US connection to the contra resupply mission, as did the president himself. However, the downed supply plane soon precipitated a political scandal, when the Justice Department's investigation unearthed a memo from Oliver North which outlined the use of $12 million, from the arms-for-hostages deal with Iran, to purchase arms for the contras. This confirmed suspicions that the administration was bypassing Congress in order to bankroll its policy of toppling the Sandinistas, and led to the Iran-Contra hearings in the middle of 1987.[27]

Following months of testimony, the Iran-Contra committees delivered their final report in mid-November 1987. The initial impact of the Iran-Contra affair, when the story first broke at the end of 1986, had been to stimulate a move in the House of Representatives in early 1987 to put a hold on unspent portions of the $100 million in contra aid which had been approved in 1986. This initiative was unsuccessful; however, the scandal undermined Reagan's prestige in Congress and in the country as a whole. The final report in late 1987 further weakened the president's credibility. The Iran-Contra Report criticized the operation's "secrecy, deception, and disdain for the law". It represented the policy process as "seriously flawed" and tainted by a "pervasive dishonesty". It insisted that even if the President had not been aware of the diversion of money to the contras he had to take "ultimate responsibility" for permitting a "cabal of zealots" to dominate the levers of foreign policy in this area.[28]

In early 1988 Reagan appealed for more aid for the contras in his twentieth major speech on the subject in five years. However, at the beginning of February 1988 Congress defeated an administration request for more contra aid. The actual delivery of US aid had ceased by the end of February, to dire warnings from Elliot Abrams that cutting off the contras would lead to a dramatic reduction in US influence in Central America and to military coups in Guatemala, Honduras and El Salvador by the end of 1988. The contras began to withdraw from Nicaragua, and the Sandinistas launched a major offensive against them. In mid-March the Reagan administration warned that over 2,000 Sandinista soldiers had entered Honduras and were headed for the contras' major strategic and supply posts. On March 16, the same day that Oliver North, Poindexter, Secord and Hakim were indicted on criminal charges, Reagan sent 3,200 soldiers to Honduras for a "training exercise". This move came under attack from many in Washington, even some of the President's supporters. On March 23, before the US could do anything else, representatives of the Sandinistas and the contras met; after both sides made significant concessions, they agreed to a preliminary two-month cease-fire. While Secretary of State George Shultz greeted the truce approvingly, and even alluded to the opening up of direct talks between Managua and Washington, Reagan voiced doubts about a contra-Sandinista settlement, while Abrams displayed his usual intransigence.[29]

Despite the Iran-Contra scandal, Howard Wiarda was already pointing in 1987 to the emergence of a "new consensus" on US policy in Central America. This was qualified by his concern that Washington might fail to implement the prescriptions of the Kissinger Commission and lapse into a policy of "benign neglect", at the same time as the Iran-Contra scandal appeared to have "damaged" the presidency and left foreign policy in "disarray". However, in contrast to what he characterized as his earlier "pessimistic" view on US policy in Central and South America, by 1987 he perceived a "firmer hand" guiding US policy in the region and a "coherent and rational strategy for carrying it out".[30] While Wiarda acknowledged what he called the "paralysis of policy" in the Reagan years, he was adamant that US foreign-policy "accomplishments" in the 1980s were numerous and "profound". He emphasized the enhanced "military preparedness", a "stronger defense", the "restored economy", and "the renewed confidence and faith in ourselves and our system". He argued that US foreign-policy successes included El Salvador, which was a "model of stability and democracy" as compared with six years before. He also celebrated the intervention in Grenada. While the US policy towards Nicaragua remained "unsuccessful" in rolling back the revolution, Wiarda emphasized that the US had prevented the Sandinista "revolution from succeeding or from being freely exported to neighboring countries".[31]

Wiarda insisted that the Reagan administration had already "won" its case on Central America by the end of 1985. And writing in early 1987 he was confident that the US was on the verge of entering into "a mature relationship" with Latin America. Wiarda criticized the intemperance of the early Reagan years, particularly the "exaggerated comments" made by Alexander Haig about "going to the source". However, he argued that the rhetoric of the domestic debate, particularly during the election years of 1980 and 1984, had obscured the growing sophistication of US policy. In the same way that the Carter administration had grown "more realistic and pragmatic and less romantic", he took the view that, in the Reagan years, US policy was "quite measured and restrained--despite the president's sometimes exaggerated hyperbole" for the "home audience". In Wiarda's view, Reagan's "charisma" and "sheer force of personality", had successfully overcome the foreign-policy system's "natural tendency" in the direction of "paralysis" and had focused "unprecedented" attention on the republics to the south. At the same time, the administration's learning process--facilitated by the Kissinger Commission and the publications of "such moderate and influential think tanks" as the American Enterprise Institute--had resulted in a "more realistic grasp of what it can and cannot do in Latin America and of what the area is all about".[32] Although Wiarda defended a corporatist, or political-cultural approach and emphasized the importance of the Iberian heritage as a key to the lack of democratic government in the region, he perceived "a trend from closed to more open forms of corporatism in some countries and from open corporatism to a genuine civic culture in others". In his view "open corporatist regimes have the advantage both of being closer to the historical traditions of Latin America and of representing an opening toward democracy". He claimed that in Central America "an open corporatist regime may be the best that we can realistically hope for in the present circumstances".[33]

At the end of the 1980s, Wiarda sought to deflect criticism of his work, particularly of his analysis of the transition to democracy, by focusing debate on his intentions and arguing that his books were the product of unbiased and "serious" scholarship.[34] But, regardless of how Wiarda understands his own intentions, his work served to legitimate the twists and turns in Reagan's foreign policy in Latin America in the 1980s. He and his writing were important in bringing the American Enterprise Institute closer to the center of the foreign-policy debate in Washington, and in shifting the foreign-policy debate in a conservative direction. The position of Wiarda and AEI in the ascent and descent of a conservative discourse on Latin America and the practice of a conservative foreign policy, can be illuminated by the way Wiarda has represented AEI's position in the foreign-policy process. In 1987 he characterized it as one of the five most influential foreign-policy think tanks in Washington. The other four were the Brookings Institution, the Center for Strategic and International Studies, the Heritage Foundation and Institute for Policy Studies. He also assigned a supporting role to the Carnegie Endowment for International Peace. What is significant, however, is his representation of the Heritage Foundation as conservative, the IPS as radical and the AEI, along with Brookings and CSIS as "middle-of-the-road".[35] Many observers would not so readily distinguish AEI from the Heritage Foundation, and AEI and CSIS can be seen as being at the political center only because domestic politics and foreign policy shifted in a conservative direction in the late 1970s, and AEI was instrumental in facilitating that shift. And with the shift back to a more managerial approach, the more moderate conservative perspective reflected in Wiarda's interpretations and policy prescriptions in the second half of the 1980s ensured that the American Enterprise Institute remained an important force in foreign-policy debates. Wiarda's approach reflected the way the conservative discourses on Latin America were partially incorporated into the liberal professional discourses by the late 1980s. At the end of the Reagan era, his work complemented the pragmatic trend in US foreign policy and the emerging consensus which was consolidated when George Bush became president.

The Transition to Socialism 1985-1990

In the shadow of the shift to a more pragmatic and managerial foreign policy and the resurgence of the dominant liberal professional discourses on Latin America, the work of many radical Latin Americanists continued to be shaped by the problems associated with dependent capitalism and the transition to socialism. Radical work on Central America and Latin America generally was strongly influenced by the Nicaraguan revolution, and the radicals continued to attack Reagan's policy in Central America. At the same time, the political and theoretical alliance and interaction between radicals and liberals continued into the second half of the 1980s in the context of the continued Central American crisis and the relative optimism surrounding the gains of the Nicaraguan revolution. Partly as a result of the relatively heterodox character of the Nicaraguan revolution and the important linkages between liberal and radical scholarship, the radical work on Central America and Latin America reflected the continued diversification of theoretical approaches which built on classic dependency theory and marxism. The radical discourses of the 1980s were shaped by concerns about the relative significance of external and internal factors as reflected in the debate between world-system theory and the modes of production approach. The radical historiography also pointed to continuing disagreements over the relationship between class, race, ethnicity, sexual difference, the environment, and the role of traditional classes, the new social movements and the state in social and political change.[36]

At the same time, the work of some radical Latin Americanists--those who had been at the center of the dependency theory debate and the debates over socio-economic class--reflected only limited theoretical or political changes. For example, Ronald Chilcote and Joel Edelstein's understanding of dependent capitalism and the transition to socialism was characterized by considerable continuity with the marxist and classic dependency theory synthesis of the early 1970s. In 1986, they argued that the people of the Third World needed to regain "control of their resources", and this "requires revolutionary struggle against domestic ruling classes and their foreign supporters". From their perspective, much of the Third World was still ruled by comprador elites, some of which were highly resilient, while some were so fragile that they would collapse rapidly if they were not backed by "imperialist military strength". They emphasized that throughout the Third World "the struggle continues, more advanced in some areas and using different forms and tactics in different contexts". From their perspective, "revolution" would probably be the "dominant force" in world history until the end of the century. The "prospects for socialism" in Central and South America were represented as being shaped by the degree of conflict among sectors of the ruling class and by shifts in the "new international strategy of trilateralism". However, in their view, socialism's success "ultimately" flowed from "revolutionary developments" and the "degree" to which the oppressed of Latin America were "willing" and "able" to gain power, meet "basic needs", reverse injustice and facilitate the "material progress and commitment of all people".[37]

Another Latin American specialist whose research focused on dependent capitalism and the transition to socialism, but reflected the methodological and political changes of the previous two decades to a far greater degree, was Richard R. Fagen. He is Professor of Latin American Studies at Stanford University, and served as president of LASA in 1975. He was at the center of the academic attack on Reagan's foreign policy. Fagen emerged as a major figure in PACCA in the 1980s, and his work and career reflected the important intersection between the radical and liberal professional discourses on Latin America. In 1986, Accuracy in Academia, a group which supported the Reagan administration, added Fagen (along with Cynthia McClintock of George Washington University, John Weeks of American University, John Womack at Harvard, and Howard Zinn at Boston University) to its list of academics providing students with "incorrect information".[38] Fagen worked as a visiting professor in Mexico in the 1960s and was in Chile in the early 1970s. He has produced books and articles on Cuba and other parts of Latin America, and by the 1970s his work was based on serious engagement with dependency theory.[39] When the crisis erupted at the end of the 1970s, the focus of his attention turned to Central America and remained there throughout the 1980s.[40] In 1986 Fagen represented the crisis in the region as an attempt by popular revolutionary movements to break with exploitative politico-economic modes of organization and socio-economic structures. He emphasized that this effort was being met by the US and the region's elite with as much force as was necessary, while they blamed the crisis on international communism.[41]

Fagen's support for the transition to socialism in Central America was apparent in **Transition and Development: Problems of Third World Socialism**, published in 1986 and co-edited by Fagen. It demonstrated the important relationship between radicalism in Latin American studies and the Nicaraguan revolution. This book was co-sponsored by the Center for the Study of the Americas (CENSA), Policy Alternatives for the Caribbean and Central America (PACCA) and the Managua-based Regional Co-ordinator of Socio-Economic Research (CRIES). Unlike PACCA's policy publications, this book was clearly located in the radical professional discourses on Latin America. Fagen and his co-editors, Carmen Diana Deere and Jose Luis Coraggio, represented the post-1945 era as the "third age of revolution". They argued that the "socialist experiments in the periphery" were the "logical outcome of the failures of dependent capitalism" and the earlier "nationalist reactions to imperialism and underdevelopment". They emphasized the complexity of the transition process. An emergent socialism, they noted, would be "deeply marked" by the "historical specificity" of those societies which "attempt to transform the model of accumulation and the associated social formation" from "dependent capitalism" to a "socialist model". The definition of socialist transition they proposed was a process whereby "the logic of capital (the profit motive)" was "subordinated to and eventually replaced by a socially determined rationality of production and distribution". From their perspective a socialist transition sought the "reconstitution of state-society relations" in a way that ensured "that the 'popular classes' have a high degree of participation in determining public policy at all levels". They argued that although such a transformation implied the "social ownership of the commanding heights of the economy and a relatively comprehensive system of planning" these structural changes were not sufficient as a definition of socialism.[42]

The book as a whole emphasized the limits imposed on small peripheral capitalist countries which were seeking to effect a transition to socialism and were made to "suffer for their audacity".[43] A number of aspects of the theme of limits were addressed in Fagen's contribution on "The Politics of Transition". He noted that all national attempts at socialist transition have occurred within the ambit of "inherited structures of underdevelopment", and that "if the history of revolutionary movements in this century teaches any consistent lesson, it is that these old structures do not quickly or easily yield to new ones". Although the political structures of the past could often be overturned more readily than deeply rooted economic and cultural structures, the current political situation continued to be shaped by the past, in part because of the close connection between politics and economics. At the same time, he argued that the "transition" can take place in what are apparently "unfavorable objective circumstances", but for this to happen "the politics of the transition" have to be regarded, "not as superstructural", but as the "necessary foundation and sustaining framework on which a new economic base must be constructed". In an effort to highlight the relationship between economics and politics and the types of tensions and contradictions which flow from the "political" character of the "economic transition", Fagen emphasized two aspects of virtually all small peripheral economies which were trying to make a transition to socialism. The small dependent economy had to continue to rely on the export of basic or "semiprocessed" commodities, at the same time as a central tenet of the new government's economic strategy needed to be the expansion of the population's "basic needs". The need for the revolutionaries to find "political solutions" to "economic impossibilities" was represented as "central to the drama of the struggle for socialism".[44]

The work of Morris Morley and James Petras also reflected an effort to engage with the problems associated with earlier approaches to dependency and imperialism and the transition to socialism.[45] At the end of the 1980s, they explicitly represented the crisis in Central America as a crisis of dependent capitalism: the authoritarian development model, Guatemala being the classic example, and the democratic dependent-welfare model embodied by Costa Rica, had been challenged by a revolutionary development model, as represented by Nicaragua under the Sandinistas. They argued that since 1979 Nicaragua had offered a development model which combined independent economic policy, welfarism, popular participation, with opposition to "subordination" by the "dominant hegemonic power". This model was emerging at a time when the earlier models were responding to the crisis by converging in a "repressive, elitist direction". An examination of the "long-term" patterns in Central America and the Third World pointed, in their view, to the conclusion that, dependent capitalism was "neither inherently democratic or authoritarian". At the same time, however, there was "implicit" in dependent capitalism, in the longer term, a trend toward extended crisis, the erosion of the "basis for growth", the reversal of social gains, and the homogenization of socio-economic alternatives. And when dependent capitalism was "linked to authoritarian structures", the "basis for social revolution" was created. They argued further that "revolutionary societies" could not "crystalize" a development model until they had ensured their "survival" against outside threats, and the successful defense of the revolution was connected to the "deepening of the process of social transformation". They concluded that, in the context of continued war, Central America was the focus for the "emergence of polarized conceptions of development: either the re-distributive participatory model, based on popular politico-military power, or a model which reconcentrates income at the top, extends state control over civil society, and subordinates the nation to the hegemonic power".[46] Overall, Morley and Petras continued to articulate a perspective that centered on state and class and sympathized with revolution, although they had broadened their analytical framework to take account of the unorthodox aspects of the Nicaraguan revolution and the emergence of new social movements.[47]

The growing radical emphasis on a more nuanced analysis of state and class on the periphery meshed with the concept of reactionary despotism as a way of explaining the obstacles to socialism and economic development which existed in Central America. For example, John Weeks expanded on reactionary despotism, which had first been adapted to Central America by Enrique Baloyra, to explain the uneven development and the ongoing crisis in the region.[48] Weeks was an economist and Latin American specialist at American University in Washington who, like Fagen, had been listed by Accuracy in Academia in the mid-1980s as a purveyor of "incorrect information".[49] Weeks, whose work in the 1970s was clearly located in the radical professional discourses on Latin America, after 1979 had turned his attention to Central America, especially Nicaragua.[50] He worked for the Nicaraguan Ministry of Planning in 1981-1982, as well as acting as a consultant for a number of international development agencies. In an important article in the **Latin American Research Review** in 1986, he traced the current crisis to the continued existence of "reactionary despotism" in the region. Reactionary despotism was defined as a particular type of socio-economic structure in which a landed elite continued to play a crucial role. In his view the history of Central America over the past century had been shaped primarily by two forces: "the power of landed property and domination by the US government". Over the years the US was able to intervene as much as it did, and determine the direction of political disputes, because of the relative weakness of Central American despotism. As a result the landed elite became increasingly dependent on the US, usually responding with repression to any demands for reform from below. In Weeks's interpretation the preponderance of the landed oligarchy backed by the US had blocked the development of liberal political reform despite the appearance of allegedly liberal regimes by the end of the nineteenth century. Ultimately the region's land-holding system, inherited from the colonial era "has been repeatedly adapted to changing conditions, but neither transformed nor reformed".[51]

The concept of reactionary despotism, and its emphasis on the specific historical character of Central America's socio-economic and state structures, was located at the intersection of the radical and liberal professional discourses in the 1980s. For example, the radical insights which flowed from the notion of reactionary despotism and the liberal ambivalence towards revolution were both demonstrated by political scientist Charles Brockett in a major synthesis which was first published in 1988. This book was firmly located in the liberal discourses and sought to draw attention to the need to see Central America in terms of the historical evolution of the region's socio-economic structures. He argued that a "sensitivity to this history" was "necessary", although "not sufficient", for the development of "solutions" that would bring about "peace and justice" in the region. His book articulated the view that "no lasting stability" could come to pass in Central America unless there was a "significant change in the social structures that have created and perpetuated incredible levels of poverty and suffering for much of the region's rural population". He concluded that because of the power of these structures and of the regional elites who benefit from them, change would flow only from "substantial popular mobilization" and "committed governments". At the same time, the emergence of popular movements, and/or governments, intent on structural change has "invariably" come up against the "stiff resistance" of the US.[52] Despite the resistance to change manifested by the authoritarian political and economic structures of Central America, some ground was perceived to have been given by the late 1980s, and the emergence of successful reformist political transitions elsewhere in Latin America complemented the liberal preference for gradual change and facilitated a growing interest in the transition to democracy. The failure of revolutionaries to emerge victorious in Central America shifted attention away from the transition to socialism and towards a renewed emphasis on the transition to democracy.

The Transition to Democracy 1985-1990

Unlike the radical discourses, the research agenda of the liberal discourses was always shaped more by a concern with authoritarian politics and the transition to democracy than it was with dependent capitalism and the transition to socialism. This simply became more apparent as the compromised conservatism of US policy embraced the transition to democracy. By the mid-1980s, liberal analysis of the democratic transition reflected both the relative resurgence of liberalism in US foreign policy and the relative diffusion of radical analytical perspectives into reconsolidated liberal professional discourses on Latin America.[53] The growing academic interest in liberalization and democratization served to bolster the shift in US foreign policy towards support for democratization as a means of preserving US hegemony in Central America and beyond. Political scientists did not return to the formulations of classic modernization theory.[54] However, what was reminiscent of an earlier era was the widespread privileging of democracy as liberal representative democracy. Although some academics were pessimistic about the prospects for democracy, particularly in Central America, their theoretical point of departure was still a revised liberal developmentalism. Despite efforts to expand the definition of the term, there were a limited number of liberals who challenged the assumption that democracy, as understood by Washington policy-makers, was a desirable or, in the long term, an attainable goal. During the final years of the Reagan administration, liberals increasingly articulated their support for economic liberalism and the transition to democracy in Latin America, complementing the direction of US foreign policy to a greater degree than a few years earlier.

Another important point of departure for liberal students of the transition to democracy was the concept of bureaucratic-authoritarianism, which originated with the work of Guillermo O'Donnell.[55] In the early 1970s, bureaucratic-authoritarianism had emerged critically out of modernization theory, in the context of O'Donnell's efforts to explain the emergence of the new authoritarianism in Argentina and Brazil. He noted that the rise of the new authoritarianism contradicted the idea, associated with classic modernization theory, that there was a causal link between economic and social modernization and democratization. As a result, O'Donnell suggested that, in late industrializing countries, economic development intersected with the end of democracy and greater, rather than less, inequality. His approach drew on Weber, historical materialism and on corporatist concepts. He also built critically on Huntington's politics of order approach and the early historical critique of modernization theory articulated by Barrington Moore.[56] He pointed to the way in which a bureaucratic-authoritarian state emerged from an historical context in which an agrarian-based oligarchy was sidelined by an early form of capitalist industrialization, based on import-substitution, operating with widespread popular and nationalist support, such as the regimes of Juan Perón in Argentina and Getulio Vargas of Brazil. When the limits of import-substitution industrialization were reached, the alliance, forged between the working class and the bourgeoisie broke down and the national bourgeoisie moved to form an alliance with the military and the technocracy. This type of regime, which replaced the earlier populist-nationalist governments, was characterized as bureaucratic-authoritarianism. A central characteristic of a bureaucratic-authoritarian regime was that it was an attempt by the national bourgeoisie, linked to transnational capital, to protect their interests and guide the economy in a direction commensurate with their needs.[57]

Although by the late 1970s O'Donnell's analysis had gone well beyond a crude state-society dichotomy associated with many liberal and radical approaches, the central contradiction articulated by his work still appeared to be the contradiction between the projection of the authoritarian state as the legitimate representative of the national and popular will on the one hand, while primarily serving the needs of transnational capitalism and the local elite on the other hand. And despite bureaucratic-authoritarianism's use of a marxist analytical perspective, it subscribed to an evolutionary conception of history and a liberal teleology in which change came about through the resurgence of the middle sectors and the retaking of the state. This would eventually lead to the return to democracy and the restoration of the legitimacy of the state, rather than to a violent revolutionary overthrow of the state. This emphasis on the contradiction between the state and civil society made bureaucratic-authoritarianism attractive to the liberal professional discourses on Latin America. And O'Donnell's ideas were taken up by liberal and radical Latin American specialists who expanded and diversified the concept of bureaucratic-authoritarianism. By the end of the 1970s it was used as an open conceptual framework which provided a guide for research rather than as a predictive theory.[58] The bureaucratic-authoritarianism debate and the understanding of political change as a reformist project, in which civil society eventually regained control of the state and authoritarianism was gradually replaced by democracy (a perspective that emphasizes regime change rather than more profound changes to state structures themselves), were central to the liberal professional discourses on Latin America by the second half of the 1980s.[59] And the emphasis on civil society regaining control of the state (and the related preference for regime change rather than state change) also enjoyed a resurgence as an element of US foreign policy.[60]

The important position of bureaucratic-authoritarianism and the preference in the liberal discourses for regime change rather than state change is highlighted by O'Donnell's own career and work. By the end of the 1970s, O'Donnell was involved with a major project on "Transitions from Authoritarian Rule: Prospects for Democracy in Latin America and Southern Europe" at the Woodrow Wilson International Center for Scholars. The Transitions Program, which was set up and carried out during Abraham Lowenthal's tenure as Latin American Program secretary, resulted in the publication in 1986 of **Transitions from Authoritarian Rule: Prospects for Democracy** co-edited and co-authored by O'Donnell.[61] The over-all project reflected a retreat from the greater preoccupation with general theory which characterized earlier debates of which O'Donnell was a part. It also privileged reformist strategies over revolutionary efforts at political change, lending legitimacy to an emphasis on transitions to democracy which are negotiated within existing social and political structures (regime changes) rather than efforts to bring about more profound structural change (state changes). The approach laid out in this work emphasized a whole range of non-systemic factors, including individual leaders rather than wider historical and political structures. They insightfully emphasize the possibility that a given regime sometimes disappears primarily as a result of a range of internal problems which are not directly related to the wider historical and socio-economic context and pay well-placed attention to the role of significant actors. However, the transitions approach still tends to confuse regime and state. And their apparent reaction against overdetermined theoretical approaches to political transitions has led to a reliance on a voluntarist framework which pays insufficient attention to historically specific social formations and their relationship to state and class structures and political transitions.[62]

The trend toward democratization in southern Europe by the second half of the 1970s was their initial point of departure, and according to O'Donnell's co-editor, Philippe Schmitter, by the second half of the 1980s virtually all of southern Europe would probably operate within, an institutional and political context similar to that of western Europe. All the contributions to the volume on southern Europe, with the exception of the section on Turkey, were optimistic that, although "unresolved problems" and a degree of uncertainty remained, the emergent "political democracies" had a "reasonable chance of surviving". However, the prognosis for Latin America was not as optimistic. Some writers doubted that a "transition" had really started in Latin America. Others were unwilling to speculate what type of political system would follow from the demise of authoritarianism, while some contributors were doubtful about the ability of the "fledgling successor democracies" to successfully "consolidate themselves in the near future".[63] A 1986 edited volume on Central America by Giuseppe DiPalma and Laurence Whitehead, who was also a co-editor of **Transitions from Authoritarian Rule**, reflected a similar approach. They argued that the "prospects for democratization" in Central America were "quite bleak".[64]

Pessimism about democratization in Central America, and the transition to democracy generally, was also apparent in the work of Samuel Huntington. Despite his initial support for the Reagan administration, his tone had moderated by the end of Reagan's first term, by which time the White House had embraced the transition to democracy. In 1984, Huntington, who clearly privileged a liberal parliamentary definition of democracy, argued that "the substantial power of anti-democratic governments", especially the USSR, the "resistance to democracy" of a number of the main "cultural traditions", combined with widespread poverty in many regions and the "high levels of polarization and violence in many societies" meant that in most cases the "limits of democratic development in the world may well have been reached".[65] In 1987, Huntington was critical of the Kissinger **Report**, which he felt suffered from all the shortcomings of the Alliance for Progress, including the same uncritical assumption of a causal link between social and economic reform and political democracy. This was an assumption which Huntington felt underpinned US policy in El Salvador under Carter as well as Reagan.[66] In his presidential address to the American Political Science Association in late 1987, after pointing to the centrality of democracy in the rise and development of political science, Huntington argued that the "most fundamental lesson" which could be extracted from "the study of politics" was that there were "no shortcuts to political salvation". Reflecting the voluntarism of the liberal transitions approach associated with O'Donnell and Schmitter, Huntington concluded by emphasizing that "if the world is to be saved and stable democratic institutions created, it will be done through *incremental* political reform undertaken by moderate, realistic men and women in the spirit of one-soul-at-a-time".[67]

Jorge I. Domínguez, who served as president of LASA in 1982-83, also remained pessimistic about the short-term prospects for democracy in Central America and the rest of the region. Cuban-born Domínguez, who is Professor of Government at Harvard University, is a particularly influential expert on Cuba and Latin America.[68] He was critical of Reagan's policy in Central America, but not openly hostile. Domínguez emphasized that the conservatives exaggerated the communist threat and his preoccupation was with redirecting US policy in a direction that would be more successful in maintaining US hegemony in the region.[69] In 1987 he argued that Latin America had experienced considerable economic growth and diversification over the previous two decades, refuting the predictions of dependency theorists that foresaw the "development of underdevelopment"; however, the expectation that economic growth would lead to political democracy had not been realized either. He took the view that there was "a correlation between democracy and very high levels of economic development for market-economy countries", but "the relationship was "indeterminate for middle-income developing countries such as those of Latin America and East Asia". Domínguez located himself with Huntington and argued that what was "predictable" in the case of Latin America was "not the advent of democracy but rather the demise of previously existing political forms".[70]

Unlike Huntington and Domínguez, Enrique Baloyra, a former consultant to the Carter administration, took an optimistic view on the transition to democracy in Latin America as a whole. At the same time he shared their

reservations about Central America. The focus of his 1987 book was on southern
Europe and South America, but he discussed Central America as a negative
example. He criticized the continued assumption in Washington, and among many
Latin American specialists, that "nothing politically relevant" could take place in
the region without "active" US involvement. Baloyra also argued that the US
"obsession" with Central America distracted attention from the "significance" of the
transition to democracy in South America, which he characterized as "the most
significant political trend" in Latin America in over twenty years.[71] He concluded
that the bureaucratic-authoritarian regimes of South America had not been as
resistant to change as had been anticipated in the early 1970s, when the concept
was first introduced by Guillermo O'Donnell. However, the "more 'primitive' forms
of authoritarian domination, such as the classical personalistic dictatorships and
oligarchic regimes of 'reactionary despotism'", in Central America, proved to be
"particularly resistant to change and have lasted much longer than bureaucratic
authoritarianism". He concluded that the "more advanced" and apparently "less
stable forms of authoritarian domination" all eventually "deteriorate and
breakdown". At the same time he emphasized that the "impulse" for change was
internal, and external "variables" were generally not that significant. The two main
variables he pointed to were the role of the US and "international economic
disequilibria". He argued that the US was far more significant, either positively or
negatively, in the case of Central America, Haiti and the Philippines than in South
America. He also emphasized that the transition to democracy had occurred during a
series of profound economic crises, which demonstrated, among other things, that
authoritarian regimes were as likely to generate "economic crises" and were as
"vulnerable to economic deterioration" as democratic governments. This had
resulted in a "lesson", which he represented as a "major political and ideological
defeat" for conservatives who had asserted that "effective" development was
"incompatible" with democracy.[72] As with Baloyra, other liberal Latin American
specialists continued to be more interested in democratization in the southern cone
and southern Europe. And in the case of South America, the predominant view was
that the democratization process remained relatively fragile.[73]

Despite the cautious assessments of the transition to democracy in South
America and the particularly pessimistic prognosis for Central America, the
understanding of Latin America generated by the liberal discourses continued to
depend on the assumption that democracy would inevitably triumph, even in
Central America. For example, in his revised edition of **Central America: A
Nation Divided**, Ralph Lee Woodward, Jr., argued that the "social revolutions"
which had shaped Central American history for the previous fifty years were not
close to completion. However, in his view, the reformist parties, such as the
Christian Democrats and the Social Democrats, were still "quite strong and if peace
can be restored there is room for optimism that those elements can begin to solve
Central America's formidable problems".[74] A similar outlook can be found in an
article by Mitchell Seligson in a 1987 volume on the transition to democracy in
Latin America, which he co-edited with Mark Rosenberg. Both Seligson and

Rosenberg, whose contributions to the edited collection were on Central America, were important LASA members in the 1980s. They served as members of the LASA Commission on Compliance with the Central America Peace Accord in early 1988. Although their work was critical, they clearly supported a gradualist and reformist political transition in Central America. In an introductory essay, Seligson argued that "the present cycle of democracy" in Latin America generally was different from earlier turns to democracy and was "probably more durable". He based this conclusion on the apparently greater unwillingness of civilian governments to regard the "military option" as an easy exit from growing political and economic "problems", primarily because the military had proven unwilling to step down once it had come into power. The military had also demonstrated that it was not any better at managing the economy than civilian politicians. Furthermore, according to Seligson, "civilian governments have taken power in Latin America at a time when almost everywhere in the region the minimum necessary levels of socio-economic development appear to have been attained". Seligson also challenged the widespread notion that Latin America's political culture was authoritarian and that this led to authoritarian regimes, pointing to two recent studies which suggested "contemporary political culture and regime type" were not as "closely linked" as the political-cultural interpretation implied.[75]

In the case of Central America, Seligson characterized the region as being midway through a "transition" from the "authoritarian past" to its "potentially democratic future". However, he emphasized the short-term obstacles, arguing that if the current policies of political and economic liberalization were "reversed", the "unrest and political violence" would continue. Furthermore, if the US again began supporting "military strongmen", the "prospects for democracy" would be "greatly dimmed".[76] Rosenberg took a less optimistic view than Seligson, and argued that if it was Central America's 'moment', this "was not reflected in the structural arrangements that characterize the political organization of most Central American countries". He took the view that, generally, "political organization" in Central America was not at a stage which would facilitate the setting up of "democratic institutions", and this situation would continue until an underlying political consensus in the region was achieved. In his view, the lack of consensus would not change as long as the economic situation continued to deteriorate. Conflicting interests had to establish greater room for negotiation, and the civil war and armed insurrection (Rosenberg argued that "the extremism of the far right led to the brutal response of the extreme left") had to come to an end. He concluded that the US remained a "critical element in Central America's search for democracy", and that the "support" of the US was "a necessary but not a sufficient condition for democracy in the region". In his view the US would face an "almost insurmountable task if it pushes democracy too hard and too fast", especially if Washington took "too rigid a view of what constitutes democracy" at the same time as it overlooked the history of US involvement in Central America.[77]

Rosenberg also contributed to a 1989 volume edited by John Booth and Mitchell Seligson. In his essay a liberal commitment to the transition to democracy was combined with considerable pessimism about the short-term prospects for democratization in Central America. This book addressed the definitional problem surrounding the term democracy more explicitly than most other studies. John Booth attempted to shift the definition away from the "pluralist-elitist conception of democracy" towards an emphasis on "popular participation" and on the degree of public involvement in decision making.[78] Most of the essays in the book had originally been presented at a LASA Conference in 1986. They were aimed at challenging the Reagan administration's celebratory assessment of the El Salvadoran elections in 1984 and 1985, the presidential elections in Guatemala and Honduras in 1985, and Reagan's dismissal of the 1984 election in Nicaragua as a fake. Although the contributors disagreed on important points--and there was, in particular, a difference between the approach of Susanne Jonas and most of the other contributors--overall the volume highlighted the region's fundamental historical, structural, political and economic problems which continued to pose obstacles to democratization regardless of how the term was defined. Although it supported a liberal reformist policy agenda, the book made apparent the limited possibility of elections leading to democracy when power was so unequally shared and jealously guarded with US support.

By the end of the 1980s, Howard Wiarda was one of the Latin American specialists most optimistic about the transition to democracy, even in Central America. Unlike liberals such as Seligson and Booth, Wiarda embraced a particularly fluid and elitist definition of democracy. At the same time, they shared the assumption that a gradual transition to democracy was both possible and desirable. Although he is well known as a proponent of the political-cultural approach explicitly criticized by Seligson, Booth and others, Wiarda's later work reflected the way the distance between conservative and liberal approaches to US policy in the region had decreased. Unlike his earlier work, which emphasized the limits that the dominant political-cultural tradition imposed on democratization in Latin America, Wiarda argued at the beginning of 1990 that "evidence" was emerging that "the recent evolution toward democracy in Latin America may be long-lasting and even permanent". He noted that in his earlier writing he had questioned whether democracy was an appropriate or even an attainable goal, given the region's corporatist and authoritarian traditions. However, he argued that although his early work was "interpreted" as support for both "the 'normalcy' of repressive regimes" and the legitimacy of US backed dictatorships, this was a "misreading" of his "views". Latin America, according to Wiarda, continued to be characterized by strong authoritarian, corporatist and "nondemocratic features". At the same time, he emphasized that at least since Latin American independence there had appeared, "alongside" the "authoritarian tradition", a "liberal democratic" and "egalitarian" approach to political and social organization. According to Wiarda this liberal tradition was often "submerged under authoritarianism"; however, the liberal strain re-emerged at various times and was "even growing gradually in strength"; however, this growth was often obscured by the power and resilience of "authoritarianism". In 1990 he argued that the "democratic ethos and institutions that were always present in Latin America had resurfaced", while the "authoritarian tradition" was "currently in headlong retreat". According to Wiarda, only Paraguay (where there were "some political openings") and Cuba and Nicaragua (where he apparently saw no "political openings") were outside the "democratic camp". The rest of the region was categorized as democratic or as "evolving-toward-democracy". At the center of Wiarda's book was a concern about whether US foreign policy, in the context of the "the new democratic openings", could be redirected in a "prudent and appropriate way" so that the US could "better secure and cement its relations with the continent". He warned that the US needed to start "understanding Latin America on its own terms, in its own context", which included its "own sometimes distinctive meanings of democracy".[79] Wiarda's work reflected the way the conservative discourses on Latin America were partially absorbed by the liberal discourses by the late 1980s. Washington's growing support for the transition to democracy facilitated the gradual consolidation of a new consensus which extended from conservatives such as Wiarda to a growing number of liberal Latin American specialists who had been openly hostile to Reagan in the early and mid-1980s.

Managing the New Pan American Partnership 1985-1990

The growing US support for the transition to democracy and the resurgence of a managerial approach in US foreign policy after 1985 was linked to the way in which the liberal professional discourses on Latin America gradually shifted from their position of antagonism towards Washington's policy in Central America to one of cautious support. By the end of the 1980s liberal criticisms were framed in terms of policy implementation rather than their earlier critique of foreign-policy assumptions. The distance that had to be travelled towards a liberal managerial policy in Central America at the beginning of Reagan's second term was demonstrated by the resolutions passed at the Latin American Studies Association's 12th Congress in Albuquerque in April 1985. The association passed five resolutions which related to US policy in Central America; these were later consolidated and revised by the resolution sub-committee, which included Cole Blasier and William LeoGrande. One of the resolutions opposed US aid to anti-Sandinista forces. A second resolution called "for an end to US military intervention in the conflict in El Salvador", the stopping of "the military build-up in Honduras" and halting of "all efforts to destabilize or overthrow the government of Nicaragua". It also called "upon the US government to support the Contadora process and other constructive efforts to bring about a negotiated settlement to the conflicts in the region". A third resolution expressed concern about the status of Guatemalan and El Salvadoran refugees in the United States. Two more focused on human rights in Guatemala and expressed a desire that the US seek to improve diplomatic and economic relations with Cuba. All resolutions passed with only 1 or 2 opposed and virtually no abstentions.[80] The following year at LASA's 13th Annual Congress in Boston, a resolution opposed to US aid to the contras, and a resolution which demanded "an end to US military intervention in Central

America", were again passed. These resolutions--along with a plea that Congress "reassert its human rights responsibilities in Central America through certification limitations on nonmilitary aid programs" and that the US "openly and energetically support the Contadora process"--were subsequently ratified by a mail vote, with over 90% of the membership voting in favor of the resolutions.[81]

The motions passed by LASA clearly reflected the hostility which US policy in Central America had engendered in the Latin American studies profession, not to mention the wider liberal frustration with Reagan's Cold War revivalism.[82] The LASA motions also reflected the alliance between liberals and radicals which characterized the Reagan years. The alliance of the 1980s was made possible by the partial incorporation of radical political and theoretical approaches into the liberal discourses in the 1970s. And throughout the 1980s the assault on the Reagan administration by the liberal Latin Americanists was supported directly and indirectly by the radical discourses on Latin America, which produced numerous critiques of US policy in Central America.[83] A prominent contributor to this literature was Noam Chomsky, a major critic of the Reagan administration.[84] His work on US policy in Central America was as unrelenting as his earlier books on US foreign policy in Southeast Asia. Chomsky sought to provoke a sense of personal responsibility in the North American public, who might in turn call the policy-makers to account.[85] His first book on Central America can be seen as representative of the more popular radical attacks on US intervention, displaying considerable continuity with the overdetermined analysis of US imperialism associated with the activist New Left of the 1960s and early 1970s. Chomsky argued that "our role in perpetuating misery and oppression, even barbaric torture and mass slaughter" was "significant in scale" and flowed directly from US policy. He emphasized that US "national security policy" and the "Cold War system of global management" were, to a great degree, "a result of US government programs that have little to do with security, but are deeply rooted in the structure of power in our society and the global concerns of dominant institutions".[86] For Chomsky the driving force behind US foreign policy was unequivocal: the "first principle" was "to ensure a favorable global environment for US-based industry, commerce, agribusiness and finance", and the "major enemy" in the Third World, as far as US policy-makers were concerned, was "primarily" the "indigenous population", because of their "unfortunate tendency to succumb to strange and unacceptable ideas about using their resources for their own purposes", resulting in the need to teach them "regular lessons in obedience".[87]

By the second half of the 1980s there also appeared more specialized radical work on the web of covert and indirect military connections the Reagan administration had relied on to pursue its anti-communist policy in Central America.[88] Reagan's contra war and the increasing reliance on a revised form of counterinsurgency in El Salvador and Guatemala were also the focus of a growing quantity of radical work (and debate).[89] The role of economic aid in the US policy of reconquest emerged as the subject of critical study by radicals such as Tom Barry and Deb Preusch, both of whom are founding directors of the Inter-Hemispheric

Education Resource Center in Albuquerque.[90] The Resource Center also produced numerous pamphlets through the 1980s which explicitly sought to influence Congress as well as the general public.[91] Despite this body of radical anti-interventionist work and the alliance between radicals and liberals, the radical discourses remained in the shadow of the dominant liberal discourses on Latin America. And the preponderance and influence of liberal critiques made clear that, as in the 1960s and 1970s, the political and theoretical intersection of the radical and the liberal discourses was on liberal terms.[92] Radical approaches and the radicals themselves were domesticated to the historically liberal structures and discourses of both the North American university system and the wide range of organizational expressions of the Latin American studies profession. This occurred in the context of a wider field of forces centered on the national political and foreign-policy process (forces which were rooted historically in liberal pluralist and/or instrumental structures and ideas) that complemented efforts to manage US hegemony in Central America and beyond. In this situation it was not surprising that critical literature, which directly or indirectly supported a liberal foreign-policy trajectory, continued to predominate.[93] This work still tended to flow more from political scientists and international-relations specialists.[94]

The continued dominance of the liberal discourses on Latin America and the central role of political scientists and international-relations specialists in the debate over Central America was clearly demonstrated by the work and position of Cole Blasier in the 1980s. He also served as a good indication of how broad a group of Latin American specialists had been alienated by Reagan's conservative militarism. Blasier was an active member of the Latin American Studies Association in this period, serving as vice-president (1985-1986) and later president (1986-1987). In 1985 he published a revised edition of **The Hovering Giant** which included a new chapter on the period from 1975 to the mid-1980s and looked at El Salvador and Nicaragua. Blasier continued to locate inter-American relations in the context of the international system as a whole. At the same time, in contrast to his approach in the mid-1970s, he took the view that, in the light of recent developments in Central America, more emphasis should be placed on seeing US policy as an attempt "to maintain control and influence over countries within its sphere" rather than as a politico-strategic response to "perceived" dangers from "rival" powers. Articulating a position which reflected the partial incorporation of a dependency perspective into the professional liberal discourse, he argued that, although the particular mix of military intervention, "political interference", aid packages and covert operations varies, in the long term US "hegemonic policies" were aimed at stopping the region's "political systems from diverging too far from approved norms". Blasier did not dismiss economic motives for US foreign policy, although, unlike radical Latin American specialists, he "subordinated" economic considerations to the politico-strategic motives of great power rivalry. At the same time, he argued that "no one should be surprised" about the US being a "hegemonic state".[95]

The historical lessons that Blasier drew in the mid-1980s supported a liberal policy agenda. He warned that the formulators of US foreign policy had "to face up to realities" and, in a comment clearly directed at the Reagan administration, he argued that policy-makers cannot "afford to ignore the claims of revolutionary movements in the idle hope that they will somehow go away". He emphasized that "suppression" only worked "in the short run". At the same time, the Alliance for Progress's "fate", said Blasier, had demonstrated the obstacles involved in any US effort to "manipulate social change"; since the 1960s changes in the US, Latin America, and around world have further limited Washington's "capacities" in this direction[96] He argued, as he had in the 1970s, that the US in Latin America had been "its own worst enemy".[97] The governments of the region did not usually ask for outside help, particularly military aid, "without good reason", and that "reason" had often been a desire to guard their "independence" from US "pressures". US "errors" in its policies towards Guatemala and Cuba facilitated, in Blasier's view, the emergence of "guerrilla movements" in the 1960s, and these movements' only chance of "victory" lay in the expansion of Washington's "suppressive military activities" in the hemisphere to such an extent that a widespread "popular reaction" would "sweep them into power". Fortunately for the US, said Blasier, the guerrillas failed to gain a wide enough popular base, or sufficient foreign aid, while US-backed counterinsurgency programs made some "temporary" and "limited" gains at "immense long-term political and other costs". Blasier emphasized that, in the early 1980s, the Reagan administration more or less "drove" the Sandinistas into an ever-tighter alliance with Moscow. He pointed to the need for a diplomatic and managerial approach to revolution, when he concluded that, although the new government in Nicaragua acknowledged its "long-term socialist objectives and its ties to the USSR, it was also intent on following an independent path in foreign and domestic policy", and it explicitly pursued "close" political and economic ties with the US, western Europe, Third World nations, as well as the socialist bloc.[98]

The idea that diplomacy could lead to the resolution of the crisis was even more explicit in the work of political scientist William LeoGrande. He emphasized the multilateral management of revolution and the diplomatic containment of Central America. LeoGrande, who was named American University's Scholar/Teacher of the Year in 1989, was involved in both the Latin American Studies Association's opposition to Reagan's policy and the PACCA initiative. He is a graduate of Syracuse University and Associate Professor of Political Science at the American University in Washington. He symbolized the alliance that developed between liberals and radicals as a result of Reagan's policy in Central America. He is on the editorial board of **NACLA Report on the Americas** and the **World Policy Journal**, and has contributed to **Foreign Affairs**; LeoGrande also served on the US House of Representatives' Democratic Caucus Task Force on Central America in 1985 and 1986. In the 1970s his research was on Cuban foreign policy.[99] But, with the revolution in Nicaragua his attention was drawn to Central America.[100]

In 1986 LeoGrande and co-editors Morris J. Blachman and Kenneth Sharpe produced **Confronting Revolution: Security Through Diplomacy in Central America**, which included a chapter on the Soviet Union by Cole Blasier. The book as a whole, like a number of other liberal efforts, sought to develop a thorough critique of US policy based on country-by-country analysis. It also sought to propose an alternative policy that would reflect its overall liberal orientation, with an emphasis on political and economic reform, multilateral diplomacy and the management of political and social change in Central America.[101] More broadly, LeoGrande and his co-editors saw their book as flowing from the "dual goals" of providing "objective analysis of the impact of US policy in Central America and the formulation of sound policy alternatives".[102] The continued centrality of objectivity to the professional liberal discourses, and the need for the opponents of Reagan's policy to project themselves as exemplars of rationality, was also apparent in LeoGrande's earlier criticism of the Kissinger **Report**. He argued that one of the **Report's** shortcomings was that it made "no effort to present an objective account of the region's history or its present agony".[103] This highlights the way in which the language, categories, and even many of the assumptions, are common to both the dominant professional discourses on Latin American and the practice of US foreign policy. The policy-makers and most Latin American specialists are still committed to objectivity and to the possibility of understanding Latin America as an object outside the imperatives of US hegemony in Latin America.

In the year following the publication of **Confronting Revolution**, PACCA (with which LeoGrande, Blachman, and Sharpe's book was also involved) published a second alternative policy statement. This book also explicitly sought to influence the foreign-policy process. It emphasized diplomacy, working with the regional powers, and respect for the initiatives of the governments of Central America. It also manifested a preoccupation with restoring conditions conducive to development. **Forging Peace: The Challenge of Central America**, authored by Richard Fagen with the extensive collaboration of the large number of Latin American specialists involved with PACCA, was far less radical in tone and content than Fagen's other work. Like **Changing Course**, which was published three years earlier, **Forging Peace** provided an alternative history of the region, emphasizing the socio-economic roots of the crisis and the central importance of nationalism and the long-term US role in aggravating the crisis. Fagen and the other contributors argued that an essentially military policy had resulted in massive human and economic costs in Central America as well as major economic, political, social and moral costs to the United States. **Forging Peace** proposed an alternative policy based on demilitarization and diplomacy, which pursued the goal of peaceful and more equitable development. Although **Forging Peace** warned that the crisis itself was rooted in inequitable development, and that "in the long run, development that does not combine social justice with growth" will only lead to instability, the model they proposed was basically a reformed liberal development model, which saw foreign aid and foreign investment, and some restructuring and diversification of the economy, as a way out of the crisis.[104]

The development model proposed by PACCA was similar to the one outlined most explicitly by writers such as Richard Feinberg, another member of PACCA who emerged in the 1980s as a high-profile critic of the Reagan administration who now serves as Latin America specialist on the National Security Council in the Clinton administration. As a young man he served in the Peace Corps in Chile from mid-1969 to mid-1971. In the early 1970s, Feinberg adopted a sympathetic view of the rise of Allende.[105] Between 1977 and 1979 he was employed by the Carter administration as a Latin American expert on the State Department's Policy Planning Staff. Feinberg has also worked for the Treasury Department and the House Banking Committee. In the late 1970s and early 1980s, he was associated, as a visiting fellow, with the Council on Foreign Relations, the Woodrow Wilson International Center for Scholars, and as an adjunct professor at the Georgetown University School of Foreign Service. He went on to become vice-president at the Overseas Development Council, a private non-profit research and policy institute which was founded in Washington in 1969. By the late 1970s, following his tenure at the State Department, Feinberg had concluded that, as far as the circum-Caribbean was concerned, Washington had "so much influence" that there was "no such thing as non-intervention; doing nothing isn't doing nothing, because it actually favors certain internal forces over others; and the weight of the (US foreign policy) bureaucracy is toward action, toward choosing sides, and toward intervention".[106] At the same time, in the early 1980s, Feinberg criticized the Reagan approach to Central America and the Third World, proposing that US policy-makers adopt a "new approach" drawing on the realist critique of global containment and on what he took to be the "virtues of economic liberalism". He argued in favor of "neo-realism" which recognized the "important changes" in terms of international economic relations and US "capabilities". He criticized the Reagan administration's reliance on "old formulae" to regain "control" in Central America, taking the view that Reagan's backward-looking approach was "increasingly ineffective" and "increasingly costly". He warned that the Reagan administration was too optimistic about its capacity to determine developments around the globe, even in "small" and "nearby" Central America. Also, in his view, the Reagan administration failed to appreciate the need to work with other regional powers, such as Mexico, and remained "trapped by ideological pre-conceptions".[107] Throughout the 1980s, Feinberg increasingly focused on Central America and on economic development and debt in the Third World.[108]

In the mid-1980s, in a book written with Bruce M. Bagley (who was Associate Professor of Comparative Politics and Acting Director of the Latin American Studies Program at the Johns Hopkins University School of Advanced International Studies at the time), Feinberg argued that the roots of the crisis in Central America were to be found in the "structurally flawed" and "inequitable development models pursued during the high growth past". They argued that "rapid but uneven economic expansion within the framework of exclusionary and illegitimate political systems" had resulted in a continued rise in violence and political polarization in Guatemala, El Salvador and Nicaragua. Furthermore, the "global recession" between 1980 and 1982, along with growing debts and civil war, contributed to the region's problems. They represented economic and political problems as reinforcing one another, resulting in a "downward spiral", arguing that any reversal of these trends necessitated a policy which dealt with the economic and political causes. At the same time, they still viewed economic and political variables as independent. And by 1986 they were confident that the "debate" in Central America about "long-term economic strategies" was not as "polarized" as the struggle for "political power". In their view Central American economic development strategies had to build on a capitalist export model which relied on the region's "good land and inexpensive labor". Feinberg and Bagley argued for the adoption of strategies of development which relied to a greater extent on "national comparative advantage", on those productive sectors already in place, and on market "access" instead of "ideological preferences". They warned that Central America would have to "sacrifice" its "future consumption" to satisfy "its debt obligations", and that foreign investors and the banks would wait for "political peace before risking more capital". The assumption on which their work rested was that 'dependent capitalism' still held out the best chance at mitigating the poverty and socio-economic inequality in the region, while economic growth could facilitate social change and democratization. And in contrast to a number of liberals in the mid-1980s, they embraced the transition to democracy. Feinberg and Bagley noted that regardless of how weak the "democratizing winds" were, their very existence was "a positive shift away from decades of personalist and military dictatorship". They characterized a "democracy-with-justice model", undergirded by a selectively interventionist state, as the most stable "regime type" for Central America. They rejected the "democracy-with-liberty" model, associated with the first Reagan administration. They also had doubts about what they called the "revolutionary democracy paradigm" (Nicaragua), which faced "internal legitimacy problems"; however, they acknowledged that 'revolutionary democracy' was "most severely constrained" in the 1980s by US efforts to "reassert its hegemony" in the area and its disregard for the Contadora process.[109]

Feinberg and Bagley warned that a lack of US support for the Contadora accord (at the same time as Washington appeared "unable or unwilling to impose political homogeneity in Central America") meant that the "extensive, if low-intensity, political violence and a chilly business environment" would continue, and that while "such conditions persist self-sustaining economic growth" would be "elusive" and "democratic impulses" would be "in danger of being short-circuited".[110] The emphasis on the Contadora process as a solution to the crisis in Central America was reflected in PACCA's 1987 policy alternative, which like Feinberg and Bagley's work regarded Washington as the main short-term obstacle.[111] Support for Contadora was also reflected in a 1987 volume edited by Bagley, which included contributions by Cynthia Arnson, Roy Gutman, Wayne S. Smith and William LeoGrande. However, some contributors remained committed to a Cold War perspective and pessimistic about the peace process.[112] For example, Margaret Daly Hayes, whose work, like Wiarda's, reflected the intersection of conservatism and liberalism, was critical of the Contadora process and continued to express reservations, particularly with regard to its ability to deal with "subversives and insurgencies".[113]

By 1987 the Latin American Studies Association's support for Contadora had manifested itself in the establishment of the Commission on Compliance with the Central America Peace Accord which visited Central America in January 1988. The idea for the Commission originated with Martin Diskin and Thomas W. Walker, and included Dario Moreno, Charles Stansifer, Richard N. Adams, John Booth, Margaret Crahan, Thomas J. Farer, Mark Rosenberg and Mitchell Seligson. They went to Central America to observe what changes had occurred since the signing of the Central American Peace Accord, known as Esquipulas II, in August 1987. The idea for the Peace Accord had first been suggested by Oscar Arias, president of Costa Rica, and it was hoped such an agreement would "lay the basis for the progressive democratization of the region". In its Final Report the LASA Commission characterized the peace process initiated by the Peace Accord in August 1987 as "a dramatic shift in the conflicts wracking the Central American region". It expressed concern that Central America's "history" remained an obstacle and President Reagan's "coolness makes the plan eminently more difficult to effect, particularly given his unswerving support for an alternative project for the region: the use of the supposed eventual military prowess of the contra as the principal means to guarantee United States security interests". They also emphasized that the fundamental economic problems which plagued the isthmus remained and that democratization was "nascent and incomplete". However, they took the view that the Peace Accord had "strengthened the prospects for democracy, civilian governments and negotiations among the Central American governments as principal vehicles for social, political and economic change in the future". They also emphasized that it had "reaffirmed Central America's desire to take charge of its own destiny".[114]

Support for Contadora, and a general emphasis on diplomacy, on a managerial approach and on a liberal reformist political and economic development model, can be found in the work of Abraham Lowenthal, one of the most prominent Latin Americanists in the United States. He produced a book in the late 1980s which articulated an extremely detailed alternative policy proposal. In 1962-1964 Lowenthal had worked as a Training Associate for the Ford Foundation in the Dominican Republic and then as a Ford Foundation Assistant Representative in Peru in 1969-1972, gaining a PhD from Harvard in 1971. Between 1974 and 1976 he served as Assistant Director and subsequently director of studies for the Council on Foreign Relations in New York. Lowenthal also worked as a consultant to the US government in the mid-1970s.[115] In 1977 he moved to the Woodrow Wilson International Center for Scholars in Washington, where he was director of the Latin American program until 1983. In the 1970s and into the 1980s, Lowenthal, whose early work focused on the Dominican Republic and Peru, also produced numerous articles about Latin America and US foreign policy generally.[116] Throughout the Reagan years, Lowenthal was highly critical of Washington's policy in Central

America and the rest of the region.[117] He served on the Latin American Studies Association's executive council, and is currently Professor of International Relations at the University of Southern California. He worked as the executive director of the Washington based Inter-American Dialogue in the early 1980s, supervising the Dialogue sessions which led to the publication of the report **The Americas in 1984: Year for Decisions.**[118] The Inter-American Dialogue report was excerpted in the Latin American Studies Association's newsletter the same year.[119] It emphasized what was also a major theme in Lowenthal's work in this period, that Reagan's Nicaraguan policy and his preoccupation with Central America was counter-productive. The Inter-American Dialogue argued that Reagan's Cold War revivalism had undermined US prestige, alienated other governments in the region, hardened the Sandinistas's position, and legitimated their relations with Cuba and Moscow.[120]

In **Partners in Conflict**, which first appeared in 1987, Lowenthal expanded the Inter-American Dialogue critique arguing that the Reagan administration's "obsession" with Central America was misguided and that Central and South American "realities" had changed in the past quarter century at a faster rate than the "perceptions" and "concepts" which emanated from Washington.[121] The main lesson that Lowenthal drew from Reagan's revival of the Cold War was that the deterioration of Washington's "influence" in Latin America could not be readily altered. This was a lesson that he felt the administration itself might have begun to learn by the mid-1980s. He argued that ultimately, if the US wanted to preserve its "interests" in Latin America on an "enduring basis", it had to "accept the end of US hegemony" and "move from a stance of dominance to one of cooperation". In his view, although the Reagan administration discussed the "crisis" in Central America with primary reference to US national security, the "main concern" was "psychopolitical". He argued that what was involved was "national insecurity", and an inability to deal "with loss of control". Lowenthal emphasized that while the US had maintained a great deal of influence in the region historically, direct US investment in Central America was no more than 0.3% of US investment worldwide. He concluded that Washington's "economic stake" in Central America was "modest", especially in contrast to its "economic stake" in Mexico and Brazil or even the "insular Caribbean". This brought Lowenthal to his "central argument", which was that US interests would be best served "if Washington looked beyond the current (and partly self-imposed) crisis of credibility in Central America". He argued that the "security" and "stability" of the hemisphere were "more deeply threatened" by region-wide "economic problems" than by civil wars in Central America. The "transformation" of Latin America over the course of the past quarter-century had generated "significant opportunities for inter-American cooperation"; however, these "opportunities" were being ignored because of the US "obsession" with Central America. His work rested on the assumption that the US and the nations of Central and South America were "potential partners". Lowenthal advocated that the US must develop "new approaches" to Latin America as a whole in order to deal with problems of economic growth, finance, debt, trade and migration and to "reinforce" what he characterized as "the regionwide turn toward democracy".[122]

In Lowenthal's view there were four major options, or approaches, which the US could consider to further its "core interests" in Central America and the Caribbean.[123] The approach which Lowenthal favoured was the "developmental alternative". While this approach was based on the assumption that a key concern of the US was still the exclusion of "tangible security threats", he argued that the US should be willing to work with differing political and economic approaches, "even Marxist ones", if they did not represent a "direct security threat". A major assumption of the "development approach" was that history, geography and economics would continue to link the Central American and Caribbean republics to the US. This approach focused on "long-term economic and social progress", not short-term political orientation. It differentiated between those nations "ready for significant economic advance" (virtually every country but El Salvador and Nicaragua in Lowenthal's view) and the nations where "civil turmoil" still represented an obstacle to "effective economic progress" in the short term. Lowenthal advocated that the US provide "free access" to North American markets, as outlined in the original version of the Caribbean Basin Initiative, to all the countries in Central America and the Caribbean (no matter what their foreign policy, ideology, internal political organization or socio-economic structure) except El Salvador and Nicaragua, with the only proviso being that they avoid any "military alliance" with the USSR. Also, according to this model, the US would extend foreign aid for the development of human resources and infrastructure within a multilateral instead of a bilateral context. In the case of the Central American countries Washington's primary objective should be to prevent the conflict in the region from growing. And it should, according to his model, seek to do this diplomatically, by supporting the Contadora process. In Lowenthal's view the "developmental approach" would safeguard the "core interests" of the US while it avoided involvement in domestic conflicts in the region. Most importantly, it would allow the US to deal with the circum-Caribbean without distracting it from its relations with Mexico and the rest of Latin America. He expressed some doubt as to Washington's ability to "sustain" the "developmental approach"; however, he emphasized that the "turn toward democracy" by the mid-1980s offered "exceptional opportunities". He argued that the US and the "other democratic nations" of the hemisphere had a shared "interest in fostering open, constitutional, and participatory politics", since a "democratic Hemisphere" would "be more humane and peaceful" and it would "also be more stable". Lowenthal argued that the time had arrived for the US to "adopt a different stance", one based on "confidence and trust"--that is, "**confianza**". In his view if Washington could "abandon the habits of dominance", Latin America and the US could replace "conflict" with "partnership".[124]

Apart from Lowenthal's work, which was one of the most exhaustive liberal critiques and alternative policy proposals, a number of other important liberals continued to generate work which challenged the Reagan administration's policy. Lars Schoultz--Professor of Political Science and Director of the Institute of Latin American Studies at the University of North Carolina, and an important member of the Latin American Studies Association (who was president of the organization in 1991-1992)--also wrote critically of the Reagan administration in the 1980s.[125] Schoultz, along with Enrique Baloyra and Federico Gil, had worked as a consultant to the State Department during the Carter administration. By the late 1980s former Carter officials--such as Anthony Lake, who was Carter's head of policy planning at the State Department (and is now Clinton's National Security Advisor), and Robert A. Pastor, who was Carter's Director of Latin American and Caribbean Affairs on the National Security Council--had both produced books on US-Nicaraguan relations and the crisis in Central America.[126] Lake's book focused closely on the events of 1978 and 1979.[127] Both writers went beyond a straightforward defense of US actions during the Carter years, but Pastor's book was a far more detailed and influential study. And, like Lowenthal, his preoccupation was with redirecting US foreign policy to better protect US interests.[128]

Also like Lowenthal's work, Pastor's 1987 book, and his work throughout the 1980s, was firmly located in the liberal discourses and rested on the idea that there was no fundamental conflict between the interests of the United States and the interests of the government and people of Nicaragua, or Latin America generally.[129] Unlike some liberals, Pastor reflected only the most limited influence of dependency theory. From his perspective the reason for friction between Nicaragua (and Central America) and the US was rooted in culture, ideology and psychology. He argued that these non-structural differences could be overcome, and the US could still be a basically positive force in the region without a fundamental altering of the character of political and economic development in Central America or the terms of the region's relations with the United States. Pastor argued that the "mistrust" between Washington and its "friends"--which was the result of "different histories", attitudes and "interests"--had "undermined their common objectives". In particular, Pastor concluded that the "roots" of the Nicaraguan revolution's "radicalization" could be found in the "minds" of both the Washington policy-makers and the Sandinistas, insofar as the "different histories" and "deep suspicions" caused each side to see "defensive actions as provocative ones". In his view Washington and Managua each formulated policies, based on different "psychological baggage", that "consistently evoked the worst in the other". Pastor emphasized that, although the US had for many years been regarded as the major player in Nicaraguan affairs, its position was not determinant, and the revolution and the country's "radicalization" after 1979 cannot be understood in terms of Washington's "actions". He asserted that the Nicaraguan revolution had developed in a direction that was "strikingly reminiscent" of the revolution in Cuba two decades earlier. Although Pastor acknowledged that Castro and the Sandinistas worried in 1980, or earlier, that Nicaragua might become "another Cuba", he was convinced that by the mid-1980s, the resemblance between Cuba and Nicaragua was becoming increasingly marked. What concerned Pastor most was that this happened even though virtually all the major actors in the United States, Nicaragua, and the other countries in the region, wanted to avoid "another Cuba". He invoked George Santayana's famous line about "those who cannot remember the past" being "condemned to repeat it". He lamented further that, in the case of Nicaragua, all those involved "remembered the outlines, if not the details, of the history", but they still "could not avoid repeating it".[130]

Pastor's approach clearly rested on the ideas which guided the practice of US foreign policy and moulded the liberal professional discourses on Latin America. Pastor emphasized the limits of US power in the region, and its increasing inability to influence events since at least the early 1960s. At the same time as Pastor argued in favor of an approach that did not put the US at the "center of events", and although he did not characterize the role of Moscow and Havana as the major factor in explaining the crisis in Central America, there was still a tendency in his work to attribute considerable explanatory power to external threats. While Pastor down-played the importance of the role of the US generally, and emphasized Washington's impotence in the Nicaraguan case specifically, he still emphasized that, despite the limitations on US efforts to influence events in Central America, a better policy could help restore and maintain the US position in the region. This is a theme which runs through most liberal work. In the case of the events of the late 1970s, Pastor took the view that the US could identify and support the moderates at an earlier and more salvageable stage. Pastor assumed that a relatively minor shift in US foreign policy could meet national security and politico-strategic goals and prevent debacles such as the Nicaraguan episode; this assumption was central to liberal foreign-policy prescriptions.

As with Pastor's writings, the work produced by the dominant liberal discourses continued to be shaped by the view that a more benevolent foreign policy, in many ways a new version of the Alliance for Progress, could achieve US objectives in Latin America.[131] It was assumed that this could be done without a fundamental restructuring of Latin America's relationship with the US. For liberals such as Pastor, the right policy still meant successfully imposing some sort of liberal capitalist model of political and economic development on the Nicaraguans and on the people and governments of Latin America. This was the policy articulated by Pastor in 1989 when he argued that the US should commit itself to "a long-term aid program", as outlined by the Kissinger Commission, on the condition that the governments and the rebels in El Salvador, Nicaragua and Guatemala negotiate a cease-fire and move towards a situation in which all political organizations can participate "fully in electoral politics" and that the various governments "agree to a precise plan for invigorating the Central American Common Market". Pastor argued that Washington "should use its resources and influence as an incentive for the Central Americans to work out their problems themselves". He saw this as the "essence of the Marshall Plan", which encouraged "cooperation among governments that had fought two catastrophic wars". He warned, somewhat menacingly, that "if Central America fails to cooperate US aid may keep its friends from declining, but it will not help the region lift itself up".[132] As we have seen, although Lowenthal was unpersuaded by much of the Kissinger Commission's strategy, like Pastor, he argued in favor of a "developmental policy". Lowenthal made a contradictory call for "a sustained US commitment to the economic and social development" of the countries of Central America and the Caribbean "without a corresponding attempt to exercise tight control of their internal affairs".[133]

By the time Pastor and Lowenthal had published their major book-length contributions to the historiography and had mapped out their policy alternatives, the Reagan administration had entered its final year. Although Reagan and his supporters had been damaged by the Iran-Contra affair, they continued to be preoccupied with Nicaragua. And their hostility to the Central American Peace Plan was justified primarily in terms of its failure to address Soviet aid to Nicaragua. At the same time even Latin America specialists who had been sympathetic to Reagan's policy throughout the 1980s often regarded Nicaragua as the major failure of the Reagan years. For example, in 1988 Margaret Daly Hayes--who has taught at the School of Advanced International Studies at Johns Hopkins University and served as a lead consultant to the Kissinger Commission--voiced qualified support for the Contadora process, while continuing to argue that Washington's policy had evolved over the Reagan years. In her view, the Reagan administration had, most importantly, achieved its main goal of containing communism. Hayes argued that by 1985, with the "encouragement" of Washington, "democratic governments have emerged in every Latin American country", apart from Paraguay, Chile, Nicaragua and Cuba, while "democratic forces dominate in both Guatemala and El Salvador, where five years ago it appeared that the guerrilla forces were facing certain victory". She asserted that "after five years of Reagan government, Nicaragua appeared to be the only crisis with which the Reagan team had not been able to cope adequately".[134]

Other Latin American specialists were not so enthusiastic. From Richard Millett's perspective, for example, Washington's policy in Central America "seemed to have been largely cast adrift", and US influence over allies and enemies was in decline by the end of 1988. The disarray of the final year of the Reagan administration flowed, in part, from "uncertainty" on all sides about the direction US policy would take once Reagan left office. Regardless of what path the incoming administration pursued "it seemed clear", to Millett, that Central America "would pose major problems for the next United States administration, problems that would offer many more dangers than opportunities".[135] At the same time, the overall retreat of conservatism and the reassertion of a more managerial foreign policy and the resurgence of the liberal professional discourses on Latin America pointed to the possibility of further shifts in policy. Although criticism of US policy, particularly towards Nicaragua, remained widespread, by the end of the Reagan years a degree of consensus was re-emerging among Latin American studies specialists and foreign-policy analysts, and it was hoped this would be consolidated during the Bush administration.[136]

The growing rapprochement with the Soviet Union, symbolized by Bush's summit meeting on Malta with Gorbachev in December 1989, facilitated the consolidation of the new consensus around the new administration's 'pragmatic' approach to foreign affairs. By the time the regimes in Eastern Europe were crumbling, even the decade-long disagreement over Central America appeared to be coming to an end. Following his election, Bush had moved quickly to deal with Reagan's Central American legacy. At a number of levels there were clear indications that, as elsewhere, the Bush administration's approach would be more pragmatic than its predecessors. Although Bush continued to back the contras and berate Nicaragua for supporting the FMLN in El Salvador, the administration also sought to shift US policy in Central America towards a multilateral and managerial approach. The change was clearly symbolized by the disappearance of the conservative ideologue Elliot Abrams, who had served as Reagan's Assistant Secretary of State for Inter-American Affairs. The position, which was initially left vacant, was eventually filled by Bernard Aronson, a conservative Democrat who had no Latin American expertise but was known for his facility as an honest broker who could heal the divisions in Congress over Central American policy. By the end of March 1989 Secretary of State Baker had solidified a bipartisan accord on Central America which provided for negotiations with the Sandinistas and humanitarian aid to the contras. Bush vowed to support the Arias Peace Plan. These initiatives made clear that Washington would neither cut the contras loose nor give them military support until after the Nicaraguan elections in February 1990. With these consensus-building efforts in the wider context of the end of the Cold War, US policy towards Central America was soon submerged by broader hemispheric and global issues.

As Washington sought to end its decade-long obsession with Central America, evidence of growing optimism among liberal Latin American specialists about the future of inter-American relations was provided by Lester D. Langley.[137] He is a prominent diplomatic historian and the author of numerous works on US relations with the circum-Caribbean.[138] In 1989 he invoked an idealistic vision of a hemispheric partnership which complemented the Pan American partnership articulated by writers such as Lowenthal, Pastor and Feinberg. In the late 1980s, Langley lamented that the current generation of scholars was "less persuaded by the power of ideas in the hemispheric experience" than earlier Latin American specialists. In contrast to this trend, he was more concerned with "the *idea* of the Western Hemisphere", than with the "formal structure of the inter-American system".[139] Langley's approach to inter-American history represented ideas and culture as an important, but neglected, axis of history in the Americas. As we have seen, in his view, a major factor which complicated US relations with Latin America revolved around the divergent "images" embodied by the "United States" (a "political entity") and "America" (both a "place" and a belief in "human betterment and community"). The "United States" and "America", argued Langley, have pursued historical trajectories which have been both "reinforcing" and "contradictory". He argued that harmonious inter-American relations were also impeded by the "crucial differences" which stemmed from the North American "belief" in a "just political order and economic opportunity for the individual", in contrast to Latin America's "faith in the centrality of the social order and an apparent resignation to a failed political tradition and an unfair economic system". Langley asserted his "liberal American's faith" that US relations with Latin America would "be better served by negotiation of disputes" and by the "reaffirmation of hemispheric unity". However, he had also come to the conclusion that "all [North] Americans (including policy-makers) who want to improve our relations with Latin America must consider the irrational forces and changeless realities that appear not only in Latin America's history but also in our own". And while Latin America has changed dramatically in the past quarter-century, there were numerous ways in which the US and Latin America had not discarded those aspects of their respective "past(s)" which "frustrate the cause of hemispheric understanding". Langley argued that, the "formal hemispheric organization", was of "less" significance for the "future" of the Americas, "than the informal but no less vital 'new' hemisphere", which rested on "the inspiration of the peoples of the Western Hemisphere" and on "their faith that they and not their governments retain the hemispheric vision". He insisted that, while government officials were preoccupied with political, economic and military concerns and the US focused on its "security interests", the "peoples of the diverse cultures of the Americas anticipate a new hemisphere in their future and in their myriad religious and humanitarian bonds are trying to achieve it".[140]

Langley's work reaffirmed, and appeared to put great emphasis on, the exceptionalism and idealism which runs through the North American understanding of US history and continues to legitimate the dominant US position in the region. His approach reflected the powerful Pan American ideas about a common history and a common destiny, which remained central to the liberal discourses on Latin America. Langley's preoccupation with culture and a vision of hemispheric harmony, which was clearly built around a US model, also referred back to the work of earlier Pan Americanists who emphasized cultural understanding, and to the liberal emphasis on culture devoid of any analysis of power relations which had shaped Latin American studies prior to the 1960s. A central work in this approach was John Crow's **The Epic of Latin America**, which was first published in 1946. Significantly the fourth edition, which appeared in 1992, complemented Langley's emphasis on culture as the key to understanding inter-American relations. Crow expressed some concern that "longstanding inequities south of the border point to a coming explosion in Latin America". He argued that "our hemisphere is now sitting on a time bomb of threatening proportions" and "if those who hold power make peaceful revolution impossible, violent revolution will become inevitable". He took the view that "the cultural achievements of the Latin American nations have always been ahead of their erratic political and economic development" and "it will be no easy task for the two Americas to work out an ongoing and productive partnership". He saw his book as a contribution to "help all Americans to understand better our southern neighbors" at a time when "the future of this hemisphere" is "hanging in a precarious imbalance" and "depends on cooperation, understanding and mutual respect".[141] Despite Crow's identification of profound socio-economic inequities and the inevitability of revolution, he continued to presume that gradual political change was still possible in Latin America and that the solution to better inter-American relations lay in greater cultural understanding rather than in any attempt to understand and address the unequal power relations which underpinned the social formations of the region and inter-American relations as a whole. Crow's and Langley's approach also intersected with the work of conservatives such as Michael Novak. He has been a resident fellow at the American Enterprise Institute for many years and held temporary diplomatic posts in the Reagan administration. Although Novak's work was clearly located in the conservative discourses throughout the 1980s, and the works of Crow and Langley are best located in the dominant liberal discourses, their similarities are important. Novak emphasized that the historical divergence of the hemisphere flowed from the Latin and Catholic tradition of the South and the Anglo-Saxon and Protestant tradition of the North. At the same time, he found considerable commonality in these traditions and invoked a common destiny in explicitly religio-historical terms. In 1990 Novak asserted that "my overriding conviction is that the Creator has tied our continents together, North and South, and instilled in us a profound passion for liberty. We have not yet achieved the full liberation of our peoples, especially the poor", but "(l)iberty is the true destiny of this hemisphere and, through it, of the world".[142] This optimism and the emphasis on the possibility of hemispheric harmony built around a shared commitment to liberty and democracy (an 'American' exceptionalism rather than a North American exceptionalism) was also characteristic of the work of Novak's former colleague at the American Enterprise Institute, Howard Wiarda.

As we have seen, Wiarda spent most of the 1980s as director of AEI's Center for Hemispheric Affairs. In 1987 Wiarda left AEI, although he retained his links with the Institute as an adjunct scholar. He spent a year at the Foreign Policy Research Institute in Philadelphia, before returning to Amherst as professor of political science. (He is also a research associate of the Center for International Affairs at Harvard.) By 1990 he had produced **Foreign Policy Without Illusion**, in which he argued that the "fragmentation" and "paralysis" which was apparent in US foreign policy was, to a considerable degree, a "reflection" of the increasing fragmentation, division and politicization which characterized North American "society". At the same time, he saw "some signs of national change", what he described as "more hope, more vigor, more confidence, greater prudence and centrism", but they were "still weak and incomplete". He lamented that it was increasingly difficult for a president to "weld a coherent sensible foreign policy out of the myriad of actors and voices now participating in the foreign policy arena". Wiarda was not optimistic about changing this situation, and he argued that the division and chaos might "be the normal workings of the democratic process", and that the current "system", regardless of its shortcomings, could be "made to function effectively". One strength of the "system", in his view, was that it had "returned Jimmy Carter to the center from an early left-wing position" and then "returned Ronald Reagan to the center from a right-wing position".[143]

Wiarda's entire approach, like the dominant professional discourses on Latin America and the practice of US foreign policy in the region, was guided by the idea that the US and Latin America shared common goals and that no significant conflict of interest existed between North and South. For example, in a second book, which also appeared in 1990, Wiarda argued that "a common democracy agenda" would provide the basis for both development in Latin America, and for US foreign-policy goals to be pursued in "relative harmony, not contradiction". He emphasized that US "interests" and Latin American "development" were "complementary": Latin America "needs the United States economically, politically, and strategically; the United States needs Latin America for the same reasons". In his view the overall complementarity was "striking". And a foreign policy which rested on "democracy, development, human rights and mutual understanding" resolved the problems associated with a "more narrowly drawn conception of US interests and security". He emphasized the "new consensus" on US foreign policy, and an "era of greater convergence" in inter-American relations. Significantly, Wiarda's emphasis on a "democracy agenda" relied explicitly on a policy position articulated in a 1987 Department of State Report entitled **Democracy in Latin America and the Caribbean: The Promise and the Challenge**. He cited, with approval, its assertion that "support for democracy, the very essence of American society, is becoming the new organizing principle for American foreign policy". Following what Wiarda described as "some earlier romantic episodes", US foreign policy had returned "to the mainstream of supporting democracy and human rights". At the same time, he emphasized that, following "earlier flirtations" with nationalist and statist approaches to political and economic development, many of Latin America's "elected, centrist, democratic political leaders" have reached the conclusion that they have to "come to grips realistically and make their accommodation with the United States". Wiarda argued that this new inter-American "embrace" was grounded "far more on genuine and mutual interdependence" than previously. He concluded that the prospect of "a community of democratic nations" was "better than ever--better even than during the heady days of the Alliance for Progress". In the context of the "the new democratic openings", he insisted that US policy could be redirected in a "prudent and appropriate way" so that the US could "better secure and cement its relations with the continent". He called for a "more enlightened, consistent and 'normal' relationship with the Latin American countries".[144] Despite his optimism about the "new democratic openings", and despite the intersection between his work and the liberal discourses, Wiarda's overall approach to Latin America is clearly located in the conservative tradition. The key to Latin American history, in Wiarda's view, was still the political traditions which originated in late medieval and early modern Iberia.[145] Wiarda's moderate conservatism reinforced the new consensus on US foreign policy, which had been consolidated by the time Bush entered office, and was eventually expanded to Central America by the time of the Nicaraguan elections in early 1990.

The February 1990 elections in Nicaragua were a crucial turning point, ushering in an era when Central America once again drifted into obscurity for most North Americans. The Latin American Studies Association sent a 12-member delegation to observe the elections. Apart from John Booth, Thomas Walker and Martin Diskin, the delegation also included Charles Stansifer, Rose Spalding, Jack Spence, Margaret Crahan, Michael Conroy and Richard R. Fagen. Most of these delegates not only observed the election in February, but had made an earlier trip to Nicaragua for a week in late November 1989. This was followed by a return trip in January and then in late February to observe the elections themselves.[146] The LASA Commission's 50-page report came to the conclusion that the elections "represented a 'free and fair' electoral process within a climate of United States-generated military and economic pressure". They were critical of the US, noting that "a review of the dreary, often illegal, behavior of the United States in marshalling military, economic and diplomatic power against a small, weak country suggests that US foreign policy has altered its modalities but not its fundamental intentions toward Latin America". Nevertheless, the "great difficulty it had in pursuing this policy of undermining a sovereign nation shows that such behavior is increasingly subject to the criticism of North American citizens as well as other countries". They were relatively optimistic, however, about the ability of the elections to facilitate a return to peace and civilian government for the region as a whole, insofar as "in the Nicaraguan case, as of March 15 1990, an incumbent government with a powerful military appears to be moving toward a peaceful transition after losing an election". At the same time they argued that the Nicaraguan elections would surely play a "broader role" in the democratization of the region. They emphasized that given the FSLN 's respect for "the results of the election, the United States must not distort the political future of Nicaragua" and it needs to "lend its weight to negotiating preconditions for free and fair elections, international monitoring of the electoral process and civilian control of the military in neighboring states of the region".[147]

As was apparent with the LASA report, many Latin American specialists remained critical of US policy in Central America. However, in the wake of the Nicaraguan election, widespread dissatisfaction was a thing of the past and the new consensus began to strengthen its hold over the dominant professional discourses on Latin America. In contrast to the Reagan years, liberal criticism increasingly focused on questions of implementation rather than challenging the assumptions on which US foreign policy in Latin America rested. The growing support for the Bush administration's pragmatic and managerial approach to foreign policy was apparent in a book by Dario Moreno, Assistant Professor of political science at Florida International University and a member of the Latin American Studies Association's Commission on Compliance with the Central America Peace Accord. In 1990 he published a study of US foreign policy in Central America which focused on the disagreement between "liberal internationalists" and "cold warriors". He argued that the "failure" of US policy in the Reagan era flowed from a "lack of consensus" in the foreign-policy establishment, and that the Central American crisis was "a reflection of the larger loss of consensus" which was a legacy of Vietnam. Moreno, who described Abraham Lowenthal as his "mentor", was firmly located in the liberal professional discourses on Latin America and clearly in sympathy with a resurgent liberal foreign policy. He pointed to the Bush administration's shift from a military to a political-diplomatic approach, in combination with attempts to appease both Congress and Cold Warriors, as "the first step in the administration's plan to rebuild the foreign policy consensus that has eluded all US administrations since Vietnam".[148]

In early 1990, Lowenthal, the pre-eminent liberal advocate of a Pan American partnership, was still reluctant to look to the future with very much optimism. But his approach reflected a complementary rather than an oppositional position. In a revised edition of **Partners in Conflict**, he argued that although "the striking triumph of democratic politics and market economics has brought on talk of the 'end of history', or at least the end of the Cold War as the organizing concept of international relations", he found it "hard to be optimistic" about Latin America. The region was entering the 1990s in "deep trouble". In his view, "economic and social conditions" were "desperate in many countries" and "political tensions" were on the rise following the "Lost Decade". He argued that Cuba was "the only country in the Hemisphere openly defying the regional commitment to democracy". However, the transition to democracy in some of the republics of Central America was "less inclusionary or robust" than elsewhere. In his view Central America was "poised uncertainly between the possibility of peace through utter exhaustion, the prospect of renewed and more violent confrontation, or years more of low-level but deadly conflict". At the same time, Washington's apparent recognition that its "preoccupation" with Central America was "misplaced" meant that it "may finally be ready in the 1990s to redirect its concerns away from Central America". However, Lowenthal was concerned that the US might "revert to pervasive neglect of Latin America" rather than turning "to such problems as drugs, migration, trade and environmental protection" and the task of "building effective partnerships with its neighbors in the Americas".[149]

Some of Lowenthal's concerns were soon addressed by George Bush's 'Enterprise for the Americas Initiative', which was launched on June 27 1990. The 'Initiative' clearly symbolized the triumph of economic and political liberalism, the fading of the Central American debate, and the consolidation of the new consensus. According to Roger B. Porter, Assistant to the President for Economic and Domestic Policy, this was "part of (Bush's) longstanding interest in encouraging democracy and economic growth in Latin America and the Caribbean". Significantly, Porter's article (speech) on the 'Initiative' appeared in the University of Miami-based **Journal of Interamerican Studies and World Affairs**, a key professional Latin American journal which reflected a more conservative liberalism than the **Latin American Research Review**. (The Board of Editors of the **Journal of Interamerican Studies and World Affairs** in 1990 included Jorge I. Domínguez, Federico G. Gil, Irving Louis Horowitz, Robert Pastor, Viron Vaky, Robert Wesson and Howard Wiarda.) Porter argued that "the global transformation of the last decade symbolizes the triumph" of "a preference for governments based on democratic political institutions and market-oriented economic arrangements". He represented these as "two ideals the United States has championed during the twentieth century" and "while the 'end of history' may not have arrived yet, the terms of international debate over politics and economics have certainly changed". He emphasized that from the early day of his presidency, Bush had "articulated a vision for Latin America that is built on the foundation of partnership". Porter held the 'Enterprise for the Americas Initiative' up as a "turning point" in inter-American relations. And, in contrast to an earlier watershed, the Alliance for Progress, which had emphasized the "importance of governments", the 'Enterprise for the Americas Initiative', according to Porter, was focused on markets. The 'Initiative' was concerned particularly with trade, investment and debt reduction. It would seek to encourage the negotiation of trade agreements directed at the long-term "vision" of a "free-trade area" stretching throughout the hemisphere. It also hoped to "unlock the potential for domestic and foreign investment and encourage capital flows", while ensuring the provision of extra debt support and debt-service reduction. He characterized the 'Initiative' as a "new approach to building a stronger economic partnership between the United States, Latin America and the Caribbean" and as "a vital tool for Latin leaders in achieving higher standards of living and meeting the challenges of an increasingly inter-related global economy".[150]

The response of Latin American leaders to the 'Enterprise for the Americas Initiative', following their conversion to neo-liberal economics over the preceding decades, was relatively enthusiastic.[151] The response from the dominant professional discourse on Latin America was also positive, and criticisms focused on implementation. As Sidney Weintraub, a former diplomat and Professor of Public Affairs at the University of Texas, noted that if the Bush Initiative had appeared in the late 1970s or early 1980s "it would have been greeted with suspicion, perhaps even derision, as just another neocolonial US maneuver". Weintraub was not convinced that US "free trade agreements" with any country other than Mexico were likely in the near future. However, he saw an overall trend in that "direction". His own problems with the 'Initiative', mapped out in a lead article in the **Journal of Interamerican Studies and World Affairs**, were framed entirely in terms of how to carry out the 'Initiative' successfully. His main criticism was directed at the decision to work towards bilateral "free-trade" agreements. Instead, he argued that the US should encourage the formation of sub-regional "free-trade" blocs based on Central America and the Andean countries, for example, and then negotiate free-trade agreements with these regional blocs.[152] On the other hand, Wayne S. Smith of the School of Advanced International Studies at Johns Hopkins University was still pessimistic about the future of inter-American relations in the wake of the invasion of Panama and the apparent failure of the US to take some responsibility for Nicaragua's economic difficulties. Although he welcomed the 'Initiative', which was "so far only a point of light on the horizon", he took the view that the Bush administration had not yet taken sufficient "advantage of the tremendous possibilities created by the end of the Cold War and the beginning of an era in which there is no enemy to threaten the United States from Latin America".[153] Like Smith, Associate Director of Americas Watch Cynthia Arnson and Johanna Mendelson Forman of American University, articulated their criticisms of the 'Initiative' in terms of implementation. They also worried that Central America would be forgotten in the wider regional push, and that the "ghosts of the past" might overshadow the US "desire for peace, multilaterialism and economic development".[154]

In the first half of 1991, Congress approved some debt relief and gave the authority for US representatives to enter into negotiations with Mexico and Canada to establish a North American Free Trade Agreement (NAFTA which came into effect on January 1 1994). By mid-1991 the US had signed a framework agreement with CARICOM and 15 framework agreements with various Latin American republics. These agreements are to form the basis for the eventual expansion of free-trade areas throughout the hemisphere. At the end of 1991, Robert Pastor voiced critical but sympathetic support for Bush's overall policy. He applauded the trajectory of the Bush administration in Latin America and was primarily concerned that rhetoric be backed up with more substantive initiatives. He concluded that Bush's "pragmatic pursuit of the regionalist option" could lead to the realization of "a century-old dream, a democratic community of the Americas". This would "combine the technology, skills, and capital of North America with the market, resources and labor of the south, creating a formidable new economic and democratic giant".[155] Pastor's vision of a Pan American partnership, which has continued to be central to the dominant professional discourses on Latin America, rested on the assumption that the continued extension throughout the Americas of liberal economic and political ideas and structures would bring prosperity and democracy for everyone. However, the primary objective was the protection and enhancement of US hegemony, the safeguarding of the interests of transnational capital and the stabilization of the privileged political and economic position of the elites and middle classes of the Americas.

Conclusion: The Triumph of Democracy 1985-1990

Throughout the 1980s the US foreign-policy debate, which focused on Central America but reflected a wider debate about the US role in the world, was framed in the context of powerful conservative discourses; however, the influence of the New Cold Warriors declined dramatically in the second half of the Reagan years. The shift away from conservative revivalism was highlighted by James Baker's emergence as Treasury Secretary in 1985. In this position, Baker, who went on to be Secretary of State under Bush, was far less opposed to economic intervention than his predecessor had been. Baker looked favorably on international economic cooperation with the major economic and financial powers and began to pursue a series of initiatives to secure agreements with them, resulting in the 1985 Plaza Agreement and the Louvre Accord of 1987. These agreements were aimed at mitigating the negative effects of Reaganomics on the international market, Third World debt repayment, and the decline in world investment. The Baker initiatives flowed from a perceived need for greater cooperation between the major capitalist powers in the management of the international economic order. When Baker emerged as Bush's Secretary of State in 1989, his appointment was very popular in the Democratic Congress. And the trend towards a new consensus accelerated once Bush entered the White House intent on a pragmatic and managerial approach to foreign policy and international economic relations.[156]

However, as we have seen, this shift was less noticeable in the case of Central America, where the conservative hold on policy remained even beyond the Reagan years. Although the US was unable to overthrow the Sandinistas militarily, Washington's support for the contras inexorably undermined the FSLN, contributing to its electoral defeat in early 1990. The February 25th election victory of the United Nicaraguan Opposition (UNO) was not just a rejection of the Sandinistas, but also a rejection of years of war and of economic devastation fueled by Washington's ongoing support for the contras and the continued economic blockade of the country.[157] By the end of the 1980s the economic circumstances of the majority of the population in Nicaragua had deteriorated precipitously. And although Nicaragua had probably been most seriously affected by the crisis of the 1980s, throughout Central America the percentage of the population living in poverty was higher than had been the case since at least the Second World War. Levels of production had declined, trade within the region had fallen dramatically and the economic circumstances of the majority of the population had deteriorated following a decade of civil war and international recession. In addition, the economic stabilization and structural adjustment policies of the second half of the 1980s contributed to the continued concentration of wealth.[158] This was the underside to the triumph of democracy and the apparent restoration of consensus in North America about the direction of US policy in Central America at the end of the 1980s.

In the wake of the electoral defeat of the Sandinistas in early 1990 (and despite the invasion of Panama at the end of 1989), the new foreign-policy consensus in the US was extended to the dominant professional discourses on Latin America. In the context of the more pragmatic foreign policy under Bush, as well as the shift in Washington's focus to Latin America as a whole, and most important, the end of the Cold War, the level of opposition to US policy emanating from Latin American specialists declined precipitously, relative to the Reagan years. As the broad alliance of professional Latin American specialists which had emerged against Reagan lost critical mass, criticisms of US policy in Central America were contained by the language, categories, ideas and liberal pluralism of the dominant professional discourses and the organizations and institutions to which they were linked. Liberals increasingly articulated mild instrumental criticisms of US foreign policy in the context of the new consensus and the declining emphasis on Central America by the Bush administration. As for radicals, the very structure of the university system and the various institutional expressions of the dominant professional discourses on Latin America ensured that radical perspectives on Central America were contained. A resurgent liberalism shaped the dominant professional discourses on Latin America and was connected to the restoration of a more pragmatic and managerial approach guiding the practice of US foreign policy. At the beginning of the 1990s, Washington's hegemony in Central America was reconstituted around an emphasis on managerial diplomacy, democratization and economic liberalization, supported by a more selective and multilateral use of direct military intervention and covert activities.

Conclusion

MANAGING LATIN AMERICA AND CONTAINING CENTRAL AMERICA

This study has traced the way in which the US emerged as the hegemonic power in the circum-Caribbean by the 1920s, followed by its rise to hemispheric and then global hegemony by 1945. It has been emphasized that connected to the US rise to predominance in Latin America between 1898 and 1945 was the appearance of professional discourses on Latin America dominated initially by historians. As we have seen, the emergent Latin American studies profession gained its authority from US power, and throughout the pre-World War II era the connection between US foreign policy and the dominant professional discourses on Latin America was even closer than in subsequent years. Although part of the professionalization process involved the growth of academic employment at North American universities, many Latin American specialists took up positions with the State Department or other departments of the US government for a considerable part of their career, as well as working closely with philanthropic organizations and foundations, like the Carnegie Foundation. At the same time, the Good Neighbor Policy and the end of direct US politico-military intervention and control in the circum-Caribbean, followed by the Second World War, facilitated a growing shift in the professional discourses on Latin America from Anglo-Saxonism to more liberal assumptions that Latin America would eventually progress along North American lines. By the 1930s powerful notions about a US civilizing role were increasingly complemented by Pan American ideas about the common history and common destiny of the Americas. But regardless of the strength of Pan Americanism, the Latin American studies profession continued to be influenced by nationalistic and racist attitudes about a US civilizing mission. And it was taken for granted that Latin America's increasing political and economic linkages with the US brought considerable benefits to all concerned.

The emphasis on the benefits to Latin America which flowed from its growing connections with North America meshed with the wider Cold War imperatives of US imperial-state policy after 1945. The Cold War saw the appearance of a more methodologically sophisticated and multidisciplinary North American social science and the dramatic growth of professional academic interest in what became known as the Third World. In the Cold War era the influence of historians on Latin American studies as a whole declined in relation to political scientists and international-relations specialists. Latin American studies between

1945 and 1968 rested on modernization theory and reflected a more secular social-scientific approach to historical change which saw Latin American countries as eventually emerging as democratic industrial nation-states similar to North America and Western Europe. However, Cold War development theory continued to rest on cultural and even racial ideas about the superiority of North American history, as a political and economic model. In the 1960s, following a period of relative neglect on the part of Washington in the 1950s, the US-sponsored Alliance for Progress attempted to bring democracy and economic well-being to Latin America. However, as revolutionary and reactionary political trends in Latin America accelerated, modernization theorists were more concerned with the management of social change and the politics of order than with democracy and greater economic equality. By the end of the 1960s, US foreign policy in Latin America had returned to the relative neglect which characterized the period prior to the Cuban revolution. However, the expansion of area studies after World War II had stimulated sufficient momentum by the end of the 1960s for Latin American studies to gain a solid position within the North American university system. In the context of the US crisis of hegemony after 1968 or so, this strong institutional base provided the foundation for the theoretical and political diversification of Latin American studies in the 1970s and allowed the dominant professional discourses on Latin America to achieve a position of greater autonomy from the policies and practices of the US imperial state.

By 1968 there was growing emphasis on the theoretical bankruptcy of North American social science generally, and Latin American studies more specifically, and dependency theory had appeared at the center of a wider radical challenge to the dominant liberal professional discourses. By the end of the 1970s, however, dependency theory was domesticated; at the same time a conservative position emerged within and outside the Latin American studies profession. Throughout this period the liberal professional discourses on Latin America maintained their position of dominance. The incorporation of various elements of the radical approach into the liberal discourses served to contain the radical assault and was central to the continued dominance of the liberal professional discourses on Latin America. Unlike the radical emphasis on a conflict model of inter-American relations, the dominant professional discourses continued to rest on the liberal idea that there was no fundamental conflict of interest between Latin American aspirations and US interests. In the wake of Vietnam there was also greater direct involvement on the part of Latin American specialists in foreign policy issues as reformist academics sought to encourage the formulation of a foreign policy which downplayed the significance of East-West relations in understanding Latin America, and took a managerial approach to North-South relations. But although liberals writing after Vietnam were far more critical of US foreign policy than earlier scholars had been, the work of those who sought to shape foreign policy directly, as well as the writing of those whose involvement was more indirect, played an important part in the strength and resilience of US hegemony. At the end of the 1970s the liberal professional discourses on Latin America intersected with and complemented the managerial foreign policy pursued in the Carter years. By 1979, however, Carter's foreign policy had already begun to shift back to a more traditional Cold War approach, while an increasingly influential group of conservative critics of Carter's policy rose to prominence.

These conservatives (often called neo-conservatives) called for a revival of the anti-communist crusade, and emphasized that a Moscow-directed communist threat was behind the problems in Central America and around the world. By 1981 the Carter administration had been replaced by Ronald Reagan and his conservative supporters, and Central America, especially Nicaragua, had emerged as a key battleground in the New Cold War. Reagan's attempt to reconquer Central America quickly emerged as a crucial focus for the Latin American studies profession. In the early 1980s, an alliance between liberals and radicals opposed to Reagan's policy in Central America was forged. As the Reagan administration failed to gain the Congressional support (as well as the wider domestic and international support) it wanted for a conservative and militaristic policy in Central America, the liberal professional discourses on Latin America regained a position of influence. The relative decline of the New Cold War highlighted the continuing dominance of the liberal professional discourses and pointed to the way the alliance between liberal and radicals had been on liberal terms. The overall orientation of Washington's policy changed during Reagan's second term. This shift was reinforced by the growing amount of work produced in North America on Central America and Latin America generally and by the organizational initiatives taken by numerous Latin American studies specialists after 1985. While still using counterinsurgency and proxy warfare, the Reagan administration increasingly embraced the transition to democracy in Latin America. In the second half of the 1980s, a managerial approach, which had been emphasized by the liberal critics of the Reagan administration, began to reappear in US foreign policy.

In Central America this shift was reflected in the way US policy moved away from low-intensity conflict, and military spending towards the imposition of a neo-liberal economic model. However, Reagan's approach continued to be based on the idea that the challenge to US hegemony in the region came from international communism and that US prestige around the globe was at stake in Central America. And despite the end of the Cold War and the more pragmatic approach of the Bush administration by 1989, the emergence of a new consensus on Central America (and especially Nicaragua) did not occur until after the February 1990 elections in Nicaragua. At the same time, the reconsolidation by 1990 of political processes and economic policies in Central America acceptable to the US was the direct result of a decade of unprecedented US military involvement and political and economic interference. This is not to suggest that the US plays a determining role in Central American history. However, the assumption that it can play a determining role, and that other external forces (particularly Cuba and the Soviet Union) were playing a determining role, was an important cause of the crisis of the 1980s. The growing stability in Central America by the end of the 1980s was brought about without any significant effort to address the problems in which the revolutions of the late 1970s and 1980s were rooted. At the beginning of the 1990s, repression and exploitation continued in Guatemala and El Salvador underneath an economic liberalization and political democratization process erected on bloodshed and intimidation. In Nicaragua, the Chamorro government was confronted with the economic and political legacy of a popular revolution which was rolled back after ten years of military and economic warfare. By 1990, after a decade of unrelenting attention from Washington, Central America had been contained.

The extension of the new consensus to the dominant professional discourses on Latin America and the continued liberalism of these discourses flows from a long-standing set of power relations. This is something that has been overlooked by many North American observers who often represent liberal and radical positions as equal competitors and talk of convergence rather than incorporation or domestication. Despite the idea that political or theoretical consensus is something arrived at through the give-and-take of equal participants, this book has argued that political consensus and theoretical convergence within the Latin American studies profession and a wider consensus on US foreign policy in Central America and beyond occurred in the context of power relations that preclude, and actively work against, the possibility of an equal exchange. Furthermore, it has also been maintained that even where there has appeared to be a lack of consensus, the institutional power relations and the dominant discourses have ensured the relative containment of political and theoretical dissent. The restoration of consensus by the end of the 1980s and the partial incorporation of the radical and the conservative discourses into the liberal professional discourses over the previous two decades occurred on terms set by liberalism.

The transition to democracy in Central America and in the rest of Latin America is taking place in the context of political and socio-economic structures which allow the military, the oligarchies and the national bourgeoisie to set the terms of the transition. In the same way the political consensus and theoretical convergence in Latin American studies emerged in the context of political and professional institutions and organizations that rest on liberal assumptions. As was emphasized at the outset, North American universities are structured around liberal pluralism and the rejection of the legitimacy of intellectual conflict and the rejection of ideas that rest on a conflict model of social and political change. By the 1960s, radical ideas began to make their way into the North American tertiary system in an unprecedented fashion. But this process occurred at a time when the acceptable boundaries for interpretive conflict had already been laid down. The universities provide a series of interconnected liberal pluralist arenas in which political and theoretical perspectives can be used and viewed as relatively equal positions, rather than positions whose relationship to each other is embedded in an array of historically unequal power relations.

The liberal pluralist structures and discourses of the North American university system are linked to the wider liberalism of the institutions and ideas of national political life. The deeply rooted liberal pluralism of the universities, and

North American institutions generally, has helped to ensure that liberal concepts and assumptions continue to structure the Latin American studies profession. More broadly, it is abundantly clear that liberal development theory has continued to provide the most influential set of assumptions about Latin America in terms of the analysis, the policies and the perceptions generated by those academics, officials, politicians, international bankers, journalists, and business people who work with or write about Latin America--as well as the Middle East, Asia, Africa and Oceania. At the end of the 1980s, liberal economic and political development ideas continued to provide the overall context in which US foreign policy was formulated and executed, not to mention the importance of liberal development theory to the IMF and the World Bank. The Enterprise for the Americas Initiative launched by the Bush administration and the recently ratified North American Free Trade Agreement (which is seen by many inside and outside of Washington as presaging a series of free-trade agreements for the Americas as a whole) clearly reflects the assumption that economic and political liberalism are the ultimate goals of all the republics in the hemisphere. And the reception given the Initiative and NAFTA by the governments in Latin America and by the dominant professional discourses on Latin America points to the continued strength of liberal assumptions.

This study has used an approach derived from imperial-state theory and Gramscian international-relations theory, and a conception of discourse adapted from a growing body of post-structuralist analysis, to represent US hegemony in a way which emphasizes the fundamental connection between the production of North American knowledge about Latin America and the projection and management of US hegemony in the region. This approach has allowed for a reconceptualization of the links between US power and North American knowledge, a perspective that points to a more diffuse understanding of US hegemony and a complicated but profoundly complementary relationship between Latin American specialists and the US imperial state. Since the early twentieth century, US foreign policy has flowed from a commitment to a powerful liberal teleology which understands history as progress towards liberal capitalist democracy. The practice of US foreign policy in Latin America has continued to be shaped by the idea that North American political and economic development provides both a measure and a model for the history of Latin America. The policies of the US imperial state have also been influenced by pragmatic considerations and by the political and economic assumptions policy-makers share with US and international capitalist elites. The core interests of capital accumulation and expansion and various conceptions of national security have been central to policy-making, yet the assumption that long-term US interests are not necessarily in significant conflict with Latin American interests has also guided the practice of US foreign policy. Furthermore foreign policy has been moulded over the years by powerful Pan American assumptions about the common history and common destiny of all the republics in the Americas, which imposes a North American understanding of a common past and a common future on the hemisphere. Despite the sometimes critical perspective of

Latin American specialists, the liberal professional discourses on Latin America have also been shaped by these assumptions, and they have facilitated the practice of US foreign policy in Latin America. Prior to the late 1960s, Latin American studies in North America was characterized by a far greater degree of dependence on the US government and its agencies than in the 1970s and 1980s, when competing professional discourses emerged. Nevertheless, both the rise and continued transformation of Latin American studies is fundamentally linked to US hegemony. This book has emphasized that power was located not just in an array of institutional structures which underpin US hegemony, but in the assumptions, categories and images which shaped the North American study of Latin America. This contributed to and was a result of the diffuse character of US hegemony, and ensured its resilience. The dominant professional discourses have complemented US hegemony and played an important role in the ongoing efforts of the US imperial state to manage Latin America and in the more recent attempt to contain Central America.

NOTES

Notes to Preface

1. Stephan Haggard, **Pathways from the Periphery: The Politics of Growth in the Newly Industrializing Countries** [1990]. Gary Gereffi, "Paths of Industrialization: An Overview" in Gary Gereffi and Donald L. Wyman, eds., **Manufacturing Miracles: Paths of Industrialization in Latin America and East Asia** [1990]. Rhys Jenkins, "Learning from the Gang: Are There Lessons for Latin America from East Asia" **Bulletin of Latin American Research** vol. 10. no. 1. 1991. Rhys Jenkins, "The Political Economy of Industrialization: A Comparison of Latin American and East Asian Newly Industrializing Countries" **Development and Change** vol. 22. no. 2. 1991. Gary Gereffi, "Rethinking Development Theory: Insights from East Asia and Latin America" in A. Douglas Kincaid and Alejandro Portes, eds., **Comparative National Development: Society and Economy in the New Global Order** [1994].

2. For example see Florencia E. Mallon, "Dialogues Among the Fragments: Retrospect and Prospect" and Steve J. Stern, "Africa, Latin America, and the Splintering of Historical Knowledge: From Fragmentation to Reverberation" in Frederick Cooper, Allen F. Isaacman, Florencia E. Mallon, William Rosebery and Steve J. Stern, **Confronting Historical Paradigms: Peasants, Labor, and the Capitalist World System in Africa and Latin America** [1993]. Orin Starn, "Rethinking the Politics of Anthropology: The Case of the Andes" **Current Anthropology** vol. 35. no. 1. 1994. Florencia E. Mallon, **Peasant and Nation: The Making of Postcolonial Mexico and Peru** [1994]. Florencia E. Mallon, "The Promise and Dilemma of Subaltern Studies: Perspectives from Latin American History" **American Historical Review** vol. 99. no. 5. 1994.

3. Patricia Seed, "Colonial and Postcolonial Discourse" **Latin American Research Review** vol. 26. no. 3. 1991. J. Jorge Klor de Alva, "The Postcolonization of the (Latin) American Experience: A Reconsideration of 'Colonialism', 'Postcolonialism' and 'Mestizaje'" in Gyan Prakash, ed., **After Colonialism: Imperial Histories and Postcolonial Displacements** [1995].

4. Ruth Berins Collier and David Collier, **Shaping the Political Arena: Critical Junctures, The Labor Movement, and Regime Dynamics in Latin America** [1991]. Jorge I. Domínguez, "On Understanding the Present by Analyzing the Past in Latin America: A Review Essay" **Political Science Quarterly** vol. 107. no. 2. 1992.

5. Timothy P. Wickham-Crowley, **Guerrillas and Revolution in Latin America: A Comparative Study of Insurgents and Regimes Since 1956** [1992]. Barry Carr and Steve Ellner, eds., **The Latin American Left: From the Fall of Allende to Perestroika** [1993]. Jorge Castañeda, **Utopia Unarmed: The Latin American Left after the Cold War** [1993]. James Dunkerley, "Beyond Utopia: The State of the Left in Latin America" **New Left Review** no. 206. 1994.

6. Arturo Escobar and Sonia E. Alvarez, eds., **The Making of Social Movements in Latin America: Identity, Strategy and Democracy** [1992].

Introduction

1. For an early radical work see Noam Chomsky, **American Power and the New Mandarins** [1968]. A recent and sophisticated approach to this question, also from a radical perspective, is Stephen Gill, **American Hegemony and the Trilateral Commission** [1990]. Examples of less critical, more instrumental, work on this subject include: Irving Louis Horowitz, ed., **The Rise and Fall of Project Camelot: Studies in the Relationship between Social Science and Practical Politics** [1967]. Ernest R. May, **"Lessons" of the Past: The Use and Misuse of History in American Foreign Policy** [1973]. Richard A. Melanson, **Writing History and Making Policy: The Cold War, Vietnam and Revisionism** [1983]. Richard E. Neustadt and Ernest R. May, **Thinking in Time: The Uses of History for Decision Makers** [1986].

2. Julia R. Schwendinger and Herman Schwendinger, **The Sociologists of the Chair: A Radical Analysis of the Formative Years of North American Sociology** [1974]. Thomas L. Haskell, **The Emergence of Professional Social Science: The American Social Science Association and the Nineteenth-Century Crisis of Authority** [1977]. Edward T. Silva and Sheila A. Slaughter, **Serving Power: The**

3. Marvin Surkin and Alan Wolfe, eds., **An End to Political Science: The Caucus Papers** [1970]. David M. Ricci, **The Tragedy of Political Science: Politics, Scholarship and Democracy** [1984].

4. See Barton Bernstein, ed., **Towards a New Past: Dissenting Essays in American History** [1968]. Gene Wise, **American Historical Explanations: A Strategy for Grounded Inquiry** [1980]. David W. Noble, **The End of American History: Democracy, Capitalism, and the Metaphor of Two Worlds in Anglo-American Historical Writing 1880-1980** [1985]. Ian Tyrrell, **The Absent Marx: Class Analysis and Liberal History in Twentieth Century America** [1986]. Peter Novick, **That Noble Dream: The "Objectivity Question" and the American Historical Profession** [1988]. Less critical analysis would include John Higham, Leonard Krieger and Felix Gilbert, **History: The Development of Historical Studies in the United States** [1965]. John Higham, **Writing American History: Essays on Modern Scholarship** [1970]. Bernard Sternsher, **Consensus, Conflict, and American Historians** [1975]. Michael Kammen, ed., **The Past Before Us: Historical Writing in the United States** [1980].

5. For example see Alexander DeConde, **American Diplomatic History in Transformation** [1976]. Robert W. Tucker, **The Radical Left and American Foreign Policy** [1971]. Joseph M. Siracusa, **New Left Diplomatic Histories and Historians: The American Revisionists** [1973]. Gerald K. Haines and J. Samuel Walker, eds., **American Foreign Relations: An Historiographical Review** [1981]. Jerald A. Combs, **American Diplomatic History: Two Centuries of Changing Interpretations** [1983].

6. See, for example, Robert A. Packenham, **Liberal America and the Third World: Political Development Ideas in Foreign Aid and Social Science** [1973]. John G. Taylor, **From Modernization to Modes of Production: A Critique of the Sociologies of Development and Underdevelopment** [1979]. Elbaki Hermassi, **The Third World Reassessed** [1980]. Peter Worsley, **The Three Worlds: Culture and World Development** [1984]. George Rosen, **Western Economists and Eastern Societies: Agents of Change in South Asia 1950-1970** [1985]. Ian Roxborough, **Theories of Underdevelopment** [1979]. Irene L. Gendzier, **Managing Political Change: Social Scientists and the Third World** [1985]. Vicky Randall and Robin

Theobald, **Political Change and Underdevelopment: A Critical Introduction to Third World Politics** [1985]. David E. Apter, **Rethinking Development: Modernization, Dependency and Postmodern Politics** [1987]. David Harrison, **The Sociology of Modernization and Development** [1988]. Diana Hunt, **Economic Theories of Development: An Analysis of Competing Paradigms** [1989]. Bjorne Hettne, **Development Theory and the Three Worlds** [1990]. Alvin Y. So, **Social Change and Development: Modernization, Dependency and World-System Theories** [1990]. Carlos Ramirez-Faria, **The Origins of Economic Inequality Between Nations: A Critique of Western Theories of Development and nderdevelopment** [1991]. Richard Peet, **Global Capitalism: Theories of Societal Development** [199U1]. Robert A. Packenham, **The Dependency Movement: Scholarship and Politics in Development Studies** [1992].
7. Robert A. McCaughey, **International Studies and Academic Enterprise: A Chapter in the Enclosure of American Learning** [1984]. The politics of Asian Studies (especially China) has attracted some attention. For example, see John N. Thomas, **The Institute of Pacific Relations: Asian Scholars and American Politics** [1974]. Paul Evans, **John King Fairbank and the American Understanding of Modern China** [1988].
8. Susanne Jonas Bodenheimer, **The Ideology of Developmentalism: The American Paradigm-Surrogate for Latin American Studies** [1971]. Ronaldo Munck, **Politics and Dependency in the Third World: The Case of Latin America** [1984]. Peter F. Klarén and Thomas J. Bossert, eds., **Promise of Development: Theories of Change in Latin America** [1986]. Jorge Larrain, **Theories of Development: Capitalism, Colonialism and Dependency** [1989]. Cristobal Kay, **Latin American Theories of Development and Underdevelopment** [1989]. David Lehmann, **Democracy and Development in Latin America: Economics, Politics and Religion in the Post-war Period** [1990].
9. See, for example, Charles Wagley, "Introduction" in Charles Wagley, ed., **Social Science Research on Latin America** [1964]. Merle Kling, "The State of Research on Latin America: Political Science" in Wagley, ed., **Social Science Research on Latin America** [1964]. Richard M. Morse, "The Strange Career of 'Latin-American Studies'" **Annals of the American Academy of Political and Social Science** vol. 356. November 1964. James Petras, "Latin American Studies in the US: A Critical Assessment" **Science and Society** vol. 32. no. 2. 1968. reprinted in James Petras, **Politics and Social Structure in Latin America** [1970]. Roger R. Trask, "Inter-American Relations" in Roberto Esquenazi-Mayo and Michael C. Meyer, eds., **Latin American Scholarship Since World War II: Trends in History, Political Science, Literature, Geography and Economics** [1971]. John D. Martz, "Political Science and Latin American Studies: A Discipline in Search of a Region" **Latin American Research Review** vol. 6. no. 1. 1971. Abraham F. Lowenthal, "'Liberal', 'Radical' and 'Bureaucratic' Perspectives on US Latin American Policy: The Alliance for Progress in Retrospect" in Julio Cotler and Richard R. Fagen, eds., **Latin America and the United States: The Changing Political Realities** [1974]. Charles W. Bergquist, "Recent United States Studies in Latin American History: Trends Since 1965" **Latin American Research Review** vol. 9. no. 1. 1974. Woodrow Borah, "Latin American History in World Perspective" in Charles F. Delzell, ed., **The Future of History** [1977]. Jorge I. Domínguez, "Consensus and Divergence: The State of the Literature on Inter-American Relations in the 1970s" **Latin American Research Review** vol. 13. no. 1. 1978. Charles Bergquist, "Latin America: A Dissenting View of 'Latin American History in World Perspective'" in Georg G. Iggers and Harold T. Parker, **International Handbook of**

Historical Studies: Contemporary Research and Theory [1979]. Steven W. Hughes and Kenneth J. Mijeski, "Contemporary Paradigms in the Study of Inter-American Relations" in John D. Martz and Lars Schoultz, eds., **Latin America, the United States and the Inter-American System** [1980]. Richard V. Salisbury, "Good Neighbors?: The United States and Latin America in the Twentieth Century" in Gerald K. Haines and J. Samuel Walker, eds., **American Foreign Relations: A Historiographical Review** [1981]. Louis Pérez, "Intervention, Hegemony and Dependency: The United States in the Circum-Caribbean 1898-1980" **Pacific Historical Review** vol. 51. no. 2. 1982. Joseph S. Tulchin, "Emerging Patterns of Research in the Study of Latin America" **Latin American Research Review** vol. 18. no. 1. 1983. Benjamin Keen, "Main Currents in United States Writings on Colonial Spanish America 1884-1984" **Hispanic American Historical Review** vol. 65. no. 4. 1985. John J. Johnson, "One Hundred Years of Historical Writing on Modern Latin America by United States Historians" **Hispanic American Historical Review** vol. 65. no. 4. 1985. Ralph Lee Woodward, Jr., "The Historiography of Modern Central America Since 1960" **Hispanic American Historical Review** vol. 67. no. 3. 1987. Stephen G. Rabe, "Marching Ahead (Slowly): The Historiography of Inter-American Relations" **Diplomatic History** vol. 13. no. 3. 1989. John D. Martz, "Political Science and Latin American Studies: Patterns and Asymmetries of Research and Publication" **Latin American Research Review** vol. 25. no. 1. 1990. Thomas M. Leonard, "Search for Security: The United States and Central America in the Twentieth Century" **The Americas: A Quarterly Review of Inter-American Cultural History** vol. 47. no. 4. 1991. Steve J. Stern, "Africa, Latin America, and the Splintering of Historical Knowledge: From Fragmentation to Reverberation" in Frederick Cooper, Allen F. Isaacman, Florencia E. Mallon, William Roseberry, Steve J. Stern, **Confronting Historical Paradigms: Peasants, Labor, and the Capitalist World System in Africa and Latin America** [1993]. Steve J. Stern, "Feudalism, Capitalism, and the World-System in the Perspective of Latin America and the Caribbean" **American Historical Review** vol. 93. no. 4. 1988. reprinted in Frederick Cooper, Allen F. Isaacman, Florencia E. Mallon, William Roseberry, Steve J. Stern, **Confronting Historical Paradigms: Peasants, Labor, and the Capitalist World System in Africa and Latin America** [1993]. Florencia E. Mallon "Dialogues Among the Fragments: Retrospect and Prospect" in Frederick Cooper, Allen F. Isaacman, Florencia E. Mallon, William Roseberry, Steve J. Stern, **Confronting Historical Paradigms: Peasants, Labor, and the Capitalist World System in Africa and Latin America** [1993].

10. A recent book by Fredrick Pike attempts to address the myths and stereotypes which have been important to US relations with Latin America since the nineteenth century. Although it contains a very good discussion of the relationship between perceptions and policies towards native peoples in North America and subsequent US approaches to Latin America, it focuses primarily on the nineteenth and early twentieth centuries and is preoccupied with the understanding of Latin America articulated by successive North American counter-cultures. Furthermore, although he attempts to incorporate gender questions into his approach he fails to put power at the center of his inquiry. Pike is apparently familiar with many of the recent debates within cultural studies and social theory; however, he ultimately situates his analysis of racial and cultural stereotypes within a revised liberal voluntarist framework. See Fredrick B. Pike, **The United States and Latin America: Myths and Stereotypes of Civlization and Nature** [1992]. For a study that is both more sophisticated and more tightly focused than Pike's see Helen Delpar, **The Enormous Vogue of Things Mexican: Cultural Relations Between the United States and Mexico 1920-1935** [1992]. For a study which focuses on US perceptions of the

temperate lands of South America from the mid-nineteenth century to the 1920s see J. Valerie Fifer, **United States' Perceptions of Latin America, 1850-1930: A 'New West' South of Capricorn?** [1991].

11. The main disciplines which will be focused on in this study are history (especially diplomatic history) and political science (especially international relations); however, disciplinary boundaries are increasingly difficult to identify, and an underlying theme of this work is the inter-disciplinary character of the approaches to Latin America adopted by North American historians and social scientists. Apart from the disciplines already mentioned, sociology, anthropology and archeology are also important, but have been excluded from sustained or direct consideration. Archaeology and anthropology, in particular, have been closely connected with colonial and neo-colonial expansion, and many North American anthropologists and archaeologists have had strong links with the US government, while their professional discourses have been linked to the wider discourses on Latin America. North American archaeology and anthropology have traditionally been the most involved in the study of the indigenous populations of Latin America, and their development as disciplines deserves separate treatment. On North American anthropology and the Maya see Paul Sullivan, **Unfinished Conversations: Mayas and Foreigners Between Two Wars** [1989]. This study will not attempt to address the way indigenous Americans have been written out of history over the past 500 years. There is a growing literature, much of it by anthropologists, which attempts to restore the indigenous inhabitants of the Americas to history. See, for example, W. George Lovell, "Surviving Conquest: The Maya of Guatemala in Historical Perspective" **Latin American Research Review** vol. 23. no. 2. 1988. Carol A. Smith, ed., **Guatemalan Indians and the State: 1540 to 1988** [1990]. Greg Urban and Joel Sherzer, eds., **Nation-States and Indians in Latin America** [1991]. There are also important first-person testimonies. See Rigoberta Menchu (edited and introduced by Elisabeth Burgos-Debray), **I Rigoberta Menchu: An Indian Woman in Guatemala** [1984].

12. The idea of a Third World emerged after World War II as an explicitly political category referring to the growing number of non-aligned nations which were reluctant to take sides in the Cold War. The term 'Third World' gained popular currency as the ranks of the non-aligned movement were strengthened throughout the 1950s and 1960s, when numerous European colonies in Asia and Africa gained their political independence. At least one tendency had evolved by the 1960s into a revolutionary approach committed to movements of national liberation on three continents. At the same time the Third World rapidly came to be more than a description of governmental coalitions and/or allied revolutionary movements in the context of the Cold War. The apparent gulf between the industrialized nations and the rest of the world in the 1950s suggested that a distinguishing characteristic of Third World countries was a shared poverty. Despite the scope of the Third World development debate, the most widespread approach to determining whether a country or region is part of the Third World continues to be based on what stage of North American or Western European-style industrialization and economic development the country has reached and whether it has completed the transition to electoral democracy. Although 'Third World' is thoroughly entrenched in popular and academic discourses, it now possesses only limited utility as a analytical concept or a political category. A number of factors have undermined the relevance of the term: the disappearance of the Second World, the rise of the Asian Tigers and the continued economic diversity and politico-military conflict within and between various countries and regions of the Third World, the globalization of political and economic elites, the emergence of an international division of labor which is shaped by the greater and greater movement of capital, labour and goods across borders, along with the existence and expansion of Third World conditions within the borders of the industrialized countries. Furthermore, although 'Third World' continues to be

primarily an economic and political (and sociological) category, it is now used at the popular and academic level as a cultural category. Under these circumstances it explains very little and serves to mask the diversity and historical particularity which characterizes the various regions that have been consigned to the Third World. On the origins and utility of the term see Nigel Harris, **The End of the Third World: Newly Industrializing Countries and the Decline of an Ideology** [1986]. pp. 7, 11-18. Leslie Wolf-Phillips, "Why 'Third World'?: Origin, Definition and Usage" **Third World Quarterly: Journal of Emerging Areas** vol. 9. no. 4. 1987. Aijaz Ahmad, **In Theory: Nations, Classes, Literatures** [1992]. pp. 293-304. Mark T. Berger, "The End of the 'Third World'?" **Third World Quarterly: Journal of Emerging Areas** vol. 15. no. 2. 1994.

13. North American political scientist D. Michael Shafer has observed that "the notion that social scientists and policy makers engage in fundamentally different activities betrays a naive view of the social scientific endeavor and social scientists' relationship to society". He argued that "what is striking is the embeddedness of policy-making in the intellectual milieu and social science in the policy concerns of the day", emphasizing that the "relationship is recursive, not dichotomous". D. Michael Shafer, **Deadly Paradigms: The Failure of US Counterinsurgency Policy** [1988]. p. 12.

14. Central America is taken here to include Guatemala, Honduras, El Salvador, Nicaragua and Costa Rica. Although these countries are not homogeneous, they do share a relatively common history, before and after their independence from Spain. Although Belize is cartographically part of Central America its historical link to the British Empire, and its complete marginality as a focus of North American interest, allows for its exclusion here. The opening of the Panama Canal in the early twentieth century, and Panama's previous links to South America, has meant that Panama's history and the history of US relations with Panama can be set somewhat apart from the rest of Central America. Mexico has a close geographical and historical relationship to Central America, but for a number of reasons it stands as a unique case in US-Latin American relations. Because of Mexico's long border and intimate association with the United States, its much bigger size in contrast to the republics of Central America, and its 'post-revolutionary' status, a separate examination of the North American study of Mexico is necessary. For example, see John A. Britton, **Revolution and Ideology: The Image of the Mexican Revolution in the United States 1910-1960.**

15. There are different approaches to the periodization of the Cold War. Walter LaFeber has talked about a New Cold War beginning in the late 1970s, as has Noam Chomsky. See Walter LaFeber, **America, Russia and the Cold War 1945-1980** [1980]. Noam Chomsky, **Towards a New Cold War: Essays on the Current Crisis and How We Got There** [1982]. Fred Halliday developed one of the clearest demarcations between Cold War (I) and Cold War (II). He divided US-Soviet relations since World War II into four phases. The First Cold War covered the period 1946-1953, while 1953-1969 is described as a "period of Oscillatory Antagonism". Détente was the period 1969-1979, while the Second Cold War was, of course, seen to have begun in 1979. See Fred Halliday, **The Making of the Second Cold War** [1986]. p. 3. For the purposes of this study, the period from 1946 to 1990 is defined as the Cold War, but the first half of the 1980s will also be referred to as the New Cold War.

16. The profound investment in empiricism which continues to characterize the historical profession and the strong commitment to quantitative analysis which guides political science, combined with their close proximity historically to political power and policy processes, has been central to the still limited impact of critical theory on the disciplines of history and political science. However, by the end of the 1980s, in the wake of (or in tandem with) marxist and feminist incursions, the debate had been joined, even if history (especially diplomatic history) and political science

(especially international relations) remain particularly resistant to 'contamination'. See Mark Poster, **Foucault, Marxism and History: Mode of Production Versus Mode of Information** [1984]. Joan Wallach Scott, **Gender and the Politics of History** [1988]. Andrew Linklater, **Beyond Realism and Marxism: Critical Theory and International Relations** [1990]. James Der Derian, **O n Diplomacy: A Genealogy of Western Estrangement** [1991].

17. J. A. Hobson, **Imperialism: A Study** [1902]. V. I. Lenin, **Imperialism, the Highest Stage of Capitalism: A Popular Outline** [1917].

18. While the imperialism debate remains centered on political and economic theories there are, of course, many studies which have focused on the cultural and technological aspects of imperialism over the years. See for example Martin Green, **Dreams of Adventure, Deeds of Empire** [1979]. Michael Adas, **Machines as the Measure of Men: Science, Technology and Ideologies of Western Dominance** [1989].

19. Although the idea of 'semi-colonialism' and the notion of 'informal imperialism' have a long lineage, it was Gallager and Robinson's work on 'free trade' imperialism in the early 1950s which stimulated the spread of the definition of imperialism as both formal and informal colonialism. See John A. Gallager and Ronald E. Robinson, "The Imperialism of Free Trade" **Economic History Review** vol. 6. no. 1. second series 1953.

20. For example, see Robert Gilpin, **US Power and the Multinational Corporation: The Political Economy of Foreign Direct Investment** [1975]. Edy Kaufman, **The Superpowers and Their Spheres of Influence: The United States and the Soviet Union in Eastern Europe and Latin America** [1976]. Robert A. Keohane and Joseph S. Nye, **Power and Interdependence: World Politics in Transition** [1977]. C. Fred Bergsten, Thomas Horst and Theodore Moran, **American Multinationals and American Interests** [1978].

21. As Eric Hobsbawm has emphasized, the imperialism debate is effectively a debate about marxism. Hobsbawm, **The Age of Empire 1875-1914** [1987]. p. 60.

22. Donald W. White, "History and American Internationalism: The Formulation from the Past after World War II" **Pacific Historical Review** vol. 58. no. 2. 1989. pp. 147-156, 167-169.

23. A particularly good example of this interpretation can be found in Julius W. Pratt, **America's Colonial Experiment: How the United States Gained, Governed, and in Part Gave Away a Colonial Empire** [1950].

24. William Roger Louis, **Imperialism at Bay: The United States and the Decolonization of the British Empire 1941-1945** [1978].

25. Andrew J. Rotter, **The Path to Vietnam: Origins of the American Commitment to Southeast Asia** [1987]. Lloyd C. Gardner, **Approaching Vietnam: From World War II Through Dienbienphu 1941-1954** [1988].

26. William Appleman Williams, **The Tragedy of American Diplomacy** [1959].

27. By the 1970s New Left interpretations and an economic understanding of the term 'imperialism' had been partially incorporated into the dominant academic discourses. At the same time, some realist writers embraced the term 'imperial' but eschewed 'imperialism' because of its use by radical exponents of economic theories of imperialism. The realist emphasis on 'imperial' rather than 'imperialism' gave support to the image of the US as the inheritor of the British empire-civilization, not the successor of exploitative British imperialism. George Liska, **Imperial America: The International Politics of Primacy** [1967]. Robert W. Tucker, **Nation or**

Empire? [1968]. Raymond Aron, **The Imperial Republic** [1974]. George Liska, **Career of Empire: America and Imperial Expansion Over Land and Sea** [1978], For a discussion of these changes see Jerome Slater, "Is United States Foreign Policy 'Imperialist' or 'Imperial'?" **Political Science Quarterly** vol. 91. no. 1. 1976. pp. 65-67.

28.   At the end of 1988, in his presidential address to the Society for Historians of American Foreign Relations, Lloyd C. Gardner, a former student of William Appleman Williams, noted that, while the Soviets were "busy rewriting their history to fill in the 'white spaces' of Stalin's era", North Americans "have set out to discover the forces behind the decline of the 'empire' we never previously acknowledged". Lloyd C. Gardner, "Lost Empires" **Diplomatic History** vol. 13. no. 1. 1989. p. 1. Roger Bell has argued that the greater acceptance of the term 'imperialism', which attended the widespread public debate following the publication of Paul Kennedy's book may indicate that many North Americans now regard the notion of US "empire" and US "hegemony" as "accurate and comforting descriptions of their nation's global position throughout this century". Roger Bell, "The Debate over American Empire in the Late Twentieth Century" **Australian Journal of International Affairs** vol. 45. no. 1. 1991. p. 87. See Paul Kennedy, **The Rise and Fall of the Great Powers: Economic Change and Military Conflict from 1500 to 2000** [1987].

29.   Tony Smith, **The Pattern of Imperialism: The United States, Great Britain and the Late Industrializing World Since 1815** [1981]. p. 6.

30.   Tony Smith, "American Imperialism is Anti-Communism" in Mommsen and Osterhammel, eds., **Imperialism and After** [1986]. pp. 41, 46-48. More recently see Tony Smith, **America's Mission: The United States and the Worldwide Struggle for Democracy in the Twentieth Century** .

31.   See for example, Bernard A. Weisberger, **Cold War Cold Peace: The United States and Russia Since 1945** [1984]. John Lewis Gaddis, **The Long Peace: Inquiries into the History of the Cold War** [1987]. Stephen E. Ambrose, **Rise to Globalism: American Foreign Policy Since 1938** [1991]. Melvyn P. Leffler, **A Preponderance of Power: National Security, the Truman Administration and the Cold War** [1992]. Examples of Latin American specialists who acknowledge economic considerations but treat politico-strategic factors as separate from, and usually more important than, economic variables, include Cole Blasier, **The Hovering Giant: US Responses to Revolutionary Change in Latin America 1910-1985** [1985]. Richard H. Immerman, **The CIA in Guatemala: The Foreign Policy of Intervention** [1982]. Stephen G. Rabe, **Eisenhower and Latin America: The Foreign Policy of Anticommunism** [1988].

32.   For example, writing in the second half of the 1980s, David Calleo emphasized that "Pax Americana is used in this book with some pride". David P. Calleo, **Beyond American Hegemony: The Future of the Western Alliance** [1987]. pp. 13, 223.

33.   Richard J. Barnet, **The Roots of War: Men and Institutions Behind US Foreign Policy** [1973].

34.   See Raymond Vernon, **Sovereignty at Bay: The Multinational Spread of US Enterprises** [1971]. Louis Turner, **Multinational Companies and the Third World** [1973]. Richard J. Barnet and Ronald E. Müller, **Global Reach: The Power of the Multinational Corporations** [1975].

35.   Morris H. Morley, "The US Imperial State in Cuba 1952-1958: Policymakng and Capitalist Interests" **Journal of Latin American Studies** vol. 14. no. 1. 1982. p. 143. James Petras and Morris Morley, **US Hegemony Under**

Siege: Class, Politics and Development in Latin America [1990]. pp. 65-86, 190-210. James Petras and Morris Morley, **Latin America in the Time of Cholera: Electoral Politics, Market Economics and Permanent Crisis** [1992]. pp. 1-31, 47-78. See also James F. Petras and Morris H. Morley, "The US Imperial State" **Review** (Fernand Braudel Center for the Study of Economies, Historical Systems and Civilizations) vol. 4. no. 2. 1980. The governments and elites of Latin America (as well as the Middle East, Africa, Asia and Oceania) have inserted themselves into the global political-economic order on favourable terms at the same time as they often enthusiastically claim to speak for the rural and urban poor of the 'Third World' who have clearly not been incorporated into the current international order on favourable terms. In Latin America, and elsewhere, certain sectors of the elite are economically, socially and culturally oriented towards North America and Western Europe, where they have bank accounts, maintain business links, own homes and send their children to school. Internationalization or globalization has meant the increasingly tight interlocking of transnational capital and national capitalist classes. Over the past decade and a half, the Debt Crisis, "the generalized economic recession" and IMF-backed structural adjustment, has contributed to greater concentration of income, high rates of unemployment, widespread poverty and the marginalization of a growing number of rural and urban poor around the globe. And as Jorge Nef emphasized at the beginning of the 1990s, for much of Latin America, "the state has become the receiver and debt-collector of a bankrupt economy on behalf of transnational creditors". In this situation, states in Latin America have been drawn into service by interlocking national and global elites. Jorge Nef, "'Normalization', Popular Struggles and the Receiver State" in Jan Knippers Black, ed., **Latin America, Its Problems and Its Promise: A Multidisciplinary Introduction,** [1991]. p. 199.

      36. Morris H. Morley, **Imperial State and Revolution: The United States and Cuba 1952-1986** [1987]. pp. 6-10.

      37. Morley, **Imperial State and Revolution** [1987]. pp. 10-15.

      38. Morley, "The US Imperial State in Cuba 1952-1958" **Journal of Latin American Studies** [1982]. pp. 143-146. Morley, **Imperial State and Revolution** [1987]. pp. 29-30.

      39. The application of a Gramsci's conception of hegemony to contemporary international relations was spearheaded by Robert W. Cox. See Robert W. Cox, "Social Forces, States and World Order: Beyond International Relations Theory" **Millennium: Journal of International Studies** vol. 10. no. 2. 1981. Robert W. Cox, "Production and Hegemony: Toward a Political Economy of World Order" in Harold K. Jacobson and Dusan Sidjanski, eds., **The Emerging International Economic Order: Dynamic Processes, Constraints and Opportunities** [1982]. Robert W. Cox, "Gramsci, Hegemony and International Relations: An Essay in Method" **Millennium: Journal of International Studies** vol. 12. no. 2. 1983. Robert W. Cox, **Production, Power and World Order: Social Forces in the Making of History** [1987].

      40. Gill, **American Hegemony and the Trilateral Commission** [1990]. pp. 46-48.

      41. It should be emphasized that even in the 1920s US hegemony was achieved at a price. This is a theme pursued by Richard Salisbury, who has pointed out that the "stability" achieved at the end of the 1920s was based primarily on "externally imposed solutions" to Central American "problems". Salisbury argued further that a basic connection between the crisis of the 1920s and the crisis of the 1980s was the US "failure to understand Central American nationalism". Not surprisingly, he concluded that Washington policymakers failed to "understand the dynamics of Central American revolutionary nationalism and anti-imperialism". Richard V. Salisbury, **Anti-Imperialism and International Competition in Central America 1920-**

1929 [1989]. pp. ix-xi, 166-172.

42. See for example Gill, **American Hegemony and the Trilateral Commission** [1990]. pp. 51-54. Stephen Gill, "Intellectuals and Transnational Capital" **The Socialist Register 1990** [1990]. On ideology see Jorge Larrain, **The Concept of Ideology** [1984]. Goran Therborn, **The Ideology of Power and the Power of Ideology** [1980]. Jorge Larrain, **Marxism and Ideology** [1983]. The marxist conception of ideology has been countered by liberal approaches to ideology as well as the liberal idea of differing "belief systems". Various conceptualizations of social science and foreign policy paradigms have also been used to highlight the assumptions and attitudes shared by the majority of North American historians, social scientists and/or US policy makers. For a liberal approach to 'ideology' and US foreign policy see Michael H. Hunt, **Ideology and US Foreign Policy** [1987]. For "belief systems" see J. R. Rosenau and O. R. Holsti, "US Leadership in a Shrinking World: The Breakdown of Consensuses and the Emergence of Conflicting Belief Systems" **World Politics** vol. 35. no. 3. 1983. The classic definition of paradigm is, of course, the one provided by Thomas Kuhn. He characterized a paradigm as "the entire constellation of beliefs, values, techniques and so on shared by the members of a given community". Thomas S. Kuhn, **The Structure of Scientific Revolutions** [1970]. p. 175.

43. It is in Foucault's most recent books that the concept of discourse and the relationship between power and knowledge are most fully developed. See Michel Foucault, **Discipline and Punish: The Birth of the Prison** [1979] and Michel Foucault, **The History of Sexuality: Volume One--An Introduction** [1979]. In his earlier writing he was concerned with interrogating the social sciences' pretensions to rationality and to authority; however, these books did not seek to conceptualize authority or demonstrate the means by which authority was exercised. Michel Foucault, **The Order of Things: An Archeology of the Human Sciences** [1970]. Michel Foucault, **The Archeology of Knowledge** [1972]. Said's pioneering work, which focused initially on the Middle East, provides an important point of departure for any study of the relationship between North American and Western European hegemony in, and North American and Western European discourses on, the Middle East, Africa, Asia, Latin America and Oceania. See Edward Said, **Orientalism** [1978]. and **Culture and Imperialism** [1993]. While Said's first book quickly became a canonical text, related territory had been charted in Victor G. Kiernan, **The Lords of Humankind: European Attitudes to the Outside World in the Imperial Age** [1972]. and Bryan S. Turner, **Marx and the End of Orientalism** [1978]. More recently see Michael Adas, **Machines as the Measure of Men: Science, Technology and Ideologies of Western Dominance** [1989]. For work on US hegemony in Latin America which builds on Foucault and/or Said see Jorge Nef, "The Trend Toward Democratization and Redemocratization in Latin America: Shadow and Substance" **Latin American Research Review** vol. 22. no. 3. 1988. Deborah Poole and Gerardo Renique, "The New Chroniclers of Peru: US Scholars and their 'Shining Path' of Peasant Rebellion" **Bulletin of Latin American Research** vol. 10. no. 2. 1991. For discussion and/or critique of Said and Foucault in relation to the Third World see Arturo Escobar, "Discourse and Power in Development: Michel Foucault and the Relevance of His Work to the Third World" **Alternatives** no. 10. 1984-1985. Arturo Escobar, "Power and Visibility: Development and the Invention and Management of the Third World" **Cultural Anthropology** vol. 3. no. 4. 1988. Arturo Escobar, **Encountering Development : The Making and Unmaking of the Third World** [1995]. Robert Young, **White Mythologies: Writing History and the West** [1990]. Aijaz Ahmad, **In Theory** [1992]. Gyan Prakash, "Writing Post-Orientalist Histories of the Third World: Perspectives from Indian Historiography" **Comparative Studies**

in Society and History vol. 32. no. 2. 1990. revised and reprinted as Gyan Prakash, "Writing Post-Orientalist Histories of the Third World: Indian Historiography Is Good to Think" in Nicholas B. Dirks, ed., **Colonialism and Culture** [1993]. Ali Behdad, **Belated Travelers: Orientalism in the Age of Colonial Dissolution** [1994]. Bryan S. Turner, **Orientalism, Postmodernism and Globalism** [1994].

44. Samuel Weber, **Institution and Interpretation** [1987]. pp. 24-27.

45. A good example of a marxist approach to ideology can be found in Edward H. Berman, **The Influence of the Carnegie, Ford and Rockefeller Foundations on American Foreign Policy: The Ideology of Philanthropy** [1983]. Ideology has been defined by Stephen Gill, following Therborn, as the "world view" of a particular class, or class fragment. He goes on to note that ideologies evolve in a continuous political and social process within groups and classes, as well as at the national and international level. Differing ideologies challenge, interact, influence and "contaminate" each other. In this struggle an ideology needs to gain the "right to speak" and then to "assert the overriding relevance of a particular kind of identity". The ideology seeks to represent "certain features of the world" as "more important than others", such as "exploitation rather than inter-dependence". Gill, **American Hegemony and the Trilateral Commission** [1990]. pp. 6-7, 245. Therborn, **The Ideology of Power and the Power of Ideology** [1980]. pp. 79-80. For example, Gill characterized the debate over US foreign policy in Central America and the Third World in the 1970s and 1980s as a debate which pitted distinct ideologies against each other. According to his interpretation there were the 'conservatives', who emphasized the importance of "rival national interests" ("national capital", sections of organized labor, the military industrial complex) and the liberal perspective, which emphasized an "interdependent world" and the "high degree of mutuality of interest among nations" ("transnational capital"), against each other. In his view both ideologies could be identified with "historic blocs of political forces". Gill, **American Hegemony and the Trilateral Commission** [1990]. p. 7.

46. Chatterjee has argued that, in the case of nationalism in the Third World, there is "an inherent contradictoriness in nationalist thinking, because it reasons within a framework of knowledge whose representational structure corresponds to the very structure of power nationalist thought seeks to repudiate....Furthermore, it is this contradictoriness which signifies, in the domain of thought, the theoretical insolubility of the national question in a colonial country, or for that matter, of the extended problem of social transformation in a post-colonial country, within a strictly nationalist framework". Partha Chatterjee, **Nationalist Thought and the Colonial World: A Derivative Discourse** [1986]. pp. 38-39.

47. Novick, **That Noble Dream** [1988]. p. 8.

48. There is, of course, considerable debate about the relationship between author and text. See Roland Barthes, "The Death of the Author" in Roland Barthes, **Image-Music-Text** [1979]. Edward Said has attempted to reinstate the individual writer, in contrast to Foucault, who Said felt had gone too far in subordinating the author to the discourse. See particularly Edward Said, **Beginnings: Intention and Method** [1985]. Also see Edward Said, **The World, the Text and the Critic** [1984].

49. Louis Hartz, "United States History in a New Perspective" in Louis Hartz, ed., **The Founding of New Societies: Studies in the History of the United States, Latin America, South Africa, Canada and Australia** [1964].

50. Weber, **Institution and Interpretation** [1987]. pp. 40-46.

51. The main difference between 'radicalism' and 'liberalism', as the terms are

used here, is that radicalism rests on a conflict model of social and political change and supports revolution, while liberalism is centered on gradual change and the assumption that conflict between divergent 'interests' can and ought to be resolved through reform rather than revolution.

52. Hughes and Mijenski "Contemporary Paradigms in the Study of Inter-American Relations" in Martz and Schoultz eds., **Latin America, the United States and the Inter-American System** [1980]. pp. 19-22.

53. Thomas J. Bossert, "The Promise of Theory" in Klarén and Bossert, eds., **Promise of Development** [1986]. p. 320. Ronald Chilcote and Joel Edelstein have also discussed liberal and radical theory in a way which implies that they are 'equal' theoretical competitors. Capitalist and socialist models of development were, in their view, both "part of the mainstream of thinking of contemporary social science and history". Ronald H. Chilcote and Joel C. Edelstein, **Latin America: Capitalist and Socialist Perspectives of Development and Underdevelopment** [1986]. pp. xiii, 5-6.

54. Alvin Y. So, **Social Change and Development** [1990]. pp. 12, 266-268.

55. Thomas G. Paterson, "Introduction" **Journal of American History** vol. 77. no. 1. 1990. p. 96. Akira Iriye, "Culture" **Journal of American History** vol. 77. no. 1. 1990. Michael H. Hunt, "Ideology" **Journal of American History** vol. 77. no. 1. 1990. Emily S. Rosenberg, "Gender" **Journal of American History** vol. 77. no. 1. 1990. Thomas J. McCormick, "World Systems" **Journal of American History** vol. 77. no. 1. 1990. Louis A. Pérez, "Dependency" **Journal of American History** vol. 77. no. 1. 1990. Melvyn P. Leffler, "National Security" **Journal of American History** vol. 77. no. 1. 1990. Michael J. Hogan, "Corporatism" **Journal of American History** vol. 77. no. 1. 1990. J. Garry Clifford, "Bureaucratic Politics" **Journal of American History** vol. 77. no. 1. 1990. Richard H. Immerman, "Psychology" **Journal of American History** vol. 77. no. 1. 1990.

56. Michael J. Hogan and Thomas G. Paterson, eds., **Explaining the History of Ame8ican Foreign Relations** [1991].

57. Louis Hartz, **The Liberal Tradition in America: An Interpretation of American Political Thought Since the Revolution** [1955]. p. 51. This is Hartz's classic statement of the 'fragment' theory. As Ian Tyrrell has pointed out, although it lacks the comparative breadth and refinement of his later work, it is the earlier book which has exercised the greatest influence on North American historians. While his later book approached US history as one European 'fragment' among many, the earlier work reinforced North American 'exceptionalism' insofar as it examined the US as a "unique case" in contrast to Europe. See Ian Tyrrell, "American Exceptionalism in an Age of International History" **American Historical Review** vol. 96. no. 4. 1991. p. 1031.

58. Immanuel Wallerstein has argued that "the concept of development" is not just a "central component" in the ideology of North American and Western "civilization" and social science, "but is in fact the central organizing concept upon which all else is hinged". Immanuel Wallerstein, "The Development of the Concept of Development" in Immanuel Wallerstein, **The Politics of the World-Economy: The States, the Movements and the Civilizations** [1984]. p. 173.

59. Arturo Escobar, "Culture, Economics and Politics in Latin American Social Movements Theory and Research" in Arturo Escobar and Sonia E. Alvarez, eds., **The Making of Social Movements in Latin America: Identity, Strategy and Democracy** (1992). p. 62.

60. Even though Latin America has often been treated as a single unit of analysis North American academics have, of course, not been unaware of the great

diversity of Latin America. Frank Tannenbaum noted in the early 1960s that the term 'Latin America' was "deceptive because it carried with it the notion of uniformity and similarity". He emphasized that in contrast to Europe, for example, the difference between two Latin American countries was greater than between any two European nations. In Tannenbaum's view "despite the many similarities in historical experience, no two countries in South America were sufficiently alike for anyone to assume that, knowing one, he (sic) may speak confidently about its neighbors". This was the case even for the republics of Central America. For example, Guatemala and Costa Rica, in his view were less similar than Poland and Spain. He insisted that "lumping them together" was a "matter of convenience for literary purposes rather than a methodologically permissible device". Frank Tannenbaum, "Latin America as a Field of Study for the Social Scientist" (1964) in Joseph Maier and Richard W. Weatherhead, eds., **The Future of Democracy in Latin America: Essays by Frank Tannenbaum** [1974]. Also see John D. Martz, "Political Science and Latin American Studies: A Discipline in Search of a Region" **Latin American Research Review** vol. 6. no. 1. 1971. pp. 79-80. David Bronheim, "Latin American Diversity and United States Foreign Policy" in Douglas A. Chalmers, ed., **Changing Latin America: New Interpretations of Its Politics and Society** [1972].

61. William B. Taylor, "Between Global Process and Local Knowledge: An Inquiry into Early Latin American Social History 1500-1900" in Olivier Zunz, ed., **Reliving the Past: The Worlds of Social History** [1985]. p 116. On the representation and invention of the New World in the early years of discovery and conquest see J. H. Elliot, **The Old World and the New 1492-1650** [1970]. Tzvetan Todorov, **The Conquest of America: The Question of the Other** [1984]. Stephen Greenblatt, **Marvelous Possessions: The Wonder of the New World** [1991].

62. On the Black Legend see Benjamin Keen, "The Black Legend Revisited: Assumptions and Realities" **Hispanic American Historical Review** vol. 49. no. 4. 1969. Lewis Hanke, "A Modest Proposal for a Moratorium on Grand Generalizations: Some Thoughts on the Black Legend" **Hispanic American Historical Review** vol. 51. no. 1. 1971. Benjamin Keen, "The White Legend Revisited: A Reply to Professor Hanke's 'Modest Proposal'" **Hispanic American Historical Review** vol. 51. no. 2. 1971. Charles Gibson, ed., **The Black Legend: Anti-Spanish Attitudes in the Old World and the New** [1971].

63. See Charles Gibson, "Latin America and the Americas" in Kammen, ed., **The Past Before Us** [1980]. pp. 200-201.

64. See, for example, the perspective articulated by George W. Crichfield in a two-volume work which appeared in the first decade of the twentieth century: "I have shown, by a thousand facts and arguments, that the barbarisms of Haiti, Santo Domingo, Central America, Venezuela, Colombia, Ecuador, and Bolivia are outrages on the civilization and progress of the human race; that they are utterly devoid of internal elements of regeneration; that the only hope for betterment lies in the influence of exterior civilization; that the Monroe Doctrine has stood as a wall of fire for a century between savagery and the possibility of outside help; that this state of affairs is a disgrace to the world; that it is incumbent on civilization to wipe out this black spot on the face of the earth; and that the United States, in virtue of its geographical location, self-interests, and moral and physical power, is the one nation of all the world to undertake this task". George W. Crichfield, **American Supremacy: The Rise and Progress of the Latin American Republics and Their Relations to the United States Under the Monroe Doctrine** [1908] vol. 2. p. 645.

65. By the end of the 1930s Pan Americanism was generally understood in North America as "the cooperative activity of the American states in the political, economic or cultural spheres". Dexter Perkins, "Bringing the Monroe Doctrine up to

Date" **Foreign Affairs** vol. 20. no. 2. 1942. p. 261.

66. In the early 1960s Richard M. Morse argued that this was further compounded insofar as North Americans, who turned their gaze southward, "wrestle(d) with an insidious doubt", because, "even in the fact of the cruelty, poverty, and tumult of Latin America" they were unable to "escape the lurking suspicion that *it is just barely conceivable*" that their "*own ancestors may have taken a wrong turn in the sixteenth and seventeenth centuries*". Anglo-Saxon Protestant North Americans "never had the opportunity to be Japanese or Hindu"; however, "once upon a time we *were* within the mother Church". According to Morse Latin America "confronts" North Americans "with much that we swept under the rug, with much that might still have been ours". He speculated further that the various "strategies" North Americans have adopted in order to keep the region "at an intellectual and psychic remove" have been "devised so as to obscure this simple fact". Morse, "The Strange Career of 'Latin-American Studies'" **The Annals of the American Academy of Political and Social Science** 1964. p. 112. (Morse's italics).

67. Eduardo Galeano, **Open Veins of Latin America: Five Centuries of the Pillage of a Continent** [1973]. p. 12. As Benedict Anderson has suggested the original adoption of the term 'America' by the creoles of North America lies in the timing of the distinct nationalist trajectories followed in the North and in the South. While England's thirteen colonies in North America, for geographical and commercial as well as political reasons, managed to break the bonds of British colonialism while remaining united as a federal political unit, the economics and geography were not conducive to the emergence of united American states in Latin America. As Anderson points out "the 'failure' of the Spanish-American experience to generate a permanent Spanish-America-wide nationalism reflects both the general level of development of capitalism and technology in the late eighteenth century and the 'local' backwardness of Spanish capitalism and technology in relation to the administrative stretch of the empire....The Protestant, English-speaking creoles to the north were much more favourably situated for realizing the idea of 'America' and indeed eventually succeeded in appropriating the everyday title of 'Americans'. The original Thirteen Colonies comprised an area smaller than Venezuela, and one third the size of Argentina. Bunched geographically together, their market-centres in Boston, New York and Philadelphia were readily accessible to one another and their populations were relatively tightly linked by print as well as commerce. The 'United States' could gradually multiply in numbers over the next 183 years, as old and new populations moved westward out of the old east coast core....Had a sizeable English-speaking community existed in California in the eighteenth century, is it not likely that an independent state would have arisen there to play Argentina to the Thirteen Colonies' Peru? Even in the USA, the affective bonds of nationalism were elastic enough, combined with the rapid expansion of the western frontier and the contradictions generated between the economies of North and South, to precipitate a war of secession almost a century after the Declaration of Independence; and this war today sharply reminds us of those that tore Venezuela and Ecuador off from Gran Colombia, and Uruguay and Paraguay from the United Provinces of the Rio de la Plata". Benedict Anderson, **Imagined Communities: Reflections on the Origins and Spread of Nationalism** [1991]. pp. 63-64.

68. Samuel Flagg Bemis, **The Latin American Policy of the United States: An Historical Interpretation** [1943]. p. x.

69. Robert N. Seidel, **Progressive Pan Americanism: Development and United States Policy Toward South America 1906-1931** [1973]. p. 1.

70. Jonathan Kwitny, **Endless Enemies: The United States and the Making of an Unfriendly World** [1987]. p. i.

71. In the mid-1960s Stanislav Andreski used Northamerica and Northamerican to describe the US and its citizens. He argued that it was a better translation of

norteamericano, which refers to people from the US specifically, emphasizing that while Canadians are North Americans they are not 'Northamericans'. Stanislav Andreski, **Parasitism and Subversion: The Case of Latin America** [1966]. p. 1.

72. Lester D. Langley, **America and the Americas: The United States in the Western Hemisphere** [1989]. pp. xvi-xviii.

73. At the same time, the term 'US' will be used to mean the government of the United States unless another meaning is clear. Further, the term 'US' will be used interchangeably with 'Washington', without presuming that the US government, or Washington, is some sort of unitary focus of power, or an undifferentiated policy-generating matrix.

74. Jorge Nef, "Latin American and Caribbean Studies in Canada: A Developmental Perspective" **Canadian Journal of Development Studies** vol. 3. no. 1. 1982. pp. 179-180, 183-184. Also see Jorge Nef, "Canada and Latin America: Solitudes in Search of a Paradigm" in Jorge Nef, ed., **Canada and the Latin American Challenge** [1978].

75. For a good analysis of the domestication of Latin American intellectuals by North American and Western European foundations and by transnational capital over the past twenty-five years see James Petras, "The Metamorphosis of Latin America's Intellectuals" **Latin American Perspectives** vol. 17. no. 2. 1990. reprinted in Petras and Morley, **US Hegemony Under Siege** [1990]. pp. 147-156. Also see their discussion of "The Retreat of the Intellectuals" in Petras and Morley, **Latin America in the Time of Cholera** [1992]. pp. 145-176.

76. For a succinct analysis of the symbiotic relationship between high level policy-makers and US corporate executives, particularly executives of transnational corporations, see Morley, **Imperial State and Revolution** [1987]. pp. 26-29.

77. Drawing a distinction between internal and external factors runs into the problem of defining external and internal. William Roseberry has recently argued, that "the more important challenge is to grasp through a variety of historical processes, the 'internalization of the external'". See William Roseberry, "Americanization in the Americas" in William Roseberry, **Anthropologies and Histories: Essays in Culture, History and Political Economy** [1989]. pp. 88-89.

78. The emphasis here on a relative victory for liberalism by the end of the 1980s contrasts sharply with the idea, articulated by Immanuel Wallerstein, that 1968 demarcated the onset of the decline of liberalism and that the end of the Cold War in 1989 represented the end of the liberal era in world-systemic terms. Wallerstein has argued that by the second half of the nineteenth century the dominant ideology of the expanding world-system was liberal and it remained dominant into the second half of the twentieth century by partially incorporating its conservative and socialist challengers. From 1848, and "at least until 1968, under the guise of three ideologies in conflict with each other we really had only one, the overwhelmingly dominant ideology of liberalism". From his perspective, while "the revolution of 1848, via its successes and its failures, ensured the triumph of liberalism as an ideology and the eventual transformation of its two rivals--conservativism and socialism--into mere adjuncts, the revolution of 1968, via its successes and failures, undid the liberal consensus" and "the period from 1968 to 1989 has seen the steady crumbling of what remained of the liberal consensus". Immanuel Wallerstein, "The Collapse of Liberalism" **The Socialist Register 1992** [1992]. pp. 96-104.

79. The classic triumphalist perspective has been articulated by Francis Fukuyama, a former RAND consultant, and a State Department employee. In 1989 he suggested that the end of the Cold War might be the 'end of history?'. He characterized the waning of the conflict between Washington and Moscow as the "end point of mankind's ideological evolution and the universalization of Western liberal democracy as the final form of human government". He emphasized that the triumph of liberalism

was still unfinished, and "victory" had occurred mainly "in the realm of ideas or consciousness". The process was "as yet incomplete in the real or material world". And according to Fukuyama's scenario, much of the Third World was still "mired in history" and would be "a terrain of conflict for many years to come". At the same time he was confident that economic and political liberalism would "govern the material world in the long run". Francis Fukuyama, "The End of History?" **The National Interest** vol. 16. no. 8. 1989. pp. 3-4, 15. Francis Fukuyama **The End of History and the Last Man** [1992]. See also Zbigniew Brzezinski, **The Grand Failure: The Birth and Death of Communism in the Twentieth Century** [1990]. Joshua Muravchik, **Exporting Democracy: Fulfilling America's Destiny** [1991]. Richard Nixon, **Seize the Moment: America's Challenge in a One-Superpower World** [1992].

80. There are many indications that the expansion of market economics and electoral politics associated with the so-called New World Order bears the seeds of its own destruction. See especially Benedict Anderson, "The Last Empires: The New World Disorder" **New Left Review** no. 193. 1992. Giovanni Arrighi, "Marxist Century, American Century: The Making and Remaking of the World Labour Movement" **New Left Review** no. 179. 1990. Robin Blackburn, "Fin de Siecle: Socialism after the Crash" **New Left Review** no. 185. 1991. Both these articles are reprinted in Robin Blackburn, ed., **After the Fall: The Failure of Communism and the Future of Socialism** [1991]. See also Alex Callinicos, **The Revenge of History: Marxism and the Eastern European Revolutions** [1991]. Robert W. Cox, "Global Perestroika" **The Socialist Register 1992** [1992].

1. Civilising the South 1898-1945

1. Frederick Merk, **Manifest Destiny and Mission in American History: A Reinterpretation** [1963]. pp. 3-4. James C. Thomson, Peter W. Stanley and John Curtis Perry, **Sentimental Imperialists: The American Experience in East Asia** [1981]. pp. 93-94.

2. John E. Findling, **Close Neighbors, Distant Friends: United States-Central American Relations** [1987]. pp. 7-9.

3. See John Lloyd Stephens, **Incidents of Travel in Central America, Chiapas and Yucatan** [1841]. See also John Lloyd Stephens, **Incidents of Travel in Yucatan** (2 vols) [1843]. For Stephens's role in archaeology's discovery of the ancient Maya see Paul Sullivan, **Unfinished Conversations: Mayas and Foreigners Between Two Wars** [1989]. pp. xix, 7-11, 14.

4. Frederick Merk, **Manifest Destiny and Mission in American History** [1963]. pp. viii-ix. 24-227. Michael H. Hunt, **Ideology and US Foreign Policy** [1987]. pp. 29-36. Albert K. Weinberg, **Manifest Destiny: A Study of Nationalist Expansionism in American History** [1935]. Reginald Horsman, **Race and Manifest Destiny: The Origins of American Racial Anglo-Saxonism** [1981].

5. See William Walker, **The War in Nicaragua** [1860]. See Charles H. Brown, **Agents of Manifest Destiny: The Lives and Times of the Filibusters** [1980].

6. See Robert E. May, **The Southern Dream of Caribbean Empire 1854-1861** [1973].

7. Ralph Lee Woodward, Jr., **Central America: A Nation Divided** [1985]. pp. 184-186.

8. Victor Bulmer-Thomas, **The Political Economy of Central America Since 1920** [1987]. p. xiv.

9. Between 1898 and 1920 the US Marines were sent ashore in Central America and the Caribbean on at least twenty separate occasions, often remaining for long periods. Walter LaFeber, **Inevitable Revolutions: The United States in Central America** [1984]. pp. 78-79.

10. William R. Keylor, **The Twentieth Century World: An International History** [1992]. pp. 209-211.

11. Prior to 1918, important articles on Central America, for example, were most likely to be written by officials of the US government who had served, or were serving, in the region. See Philip Marshall Brown, "American Intervention in Central America" **The Journal of Race Development** vol. 4. 1913-1914. Clifford D. Ham, Americanizing Nicaragua: How Yankee Marines, Financial Oversight and Baseball Are Stabilizing Central America" **The American Review of Reviews** vol. 53. 1916. Brown was Assistant Professor of International Law and Diplomacy at Princeton and former US Minister to Honduras. Ham was Collector-General of Customs in Nicaragua. Both articles legitimated US intervention in the region.

12. William J. Griffith, "The Historiography of Central America Since 1830" **Hispanic American Historical Review** vol. 40. no. 4. 1960. p. 552. See Hubert Howe Bancroft, **History of Central America** (3 vols.) [1882-1887]. See Arthur Morelet, **Travels in Central America** [1871]. Henry R. Blaney, **The Golden Caribbean: A Winter Visit to the Republics of Colombia, Costa Rica, Spanish Honduras, Belize and the Spanish Main Via Boston and New Orleans** [1900]. J. G. Walker, **Ocean to Ocean: An Account Personal and Historical of Nicaragua and Its People** [1902]. Frederick Palmer, **Central America and Its Problems** [1910].

13. John J. Johnson, "One Hundred Years of Historical Writing on Modern Latin America by United States Historians" **Hispanic American Historical Review** vol. 65. no. 4. 1985. pp. 745-747.

14. See, for example, James Morton Callahan, **An Introduction to American Expansion Policy** [1908]. George W. Crichfield, **American Supremacy: The Rise and Progress of the Latin American Republics and Their Relations to the United States Under the Monroe Doctrine** (2 vols) [1908]. See also the work of Albert Bushnell Hart, Professor of Government at Harvard University. He was in favor of the US retaining the Philippines and vigorously protecting US interests in the Caribbean, and Latin America more generally, as well as in Asia. He characterized the drive across the Pacific and southward into the Caribbean as "inevitable", and as part of the same process which had seen the earlier US absorption of California and Texas insofar as the islands of the Pacific and the Caribbean, like the territories absorbed earlier, were "badly ruled, rich and strategically important". Hart was not entirely happy about having to rule people without their consent; however, strategic and commercial interests were paramount. At the same time he argued that US influence and rule would benefit the locals, regardless of their opposition to it, since ultimately the "general tendency" of US "expansion" was "toward freedom". Albert Bushnell Hart, **The Foundations of American Foreign Policy** [1901]. pp. 51, 169-170. See Albert Bushnell Hart, **The Monroe Doctrine: An Interpretation** [1916]. See Jerald A. Combs, **American Diplomatic History: Two Centuries of Changing Interpretations** [1983]. pp 88-89.

15. See John H. Latané, **The Diplomatic Relations of the United States and Spanish America** [1900] and John H. Latané, **The United States and Latin America** [1920]. pp. 287-288, 318-319. J. Fred Rippy's 1920 review of Latané's book was quite critical for the time. Rippy pointed to inadequate enlargement and revision, especially Latané's failure to use numerous works which related to his topic and had been produced in the intervening twenty years. See the **Hispanic American Historical Review** vol. 3. no. 4. 1920. pp. 571-574. However, Rippy was not challenging the book's central assumptions so much as acting as a representative of the emergent 'Latin American studies' profession and demanding that its author adopt a more professional approach to his work.

16. Combs, **American Diplomatic History** [1983]. pp. 75, 84, 115. John Higham, Leonard Krieger and Felix Gilbert, **History: The Development of Historical Studies in the United States** [1965]. pp. 187-189.

17. Hunt, **Ideology and US Foreign Policy** [1987]. pp. 17-18.

18. Peter Novick, **That Noble Dream: The "Objectivity Question" and the American Historical Profession** [1988]. pp. 72, 80-85. Also see Higham, Krieger and Gilbert, **History** [1965]. pp. 158-160.

19. Warren F. Kuehl, "Webs of Common Interests Revisited: Nationalism, Internationalism, and Historians of American Foreign Relations" **Diplomatic History** vol. 10. no. 2. 1986. pp. 107-108, 111, 113, 117.

20. William Spence Robertson wrote a major book on Spanish American independence, and one on US-Latin American relations. See William Spence Robertson, **The Rise of the Spanish American Republics as Told in the Lives of Their Liberators** [1918] and William Spence Robertson, **Hispanic-American Relations with the United States** [1923].

21. In the late 1940s this situation was criticized by members of the profession itself, although little appears to have come of it. In Lesley Byrd Simpson's view it was "extraordinary" that the main forum for the study of Latin American history in North America "should give such prominence to the correspondence and quarrels of diplomats and state departments". He argued that it was "another instance of

historiography conditioned by the availability of documents". He also expressed concern over the fact that Latin American history as written by North Americans was "in danger of depending upon a premise which we may find it embarrassing to defend, namely, that the importance given to a country varies directly as it affects the interests of the United States". He argued that "such parochialism violate(d) the canons of historiography" insofar as North American historians of Latin America were "trying to piece together the history of Latin America, not that of the United States". See Lesley Byrd Simpson, "Thirty Years of the *Hispanic American Historical Review*" **Hispanic American Historical Review** vol. 29. no. 2. 1949. pp. 192-195.

22. Charles Gibson and Benjamin Keen, "Trends of United States Studies in Latin American History" (1957) in Howard F. Cline, ed., **Latin American History: Essays on Its Study and Teaching 1898-1965** (2 vols.) [1967]. pp. 528, 540-541. R. A. Humphreys, "William Hickling Prescott: The Man and the Historian" in Howard F. Cline, ed., **William Hickling Prescott: A Memorial** [1959].

23. Arthur P. Whitaker, "The Commerce of Louisiana and the Floridas at the End of the Eighteenth Century" **Hispanic American Historical Review** vol. 8. no. 2. 1928. Arthur P. Whitaker, **The Spanish American Frontier 1783-1795: The Westward Movement and the Spanish Retreat in the Mississippi Valley** [1927]. Arthur P. Whitaker, **The Mississippi Question 1795-1803: A Study in Trade, Politics and Diplomacy** [1932]. Arthur P. Whitaker, **The United States and the Independence of Latin America 1800-1830** [1941].

24. One commentator has estimated that between 1920 and 1945 there was an average of only one academic political science article a year on Latin America published in North American scholarly journals, and most of those were in the **Hispanic American Historical Review**, which published thirteen in this period, or in the **American Political Science Review**, which published six. Rosendo A. Gomez, **The Study of Latin American Politics in University Programs in the United States** [1967]. p. 11. John D. Martz, "Political Science and Latin American Studies: Patterns and Asymmetries of Research and Publication" **Latin American Research Review** vol. 25. no. 1. 1990. p. 68. See also Federico G. Gil, "Latin American Studies and Political Science: A Historical Sketch" **LASA Forum** vol. 16. no. 2. 1985. pp. 8-9.

25. The **Hispanic American Historical Review** began publication after Charles E. Chapman, with the encouragement of William Spence Robertson, William R. Shepherd and J. Franklin Jameson (the Managing Editor of the **American Historical Review**), along with "unofficial declarations of interest" from the Pan American Union, the State Department and the Treasury Department, held a meeting to discuss a new Hispanic American History journal at the annual American Historical Association's conference in Cincinnati in December 1916. Following further support from Leo S. Rowe, James A. Robertson, Hiram Bingham, Herbert E. Bolton, Frederick Jackson Turner among others, as well as the written encouragement of Secretary of State Robert Lansing and President Woodrow Wilson, and financial support from Charles E. Chapman, Charles W. Hackett and William R. Shepherd, the **Hispanic American Historical Review** was born and the first issue appeared in February 1918. The first Board of Editors included Charles E. Chapman, Isaac J. Cox and William Spence Robertson, while Herbert E. Bolton and William R. Shepherd were the first advisory editors. Charles E. Chapman, "The Founding of The Review" **Hispanic American Historical Review** vol. 1. no. 1. 1918. pp. 8-23. See "A Letter from President Wilson" **Hispanic American Historical Review** vol. 1. no. 1. 1918. p. 1. The **Hispanic American Historical Review** published regularly for five years (1918-1922), but financial problems led to a halt in publication from 1923 until

1926, when Duke University took over the journal and appointed J. Fred Rippy as the Associate Managing Editor and the University's "permanent representative" on the editorial board. At the time of its reappearance the editors asserted without equivocation that the **Hispanic American Historical Review** was "devoted to no 'ism'" and was "the organ of no special section or group". The editors reconfirmed that the new journal would help "in the drawing together of the intellectual forces of all the Americas", while being of "service to the greatest number possible throughout the Americas", although they adamantly refused to involve the journal in "controversies" of any kind. "Editorial Note" **Hispanic American Historical Review** vol. 6. nos. 1-3. 1926. pp. 1-4.

26. Novick, **That Noble Dream** [1988]. p. 21. On the emergence and role of scientific method and objectivity in structuring twentieth-century North American sociological discourse see Robert C. Bannister, **Sociology and Scientism: The American Quest for Objectivity 1880-1940** [1987]. North American historians of the late nineteenth and early twentieth century, particularly those who had done their higher degrees in Germany, adopted and distorted German historical methodology and made it their own. The North Americanization of the German historical model was particularly obvious in the use of Leopold von Ranke who was regarded as a major "inspirational model". Most German historians viewed Ranke's work as the complete opposite of "nonphilosophical empiricism"; however, North American advocates of scientific history held him up as a model of empiricism and objectivity. The scientific method, which structured the emerging professional discourse of North American historians, was a simplistic inductionism which recommended that the facts speak for themselves. The scientific method was understood to mean that science had to be overwhelmingly empirical and avoid speculation. It had to be "scrupulously neutral on larger questions of end and meaning" and when "systematically pursued, it might ultimately produce a comprehensive, 'definitive' history". Ranke's famous dictum that the goal of the historian was to discover "*wie es eigentlich gewesen*" has usually been translated to mean--"as it really was" or "as it actually was". However, in the nineteenth century, at the time when Ranke used the term, *eigentlich* possessed a double meaning which it has subsequently lost. In Ranke's era it also meant "essentially" and he regarded the main task of the historian as being to "penetrate" to the "essences". Novick, **That Noble Dream** [1988]. pp. 25-38.

27. After 1870, the "first wave" of professional North American historians were convinced that an emphasis on the "facts" and the generation of historical laws were "indissolubly linked." But it was the second wave of professional historians, led by John Franklin Jameson and Frederick Jackson Turner, who were "moved even more strongly than their elders by the desire to attain the modern authority of science" that truly vulgarized Leopold von Ranke. As North Americans it was "easy" for them to turn to a "nominalistic empiricism" founded on "common sense realism". The "second wave" of professional historians were also far more "influenced" by "historicism" than the "first wave". Modern historicism, which conceived of history as "a self-contained and continuous process of qualitative change", did not have much purchase in North America until the end of the nineteenth century. The ability to distinguish between past and future had been curbed by what Ross called "a millennial conception of the American republic in which the past appeared as prologue and the future as fulfillment of America's republican destiny". The second wave historians discarded the "millennial framework" and asserted the difference between past and future opting for a more scientific and empirical approach than their elders. Dorothy Ross, "On the Misunderstanding of Ranke and the Origins of the Historical Profession in America" in Georg G. Iggers and James M. Powell, eds., **Leopold von Ranke and the Shaping of the Historical Discipline** [1990]. pp. 154-157, 162-163, 166-

169. See also Dorothy Ross, **The Origins of American Social Science** [1991].

28. Novick, **That Noble Dream** [1988]. pp. 47-51.

29. The formation of the American Political Science Association (APSA) was a conscious break from the non-disciplinary approach to the social sciences as articulated by the American Social Science Association, which had been established in 1865. But the immediate reason behind the formation of the APSA was the preoccupation, on the part of a number of political scientists, with clearlyly separating themselves from the discipline of history and from its national organization the American Historical Association (1884). APSA's membership rose to 4,000 at the end of World War II. In 1960 there were over 7,000 members and in excess of 14,000 by 1976. See David M. Ricci, **The Tragedy of Political Science: Politics, Scholarship and Democracy** [1984]. pp. 63-64. For the wider context of the emergence of APSA see Ross, **The Origins of American Social Science** [1991]. pp. 257-300. See also Thomas L. Haskell, **The Emergence of Professional Social Science: The American Social Science Association and the Nineteenth-Century Crisis of Authority** [1977].

30. Gil, "Latin American Studies and Political Science" **LASA Forum** 1985. p. 8.

31. James Allen Smith, **The Idea Brokers: Think Tanks and the Rise of the New Policy Elite** [1991]. pp. 271-273, 280-281, 290. Paul Dickson, **Think Tanks** [1971]. pp. 300-304.

32. The British branch became known as the Royal Institute of International Affairs and provided a major focus for the emergence of international relations as a discrete discipline in Britain after 1919. Laurence H. Shoup and William Minter, **Imperial Brain Trust: The Council on Foreign Relations and United States Foreign Policy** [1977]. pp. 11-16.

33. The President of the Rockefeller Foundation is cited in Frank A. Ninkovich, **The Diplomacy of Ideas: US Foreign Policy and Cultural Relations 1938-1950** [1981]. pp. 14-15, 22-23, 187. See also Barbara Howe, "The Emergence of Scientific Philanthropy 1900-1920: Origins, Issues and Outcomes" in Robert F. Arnove, ed., **Philanthropy and Cultural Imperialism: The Foundations at Home and Abroad** [1980]. pp. 27-30.

34. Nicholas Murray Butler, cited in Kuehl, "Webs of Common Interests Revisited" **Diplomatic History** 1986. pp. 108-109. Ninkovich, **The Diplomacy of Ideas** [1981]. pp. 8-14. Howe, "The Emergence of Scientific Philanthropy 1900-1920" in Arnove, ed., **Philanthropy and Cultural Imperialism** [1982].

35. LaFeber, **Inevitable Revolutions** [1984]. p. 41. Ninkovich, **The Diplomacy of Ideas** [1981]. pp. 8-9.

36. Novick, **That Noble Dream** [1988]. pp. 63-68. On the particularly tenuous character of "academic freedom" between the 1880s and 1918, see Ellen W. Schrecker, **No Ivory Tower: McCarthyism and the Universities** [1986]. pp. 12-23.

37. Richard M. Morse, "The Strange Career of 'Latin American Studies'" **The Annals of the American Academy of Political and Social Science** vol. 356. November 1964. p. 111.

38. Rowe was born in 1872, and completed his undergraduate degrees at the University of Pennsylvania in the early 1890s. After two years in Germany he received his PhD from the University of Halle and entered the political science department at the University of Pennsylvania in 1896. By 1904 he was a full professor and department head and continued in that capacity until 1917. During a leave of absence he served on the US government's legal commission in Puerto Rico in 1900 and 1901 and went on

to be chairman of the Puerto Rican Code Commission from 1901 to 1902. From 1915-1917 he served as secretary general of the Inter-American High Commission. With the US entry into World War I in 1917 he moved into government service completely, working as Assistant Secretary of the US Treasury from 1917 to 1919, during which time he devoted considerable attention to Latin America's economic and financial "problems", and as Chief of the State Department's Latin American Division from November 1919 to September 1920. In the 1920s, 1930s and early 1940s, Rowe represented the United States government at numerous Pan American and Inter-American conferences in his capacity as Director General of the Pan-American Union from 1920 until his death on 5 December 1946. Roscoe R. Hill, "Leo S. Rowe" **Hispanic American Historical Review** vol. 27. no. 2. 1947. pp. 187-188.

    39. Leo S. Rowe, **The United States and Porto Rico: With Special Reference to the Problems Arising Out of Our Contact with the Spanish-American Civilization** [1904]. pp. vii, xi-xiv, 10-13, 17-19, 261.

    40. Michael Adas, **Machines as the Measure of Men: Science, Technology and Ideologies of Western Dominance** [1989]. pp. 133-401.

    41. Jules R. Benjamin, "The Framework of US Relations with Latin America in the Twentieth Century: An Interpretive Essay" **Diplomatic History** vol. 11. no. 2. 1987. p. 94. On the relationship between US policy towards and perceptions of Indians in North America and Washington's approach to the circum-Caribbean and Latin America see Fredrick B. Pike, **The United States and Latin America: Myths and Stereotypes of Civilization and Nature** [1992]. pp. 86-112, 155-192.

    42. Donald W. White, "History and American Internationalism: The Formulation from the Past After World War II" **The Pacific Historical Review** vol. 58. no. 2. 1989. pp. 147-148.

    43. On North American attitudes in relation to Central America and the Caribbean in this period, see David Healy, **Drive to Hegemony: The United States in the Caribbean 1898-1917** [1988]. pp. 58-76, 287-290. Hunt, **Ideology and US Foreign Policy** [1987]. 58-62, 127, 131-132.

    44. Benjamin, "The Framework of US Relations with Latin America in the Twentieth Century" **Diplomatic History** 1987. pp. 97-98. On the relationship between reform Darwinism, progressivism and imperialism, see Robert C. Bannister, **Social Darwinism: Science and Myth in Anglo American Social Thought** [1988]. pp. 226-242.

    45. Benjamin, The Framework of US Relations with Latin America in the Twentieth Century" **Diplomatic History** 1987. p. 98.

    46. An important contemporary of Munro was the academic and diplomat Chester Lloyd Jones. He also wrote about US relations with Central America and the Caribbean in this period. Like Munro he spent almost a decade working directly for the State Department; however, unlike Munro and others who took a more conventional diplomatic history and political relations approach, Jones focused on the commercial aspect of US relations with the circum-Caribbean. At the same time, he emphasized the exceptional character of US politico-military and economic expansion and its anti-imperialism, as evidenced by the Monroe Doctrine, which he viewed as an increasingly economic as well as a political policy. Jones did not see the US as anti-imperial just in the western hemisphere, but around the world. For example, he emphasized the anti-imperial role of the United States's 'Open Door' policy in China. See Chester Lloyd Jones, **Caribbean Interests of the United States** [1916]. p. 2. Chester Lloyd Jones, **The Caribbean Since 1900** [1936]. p. 462. Jones completed his PhD at the University of Pennsylvania in 1906. From 1906 to 1910 he worked as an instructor in political science at the University of Pennsylvania. In 1910 he took up the post of Professor of Political Science and Commerce at the University of

Wisconsin, remaining there until 1920. During the 1920s he worked for the US State Department serving as the commercial attaché at the US Embassy in Madrid Spain. He then worked at the US Legation in Havana in 1921 and 1922 and was subsequently posted to the US Embassy in Paris from 1922 to 1927. He served as an adviser at the Pan American Conference in Havana in 1928 and as the US Department of Commerce's special representative in Mexico in that year. In 1929 he returned to the University of Wisconsin, taking up the post of Professor of Economics until his death in 1941. See Chester Lloyd Jones, "The Development of the Caribbean" in Chester Lloyd Jones, Henry Kittredge Norton and Parker Thomas Moon, **The United States and the Caribbean** [1929]. Chester Lloyd Jones, **Caribbean Background and Prospects** [1931]. Chester Lloyd Jones, **Costa Rica and Civilization in the Caribbean** [1935]. Chester Lloyd Jones, **Guatemala: Past and Present** [1940]. See also Chester Lloyd Jones, **Mexico and Its Reconstruction** [1921].

47. Munro was born in Providence, Rhode Island, in 1892. He studied for a bachelor's degree in arts at Brown University and then went to the University of Wisconsin for a year, completing a second bachelor of arts degree. Richard V. Salisbury, "Good Neighbors?: The United States and Latin America in the Twentieth Century" in Gerald K. Haines and J. Samuel Walker, eds., **American Foreign Relations: A Historiographical Review** [1981]. pp. 316-317. Griffith, "The Historiography of Central America Since 1830" **Hispanic American Historical Review** 1960. p. 552. Ninkovich, **The Diplomacy of Ideas** [1981]. p. 12.

48. Munro, **A Student in Central America 1914-1916** [1983]. p. xi.

49. Dana Gardner Munro, **The Five Republics of Central America: Their Political and Economic Development and Their Relations with the United States** [1918]. This is the published version of his 1917 University of Pennsylvania PhD dissertation.

50. See Johnson, "One Hundred Years of Historical Writing on Modern Latin America by United States Historians" **Hispanic American Historical Review** 1985. p. 746.

51. Both Richard Salisbury and William Griffith described Munro's 1918 book as a "standard work". See Salisbury, "Good Neighbors?: The United States and Latin America in the Twentieth Century" in Haines and Walker, eds., **American Foreign Relations** [1981]. pp. 316-317. Griffith, "The Historiography of Central America Since 1830" **Hispanic American Historical Review** 1960. p. 552.

52. See Munro, **A Student in Central America 1914-1916** [1983]. p. ix. Elsewhere Woodward has argued that Munro's later books provide "excellent coverage of Central America". See Woodward, **Central America** [1985]. pp. 338-339. This view has been echoed by Lester D. Langley who noted that Munro's more recent work was particularly important and useful for his own work. Lester D. Langley, **The United States and the Caribbean in the Twentieth Century** [1982]. p. ix.

53. Of course, not all North American writers still profess respect for Munro, and even in the 1920s and 1930s his work came under fire from some quarters. Writing in the 1930s, Carleton Beals argued that **The Five Republics of Central America** had been published by the Carnegie Endowment for International Peace, two decades earlier, as part of an effort to advance an "interventionist" policy line. Carleton Beals, **The Coming Struggle for Latin America** [1937]. pp. 212-216. cited in John A. Britton, **Carleton Beals: A Radical Journalist in Latin America** [1987]. pp. 155, 268.

54. Munro, **The Five Republics of Central America** [1918]. pp. xiii-xiv, 183, 185, 191-192, 196-198. Munro's work still relied on reductionist national and racial images. Munro characterized the majority of Guatemalans as "docile and ignorant pure-blooded Indians" who had "never shown any liking or capacity for war"

and had "a deep-rooted respect and fear" of authority. And it was because of this that it was far harder to shape them into a "revolutionary army" than "the turbulent half-breeds" of the other republics of Central America. The "half-breed", or ladino, was characterized elsewhere as "intelligent but unstable" and "little inclined to steady manual or intellectual labor". For this reason many of them, according to Munro, sought "wealth and influence" through "the pursuit of politics"; however, they still "played a less prominent part in affairs than the members of the white aristocracy". He characterized "the people" of El Salvador as "fairly industrious considering the climate", while the citizens of Honduras were "naturally quick and intelligent". According to Munro the early Spanish settlers of what was to become Costa Rica "sank into a state of dense ignorance and were forced to adopt most primitive ways of living", but they eventually "acquired industrious habits which still distinguished them from their neighbors". Munro attributed this, in part, to the fact that "the majority of the people of Costa Rica" were believed to be descendants of the *Gallegos*, "one of the most law-abiding and hard-working of the numerous races that occupy the Iberian Peninsula, while those of the other countries are predominantly Andalusian". However, lamented Munro, the Pacific Coast of Costa Rica was "sparsely inhabited by an unprogressive race who are largely of Indian descent". Munro, **The Five Republics of Central America** [1918]. pp. 57-58, 60 62-64, 100-101, 131, 138, 140-141, 195. The emergence of a more democratic social structure in Costa Rica was not linked to race but to the historical scarcity of land, labor, and capital in the southern part of the isthmus, in contrast to the other republics. Samuel Z. Stone, **The Heritage of the Conquistadors: Ruling Classes in Central America from Conquest to the Sandinistas** [1990]. pp. 1-28.

55. When Munro was posted to Haiti in 1930 as US Minister (Ambassador), North American-Haitian relations on the island were plagued by racial tension. After his arrival Munro made a point of not becoming a member of the American Club in Port-au-Prince, which was a segregated club. This and other efforts on the part of Munro and the US military commander, Colonel Louis McCarty, were thought to have improved relations somewhat. Hans Schmidt, **The United States Occupation of Haiti 1915-1934** [1971]. p. 220.

56. Dana Gardner Munro, **The Five Republics of Central America** [1918]. pp. xiii-xiv, 204-206, 304-305, 316-319.

57.Salisbury, "Good Neighbors?: The United States and Latin America in the Twentieth Century" in Haines and Walker, eds., **American Foreign Relations** [1981]. pp. 316-317. Griffith, "The Historiography of Central America Since 1830" **Hispanic American Historical Review** 1960. p. 552. Munro, **The United States and the Caribbean Republics 1921-1933** [1974]. p. ix.

58. Walter LaFeber, **The American Age: United States Foreign Policy at Home and Abroad Since 1750** [1989]. pp. 341-342.

59. Robert D. Schulzinger, **The Wise Men of Foreign Affairs: The History of the Council on Foreign Relations** [1984]. pp. 28-29, 255, 266-267. William Shepherd contributed funds to the initial **Hispanic American Historical Review** project, served on the **Hispanic American Historical Review**'s Committee of Organization in the year prior to the appearance of the first issue, and he and Herbert E. Bolton acted as the journal's first two advisory editors. At the same time, from 1921-1927, before he became chair of the Council on Foreign Relations' Committee on Latin American Affairs, Shepherd served as one of the Council's directors. Charles E. Chapman, "The Founding of the Review" **Hispanic American Historical Review** vol. 1. no. 1. 1918. pp. 11, 14, 16, 19. Schulzinger, **The Wise Men of Foreign Affairs** [1984]. pp. 28-29, 255.

60. Schulzinger, **The Wise Men of Foreign Affairs** [1984]. pp. 29-31, 267. The Council's support for US policy in the region was also reflected in the

1929 publication of **American Relations in the Caribbean**, by Charles P. Howland, a research associate in government at Yale University and director of research for the Council of Foreign Relations. This was the first part of what became the Council's annual **Survey of American Foreign Relations**. Over half of the Caribbean section was devoted to Central America, especially Nicaragua. Charles P. Howland, **American Relations in the Caribbean: A Preliminary Issue of Section I of the Annual Survey of American Foreign Relations 1929** [1929]. Kuehl, "Webs of Common Interests Revisited" **Diplomatic History 1986.** p. 111. With the Depression in the 1930s, the Council itself began to suffer financially. At the same time, the New York bankers in the Council, and there were a number of them, were seriously affected by the Depression, and their Latin American loans were almost all defaulted on by the debtor governments in the region. The Council on Foreign Relations' weakened financial position made it less influential with the US government and the North American public, while the bankers launched more direct initiatives and established bondholders' protective committees to lobby Washington and assist in the recovery of their investment. Throughout the 1930s the Council's total membership remained stagnant at approximately 500, despite efforts to recruit new members. In the 1920s the Rockefeller and Carnegie foundations had been lavish financial backers; however, following the Depression they curtailed their financial support and began to give more money to the Institute of Pacific Relations and the Foreign Policy Association. Schulzinger, **The Wise Men of Foreign Affairs** [1984]. pp. 30-31.

61. George T. Weitzel, "The United States and Central America--Policy of Clay and Knox" **The Annals of the American Academy of Political and Social Science** vol. 132. July 1927. Victor M. Cutter, "Relations of United States Companies with Latin America" **The Annals of the American Academy of Political and Social Science** vol. 132. July 1927. H. W. Dodds, "The United States and Nicaragua" **The Annals of the American Academy of Political and Social Science** vol. 132. July 1927. William R. Shepherd, "The Reconciliation of Fact with Sentiment in Our Dealings with Latin America" **The Annals of the American Academy of Political and Social Science** vol. 132. July 1927. C. H. Haring, "South America and Our Policy in the Caribbean" **The Annals of the American Academy of Political and Social Science** vol. 132. July 1927. Whiting Williams, "Geographic Determinism in Nicaragua" **The Annals of the American Academy of Political and Social Science** vol. 132. July 1927. Wallace Thompson, "The Doctrine of the 'Special Interest' of the United States in the Region of the Caribbean Sea" **The Annals of the American Academy of Political and Social Science** vol. 132. July 1927. The growing interest in Nicaragua and Central America and the Caribbean more generally was also reflected in the contributions to the **Hispanic American Historical Review** in the late 1920s. See Charles E. Chapman, "The United States and the Dominican Republic" **Hispanic American Historical Review** vol. 7. no. 1. 1927. Charles E. Chapman, "The Development of the Intervention in Haiti" **Hispanic American Historical Review** vol. 7. no. 3. 1927. Anna I. Powell, "Relations Between the United States and Nicaragua, 1898-1916" **Hispanic American Historical Review** vol. 8. no. 1. 1928. Joseph B. Lockey of the University of California (Los Angeles) explored the early relations of the US with Central America. See Joseph B. Lockey, "Diplomatic Futility" **Hispanic American Historical Review** vol. 10. no. 3. 1930.

62. See **Hispanic American Historical Review** vol. 9. no. 2. 1929. pp. 224-230. Leland H. Jenks, **Our Cuban Colony** [1928]. Melvin M. Knight, **The Americans in Santo Domingo** [1928].

63. Chapman's book on Cuba, which was published in 1927, had been

encouraged by the State Department and the funding for the project, which was provided by the Carnegie Foundation, was organized by Enoch H. Crowder, who was then US Minister (Ambassador) to Cuba. Louis A. Pérez, Jr., "Intervention, Hegemony, and Dependency: The United States in the Circum-Caribbean 1898-1980" **Pacific Historical Review** vol. 51. no. 2. 1982. pp. 171-172. See Charles E. Chapman, **A History of the Cuban Republic** [1927]. Louis A. Pérez, Jr., "Scholarship and the State: Notes on 'A History of the Cuban Republic'" **Hispanic American Historical Review** vol. 54. no. 4. 1974. pp. 682-690.

64. **Hispanic American Historical Review** vol. 9. no. 1. 1929. pp. 99-103.

65. Henry L. Stimson, "Future Philippine Policy Under the Jones Act" **Foreign Affairs** vol. 5 no. 4. 1927. Henry L. Stimson, "Bases of American Foreign Policy During the Past Four Years" **Foreign Affairs** vol. 11. no. 4. 1933. Henry L. Stimson, **The Far Eastern Crisis: Recollections and Observations** [1936]. On Stimson see Godfrey Hodgson, **The Colonel: The Life and Wars of Henry Stimson 1867-1950** [1990]. See also Larry G. Gerber, **The Limits of Liberalism: Josephus Daniels, Henry Stimson, Bernard Baruch, Donald Richberg, Felix Frankfurter and the Development of the Modern American Political Economy** [1984].

66. Stimson relied heavily on Dana Munro's **The Five Republics of Central America** for both historical background and analysis. Following Munro, he pointed to racial and geographic differences between Nicaragua and the US to help understand relations between the two countries. He also emphasized historical differences, by which he meant primarily cultural differences, focusing on the Spanish colonial heritage. In his view the "central cause" of the collapse of "popular government" in Nicaragua and elsewhere in the region was the "failure" of the people to manage "the system of popular election". Because the voters were mainly illiterate, and because the Indians "occupied a position" resembling serfdom or slavery, the "results of the elections" in all the republics of Central America were completely dominated by those individuals who "controlled" the "machinery of government"--the military and the police. He also lamented that the central government had too much power and there was, as a result, a very limited amount of "local self-government", which he eulogized as "that great school of democracy". Henry L. Stimson, **American Policy in Nicaragua** [1927]. pp. 1, 4-5, 7-9, 92-102.

67. Stimson, **American Policy in Nicaragua** [1927]. pp. 120-126.

68. Roscoe R. Hill was born in Illinois in 1880. In 1904 he went to Cuba as director of the American School in Matanzas. After half a dozen years in Cuba he returned to the US and studied history at the University of Chicago and Columbia University in New York. From 1913 to 1915 he worked as a history instructor at Columbia. From 1915 until 1919 he taught history at the University of New Mexico and worked as President of the Spanish American Normal School of New Mexico. In 1920 he entered government service as a regional economist for Latin America in the Office of the Foreign Trade Adviser at the State Department. He was soon appointed commissioner of the Nicaraguan High Commission, a post he occupied from 1920 to 1928. From 1928 to 1930 he worked at the Library of Congress. He continued to serve as a member of the Inter-American High Commission's Nicaraguan Group, while working on his doctoral dissertation at Columbia under the supervision of political scientist William R. Shepherd. Hill received his PhD in 1933, and in that year he took up the post of assistant chief of the Manuscript Division of the Library of Congress and held that position until 1935. From 1935 until 1941 he served as chief of the Classification Division of the National Archives. Hill then took up the post of chief of the State Department Archives in the National Archives in Washington until his retirement in December 1946. Hill, who died in 1960, was closely associated with the

Hispanic American Historical Review for much of his career, serving on the board of editors from the mid-1930s to 1947 and holding the post of Associate for Archives from 1951 to 1953. Manoel Cardozo, "Roscoe R. Hill" **Hispanic American Historical Review** vol. 27. no. 1 1947. pp. 170-173. Hill wrote one of the **Hispanic American Historical Review's** articles on Nicaragua in the pre-1959 era and also contributed a number of articles on "archivology" in the early 1950s as well as being the author of the "standard work" on Latin American archives. See Roscoe R. Hill, "The Nicaraguan Canal Idea to 1913" **Hispanic American Historical Review** vol. 28. no. 2. 1948. See Roscoe R. Hill, **The National Archives of Latin America** [1945].

69. Roscoe R. Hill, **Fiscal Intervention in Nicaragua** [1933]. p. v. Ralph Lee Woodward, Jr., described Hill's book as having been written from "the bankers' point of view". See Woodward, **Central America** [1985]. p. 340.

70. Cox held a fellowship in American History at the University of Pennsylvania from 1902 until 1904, receiving his PhD in that year. Cox was one of the founders of the **Hispanic American Historical Review**, a member of the journal's first board of editors, and a professor of history at Northwestern University for much of his career. He served as an advisory editor for the **Hispanic American Historical Review** from 1934-1955, to which he had already contributed a couple of articles by the early 1930s. He taught in the history department at the University of Cincinnati from 1904 until 1919 when he took up the post of professor of history at Northwestern University, becoming professor emeritus at Northwestern in 1941. He died in October 1956. Harris Gaylord Warren, "Isaac Joslin Cox 1873-1956" **Hispanic American Historical Review** vol. 37. no. 1. 1957. pp. 138-139. Charles Gibson, ed., **Guide to the Hispanic American Historical Review 1946-1955** [1958]. p. 172. Like a number of other North American Latin Americanists in this era, such as Charles Wilson Hackett and Arthur Preston Whitaker, he gained his reputation (and gravitated to diplomatic history and the history of inter-American relations) via his interest in and work on the history of the Spanish borderlands. See Isaac Joslin Cox, **The Early Exploration of Louisiana** [1906]. Isaac Joslin Cox, **The West Florida Controversy 1798-1813: A Study in American Diplomacy** [1918]. See Charles Wilson Hackett, **The Mexican Revolution and the United States 1910-1926** [1926].

71. Isaac Joslin Cox, **Nicaragua and the United States 1909-1927** [1927]. pp. 703, 738, 808. It was reviewed in 1928 in the pages of the **Hispanic American Historical Review** by Alfred Hasbrouck, who heaped praise on Cox and his book. He characterized it as the "work of a trained historian who tells the whole story in an impartial manner giving credit or blame to both sides whenever it becomes due, but generally stating the facts and leaving the reader to form his own conclusions". The book was further eulogized as "extremely accurate" and its author, who was described as both a "straight thinker" and "an impartial historian", was fulsomely praised for telling the "difficult and complicated story of political and financial intrigue in a vivid and interesting way". **Hispanic American Historical Review** vol. 9. no. 1. 1929. pp. 99-100. Ralph Lee Woodward, Jr., has characterized Stimson and Cox's books as "carefully written defenses of US policy". See Woodward, **Central America** [1985]. p. 340.

72. Harold Norman Denny, **Dollars for Bullets: The Story of American Rule in Nicaragua** [1929]. Other work on Central America generally, and US policy in Nicaragua more specifically, which was relatively sympathetic to Washington included a 1928 travel book by the veteran war correspondent Arthur Ruhl. He characterized the differences between the US and Central America as primarily cultural and psychological, and he was confident that the differences could be overcome with diplomacy. At the same time he argued that the US should have re-intervened more

quickly in Nicaragua following the return to civil war after the withdrawal of the
Marines in 1925. He was very sympathetic to Henry Stimson, describing him as an
"altruistic American" of "first rate ability" who took a "definite and authoritative
stand" in 1927 which "was undoubtedly refreshing to the Nicaraguans". On the
question of "dollar diplomacy" he criticized the view that "some vague 'Wall Street'"
was responsible for Nicaragua's "ills". His refutation of this interpretation was based
on what Ruhl called Dana Munro's "common sense" view that the limited amount of
money made by Brown Brothers and Seligman and Company clearly suggested that
their motives were not avariciously pecuniary. He invoked a sort of innocent-abroad
theme when he argued that the United States' "faults" in its treatment of Nicaragua,
Central America, and the Caribbean generally, stemmed more from a "lack of policy"
than from the policy that existed. According to Ruhl the US had conducted itself badly
on occasion because of "ignorance and ineptitude", not because of "malice or
unfriendliness". In his view this could be rectified if the US established a "suitable
colonial office" to deal with Washington's growing number of colonies and
dependencies. Arthur Ruhl, **The Central Americans: Adventures and
Impressions Between Mexico and Panama** [1928]. pp. 86-90, 105-110.
Other books which were more straightforward travelogues included: Rhys Carpenter,
The Land Beyond Mexico [1920]. Eugene Cunningham, **Gypsing Through
Central America** [1922]. Frank G. Carpenter, **Lands of the Caribbean: The
Canal Zone, Panama, Costa Rica, Nicaragua, Salvador, Honduras,
Guatemala, Cuba, Jamaica, Haiti, Santo Domingo, Porto Rico, and
the Virgin Islands** [1925]. Wallace Thompson, **Rainbow Countries of
Central America** [1926]. Thomas W. Gann, **Discoveries and Adventures in
Central America** [1929].

     73. J. Fred Rippy, **The Caribbean Danger Zone** [1940]. p. 274.

     74. Carleton Beals, **Banana Gold** [1932]. p. 305.

     75. Denny, **Dollars for Bullets** [1929]. pp. i-ii., 400.

     76. Buell received his MA in 1920 and his PhD in 1923 from Princeton
University. He worked as an instructor and then assistant professor in government at
Harvard from 1922 to 1927. In the late 1920s and early 1930s, he worked briefly at
Columbia University, the University of California, Yale, and Princeton, as well as the
New School of Social Research in New York. Buell became president of the Foreign
Policy Association in 1933 and continued in that position until 1939. In 1934 he
served as the chairman of the Commission on Cuba Affairs. He was also a member of
American Political Science Association and the Council on Foreign Relations. His last
book was a study of Liberia on the occasion of its centenary as an 'independent'
republic. See Raymond Leslie Buell, **Liberia: Century of Survival** [1947].

     77. The Association's research and education work was premised on the
assumption that the US was inextricably linked to the wider world and its problems,
that there was a need for greater international understanding, and that social scientists
could contribute to this by careful and scientific study, and then make their findings
known to the general public, who would influence policy in a constructive direction.
Kuehl, "Webs of Common Interests Revisited" **Diplomatic History** 1986. pp.
108-110.

     78. Buell praised the United Fruit Company as both the "largest and certainly
the best employer of labor" in Central America, concluding that overall foreign
business and investment had "bestowed a large number of material benefits" on the
region. He asserted that it had improved the region's communications network,
encouraged economic development, provided thousands of jobs, increased government
tax revenues as well as teaching the "native population something of modern industrial
methods and hygiene". At the same time, he warned that, despite the catalogue of
benefits, the "disputes in Central America over foreign capital will increase rather than

diminish". Under these circumstances he advocated that foreign capitalists in Central America pursue a policy of "enlightened self-interest", arguing that there were "a number of gestures which foreign enterprise might make which would increase its popularity". Raymond Leslie Buell, **The Central Americas** [New York: Foreign Policy Association, 1930]. pp. 3-4, 10, 12, 16-17, 22-23.

    79. Buell, **The Central Americas** [1930]. pp. 27-31. Similar themes were pursued in a 1931 article by Buell, in which he welcomed the trend in US foreign policy away from intervention. He argued that the dramatic increase in US naval and military power in the past three decades and emergence of international organizations such as the World Court ensured the protection of US "security" interests in the region and meant the US no longer had any need to follow a policy of "preventive intervention" in Central America and the Caribbean. See Raymond Leslie Buell, "Changes in Our Latin American Policy" **The Annals of the American Academy of Political and Social Science** vol. 156. July 1931. pp. 126, 131-132. See also Raymond Leslie Buell, "The United States and Central American Stability" **Foreign Policy Reports** vol. 7. no. 9. 1931. Raymond Leslie Buell, "The United States and Central American Revolutions" **Foreign Policy Reports** vol. 7. no. 10. 1931. In 1933 an article by Buell, which appeared in **Foreign Affairs**, underlined the politico-strategic importance of Central America in US foreign policy insofar as an "accident of geography" had placed them close to the Panama Canal. He argued that the "maintenance of the 'independence'" of the Central American republics was in Washington's "vital interest". He invoked the hegemonic presumption, and even an imperial imperative, when he asserted that Central America had "much the same political importance" for the US that Egypt had in the British Empire and Manchuria had for Japan. In this article Buell again raised the issue of a Central American Union as a solution to political instability and economic stagnation. He again emphasized, as he had three years earlier, that "a magnificent impetus to Central American union" would be revision of the Bryan-Chamorro treaty, eliminating all those provisions which related to naval bases, and transforming it into an "agreement" between Washington and all five republics of Central America. He also recommended that the US "lend its influence" to "debt consolidation" and the raising of "new funds to construct desirable public works". Buell conceded that "serious difficulties" continued to plague the movement for Central American Union; however, he insisted that the major alternatives to Union, the US policies of non-recognition and no-revolution, "besides being of dubious legal validity, have a sterile, negative character which have often accentuated destructive dictatorship on the one hand and chronic disorder on the other." He concluded that, following the expiration of the Central American treaties of 1923, in 1934 "the only wise course" for the Central American republics to pursue was "not to denounce these agreements entirely, but to remould them in the light of the unionist ideal" and, to facilitate that goal, the US "should extend every legitimate aid". Raymond Leslie Buell, "Union or Disunion in Central America" **Foreign Affairs** vol. 11. no. 3. 1933. pp. 478, 488-489.

    80. LaFeber, **Inevitable Revolutions** [1984]. pp. 61-69, 79-80. LaFeber, **The American Age** [1989]. pp. 339-344. Keylor, **The Twentieth Century World** [1992]. p. 211.

    81. Dana G. Munro, "The Establishment of Peace in Nicaragua" **Foreign Affairs** vol. 11. no. 4. 1933. pp. 704-705.

    82. Dana Munro, **The United States and the Caribbean Area** [1934]. pp. 201-206, 216, 225-226.

    83. Lawrence Dennis, a former US government official who had served in Nicaragua, developed a sympathetic but critical position on US foreign policy in Nicaragua in particular, and Latin America in general, in the pages of **Foreign Affairs** in 1931. Dennis, who had fascist sympathies, was an isolationist; however,

his critique of US policy in Nicaragua was premised mainly on a 'limits of power' argument which doubted the ability of the US to achieve its goals by continuing the occupation. See Lawrence Dennis, "Revolution, Recognition and Intervention" **Foreign Affairs** vol. 9. no. 2. 1931. Lawrence Dennis, "Nicaragua: In Again, Out Again" **Foreign Affairs** vol. 9. no. 3. 1931.

84. Dexter Perkins, "Bringing the Monroe Doctrine up to Date" **Foreign Affairs** vol. 20. no. 2. 1942. p. 261.

85. Combs, **American Diplomatic History** [1983]. pp. 188-189.

86. Beals's perspective was often at odds with the editorial outlook of the majority of North American magazines, newspapers and publishers and with the "preconceptions" of the North American readership. Britton, **Carleton Beals** [1987]. pp. 2-5. While still a student at the University of California (Berkeley), Beals was an admirer of the famous socialist Eugene Debs. Debs' commitment to the farmers and workers of North America in the face of the inequitable and rigid class structure which industrialization was bringing to the United States was shared by Beals, who carried that commitment to Central and South America, where the "masses" were not only struggling against the captains of industry and the onslaught of industrialization but against agrarian feudalism. While Beals's experiences in Latin America exposed him to new types of resistance and rebellion, his "Debsian left-wing populism" continued to shape his outlook. Britton, **Carleton Beals** [1987]. pp. 8-9, 12-13.

87. The overall perspective taken in the articles he produced on Mexico in the early 1920s has been compared to the approach found in the work of John Reed and John Kenneth Turner, who wrote about Mexico a decade earlier. Britton, **Carleton Beals** [1987]. pp. 14-15, 18-23. John Reed, **Insurgent Mexico** [1914]. John Kenneth Turner, **Barbarous Mexico** [1911].

88. Carleton Beals, **Mexico: An Interpretation** (1923). Carleton Beals, **Brimston and Chili** [1927]. Carleton Beals, **Mexican Maze** [1931]. Carleton Beals, **Porfirio Diaz: Dictator of Mexico** [1932]. Carleton Beals, **Glass Houses** [1938]. He also wrote a novel about life in the Mexican oil fields. Carleton Beals, **Black River** [1934]. He wrote three other novels during his career. Carleton Beals, **Destroying Victor** [1929]. Carleton Beals, **The Stones Awake** [1936]. Beals' last novel was the most successful financially, but unlike the other three was virtually devoid of social or political comment. See Carleton Beals, **Dawn Over the Amazon** [1943]. Britton, **Carleton Beals** [1987]. pp. 197-198.

89. Britton, **Carleton Beals** [1987]. pp. 30-31, 37. Ernest H. Gruening, **México and Its Heritage** [1928]. Frank Tannenbaum, **The Mexican Agrarian Revolution** [1928]. Frank Tannenbaum, **Peace by Revolution: An Interpretation of Mexico** [1933]. Frank Tannenbaum, **Mexico: The Struggle for Peace and Bread** [1950]. Although Tannenbaum gained significant influence by the 1930s as a Mexico specialist, he did not achieve his position of leadership in the professional study of Latin America, and his work was not clearly situated in the dominant professional discourses on Latin America, until the years after 1945, by which time his writing no longer reflected the radicalism of his early years. Tannenbaum, who was born in Eastern Europe in 1893 and arrived in the United States in 1905, spent his formative years (as well as much of his adult life) in New York City, where he was involved with the Industrial Workers of the World prior to the First World War. He graduated from Columbia College in 1921 and then spent three years travelling around Mexico working as a journalist for **Survey**. He gained his PhD in economics in 1927 (his thesis was on Mexican land reform) at the Brookings Institution in Washington. For the rest of the 1920s he worked at the Brookings Institution on a social and economic survey of Puerto Rico. In 1931 he returned to Mexico to work on a survey of rural education for the Mexican government, and then went on to the rest of Latin America to travel for two years on a fellowship from the

New York-based John Simon Guggenheim Foundation. In 1935-36, following brief periods of teaching at Yale and Cornell, Tannenbaum gained a position as a lecturer at Columbia University. By 1945 he had become Professor of Latin American History at Columbia, a post he held until he retired in 1961. Although Tannenbaum wrote on a wide range of topics, he was first and foremost a Mexico specialist. Like Charles Beard and other progressives, Tannenbaum took an approach structured by some version of North American exceptionalism, and as the Cold War unfolded his work increasingly emphasized the exceptionalism of North American history and US foreign policy, and the positive impact the US could have on Latin America. Tannenbaum's teaching and writing also pointed to his interest in an "interdisciplinary approach" to the study of Latin America, and he was the major force behind the University Seminar Program at Columbia University after World War II. Using the seminar program to emphasize an interdisciplinary approach, and to focus learning and knowledge on specific problems, Tannenbaum hoped to integrate the "practical world" with "the university". Stanley R. Ross, "Frank Tannebaum 1893-1969" **Hispanic American Historical Review** vol. 40. no. 2. 1970. pp. 345-347. Helen Delpar, "Frank Tannenbaum: The Making of a Mexicanist, 1914-1933" **The Americas: A Quarterly Review of Inter-American Cultural History** vol. 65. no. 2. 1988. pp. 153-171. On Beals and Tannenbaum, see also Jefferson R. Cowie, **The Emergence of Alternative Views of Latin America: The Thought of Three US Intellectuals, 1920-1935** [1992]. Frank Tannenbaum, **Slave and Citizen: The Negro in the Americas** [1947]. Frank Tannenbaum, **The American Tradition in Foreign Policy** [1955]. Frank Tannenbaum, **Ten Keys to Latin America** [1962].

90. Carleton Beals, **Banana Gold** [1932]. pp. 117-118, 120-123, 286, 294-296.

91. Beals, **Banana Gold** [1932]. pp. 102-103. In the 1930s Carleton Beals continued to write about Latin America, although his focus moved even further south, and he developed a particular interest in Peru. By 1938, Beals's attention, like that of most North American journalists, had turned to the looming war in Europe and Asia. There was a growing interest in North America for information on the rise and expansion of Nazi Germany, fascist Italy and imperial Japan. In relation to Latin America there was growing concern about the "influence" of the Axis powers in the region. As a recognized expert on Latin America, Beals was well placed to address this question. In late 1938 he published a book which bordered on the sensationalist, but overall alleviated concerns about German and Japanese influence in the Western Hemisphere, rather than fueling them. See Britton, **Carleton Beals**. [1987]. pp. 166-189. See Carleton Beals, **The Coming Struggle for Latin America** [1938]. While **The Coming Struggle for Latin America** articulated an anti-fascism similar to the anti-fascism of the North American Communists in the post-1935 popular-front era, Beals' work continued to reflect a distrust of Stalin, Trotsky and the Communist movement as a whole. At the same time, he continued to adopt a critical position with regard to Roosevelt's Latin American policy and the New Deal, despite the reforms which had been undertaken, and he was unwilling to subordinate the need for land reform, trade unions and greater economic sovereignty in Latin America to the calls for unity against the fascist threat emanating from North American radicals. Britton, **Carleton Beals** [1987]. pp. 193-194. In the Cold War era, Beals found that his emphasis on the prospects for radical economic and social change and his criticism of US policy meant that newspapers and publishers were unwilling to publish his work. In the 1950s he turned to writing text books and local histories because he had so much trouble getting his articles and his books published. Even then his local history of Bristol, Connecticut, which was hardly controversial, drew the attention of the FBI, who then began a secret investigation which, after finding that

although he had been affiliated with Left and Communist groups he had never been a CPUSA member, decided the case should not be pursued further. In mid-1955, after reading one of Beal's articles on Guatemala, which had presented an unfavorable portrait of Castillo Armas, vice president Richard Nixon, asked the FBI to start another investigation; however, after being made aware of the result of their earlier findings, Nixon did not press the issue. Britton, **Carleton Beals** [1987]. pp. 201-209.

92. Schrecker, **No Ivory Tower** [1986]. pp. 19-20. Novick, **That Noble Dream** [1988]. p. 64. Nearing wrote one of the few major books opposed to US entry into World War I; however, his views had been marginal before 1917, and after the US joined the war most North American academics were eager for many years to write books which supported US involvement. Combs, **American Diplomatic History** [1983]. p. 93.

93. Schrecker, **No Ivory Tower** [1986]. pp. 26-27. Scott Nearing, **The Making of a Radical: A Political Autobiography** [1972]. pp. 145-154. Scott Nearing, **The Twilight of Empire: An Economic Interpretation of Imperialist Cycles** [1930].

94. Scott Nearing, **The American Empire** [1921]. Scott Nearing, **The Tragedy of Empire** [1945].

95. Scott Nearing and Joseph Freeman, **Dollar Diplomacy: A Study in American Imperialism** [1925]. Joseph Freeman was born in the Ukraine in 1897 and arrived in the US in 1904, eventually becoming a US citizen in 1920. He completed a bachelor of arts degree at Columbia University in 1919 and went on to pursue a career as a journalist, editor and political activist. In 1920 he worked for the **Chicago Tribune** in Paris, becoming the **Chicago Tribune** and London correspondent of the **New York Daily News** in 1921. In 1922-1923 he became the assistant editor of **The Liberator** in New York, and in 1924 he worked as the publicity director for the American Civil Liberties Union. From the mid-1920s to the early 1930s, he was the New York correspondent for the Soviet Telegraph Agency. In the same period he was co-founder and editor in 1926 of **New Masses**, going on to serve as the paper's Moscow correspondent in 1926-1927 and as Mexico correspondent in 1929. He returned to his post as editor of **New Masses** from 1931 to 1933 and from 1936 to 1937. In 1934 he was co-founder of **Partisan Review** serving as co-editor until 1936.

96. Nearing and Freeman, **Dollar Diplomacy** [1925]. pp. xiv-xv, 17-18, 122-124, 133, 151, 160, 169-172, 233, 244-246, 260-266, 271-272, 277.

97. Combs, **American Diplomatic History** [1983]. pp. 183-186. After the publication of **Dollar Diplomacy**, Nearing continued to write about imperialism, but none of his books ever focused on Latin America to the degree that **Dollar Diplomacy** had; however, he did maintain some interest in the region and, along with C. Wright Mills and I. F. Stone, he was a founding member of the Fair Play for Cuba Committee in November 1960, which also numbered Carleton Beals among its enthusiastic membership. Britton, **Carleton Beals** [1987]. pp. 217-218. Scott Nearing, **Cuba and Latin America: An Eyewitness Report on the Continental Congress for Solidarity with Cuba** [1963].

98. Novick, **That Noble Dream** [1988]. pp. 92-108, 178. Combs, **American Diplomatic History** [1983]. p. 115.

99. Leland Hamilton Jenks, **Our Cuban Colony: A Study in Sugar** [1928]. Melvin M. Knight, **The Americans in Santo Domingo** [1928]. J. Fred Rippy, **The Capitalists and Colombia** [1931]. Other books in the series included Margaret Alexander Marsh, **The Bankers in Bolivia** [1928]. Bailey W. Diffie and J. W. Diffie, **Porto Rico: A Broken Pledge** [1931]. See also Melvin M. Knight, **Morocco as a French Economic Venture** [1937].

100. Combs, **American Diplomatic History** [1983]. p. 186. Norman

Etherington has described Barnes's economic determinism as a "grossly oversimplified monocausal explanation of the growth of modern colonial empires". Norman Etherington, **Theories of Imperialism: War, Conquest and Capital** [1983]. p. 191. A prolific and industrious academic, Barnes gravitated to the center of controversy, but despite his radical credentials, and his commitment to revisionism and progressivism, he never ceased to subscribe to the idea that there was an "objective historical truth". Barnes' polemical and simplistic style, and his conviction that an "objective historical truth" existed and he possessed it, has been thoroughly evaluated in Novick, **That Noble Dream** [1988]. pp. 178, 208-224.

101. For example, the work of Charles David Kepner was far more sophisticated than Barnes's approach to 'economic imperialism'. Charles David Kepner, Jr., and Jay Henry Soothill, **The Banana Empire: A Case Study of Economic Imperialism** [1935]. Charles David Kepner, Jr., **Social Aspects of the Banana Industry** [1936].

102. Combs, **American Diplomatic History** [1983]. p. 186. Apart from the Barnes series, which probably represented the majority of radical work on US imperialism in Latin America, radical critiques of US imperialism by the late 1920s also included a book entitled **Machine-Gun Diplomacy**, by J. A. H. Hopkins and Melinda Alexander, which looked at US intervention in Nicaragua and in the region more generally. It styled the US as "imperialistic America", emphasized the importance of dollar-diplomacy, and called for greater emphasis on self-determination in practice, as well as in theory. J. A. H. Hopkins and Melinda Alexander, **Machine-Gun Diplomacy** [1928]. pp. 9-13, 107-142, 178-184.

103. Robert Young, **White Mythologies: Writing History and the West** [1990]. pp. 2-3.

104. This view can be found in Gene Wise, **American Historical Explanations: A Strategy for Grounded Inquiry** [1980]. Bernard Sternsher, **Consensus, Conflict and American Historians** [1975]. pp. 1-4. and in David W. Noble, **The End of American History: Democracy, Capitalism, and the Metaphor of Two Worlds in Anglo-American Historical Writing 1880-1980** [1985]. pp. 41-64. David W. Noble, "The Reconstruction of Progress: Charles Beard, Richard Hofstadter and Postwar Historical Thought" in Lary May, ed., **Recasting America: Culture and Politics in the Age of Cold War** [1989]. pp. 61-62.

105. The progressive discourses took on new significance with the emergence of the so-called neo-progressives (the New Left) in the 1960s. Novick, **That Noble Dream** [1988]. p. 332. Sternsher, **Consensus, Conflict, and American Historians** [1975]. pp. 276-279. For an analysis of Beard and the progressives which emphasizes that their impact was limited in the 1930s and that their long term significance is to be found in the rise of New Left historiography in the 1960s, see Ian Tyrrell, **The Absent Marx: Class Analysis and Liberal History in Twentieth Century America** [1986]. pp. 15-70.

106. Typical was the recommendation made to the Latin American study group on January 17, 1933, by Harold Roig, the vice-president of W. R. Grace and Company. He argued that the US ought to try and stimulate "economic diversification" in the region. If the Latin Americans could make more money, they could in turn take out new loans with greater likelihood of repayment. The Council on Foreign Relations was associated with the view that a more industrialized and economically diverse Latin America might not require the same quantity of manufactured and finished goods, but would still encourage significantly larger purchases from the US, alleviating the Depression era economic problems in North America. This view also rested on the assumption that this could be achieved without dramatic structural changes. In the second half of the 1930s the secretary of the Council on Foreign Relations' Latin

American Studies Committee, Edgar P. Dean, criticized Frank Tannenbaum's book **Whither Latin America?**, which emphasized that dramatic economic and political changes flowed from revolutionary rather than evolutionary politics and policies, and that 'progress' could often be an illusion. More specifically, Tannenbaum's book articulated a pessimistic view of Latin America's ability to industrialize. After reading **Whither Latin America?**, Dean wrote a letter to US Commerce Department official George Whyte saying that "although" he was not optimistic "that certain Latin American countries will ever attain the industry of Great Britain", he felt that "they have much more of an industrial future than Tannenbaum" who "believes" that "they have no future at all". Whyte agreed with Dean and argued that, although many people in Latin America continued to live in poverty, the current "boom" in Brazil and Argentina suggested that Tannenbaum was a "poor prophet". Nevertheless Tannenbaum continued to question the likelihood of rapid, or widespread, economic development in Latin America, at seminars and in his writing. Frank Tannenbaum, **Whither Latin America?: An Introduction to Its Economic and Social Problems** [1934]. Joseph Maier and Richard W. Weatherhead, "Introduction" in Joseph Maier and Richard W. Weatherhead, eds., **The Future of Democracy in Latin America: Essays by Frank Tannenbaum** [1974]. pp. 34-35. Edgar P. Dean to George Whyte, March 12, 1937, and George Whyte to Edgar P. Dean, March 15, 1937, cited in Schulzinger, **The Wise Men of Foreign Affairs** [1984]. pp. 47-49, 52-53. See H. Foster Bain, **Ores and Industry in South America** [1934]. Willy Feuerlein and Elizabeth Hannan, **Dollars in Latin America** [1941]. William A. M. Burden, **The Struggle for Airways in Latin America** [1943].

107. Gil, "Latin American Studies and Political Science" **LASA Forum** 1985 p. 8. Gibson and Keen, "Trends of United States Studies in Latin American History" (1957) in Cline, ed., **Latin American History** [1967]. pp. 532-533. M. M. Wise, "Development of Bibliographical Activity During the Past Five Years: A Tentative Survey" **Handbook of Latin American Studies: 1939** [1940].

108. LaFeber, **Inevitable Revolutions** [1984]. pp. 81-82.

109. LaFeber, **Inevitable Revolutions** [1984]. pp. 82-83.

110. Benjamin, "The Framework of US Relations with Latin America in the Twentieth Century" **Diplomatic History** 1987. p. 100.

111. Benjamin, "The Framework of US Relations with Latin America in the Twentieth Century" **Diplomatic History** 1987. pp. 101-102.

112. See Benjamin, "The Framework of US Relations with Latin America in the Twentieth Century" **Diplomatic History** 1987. pp. 102-104. Gordon Connell-Smith, **The Inter-American System** [1966]. Gordon Connell-Smith, **The United States and Latin America: An Historical Analysis of Inter-American Relations** [1974]. On the Office of the Coordinator of Inter-American Affairs see Frank Ninkovich, **The Diplomacy of Ideas** [1981]. pp. 35-39.

113. Sumner Welles, **The Roosevelt Administration and Its Dealings with the Republics of the Western Hemisphere** [1935]. pp. 1, 16. Sumner Welles, **Pan American Cooperation** [1935]. pp. 2, 7. Cited in Ninkovich, **The Diplomacy of Ideas** [1981]. pp. 19, 22-24, 189.

114. Duggan cited in Ninkovich, **The Diplomacy of Ideas** [1981]. pp. 24-25.

115. Ninkovich, **The Diplomacy of Ideas** [1981]. pp. 26-30, 34.

116. Benjamin, "The Framework of US Relations with Latin America in the Twentieth Century" **Diplomatic History** 1987. p. 102.

117. Wallace Thompson, **Greater America: An Interpretation of Latin America in Relation to Anglo-Saxon America** [1932]. pp. 214-216, 245-248.

118. On Bolton's importance to the study of the Spanish borderlands see

David J. Weber, "Turner, the Boltonians and the Borderlands" **American Historical Review** vol. 91. no. 1. 1986. Albert L. Hurtado, "Herbert E. Bolton, Racism and American History" **Pacific Historical Review** vol. 62. no. 2. 1993.

    119. Herbert Eugene Bolton, "The Epic of Greater America" **American Historical Review** vol. 38. no. 3. 1933. See Charles Gibson, "Latin America and the Americas" in Kammen, ed., **The Past Before Us** [1980]. pp. 200-201. John F. Bannon, **Herbert Eugene Bolton: The Historian and the Man 1870-1953** [1978]. pp. 110, 182-189, 255-256.

    120. See Lewis Hanke, ed., **Do the Americas Have a Common History?: A Critique of the Bolton Theory** [1964]. Louis Hartz's edited volume represents an important point of departure for the comparative study of the history of the Americas. See Louis Hartz, "A Theory of the Development of the New Societies" in Louis Hartz, ed., **The Founding of New Societies: Studies in the History of the United States, Latin America, South Africa, Canada and Australia** [1964]. Louis Hartz, "United States History in a New Perspective" in Hartz, ed., **The Founding of New Societies** [1964]. Richard M. Morse, "The Heritage of Latin America" in Hartz, ed., **The Founding of New Societies** [1964]. There are very few explicit attempts to compare the colonial histories of North and South America. See, for example, James Lang, **Conquest and Commerce: Spain and England in the Americas** [1975]. Claudio Véliz, **The New World of the Gothic Fox: Culture and Economy in English and Spanish America** [1994]. Slavery generally has been the subject of important comparative work. See George M. Fredrickson, **White Supremacy: A Comparative Study in American and South African History** [1981]. Peter Kolchin, **Unfree Labor: American Slavery and Russian Serfdom** [1987]. And slavery in the Americas has probably been a focus of more comparative work than almost any other aspect of hemispheric history. See Herbert S. Klein, **Slavery in the Americas: A Comparative Study of Virginia and Cuba** [1967]. David Brion Davis, **The Problem of Slavery in Western Culture** [1966]. Laura Foner and Eugene D. Genovese, eds., **Slavery in the New World: A Reader in Comparative History** [1969]. Carl N. Degler, **Neither Black nor White: Slavery and Race Relations in Brazil and the United States** [1971]. S. L. Engerman and Eugene D. Genovese, eds., **Race and Slavery in the Western Hemisphere: Quantitative Studies** [1974]. Eugene D. Genovese, **From Rebellion to Revolution: Afro-American Slave Revolts in the Making of the New World** [1979]. C. Duncan Rice, **The Rise and Fall of Black Slavery** [1975]. David Brion Davis, **The Problem of Slavery in the Age of Revolution 1770-1823** [1975]. David Eltis, "Europeans and the Rise and Fall of African Slavery in the Americas: An Interpretation" **American Historical Review** vol. 98. no. 5. 1993. For a recent unitary/comparative synthesis by a British writer, see Robin Blackburn, **The Overthrow of Colonial Slavery 1776-1848** [1988]. The comparative study of the frontier generally, and the frontier in the Western Hemisphere specifically, is considerably weaker than the comparative work on slavery. Leonard Thompson and Howard Lamar, "Comparative Frontier History" in Howard Lamar and Leonard Thompson, eds., **The Frontier in History: North America and Southern Africa Compared** [1981]. p. 6. Michael T. Katzman, "The Brazilian Frontier in Comparative Perspective" **Comparative Studies in Society and History** vol. 17. 1975. Alastair Hennessy, **The Frontier in Latin American History** [1978]. pp. 6-27, 138-159. For a recent discussion of the still limited scope of the comparative history of the frontier in the Americas in the context of the influence of the Turner thesis and of Bolton's own work on the Borderlands as well as his emphasis on hemispheric history, see Weber, "Turner, the Boltonians, and the Borderlands" **American Historical Review** 1986. pp. 71-74. For a

comparative/unitary analysis of decolonization in the Americas see Benedict Anderson's chapter on the "Creole Pioneers" in Benedict Anderson, **Imagined Communities: Reflections on the Origin and Spread of Nationalism** [1991]. pp. 47-65. See also Immanuel Wallerstein's chapter "The Settler Decolonization of the Americas: 1763-1833" in Immanuel Wallerstein, **The Modern World-System III: The Second Era of Great Expansion of the Capitalist World-Economy 1730-1840s** [1989]. pp. 191-256. For a more general comparative/unitary analysis see Anibal Quijano and Immanuel Wallerstein, "Americanity as a concept, or the Americas in the modern world-system" **International Social Science Journal** no. 134. 1992. S. N. Eisenstadt, "Culture, religions and development in North American and Latin American civilizations" **International Social Science Journal** no. 134. 1992. For a recent attempt to contrast 'economic development', the politics of industrialization, militarism and the Indian 'problem' in Latin American and US history see Jim Levy and Peter Ross, "A Common History? Two Latin Americanists View the Writing of US History in Hemispheric Perspective" **Australasian Journal of American Studies** vol. 12. no. 1. 1993.

121. After 1945 the colonial history of North America was important to the US because of its significance in the United States' rise to "national greatness" rather than because of its possible similarities to colonial Latin America. Ian Tyrrell, "American Exceptionalism in an Age of International History" **The American Historical Review** vol. 96. no. 4. 1991. pp. 1039-1040.

122. Lester D. Langley, **America and the Americas: The United States in the Western Hemisphere** [1989]. p. 152. Ninkovich, **The Diplomacy of Ideas** [1981]. p. 25. See Samuel Guy Inman, **Building an Inter-American Neighborhood** [1937]. Samuel Guy Inman, **Latin America: Its Place in World Life** [1937].

123. Laurence Duggan, **The Americas: The Search for Hemispheric Security** [1949]. Duggan worked in the State Department's Latin American Division until his death at the end of the 1940s. See also John Moors Cabot, **Towards Our Common American Destiny** [1954].

124. In the mid-1950s the historian Arthur P. Whitaker wrote a book which sympathetically sought to chart the development of the idea that the inhabitants of the Americas had a "special relationship" which set "them apart from the rest of the world". See Arthur P. Whitaker, **The Western Hemisphere Idea: Its Rise and Decline** [1954]. p. 1. See also, for example, the work in the early 1960s of J. Lloyd Mecham, who was one of Bolton's PhD students, and the work of Lester D. Langley in the 1980s. J. Lloyd Mecham, **The United States and Inter-American Security** [1961]. J. Lloyd Mecham, **A Survey of United States-Latin American Relations** [1965]. Lester D. Langley, **America and the Americas: The United States in the Western Hemisphere** [1989]. p. xxii.

125. Bolton, born in 1870 in rural Wisconsin, did most of his work for his PhD at the University of Wisconsin under Frederick Jackson Turner and then finished the degree in 1899 at Pennsylvania under the supervision of John B. McMaster. Bolton's dissertation was on the pre-Civil War South and he began his academic career as a student of US history. After six years he took up a post at Stanford and then Berkeley. Robert A. McCaughey, **International Studies and Academic Enterprise: A Chapter in the Enclosure of American Learning** [1984]. pp. 89-93. Bannon, **Herbert Eugene Bolton** [1978]. pp. 143-144, 283-290.

126. Herbert Eugene Bolton, **Athanase De Mézieres and the Louisiana-Texas Frontier 1768-1780** (2 vols.) [1914]. Herbert Eugene Bolton, **Texas in the Middle Eighteenth Century: Studies in Spanish Colonial History and Administration** [1915]. Herbert Eugene Bolton,

Spanish Exploration in the Southwest 1542-1706 [1916]. Herbert Eugene Bolton, with Thomas Maitland Marshall, **The Colonization of North America 1492-1783** [1920]. Herbert Eugene Bolton, **The Spanish Borderlands: A Chronicle of Old Florida and the Southwest** [1921]. Herbert Eugene Bolton, with Ephraim Douglass Adams, **California's Story** [1922]. Herbert Eugene Bolton, **Fray Juan Crespi: Missionary Explorer on the Pacific Coast 1769-1774** [1927]. Herbert Eugene Bolton, **History of the Americas: A Syllabus with Maps** [1928]. Herbert Eugene Bolton, **Outpost of Empire: The Story of the Founding of San Francisco** [1931]. Herbert Eugene Bolton, **Rim of Christendom: A Biography of Eusebio Francisco Kino, Pacific Coast Pioneer** [1936]. Herbert Eugene Bolton, **Wider Horizons of American History** [1939]. For a complete list of Bolton's work see Adele Ogden, "A Bibliography of the Writings of Herbert Eugene Bolton" in Adele Ogden, ed., **Greater America: Essays in Honour of Herbert Eugene Bolton** [1945].

127. Clarence H. Haring, **The Buccaneers in the West Indies in the 17th Century** [1910]. Clarence H. Haring, **Trade and Navigation Between Spain and the Indies in the Time of the Hapsburgs** [1918]. Clarence H. Haring, **The Spanish Empire in America** [1947]. Clarence H. Haring, **Empire in Brazil: A New World Experiment in Monarchy** [1965].

128. McCaughey, **International Studies and Academic Enterprise** [1984]. pp. 92-94. Bannon, **Herbert Eugene Bolton** [1978]. pp. 283-290. John Francis Bannon, "Alfred Barnaby Thomas" in Eugene R. Huck and Edward H. Moseley, eds., **Militarists, Merchants and Missionaries: United States Expansion in Middle America** (Essays Written in Honor of Alfred Barnaby Thomas) [1970]. pp. ix-xi. For a complete list of the work of Bolton's students see Gregory Crampton, "A Bibliography of the Historical Writings of the Students of Herbert Eugene Bolton" in Ogden, ed., **Greater America** [1945].

129.McCa ughey, **International Studies and Academic Enterprise** [1984]. pp. 93-95, 105.

130. Rockefeller cited in Ninkovich, **The Diplomacy of Ideas** [1981]. pp. 35-36.

131. Ninkovich, **The Diplomacy of Ideas** [1981]. pp. 40-41, 194.

132. Preston James, "Outline of Research in the Study of Contemporary Culture Patterns in Latin America" cited in Ninkovich, **The Diplomacy of Ideas** [1981]. p. 42. Preston James was the author of a standard text on the geography and history of Latin America. See Preston James, **Introduction to Latin America** [1959].

133. In the latter stages of the war the Joint Committee on Latin American Studies began to entertain ideas about becoming a planning organization when the war ended. However, the government lost interest in the Committee after 1945 and its significance, and its operations, declined dramatically. Ninkovich, **The Diplomacy of Ideas** [1981]. p. 42.

134. For a work which combined colonial and diplomatic history and reflected the way an interest in the Spanish borderlands meshed with diplomatic history, see Charles C. Griffin, **The United States and the Disruption of the Spanish Empire 1810-1822** [1937].

135. Rippy was born in Tennessee in 1892. After receiving a BA from the Southwestern University of Texas in 1913 and a master's degree from Vanderbilt University in 1915, he went on to study at the University of California (Berkeley), where he completed his PhD in 1920 under Bolton. From Berkeley Rippy proceeded to the University of Chicago as a history instructor and by 1924 had risen to the rank of associate professor. From 1926 to 1936 he was professor of history at Duke University, returning as professor to University of Chicago where he remained,

becoming professor emeritus in 1958. In 1927 he went to Central America on a Guggenheim fellowship and in 1928 he visited Colombia as a Carnegie fellow. Hispanic Foundation, **National Directory of Latin Americanists** [1971]. p. 464. J. Fred Rippy, **Bygones I Cannot Help Recalling: The Memoirs of a Mobile Scholar** [1966].

136. See J. Fred Rippy, "Notes on the Early Telephone Companies of Latin America" **Hispanic American Historical Review** vol. 26. no. 1. 1946. J. Fred Rippy, "The British Investment 'Boom' of the 1880s in Latin America" **Hispanic American Historical Review** vol. 29. no. 2. 1949. J. Fred Rippy, "Notes on Early British Gas Companies in Latin America" **Hispanic American Historical Review** vol. 30. no. 1. 1950. J. Fred Rippy, "British Investments in Latin America: A Decade of Rapid Reduction, 1940-1950" **Hispanic American Historical Review** vol. 32. no. 2. 1952. J. Fred Rippy, "British Investments in Latin America at Their Peak" **Hispanic American Historical Review** vol. 34. no. 1. 1954. J. Fred Rippy, "British Investments in Latin-American Electrical Utilities" **Hispanic American Historical Review** vol. 34. no. 2. 1954. Gibson, ed., **Guide to the Hispanic American Historical Review** [1958]. pp. 38-39, 172. Charles W. Hackett, "Discussion of Lesley Byrd Simpson, 'Thirty Years of the *Hispanic American Historical Review*' and Charles C. Griffin, 'Economic and Social Aspects of the Era of Spanish-American Independence'" **Hispanic American Historical Review** vol. 29. no. 2. 1949. p. 214. Rippy also contributed to the first issue of the **Journal of Interamerican Studies**, which later became the **Journal of Interamerican Studies and World Affairs**. See J. Fred Rippy, "US Aid to Latin America" **Journal of Interamerican Studies** vol. 1. no. 1. 1959.

137. J. Fred Rippy, **The United States and Mexico** [1926]. J. Fred Rippy, **Latin America in World Politics: An Outline Survey** [1928]. J. Fred Rippy, **Rivalry of the United States and Great Britain over Latin America 1808-1830** [1929]. J. Fred Rippy, **The Capitalists and Colombia** [1931]. J. Fred Rippy, **Historical Evolution of Hispanic America** [1932]. J. Fred Rippy and Jean Thomas Nelson, **Crusaders of the Jungle** [1936]. J. Fred Rippy, **America and the Strife of Europe** [1938]. J. Fred Rippy, **Latin America in World Politics** [1938]. J. Fred Rippy, **South America and Hemisphere Defense** [1941]. J. Fred Rippy, **Latin America and the Industrial Age** [1944]. J. Fred Rippy, **Globe and Hemisphere: Latin America's Place in the Postwar Foreign Relations of the United States** [1958]. J. Fred Rippy, **Latin America: A Modern History** [1958]. J. Fred Rippy, **British Investments in Latin America 1822-1949: A Case Study in the Operations of Private Enterprise in Retarded Regions** [1959].

138. Schulzinger, **The Wise Men of Foreign Affairs** [1984]. pp. 49-51. Although Rippy looked favorably on the Good Neighbor Policy, he was more concerned with the cooperative side of the policy than he was with its retreat from unilateral intervention. Rippy articulated the view that intervention in the past had been crucial in order to protect US interests, and that in the future the negative response to such intervention would be overcome, not by completely avoiding intervention but by intervening with the multi-lateral support and assistance of the majority of Latin American countries. Combs, **American Diplomatic History** [1983]. p. 189.

139. J. Fred Rippy, **The Caribbean Danger Zone** [1940]. pp. 134-137. Rippy's analysis of US intervention in Nicaragua represented a relatively sophisticated approach that combined an emphasis on the interplay of economic and strategic motives and the specific motives and actions of actors on the spot--what has more recently been codified as 'sub-imperialism'. ('Sub-imperialism' is used here to refer to

the 'independent' activity of the European and North American military men and traders on the spot, engaging in political and military intervention and territorial expansion in order to gain new advantages, usually economic, for themselves personally, or for some other interest group such as the United Fruit Company, without the direct approval or authorization of either their home government or their head office.) In the last few years the concept of 'sub-imperialism' has been used by historians of both European and US imperialism. See Barry Rigby, "The Origins of American Expansion in Hawaii and Samoa 1865-1900" **International History Review** vol. 10. no. 2. 1988. According to Rippy the US invasion and occupation of Nicaragua can be traced to the instigation of the revolt against Zelaya, at the end of 1909, on the part of the North Americans who had investments on Nicaragua's eastern seaboard, the officers in charge of the US naval vessels in the area, and the Nicaraguan Conservatives and dissident Liberals led by Juan J. Estrada, Adolfo Díaz and Emiliano Chamorro. Rippy, **The Caribbean Danger Zone** [1940]. pp. 166-179, 180-182, 206-223. A more popular study, which emphasized dollar diplomacy more than Rippy was Adolphe W. Roberts's popular history of the Caribbean. He was critical of Theodore Roosevelt and the dollar diplomacy of the first two or three decades of the twentieth century, but he felt that US policy since the rise of the Good Neighbor Policy had improved. He portrayed the United Fruit Company as a practitioner of "commercial imperialism". And he asserted that Sandino "personified" all that remained of "independent patriotism". See Adolphe W. Roberts, **The Caribbean: The Story of Our Sea of Destiny** [1940]. pp. 317-321, 329, 331.

140. Rippy, **The Caribbean Danger Zone** [1940]. pp. 242-244. Rippy noted that, while the full importance of the "totalitarian threat" was not yet apparent, "defensive precautions" against totalitarianism did not have to precipitate the reappearance of Latin American "distrust and bitterness". He believed that "fair treatment and honorable diplomacy" would "secure the cordial collaboration of the Latin Americans in our defense and theirs". He concluded that the rulers of Central and South America would be most willing to cooperate with the nation that displays the "most respect for their interests and sensibilities". In his view, there was no question that the United States was the most likely candidate in this regard, and he argued that the Latin Americans would withdraw their support only if they believed that the US was unable to defeat totalitarianism. Rippy argued that it was abundantly clear that the US "should continue the Good Neighbor Policy, perhaps expand its scope, and look after the political, economic, moral and military defenses of the nation". Rippy, **The Caribbean Danger Zone** [1940]. pp. 250-254, 261.

141. Rippy, **The Caribbean Danger Zone** [1940]. pp. v, 4, 7-8, 14, 55.

142. See Wilfrid Hardy Callcott, **The Caribbean Policy of the United States 1890-1920** [1942]. Woodward, **Central America** [1985]. p. 339. Calcott was born in Texas in the 1890s. In 1919 he graduated from Southwestern College in Georgetown, Texas, and went on to obtain his PhD from Columbia University in 1926. Three years before completing his PhD he took up a teaching position in the Department of History at the University of South Carolina where he remained until 1965. During his years at South Carolina, he was actively involved with university administration, eventually rising to the position of Dean of the University. C. Alan Hutchinson, "Wilfrid Hardy Callcott 1895-1969" **Hispanic American Historical Review** vol. 50. no. 2. 1970. pp. 349-350.

143. Calcott, **The Caribbean Policy of the United States 1890-1920** [1942]. pp. ix-xi. Also see Wilfrid Hardy Callcott, **Church and State in Mexico 1822-1857** [1926]. Wilfrid Hardy Callcott, **Liberalism in Mexico 1857-1929** [1931]. Wilfrid Hardy Callcott, **Santa Anna, The Story of an Enigma Who Once Was Mexico** [1936]. Wilfrid Hardy Callcott, **The Western**

Hemisphere: Its Influence on United States Policies to the End of
World War Two [1968].

144. Samuel Flagg Bemis, **The Latin American Policy of the United
States: An Historical Interpretation** [1943]. It was published under the
auspices of the Yale Institute of International Studies, set up in 1935 with the financial
assistance of the Rockefeller Foundation. The Institute's research program was aimed at
the study and clarification of "contemporary problems in the foreign policy of the
United States". Robin Winks has characterized the work of the academics associated
with the Institute after 1940 as directed towards the question of "how the world might
be reorganized to fit American needs". He concluded that, "though they would not have
said so, these scholars were working on a history of imperial America, and all their
efforts were of interest to the State Department", and "most received assistance from
it". Robin W. Winks, **Cloak and Gown: Scholars in the Secret War 1939-
1961** [1987]. pp. 42-43.

145. It has been compared to A. Whitney Griswold's highly influential **The
Far Eastern Policy of the United States**, also published by the Yale Institute
of International Studies. See A. Whitney Griswold's **The Far Eastern Policy of
the United States** [1938]. Salisbury, "Good Neighbors?: The United States and
Latin America in the Twentieth Century" in Haines and Walker, eds., **American
Foreign Relations** [1981]. p. 311. Lester D. Langley, "The Diplomatic
Historians: Bailey and Bemis" **The History Teacher** vol. 6. no. 1. 1972. p. 65.
Combs, **American Diplomatic History** [1983]. p. 273.

146. Langley, **America and the Americas** [1989]. pp. xv, 290. Twenty
years earlier Langley noted that, although the book was "tendentious and didactic", it
had "never been completely supplanted by more recent books on the same topic".
Langley, "The Diplomatic Historians: Bailey and Bemis" **The History Teacher**
1972. p. 65.

147. Salisbury, "Good Neighbors?" in Haines and Walker, eds., **American
Foreign Relations** [1981]. p. 311. Jerald A. Combs has called him "the greatest of
all historians of early American diplomacy". See Combs, **American Diplomatic
History** [1983]. p. 156.

148. Bemis received a BA and an MA from Clark University. While at Harvard
he finished a second master's degree and completed a PhD under the supervision of
Edward Channing after a period of research in England and France. Between 1917 and
1923 he taught history at colleges in Colorado Springs and Walla Walla, Washington.
He then moved to Washington, D.C., first as a research associate at the Carnegie
Institute (1923-1924) and then as Professor of History at George Washington
University (1924-1934). After a year as a visiting lecturer at Harvard in 1934-1935, he
took up his post at Yale. He served as President of the American Historical Association
in 1961, and he died in 1973. Langley, "The Diplomatic Historians: Bailey and Bemis"
The History Teacher 1972. p. 61. Throughout his career Bemis was a prolific
historian of US diplomatic history, writing monographs, influential general texts and
reference works. Much of his monograph work focused on eighteenth- and nineteenth-
century US diplomatic history. See Samuel Flagg Bemis, **Jay's Treaty: A Study in
Commerce and Diplomacy** [1923]. Samuel Flagg Bemis, **Pinckney's Treaty:
A Study of America's Advantage from Europe's Distress, 1783-1800**
[1926]. Samuel Flagg Bemis, ed., **The American Secretaries of State and
Their Diplomacy** (10 vols.) [1927-1929]. Samuel Flagg Bemis, **The Hussey-
Cumberland Mission and American Independence: An Essay in the
Diplomacy of the American Revolution** [1931]. Samuel Flagg Bemis and
Grace Gardner Griffin, **Guide to the Diplomatic History of the United
States 1775-1921** [1935]. Samuel Flagg Bemis, **The Diplomacy of the
American Revolution** [1935]. Samuel Flagg Bemis, **A Diplomatic History**

of the United States [1936]. Samuel Flagg Bemis, **The United States as a World Power: A Diplomatic History 1900-1950** [1950]. Samuel Flagg Bemis, **John Quincy Adams and the Foundations of American Foreign Policy** [1949]. Samuel Flagg Bemis, **John Quincy Adams and the Union** [1956]. Samuel Flagg Bemis, **A Short History of American Foreign Policy and Diplomacy** [1959]. Samuel Flagg Bemis, **American Foreign Policy and the Blessings of Liberty and Other Essays** [1962].

149. He had supported US intervention in World War I, but would have preferred Washington's involvement to be more conditional. He was opposed to US involvement in the League of Nations for fear that participation would drag the US into European conflicts; however, he did not think the US should obstruct the League of Nations. The root of Bemis's ambivalence with regard to US involvement in Europe and elsewhere can be found in his view that modern twentieth-century US diplomacy was inferior in quality to that conducted for the first one hundred years or more of the republic's existence. He argued that between the declaration of independence in 1776 and the war with Spain in 1898 the US had "made no serious mistakes in its diplomacy and committed few minor errors". In this period the US, as a result of geography had been able to remain isolated from European conflicts and pursue its interests. However, at the outset of the twentieth century, when the US had set out to acquire an overseas empire, its problems began. In his writing he criticized US annexation of the Philippines, because it was in just such a place that the US "was most likely to become entangled in international rivalries alien to its interests". The annexation of the Philippines was followed, in his view, by a series of "deplorable diplomatic blunders", such as the Open Door Policy, which assisted Great Britain more than the United States, while the diplomatic excesses of Theodore Roosevelt had done more harm than good. He argued that the Roosevelt Corollary and the intervention in Panama had been completely uncalled for, since the establishment of a protectorate over Cuba and the annexation of Puerto Rico were sufficient to safeguard US interests in the Caribbean. Samuel Flagg Bemis, **A Diplomatic History of the United States** [1936]. pp. 802-805. Combs, **American Diplomatic History** [1983]. pp. 157-159.

150. Bemis cited in Novick, **That Noble Dream** [1988]. p. 243-244.

151. Bemis cited in Gaddis Smith, "The Two Worlds of Samuel Flagg Bemis" **Diplomatic History** vol. 9. no. 4. 1985. pp. 297-299.

152. Bemis cited in Smith, "The Two Worlds of Samuel Flagg Bemis" **Diplomatic History** 1985. p. 298.

153. Bemis, **The Latin American Policy of the United States**, [1943]. pp. 123-124.

154. Bemis, **The Latin American Policy of the United States** [1943]. pp. x, 124-125, 139, 209-213, 386.

155. In his work Pratt, who was chairman of the University of Buffalo [New York] History Department for over twenty years after World War I, interpreted the US establishment of protectorates over, and annexation of, countries in Central America, the Caribbean and Southeast Asia as a "passing phase" for which the US need not feel ashamed. In Pratt's view, these countries had been in need of "guardianship" until such time as they were able to govern themselves. The impact of US rule had on balance been beneficial and benevolent. The US had withdrawn from its protectorates and colonies, remaining in only those territories, or parts of territories which were of the utmost strategic significance. Pratt argued that this was entirely "legitimate", especially since the colonies that were retained were of no economic importance and were often liabilities in economic terms. In Pratt's view, the US had shown great restraint, insofar as it had possessed the power since the beginning of the century to make more conquests and hold more territory. If the US had taken full advantage of its global power, it would have deserved to be branded imperialist. Julius W. Pratt,

America's Colonial Experiment: How the United States Gained, Governed, and in Part Gave Away a Colonial Empire [1950]. pp. 1-3, 331-369. Combs, **American Diplomatic History** [1983] p. 272. Klaus Schwabe, "The Global Role of the United States and Its Imperial Consequences, 1898-1973" in Wolfgang J. Mommsen and Jurgen Osterhammel, eds., **Imperialism and After: Continuities and Discontinuities** [1986]. pp. 13, 30. In the Preface to his 1943 book, Bemis thanked Julius Pratt, along with Dexter Perkins, for reading and criticizing the manuscript. Bemis, **The Latin American Policy of the United States** [1943]. pp. xi-xii. Novick, **That Noble Dream** [1988]. p. 170.

156. Bemis, **The Latin American Policy of the United States** [1943]. p. 161. Bemis dismissed Charles Beard's attempt to "make of Nicaragua an illustration *par excellence* of how private interests supplanted public interests", because his conclusions were based on the "testimony of Toribio Tijerno, an ex Nicaraguan financial agent in New York and Thomas P. Moffat, a critical and discontented former United States consul-general in Nicaragua", both of whom appeared before the Senate Subcommittee on Foreign Relations in early 1927. Rippy, on the other hand, in Bemis's words, made a "more temperate analysis of 'dollar diplomacy' and strategical factors in Nicaragua"; however, he gave "almost no consideration" to the 1907 and 1923 Central American treaties, which in his view explained US foreign policy "more" than "dollar diplomacy" did. See Bemis, **The Latin American Policy of the United States**, [1943]. p. 412. note 42.

157. As further proof that the US intervention in Nicaragua was not motivated by economic factors, Bemis pointed out that at the time of intervention Nicaragua actually had a very low level of US investment. Prior to World War I, US capital was still invested mainly in the United States itself, and the US government often had trouble encouraging North American banks to invest overseas. He then attempted to generate a broader, even theoretical, conclusion from this by arguing that because the US had more capital invested in Cuba, Mexico, Canada and the larger republics of South America, "it seems to be an historical fact that the more capital a country of the New World has accepted from private investors in the United States the less danger there has been of intervention". According to Bemis, US investment "brought a wealth of good" to the republics of Latin America; however, in general he doubted that the North American economy, generally, or the North American investors specifically reaped significant benefits. The reason for this, said Bemis, was because the investments were not really "safe". He argued that this was due to the 'fact' that, in contrast to the European powers, the United States, "with its deep continental instincts of nonintervention", had been unwilling to use force to guarantee North American investment. Bemis, **The Latin American Policy of the United States** [1943]. pp. 165-166.

158. Bemis, **The Latin American Policy of the United States** [1943]. pp. 162-165, 187-188. By the 1940s, some writers, such as the North American fascist Lawrence Dennis, had become confirmed non-interventionists, even when it came to Central America. He took a position which was more isolationist, and more critical of the Nicaraguan affair than Bemis. Dennis, like Dana Munro, had been in Nicaragua with the US Foreign Service during the US occupation. He described the pretexts for the occupation as "hollow", and characterized the Nicaraguan intervention as just another instance in the "many bloody phases" of Washington's "prolonged adventures in dollar diplomacy". Lawrence Dennis, **The Dynamics of War and Revolution** [1940]. p. 108. For an analysis of Dennis and his writing see Ronald Radosh, **Prophets on the Right: Profiles of Conservative Critics of American Globalism** [1974]. pp. 275-295, especially 276-277.

159. Bemis, **The Latin American Policy of the United States** [1943]. pp. 331-332, 343-344, 350.

160. See Frederick Upham Adams, **The Conquest of the Tropics: The Story of the Creative Enterprises Conducted by the United Fruit Company** [1914]. Samuel Crowther, **The Romance and Rise of the American Tropics** [1929].

161. Wilson insisted that, "in terms of inter-American relations in general, good salesmanship, good investment, and good merchandising can accomplish more in six months than an entire circus parade of pinkos and abstruse proponents of 'cultural relations' between the Americas can accomplish in sixteen thousand years". Charles Morrow Wilson, **Central America: Challenge and Opportunity** [1942]. Charles Morrow Wilson, **Middle America** [1944]. This was followed by an even more explicit celebration of the United Fruit Company's activities in Central America. See Charles Morrow Wilson, **Empire in Green and Gold: The Story of the American Banana Trade** [1947]. Ralph Lee Woodward, Jr., characterized Wilson as the United Fruit Company's "principal apologist". Woodward, **Central America** [1985]. p. 348. Following his time in Latin America with the United Fruit Company, Wilson worked in Liberia for the Firestone Plantations Company, and with the Liberian government for over four years. He has also worked as a consultant on tropic relations and affairs to the State Department, and by the early 1970s was working as a counselor for various members of the US Senate's Foreign Relations Committee. He was also a life-long friend of J. William Fulbright, who wrote the foreword to Wilson's book on Liberia. See Charles Morrow Wilson, **Liberia: Black Africa in Microcosm** [1971].

162. Adolf A. Berle, Jr., cited in Bemis, **The Latin American Policy of the United States** [1943]. pp. 350-353. (Bemis's italics).

163. Bemis, **The Latin American Policy of the United States** [1943]. p. 6. Ellsworth Huntington, **Civilization and Climate** [1915]. For a recent critique of Huntington's ideas, see Richard Peet, **Global Capitalism: Theories of Societal Development** [1991]. pp. 14-20.

164. Bemis, **The Latin American Policy of the United States** [1943]. pp. 6-7, 395.

165. Peter Worsley, **The Three Worlds: Culture and World Development** [1984]. p. 1.

166. Merk, **Manifest Destiny and Mission in American History** [1963]. pp. 243-244. See Carl Schurz, **American Imperialism: The Convocation Address Delivered on the Occasion of the Twenty Seventh Convocation of the University of Chicago** [1899]. Carl Schurz, **The Policy of Imperialism: Address by Carl Schurz** [1899].

167. Schwabe, "The Global Role of the United States and Its Imperial Consequences 1898-1973" in Mommsen and Osterhammel, **Imperialism and After** [1986]. pp. 13-14.

168. Noble, **The End of American History** [1985]. pp. 57-59.

169. Thomas C. Kennedy, **Charles A. Beard and American Foreign Policy** [1975]. pp. 160, 163-164. See Charles A. Beard (and George H. E. Smith), **The Idea of National Interest: An Analytical Study in American Foreign Policy** [1934]. Charles A. Beard (and George H. E. Smith), **The Open Door at Home** [1934]. See also Charles A. Beard, **American Foreign Policy in the Making 1932-1940: A Study in Responsibilities** [1944].

2. Modernization and Development 1945-1968

1.   US industry was responsible for at least 60% of global manufacturing in the years immediately after World War II. Daniel Chirot, **Social Change in the Modern Era** (1986). p. 194. Also see Andrew Glyn, Alan Hughes, Alain Lipietz and Ajit Singh, "The Rise and Fall of the Golden Age" in Stephen Marglin and Juliet B. Schor, eds., **The Golden Age of Capitalism:Reinterpreting the Postwar Experience** (Oxford: Oxford University Press, 1990).

2.   Dean C. Tipps, "Modernization Theory and the Comparative Study of Societies: A Critical Perspective" in Cyril E. Black, ed., **Comparative Modernization: A Reader** [1976]. p. 71. Gabriel Kolko, **Confronting the Third World: United States Foreign Policy 1945-1980** [1988]. p. 44. Jules Benjamin, "The Framework of US Relations with Latin America in the Twentieth Century: An Interpretive Essay" **Diplomatic History** vol. 11. no. 2. 1987. p. 105.

3.   Chirot, **Social Change in the Modern Era** [1986]. pp. 198-199.

4.   Michael J. Hogan, **The Marshall Plan: America, Britain, and the Reconstruction of Western Europe, 1947-1952** [1987].

5.   . Benjamin, "The Framework of US Relations with Latin America in the Twentieth Century" **Diplomatic History** 1987. pp. 105-106. Thomas G. Paterson, **Meeting the Communist Threat: Truman to Reagan** [1988]. pp. 147-158.

6.   Samuel L. Baily, **The United States and the Development of South America 1945-1975** [1976]. pp. 64-67.

7.   Walter LaFeber, **Inevitable Revolutions: The United States in Central America** [1984]. pp. 92-93.

8.   Baily, **The United States and the Development of South America 1945-1975** [1976]. pp. 73-74.

9.   Benjamin, "The Framework of US Relations with Latin America in the Twentieth Century" **Diplomatic History** 1987. pp. 106-107. Kolko, **Confronting the Third World** [1988]. pp. 93-105.

10.   Right up to the present day, the period between the end of World War II, if not earlier, and the Cuban Revolution, has continued to be an era in US-Latin American relations of minimal interest to North American academics. As Stephen G. Rabe has observed recently, historians of US-Latin American relations usually view the period from 1945 to 1960 "as an unhappy, dull and insignificant interregnum between the Good Neighbor and the Alliance for Progress", with "the one notable exception to scholarly disinterest" being the Guatemalan episode. Stephen G. Rabe, **Eisenhower and Latin America: The Foreign Policy of Anticommunism** [1988]. p. 4.

11.   LaFeber, **Inevitable Revolutions** [1984]. pp. 90-93, 126, 136-137, 148.

12.   Peter Novick, **That Noble Dream: The "Objectivity Question" and the American Historical Profession** [1988]. p. 281. Robert A. McCaughey, **International Studies and Academic Enterprise: A Chapter in the Enclosure of American Learning** [1984]. pp. 102-103.

13.   McCaughey, **International Studies and Academic Enterprise** [1984]. p. 114. Novick, **That Noble Dream** [1988]. pp. 301-302. Robin W. Winks, **Cloak and Gown: Scholars in the Secret War 1939-1961** [1987]. pp. 60-115.

14.   Novick, **That Noble Dream** [1988]. pp. 303-308.

15.   Ernest R. May, "The Decline of Diplomatic History" in George Athan Billias and Gerald N. Grob, eds., **American History: Retrospect and Prospect** [1971]. pp. 400-402.

16.   For example, just after World War II, William W. Kaufmann, a student of

Samuel Flagg Bemis, wrote an important work of diplomatic history on British-Latin American relations but subsequently changed the focus of his research dramatically. Initially taking a position with the RAND Corporation, he established himself as a defense policy analyst of some importance. See William W. Kaufmann, **British Policy and the Independence of Latin America 1804-1828** [1951]. May, "The Decline of Diplomatic History" in Billias and Grob, eds., **American History** [1971]. p. 402.

17. May, "The Decline of Diplomatic History" in Billias and Grob, eds., **American History** [1971]. pp. 402-403. The opening up of new fields of study in history and the social sciences, and the expansion of government and government-related jobs, does not explain entirely why diplomatic historians no longer led the historical profession in the US by the 1960s. The decline of diplomatic history also had its origins within the discipline itself. Diplomatic history evolved in the nineteenth century as a specialized field which concerned itself with the examination and study of diplomatic documents and records. By the beginning of the twentieth century, historians in other fields had already rejected an approach which relied exclusively for its sources on formal documents. In diplomatic history, however, the "traditional approach" continued. And diplomatic history's methodological shortcomings were compounded when, following World War I, diplomatic historians were overwhelmed by vast quantities of new official government documents. And in the years between the two World Wars, diplomatic historians continued to approach their sources in virtually the same way that Ranke had gone through the Venetian archives. And they produced a "close reconstruction of negotiations between courts". May, "The Decline of Diplomatic History" in Billias and Grob, eds., **American History** [1971]. pp. 403-405.

18. See Barry M. Katz, "The Criticism of Arms: The Frankfurt School Goes to War" **Journal of Modern History** vol. 59. no. 3. 1987. pp. 439, 446-447.

19. See Winks, **Cloak and Gown** [1987]. pp. 495-498. Katz, "The Criticism of Arms" **Journal of Modern History** 1987. pp. 446-447. Novick, **That Noble Dream** [1988]. pp. 309-310. McCaughey, **International Studies and Academic Enterprise** [1984]. pp. 115-117. Richard D. Lambert, et al., **Beyond Growth: The Next Stage in Language and Area Studies** [1984]. pp. 4-8. Michael N. Pearson, "Introduction" in Michael N. Pearson and Blair B. Kling, eds., **The Age of Partnership: Europeans in Asia before Dominion** [1979]. p. 1. On Stavrianos and global history see Gilbert Allardyce, "Toward World History: American Historians and the Coming of the World History Course" **Journal of World History** vol. 1. no. 1. 1990. On Fairbank and the North American study of China, see Paul Evans, **John King Fairbank and the American Understanding of Modern China** [1988]. McGeorge Bundy, one-time president of the Ford Foundation, which provided considerable support for area studies in the 1950s and 1960s through its International Training and Research Program, characterized the Office of Strategic Services as the "first great center of area studies in the United States". McGeorge Bundy, "The Battlefields of Power and the Searchlights of the Academy" in Edgar A. G. Johnson, ed., **Dimensions of Diplomacy** [1964]. pp. 2-3. Barry Katz has called the research and analysis branch of the OSS the "social science equivalent of the Manhattan Project". Bundy and Katz are cited in Winks, **Cloak and Gown** [1987]. pp. 115, 501.

20. John King Fairbank, **The United States and China** [1948]. W. Norman Brown, **The United States and India and Pakistan** [1953].

21. In the late 1950s Dozer wrote a book which covered the emergence and decline of the Good Neighbor Policy. He was particularly concerned to illuminate Latin American attitudes towards the US. Donald Marquand Dozer, **Are We Good Neighbors: Three Decades of Inter-American Relations 1930-1960**

278 *Notes to pages 66-97*

[1959]. He produced a number of other works on Latin America and inter-American history over the years. See Donald Marquand Dozer, **Latin America: An Interpretive History** [1962]. Donald Marquand Dozer, **The Monroe Doctrine: Its Modern Significance** [1965]. Donald Marquand Dozer, **The Challenge to Pan Americanism** [1972]. Donald Marquand Dozer, **The Panama Canal in Perspective** [1978].

22. In 1951 30% of all area-studies PhDs from sample universities were on Latin America, while East Asia and South Asia together totaled 25%. By 1960 Latin America was 18% and East and South Asia totaled 33%, with the Middle East remaining steady at 13% in 1951 and 12% in 1960. McCaughey, **International Studies and Academic Enterprise** [1984]. pp. 139-140, 198-201.

23. Winks, **Cloak and Gown** [1987]. pp. 114-115, 447-448, 495.

24. Peggy K. Liss, "Arthur Preston Whitaker (1895-1979)" **Hispanic American Historical Review** vol. 60. no. 3. 1980. pp. 473-475. Hispanic Foundation, Library of Congress, **National Directory of Latin Americanists** [1971]. pp. 590-591. Lewis Hanke, "The Development of Latin American Studies in the United States 1939-1945" **The Americas: A Quarterly Review of Inter-American Cultural History** vol. 4. no. 1. 1947. reprinted in Howard F. Cline, ed., **Latin American History: Essays on Its Study and Teaching 1898-1965** [1967]. pp. 317-320.

25. McCaughey, **International Studies and Academic Enterprise** [1984]. p. 116. Edwin Lieuwen, "Bryce Wood (1909-1986)" **Hispanic American Historical Review** vol. 67. no. 1. 1987. p. 143. Hispanic Foundation, **National Directory of Latin Americanists** [1971]. pp. 603-604.

26. Harold F. Peterson, **Argentina and the United States 1810-1960** [1964].

27. Guerrant was born in Danville, Virgina, in 1911 and gained his PhD from the University of Southern California in 1942. He worked as an Instructor in History at the California Institute of Technology from 1942 to 1944, and then from 1944 to 1945 he was a political analyst in the Office of the Co-ordinator of Inter-American Affairs in Washington under Donald W. Rowland, chief of the Political Research Unit Office of the Co-ordinator of Inter-American Affairs. (Rowland went on to be chairman of the Department of History at the University of Southern California.) From 1945 to 1946 Guerrant served in the American Republics Division of the Department of State under Dr. Roland D. Hussey (Chief of the Research and Analysis Section of the American Republics Division of the Department of State) who went on to be Professor of History at the University of California [Los Angeles]. In his 1951 study of the Good Neighbor Policy, Guerrant characterized Roosevelt's approach to Latin America as a "hands off policy". According to Guerrant, the commitment to "non-intervention" was the "keystone" of Good Neighbor Policy. In his view the Good Neighbor Policy ushered in a "new epoch in Inter-American relations" and once the Latin Americans had determined that the US was "sincere", there emerged a new optimism in the southern republics. As far as Guerrant was concerned, Roosevelt's only significant failure was to treat democracies differently than dictatorships. Using guarded language, Guerrant characterized US policy in Latin America since 1945 as following a course which "differed considerably" from the line pursued by Roosevelt's government. Edward O. Guerrant, **Roosevelt's Good Neighbour Policy** [1950]. pp. viii, 1-2, 8-10, 17-18, 237. A far more analytically sophisticated and interpretive work than Guerrant's highly descriptive study, was Alexander DeConde's book which appeared in 1951. Like earlier writers, DeConde traced the origins of the Good Neighbor Policy to the Hoover administration. Alexander DeConde, **Herbert Hoover's Latin American Policy** [1951]. See Roger R. Trask, "Inter-American Relations" in Roberto Esquenazi-Mayo and Michael C. Meyer, eds., **Latin American Scholarship since World War**

Two: Trends in History, Political Science, Literature, Geography and Economics [1971]. pp. 206-207.

28. Hanke, "The Development of Latin American Studies in the United States 1939-1945" The Americas 1947. reprinted in Cline, ed., Latin American History [1967]. p. 318.

29. Hanke, "The Development of Latin American Studies in the United States 1939-1945" The Americas 1947. reprinted in Cline, ed., Latin American History [1967]. pp. 319-320.

30. Novick, That Noble Dream [1988]. p. 311.

31.The significance of Brown's work is discussed in Ronald Inden, "Orientalist Constructions of India" Modern Asian Studies vol. 20. no. 3. 1986. p. 438.

32. Ninkovich, The Diplomacy of Ideas [1981]. pp. 40-42, 194.

33. Robert Redfield, Tepoztlan, A Mexican Village: A Study of Folk Life [1930]. Robert Redfield and Alfonso Villa Rojas, Chan Kom: A Maya Village [1934]. Robert Redfield, The Folk Culture of Yucatan [1940]. Robert Redfield, A Village That Chose Progress: Chan Kom Revisited [1950]. Robert Redfield, The Primitive World and Its Transformation [1953].

34. William Roseberry, Anthropologies and Histories: Essays in Culture, History, and Political Economy [1989]. pp. 148, 212-215. Eric R. Wolf, Europe and the People Without History [1982]. pp. 11, 14. Paul Sullivan, Unfinished Conversations: Mayas and Foreigners Between Two Wars [1989]. pp. 156-159.

35. John Crow, The Epic of Latin America [1946]. William L. Schurz, This New World: The Civilization of Latin America [1954].

36. On the "exclusion" of marxism from North American historiography, see Ian Tyrrell, The Absent Marx: Class Analysis and Liberal History in Twentieth Century America [1986].

37. The anonymous former SSRCC member is cited in Howard Wiarda, Ethnocentrism in Foreign Policy: Can We Understand the Third World? [1985]. p. 63.

38. Tipps, "Modernization Theory and the Comparative Study of Societies" in Black, ed., Comparative Modernization [1976]. pp. 71-72.

39. Many US policy makers continued to presume, well into the 1960s, that there was a direct causal link between poverty and revolution. See Robert A. Packenham, Liberal America and the Third World: Political Development Ideas in Foreign Aid and Social Science [1973]. pp. 52-53.

40. Irving Louis Horowitz, Beyond Empire and Revolution: Militarization and Consolidation in the Third World [1982]. pp. 76-77.

41. For a discussion of this see Immanuel Wallerstein, The Modern World-System III: The Second Era of Great Expansion of the Capitalist World-Economy 1730-1840s [1989]. pp. 3-53.

42. Michael Adas, Machines as the Measure of Men: Science Technology and Ideologies of Wester Dominance [1989]. pp. 402-403, 411-415.

43. Elbaki Hermassi, The Third World Reassessed [1980]. pp. 17-19. Peter Worsley, The Three Worlds: Culture and World Development [1984]. p. 20.

44. Walt Whitman Rostow, The Stages of Economic Growth: A Non-Communist Manifesto [1960]. A second edition appeared in the early 1970s. Rostow added a new appendix and a new preface in which he argued that the events of the past ten years, the response to his book, as well as the expansion of knowledge about the past had, in his view, vindicated his conceptual framework. See

Walt Whitman Rostow, **The Stages of Economic Growth: A Non-Communist Manifesto** [1971]. See also the third edition, which appeared in the context of the end of the Cold War. Walt Whitman Rostow, **The Stages of Economic Growth: A Non-Communist Manifesto** [1990]. Rostow also addressed the question of political modernization in a book which was published in the early 1970s. See Walt Whitman Rostow, **Politics and the Stages of Growth** [1971]. Carlos Ramirz-Faria observed recently that Rostow "brings together all the main strands of development studies" and "is also the most controversial because of his theoretical contentions and because of his political clout". Carlos Ramirez-Faria, **The Origins of Economic Inequality Between Nations: A Critique of Western Theories on Development and Underdevelopment** [1991]. p. 118.

45. Winks, **Cloak and Gown** [1987]. pp. 87, 497.

46. This view was articulated in another influential book by Rostow. See Walt Whitman Rostow, **The United States in the World Arena: An Essay in Recent History** [1959]. Jerald Combs, **American Diplomatic History: Two Centuries of Changing Interpretations** [1983]. pp. 249-250. Richard A. Melanson, **Writing History and Making Policy: The Cold War and Revisionism** [1983]. pp. 41-42. See also Walt Whitman Rostow, **Eisenhower, Kennedy and Foreign Aid** [1985].

47. Almond's classic behaviouralist work was Gabriel A. Almond, H. E. Krugman, E. Lewin and H. Wriggins, **The Appeals of Communism** [1954]. On behaviouralism in North America in the 1950s see Peter J. Seybold, "The Ford Foundation and the Triumph of Behavioralism in American Political Science" in Robert F. Arnove, **Philanthropy and Cultural Imperialism: The Foundations at Home and Abroad** [1982]. pp. 269-303. Also see David M. Ricci, **The Tragedy of Political Science: Politics, Scholarship and Democracy** [1984]. pp. 133-175. Irene L. Gendzier, **Managing Political Change: Social Scientists and the Third World** [1985]. pp. 84-85, 109-147.

48. Gabriel Almond and James S. Coleman, eds., **The Politics of Developing Areas** [1960].

49. See George I. Blanksten, "The Politics of Latin America" in Almond and Coleman, eds., **The Politics of Developing Areas** [1960]. pp. 455-531. For subsequent work by Blanksten and other Latin American specialists more or less reflecting the dominant approach to political development of the late 1950s and early 1960s, see George I. Blanksten, "Political Groups in Latin America" in John H. Kautsky, ed., **Political Change in Underdeveloped Countries: Nationalism and Communism** [1962]. Merle Kling, "Towards a Theory of Power and Political Instability in Latin America" in Kautsky, ed., **Political Change in Underdeveloped Countries** [1962]. Kalman H. Silvert, "Political Change in Latin America" in Herbert L. Matthews, ed., **The United States and Latin America** [1959].

50. For a succinct summary of the application of classic modernization theory to Latin America see Thomas E. Skidmore and Peter H. Smith, **Modern Latin America** [1984]. pp. 7-12. See also Peter F. Klarén, "Lost Promise: Explaining Latin American Underdevelopment" in Peter F. Klarén and Thomas J. Bossert, eds., **Promise of Development: Theories of Change in Latin America** [1986]. pp. 3-14.

51. John Johnson, **Political Change in Latin America: The Emergence of the Middle Sectors** [1958]. See also John Johnson, "Political Change in Latin America: The Emergence of the Middle Sectors (1958)" in Klarén and Bossert, eds., **Promise of Development** [1986].

52. Baily, **The United States and the Development of South America** [1976]. p. 70. James Dunkerley, **Rebellion in the Veins: Political Struggle in Bolivia 1952-1982** [1984]. pp. 38-82.

53. Schulzinger, **The Wise Men of Foreign Affairs** [1984]. p. 146.

54. Spruille Braden, **Syllabus on the Communist Threat to the Americas** [1953].

55. Robert J. Alexander, **Communism in Latin America** [1957]. Important studies of the communist threat, with a focus other than Latin America, include R. Swearingen and P. Langer, **Red Flag in Japan: International Communism in Action 1919-1951** [1952]. Anthony T. Bouscaren, **Imperial Communism** [1953]. John H. Kautsky, **Moscow and the Communist Party of India: A Study of the Postwar Evolution of International Communist Strategy** [1956]. Lucian W. Pye, **Guerrilla Communism in Malaya** [1956]. Frank N. Trager, ed., **Marxism in Southeast Asia: A Study of Four Countries** [1959]. Gene Overstreet and Marshall Windmiller, **Communism in India** [1959]. Kermit E. Mckenzie, **Comintern and World Revolution 1928-1943: The Shaping of Doctrine** [1964]. Cyril E. Black and T. P. Thornton, eds., **Communism and Revolution: The Strategic Uses of Political Violence** [1964].

56. "Interview with Dr. Robert J. Alexander Conducted by Dr. John French" (October 29, 1989) in John D. French, **Robert J. Alexander: The Complete Bibliography of a Pioneering Latin Americanist** [1991]. pp. 3-11. Baily, **The United States and the Development of South America** [1976]. pp. 59-60.

57. Robert J. Alexander, **The Bolivian National Revolution** [1958]. Robert J. Alexander, **Prophets of the Revolution: Profiles of Latin American Leaders** [1962]. Robert J. Alexander, **Labor Relations in Argentina, Brazil and Chile** [1962]. Robert J. Alexander, **The Venezuelan Democratic Revolution** [1964]. Robert J. Alexander, **Organized Labor in Latin America** [1965]. Robert J. Alexander, **The Communist Party of Venezuela** [1969]. Robert J. Alexander, **Trotskyism in Latin America** [1973]. Robert J. Alexander, **Agrarian Reform in Latin America** [1974]. Robert J. Alexander, **The Right Opposition: The Lovestoneites and the International Communist Opposition of the 1930s** [1981]. For the complete bibliography, see French, **Robert J. Alexander** [1991].

58. In 1953 Theodore Geiger warned that "since 1944 the Communist party of Guatemala--a working arm of Soviet imperialism--has entrenched itself so successfully within the government, the majority political parties, the trade-union and peasant organizations, and the press and radio, that it is today the most powerful active influence in Guatemalan public life". Theodore Geiger, **Communism Versus Progress in Guatemala** [1953]. p. 1. The US government's own contribution to the literature included US Department of State, **Intervention of International Communism in Guatemala** [1954]. A work which clearly reflected the view that events in Guatemala had to be understood in the context of the communist conspiracy to take over Latin America as a whole, was Daniel James, **Red Design for the Americas: Guatemalan Prelude** [1954]. James later wrote a similar book on Cuba. See Daniel James, **Cuba: The First Soviet Satellite in the Americas** [1961]. Writing in the early 1960s, journalist Mario Rosenthal took the view that Guatemala had been on the verge of a "Communist takeover" in the mid-1950s and had been saved from that fate by Washington. He argued that "the genuine concern for all mankind in the US, official and private, has gone beyond anything ever before seen in the world. It could almost be said that humanitarianism has reached its apex in the United States". See Mario Rosenthal, **Guatemala: The Story of an Emergent**

282 *Notes to pages 66-97*

Latin American Democracy [1962]. p. 37.

59. Stokes Newbold (Richard N. Adams), **A Study of Receptivity to Communism in Rural Guatemala** [1954]. Stokes Newbold (Richard N. Adams), "Receptivity to Communist-Fomented Agitation in Rural Guatemala" **Economic Development and Cultural Change** vol. 5. no. 4. 1957. Schlesinger and Stephen Kinzer, **Bitter Fruit: The Untold Story of the American Coup in Guatemala** [1983]. p. 220. See also Richard N. Adams, "Social Change in Guatemala and US Policy" in Richard N. Adams, John P. Gillin, Allan R. Holmberg, Oscar Lewis, Richard W. Patch and Charles Wagley, **Social Change in Latin America Today: Its Implications for United States Policy** [1960].

60. Ronald M. Schneider, **Communism in Guatemala: 1944-1954** [1959]. For example, in the mid-1960s, J. Lloyd Mecham characterized it as "the best work for this period". See J. Lloyd Mecham, **A Survey of United States-Latin American Relations** [1965]. p. 213.

61. Schneider, **Communism in Guatemala: 1944-1954** [1959]. pp. 323-325. Schlesinger and Kinzer, **Bitter Fruit** [1983]. p. 220.

62. Schneider, **Communism in Guatemala: 1944-1954** [1959]. pp. viii-ix, xii-xiii, 321-322. In the 1970s, Schneider revised his analysis, but he still characterized the 1944 to 1954 period as an unsuccessful attempt at a "communist takeover". See Ronald M. Schneider, "Guatemala: An Aborted Communist Takeover" in Thomas T. Hammond, ed., **The Anatomy of Communist Takeovers** [1975]. pp. 563-582.

63. Martz was born in Pennsylvania in 1934 and began his PhD at the University of North Carolina in 1960, after having completed a BA at Harvard in 1955 and an MA at George Washington University in 1960. He finished his PhD in 1963 with the help of a fellowship under the National Defense Education Act (1960-1962) and a Ford Foundation Foreign Area fellowship (1962-1963). Martz became an assistant professor in the Department of Political Science at the University of North Carolina in that year. By 1966 he had risen to associate professor and had become the associate director of the University of North Carolina's Latin American Institute (holding the latter post until 1978). By 1970 he was professor and chairman of the Department of Political Science at the University of North Carolina. Then in 1978 he took up the post of professor and head of the Department of Political Science at Pennsylvania State University, where he remains as professor. Martz was president of the Latin American Studies Association in 1973-1974 and served as editor of the **Latin American Research Review** from 1975 to 1980. Hispanic Foundation, **National Directory of Latin Americanists** [1971]. p. 357.

64. John D. Martz, **Colombia: A Contemporary Political Study** [1962]. John D. Martz, **Justo Rufino Barrios and Central American Union** [1963]. John D. Martz, ed., **The Dynamics of Change in Latin American Politics** [1965]. John D. Martz, *Accion Democratica*: **Evolution of a Modern Political Party in Venezuela** [1966]. John D. Martz and Miguel Jorrin, **Latin-American Political Thought and Ideology** [1970]. John D. Martz, **Ecuador: Conflicting Political Culture and the Quest for Progress** [1972]. John D. Martz and Enrique A. Baloyra, **Electoral Mobilization and Public Opinion: The Venezuela Campaign of 1973** [1976]. John D. Martz and David J. Myers, eds., **Venezuela: The Democratic Experience** [1977]. John D. Martz and Enrique Baloyra, **Political Attitudes in Venezuela: Societal Cleavages and Political Opinion** [1979]. John D. Martz and Lars Schoultz, eds., **Latin America, The United States and the Inter-American System** [1980]. John D. Martz and E. Michael Erisman, eds., **Colossus Challenged: The Struggle for Caribbean Influence** [1982]. John D. Martz, **Politics and Petroleum in Ecuador** [1987]. John D. Martz, ed.,

United States Policy in Latin America: A Quarter Century of Crisis and Challenge [1988].

65. John D. Martz, **Communist Infiltration in Guatemala: A Study of Subversion** [1956].

66. John D. Martz, **Central America: The Crisis and the Challenge** [1959].

67. In 1966 Dexter Perkins described **Central America: The Crisis and the Challenge** as "very useful", and as one of only "two key works" of a "general" nature on Central America. The other "key work" was Franklin D. Parker, **The Central American Republics** [1964]. See Dexter Perkins, **The United States and the Caribbean** [1966]. pp. 185-186.

68. Martz, **Central America** [1959]. pp. 3-4, 8-11.

69. He also pointed to Jorge Ubico of Guatemala whose thirteen-year rule led to a "number of improvements". According to Martz, Ubico facilitated the emergence of a level of economic development which "aroused" an increased "desire for democratic ideals" and his rule was succeeded by almost ten years of "continuous" government and even a "free election", until "communist infiltration upset the picture". Martz, **Central America** [1959]. 18-22.

70. Martz, **Central America** [1959]. pp. 321-323, 324. Martz conceded that the United Fruit Company was larger and more powerful than the various governments of Central America and he acknowledged that UFCO had historically been far less "paternalistic" and benevolent than it was in 1959. However, he argued that by the late 1950s UFCO workers were always paid at a higher rate than labourers who worked for local businessmen and plantation owners, and that their education, recreation, health and sanitation facilities were "superior" to those provided to Central American workers not employed by the United Fruit Company. Also the mid-1950s saw a renegotiation of UFCO contracts on more favourable terms for Costa Rica, Guatemala and Honduras. The United Fruit Company, insisted Martz,"for all its shady past and present reluctance, is generally operating to the advantage of the countries with which it deals", while UFCO gets "fewer tangible benefits" not also received by other foreign firms. Martz, **Central America** [1959]. pp. 324-326.

71. Marshall cited in David Green, "The Cold War Comes to Latin America" in Barton J. Bernstein, ed., **Politics and Policies of the Truman Administration** [1970]. p. 176.

72. Stacy May and Galo Plaza, **The United Fruit Company in Latin America** [1958]. pp. 249-250. This study was characterized by William J. Griffith in 1960 as "a more objective evaluation" of United Fruit's operations than the work of Charles Morrow Wilson and the critical work of Charles David Kepner and Jay Henry Soothill. See Charles Morrow Wilson, **Empire in Green and Gold: The Story of the American Banana Trade** [1947]. Charles David Kepner and Jay Henry Soothill, **The Banana Empire** [1931]. Charles David Kepner, **Social Aspects of the Banana Industry** [1936]. Griffith, "The Historiography of Central America Since 1830" **Hispanic American Historical Review** 1960. p. 566.

73. R. A. Labarge, **Impact of the United Fruit Company on the Economic Development of Guatemala 1946-1954** [1960]. reprinted as R. A. Labarge, "Impact of the United Fruit Company on the Economic Development of Guatemala 1946-1954" in **Studies in Middle American Economics** [1968].

74. Martz, **Central America** [1959]. pp. 337-339. John Moors Cabot, **Toward Our Common American Destiny** [1954]. cited in Martz, **Central America** [1959]. p. 340. Martz's inclusion of Cabot's statement further underlined the close connection between the dominant professional discourses and the foreign-policy process. **Towards Our Common American Destiny** is a collection of speeches and interviews Cabot made during his tenure as Assistant Secretary of State

for Inter-American Affairs. Throughout his work, Martz relied uncritically on official sources. For example, he noted that El Salvador, which by the 1950s was progressing economically under President Osorio, was also "confronted" with a "communist problem of serious proportions", and Osorio's eventual "success" was "ample testimony" to the strength of his anti-communism. To support his positive portrayal of Osorio the anti-communist, Martz relied on the former US ambassador to El Salvador, who in June 1954 praised the Osorio government for "taking 'positive action' against the blandishments of communism". The US Ambassador was then quoted by Martz as having said that Osorio's approach was "based on a frank program of true social progress" and that Honduras was "already well along the road to making itself a small nation's example of democracy in action". Martz, **Central America** [1959]. pp. 91-94. Martz also relied heavily and uncritically on the writings and utterances of other important actors, such as John Foster Dulles and the US ambassador to Guatemala, John Peurifoy.

75. For example he argued that El Salvador was leading the region in political and economic cooperation, and according to Martz, El Salvador's "reasoned approach" was "the very antithesis of the usual breast-beating Latin volatility". Martz, **Central America** [1959]. p. 80.

76. According to Martz, a number of critics of US foreign policy would have taken a "somewhat more sympathetic" view if they had "believed that communism precipitated the US intervention"; however, they were "convinced" that Washington's preoccupation "with communism was but a screen behind which the vultures of yankee imperialism might swoop down and pick the bones of Guatemalans". He insisted that "few" Latin Americans were "ever likely to appreciate the deep concern of the US government--legislative as well as executive--with the growth of communism in the very backyard of the nation". Martz, **Central America**, [1959]. pp. 335-337. Martz did not mention the titles of the books by Toriello and Arévalo, but presumably he was referring to Guillermo Toriello, **La batalla de Guatemala** [1955]. Guillermo Toriello, **A donde va Guatemala?** [1956]. Juan Jose Arévalo, **La democracia y el imperio** [1954]. Juan Jose Arévalo, **Fabula del tiburón y las sardinas: América Latina estrangulada** [1956]. This was later published as Juan Jose Arévalo, **The Shark and the Sardines** [1961]. Other books by former government officials include Manuel Galich, **Por que lucha Guatemala, Arévalo y Arbenz: Dos hombres contra un imperio** [1956]. Alfonso Bauer Paíz, **Como opera el capital yanqui en Centro-america: El caso de Guatemala** [1956].

77. Evidence of the continuing effort to draw attention to the communist threat in Central America can be found in the work of Thorsten V. Kalijarvi, Professor of International and Public Affairs at Pennsylvania State University and former US Ambassador to El Salvador. In 1962 he warned that "a political ground fire" was sweeping Central America. The Communists, according to Kalijarvi, had "fertile ground in which to sow their ideas". He characterized the situation as one in which "many of the poor in Central America feel that Castro is a hero, whose lead they would willingly follow", in part because "they have little or nothing to lose from a take-over". According to the former ambassador, there had "been relatively little change in the ways of life except in the large cities" since the middle of the nineteenth century, and for this reason John Lloyd Stephens's travel volumes were still "surprisingly modern and accurate", and therefore "basic to an understanding of the region". Thorsten, V. Kalijarvi, **Central America: Land of Lords and Lizards** [1962]. pp. 3-4, 11-12.

78. Samuel Guy Inman, **A New Day in Guatemala: A Study of the Present Social Revolution** [1951].

79. In 1967 he was appointed Professor of Government and Director of the Ibero-American Center at New York University. Also in 1967 Silvert, who had worked

as a consultant to the Ford Foundation, took up the post of Program Adviser at the Ford Foundation's International Division. In the early to mid-1970s Silvert, who died in 1976, was a member of the Linowitz Commission. Richard M. Morse, "Kalman H. Silvert (1921-1976): A Reminiscence" **Hispanic American Historical Review** vol. 57. no. 3. 1977. pp. 504-507. He wrote a number of books during his career. See, for example, Kalman H. Silvert, **The Conflict Society: Reaction and Revolution in Latin America** [1961]. Kalman H. Silvert, **Man's Power: A Biased Guide to Political Thought** [1970]. Kalman H. Silvert, **The Relevance of Latin American Domestic Politics to North American Foreign Policy** [1974]. Kalman H. Silvert, **The Reason for Democracy** [1977]. Kalman H. Silvert, **Essays in Understanding Latin America** [1977].

80. Kalman H. Silvert, **A Study in Government: Guatemala** [1954]. pp. 12-13, 58-59, 93. In a 1956 article with John Gillin, Silvert found the major source of the dynamics of the 1944-1954 period in national political and economic developments rather than in the international struggle between the US and international communism. See John Gillin and Kalman H. Silvert, "Ambiguities in Guatemala" **Foreign Affairs** vol. 34. no. 3. 1956.

81. See Philip B. Taylor, Jr., "The Guatemalan Affair: A Critique of United States Foreign Policy" **American Political Science Review** vol. 50. no. 3. 1956.

82. Two North American journalists who were prominent in the rediscovery of Latin America in the late 1950s were Tad Szulc and Herbert L. Matthews. In early 1959 Szulc made a less than prophetic assessment of what the future held for the region when he characterized the assassination of Anastasio Somoza in 1956, the overthrow of Batista in Cuba in 1959, along with the collapse of dictatorships in Argentina, Venezuela, Peru, Brazil and Colombia in the late 1950s, as evidence that "democracy, so late in coming and still taking its first shaky and tentative steps forward, is here to stay in Latin America". He argued that "the pattern of events in the late 1950s suggests unmistakably that the republics of the south, so recently emancipated from the regimes of force, have finally crossed the great divide of their political destinies and taken the road toward constitutional order and stability". Tad Szulc, **Twilight of the Tyrants** [1959]. pp. 3-4. Matthews, a journalist and later editor for the **New York Times**, adopted an encouraging and sympathetic perspective on the Cuban Revolution of 1959. He interviewed Castro in the Sierra Maestra in February 1957, and is often blamed for, or credited with, attracting international attention to the Cuban cause. See Herbert L. Matthews, **The Cuban Story** [1961].

83. President Eisenhower's brother Milton had been warning for years that US policy had to pay greater attention to Latin America, and he had pushed particularly for greater economic assistance. Milton Eisenhower was one of his brother's closest advisors on Latin America, undertaking a 'fact finding mission' to the region for the President in 1953 and again visiting Central America in 1958. However, throughout the 1950s his proposals, particularly in the economic field, were not acted upon. In his major book on US relations with the region, which was published in 1963, he anticipated revolution in Latin America, but argued that it could be peaceful if the US and the people of Latin America worked together. He argued that US "aid can be decisive in helping Latin Americans build better institutions, increase income, and purge injustice from their society"; however, "we must be swift and generous". Milton Eisenhower, **The Wine is Bitter: The United States and Latin America** [1963]. pp. xii-xiii. See also H. W. Brands, Jr., **Cold Warriors: Eisenhower's Generation and American Foreign Policy** [1988]. pp. 27-47.

84. A partial exception to this statement was J. Fred Rippy, **Globe and Hemisphere: Latin America's Place in the Postwar Foreign Relations of the United States** [1958]. Another general book which demonstrates the

limited amount of interest in writing about inter-American relations in the 1950s was Laurence Duggan, **The Americas: The Search for Hemispheric Security** [1949]. Another partial exception was Wilfrid H. Callcott's **The Western Hemisphere: Its Influence on United States Policies to the End of World War II** [1968].

85. Graham H. Stuart, **Latin America and the United States** [1955]. Graham H. Stuart and James L. Tigner, **Latin America and the United States** [1975].

86. See Perkins, **The United States and the Caribbean** [1966]. Howard F. Cline, **The United States and Mexico** [1965]. Thomas F. McGann, **Argentina, the United States, and the Inter-American System 1880-1914** [1958]. Frederick B. Pike, **Chile and the United States 1880-1962: The Emergence of Chile's Social Crisis and the Challenge to United States Diplomacy** [1963]. James C. Carey, **Peru and the United States 1900-1962** [1963]. E. Bradford Burns, **The Unwritten Alliance: Rio Branco and Brazilian-American Relations** [1966].

87. Trask, "Inter-American Relations" in Esquenazi-Mayo and Meyer, eds., **Latin American Scholarship Since World War Two** [1971]. p. 206. In 1965 J. Lloyd Mecham praised **The Latin American Policy of the United States** as an "excellent study" of the historical evolution of US policy towards Latin America. J. Lloyd Mecham, **A Survey of United States-Latin American Relations** [1965]. pp. vii-viii. Writing in the mid-1960s Dexter Perkins, like Mecham, also directed his readers to Bemis's book as a "classic". See Perkins, **The United States and the Caribbean** [1966]. p. 186.

88. Samuel Flagg Bemis, **A Diplomatic History of the United States** [1965]. p. 980. cited in Combs, **American Diplomatic History** [1986]. pp. 226-227, 248.

89. Winks, **Cloak and Gown** [1987]. pp. 382-383. Further evidence of Bemis's Cold Warrior credentials can be found in his position in the debate among academics about whether Communist Party members should be permitted to hold positions at North American universities. In the 1950s Bemis went so far as to resign from the American Association of University Professors when it failed to support an effort to make membership of the Communist Party sufficient reason for the immediate dismissal of academics. Novick, **That Noble Dream** [1988]. p. 326.

90. Samuel Flagg Bemis, "American Foreign Policy and the Blessings of Liberty" in Samuel Flagg Bemis, **American Foreign Policy and the Blessings of Liberty and Other Essays** [1962]. pp. 10-14. Kennedy's Secretary of State, Dean Rusk, was present when Bemis addressed the American Historical Association. Although Bemis's general interpretation of the Cold War and his criticisms of containment represented the most conservative Republicanism, Rusk publicly praised Bemis's speech as "a lucid review of the course we have travelled". Rusk did not take issue with Bemis's interpretation of how the Cold War originated, or the assertion that China was "betrayed". Rusk was quick to assure Bemis that the Kennedy administration was ready to take on the USSR in those parts of the strategically important Third World where 'international communism' had not staked its claim. Melanson, **Writing History and Making Policy** [1983]. pp. 38-39. Undoubtedly Rusk was being diplomatic in his comments on Bemis's address, since he did not share Bemis's commmitment to "rollback". See Thomas J. Schoenbaum, **Waging Peace and War: Dean Rusk in the Truman, Kennedy and Johnson Years** [1988]. pp. 264-267.

91. Dexter Perkins, **The Monroe Doctrine 1823-1826** [1927]. Dexter Perkins, **The Monroe Doctrine 1826-1867** [1933]. Dexter Perkins, **The Monroe Doctrine 1867-1907** [1937]. Dexter Perkins, **Hands Off: A History**

of the Monroe Doctrine [1941]. Dexter Perkins, **A History of the Monroe Doctrine** [1955]. Dexter Perkins, **America and Two Wars** [1944]. Dexter Perkins, **The Evolution of American Foreign Policy** [1948]. Dexter Perkins, **The American Approach to Foreign Policy** [1951]. Dexter Perkins, **Charles Evans Hughes and American Democratic Statesmanship** [1956]. Dexter Perkins, **The New Age of Franklin Roosevelt 1932-1945** [1957]. Dexter Perkins, **The American Way** [1957]. Dexter Perkins, **The United States and Latin America** [1961]. Dexter Perkins, **America's Quest for Peace** [1962]. Dexter Perkins and Glyndon G. Van Deusen, **The United States of America: A History** [1962]. Dexter Perkins and John L. Snell and the Committee on Graduate Education of the American Historical Association, **The Education of Historians in the United States** [1962]. Dexter Perkins, **A History of the Monroe Doctrine** [1963]. Dexter Perkins, **The American Democracy: Its Rise to Power** [1964]. Dexter Perkins, **The Evolution of American Foreign Policy** [1966]. Dexter Perkins, **The Diplomacy of a New Age: Major Issues in US Policy Since 1945** [1967]. Dexter Perkins and Glyndon G. Van Deusen, **The United States of America: A History** [1968].

92. Dexter Perkins, **The American Approach to Foreign Policy** [1962]. Dexter Perkins, **Foreign Policy and the American Spirit: Essays** [1957]. Donald W. White, "History and American Internationalism: The Formulation from the Past after World War II" **Pacific Historical Review** vol. 58. no. 2. 1989. p. 162-163.

93. He also argued that the Good Neighbor Policy was still alive and well. Dexter Perkins, **The United States and the Caribbean** [1947]. pp. x-xi. Although he welcomed the Good Neighbor Policy's renunciation of unilateral intervention he appeared, as one historian noted, to be "opposed" to Washington's intervention primarily because he regarded it as "useless", not because he though it was "wrong". Trask, "Inter-American Relations" in Esquenazi-Mayo and Meyer, eds., **Latin American Scholarship Since World War Two** [1971]. p. 210.

94. Perkins cited in Novick, **That Noble Dream** [1988]. p. 309.

95. In the late 1960s he asserted, "(I)s not the Cold War, with all its human and economic costs, largely their (the Soviet Union's) responsibility?" See Dexter Perkins, **Yield of the Years: An Autobiography** [1969]. pp. 144-145.

96. Dexter Perkins, **The United States and Latin America** [1961]. pp. 84-86. In this book Perkins insisted that the "real enemy" in the Americas was "the penetration of the alien and vicious ideas that emanate from the Kremlin". He characterized the reformist government, which was elected to office in Guatemala in 1944, as "heavily infiltrated" by Communists who "speedily perverted" the government's land-reform program. Perkins dismissed any direct US role in the overthrow of Arbenz in 1954 and emphasized the growing lack of support for the Arbenz regime within the Guatemalan army and on the part of other Latin American governments. He points to the Organization of American States' eventual recognition of the Communist "menace" and concluded that the Guatemalan affair demonstrated that any subsequent attempts by the Communists to "take over the government of an American state" would prove very difficult. He even predicted that Communism had "ebbed" in the region during the 1950s. He stood by this statement in his preface, when he noted that his comments on Latin America's "political development" could appear "over optimistic" following Cuba's increasingly close ties to the Soviet Union, but he felt that in the longer term he would be vindicated. Perkins, **The United States and Latin America** [1961]. pp. ix, 43, 81-83.

97. Perkins, **The United States and Latin America** [1961]. pp. 122-124.

98. Mecham was born in the early 1890s. He completed his PhD under

Herbert Eugene Bolton at the University of California (Berkeley) before taking a position at the University of Texas, where Charles Hackett, another former student of Bolton's, was also based. McCaughey, **International Studies and Academic Enterprise** [1984]. p. 93.

99. Mecham's early published work was on colonial and religious history. J. Lloyd Mecham, **Francisco de Ibarra and Nueva Vizcaya** [1927]. J. Lloyd Mecham, **Church and State in Latin America: A History of Politicoecclesiastical Relations** [1934].

100. Federico Gil, **Latin American-United States Relations** [1971]. p. 143.

101. Abraham F. Lowenthal, "The United States and Latin America: Ending the Hegemonic Presumption" **Foreign Affairs** vol. 55. no. 1. 1976.

102. J. Lloyd Mecham, **The United States and Inter-American Security, 1889-1960** [1961]. p. 424. A shorter and updated version of his chapter on 'international communism', where the general thrust remained unchanged, can also be found in J. Lloyd Mecham, **A Survey of United States Latin American Relations** [1965]. pp. 208-235.

103. Mecham, **The United States and Inter-American Security** [1961]. p. 426. Mecham quoted Robert J. Alexander approvingly as a "well-informed scholar" to support his analysis of international communism. See Alexander, **Communism in Latin America** [1957]. Another work which approached 'international communism' in Latin America in a fashion similar to Mecham's was the work of Dorothy Dillon, who was an employee on the Planning Staff of the State Department's Bureau of Educational and Cultural Affairs. In 1962 Dillon argued that "complete Communist domination of Guatemala" had been "forestalled by the overthrow of the Arbenz regime". She warned, however, that since the mid-1950s Latin America "has become an important target in the judgement of the leaders of international communism". Dorothy Dillon, **International Communism and Latin America: Perspectives and Prospects** [1962]. p. 14. In 1965 Mecham cited Dillon, along with Alexander's **Communism in Latin America** and a 1960 US Senate Committee on Foreign Relations publication, as "the best references on Communism in Latin America". See J. Lloyd Mecham, **A Survey of United States-Latin American Relations** [1965]. pp. 208-209. In 1966 Alexander's book was described by Dexter Perkins as "the key work on Communism" for the region. See Perkins, **The United States and the Caribbean** [1966]. pp. 184-185.

104. Mecham, **The United States and Inter-American Security**, pp. 436-437. The main secondary sources for his section on Guatemala are Robert J. Alexander, anti-communist journalist Daniel James's **Red Design for the Americas** [1954], and Ronald Schneider's **Communism in Guatemala: 1944-1954** [1959]. Mecham argued that the 'international communist' movement gained control of the Guatemalan government primarily because of the "indulgent attitude" of Arbenz and that the debate over whether Arbenz himself was a communist was unimportant: what was important was Arbenz's unwavering "support and loyalty to his communist friends". To support his interpretation of Arbenz, Mecham relied uncritically on US Ambassador Peurifoy, who stated that he was unable to get anywhere with Arbenz "in his efforts to point out the dangers of Communist infiltration". According to Peurifoy, Arbenz argued that "many notorious Reds" were either not Communists or "were not dangerous"; furthermore, insisted Peurifoy, Arbenz "thought and talked like a Communist". Mecham also emphasized that, despite Arbenz's denial that the Soviet Union had any "designs" on Guatemala, the "Reds in Guatemala were working for Soviet aims under consistent and disciplined Soviet control". This interpretation was apparently based entirely on Peurifoy's comment that most of the

Communist leaders in Guatemala had made at least one trip to the USSR or another eastern-bloc country. Mecham concluded that in the mid-1950s the United States' "own security" as well as that of the other countries of Central and South America had been in "jeopardy" from "the agents of international Communism" who sought to use "Guatemala as a base". Mecham, **The United States and Inter-American Security** [1961]. pp. 438-440. Peurifoy's claim that the Guatemalan Communist leadership had almost all made trips to the Communist bloc was in the US Department of State **Bulletin** no. 31. September 6, 1954, p. 334; cited in Mecham, **The United States and Inter-American Security** [1961]. p. 440. Much the same interpretation of events, minus the overt reference to Peurifoy, can be found in J. Lloyd Mecham, **A Survey of United States-Latin American Relations** [1965]. pp. 215-216. It is worth noting, however, that according to Silvert no Guatemalan Communists visited the eastern bloc for what he called "international conferences" until 1952, by which time the Guatemalan Communist Party's position in the country was "secure". Silvert, **A Study in Government: Guatemala** [1954]. p. 59.

105. Mecham, **The United States and Inter-American Security** [1961]. pp. 453-455, 462. In 1965 Mecham devoted considerable attention to Cuba, particularly in a section entitled "The Cuban Problem". See J. Lloyd Mecham, **A Survey of United States-Latin American Relations** [1965]. pp. 220-235.

106. Mecham, **The United States and Inter-American Security** [1961]. pp. 474-475.

107. Mecham, **The United States and Inter-American Security** [1961]. pp.462-464.

108. Arthur Preston Whitaker, **The United States and South America: The Northern Republics** [1948]. Arthur Preston Whitaker, **The Western Hemisphere Idea: Its Rise and Decline** [1954]. Arthur Preston Whitaker, **The United States and Argentina** [1954]. Arthur Preston Whitaker, **The United States and the Southern Cone: Argentina, Chile and Uruguay** [1976].

109. Examples of sophisticated anthropological and historical work include Eric Wolf, **Sons of the Shaking Earth: The People of Mexico and Guatemala--Their Land, History and Culture** [1959]. Charles Gibson, **The Aztecs Under Spanish Rule: A History of the Indians of the Valley of Mexico 1519-1810** [1964].

110. Wood was born in Everett, Washington, in 1909 and studied for his BA and MA at Reed College in the early 1930s. He gained a PhD in political science from Columbia University in 1940, and he worked as an instructor there from 1936 until 1942. As already noted, in 1942 and 1943 he worked as Senior Administrative Assistant in the Division of Special Political Affairs of the Department of State, before taking up the position of Assistant Professor and later Professor at Swarthmore College from 1943 to 1950, as well as serving as Assistant Director of the Division of Social Sciences at the Rockefeller Foundation during much of this period. In 1950 he took up the full-time post of Staff and Executive Associate of the Social Science Research Council in New York. For twenty-five years thereafter he ardently supported North American research on Latin America, making sure that grants and fellowships were available for young North Americans, and organizing and sponsoring seminars and conferences in North and South America. From 1973, when he retired from the SSRC, until his death in 1986, he devoted himself to archival research in the National Archives in Washington, the results of which were a book on Ecuador and Peru and his final book on the fate of the Good Neighbor Policy after 1945. Lieuwen, "Bryce Wood (1909-1986)" **Hispanic American Historical Review** 1987. p. 143. Hispanic Foundation, Library of Congress, **National Directory of Latin Americanists** [1971]. pp. 603-604. See, for example, Bryce Wood, "The Department of State and the

Non-national Interest: The Cases of Argentine Meat and Paraguayan Tea" **Inter-American Economic Affairs** vol. 15. no. 2. 1961. Bryce Wood, "External Restraints on the Good Neighbor Policy" **Inter-American Economic Affairs** vol. 16. no. 2. 1962. **The United States and Latin American Wars 1932-1942** [1966]. Bryce Wood, "Self-Plagiarism and Foreign Policy" **Latin American Research Review** vol. 3. no. 3. 1968. Bryce Wood, "How Wars End in Latin America" **Annals of the American Academy of Political and Social Science** no. 392. 1972. Bryce Wood, **Aggression and History: The Case of Ecuador and Peru** [1978]. Bryce Wood, "The End of the Good Neighbor Policy: Changing Patterns of US Influence" **Caribbean Review** vol. 11. no. 2. 1982. Bryce Wood, **The Dismantling of the Good Neighbor Policy** [1985].

111. Johnson saw it as standing out among a "disappointing" field in the early 1960s. Johnson, "One Hundred Years of Historical Writing on Modern Latin America" **Hispanic American Historical Review** 1985. pp. 748-749, 753. See also Combs, **American Diplomatic History** [1983]. pp. 273-274.

112. Bryce Wood, **The Making of the Good Neighbor Policy** [1961]. pp. 132-135.

113. Wood, **The Making of the Good Neighbor Policy** [1961]. pp. 167, 361. See Abraham F. Lowenthal, "'Liberal', 'Radical' and 'Bureaucratic' Perspectives on US Latin American Policy: The Alliance for Progress in Retrospect" in Julio Cotler and Richard R. Fagen, eds., **Latin America and the United States: The Changing Political Realities** [1974]. p. 215.

114. Novick, **That Noble Dream** [1988]. p. 310.

115. See Barbara Barksdale Clouse, **Brainpower for the Cold War: The Sputnik Crisis and the National Defense Education Act of 1958** [1981].

116. Richard R. Fagen, "Studying Latin American Politics: Some Implications of a *Dependencia* Approach" **Latin American Research Review** vol. 12. no. 2. 1977. p. 4. Martin C. Needler and Thomas W. Walker linked the dramatic growth of Latin American studies in the 1960s to the rise of Castro, and the greater emphasis put on the region by the Kennedy administration. See Martin C. Needler and Thomas W. Walker, "The Current Status of Latin American Studies Programs" **Latin American Research Review** vol. 6. no. 1. 1971. pp. 133-134. John J. Johnson noted that following the rise of Castro "there was a stampede of students into the field". He described the funding and infrastructure for Latin American studies as being provided by "Washington, in the interest of national security"; by "the foundations, as they have tended to be, enamoured of the exotic; and the colleges and universities, to reaffirm their proclaimed dedication to public service". Johnson, "One Hundred Years of Historical Writing on Modern Latin America" **Hispanic American Historical Review** 1985. pp. 749-750.

117. Benjamin, "The Framework of US Relations with Latin America in the Twentieth Century" **Diplomatic History** 1987. p. 107. Wiarda, **Ethnocentrism in Foreign Policy** [1985]. p. 21. As Robert Packenham has argued, the Alliance for Progress represented one of "the most sustained" and "explicit" efforts to bring democracy to the Third World. According to Packenham, President Kennedy defined democracy as constitutional democracy, and was apparently convinced that "economic and social progress" would dramatically increase the possibility of North American style democracy taking root in Latin America. Packenham, **Liberal America and the Third World** [1973]. pp. 69-70.

118. Lyman Bryson, "Introduction" in Adams et al., **Social Change in Latin America Today: The Implications for United States Policy** [1960]. p. 1.

119. Benjamin, "The Framework of US Relations with Latin America in the

Twentieth Century" **Diplomatic History** 1987. p. 107. Wiarda, **Ethnocentrism in Foreign Policy** [1985]. p. 5. Max Millikan and Walt Whitman Rostow, **A Proposal: Key to an Effective Foreign Policy** [1957]. Max F. Millikan and Donald L. Blackmer et al., **The Emerging Nations: Their Growth and United States Policy** [1961]. Adolf A. Berle, **Latin America: Diplomacy and Reality** [New York: Harper and Row, 1962, published for the Council on Foreign Relations]. Cyril E. Black, **The Dynamics of Modernization: A Study in Comparative History** [1966]. For an analysis of the particularly close fit between modernization theory and US foreign policy in the early 1960s, see Ramirez-Faria, **The Origins of Economic Inequality Between Nations** [1991]. pp. 119-120.

120. Gordon published an appraisal of the Alliance for Progress in 1963. He articulated a view that put considerable emphasis on the social and political benefits which flow from encouraging private enterprise. Although he accepted that Latin America's economies would be mixed, he argued that the role of the public sector needed to be clearly demarcated. He was concerned that government-run enterprises would become top heavy and inefficient. He was convinced that the terms of trade between North and South had not been as disadvantageous as many Latin Americans believed, and he injected a note of caution into the expectations held out for the Alliance, warning that it would be unadvisable to expect too much too quickly. See Lincoln Gordon, **A New Deal for Latin America: The Alliance for Progress** [1963]. Gordon's cautious but optimistic analysis had been preceded by a collection of articles edited by longtime US Ambassador to the OAS John C. Dreier, which included contributions from Milton Eisenhower and Dean Rusk as well as Raul Prebisch. The overall tone was, of course, supportive. See John C. Dreier, ed., **The Alliance for Progress: Problems and Perspectives** [1962]. See also John C. Dreier, **The Organization of American States and the Hemisphere Crisis** [1962].

121. Abraham F. Lowenthal, "'Liberal', 'Radical' and 'Bureaucratic' Perspectives on US Latin American Policy: The Alliance for Progress in Retrospect" in Cotler and Fagen, eds., **Latin America and the United States** [1974]. pp. 230-232. Baily, **The United States and the Development of South America 1945-1975** [1976]. pp. 84-96. For an insider's account, see Arthur M. Schlesinger, Jr., **A Thousand Days: John F. Kennedy in the White House** [1965]. pp. 168-185. And for programmatic support at the time of the Alliance for Progress's launch, see Charles O. Porter and Robert J. Alexander, **The Struggle for Democracy in Latin America** [1961].

122. Berle cited in Benjamin, "The Framework of US Relations with Latin America in the Twentieth Century" **Diplomatic History** 1987. pp. 107-108.

123. Mecham, **The United States and Inter-American Security** [1961]. p. 388.

124. Frank Tannenbaum, **Ten Keys to Latin America** [1962]. pp. 227-237.

125. L. S. Stavrianos, **Global Rift: The Third World Comes of Age** [1981]. pp. 685-686.

126. Delesseps S. Morrison, **Latin American Mission** [1965]. pp. 34, 97-105, 199. See Baily, **The United States and the Development of South America 1945-1975** [1976]. pp. 88-89.

127. Kolko, **Confronting the Third World** [1988]. pp. 132-133.

128. John J. Johnson, ed., **The Role of the Military in Underdeveloped Countries** [1962]. Gendzier, **Managing Political Change** [1985]. pp. 63-67. For a similar concern and approach, see Samuel P. Huntington, ed., **Changing Patterns of Military Politics** [1962]. John J. Johnson, **T h e**

Military and Society in Latin America [1964]. Morris Janowitz, **The Military in the Political Development of New Nations: An Essay in Comparative Analysis** [1964]. Morris Janowitz, ed., **The New Military: Changing Patterns of Organization** [1964].

129. National Security Council, "US Overseas Internal Defense Policy" August 1, 1962, 80: 281A., pp. 12, 16; cited in Kolko, **Confronting the Third World** [1988]. p. 133.

130. See Edwin Lieuwen, **Arms and Politics in Latin America** [1960]. Edwin Lieuwen, **Generals versus Presidents: Neo-Militarism in Latin America** [1964]. Edwin Lieuwen, **US Policy in Latin America: A Short History** [1965]. Edwin Lieuwen, **The United States and the Challenge to Security in Latin America** [1966]. Johnson, "One Hundred Years of Historical Writing on Modern Latin America" **Hispanic American Historical Review** 1985. p. 756.

131. Simon G. Hanson, **Five Years of the Alliance for Progress: An Appraisal** [1967]. See also Simon G. Hanson, **Dollar Diplomacy Modern Style: Chapters in the Failure of the Alliance for Progress** [1970]. Hanson wrote an important study of Latin American economics in the early 1950s. See Simon G. Hanson, **Economic Development in Latin America** [1951]. Latin America based critics included Victor Alba, **Alliance Without Allies: The Mythology of Progress in Latin America** [1965]. Even J. Lloyd Mecham struck a critical note with regard to the Alliance for Progress, although his views foreshadowed the rise of conservative development theory. In 1965, he asserted that, although Washington's financial commitment had not wavered, the Alliance's "status" some three years after it had been launched "was not encouraging". Mecham outlined four "obstacles" to the Alliance. He argued that it had been "oversold" at the start seeking "to accomplish in a decade what no nation has every accomplished in less than a generation". In particular he asserted that no account had been taken of the region's "basic problem"--the "population explosion". Second, the early 1960s in Latin America were notable for the "exceptional number of political upheavals", at a time when "political stability" was what the region "need(ed) most", if "any economic program" was going to "succeed". Third, the amount of foreign and domestic private capital invested in the region "fell far below expectations". Inflation, political instability, and fear of expropriation, caused a "lack of confidence" which "greatly retarded the inflow of American capital", while private investment on the part of Latin Americans was also disappointing. The fourth "obstacle", which Mecham regarded, with some accuracy, as "probably the most important reason", was that the "landowning aristocracy" and the "conservative class" who traditionally controlled the region's political and economic life, had a "psychotic fear" of the Alliance. Mecham was confident, however, that the "oligarchic reaction" would be unable to "indefinitely hold back the tide of reform"; however, he was less certain whether the elite would embrace reform or be swept aside by revolution. In his view the Alliance's "future" depended "greatly" on this decision. Mecham concluded his discussion of the Alliance by emphasizing its "dependence" on the Latin Americans. He quoted sympathetically from a government report which argued that "no matter what the amount of outside assistance, nothing will avail to promote rapid progress if Latin-American leaders do not stimulate the will for development, mobilize internal savings, encourage the massive flow of private investment, and promote other economic, social and administrative change". Mecham, **A Survey of United States-Latin American Relations** [1965]. pp. 204-206.

132. Irving Louis Horowitz, "The Rise and Fall of Project Camelot" in Irving Louis Horowitz, **Ideology and Utopia in the United States 1956-1976** [1977]. pp. 226, 231, 236, 244. Michael T. Klare, **The University-Military-**

Police Complex [1977]. pp. 49-62. Gendzier, **Managing Political Change** [1985]. pp. 60-63. See also Irving Louis Horowitz, ed., **The Rise and Fall of Project Camelot: Studies in the Relationship Between Social Science and Practical Politics** [1967]. Kalman H. Silvert, "Politics and Studying Societies: The United States and Latin America" in Silvert, ed., **Essays in Understanding Latin America** [1977]. pp. 131-141.

133. Willard F. Barber and C. Neale Ronning, **Internal Security and Military Power: Counterinsurgency and Civic Action in Latin America** [1966]. Gendzier, **Managing Political Change** [1985]. pp. 63, 77.

134. Samuel P. Huntington, **Political Order in Changing Societies** [1968].

135. William D. Rogers, **The Twilight Struggle: The Alliance for Progress and the Politics of Development in Latin America** [1967]. See also J. Warren Nystrom and Nathan A. Haverstock, **The Alliance for Progress: Key to Latin American Development** [1966].

136. Robert N. Burr, **Our Troubled Hemisphere: Perspectives on US-Latin American Relations** [1967].

137. Robert J. Alexander, **Today's Latin America** [1968]. pp. vii-viii, 12-13, 236-239.

138. McCaughey, **International Studies and Academic Enterprise** [1984]. pp. 105, 200, 250.

139. Needler and Walker, "The Current Status of Latin American Studies Programs" **Latin American Research Review** 1971. pp. 119-120, 133. Major centres for Latin American studies in the US include The Institute of Latin America and Iberian Studies at Columbia University, Latin American Studies at Cornell University, the Latin American Studies Program at Georgetown University, and the Latin American Studies Program at Indiana University. There is a Latin American Studies Program in the School of Advanced International Studies at Johns Hopkins University, at the New School for Social Research (New York) and at The Ohio State University. There is the Ibero-American Language and Area Center at New York University and the well-known and highly regarded Center for Latin American Studies at Stanford University as well as the Latin America Area Center at the University of Arizona. The University of California has the Center for Latin American Studies at Berkeley and the Latin American Center at Los Angeles, not to mention its Center for US-Mexican Studies in San Diego. The University of Chicago, the University of Connecticut, the Unversity of Florida, the University of Illinois and the University of Pittsburgh all boast centers for Latin American studies, while the University of Texas is well-known for its Institute of Latin American Studies in Austin. The School of International Studies at the University of Washington has a Latin American Studies department and there are also the Council on Latin American Studies at Yale University and the Center for Latin America at the University of Wisconsin. In Canada there are York University's Research Program for Latin America and Caribbean Studies, the Latin American Studies Committee at the University of Toronto, while the Center for Developing Area Studies at McGill University is well-known for its Latin American program. See Thomas P. Fenton and Mary J. Heffron, eds., **Latin America and Caribbean: A Directory of Resources** [1986]. pp. 118-120. For a comprehensive list, up to the end of the 1960s, see Robert P. Haro, **Latin American Research in the United States and Canada: A Guide and Directory** [1971]. pp. 73-102.

140. Hispanic Foundation, **National Directory of Latin Americanists** [1971]. pp. 1, 3. Richard Graham and Peter H. Smith, "Introduction" in Richard Graham and Peter H. Smith, eds., **New Approaches to Latin American History** [1974]. p. ix.

141. In 1960 a total of three PhDs on social change and development in

Central America were awarded by the fifteen major North American universities, which produced almost 100 of the 140 PhDs granted to the mid-1970s. This was followed by only 1 in 1961, 0 in 1962, 4 in 1963 and 2 in 1964. The total picked up substantially by the mid-1960s, with 8 being granted in 1965, 8 in 1966, 10 in 1967, 11 in 1968, 9 in 1969, 9 in 1970, 6 in 1971 and 19 in 1972, dropping off dramatically to 1 in 1973 and 2 in 1974. See D. Neil Snarr and E. Leonard Brown, "An Analysis of PhD Dissertations on Central America 1960-1974" **Latin American Research Review** vol. 12. no. 2. 1977. pp. 187-195.

142. See **Latin American Research Review** vol. 1. no. 1. 1965. p. 5.

143. Johnson, "One Hundred Years of Historical Writing on Modern Latin America" **Hispanic American Historical Review** 1985. pp. 750-751. McCaughey, **International Studies and Academic Enterprise** [1984]. p. 222. The **Journal of Interamerican Studies** moved to the University of Miami (Coral Gables) in 1964 and in 1967 the connection with the Pan American Foundation was terminated when the University of Miami assumed complete financial and publishing responsibility for the journal, and the Institute of Interamerican Studies at the Center for Advanced International Studies at the University of Miami assumed editorial control. In the early 1970s the journal changed its name to the **Journal of Interamerican Studies and World Affairs**, although its focus remained on Latin America. See, John P. Harrison, "History of the **Journal**" in **Cumulative Index Journal of Interamerican Studies and World Affairs, 1959-1989** [1989]. pp. 5-6. On the foundation of the Latin American Studies Association, see Howard F. Cline, "The Latin American Studies Association: A Summary Survey with Appendix" **Latin American Research Review** vol. 2. no. 1. 1966. pp. 57-79. Also see Robert A. Packenham, **The Dependency Movement: Scholarship and Politics in Development Studies** [1992]. pp. 268-273.

144. Kalman H. Silvert, "Politics and Studying Societies: The United States and Latin America" in Silvert, **Essays in Understanding Latin America** [1977]. p. 132.

145. Richard Lambert et al., **Beyond Growth: The Next Stage in Language and Area Studies** [1984]. pp. 10-11. The growing number of specialists, research centers and increasing quantities of research money pumped into Latin American studies programs by the 1960s, were complimented by a coordinated effort to build up Latin American material in North American libraries. In 1947 the Association of Research Libraries formally adopted what was known as the Farmington Plan. The Plan had begun to emerge in the late 1930s when the Library of Congress became worried that the outbreak of war in Europe would curtail North American access to important European archives and research materials. Following a series of meetings convened in Farmington, Connecticut, during World War II, by Wilmarth Sheldon Lewis, chief of the Central Information Division of the Research and Analysis branch of the OSS, the Farmington Plan was finally implemented in 1948, when the systematic acquisition of French, Swedish and Swiss publications for that year was undertaken. The Plan was gradually expanded and by the 1960s it extended to most areas of the world, encompassing 145 countries by 1961. The Farmington Plan was essentially a voluntary agreement between over sixty North American libraries to be responsible for the collection and maintenance of overseas publications. North American libraries usually agreed to take responsibility for particular countries. For example, Tulane University Library emerged as the major depository for material related to Central America, taking responsibility for El Salvador, Guatemala, Honduras and Nicaragua, while Costa Rica fell to the University of Kansas Library. The Association of Research Libraries Farmington Plan was further complemented by the Seminar on the Acquisition of Latin American Library Materials (SALALM), held in 1956 under the auspices of the University of Florida and the Pan American Union,

which sought to expand the systematic acquisition of Latin American research material. SALALM evolved into an annual meeting of librarians and Latin American specialists and successfully gained financial support from the Organization of American States and the Rockefeller Foundation. By the 1960s SALALM had organized the Latin American Cooperative Acquisitions Program (LACAP), which was a cooperative commercial acquisitions program run by the Stechert-Hafner Corporation, which gradually embraced research libraries across North America. Haro, **Latin American Research in the United States and Canada** [1971]. pp. 1-5. Winks, **Cloak and Gown** [1987]. pp. 96, 108-109.

146. Thomas L. Karnes, **The Failure of Union: Central America 1824-1960** [1961]. Franklin D. Parker, **The Central American Republics** [1964].

147. Mario Rodríguez, **Central America** [1965]. pp. 148-156. 168.

148. The first studies by economic development specialists focusing on Central America were also beginning to appear in this period. See John F. McCamant, **Development Assistance in Central America** [1967]. McCamant's book was narrow in focus and argued that the main obstacle to Central American 'development' was the weakness of the public sector, a situation which he perceived as having improved over the course of the 1960s as a result of the Alliance for Progress. It was based on his 1965 PhD dissertation. John F. McCamant, **The Role of International Economic Assistance Programs in Economic and Political Change in Central America** [1965]. See also Roger D. Hansen, **Central America: Regional Integration and Economic Development** [1967]. Gary W. Wynia, **Politics and Planners: Economic Development Policy in Central America** [1972].

149. Dana G. Munro, **Intervention and Dollar Diplomacy in the Caribbean, 1900-1921** [1964]. Dana G. Munro, **The United States and the Caribbean Republics 1921-1933** [1974]. Richard V. Salisbury, "Good Neighbors?: The United States and Latin America in the Twentieth Century" in Haines and Walker, eds., **American Foreign Relations** [1984]. pp. 316-317. John J. Johnson described Munro's 1964 volume as "the best defense of the United States' Caribbean policy". See John J. Johnson, "One Hundred Years of Historical Writing on Modern Latin America" **Hispanic American Historical Review** vol. 65. no. 4. 1985. p. 754.

150. Munro, **The United States and the Caribbean Republics** [1974]. pp. 379-381.

151. He argued that the dictatorships in El Salvador and Guatemala in the 1930s "were not necessarily unpopular" and "undemocratic procedures did not prevent them from being accepted, more or less willingly, by the majority of the people". Munro insisted that the State Department "usually maintained normal diplomatic relations with governments of this sort", while hoping that "the relative stability which they provided would encourage progress toward more democratic government". Writing in 1974, he argued that this hope "seems to have been justified", since El Salvador and Guatemala, "have elections today in which most of the citizens seem to participate". Munro, **The United States and the Caribbean Republics** [1974]. pp. 381-383.

152. Marvin Goldwert, **The Constabulary in the Dominican Republic and Nicaragua: Progeny and Legacy of United States Intervention** [1962]. Interest in the history of US involvement was apparent in some PhD research topics. For example, see T. J. Dodd, **The United States in Nicaraguan Politics: Supervised Elections 1927-32** [1966]. R. B. Chardkoff, **Communist Toehold in the Americas: A History of Official United States Involvement in the Guatemalan Crisis 1954** [1967].

153. Neill Macaulay, **The Sandino Affair** [1967].

154. For earlier studies which focused explicitly on the Marines, see Roscoe R. Hill "American Marines in Nicaragua 1912-1925" in A. Curtis Wilgus, ed., **Hispanic American Essays: A Memorial to James Alexander Robertson** [1942]. Bernard C. Nalty, **The United States Marines in Nicaragua** [1962].

155. A good example of his tendency to romanticize both sides in the conflict was his description of a battle at Ocotal between Sandino's guerrillas and the Marines in mid-July 1927. According to Macaulay "the Marines at Ocotal held their ground masterfully. They fought with all the tenacity, courage and skill for which the Corps was famous. Sandino's scrawny brown peasants fought less skilfully, but no less bravely. If nothing else they showed they knew how to die. Eventually they would develop their own unique and effective style of warfare and prove themselves worthy opponents of the US Marines". Macaulay, **The Sandino Affair** [1967]. p. 82. Macaulay's apparent sympathy for both sides no doubt grew from his own experience as a soldier both in the US Army in Korea and with Castro's guerrilla army in the late 1950s. This is illustrated by a second book about his time in Cuba on the eve of the revolution. The book is not sentimental, but Macaulay quite clearly emerges as a romantic adventurer, in love with soldiering, a patriot who believes in democracy and capitalism, but committed to eradicating social and economic injustice. Neil Macaulay, **A Rebel in Cuba** [1970]. See Charles W. Bergquist, "Recent United States Studies in Latin American History: Trends Since 1965" **Latin American Research Review** vol. 9. no. 1. 1974. p. 13. Neill Macaulay was born and raised in South Carolina and served as an officer in the US Army for two years in the early 1950s. In 1958 he went to Cuba and joined Fidel Castro's rebel army (Ejército Rebelde de Movimiento 26 de Julio) serving in the Sierra de Los Organos, Pinar del Río Province. He initially worked as a first lieutenant and staff officer, subsequently commanding a heavy weapons platoon. In 1960 he went back to the US and embarked on graduate work in history. He gained an MA from the University of South Carolina and a PhD from the University of Texas. In the mid 1960s he went to Brazil as a Ford Foundation Fellow. By the late 1960s he was working as Assistant Professor of History at the University of Florida in Gainesville.

156. Wood, **The Rise of the Good Neighbor Policy** [1961]. p. 15. Cited in Macaulay, **The Sandino Affair** [1967]. p. 26.

157. William Kamman, **A Search for Stability: United States Diplomacy Toward Nicaragua 1925-1933** [1968].

158. Kamman, **A Search for Stability** [1968]. pp. 2, 7-8, 136-137, 186.

159. Kamman, **A Search for Stability** [1968]. pp. 1, 7-8.

160. Kamman, **A Search for Stability** [1968]. pp. 1, 17, 19-20. In the case of the elections of 1928, Kamman was at pains to minimize the role of the US in securing the presidency for the Liberal General Moncada. He argued that there was "no evidence" that the State Department "intentionally boosted" the General. He conceded that Moncada "made the most" of his visit to, and his various "contacts" in, Washington, especially Secretary of State Stimson, and that the people of Nicaragua were certainly convinced that he had been anointed by Washington. However, Kamman insisted that US "design" did not bring about these "attitudes and events". Kamman, **A Search for Stability** [1968]. pp. 153.

161. Kamman, **A Search for Stability** [1968]. p. 218.

3. The Limits of Power 1968-1979

1. Containment, from 1947 to 1968, was followed by a weaker consensus around détente, which began to form in late 1969 and was at its height from mid-1971 to late 1973 and had begun to collapse by early 1975. No foreign policy consensus emerged under Ford or Carter, and Reagan's presidency was not characterized by anything resembling a national consensus on foreign policy until its final years. This particular periodization is from Richard A. Melanson, **Writing History and Making Policy: The Cold War, Vietnam and Revisionism** [1983]. p. 9. See also Richard A. Melanson, **Reconstructing Consensus: American Foreign Policy Since the Vietnam War** [1991]. On the breakdown of 'consensus' see Ole R. Holsti and James R. Rosenau, **American Leadership in World Affairs: Vietnam and the Breakdown of Consensus** [1984]. On the crisis of hegemony, see Stephen Gill, **American Hegemony and the Trilateral Commission** [1990]. pp. 3, 48, 86-88.

2. In 1967 Senator Eugene J. McCarthy, who sought the Democratic Party's nomination for President in 1968, called for a "more restrained" US foreign policy. He asserted that if the US was going to "meet its historical obligations" in Latin America and "fulfill the promise" of the Alliance for Progress, Washington had to "close the gap between myth and reality" in its policy in the region. In the case of Vietnam he pushed for greater U.N. involvement in seeking a settlement, and a US military strategy to control certain strong points at the same time as the US sought negotiations with the NLF. See Eugene McCarthy, **The Limits of Power: America's Role in the World** [1967]. pp. vii, 115-116, 195-196. Also see, for example, Arthur M. Schlesinger, Jr., **The Bitter Heritage: Vietnam and American Democracy** [1966]. J. William Fulbright, **The Arrogance of Power** [1967]. Theodore Draper, **Abuse of Power** [1967]. William J. Lederer, **Our Own Worst Enemy** [1968]. See also Charles Gati, "Another Grand Debate?: The Limitationist Critique of American Foreign Policy" **World Politics** vol. 21. no. 1. 1968.

3. Theodore Roszak, ed., **The Dissenting Academy: Critical Essays on the American Intellectual Establishment** [1968]. See also Barton Berstein, ed., **Towards a New Past: Dissenting Essays in American History** [1968]. Also see the overall critique of North American political science articulated by the Caucus for a New Political Science (CNPS), which was established in 1967 within the American Political Science Association. See Marvin Surkin and Alan Wolfe, "Introduction: An End to Political Science" in Marvin Surkin and Alan Wolfe, eds., **An End to Political Science: The Caucus Papers** [1970]. For a discussion of CNPS see David M. Ricci, **The Tragedy of Political Science: Politics, Scholarship and Democracy** [1984]. pp. 188-190. See also Peter Novick, **That Noble Dream: The "Objectivity Question" and the American Historical Profession** [1988]. pp. 415-417. Bernard Sternsher, **Consensus, Conflict and American Historians** [1975]. Jonathan M. Wiener, "Radical Historians and the Crisis in American History 1959-1980" **Journal of American History** vol. 76. no. 2. 1989. John Higham, "Changing Paradigms: The Collapse of Consensus History" **Journal of American History** vol. 76. no. 2. 1989. Gerda Lerner, has argued that "what we now perceive as the 'crisis of history'" was "merely the coming to an end of the function of history as elite ideology". Gerda Lerner, "The Necessity of History and the Professional Historian" **Journal of American History** vol. 69. no. 1. 1982. p. 19. William Roseberry has argued that there was an ongoing "theoretical and methodological crisis" in anthropology from the mid-1960s. William Roseberry, "Anthropology, History and Modes of Production" in William Roseberry, **Anthropologies and Histories: Essays in Culture, History, and Political Economy** [1989]. p. 148.

4.   James Petras, "Ideology and the United States Political Scientists" **Science and Society** vol. 29. no. 2. 1965. André Gunder Frank, "Sociology of Development and Underdevelopment of Sociology" (1967) reprinted in André Gunder Frank, **Latin America: Underdevelopment or Revolution-Essays on the Development of Underdevelopment and the Immediate Enemy** [1969]. pp. 21-94. James Petras, "Latin American Studies in the US: A Critical Assessment" **Science and Society** vol. 32. no. 2. 1968; reprinted in James Petras, **Politics and Social Structure in Latin America** [1970]. Susanne Jonas Bodenheimer, **The Ideology of Developmentalism: The American Paradigm Surrogate for Latin American Studies** [1971]. From a liberal perspective the theoretical poverty of political science, in relation to Latin America, had already been lamented in the early 1960s by Merle Kling who noted that, like Latin America itself, political research on Latin America was characterized by underdevelopment and traditionalism and was under "internal and external pressures to modernize". See Merle Kling, "The State of Research on Latin America: Political Science" in Charles Wagley, ed., **Social Science Research on Latin America** [1964]. p. 168.

5.   Many practitioners, and critics, emphasize that dependency theory is not a theory but an approach. For example, David Becker has argued in favour of the terms **dependencismo** and **dependencista**, which he feels "better capture the sense that dependency is primarily a world view and an approach to the study of development". In his view the use of Spanish terminology also acknowledges "the Latin American origins of many who have made major contributions to the intellectual development of the dependency viewpoint". See David G. Becker, **The New Bourgeoisie and the Limits of Dependency: Mining, Class and Power in 'Revolutionary' Peru** [1983]. p. 3. See also Fernando Henrique Cardoso, "The Consumption of Dependency Theory in the United States" **Latin American Research Review** vol. 12. no. 3. 1977. In this study the terms 'theory' and 'approach' will be used interchangeably when talking about dependency. Although it may be inaccurate to characterize dependency, as a theory it is still widely represented in North America as a theory. Furthermore, by relying on the English terminology, this study seeks to emphasize that dependency theory, despite its Latin American background, has been thoroughly domesticated by the North American radical and liberal professional discourses.

6.   By the mid-1970s a group of neo-conservative historians, political scientists and political activists had emerged as part of a wider 'conservative' revival which elected Ronald Reagan to the White House at the end of 1980. The 'conservatives', who will be discussed in Chapter 4, included neo-conservatives, traditional conservatives, religious fundamentalists, and even individuals who regarded themselves as liberals. Despite differences, they can be located in the 'conservative' discourses as they emerged in the late 1970s. Sydney Blumenthal has characterized the neo-conservatives as the "counter-establishment", which underlines the position of many of them on the fringes of the liberal discourse. Sidney Blumenthal, **The Rise of the Counter Establishment: From Conservative Ideology to Political Power** [1986]. For a discussion of neo-conservatism, see Gillian Peele, **Revival and Reaction: The Right in Contemporary America** [1984]. pp. 5, 19-50. Also see John S. Saloma III, **Ominous Politics: The New Conservative Labyrinth** [1984]. Liberalism and 'conservatism' in North America have often intersected. At the beginning of the 1980s, for example, Peter Steinfels represented both Brzezinski and Kirkpatrick as neo-conservatives, and organizations such as the Trilateral Commission, of which Brzezinski was Director from 1973-1976, as being linked to the neo-conservative movement. However, the Carter administration was very well connected to the Trilateral Commission which was initially criticized by the Reagan administration. Peter Steinfels, **The Neoconservatives: The Men Who**

Are Changing America's Politics [1979]. p. 9.

7. Jorge I. Domínguez, "Consensus and Divergence: The State of the Literature on Inter-American Relations in the 1970s" **Latin American Research Review** vol. 13. no. 1. 1978. p. 113. More recently, in the case of 'Third World studies', Tony Smith has argued that dependency theory "raised" a "wide range of new issues" in an area that was "relatively moribund" by 1970. And "thanks to the vigor of the dependency school's attack on the established 'developmentalist' framework for studying change in the Third World, debates going on today in development studies are perhaps the most interesting and important in the field of comparative politics". However, he emphasized that "no matter how interesting and important these debates, it should be apparent that the field of Third World studies is in a state of crisis". See Tony Smith, "Requiem or New Agenda for Third World Studies" **World Politics** vol. 37. no. 4. 1985; reprinted in Ikuo Kabashima and Lynn T. White III, eds., **Political System and Change** [1986]. p. 347.

8. It should be emphasized that the line between radicalism and liberalism is not always clear. For example, the distinction between radicals and liberals was often blurred in the 1970s as liberalism was reinvigorated by radical analysis and methodology. In the 1980s, Reagan's policies facilitated a political 'alliance' between radicals and liberals which reinforced the theoretical commonality between the radical and the liberal discourse. The central difference between radicalism and liberalism, as the terms are used here, is that radicalism relies on a conflict model of social and political change and generally supports revolution, while a preference for gradual change and the assumption that conflict between divergent interests can and ought to be resolved through reform rather than revolution is central to the liberal discourses.

9. Kalman H. Silvert, "American Academic Ethics and Social Research Abroad: The Lesson of Project Camelot" in Irving Louis Horowitz, ed., **The Rise and Fall of Project Camelot: Studies in the Relationship between Social Science and Practical Politics** [1967]. In 1970 Stanley Ross argued that "the key point is that any discussion of US academic endeavours in Latin America must take into consideration the general role of the US in Latin American history. Successful intellectual activity must be based on respect not paternalism, intellectual autonomy and not cultural imperialism". Stanley R. Ross, "Introduction" in Stanley R. Ross, ed., **Latin America in Transition: Problems in Training and Research** [1970]. p. xiii. In 1971 William N. Dunn suggested that "(i)t may even be worthwhile reflecting on the proposition that, given the present state of North American knowledge, understanding and appreciation for Latin America, major problems of United States-Latin American relations may be irrevocably beyond solution, at least in terms of traditional values, beliefs, and attitudes toward the conduct of United States foreign policy". William N. Dunn, "The Scholar-Diplomat Seminar on Latin American Affairs: The Promise and Illusion of the State Department Reform Movement" **Latin American Research Review** vol. 6. no. 2. 1971. p. 83.

10. A particularly good example of this approach is the work of Ernest R. May. He is Professor of History at Harvard, a member of the Council on Foreign Relations and has worked as a consultant to the US government on a number of occasions. He also worked for the Joint Chiefs of Staff during World War II, and since the 1970s has taught a course (entitled the "Uses of History") at Harvard with Richard Neustadt (Professor of Public Administration in the John F. Kennedy School of Government at Harvard). This course is attended mainly by professionals in mid-career, including a number of relatively senior officials from a variety of government departments. Writing in the early 1970s, May argued that "people in government who see value in more critical and systematic reasoning from past experience will need help from men and women who have studied history and given some thought to how work by professional historians can best be exploited". Ernest R. May, **"Lessons" of the**

Past: The Use and Misuse of History in American Foreign Policy
[1973]. p. 172. See also Richard E. Neustadt and Ernest R. May, **Thinking in Time:
The Uses of History for Decision Makers** [1986]. For a sympathetic but
pessimistic evaluation of the likelihood of US policy-makers learning anything but the
most simplistic lessons from history see Melanson, **Writing History and
Making Policy** [1985]. pp. 5-6, 221-226.

11. As Richard Fagen has argued, a "leap of faith" is required in order to
subscribe to the "belief that knowledge correctly generated, framed, and presented will
have some impact on the conduct of public affairs. The leap is perhaps a bit longer in
the field of international politics and foreign policy than elsewhere. According to
Fagen the "foreign policy process (again, at least in the United States) tends to define
useful knowledge as *intelligence*....There is a resulting vulgarization of the concept
of knowledge, a closing-off of alternative understandings of reality, and a confusion of
data on 'events' with knowledge of the more enduring forces at work both domestically
and internationally". Richard R. Fagen, "Introduction" in Richard R. Fagen, ed.,
Capitalism and the State in US-Latin American Relations [1979]. p. 2.

12. For example, Lester Langley reported being told by "a distinguished
political scientist", who served as a consultant to the Kissinger Commission, that it
was necessary to "remember that the Kissinger Report was, fundamentally, a *political*
document designed *for* the President of the United States. I tried to tell members of the
Commission early on that there were limits to what the US could do in Central America,
but *not one* wanted to hear such negative talk. I realized then and there that if I wanted
to have any influence I had to sound more positive". Lester D. Langley, "Fire Down
Below: A Review Essay on the Central American Crisis" **Diplomatic History** vol.
9. no. 2. 1985. p. 162.

13. Gabriel Kolko, **Confronting the Third World: United States
Foreign Policy 1945-1980** [1988]. pp. 205-209.

14. Gabriel Kolko, **Confronting the Third World** [1988]. pp. 209-211.
The continuity between the Nixon Doctrine and the objectives, if not the means, of US
policy between 1945 and 1968 is emphasized in Robert S. Litwak, **Détente and the
Nixon Doctrine: American Foreign Policy and the Pursuit of Stability
1969-1976** [1984]. pp. 193-194.

15. Enrico Augelli and Craig Murphy, **America's Quest for Supremacy
and the Third World: An Essay in Gramscian Analysis** [1988]. p. 144.

16. Rockefeller cited in Walter LaFeber, **Inevitable Revolutions: The
United States in Central America** [1984]. pp. 201-202. See Nelson A.
Rockefeller, **The Rockefeller Report on the Americas: The Official
Report of a United States Presidential Mission for the Western
Hemisphere** [1969]. More or less the same perspective as was articulated in the 1969
Report can be found in the Latin American Report of Nelson Rockefeller's Commission
on Critical Choices for Americans, produced while he was serving as Gerald Ford's vice-
president in the mid-1970s. See James D. Theberge and Roger W. Fontaine, **Latin
America: Struggle for Progress** (Critical Choices for Americans vol. 14.)
[1977].

17. Jorge Nef, "The Trend Toward Democratization and Redemocratization in
Latin America: Shadow and Substance" **Latin American Research Review** vol.
23. no. 3. 1988. p. 132.

18. Samuel L. Baily, **The United States and the Development of
South America 1945-1975** [1976]. pp. 118-123. The "Action for Progress in the
Americas" was launched in an October 1969 speech at the Inter-American Press Club in
Washington in which Nixon called for "a more mature partnership in which all voices
are heard and none is predominant". It is the only general official statement on US
policy toward Central and South America Nixon is known to have made. Nixon, and of

course Kissinger's, approach rested on the assumption that if developments in Latin America were devoid of major domestic implications, or Cold War consequences, then they were left to the foreign policy bureaucrats at the Department of State. When a situation in the region was perceived as a Cold War problem, such as the rise of Allende in Chile, Nixon himself became involved and was "willing to play very rough". As Michael Francis has argued, in this situation, the objective of "good relations" with Latin America was "not highly valued". While Kennedy, and even Johnson under the influence of Kennedy's advisers, at least saw Latin America as an arena of ongoing importance in the United States' struggle with the Soviet Union, Nixon, along with Kissinger, saw Latin America as important only if what was perceived as an East-West crisis occurred in the region. Their outlook was that Central and South America "counted for little in the world of power politics and should remain the passive supplicant of Washington's favors and wishes". Michael J. Francis, "United States Policy Toward Latin America during the Kissinger Years" in John D. Martz, ed., **United States Policy in Latin America: A Quarter Century of Crisis and Challenge 1961-1986** [1988]. pp. 28-29, 55. The text of the address is reprinted in Martin C. Needler, **The United States and the Latin American Revolution** [1972]. pp. 155-162.

19. Under Nixon the US Southern Command also sought to resurrect CONDECA (the Central American Defense group) which had fallen apart after the Soccer War in 1969. However, the generals were not particularly interested in regional cooperation, and CONDECA died by the mid-1970s. LaFeber, **Inevitable Revolutions** [1984]. pp. 202-204.

20. Gabriel Kolko, **Confronting the Third World** [1988]. pp. 213-222, 277.

21. Paul Buhle, **Marxism in the USA: From 1870 to the Present Day** [1987]. pp. 198-199. Russell Jacoby, **The Last Intellectuals: American Culture in the Age of Academe** [1987]. pp. 177-178. In the early 1940s Sweezy produced an important marxist economics textbook which served as a bridge between classical marxism and neo-marxism. Paul Sweezy, **The Theory of Capitalist Development** [1942]. Anthony Brewer, **Marxist Theories of Imperialism: A Critical Survey** [London: Routledge and Kegan Paul, 1980]. p. 132.

22. Jacoby, **The Last Intellectuals: American Culture in the Age of Academe** [1987]. pp. 178-179.

23. Paul A. Baran, **The Political Economy of Growth** [1957]. Paul Baran was born in the Soviet Union and educated at the Plekhanov Institute in Moscow and in Germany. He arrived in the United States in 1939 and received an MA from Harvard in 1941. After his wartime service with the OSS, he worked for the New York Federal Reserve Bank, and in 1949 he took up the post of Professor of Economics at Stanford University. During the 1950s Baran, like many other critics of US foreign policy, was denied a passport under the Internal Security Act. Throughout the 1950s the Stanford administration was petitioned by alumni to fire Baran, and Baran himself was subject to various forms of harassment which made it clear the University wanted him to leave. This only intensified after 1959, when he became openly enthusiastic about the Cuban revolution (he visited Cuba in 1960 and met personally with Castro); however, the administration, although it wanted to, could not fire him because he had tenure. Jacoby, **The Last Intellectuals** [1987]. pp. 176-178. David Caute, **The Great Fear: The Anti-Communist Purge Under Truman and Eisenhower** [1978]. p. 248.

24. See especialy Baran, **The Political Economy of Growth** [1957]. pp. 107-131, 265-277, 298-299, 300-463. Buhle, **Marxism in the USA** [1987]. p. 199. Brewer, **Marxist Theories of Imperialism** [1980]. pp. 131-157.

25. Norman Etherington, **Theories of Imperialism: War, Conquest**

and Capital [1983]. pp. 238-241. For a number of essays representative of Sweezy's work in the 1950s, see Paul M. Sweezy, **Modern Capitalism and Other Essays** [1971]. Paul Buhle, **Marxism in the USA** [1987]. pp. 199, 287. For collected essays from the 1960s and early 1970s, see Paul M. Sweezy and Harry Magdoff, **The Dynamics of US Capitalism: Corporate Structure, Inflation, Credit, Gold and the Dollar** [1972]. See also Paul A. Baran and Paul M. Sweezy, **Monopoly Capital: An Essay on the American Economic and Social Order** [1966].

26. Harry Magdoff, **The Age of Imperialism: The Economics of US Foreign Policy** [1966]. Harry Magdoff, **Imperialism: From the Colonial Age to the Present** [1978].

27. Paul M. Sweezy and Leo Huberman, **Cuba: Anatomy of a Revolution** [1960]. In 1963, Sweezy and Huberman brought together articles (by Carlos Fuentes, André Gunder Frank and others) which had appeared previously in **Monthly Review**, and published them in book form. See Paul M. Sweezy and Leo Huberman, eds., **Whither Latin America?** [1963]. Also see Paul M. Sweezy and Leo Huberman, **Socialism in Cuba** [1969]. Paul M. Sweezy and Harry Magdoff, **Revolution and Counter-Revolution in Chile** [1974]. In a 1963 book John Gerassi, the onetime Latin American correspondent for **Time**, and later editor of **Newsweek**, roundly criticized both US policy and the Latin American elites. He argued that violent revolution was virtually inevitable in Latin America. See John Gerassi, **The Great Fear: The Reconquest of Latin America by Latin Americans** [1963]. See also the revised edition John Gerassi, **The Great Fear in Latin America** [1971].

28. Raul Prebisch (United Nations Economic Commission for Latin America), **The Economic Development of Latin America and Its Principal Problems** [1949]. On Prebisch see Kathryn Sikkink, "The Influence of Raul Prebisch on Economic Policy-Making in Argentina, 1950-1962" **Latin American Research Review** vol. 23. no. 2. 1988. Adalbert Krieger Vasena, "Comments on the Influence of Raul Prebisch on Economic Policy-Making in Argentina 1950-1962" **Latin American Research Review** vol. 23. no. 2. 1988. Richard D. Mallon, "The Influence of Raul Prebisch on Argentine Economic Policy-Making 1950-1962: A Comment" **Latin American Research Review** vol. 23. no. 2. 1988. Hugh Schwartz, "Raul Prebisch and Argentine Economic Policy-Making 1950-1962: A Comment" **Latin American Research Review** vol. 23. no. 2. 1988. David Lehmann, **Democracy and Development in Latin America: Economics, Politics and Religion in the Post-war Period** [1990]. pp. 3-11.

29. C. Richard Bath and Dilmus D. James, "Dependency Analysis of Latin America" **Latin American Research Review** vol. 11. no. 3. 1976. pp. 6-7. Charles Bergquist, "Latin America: A Dissenting View of 'Latin American History in World Perspective'" in Georg G. Iggers and Harold T. Parker, eds., **International Handbook of Historical Studies: Contemporary Research and Theory** [1979]. pp. 374-375. On the roots of dependency theory, see Joseph L. Love, "The Origins of Dependency Analysis" **Journal of Latin American Studies** vol. 22. no. 1. 1990. Cristobal Kay, **Latin American Theories of Development and Underdevelopment** [1989]. pp. 1-57, 125-162. Jorge Larrain, **Theories of Development: Capitalism, Colonialism and Dependency** [1989]. pp. 85-174.

30. David Harrison, **The Sociology of Modernization and Development** [1988]. p. 78. Brewer, **Marxist Theories of Imperialism** [1980]. p. 158. Carlos Ramirez-Faria, **The Origins of Economic Inequality Between Nations: A Critique of Western Theories on Development and Underdevelopment** [1991]. p. 178.

31. Fernando Henrique Cardoso and Enzo Falleto, **Dependencia y desarrollo en América Latina** [México: Siglo XXI, 1969]. Love, "The Origins of Dependency Analysis" **Journal of Latin American Studies** 1990. p. 143. Larrain, **Theories of Development** [1989]. pp. 111-112. Brewer, **Marxist Theories of Imperialism** [1980]. p. 158. Tulio Halperin-Donghi, "'Dependency Theory' and Latin American Historiography" **Latin American Research Review** vol. 17. no. 1. 1982. p. 116.

32. André Gunder Frank, **Capitalism and Underdevelopment in Latin America: Historical Studies of Chile and Brazil** [1967]. p. xi. Brewer, **Marxist Theories of Imperialism** [1980]. p. 158.

33. André Gunder Frank, **Latin America: Underdevelopment or Revolution-Essays on the Development of Underdevelopment and the Immediate Enemy** [1969]. pp. ix-x, 4. See also André Gunder Frank, **Lumpen-Bourgeoisie, Lumpen-Development: Dependence, Class and Politics in Latin America** [1972]. Frank's most famous essay in North America is probably "The Development of Underdevelopment", which originally appeared in **Monthly Review** in September 1966, was reprinted in **Latin America: Underdevelopment or Revolution** in 1969, again in Robert I. Rhodes, ed., **Imperialism and Underdevelopment: A Reader** [1970] and again in an abridged form in James D Cockcroft, André Gunder Frank and Dale L. Johnson, **Dependence and Underdevelopment: Latin America's Political Economy** [1972].

34. Fernando Henrique Cardoso, "The Consumption of Dependency Theory in the United States" **Latin American Research Review** vol. 12. no. 3. 1977. pp. 12-13.

35. Some observers have emphasized that in Middle Eastern studies, for example, the crisis of the 1960s was contained to a much greater degree than in other sectors of area studies. Irene Gendzier, **Managing Political Change: Social Scientists and the Third World** [1985]. pp. 9-10.

36. See Dadabhai Naoroji, **Poverty and Un-British Rule in India** [1901]. See Bjorn Hettne, **Development Theory and the Three Worlds** [1991]. pp. 103-108.

37. Richard Higgott and Richard Robison, "Introduction" in Richard Higgott and Richard Robison, ed., **Southeast Asia: Essays in the Political Economy of Structural Change** [1985]. p. 13.

38. Peter Duignan and L. H. Gann, **The United States and Africa: A History** [1984]. pp. 325-334. William Minter, **King Solomon's Mines Revisited: Western Interests and the Burdened History of Southern Africa** [1986]. pp. 179-304.

39. Walter Rodney, **How Europe Underdeveloped Africa** [1972]. See Florencia Mallon, "Dialogues Among the Fragments: Retrospect and Prospect" in Frederick Cooper, Florencia E. Mallon, Allen F. Isaacman, William Roseberry and Steve J. Stern, **Confronting Historical Paradigms: Peasants, Labor and the Capitalist World System in Africa and Latin America** [1993]. p. 382.

40. Hettne, **Development Theory and the Three Worlds** [1991]. p. 108. On Oceania see Vijay Naidu, **Development, State and Class Theories: An Introductory Survey** [1991]. pp. 16-17.

41. Bath and James, "Dependency Analysis of Latin America" **Latin American Research Review** 1976. pp. 10-11.

42. See for example Susanne Jonas and David Tobis, eds., **Guatemala** [1974]. Roger Burbach and Patricia Flynn, **Agribusiness in the Americas** [1980].

43. Edelstein, who gained a BA and an MA from the New School of Social

Research in New York, was the founder of the now defunct Union of Radical Latin Americanists. In the mid-1970s he completed a PhD in political science at the University of California (Riverside) on development theory and the Cuban Revolution. He went on to become associate professor of political science at the University of Colorado (Denver).

44. Fernando Henrique Cardoso, "Dependency and Development in Latin America" **New Left Review** no. 74. 1972. Fernando Henrique Cardoso, "Imperialism and Dependency in Latin America" in F. Bonilla and R. Girling, eds., **Structures of Dependency** [1973]. John Saxe Fernandez, "The Central American Defense Council and Pax Americana" in Irving Louis Horowitz, Josué de Castro and John Gerassi, eds., **Latin American Radicalism: A Documentary Report on Left and Nationalist Movements** [1969]. Rodolfo Stavenhagen, "Classes, Colonialism and Acculturation: A System of Inter-Ethnic Relations in Mesoamerica" **Studies in Comparative International Development** vol. 1. no. 6. 1965; reprinted in Irving Louis Horowitz, ed., **Masses in Latin America** [1970]. Rodolfo Stavenhagen, "Seven Erroneous Theses About Latin America" **New University Thought** vol. 4. no. 4. 1966-1967; reprinted in Horowitz, de Castro and Gerassi, eds., **Latin American Radicalism** [1969]. Rodolfo Stavenhagen, "Decolonializing Applied Social Sciences" **Human Organization** vol. 30. no. 4. 1971; reprinted in Rodolfo Stavenhagen, **Between Underdevelopment and Revolution: A Latin American Perspective** [1981]. Rodolfo Stavenhagen, "The Future of Latin America: Between Underdevelopment and Revolution" **Latin American Perspectives** vol. 1. no. 1. 1974.

45. This exposition is from Ronald C. Chilcote and Joel C. Edelstein, "Introduction: Alternative Perspectives of Development and Underdevelopment in Latin America" in Ronald C. Chilcote and Joel C. Edelstein, eds., **Latin America: The Struggle with Dependency and Beyond** [1974]. pp. 49, 53. This summary can also be found in Bath and James, "Dependency Analysis of Latin America" **Latin American Research Review** 1976. p. 5; and Ronaldo Munck, **Politics and Dependency in the Third World: The Case of Latin America** [1984]. p. 9.

46. For a critique of classic dependency theory, see Bath and James, "Dependency Analysis of Latin America" **Latin American Research Review** 1976. pp. 13-19. C. Richard Bath was a one time member of NACLA, and a former member of the Union of Radical Latin Americanists, who expressed sympathy for a radical perspective in 1976, but "would accept any political and/or economic approach to the solution of general problems of income distribution and social justice in Latin America". Bath and James, "Dependency Analysis of Latin America" **Latin American Research Review** 1976. p. 4.

47. André Gunder Frank, **Critique and Anti-Critique: Essays on Dependence and Reformism** [1984]. p. vii.

48. See, for example, André Gunder Frank, "Dependence is Dead, Long Live Dependence and the Class Struggle: A Reply to Critics" **Latin American Perspectives** vol. 1. no. 1. 1974. Ronald H. Chilcote, "Dependency: A Critical Synthesis of the Literature" **Latin American Perspectives** vol. 1. no. 1. 1974. See also the rest of the articles in this and subsequent issues of **Latin American Perspectives**. In 1982 a number of important contributions to the debate, which had appeared in **Latin American Perspectives**, were brought together in an edited collection. See Ronald H. Chilcote, ed., **Dependency and Marxism: Toward a Resolution of the Debate** [1982].

49. This point is made in Bath and James "Dependency Analysis of Latin America" **Latin American Research Review** 1976. p. 19.

50. James Petras and Maurice Zeitlin, "Introduction", in James Petras and Maurice Zeitlin, eds., **Latin America: Reform or Revolution?** [1968].

51. See for example James Petras, **Politics and Social Structure in Latin America** [1970]. James Petras and Robert LaPorte, **Cultivating Revolution: The United States and Agrarian Reform in Latin America** [1971]. James Petras, ed., **Latin America: From Dependence to Revolution** [1973]. James Petras, ed., **Critical Perspectives on Imperialism and Social Class in the Third World** [1978].

52. James Petras, **Politics and Social Forces in Chilean Development** [1969]. James Petras and Hugo Zemelman Merino, **Peasants in Revolt: A Chilean Case Study 1965-1971** [1972]. James Petras, "Political and Social Change in Chile" in Petras, ed., **Latin America: From Dependence to Revolution** [1973]. James Petras, "Chile: Nationalization, Socioeconomic Change and Popular Participation" in Petras, ed., **Latin America: From Dependence to Revolution** [1973]. James Petras and Robert LaPorte, Jr., "US Response to Economic Nationalism in Chile" in Petras, ed., **Latin America: From Dependence to Revolution** [1973]. Marcelo J. Cavarozzi and James F. Petras, "Chile" in Chilcote and Edelstein, eds., **Latin America** [1974].

53. James Petras, "Preface" in Petras, ed., **Latin America: From Dependence to Revolution** [1973]. pp. vii-viii. James Petras, "Introduction" in Petras, ed., **Latin America: From Dependence to Revolution** [1973]. pp. 3-4.

54. James Petras and Morris Morley, **The United States and Chile: Imperialism and the Overthrow of the Allende Government** [1975].

55. See, for example, the articles in Cockcroft, Frank and Johnson, **Dependence and Underdevelopment** [1972]. Petras, ed., **Latin America: From Dependence to Revolution** [1973]. Chilcote and Edelstein, eds., **Latin America** [1974]. Petras, ed., **Critical Perspectives on Imperialism and Social Class in the Third World** [1978].

56. An early 'radical' publication on Guatemala was Thomas and Marjorie Melville, **Guatemala: Another Vietnam?** [1971]. This was a slightly revised version of **Guatemala: The Politics of Land Ownership** [1971]. Marjorie Melville and Thomas Melville, both US citizens, were Catholic Missionaries based in Guatemala from the mid 1950s. Marjorie Melville first arrived in the country in 1954 and served as a nun and a sociology teacher in Guatemala City as well as working with students in "social improvement organizations". From 1957 Thomas Melville worked as a parish priest and helped in the organization of peasant cooperatives. In December 1967 they were forced to leave Guatemala. They returned to the United States, where they began graduate work on US relations with Latin America in the School of International Service at the American University in Washington, DC. In 1970 the Melvilles were imprisoned in the United States for anti-war activity following their participation in the destruction of files at a draft induction center.

57. Jamail went on to a professorship in the Department of Government, and a research associate position with the Institute of Latin American Studies, at the University of Texas at Austin. See Milton Henry Jamail, **Guatemala 1944-1972: The Politics of Aborted Revolution** [1972]. D. Neil Snarr and E. Leonard Brown, "An Analysis of PhD Dissertations on Central America: 1960-1974" **Latin American Research Review** vol. 12. no. 2. 1977. p. 198. In the early 1980s Jamail collaborated with George Black, of NACLA, to produce **Garrison Guatemala**, as well as a book on Israel's role in Central America. George Black, with Milton Jamail and Norma Stoltz Chinchilla, **Garrison Guatemala** [1984]. Milton Jamail and Margo Gutiérrez, **It's No Secret: Israel's Military Involvement in Central America** [1986]. See also Milton Jamail and Margo Gutiérrez, "Israel's Military Role in Central America" in Damian J. Fernandez, ed., **Central America and the Middle East: The Internationalization of the Crises** [1990].

58. Jonas was a graduate of Radcliffe College. She has an MA from Harvard

and an MA from the Massachusetts Institute of Technology. Her PhD dissertation was on US foreign policy, foreign aid and 'development' in Guatemala. See Susanne Jonas, **Test Case for the Hemisphere: United States Strategy in Guatemala 1950-1974** [1974]. Part of her thesis was published in Spanish as Susanne Jonas, **Guatemala: plan piloto para el continente** [1981].

59. Bodenheimer **The Ideology of Developmentalism** [1971].

60. Susanne Jonas Bodenheimer, "Dependency and Imperialism: The Roots of Latin American Underdevelopment" **Politics and Society** vol. 1. no. 3. 1971; reprinted in K. T. Fann and Donald C. Hodges, eds., **Readings in US Imperialism** [1971].

61. Susanne Jonas, "Guatemala: Land of Eternal Struggle" in Chilcote and Edelstein, eds., **Latin America: The Struggle with Dependency and Beyond** [1974]. pp. 93-94, 96, 100.

62. The "vulnerability" of the "Guatemalan Revolution" (1944-1954) was explained by Jonas as being due--apart from the limited socialist bloc support and the "overwhelming power" of the US--to it not being a revolution. She argued that "structural changes were incomplete" and the "class base was inadequate to sustain a revolution or to permit the development of revolutionary consciousness". She held up Cuba as a model, noting that the reversal of over 400 years of "dependent capitalism and underdevelopment", especially during a decade of "active expansion by US capital" was a "monumental task"; however, Cuba, "faced with essentially the same obstacles, came much closer to succeeding in the first ten years of its Revolution". What Cuba did, and Guatemala failed to do, was break the country's "fundamental relation to the capitalist world market and specifically to the United States", and Guatemala's "failure" to do this was "directly related to the urban petty bourgeois class base of the Revolution", which "remained more interested in consolidating their own political and economic power than in sharing it with the masses". According to Jonas, they were motivated by the "desire to promote their own careers through the Revolution", and by the "fear of any alliance which might entail an independent power base for the proletariat and peasantry and a consequent weakening of petty bourgeois hegemony". Jonas argued that while the Revolution, despite its limited nature, "brought real gains to the male proletariat and peasants", it "did very little for Indians generally, or for women and particularly Indian women". According to Jonas the "experience of the Revolution made clear to Indians and to women that they could never be given their equality by an urban, **ladino** male petty bourgeoisie, but would have to demand it", and the "final overthrow of the Revolution was merely the concrete expression of these latent contradictions". Jonas, "Guatemala" in Chilcote and Edelstein, eds., **Latin America** [1974]. pp. 166-169.

63. Jonas, "Guatemala" in Chilcote and Edelstein, eds., **Latin America** [1974]. pp. 172, 176-177, 194-195, 197-200, 204-206, 211-214.

64. James Petras and Morris Morley, **US Hegemony Under Siege: Class, Politics and Development in Latin America** [1990]. pp. 31, 34-35, 40.

65. Vicky Randall and Robin Theobald, **Political Change and Underdevelopment: A Critical Introduction to Third World Politics** [1985]. pp. 137-138, 148-171. Nicos Poulantzas, **Political Power and Social Classes** [1968]. Ralph Miliband, **The State in Capitalist Society** [1969]. For a critical review of theories of the capitalist state see Bob Jessop, **State Theory: Putting Capitalist States in Their Place** [1990].

66. For example, see Hamza Alavi, "The State in Post-Colonial Societies: Pakistan and Bangladesh" **New Left Review** no. 74. 1972; reprinted in Kathleen Gough and Hari P. Sharma, eds., **Imperialism and Revolution in South Asia** [1973]. Colin Leys, **Underdevelopment in Kenya: The Political Economy**

of Neo-Colonialism 1964-1971 [1975]. Anupam Sen, **The State, Industrialization and Class Formations in India: A Neo-Marxist Perspective on Colonialism, Underdevelopment and Development** [1982]. Amiya Kumar Bagchi, **The Political Economy of Development** [1982]. Richard Robison, **Indonesia: The Rise of Capital** [1986]. A particularly orthodox marxist perspective also emerged to challenge dependency theory. See Bill Warren, **Imperialism: Pioneer of Capitalism** [1980]. Also see Geoffrey Kay, **Development and Underdevelopment: A Marxist Analysis** [1975].

67. Perry Anderson, **Passages from Antiquity to Feudalism** [1974]. Perry Anderson, **Lineages of the Absolutist State** [1974]. Barry Hindess and Paul Hirst, **Pre-Capitalist Modes of Production** [1975]. Two particularly important debates which paved the way for the modes of production approach were the 'Transition Debate', which appeared primarily in the North American journal **Science and Society** in the 1950s but also included work in **Past and Present**, and later in **Marxism Today** and the **New Left Review**, and what became known as the 'Brenner Debate', which was initiated with an article by Robert Brenner in **Past and Present** in the mid-1970s. See Rodney Hilton, ed., **The Transition from Feudalism to Capitalism** [1976]. T. H. Aston and C. H. E. Philpin, eds., **The Brenner Debate: Agrarian Class Structure and Economic Development in Pre-Industrial Europe** [1985]. Probably the key French writer in the modes of production tradition is Pierre-Philippe Rey, **Colonialisme, néo-colonialisme, et transition au capitalisme** [1971]. Pierre-Philippe Rey, **Les Alliances de Classes: Sur l'articulation des modes de production** [1973]. For a good critique and discussion of the modes of production debate see Aidan Foster-Carter, "The Modes of Production Controversy" **New Left Review** no. 107. 1978. pp. 47-78. Also see John G. Taylor, **From Modernization to Modes of Production: A Critique of Sociologies of Development and Underdevelopment** [1983].

68. Ernesto Laclau, "Feudalism and Capitalism in Latin America" **New Left Review** no. 67. 1971; reprinted in Ernesto Laclau, **Politics and Ideology in Marxist Theory** [1979]. pp. 15-50. (In a postscript Laclau extends his critique to Wallerstein's work.) Laclau's original article is also reprinted in Peter F. Klarén and Thomas J. Bossert, eds., **Promise of Development: Theories of Change in Latin America** [1986]. pp. 166-188. Ian Roxborough, **Theories of Underdevelopment** [1979]. pp. 47-49.

69. Petras and Morley, **US Hegemony Under Siege** [1990]. pp. 41-42. Peter F. Klarén, "Lost Promise: Explaining Latin American Underdevelopment" in Klarén and Bossert, eds., **Promise of Development** [1986]. pp. 24-25. Harrison, **The Sociology of Modernization and Development** [1988]. pp. 123-138.

70. For example, Enrique Semo's book on Mexico (which is clearly reacting against dependency theory in favour of a modes of production approach) was published in Spanish in 1973, but was not translated into English until 1993. Enrique Semo, **The History of Capitalism in Mexico: Its Origins 1521-1763** [Austin: University of Texas Press, 1993, first published in Spanish in 1973 as **Historia del capitalismo en México. Los orígenes 1521-1763**].

71. Colin Henfrey, "Dependency, Modes of Production and the Class Analysis of Latin America" **Latin American Perspectives** vol. 8. nos. 3-4. 1981. Norma Stoltz Chinchilla, "Interpreting Social Change in Guatemala: Modernization, Dependency and Articulation of Modes of Production" in Ronald H. Chilcote and Dale L. Johnson, eds., **Theories of Development: Mode of Production or Dependency?** [1983].

72. See, for example, Brooke Larson, "Rural Rhythms of Class Conflict in Eighteenth Century Cochabamba" **Hispanic American Historical Review** vol. 60. 1980. Steve J. Stern, "The Rise and Fall of Indian-White Alliances: A Regional

View of 'Conquest' History" **Hispanic American Historical Review** vol. 61. August 1981. Steve J. Stern, **Peru's Indian Peoples and the Challenge of Spanish Conquest: Huamanga to 1640** [1982]. Steve J. Stern, "The Struggle for Solidarity: Class, Culture and Community in Highland Indian America" **Radical History Review** no. 27. 1983. Florencia E. Mallon, **The Defense of Community in Peru's Central Highlands: Peasant Struggle and Capitalist Transition 1860-1940** [1983]. William Roseberry, **Coffee and Capitalism in the Venezuelan Andes** [1983]. Steve J. Stern, "New Approaches to the Study of Peasant Rebellion and Consciousness: Implications of the Andean Experience" in Steve J. Stern, ed., **Resistance, Rebellion and Consciousness in the Andean Peasant World, 18th to 20th Centuries** [1987]. Brooke Larson, **Colonialism and Agrarian Transformation in Bolivia: Cochabamba 1550-1900** [1988]. For a summary and discussion of the modes of production debate in relation to anthropology and Latin America see Roseberry, **Anthropologies and Histories** [1989]. pp. 145-174.

73. See Alvin Y. So, **Social Change and Development: Modernization, Dependency and World-System Theories** [1990].

74. The work of Samir Amin, an Egyptian economic historian whose work has focused primarily on Africa, is also often located within the dependency theory, world-system and unequal exchange tradition. However, by the 1970s his work as a whole reflected a synthesis of modes of production and the theory of unequal exchange with insights drawn from dependency and world-system theory. For a good discussion of Amin and his work, see David F. Ruccio and Lawrence H. Simon, "Perspectives on Underdevelopment: Frank, the Modes of Production School and Amin" in Charles K. Wilber and Kenneth P. Jameson, eds., **The Political Economic of Development and Underdevelopment** [1992]. Samir Amin, **Accumulation on a World Scale: A Critique of the Theory of Underdevelopment** [1974]. Samir Amin, **Unequal Development: An Essay on the Social Formations of Peripheral Capitalism** [1976]. Samir Amin, **Imperialism and Unequal Development** [1977].

75. The influence was a two-way affair insofar as volume three of Braudel's Civilization and Capitalism drew heavily on Wallerstein's modern world-system. Fernand Braudel, **The Perspective of the World: Civilization and Capitalism 15th-18th Century, Volume 3** [1984]. pp. 69-70. See also Fernand Braudel, **The Structures of Everyday Life: Civilization and Capitalism 15th-18th Century, Volume 1** [1981]. Fernand Braudel, **The Wheels of Commerce: Civilization and Capitalism 15th-18th Century, Volume 2** [1982]. On the Annales School generally, see Peter Burke, **The French Historical Revolution: The Annales School 1929-1989** [1990].

76. Buhle, **Marxism in the USA** [1987]. p. 265.

77. Immanuel Wallerstein, **Africa: The Politics of Independence** [1961]. Immanuel Wallerstein, ed., **Social Change: The Colonial Situation** [1966]. Immanuel Wallerstein, **Africa: The Politics of Unity** [1967]. Immanuel Wallerstein, **Universities in Turmoil: The Politics of Change** [1969]. Charles Ragin and Daniel Chirot, "The World System of Immanuel Wallerstein: Sociology and Politics as History" in Theda Skocpol, ed., **Vision and Method in Historical Sociology** [1984]. pp. 276-283, 311.

78. Ragin and Chirot, "The World System of Immanuel Wallerstein" in Skocpol, ed., **Vision and Method in Historical Sociology** [1985]. pp. 284-290. Immanuel Wallerstein, **The Modern World System: Capitalist Agriculture and the Origins of the European World-Economy in the Sixteenth Century** [1974]. Immanuel Wallerstein, **The Modern World System II: Mercantilism and the Consolidation of the European World-**

Economy **1600-1750** [1980]. See also Immanuel Wallerstein, **Historical Capitalism** [1983]. Immanuel Wallerstein, **The Modern World-System III: The Second Era of Great Expansion of the Capitalist World-Economy 1730s-1840s** [1989].

79. Ragin and Chirot, "The World System of Immanuel Wallerstein" in Skocpol, ed., **Vision and Method in Historical Sociology** [1985]. pp. 288-290, 309-310.

80. See, for example, Robert Brenner, "The Origins of Capitalist Development: A Critique of Neo-Smithian Marxism" **New Left Review** no. 104. 1977. Theda Skocpol, "Wallerstein's World Capitalist System: A Theoretical and Historical Critique" **American Journal of Sociology** vol. 82. no. 5. 1977. Anthony Brewer, **Marxist Theories of Imperialism: A Critical Survey** [1980]. pp. 158-181. C. H. George, "The Origins of Capitalism: A Marxist Epitome and a Critique of Immanuel Wallerstein's Modern World-System" **Marxist Perspectives**, vol. 3. no. 2. 1980. Peter Worsley, "One World or Three?: A Critique of the World-System Theory of Immanuel Wallerstein" **The Socialist Register 1980** [1980]. Rex Mortimer "Wallerstein, Dependency, Passion and Vision: The Search for Class in the Capitalist Periphery" in Rex Mortimer (H. Feith and R. Tiffin, eds.), **Stubborn Survivors: Dissenting Essays on Peasants and Third World Development** [1984].

81. A recent book by Wallerstein and his colleagues has partially addressed this problem and gives greater agency to a range of actors in the modern world-system. Giovanni Arrighi, Terence K. Hopkins and Immanuel Wallerstein, **Antisystemic Movements** [1989].

82. Petras and Morley, **US Hegemony Under Siege** [1990]. pp. 40-41.

83. Ragin and Chirot, "The World System of Immanuel Wallerstein" in Skocpol, ed., **Vision and Method in Historical Sociology** [1985]. pp. 306, 311. See Michael Hechter, **Internal Colonialism: The Celtic Fringe in British National Development 1536-1966** [1975]. Daniel Chirot, **Social Change in a Peripheral Society: The Creation of a Balkan Colony** [1976]. Frances Moulder, **Japan, China and the Modern World-Economy: Towards a Reinterpretation of East Asian Development ca. 1600 to ca. 1918** [1977]. Daniel Chirot, **Social Change in the Twentieth Century** [1977]. Barbara Kaplan, ed., **Social Change in the Capitalist World Economy** [1978]. Walter Goldfrank, ed., **The World-System of Capitalism: Past and Present** [1979]. Terrence Hopkins and Immanuel Wallerstein, **Processes of the World-System** [1980]. Albert Bergesen, "Long Waves of Colonial Expansion and Contraction 1415-1969" in Albert Bergesen, ed., **Studies of the Modern World-System** [1980]. W. Ladd Hollist and Robert J. Boydston, eds., **World-System Structure** [1981]. L. S. Stavrianos, **Global Rift: The Third World Comes of Age** [1981]. Edward Friedman, **Ascent and Decline in the World-System** [1982]. Albert Bergesen, **The Crises of the Capitalist World-Economy** [1983]. Daniel Chirot, **Social Change in the Modern Era** [1986]. Christopher Chase-Dunn, **Global Formation: Structure of the World Economy** [1989].

84. Eric R. Wolf, **Sons of the Shaking Earth: The People of Mexico and Guatemala--Their Land, History and Culture** [1959]. Eric R. Wolf, **Peasants** [1966]. Eric R. Wolf, **Peasant Wars of the Twentieth Century** [1969].

85. Eric R. Wolf, **Europe and the People Without History** [1982]. pp. 3, 23.

86. Steve J. Stern, "Feudalism, Capitalism, and the World-System in the Perspective of Latin America and the Caribbean" **American Historical Review**

vol. 93. no. 4. 1988; reprinted in Cooper, Mallon, Isaacman, Roseberry and Stern, **Confronting Historical Paradigms** [1993]. p. 55. Wallerstein's response to Stern's criticisms clearly demonstrated Wallerstein's unwillingness to give any ground to his critics. See Immanuel Wallerstein, "Comments on Stern's Critical Tests" **American Historical Review** vol. 93. no. 4. 1988. Steve J. Stern, "Reply: 'Ever More Solitary'" **American Historical Review** vol. 93. no. 4. 1988.

87. For example, see Bradford E. Burns, **Latin America: A Concise Interpretive History** [1972]. Eric R. Wolf and Edward C. Hansen, **The Human Condition in Latin America** [1972]. Benjamin Keen and Mark Wasserman, **A Short History of Latin America** [1980]. Thomas E. Skidmore and Peter H. Smith, **Modern Latin America** [1984]. Stern, "Feudalism, Capitalism, and the World-System in the Perspective of Latin America and the Caribbean" in Cooper, Mallon, Isaacman, Roseberry and Stern, **Confronting Historical Paradigms** [1993]. pp. 27, 58-59.

88. A good example of a liberal revision of classic dependency theory is Baily, **The United States and the Development of South America, 1945-1975** [1976]. Also, see a 1978 study of Guatmala in which the author, José M. Aybar de Soto, argued that in "long term historical perspective" an "historical break" foreshadowed by the 1944-1954 period could be repeated successfully only "as a result of a total system transformation headed by the metropole", and "herein, may lie the hope for Guatemala and the pressing problems of the underdeveloped world". José M. Aybar de Soto, **Dependency and Intervention: The Case of Guatemala in 1954** [1978]. pp. 290, 312.

89. Richard R. Fagen, "Studying Latin American Politics: Some Implications of a Dependencia Approach" **Latin American Research Review** vol. 12. no. 2. 1977. p. 3, 22.

90. Jorge I. Domínguez, "Consensus and Divergence: The State of the Literature on Inter-American Relations in the 1970s" **Latin American Research Review** 1978. p. 115.

91. Fernando Henrique Cardoso, "Associated Dependent Development: Theoretical and Practical Implications" in Alfred Stepan, ed., **Authoritarian Brazil** [1973]. On the new dependency studies, which is used in the broadest sense of the term by some writers to include bureaucratic-authoritarianism, see So, **Social Change and Development** [1990]. pp. 135-165.

92. Peter Evans, **Dependent Development: The Alliance of Multinational, State and Local Capital in Brazil** [1979]. Stephan Haggard, **Pathways from the Periphery: The Politics of Growth in the Newly Industrializing Countries** [1990]. pp. 17-18. By the 1980s other important new dependency work included the 'post-imperialism' school of writers; see Becker, **The New Bourgeoisie and the Limits of Dependency** [1983]. David G. Becker, "Development, Democracy and Dependency in Latin America: A Post-Imperialist View" **Third World Quarterly: Journal of Emerging Areas** vol. 6. no. 2. 1984.

93. In 1976 two North American Latin American specialists argued that "it is now evident that dependency analysis has emerged as a legitimate field of inquiry for Latin Americanists, even if some scholars refuse to acknowledge its existence". Bath and James, "Dependency Analysis of Latin America" **Latin American Research Review** 1976. p. 3. In 1979 Charles Bergquist argued that "there has emerged a new paradigm which challenges the conceptual framework, basic assumptions, and methodology of the liberal historiography long dominant in Latin America, and indeed, the West as a whole". See Bergquist, "Latin America: A Dissenting View of 'Latin American History in World Perspective'" in Iggers and Parker, **International Handbook of Historical Studies** [1979]. pp. 371-372. Some North American Latin American specialists advocated "a union of positivist method and progressive

theory". See Steven Jackson, Bruce Russet, Duncan Snidal and David Sylvan, "An Assessment of Empirical Research on *Dependencia*" **Latin American Research Review** vol. 14. no. 3. 1979. pp. 25-26. In 1980, Steven W. Hughes and Kenneth J. Mijeski argued that a "third paradigm" was emerging in the study of inter-American relations, which synthesized dependency theory and modernization theory. See Steven W. Hughes and Kenneth J. Mijeski, "Contemporary Paradigms in the Study of Inter-American Relations" in Martz and Schoultz, eds., **Latin America, The United States and the Inter-American System** [1980]. pp. 19-22. See also John S. Gitlitz and Henry A. Landsberger, "The Inter-American Political Economy: How Dependable is Dependency Theory?" in Martz and Schoultz, eds., **Latin America, the United States and the Inter-American System** [1980]. pp. 65-69. Leonard Binder, "The Natural History of Development Theory" **Comparative Studies in Society and History** vol. 28. no. 1. 1987. pp. 22-24.

94. Joseph S. Tulchin, "Emerging Patterns of Research in the Study of Latin America" **Latin America Research Review** vol. 18. no. 1. 1983. pp. 87-90. See also Abraham F. Lowenthal, "Research in Latin America and the Caribbean on International Relations and Foreign Policy: Some Impressions" **Latin American Research Review** vol. 18. no. 1. 1983. pp. 161-163. Richard Graham and Peter H. Smith, "Introduction" in Graham and Smith, eds., **New Approaches to Latin American History** [1974]. p. xiii.

95. Ronald H. Chilcote, "A Question of Dependency" **Latin American Research Review** vol. 13. no. 2. 1978. p. 55.

96. Chilcote, "A Question of Dependency" **Latin American Research Review** 1978. pp. 60-67.

97. Interestingly it has been argued that the New Left's attempt to identify with--and distill a whole range of 'Third World' struggles (in Latin America, Asia and Africa) into--a radical Third Worldism helped to detach the movement from its domestic roots in North America and Western Europe and facilitated its sharp decline by the end of the 1960s. Nigel Young, **An Infantile Disorder?: The Crisis and Decline of the New Left** [1977]. pp. 103, 133, 158-159, 163-164, 179, 183-188, 205-206, 256-259.

98. Novick, **That Noble Dream** [1988]. pp. 345-347, 420-421. Paul Buhle, "Madison: An Introduction" in Paul Buhle, ed., **History and the New Left: Madison Wisconsin 1950-1970** [Philadelphia: Temple University Press, 1990]. pp. 18-22. Jonathan M. Wiener, "Radical Historians and the Crisis in American History 1959-1980" **Journal of American History** vol. 76. no. 2. 1989. pp. 405-407.

99. Combs, **American Diplomatic History** [1983]. pp. 280-281. Bradford Perkins, "The Tragedy of American Diplomacy: Twenty-Five Years After" **Reviews in American History** vol. 12. no. 1. 1984. pp. 3, 16. Robert Freeman Smith, **The United States and Cuba: Business and Diplomacy 1917-1960** [1960]. Robert Freeman Smith, "American Foreign Relations 1920-1942" in Bernstein, ed., **Towards a New Past** [1968]. Robert Freeman Smith, "The Morrow Mission and the International Committee of Bankers on Mexico: The Interaction of Finance Diplomacy and the New Mexican Elite" **Journal of Latin American Studies** vol. 1. no. 2. 1969. Robert Freeman Smith, **The United States and Revolutionary Nationalism in Mexico 1916-1932** [1972]. Robert Freeman Smith, "The American Revolution and Latin America: An Essay in Imagery, Perceptions and Ideological Influence" **Journal of Interamerican Studies and World Affairs** vol. 20. no. 4. 1978. David Healy went on to become Professor of History at the University of Wisconsin (Milwaukee), and he has produced a number of diplomatic works focusing on US relations with Cuba and the Caribbean over the years, all of which which can be represented as reflecting a 'neo-progressive' approach to US diplomatic history. David Healy, **The United States in Cuba 1898-1902:**

Generals, Politicians and the Search for Policy [1963]. David Healy, U S Expansionism: The Imperialist Urge in the 1890s [1970]. David Healy, Gunboat Diplomacy in the Wilson Era: The US Navy in Haiti 1915-1916 [1976]. David Healy, Drive to Hegemony: The United States in the Caribbean 1898-1917 [1988].

100. William Appleman Williams, The Tragedy of American Diplomacy [1959]. Buhle, "Madison: An Introduction" in Buhle, ed., History and the New Left [1990]. pp. 3-4. William Appleman Williams, "My Life in Madison" in Buhle, ed., History and the New Left [1990]. Wiener, "Radical Historians and the Crisis in American History 1959-1980" Journal of American History 1989. pp. 405-407. On the influence of Williams's work on other historians, see also J. A. Thompson, "William Appleman Williams and the 'American Empire'" Journal of American Studies vol. 7. no. 1. 1973. p. 91. Ian Tyrrell, The Absent Marx: Class Analysis and Liberal History in Twentieth Century America [1986]. pp. 133-140. Bradford Perkins, "The Tragedy of American Diplomacy: Twenty-Five Years After" Reviews in American History vol. 12. no. 1. 1984. See David W. Noble, The End of American History: Democracy, Capitalism, and the Metaphor of Two Worlds in Anglo-American Historical Writing 1880-1980 [1985]. pp. 115-140. David W. Noble, "William Appleman Williams and the Crisis of Public History" in Lloyd C. Gardner, ed., Redefining the Past: Essays in Diplomatic History in Honor of William Appleman Williams [1986]. pp. 45-62.

101. William Appleman Williams, American-Russian Relations 1781-1947 [1952]. William Appleman Williams, The Contours of American History [1961]. William Appleman Williams, The United States, Cuba and Castro: An Essay on the Dynamics of Revolution and the Dissolution of Empire [1962]. William Appleman Williams, The Great Evasion: An Essay on the Contemporary Relevance of Karl Marx and on the Wisdom of Admitting the Heretic into the Dialogue about America's Future [1964]. William Appleman Williams, The Roots of the Modern American Empire: A Study of the Growth and Shaping of Social Consciousness in a Marketplace Society [1969]. William Appleman Williams, History as a Way of Learning [1974]. William Appleman Williams, America Confronts a Revolutionary World 1776-1976 [1976]. William Appleman Williams, Americans in a Changing World: A History of the United Sates in the Twentieth Century [1978].

102. Ronald Robinson and John Gallagher, "The Imperialism of Free Trade" Economic History Review vol. 6. no. 1. second series 1953.

103. Novick, That Noble Dream [1988]. p. 446. For critiques of the Wisconsin 'school', see Thompson, "William Appleman Williams and the 'American Empire'" 1973. pp. 92-104. Sternsher, Consensus, Conflict and American Historians [1975]. pp. 279-280, 307-334. Also see Bradford Perkins, "The Tragedy of American Diplomacy: Twenty-five Years Later" Reviews in American History vol. 12. March 1984. Combs, American Diplomatic History [1983]. pp. 255-256. For less credible critiques, which empitomize the problems associated with identifying a school of New Left diplomatic history, see Robert W. Tucker, The Radical Left and American Foreign Policy [1971]. Joseph M. Siracusa, New Left Diplomatic Histories and Historians: The American Revisionists [1973]. Robert J. Maddox, The New Left and the Origins of the Cold War [1973].

104. Gar Alperovitz, Atomic Diplomacy: Hiroshima and Potsdam [1965]. Thomas McCormick, China Market: America's Quest for Informal Empire 1893-1901 [1967]. Walter LaFeber, America, Russia and the Cold

War, 1945-1966 [New York: Alfred A. Knopf, 1967]. N. Gordon Levin, Jr., **Woodrow Wilson and World Politics: America's Response to War and Revolution** [1968]. Carl Parrini, **Heir to Empire: United States Economic Diplomacy 1916-1923** [1969]. Lloyd C. Gardner, **Architects of Illusion: Men and Ideas in American Foreign Policy 1941-1949** [1970]. Jerry Israel, **Progressives and the Open Door: America and China 1905-1921** [1971].

    105. Walter LaFeber, **The New Empire: An Interpretation of American Expansion 1860-1898** [1963]. Combs, **American Diplomatic History** [1983]. pp. 278-279.

    106. Tyrrell, **The Absent Marx** [1986]. pp.133-134.

    107. See Lloyd C. Gardner, **Economic Aspects of New Deal Diplomacy** [1964]. Combs, **American Diplomatic History** [1983]. p. 280. Gardner, who completed his PhD at Wisconsin in 1960, contributed to one of the volumes in the now classic 'Dissenting Essays' series. See Lloyd C. Gardner, "American Foreign Policy 1900-1921: A Second Look at the Realist Critique of American Diplomacy" in Bernstein, ed., **Towards a New Past** [1968].

    108. David Horowitz, "The Alliance for Progress" **The Socialist Register 1964** [1964]; reprinted in Robert I. Rhodes, ed., **Imperialism and Underdevelopment: A Reader** [1970]. pp. 58-59.

    109. David Green, **The Containment of Latin America: A History of the Myths and Realities of the Good Neighbor Policy** [1971]. pp. vii-viii, 121, 255, 290-291, 295-297. See also David Green, The Cold War Comes to Latin America" in Barton J. Bernstein, ed., **Politics and Policies of the Truman Administration** [1970].

    110. Novick, **That Noble Dream** [1988]. p. 448, 453.

    111. Combs, **American Diplomatic History** [1983]. p. 257.

    112. Melanson, **Writing History and Making Policy** [1983]. pp. 60-61. Novick also perceived a "recurring ambiguity" in Williams's analysis of US expansion, over whether it was "the inevitable consequence of the structure of American capitalism or a 'cruel convenience' which could be reversed by a political act of will". According to Novick this "reflected the tension" between the "pessimistic streak" to be found in Frederick Jackson Turner's work, and the "reforming zeal" of John A. Hobson, both of whom stood as precursors to Williams's own work. Novick, **That Noble Dream** [1988]. p. 446.

    113. William Appleman Williams, **Empire as a Way of Life: An Essay on the Causes and Character of America's Present Predicament Along with a Few Thoughts About an Alternative** [1980]. pp. 225-226.

    114. A critical view of the state of diplomatic history at the beginning of the 1970s can be found in Thomas J. McCormick, "The State of American Diplomatic History" in H. J. Bass, ed., **The State of American History** [1970]. pp. 119, 140. Laurence Evans, "The Dangers of Diplomatic History" in H. J. Bass, ed., **The State of American History** [1970]. pp. 155-156. Ernest R. May, "The Decline of Diplomatic History" in George Athan Billias and Gerald N. Grob, eds., **American History: Retrospect and Prospect** [1971]. p. 400.

    115. Important diplomatic historians connected with the association and the journal in an administrative or editorial capacity have included Akira Iriye, Alexander DeConde, John Gaddis, Lester L. Langley, Thomas G. Paterson, Warren I. Cohen, George C. Herring, Robert Freeman Smith, Gary R. Hess, Walter LaFeber, Roger R. Trask, Michael H. Hunt, Ernest R. May, Lloyd C. Gardner and Jerald A. Combs.

    116. A relatively distinct theoretical approach to diplomatic history which emerged in the 1970s and points to the theoretical revision and reinvigoration of the liberal professional discourses by New Left historiography was the corporatist

approach. This is not to be confused with the corporatist approach to Latin American history exemplified by academics such as Howard Wiarda, although there is a connection. In some cases, historians who subscribed to this approach used the concept of corporate liberalism, developed in the late 1950s by William Appleman Williams, to explain the motives for US politico-economic and military expansion, and the structure of US hegemony. They defined corporate liberalism, or corporatism, as a politico-economic system that was organized around officially sanctioned functional or economic groups, such as business, agriculture and organized labor. These various corporate interests are integrated into an organic whole via various planning, coordinating and regulating institutions. Private and public sector elites collaborate to ensure order and progress and the increasingly overlapping interests of the various groups are bound. Diplomatic historians who advocate this approach have drawn attention to the way in which US leaders have attempted to adapt North American liberal institutions of an earlier era to the imperatives of changing world capitalism. The corporate liberal 'state' is distinguished by a particular organizational structure and an identifiable ideology which seeks to rationalize and justify that structure. US corporate liberalism has been found to be based on the liberal idea of a "middle way" between laissez-faire liberalism and paternalistic statism. Michael J. Hogan, "Corporatism: A Positive Appraisal" **Diplomatic History** vol. 10. no. 4. 1986. pp. 363-364. Ellis W. Hawley, "The Discovery and Study of 'Corporate Liberalism'" **Business History Review** vol. 52. no. 3. 1978. See also John Lewis Gaddis, "The Corporatist Synthesis: A Skeptical View" **Diplomatic History** vol. 10. no. 4. 1986. Michael J. Hogan, "Corporatism" **The Journal of American History** vol. 77. no. 1. 1990.

117. No New Left diplomatic historian reflected the moderate political character of New Left revisionism more than Robert Freeman Smith. His work makes it clear why 'neo-progressivism' as a perspective, and New Left diplomatic historians as individuals, were almost completely incorporated into the liberal discourse in the 1970s. For example, writing in the mid-1970s, although Smith represented the Good Neighbor Policy as part of the historic effort by the United States to build an economic and ideological "system" in the Western Hemisphere under US leadership, his overall approach to the end of the Good Neighbor Policy resembled the outlook of, and reflected the concerns of, a liberal Washington policy-maker, rather than those of a 'radical' diplomatic historian. He interpreted the failure of the Good Neighbor Policy, and the worsening of inter-American relations in its wake, as stemming from "the messianic benevolence of elements of the Good Neighbor Policy", which had led to the development of "false expectations" in North and South America. He argued that "whatever one thinks about the policies of the United States, the vast power differential between the United States and Latin American nations is a fact of life and will produce charges of imperialism regardless of what the United States does or does not do". He concluded that the Good Neighbor Policy "had both positive" and "negative" aspects", and "with all its contradictions it represented an attempt (in part successful) to place United States-Latin American relations on a higher plane by stressing peaceful settlement of disputes, reciprocity as a standard of international relations, and mutual understanding". He also noted, however, that the Good Neighbor Policy "could be excessively paternalistic", while the "idea" that the US "could solve all of the problems of the hemisphere through governmental programs led to frustration and hostility". In his view the Good Neighbor Policy reflected "the ambiguity and paradoxical nature of all United States foreign policy". Robert Freeman Smith, "The Good Neighbour Policy: The Liberal Paradox in US Relations with Latin America" in Leonard Liggio and James J. Martin, eds., **Watershed of Empire: Essays on New Deal Foreign Policy** [1976]. pp. 65, 90-91. Although Smith's work in the 1970s can be described as liberal, by the 1980s Smith himself (along with another former Wisconsin school historian, Ronald Radosh) had shifted to a position of support for Reagan's 'conservative' policy

in Central America. Novick, **That Noble Dream** [1988]. p. 457. See Robert Freeman Smith, **The United States and the Latin American Sphere of Influence: Volume I--The Era of Caribbean Intervention, 1890-1930** [1983]. Robert Freeman Smith, **The United States and the Latin American Sphere of Influence: Volume II--Era of Good Neighbors, Cold Warriors and Hairshirts, 1930-1982** [1983].

118. LaFeber's best-known work is his revisionist history of the Cold War, which has gone through at least five or six editions. Walter LaFeber, **America, Russia and the Cold War 1945-1984** [1985]. Also see, Lloyd C. Gardner, Walter LaFeber, and Thomas J. McCormick, **Creation of the American Empire: US Diplomatic History** (2 vols.) [1976]. Walter LaFeber, **The American Age: US Foreign Policy at Home and Abroad Since 1750** [1989].

119. This point is made in Tyrrell, **The Absent Marx** [1986]. pp. 179-180.

120. Melanson, **Writing History and Making Policy** [1983]. p. 74.

121. Gabriel Kolko, **The Politics of War: The World and US Foreign Policy 1943-1945** [1968]. Gabriel Kolko, **The Roots of American Foreign Policy: An Analysis of Power and Purpose** [1969].

122. Gabriel Kolko and Joyce Kolko, **The Limits of Power: The World and United States Foreign Policy 1945-1954** [1972]. Gabriel Kolko, **Main Currents in Modern American History** [1976]. Gabriel Kolko, **Anatomy of a War: Vietnam, the United States and the Modern Historical Experience** [1985]. Kolko's most recent book is probably one of the few efforts to synthesize the history of US relations with the 'Third World' to date. Gabriel Kolko, **Confronting the Third World: United States Foreign Policy 1945-1980** [1988].

123. Kolko, **Anatomy of a War** [1985], p. xiv.

124. For a review of Kolko's latest book, and a discussion of the way Kolko's work continues to be excluded from serious consideration by a majority of North American diplomatic historians, see Robert J. McMahon, "Interpreting America's Failures in the Third World" **Diplomatic History** vol. 15. no. 1. 1991. pp. 131-136.

125. Noam Chomsky, **American Power and the New Mandarins** [1968]. Noam Chomsky, The Responsibility of Intellectuals" in Roszak, ed., **The Dissenting Academy** [1968]. Noam Chomsky, **At War with Asia** [1969]. Noam Chomsky, **For Reasons of State** [1970]. Noam Chomsky, **The Political Economy of Human Rights: Volume 1--The Washington Connection and Third World Fascism** [1980]. Noam Chomsky, **The Political Economy of Human Rights: Volume 2--After the Cataclysm** [1980].

126. Novick, **That Noble Dream** [1988]. p. 417. Joshua Cohen and Joel Rogers, "Knowledge, Morality and Hope: The Social Thought of Noam Chomsky" **New Left Review** no. 187. 1991. pp. 26-27.

127. Gill, **American Hegemony and the Trilateral Commission** [1990]. p. 159. On Chomsky see Russell Jacoby, **The Last Intellectuals: American Culture in the Age of Academe** [1987]. pp. 96-97, 182-183, 199-200.

128. See, for example, Carl Oglesby, "Vietnamese Crucible: An Essay on the Meanings of the Cold War" in Carl Oglesby and Richard Shaull, eds., **Containment and Change** [1967].

129. David Horowitz wrote one of the most popular radical critiques of the Vietnam era. See David Horowitz, **From Yalta to Vietnam: American Foreign Policy in the Cold War** [1965]. See also David Horowitz, **The Free World Colossus: A Critique of American Foreign Policy in the Cold War**

[1971]. And see David Horowitz, **Imperialism and Revolution** [1969].
130. Michael T. Klare, **War Without End: American Planning for the Next Vietnams** [1970].
131. See Michael T. Klare, **The University-Military-Police Complex** [1977].
132. Michael T. Klare, **Beyond the "Vietnam Syndrome": US Intervention in the 1980s** [1981]. Michael T. Klare and Cynthia Arnson, **Supplying Repression: US Support for Authoritarian Regimes Abroad** [1981].
133. Marcus G. Raskin and Bernard B. Fall, eds., **The Viet-Nam Reader: Articles and Documents on American Foreign Policy and the Viet-Nam Crisis** [1965]. Subsidiaries of IPS were eventually set up in Cambridge (Massachusetts), San Francisco and Atlanta, followed by the establishment of the Transnational Institute in London and Amsterdam in 1973. John S. Friedman, "Introduction" in John S. Friedman, ed., **First Harvest: The Institute for Policy Studies 1963-1983** [1983]. pp. xi-xii. See James Allen Smith, **The Idea Brokers: Think Tanks and the Rise of the New Policy Elite** [1991]. pp. 159-166. Paul Dickson, **Think Tanks** [1971]. pp. 276-289.
134. Richard J. Barnet, **Intervention and Revolution: The United States in the Third World** [1968]. p. 284.
135. Richard J. Barnet, **Roots of War: The Men and Institutions Behind US Foreign Policy** [1973]. Richard J. Barnet and Ronald E. Müller, **Global Reach: The Power of the Multinational Corporations** [1974]. Howard Wachtel, **The New Gnomes: Multinational Banks in the Third World** [1977]. Richard J. Barnet, **The Giants: Russia and America** [1977]. Richard J. Barnet, **The Lean Years: Politics in the Age of Scarcity** [1980]. Richard J. Barnet, **Real Security: Restoring American Power in a Dangerous Decade** [1981]. Richard J. Barnet, **Allies: America, Europe and Japan Since the War** [1984]. Alan Wolfe, **The Rise and Fall of the "Soviet Threat": Domestic Sources of the Cold War Consensus** [1979]. Eqbal Ahmad, **Political Culture and Foreign Policy** [1980]. Fred Halliday is a fellow of the Transnational Institute in London; See his **Iran: Dictatorship and Development** [1979], **The Making of the Second Cold War** [1983], **Beyond Irangate: The Reagan Doctrine and the Third World** [1987], **Cold War, Third World: An Essay on Soviet-American Relations** [1989]. See also these works by Susan George: **How the Other Half Dies: The Real Reasons for World Hunger** [1976], **Feeding the Few: Corporate Control of Food** [1979], **Ill Fares the Land: Essays on Food, Hunger and Power** [1985], **A Fate Worse than Debt** [1988], **The Debt Boomerang** [1992].
136. Paul Cowan **The Making of an Un-American: A Dialogue with Experience** [1970].
137. David Morris, **We Must Make Haste-Slowly: The Process of Revolution in Chile** [1973]. Saul Landau and John Dinges, **Assassination on Embassy Row** [1980]. John Dinges and Saul Landau, "An Act of Terror" in Friedman, **First Harvest** [1983]. p. 3.
138. See The Institute for Policy Studies' Ad Hoc Working Group on Latin America, **The Southern Connection: Recommendations for a New Approach to Inter-American Relations** [1977].
139. Cynthia Arnson, who was a fellow of IPS in the late 1970s and early 1980 eventually took up a position as foreign policy aide to Democratic Congressional representative George Miller from California, a post she held from 1983 to 1988. Cynthia Arnson, **El Salvador: A Revolution Confronts the United States**

[1982]. Cynthia J. Arnson, **Crossroads: Congress, the Reagan Administration and Central America** [1989].

140. For a good discussion of this shift, see Randall and Theobald, **Political Change and Underdevelopment** [1985]. pp. 67-98.

141. Irving Louis Horowitz, **Beyond Empire and Revolution: Militarization and Consolidation in the Third World** [1982]. pp. 22, 77-78. Binder, "The Natural History of Development Theory" **Comparative Studies in Society and History** 1986. pp. 14-18. D. C. O'Brien, "Modernization, Order, and the Erosion of a Democratic Ideal: American Political Science 1960-1970" in David Lehmann, ed., **Development Theory: Four Critical Essays** [1979]. p. 50.

142. Chomsky, **American Power and the New Mandarins** [1968]. Marshall Windmiller, "International Relations: The New American Mandarins" in Roszak, ed., **The Dissenting Academy** [1969]. pp. 110-134.

143. Samuel Huntington, **Political Order in Changing Societies** [1968]. Henry C. Kenski, "Teaching Latin American Politics at American Universities: A Survey" **Latin American Research Review** vol. 10. no. 1. 1975. pp. 90, 96-97. Henry C. Kenski and Margaret Gorgan Kenski, **Teaching Political Development and Modernization at American Universities: A Survey** [1974]. pp. 9-10. The influence of Huntington's book outside the US was also significant. For example, as Bruce Cumings has noted, "the book was translated into Korean and is widely read there". Bruce Cumings, "The Origins and Development of the Northeast Asian Political Economy: Industrial Sectors, Product Cycles and Political Consequences" **International Organization** vol. 38. no. 1. 1984. reprinted in Frederic C. Deyo, **The Political Economy of the New Asian Industrialism** [1987]. p. 72.

144. Huntington, **Political Order in Changing Societies** [1968]. pp. vii, 4-5.

145. Huntington, **Political Order in Changing Societies** [1968]. pp. 41, 43-45, 52-53, 56, 144-145.

146. Samuel P. Huntington, "The Bases of Accommodation" **Foreign Affairs** vol. 46. no. 3. 1968. p. 644. See Colin Leys, "Samuel Huntington and the End of Classical Modernization Theory" in Hamza Alavi and Teodor Shanin, eds., **Introduction to the Sociology of "Developing Societies"** [1983]. pp. 342-343. On Kissinger's view on the NLF in 1966 see Seymour Hersch, **The Price of Power: Kissinger in the Nixon White House** [1983]. p. 47. "Urban revolution" and "forced-draft urbanization" were euphemisms for the "saturation-bombing and scorched-earth techniques by which the United States and the Saigon regime attempted to deny the countryside to the NLF, at an estimated cost of 2 million killed or wounded and 8 million refugees--out of a total South Vietnamese population of some 16 million". Huntington's article, which highlighted the political direction of **Political Order in Changing Societies**, also stressed that "defeating the revolution in Vietnam" could be accomplished without "defeating" the Vietnamese Communists. In fact, Huntington more or less acknowledged that Communist strength in rural Vietnam could not be seriously undermined, and he suggested that a "peace settlement" recognize this and allow the NLF to participate in the electoral process locally and nationally. He even claimed that in the eventuality of the NLF gaining control of the government of South Vietnam the "US would obviously regret the outcome but could also accept it and feel little compulsion to re-intervene." Thus, as Leys has noted, Huntington carried "his anti-revolutionary outlook to its logical conclusion by separating it from anti-communism". For Huntington communist regimes were less "pernicious" than a lack of political order. Leys, "Samuel Huntington and the End of Classical Modernization Theory" in Alavi and Shanin, eds., **Introduction to the Sociology of "Developing Societies"** [1983]. pp. 342-344, 349.

318 *Notes to pages 101-153*

147. By the end of the 1970s **Foreign Policy**'s editorial board had included at various times, C. Fred Bergsten, Frances FitzGerald, Lawrence Freedman, Morton H. Halperin, Joseph S. Nye, Jr., William D. Rogers (former US Deputy Co-ordinator of the Alliance for Progress) and Tad Szulc.

148. Robert D. Schulzinger, **The Wise Men of Foreign Affairs: The History of the Council on Foreign Relations** [1984]. p. 210.

149. Samuel Huntington, Michael Crozier and Joji Watanuki, **The Crisis of Democracy: Report on the Governability of Democracies to the Trilateral Commission** [1975]. Holly Sklar, "Trilateralism: Managing Dependence and Democracy" in Holly Sklar, ed., **Trilateralism: The Trilateral Commission and Elite Planning for World Management** [1980]. pp. 36-39. Holly Sklar and Ros Everdell, "Who's Who on the Trilateral Commission" in Sklar, ed., **Trilateralism** [1980]. pp. 92, 111.

150. Elbaki Hermassi, **The Third World Reassessed** [1980]. pp. 23-25.

151. Paul Cammack, "Brazil: The Long March to the New Republic" **New Left Review** no. 190. 1991. pp. 38-39. Thomas E. Skidmore, "Brazil's Slow Road to Democratization: 1974-1985" in Alfred Stepan, ed., **Democratizing Brazil: Problems of Transition and Consolidation** [1989]. pp. 7-8, 37.

152. Samuel Huntington and Joan M. Nelson, **No Easy Choice: Political Participation in Developing Countries** [1976].

153. Binder, "The Natural History of Development Theory" **Comparative Studies in Society and History** 1986. pp. 14-15. See for example, Reinhard Bendix, **Nation Building and Citizenship** [1964]. Edward Shils, **Political Development in the New States** [1965]. Joseph G. LaPalombra and Myron Weiner, **Political Parties and Political Development** [1966]. Gabriel A. Almond and G. Bingham Powell, **Comparative Politics: A Developmental Approach** [1966]. Lloyd Rudolph and Suzanne Rudolph, **The Modernity of Tradition: Political Development in India** [1967]. Robert A. Nisbet, **Social Change and History** [1969]. Gabriel A. Almond and Scott C. Flanagan et al., **Crises, Choice, and Change: Historical Studies of Political Development** [1973]. Morris Janowitz, **Military Institutions and Coercion in the Developing Nations** [1977].

154. A belief in the middle sectors is criticized in Lowenthal, "'Liberal', 'Radical' and 'Bureaucratic' Perspectives on US Latin American Policy" in Cotler and Fagen, eds., **Latin America and the United States** [1974]. pp. 218-219.

155. This approach was foreshadowed in Albert O. Hirschman, **Journeys Toward Progress** [1963]. Charles Bergquist, "Recent United States Studies in Latin American History: Trends Since 1965" **Latin American Research Review** vol. 9. no. 1. 1974. pp. 19-20, 34.

156. Charles W. Anderson, **Politics and Economic Change in Latin America: The Governing of Restless Nations** [1967]. Kenski, "Teaching Latin American Politics at American Universities" **Latin American Research Review** 1975. pp. 90, 94-95.

157. Klarén, "Lost Promise: Explaining Latin American Underdevelopment" in Klarén and Bossert, ed., **Promise of Development** [1986]. pp. 26-29. Thomas J. Bossert, "The Promise of Theory" in Klarén and Bossert, ed., **Promise of Development** [1986]. pp. 316-317. Bergquist, "Recent United States Studies in Latin American History" **Latin American Research Review** 1974. p. 23.

158. Richard M. Morse, "The Heritage of Latin America" in Louis Hartz, ed., **The Founding of New Societies** [1964]. Claudio Véliz, "Introduction" in Claudio Véliz, ed., **The Politics of Conformity in Latin America** [1967]. Philippe Schmitter, "Paths to Political Development in Latin America" in Douglas A. Chalmers, ed., **Changing Latin America: New Interpretations of Its Politics and**

Society [1972]. Howard J. Wiarda, "Toward a Framework for the Study of Political Change in the Iberic-Latin Tradition: The Corporative Model" **World Politics** vol. 25. no. 2. 1973. Howard J. Wiarda, "Social Change, Political Development and the Latin American Tradition" in Howard J. Wiarda, ed., **Politics and Social Change in Latin America: The Distinct Tradition** [1982]; reprinted in Klarén and Bossert, ed., **Promise of Development** [1986]. Howard J. Wiarda, **Corporatism and Development: The Portuguese Experience** [1977]. Claudio Véliz, **The Centralist Tradition in Latin America** [1980]. Howard J. Wiarda, **Corporatism and National Development in Latin America** [1981]. See also Alfred Stepan, **The State and Society: Peru in Comparative Perspective** [1978].

159. Bergquist, "Recent United States Studies in Latin American History" **Latin American Research Review** 1974. pp. 23-27. Books which were informed by a corporatist approach in the late 1960s and 1970s might include Warren Dean, **The Industrialization of Sao Paulo 1880-1945** [1969]. John D. Wirth, **The Politics of Brazilian Development 1930-1954** [1970]. Roger D. Hansen, **The Politics of Mexican Development** [1971]. William Paul McGreevey, **An Economic History of Colombia 1845-1930** [1971].

160. An early example of the adaptation by North American historians of both dependency theory and the corporatist approach was Stanley and Barbara Stein's study of colonial Latin America. They emphasized a colonial legacy of political, social and economic institutions and structures which blocked social change and political and economic development. Stanley J. Stein and Barbara H. Stein, **The Colonial Heritage of Latin America: Essays on Economic Dependence in Perspective** [1970]. The importance of Stein's book is emphasized in Bergquist, "Recent United States Studies in Latin American History" **Latin American Research Review** 1974. p. 26. Bergquist, "Latin America: A Dissenting View of 'Latin American History in World Perspective'" in Iggers and Parker, eds., **International Handbook of Historical Studies** [1979]. pp. 379-380. By the late 1970s Brian Loveman's work on Chile, for example, also reflected the effect of the dependency approach and the corporatist approach on the North American discourses on Latin America. He argued that in contrast to the "principal colonial centers" the "relative geographical isolation, poverty, and lack of significant gold and silver mines contributed to the development of an agrarian-based economy in Chile". Geographic and demographic factors facilitated the emergence in Chile of "a colonial elite with strong localistic orientations, a fortress mentality, and a significant military tradition". Over the years "intermarriage, shared social values, and dependence for economic well-being upon the exploitation of the rural labor force unified the Chilean upper classes and helped forge a unique variant of Hispanic capitalism on the periphery of the Spanish empire". And, even after independence in the early years of the nineteenth century, Chile retained "the indelible markings of Hispanic capitalism". Brian Loveman, **Chile: The Legacy of Hispanic Capitalism** [1979]. pp. 74, 115.

161. Klarén, "Lost Promise: Explaining Latin American Underdevelopment" in Klarén and Bossert, ed., **Promise of Development** [1986]. pp. 29-30. Peter H. Smith, "Political Legitimacy in Spanish America" in Richard Graham and Peter H. Smith, eds., **New Approaches to Latin American History** [1974]. pp. 253-254. See Guillermo O'Donnell, **Modernization and Bureaucratic-Authoritarianism: Studies in South American Politics** [1973].

162. George C. Lodge, **Engines of Change: United States Interests and Revolution in Latin America** [1970].

163. Sklar and Everdell, "Who's Who on the Trilateral Commission" in Sklar, ed., **Trilateralism** [1980]. p. 111. Benjamin C. Roberts, George C. Lodge and

Hideaki Okamoto, **Collective Bargaining and Employee Participation in Western Europe, North America and Japan** [1979].

164. Lodge, **Engines of Change** [1970]. pp. vii-viii.

165. Lodge, **Engines of Change** [1970]. pp. 3, 8, 10-11. Huntington, **Political Order in Changing Societies** [1968]. p. 6.

166. He also warned that "if the revolution is inevitable, then the protection of United States economic interests requires that United States companies perceive their revolutionary role". He warned that North American corporations "should explore new formulas for sharing control, new ways of allocating their power and new criteria for appraising their activities, all of which must be consistent with the revolutionary process itself". Ultimately, "the protection of American economic interests depends upon the effectiveness with which American enterprise can move within the revolutionary circuit; the speed with which it can create new designs and procedures for becoming a part of the winning combination of engines of change". Lodge, **Engines of Change** [1970]. pp. 331-332, 336.

167. Lodge, **Engines of Change** [1970]. pp. 341-342, 354, 362-363, 368-370.

168. Herbert K. May, **Problems and Prospects of the Alliance for Progress: A Critical Examination** [1968]. Robert J. Alexander, **Today's Latin America** [1968]. Harvey S. Perloff, **Alliance for Progress: A Social Invention in the Making** [1969]. Perloff was a former US government official directly associated with the Alliance. Jerome Levinson and Juan de Onis, **The Alliance that Lost Its Way: A Critical Report on the Alliance for Progress** [1970]. Jerome I. Levinson, "After the Alliance for Progress: Implications for Inter-American Relations" in Douglas A. Chalmers, ed., **Changing Latin America: New Interpretations of Its Politics and Society** [1972]. Federico Gil, **Latin American-United States Relations** [1971]. pp. 238-250, 267-281. See Lowenthal, "'Liberal', 'Radical' and 'Bureaucratic' Perspectives on US Latin American Policy: The Alliance for Progress in Retrospect" in Cotler and Fagen, eds., **Latin America and the United States** [1974]. p. 215.

169. Lowenthal, "'Liberal', 'Radical' and 'Bureaucratic' Perspectives on US Latin American Policy: The Alliance for Progress in Retrospect" in Cotler and Fagen, eds., **Latin America and the United States** [1974]. p. 215.

170. The existence of "pervasive, serious and persistent misunderstanding" between Latin America and the US had been central to Milton Eisenhower's book, which also argued that the "welfare" of the US and the "welfare" of the nations of Latin America were "inextricably bound together". See Milton Eisenhower, **The Wine is Bitter: The United States and Latin America** [1963]. pp. 6, 45. Lowenthal, "'Liberal', 'Radical' and 'Bureaucratic' Perspectives on US Latin American Policy" in Cotler and Fagen, eds., **Latin America and the United States** [1974]. pp. 215-216.

171. Harvey S. Perloff, **Alliance for Progress: A Social Invention in the Making** [1969]. p. ix. Lowenthal "'Liberal', 'Radical' and 'Bureaucratic' Perspectives on US Latin American Policy" in Cotler and Fagen, eds., **Latin America and the United States** [1974]. pp. 216-218.

172. Martin C. Needler, **The United States and the Latin American Revolution** [1977]. pp. 53-54, 112. See Martin C. Needler, **The United States and the Latin American Revolution** [1972]. See also Martin C. Needler, **Political Development in Latin America: Instability, Violence and Evolutionary Change** [1968]. A revised liberal perspective is also reflected in Martin C. Needler, "Toward a Reappraisal of United States Foreign Policy in Latin America After Vietnam" in Gregg and Kegley, **After Vietnam: The Future of American Foreign Policy** [1971]. Martin C. Needler, "The Influence of American

Institutions in Latin America" **The Annals of the American Academy of Political and Social Science** vol. 428. 1976. Martin C. Needler, **A n Introduction to Latin American Politics: The Structure of Conflict** [1977].

173. Maier, "Marking Time" in Kammen, ed., **The Past Before Us** [1980]. pp. 358-359. J. Garry Clifford, "Bureaucratic Politics" **Journal of American History** vol. 77. no. 1. 1990. pp. 161-162. The first application of bureaucratic politics to foreign policy was Richard C. Snyder, H. W. Bruck and Burton M. Sapin, eds., **Decision Making as an Approach to the Study of International Politics** [1954]. Graham T. Allison **Essence of Decision: Explaining the Cuban Missile Crisis** [1971]. See also Graham T. Allison and Morton H. Halperin, "Bureaucratic Politics: A Paradigm and Some Policy Implications" in Raymond Tanter and Richard H. Ullman, eds., **Theory and Politics in International Relations** [1972]. Morton H. Halperin and Arnold Kanter, "The Bureaucratic Perspective: A Preliminary Framework" in Morton H. Halperin and Arnold Kanter, eds., **Readings in American Foreign Policy: A Bureaucratic Perspective** [1973]. Hadley Arkes, **Bureaucracy, the Marshall Plan, and the National Interest** [1973]. Ernest R. May, "The 'Bureaucratic-Politics' Approach: US-Argentine Relations, 1942-47" in Cotler and Fagen, eds., **Latin America and the United States** [1974]. I. M. Destler, **Presidents, Bureaucrats, and Foreign Policy: The Politics of Organization Reform** [1974]. Jerel A. Rosati, "Developing a Systematic Decision-Making Framework: Bureaucratic Politics in Perspective" **World Politics** vol. 33. no. 2. 1981.

174. Abraham F. Lowenthal, "'Liberal', 'Radical' and 'Bureaucratic' Perspectives on US Latin American Policy: The Alliance for Progress in Retrospect" in Julio Cotler and Richard R. Fagen, eds., **Latin America and the United States** [1974]. pp. 212-215, 225-227. Also see the earlier version, which appeared as Abraham F. Lowenthal, "United States Policy Toward Latin America: 'Liberal', 'Radical' and 'Bureaucratic' Perspectives" **Latin American Research Review** vol. 8. no. 3. 1973.

175. Abraham F. Lowenthal, **The Dominican Intervention** [1972]. Apart from Lowenthal's work one early study that reflected a 'bureaucratic politics' approach to inter-American relations was R. Harrison Wagner, **United States Policy Toward Latin America: A Study in Domestic and International Politics** [1970]. Lowenthal, "'Liberal', 'Radical' and 'Bureaucratic' Perspectives on US Latin American Policy" Cotler and Fagen, eds., **Latin America and the United States** [1974]. p. 227.

176. Explicit analytical perspectives, apart from bureaucratic politics, which informed his work included a focus on the influence of North American domestic politics on US foreign policy and the "transnational relations" paradigm which argues that the study of the relations between governments and international organizations such as the OAS was not sufficient and the "interactions" of "nongovernmental groups" and their "interaction" with governments and parts of governments must also be considered. Blasier, **The Hovering Giant** [1976] pp. 6-9. The leading advocates of the transnational relations perspective in the 1970s were Robert O. Keohane and Joseph S. Nye, Jr. See Robert O. Keohane and Joseph S. Nye, Jr., eds., **Transnational Relations and World Politics** [1972].

177. Cole Blasier, "The US/USSR Exchange in Latin American Studies Studies" **LASA Forum** vol. 20. no. 3. 1989. pp. 14-15.

178. Cole Blasier, "The United States and the Revolution" in James M. Malloy and Richard S. Thorn, eds., **Beyond the Revolution: Bolivia Since 1952** [1971]. Cole Blasier, "The Elimination of United States Influence" in Carmelo Mesa-Lago, ed., **Revolutionary Change in Cuba** [1971]. Cole Blasier, "The

United States, Germany and the Bolivian Revolutionaries 1941-1946" **Hispanic American Historical Review** vol. 52. no. 1. 1972. Cole Blasier, "The United States and Madero" **Journal of Latin American Studies** vol. 4. no. 2. 1972. Cole Blasier, "Security: The Extracontinental Dimension" in Kevin J. Middlebrook and Carlos Rico, eds., **The United States and Latin America in the 1980s: Contending Perspectives on a Decade of Crisis** [1986]. Cole Blasier, "The Soviet Union" in Morris J. Blachman, William LeoGrande and Kenneth Sharpe, eds., **Confronting Revolution: Security Through Diplomacy in Central America** [1986]. Cole Blasier, "The United States and Democracy in Latin America" in James M. Malloy and Mitchell A. Seligson, eds., **Authoritarians and Democrats: Regime Transition in Latin America** [1987].

179. Cole Blasier, **The Hovering Giant: US Responses to Revolutionary Change in Latin America** [1976]. p. xviii. Commission on United States-Latin American Relations (Sol Linowitz, chair), **The Americas in a Changing World** [1975].

180. In Blasier's estimation his book's "most important contributions to the historical record" were the "disclosures" about Guatemala and Bolivia, which, unlike US relations with Mexico and Cuba, "have received far less scholarly attention". Blasier, **The Hovering Giant** [1976]. pp. xv-xvii. He later produced a book on Soviet relations with Latin America. See Cole Blasier, **The Giant's Rival: The USSR and Latin America** [1983].

181. Blasier defined revolution as "an exceptionally rapid, comprehensive and profound form of social change, usually accompanied by violence and resulting in an abrupt and explosive break with the past". In his view, the nations of Latin America which have been "most transformed by revolutionary change" were Mexico, Bolivia and Cuba, and possibly even Peru and Chile. Blasier, **The Hovering Giant** [1976] pp. 3-4. A decade later, in the second edition of his book he had reduced the list to Mexico, Cuba and Nicaragua. See Cole Blasier, **The Hovering Giant: US Responses to Revolutionary Change in Latin America 1910-1985** [1985]. p. 4.

182. Blasier, **The Hovering Giant** [1976] pp. 5-6.

183. Blasier, **The Hovering Giant** [1976] p. 9. The second edition of his book, which will be discussed in Chapter 5, brought this generalization forward to include the ouster of Somoza in 1979. See Blasier, **The Hovering Giant** [1985] p. 9.

184. Blasier, **The Hovering Giant** [1976]. pp. 9-11.

185. Blasier, **The Hovering Giant** [1976]. pp. 221-225. Although Blasier emphasized that the United States' had long been engaged in an effort to dominate the Western Hemisphere, he sought to distinguish his analysis from "radical scholars" and "polemicists". He asserted that marxists interpret US responses to revolution as primarily "an expression of the interests of trading and investing companies", particularly of "multinational corporations". He argued that, although the "more sophisticated Marxist critics" did not represent every move of the US government as a result of "corporate pressures", they did hold the view that foreign policy emanating from Washington was "fundamentally" concerned with "maintaining the regional status quo for continued capitalist exploitation". While, in the case of Guatemala, an economic interpretation had "more plausibility" than in other instances, due to the presence and role of the United Fruit Company, he still saw "strategic reasons" as "more plausible". In response to "marxist critics", who argued that Washington's "official hostility" toward the Guatemalan government "tended to coincide with US private interests", he argued that, although UFCO retrieved most its lost property following the overthrow of Arbenz, this did not necessarily "prove" that North American "private interests" were "decisive" in the decision to intervene. And he insisted that his "point"

was "not that private interest played no role at all", but "only that strategic considerations were more important". At the same time, in Blasier's view, the marxists were "right" regarding the United States' preoccupation with protecting its "position" in the hemisphere; however, he was quick to assert that the drive for political domination was "a fact of life long before the rise of modern capitalism", while it was also clearly evident in the Soviet Union's political dominance in Eastern Europe. Blasier, **The Hovering Giant** [1976]. p. 219-221, 225.

186. Blasier, **The Hovering Giant** [1976]. pp. 270-273.

187. Schulzinger, **The Wise Men of Foreign Affairs** [1984]. pp. 225-227.

188. Albert Fishlow, Carlos Diaz-Alejandro, Richard R. Fagen and Roger D. Hansen, **Rich and Poor Nations in the World Economy** [1978]. pp. 204-205. Roger D. Hansen, **Beyond the North-South Stalemate** [1979]. pp. 286, 290. Lincoln Gordon, **Growth Policies and the International Order** [1979]. p. 167. See Jorge I. Domínguez, Nigel S. Rodley, Bryce Wood and Richard A. Falk, **Enhancing Global Human Rights** [1979]. For a discussion of the 1980s Project, see Schulzinger, **The Wise Men of Foreign Affairs** [1984]. pp. 228-230, 234-235.

189. Meyer cited in LaFeber, **Inevitable Revolutions** [1984]. pp. 200-201. Timothy P. Wickham-Crowley, **Guerrillas and Revolution in Latin America A Comparative Study of Insurgents and Regimes Since 1956** [1992]. pp. 209-213.

190. Victor Bulmer-Thomas, **The Political Economy of Central America Since 1920** [1987]. pp. 200-229.

191. LaFeber, **Inevitable Revolutions** [1984]. pp. 207-209. James Dunkerley, **Power in the Isthmus: A Political History of Modern Central America** [1988]. pp. 556-557. Bulmer-Thomas, **The Political Economy of Central America Since 1920** [1987]. pp. 207-212.

192. Zbigniew Brzezinski, **Power and Principle: Memoirs of the National Security Advisor 1977-1981** [1983]. pp. 5-6, 49, 288-289. Holly Sklar and Ros Everdell, "Who's Who on the Trilateral Commission" in Holly Sklar, ed., **Trilateralism: The Trilateral Commission and Elite Planning for World Management** [1980]. pp. 91, 99-109.

193. Gill, **American Hegemony and the Trilateral Commission** [1990] p. 1.

194. Willy Brandt, **North-South: A Programme for Survival-- Report of the Independent Commission on International Development Issues** [1980].

195. Holly Sklar, **Washington's War on Nicaragua** [1988]. p. 8. Commission on United States-Latin American Relations (Sol Linowitz, chair), **The Americas in a Changing World** [1975]. Commission on United States-Latin American Relations (Sol Linowitz, chair), **The United States and Latin America: Next Steps** [1976].

196. Robert A. Pastor, **Condemned to Repetition: The United States and Nicaragua** [1987]. pp. 50-52, 183-187. For detailed analysis of the Carter administration and Nicaragua see Morris H. Morley, **Washington, Somoza, and the Sandinistas: State and Regime in US Policy 1969-1981** [1994].

197. LaFeber, **Inevitable Revolutions** [1984]. pp. 210-213.

198. The debate within the Carter administration itself, which had ranged Brzezinski, the National Security Advisor, and Pastor, the top Latin American expert on the National Security Council, on one side, and Secretary of State Cyrus Vance and US Ambassador to the UN Andrew Young on the other, had actually ended not long after Somoza's overthrow, which had been preceded by the ouster of the Shah of Iran (January

1979) and followed by the Soviet invasion of Afghanistan (December 1979). Brzezinski and Pastor, with their increasing emphasis on, or return to, Cold War verities and the external roots of the crisis in Central America, had won out over the latters' emphasis on the internal origins of the crisis. Young left the administration and was soon followed by Vance. LaFeber, **Inevitable Revolutions** [1984]. p. 210. Dario Moreno, **US Policy in Central America: The Endless Debate** [Miami: Florida International University Press, 1990]. pp. 22-30.

199. Murdo Macleod, **Spanish Central America: A Socioeconomic History 1520-1720** [1973]. J. P. Bell, **Crisis in Costa Rica** [1971]. David Browning, **El Salvador: Landscape and Society** [1971]. Alaster White, **El Salvador** [1973]. Thomas L. Karnes, **Failure of Union: Central America 1824-1975** [1975]. This is a revised and updated version of Thomas L. Karnes, **The Failure of Union: Central America 1824-1960** [1961]. Thomas L. Karnes, **Tropical Enterprise: The Standard Fruit and Steamship Company in Latin America** [1978]. Thomas F. Anderson, **Matanza: El Salvador's Communist Revolt of 1932** [1971]. Thomas F. Anderson, **The War of the Dispossessed** [1981]. William Durham, **Scarcity and Survival in Central America: Ecological Origins of the Soccer War** [1979]. Thomas W. Walker, **The Christian Democratic Movement in Nicaragua** [1970]. Stephen A. Webre, **José Napoleon Duarte and the Christian Democratic Party in Salvadoran Politics 1960-1972** [1979]. See also Miles L. Wortman, **Government and Society in Central America 1680-1840** [1982].

200. Ralph Lee Woodward, Jr., **Central America: A Nation Divided** [1976].

201. Louis J. Pérez, Jr., "Intervention, Hegemony and Dependency: The United States in the Circum-Caribbean 1898-1980" **Pacific Historical Review** vol. 51. no. 2. 1982. pp. 175-176. Stephen G. Rabe, "Marching Ahead (Slowly): The Historiography of Inter-American Relations" **Diplomatic History** vol. 13. no. 3. 1989. pp. 304-305.

202. Robert D. Crassweller, **The Caribbean Community: Changing Societies and US Policy** [1972]. John Bartlow Martin, **US Policy in the Caribbean** [1978].

203. Lester D. Langley, **Struggle for the American Mediterranean: United States-European Rivalry 1776-1904** [1976]. Lester D. Langley, **The United States and the Caribbean 1900-1970** [1980].

204. See Lester Langley, **The Cuban Policy of the United States: A Brief History** [New York: John Wiley and Sons, 1968]. Allan Reed Millett, **The Politics of Intervention: The Military Occupation of Cuba 1906-1909** [1968]. Louis A. Pérez, Jr., "Supervision of a Protectorate: The United States and the Cuban Army 1898-1908" **Hispanic American Historical Review** vol. 52. no. 2. 1972. Irwin Gellman, **Batista and Roosevelt: Good Neighbor Diplomacy in Cuba 1933-1945** [1973]. Louis A. Pérez, Jr., **Intervention, Revolution and Politics in Cuba 1913-1921** [1978]. Jules Robert Benjamin, **The United States and Cuba: Hegemony and Dependent Development 1880-1934** [1978]. Louis A. Pérez, Jr., "Cuba Between Empires 1878-1902" **Pacific Historical Review** vol. 40. no. 4. 1979. Also see Louis A. Pérez, Jr., **Cuba Between Empires 1878-1902** [1983]. Louis A. Pérez, Jr., **Cuba: Between Reform and Revolution** [1988]. Jules Robert Benjamin, **The United States and the Origins of the Cuban Revolution: An Empire of Liberty in an Age of National Liberation** [1990]. There was also renewed interest in US relations with the Dominican Republic and Haiti, both of which have been directly affected by the United States assertion and maintenance of its hegemony in the region. See Theodore Draper, **The Dominican Revolt: A Case Study in American Policy** [1968].

Kenneth J. Grieb, "Warren G. Harding and the Dominican Republic: US Withdrawal 1921-1923" **Journal of Inter-American Studies** vol. 11. no. 3. 1969. Jerome Slater, **Intervention and Negotiation: The United States and the Dominican Revolution** [1970]. Abraham F. Lowenthal, "The United States and the Dominican Republic to 1965: Background to Intervention" **Caribbean Studies** vol. 10. no. 1. 1970. Hans Schmidt, **The United States Occupation of Haiti 1915-1934** [1971]. Abraham Lowenthal, **The Dominican Intervention** [1972]. G. Pope Atkins and Larman C. Wilson, **The United States and The Trujillo Regime** [1972]. David Healy, **Gunboat Diplomacy in the Wilson Era: The US Navy in Haiti 1915-1916** [1976]. Piero Gleijeses, **The Dominican Crisis: The 1965 Constitutionalist Revolt and American Intervention** [1978]. Bruce J. Calder, "Caudillos and Gavrilleros versus the United States: Guerilla Insurgency during the Dominican Intervention 1916-1924" **Hispanic American Historical Review** vol. 58. no. 4. 1978. See also Bruce J. Calder, **The Impact of Intervention: The Dominican Republic During the US Occupation of 1916-1924** [1984]. New literature on US-Panamanian relations also began to appear in the 1970s, and was given new impetus by the Carter administration's Panama Treaty initiative. Sheldon B. Liss, **The Canal: Aspects of United States-Panamanian Relations** [1969]. Walter LaFeber, **The Panama Canal: The Crisis in Historical Perspective** [1978].

    205. Richard Millet, **Guardians of the Dynasty: A History of the US Created** *Guardia Nacional de Nicaragua* **and the Somoza Family** [1977]. Millet's original thesis on the Guardia was submitted as Richard Millet, **The History of the Guardia Nacional de Nicaragua 1925-1965** [Unpublished PhD dissertation, University of New Mexico, 1966]. US-Nicaraguan relations was a focus of interest for other North American PhD students in the 1960s. See, for example, Thomas Joseph Dodd, Jr., **The United States in Nicaraguan Politics: Supervised Elections 1927-1932** [Unpublished PhD dissertation, George Washington University, 1966]. John J. Tierney, Jr., **The United States and Nicaragua 1927-1932: Decisions for De-Escalation and Withdrawal** [Unpublished PhD dissertation, University of Pennsylvania, 1969]. Ralph Lee Woodward singled Millet's book out as "the most influential" and "one of the most important contributions to twentieth century Central American historiography" in part because it was "well-researched" and because it dealt "scientifically with the history of military institutions on the isthmus". Ralph Lee Woodward, Jr., "The Historiography of Modern Central America Since 1960" **Hispanic American Historical Review** vol. 67. no. 3. 1987. p. 490.

    206. Richard L. Millet, "Central American Paralysis" **Foreign Policy** no. 39. 1980. Richard L. Millett, "From Somoza to the Sandinistas: The Roots of Revolution in Nicaragua" in Wolf Grabendorff, Heinrich W. Krumwiede and Jorg Todt, eds., **Political Change in Central America: Internal and External Dimensions** [1984]. Richard L. Millet, "Historical Setting" in James A. Rudolph, ed., **Honduras: A Country Study** [1984]. Richard L. Millett, "The Central American Region" in Jan Knippers Black, ed., **Latin America: Its Problems and Its Promise** [1984]. Richard L. Millett, "Praetorians or Patriots? The Central American Military" in Robert S. Leiken, ed., **Central America: Anatomy of Conflict** [1984]. Richard L. Millet, "Honduras: An Emerging Dilemma" in Richard S. Newfarmer, ed., **From Gunboats to Diplomacy: New US Policies for Latin America** [Baltimore: Johns Hopkins University Press, 1984]. Richard L. Millett, "The United States and Central America: A Policy Adrift" **Current History** vol. 87. no. 533. 1988. Richard L. Millett, "An Unclear Menace: US Perceptions of Soviet Strategy in Latin America" in Eusebio Mujal-Leon, ed., **The USSR and Latin America: A Developing Relationship** [1989]. Richard L. Millett, "Limited

Hopes and Fears in Guatemala" **Current History** vol. 90. no. 554. 1991. Richard Millet, "Central America: Background to the Crisis" in Jan Knippers Black, ed., **Latin America, Its Problems and Its Promise: A Multidisciplinary Introduction** [1991].

207. Millet's work also still relied on crude cultural and national categories, which perpetuated images of a dynamic North America in contrast to a corrupt and stagnating Central America. See his reference to the "typical American drive for efficiency and modernization" and the assertion that Nicaragua was "hardly famous for its healthful climate or high morals". His book was relatively sympathetic with the actions of US marine officers on the ground, but he also criticized US efforts to represent Sandino as a "bandit", noting that "the wishful speculation that his movement would soon evaporate proved grossly inaccurate". Millet, **Guardians of the Dynasty** [1977]. pp. 74-76, 85.

208. Millet, **Guardians of the Dynasty** [1977]. pp. 20, 26, 183-185, 137-139, 251, 261. The overall importance of the military relationship in the foundation and maintenance of US hegemony was addressed in Don L. Etchison, **The United States and Militarism in Central America** [1975].

209. Kenneth J. Grieb, "American Involvement in the Rise of Jorge Ubico" **Caribbean Studies** vol. 10. no. 1. 1970. Kenneth Grieb, **Guatemalan Caudillo: The Regime of Jorge Ubico 1931-1944** [1979]. Also see Kenneth J. Grieb, "The United States and the Rise of General Maximiliano Hernandez Martínez" **Journal of Latin American Studies** vol. 3. no. 2. 1971.

210. Immerman's study was awarded the Society for Historians of American Foreign Relations' Bernath Memorial Book Award in 1983. Rabe, "Marching Ahead (Slowly)" **Diplomatic History** [1989]. p. 308.

211. Richard H. Immerman, **The CIA in Guatemala: The Foreign Policy of Intervention** [1982]. pp. ix, 6. See Richard Immerman, **Guatemala and the United States, 1954: A Cold War Strategy for the Americas** [Unpublished PhD dissertation, Boston College, 1978].

212. Immerman, **The CIA in Guatemala** [1988]. pp. 8-9. Robert J. Alexander, "Guatemalan Communists" **The Canadian Forum** vol. 34. July 1954. p. 81; cited in Immerman, **The CIA in Guatemala** [1988]. pp. 101, 105, 232-233. See also Robert J. Alexander, "The Guatemalan Revolution and Communism" **Foreign Policy Bulletin (Report?)** vol. 33. April 1, 1954.

213. Immerman, **The CIA in Guatemala** [1988]. pp. 167-168, 197-201. Immerman's book on Guatemala was followed by a book by Stephen Schlesinger and Stephen Kinzer which focused on the 1954 intervention. Like Immerman, Kinzer (a long-time Latin American correspondent for the **Boston Globe**) and Schlesinger concluded that Cold War myopia had spurred on Washington policy-makers, who failed to see that nationalism, not communism, was the driving force behind the Guatemalan revolution, and as a result of US intervention in 1954 Guatemala has remained one of the most unstable and inequitable republics in Central America for almost thirty years. Stephen Schlesinger and Stephen Kinzer, **Bitter Fruit: The Untold Story of the American Coup in Guatemala** [1983]. pp. 227-228, 254-255. Writing in the early 1980s about Guatemala in the 1950s, Stephen Kinzer adopted a critical position with regard to US intervention in Guatemala; however, Kinzer, who became the **New York Times** main journalist in Nicaragua in 1983, gradually grew disenchanted with the Sandinistas. His reportage for the **Times** on Nicaragua and the rest of Central America, increasingly fell into line with Washington. In late 1985 he more or less suggested that a recent "election" in Guatemala, might provide a model for beleaguered Nicaragua. Edward S. Herman and Noam Chomsky, **Manufacturing Consent: The Political Economy of the Mass Media** [1988]. pp. 83-85, 112-128. This was no doubt in part because of the influence of his editors, but his own disillusionment

with the Sandinistas was equally important. In **Blood of Brothers** he argued that the Sandinistas on the one hand, and the contras and their North American supporters on the other, were virtual mirror images. He wrote admiringly of Oliver North and even asserted that "North would have made a fine Sandinista". Stephen Kinzer, **Blood of Brothers: Life and War in Nicaragua. A New York Times Correspondent's Eyewitness Account** [1990]; cited in Michael Rosenfeld, "How Kinzer Changed with the **Times**" In **These Times** vol. 15. no. 26. 1991. pp. 18-19. Kinzer avoided any discussion of power relations and saw no difference between the singlemindedness and ideological fervor of Oliver North, with the US military machine behind him, and the increasingly narrow options of Central American revolutionaries trying to introduce structural changes to a country of 3 million people under the unrelenting gaze of Washington.

214. In 1962, Perkins argued that if the US accepted its 'imperial' history, its global role would be easier to carry out. North Americans could not "disavow principle" or "evade the logic of power", and there was "no way to prevent the blunting of the instruments of power and the tarnishing of ideals". In his examination of a number of the United States' direct dependencies (Hawaii, Puerto Rico, the Philippines, the Virgin Islands and its main Pacific Island territories), he argued for a current policy which accepted that, given the United States' position, a certain amount of imperialism was inevitable. He asserted that US security and interests were more important than the aspirations of Third World nations. He also argued that a willingness on the part of the US to acknowledge that it was an imperial power might lead to a greater understanding of "the dilemmas of relations between those who have and those who have not achieved the metamorphosis of industrialization". In the case of historical dependencies, he took the position that "good intentions did not prevent the dependencies from being deeply shaken and firmly shaped by American control into forms sometimes grotesque and unexpected". He argued that US leaders had been prevented from "facing the situations of dependencies frankly" because they were unable to "admit that dependency was more than a passing phase". In his view, US recognition of the long-term character of Washington's dominance, and of the need to combine an emphasis on political reform and an awareness of the "difficulty of transplanting" North American "principles and institutions of government" with economic planning, could help solve future policy problems. Whitney T. Perkins, **Denial of Empire: The United States and Its Dependencies** [1962]. pp. 7-10, 341-345. The US acceptance of its imperial role as the only way of maintaining global order was a theme of George Liska's work by the late 1960s. George Liska, **Imperial America: The International Politics of Primacy** [1967]. George Liska, **War and Order: Reflections on Vietnam and History** [1968]. See Jerome Slater, "Is United States Foreign Policy 'Imperialist' or 'Imperial'?" **Political Science Quarterly** vol. 91. no.1. 1976. pp. 65-67.

215. Tony Smith, **The Pattern of Imperialism: The United States, Great Britain and the late-industrializing World Since 1815** [1981].

216. Fieldhouse argued that British imperialism was generally "the consequence of instability generated on the frontiers of empire by advancing parties of traders, missionaries and other Europeans coming into conflict with indigenous societies". In his view "Europe was pulled into imperialism by the magnetic force of the periphery". D. K. Fieldhouse, **Economics and Empire: 1830-1914** [1973]. pp. 76-84, 463. See also D. K. Fieldhouse, **The Colonial Empires: A Comparative Survey from the Eighteenth Century** [1966]. D. K. Fieldhouse, **Colonialism 1870-1945: An Introduction** [1981]. See also J. S. Galbraith, "'The Turbulent Frontier' as a Factor in British Expansion" **Comparative Studies in Society and History**, vol. 2. no. 2. 1960.

217. Whitney T. Perkins, **Constraint of Empire: The United States and Caribbean Interventions** [1981]. pp. x-xiii. Ronald Robinson, "The Non-

European Foundations of European Imperialism: Sketch for a Theory of Collaboration" in Roger Owen and Bob Sutcliffe, eds., **Studies in the Theory of Imperialism** [1972]. Ronald Robinson and John Gallagher, **Africa and the Victorians: The Official Mind of Imperialism** [1965]. See William Roger Louis ed., **Imperialism: The Robinson and Gallagher Controversy** [1976].

218. Perkins, **Constraint of Empire** [1981]. pp. x, xiv, 2, 4, 75-76.

219. Dana Gardner Munro, **Intervention and Dollar Diplomacy in the Caribbean 1900-1921** [1964]. Dana Gardner Munro, **The United States and the Caribbean Republics 1921-1933** [1974].

220. Perkins, **Constraint of Empire** [1981]. pp. 2, 4, 139, 194.

221. By the late 1970s the overall understanding of US relations with Central America apparent in Perkins's work was being further refined by diplomatic historians who had begun to argue that US relations with the southern republics could be understood only in a global framework and emphasized a multi-archival methodology and a 'multi-dimensional systemic' approach. Richard V. Salisbury, "Good Neighbours: The United States and Latin America in the Twentieth Century" in Gerald K. Haines and J. Samuel Walker, eds., **American Foreign Relations: An Historiographical Review** [1981]. p. 315. See the work on Central America by Richard V. Salisbury and Thomas D. Schoonover, which represents a refinement of the 'multi-dimensional systemic' model and clearly reflects the influence of dependency theory and world-system theory on liberal scholarship. Richard V. Salisbury, "Domestic Politics and Foreign Policy: Costa Rica's Stand on Recognition" **Hispanic American Historican Review** vol. 54. no. 3. 1974. Richard V. Salisbury, "Costa Rica and the 1920-1921 Union Movement: A Reassessment" **Journal of Interamerican Studies and World Affairs** vol. 19. no. 3. 1977. Richard V. Salisbury, "United States Intervention in Nicaragua: The Costa Rican Role" **Prologue: The Journal of the National Archives** vol. 9. no. 4. 1977. Richard V. Salisbury, "The Anti-Imperialist Career of Alejandro Alvarado Quiros" **Hispanic American Historical Review** vol. 57. no. 4. 1977. Richard V. Salisbury, "Jorge Volio and Isthmian Revolutionary Politics" **Red River Valley Historical Journal of World History** vol. 4. no. 4. 1980. Richard V. Salisbury, "The Middle American Exile of Víctor Raul Haya de la Torre" **The Americas: A Quarterly Review of Inter-American Cultural History** vol. 40. no. 1. 1983. Richard V. Salisbury, "Mexico, The United States, and the 1926-1927 Nicaraguan Crisis" **Hispanic American Historical Review** vol. 66. no. 2. 1986. Richard V. Salisbury, **Anti-Imperialism and International Competition in Central America 1920-1929** [1989]. Richard V. Salisbury, "Revolution and Recognition: A British Perspective on Isthmian Affairs During the 1920s" **The Americas: A Quarterly Review of Inter-American Cultural History** vol. 48. no. 3. 1992. Thomas D. Schoonover, "Central American Commerce and Maritime Activity in the 19th Century: A Quantitative Approach" **Latin American Research Review** vol. 13. no. 2. 1978. Thomas D. Schoonover, "Misconstrued Mission: Expansionism and Black Colonization in Mexico and Central America during the Civil War" **Pacific Historical Review** vol. 49. no. 4. 1980. Thomas D. Schoonover, "Imperialism in Middle America: United States, Britain, Germany and France Compete for Transit Rights and Trade 1820s-1920s" in Rhodri Jeffreys-Jones, ed., **Eagle Against Empire: American Opposition to European Imperialism 1914-1982** [1983]. Thomas D. Schoonover, "Prussia and the Protection of German Transit Through Middle America and Commerce with the Pacific Basin 1848-1851" **Jahrbuch für Geschichte von Staat, Wirtschaft und Gesellschaft Lateinamerikas** vol. 22. 1985. Thomas D. Schoonover, "Metropole Rivalry in Central America 1820-1929: An Overview" in Ralph Lee Woodward, Jr., ed., **Central America: Historical Perspectives on the Contemporary Crisis** [1988]. Thomas D. Schoonover, "A

United States Dilemma: Economic Opportunity and Anti-Americanism in El Salvador 1901-1911" **Pacific Historical Review** vol. 58. no. 4. 1989. Thomas D. Schoonover, **The United States in Central America, 1860-1911: Episodes in Social Imperialism and Imperial Rivalry in the World System** [1992].

4. The New Cold War 1979-1990

1. Morris H. Morley, **Washington, Somoza, and the Sandinistas: State and Regime in US Policy 1969-1981** [1994]. pp. 172-307.

2. Roger Burbach, "Central America: The End of US Hegemony?" **Monthly Review** vol. 34. no. 1. 1982. p. 2.

3. Cynthia J. Arnson, **Crossroads: Congress, the Reagan Administration and Central America** [1989]. Dario Moreno, **US Policy in Central America: The Endless Debate** [1990].

4. Prominent neo-conservative, and self-styled new nationalist, Norman Podhoretz, argued that new nationalism first appeared as a significant force in 1972, when Richard Nixon was voted back into the White House by those North Americans hostile to the increasingly "negative attitude" toward US power. The new nationalism "reached the dimensions of a tidal wave", said Podhoretz, at the time of the Iranian hostage crisis. Norman Podhoretz, **The Present Danger: "Do We Have the Will to Reverse the Decline of American Power"** [1980]. pp. 86-88. The conservatism of the 1970s and 1980s had links that went back to pre-1945 conservatism and has been traced to the conservative reaction to Roosevelt's New Deal in the 1930s. Jerome L. Himmelstein has argued that the New Right, allied with neo-conservatism and the Religious Right, which swept Reagan into the White House, did so not by breaking with conservative tradition in the United States, but by remaining faithful to it. Jerome L. Himmelstein, **To the Right: The Transformation of American Conservatism** [1990]. This point is also made by Alan Wolfe, "The Ideology of US Conservatism: Sociology, Liberalism and the Radical Right" **New Left Review** no. 128. 1981. pp. 17-27. See also Jonathan Martin Kolkey, **The New Right 1960-1968** (with epilogue 1969-1980) [1983]. pp. 337-339. Harvey J. Kaye, "The Use and Abuse of the Past: The New Right and the Crisis of History" **The Socialist Register 1987** [1987]. pp. 336, 340-343. On Reagan's rise to power see Mike Davis, "The New Right's Road to Power" **New Left Review** no. 128. 1981; reprinted in Mike Davis, **Prisoners of the American Dream: Politics and Economy in the History of the US Working Class** [1986]. pp. 157-180. Joel Krieger, **Reagan, Thatcher and the Politics of Decline** [1986]. pp. 130-153. Sidney Blumenthal, **The Rise of the Counter Establishment: From Conservative Ideology to Political Power** [1986]. pp. 12-86.

5. Richard Melanson talked about the emergence in the late 1970s of a "conservative nationalism" which "rejected the introspective guilt of the post-Vietnam period without, however, fully embracing the liberal internationalism of the Cold War consensus". Richard A. Melanson, **Writing History and Making Policy: The Cold War, Vietnam and Revisionism** [1983]. pp. 199-201.

6. See Steven Rose, Richard Lewontin and Leon J. Kamin, **Not in Our Genes: Biology, Ideology and Human Nature** [1984]. pp. 3-36, 265-290.

7. North American and Western European governments were able to back up these recommendations with their determining influence over the International Monetary Fund (IMF) and the World Bank, the two most influential international financial organizations in the world. This was enhanced by the weakened impact of the United Nations and related organizations such as the International Labour Organization (ILO), the United Nations Conference on Trade and Development (UNCTAD) and the United Nations Development Program (UNDP), where Third World views have had more weight. The central prescription for the Third World that flowed from free market ideology was that underdevelopment was caused by "poor resource allocation due to incorrect pricing policies and to too much state intervention by overly active Third World governments". Neo-classical economics rests on the assumption that state intervention acts as a brake on economic growth and that by adopting a free market/free

trade approach, selling off state-owned corporations, opening up the countries to foreign investment and getting rid of government regulations on prices and markets, governments would encourage economic growth and economic efficiency. Neo-classical economics and the conservative discourses were structured by the assumption that the cause of Third World underdevelopment is not a result of the "predatory" activity of North America and Western Europe, but of the inefficiency, corruption and interventionist activities of the Third World states, and that the solution lies not in the dramatic reformation of the world economic order but in the promotion of free trade and laissez-faire economic policies. To support their argument they pointed to countries such as South Korea, Taiwan, Hong Kong and Singapore, which they characterized as examples of the success of the free-market model (these countries do not, of course, upon close scrutiny, resemble the laissez-faire model, nor can their developmental success necessarily be attributed to free market policies), while pointing to the apparent failure of the public-interventionist model adopted by most governments in Africa and Latin America. The neo-classical counter-revolution, like North American 'conservatism', assumed that an idealized representation of how economic development proceeded in the West was applicable to a completely different cultural, institutional and historical context. North American and Western European assumptions about economics are often irrelevant in North America and Western Europe, and in the case of the Third World the mechanical application of free market economics--especially to a country or region in which markets are still fragmented, information is often limited and significant aspects of economic exchange are still outside the money economy-- could not be expected to have a beneficial impact. See Michael P. Todaro, **Economic Development in the Third World** [1989]. pp. 82-84. The most famous exponent of conservative development economics is probably the British academic P. T. Bauer. See P. T. Bauer, **Equality, the Third World, and Economic Delusion** [1981]. P. T. Bauer, **Reality and Rhetoric: Studies in the Economics of Development** [1984]. P. T. Bauer, "Foreign Aid and the Third World" in Peter Duignan and Alvin Rabushka, eds., **The United States in the 1980s** [1980]. P. T. Bauer, "The Vicious Circle of Poverty" in Mitchel A. Seligson, ed., **The Gap Between Rich and Poor: Contending Perspectives on the Political Economy of Development** [1984].

    8. The rise of Reagan also affected Latin American studies (and area studies) in financial terms. The Reagan administration's commitment to reducing federal spending, in all areas except defense spending, combined with stable or declining university enrollments, so that many area studies and language programs, including Latin American studies (the growth of which had begun to level out, or contract, by the late 1970s), were even less likely to recover in the 1980s. Washington's renewed commitment to intervention around the world was not complemented by an interest in language programs or area studies. At the same time, the Reagan administration sought to rely on academic expertise located outside of the university-based area-studies programs, turning to the growing number of think tanks that had emerged by the late 1970s. This trend continued throughout the 1980s; however, it should be emphasized that the limited expansion, leveling out or even decline, was not confined to area studies, but was part of the decline of university-based "academic enterprise" generally, in contrast to the 1960s. Peter H. Smith, "The Intellectual Integrity of Latin American Studies" **LASA Forum** vol. 12. no. 4. 1982. pp. 11-12. Gilbert Merkx, "The Washington Policy Process: Implications for Latin American Studies" **LASA Forum** vol. 12. no. 4. 1982. pp. 12-13. Hugh M. Hamill, Jr., "Title VI Funding: A Commentary" **LASA Forum** vol. 15. no. 3. 1984. p. 11. Gilbert Merkx, "Research Manpower Needs for Latin America and the Caribbean: An Assessment" **LASA Forum** vol. 15. no. 3. 1984. pp. 11, 19. Richard D. Lambert et al., **Beyond Growth: The Next Stage in Language and Area Studies** [1984]. pp. 11-13. Robert A.

McCaughey, **International Studies and Academic Enterprise: A Chapter in the Enclosure of American Learning** [1984]. pp. 237-255. Gilbert Merkx, "Title VI Accomplishments, Problems and New Directions" **LASA Forum** vol. 21. no. 2. 1990. pp. 1, 18-23.

   9. The most well-known liberal and radical revisionist works, which began to appear in the 1970s, include David Halberstram, **The Best and the Brightest** [1972]. Frances Fitzgerald, **Fire in the Lake: The Vietnamese and the Americans in Vietnam** [1972]. George C. Herring, **America's Longest War: The United States and Vietnam 1950-1975** [1979]. Archimedes Patti, **Why Vietnam?: Prelude to America's Albatross** [1980]. Stanley Karnow, **Vietnam: A History** [1983]. James William Gibson, **The Perfect War: Technowar in Vietnam** [1986]. George McT. Kahin, **Intervention: How America Became Involved in Vietnam** [1987]. Andrew J. Rotter, **The Path to Vietnam: Origins of the American Commitment to Southeast Asia** [1987]. Lloyd C. Gardner, **Approaching Vietnam: From World War II Through Dienbienphu 1941-1954** [1988]. Neil Sheehan, **A Bright Shining Lie: John Paul Vann and America in Vietnam** [1988]. Marilyn B. Young, **The Vietnam Wars 1945-1990** [1991]. As Marvin Gettleman has pointed out, by the 1980s this literature represented the "outer limits" of the attempt to understand why the US lost. Marvin Gettleman, "Against Cartesianism: Preliminary Notes on Three Generations of English-Language Political Discourse on Vietnam" **Bulletin of Concerned Asian Scholars** vol. 21. nos. 2-4. 1989. pp. 142-143. To go beyond these limits researchers have to focus on why the Vietnamese Communists won. This has been done most recently by Gabriel Kolko in what will undoubtedly stand for many years as a classic radical study of the war. Gabriel Kolko, **Anatomy of a War: Vietnam, the United States and the Modern Historical Experience** [1985]. The trail was blazed for Kolko by North Americans such as David Marr, Jayne Werner and Alexander Woodside as well as North American based Vietnamese historians such as Huynh Kim Kanh. See David Marr, **Vietnamese Anticolonialism 1885-1925** [1971]. David Marr, **Vietnamese Tradition on Trial 1920-1945** [1981]. Jayne Werner, **Peasant Politics and Religious Sectarianism** [1981]. Alexander Woodside, **Vietnam and the Chinese Model: A Comparative Study of Vietnamese and Chinese Government in the First Half of the Nineteenth Century** [1971]. Alexander Woodside, **Community and Revolution in Modern Vietnam** [1976]. Huyhn Kim Khanh, **Vietnamese Communism 1925-1945** [1982].

   10. Most of the books which reflect the conservative perspective on the Vietnam war have been written by unrepentant participants. According to Admiral Ulysses S. Grant Sharp, the US war in Vietnam could have been won if Lyndon Johnson had initiated the saturation bombing of the North at a much earlier date. General William Westmoreland, who was the top US military man in Vietnam at the time of the Tet Offensive in early 1968, asserted that the war was lost in Washington, where politically sensitive politicians pursued a "no-win policy" to appease "a misguided minority opposition" which was "masterfully manipulated by Hanoi and Moscow". Westmoreland's argument was refined by Leslie Gelb and Richard Betts. They argued that the US "Cold War national security establishment" actually worked, but the people of the United States, who were increasingly tired of a conflict they had not really understood, caused presidents and politicians in Washington to lose the war because the politicians were ultimately more concerned with gaining votes than winning wars in Southeast Asia. Colonel Harry Summers looked at the evidence and concluded that it was a noble cause, and the only real error was that the US failed. A similar interpretation was offered by Guenter Lewy in 1978, when he lamented "the impairment of national pride and self confidence that has beset this country since the fall of Vietnam". He argued

that, based on his analysis of battlefield practices, "the sense of guilt created by the Vietnam War in the minds of many Americans is not warranted and that charges of officially condoned illegal and grossly immoral conduct are without substance". Lewy also defended the domino theory. Another participant, Lieutenant-General Phillip B. Davidson has argued in a massive book that Washington's defeat was due to a number of factors, but the major cause was the United State's failure to actually declare war and seek not only the preservation of South Vietnam, but the defeat of the North. Ulysses S. Grant Sharp, **Strategy for Defeat: Vietnam in Retrospect** [1978]. William Westmoreland, **A Soldier Reports** [1976]. Guenter Lewy **America in Vietnam** [1978]. Leslie Gelb and Richard Betts, **The Irony of Vietnam: The System Worked** [1979]. Harry G. Summers, Jr., **On Strategy: The Vietnam War in Context** [1981]. Phillip B. Davidson, **Vietnam at War: The History 1946-1975** [1988].

11. Reagan's assertion that the war was a "noble cause" can be found in the **New York Times**, 19 August 1980; cited in Melanson, **Writing History and Making Policy** [1983]. pp. 205, 251.

12. Walter LaFeber, "The Last War, the Next War, and the New Revisionists" **Democracy** vol. 1 no. 1. 1981. The Vietnam Syndrome is usually defined as the unwillingness of the North American public to support US military intervention and involvement, especially in the form of US military presence, in the Third World. See Michael T. Klare, **Beyond the "Vietnam Syndrome": US Interventionism in the 1980s** [1981]. p. 1.

13. Norman Pohoretz, **Breaking Ranks: A Political Memoir** [1979]. pp. 16, 21. See also Norman Podhoretz, **Making It** [1967].

14. Blumenthal, **The Rise of the Counter-Establishment** [1986]. pp. 144-146.

15. Podhoretz, **The Present Danger** [1980]. pp. 12, 30-31. See also pp. 25-38 and pp. 79-85. See Blumenthal, **The Rise of the Counter-Establishment** [1986]. pp. 142-146.

16. Podhoretz argued that one of the basic causes of the US loss of will was homosexuality, which he also saw as a basic cause of appeasement in England in the 1930s. See Norman Podhoretz, "The Culture of Appeasement" **Harper's** vol. 255. no. 1529. 1977. p. 32. reprinted in Podhoretz, **The Present Danger** [1980] with some apparent changes so that the connection between lack of will and homosexuality can only be inferred since it is not stated explicitly. See Jerry Sanders **Peddlers of Crisis: The Committee on the Present Danger and the Politics of Containment** [1983]. p. 216.

17. Norman Podhoretz, **Why We Were in Vietnam** [1982]. p. 205. Blumenthal, **The Rise of the Counter-Establishment** [1986]. pp. 146-147.

18. Marvin R. Zahniser and W. Michael Weis, "A Diplomatic Pearl Harbor?: Richard Nixon's Goodwill Mission to Latin America in 1958" **Diplomatic History** vol. 13. no. 2. 1989. John Martz has argued that Nixon was never able to overcome his suspicion of Latin America, which was stimulated by the hostile reception he received in Peru and Venezuela in 1958. See John D. Martz, "Introduction" in John D. Martz, ed., **United States Policy in Latin America: A Quarter Century of Crisis and Challenge** [1988]. p. xv.

19. Robert Pastor, **Condemned to Repetition: The United States and Nicaragua** [1987]. p. 11.

20. Tom Wicker, **One of Us: Richard Nixon and the American Dream** [1990].

21. His view of Washington's historical role south of the border was summed up in **The Real War** when he asserted that the US "had the great power responsibility for keeping the peace in Central and South America, assumed under the Monroe

Doctrine". Richard Nixon, **The Real War** [1980]. p. 308. Richard Nixon, **Leaders** [1982]. Richard Nixon, **Real Peace: Strategy for the West** [1984]. Richard Nixon, **1990: Victory Without War** [1988]. Richard Nixon, **Seize the Moment: America's Challenge in a One-Superpower World** [1992]. See also Richard Nixon, **RN: The Memoirs of Richard Nixon** [1978].

22. Richard Nixon, **No More Vietnams** [1985]. pp. 20, 164-166, 212-213, 237. Susan Jeffords has located Nixon's book within the larger effort to "remasculinize" the United States after Vietnam. Significantly, her analysis focused on novels and movies; Nixon's book, was the only non-fiction text which she examined. She argued that in **No More Vietnams**, as well as numerous movies in the Rambo mold, "women or what are perceived as the feminine characteristics of weakness, passivity, nonaggression, and negotiation are shown to be responsible for America's loss of the war in Vietnam". Her analysis represented Nixon's **No More Vietnams** as part of the self-mythologization of the war, and the celebration and reassertion of masculine virtues as part of the "remasculinization of America" after the assault on patriarchal structures which occurred in the 1960s. See Susan Jeffords **The Remasculinization of America: Gender and the Vietnam War** [1989]. pp. 22-30, 156-160, 168-169.

23. Gabriel Kolko, **Anatomy of a War: Vietnam, the United States and the Modern Historical Experience** [1985]. p. 545. For a recent liberal analysis of why the war was unwinnable, see Thomas G. Paterson, **Meeting the Communist Threat: From Truman to Reagan** [1988]. pp. 259-269.

24. See, for example, Lucian Pye, **Redefining American Policy in Southeast Asia** [1982]. Jorge I. Domínguez, **US Interests and Policies in the Caribbean and Central America** [1982].

25. Another conservative think tank, the Heritage Foundation, which was established in 1973, provided the Reagan administration with thirty-six staff members in 1981, while eighteen people from the Center for Strategic and International Studies (CSIS) moved up the street to the White House. The much older conservative think tank, the Hoover Institution, by which Reagan was named an honorary fellow in 1974, had provided the administration with at least fifty academics or former academics by 1985. Blumenthal, **The Rise of the Counter-Establishment** [1986]. pp. 4-5, 32-45. Steinfels, **The Neoconservatives** [1980]. pp. 11-12. Sanders, **Peddlers of Crisis** [1983]. pp. 217-218. John S. Saloma III, **Ominous Politics: The New Conservative Labyrinth** [1984]. pp. 7-12. James A. Smith, **The Idea Brokers: Think Tanks and the Rise of the New Policy Elite** [1991]. pp. 174-180, 270-271.

26. Kirkpatrick has written widely on US politics and foreign policy. See, for example, Jeane J. Kirkpatrick, **The New Presidential Elite: Men and Women in National Politics** [1976], **Dismantling the Parties: Reflections on Party Reform and Party Decomposition** [1978], **Dictatorships and Double Standards: Rationalism and Reason in Politics** [1982], **The Reagan Phenomenon-And Other Speeches on Foreign Policy** [1983], **"This very human institution": Commentaries and Addresses on the United Nations and US Foreign Policy** [1984] and **Idealism, Realism and the Myth of Appeasement** [1984].

27. Jeane J. Kirkpatrick, **Leader and Vanguard in Mass Society: A Study of Peronist Argentina** [1971].

28. Sanders, **Peddlers of Crisis** [1983]. pp. 8, 13, 150. Sanders's interview with Kirkpatrick, August 31, 1977, cited in Sanders, **Peddlers of Crisis** [1983]. pp. 162, 169. Blumenthal, **The Rise of the Counter-Establishment** [1986]. pp. 126-127, 140-141. On the Committee for the Present Danger see Charles Tyroler, ed., **Alerting America: The Papers of the Committee on THE**

PRESENT DANGER [1984].
    29. Blumenthal, **The Rise of the Counter-Establishment** [1986]. p. 141. After 1978, **The Washington Quarterly**, under the editorship of Michael Ledeen, also provided a forum in which conservatives challenged the Carter administration and the liberal 'establishment'. Pedro Sanjuan, "To See Ourselves as Others See Us: Some Latin American Perspectives on US Policy" **The Washington Quarterly: A Review of Strategic and International Issues** vol. 2. no. 2. 1979. Roger W. Fontaine, "Fidel Castro: Front and Center" **The Washington Quarterly: A Review of Strategic and International Issues** vol. 2. no. 2. 1979. Michael Ledeen and William H. Lewis, "Carter and the Fall of the Shah: The Inside Story" **The Washington Quarterly: A Review of Strategic and International Issues** vol. 3. no. 2. 1980. Roger W. Fontaine, Cleto DiGiovanni, Jr., and Alexander Kruger, "Castro's Specter" **The Washington Quarterly: A Review of Strategic and International Issues** vol. 3. no. 4. 1980. Pedro Sanjuan, "Why We Don't Have a Latin American Policy" **The Washington Quarterly: A Review of Strategic and International Issues** vol. 3. no. 4. 1980.
    30. The Report of the Committee of Santa Fe also influenced the Reagan Administration's Latin American Policy at the beginning of the decade. See Committee of Santa Fe, **A New Inter-American Policy for the Eighties** [1980]. The Committee of Santa Fe included L. Francis Bouchey, Executive Vice President of the Council for Inter-American Security (a small conservative think tank), David Jordan, Professor of Government at the University of Virginia, Lewis Tambs, Professor of History at Arizona State University, and Gordon Sumner, retired Lieutenant General. All went on to be ambassadors to Latin America during the Reagan administration, while Sumner gained a post as an adviser to the Assistant Secretary of State for Inter-American Affairs. The most influential member of the Committee was Roger W. Fontaine. A graduate of Johns Hopkins School of Advanced International Studies, Fontaine was the director of Latin American Studies at the Center for Strategic and International Studies (CSIS) at Georgetown from 1975 until he took up a post with the National Security Council under Reagan. The director of Latin American Studies at CSIS before Fontaine was James D. Theberge, who held the post from 1970 to 1975, before becoming Gerald Ford's ambassador to Nicaragua. Theberge and Fontaine prepared the 1977 report on Latin America for Nelson A. Rockefeller's Commission on Critical Choices for Americans. In 1980 Theberge headed a Latin American study group set up by the Republican National Committee. Roy Gutman, **Banana Diplomacy: The Making of American Policy in Nicaragua** [1988]. pp. 21, 27, 132. Holly Sklar, **Washington's War on Nicaragua** [1988]. pp. 58-59. See Roger W. Fontaine, **Brazil and the United States: Toward a Maturing Relationship** [1974]. Roger W. Fontaine, **On Negotiating with Cuba** [1975]. James D. Theberge and Roger W. Fontaine, eds., **Latin America's New Internationalism: The End of Hemispheric Isolation** [1976]. James D. Theberge and Roger W. Fontaine, **Latin America: Struggle for Progress** [1977].
    31. Jeane J. Kirkpatrick, "Dictatorships and Double Standards" **Commentary** vol. 68. no. 5. 1979; reprinted in Kirkpatrick, **Dictatorships and Double Standards** [1982].
    32. In another article in **Commentary** on the eve of Reagan's entry into the White House, Kirkpatrick again lambasted Carter's Latin American policy, arguing that it had facilitated the destablization of "friendly governments", the expansion of Cuba's influence, and the "decline" of Washington's power in Latin America. See Jeane J. Kirkpatrick, US Security and Latin America" **Commentary** vol. 70. no. 1. 1981; reprinted in Kirkpatrick, **Dictatorships and Double Standards** [1982]. Also revised and reprinted in Howard J. Wiarda, ed., **Rift and Revolution: The Central**

American Imbroglio [1984].

33. Kirkpatrick, "Dictatorships and Double Standards" in Kirkpatrick, **Dictatorships and Double Standards** [1982]. pp. 23-24. She argued that the series of events in Nicaragua in the late 1970s was characterized by a "suggestive resemblance" to both contemporaneous developments in Iran and to US policy towards China prior to Chiang Kai-shek's withdrawal to Taiwan, towards Cuba before Castro's rise to power, towards developments at key moments during the war in Vietnam, and towards recent events in Angola. The pattern she perceived was that in all of these situations the US attempted "to impose liberalization and democratization on a government confronted with violent internal opposition" and this "not only failed, but actually assisted the coming to power of new regimes in which ordinary people enjoy fewer freedoms and less personal security than under the previous autocracy". Jeane J. Kirkpatrick, "Dictatorships and Double Standards" in Kirkpatrick, **Dictatorships and Double Standards** [1982]. pp. 26-27.

34. Kirkpatrick, "Dictatorships and Double Standards" in Kirkpatrick, **Dictatorships and Double Standards** [1982]. pp. 24-26. The authoritarian-totalitarian distinction, justifying US support for the Somoza dynasty, had actually been articulated in North American foreign policy circles as early as 1949. At a Council on Foreign Relations meeting in New York at the beginning of 1949, the meeting's chairman, Francis Adams Truslow--a prominent businessman and lawyer--asserted that support for Somoza as a bulwark against the spread of "totalitarianism" in the Americas was based on the fact that although Somoza's rule was "autocratic", it was preferable to a totalitarian regime, which would involve "autocratic rule, plus total, absolute control of economic life, as for example, communism". Cited in Walter LaFeber, **Inevitable Revolutions: The United States in Central America** [1984]. pp. 103-104.

35. According to Kirkpatrick, "because the miseries of traditional life are familiar, they are bearable to ordinary people who, growing up in the society, learn to cope, as children born to untouchables in India acquire the skills and attitudes necessary for survival in the miserable roles they are destined to fill". She also asserted, apparently unaware of the tens of thousands of Guatemalans and El Salvadorans languishing in refugee camps in Mexico and elsewhere (not to mention the internal refugees), that her traditional autocracies "create no refugees", while "precisely the opposite is true of revolutionary Communist regimes" which "create refugees by the millions because they claim jurisdiction over the whole life of the society and make demands for change that so violate internalized values and habits that inhabitants flee in the remarkable expectation that their attitudes, values and goals will 'fit' better in a foreign country than in their native land." Kirkpatrick, "Dictatorships and Double Standards" in Kirkpatrick, **Dictatorships and Double Standards** [1982]. pp. 49-50. By 1986-1987 there were at least 1.5 million Central Americans who had been displaced by civil strife and were, in effect, internal refugees. See Abraham F. Lowenthal, **Partners in Conflict: The United States and Latin America** [1987]. pp. 6-7. John Booth estimated that by 1991 there were over 2 million internal and external Central American refugees. John A. Booth, "Socioeconomic and Political Roots of National Revolts in Central America" **Latin American Research Review** vol. 26. no. 1. 1991. p. 33.

36. Kirkpatrick, "Dictatorships and Double Standards" in Kirkpatrick, **Dictatorships and Double Standards** [1982]. pp. 50-51.

37. In support of this argument Kirkpatrick pointed to the work of Zbigniew Brzezinski, the Carter administration's chief ideologue and National Security Adviser. She asserted that the intellectual framework for US foreign policy in the Carter era can be found in Zbigniew Brzezinski's **Between Two Ages: America's Role in the Technetronic Era** [1970]. At the end of the 1960s Brzezinski, according to Kirkpatrick, looked beyond the Cold War and foresaw that a "new approach" was going

to be needed in international affairs. The "new approach", which he called "rational humanism", would consign the traditional focus on "national supremacy" to the dustbin of history, and take a global perspective on international problems which had to be regarded as "human issues" rather than "political confrontations". Kirkpatrick, "Dictatorships and Double Standards" in Kirkpatrick, **Dictatorships and Double Standards** [1982]. pp. 32-35. See also Kirkpatrick, "US Security and Latin America" in Kirkpatrick, **Dictatorships and Double Standards** [1982]. p. 56. Kirkpatrick has also argued that the views of the New Left were at the heart of Washington's foreign policy in the late 1970s. In particular she pointed to Robert Pastor, who was the Director of Latin American and Caribbean Affairs on the National Security Council in the Carter administration. Given Pastor's links with Brzezinski, and his own relatively 'hard-line' reputation, it is ironic that he was one of the individuals in the Carter administration whom she sought to single out. She stressed that before joining the Carter administration Pastor had been associated with the 1977 report prepared by the Institute for Policy Studies Ad Hoc Working Group on Latin America. She argued that, although this report was more radical than the report on US-Latin American relations prepared by the Linowitz Commission, with which Pastor was also connected as Executive Director, it incorporated many of the Linowitz Report's recommendations. This, for Kirkpatrick, was unescapable evidence of "the affinity between the views of the foreign policy establishment and the New Left", and it clearly demonstrated "how readily the categories of the new liberalism could be translated into those of revolutionary 'socialism' and how short a step it was from utopian globalism and the expectation of change to anti-American perspectives and revolutionary activism". See Kirkpatrick, "US Security and Latin America" in Kirkpatrick, **Dictatorships and Double Standards** [1982]. p. 60. See also Sol M. Linowitz, **The Americas in a Changing World: A Report of the Commission on United States-Latin American Relations** [1975]. Institute for Policy Studies' Ad Hoc Working Group on Latin America, **The Southern Connection: Recommendations for a New Approach to Inter-American Relations** [1977].

38. Kirkpatrick, "Dictatorships and Double Standards" in Kirkpatrick, **Dictatorships and Double Standards** [1982]. pp. 36-37. "So what", she said, "if the 'deep historical forces' at work" in Central America "look a lot like Russians or Cubans?" Kirkpatrick, "Dictatorships and Double Standards" in Kirkpatrick, **Dictatorships and Double Standards** [1982]. pp. 38-39.

39. Kirkpatrick, "Dictatorships and Double Standards" in Kirkpatrick, **Dictatorships and Double Standards** [1982]. pp. 36-37.

40. In early 1981 Kirkpatrick hoped that in its approach to human rights and foreign policy generally, the Reagan administration would take what she called "the cure of history". In her view "the cure of history" was "nothing more or less than the cure of reality". She emphasized that rights were "embodied in institutions, not in rhetoric" and that if the US took "the cure of history" it would discover that "force" was "sometimes necessary" in "the real world", in order to protect human rights, and that US power was "necessary to protect and expand the frontier of human rights in our time". Jeane J. Kirkpatrick, "Ideas and Institutions" (1981), reprinted in Kirkpatrick, **The Reagan Phenomenon** [1983]. pp. 44-45.

41. Kirkpatrick, "Dictatorships and Double Standards" in Kirkpatrick, **Dictatorships and Double Standards** [1982]. pp. 31-32, 52.

42. Jeane J. Kirkpatrick, "Reagan Policies and Black American Goals for Africa" in Kirkpatrick, **The Reagan Phenomenon** [1983]; cited in Kaye, "The Use and Abuse of the Past: The New Right and the Crisis of History" **The Socialist Register 1987** [1987]. pp. 341-342.

43. Samuel P. Huntington, **The Dilemma of American Ideals and Institutions in Foreign Policy** [1981]. pp. 4-9, 13-14. See also Samuel P.

Huntington, **American Politics: The Promise of Disharmony** [1981]. pp. 247-253, 257-259.

44. In 1981 Reagan asserted: "Let's not delude ourselves. The Soviet Union underlies all the unrest that is going on. If they weren't engaged in this game of dominoes, there wouldn't be any hot spots in the world". **New York Magazine**, 9 March 1981; cited in Fred Halliday, **The Making of the Second Cold War** [1983]. p. 15.

45. **New York Times**, 13 July 1980. p. 14; cited in LaFeber, **Inevitable Revolutions** [1984]. p. 271.

46. Pastor, **Condemned to Repetition** [1987]. pp. 230, 243.

47. LaFeber, **Inevitable Revolutions** [1984]. pp. 280, 303. Tom Barry and Deb Preusch, **The Soft War: The Uses and Abuses of US Economic Aid in Central America** [1988]. pp. xiii-ix, 3, 15-16, 34-35.

48. George C. Herring, "Vietnam, El Salvador, and the Uses of History" in Kenneth M. Coleman and George C. Herring, eds., **The Central American Crisis: Sources of Conflict and the Failure of US Policy** [1985]. pp. 97-98.

49. LaFeber, **Inevitable Revolutions** [1984]. pp. 284-286.

50. As Walter LaFeber has noted, the democratic legitimacy of the elections remains doubtful in a country where the military and the death squads had been intimidating the population for years. Many of the electoral procedures, such as stamping voters' thumbs with ink, transparent ballot boxes and voting receipts generated fear among the peasantry that their vote was less than secret. LaFeber, **Inevitable Revolutions** [1984]. pp. 286-290.

51. LaFeber, **Inevitable Revolutions** [1984]. pp. 289-293. Gutman, **Banana Diplomacy** [1988]. pp. 58-146.

52. Pastor, **Condemned to Repetition** [1987]. pp. 244-246.

53. LaFeber, **Inevitable Revolutions** [1984]. pp. 304-305. Thomas W. Walker, "Nicaraguan-US Friction: The First Four Years 1979-1983" in Coleman and Herring, eds., **The Central American Crisis** [1985]. p. 159.

54. LaFeber, **Inevitable Revolutions** [1984]. pp. 305-306. Gutman, **Banana Diplomacy** [1988]. pp. 90-91, 146-148. Jonathan Marshall, Peter Dale Scott and Jane Hunter, **The Iran-Contra Connection: Secret Teams and Covert Operations in the Reagan Era** [1987]. p. 199.

55. Nestor Sanchez, "The Communist Threat" **Foreign Policy** no. 52. 1983. pp. 45, 47, 50.

56. Reagan cited in Cynthia J. Arnson, "The Reagan Administration, Congress, and Central America: The Search for Consensus" in Nora Hamilton, Jeffry A. Frieden, Linda Fuller and Manuel Pastor, Jr., eds., **Crisis in Central America: Regional Dynamics and US Policy in the 1980s** [1988]. pp. 41-42, 54.

57. Gutman, **Banana Diplomacy** [1988]. pp. 141-142. The origins of the Commission are discussed in Howard J. Wiarda "The Kissinger Commission Report: Background and Political Dimensions" in **American Enterprise Institute Foreign Policy and Defense Review** vol. 5. no. 1. 1984. p. 3. A revised version of this article appeared as Howard J. Wiarda, "The Kissinger Commission Report on Central America" in Howard J. Wiarda, **Finding Our Way?: Toward Maturity in US-Latin American Relations** [1987]. pp. 201-208.

58. Kissinger's career began during the final stages of the Second World War, when he served in the US Army's Counterintelligence Corps (CIC). He remained on active duty in West Germany after 1945, working as an instructor at the Army's European Command Intelligence School in Oberammergau. In May 1946 he left the Army, but he continued to work as a civilian instructor at Oberammergau until mid-1947. Later that year Kissinger, still an officer in the army reserve, enrolled as an undergraduate at Harvard. He began graduate studies at Harvard in 1950, while also

working part time for the Defense Department's Operations Research Office. Kissinger became a consultant to the director of the Psychological Strategy Board in 1952. The Psychological Strategy Board was an arm of the NSC which dealt with clandestine paramilitary and psychological operations. In 1954 Nelson A. Rockefeller, a close associate of Kissinger who was already known to rely on Kissinger for advice, was made Eisenhower's Special Assistant for Cold War Planning. This post included both the approval and monitoring of the CIA's covert operations in the very year when the Agency was instrumental in ousting the Arbenz government in Guatemala. The following year (1955), Kissinger became a consultant to the National Security Council's Operations Coordination Board, which was the most important clandestine policy-making arm of the NSC. Prior to 1955 Kissinger had already attracted the notice of Allen Dulles, the influential head of the Central Intelligence Agency. According to one top official at the Operations Coordination Board, in the mid-1950s Kissinger was held in high esteem by Allen Dulles, who considered Kissinger and Walt Whitman Rostow, then a professor at MIT, as "kind of a team". Despite his connections with the Eisenhower administration, Kissinger was a member of the Democratic Party until 1963 or 1964, and his contacts in the Party and in the academic world were sufficient to gain him part-time consultancy work at the National Security Council during the Kennedy administration. His move to the Republican Party had occurred by 1964, when he acted as a foreign-policy consultant for the Republican Platform Committee; however, he continued to serve as a consultant on Vietnam during Lyndon Johnson's years as President. His position at Harvard, and his connections with the Kennedy administration, had put him in contact with State Department officials and advisors involved with Western Europe, while his work for the Johnson administration further extended his network of contacts to encompass high-level officials at the Pentagon and the White House, as well as the State Department. When Richard Nixon was elected to the presidency in 1968, Kissinger became his Secretary of State. Following Nixon's resignation on August 9, 1974, Kissinger served as Secretary of State to President Gerald Ford. And at the end of his tenure as Secretary of State in 1977, Kissinger emerged as an international consultant, part-time university lecturer and author. He joined the executive of the Trilateral Commission in 1977, and acted as a private consultant to the Shah of Iran after his overthrow in 1979. He continues to be associated, as a consultant and advisor, with a number of important US and overseas businesses, including Chase Manhattan Bank, Goldman, Sachs and Co., and the General Electric Company of Britain. In the early 1980s Kissinger was regularly reported by the US media to be acting as a foreign-policy consultant and advisor to the Reagan administration. Seymour M. Hersh, **The Price of Power: Henry Kissinger in the Nixon White House** [1983]. pp. 13, 26-27, 642.

59. Norman Birnbaum has argued that Kissinger can be seen "as the supreme student of empire". Kissinger has always advanced his career by speaking directly to, and working directly for, the North American foreign-policy, corporate and military establishments, while his writings, especially his memoirs, unrelentingly articulate a theoretical perspective which regards power as the essential aspect of international relations. Norman Birnbaum, **The Radical Renewal: The Politics of Ideas in Modern America** [1988]. pp. 39, 162-163.

60. See Henry Kissinger, **Nuclear Weapons and Foreign Policy** [1957]. Henry Kissinger, **A World Restored: Metternich, Castlereagh, and the Problems of Peace, 1812-1822** [1957]. Henry Kissinger, **The Necessity for Choice: Prospects of American Foreign Policy** [1961]. Henry Kissinger, **The Troubled Partnership: A Reappraisal of the Atlantic Alliance** [1965]. Henry Kissinger, ed., **Problems of National Strategy: A Book of Readings** [1965]. Henry Kissinger, **American Foreign Policy: Three Essays** [1969]. Kissinger has also written numerous academic articles over the

years, particularly for the Council on Foreign Relations' prestigious journal **Foreign Affairs**. He has also published two large volumes of memoirs: **The White House Years** [1979] and **Years of Upheaval** [1982].

61. Hersh, **The Price of Power** [1983]. p. 263. This famous conversation is also discussed in Michael J. Francis, "United States Policy toward Latin America During the Kissinger Years" in Martz, ed., **United States Policy in Latin America** [1988]. pp. 30-31.

62. Hersh, **The Price of Power** [1983]. pp. 270-271.

63. Kissinger was explicit about the **Report's** role in facilitating the establishment of a "national consensus" on Central America. He argued, in the **Report's** introductory letter, that "the best route to consensus" was "by exposure to the realities of Central America". See Henry Kissinger [Chairman of the National Bipartisan Commission on Central America], **Report of the National Bipartisan Commission on Central America** [1984]. pp. i, 1-3. English and Spanish language editions of the **Report** were also published commercially. See **The Report of the President's National Bipartisan Commission on Central America** [1984]. There is also the **Appendix to the Report of the National Bipartisan Commission on Central America** [1984], which contains the various submissions solicited from Latin American specialists.

64. Howard J. Wiarda, "The Kissinger Commission Report: Background and Political Dimensions" **American Enterprise Institute Foreign Policy and Defense Review** vol. 5. no. 1. 1984. p. 2.

65. William M. LeoGrande "Through the Looking Glass: The Kissinger Report on Central America" **World Policy** vol. 1. no. 2. 1984. pp. 252-253. See also Lloyd S. Etheredge, **Can Governments Learn?: American Foreign Policy and Central American Revolutions** [1985]. pp. 183-195.

66. Kissinger, **Report of the National Bipartisan Commission on Central America** [1984]. pp. 2, 5, 37.

67. Kissinger, **Report of the National Bipartisan Commission on Central America** [1984]. pp. 7-9.

68. Wiarda was born in Michigan in 1939. He received a BA from the University of Michigan in 1961 and he went on to the University of Florida, gaining an MA in 1962 and a PhD in 1965. In 1965 he took up a post as Assistant Professor of Political Science at the University of Massachusetts, eventually rising to a professorship. Although he was based at AEI for much of the 1980s, he continued to hold his post at the University of Massachusetts, and was formerly director of the University of Massachusetts's Center for Latin American Studies. Wiarda has written, coauthored and edited numerous books on Latin American history and politics and US foreign policy. For example, see Howard J. Wiarda, **Dictatorship and Development: The Methods of Control in Trujillo's Dominican Republic** [1968]. Howard J. Wiarda, **The Dominican Republic: Nation in Transition** [1969]. Howard J. Wiarda, **The Brazilian Catholic Labor Movement: The Dilemmas of National Development** [1969]. Howard J. Wiarda, **Dictatorship, Development and Disintegration: Politics and Social Change in the Dominican Republic** [1975]. Howard J. Wiarda, **Critical Elections and Critical Coups: State, Society and the Military in the Processes of Latin American Development** [1979]. Howard J. Wiarda, ed., **The Continuing Struggle for Democracy in Latin America** [1980]. Howard J. Wiarda, **Corporatism and National Development in Latin America** [1981]. Howard, J. Wiarda, ed., **Human Rights and US Human Rights Policy: Theoretical Approaches and Some Perspectives on Latin America** [1982]. Howard J. Wiarda, **Trade, Aid and US Policy** [1983]. Howard J. Wiarda, ed., **The Crisis in Latin America: Strategic, Economic and**

Political Dimensions [1984]. Howard J. Wiarda, ed., **The Iberian-Latin American Connection: Implications for US Foreign Policy** [1986]. Howard J. Wiarda, **Population, Internal Unrest and US Security in Latin America** [1986]. Howard J. Wiarda, **Latin America at the Crossroads: Debt, Development and the Future** [1987].

69. Kissinger, **Report of the National Bipartisan Commission on Central America** [1984]. pp. 17-20. This interpretation, word for word, can be found in the submission to the Commission by Wiarda. See Howard J. Wiarda, "Political Development in Central America: Options and Possibilities", Statement presented to the National Bipartisan Commission on Central America, US Department of State, Washington November 9, 1983; reprinted in **American Enterprise Institute Foreign Policy and Defense Review** vol. 5. no. 1. 1984. reprinted as Chapter 15 in Howard J. Wiarda, **Finding Our Way?: Toward Maturity in US-Latin American Relations** [1987]. Wiarda prepared two submissions for the Kissinger Commission. See also Howard J. Wiarda "US Policy in Central America: Toward a New Relationship", Statement presented to the National Bipartisan Commission on Central America, US Department of State, Washington, DC, September 28-29, 1983. Printed in **Appendix to the Report of the National Bipartisan Commission on Central America** [1984]; reprinted as Chapter 8 in Howard J. Wiarda, **In Search of Policy: The United States and Latin America** [1984].

70. Kissinger, **Report of the National Bipartisan Commission on Central America** [1984]. pp. 20-22, 24-25. Wiarda, "Political Development in Central America" **American Enterprise Institute Foreign Policy and Defense Review** 1984. pp. 8-10.

71. Kissinger, **Report of the National Bipartisan Commission on Central America** [1984]. p. 25. See LeoGrande "Through the Looking Glass" **World Policy Journal** 1984. pp. 255-256.

72. The Kissinger Report's failure to understand "the intense nationalism that fuels today's crisis" was emphasized in Abraham F. Lowenthal, "The United States and Central America: Reflections on the Kissinger Commission Report" in Coleman and Herring, eds., **The Central American Crisis** [1985]. p. 205.

73. Kissinger, **Report of the National Bipartisan Commission on Central America** [1984]. pp. 34-35.

74. The Report emphasized that throughout the 1960s Central America had a per capita growth rate in excess of 5% which "far surpassed" the Alliance for Progress target of 2.5%, while what it believed was "an impressive inventory of physical infrastructure was constructed in the five Central American countries during this period, including schools, hospitals, low-cost housing, and sewage systems". The **Report** argued that US direct private investment in Central America, which "continued to grow" in the 1960s, following the establishment of the Alliance for Progress, had "contributed substantially to the region's growth". The Commission lamented that this investment "has been a constant target of the propaganda of the radical left, which has played upon the theme of economic hegemony and 'imperialism'". The **Report** acknowleged that Central America's "dependence on trade" with the US has "always been high" and the US continues to be the main market for Central American exports; however, it insisted that, while "such dependence remains a sensitive issue, investment from the US and trade relations with the US are critically important to the economies of Central America". There was no doubt, as far as the Commission was concerned, that "whatever the mistakes of the past, private US investment in the region now plays a vital and constructive role", while the Alliance for Progress had been "a major force for modernization and development" and "US assistance programs have made and continue to make an important contribution". The **Report** was adamant that while the US may not have paid enough "attention" to Central America and it had been "insensitive" and

"interfering" on other occasions, this was not the same as saying that Washington's policies were "the principal cause of the region's afflictions", a view the **Report** attributed to the Sandinistas. Kissinger, **Report of the National Bipartisan Commission on Central America** [1984]. pp. 35-37.

75. Kissinger, **Report of the National Bipartisan Commission on Central America** [1984]. pp. 46, 50-63. The **Report** argued further that "a comprehensive effort to promote democracy and prosperity" in Central America must not only be based on economic development but also follow a policy of "accelerated 'human development'". The specific recommendations to accelerate "human development" were that the US "increase food aid on an emergency basis", that the Peace Corps "expand its recruitment of front line teachers to serve in a new Literacy Corps", and that Peace Corps operations "be expanded at the primary, secondary and technical levels in part by establishing a Central American Teacher Corps, recruited from the Spanish-speaking population of the United States". Kissinger, **Report of the National Bipartisan Commission on Central America** [1984]. pp. 69-70. As Abraham Lowenthal has noted, the advocacy of a Literacy Corps, is an impractical "tribute" to a similar Cuban and Nicarguan policy. Lowenthal, "The United States and Central America: Reflections on the Kissinger Commission Report" [1985]. p. 208. The **Report** also recommended that "an expanded program of secondary level technical and vocational education" be established and the "expansion of the International Executive Service Corps (IESC)". The IESC is a nongovernmental "voluntary organization of retired American business executives" which with "some support from the US government" could "give particular attention to training managers of small businesses" which "would strengthen the economy, while also contributing to the development of the middle class". The **Report** also recommended the disbursement of 10,000 government scholarships to allow students from Central America to study in the United States. It suggested that the US work with the universities and goverments of Central America to "strengthen" the major universities in Central America. The **Report** advised that the US help improve the judicial systems of Central America and that a program to translate and publish "important books" in Spanish and English be developed. In the area of heath and medical care, the **Report** called for the expansion of AID (Agency for International Development) technical assistance programs which dealt with childhood disease and mortality and the re-establishment of programs to fight malaria and related diseases. It also recommended that the "population and family planning programs" supported at the moment by AID be continued. According to the **Report** US companies "active in the region, have a particular responsibility to provide leadership in creating safe and healthy conditions, as well as to introduce appropriate standards of environmental pollution control in their own operations". They emphasized the need for "an enlarged housing and infrastructure construction program" and the need for Washington's "support for accelerated education and training of professionals in public administration". With regard to refugees the **Report** claimed that while the "one million displaced persons" in the region who are in Costa Rica, Honduras or Mexico "are being adequately cared for under the auspices of the United Nations High Commissioner for Refugees" the "hundreds of thousands" who are in Guatemala and El Salvador continue to live "under the most miserable conditions". In this situation the Report recommends "expanded support for adequate relief efforts" carried out by AID and the US State Department. Kissinger, **Report of the National Bipartisan Commission on Central America** [1984]. pp. 70-82.

76. LeoGrande, "Through the Looking Glass" **World Policy Journal** 1984. p. 254.

77. Kissinger, **Report of the National Bipartisan Commission on Central America** [1984]. pp. 86-88.

78. LeoGrande, "Through the Looking Glass" **World Policy Journal**

1984. p. 257. The **Report** emphasized that by 1979, Cuba had emerged, in military terms, as "perhaps the strongest power in the Western Hemisphere" apart from the US itself, and "it was also the country best prepared and most eager to exploit the intensifying crisis in Central America". Pointing to Nicaragua in the late 1970s, the **Report** turned Cuba into a major, if not determining, factor when it asserted that-- although a number of Latin American governments aided the Nicaraguan revolutionaries, and the suspension of US military aid "helped precipitate Somoza's fall"--it was the support of Cuba that "was a particularly important factor in the Sandinista triumph". Kissinger, **Report of the National Bipartisan Commission on Central America** [1984]. pp. 25-27.

79. Kissinger, **Report of the National Bipartisan Commission on Central America** [1984]. pp. 90-93.

80. Arnson, "The Reagan Administration, Congress and Central America: The Search for Consensus" in Hamilton et al., eds., **Crisis in Central America** [1988]. pp. 42-43, 51. See also Arnson, **Crossroads** [1989]. pp. 139-154.

81. He argued that the Sandinstas were "not content to brutalize their own land", where they were carrying out a "Communist reign of terror", but also sought to "export their terror to every other country in the region"; reprinted in **New York Times** May 10, 1984; cited in Holly Sklar, **Washington's War on Nicaragua** [1988]. pp. 173-175.

82. Arnson, "The Reagan Administration, Congress and Central America: The Search for Consensus" in Hamilton et al., eds., **Crisis in Central America** [1988]. pp. 43-46. Arnson, **Crossroads** [1989]. pp. 154-168.

83. Mark Falcoff and Robert Royal, eds., **Crisis and Opportunity: US Policy in Central America and the Caribbean** [1984]. This volume was revised as Mark Falcoff and Robert Royal, eds., **The Continuing Crisis: US Policy in Central America and the Caribbean** [1987].

84. Edward Gonzalez, Brian Michael Jenkins, David Ronfeldt and Caesar Sereseres, **US Policy for Central America: A Briefing** [1984]. See also David Ronfeldt, **Geopolitics, Security and US Strategy in the Caribbean Basin** [1983].

85. Margaret Daly Hayes, **Latin America and the US National Interest: A Basis for US Foreign Policy** [1984]. p. 81.

86. Mark Falcoff, "Arms and Politics Revisited: Latin America as a Military and Strategic Theater" in Howard J. Wiarda, ed., **The Crisis in Latin America: Strategic, Economic and Political Dimensions** [1984]. Howard J. Wiarda, "Conceptual and Political Dimensions of the Crisis in US-Latin American Relations: Towards a New Policy Formulation" in Wiarda, ed., **The Crisis in Latin America** [1984]. Wiarda, **In Search of Policy** [1984].

87. In the foreword to **Rift and Revolution**, the President of the American Enterprise Institute, William J. Baroody, Jr., claimed that "some of the best studies of the area" had been written by past and current AEI scholars who had also "been strongly involved in influencing the policy process". He boasted that almost every contributor to Wiarda's volume had testifed to the Kissinger Commission. Wiarda, ed., **Rift and Revolution** [1984]. p. xi.

88. Apart from Wiarda's introduction the first two hundred pages of the book were historical background which focused on internal developments in Central America. The contributors included 'moderate' Central American specialists such as Thomas P. Anderson and Thomas L. Karnes. These chapters generated a cumulative impression of a crisis that gestated over a long period of time. However, the second half of the book, which focused on the "international dimensions of the crisis", encompassed articles by Kremlinologists, a terrorism 'expert' and a specialist on European communism (Jiri Valenta and Virginia Valenta, Ernest Evans and Eusebio Mujal-Leon), as well as

prominent conservatives like Jeane Kirkpatrick and Mark Falcoff. Wiarda later joined forces with Falcoff, Jiri Valenta, Virginia Valenta, and Ernest Evans to produce a book on the "communist challenge" and the "rising presence" of the Soviet Union in Latin America and the danger represented by the marxist-leninist government in Nicaragua. See Howard J. Wiarda, Mark Falcoff, Ernest Evans, Jiri Valenta, Virginia Valenta, eds., **The Communist Challenge in the Caribbean and Central America** [1987]. p. xi.

89. Ernest Evans, the author of this particular section cautioned that, unlike the revolutionary movements in Latin America in the 1960s and early 1970s, these would be much more of a challenge to the US, and "any sort of US military intervention" would "have much higher costs and risks" than previously. Ernest Evans, "Revolutionary Movements in Central America: The Development of a New Strategy" in Wiarda, ed., **Rift and Revolution** [1984]. p. 189; revised in Wiarda et al., eds., **The Communist Challenge in the Caribbean and Central America** [1987].

90. See William Theodore De Bary, "The Association for Asian Studies: Nonpolitical but Not Unconcerned" **Journal of Asian Studies** vol. 29. no. 4. 1970.

91. Douglas Allen, "Antiwar Asian Scholars and the Vietnam/Indochina War" **Bulletin of Concerned Asian Scholars** vol. 21. nos. 2-4. 1989.

92. The Association for Asian Studies came into existence in the late 1940s (as the Far Eastern Association) around the **Far Eastern Quarterly**, which first appeared in 1941 (the Far Eastern Association became the Association for Asian Studies in 1958). Although the poor relationship between LASA and the Reagan administration had few precedents, many Asian studies specialists were badly treated by the government in the early Cold War era. In the 1950s, the Institute for Pacific Relations' reputation suffered irreparable damage, after the Senate Internal Security Subcommittee concluded that the organization had been instrumental in the loss of China. The tensions surrounding the debate over the 'loss' of China, and the Institute for Pacific Relations controversy, complicated the emergence of the Association for Asian Studies in the 1950s. Certainly, John King Fairbank, who was a major figure in the OSS and in the institutionalization of Asian studies in North America, had come under some scrutiny in the McCarthy years and did not have a particularly good relationship with the State Department until the 1960s. In the early 1950s Fairbank's services as a State Department consultant were discontinued, and he was refused entry into Japan in 1951. Paul M. Evans, **John Fairbank and the American Understanding of Modern China** [1988]. pp. 64, 206-213. David Caute, **The Fellow-Travellers: Intellectual Friends of Communism** [1988]. pp. 359-361. See also John N. Thomas, **The Institute of Pacific Relations: Asian Scholars and American Politics** [1974]. Robert P. Newman, **Owen Lattimore and the "Loss" of China** [1992].

93. Kalman Silvert, "Politics and Studying Societies: The United States and Latin America" in Kalman Silvert, **Essays in Understanding Latin America** [1977]. p. 132. Howard Cline, one of LASA's founders, also characterized Fidel Castro as the organization's "remote godfather". Howard F. Cline, "The Latin American Studies Association: A Summary Survey with Appendix" **Latin American Research Review** vol. 2. no. 1. 1966. p. 64. Robert Packenham, whose recent critique of the 'dependency movement' rests on the assumption that the academy can operate outside of politics, lamented the "politicization" of LASA and the shift towards the assumption that "the fusion of academic work and political struggles is considered desirable and necessary". Robert Packenham, **The Dependency Movement: Scholarship and Politics in Development Studies** [1992]. pp. 268, 295.

94. See "Suggested Guidelines for the Relations Between US Scholars and

Universities and Latin American Scholars and Universities Under Repressive Regimes" reprinted as Appendix I in Jan Knippers Black, ed., **Latin America: Its Problems and Its Promises** [1984]. pp. 515-517. See also Jorge I Domínguez, "The Nature of Professional Scholarly Responsibility" LASA Forum vol. 14. no. 1. 1983; reprinted as Appendix II in Knippers Black, ed., **Latin America** [1984].

95. In 1980 Richard L. Clinton and R. Kenneth Godwin argued that a broadly conceived conception of "human rights" was the "most realistic" basis for US foreign policy in Latin America. Richard L. Clinton and R. Kenneth Godwin, "Human Rights and Development: Lessons from Latin America" in John D. Martz and Lars Schoultz, eds., **Latin America, the United States and the Inter-American System** [1980]. p. 235. See also John D. Martz, "Democracy and the Imposition of Values: Definitions and Diplomacy" in Martz and Schoultz, eds., **Latin America, the United States and the Inter-American System** [1980]. Prominent Latin Americanists Jorge I. Domínguez and Bryce Wood contributed to a study for the 1980s Project which sought to address Washington's neglect of human-rights abuses by governments friendly to the United States. The 1980s Project sought to chart a new course beyond Cold War globalism, and at least some of its views were reflected in the Carter administration's policies. Jorge I. Domínguez, Nigel S. Rodley, Bryce Wood and Richard A. Falk, **Enhancing Global Human Rights** [1979].

96. Richard E. Feinberg, ed., **Central America: International Dimensions of the Crisis** [1982].

97. H. Michael Erisman and John D. Martz, eds., **Colossus Challenged: The Struggle for Caribbean Influence** [1982].

98. Richard R. Fagen and Olga Pellicer, eds., **The Future of Central America: Policy Choices for the US and Mexico** [1983]. See also Piero Gleijeses, **Tilting at Windmills: Reagan and Central America** [1982].

99. Thomas W. Walker, **Nicaragua: Land of Sandino** [1981] (a second edition appeared in 1986). Thomas W. Walker, ed., **Nicaragua in Revolution** [1982]. See also Thomas W. Walker, ed., **Nicaragua: The First Five Years** [1985]. Thomas W. Walker, ed., **Reagan Versus the Sandinistas: The Undeclared War on Nicaragua** [1987].

100. John A. Booth, **The End and the Beginning: The Nicaraguan Revolution** [1982] (a second edition appeared in 1985). John A. Booth, "A Guatemalan Nightmare: Levels of Political Violence 1966-1972" **Journal of Interamerican Studies and World Affairs** vol. 22. no. 1. 1980. John A. Booth, "The Revolution in Nicaragua: Through a Frontier in History" in Donald E. Schulz and Douglas H. Graham, eds., **Revolution and Counterrevolution in Central America and the Caribbean** [1984]. John A. Booth, "'Trickle-up' Income Redistribution and Development in Central America During the 1960s and 1970s" in Mitchel A. Seligson, ed., **The Gap Between Rich and Poor: Contending Perspectives on the Political Economy of Development** [1984]. John A. Booth, "War and the Nicaraguan Revolution" **Current History** vol. 85. no. 515. 1986. Also see John A. Booth and Thomas W. Walker, **Understanding Central America** [1989].

101. John A. Booth, Anne L. Howar, Lord Kennet, David Pfrimmer and Margaret Ellen Roggensack, **The 1985 Guatemalan National Elections: Will the Military Relinquish Power?** [1985]. John A. Booth, David Carliner, Joseph Eldridge, Margaret Ellen Roggensack and Bonnie Teneriello, **Political Transition and the Rule of Law in Guatemala** [1988].

102. Thomas W. Walker and Harvey Williams, "Research Seminar in Nicaragua" **LASA Forum** vol. 19. no. 2. 1988. pp. 1, 7-8.

103. Enrique A. Baloyra, **El Salvador in Transition** [1982]. p. 76. See Enrique Baloyra, Federico G. Gil and Lars Schoultz, "The Peaceful Transition to

Democracy: Elections and the Restorations of Rights" Democracy in Latin America: Prospects and Implications Paper no. 1. [Washington: Department of State Contract 1722-020083, August 1981]. Enrique Baloyra, Federico G. Gil and Lars Schoultz, "The Deterioration and Breakdown of Reactionary Despotism in Central America" Democracy in Latin America: Prospects and Implications Paper no. 2. [Washington: Department of State Contract 1722-020083, August 1981].

104. Enrique A. Baloyra, "Political Change in El Salvador?" **Current History** vol. 83. no. 490. 1984. Enrique A. Baloyra, "Dilemmas of Political Transition in El Salvador" **Journal of International Affairs** vol. 38. no. 2. 1985. Enrique A. Baloyra, "Central America on the Reagan Watch: Rhetoric and Reality" **Journal of Interamerican Studies and World Affairs** vol. 27. no. 1. 1985. Enrique A. Baloyra, "Negotiating War in El Salvador: The Politics of Endgame" **Journal of Interamerican Studies and World Affairs** vol. 28. no. 1. 1986.

105. Enrique A. Baloyra, "Reactionary Despotism in Central America: An Impediment to Democratic Transition" in Martin Diskin, ed., **Trouble in Our Backyard: Central America and the United States in the Eighties** [1983]. Enrique Baloyra-Herp, "Reactionary Despotism in Central America" **Journal of Latin American Studies** vol. 15. no. 2. 1983.

106. See, for example, Edelberto Torres-Rivas, "Guatemala: Crisis and Political Violence" **NACLA-Report on the Americas** vol. 14. no. 1. 1980. Robert Armstrong and Janet Shenk, "El Salvador: Why Revolution" **NACLA-Report on the Americas** vol. 14. no. 2. 1980. Robert Armstrong and Janet Shenk, "El Salvador: A Revolution Brews" **NACLA-Report on the Americas** vol. 14. no. 4. 1980. Janet Shenk, "Central America: No Road Back--El Salvador" **NACLA-Report on the Americas** vol. 15. no. 3. 1981. Judy Butler, "Central America: No Road Back--The Wider War" **NACLA-Report on the Americas** vol. 15. no. 3. 1981. Robert C. Armstrong (with Holly Sklar), "Reagan's Policy in Crisis: Will the Empire Strike Back?" **NACLA-Report on the Americas** vol. 15. no. 4. 1981. Steven Volk, "Honduras: On the Border of War" **NACLA-Report on the Americas** vol. 15. no. 6. 1981. George Black and Judy Butler "Target Nicaragua" **NACLA-Report on the Americas** vol. 16. no. 1. 1982. Robert Armstrong, "El Salvador: Beyond Elections" **NACLA-Report on the Americas** vol. 16. no. 2. 1982. George Black (with Milton Jamail and Norma Stoltz Chinchilla), "Garrison Guatemala" **NACLA-Report on the Americas** vol. 17. no. 1. 1983. George Black (with Milton Jamail and Norma Stoltz Chinchilla), "Guatemala: The War Is Not Over" **NACLA-Report on the Americas** vol. 17. no. 2. 1983. Robert Armstrong, "By What Right?: US Foreign Policy 1945-1983" **NACLA-Report on the Americas** vol. 17. no. 6. 1983.

107. See "Why the FSLN Struggles in Unity with the People" **Latin American Perspectives** vol. 6. no. 1. 1979. "Sandinista Perspectives: Three Differing Views" **Latin American Perspectives** vol. 6. no. 1. 1979. "Communique to the Nicaraguan People" **Latin American Perspectives** vol. 6. no. 1. 1979. See also Norma Stoltz Chinchilla, "Class Struggle in Central America: Background and Overview" **Latin American Perspectives** vol. 7. nos. 2-3. 1980. Edelberto Torres-Rivas, "The Central American Model of Growth: Crisis for Whom?" **Latin American Perspectives** vol. 7. nos. 2-3. 1980. Mario Posas, "Honduras at the Crossroads" **Latin American Perspectives** vol. 7. nos. 2-3. 1980. Gabriel Aguilera Peralta, "Terror and Violence as Weapons of Counter-Insurgency in Guatemala" **Latin American Perspectives** vol. 7. nos. 2-3. 1980. Ernesto Richter, "Social Classes, Accumulation, and the Crisis of 'Overpopulation' in El Salvador" **Latin American Perspectives** vol. 7. nos. 2-3. 1980. Blase Bonpane, "The Church and Revolutionary Struggle in Central America" **Latin American Perspectives** vol. 7. nos. 2-3. 1980. Milton H. Jamail, "The Strongmen are Shaking" **Latin American**

Perspectives vol. 7. nos. 2-3. 1980. Carmen Diana Deere and Peter Marchetti, "The Worker-Peasant Alliance in the First Year of the Nicaraguan Agrarian Reform" **Latin American Perspectives** vol. 8. no. 2. 1981.

108. Marvin E. Gettleman, Patrick Lacefield, Louis Menashe, David Mermelstein and Ronald Radosh, eds., **El Salvador: Central America in the New Cold War** [1981].

109. Eldon Kenworthy, "The US and Latin America: Empire vs. Social Change" **Democracy** vol. 1. no. 3. 1981. Eldon Kenworthy, "Reagan Rediscovers Monroe" **Democracy** vol. 2. no. 3. 1982. Eldon Kenworthy, "Why the United States is in Central America" **Bulletin of the Atomic Scientists** vol. 39. no. 8. 1983. Eldon Kenworthy, "Central America: Beyond the Credibility Trap" **World Policy Journal** vol. 1. no. 1. 1983. This article is updated and reprinted in Coleman and Herring, eds. **The Central American Crisis** [1985]. Also see Eldon Kenworthy, "Grenada as Theater" **World Policy Journal** vol. 1. no. 3. 1984.

110. James Petras, "Nicaragua: The Transition to a New Society" **Latin American Perspectives** vol. 8. no. 2. 1981. James F. Petras and Morris H. Morley, "Supporting Repression: US Policy and the Demise of Human Rights in El Salvador 1979-1981" **The Socialist Register 1981** [1981]. James F. Petras and Morris H. Morley, "Imperialism and Intervention in Third World: US Foreign Policy and Central America" **The Socialist Register 1983** [1983]. James F. Petras and Morris H. Morley, "Anti-Communism in Guatemala: Washington's Alliance with Generals and Death Squads" **The Socialist Register 1984** [London: Merlin Press, 1984]. See also Philip Brenner, "Waging Ideological War: Anti-Communism and US Foreign Policy in Central America" **The Socialist Register 1984** [1984].

111. Susanne Jonas, "Central America as a Theater of US Cold War Politics" **Latin American Perspectives** vol. 9. no. 3. 1982. Marlene Dixon and Susanne Jonas, eds., **Revolution and Intervention in Central America** [1983].

112. George Black, **Triumph of the People: The Sandinista Revolution in Nicaragua** [1981]. Arnon Hadar, **The United States and El Salvador: Political and Military Involvement** [1981]. Tom Barry, Beth Wood and Deb Preusch, **Dollars and Dictators: A Guide to Central America** [1982]. Joseph Collins, **Nicaragua: What Difference Could a Revolution Make?** [1982] Cynthia J. Arnson, **El Salvador: A Revolution Confronts the United States** [1982]. Tommie Sue Montgomery, **Revolution in El Salvador: Origins and Evolution** [1982]. Robert Armstrong and Janet Shenk, **E l Salvador: The Face of Revolution** [1982]. George Black (with Milton Jamail and Norma Stoltz Chinchilla), **Garrison Guatemala** [1984]. Jim Handy, **Gift of the Devil: A History of Guatemala** [1984]. Richard Alan White, **The Morass: United States Intervention in Central America** [1984]. Phillip Berryman, **What's Wrong in Central America and What to Do About It** [1983]. Phillip Berryman, **The Religious Roots of Rebellion: Christians in the Central American Revolutions** [1984]. Phillip Berryman, **Christians in Guatemala's Struggle** [1984]. Phillip Berryman, **Inside Central America: The Essential Facts Past and Present on El Salvador, Nicaragua, Honduras, Guatemala and Costa Rica** [1985]. Also published as Phillip Berryman, **Inside Central America: US Policy in Its New Vietnam** [1985].

113. Walter LaFeber, **The Panama Canal: The Crisis in Historical Perspective** [1978].

114. Walter LaFeber, **Inevitable Revolutions: The United States in Central America** [1984]. p. 361. He continued to write about US policy in Latin America throughout the 1980s. See Walter LaFeber, "Latin American Policy" in Robert A. Divine, ed., **Exploring the Johnson Years** [1981]. Walter LaFeber, "An Overview of Central America" **Bulletin of the Atomic Scientists** vol. 39. no. 8.

1983. Walter LaFeber, "The Reagan Administration and Revolution in Central America" **Political Science Quarterly** vol. 99. no. 1. 1984. Walter LaFeber, "The Burdens of the Past" in Robert S. Leiken, ed., **Central America: Anatomy of Conflict** [1984]. Walter LaFeber, "The Reagan Policy in Historical Perspective" in Coleman and Herring, eds. **The Central American Crisis** [1985]. Walter LaFeber, "The Evolution of the Monroe Doctrine from Monroe to Reagan" in Lloyd C. Gardner, ed., **Redefining the Past: Essays in Diplomatic History in Honor of William Appleman Williams** [1986]. Walter LaFeber, "Four Themes and an Irony" in John M. Kirk and George W. Schuyler, eds., **Central America: Democracy, Development and Change** [1988]. Also see the second edition, Walter LaFeber, **Inevitable Revolutions: The United States in Central America** [1993].

115. LaFeber, **Inevitable Revolutions** [1984]. pp. 16-18, 302.

116. Walter LaFeber, "Inevitable Revolutions" **The Atlantic Monthly** vol. 249. no. 6. 1982. p. 83.

117. See Steve C. Ropp and James A. Morris, eds., **Central America: Crisis and Adaptation** [1984]. Martin Diskin, ed., **Trouble in Our Backyard: Central America and the United States in the 1980s** [1983]. James A. Morris, **Honduras: Caudillo Politics and Military Rulers** [Boulder: Westview Press, 1984].

118. H. Michael Erisman, ed., **The Caribbean Challenge: US Policy in a Volatile Region** [1984]. Alan Adelman and Reid Reading, ed., **Confrontation in the Caribbean Basin** [1984].

119. Richard Newfarmer, ed., **From Gunboats to Diplomacy: New US Policies for Latin America** [1984].

120. Latin American Studies Association, **The Electoral Process in Nicaragua: Domestic and International Influences: Report of the Latin American Studies Association Delegation to Observe the Nicaraguan General Elections of November 4, 1984** [1984]. p. 1. See also Thomas W. Walker, "Introduction" in Walker, ed., **Reagan Versus the Sandinistas** [1987]. pp. 10-11.

121. See "Nicaragua Report Stirs Controversy" **LASA Forum** vol. 16. no. 1. 1985. pp. 8-11. Wayne A. Cornelius, "The 1984 Elections Revisited" **LASA Forum** vol. 16. no. 3. 1986. pp. 22-28. Daniel C. Levy, "LASA's Election Coverage: Reflections and Suggestions" **LASA Forum** vol. 16. no. 4. 1986. pp. 24-27. See James Petras's letter to the editor in " **LASA Forum** vol. 16. no. 4. 1986. pp. 31-32. David G. Becker, "LASA's Election Coverage: An Effort Misplaced?" **LASA Forum** vol. 17. no. 3. 1986. pp. 7-9. Wayne A. Cornelius, "The 1984 Nicaraguan Election Observation: A Final Comment" **LASA Forum** vol. 19. no. 2. 1988. p. 16. Roy Gutman, "Nicaraguan Turning Point: How the 1984 Vote Was Sabotaged" **LASA Forum** vol. 19. no. 2. 1988. pp. 16-19. In the mid-1980s LASA's Task Force on Human Rights and Academic Freedom prepared a report on Nicaragua's Atlantic Coast. See Martin Diskin, Thomas Bossert, Salomon Nahmad S. and Stéfano Varese, **Peace and Autonomy on the Atlantic Coast of Nicaragua: A Report of the LASA Task Force on Human Rights and Academic Freedom** [1986].

122. Margaret E. Leahy, "The Harassment of Nicaraguanists and Fellow Travelers" in Walker, ed., **Reagan Versus the Sandinistas** [1987]. pp. 232-233. See Susanne Jonas's motion, to the annual LASA business meeting, on US government harassment of travelling academics and the FBI's efforts to question Latin American specialists who had returned from Nicaragua. **LASA Forum** vol. 16. no. 2. 1985. p. 5.

123. See "Defending Freedom of Inquiry: LASA vs. the US Customs Service" **LASA Forum** vol. 17. no. 2. 1986. "Defending Freedom of Inquiry: LASA vs. the US Customs Service an Update" **LASA Forum** vol. 17. no. 3. 1986. pp. 11-12. "LASA

vs. the US Customs Service: Final Resolution" **LASA Forum** vol. 19. no. 2. 1988. p. 15.

124. Roger Burbach and Patricia Flynn, eds., **The Politics of Intervention: The United States in Central America** [1984]. See also Enrique Domínguez and Deborah Huntington, "The Salvation Brokers: Conservative Evangelicals in Central America" **NACLA Report on the Americas** vol. 18. no. 1. 1984. Estudios Centroamericanos, "El Salvador 1984" **NACLA Report on the Americas** vol. 18. no. 2. 1984. Allan Nairn, "Endgame: US Military Strategy in Central America" **NACLA Report on the Americas** vol. 18. no. 3. 1984.

125. Roger Burbach and Orlando Nuñez, **Fire in the Americas: Forging a Revolutionary Agenda** [1987]. pp. 7-8, 12-15, 17, 83-106.

126. Policy Alternatives for the Caribbean and Central America, **Changing Course: Blueprint for Peace in Central America and the Caribbean** [1984]. The authors of **Changing Course** included Robert Armstrong, Richard Barnet, Phillip Berryman, Robert Borosage, Saul Landau and Richard Fagen. They were assisted by Cynthia Arnson, Roger Burbach, Richard E. Feinberg, Walter LaFeber and William LeoGrande, as well as Nora Hamilton, Mark Hansen, David Landes, Richard Newfarmer, Marcus Raskin and John Weeks.

127. PACCA, **Changing Course** [1984]. pp. 18, 63-70, 72-78.

128. PACCA, **Changing Course** [1984]. pp. 52-55. PACCA was clearly aimed at mobilizing domestic opposition, and a number of their publications sought to focus on the way US foreign policy related to domestic politics, institutions and issues. Joshua Cohen and Joel Rogers, **Rules of the Game: American Politics and the Central American Movement** [1986]. Joshua Cohen and Joel Rogers, **Inequity and Intervention: The Federal Budget and Central America** [1986]. Daniel Cantor and Juliet Schor, **Tunnel Vision: Labor, the World Economy, and Central America** [1987]. Mark Tushnet, **Central America and the Law: The Constitution, Civil Liberties and the Courts** [1988].

129. This is further highlighted, for example, by the more explicitly radical analytical perspective and tone of most of the contributions to another PACCA publication, which was not attempting to put forward specific policy proposals. See Richard R. Fagen, Carmen Diana Deere and Jose Luis Coraggio, eds., **Transition and Development: Problems of Third World Socialism** [1986].

130. James Chace, **Endless War: How We Got involved In Central America--And What Can Be Done** [1984].

131. James Chace, **Solvency: The Price of Survival--An Essay on American Foreign Policy** [1981]. Richard J. Barnet, **Real Security: Restoring American Power in a Dangerous Decade** [1981]. Robert D. Schulzinger, **The Wise Men of Foreign Affairs: The History of the Council on Foreign Relations** [1984]. pp. 235-236.

132. James Chace, "Getting Out of the Central American Maze" **The New York Review of Books** June 24, 1982. James Chace, "The Endless War" **The New York Review of Books** December 8, 1983.

133. Raymond Bonner, **Weakness and Deceit: US Policy in El Salvador** [1984]. p. 15. Bonner later produced a book about US policy in the Philippines. Raymond Bonner, **Waltzing with a Dictator: The Marcoses and the Making of American Policy** [1987]. There was also a critique of US policy in El Salvador by Charles Clements, a medical doctor who served with the US Air Force in Vietnam and eventually became disillusioned with the Southeast Asian war. Clements spent months behind guerrilla lines in El Salvador. Charles Clements, **Witness to War: An American Doctor in El Salvador** [1984].

134. See, for example, Tom Buckley, **Violent Neighbors: El Salvador, Central America and the United States** [1984]. Karl Grossman, **Nicaragua:**

America's New Vietnam [1984]. Jonathan Kwitny, **Endless Enemies: The Making of an Unfriendly World** [1984]. pp. 219-251. T. D. Allman, **Unmanifest Destiny: Mayhem and Illusion in American Foreign Policy--From the Monroe Doctrine to Reagan's War in El Salvador** [1984].

135. Richard Melanson pointed to the gap between grandiose rhetoric and actual policy in 1983. Melanson, **Writing History and Making Policy** [1983]. p. 209.

5. The Triumph of Democracy 1985-1990

1. US Department of State, **Democracy in Latin America and the Caribbean: The Promise and the Challenge** [1987].
2. Some writers have characterized the shift towards classic liberal economic development policies in the 1970s as the rise of neo-conservative economics. Other writers have characterized the change as the "Neoclassical Counter-Revolution", which was part of the ascendancy in the early 1980s of conservative governments in North America and Western Europe. By the 1980s the term 'neo-liberal economics' was also being used. A neo-liberal economic model can be defined as a combination of "orthodox stabilization measures" and a sustained effort to restructure the economy in a way which curtails the role of the state and emphasizes the role of market forces. Catherine M. Conaghan, James M. Malloy and Luis A. Abugattas, "Business and the 'Boys': The Politics of Neoliberalism in the Central Andes" **Latin American Research Review** vol. 25. no. 2. 1990. p. 28. Michael P. Todaro, **Economic Development in the Third World** [1989]. pp. 82-83.
3. Reagan cited in Robert A. Pastor, **Condemned to Repetition: The United States and Nicaragua** [1987]. p. 250. Walter LaFeber, **The American Age: United States Foreign Policy at Home and Abroad Since 1750** [1989]. p. 677. See Fred Halliday, **Beyond Irangate: The Reagan Doctrine and the Third World** [1987].
4. Cynthia Arnson, "The Reagan Administration, Congress and Central America: The Search for Consensus" in Nora Hamilton, Jeffry A. Frieden, Linda Fuller and Manuel Pastor, Jr., eds., **Crisis in Central America: Regional Dynamics and US Policy in the 1980s** [1988]. pp. 46-50, 56. Cynthia J. Arnson, **Crossroads: Congress, the Reagan Administration and Central America** [1989]. pp. 169-184.
5. Arnson, "The Reagan Administration, Congress and Central America: The Search for Consensus" in Hamilton et al., eds., **Crisis in Central America** [1988]. pp. 50-52. Arnson, **Crossroads** [1989]. pp. 184-200.
6. Roy Gutman, **Banana Diplomacy: The Making of American Policy in Nicaragua 1981-1987** [1988]. pp. 33, 331-332. Robert S. Leiken, "Sins of the Sandinistas: Nicaragua's Untold Stories" **The New Republic** October 8, 1984. Leiken explained his dramatic shift during the 1980s as a result of his realization "that the Left was no longer consistently anti-imperialist (if it ever had been) but merely anti-American", at the same time as "Soviet expansionism in the Third World was driving me to the conclusion that the United States could be a defender of national independence and a positive force in world politics"; however, his "evolution to a thorough-going anti-totalitarian required the direct experience of Sandinista Nicaragua". Robert S. Leiken, "The Charmed Circle" in Peter Collier and David Horowitz, eds., **Second Thoughts: Former Radicals Look Back at the Sixties** [1989]. pp. 30-31. See also Robert S. Leiken, "Truth and Consequences" in Collier and Horowitz, eds., **Second Thoughts** [1989]. Robert S. Leiken, ed., **Central America: Anatomy of a Conflict** [1984]. Robert S. Leiken and Barry Rubin, eds., **The Central American Crisis Reader** [1987].
7. See David Horowitz, "Why I Am No Longer a Leftist" in Collier and Horowitz, eds., **Second Thoughts** [1989]. Ronald Radosh, "Darkening Nicaragua" **The New Republic** October 24, 1983. Ronald Radosh, "Cuba Then, Nicaragua Now" in Collier and Horowitz, eds., **Second Thoughts** [1989]. Barry Rubin, "Learning from Experience", in Collier and Horowitz, eds., **Second Thoughts** [1989]. Barry Rubin, **Modern Dictators: A History of Tyranny in the Third World** [1987].
8. Joshua Muravchik, "A Cure Worse Than the Disease" in Collier and

Horowitz, eds., **Second Thoughts** [1989]. p. 165. See also Joshua Muravchik, **The Uncertain Crusade: Jimmy Carter and the Dilemmas of Human Rights Policy** [1986]. Joshua Muravchik, "The Slow Road to Communism" in Mark Falcoff and Robert Royal, eds., **The Continuing Crisis: US Policy in Central America and the Caribbean--Thirty Essays by Statesmen, Scholars, Religious Leaders and Journalists** [1987]. Joshua Muravchik, **News Coverage of the Sandinista Revolution** [1988]. Joshua Muravchik, **Exporting Democracy: Fulfilling America's Destiny** [1991].

9. Norman Podhoretz, "The Neo-Conservative Anguish over Reagan's Foreign Policy" **New York Times Magazine** May 2 1982; cited in Gillian Peele, **Revival and Reaction: The Right in Contemporary America** [1984]. pp. 167, 221. Also see Norman Podhoretz, "The Reagan Road to Détente" **Foreign Affairs** vol. 63. no. 3. 1984; cited in Garry Wills, **Reagan's America: Innocents at Home** [1985]. p. 462. In 1983 Pohoretz wrote in a celebratory tone about how the "inspiriting" US invasion of Grenada had countered "the sickly inhibitions against the use of military force". Norman Podhoretz, **New York Times** October 30 1985. Cited in Noam Chomsky, **Turning the Tide: The United States and Latin America** [1987]. pp. 216, 317.

10. Jeane J. Kirkpatrick, "Reagan's Puzzling Strategy" **Chicago Tribune** January 19, 1986; cited in Wills, **Innocents at Home** [1988]. pp. 354, 462.

11. See Jeane J. Kirkpatrick, **The Reagan Doctrine and US Foreign Policy** [1985]. Jeane J. Kirkpatrick, **The United States and the World: Setting Limits** [1986]. Jeane J. Kirkpatrick, **The Withering Away of the Totalitarian State...And Other Surprises** [1991].

12. He completed a PhD in modern European history under George Mosse at the University of Wisconsin in the late 1960s. In the early 1970s he taught history at Washington University in Saint Louis and at the University of Rome. In the mid-1970s he covered Italy for **The New Republic** while his research increasingly focused on "terrorism" in Italy and more generally. Michael A. Ledeen, **Perilous Statecraft: An Insider's Account of the Iran-Contra Affair** [1988]. pp. ix-x. George Mosse, "New Left Intellectuals/New Left Politics" in Paul Buhle, ed. **History and the New Left: Madison, Wisconsin 1950-1970** [Philadelphia: Temple University Press, 1990]. p. 233. Also see Michael A. Ledeen and William Lewis, **Debacle: The American Failure in Iran** [1981].

13. Sidney Blumenthal, **The Rise of the Counter-Establishment: From Conservative Ideology to Political Power** [1986]. pp. 35-36. Paul Dickson, **Think Tanks** [1971]. pp. 303-305. James Allen Smith, **The Idea Brokers: Think Tanks and the Rise of the New Policy Elite** [1991]. pp. 208-212, 276-277. Another fellow at CSIS, beginning in the late 1970s, was Georges A. Fauriol. By the end of the Reagan era, Fauriol, formerly associated with the US Information Agency and the Inter-American Development Bank, was director of CSIS's Latin American Studies Program and had produced a number of books on Central and South America that clearly reflected a conservative perspective. Georges A. Fauriol, **Foreign Policy Behaviour of Caribbean States: Guyana, Haiti and Jamaica** [1984]. Georges A. Fauriol, **Latin American Insurgencies** [1985]. Georges A. Fauriol and Eva Loser, **Guatemala Election Study Report** [1986]. Georges A. Fauriol and Eva Loser, **Guatemala: A Political Puzzle** [1988]. Georges A. Fauriol, **The Third Century: US Latin American Policy Choices for the 1990s** [1988].

14. In 1983, after his resignation as Secretary of State, Haig became a senior fellow at the Hudson Institute for Policy Research, and a consultant to United Technologies. The chapter on Central America in his memoirs, which first appeared in 1984, was a defense of the 'domino theory' and of the 1981 **White Paper** on El

Salvador. See Alexander Haig, **Caveat: Realism, Reagan and Foreign Policy** [1984]. pp. 117-140.

15. Hedrick Smith, **The Power Game: How Washington Works** [1988]. pp. 628-629. Ben Bradlee, **Guts and Glory: The Rise and Fall of Oliver North** [1988]. pp. 308-312. Ledeen, **Perilous Statecraft** [1988]. p. x.

16. Michael A. Ledeen, **Grave New World** [1985]. pp. vii-viii, 3-4, 101, 210-213.

17. Ledeen, **Grave New World** [1985]. pp. 96, 230. Ledeen's analysis of Latin American studies was based on Ernst Halperin, "Area Studies in America: The State of Latin American Studies" **The Washington Quarterly: A Review of Strategic and International Issues** vol. 1. no. 2. 1978. Ledeen argued that Latin Americanists in the State Department were probably the "weakest" of the government's entire staff of area-studies experts, while "intelligence assessments" on Latin America were also poor, and part of the reason Washington was unable to plan and execute a "wise" foreign policy in the region was a result of the "conventional wisdom" which predominated in Latin American studies. Ledeen, **Grave New World** [1985]. pp. 96-99.

18. He emphasized that "(p)resent-day anti-Americanism is ironically an attribute much more likely to be found and celebrated in elite intellectual circles of North America than in the hovels of Latin America". Irving Louis Horowitz, "Latin America, Anti-Americanism and Intellectual Hubris" in Alvin Z. Rubinstein and Donald E. Smith, eds., **Anti-Americanism in the Third World: Implications for US Foreign Policy** [1985]. pp. 49-65. Also see Irving Louis Horowitz, **The Decomposition of Sociology** [1993]. In a book which devoted a chapter to Nicaragua, Paul Hollander also diagnosed 'anti-Americanism' as a psychosocial disorder. See Paul Hollander, **Anti-Americanism: Critiques at Home and Abroad 1965-1990** [1990]. pp. 259-306.

19. Mark Falcoff, "Struggle for Central America" **Problems of Communism** vol. 33. no. 2. 1984. p. 65. Thomas W. Walker, ed., **Nicaragua in Revolution** [1982]. John A. Booth, **The End and the Beginning: The Nicaraguan Revolution** [1982]. Mark Falcoff was a resident fellow at the American Enterprise Institute's Center for Hemispheric Studies in the first part of the 1980s, and went on to work as a staff member for the Senate Foreign Relations Committee. Falcoff did his master's and doctoral study at Princeton University, and has held teaching positions at the University of Illinois, the University of Oregon, the University of California (Los Angeles) and the US Foreign Service Institute. In the late 1980s he was an international-affairs fellow at the Council on Foreign Relations, and continued to maintain his links with the American Enterprise Institute. He is listed as a resident scholar at AEI as of 1990. See Mark Falcoff, "Latin America" in Peter Duignan and Alvin Rabushka, eds., **The United States in the 1980s** [1980]. Mark Falcoff, "The Timerman Case" **Commentary** vol. 72. no. 1. 1981. Mark Falcoff, " The Apple of Discord: Central America in US Politics" in Howard J. Wiarda, ed., **Rift and Revolution: The Central American Imbroglio** [1984]. Mark Falcoff, "Regional Diplomatic Options in Central America" **American Enterprise Institute Foreign Policy and Defense Review** vol. 5. no. 1. 1984. Mark Falcoff, "Cuba's Strategy in Exporting Revolution", in Dennis L. Bark, ed., **The Red Orchestra: Instruments of Soviet Policy in Latin America and the Caribbean** [1985]. Mark Falcoff, "Communism in Central America and the Caribbean" in Howard J. Wiarda et al., **The Communist Challenge in the Caribbean and Central America** [1987]. Mark Falcoff, "Nicaraguan Harvest" in Wiarda, Falcoff, Evans, Valenta and Valenta, **The Communist Challenge in the Caribbean and Central America** [1987]. Mark Falcoff, "Somoza, Sandino and the United States" in Mark Falcoff and Robert Royal, eds., **The Continuing Crisis:**

US Policy in Central America and the Caribbean [1987].

20. Joyce Garver Keller, Director, People for the American Way, cited in Margaret E. Leahy, "The Harassment of Nicaraguanists and Fellow Travelers" in Thomas W. Walker, ed., **Reagan Versus the Sandinistas: The Undeclared War on Nicaragua** [1987]. pp. 239, 241.

21. Reagan cited in Leahy, "The Harassment of Nicaraguanists and Fellow Travelers" in Walker, ed., **Reagan Versus the Sandinistas** [1987]. pp. 239-241, 243. See E. Bradford Burns, **At War in Nicaragua: The Reagan Doctrine and the Politics of Nostalgia** [1987]. Burns is most well-known for his work on Brazil, but his interest in Central America, particularly El Salvador, had grown by the 1980s. See E. Bradford Burns, **A History of Brazil** [New York: Columbia University Press, 1980, first published 1970]. E. Bradford Burns, "The Modernization of Underdevelopment: El Salvador 1858-1931" **Journal of Developing Areas** vol. 18. no. 3. 1984. E. Bradford Burns, "The Intellectual Infrastructure of Modernization in El Salvador 1870-1900" **The Americas: A Quarterly Review of Inter-American Cultural History** vol. 41. no. 1. 1985. E. Bradford Burns, "Establishing the Patterns of Progress and Poverty in Central America" in Michael T. Martin and Terry R. Kandal, eds., **Studies of Development and Change in the Modern World** [1989].

22. Howard J. Wiarda, **Ethnocentrism in Foreign Policy: Can We Understand the Third World?** [1985]. This short book incorporated two earlier articles by Wiarda on the subject. See Howard J. Wiarda, "The Ethnocentrism of the Social Sciences: Implications for Research and Policy" **The Review of Politics** vol. 43. no. 2. 1981. Howard J. Wiarda, "Toward a Nonethnocentric Theory of Development: Alternative Conceptions from the Third World" **The Journal of Developing Areas** vol. 17. no. 4. 1983.

23. Wiarda, **Ethnocentrism in Foreign Policy** [1985]. pp. 4, 14-15, 28-31, 48.

24. Irving Louis Horowitz, "Masses in Latin America" in Irving Louis Horowitz, ed., **Masses in Latin America** [1970]. p. 3.

25. Wiarda, **Ethnocentrism in Foreign Policy** [1985]. pp. 31, 47.

26. Wiarda, **Ethnocentrism in Foreign Policy: Can We Understand the Third World?** [1985]. pp. 34-36. In a 1984 article, in the midst of the policy debate over Central America, Wiarda argued that "the key reason for our poverty of policy in Central America derives from the poverty of the theories undergirding them". The North American and Western European model was not only ethnocentric and rigid, but it "had the additional negative effect of undermining many existing and transitional institutions and thus have contributed further to the very instability our policies have consistently sought to prevent." His solution was that unless the US began "to treat Central America seriously, on its own terms, in its own institutional context, empathetically and without the condescension and ethnocentrism of the past, the new and worthwhile policy proposals recently put forward such as Project Democracy, a Marshall Plan for Central America, and other suggestions offered in the reports of the Atlantic Council and the Kissinger Commission, have almost no possibility of achieving success". Howard J. Wiarda, "At the Root of the Problem: Conceptual Failures in US-Central American Relations" in Robert S. Leiken, ed., **Central America: Anatomy of Conflict** [1984]. especially pp. 259-264, 270-271, 273, 276.

27. Arnson, **Crossroads** [1989]. pp. 198-201. Gutman, **Banana Diplomacy** [1988]. pp. 293-295, 331-357. See Congressional Committees Investigating the Iran-Contra Affair (chaired by Daniel K. Inouye and Lee H. Hamilton) (edited by Joel Brinkley and Stephen Engelberg), **Report of the Congressional Committees Investigating the Iran-Contra Affair** [1988]. It has been

estimated by Robert Pastor that the total US military aid to the contras between 1982 and 1987 was $142 million dollars (US) in comparison to $131.6 million dollars in military aid to Guatemala, El Salvador, Nicaragua, Honduras and Costa Rica combined between 1962 and 1980. This does not include the $57 million dollars in "nonlethal" military assistance to the contras or the money from private sources and foreign governments. Pastor, **Condemned to Repetition** [1987] pp. 256-257, 367.

28. Cited in Arnson, **Crossroads** [1989]. pp. 201-202.

29. Gutman, **Banana Diplomacy** [1988]. pp. 358-360.

30. Howard J. Wiarda, **Finding Our Way: Toward Maturity in US-Latin American Relations** [1987]. pp. xiii-xiv, 1-8, 209, 229-233.

31. Wiarda, **Finding Our Way** [1987]. pp. 229-230. A concerted defense of the Reagan administration's effort to roll back the Nicaraguan revolution was provided by Robert F. Turner in 1987. He had worked under contract for the Office of the Legal Adviser to the Department of State in 1985. Robert F. Turner, **Nicaragua vs. the United States: A Look at the Facts** [Washington: Pergamon, 1987].

32. Wiarda, **Finding Our Way** [1987]. pp. xiii-xiv, 1-8, 230-233.

33. Wiarda, **Finding Our Way** [1987]. pp. 25-31.

34. In 1989 Wiarda argued that "I think of myself as a serious scholar" and "I have been among the State Department's foremost critics". The "more recent trend toward democratization corresponds to my own personal political preferences--though as a scholar...I try not to force these personal biases on my readers". Howard J. Wiarda, "Response to Keith A. Haynes's 'Authoritarianism, Democracy and Development: The Corporative Theories of Howard J. Wiarda Revisited'" **Latin American Perspectives** vol. 16. no. 4. 1989. pp. 61-62. See also Keith A. Haynes, "Authoritarianism, Democracy and Development: The Corporative Theories of Howard J. Wiarda Revisited" **Latin American Perspectives** vol. 15. no. 3. 1988. Keith A. Haynes, "Reply to Howard J. Wiarda: Democracy, Serious Scholarship and Class Struggle" **Latin American Perspectives** vol. 16. no. 4. 1989.

35. He argued that when a "liberal Democratic administration" was in office IPS experienced "some added legitimacy", while the Heritage Foundation enjoyed "increased influence" with a "conservative Republican administration", but that the American Enterprise Institute, CSIS and Brookings "command the broad center of the political spectrum and therefore have influence no matter what the politics of the administration in power". Wiarda, **Finding Our Way** [1987]. p. 221. Elsewhere he characterized AEI as "a pluralist Think Tank genuinely dedicated as its motto states to the 'competition of ideas in a free society'" Wiarda, "Response to Keith A. Haynes's 'Authoritarianism, Democracy, and Development'" **Latin American Perspectives** 1989. p. 61.

36. See, for example, Forest D. Colburn, **Post-Revolutionary Nicaragua: State, Class, and the Dilemmas of Agrarian Policy** [1986]. Robert Williams, **Export Agriculture and the Crisis in Central America** [1986]. José Luis Coraggio, **Nicaragua: Revolution and Democracy** [1986]. Rose J. Spalding, ed., **The Political Economy of Revolutionary Nicaragua** [1987]. Tom Barry, **Roots of Rebellion: Land and Hunger in Central America** [1987]. Roger Burbach and Orlando Nuñez, **Fire in the Americas: Forging a Revolutionary Agenda** [1987]. Gary Ruchwarger, **People in Power: Forging a Grassroots Democracy in Nicaragua** [1987]. Dennis Gilbert, **Sandinistas: The Party and the Revolution** [1988]. Roger N. Lancaster, **Thanks to God and the Revolution: Popular Religion and Class Consciousness in the New Nicaragua** [1988]. Jim Handy, "Democracy, Military Rule and Agrarian Reform in Guatemala" in John M. Kirk and George W. Schuyler, eds., **Central America: Democracy, Development and Change** [1988]. W. George Lovell, "Resisting Conquest: Development and the Guatemalan

Indian" in Kirk and Schuyler, eds., **Central America** [1988]. Richard L. Harris, "Marxism and the Transition to Socialism in Latin America" **Latin American Perspectives** vol. 15. no. 1. 1988. Carlos M. Vilas, "Popular Insurgency and Social Revolution in Central America" **Latin American Perspectives** vol. 15. no. 1. 1988. Francisco A. Alvarez, "Transition Before the Transition: The Case of El Salvador" **Latin American Perspectives** vol. 15. no. 1. 1988. James F. Petras and Frank T. Fitzgerald, "Authoritarianism and Democracy in the Transition to Socialism" **Latin American Perspectives** vol. 15. no. 1. 1988. Keith A. Haynes, "Mass Participation and the Transition to Socialism: A Critique of Petras and Fitzgerald" **Latin American Perspectives** vol. 15. no. 1. 1988. Frank T. Fitzgerald and James F. Petras, "Confusion About the Transition to Socialism: A Rejoinder to Haynes" **Latin American Perspectives** vol. 15. no. 1. 1988. William I. Robinson and Kent Norsworthy, "A Critique of the 'Antidemocratic Tendency' Argument: The Case of Mass Organizations and Popular Participation in Nicaragua" **Latin American Perspectives** vol. 15. no. 1. 1988. Jan L. Flora and Edelberto Torres-Rivas "Historical Bases of Insurgency in Central America" in Jan L. Flora and Edelberto Torres-Rivas eds., **Sociology of "Developing Societies": Central America** [1989]. Carlos M. Vilas, "The Impact of Revolutionary Transition on the Popular Classes: The Working Class in the Sandinista Revolution" in Flora and Torres-Rivas eds., **Sociology of "Developing Societies": Central America** [1989]. Richard Stahler Sholk, "Stabilization, Destabilization, and the Popular Classes in Nicaragua 1979-1988" **Latin American Research Review** vol. 25. no. 3. 1990. Susanne Jonas and Nancy Stein, "The Construction of Democracy in Nicaragua" **Latin American Perspectives** vol. 17. no. 3. 1990. Bruce E. Wright, "Pluralism and Vanguardism in the Nicaraguan Revolution" **Latin American Perspectives** vol. 17. no. 3. 1990. Ilja A. Luciak, "Democracy in the Nicaraguan Countryside: A Comparative Analysis of Sandinista Grassroots Movements" **Latin American Perspectives** vol. 17. no. 3. 1990. Laura J. Enríquez, **Harvesting Change: Labor and Agrarian Reform in Nicaragua 1979-1990** [1991].

37. Although they noted the differences between conservatives and trilateralists in the Reagan years, they concluded that trilateralism remained a major force in US policy. Ronald H. Chilcote and Joel C. Edelstein, **Latin America: Capitalist and Socialist Perspectives of Development and Underdevelopment** [1986]. pp. xiii, 5-6, 140-141.

38. Joyce Garver Keller, Director, People for the American Way, cited in Leahy, "The Harassment of Nicaraguanists and Fellow Travelers" in Walker ed., **Reagan Versus the Sandinistas** [1987]. pp. 239, 242.

39. Richard R. Fagen, **Cuba: The Political Content of Adult Education** [1964]. Richard R. Fagen, "Charismatic Authority and the Leadership of Fidel Castro" **Western Political Quarterly** vol. 18. no. 2. 1965. Richard R. Fagen, **The Transformation of Political Culture in Cuba** [1969]. Richard R. Fagen, "US-Cuban Relations" in David S. Smith, ed., **Prospects for Latin America** [1970]. Richard R. Fagen, "The United States and Chile: Roots and Branches" **Foreign Affairs** vol. 53. no. 2. 1975. Richard R. Fagen, "Studying Latin American Politics: Some Implications of a *Dependencia* Approach" **Latin American Research Review** vol. 12. no. 2. 1977. Richard R. Fagen, "A Funny Thing Happened on the Way to the Market: Thoughts on Extending Dependency Ideas" **International Organization** vol. 32. Winter 1978. Richard R. Fagen, "Introduction" in Richard R. Fagen, ed., **Capitalism and the State in US-Latin American Relations** [1979].

40. Richard R. Fagen, **The Nicaraguan Revolution: A Personal Report** [1981]. See also Richard R. Fagen, "The End of the Affair" **Foreign Policy** no. 36. 1979. Richard R. Fagen, "The Carter Administration and Latin America:

Business as Usual?" **Foreign Affairs** vol. 57. no. 3. 1979. Richard R. Fagen and Olga Pellicer, "Introduction" in Richard R. Fagen and Olga Pellicer, eds., **The Future of Central America: Policy Choices for the US and Mexico** [1983]. Richard R. Fagen, "Revolution and Crisis in Nicaragua" in Martin Diskin, ed., **Trouble in Our Backyard: Central America and the United States in the 1980s** [1983]. Richard R. Fagen, "United States Policy in Central America" **Millennium: Journal of International Studies** vol. 13. no. 2. 1984. Fagen was eventually inspired to write a novel about the crisis. See Richard R. Fagen, **Closer to Houston** [1990].

41. Terry Karl and Richard R. Fagen, "The Logic of Hegemony: The United States as a Superpower in Central America" in Jan F. Triska, ed., **Dominant Powers and Subordinate States: The United States in Latin America and the Soviet Union in Eastern Europe** [1986]. p. 238.

42. Richard R. Fagen, Carmen Diana Deere and Jose Luis Coraggio, "Introduction" in Richard R. Fagen, Carmen Diana Deere and Jose Luis Coraggio, eds., **Transition and Development: Problems of Third World Socialism** [1986]. pp. 9-10.

43. Fagen, Deere and Coraggio, "Introduction" in Fagen, Deere and Coraggio, eds., **Transition and Development** [1986]. pp. 11-21, 27.

44. Richard R. Fagen, "The Politics of Transition" in Fagen, Deere and Coraggio, eds., **Transition and Development** [1986]. pp. 249-250, 253, 257-258.

45. By the second half of the 1980s their theory of the imperial state had been thoroughly mapped out, particularly in Morley's work on US-Cuban relations. Morris H. Morley, **Imperial State and Revolution: The United States and Cuba 1952-1986** [1987]. See also James F. Petras and Morris H. Morley, "The US Imperial State" **Review** vol. 4. no. 2. 1980. Morris H. Morley, "The US Imperial State in Cuba 1952-1958: Policymaking and Capitalist Interests" **Journal of Latin American Studies** vol. 14. no. 1. 1982. Morris H. Morley, **Washington, Somoza, and the Sandinistas: State and Regime in US Policy 1969-1981** [1994].

46. James Petras and Morris H. Morley, "Central America: Dependent-Welfare, Authoritarian and Revolutionary Concepts of Development" in Kirk and Schuyler, eds., **Central America** [1988]. pp. 63-65, 86-87.

47. In 1990 Morley and Petras linked their understanding of dependent capitalism and the transition to socialism to a revised class struggle model of social change when they assigned central importance to the new social movements, "which combine with and transcend the action of organized labor movements", in both the urban centers and in rural areas where modernized agriculture has taken hold. In the context of an international system of capital accumulation and economic cycles, dominated by powerful states in affiliation with transnational capital, Petras and Morley represented the new social movements, and the growing number of individuals and communities uprooted by both imperial state terrorism and state terrorism, as a major dynamic for social and political change. James F. Petras and Morris Morley, **US Hegemony Under Siege: Class, Politics and Development in Latin America** [1990]. pp. 52-53, 58-60. See also James Petras, "New Social Movements in Central America: Perspectives on Democratic Social Transformations" in Kirk and Schuyler, eds., **Central America** [1988].

48. Enrique Baloyra, Federico G. Gil and Lars Schoultz, "The Deterioration and Breakdown of Reactionary Despotism in Central America" Democracy in Latin America: Prospects and Implications Paper no. 2. [Washington: Department of State, Contract 1722-020083, August 1981]. Enrique A. Baloyra, "Reactionary Despotism in Central America: An Impediment to Democratic Transition" in Martin Diskin, ed., **Trouble in Our Backyard: Central America and the United States in the Eighties**

[1983]. Enrique Baloyra-Herp, "Reactionary Despotism in Central America" **Journal of Latin American Studies** vol. 15. no. 2. 1983.

49. Leahy, "The Harassment of Nicaraguanists and Fellow Travelers" in Walker, ed., **Reagan Versus the Sandinistas** [1987]. p. 239.

50. John Weeks's other work included Elizabeth Dore and John Weeks, "The Intensification of the Attack against the Working Class in 'Revolutionary' Peru" **Latin American Perspectives** vol. 3. no. 2. 1976. Elizabeth Dore and John Weeks, "International Exchange and the Causes of Backwardness" **Latin American Perspectives** vol. 6. no. 2. 1979. John Weeks, "The Industrial Sector" in Thomas W. Walker, ed., **Nicaragua: The First Five Years** [1985]. John Weeks, "The Mixed Economy in Nicaragua: The Economic Battlefield" in Spalding, ed., **The Political Economy of Revolutionary Nicaragua** [1987]. John Weeks and Andrew Zimbalist, **Panama at the Crossroads: Economic Development and Political Change in the Twentieth Century** [1991].

51. John Weeks, **The Economies of Central America** [1985]. p. 4. John Weeks, "An Interpretation of the Central American Crisis" **Latin American Research Review** vol. 21. no. 3. 1986. pp. 32, 35. See also John Weeks, "Land, Labour and Despotism in Central America" in Giuseppe Di Palma and Laurence Whitehead, eds., **The Central American Impasse** [1986]. For a marxist critique of Weeks's framework, see Patricia Howard Borjas, "Perspectives on the Central American Crisis: 'Reactionary Despotism' or Monopoly Capital?" **Capital and Class** no. 39. 1989. pp. 51-81.

52. Charles D. Brockett, **Land, Power and Poverty: Agrarian Transformation and Political Conflict in Central America** [1990]. pp. ix, 8. See also William C. Thiesenhusen, "Introduction: Searching for Agrarian Reform in Latin America" in William C. Thiesenhusen, ed., **Searching for Agrarian Reform in Latin America** [1989]. John A. Booth, "Socioeconomic and Political Roots of National Revolts in Central America" **Latin American Research Review** vol. 26. no. 2. 1991.

53. Radicals challenged the **bona fides** of the democratic transition, and debated the significance of a policy of contained liberalization and democratization. See Edward S. Herman and Frank Brodhead, **Demonstration Elections: US-Staged Elections in the Dominican Republic, Vietnam and El Salvador** [1984]. Edward S. Herman and James Petras, "'Resurgent Democracy': Rhetoric and Reality" **New Left Review** no. 154. 1985. See also Paul Cammack, "Resurgent Democracy: Threat and Promise" **New Left Review** no. 157. 1986. Jim Handy, "Resurgent Democracy and the Guatemalan Military" **Journal of Latin American Studies** vol. 18. no. 2. 1986. Timothy Harding and James Petras, "Democratization and Class Struggle" **Latin American Perspectives** vol. 15. no. 3. 1988. Susanne Jonas, "Contradictions of Guatemala's 'Political Opening'" **Latin American Perspectives** vol. 15. no. 3. 1988. James Petras and Fernando Ignacio Leiva, "Chile: The Authoritarian Transition to Electoral Politics: A Critique" **Latin American Perspectives** vol. 15. no. 3. 1988.

54. A good example of a liberal approach to democracy in Latin America, which reflected two decades of debate and interaction between liberal and radical perspectives was Martin C. Needler's 1987 study. He explicitly addressed what he saw as the resuscitation of the historical-cultural approach, which he felt was being allowed to again carry "the principal burden of social explanation". He was concerned that as the emphasis on historical-cultural factors gained influence it could "become a pretext for acquiescing in situations which strenuous efforts should be made to change". He argued that "the authoritarianism that has characterized Latin America has been due primarily not to culture, but to structure; not to what the Iberian conquerors and settlers brought with them, but what they found in the New World; not to the heritage of the past, but to

the conditions of the present; not to the beliefs of the majority but to the interests of the minority". He emphasized that "the problem of democracy in Latin America is thus not primarily a problem of distribution of attitudes and beliefs but a problem of the distribution of economic and political power". Martin C. Needler, **The Problem of Democracy in Latin America** [1987]. pp. xi-xii, 161-165.

55. David Lehmann, "A Latin American Political Scientist: Guillermo O'Donnell" **Latin American Research Review** vol. 24. no. 2. 1989. David Lehmann, **Democracy and Development in Latin America: Economics, Politics and Religion in the Post-war Period** [1990]. pp. 51-59. Thomas J. Bossert, "The Promise of Theory" in Peter F. Klarén and Thomas J. Bossert, eds., **Promise of Development: Theories of Change in Latin America** [Boulder: Westview Press, 1986]. pp. 318-331. Guillermo A. O'Donnell, **Modernization and Bureaucratic-Authoritarianism: Studies in South American Politics** [1973]. Guillermo A. O'Donnell, "Corporatism and the Question of the State" in James M. Malloy, ed., **Authoritarianism and Corporatism in Latin America** [1977]. Guillermo A. O'Donnell, "Reflections on the Patterns of Change in the Bureaucratic-Authoritarian State" **Latin American Research Review** vol. 13. no. 1. 1978. Guillermo O'Donnell, "State and Alliances in Argentina" **Journal of Development Studies** vol. 15. no. 1. 1978. Guillermo O'Donnell, "Tensions in the Bureaucratic-Authoritarian State and the Question of Democracy" in David Collier, ed., **The New Authoritarianism in Latin America** [1979]; reprinted in Klarén and Bossert, eds., **Promise of Development** [1986]. Guillermo O'Donnell, **1966-1973, El estado burocratico autoritario: triunfos, derrotas y crisis** [1982]. Guillermo O'Donnell, **Bureaucratic Authoritarianism: Argentina, 1966-1973 in Comparative Perspective** [1988].

56. Barrington Moore, Jr., **Social Origins of Dictatorship and Democracy: Lord and Peasant in the Making of the Modern World** [1966].

57. Peter F. Klarén, "Lost Promise: Explaining Latin American Underdevelopment" in Klarén and Bossert, eds., **Promise of Development** [1986]. pp. 29-30. See Karen L. Remmer and Gilbert W. Merkx, "Bureaucratic-Authoritarianism Revisited" **Latin American Research Review** vol. 17. no. 2. 1982. p. 5. Leonard Binder, "The Natural History of Development Theory" **Comparative Studies in Society and History** vol. 28. no. 1. 1986. pp. 23-26.

58. Binder, "The Natural History of Development Theory" **Comparative Studies in Society and History** 1986. p. 26. See David Collier, "The Bureaucratic-Authoritarian Model: Synthesis and Priorities for Future Research" in Collier, ed., **The New Authoritarianism in Latin America** [1979]. Paul Cammack, "The Political Economy of Contemporary Military Regimes in Latin America: From Bureaucratic Authoritarianism to Restructuring" in Philip O'Brien and Paul Cammack, eds., **Generals in Retreat: The Crisis of Military Rule in Latin America** [1985]. pp. 1-31. Paul Cammack and Philip O'Brien, "Conclusion: The Retreat of the Generals" in O'Brien and Cammack, eds., **Generals in Retreat** [1985]. pp. 184-200. George A. Lopez and Michael Stohl, "Liberalization and Redemocratization in Latin America: The Search for Models and Meanings" in George A. Lopez and Michael Stohl, eds., **Liberalization and Redemocratization in Latin America** [1987]. pp. 1-2. Stephan Haggard, **Pathways from the Periphery: The Politics of Growth in the Newly Industrializing Countries** [1990], especially pp. 254-270.

59. Alfred Stepan, "State Power and the Strength of Civil Society in the Southern Cone of Latin America" in Peter B. Evans, Dietrich Rueschemeyer and Theda Skocpol, eds., **Bringing the State Back In** [1985]. See also Alfred Stepan, **The**

Notes to pages 185-227

State and Society: Peru in Comparative Perspective [1978].

60. As Petras and Morley have argued, US policy-makers view a shift from dictatorship to democracy, primarily as a means to protect the state, not as a way of "promoting democratization". For example, El Salvador and Guatemala in the 1980s were indicative of the "distinction" Washington drew between "regime and state changes". In these and other cases it was clear that US foreign policy toward "political transitions" was preoccupied with bringing about "regime changes" to safeguard the "continuity" of the state. From their perspective, the "key issue" facing US policy-makers was not whether to support dictators or democrats, but the need to formulate policy in support of the best "type of regime" to protect those "existing state institutions" which complemented the "permanent" interests of the United States. Petras and Morley, **US Hegemony Under Siege** [1990]. pp. 113-114, 128-135, 140-141.

61. Guillermo O'Donnell, Philippe C. Schmitter and Laurence Whitehead, eds., **Transitions from Authoritarian Rule: Prospects for Democracy** [1986]. (It was also published as four volumes in paperback.) All references are to the paperback editions.

62. For a recent marxist critique of the transitions approach see Richard Robison, Kevin Hewison and Garry Rodan, "Political Power in Industrializing Capitalist Societies: Theoretical Approaches" in Kevin Hewison, Richard Robison and Garry Rodan, eds., **Southeast Asia in the 1990s: Authoritarianism, Democracy and Capitalism** [1993]. pp. 20-24. Also see James F. Petras, State, Regime and the Democratization Muddle" **LASA Forum** vol. 18. no. 4. 1988. James F. Petras, "State, Regime and the Democratization Muddle" **Journal of Contemporary Asia** vol. 19. no. 1. 1989.

63. Schmitter argued that the democratization process in Southern Europe got off to a more promising start than in Latin America, in part because the US was more consistently supportive of democratization in Southern Europe, while in Latin America its policy was ambiguous and varied from one case to another. At the same time, "transitions from authoritarian rule and immediate prospects for political democracy were largely to be explained in terms of national forces and calculations". He speculated as to whether some of the countries in southern Europe "possess more viable civil societies and hegemonic blocs than those of Latin America" and whether "certain historical factors" which varied from country to country and region to region explained the "more resilient and viable civil societies in Southern Europe than in Latin America". Philippe C. Schmitter, "An Introduction to Southern European Transitions from Authoritarian Rule: Italy, Greece, Portugal, Spain and Turkey" in Guillermo O'Donnell, Philippe C. Schmitter and Laurence Whitehead, eds., **Transitions from Authoritarian Rule: Southern Europe** [1986]. pp. 3-7. See also Guillermo O'Donnell, "Introduction to the Latin American Cases" in Guillermo O'Donnell, Philippe C. Schmitter and Laurence Whitehead, ed., **Transitions from Authoritarian Rule: Latin America** [1986]. Guillermo O'Donnell and Philippe C. Schmitter, **Transitions from Authoritarian Rule: Tentative Conclusions and Uncertain Democracies** [1986].

64. Giuseppe Di Palma and Laurence Whitehead, "Introduction" in Giuseppe Di Palma and Laurence Whitehead, eds., **The Central American Impasse** [1986]. p. 5.

65. Samuel P. Huntington, "Will More Countries Become Democratic?" **Political Science Quarterly** vol. 99. no. 2. 1984. p. 218.

66. Samuel P. Huntington, "The Goals of Development" in Myron Weiner and Samuel P. Huntington, eds., **Understanding Political Development** [1987]. pp. 9-10.

67. Samuel P. Huntington, "One Soul at a Time: Political Science and Political

Reform" **American Political Science Review** vol. 82. no. 1. 1988. p. 9. Huntington's voluntarism and realism about the prospects for democracy was also apparent in Samuel P. Huntington, "The Modest Meaning of Democracy" in Robert A. Pastor, ed., **Democracy in the Americas: Stopping the Pendulum** [1989]. pp. 11-28.

    68. Jorge I. Domínguez, **Cuba: Order and Revolution** [1978]. Jorge I. Domínguez, **Cuba: Internal and International Affairs** [1982]. Jorge I. Domínguez, "US, Soviet and Cuban Policies Toward Latin America" in Marshall D. Shulman, ed. **East-West Tensions in the Third World** [1986]. Jorge I. Domínguez, **To Make a World Safe for Revolution: Cuba's Foreign Policy** [1989].

    69. Jorge I. Domínguez, **US Interests and Policies in Central America and the Caribbean** [1982]. pp. 49-50. Jorge I. Domínguez and Virginia Domínguez, **The Caribbean: Its Implications for the United States** [1981]. Jorge I. Domínguez and Marc Lindenberg, **Central America: Current Crisis and Future Prospects** [1984].

    70. Huntington, "Will More Countries Become Democratic?" **Political Science Quarterly** 1984. p. 201; cited in Jorge I. Dominguez, "Political Change: Central America, South America and the Caribbean" in Weiner and Huntington, eds., **Understanding Political Development** [1987]. pp. 91-92.

    71. Enrique A. Baloyra, "Introduction" in Enrique A. Baloyra, ed., **Comparing New Democracies: Transition and Consolidation in Mediterranean Europe and the Southern Cone** [1987]. pp. 1-3. See also Baloyra, "Democratic Transition in Comparative Perspective" in Baloyra, ed., **Comparing New Democracies** [1987]. He underlined the importance of elections, arguing that "free and competitive elections appear to be one of the indispensable requirements of a genuine democratic transition". He emphasized that "even under the dire and ominous conditions of El Salvador, where the context of the transition is civil war, a series of elections may and in fact does have a positive impact". Also in most cases transitions occur without an agreement on reform being worked out beforehand, and the transitions are, in effect, "transitions without reconciliation". In all the South American cases it was the military government itself which managed the transition and "eventually accepted the outcome of the electoral competitions". He also emphasized that, apart from Nicaragua and El Salvador, the "recent transitions" had not occurred "in the middle of a civil war, nor have they been accompanied by very substantial changes in the political economy of the state". He concluded, however, that despite the lack of consolidation in many cases, "electoral competition, even in the case of El Salvador, has produced outcomes favorable to democratization". He argued that "obstructionism and continuism *always*" lost at election time and this was accompanied by "very marked preferences" among the public "in favor of peaceful solutions to political problems, a condemnation of military rule and a new spirit of accommodation". At the same time he did not regard this as necessarily reflecting a change in "political culture", especially in El Salvador. Baloyra, "Conclusion: Toward a Framework for the Study of Democratic Consolidation" in Baloyra, ed., **Comparing New Democracies** [1987]. pp. 298-301. This point was also made more recently in Enrique Baloyra-Herp, "The Persistent Conflict in El Salvador" **Current History** vol. 90. no. 554. 1991. pp. 121, 132.

    72. While he did not see external factors as determinant, he did note that the transition in Argentina and Portugal had followed the external defeat of the regime, by the British in the Falklands on the one hand and by nationalist revolts in their African colonies on the other hand. Baloyra, "Conclusion: Toward a Framework for the Study of Democratic Consolidation" in Baloyra, ed., **Comparing New Democracies** [1987]. pp. 297-298.

73. See, for example, Larry Diamond and Juan J. Linz, "Introduction: Politics, Society and Democracy in Latin America" in Larry Diamond, Juan J. Linz and Seymour Martin Lipset, eds., **Democracy in Developing Countries--Volume Four: Latin America** [1989]. p, 52. Diane Ethier, "Processes of Transition and Democratic Consolidation: Theoretical Indicators" in Diane Ethier, ed., **Democratic Transition and Consolidation in Southern Europe, Latin America and Southeast Asia** [1990].

74. Ralph Lee Woodward, Jr., **Central America: A Nation Divided** [1985]. pp. 281-283. See also Ralph Lee Woodward, Jr., "The Rise and Decline of Liberalism in Central America: Historical Perspectives on the Contemporary Crisis" **Journal of Interamerican Studies and World Affairs** vol. 26. no. 3. 1984. See also Ralph Lee Woodward, Jr., "Introduction: Central America and Historical Perspective" in Ralph Lee Woodward, Jr., ed., **Central America: Historical Perspectives on the Contemporary Crises** [1988].

75. Mitchell A. Seligson, "Democratization in Latin America: The Current Cycle" in James M. Malloy and Mitchell A. Seligson, eds., **Authoritarians and Democrats: Regime Transition in Latin America** [1987]. pp. 9-10. John A. Booth and Mitchell A. Seligson, "The Political Culture of Authoritarianism in Mexico: A Reexamination" **Latin American Research Review** vol. 19. no. 1. 1984. Susan Tiano, "Authoritarianism and Political Culture in Argentina and Chile in the Mid-1960s" **Latin American Research Review** vol. 21. no. 1. 1986.

76. Mitchell A. Seligson, "Development, Democratization and Decay: Central America at the Crossroads" in Malloy and Seligson, eds., **Authoritarians and Democrats** [1987]. p. 187. Other studies critical of the transition to democracy in Central America included Gordon L. Bowen, "Prospects for Liberalization by Way of Democratization in Guatemala" in Lopez and Stohl, eds., **Liberalization and Redemocratization in Latin America** [1987]. pp. 48-50.

77. Mark B. Rosenberg, "Political Obstacles to Democracy in Central America" in Malloy and Seligson, eds., **Authoritarians and Democrats** [1987]. pp. 193, 209-212.

78. John A. Booth, "Elections and Democracy in Central America: A Framework for Analysis" in John A. Booth and Mitchell A. Seligson, eds., **Elections and Democracy in Central America** [1989]. pp. 11-13.

79. Howard J. Wiarda, **The Democratic Revolution in Latin America: History, Politics and US Policy** [1990]. pp. xii-xiii, xiv-xv, xxvii. See also Howard J. Wiarda, "Response to Keith A. Haynes's 'Authoritarianism, Democracy and Development: The Corporative Theories of Howard J. Wiarda Revisited'" **Latin American Perspectives** vol. 16. no. 4. 1989. pp. 60-62.

80. They were subsequently ratified by mail ballot to all LASA membership and sent to the various sections of the government. "Resolution Against US Aid to Anti-Sandinista Forces" **LASA Forum** vol. 16. no. 2. 1985. p. 3. "Resolution on US Policy in Central America" **LASA Forum** vol. 16. no. 2. 1985. p. 3. "Resolution on Salvadoran and Guatemalan Refugees in the United States" **LASA Forum** vol. 16. no. 2. 1985. p. 3. "Resolution on Guatemala" **LASA Forum** vol. 16. no. 2. 1985. p. 4. "Resolution on Cuba" **LASA Forum** vol. 16. no. 2. 1985. p. 4.

81. See "Resolution Against US Aid to Anti-Nicaraguan Forces" **LASA Forum** vol. 17. no. 4. 1987. pp. 25. "Resolution on US Policy in Central America" **LASA Forum** vol. 17. no. 4. 1987. pp. 25-26.

82. The liberal frustration was clear in a book published under the auspices of the Carnegie Endowment in 1985, and edited by Sanford J. Ungar, former managing editor of **Foreign Policy**. Sanford J. Ungar, ed., **Estrangement: America and the World** [1985].

83. Marlene Dixon, ed., **On Trial: Reagan's War Against Nicaragua-**

-Testimony of the Permanent People's Tribunal [1985]. Karl Bermann, **Under the Big Stick: Nicaragua and the United States Since 1848** [1986]. Holly Sklar, **Reagan, Trilateralism and the Neoliberals: Containment and Intervention in the 1980s** [1986]. George Black, **The Good Neighbor: How the United States Wrote the History of Central America and the Caribbean** [1988]. John Lamperti, **What Are We Afraid Of?: An Assessment of the Communist Threat in Central America** [1988].

84. Noam Chomsky, **Towards a New Cold War: Essays on the Current Crisis and How We Got There** [1982]. Noam Chomsky, **The Fateful Triangle: Israel, the United States and the Palestinians** [1984]. Noam Chomsky, **Pirates and Emperors: International Terrorism in the Real World** [1987]. Noam Chomsky and Edward S. Herman, **Manufacturing Consent: The Political Economy of the Mass Media** [1988]. Noam Chomsky, **Necessary Illusions: Thought Control in Democratic Societies** [1989]. Noam Chomsky, **Deterring Democracy** [1991].

85. For example, he argued that "there is no way to give a precise measure of the scale of our responsibility in each particular case, but whether we conclude that our share is 90%, or 40%, or 2%, it is that factor that should primarily concern us, since it is that factor that we can directly influence". See Noam Chomsky, **Turning the Tide: The US and Latin America** [1987]. p. 2. This was first published as Noam Chomsky, **Turning the Tide: US Intervention in Central America and the Struggle for Peace** [1985].

86. Chomsky, **Turning the Tide** [1987]. pp. 1-2.

87. Noam Chomsky, **On Power and Ideology** [1987]. pp. 9-10. See also Noam Chomsky, **The Culture of Terrorism** [1988]. Noam Chomsky, **The Chomsky Reader** (edited by James Peck) [1987]. pp. 315-367. On Chomsky's ideas see Joshua Cohen and Joel Rogers, "Knowledge, Morality and Hope: The Social Thought of Noam Chomsky" **New Left Review** no. 187. 1991.

88. Jonathan Marshall, Peter Dale Scott and Jane Hunter, **The Iran Contra Connection: Secret Teams and Covert Operations in the Reagan Era** [1987]. See Cheryl A. Rubenberg, "Israeli Foreign Policy in Central America" **Third World Quarterly** vol. 8. no. 3. 1986. Milton Jamail and Margo Gutierrez, **It's No Secret: Israel's Military Involvement in Central America** [1986]. Bishara Bahbah, **Israel and Latin America: The Military Connection** [1986]. Jane Hunter, **Israeli Foreign Policy: South Africa and Central America** [1987]. Damian J. Fernandez, ed., **Central America and the Middle East: The Internationalization of the Crises** [1990]. See also Peter Dale Scott and Jonathan Marshall, **Cocaine Politics: Drugs, Armies and the CIA in Central America** [Berkeley: University of California Press, 1991].

89. Michael McClintoch, **The American Connection: State Terror and Popular Resistance in El Salvador** [1985]. Michael McClintoch, **The American Connection: State Terror and Popular Resistance in Guatemala** [1985]. Peter Kornbluh, **Nicaragua: The Price of Intervention-- Reagan's War Against the Sandinistas** [1987]. William I. Robinson and Kent Norsworthy, **David and Goliath: Washington's War Against Nicaragua** [1987]. Holly Sklar, **Washington's War on Nicaragua** [1988]. Tom Barry, **Low-Intensity Conflict: The New Battlefield in Central America** [1986]. Tom Barry, **Guatemala: The Politics of Counterinsurgency** [1986]. Sara Miles, "The Real War: Low-Intensity Conflict in Central America" **NACLA Report on the Americas** vol. 20. no. 2. 1986. Allan Nairn, "Low-Intensity Conflict: A Debate--One Hit, Two Misses" **NACLA Report on the Americas** vol. 20. no. 3. 1986. Peter Kornbluh and Joy Hackel, "Low-Intensity Conflict: A Debate--Is it Live or is it

Memorex?" **NACLA Report on the Americas** vol. 20. no. 3. 1986. Robert
Matthews, "Sowing Dragon's Teeth: The US War Against Nicaragua" **NACLA Report
on the Americas** vol. 20. no. 4. 1986. **NACLA Report on the Americas** vol.
21. no. 1. 1987. William M. LeoGrande, "Central America: Counterinsurgency
Revisited" **NACLA Report on the Americas** vol. 21. no. 1. 1987. Holly Sklar,
"Born-Again War: The Low-Intensity Mystique" **NACLA Report on the Americas**
vol. 21. no. 2. 1987. Peter Kornbluh, "Test Case for the Reagan Doctrine: The Contra
War" **Third World Quarterly: Journal of Emerging Areas** vol. 9. no. 4.
1987. Jane Hunter and Sara Diamond, "The Show Goes On: The Right After Reagan"
NACLA Report on the Americas vol. 22. no. 5. 1988. Michael T. Klare and Peter
Kornbluh, eds., **Low Intensity Warfare: How the USA Fights Wars
Without Declaring Them** [1988].

90. Tom Barry and Deb Preusch, **The Soft War: The Uses and Abuses
of US Economic Aid in Central America** [1988]. See also Kevin Danaher,
Phillip Berryman and Medea Benjamin, **Help or Hindrance?: United States
Economic Aid in Central America** [1987]. Tom Barry and Rachel Garst,
Feeding the Crisis: US Food Aid and Farm Policy in Central America
[1990]. See also books which focused on the role of North American labor
organizations in furthering US foreign-policy goals in Central America. Tom Barry and
Deb Preusch, **AIFLD in Central America: Agents as Organizers** [1987].
Daniel Cantor and Juliet Schor, **Tunnel Vision: Labor, the World Economy,
and Central America** [1987]. Al Weinrub and William Bollinger, **The AFL-CIO
in Central America: A Look at the American Institute for Free Labor
Development (AIFLD)** [1987]. Robert Armstrong, Hank Frundt, Hobart Spalding
and Sean Sweeney, **Working Against US: The American Institute for Free
Labour Development (AIFLD) in El Salvador and the International
Policy of the AFL-CIO** [1988].

91. See Inter-Hemispheric Education Resource Center, **AIFLD in Central
America: Agents as Organizers** [1987]. Inter-Hemispheric Education Resource
Center, **US Food Aid and Farm Policy in Central America** [1989]. Inter-
Hemispheric Education Resource Center, **Food Aid in Central America:
Feeding the Crisis** [1989]. Inter-Hemispheric Education Resource Center,
**National Endowment for Democracy (NED): A Foreign Policy Branch
Gone Awry** [1990].

92. Cynthia Arnson's career as an aide to a democratic member of Congress in
the 1980s and her book on the relationship between the White House and Congress,
were indicative of the terms of the alliance between radicals and liberals. She had also
worked at the IPS, was involved with NACLA and had been a part of PACCA. At the
beginning of the 1990s she was working as Associate Director of Americas Watch. See
Cynthia J. Arnson, **Crossroads: Congress, the Reagan Administration and
Central America** [1989].

93. For example, a substantial edited volume, which appeared in 1986,
included contributions by radicals, as well as Howard Wiarda and Margaret Daly Hayes,
but its cumulative perspective was liberal. See Kevin J. Middlebrook and Carlos Rico,
eds., **The United States and Latin America in the 1980s: Contending
Perspectives on a Decade of Crisis** [1986]. Kenneth M. Coleman and George
C. Herring, eds., **The Central American Crisis: Sources of Conflict and
the Failure of US Policy** [1985]. Lester D. Langley, **Central America: The
Real Stakes--Understanding Central America Before It's Too Late**
[1985]. Daniel Siegel and Tom Spaulding, with Peter Kornbluh, **Outcast Among
Allies: The International Costs of Reagan's War Against Nicaragua**
[1985]. Cynthia Brown, Alfred Stepan, Holly Burkhalter, Robert K. Goldman, Juan
Mendez, Allan Nairn and Aryeh Neier, **With Friends Like These: The Americas**

Watch Report on Human Rights and US Policy in Latin America [1985], especially pp. xv-xxii, 112-204. Lloyd S. Etheredge, **Can Governments Learn?: American Foreign Policy and Central American Revolutions** [1985]. Jan Knippers Black, **Sentinels of Empire: The United States and Latin American Militarism** [1986]. Harold Molineu, **US Policy Toward Latin America: From Regionalism to Globalism** [1986], especially pp. 1-12, 176-207, 213-232. Edward Best, **US Policy and Regional Security in Central America** [1987]. Guy Poitras, **The Ordeal of Hegemony: The United States and Latin America** [1990]. Tom J. Farer, **The Grand Strategy of the United States in Latin America** [1988]. Tom Farer, who testified to the Kissinger Commission, also made a number of earlier contributions to the debate. See Tom J. Farer, "Searching for Defeat" **Foreign Policy** no. 40. 1980. Tom J. Farer, "Manage the Revolution?" **Foreign Policy** no. 52. 1983. Tom J. Farer, "At Sea in Central America: Can We Negotiate Our Way to Shore?" in Robert S. Leiken, ed., **Central America: Anatomy of Conflict** [1984]. Tom J. Farer, "Contadora: The Hidden Agenda" **Foreign Policy** no. 59. 1985. Other journalistic liberal work included Peter Davis, **Where Is Nicaragua?** [1987]. Edward R. F. Sheehan, **Agony in the Garden: A Stranger in Central America** [1989]. See also Gutman's critique of the Reagan administration's policy, which implicitly supported a bureaucratic politics approach. He detailed how US policy towards Central America unfolded in part as a struggle between 'conservatives' and more moderate officials in the White House, the State Department, the CIA and the Department of Defense. Roy Gutman, **Banana Diplomacy: The Making of American Policy in Nicaragua 1981-1987** [1988].

94. However, even the diplomatic historian Thomas Leonard, whose work appeared to be relatively impervious to political and theoretical changes produced a reference work which was clearly provoked by the Central American crisis. Thomas M. Leonard, **Central America and United States Policies 1820s-1980s: A Guide to Issues and References** [1985]. See also Thomas M. Leonard, **The United States and Central America 1944-1949: Perceptions of Political Dynamics** [1984]. Thomas M. Leonard, "The United States and Central America 1955-1960" **The Valley Forge Journal: A Record of Patriotism and American Culture** vol. 3. no. 1. 1986. Thomas M. Leonard, "'Keeping the Europeans Out': The United States and Central America Since 1823" in Woodward, ed., **Central America** [1988]. Thomas M. Leonard, "Nationalism or Communism: The Truman Administration and Guatemala 1945-1952" **Journal of Third World Studies** vol. 7. no. 1. 1990. Thomas M. Leonard, "Search for Security: The United States and Central America in the Twentieth Century" **The Americas: A Quarterly Review of Inter-American Cultural History** vol. 47. no. 4. 1991. A concern about the situation in the mid-1980s also appeared to inform Bryce Wood's study of the demise of the Good Neighbor Policy, which he traced to the 1954 US intervention in Guatemala. Wood argued that the US "lost" its "credibility" and its "honorable reputation" in Latin America and around the world in 1954, and that they had not been "regained". His commitment to the restoration of a hemispheric 'partnership' was apparent when he emphasized that the Guatemalans "lost" the chance of a "freer and fairer social and economic order (which they are still fighting for)" and the republics of the western hemisphere "jointly lost a chance to face a Soviet threat and to forge a new political order". Bryce Wood, **The Dismantling of the Good Neighbor Policy** [1985]. pp. 157, 169, 173, 189-192, 198, 207-209. In 1987, John Findling, an exceedingly conventional diplomatic historian, lamented that the Reagan administration demonstrated "little understanding or appreciation of the nearly two hundred years of history" linking the US and Central America, and he criticized the "perfunctory" treatment of the United States' historical role in Central America by the

Kissinger Commission's **Report**. He noted the problems involved in identifying US interests in the region; however, he found it "difficult to see how Nicaragua, an economically impoverished country with just one percent of the population of the United States, can represent the apocalyptic threat the more shrill voices in Washington declare it to be". John E. Findling, **Close Neighbors, Distant Friends: United States-Central American Relations** [1987]. pp. xvi, 181.

95. Cole Blasier, **The Hovering Giant: US Responses to Revolutionary Change in Latin America 1910-1985** [1985]. pp. xv, 296-298. See also Cole Blasier, "Security: The Extracontinental Dimension" in Middlebrook and Rico, eds., **The United States and Latin America in the 1980s** [1986]. Cole Blasier, "The Soviet Union" in Morris J. Blachman, William LeoGrande and Kenneth Sharpe, eds., **Confronting Revolution: Security Through Diplomacy in Central America** [1986].

96. Blasier, **The Hovering Giant** [1985]. pp. 301-302.

97. Blasier, **The Hovering Giant** [1985]. p. 302. The idea of the US being its "own worst enemy" is a long-standing liberal theme. See, for example, Eugene Burdick and William J. Lederer, **The Ugly American** [1958]. William J. Lederer, **Our Own Worst Enemy** [1968]. Anthony Lake, I. M. Destler and Leslie H. Gelb, **Our Own Worst Enemy: The Unmaking of American Foreign Policy** [1984].

98. Blasier, **The Hovering Giant** [1985]. pp. 302-303.

99. William M. LeoGrande, "The Evolution of Nonalignment" **Problems of Communism** vol. 29. no. 1. 1980. William M. LeoGrande, "Cuban-Soviet Relations and Cuban Policy in Africa" **Cuban Studies** vol. 10. no. 1. 1980. William LeoGrande, **Cuba's Policy in Africa 1959-1980** [1980].

100. William M. LeoGrande, "The Revolution in Nicaragua: Another Cuba?" **Foreign Affairs** vol. 58. no. 1. 1979. William M. LeoGrande and Carole Ann Robbins, "Oligarchs and Officers: The Crisis in El Salvador" **Foreign Affairs** vol. 58. no. 5. 1980. William M. LeoGrande, "Cuba Policy Recycled" **Foreign Policy** no. 46. 1982. William M. LeoGrande, "The United States and the Nicaraguan Revolution" in Thomas W. Walker, ed., **Nicaragua in Revolution** [1982]. William M. LeoGrande, "US Policy Options in Central America" Richard R. Fagen and Olga Pellicer, eds., **The Future of Central America: Policy Choices for the US and Mexico** [1983]. William M. LeoGrande, "Through the Looking Glass: The Kissinger Report on Central America" **World Policy Journal** vol. 1. no. 2. 1984. William M. LeoGrande, "Cuba: Going to the Source" in Richard S. Newfarmer, ed., **From Gunboats to Diplomacy: New US Policies for Latin America** [1984]. William M. LeoGrande, "The Contras and Congress" in Walker, ed., **Reagan Versus the Sandinistas** [1987]. William M. LeoGrande, "Roll-back or Containment?: The United States, Nicaragua and the Search for Peace in Central America" **International Security** vol. 11. no. 2. 1986. William M. LeoGrande, "Regime Illegitimacy and Revolutionary Movements: Central America" in Barry M. Schutz and Robert O. Slater, eds., **Revolution and Political Change in the Third World** [Boulder: Lynne Rienner Publishers, 1990]. William M. LeoGrande, "After the Battle of San Salvador: Breaking the Deadlock" **World Policy Journal** vol. 7. no. 2. 1990. William M. LeoGrande, "From Reagan to Bush: The Transition in US Policy Towards Central America" **Journal of Latin American Studies** vol. 22. no. 3. 1990.

101. Morris J. Blachman, William LeoGrande, and Kenneth Sharpe **Confronting Revolution: Security Through Diplomacy in Central America** [1986].

102. Morris J. Blachman, William LeoGrande, and Kenneth Sharpe, "Preface" in Blachman, LeoGrande, and Sharpe **Confronting Revolution** [1986]. p. vii.

103. LeoGrande, "Through the Looking Glass" **World Policy Journal** 1984. p. 254.

104. Richard Fagen, **Forging Peace: The Challenge of Central America** [1987]. pp. 17-33, 36-56, 119-132. In the second half of the 1980s, PACCA also sponsored a number of short books on the domestic linkages and domestic costs of US foreign policy in Central America. Joshua Cohen and Joel Rogers, **Inequity and Intervention: The Federal Budget and Central America** [1986]. Joshua Cohen and Joel Rogers, **The Rules of the Game: American Politics and the Central American Movement** [1986]. Mark Tushnet, **Central America and the Law: The Constitution, Civil Liberties and the Courts** [1988].

105. Richard E. Feinberg, **The Triumph of Allende: Chile's Legal Revolution** [1972].

106. Feinberg cited in Richard Melanson, **Writing History and Making Policy: The Cold War, Vietnam and Revisionism** [1983]. pp. 190-191.

107. Richard E. Feinberg, **The Intemperate Zone: The Third World Challenge to US Foreign Policy** [1983]. pp. 16-19, 22-23, 230-231, 257.

108. Richard E. Feinberg, **Subsidizing Success: The Export-Import Bank in the US Economy** [Cambridge: Cambridge University Press, 1982]. Richard E. Feinberg, "Central America: No Easy Answers" **Foreign Affairs** vol. 59. no. 5. 1981. Richard E. Feinberg, "Introduction and Overview" in Richard E. Feinberg, ed., **Central America: International Dimensions of the Crisis** [1982]. Richard E. Feinberg, "The Recent Rapid Redefinitions of US Interests and Diplomacy in Central America" in Feinberg, ed., **Central America: International Dimensions of the Crisis** [1982]. Richard E. Feinberg,"United States' Interests and Options in Central America" in Wolf Grabendorff, Jorg Todt and H. W. Krumwiede, eds., **Political Change in Central America: Internal and External Dimensions** [1984]. Richard E. Feinberg and Robert A. Pastor, "Far from Hopeless: An Economic Program for Post-War Central America" in Robert S. Leiken, ed., **Central America: Anatomy of Conflict** [1984]. Richard E. Feinberg, "Costa Rica: End of the Fiesta" in Richard Newfarmer, ed., **From Gunboats to Diplomacy: New US Policies for Latin America** [1984]. Richard E. Feinberg, "Comment: Debt and Trade in US-Latin American Relations" in Kevin J. Middlebrook and Carlos Rico, eds., **The United States and Latin America in the 1980s: Contending Perspectives on a Decade of Crisis** [1986]. Richard E. Feinberg, "Third World Debt: Toward a More Balanced Adjustment" **Journal of Interamerican Studies and World Affairs** vol. 29. no. 1. 1987. Richard E. Feinberg, "Multilateral Lending and Latin America" **The World Economy** vol. 10. no. 2. 1987. Richard E. Feinberg, "Central American Debt: Genuine Case-by-Case Studies" in William Ascher and Ann Hubbard, eds., **Central American Recovery and Development: Task Force Report to the International Commission for Central American Recovery and Development** [1989].

109. Richard E. Feinberg and Bruce M. Bagley, **Development Postponed: The Political Economy of Central America in the 1980s** [1986]. pp. 33-41, 47-50.

110. Feinberg and Bagley, **Development Postponed** [1986]. pp. 49-50.

111. Fagen, **Forging Peace** [1987]. pp. 40-42.

112. Bruce M. Bagley, ed., **Contadora and the Diplomacy of Peace in Central America--vol. 1: The United States, Central America and Contadora** [1987].

113. Margaret Daly Hayes, "US Security Interests in Central America" in Bagley, ed., **Contadora and the Diplomacy of Peace in Central America** [1987]. pp. 11-12.

114. LASA Commission on Compliance with the Central American Peace

Accord, **Final Report of the LASA Commission on the Central America Peace Accord** [March 1988]; reprinted as "Appendix-Extraordinary Opportunities...And New Risks: Final Report of the LASA Commission on the Central America Peace Accord" **LASA Forum** vol. 19. no. 1. 1988. pp. 1, 3, 35-38.

115. See Abraham F. Lowenthal et al., "The Conduct of Routine Relations: The United States and Latin America" (Appendix 1). **Report of the Commission on the Organization of the Government for the Conduct of Foreign Policy** [1975].

116. Abraham F. Lowenthal, "The Dominican Republic: The Politics of Chaos" in A. Van Lazar and R. R. Kaufman, eds., **Reform and Revolution: Readings in Latin American Politics** [1969]. Abraham F. Lowenthal, "The United States and the Dominican Republic to 1965: Background to Intervention" **Caribbean Studies** vol. 10. no. 2. 1970. Abraham F. Lowenthal, "The Political Role of the Dominican Armed Forces: A Note on the 1963 Overthrow of Juan Bosch and on the 1965 Dominican Revolution" **Journal of Interamerican Studies and World Affairs** vol. 15. no. 3. 1973; reprinted in Abraham F. Lowenthal, ed., **Armies and Politics in Latin America** [1976]. Abraham F. Lowenthal, **The Dominican Intervention** [1972]. Abraham F. Lowenthal, "United States Policy Towards Latin America: 'Liberal', 'Radical' and 'Bureaucratic' Perspectives" **Latin American Research Review** vol. 8. no. 3. 1973; revised and reprinted as Abraham F. Lowenthal, "'Liberal', 'Radical' and 'Bueaucratic' Perspectives on US Latin American Policy: The Alliance for Progress in Retrospect" in Julio Cotler and Richard R. Fagen, eds., **Latin America and the United States: The Changing Political Realities** [1974]. Abraham F. Lowenthal, "Peru's Ambiguous Revolution" **Foreign Affairs** vol. 52. no. 4. 1974. Abraham F. Lowenthal, "Armies and Politics in Latin America" **World Politics** vol. 27. no. 1. 1974; reprinted in Abraham F. Lowenthal, ed., **Armies and Politics in Latin America** [1976]. Abraham F. Lowenthal, "The United States and Latin America: Ending the Hegemonic Presumption" **Foreign Affairs** vol. 55. no. 1. 1976. Abraham F. Lowenthal, "Cuba's African Adventure" **International Security** vol. 2. no. 1. 1977. Abraham F. Lowenthal and Milton Charlton, "The United States and Panama: Confrontation or Cooperation?" **American Enterprise Institute (Foreign Policy and) Defense Review** vol. 1. no. 4. 1977. Abraham F. Lowenthal, "Latin America: A Not So Special Relationship" **Foreign Policy** no. 32. 1978. Abraham F. Lowenthal, "The Peruvian Experiment Reconsidered" in Cynthia McClintock and Abraham F. Lowenthal, eds., **The Peruvian Experiment Reconsidered** [Princeton: Princeton University Press, 1983]. Abraham F. Lowenthal, "Research in Latin America and the Caribbean on International Relations and Foreign Policy: Some Impressions" **Latin American Research Review** vol. 18. no. 1. 1983.

117. Abraham F. Lowenthal, "Changing Patterns in Inter-American Relations" **Washington Quarterly: A Review of Strategic and International Issues** vol. 4. no. 1. 1981. Abraham F. Lowenthal, "Ronald Reagan and Latin America: Coping with Hegemony in Decline" in Kenneth A. Oye, Robert J. Lieber and Donald S. Rothchild, eds., **Eagle Defiant?: United States Foreign Policy in the 1980s** [1983]. Abraham F. Lowenthal, "Changing the Agenda" **Foreign Policy** no. 52. 1983. Abraham F. Lowenthal, "The Insular Caribbean as a Crucial Test for US Policy" in H. Michael Erisman, ed., **The Caribbean Challenge: US Policy in a Volatile Region** [1984]. Abraham F. Lowenthal, "The United States and Central America: Reflections on the Kissinger Commission Report" in Coleman and Herring, eds., **The Central American Crisis** [1985]. Abraham F. Lowenthal, "Rethinking US Interests in the Western Hemisphere" **Journal of Interamerican Studies and World Affairs** vol. 29. no. 1. 1987. Abraham F. Lowenthal, "The United States and South America" **Current History** vol. 87. no.

525. 1988. Abraham F. Lowenthal, "The United States, Central America and the Caribbean" in Martz, ed., **United States Policy in Latin America** [1988].

118. Inter-American Dialogue (Sol M. Linowitz, chair), **The Americas in 1984: Year for Decisions** (Report of the Inter-American Dialogue) [1984].

119. Inter-American Dialogue (Sol M. Linowitz, chair), "The Americas in 1984: A Year for Decisions" **LASA Forum** vol. 15. no. 3. 1984.

120. This view was, of course, widespread by the second half of the 1980s. See, for example, the work of Gregory F. Treverton, of the John F. Kennedy School of Government at Harvard, and a consultant to both the Kissinger Commission and the Inter-American Dialogue. Gregory F. Treverton, "US Strategy in Central America" **Survival** vol. 28. no. 2. 1986.

121. Abraham F. Lowenthal, **Partners in Conflict: The United States and Latin America** [1987]. pp. ix-x.

122. Lowenthal, **Partners in Conflict** [1987]. pp. 45-47, 64-65, 150.

123. One option was what he called "intermittent intervention", which was the "traditional" US policy towards the region, and was based on limited concern with social and economic development and a narrow understanding of national security. Another was "sustained disengagement", which was characterized by a low level of interest in both socio-economic development and historical security concerns. A third was the "activist expansion" approach, which entailed a focus on national security and issues of socio-economic development. The fourth was a "long-term developmental" approach, which encompassed increased US interest in social and economic "questions" and a reduction in interest in conventional "security issues". The Kissinger Commission's recommendations, which outlined Washington's need to intervene on virtually all fronts in Central America and the Caribbean, symbolized, for Lowenthal, the "activist expansion" approach. The Commission, in his view, recommended that the US lead the "process of regional transformation" in an effort to "preempt revolutionary movements". Lowenthal directly challenged the Kissinger **Report**, characterizing its assertion that the "correct aim of US policy in Central America" ought to be to secure and support "peaceful, democratic, reform-oriented, stable, prosperous, and congenial neighbors" as "utterly unrealistic". He argued that, apart from Costa Rica the Central American republics were "conflict wracked, repressive, polarized, economically depressed, and unstable", as well as containing considerable anti-US sentiment, and no foreign policy emerging from Washington "could soon change these grim realities". In fact, part of Washington's "problem" in Central America was rooted in "the paradox that an increased US presence may well heighten the very nationalist and revolutionary sentiments that make Washington uncomfortable". Lowenthal, **Partners in Conflict** [1987]. pp. 155, 157, 164-165.

124. Lowenthal, **Partners in Conflict** [1987]. pp. 165-170, 187-189, 196-197, 199-200.

125. Lars Schoultz, **National Security and United States Policy Towards Latin America** [1987]. See also his earlier work: Lars Schoultz, "US Diplomacy and Human Rights in Latin America" in John D. Martz and Lars Schoultz, eds., **Latin America, the United States and the Inter-American System** [1980]. Lars Schoultz, **Human Rights and United States Policy Towards Latin America** [1981].

126. Anthony Lake, **Somoza Falling--The Nicaraguan Dilemma: A Portrait of Washington at Work** [1989]. Robert Pastor, **Condemned to Repetition: The United States and Nicaragua** [1987]. It was reprinted with a new epilogue in 1988. Other liberal studies by former officials or diplomat, included a book by Frank McNeil, who was US Ambassador to Costa Rica during the Carter and Reagan administrations. See Frank McNeil, **War and Peace in Central America** [1988]. See also the work of Wayne S. Smith, of the Johns Hopkins University's

School of Advanced International Studies in Washington. He spent 25 years as a diplomat, including four years as chief of the US Interests Section in Cuba, until his resignation in 1982 in protest over Reagan's foreign policy in the region. Wayne S. Smith, **The Closest of Enemies: A Personal and Diplomatic Account of US-Cuban Relations Since 1957** [1987]. Wayne S. Smith, "Bringing Diplomacy Back In: A Critique of US Policy in Central America" in Bagley, ed., **Contadora and the Diplomacy of Peace in Central America** [1987]. Wayne S. Smith, "The Reagan Administration and Its Attempt to Thwart Change" in Kirk and Schuyler, eds., **Central America** [1988].

127. Lake completed a PhD at Princeton in the mid-1970s. Lake's other work includes Anthony Lake, **The "Tar Baby" Option: American Policy Toward Southern Rhodesia** [1976]. Anthony Lake, **Third World Radical Regimes: US Policy Under Carter and Reagan** [1985].

128. Pastor acknowledged that "the advantage of having participated in making a policy often carries with it the disadvantages--from a scholarly standpoint--of having a stake in defending that policy"; however, he insisted that his book was "neither a memoir nor an apologia for the Carter Administration's actions". Pastor, **Condemned to Repetition** [1987]. p. xii. Robert Pastor entered the Carter administration as the National Security Council's Latin American expert at the age of 29, only days after graduating with a PhD from Harvard. Although he had no previous governmental or diplomatic experience, he had served as Executive Director of the Linowitz Commission and also had links with the Institute for Policy Studies major policy paper on inter-American relations in the mid-1970s. Currently Professor of Political Science at Emory University, and Director of the Carter Center's Latin American and Caribbean Program at Emory, he is generally regarded as a major liberal authority on US-Latin American relations. In an interview in 1981 he described himself as "very much a product of the Vietnam generation". Pastor 'confessed' to being influenced by David Horowitz's **From Yalta to Vietnam**; however, he found Horowitz's "psychological critique" of the US "Cold War mentality" more persuasive than his analysis of the economic forces behind US involvement in Vietnam. While he was certainly not an avid supporter of Horowitz's analysis, even as a student in the 1960s and early 1970s, Pastor claimed that his time in the Carter administration changed his perspective markedly. For example, he stated that while his outlook towards Cuba had never been "favorable", prior to taking up the NSC position he had "tried to find some things, particularly internally, that the Cubans did which were not bad". By the end of the Carter years, Pastor's limited sympathy for Cuba had disappeared. He had become convinced that Cuba's activities and goals in the region exacerbated Washington's inability to achieve its "legitimate" objectives. Melanson, **Writing History and Making Policy** [1983]. pp. 153-154. (Melanson interviewed Pastor on April 20, 1981). Pastor was regarded by many in the Carter administration, and outside of it, as a 'hard-liner'. The State Department's Patt Derian, who held the top human-rights post in the Carter administration, certainly thought so. Derian was opposed to US military aid to El Salvador, in particular a highly contended $5.7 million package which in early 1980 Archbishop Romero had asked Washington not to send. Derian regarded Pastor's unequivocal support for the aid, and his hard-line towards El Salvador, as "a real roadblock" to the administration's efforts to improve the human-rights situation in the war-torn country. Those who defended Pastor argued that his views were simply a reflection of the outlook of "hard-line anti-communist" National Security Advisor Zbigniew Brzezinski, who was Pastor's boss. Raymond Bonner, **Weakness and Deceit: US Policy in El Salvador** [1984]. pp. 174-176. Ironically, despite Pastor's links with Brzezinski, and his "hard-line" reputation, he was one of the individuals in the Carter administration whom Jeane Kirkpatrick pointed to as evidence that the views of the New Left were at the heart of Washington's

foreign policy in the late 1970s. See Jeane J. Kirkpatrick, "US Security and Latin America" **Commentary** vol. 71. no. 1. 1981; reprinted in Jeane J. Kirkpatrick, **Dictatorship and Double Standards: Rationalism and Reason in Politics** [1982]. p. 60.

129. Robert A. Pastor, **Congress and the Politics of US Foreign Economic Policy 1929-1976** [1980]. Robert A. Pastor, "Our Real Interests in Central America" **The Atlantic Monthly** vol. 250. no. 1. 1982. Robert A. Pastor, "The Target and the Source: El Salvador and Nicaragua" **Washington Quarterly: A Review of Strategic and International Issues** vol. 5. no. 3. 1982. Robert A. Pastor, "Sinking in the Caribbean Basin" **Foreign Affairs** vol. 60. no. 5. 1982. Robert A. Pastor, "Cuba and the Soviet Union: Does Cuba Act Alone?" in Barry B. Levine, ed., **The New Cuban Presence in the Caribbean** [1983]. Robert A. Pastor, "A Question of US National Interests in Central America" in Wolf Grabendorff, Heinrich W. Krumwiede and Jorg Todt, eds., **Political Change in Central America: Internal and External Dimensions** [Boulder: Westview, 1984]. Robert A. Pastor, "Continuity and Change in US Foreign Policy: Carter and Reagan on El Salvador" **Journal of Policy Analysis and Management** vol. 3. no. 2. 1984. Robert A. Pastor, **Migration and Development in the Caribbean: The Unexplored Connection** [1985]. Robert A. Pastor, "Explaining US Policy Toward the Caribbean Basin" **World Politics** vol. 38. no. 3. 1986. Robert A. Pastor, "Does the United States Push Revolutions to Cuba?: The Case of Grenada" **Journal of Interamerican Studies and World Affairs** vol. 28. no. 1. 1986. Robert A. Pastor, "The Reagan Administration and Latin America: Eagle Insurgent" in Kenneth A. Oye, Robert J. Lieber and Donald Rothchild, eds., **Eagle Resurgent?: The Reagan Era in American Foreign Policy** [1987]. Robert A. Pastor, **Latin America's Debt Crisis: Adjusting to the Past or Planning for the Future** [1987]. Robert A. Pastor and Jorge G. Castaneda, **Limits to Friendship: The United States and Mexico** [1988]. Robert A. Pastor, "The Carter Administration and Latin America: A Test of Principle" in John D. Martz, ed., **United States Policy in Latin America: A Quarter Century of Crisis and Challenge 1961-1986** [1988]. Robert A. Pastor, "Securing a Democratic Hemispheric" **Foreign Policy** no. 73. 1988-1989. Robert A. Pastor, "Forging a Hemispheric Bargain: The Bush Opportunity" **Journal of International Affairs** vol. 43. no. 1. 1989. Robert A. Pastor, "Introduction: The Swing of the Pendulum" in Robert A. Pastor, ed., **Democracy in the Americas: Stopping the Pendulum** [1989]. Robert A. Pastor, "How to Reinforce Democracy in the Americas: Seven Proposals" in Pastor, ed., **Democracy in the Americas** [1989]. Robert A. Pastor, "Nicaragua's Choice: The Making of a Free Election" **Journal of Democracy** vol. 1. no. 3. 1990.

130. Pastor, **Condemned to Repetition** [1987]. pp. xi., 6-7, 14-15. Pastor argued that the United States' Nicaraguan policy between 1974 and 1982 went through all of the "seven stages" which Washington's relations with Cuba had gone through two decades earlier. See Pastor, **Condemned to Repetition** [1987]. pp. 266-269.

131. Significantly, Lowenthal contrasted the late 1980s with the early 1960s when, during "another time of troubles in Latin America", the Alliance for Progress was launched by President Kennedy. In the 1950s the region "had experienced severe economic problems, mounting social pressures and the growth of revolutionary movments". In the final years of the 1980s, as in the 1950s, Latin America is again in "a time of great ferment" as massive urbanization, rapid industrialization and the population explosion have wrought an incredible transformation in the hemisphere. The "crux" of the region's "problem" is economic, and according to Lowenthal "it can only be solved if the US government makes a political decision to give priority to facing the hemispheric crisis of debt and trade". In Lowenthal's view "only if

Washington recognizes the urgency of promoting hemispheric cooperation as a political priority can the present vicious cycle be broken". Lowenthal, **Partners in Conflict** [1987]. pp. 181, 185.

132. Robert A. Pastor, "Forging a Hemispheric Bargain: The Bush Opportunity" **Journal of International Affairs** vol. 43. no. 1. 1989. pp. 71-73.

133. See Lowenthal, **Partners in Conflict** [1987]. pp. 157-170, especially pp. 165-170.

134. Margaret Daly Hayes, "Not What I Say, But What I Do: Latin American Policy in the Reagan Administration" in Martz, ed., **United States Policy in Latin America** [1988]. pp. 99, 127. Hayes's earlier work included Margaret Daly Hayes, "Security to the South: US Interests in Latin America" **International Security** vol. 5. no. 1. 1980. Margaret Daly Hayes, "The Stakes in Central America and US Policy Responses" **American Enterprise Institute Foreign Policy and Defense Review** vol. 4. no. 2. 1982. Margaret Daly Hayes, "US Security in Central America" **American Enterprise Institute Foreign Policy and Defense Review** vol. 5. no. 1. 1984. Margaret Daly Hayes, **Latin America and the US National Interest: A Basis for US Foreign Policy** [1984].

135. Richard L. Millett, "The United States and Central America: A Policy Adrift" **Current History** vol. 87. no. 533. 1988. p. 448.

136. George McGovern, "The 1988 Election: US Foreign Policy at a Watershed" **Foreign Affairs** vol. 66. no. 3. 1988. Samuel P. Huntington, "Coping with the Lippman Gap" **Foreign Affairs** vol. 66. no. 3. 1988. Zbigniew Brzezinski, "America's New Geostrategy" **Foreign Affairs** vol. 66. no. 4. 1988. Richard N. Gardner, "The Case for Practical Internationalism" **Foreign Affairs** vol. 66. no. 4. 1988. Henry Kissinger and Cyrus Vance, "Bipartisan Objectives for American Foreign Policy" **Foreign Affairs** vol. 66. no. 5. 1988. James Chace, "A New Grand Strategy" **Foreign Policy** no. 70. 1988. Sol M. Linowitz, "Latin America: The President's Agenda" **Foreign Affairs** vol. 67. no. 2. 1988/1989. Robert Pastor, "Securing a Democratic Hemisphere" **Foreign Policy** no. 73. 1988/89. Inter-American Dialogue, **The Americas in 1989: Consensus for Action** (Report of the Inter-American Dialogue) [1989]. Margaret Daly Hayes, "The United States and Latin America: A Lost Decade" **Foreign Affairs** vol. 68. no. 1. 1989. Robert W. Tucker, "Reagan's Foreign Policy" **Foreign Affairs** vol. 68. no. 1. 1989. Richard Nixon, "American Foreign Policy: The Bush Agenda" **Foreign Affairs** vol. 68. no. 1. 1989.

137. Langley, a Research Professor of History at the University of Georgia, was born in Clarksville, Texas, in August 1940. He received a PhD in history from the University of Kansas in 1965. He worked briefly as a history instructor at the University of Kansas, then as an assistant professor from 1965 to 1969 in tertiary institutions in Texas and Washington State. By 1970 he had taken up the post of Associate Professor of Foreign Relations at the University of Georgia. Hispanic Foundation Library of Congress, **National Directory of Latin Americanists** [1971]. p. 320.

138. See Lester D. Langley, **The Cuban Policy of the United States: A Brief History** [1968]. Lester D. Langley, **The Struggle for the American Mediterranean: United States-European Rivalry in the Gulf-Caribbean 1776-1904** [1976]. Lester D. Langley, **The United States and the Caribbean in the Twentieth Century** [1982]. One of Langley's more recent books focused on the US consuls and military men directly involved in US intervention in the circum-Caribbean in the first three decades of this century. His examination of the 1920s and 1930s represented the US impact as primarily negative; however, his interpretation suggested that the negative impact flowed from the US failure to be a more explicitly colonial power. He noted that, because the US government did not have a colonial office, the policy was often carried out by the military. And he concluded that, although

the military men were successful as "conquerors", they failed as "rulers of conquered places". Lester D. Langley, **The Banana Wars: US Intervention in the Caribbean 1898-1934** [1985]. pp. 221-223. See also Lester D. Langley and Thomas D. Schoonover, **The Banana Men: American Mercenaries and Entrepreneurs in Central America 1880-1930** [1994]. A forerunner of Langley's work was Richard Challener, **Admirals, Generals and American Foreign Policy 1898-1914** [1973]. There is also Ivan Musicant's celebratory military history. See Ivan Musicant, **The Banana Wars: A History of United States Military Intervention in Latin America from the Spanish-American War to the Invasion of Panama** [1990].

139. Langley defined the idea of the Western Hemisphere with reference to the definition articulated by Arthur Preston Whitaker thirty years earlier. For Whitaker the idea of the Western Hemisphere was founded on the notion that the inhabitants of North and South America have a "special relationship to one another that sets them apart from the rest of the world". Lester D. Langley, **America and the Americas: The United States in the Western Hemisphere** [1989]. pp. xiii, 248-250, 291-292. Arthur Preston Whitaker, **The Western Hemisphere Idea: Its Rise and Decline** [1954]. p. 1. Langley noted that at the outset of his career he approached the study of inter-American relations from the "perspective of a US diplomatic historian", which meant an "inevitable focus" on policy issues and formal relations between states. He argued that in this stage of his career he had been convinced that "greater understanding and sympathy with Latin America, its peoples, and their problems would do more to advance US interests in the hemisphere than a Latin American policy that relied on forceful diplomacy, economic pressure, or the dispatching of troops". He argued that, although he had moved "much more to a Latin American view", he still subscribed to his earlier "belief" that increased understanding could lead to greater harmony in the hemisphere; however, this view was now "tempered" by his "realization that the impulses working on Latin America have largely come from within, not from the United States". Langley, **America and the Americas** [1989]. pp. xv-xvi.

140. Langley, **America and the Americas** [1989]. pp. xvi-xvii, xix-xx, xxii.

141. John A. Crow, **The Epic of Latin America** [1992]. pp. xi-xiii.

142. Michael Novak, **This Hemisphere of Liberty: A Philosophy of the Americas** [1990]. p. 6. See also Michael Novak, **The American Vision: An Essay on the Future of Democratic Capitalism** [1978]. Michael Novak, ed., **Liberation South, Liberation North** [1981]. Michael Novak, **The Spirit of Democratic Capitalism** [1982]. Michael Novak, ed., **Latin America: Dependency or Interdependence** [1985]. Peter L. Berger and Michael Novak, **Speaking to the Third World: Essays on Democracy and Development** [1985]. Michael Novak, **Taking Glasnost Seriously: Toward an Open Soviet Union** [1988].

143. Howard J. Wiarda, **Foreign Policy Without Illusion: How Foreign Policy Making Works and Fails to Work in the United States** [1990]. pp. vii, 1-17, 322-327.

144. Wiarda, **The Democratic Revolution in Latin America** [1990]. pp. xiv-xv, 108-109, 263-264, 278-282. US State Department, **Democracy in Latin America and the Caribbean** [1987]. p. 13; cited in Wiarda, **The Democratic Revolution in Latin America** [1990]. p. 279. Wiarda's specific recommendations as to how US policy was to achieve its "democracy agenda" in Central and South America were not new. He had made all of them before, and he sought to revive and rehabilitate previous US programs. He advocated the continued use of diplomacy and political pressure, albeit in an "enlightened and skillful" way. He invoked the idea of a Marshall Plan, as outlined in the Kissinger Report, and he warned

that military aid needed to continue especially to countries such as El Salvador, where strong guerrilla insurrections existed, "otherwise the entire country may be lost indefinitely for democracy". He advocated the importance and expansion of cultural exchanges, the Peace Corps and the National Endowment for Democracy, which was established in 1983. Wiarda, **The Democratic Revolution in Latin America** [1990]. pp. 274-278, 143-168. In 1990 Wiarda also produced an edited collection of articles and documents on US foreign policy to be used as a university text. He explained at the beginning that in deciding what to put in the book he had "tried to include balanced and sensible points of view". Howard J. Wiarda, "Preface" in Howard J. Wiarda, **On the Agenda: Current Issues and Conflicts in US Foreign Policy** [1990]. p. iii. The section of the book specifically on Latin America contained four articles: two by Wiarda, as well as an excerpt from the 1989 Inter-American Dialogue Report and an excerpt from a 1989 report by the Committee of Santa Fe. See the Committee of Santa Fe, **Santa Fe II: A Strategy for Latin America in the Nineties** [1989]. Inter-American Dialogue, **The Americas in 1989: Consensus for Action** [1989].

145. For example, see his comment that "(w)e are often ignorant about Latin American history. Many of our students seem to believe Latin America either has no history or else that its history began in 1979 with the Nicaraguan revolution. We need to know the roots and background of Latin America, why the weight of history and the past remains so heavy there, and why it has been so difficult to establish democracy in the region. We must therefore study not just Latin America's recent politics but its origins in medieval Iberia and in the system Spain and Portugal transferred to the New World". Wiarda, **The Democratic Revolution in Latin America** [1990]. p. xvi.

146. Latin American Studies Association, "International Commission of the Latin American Studies Association to Observe the February 25, 1990, Nicaraguan Election: Interim Report December 15, 1989" **LASA Forum** vol. 20. no. 4. 1990. pp. 33, 42.

147. Latin American Studies Association Commission to Observe the 1990 Nicaraguan Election, **Electoral Democracy Under International Pressure: The Report of the Latin American Studies Association Commission to Observe the 1990 Nicaraguan Election March 15, 1990** [1990]. pp. 45-46. The Latin American Studies Association also kept up the pressure on Washington with regard to its policy towards El Salvador, passing a resolution on El Salvador and also expressing concern about the slaying of the Jesuits at the Central American University in El Salvador in November 1989. See "Report of the LASA Business Meeting, XV International Congress, Miami, December 5 1989" **LASA Forum** vol. 20. no. 4. 1990. pp. 11-12. "US Government Officials Respond to LASA Statement on Murder of Jesuit Priests" **LASA Forum** vol. 21. no. 1. 1990. pp. 6-8. "LASA Membership Ratifies El Salvador Resolution" **LASA Forum** vol. 21. no. 1. 1990. p. 12.

148. Dario Moreno, **US Policy in Central America: The Endless Debate** [1990]. pp. ix, 16-19, 148-149. See also Dario Moreno, "Thunder on the Left: Radical Critiques of US Central American Policy" **Latin American Research Review** vol. 26. no. 3. 1991.

149. Abraham F. Lowenthal, **Partners in Conflict: The US and Latin America in the 1990s** [1990]. pp. 215-216, 218, 220-222.

150. Roger B. Porter, "The Enterprise for the Americas Initiative: A New Approach" **Journal of Interamerican Studies and World Affairs** vol. 32. no. 4. 1990. pp. 1-2, 4-7, 11.

151. On economic liberalism in Latin America, see Alejandro Foxley, **Latin American Experiments in Neoconservative Economics** [1983]. Joseph

Ramos, **Neoconservative Economics in the Southern Cone of Latin America** [1986]. James F. Petras and Steve Vieux, "Twentieth-Century Neoliberals: Inheritors of the Exploits of Columbus" **Latin American Perspectives** vol. 19. no. 3. 1992. Ian Roxborough, "Neo-liberalism in Latin America: Limits and Alternatives" **Third World Quarterly: Journal of Emerging Areas** vol. 13. no. 3. 1992. James Petras and Morris Morley, **Latin America in the Time of Cholera: Electoral Politics, Market Economics and Permanent Crisis** [1992].

      152. Sidney Weintraub, "The New US Initiative Toward Latin America" **Journal of Interamerican Studies and World Affairs** vol. 33. no. 1. 1991. pp. 1-2, 12-16. See Sidney Weintraub, **A Marriage of Convenience: Relations Between Mexico and the United States** [1990].

      153. Wayne S. Smith, "The United States and South America: Beyond the Monroe Doctrine" **Current History** vol. 90. no. 553. p. 90.

      154. Cynthia J. Arnson and Johanna Mendelson "United States Policy in Central America" **Current History** vol. 90 no. 554. 1991. p. 137.

      155. Robert A. Pastor, The Bush Administration and Latin America: The Pragmatic Style and the Regionalist Option" **Journal of Interamerican Studies and World Affairs** vol. 33. no. 3. 1991. pp. 22-24, 29.

      156. Stephen Gill, **American Hegemony and the Trilateral Commission** [1990]. pp. 108, 119-121.

      157. William I. Robinson, "Nicaragua: The Making of a 'Democratic' Opposition" **NACLA-Report on the Americas** vol. 23. no. 5. 1990. p. 7. Also see James Dunkerley, "Refelections on the Nicaraguan Election" **New Left Review** no. 182. 1990. Philip J. Williams, "Elections and Democratization in Nicaragua: The 1990 Elections in Perspective" **Journal of Interamerican Studies and World Affairs** vol. 32. no. 4. 1990. Antoni Kapcia, "What Went Wrong? The Sandinista Revolution" **Bulletin of Latin American Research** vol. 13. no. 3. 1994.

      158. While 60% of Central America's population was seen to be living below the poverty line in 1986, the figure had risen to 76% by 1989. "Increasing Poverty in the Region" **Mexico and Central America Report** 16 January 1992. p. 4. Between 1980 and 1988 the percentage of export earnings required to service the foreign debts of the countries of Central America had risen from 12% to 40%. Between 1980 and 1988 regional trade declined by 50% at the same time as Central America continued to have high rates of unemployment, underemployment, with at least half the population of the region, apart from Costa Rica, carving out an existence beyond the formal market economy and the rights and obligations provided by legislation and taxation. Eldon Kenworthy, "Central America's Lost Decade" in Jan Knippers Black, ed., **Latin America, Its Problems and Its Promise: A Multidisciplinary Introduction** [1991]. pp. 346-348. Also see James Dunkerley, **The Pacification of Central America: Political Change in the Isthmus 1987-1993** [1994].

BIBLIOGRAPHY

Books

Alison Acker, **Honduras: The Making of a Banana Republic** [Boston: South End Press, 1988].

Frederick Adams, **The Conquest of the Tropics: The Story of the Creative Enterprises Conducted by the United Fruit Company** [Garden City: Doubleday, 1914; reprinted New York: Arno Press, 1976].

Richard N. Adams (Stokes Newbold), **A Study of Receptivity to Communism in Rural Guatemala** [Washington: Department of State, 1954, External Research Paper no. 116].

Richard Newbold Adams, **Cultural Surveys of Panama-Nicaragua-Guatemala-El Salvador-Honduras** [Washington: Pan-American Sanitary Bureau, 1957].

Richard Newbold Adams, **Crucifixion by Power: Essays on Guatemalan National Social Structure 1944-1966** [Austin: University of Texas Press, 1970].

Michael Adas, **Machines as the Measure of Men: Science, Technology, and Ideologies of Western Dominance** [Ithaca: Cornell University Press, 1989].

Philip Agee, **Inside the Company: CIA Diary** [Harmondsworth: Penguin Books, 1975].

John Agnew, **The United States in the World-Economy: A Regional Geography** [Cambridge: Cambridge University Press, 1988; first published 1987].

Aijaz Ahmad, **In Theory: Classes, Nations, Literatures** [London: Verso, 1992].

Eqbal Ahmad, **Political Culture and Foreign Policy** [Washington: Institute for Policy Studies, 1980].

Victor Alba, **Alliance Without Allies: The Mythology of Progress in Latin America** [New York: Praeger, 1965; first published in 1964 in Spanish as **Parasitos, mitos y sordomudos**].

Victor Alba, **Politics and the Labor Movement in Latin America** [Stanford: Stanford University Press, 1968].

Robert J. Alexander, **Communism in Latin America** [New Brunswick: Rutgers University Press, 1957].

Robert J. Alexander, **The Bolivian National Revolution** [New Brunswick: Rutgers University Press, 1958].

Robert J. Alexander and Charles O. Porter, **The Struggle for Democracy in Latin America** [New York: Macmillan, 1961].

Robert J. Alexander, **Prophets of the Revolution: Profiles of Latin American Leaders** [New York: Macmillan, 1962].

Robert J. Alexander, **Labor Relations in Argentina, Brazil and Chile** [New York: McGraw Hill, 1962].

Robert J. Alexander, **Today's Latin America** [Garden City: Anchor Books, 1962].

Robert J. Alexander, **Today's Latin America** [Garden City: Anchor Books, second revised edition 1968; first published 1962].

Robert J. Alexander, **The Venezuelan Democratic Revolution** [New Brunswick: Rutgers University Press, 1964].

Robert J. Alexander, **Organized Labor in Latin America** [New York: Free Press, 1965].

Robert J. Alexander, **The Communist Party of Venezuela** [Stanford: Hoover Institution Press-Stanford University, 1969].

Robert J. Alexander, **Trotskyism in Latin America** [Stanford: Hoover Institution Press-Stanford University, 1973].

Robert J. Alexander, **Agrarian Reform in Latin America** [New York: Macmillan, 1974].

Robert J. Alexander, **The Right Opposition: The Lovestoneites and the International Communist Opposition of the 1930s** [Westport: Greenwood Press, 1981].

Graham T. Allison, **Essence of Decision: Explaining the Cuban Missile Crisis** [Boston: Little Brown, 1971].

T. D. Allman, **Unmanifest Destiny: Mayhem and Illusion in American Foreign Policy: From the Monroe Doctrine to Reagan's War in El Salvador** [Garden City: Doubleday, 1984].

Gabriel A. Almond et al., **The Appeals of Communism** [Princeton University Press, 1965; first published 1954].

Gabriel A. Almond, **The American People and Foreign Policy** [New York: Praeger, 1965].

Gabriel A. Almond and G. Bingham Powell, **Comparative Politics: A Developmental Approach** [Boston: Little Brown, 1966].

Gabriel A. Almond, Scott C. Flanagan et al., **Crises, Choice, and Change: Historical Studies of Political Development** [Boston: Little Brown, 1973].

Stephen Ambrose, **Rise to Globalism: American Foreign Policy Since 1938** [London: Penguin Books, 1991, sixth revised edition; first published 1971].

Samir Amin, **Accumulation on a World Scale: A Critique of the Theory of Underdevelopment** [Sussex: Harvester Press, 1974].

Samir Amin, **Unequal Development: An Essay on the Social Formations of Peripheral Capitalism** [New York: Monthly Review Press, 1976].

Samir Amin, **Imperialism and Unequal Development** [New York: Monthly Review Press, 1977].

Benedict Anderson, **Imagined Communities: Reflections on the Origin and Spread of Nationalism** [London: Verso, revised and extended edition 1991; first published 1983].

Charles W. Anderson, **Politics and Economic Change in Latin America: The Governing of Restless Nations** [Princeton: D. Van Nostrand, 1967].

Perry Anderson, **Passages from Antiquity to Feudalism** [London: New Left

Books, 1974].

Perry Anderson, **Lineages of the Absolutist State** [London: New Left Books, 1974].

Thomas P. Anderson, **Matanza: El Salvador's Communist Revolt of 1932** [Lincoln: University of Nebraska Press, 1971].

Thomas P. Anderson, **The War of the Dispossessed** [Lincoln: University of Nebraska Press, 1981].

Thomas P. Anderson, **Politics in Central America: Guatemala, El Salvador, Honduras and Nicaragua** [New York: Praeger, 1982].

Stanislav Andreski, **Parasitism and Subversion: The Case of Latin America** [London: Weidenfeld and Nicolson, 1966].

David E. Apter, **The Gold Coast in Transition** [Princeton: Princeton University Press, 1955].

David E. Apter, **The Politics of Modernization** [Chicago: University of Chicago Press, 1969; first published 1965].

David E. Apter, **Rethinking Development: Modernization, Dependency and Postmodern Politics** [Beverly Hills: Sage Publications, 1987].

Juan José Arévalo, **Guatemala: La democracia y el imperio** [Buenos Aires: Editorial Renacimiento, revised edition 1955].

Juan José Arévalo, **Fabula del tiburon y las sardinas: América Latina estrangulada** [Buenos Aires: Meridion, 1956].

Juan José Arévalo, **The Shark and the Sardines,** [New York: Lyle Stuart, 1961; first published in 1956 in Spanish as **Fabula del tiburon y las sardinas: América Latina estrangulada**].

Juan José Arévalo, **Anti-Kommunism in Latin America** [New York: Lyle Stuart, 1964; first published in 1959 in Spanish as **Antikomunismo en América Latina**].

Hadley Arkes, **Bureaucracy, the Marshall Plan, and the National Interest** [Princeton: Princeton University Press, 1973].

Robert Armstrong, Hank Frundt, Hobart Spalding and Sean Sweeney, **Working Against US: The American Institute for Free Labour Development (AIFLD) in El Salvador and the International Policy of the AFL-CIO** [New York: Monthly Review Press, 1988].

Cynthia Arnson, Delia Miller and Roland Seeman, **Background Information on Guatemala, the Armed Forces and US Military Assistance** [Washington: Institute for Policy Studies, 1981].

Cynthia Arnson and Flora Montealegre, **Background Information on Guatemala, Human Rights and US Military Assistance** [Washington: Institute for Policy Studies, 1982].

Cynthia Arnson, **El Salvador: A Revolution Confronts the United States** [Washington: Institute for Policy Studies, 1982].

Cynthia Arnson, **Crossroads: Congress, the Reagan Administration, and Central America** [New York: Pantheon, 1989].

Giovanni Arrighi, Terence K. Hopkins and Immanuel Wallerstein, **Antisystemic Movements** [London: Verso, 1989].

Timothy Ashby, **The Bear in the Backyard: Moscow's Caribbean Strategy** [Lexington: Lexington Books, 1987].

T. H. Aston and C. H. E. Philpin, eds., **The Brenner Debate: Agrarian**

Class Structure and Economic Development in Pre-Industrial Europe [Cambridge: Cambridge University Press, 1985].

G. Pope Atkins and Larman C. Wilson, **The United States and the Trujillo Regime** [New Brunswick: Rutgers University Press, 1972].

Enrico Augelli and Craig Murphy, **America's Quest for Supremacy and the Third World: A Gramscian Analysis** [London: Pinter, 1988].

José M. Aybar de Soto, **Dependency and Intervention: The Case of Guatemala in 1954** [Boulder: Westview Press, 1978].

Amiya Kumar Bagchi, **The Political Economy of Development** [Cambridge: Cambridge University Press, 1982].

Bruce M. Bagley, Roberto Alvarez and Katherine Hagedorn, eds., **Contadora and the Central American Peace Process: Selected Documents** [Boulder: Westview Press, 1985].

Bishara Bahbah, **Israel and Latin America: The Military Connection** [New York: St. Martin's Press, 1986].

Samuel L. Baily, **The United States and the Development of South America 1945-1975** [New York: Franklin Watts, 1976].

H. Foster Bain, **Ores and Industry in South America** [New York: Harper and Row, 1934, for the Council on Foreign Relations].

David A. Baldwin, **Economic Development and American Foreign Policy 1943-1962** [Chicago: University of Chicago Press, 1966].

Enrique Baloyra, **El Salvador in Transition** [Chapel Hill: University of North Carolina Press, 1983; first published 1982].

Hubert Howe Bancroft, **History of Central America** (3 vols.) [San Francisco: A. L. Bancroft, 1882-1887].

Robert C. Bannister, **Social Darwinism: Science and Myth in Anglo-American Thought** [Philadelphia: Temple University Press, 1988; first published 1979].

Robert C. Bannister, **Sociology and Scientism: The American Quest for Objectivity** [Chapel Hill: University of North Carolina Press, 1987].

John Francis Bannon, **Herbert Eugene Bolton: The Historian and the Man 1870-1953** [Tucson: University of Arizona Press, 1978].

Paul A. Baran, **The Political Economy of Growth** [New York: Monthly Review Press, 1957].

Paul A. Baran and Paul Sweezy, **Monopoly Capital: An Essay on the American Economic and Social Order** [New York: Monthly Review Press, 1966].

Willard F. Barber and C. Neale Ronning, **Internal Security and Military Power: Counterinsurgency and Civic Action in Latin America** [Columbus: Ohio State University Press, 1966].

Richard J. Barnet, **Intervention and Revolution: The United States in the Third World** [London: MacGibbon and Kee, 1970; first published 1968].

Richard J. Barnet, **Roots of War: The Men and Institutions Behind US Foreign Policy** [Baltimore: Pelican Books, 1973].

Richard J. Barnet and Ronald E. Müller, **Global Reach: The Power of the Multinational Corporations** [London: Jonathan Cape, 1975; first published 1974].

Richard J. Barnet, **The Giants: Russia and America** [New York: Simon and Schuster, 1977].

Richard J. Barnet, **The Lean Years: Politics in the Age of Scarcity** [New York: Simon and Schuster, 1980].

Richard J. Barnet, **Real Security: Restoring American Power in a Dangerous Decade** [New York: Simon and Schuster, 1981].

Richard J. Barnet, **Allies: America, Europe and Japan Since the War** [London: Jonathan Cape, 1984].

Tom Barry, Beth Wood and Deb Preusch, **Dollars and Dictators: A Guide to Central America** [Albuquerque: Inter-Hemispheric Education Resource Center, 1982; reprinted London: Zed Press, 1982].

Tom Barry, Beth Wood and Deb Preusch, **The Other Side of Paradise: Foreign Control in the Caribbean** [New York: Grove Press, 1984].

Tom Barry, **Low-Intensity Conflict: The New Battlefield in Central America** [Albuquerque: Inter-Hemispheric Education Resource Center, 1986].

Tom Barry, **Guatemala: The Politics of Counterinsurgency** [Albuquerque: Inter-Hemispheric Education Resource Center, 1986].

Tom Barry and Deb Preusch, **The Central America Fact Book** [New York: Grove Press, 1986].

Tom Barry, **Roots of Rebellion: Land and Hunger in Central America** [Boston: South End Press, 1987].

Tom Barry and Deb Preusch, **AIFLD in Central America: Agents as Organizers** [Albuquerque: Inter-Hemispheric Education Resource Center; first published 1987, updated 1990].

Tom Barry and Deb Preusch, **The Soft War: The Uses and Abuses of US Economic Aid in Central America** [New York: Grove Press, 1988].

Tom Barry and Rachel Garst, **Feeding the Crisis: US Food Aid and Farm Policy in Central America** [Lincoln: Nebraska University Press, 1990].

Roland Barthes, **Mythologies** [London: Paladin, 1976; first published 1973].

P. T. Bauer, **Equality, the Third World, and Economic Delusion** [Cambridge: Harvard University Press, 1981].

P. T. Bauer, **Reality and Rhetoric: Studies in the Economics of Development** [London: Weidenfeld and Nicolson, 1984].

Jean-François Bayart, **The State in Africa: The Politics of the Belly** [London: Longman, 1993; first published in French in 1989 as **L'Etat en Afrique: la politique du ventre**].

Carleton Beals, **Brimstone and Chili: A Book of Personal Experiences in the Southwest and Mexico** [New York: Alfred A. Knopf, 1927].

Carleton Beals, **Mexican Maze** [Philadelphia: J. B. Lippincott, 1931].

Carleton Beals, **Banana Gold** [Philadelphia: J. B. Lippincott, 1932; reprinted New York: Arno Press, 1970].

Carleton Beals, **The Crime of Cuba** [Philadelphia: J. B. Lippincott, 1933].

Carleton Beals, **Fire on the Andes** [Philadelphia: J. B. Lippincott, 1934].

Carleton Beals, **The Coming Struggle for Latin America** [Philadelphia: J. B. Lippincott, 1937].

Carleton Beals, Bryce Oliver, Herschell Brickell, Samuel Guy Inman, **What the**

South Americans Think of Us [New York: McBride, 1945].

Charles A. Beard (and George H. E. Smith), **The Idea of National Interest: An Analytical Study in American Foreign Policy** [New York: Macmillan, 1934, reprinted Chicago: Quadrangle Books, 1966].

Charles A. Beard (and George H. E. Smith), **The Open Door at Home** [New York: Macmillan, 1934].

Charles A. Beard, **American Foreign Policy in the Making 1932-1940: A Study in Responsibilities** [New York: Harper and Brothers, 1944].

Carl L. Becker, **How New Will the Better World Be?: A Discussion of Post War Reconstruction** [New York: 1944].

David G. Becker, **The New Bourgeoisie and the Limits of Dependency: Mining, Class and Power in "Revolutionary" Peru** [Princeton: Princeton University Press, 1983].

David G. Becker, Jeff Frieden, Sayre P. Schatz and Richard L. Sklar, **Postimperialism: International Capitalism and Development in the Late Twentieth Century** [Boulder: Lynne Rienner, 1987].

Ali Behdad, **Belated Travelers: Orientalism in the Age of Colonial Dissolution** [Durham: Duke University Press, 1994].

J. P. Bell, **Crisis in Costa Rica** [Austin: University of Texas Press, 1971].

Samuel Flagg Bemis, **Jay's Treaty: A Study in Commerce and Diplomacy** [New York: Macmillan, 1923; revised edition New Haven: Yale University Press, 1962].

Samuel Flagg Bemis, **Pinckney's Treaty: A Study of America's Advantage from Europe's Distress, 1783-1800** [Baltimore: Johns Hopkins University Press, 1926].

Samuel Flagg Bemis, ed., **The American Secretaries of State and Their Diplomacy** (10 vols.) [New York: Alfred A. Knopf, 1927-1929; reprinted New York: Pageant, 1958].

Samuel Flagg Bemis, **The Hussey-Cumberland Mission and American Independence: An Essay in the Diplomacy of the American Revolution** [Princeton: Princeton University Press, 1931].

Samuel Flag Bemis and Grace Gardner Griffin, eds., **Guide to the Diplomatic History of the United States** [Washington: US Government Printing Office, 1935; reprinted Gloucester: Peter Smith, 1959].

Samuel Flagg Bemis, **The Diplomacy of the American Revolution** [New York: Appleton-Century, 1935; third edition Bloomington: Indiana University Press, 1957].

Samuel Flagg Bemis, **The United States as a World Power: A Diplomatic History 1900-1950** [New York: Henry Holt, 1950, revised and extended; first published 1936].

Samuel Flagg Bemis, **The United States as a World Power: A Diplomatic History 1900-1955** [New York: Henry Holt, revised edition 1955; first published 1936].

Samuel Flagg Bemis, **A Diplomatic History of the United States** [New York: Holt, 1936; second edition, revised and expanded 1942; third edition, revised and extended, 1950; fourth edition, revised and extended, 1955].

Samuel Flagg Bemis, **The Latin American Policy of the United States: An Historical Interpretation** [New York: Harcourt, Brace and World,

1943].

Samuel Flagg Bemis, **A Short History of American Foreign Policy and Diplomacy** [New York: Holt, 1959].

Reinhard Bendix, **Nation Building and Citizenship** [New York: John Wiley, 1964].

Jules R. Benjamin, **The United States and Cuba: Hegemony and Dependent Development 1880-1934** [Pittsburgh: University of Pittsburgh Press, 1977].

Jules R. Benjamin, **The United States and the Origins of the Cuban Revolution: An Empire of Liberty in an Age of National Liberation** [Princeton: Princeton University Press, 1990].

Peter L. Berger and Michael Novak, **Speaking to the Third World: Essays on Democracy and Development** [Washington: American Enterprise Institute, 1985].

Albert Bergesen, **The Crises of the Capitalist World-Economy** [Beverly Hills: Sage, 1983].

C. Fred Bergsten, Thomas Horst and Theodore Moran, **American Multinationals and American Interests** [Washington: Brookings Institution, 1978].

Adolf A. Berle, **Power Without Property: A Development in American Political Economy** [New York: Harcourt Brace, 1959].

Adolf A. Berle, **Latin America--Diplomacy and Reality** [New York: Harper and Row, 1962, published for the Council on Foreign Relations].

Edward H. Berman, **The Influence of the Carnegie, Ford and Rockefeller Foundations on American Foreign Policy: The Ideology of Philanthropy** [Albany: State University of New York Press, 1983].

Karl Bermann, **Under the Big Stick: Nicaragua and the United States Since 1848** [Boston: South End Press, 1986].

Phillip Berryman, **What's Wrong in Central America and What to Do About It** [Philadelphia: American Friends Service Committee, 1983].

Phillip Berryman, **The Religious Roots of Rebellion: Christians in the Central American Revolutions** [Maryknoll, New York: Orbis, 1984].

Phillip Berryman, **Christians in Guatemala's Struggle** [London: Catholic Institute for International Relations, 1984].

Phillip Berryman, **Inside Central America: The Essential Facts Past and Present on El Salvador, Nicaragua, Honduras, Guatemala and Costa Rica** [New York: Pantheon, 1985]. (Also published as **Inside Central America: US Policy in Its New Vietnam** [London: Pluto Press, 1985].)

Edward Best, **US Policy and Regional Security in Central America** [New York: St. Martin's Press, 1987].

Percy W. Bidwell, **Raw Materials: A Study of American Foreign Policy** [New York: Greenwood Press, 1974; first published New York: Harper and Row, 1958, published for the Council on Foreign Relations].

Hiram Bingham, **Across South America** [Boston: Houghton Mifflin, 1911].

Hiram Bingham, **The Monroe Doctrine: An Obsolete Shibboleth** [New Haven: Yale University Press, 1913; third printing 1915; reprinted New York: DaCapo Press, 1976].

Norman Birnbaum, **The Radical Renewal: The Politics of Ideas in Modern America** [New York: Pantheon, 1988].

Cyril E. Black, **The Dynamics of Modernization: A Study in Comparative History** [New York: Harper and Row, 1967; first published 1966].

Cyril E. Black and T. P. Thornton, eds., **Communism and Revolution: The Strategic Uses of Political Violence** [Princeton: Princeton University Press, 1964].

George Black, **The Triumph of the People: The Sandinista Revolution in Nicaragua** [London: Zed Press, 1981].

George Black (with Milton Jamail and Norma Stoltz Chinchilla), **Garrison Guatemala** [New York: Monthly Review Press, 1984].

George Black, **The Good Neighbor: How the United States Wrote the History of Central America and the Caribbean** [New York: Pantheon, 1988].

Jan Knippers Black, **The Dominican Republic: Politics and Development in an Unsovereign State** [Boston: Allen and Unwin, 1986].

Jan Knippers Black, **Sentinels of Empire: The United States and Latin American Militarism** [New York: Greenwood Press, 1986].

Robin Blackburn, **The Overthrow of Colonial Slavery 1776-1848** [London: Verso, 1988].

Henry R. Blaney, **The Golden Caribbean: A Winter Visit to the Republics of Colombia, Costa Rica, Spanish Honduras, Belize, the Spanish Main via Boston and New Orleans** [Boston: Lee and Shepard, 1900].

Cole Blasier, **The Hovering Giant: US Responses to Revolutionary Change in Latin America 1910-1976** [Pittsburgh: University of Pittsburgh Press, 1976].

Cole Blasier, **The Giant's Rival: The USSR and Latin America** [Pittsburgh: University of Pittsburgh Press, 1983].

Cole Blasier, **The Hovering Giant: US Responses to Revolutionary Change in Latin America 1910-1985** [Pittsburgh: University of Pittsburgh Press, revised edition 1985; first published 1976].

Maurice Bloch, **Marxism and Anthropology** [New York: Oxford University Press, 1985; first published 1983].

Sidney Blumenthal, **The Rise of the Counter-Establishment: From Conservative Ideology to Political Power** [New York: Times Books, 1986].

Herbert Eugene Bolton, **Athanase De Mézieres and the Louisiana-Texas Frontier 1768-1780** (2 vols.) [Cleveland: Clark, 1914].

Herbert Eugene Bolton, **Texas in the Middle Eighteenth Century: Studies in Spanish Colonial History and Administration** [Berkeley: University of California Press, 1915].

Herbert Eugene Bolton, **Spanish Exploration in the Southwest 1542-1706** [New York: Scribner's, 1916].

Herbert Eugene Bolton, with Thomas Maitland Marshall, **The Colonization of North America 1492-1783** [New York: Macmillan, 1920].

Herbert Eugene Bolton, **The Spanish Borderlands: A Chronicle of Old Florida and the Southwest** [New Haven: Yale University Press, 1921].

Herbert Eugene Bolton, with Ephraim Douglass Adams, **California's Story** [Boston: Allyn and Bacon, 1922].

Herbert Eugene Bolton, **Fray Juan Crespi: Missionary Explorer on the Pacific Coast 1769-1774** [Berkeley: University of California Press, 1927].

Herbert Eugene Bolton, **History of the Americas: A Syllabus with Maps** [Boston: Ginn, 1928].

Herbert Eugene Bolton, **Outpost of Empire: The Story of the Founding of San Francisco** [New York: Alfred A. Knopf, 1931].

Herbert Eugene Bolton, **Rim of Christendom: A Biography of Eusebio Francisco Kino, Pacific Coast Pioneer** [New York: Macmillan, 1936].

Herbert Eugene Bolton, **Wider Horizons of American History** [New York: Appleton-Century, 1939].

Raymond Bonner, **Weakness and Deceit: US Policy in El Salvador** [London: Hamish Hamilton, 1985; first published 1984].

Raymond Bonner, **Waltzing with a Dictator: The Marcoses and the Making of American Policy** [London: Macmillan, 1987].

Philip W. Bonsal, **Cuba, Castro and the United States** [Pittsburgh: University of Pittsburgh Press, 1971].

Stephen Bonsal, **The American Mediterranean** [New York: Moffat Yard, 1912].

John A. Booth, **The End and the Beginning: The Nicaraguan Revolution** [Boulder: Westview Press, 1982].

John A. Booth, **The End and the Beginning: The Nicaraguan Revolution** [Boulder: Westview Press, second edition 1985; first published 1982].

John A. Booth, Anne L. Howar, Lord Kennet, David Pfrimmer and Margaret Ellen Roggensack, **The 1985 Guatemalan National Elections: Will the Military Relinquish Power?** [Washington: International Human Rights Law Group and Washington Office on Latin America, 1985].

John A. Booth, David Carliner, Joseph Eldridge, Margaret Ellen Roggensack and Bonnie Teneriello, **Political Transition and the Rule of Law in Guatemala** [Washington: International Human Rights Law Group and Washington Office on Latin America, 1988].

John A. Booth and Thomas W. Walker, **Understanding Central America** [Boulder: Westview Press, 1989].

L. Francis Bouchey and Alberto M. Piedra, **Guatemala: A Promise in Peril** [Washington: Council for Inter-American Security, 1980].

Anthony T. Bouscaren, **Imperial Communism** [New York: Greenwood Press, 1975; first published 1953].

Spruille Braden, **Syllabus on the Communist Threat in the Americas** [New York: Lecture Before the Great Issues Course at Dartmouth College March 12, 1953, reprinted by New York Public Library].

D. A. Brading, **The First America: The Spanish Monarchy, Creole patriots and the Liberal state 1492-1867** [Cambridge: Cambridge

University Press, 1991].

Ben Bradlee, **Guts and Glory: The Rise and Fall of Oliver North** [London: Grafton, 1988].

H. W. Brands, Jr., **Cold Warriors: Eisenhower's Generation and American Foreign Policy** [New York: Columbia University Press, 1988].

Willy Brandt, **North-South: A Programme for Survival--Report of the Independent Commission on International Development Issues** [London: Pan, 1980].

Sue Branford and Bernardo Kucinski, **The Debt Squads: The US, the Banks and Latin America** [London: Zed Books, 1988].

Fernand Braudel, **The Structures of Everyday Life: Civilization and Capitalism 15th--18th Century Volume 1** [New York: Harper and Row, 1981].

Fernand Braudel, **The Wheels of Commerce: Civilization and Capitalism 15th--18th Century Volume 2** [New York: Harper and Row, 1982].

Fernand Braudel, **The Perspective of the World: Civilization and Capitalism 15th--18th Century Volume 3** [New York: Harper and Row, 1984].

Philip Brenner, **From Confrontation to Negotiation: US Relations with Cuba** [Boulder: Westview Press, 1988, a PACCA Book].

Anthony Brewer, **Marxist Theories of Imperialism: A Critical Survey** [London: Routledge and Kegan Paul, 1980].

Anthony Brewer, **Marxist Theories of Imperialism: A Critical Survey** [London: Routledge revised edition 1990; first published 1980].

John A. Britton, **Carleton Beals: A Radical Journalist in Latin America** [Albuquerque: University of New Mexico Press, 1987].

John A. Britton, **Revolution and Ideology: The Image of the Mexican Revolution in the United States 1910-1960** [Lexington: University Press of Kentucky, 1994].

Charles D. Brockett, **Land, Power, and Poverty: Agrarian Transformation and Political Conflict in Central America** [Boston: Unwin Hyman, 1988].

Charles D. Brockett, **Land, Power, and Poverty: Agrarian Transformation and Political Conflict in Central America** [Boston: Unwin Hyman, revised edition 1990; first published 1988].

Stephen Eric Bronner, **Moments of Decision: Political History and the Crises of Radicalism** [New York: Routledge, 1992].

Charles H. Brown, **Agents of Manifest Destiny: The Lives and Times of the Filibusters** [Chapel Hill: University of North Carolina Press, 1980].

Cynthia Brown, Alfred Stepan, Holly Burkhalter, Robert K. Goldman, Juan Mendez, Allan Nairn and Aryeh Neier, **With Friends Like These: The Americas Watch Report on Human Rights and US Policy in Latin America** [New York: Pantheon, 1985].

W. Norman Brown, **The United States and India and Pakistan** [Cambridge: Harvard University Press, revised edition, 1963; first published 1953].

W. Norman Brown, **The United States and India, Pakistan and Bangladesh** [Cambridge: Harvard University Press, third edition 1972].

David Browning, **El Salvador: Landscape and Society** [New York: Oxford University Press, 1971].

Zbigniew Brzezinski, **Between Two Ages: America's Role in the Technetronic Era** [London: Penguin, 1976; first published New York: Viking, 1970].

Zbigniew Brzezinski, **Power and Principle: Memoirs of the National Security Adviser 1977-1981** [London: Weidenfeld and Nicolson, 1983].

Zbigniew Brzezinski, **The Grand Failure: The Birth and Death of Communism in the Twentieth Century** [New York: Macmillan, 1990].

Tom Buckley, **Violent Neighbors: El Salvador, Central America and the United States** [New York: Times Books, 1984].

Raymond Leslie Buell, **The Central Americas** [New York: Foreign Policy Association, Pamphlet no. 69, December 1930].

Raymond Leslie Buell, **Liberia: Century of Survival** [Philadelphia: University of Pennsylvania Press, 1947].

Paul Buhle, **Marxism in the USA: From 1870 to the Present Day** [London: Verso, 1987].

Victor Bulmer-Thomas, **The Political Economy of Central America Since 1920** [Cambridge: Cambridge University Press, 1987].

Roger Burbach and Patricia Flynn, **Agribusiness in the Americas** [New York: Monthly Review Press, 1980].

Roger Burbach and Orlando Nuñez, **Fire in the Americas: Forging a Revolutionary Agenda** [London: Verso, 1987].

William A. M. Burden, **The Struggle for Airways in Latin America** [New York: Harper and Row, 1943, for the Council on Foreign Relations].

Peter Burke, **The French Historical Revolution: The Annales School 1929-1989** [Cambridge: Polity Press, 1990].

Peter Burke, **History and Social Theory** [Ithaca: Cornell University Press, 1993].

E. Bradford Burns, **The Unwritten Alliance: Rio Branco and Brazilian-American Relations** [New York: Columbia University Press, 1966].

E. Bradford Burns, **Latin America: A Concise Interpretive History** [Englewood Cliffs: Prentice Hall, 1972].

E. Bradford Burns, **A History of Brazil** [New York: Columbia University Press, 1980, second edition].

E. Bradford Burns, **The Poverty of Progress: Latin America in the 19th Century** [Berkeley: University of California Press, 1980].

E. Bradford Burns, **Eadweard Muybridge in Guatemala 1875: The Photographer as Social Recorder** [Berkeley: University of California Press, 1986].

E. Bradford Burns, **At War in Nicaragua: The Reagan Doctrine and the Politics of Nostalgia** [New York: Harper and Row, 1987].

James MacGregor Burns, **The Power to Lead: The Crisis of the American Presidency** [New York: Simon and Schuster, 1984].

Robert N. Burr, **Our Troubled Hemisphere: Perspectives on US-Latin American Relations** [Washington: Brookings Institution, 1967].

Archer C. Bush, **Organized Labor in Guatemala 1944-1949: A Case Study of an Adolescent Labor Movement in an Underdeveloped Country** [Hamilton: Colgate University, 1950].

Ruth Lapham Butler, ed., **Guide to the Hispanic American Historical Review 1918-1945** [Durham: Duke University Press, 1950; reprinted New York: Kraus Reprint, 1970].

Manuel Caballero, **Latin America and the Comintern 1919-1943** [Cambridge: Cambridge University Press, 1986].

John Moors Cabot, **Toward Our Common American Destiny** [Medford: Fletcher School of Law and Diplomacy, 1954].

Bruce J. Calder, **The Impact of Intervention: The Dominican Republic During the US Occupation of 1916-1924** [Austin: University of Texas Press, 1984].

James Morton Callahan, **An Introduction to American Expansion Policy** [Morgantown: West Virginia University Studies in American History, 1908].

James Morton Callahan, **American Foreign Policy in Mexican Relations** [New York: Cooper Square, 1967; first published 1932].

Wilfrid Hardy Callcott, **Church and State in Mexico 1822-1857** [Durham: Duke University Press, 1926].

Wilfrid Hardy Callcott, **Liberalism in Mexico 1857-1929** [Stanford: Stanford University Press, 1931].

Wilfrid Hardy Callcott, **Santa Anna, The Story of an Enigma Who Once Was Mexico** [Tulsa: Oklahoma University Press, 1936].

Wilfrid Hardy Callcott, **The Caribbean Policy of the United States 1890-1920** [Baltimore: Johns Hopkins University Press, 1942, reprinted New York: Octagon Books, 1966].

Wilfrid Hardy Callcott, **The Western Hemisphere: Its Influence on United States Policies to the End of World War II** [Austin: University of Texas Press, 1968].

David P. Calleo, **Beyond American Hegemony: The Future of the Western Alliance** [New York: Basic Books, 1987, a Twentieth Century Fund Book].

Alex Callinicos, **The Revenge of History: Marxism and the Eastern European Revolutions** [Cambridge: Polity Press, 1991].

Peter Calvert, **Guatemala: A Nation in Turmoil** [Boulder: Westview Press, 1985].

Daniel Cantor and Juliet Schor, **Tunnel Vision: Labor, the World Economy, and Central America** [Boston: South End Press, 1987].

James C. Carey, **Peru and the United States 1900-1962** [Notre Dame: University of Notre Dame Press, 1963].

Thomas Carothers, **In the Name of Democracy: US Policy Toward Latin America in the Reagan Years** [Berkeley: University of California Press, 1991].

Frank G. Carpenter, **Lands of the Caribbean: The Canal Zone, Panama, Costa Rica, Nicaragua, Salvador, Honduras, Guatemala, Cuba,**

Jamaica, Haiti, Santo Domingo, Porto Rico, and the Virgin Islands [Garden City: Doubleday, 1925].

Rhys Carpenter, **The Land Beyond Mexico** [Boston: R. G. Badger, 1920].

Jorge Castañeda, **Utopia Unarmed: The Latin American Left after the Cold War** [New York: Alfred A. Knopf, 1993].

David Caute, **The Fellow Travellers: Intellectual Friends of Communism** [New Haven: Yale University Press, revised edition 1988; first published 1973].

David Caute, **The Great Fear: The Anti-Communist Purge Under Truman and Eisenhower** [New York: Simon and Schuster, 1978].

Marta Cehelsky, **Guatemala's Frustrated Revolution: The Liberation of 1954** [Unpublished MA thesis, Columbia University, 1967].

James Chace, **Solvency: The Price of Survival--An Essay on American Foreign Policy** [New York: Random House, 1981].

James Chace, **Endless War: How We Got Involved in Central America--And What Can Be Done** [New York: Vintage Press, 1984].

James Chace, **The Consequences of the Peace: The New Internationalism and American Foreign Policy** [New York: Oxford Unviersity Press/Twentieth Century Fund, 1992].

Richard D. Challener, **Admirals, Generals and American Foreign Policy 1898-1914** [Princeton: Princeton University Press, 1973].

Charles E. Chapman, **A History of the Cuban Republic: A Study in Hispanic-American Politics** [New York: Macmillan, 1927].

Richard Bruce Chardkoff, **Communist Toehold in the Americas: A History of Official United States Involvement in the Guatemalan Crisis, 1954** [Unpublished PhD dissertation, Florida State University, 1967].

Christopher Chase-Dunn, **Global Formation: Structures of the World-Economy** [London: Basil Blackwell, 1989].

Partha Chatterjee, **Nationalist Thought and the Colonial World: A Derivative Discourse** [London: Zed Books, 1986].

Ronald H. Chilcote, **Portuguese Africa** [Englewood Cliffs: Prentice-Hall, 1967].

Ronald H. Chilcote, **Revolution and Structural Change in Latin America: A Bibliography on Ideology, Development and the Radical Left 1930-1965** (2 vols.) [Stanford: Hoover Institution, Stanford University Press, 1970].

Ronald H. Chilcote, **Protest and Resistance in Angola and Brazil** [Berkeley: University of California Press, 1972].

Ronald H. Chilcote, **The Brazilian Communist Party: Conflict and Integration 1922-1972** [New York: Oxford University Press, 1974].

Ronald H. Chilcote, **Theories of Comparative Politics: The Search for a Paradigm** [Boulder: Westview Press, 1981].

Ronald H. Chilcote, **Theories of Development and Underdevelopment** [Boulder: Westview Press, 1984].

Ronald H. Chilcote and Joel C. Edelstein, **Latin America: Capitalist and Socialist Perspectives of Development and Underdevelopment** [Boulder: Westview Press, 1986]. (This is a completely revised and expanded version of the authors' introduction to **Latin America: The Struggle with Dependency and Beyond**, published in 1974.)

Jack Child, **Geopolitics and Conflicts in South America: Quarrels Among Neighbors** [New York: Praeger, 1985].

John Child, **Unequal Alliance: The Inter-American Military System 1938-1979** [Boulder: Westview Press, 1980].

Daniel Chirot, **Social Change in a Peripheral Society: The Creation of a Balkan Colony** [New York: Academic Press, 1976].

Daniel Chirot, **Social Change in the Twentieth Century** [New York: Harcourt, Brace and Jovanovich, 1977].

Daniel Chirot, **Social Change in the Modern Era** [New York: Harcourt, Brace and Jovanovich, 1986].

Noam Chomsky, **American Power and the New Mandarins** [New York: Pantheon, 1968; second edition 1969].

Noam Chomsky, **At War with Asia** [London: Fontana, second edition 1971; first published 1969].

Noam Chomsky, **For Reasons of State** [London: Fontana, 1973; first published 1970].

Noam Chomsky, **The Political Economy of Human Rights--volume 1: The Washington Connection and Third World Fascism** [Sydney: Hale and Iremonger, 1980].

Noam Chomsky, **The Political Economy of Human Rights--volume 2: After the Cataclysm** [Sydney: Hale and Iremonger, 1980].

Noam Chomsky, **Turning the Tide: US Intervention in Central America and the Struggle for Peace** [Boston: South End Press, 1985].

Noam Chomsky, **Turning the Tide: The US and Latin America** [New York: Black Rose Books, revised edition 1987; first published 1985].

Noam Chomsky, **Pirates and Emperors: International Terrorism in the Real World** [Montreal: Black Rose Books, 1987].

Noam Chomsky, **On Power and Ideology** [Montreal: Black Rose Books, 1987].

Noam Chomsky (edited by James Peck), **The Chomsky Reader** [New York: Pantheon, 1987].

Noam Chomsky, **The Culture of Terrorism** [Montreal: Black Rose Books, 1988].

Noam Chomsky and Edward S. Herman, **Manufacturing Consent: The Political Economy of the Mass Media** [New York: Pantheon, 1988].

Noam Chomsky, **Necessary Illusions: Thought Control in Democratic Societies** [Boston: South End Press, 1989].

Noam Chomsky, **Deterring Democracy** [London: Verso, 1991].

Noam Chomsky, **Rethinking Camelot: JFK, the Vietnam War and US Political Culture** [London: Verso, 1991].

Noam Chomsky, **Year 501: The Conquest Continues** [London: Verso, 1993].

Noam Chomsky, **World Orders, Old and New** [London: Pluto, 1994].

Shirley Christian, **Nicaragua: Revolution in the Family** [New York: Random House, 1985].

Paul Coe Clark, **Diplomatic Relations Between the United States and the Somoza Regime 1933-1956** [Unpublished PhD dissertation, University of Alabama, 1988].

Charles Clements, **Witness to War: An American Doctor in El Salvador** [New York: Bantam Books, 1984].

Howard F. Cline, **The United States and Mexico** [Cambridge: Harvard University Press, 1965, revised edition].

Barbara Barksdale Close, **Brainpower for the Cold War: The Sputnik Crisis and the National Defense Education Act of 1958** [New York: Greenwood Press, 1981].

Leslie Cockburn, **Out of Control: The Story of the Reagan Administration's Secret War in Nicaragua, the Illegal Arms Pipeline, and the Contra Drug Connection** [New York: Atlantic Monthly Press, 1987].

James D. Cockcroft, **Intellectual Precursors of the Mexican Revolution** [Austin: University of Texas Press, 1968].

James D. Cockcroft, Andre Gunder Frank and Dale L. Johnson, **Dependence and Underdevelopment: Latin America's Political Economy** [Garden City: Anchor Books, 1972].

James D. Cockcroft, **Mexico: Class Formation, Capital Accumulation and the State** [New York: Monthly Review Press, 1983].

Joshua Cohen and Joel Rogers, **Inequity and Intervention: The Federal Budget and Central America** [Boston: South End Press, 1986].

Joshua Cohen and Joel Rogers, **The Rules of the Game: American Politics and the Central American Movement** [Boston: South End Press, 1986].

Paul A. Cohen, **Discovering History in China: American Historical Writing on the Recent Chinese Past** [New York: Columbia University Press, 1984].

Warren I. Cohen, **The American Revisionists: The Lessons of Intervention in World War One** [Chicago: University of Chicago Press, 1967].

Warren I. Cohen, **Empire Without Tears: American Foreign Relations 1921-1933** [Philadelphia: Temple University Press, 1987].

Forrest D. Colburn, **Post-Revolutionary Nicaragua: State, Class and the Dilemmas of Agrarian Policy** [Berkeley: University of California Press, 1986].

Ruth Berins Collier and David Collier, **Shaping the Political Arena: Critical Junctures, The Labor Movement, and Regime Dynamics in Latin America** [Princeton: Princeton University Press, 1991].

Richard H. Collin, **Theodore Roosevelt, Culture, Diplomacy and Expansion: A New View of American Imperialism** [Baton Rouge: Louisiana State University Press, 1985].

Richard H. Collin, **Theodore Roosevelt's Caribbean: The Panama Canal, The Monroe Doctrine and the Latin American Context** [Baton Rouge: Louisiana State University Press, 1990].

Joseph Collins (with Frances Moore Lappé, Nick Allen and Paul Rice),

Nicaragua: What Difference Could a Revolution Make? [San Francisco: Institute for Food and Development Policy, 1982].

Joseph Collins (with Frances Moore Lappé, Nick Allen and Paul Rice), **Nicaragua: What Difference Could a Revolution Make?--Food and Farming in the New Nicaragua** [New York: Grove Press, 1986, third edition, revised and updated; first published, 1982].

Jerald A. Combs, **American Diplomatic History: Two Centuries of Changing Interpretations** [Berkeley: University of California Press, 1983].

Jerald A. Combs, **The History of American Foreign Policy** [New York: Alfred A. Knopf, 1986].

Commission on United States-Latin American Relations (Sol M. Linowitz, chair), **The Americas in a Changing World** [Chicago: Quadrangle Press, 1976].

Commission on United States-Latin American Relations (Sol Linowitz, chair), **The United States and Latin America: Next Steps** [New York: Center for Inter-American Relations, 1976].

Committee of Santa Fe (Lewis Tambs, ed.), **A New Inter-American Policy for the Eighties: Report of the Committee of Santa Fe** [Washington: Council for Inter-American Security, 1980].

Committee of Santa Fe, **Santa Fe II: A Strategy for Latin America in the Nineties** [Washington: Council for Inter-American Security, 1989].

Gordon Connell-Smith, **The Inter-American System** [London: Oxford University Press, 1966].

Gordon Connell-Smith, **The United States and Latin America: An Historical Analysis of Inter-American Relations** [London: Heinemann, 1974].

Gray L. Cowan, **A History of the School of International Affairs and Associated Area Institutes** [New York: Columbia University Press, 1954].

Paul Cowan, **The Making of an Un-American: A Dialogue with Experience** [New York: Viking Press, 1970].

Jefferson R. Cowie, **The Emergence of Alternative Views of Latin America: The Thought of Three U.S. Intellectuals, 1920-1935** [Chapel Hill: Duke University Program in Latin American Studies, Working Paper #3, 1992].

Isaac Joslin Cox, **The Early Exploration of Louisiana** [Cincinnati: University of Cincinnati Press, 1906].

Isaac Joslin Cox, **The West Florida Controversy 1798-1813: A Study in American Diplomacy** [Baltimore: Johns Hopkins University Press, 1918].

Isaac Joslin Cox, **Nicaragua and the United States 1909-1927** [Boston: World Peace Foundation Pamphlets vol. 10. no. 7, 1927].

Robert W. Cox, **Production, Power and World Order: Social Forces in the Making of History** [New York: Columbia University Press, 1987].

Robert D. Crassweller, **The Caribbean Community: Changing Societies and US Policy** [New York: Praeger, 1972].

George W. Crichfield, **American Supremacy: The Rise and Progress of**

the Latin American Republics and Their Relations to the
United States Under the Monroe Doctrine (2 vols.) [New York:
Bentano's, 1908].

John A Crow, The Epic of Latin America [Garden City: Doubleday, 1946].

John A Crow, The Epic of Latin America [Berkeley: University of California
Press, fourth edition, 1992; first published 1946].

Samuel Crowthers, The Romance and Rise of the American Tropics
[Garden City: Doubleday Doran, 1929].

Lejeune Cummins, Quijote on a Burro: Sandino and the Marines, a
Study in the Formulation of Foreign Policy [Mexico: Impresora
Azteca, 1958].

Eugene Cunningham, Gypsing Through Central America [New York: E. P.
Dutton, 1922].

Robert Dallek, Franklin D. Roosevelt and American Foreign Policy
1932-1945 [New York: Oxford University Press, 1979].

Kevin Danaher, Philip Berryman and Medea Benjamin, Help or Hindrance?
United States Economic Aid in Central America [San Francisco:
Institute for Food and Development Policy, 1987].

Colin Danby, The Electoral Farce Ends, The War Continues: The
United States and the Salvadoran Elections [Cambridge: Central
American Information Office, 1982].

Philip Darby, The Three Faces of Imperialism: British and American
Approaches to Asia and Africa 1870-1970 [New Haven: Yale
University Press, 1987].

Phillip B. Davidson, Vietnam at War: The History 1946-1975 [London:
Pan, 1988].

David Brion Davis, The Problem of Slavery in Western Culture [Ithaca:
Cornell University Press, 1966].

David Brion Davis, The Problem of Slavery in the Age of Revolution
1770-1823 [Ithaca: Cornell University Press, 1975].

Harold Eugene Davis, John J. Finan and F. Taylor Peck, Latin American
Diplomatic History: An Introduction [Baton Rouge: Louisiana State
University Press, 1977].

Mike Davis, Prisoners of the American Dream: Politics and Economy
in the History of the US Working Class [London: Verso, 1987;
first published 1986].

Peter Davis, Where Is Nicaragua? [New York: Simon and Schuster, 1987].

Shelton H. Davis and Julie Hodson, Witness to Political Violence in
Guatemala: The Suppression of a Rural Movement [Boston:
Oxfam America, 1982].

Warren Dean, The Industrialization of Sao Paulo 1880-1945 [Austin:
University of Texas Press, 1969].

Alexander DeConde, Herbert Hoover's Latin American Policy [New York:
Octagon Books, 1970; first published Stanford University Press, 1951].

Alexander DeConde, American Diplomatic History in Transformation
[Washington: American Historical Association, 1976].

Alexander DeConde, A History of American Foreign Policy--volume II:
Global Power 1900 to the Present [New York: Charles Scribner,

third edition 1978; first published 1963].

Carmen Diana Deere, **In the Shadows of the Sun: Caribbean Development Alternatives and US Policy** [Boulder: Westview Press, 1990].

Carl N. Degler, **Neither Black nor White: Slavery and Race Relations in Brazil and the United States** [New York: Macmillan, 1971].

Helen Delpar, ed., **The Encyclopedia of Latin America** [New York: McGraw-Hill, 1974].

Helen Delpar, **The Enormous Vogue of Things Mexican: Cultural Relations Between the United States and Mexico 1920-1935** [Tuscaloosa: University of Alabama Press, 1992].

Lawrence Dennis, **The Dynamics of War and Revolution** [New York: The Weekly Foreign Letter, 1940].

Harold N. Denny, **Dollars for Bullets: The Story of American Rule in Nicaragua** [New York: Dial Press, 1929; reprinted New York: Greenwood Press, 1980].

Rafael de Nogales, **The Looting of Nicaragua** [New York: Mcbride, 1928].

James Der Derian, **On Diplomacy: A Genealogy of Western Estrangement** [Oxford: Basil Blackwell, 1991; first published 1987].

José Aybar de Soto, **Dependency and Intervention: The Case of Guatemala in 1954** [Boulder: Westview Press, 1978].

I. M. Destler, **Presidents, Bureaucrats, and Foreign Policy: The Politics of Organizational Reform** [Princeton: Princeton University Press, 1974].

Hermann B. Deutsch, **The Incredible Yanqui: The Career of Lee Christmas** [London: Longman Green, 1931].

Christopher Dickey, **With The Contras: A Reporter in the Wilds of Nicaragua** [London: Faber and Faber, 1986; first published New York: Simon and Schuster, 1985].

Paul Dickson, **Think Tanks** [New York: Atheneum, 1971].

Joan Didion, **Salvador** [London: Chatto and Windus, 1983].

Bernard Diedrich, **Somoza and the Legacy of US Involvement in Central America** [London: Junction Books, 1982].

Bailey W. Diffie and J. W. Diffie, **Porto Rico: A Broken Pledge** [New York: Vanguard Press, 1931].

John P. Diggins, **Up From Communism: Conservative Odysseys in American Intellectual History** [New York: Harper and Row, 1977; first published 1975].

John P. Diggins, **The Lost Soul of American Politics: Virtue, Self-Interest and the Foundations of Liberalism** [Chicago: University of Chicago Press, 1986; first published 1984].

Cleto DiGiovanni, Jr., **US Policy and the Marxist Threat to Central America** [Washington: Heritage Foundation, 1980].

Dorothy Dillon, **International Communism and Latin America: Perspectives and Prospects** [Gainesville: University of Florida Press, 1962].

David H. Dinwoodie, **Expedient Diplomacy: The United States and Guatemala 1898-1920** [Unpublished PhD dissertation, University of

Colorado, 1966].

Martin Diskin, **Reform Without Change in El Salvador: The Political War for the Countryside** [Boulder: Westview Press, 1990].

Robert A. Divine, **Eisenhower and the Cold War** [New York: Oxford University Press, 1981].

Marlene Dixon, **Things Which Are Done in Secret** [Montreal: Black Rose Books, 1976].

Marlene Dixon, ed., **On Trial: Reagan's War Against Nicaragua-- Testimony of the Permanent People's Tribunal** [London: Zed Books, 1985].

Thomas Joseph Dodd, Jr., **The United States in Nicaraguan Politics: Supervised Elections 1927-1932** [Unpublished PhD dissertation, George Washington University, 1966].

Michael Dodson and Laura Nuzzi O'Shaughnessy, **Nicaragua's Other Revolution: Religious Faith and Political Struggle** [Chapel Hill: University of North Carolina Press, 1990].

Jorge I. Domínguez, **Cuba: Order and Revolution** [Cambridge: Harvard University Press, 1978].

Jorge I. Domínguez, Nigel S. Rodley, Bryce Wood and Richard A. Falk, **Enhancing Global Human Rights** [New York: McGraw-Hill, 1979, published for the Council on Foreign Relations].

Jorge I. Domínguez, **Cuba: Internal and International Affairs** [Beverly Hills: Sage, 1982].

Jorge I. Domínguez, **US Interests and Policies in Central America and the Caribbean** [Washington: American Enterprise Institute, 1982].

Jorge I. Domínguez and Marc Lindenberg, **Central America: Current Crisis and Future Prospects** [New York: Foreign Policy Association, 1984, reprinted 1989].

Jorge I. Domínguez, **To Make a World Safe for Revolution: Cuba's Foreign Policy** [Cambridge: Harvard University Press, 1989].

John C. Donovan, **The Cold Warriors: A Policy Making Elite** [Lexington: D. C. Heath, 1974].

Paul Jaime Dosal, **Dependency, Revolution and Industrial Development in Guatemala 1821-1986** [Unpublished PhD dissertation, Tulane University, 1987].

Craig L. Dozier, **Nicaragua's Mosquito Shore: The Years of British and American Presence** [Tuscaloosa: University of Alabama Press, 1985].

Donald Marquand Dozer, **Are We Good Neighbours?: Three Decades of Inter-American Relations 1930-1960** [Gainesville: University of Florida Press, 1959; reprinted New York: Johnson Reprint, 1972].

Donald Marquand Dozer, **Latin America: An Interpretive History** [New York: McGraw-Hill, 1962].

Donald Marquand Dozer, **The Monroe Doctrine: Its Modern Significance** [New York: Alfred A. Knopf, 1965].

Donald Marquand Dozer, **The Challenge to Pan Americanism** [Tempe: Arizona State University, Center for Latin American Studies, 1972].

Donald Marquand Dozer, **The Panama Canal in Perspective** [Washington: Council on American Affairs, 1978].

Theodore Draper, **Abuse of Power** [New York: Viking Press, 1967]. Also published as **Abuse of Power: US Foreign Policy from Cuba to Vietnam** [London: Penguin Books, 1969].

Theodore Draper, **The Dominican Revolt: A Case Study in American Policy** [New York: A Commentary Report, 1968].

Theodore Draper, **A Very Thin Line: The Iran-Contra Affairs** [New York: Hill and Wang, 1991].

John C. Dreier, ed., **The Alliance for Progress: Problems and Perspectives** [Baltimore: Johns Hopkins University Press, 1962].

John C. Dreier, **The Organization of American States and the Hemisphere Crisis** [New York: Harper and Row, 1962, published for the Council on Foreign Relations].

Richard Drinnon, **Facing West: The Metaphysics of Indian Hating and Empire Building** [New York: Schocken Books, 1990; first published 1980].

Laurence Duggan, **The Americas: The Search for Hemispheric Security** [New York: Henry Holt, 1949].

Peter Duignan and L. H. Gann, **The United States and Africa: A History** [Cambridge: Cambridge University Press, 1984].

W. Raymond Duncan, **Latin American Politics: A Developmental Approach** [New York: Praeger, 1975].

W. Raymond Duncan, **The Soviet Union and Cuba: Interests and Influence** [New York: Praeger, 1985].

James Dunkerley, **The Long War: Dictatorship and Revolution in El Salvador** [London: Junction Books, 1982].

James Dunkerley, **Rebellion in the Veins: Political Struggle in Bolivia 1952-1982** [London: Verso, 1984].

James Dunkerley, **Power in the Isthmus: A Political History of Modern Central America** [London: Verso, 1988].

James Dunkerley, **Political Suicide in Latin America and Other Essays** [London: Verso, 1992].

James Dunkerley, **The Pacification of Central America: Political Change in the Isthmus, 1987-1993** [London: Verso, 1994].

William H. Durham, **Scarcity and Survival in Central America: Ecological Origins of the Soccer War** [Stanford: University of California Press, 1979].

John D. Early, **The Demographic Structure and Evolution of a Peasant System: The Guatemalan Population** [Boca Raton: University Presses of Florida, 1982].

Roland H. Ebel, **Political Modernization in Three Guatemalan Indian Communities** [New Orleans: Middle America Research Institute, 1969].

Nicholas Eberstadt, **Foreign Aid and American Purpose** [Washington: American Enterprise Institute, 1989].

Education and World Affairs, **The University Looks Abroad: Approaches to World Affairs at Six American Universities** [New York: Walker, 1965].

Milton S. Eisenhower, **The Wine is Bitter: The United States and Latin America** [Garden City: Doubleday, 1963].

S. N. Eisenstadt, **Modernization: Protest and Change** [Englewood Cliffs: Prentice-Hall, 1966].

S. N. Eisenstadt, **Tradition, Change and Modernity** [New York: Wiley, 1973].

S. N. Eisenstadt, **Revolution and the Transformation of Societies** [New York: Free Press, 1978].

Robert V. Elam, **Appeal to Arms: The Army and Politics in El Salvador 1931-1964** [Unpublished PhD dissertation, University of New Mexico, 1968].

J. H. Elliot, **The Old World and the New 1492-1650** [New York: Cambridge University Press, 1992; first published 1970].

S. L. Engerman and Eugene D. Genovese, eds., **Race and Slavery in the Western Hemisphere: Quantitative Studies** [Princeton: Princeton University Press, 1974].

Laura J. Enríquez, **Harvesting Change: Labor and Agrarian Reform in Nicaragua 1979-1990** [Chapel Hill: University of North Carolina Press, 1991].

H. Michael Erisman, **Cuba's International Relations: The Anatomy of a Nationalistic Foreign Policy** [Boulder: Westview Press, 1985].

Arturo Escobar, **Encountering Development: The Making and Unmaking of the Third World** [Princeton: Princeton University Press, 1995].

Donald Etchison, **The United States and Militarism in Central America** [New York: Praeger, 1975].

Lloyd S. Etheridge, **Can Governments Learn?: American Foreign Policy and Central American Revolutions** [New York: Pergamon Press, 1985].

Norman Etherington, **Theories of Imperialism: War, Conquest and Capital** [London: Croom Helm, 1983].

Paul Evans, **John King Fairbank and the American Understanding of Modern China** [Oxford: Basil Blackwell, 1988].

Peter Evans, **Dependent Development: The Alliance of Multinational, State and Local Capital in Brazil** [Princeton: Princeton University Press, 1979].

Richard R. Fagen, **Cuba: The Political Content of Adult Education** [Stanford: Hoover Institution, 1964].

Richard R. Fagen, **The Transformation of Political Culture in Cuba** [Stanford: Stanford University Press, 1969].

Richard R. Fagen, **The Nicaraguan Revolution: A Personal Report** [Washington: Institute for Policy Studies, 1981].

Richard R. Fagen, **Forging Peace: The Challenge of Central America** [New York: Basil Blackwell, 1987].

John Edwin Fagg, **Latin America: A General History** [New York: Macmillan, 1963].

John King Fairbank, **The United States and China** [Cambridge: Harvard University Press, 1983 fourth edition enlarged; first published 1948].

Mark Falcoff, **Small Countries, Large Issues: Studies in US-Latin American Asymmetries** [Washington: American Enterprise Institute,

1984].

Tom J. Farer, **The Grand Strategy of the United States in Latin America** [New Bruns

David Farnsworth and James McKenney, **US-Panama Relations 1903-1978: A Study in Linkage Politics** [Boulder: Westview Press, 1983].

Georges A. Fauriol et al., **The Cuban Revolution: 25 Years Later** [Boulder: Westview Press, 1984].

Georges A. Fauriol and Thomas H. Moorer, **Caribbean Basin Security** [New York: Praeger, 1984, The Washington Papers (CSIS)].

Georges A. Fauriol, **Foreign Policy Behaviour of Caribbean States: Guyana, Haiti and Jamaica** [New York: University Press of America, 1984].

Georges A. Fauriol, **Latin American Insurgencies** [Washington: National Defense University, 1985].

Georges A. Fauriol and Eva Loser, **Guatemala Election Study Report** [Washington: Georgetown University Center for Strategic and International Studies, 1986].

Georges A. Fauriol and Eva Loser, **Guatemala: A Political Puzzle** [New Brunswick: Transaction Books, 1988].

Georges A. Fauriol, **The Third Century: US Latin American Policy Choices for the 1990s** [Washington: Center for Strategic and International Studies, 1988].

Geoges A. Fauriol et al., **The United States and Brazil: Structuring a Mature Relationship** [Washington: Center for Strategic and International Studies Panel Reports, 1988].

Richard E. Feinberg, **The Triumph of Allende: Chile's Legal Revolution** [New York: New American Library, 1972].

Richard E. Feinberg, **Subsidizing Success: The Export-Import Bank in the US Economy** [Cambridge: Cambridge University Press, 1982].

Richard E. Feinberg, **The Intemperate Zone: The Third World Challenge to US Foreign Policy** [New York: W. W. Norton, 1983].

Richard E. Feinberg and Bruce M. Bagley, **Development Postponed: The Political Economy of Central America in the 1980s** [Boulder: Westview Press, 1986, for Central American and Caribbean Program School of Advanced International Studies, Johns Hopkins University].

Thomas P. Fenton and Mary J. Heffron, **Latin America and the Caribbean: A Directory of Resources** [London: Zed Books, 1986].

Willy Feuerlein and Elizabeth Hannan, **Dollars in Latin America** [New York: Harper and Row, 1941, for the Council on Foreign Relations].

D. K. Fieldhouse, **The Colonial Empires: A Comparative Survey from the Eighteenth Century** [London: Weidenfeld and Nicolson, 1971; first published 1966].

D. K. Fieldhouse, **Economics and Empire: 1830-1914** [London: Weidenfeld and Nicolson, 1973].

D. K. Fieldhouse, **Colonialism 1870-1945: An Introduction** [London: Weidenfeld and Nicolson, 1981].

D. K. Fieldhouse, **The Colonial Empires: A Comparative Survey from the Eighteenth Century** [London: Weidenfeld and Nicolson, second edition 1982; first published 1966].

J. Valerie Fifer, **United States' Perceptions of Latin America, 1850-1930: A 'New West' South of Capricorn?** [Manchester: Manchester University Press, 1991].

John E. Findling, **Close Neighbors, Distant Friends: United States-Central American Relations** [New York: Greenwood Press, 1987].

Albert Fishlow, Carlos Diaz-Alejandro, Richard R. Fagen and Roger D. Hansen, **Rich and Poor Nations in the World Economy** [New York: McGraw-Hill, 1978, published for the Council on Foreign Relations].

Frances Fitzgerald, **Fire in the Lake: The Vietnamese and the Americans in Vietnam** [Boston: Little Brown, 1972].

Russell H. Fitzgibbon, **Cuba and the United States 1900-1935** [Menasha: George Banta, 1935].

Ralph E. Flanders, **The American Century** [Cambridge: Harvard University Press, 1950].

Laura Foner and Eugene D. Genovese, eds., **Slavery in the New World: A Reader in Comparative History** [Englewood Cliffs: Prentice-Hall, 1969].

Roger W. Fontaine, **Brazil and the United States: Toward a Maturing Relationship** [Washington: American Enterprise Institute, 1974].

Roger W. Fontaine, **On Negotiating with Cuba** [Washington: American Enterprise Institute, 1975].

Roger W. Fontaine and James D. Theberge, **Latin America's New Internationalism: The End of Hemispheric Isolationism** [New York: Praeger, 1976].

David P. Forsythe, **Human Rights and US Foreign Policy** [Gainesville: University Presses of Florida, 1988].

Michel Foucault, **The Order of Things: An Archeology of the Human Sciences** [London: Tavistock, 1986; first published in English in 1970; originally published in French in 1966 as **Les Mots et les choses**].

Michel Foucault, **The Archaeology of Knowledge** [London: Tavistock, 1986; first published in English in 1972; originally published in French in 1969 as **L'Archéologie du savoir**].

Michel Foucault, **Discipline and Punish: The Birth of the Prison** [New York: Vintage Books, 1979; first published in 1975 in French as **Surveiller et punir: naissance de la prison**]

Michel Foucault, **The History of Sexuality--Volume One: An Introduction** [London: Allen Lane, 1979; first published in 1976 in French as **La Volonté de savoir**].

Alejandro Foxley, **Latin American Experiments in Neoconservative Economics** [Berkeley: University of California Press, 1983].

Andre Gunder Frank, **Capitalism and Underdevelopment in Latin America: Historical Studies of Chile and Brazil** [New York: Monthly Review Press, 1967, revised and enlarged edition 1969].

Andre Gunder Frank, **Latin America: Underdevelopment or Revolution: Essays on the Development of Underdevelopment and the Immediate Enemy** [New York: Monthly Review Press, 1969, second edition 1970].

Andre Gunder Frank, **Lumpen-Bourgeoisie, Lumpen-Development: Dependence, Class and Politics in Latin America** [New York: Monthly Review Press, 1972].

Andre Gunder Frank, **World Accumulation 1492-1789** [London: Macmillan, 1978].

Andre Gunder Frank, **Dependent Accumulation and Underdevelopment** [London: Macmillan, 1978].

Andre Gunder Frank, **Mexican Agriculture 1521-1630: Transformation of the Mode of Production** [Cambridge: Cambridge University Press, 1979].

Andre Gunder Frank, **Critique and Anti-Critique: Essays on Dependence and Reformism** [London: Macmillan, 1984].

George M. Fredrickson, **White Supremacy: A Comparative Study in American and South African History** [New York: Oxford University Press, 1981].

John D. French, **Robert J. Alexander: The Complete Bibliography of a Pioneering Latin Americanist** (Latin American Labor Studies Bibliographies vol. 3.) [Miami: Center for Labor Research and Studies, Florida International University, 1991].

Jonathan L. Fried, Marvin E. Gettleman, Deborah T. Levenson and Nancy Peckenham, eds., **Guatemala in Rebellion: Unfinished History** [New York: Grove Press, 1983].

Edward Friedman, **Ascent and Decline in the World-System** [Beverly Hills: Sage, 1982].

Francis Fukuyama, **The End of History and the Last Man** [London: Hamish Hamilton, 1992].

J. William Fulbright, **The Arrogance of Power** [London: Jonathan Cape, 1967].

J. William Fulbright, **The Crippled Giant: American Foreign Policy and Its Domestic Consequences** [New York: Random House, 1972].

J. William Fulbright, **The Price of Empire** [New York: Pantheon, 1989].

John Lewis Gaddis, **The United States and the Origins of the Cold War 1941-1947** [New York: Columbia University Press, 1973].

John Lewis Gaddis, **The Long Peace: Inquiries into the History of the Cold War** [New York: Oxford University Press, 1987].

John Kenneth Galbraith, **The Nature of Mass Poverty** [Cambridge: Harvard University Press, 1979].

Eduardo Galeano, **Guatemala: Occupied Country** [New York: Monthly Review Press, 1969; first published in Spanish in 1967 as **Guatemala: País Ocupado**].

Eduardo Galeano, **Open Veins of Latin America: Five Centuries of the Pillage of a Continent** [New York: Monthly Review Press, 1973; first published in Spanish in 1971 as **Las venas abiertas de América Latina**].

Manuel Galich, **Por que lucha Guatemala, Arévalo y Arbenz: Dos hombres contra un imperio** [Buenos Aires: Editora Elmer, 1956].

Thomas W. Gann, **Mystery Cities** [New York: Scribner's and Sons, 1925].

Thomas W. Gann, **Maya Cities** [New York: Scribner's and Sons, 1927].

Thomas W. Gann, **Discoveries and Adventures in Central America** [New York: Scribner's and Sons, 1929].

Thomas W. Gann, **History of the Maya** [New York: Scribner's and Sons, 1931].

Lloyd C. Gardner, **Economic Aspects of New Deal Diplomacy** [Madison: University of Wisconsin Press, 1964].

Lloyd C. Gardner, **Architects of Illusion: Men and Ideas in American Foreign Policy 1941-1949** [Chicago: Quadrangle Books, 1970, second edition 1972].

Lloyd C. Gardner, Walter LaFeber, and Thomas J. McCormick, **Creation of the American Empire: US Diplomatic History** (2 vols.) [Chicago: Rand McNally, second edition, 1976].

Lloyd C. Gardner, **Imperial America: American Foreign Policy Since 1898** [New York: Harcourt, Brace and Jovanovich, 1976].

Lloyd C. Gardner, **A Covenant with Power: America and World Order from Wilson to Reagan** [New York: Oxford University Press, 1984].

Lloyd C. Gardner, **Safe for Democracy: The Anglo-American Response to Revolution 1913-1923** [New York: Oxford University Press, 1987].

Lloyd C. Gardner, **Approaching Vietnam: From World War II Through Dienbienphu** [New York: W. W. Norton, 1988].

Edmund Gaspar, **United States-Latin America: A Special Relationship?** [Washington: American Enterprise Institute, 1978].

Theodore Geiger, **Communism Versus Progress in Guatemala** [Washington: National Planning Association Committee on International Policy, December 1953].

Theodore Geiger, **The Conflicted Relationship: The West and the Transformation of Asia, Africa and Latin America** [New York: McGraw-Hill, 1967].

Leslie H. Gelb and Richard Betts, **The Irony of Vietnam: The System Worked** [Washington: Brookings Institution, 1979].

Irwin F. Gellman, **Roosevelt and Batista: Good Neighbour Diplomacy in Cuba 1933-1945** [Albuquerque: University of New Mexico Press, 1973].

Irwin F. Gellman, **Good Neighbour Diplomacy: United States Policies in Latin America 1933-1945** [Baltimore: Johns Hopkins University Press, 1979].

Irene L. Gendzier, **Managing Political Change: Social Scientists and the Third World** [Boulder: Westview Press, 1985].

Eugene D. Genovese, **From Rebellion to Revolution: Afro-American Slave Revolts in the Making of the New World** [Baton Rouge: Louisiana State University Press, 1979].

Susan George, **How the Other Half Dies: The Real Reasons for World Hunger** [London: Penguin, revised edition 1988; first published 1976].

Susan George, **Feeding the Few: Corporate Control of Food** [Washington: Institute for Policy Studies, 1979].

Susan George, **Ill Fares the Land: Essays on Food, Hunger and Power** [Washington: Institute for Policy Studies, 1985].

Susan George, **A Fate Worse than Debt** [London: Penguin, 1988].

Susan George, **The Debt Boomerang** [London: Pluto Press, 1992].
John Gerassi, **The Great Fear: The Reconquest of Latin America by Latin Americans** [New York: Macmillan, 1963].
John Gerassi, **The Great Fear In Latin America** [London: Collier-Macmillan, 1971]. a revised version of **The Great Fear: The Reconquest of Latin America by Latin Americans** [New York: Macmillan, 1963].
Larry G. Gerber, **The Limits of Liberalism: Josephus Daniels, Henry Stimson, Bernard Baruch, Donald Richberg, Felix Frankfurter and the Development of the Modern American Political Economy** [New York: New York University Press, 1984].
Georgie Anne Geyer, **The New Latins: Fateful Change in South and Central America** [Garden City: Doubleday, 1970].
Charles Gibson, ed., **Guide to the Hispanic American Historical Review 1946-1955** [Durham: Duke University Press, 1958].
Charles Gibson, **The Aztecs Under Spanish Rule: A History of the Indians of the Valley of Mexico 1519-1810** [Stanford: Stanford University Press, 1964].
Charles Gibson, **Spain in America** [New York: Harper and Row, 1966].
Charles Gibson, ed., **The Black Legend: Anti-Spanish Attitudes in the Old World and the New** [New York: Alfred A. Knopf, 1971].
James William Gibson, **The Perfect War: Technowar in Vietnam** [New York: Atlantic Monthly, 1986].
Federico G. Gil, **Latin American-United States Relations** [New York: Harcourt, Brace and Jovanovich, 1971].
Dennis Gilbert, **Sandinistas: The Party and the Revolution** [London: Basil Blackwell, 1990; first published 1988].
Mark T. Gilderhus, **Diplomacy and Revolution: US Mexican Relations Under Wilson and Carranza** [Tucson: University of Arizona Press, 1977].
Stephen Gill, **American Hegemony and the Trilateral Commission** [Cambridge: Cambridge University Press, 1990].
Robert Gilpin, **US Power and Multinational Corporations: The Political Economy of Foreign Direct Investment** [New York: Basic Books, 1975].
Robert Gilpin, **War and Change in World Politics** [Princeton: Princeton University Press, 1981].
Robert Gilpin, **The Political Economy of International Relations** [Princeton: Princeton University Press, 1987].
Earl T. Glauert and Lester D. Langley, eds., **The United States and Latin America** [London: Addison-Wesley, 1971].
Piero Gleijeses, **The Dominican Crisis: The 1965 Constitutionalist Revolt and American Intervention** [Baltimore: Johns Hopkins University Press, 1978].
Piero Gleijeses, **Perspectives of a Regime's Transformation in Guatemala** [Bonn: Friedrich Ebert Stiftung, 1981].
Piero Gleijeses, **Tilting at Windmills: Reagan and Central America** [Washington: Johns Hopkins University School of Advanced International Studies (SAIS), Papers in International Affairs, 1982].

Piero, Gleijeses, **Politics and Culture in Guatemala** [Ann Arbor: Center for Political Studies, University of Michigan, 1988].

Piero, Gleijeses, **Shattered Hope: The Guatemalan Revolution and the United States 1944-1954** [Princeton: Princeton University Press, 1991].

Walter Goldfrank, ed., **The World-System of Capitalism: Past and Present** [Beverly Hills: Sage, 1979].

Rosendo A. Gomez, **The Study of Latin American Politics in University Programs in the United States** [Tucson: University of Arizona Press, 1967].

Edward Gonzalez, Brian Michael Jenkins, David Ronfeldt and Caesar Sereseres, US **Policy for Central America: A Briefing** [Santa Monica: Rand Corporation, 1984].

David C. Gordon, **Self-determination and History in the Third World** [Princeton: Princeton University Press, 1971].

Lincoln Gordon, **A New Deal for Latin America: The Alliance for Progress** [Cambridge: Harvard University Press, 1963].

Lincoln Gordon, **Growth Policies and the International Order** [New York: McGraw-Hill, 1979, for the Council on Foreign Relations].

Van Gosse, **Where the Boys Are: Cuba, Cold War America and the Making of a New Left** [London: Verso, 1993].

David Green, **The Containment of Latin America: A History of the Myths and Realities of the Good Neighbour Policy** [Chicago: Quadrangle Books, 1971].

Stephen Greenblatt, **Marvelous Possessions: The Wonder of the New World** [Chicago: University of Chicago Press, 1991].

John A. S. Grenville and George Berkeley Young, **Politics, Strategy and American Diplomacy: Studies in Foreign Policy 1873-1917** [New Haven: Yale University Press, 1967].

Kenneth J. Grieb, **Guatemalan Caudillo: The Regime of Jorge Ubico, Guatemala 1931-1944** [Athens: Ohio University Press, 1979].

Kenneth J. Grieb, Ralph Lee Woodward, Jr., Graeme S. Mount, Thomas Mathews, eds., **Research Guide to Central America and the Caribbean** [Madison: University of Wisconsin Press, 1985].

Kenneth J. Grieb, **Central America in the Nineteenth and Twentieth Centuries: An Annotated Bibliography** [Boston: G. K. Hall, 1988].

Charles C. Griffin, **The United States and the Disruption of the Spanish Empire 1810-1822** [New York: Columbia University Press, 1937].

Charles C. Griffin and J. Benedict Warren, eds., **Latin America: A Guide to the Historical Literature** [Austin: University of Texas Press, 1971].

Karl Grossman, **Nicaragua: America's New Vietnam** [Sag Harbour: Permanent Press, 1984].

Ernest H. Gruening, **Mexico and Its Heritage** [New York: Century, 1928].

Edward O. Guerrant, **Roosevelt's Good Neighbour Policy** [Albuquerque: University of New Mexico Press, 1950].

Melvin Gurtov, **The United States Against the Third World: Antinationalism and Intervention** [New York: Praeger, 1974].

Roy Gutman, **Banana Diplomacy: The Making of American Policy in Nicaragua 1981-1987** [New York: Simon and Schuster, 1988].

Richard N. Haass, **Conflicts Unending: The United States and Regional Disputes** [New Haven: Yale University Press, 1990].

Charles W. Hackett, **The Mexican Revolution and the United States 1910-1926** [Boston: World Peace Foundation, 1926].

Arnon Hadar, **The United States and El Salvador: Political and Military Involvement** [Berkeley: US-El Salvador Research and Information Center, 1981].

Stephan Haggard, **Pathways from the Periphery: The Politics of Growth in the Newly Industrializing Countries** [Ithaca: Cornell University Press, 1990].

David G. Haglund, **Latin America and the Transformation of US Strategic Thought 1936-1940** [Albuquerque: University of New Mexico Press, 1984].

Alexander M. Haig, Jr., **Caveat: Realism, Reagan and Foreign Policy** [London: Weidenfeld and Nicolson, 1984].

Gerald K. Haines, **The Americanization of Brazil: A Study of US Cold War Diplomacy in the Third World 1945-1954** [Wilmington: Scholarly Resources, 1989].

David Halberstam, **The Making of a Quagmire** [New York: Ballantine, 1989; first published, 1965].

David Halberstam, **The Best and the Brightest** [London: Barrie and Jenkins, 1972].

John A. Hall, **Liberalism: Politics, Ideology and the Market** [London: Paladin, 1988; first published 1987].

Louis J. Halle, **The Cold War as History** [New York: Harper and Row, 1967].

Fred Halliday, **Iran: Dictatorship and Development** [Harmondsworth, Penguin, 1979].

Fred Halliday, **The Making of the Second Cold War** [London: Verso, revised edition 1986; first published 1983].

Fred Halliday, **Beyond Irangate: The Reagan Doctrine and the Third World** [Amsterdam: Transnational Institute, 1987].

Fred Halliday, **Cold War, Third World: An Essay on Soviet American Relations** [London: Hutchinson Radius, 1989].

Morton H. Halperin and Arnold Kanter, eds., **Readings in American Foreign Policy: A Bureaucratic Perspective** [Boston: Little Brown, 1973].

Morton H. Halperin, **Bureaucratic Politics and Foreign Policy** [Washington: Brookings Institution, 1974].

Alonzo L. Hamby, **Liberalism and Its Challengers: From FDR to Bush** [New York: Oxford University Press, second edition 1992; first published 1985].

Nora Hamilton, **The Limits of State Autonomy: Post-Revolutionary Mexico** [Princeton: Princeton University Press, 1982].

Paul Y. Hammond, **The Cold War Years: American Foreign Policy Since 1945** [New York: Harcourt, Brace and World, 1969].

Jim Handy, **Gift of the Devil: A History of Guatemala** [Boston: South End Press, 1984].

Jim Handy, **Revolution and Reaction: National Policy and Rural Politics in Guatemala 1944-1954** [Unpublished PhD dissertation, University of Toronto, 1985].

Jim Handy, **Revolution in the Countryside: Rural Conflict and Agrarian Reform in Guatemala 1944-1954** [Chapel Hill: University of North Carolina Press, 1994].

Roger D. Hansen, **Central America: Regional Integration and Economic Development** [Washington: 1967].

Roger D. Hansen, **The Politics of Mexican Development** [Baltimore: Johns Hopkins University Press, 1977; first published 1971].

Roger D. Hansen, **Beyond the North-South Stalemate** [New York: McGraw-Hill, 1979, for the Council on Foreign Relations].

Simon G. Hanson, **Economic Development in Latin America** [Washington: Inter-American Affairs Press, 1951].

Simon G. Hanson, **Five Years of the Alliance for Progress: An Appraisal** [Washington: Inter-American Affairs Press, 1967].

Simon G. Hanson, **Dollar Diplomacy Modern Style: Chapters in the Failure of the Alliance for Progress** [Washington: Inter-American Affairs Press, 1970].

Clarence H. Haring, **The Buccaneers in the West Indies in the 17th Century** [London: Methuen, 1910].

Clarence H. Haring, **Trade and Navigation Between Spain and the Indies in the Time of the Hapsburgs** [Cambridge: Harvard University Press, 1918].

Clarence H. Haring, **The Spanish Empire in America** [New York: Oxford University Press, 1947].

Clarence H. Haring, **Empire in Brazil: A New World Experiment in Monarchy** [Cambridge: Harvard University Press, 1965].

Robert P. Haro, **Latin American Research in the United States and Canada: A Guide and Directory** [Chicago: American Library Association, 1971].

Nigel Harris, **The End of the Third World: Newly Industrializing Countries and the Decline of an Ideology** [London: Penguin, 1987; first published 1986].

Richard L. Harris, **Marxism, Socialism and Democracy in Latin America** [Boulder: Westview Press, 1992].

David Harrison, **The Sociology of Modernization and Development** [London: Unwin Hyman, 1990; first published 1988].

Selig S. Harrison, **The Widening Gulf: Asian Nationalism and American Policy** [New York: Free Press, 1979].

Albert Bushnell Hart, **The Foundations of American Foreign Policy** [New York: Macmillan, 1901; reprinted New York: Da Capo Press, 1970].

Albert Bushnell Hart, **The Monroe Doctrine: An Interpretation** [London: Duckworth, 1916].

Louis Hartz, **The Liberal Tradition in America: An Interpretation of American Political Thought Since the Revolution** [New York: Harcourt, Brace and World, 1955].

Thomas L. Haskell, **The Emergence of Professional Social Science:**

The American Social Science Association and the Nineteenth-Century Crisis of Authority [Urbana: University of Illinois Press, 1977].

John Hawkins, **Inverse Images: The Meaning of Culture, Ethnicity and Family in Postcolonial Guatemala** [Albuquerque: University of New Mexico Press, 1984].

Margaret Daly Hayes, **Latin America and the US National Interest: A Basis for US Foreign Policy** [Boulder: Westview Press, 1984].

David Healy, **The United States in Cuba 1898-1902: Generals, Politicians and the Search for Policy** [Madison: University of Wisconsin Press, 1963].

David Healy, **The Imperialist Urge in the 1890s** [Madison: University of Wisconsin Press, 1970].

David Healy, **Gunboat Diplomacy in the Wilson Era: The US Navy in Haiti 1915-1916** [Madison: University of Wisconsin Press, 1976].

David Healy, **Drive to Hegemony: The United States in the Caribbean 1898-1917** [Madison: University of Wisconsin Press, 1988].

Michael Hechter, **Internal Colonialism: The Celtic Fringe in British National Development 1536-1966** [London: Routledge and Kegan Paul, 1975].

Alastair Hennessy, **The Frontier in Latin American History** [Albuquerque: University of New Mexico Press, 1978].

Edward S. Herman, **The *Real* Terror Network: Terrorism in Fact and Propaganda** [Boston: South End Press, 1982].

Edward S. Herman and Frank Brodhead, **Demonstration Elections: US Staged Elections in the Dominican Republic, Vietnam and El Salvador** [Boston: Southend Press, 1984].

Elbaki Hermassi, **The Third World Reassessed** [Berkeley: University of California Press, 1980].

Thomas R. Herrick, **Economic and Political Development of Guatemala During the Barrios Period** [Unpublished PhD dissertation, University of Chicago, 1967].

George C. Herring, **America's Longest War: The United States and Vietnam 1950-1975** [New York: Alfred A. Knopf, 1979; second revised edition 1986].

Hubert Herring, **A History of Latin America: From the Beginnings to the Present** [London: Jonathan Cape, third enlarged edition 1968; first published 1955].

Bjorne Hettne, **Development Theory and the Three Worlds** [London: Longman, 1990].

John Higham, **Writing American History: Essays on Modern Scholarship** [Bloomington: Indiana University Press, 1970].

Howard C. Hill, **Roosevelt and the Caribbean** [Chicago: University of Chicago Press, 1927].

Roscoe R. Hill, **Fiscal Intervention in Nicaragua** [New York: Paul Maisel, 1933].

Roscoe R. Hill, **The National Archives of Latin America** [Cambridge: Harvard University Press, 1945].

Rodney Hilton, ed., **The Transition from Feudalism to Capitalism** [London: Verso, 1976].

Jerome L. Himmelstein, **To the Right: The Transformation of American Conservatism** [Berkeley: University of California Press, 1990].

Barry Hindess and Paul Q. Hirst, **Pre-Capitalist Modes of Production** [London: Routledge and Kegan Paul, 1975].

Albert O. Hirschman, **Journeys Toward Progress: Studies of Economic Policy Making in Latin America** [New York: The Twentieth Century Fund, 1963].

Eric J. Hobsbawm, **The Age of Empire 1875-1914** [London: Weidenfeld and Nicolson, 1987].

Donald C. Hodges, **The Latin American Revolution: Politics and Strategy from Apro-Marxism to Guevarism** [New York: William Morrow, 1974].

Donald C. Hodges, **Intellectual Foundations of the Nicaraguan Revolution** [Austin: University of Texas Press, 1986].

Donald C. Hodges, **Sandino's Communism: Spiritual Politics for the Twenty-First Century** [Austin: University of Texas Press, 1992].

Godfrey Hodgson, **The Colonel: The Life and Wars of Henry Stimson 1867-1950** [New York: Alfred A. Knopf, 1990].

Stanley Hoffmann, **Gulliver's Troubles: On the Setting of American Foreign Policy** [New York: McGraw-Hill, 1968].

Stanley Hoffmann, **Primacy or World Order: American Foreign Policy Since the Cold War** [New York: McGraw-Hill, 1978].

Michael J. Hogan, **The Marshall Plan: America, Britain, and the Reconstruction of Western Europe 1947-1952** [New York: Cambridge University Press, 1987].

Paul Hollander, **Anti-Americanism: Critiques at Home and Abroad 1965-1990** [New York: Oxford University Press, 1992].

W. Ladd Hollist and Robert J. Boydston, eds., **World-System Structure** [Beverly Hills: Sage, 1981].

Ole R. Holsti and James R. Rosenau, **American Leadership in World Affairs: Vietnam and the Breakdown of Consensus** [Boston: Allen and Unwin, 1984].

Ankie M. M. Hoogvelt, **The Sociology of Developing Societies** [London: Macmillan, 1978].

Ankie M. M. Hoogvelt, **The Third World in Global Development** [London: Macmillan, 1985; first published 1982].

Townsend Hoopes, **The Limits of Intervention: An Inside Account of How the Johnson Policy of Escalation in Vietnam Was Reversed** [New York: D. McKay, 1969].

Townsend Hoopes, **The Devil and John Foster Dulles** [Boston: Little Brown, 1973].

J. A. H. Hopkins and Melinda Alexander, **Machine-Gun Diplomacy** [New York: Lewis Copeland, 1928].

Terence K. Hopkins and Immanuel Wallerstein, **Processes of the World-System** [Beverly Hills: Sage, 1980].

David Horowitz, **From Yalta to Vietnam: American Foreign Policy in** the Cold War [Harmondsworth: Penguin, 1969; first published London: MacGibbon and Kee, 1965].

David Horowitz, **The Free World Colossus: A Critique of American Foreign Policy in the Cold War** [New York: Hill and Wang, revised edition 1971; first published as **From Yalta to Vietnam** in 1965].

David Horowitz, **Imperialism and Revolution** [London: Allen Lane, 1969].

Irving Louis Horowitz, ed., **The Rise and Fall of Project Camelot: Studies in the Relationship between Social Science and Practical Politics** [Cambridge: Massachusetts Institute of Technology Press, 1967].

Irving Louis Horowitz, **Three Worlds of Development: The Theory and Practice of International Stratification** [New York: Oxford University Press, 1972].

Irving Louis Horowitz, **Ideology and Utopia in the United States 1956-1976** [New York: Oxford University Press, 1977].

Irving Louis Horowitz, **Beyond Empire and Revolution: Militarization and Consolidation in the Third World** [New York: Oxford University Press, 1982].

Irving Louis Horowitz, **The Decomposition of Sociology** [New York: Oxford University Press, 1993].

Reginald Horsman, **Race and Manifest Destiny: The Origins of American Racial Anglo-Saxonism** [Cambridge: Cambridge University Press, 1981].

Harold A. Hovey, **United States Military Assistance: A Study of Policies and Practices** [New York: Praeger, 1965].

Charles P. Howland, **American Relations in the Caribbean** [New Haven: Yale University Press, 1929].

Charles Evan Hughes, **Our Relations to the Nations of the Western Hemisphere** [Princeton: Princeton University Press, 1928].

Richard Humphrey, **Universities and Development Assistance Abroad** [Washington: American Council on Education, 1967].

Diana Hunt, **Economic Theories of Development: An Analysis of Competing Paradigms** [Brighton: Harvester Wheatsheaf, 1989].

Michael H. Hunt, **Ideology and US Foreign Policy** [New Haven: Yale University Press, 1987].

Jane Hunter, **Israeli Foreign Policy: South Africa and Central America** [Boston: South End Press, 1987].

Ellsworth Huntington, **Civilization and Climate** [New Haven: Yale University Press, 1915].

Samuel P. Huntington, **The Soldier and the State: The Theory and Politics of Civil-Military Relations** [Cambridge: Harvard University Press, 1957].

Samuel P. Huntington, ed., **Changing Patterns of Military Politics** [New York: Free Press, 1962].

Samuel P. Huntington, **Political Order in Changing Societies** [New Haven: Yale University Press, 1968].

Samuel P. Huntington, Michael Crozier and Joji Watanuki, **The Crisis of Democracy: Report on the Governability of Democracies to** the **Trilateral Commission** [New York: New York University Press, 1975].

Samuel P. Huntington and Joan M. Nelson, **No Easy Choice: Political Participation in Developing Countries** [Cambridge: Harvard University Press, 1976].

Samuel P. Huntington, **American Politics: The Promise of Disharmony** [Cambridge: Harvard University Press, 1982; first published 1981].

Samuel P. Huntington, **The Dilemma of American Ideals and Institutions in Foreign Policy** [Washington: American Enterprise Institute, 1981].

Samuel P. Huntington, **The Third Wave: Democratization in the Late Twentieth Century** [Norman: University of Oklahoma Press, 1991].

Aldous Huxley, **Beyond the Mexique Bay: A Traveller's Journal** [Harmondsworth: Penguin Books, 1955; first published 1934].

Richard H. Immerman, **The United States and Guatemala, 1954: A Cold War Strategy for the Americas** [Unpublished PhD dissertation, Boston College, 1978].

Richard H. Immerman, **The CIA in Guatemala: The Foreign Policy of Intervention** [Austin: University of Texas Press, 1982].

Samuel Guy Inman, **Through Santo Domingo and Haiti: A Cruise with the Marines** [New York: Committee on Cooperation in Latin America, 1919].

Samuel Guy Inman, **Problems in Pan Americanism** [New York: George H. Doran, 1922].

Samuel Guy Inman, **Building an Inter-American Neighborhood** [New York: National Peace Conference, 1937].

Samuel Guy Inman, **Latin America: Its Place in World Life** [Chicago: Willet Clark, 1937].

Samuel Guy Inman, **A New Day in Guatemala** [Wilton: World-over Press, 1951].

Institute for Policy Studies, Ad Hoc Working Group on Latin America, **The Southern Connection: Recommendations for a New Approach to Inter-American Relations** [Washington: Institute for Policy Studies, 1977].

Inter-American Dialogue (Sol M. Linowitz, chair), **The Americas in 1984: Year for Decisions** (Report of the Inter-American Dialogue) [Queenstown: Aspen Institute for Humanistic Studies, 1984].

Inter-American Dialogue, **The Americas in 1989: Consensus for Action** (Report of the Inter-American Dialogue) [Queenstown: Aspen Institute for Humanistic Studies, 1989].

Inter-American Dialogue, **The Americas in a New World** (Report of the Inter-American Dialogue) [Queenstown: Aspen Institute for Humanistic Studies, 1990].

Inter-American Dialogue, **Convergence and Community: The Americas in 1993** (Report of the Inter-American Dialogue) [Queenstown: Aspen Institute for Humanistic Studies, 1992].

Inter-Hemispheric Education Resource Center, **US Food Aid and Farm Policy in Central America** [Albuquerque: Inter-Hemispheric Education Resource

Center, 1989].

Inter-Hemispheric Education Resource Center, **Food Aid in Central America: Feeding the Crisis** [Albuquerque: Inter-Hemispheric Education Resource Center, 1989].

Inter-Hemispheric Education Resource Center, **National Endowment for Democracy (NED): A Foreign Policy Branch Gone Awry** [Albuquerque: Inter-Hemispheric Education Resource Center, 1990].

International Commission for Central American Recovery and Development, **The Report of the International Commission for Central American Recovery and Development--Poverty, Conflict, and Hope: A Turning Point in Central American Recovery and Development** [Durham: Duke University Press, 1989].

Arnold R. Isaacs, **Without Honor: Defeat in Vietnam and Cambodia** [New York: Vintage Books, 1984; first published 1983].

Harold R. Isaacs, **Scratches on Our Minds: American Images of China and India** [New York: Greenwood Press, 1973; first published 1958].

Nils Jacobsen, **Mirages of Transition: The Peruvian Altiplano 1780-1930** [Berkeley: University of California Press, 1993].

Russell Jacoby, **The Last Intellectuals: American Culture in the Age of Academe** [New York: Farrar, Straus and Giroux, 1987].

Milton Jamail, **Guatemala 1944-1972: The Politics of Aborted Revolution** [Unpublished PhD dissertation, University of Arizona, 1972].

Milton Jamail and Margo Gutierrez, **It's No Secret: Israel's Military Involvement in Central America** [Belmont Maryland: Association of Arab-American University Graduates, 1986].

Daniel James, **Red Design for the Americas: Guatemalan Prelude** [New York: John Day, 1954].

Daniel James, **Cuba: The First Soviet Satellite in the Americas** [New York: Avon Book Division, 1961].

Preston James, **Introduction to Latin America** [New York: Odyssey Press, third edition, 1959].

Morris Janowitz, **The Professional Soldier: A Social and Political Portrait** [New York: Free Press, 1971; first published 1960].

Morris Janowitz, **The Military in the Political Development of New Nations: An Essay in Comparative Analysis** [Chicago: University of Chicago Press, 1964].

Morris Janowitz, ed., **The New Military: Changing Patterns of Organization** [New York: Russell Sage, 1964].

Morris Janowitz, **Military Institutions and Coercion in the Developing Nations** [Chicago: University of Chicago Press, 1977].

Susan Jeffords, **The Remasculinization of America: Gender and the Vietnam War** [Bloomington: Indiana University Press, 1989].

Leland H. Jenks, **Our Cuban Colony: A Study in Sugar** [New York: Vanguard Press, 1928].

Bob Jessop, **State Theory: Putting Capitalist States in Their Place** [University Park: Pennsylvania State University Press, 1990].

Robert W. Johannsen, **To the Halls of the Montezumas: The Mexican War in the American Imagination** [London: Oxford University Press,

1985].

Dale L. Johnson, **The Sociology of Change and Reaction in Latin America** [Indianapolis: Bobbs Merrill, 1973].

John J. Johnson, **Political Change in Latin America: The Emergence of the Middle Sectors** [Stanford: Stanford University Press, 1958].

John J. Johnson, ed., **The Role of the Military in Underdeveloped Countries** [Princeton: Princeton University Press, 1962].

John J. Johnson, **The Military and Society in Latin America** [Stanford: Stanford University Press, 1964].

John J. Johnson, **Latin America in Caricature** [Austin: University of Texas Press, 1980].

John J. Johnson, **A Hemisphere Apart: The Foundation of United States Policy Toward Latin America** [Baltimore: Johns Hopkins University Press, 1990].

William Franklin Johnston, **Some Principles of Communist Unconventional Warfare: Lessons from the Yenan and Guatemalan 'Ways'** [Unpublished MA thesis, Georgetown University, 1958].

Susanne Jonas Bodenheimer, **The Ideology of Developmentalism: The American Paradigm--Surrogate for Latin American Studies** [Berkeley: Sage, 1971].

Susanne Jonas, **Test Case for the Hemisphere: United States Strategy in Guatemala 1950-1974** [Unpublished PhD dissertation, University of California (Berkeley), 1974].

Susanne Jonas and David Tobis, eds., **Guatemala** [New York: North American Congress on Latin America, 1974].

Susanne Jonas and David Tobis, eds., **Guatemala: Una historia inmediata** [Mexico: Siglo Veintiuno Editores, 1976; first published in English 1974].

Susanne Jonas, **Guatemala: plan piloto para el continente** [San José: Editorial Universitaria Centroamericana, 1981].

Susanne Jonas, **The Battle for Guatemala: Rebels, Death Squads and US Power** [Boulder: Westview Press, 1991].

Chester Lloyd Jones, **Caribbean Interests of the United States** [New York: Arno Press, 1970; first published New York: D. Appleton, 1916].

Chester Lloyd Jones, **Mexico and Its Reconstruction** [New York: D. Appleton, 1921].

Chester Lloyd Jones, **Caribbean Background and Prospects** [New York: D. Appleton, 1931].

Chester Lloyd Jones, **Costa Rica and Civilization in the Caribbean** [Madison: University of Wisconsin Press, 1935].

Chester Lloyd Jones, **The Caribbean Since 1900** [New York: Russell and Russell, 1936, reprinted 1970].

Chester Lloyd Jones, **Guatemala: Past and Present** [New York: Russell and Russell, 1966; first published University of Minnesota Press, 1940].

Ken Jowitt, **The Leninist Response to National Dependency** [Berkeley: Institute of International Studies, University of California, 1978].

Ken Jowitt, **New World Disorder: The Leninist Extinction** [Berkeley: University of California Press, 1992].

George McT. Kahin, **Intervention: How America Became Involved in Vietnam** [Garden City: Anchor Books, 1987].

Thorsten V. Kalijarvi, **Central America: Land of Lords and Lizards** [Princeton: D. Van Nostrand, 1962].

William Kamman, **A Search for Stability: United States Diplomacy Toward Nicaragua 1925-1933** [Notre Dame: University of Notre Dame Press, 1968].

William Everett Kane, **Civil Strife in Latin America: A Legal History of US Involvement** [Baltimore: Johns Hopkins University Press, 1972].

Barbara Kaplan, ed., **Social Change in the Capitalist World Economy** [Beverly Hills: Sage, 1978].

Thomas L. Karnes, **The Failure of Union: Central America 1824-1960** [Chapel Hill: University of North Carolina Press, 1961].

Thomas L. Karnes, **Failure of Union: Central America 1824-1975** [Tempe: University of Arizona Press, 1975].

Thomas L. Karnes, **Tropical Enterprise: The Standard Fruit and Steamship Company in Latin America** [Baton Rouge: Louisiana State University Press, 1978].

Stanley Karnow, **Vietnam: A History** [New York: The Viking Press, 1983].

Paul M. Kattenberg, **The Vietnam Trauma in American Foreign Policy 1945-1975** [New Brunswick: Transaction Books, 1982; first published 1980].

David M. Kauck, **Agricultural Commercialization and State Development in Central America: The Political Economy of the Coffee Industry from 1838-1940** [Unpublished PhD dissertation, University of Washington, 1988].

Burton I. Kaufman, **Trade and Aid: Eisenhower's Foreign Economic Policy** [Baltimore: Johns Hopkins University Press, 1982].

Edy Kaufman, **The Superpowers and their Spheres of Influence: The United States and the Soviet Union in Eastern Europe and Latin America** [London: Croom Helm, 1976].

William W. Kaufmann, **British Policy and the Independence of Latin America 1804-1828** [New Haven: Yale University Press, 1951].

John H. Kautsky, **Moscow and the Communist Party of India: A Study of the Postwar Evolution of International Communist Strategy** [New York: Wiley, 1956].

Cristobal Kay, **Latin American Theories of Development and Underdevelopment** [London: Routledge, 1989].

Geoffrey Kay, **Development and Underdevelopment: A Marxist Analysis** [London: Macmillan, 1975].

Harvey J. Kaye, **The British Marxist Historians** [Cambridge: Polity Press, 1984].

Margaret E. Keck, **The Workers' Party and Democratization in Brazil** [New Haven: Yale University Press, 1992].

Benjamin Keen, ed., **Americans All: The Story of Our Latin American Neighbours** [New York: Dell, 1966].

Benjamin Keen and Mark Wasserman, **A Short History of Latin America** [Boston: Houghton Mifflin, 1980].

George F. Kennan, **American Diplomacy 1900-1950** [Chicago: University of Chicago Press, 1951].

George F. Kennan, **Realities of American Foreign Policy** [Princeton: Princeton University Press, 1954].

Paul Kennedy, **The Rise and Fall of the Great Powers: Economic Change and Military Conflict from 1500 to 2000** [New York: Random House, 1987].

Thomas C. Kennedy, **Charles A. Beard and American Foreign Policy** [Gainesville: University Presses of Florida, 1975].

Henry C. Kenski and Margaret Gorgan Kenski, **Teaching Political Development and Modernization at American Universities: A Survey** [Tucson: University of Arizona Press, 1974].

Robert O. Keohane and Joseph S. Nye, eds., **Transnational Relations and World Politics** [Cambridge: Harvard University Press, 1972].

Robert O. Keohane and Joseph S. Nye, **Power and Interdependence: World Politics in Transition** [Boston: Little Brown, 1977].

Robert O. Keohane, **After Hegemony: Cooperation and Discord in the World Political Economy** [Princeton: Princeton University Press, 1984].

Charles David Kepner, Jr., and Henry J. Soothill, **The Banana Empire: A Case Study of Economic Imperialism** [New York: Russell and Russell, 1967; first published New York: Vanguard Press, 1931].

Charles David Kepner, Jr., **Social Aspects of the Banana Industry** [New York: Columbia University Press, 1936; reprinted New York: AMS Press, 1967].

Huyhn Kim Khanh, **Vietnamese Communism 1925-1945** [Ithaca New York: Cornell University Press, 1982].

Benjamin Kidd, **The Control of the Tropics** [New York: Macmillan, 1898].

Victor G. Kiernan, **The Lords of Humankind: European Attitudes to the Outside World in the Imperial Age** [Harmondsworth: Penguin, 1972].

Stephen Kinzer, **Blood of Brothers: Life and War in Nicaragua--A New York Times Correspondent's Eyewitness Account** [New York: Putnam, 1991].

Jeane J. Kirkpatrick, **Leader and Vanguard in Mass Society: A Study of Peronist Argentina** [Cambridge: Massachusetts Institute of Technology Press, 1971].

Jeane J. Kirkpatrick, **Political Woman** [New York: Basic Books, 1974].

Jeane J. Kirkpatrick, **The New Presidential Elite: Men and Women in National Politics** [New York: Russell Sage, 1976].

Jeane J. Kirkpatrick, **Dismantling the Parties: Reflections on Party Reform and Party Decomposition** [Washington: American Enterprise Institute, 1978].

Jeane J. Kirkpatrick, **"This very human institution": Commentaries and Addresses on the United Nations and US Foreign Policy** [Washington: US Information Agency, 1984].

Jeane J. Kirkpatrick, **Idealism, Realism and the Myth of Appeasement** [London: Alliance Publishers for the Institute for European Defense and

Strategic Studies, 1984].

Jeane J. Kirkpatrick, **The Reagan Doctrine and US Foreign Policy** [Washington: The Fund for an American Renaissance, 1985].

Jeane J. Kirkpatrick, **The United States and the World: Setting Limits** [Washington: American Enterprise Institute, 1986]. (The 1985 Francis Boyer Lecture on Public Policy.)

Jeane J. Kirkpatrick, **The Withering Away of the Totalitarian State...And Other Surprises** [Washington: American Enterprise Institute Press, 1991].

Henry Kissinger, **A World Restored: Metternich, Castlereagh and the Problems of Peace 1812-1822** [Boston: Houghton and Mifflin, 1957].

Henry Kissinger, **Nuclear Weapons and Foreign Policy** [New York: Harper and Row, 1957].

Henry Kissinger, **The Necessity for Choice: Prospects of American Foreign Policy** [New York: Harper and Row, 1961].

Henry Kissinger, **The Troubled Partnership: A Reappraisal of the Atlantic Alliance** [New York: McGraw-Hill, 1965].

Henry Kissinger, ed., **Problems of National Strategy: A Book of Readings** [New York: Praeger, 1965].

Henry Kissinger, **American Foreign Policy: Three Essays** [New York: W. W. Norton, 1969].

Henry Kissinger, **The White House Years** [Boston: Little Brown, 1979].

Henry Kissinger, **Years of Upheaval** [Boston: Little Brown, 1982].

Michael T. Klare, **War Without End: American Planning for the Next Vietnams** [New York: Vintage Books, 1972].

Michael T. Klare, **The University-Military-Police Complex** [Berkeley: North American Congress on Latin America 1977].

Michael T. Klare, **Beyond the "Vietnam Syndrome": US Intervention in the 1980s** [Washington: Institute for Policy Studies, 1982; first published 1981].

Herbert S. Klein, **Slavery in the Americas: A Comparative Study of Virginia and Cuba** [Chicago: University of Chicago Press, 1967].

Herbert S. Klein, **African Slavery in Latin America and the Caribbean** [New York: Oxford University Press, 1986].

Melvin M. Knight, **The Americans in Santo Domingo** [New York: Arno Press, 1970; first published New York: Vanguard Press, 1928].

Melvin M. Knight, **Morocco as a French Economic Venture** [New York: Vanguard Press, 1937].

Walter Knut, **The Regime of Anastasio Somoza Garcia and State Formation in Nicaragua 1936-1956** [Unpublished PhD dissertation, University of North Carolina, 1987].

W. H. Koebel, **Central America: Guatemala, Nicaragua, Costa Rica, Honduras, Panama, and El Salvador** [London: T. Fisher Unwin, 1917].

Peter Kolchin, **Unfree Labor: American Slavery and Russian Serfdom** [Cambridge: Harvard University Press, 1987].

Jonathan Martin Kolkey, **The New Right 1960-1968** (with epilogue 1969-1980) [New York: University Press of America, 1983].

Gabriel Kolko, **The Roots of American Foreign Policy: An Analysis of Power and Purpose** [Boston: Beacon Press, 1969].

Gabriel Kolko and Joyce Kolko, **The Limits of Power: The World and United States Foreign Policy 1945-1954** [New York: Pantheon, 1972].

Gabriel Kolko, **Main Currents in Modern American History** [New York: Pantheon Press, 1984; first published 1976].

Gabriel Kolko, **Anatomy of a War: Vietnam, the United States and the Modern Historical Experience** [New York: Pantheon, 1985; also published by George Allen and Unwin in 1985 as **Vietnam: Anatomy of a War 1940-1975**].

Gabriel Kolko, **Confronting the Third World: United States Foreign Policy 1945-1980** [New York: Pantheon Press, 1988].

Peter Kornbluh, **Nicaragua: The Price of Intervention--Reagan's War Against the Sandinistas** [Washington: Institute for Policy Studies, 1987].

R. M. Koster and Guillermo Sanchez, **In The Time of the Tyrants--Panama: 1968-1990** [New York: W. W. Norton, 1990].

Stephen D. Krasner, **Structural Conflict: The Third World Against Global Liberalism** [Berkeley: University of California Press, 1985].

Clifford Krauss, **Inside Central America: Its People, Politics, and History** [New York: Summit Books, 1991].

William Krehm, **Democracies and Tyrannies of the Caribbean** [Westport: Lawrence Hill, 1984; first published in Spanish in 1948].

Michael L. Krenn, **US Policy Toward Economic Nationalism in Latin America 1917-1929** [Wilmington: Scholarly Resources, 1990].

Joel Krieger, **Reagan, Thatcher and the Politics of Decline** [Cambridge: Polity Press, 1986].

Michael J. Kryzanek, **US-Latin American Relations** [New York: Praeger, 1985].

Thomas S. Kuhn, **The Structure of Scientific Revolutions** [Chicago: University of Chicago Press, second enlarged edition 1970; first published 1962].

Jonathan Kwitny, **Endless Enemies: The Making of an Unfriendly World** [Harmondsworth: Penguin, 1987; first published New York: Congdon and Weed, 1984].

Richard Allen Labarge, **Impact of the United Fruit Company on the Economic Development of Guatemala 1946-1954** [New Orleans: Tulane University Press, 1960].

Ernesto Laclau and Chantal Mouffe, **Hegemony and Socialist Strategy: Towards a Radical Democratic Politics** [London: Verso, 1985].

Walter LaFeber, **The New Empire: An Interpretation of American Expansion 1860-1898** [Ithaca: Cornell University Press, 1963].

Walter LaFeber, **America, Russia and the Cold War 1945-1984** [New York: Alfred A. Knopf, fifth edition revised 1985].

Walter LaFeber, **The Panama Canal: The Crisis in Historical Perspective** [New York: Oxford University Press, 1978].

Walter LaFeber, **The Panama Canal: The Crisis in Historical**

Perspective [New York: Oxford University Press, updated edition 1989; first published 1978].

Walter LaFeber, **Inevitable Revolutions: The United States in Central America** [New York: W. W. Norton, 1983].

Walter LaFeber, **Inevitable Revolutions: The United States in Central America** [New York: W. W. Norton, expanded edition 1984; first published 1983].

Walter LaFeber, **The American Age: US Foreign Policy at Home and Abroad Since 1750** [New York: W. W. Norton, 1989].

Walter LaFeber, **Inevitable Revolutions: The United States in Central America** [New York: W. W. Norton, second edition, revised and expanded 1993, expanded edition 1984; first published 1983].

Anthony Lake, **Caution and Concern: The Making of American Policy Toward South Africa** [Unpublished PhD dissertation, Princeton University, 1974].

Anthony Lake, **The "Tar Baby" Option: American Policy Toward Southern Rhodesia** [New York: Columbia University Press, 1976].

Anthony Lake, ed., **The Vietnam Legacy: The War, American Society and the Future of American Foreign Policy** [New York: New York University Press, for the Council on Foreign Relations, 1976].

Anthony Lake, I. M. Destler and Leslie H. Gelb, **Our Own Worst Enemy: The Unmaking of American Foreign Policy** [New York: Simon and Schuster, 1984].

Anthony Lake, **Third World Radical Regimes: US Policy Under Carter and Reagan** [New York: Foreign Policy Association, 1985].

Anthony Lake, **Somoza Falling: A Portrait of Washington At Work** [Amherst: University of Massachusetts Press, 1990; first published as **Somoza Falling--The Nicaraguan Dilemma: A Portrait of Washington At Work** Boston: Houghton Mifflin, 1989].

Richard D. Lambert, **Language and Area Studies Review** [Philadelphia: American Academy of Political and Social Science, 1973].

Richard D. Lambert et al., **Beyond Growth: The Next Stage in Language and Area Studies: A Report by the Association of American Universities** [Washington: Association of American Universities, 1984].

John Lamperti, **What Are We Afraid Of?: An Assessment of the "Communist Threat" in Central America** [Boston: South End Press, 1988].

Roger N. Lancaster, **Thanks to God and the Revolution: Popular Religion and Class Consciousness in the New Nicaragua** [New York: Columbia University Press, 1988].

Saul Landau and John Dinges, **Assassination on Embassy Row** [New York: Pantheon, 1980].

Saul Landau, **The Dangerous Doctrine: National Security and US Foreign Policy** [Boulder: Westview Press, 1988].

Saul Landau, **The Guerrilla Wars of Central America: Nicaragua, El Salvador and Guatemala** [London: Weidenfeld and Nicholson, 1993].

James Lang, **Conquest and Commerce: Spain and England in the Americas** [New York: Academic Press, 1975].

James Lang, **Portuguese Brazil: The King's Plantation** [New York: Academic Press, 1975].

William L. Langer, **European Alliances and Alignments 1871-1890** [New York: Alfred A. Knopf, 1931; reprinted New York: Greenwood Press, 1977].

William L. Langer, **The Diplomacy of Imperialism 1890-1902** [New York: Alfred A. Knopf, 1935, reprinted 1951].

Lester D. Langley, **The Cuban Policy of the United States: A Brief History** [New York: Wiley, 1968].

Lester D. Langley, **The Struggle for the American Mediterranean: United States-European Rivalry in the Gulf-Caribbean 1776-1904** [Athens: University of Georgia Press, 1976].

Lester D. Langley, **The United States and the Caribbean in the Twentieth Century** [Athens: University of Georgia Press, 1982; first published in 1980 as **The United States and the Caribbean 1900-1970**].

Lester D. Langley, **The Banana Wars: An Inner History of American Empire 1900-1934** [Lexington: University Press of Kentucky, 1983].

Lester D. Langley, **The Banana Wars: US Intervention in the Caribbean 1898-1934** [Lexington: University Press of Kentucky, revised edition 1985; first published in 1983 as **The Banana Wars: An Inner History of American Empire 1900-1934**].

Lester D. Langley, **Central America: The Real Stakes--Understanding Central America Before It's Too Late** [New York: Crown, 1985].

Lester D. Langley, **America and the Americas: The United States in the Western Hemisphere** [Athens: University of Georgia Press, 1989].

Lester D. Langley and Thomas D. Schoonover, **The Banana Men: American Mercenaries and Entrepreneurs in Central America 1880-1930** [Lexington: University Press of Kentucky, 1994].

Joseph G. LaPalombra and Myron Weiner, **Political Parties and Political Development** [Princeton: Princeton University Press, 1966].

Jorge Larrain, **The Concept of Ideology** [London: Hutchinson, 1981; first published 1979].

Jorge Larrain, **Marxism and Ideology** [London: Macmillan, 1983].

Jorge Larrain, **Theories of Development: Capitalism, Colonialism and Dependency** [London: Polity Press, 1989].

Jorge Larrain, **Ideology and Cultural Identity: Modernity and the Third World Presence** [London: Polity Press, 1994].

Brooke Larson, **Colonialism and Agrarian Transformation in Bolivia: Cochabamba 1550-1900** [Princeton: Princeton University Press, 1988].

John Holladay Latané, **The Diplomatic Relations of the United States and Spanish America** [Baltimore: Johns Hopkins University Press, 1900].

John Holladay Latané, **The United States and Latin America** [Garden City: Doubleday Page, 1920].

John Holladay Latané, **History of American Foreign Policy** [New York: Doubleday Doran, 1927].

Latin American Studies Association, **The Electoral Process in Nicaragua: Domestic and International Influences: Report of the Latin**

American Studies Assocation Delegation to Observe the Nicaraguan General Election of November 4, 1984 [Pittsburgh: University of Pittsburgh, Latin American Studies Association, 1984].

Latin American Studies Association Commission on Compliance with the Central American Peace Accord, **Final Report of the LASA Commission on the Central America Peace Accord** [Pittsburgh: University of Pittsburgh, Latin American Studies Association, March 1988] (reprinted as "Appendix--Extraordinary Opportunities...And New Risks: Final Report of the LASA Commission on the Central America Peace Accord" **LASA Forum** vol. 19, no. 1, 1988).

Latin American Studies Association, **Electoral Democracy Under International Pressure: The Report of the Latin American Studies Association Commission to Observe the 1990 Nicaraguan Election** [Pittsburgh: University of Pittsburgh, Latin American Studies Association, 15 March 1990].

Latin American Studies Center, **Central America: A Bibliography** [Los Angeles: Latin American Studies Center--California State University, second revised edition, 1981].

Michael A. Ledeen and William Lewis, **Debacle: The American Failure in Iran** [New York: Alfred A. Knopf, 1981].

Michael Ledeen, **Grave New World** [New York: Oxford University Press, 1985].

Michael Ledeen, **Perilous Statecraft: An Insider's Account of the Iran-Contra Affair** [New York: Simon and Schuster, 1988].

William J. Lederer and Eugene Burdick, **The Ugly American** [London: Victor Gollancz, 1958].

William J. Lederer, **Our Own Worst Enemy** [New York: W. W. Norton, 1968] (also published as **The Anguished American** [London: Victor Gollancz, 1969]).

Melvyn P. Leffler, **A Preponderance of Power: National Security, the Truman Administration and the Cold War** [Stanford: Stanford University Press, 1992].

David Lehmann, **Democracy and Development in Latin America: Economics, Politics and Religion in the Post-war Period** [Philadelphia: Temple University Press, 1990].

Robert S. Leiken, **Soviet Strategy in Latin America** [New York: Praeger, 1982, The Washington Papers, vol. 10, no. 93].

John A. Lejeune, **The Reminiscences of a Marine** [Philadelphia: Dorrance, 1930].

Jesse Lemisch, **On Active Service in War and Peace: Politics and Ideology in the American Historical Profession** [Toronto: New Hogtown Press, 1975].

Sidney Lens, **The Forging of the American Empire: From the Revolution to Vietnam, A History of American Imperialism** [New York: Crowell, 1971].

William LeoGrande, **Cuba's Policy in Africa 1959-1980** [Berkeley: Institute of International Studies, 1980].

William LeoGrande, **Central America and the Polls** [Washington: Washington Office on Latin America, 1984].

Thomas M. Leonard, **The United States and Central America 1944-1949: Perceptions of Political Dynamics** [Tuscaloosa: University of Alabama Press, 1984].

Thomas M. Leonard, **Central America and United States Policies 1820s-1980s: A Guide to Issues and References** [Claremont California: Regina Books, 1985].

Thomas M. Leonard, **Central America and the United States: The Search for Stability** [Athens: University of Georgia Press, 1991].

Daniel Lerner, **The Passing of Traditional Society: Modernizing the Middle East** [New York: Free Press, 1958].

Penny Lernoux, **Cry of the People: United States Involvement in the Rise of Facism, Torture, and Murder and the Persecution of the Catholic Church in Latin America** [New York: Doubleday, 1980; reprinted as **Cry of the People: The Struggle for Human Rights in Latin America--The Catholic Church in Conflict with US Policy** (New York: Penguin Books, 1986)].

Jerome Levinson and Juan de Onis, **The Alliance That Lost Its Way: A Critical Report on the Alliance for Progress** [Chicago: Quadrangle Books, 1970].

Guenter Lewy, **America in Vietnam** [New York: Oxford University Press, 1978].

Colin Leys, **Underdevelopment in Kenya: The Political Economy of Neo-Colonialism 1964-1971** [London: Heinemann, 1975].

Library of Congress, Hispanic Foundation, **National Directory of Latin Americanists** [Washington: Library of Congress, second edition, 1971].

Edwin Lieuwen, **Arms and Politics in Latin America** [New York: Frederick A. Praeger, revised edition 1961; first published 1960].

Edwin Lieuwen, **Generals versus Presidents: Neo-Militarism in Latin America** [New York: Praeger, 1964].

Edwin Lieuwen, **US Policy in Latin America: A Short History** [New York: Praeger, 1965].

Edwin Lieuwen, **The United States and the Challenge to Security in Latin America** [Columbus: Ohio State University Press, 1966].

Marc Lindenberg and Benjamin Crosby, **Managing Development: The Political Dimension** [New Brunswick: Transaction Books, 1981].

Gerald F. Linderman, **The Mirror of War: American Society and the Spanish-American War** [Ann Arbor: University of Michigan Press, 1974].

Sol M. Linowitz (chair, Commission on United States-Latin American Relations), **The Americas in a Changing World** [Chicago: Quadrangle Press, 1976].

Sol Linowitz (chair, Commission on United States-Latin American Relations), **The United States and Latin America: Next Steps** [New York: Center for Inter-American Relations, 1976].

Alain Lipietz, **Mirages and Miracles: The Crises of Global Fordism** [London: Verso, 1987].

Seymour Martin Lipset and Everett Carl Ladd, Jr., **The Divided Academy: Professors and Politics** [New York: McGraw-Hill, 1975].

Charles Lipson, **Standing Guard: Protecting Foreign Capital in the Nineteenth and Twentieth Centuries** [Berkeley: University of California Press, 1985].

George Liska, **Imperial America: The International Politics of Primacy** [Baltimore: Johns Hopkins University Press, 1967].

George Liska, **War and Order: Reflections on Vietnam and History** [Baltimore: Johns Hopkins University Press, 1968].

George Liska, **Beyond Kissinger: Ways of Conservative Statecraft** [Baltimore: Johns Hopkins University Press, 1973].

George Liska, **States in Evolution: Changing Societies and Traditional Systems in World Politics** [Baltimore: Johns Hopkins University Press, 1975].

George Liska, **Quest for Equilibrium: America and the Balance of Power on Land and Sea** [Baltimore: Johns Hopkins University Press, 1977].

George Liska, **Career of Empire: America and Imperial Expansion Over Land and Sea** [Baltimore: Johns Hopkins University Press, 1978].

Sheldon B. Liss, **Marxist Thought in Latin America** [Berkeley: University of California Press, 1984].

Sheldon B. Liss, **Roots of Revolution: Radical Thought in Cuba** [Lincoln: University of Nebraska Press, 1987].

Sheldon B. Liss, **Radical Thought in Central America** [Boulder: Westview Press, 1991].

Robert S. Litwak, **Détente and the Nixon Doctrine: American Foreign Policy and the Pursuit of Stability 1969-1976** [Cambridge: Cambridge University Press, 1986; first published 1984].

Joseph B. Lockley, **Pan Americanism: Its Beginnings** [New York: Macmillan, 1920].

George Cabot Lodge, **Engines of Change: United States Interests and Revolution in Latin America** [New York: Alfred A. Knopf, 1970].

Timothy J. Lomperis, **The War Everyone Lost--And Won: America's Intervention in Viet Nam's Twin Struggles** [Baton Rouge: Louisiana State University Press, 1984].

William Roger Louis, ed., **Imperialism: The Robinson and Gallagher Controversy** [New York: Franklin Watts, 1976].

William Roger Louis, **Imperialism at Bay: The United States and the Decolonization of the British Empire 1941-1945** [New York: Oxford University Press, 1978].

Brian Loveman, **Chile: The Legacy of Hispanic Capitalism** [New York: Oxford University Press, 1979].

Abraham F. Lowenthal, **The Dominican Intervention** [Cambridge: Harvard University Press, 1972].

Abraham F. Lowenthal, **Partners in Conflict: The United States and Latin America** [Baltimore: Johns Hopkins University Press, 1987].

Abraham F. Lowenthal, **Partners in Conflict: The United States and Latin America in the 1990s** [Baltimore: Johns Hopkins University Press, 1990; revised edition of **Partners in Conflict: The United States and Latin America**, first published 1987].

Henry R. Luce, **The American Century** [New York: 1941].

Neill Macaulay, **The Sandino Affair** [Chicago: Quadrangle Books, 1967].

Colin M. MacLachlan, **Spain's Empire in the New World: The Role of Ideas in Institutional and Social Change** [Berkeley: University of California Press, 1991; first published 1988].

Murdo MacLeod, **Spanish Central America: A Socioeconomic History 1520-1720** [Berkeley: University of California Press, 1973].

Robert J. Maddox, **The New Left and the Origins of the Cold War** [Princeton: Princeton University Press, 1973].

Harry Magdoff, **The Age of Imperialism: The Economics of US Foreign Policy** [New York: Monthly Review Press, 1969].

Harry Magdoff, **Imperialism: From the Colonial Age to the Present** [London: Monthly Review Press, 1978].

Anthony P. Maingot, **US Power and Caribbean Sovereignty: Geopolitics in a Sphere of Influence** [Boulder: Lynne Rienner, 1988].

Florencia E. Mallon, **The Defense of Community in Peru's Central Highlands: Peasant Struggle and Capitalist Transition 1860-1940** [Princeton: Princeton University Press, 1983].

Florencia E. Mallon, **Peasant and Nation: The Making of Postcolonial Mexico and Peru** [Berkeley: University of California Press, 1994].

Beatrice Manz, **Refugees of a Hidden War: The Aftermath of Counterinsurgency in Guatemala** [Albany: State University of New York Press, 1988].

Patrick Marnham, **So Far from God: A Journey to Central America** [New York: Viking Penguin, 1986].

David Marr, **Vietnamese Anticolonialism 1885-1925** [Berkeley: University of California Press, 1971].

David Marr, **Vietnamese Tradition on Trial 1920-1945** [Berkeley: University of California Press, 1981].

Margaret Alexander Marsh, **The Bankers in Bolivia: A Study in American Foreign Investment** [New York: Vanguard Press, 1928].

Jonathan Marshall, Peter Dale Scott and Jane Hunter, **The Iran Contra Connection: Secret Teams and Covert Operations in the Reagan Era** [Boston: South End Press, 1987].

Jonathan Marshall, **Drug Wars: Corruption, Counterinsurgency and Covert Operations in the Third World** [Berkeley: Cohan and Cohen, 1991].

Jose Marti, **Inside the Monster: Writings on the United States and American Imperialism** [New York: Monthly Review Press, 1975].

Gerald Martin, **Journeys Through the Labyrinth: Latin American Fiction in the Twentieth Century** [London: Verso, 1989].

John Bartlow Martin, **Overtaken by Events: The Dominican Crisis from the Fall of Trujillo to the Civil War** [Garden City: Doubleday, 1966].

John Bartlow Martin, **US Policy in the Caribbean** [Boulder: Westview Press, 1978, for the Twentieth Century Fund].

John D. Martz, **Communist Infiltration in Guatemala: A Study in**

Subversion [New York: Vantage Press, 1956].

John D. Martz, **Central America: The Crisis and the Challenge** [Chapel Hill: University of North Carolina, 1959].

John D. Martz, **Colombia: A Contemporary Political Study** [Chapel Hill: University of North Carolina Press, 1962; reprinted New York: Greenwood Press, 1975].

John D. Martz, **Justo Rufino Barrios and Central American Union** [Gainesville: University of Florida Press, 1963].

John D. Martz, ed., **The Dynamics of Change in Latin American Politics** [Englewood Cliffs: Prentice-Hall, 1965, second edition 1971].

John D. Martz, *Acción Democrática*: **Evolution of a Modern Political Party in Venezuela** [Princeton: Princeton University Press, 1966].

John D. Martz and Miguel Jorrin, **Latin-American Political Thought and Ideology** [Chapel Hill: University of North Carolina Press, 1970].

John D. Martz, **Ecuador: Conflicting Political Culture and the Quest for Progress** [Boston: Allyn and Bacon, 1972].

John D. Martz and Enrique A. Baloyra, **Electoral Mobilization and Public Opinion: The Venezuela Campaign of 1973** [Chapel Hill: University of North Carolina Press, 1976].

John D. Martz and David J. Myers, eds., **Venezuela: The Democratic Experience** [New York: Praeger, 1977, second edition 1986].

John D. Martz and Enrique Baloyra, **Political Attitudes in Venezuela: Societal Cleavages and Political Opinion** [Austin: University of Texas Press, 1979].

John D. Martz, **Politics and Petroleum in Ecuador** [New Brunswick: Transaction Books, 1987].

Jonathan Evan Maslow, **Bird of Life, Bird of Death: A Naturalist's Journey Through a Land of Political Turmoil** [London: Viking, 1986].

Herbert L. Matthews, **The Cuban Story** [New York: George Braziller, 1961].

Ernest R. May, **Imperial Democracy: The Emergence of America as a Great Power** [New York: Harcourt, Brace and World, 1961].

Ernest R. May, **American Imperialism: A Speculative Essay** [New York: Atheneum, 1968].

Ernest R. May, **'Lessons of the Past': The Use and Misuse of History in American Foreign Policy** [London: Oxford University Press, 1975; first published 1973].

Ernest R. May, **The Making of the Monroe Doctrine** [Cambridge: Harvard University Press, 1975].

Ernest R. May and Richard E. Neustadt, **Thinking in Time: The Uses of History for Decision Makers** [New York: Free Press, 1986].

Herbert K. May, **Problems and Prospects of the Alliance for Progress: A Critical Examination** [New York: Praeger, 1968].

Herbert K. May, **The Role of Foreign Investment in Latin America: Some Considerations and Definitions** [New York: Fund for Multinational Management Education, 1974].

Herbert K. May, **Multinational Corporations in Latin America: A Study** [New York: Council of the Americas, 1975].

Robert E. May, **The Southern Dream of Caribbean Empire 1854-1861** [Baton Rouge: University of Louisiana Press, 1973].

Stacey May and Galo Plaza, **The United Fruit Company in Latin America** [Washington: National Planning Association, 1958; reprinted New York: Arno Press, 1976].

David Mayers, **George Kennan and the Dilemmas of US Foreign Policy** [New York: Oxford University Press, 1988].

John F. McCamant, **The Role of International Economic Assistance Programs in Economic and Political Change in Central America** [Unpublished PhD dissertation, University of Washington, 1965].

John F. McCamant, **Development Assistance in Central America** [New York: Praeger, 1967].

Thomas P. McCann, **An American Company: The Tragedy of United Fruit** [New York: Crown, 1976].

Eugene J. McCarthy, **The Limits of Power: America's Role in the World** [New York: Holt, Rinehart and Winston, 1967].

Robert A. McCaughey, **International Studies and Academic Enterprise: A Chapter in the Enclosure of American Learning** [New York: Columbia University Press, 1984].

Michael McClintock, **The American Connection--Volume 1: State Terror and Popular Resistance in El Salvador** [London: Zed Books, 1985].

Michael McClintock, **The American Connection--Volume 2: State Terror and Popular Resistance in Guatemala** [London: Zed Books, 1985].

Michael McClintock, **Instruments of Statecraft: US Guerrilla Warfare, Counter-Insurgency and Counter-Terrorism 1940-1990** [New York: Pantheon, 1992].

David McCreery, **Development and the State in Reforma Guatemala 1871-1885** [Columbus: Ohio University Center for International Studies, 1983].

Ronald H. McDonald and J. Mark Ruhl, **Party Politics and Elections in Latin America** [Boulder: Westview Press, 1989].

Thomas F. McGann, **Argentina, the United States, and the Inter-American System 1880-1914** [Notre Dame: University of Notre Dame Press, 1958].

William Paul McGreevey, **An Economic History of Colombia 1845-1930** [Cambridge: Cambridge University Press, 1971].

Kermit E. Mckenzie, **Comintern and World Revolution 1928-1943: The Shaping of Doctrine** [New York: Columbia University Press, 1964].

Frank McNeil, **War and Peace in Central America: Reality and Illusion** [New York: Charles Scribner's Sons, 1988].

J. Lloyd Mecham, **Church and State in Latin America: A History of Politico-Ecclesiastical Relations** [Chapel Hill: University of North Carolina Press, 1934, reprinted 1966].

J. Lloyd Mecham, **The United States and Inter-American Security** [Austin: University of Texas Press, 1961].

J. Lloyd Mecham, **A Survey of United States-Latin American Relations** [Boston: Houghton Mifflin, 1965].

J. Lloyd Mecham, **Francisco Ibarra and Nueva Vizcaya** [New York: Greenwood Press, 1968].

Richard A. Melanson, **Writing History and Making Policy: The Cold War, Vietnam and Revisionism** [New York: University Press of America, 1983].

Richard A. Melanson, **Reconstructing Consensus: American Foreign Policy since the Vietnam War** [London: Macmillan, 1991].

G. A. Mellander, **The United States in Panamanian Politics: The Intriguing Years** [Danville: Interstate, 1971].

Dianna Melrose, **Nicaragua: The Threat of a Good Example?** [Oxford: Oxfam, 1985].

Thomas and Marjorie Melville, **Guatemala: The Politics of Land Ownership** [New York: Free Press, 1971].

Thomas and Marjorie Melville, **Guatemala: Another Vietnam?** [Harmondsworth: Penguin Books, 1971] (a slightly revised version of **Guatemala: The Politics of Land Ownership** [New York: Free Press, 1971]).

Rigoberta Menchu (edited and introduced by Elisabeth Burgos-Debray), **I, Rigoberta Menchu: An Indian Woman in Guatemala** [London: Verso, 1984; first published as **Me llamo Rigoberta Menchu y así me nacio la conciencia**, 1983].

Frederick Merk, **Manifest Destiny and Mission in American History: A Reinterpretation** [New York: Alfred A. Knopf, 1963].

Michael C. Meyer, **Supplement to a Bibliography of United States-Latin American Relations Since 1810** [Lincoln: University of Nebraska Press, 1979].

Joel S. Migdal, **Peasants, Politics and Revolution: Pressures Toward Political Change in the Third World** [Princeton: Princeton University Press, 1974].

Joel S. Migdal, **Strong Societies and Weak States: State-Society Relations and State Capabilities in the Third World** [Princeton: Princeton University Press, 1988].

Ralph Miliband, **The State in Capitalist Society** [London: Weidenfeld and Nicolson 1969].

Max F. Milikan and Walt Whitman Rostow, **A Proposal: Key to an Effective Foreign Policy** [New York: Harper and Row, 1957].

Max F. Milikan, Donald L. Blackmer et al., **The Emerging Nations: Their Growth and United States Policy** [Boston: Little Brown, 1961].

Delia Miller, R. Seem and Cynthia Arnson, **Background Information on Guatemala, the Armed Forces and US Military Assistance** [Washington: Institute for Policy Studies, 1981].

Nicola Miller, **Soviet Relations with Latin America 1959-1987** [Cambridge: Cambridge University Press, 1989].

Allan Reed Millett, **The Politics of Intervention: The Military Occupation of Cuba 1906-1909** [Columbus: Ohio State University Press, 1968].

Richard Millett, **The History of the Guardia Nacional de Nicaragua 1925-1965** [Unpublished PhD dissertation, University of New Mexico, 1966].

Richard Millett, **Guardians of the Dynasty: A History of the US Created** *Guardia Nacional de Nicaragua* **and the Somoza Family** [Maryknoll, New York: Orbis Books, 1977].

William Minter, **King Solomon's Mines Revisited: Western Interests and the Burdened History of Southern Africa** [New York: Basic Books, 1986].

Harold Molineu, **US Policy Toward Latin America: From Regionalism to Globalism** [Boulder: Westview Press, 1986].

Tommie Sue Montgomery, **Revolution in El Salvador: Origins and Evolution** [Boulder: Westview Press, second edition revised and updated, 1990; first published 1982].

Parker T. Moon, **Imperialism and World Politics** [New York: Macmillan, 1939; first published 1926].

Barrington Moore, Jr., **Social Origins of Dictatorship and Democracy: Lord and Peasant in the Making of the Modern World** [Boston: Beacon Press, 1966].

Arthur, Morelet, **Travels in Central America** [New York: Leypoldt, Host and Williams, 1871].

Dario Moreno, **US Policy in Central America: The Endless Debate** [Miami: Florida International University Press, 1990].

Dario Moreno, **The Struggle for Peace in Central America** [Miami: University Press of Florida, 1994].

Elting E. Morison, **Turmoil and Tradition: A Study of the Life and Times of Henry L. Stimson** [New York: Atheneum, 1963].

Morris Morley and James Petras, **The Reagan Administration and Nicaragua: How Washington Constructs Its Case for Counter-revolution in Central America** [New York: Institute for Media Analysis, 1987].

Morris H. Morley, **Imperial State and Revolution: The United States and Cuba 1952-1986** [New York: Cambridge University Press, 1987].

Morris H. Morley, **Washington, Somoza, and the Sandinistas: State and Regime in US Policy 1969-1981** [New York: Cambridge University Press, 1994].

David Morris, **We Must Make Haste--Slowly: The Process of Revolution in Chile** [New York: Random House, 1973].

Delesseps S. Morrison, **Latin American Mission** [New York: 1965].

Frances Moulder, **Japan, China and the Modern World-Economy: Towards a Reinterpretation of East Asian Development ca. 1600 to ca. 1918** [Cambridge: Cambridge University Press, 1977].

Nicos P. Mouzelis, **Politics in the Semi-Periphery: Early Parliamentarism and Late Industrialisation in the Balkans and Latin America** [London: Macmillan, 1986].

Paige Elliott Mulhollan, **Philander C. Knox and Dollar Diplomacy 1909-1913** [Unpublished PhD dissertation, University of Texas, 1966].

Ronaldo Munck, **Politics and Dependency in the Third World: The**

Case of Latin America [London: Zed Press, 1984].

Ronaldo Munck, **Latin America: The Transition to Democracy** [London: Zed Press, 1987].

Dana Gardner Munro, **The Five Republics of Central America: Their Political and Economic Development and Their Relations with the United States** [Unpublished PhD dissertation, University of Pennsylvania, 1917].

Dana Gardner Munro, **The Five Republics of Central America: Their Political and Economic Development and Their Relations with the United States** [New York: Oxford University Press, 1918].

Dana Gardner Munro, **The United States and the Caribbean Area** [Boston: World Peace Foundation, 1934; reprinted New York: Johnson Reprint Corp., 1966].

Dana Gardner Munro, **The Latin American Republics: A History** [London: George G. Harrap, 1961, third edition].

Dana Gardner Munro, **Intervention and Dollar Diplomacy in the Caribbean 1900-1921** [Princeton: Princeton University Press, 1964].

Dana Gardner Munro, **The United States and the Caribbean Republics 1921-1933**. [Princeton: Princeton University Press, 1974].

Dana G. Munro, **A Student in Central America 1914-1916** [New Orleans: Tulane University Press, 1983].

Joshua Muravchik, **The Uncertain Crusade: Jimmy Carter and the Dilemmas of Human Rights Policy** [Washington: American Enterprise Institute, 1986].

Joshua Muravchik, **News Coverage of the Sandinista Revolution** [Washington: American Enterprise Institute, 1988].

Joshua Muravchik, **Exporting Democracy: Fulfilling America's Destiny** [Washington: American Enterprise Institute, 1991].

Ivan Musicant, **The Banana Wars: A History of United States Military Intervention in Latin America from the Spanish-American War to the Invasion of Grenada** [New York: Macmillan, 1990].

Vijay Naidu, **Development, State and Class Theories: An Introductory Survey** [Suva: Fiji Institute of Applied Studies, 1991].

Bernard C. Nalty, **The United States Marines in Nicaragua** [Washington: Historical Branch G-3, US Marine Corps Historical Reference Series 21, revised edition 1962].

Dadabhai Naoroji, **Poverty and Un-British Rule in India** [Delhi: Government of India Publications Division, 1962; first published in London 1901].

James A. Nathan and James K. Oliver, **United States Foreign Policy and World Order** [Boston: Little Brown, third edition 1985].

Scott Nearing, **The American Empire** [New York: Rand School of Social Science, 1921].

Scott Nearing and Joseph Freeman, **Dollar Diplomacy: A Study in American Imperialism** [New York: Monthly Review Press, 1966; first published 1925].

Scott Nearing, **The Twilight of Empire: An Economic Interpretation of Imperialist Cycles** [New York: Vanguard Press, 1930].

Scott Nearing, **The Tragedy of Empire** [New York: Island Press, 1945].

Scott Nearing, **Cuba and Latin America: An Eyewitness Report on the Continental Congress for Solidarity with Cuba** (pamphlet) [Harborside: Social Science Institute, 1963].

Scott Nearing, **The Making of a Radical: A Political Autobiography** [New York: Harper and Row, 1972].

Martin C. Needler, **Understanding Foreign Policy** [New York: Holt, Rinehart and Winston, 1966].

Martin C. Needler, **Political Development in Latin America: Instability, Violence, and Evolutionary Change** [New York: Random House, 1968].

Martin C. Needler, **The United States and the Latin American Revolution** [Berkeley: University of California Press, revised edition 1977; first published Boston: Allyn and Bacon, 1972].

Martin C. Needler, **An Introduction to Latin American Politics: The Structure of Conflict** [Englewood Cliffs: Prentice-Hall, 1977].

Martin C. Needler, **The Problem of Democracy in Latin America** [Lexington: D. C. Heath, 1987].

Martin C. Needler, **Mexican Politics: The Containment of Conflict** [New York: Praeger, second edition, revised and updated, 1990; first published 1982].

Robert P. Newman, **Owen Lattimore and the "Loss" of China** [Berkeley: University of California Press, 1992].

Frank A. Ninkovich, **The Diplomacy of Ideas: US Foreign Policy and Cultural Relations 1938-1950** [Cambridge: Cambridge University Press, 1981].

Robert A. Nisbet, **Social Change and History** [New York: Oxford University Press, 1969].

Richard Nixon, **RN: The Memoirs of Richard Nixon** [New York: Grosset and Dunlap, 1978].

Richard Nixon, **The Real War** [New York: Warner Books, 1980].

Richard Nixon, **Leaders** [New York: Warner Books, 1982].

Richard Nixon, **Real Peace: Strategy for the West** [New York: Little Brown, 1984].

Richard Nixon, **No More Vietnams** [London: W. H. Allen, 1986; first published New York: Arbor House, 1985].

Richard Nixon, **1990: Victory Without War** [London: Sidgwick and Jackson, 1988].

Richard Nixon, **Seize the Moment: America's Challenge in a One-Superpower World** [New York: Simon and Schuster, 1992].

David Nolan, **The Ideology of the Sandinistas and the Nicaraguan Revolution** [Miami: University of Miami Press, 1984].

Michael Novak, **The American Vision: An Essay on the Future of Democratic Capitalism** [Washington: American Enterprise Institute, 1978].

Michael Novak, ed., **Liberation South, Liberation North** [Washington: American Enterprise Institute, 1981].

Michael Novak, **The Spirit of Democratic Capitalism** [Washington:

American Enterprise Institute, 1982].

Michael Novak, ed., **Latin America: Dependency or Interdependence** [Washington: American Enterprise Institute, 1985].

Michael Novak, **Taking Glasnost Seriously: Toward an Open Soviet Union** [Washington: American Enterprise Institute, 1988].

Michael Novak, ed., **Liberation Theology and Liberal Society** [Washington: American Enterprise Institute, 1987].

Michael Novak, **This Hemisphere of Liberty: A Philosophy of the Americas** [Washington: American Enterprise Institute, 1990].

Peter Novick, **That Noble Dream: The "Objectivity Question" and the American Historical Profession** [Cambridge: Cambridge University Press, 1988].

Richard A. Nuccio, **What's Wrong, Who's Right in Central America?: A Citizen's Guide** [New York: Roosevelt Center for American Policy Studies, 1986].

Jeffrey B. Nugent, **Economic Integration in Central America: Empirical Investigations** [Baltimore: Johns Hopkins University Press, 1974].

J. Warren Nystrom and Nathan A. Haverstock, **The Alliance for Progress: Key to Latin America's Development** [Princeton: D. Van Nostrand, 1966].

Guillermo O'Donnell, **Modernization and Bureaucratic-Authoritarianism: Studies in South American Politics** [Berkeley: University of California Institute of International Studies, 1973].

Guillermo O'Donnell, **1966-1973, El estado burocratico autoritario: triunfos, derrotas y crisis** [Buenos Aires: Editorial Belgrano, 1982].

Guillermo O'Donnell and Philippe C. Schmitter, **Transitions from Authoritarian Rule: Tentative Conclusions and Uncertain Democracies** [Baltimore: Johns Hopkins University Press, 1986].

Guillermo O'Donnell, **Bureaucratic-Authoritarianism: Argentina 1966-1973 in Comparative Perspective** [Berkeley: University of California Press, 1988].

Gary L. Olson, **US Foreign Policy and the Third World Peasant: Land Reform in Asia and Latin America** [New York: Praeger, 1974].

Laura Nuzzi O'Shaughnessy and Luis H. Serra, **The Church and Revolution in Nicaragua** [Athens: Ohio University, International Studies Latin American Monographs Series no. 11, 1986].

Gene Overstreet and Marshall Windmiller, **Communism in India** [Berkeley: University of California Press, 1959].

PACCA (Policy Alternatives for the Caribbean and Central America), **Changing Course: Blueprint for Peace in Central America and the Caribbean** [Washington: Institute for Policy Studies, 1984].

Robert A. Packenham, **Liberal America and the Third World: Political Development Ideas in Foreign Aid and Social Science** [Princeton: Princeton University Press, 1973].

Robert A. Packenham, **The Dependency Movement: Scholarship and Politics in Development Studies** [Cambridge: Harvard University Press, 1992].

Alfonso Bauer Paíz, **Como opera el capital yanqui en Centro-américa:**

El caso de Guatemala [Mexico: Ibero-Mexicana, 1956].

Frederick Palmer, **Central America and Its Problems** [New York: Moffat Yard, 1910].

Franklin D. Parker, **The Central American Republics** [New York: Oxford University Press, 1964].

Francis Parkinson, **Latin America, the Cold War and the World Powers 1945-1973: A Study in Diplomatic History** [London: Sage, 1974].

Patricia Parkman, **Nonviolent Insurrection in El Salvador: The Fall of General Maximiliano Hernandez Martinez** [Tucson: University of Arizona Press, 1988].

Robert A. Pastor, **Congress and the Politcs of US Foreign Economic Policy 1929-1976** [Berkeley: University of California Press, 1980].

Robert A. Pastor, **Migration and Development in the Caribbean: The Unexplored Connection** [Boulder: Westview Press, 1985].

Robert A. Pastor, **Latin America's Debt Crisis: Adjusting to the Past or Planning for the Future** [Boulder: Lynne Rienner Publishers, 1987].

Robert A. Pastor, **Condemned to Repetition: The United States and Nicaragua** [Princeton: Princeton University Press, 1987].

Robert A. Pastor, **Condemned to Repetition: The United States and Nicaragua** [Princeton: Princeton University Press, reprinted with a new epilogue 1988].

Robert A. Pastor and Jorge G. Castañeda, **Limits to Friendship: The United States and Mexico** [New York: Alfred A. Knopf, 1988].

Robert A. Pastor, **Whirlpool: US Foreign Policy Toward Latin America and the Caribbean** [Princeton: Princeton University Press, 1992].

Thomas G. Paterson, **Meeting the Communist Threat: Truman to Reagan** [New York: Oxford University Press, 1988].

Thomas G. Paterson, **Contesting Castro: The United States and the Triumph of the Cuban Revolution** New York: Oxford University Press, 1994].

Archimedes Patti, **Why Vietnam?: Prelude to America's Albatross** [Berkeley: University of California Press, 1980].

Jeremy Paxman, **Through the Volcanoes: A Central American Journey** [London: Paladin, 1987; first published 1985].

Jenny Pearce, **Under the Eagle: US Intervention in Central America and the Caribbean** [London: Latin America Bureau, updated edition 1982; first published 1981].

Jenny Pearce, **Promised Land: Peasant Rebellion in Chalatenango, El Salvador** [London: Latin American Bureau, 1986].

Gillian Peele, **Revival and Reaction: The Right in Contemporary America** [New York: Oxford University Press, 1987; first published 1984].

John A. Peeler, **Latin American Democracies: Colombia, Costa Rica, Venezuela** [Chapel Hill: University of North Carolina Press, 1985].

Richard Peet, **Global Capitalism: Theories of Societal Development** [London: Routledge, 1991].

Louis A. Pérez, Jr., **Army Politics in Cuba 1898-1958** [Pittsburgh:

University of Pittsburgh Press, 1976].

Louis A. Pérez, Jr., **Cuba Between Empires 1878-1902** [Pittsburgh: University of Pittsburgh Press, 1983].

Louis A. Pérez, Jr., **Cuba Under the Platt Amendment 1902-1934** [Pittsburgh: University of Pittsburgh Press, 1986].

Louis A. Pérez, **Cuba: Between Reform and Revolution** [New York: Oxford University Press, 1988].

Louis A. Pérez, Jr., **Lords of the Mountain: Social Banditry and Peasant Protest in Cuba 1878-1918** [Pittsburg: University of Pittsburgh Press, 1989].

Hector Pérez-Brignoli, **A Brief History of Central America** [Berkeley: University of California Press, 1989].

Dexter Perkins, **The Monroe Doctrine 1823-1826** [Cambridge: Harvard University Press, 1927; reprinted Gloucester: Peter Smith, 1965].

Dexter Perkins, **The Monroe Doctrine 1826-1867** [Baltimore: Johns Hopkins University Press, 1933; reprinted Gloucester: Peter Smith, 1966].

Dexter Perkins, **The Monroe Doctrine 1867-1907** [Baltimore: Johns Hopkins University Press 1937; reprinted Gloucester: Peter Smith, 1966].

Dexter Perkins, **Hands Off: A History of the Monroe Doctrine** [Boston: Little Brown, 1941].

Dexter Perkins, **A History of the Monroe Doctrine** [Boston: Little Brown, revised 1955; first published 1941].

Dexter Perkins, **America and Two Wars** [Boston: Little Brown, 1944].

Dexter Perkins, **The United States and the Caribbean** [Cambridge: Harvard University Press, 1947].

Dexter Perkins, **The Evolution of American Foreign Policy** [New York: Oxford University Press, 1948].

Dexter Perkins, **The American Approach to Foreign Policy** [Cambridge: Harvard University Press, 1951].

Dexter Perkins, **Charles Evans Hughes and American Democratic Statesmanship** [Boston: Little, Brown, 1956 reprinted New York: Greenwood Press, 1978].

Dexter Perkins, **The New Age of Franklin Roosevelt 1932-1945** [Chicago: University of Chicago Press, 1957].

Dexter Perkins, **The American Way** [New York: Cornell University Press, 1957].

Dexter Perkins, **Foreign Policy and the American Spirit: Essays** [Port Washington New York: Kennikat Press, 1972; first published 1957].

Dexter Perkins, **The United States and Latin America** [Baton Rouge: Louisiana State University Press, 1961, reprinted 1964].

Dexter Perkins, **America's Quest for Peace** [Bloomington: Indiana University Press, 1962].

Dexter Perkins, **The American Approach to Foreign Policy** [Cambridge: Harvard University Press, revised edition 1962; first published 1951].

Dexter Perkins, **A History of the Monroe Doctrine** [Boston: Little Brown, 1963, third edition]. (This is a revised version of **Hands Off: A History of the Monroe Doctrine** first published in 1941.)

Dexter Perkins, **The American Democracy: Its Rise to Power** [New York:

Macmillan, 1964].

Dexter Perkins, **The Evolution of American Foreign Policy** [New York: Oxford University Press, 1966, second edition].

Dexter Perkins, **The United States and the Caribbean** [Cambridge: Harvard University Press, revised edition 1966].

Dexter Perkins, **The Diplomacy of a New Age: Major Issues in US Policy Since 1945** [Bloomington: Indiana University Press, 1967].

Dexter Perkins, **Yield of the Years: An Autobiography** [Boston: Little Brown, 1969].

Whitney T. Perkins, **Denial of Empire: The United States and Its Dependencies** [Leyden: A. W. Sythoff, 1962].

Whitney T. Perkins, **Constraints of Empire: The United States and Caribbean Interventions** [Oxford: Clio Press, 1981].

Harvey S. Perloff, **Alliance for Progress: A Social Invention in the Making** [Baltimore: Johns Hopkins University Press, 1969].

Stan Persky, **The Last Domino: US Foreign Policy in Central America Under Reagan** [Vancouver: New Star Books, 1984].

Harold F. Peterson, **Argentina and the United States 1810-1960** [New York: State University of New York, 1964].

James F. Petras, **Politics and Social Forces in Chilean Development** [Berkeley: University of California Press, 1969].

James F. Petras and Maurice Zeitlin, **El radicalismo de la clase trabajadora Chilena** [Buenos Aires: Centro Editor de América Latina, 1970].

James F. Petras and Robert LaPorte, **Cultivating Revolution: The United States and Agrarian Reform in Latin America** [New York: Vintage Books, 1973; first published 1971].

James F. Petras and Hugo Zemelman Merino, **Peasants in Revolt: A Chilean Case Study 1965-1971** [Austin: University of Texas Press, 1972].

James F. Petras and Morris Morley, **The United States and Chile: Imperialism and the Overthrow of the Allende Government** [New York: Monthly Review Press, 1975].

James Petras, Morris Morley and Steven Smith, **The Nationalization of Venezuelan Oil** [New York: Praeger, 1977].

James F. Petras, **Critical Perspectives on Imperialism and Social Class in the Third World** [New York: Monthly Review Press, 1978].

James F. Petras and Morris Morley, **US Hegemony Under Siege: Class, Politics and Development in Latin America** [London: Verso, 1990].

James F. Petras and Morris Morley, **Latin America in the Time of Cholera: Electoral Politics, Market Economics and Permanent Crisis** [London: Routledge, 1992].

Irving Peter Pflaum, **Tragic Island: How Communism Came to Cuba** [Englewood Cliffs: Prentice-Hall, 1961].

W. W. Pierson and Federico G. Gil, **Governments of Latin America** [New York: McGraw-Hill, 1957].

Jan Nederveen Pieterse, **Empire and Emancipation: Power and Liberation on a World Scale** [London: Pluto Press, 1990].

Fredrick B. Pike, **Chile and the United States 1880-1962: The Emergence of Chile's Social Crisis and the Challenge to United States Diplomacy** [Notre Dame: University of Notre Dame Press, 1963].

Fredrick B. Pike, **Hispanismo** [Notre Dame: University of Notre Dame Press, 1971].

Fredrick B. Pike, **Spanish America 1900-1970, Tradition and Social Innovation** [New York: W. W. Norton, 1973].

Fredrick B. Pike, **The United States and the Andean Republics** [Cambridge: Harvard University Press, 1977].

Fredrick B. Pike, **The Politics of the Miraculous in Peru: Haya de la Torre and the Spiritualist Tradition** [Lincoln: Nebraska University Press, 1986].

Fredrick B. Pike, **The United States and Latin America: Myths and Stereotypes of Civilization and Nature** [Austin: University of Texas Press, 1992].

Joseph A. Pitti, **Jorge Ubico and Guatemalan Politics in the 1920s** [Unpublished PhD dissertation, University of New Mexico, 1975].

Norman Podhoretz, **Making It** [New York: Random House, 1967].

Norman Podhoretz, **Doings and Undoings** [New York: Farrar Straus, 1964].

Norman Podhoretz, **Breaking Ranks: A Political Memoir** [London: Weidenfeld and Nicolson, 1980; first published 1979].

Norman Podhoretz, **The Present Danger: "Do We Have the Will to Reverse the Decline of American Power?"** [New York: Simon and Schuster, 1980].

Norman Podhoretz, **Why We Were in Vietnam** [New York: Simon and Schuster, 1982].

Guy E. Poitras, **Latin America: The Politics of Immobility** [Englewood Cliffs: Prentice Hall, 1974].

Guy E. Poitras, **The Ordeal of Hegemony: The United States and Latin America** [Boulder: Westview Press, 1990].

Nicos Poulantzas, **Political Power and Social Classes** [London: New Left Books, 1973; originally published in French in 1968 as **Pouvoir politique et classes sociales**].

Julius W. Pratt, **America's Colonial Experiment: How the United States Gained, Governed, and in Part Gave Away a Colonial Empire** [New York: Prentice-Hall, 1950].

Julius W. Pratt, **Expansionists of 1898: The Acquisition of Hawaii and the Spanish Islands** [Gloucester: Peter Smith, 1959].

Julius W. Pratt, **A History of United States Foreign Policy** [Englewood Cliffs: Prentice-Hall, 1965].

Julius W. Pratt, **Challenge and Rejection: The US and World Leadership 1900-1921** [New York: Macmillan, 1967].

Mary Louise Pratt, **Imperial Eyes: Travel Writing and Transculturation** [London: Routledge, 1992].

Raúl Prebisch (United Nations Economic Commission for Latin America), **The Economic Development of Latin America and Its Principal Problems** [New York: United Nations, 1949].

Roy L. Prosterman and Jeffrey M. Riedinger, **Land Reform and Democratic Development** [Baltimore: Johns Hopkins University Press, 1987].

Susan Kaufman Purcell, **Mexico in Transition: Implications for US Policy** [New York: Harper and Row, for the Council on Foreign Relations, 1988].

Lucian W. Pye, **Guerrilla Communism in Malaya** [Princeton: Princeton University Press, 1956].

Lucian Pye, **Redefining American Policy in Southeast Asia** [Washington: American Enterprise Institute, 1982].

George H. Quester, **American Foreign Policy: The Lost Consensus** [New York: Praeger, 1982].

Aníbal Quijano, **Nationalism and Colonialism in Peru: A Study in Neo-Imperialism** [New York: Monthly Review Press, 1971].

Stephen G. Rabe, **Eisenhower and Latin America: The Foreign Policy of Anti-Communism** [Chapel Hill: University of North Carolina Press, 1988].

Ronald Radosh, **American Labour and United States Foreign Policy** [New York: Random House, 1969].

Ronald Radosh, **Prophets on the Right: Profiles of Conservative Critics of American Globalism** [New York: Simon and Schuster, 1975].

Carlos Ramirez-Faria, **The Origins of Economic Inequality Between Nations: A Critique of Western Theories of Development and Underdevelopment** [London: Unwin Hyman, 1991].

Joseph Ramos, **Neoconservative Economics in the Southern Cone of Latin America** [Baltimore: Johns Hopkins University Press, 1986].

Vicky Randall and Robin Theobald, **Political Change and Underdevelopment: A Critical Introduction to Third World Politics** [London: Macmillan, 1985].

John Ranelagh, **The Agency: The Rise and Decline of the CIA** [London: Weidenfeld and Nicolson, 1986].

Carlos Rangel, **The Latin Americans: Their Love-Hate Relationship with the United States** [New Brunswick: Transaction Books, revised edition, 1987].

Marcus G. Raskin and Bernard B. Fall, eds., **The Viet-Nam Reader: Articles and Documents on American Foreign Policy and the Viet-Nam Crisis** [New York: Random House, 1965].

Robert Redfield, **Tepoztlan, A Mexican Village: A Study of Folk Life** [Chicago: University of Chicago Press, 1930].

Robert Redfield and Alfonso Villa Rojas, **Chan Kom: A Maya Village** [Washington: Carnegie Institute, 1934, publication no. 448].

Robert Redfield, **The Folk Culture of Yucatan** [Chicago: University of Chicago Press, 1940].

Robert Redfield, **A Village That Chose Progress: Chan Kom Revisited** [Chicago: University of Chicago Press, 1950].

Robert Redfield, **The Primitive World and Its Transformation** [Ithaca: Cornell University Press, 1953].

Robert Redfield, **Peasant Society and Culture** [Chicago: University of

Chicago Press, 1965].

John Reed, **Insurgent Mexico** [New York: International Publishers, 1984; first published 1914].

Pierre-Philippe Rey, **Colonialisme, néo-colonialisme, et transition au capitalisme** [Paris: Maspero, 1971].

Pierre-Philippe Rey, **Les Alliances de Classes: sur l'articulation des modes de production** [Paris: Maspero, 1973].

Darcy Ribeiro, **The Americas and Civilization** [London: George Allen and Unwin, 1971].

David M. Ricci, **The Tragedy of Political Science: Politics, Scholarship and Democracy** [New Haven: Yale University Press, 1984].

C. Duncan Rice, **The Rise and Fall of Black Slavery** [Baton Rouge: Louisiana State University Press, 1975].

Edward E. Rice, **Wars of the Third Kind: Conflict in Underdeveloped Countries** [Berkeley: University of California Press, 1988].

Susan M. Rigdon, **The Culture Facade: Art, Science and Politics in the Work of Oscar Lewis** [Urbana: University of Illinois Press, 1988].

J. Fred Rippy, **The United States and Mexico** [New York: F. S. Crofts, revised edition 1931; first published Alfred A. Knopf, 1926].

J. Fred Rippy, **Latin America in World Politics: An Outline Survey** [New York: Alfred A. Knopf, 1928].

J. Fred Rippy, **Rivalry of the United States and Great Britain over Latin America 1808-1830** [Baltimore: Johns Hopkins University Press, 1929].

J. Fred Rippy, **The Capitalists and Colombia** [New York: Vanguard Press, 1931; reprinted New York: Arno Press, 1976, American Business Abroad Series].

J. Fred Rippy, **Historical Evolution of Hispanic America** [New York: F. J. Crofts, third edition 1945; first published 1932].

J. Fred Rippy and Jean Thomas Nelson, **Crusaders of the Jungle** [New York: Greenwood Press, 1971; first published 1936].

J. Fred Rippy, **America and the Strife of Europe** [Chicago: University of Chicago Press, 1938].

J. Fred Rippy, **The Caribbean Danger Zone** [New York: G. P. Putnam's Sons, 1940].

J. Fred Rippy, **South America and Hemisphere Defense** [Baton Rouge: Louisiana State University Press, 1941].

J. Fred Rippy, **Latin America and the Industrial Age** [New York: Greenwood Press, 1971; first published New York: Putnam, 1944].

J. Fred Rippy, **Globe and Hemisphere: Latin America's Place in the Postwar Foreign Relations of the United States** [Chicago: University of Chicago Press, 1958; reprinted New York: Greenwood Press, 1972].

J. Fred Rippy, **Latin America: A Modern History** [Ann Arbor: University of Michigan Press, 1958; revised edition 1968].

J. Fred Rippy, **British Investments in Latin America 1822-1949: A Case Study in the Operations of Private Enterprise in**

Retarded Regions [Minneapolis: University of Minnesota Press, 1959; reprinted New York: Arno Press, 1977].

J. Fred Rippy, **Bygones I Cannot Help Recalling: Memoirs of a Mobile Scholar** [Austin: Steck-Vaughn, 1966].

Benjamin C. Roberts, George C. Lodge and Hideaki Okamoto, **Collective Bargaining and Employee Participation in Western Europe, North America and Japan** [New York: Trilateral Commission, 1979].

W. Adolphe Roberts, **The Caribbean: The Story of Our Sea of Destiny** [New York: Bobbs-Merrill, 1940].

William Spence Robertson, **Hispanic-American Relations with the United States** [New York: Oxford University Press, 1923].

William Spence Robertson, **History of the Latin American Nations** [New York: D. Appleton, 1925].

Richard Robison, **Indonesia: The Rise of Capital** [Sydney: Allen and Unwin, 1986].

Ronald Robinson and John Gallagher, **Africa and the Victorians: The Official Mind of Imperialism** [London: Macmillan, 1965].

William I. Robinson and Kent Norsworthy, **David and Goliath: Washington's War Against Nicaragua** [London: Zed Books, 1987].

Nelson A. Rockefeller, **The Rockefeller Report on the Americas: The Official Report of a United States Presidential Mission for the Western Hemisphere** [Chicago: Quadrangle Books, 1969].

Walter Rodney, **How Europe Underdeveloped Africa** [London: Bogle-L'Ouverture Publications, 1972].

Mario Rodríguez, **Central America** [Englewood Cliffs: Prentice-Hall, 1965].

William D. Rogers, **The Twilight Struggle: The Alliance for Progress and the Politics of Development in Latin America** [New York: Random House, 1967].

Margaret E. Roggensack and John A. Booth, **Report of the International Human Rights Law Group and the Washington Office on Latin America Advance Election Observer Mission to Guatemala** [Washington: International Human Rights Law Group and Washington Office on Latin America, 1985].

David Ronfeldt, **Geopolitics, Security and US Strategy in the Caribbean Basin** [Santa Monica: Rand Corporation, 1983].

Steven Rose, Richard Lewontin and Leon J. Kamin, **Not in Our Genes: Biology, Ideology and Human Nature** [London: Penguin, 1988; first published 1984].

William Roseberry, **Coffee and Capitalism in the Venezuelan Andes** [Austin: University of Texas Press, 1983].

George Rosen, **Western Economists and Eastern Societies: Agents of Change in South Asia 1950-1970** [Baltimore: Johns Hopkins University Press, 1985].

Emily S. Rosenberg, **Spreading the American Dream: American Economic and Cultural Expansion 1890-1945** [New York: Hill and Wang, 1982].

Mario Rosenthal, **Guatemala: The Story of an Emergent Latin American Democracy** [New York: Twayne, 1962].

Dorothy Ross, **The Origins of American Social Science** [Cambridge: Cambridge University Press, 1991].

Stanley R. Ross et al., eds., **Guide to the Hispanic American Historical Review 1955-1975** [Durham: Duke University Press, 1980].

Ernest Rossi and Jack C. Plano, **The Latin American Political Dictionary** [Santa Barbara: Clio Press, 1980].

Walt Whitman Rostow, **The United States in the World Arena: An Essay in Recent History** [New York: Harper and Brothers, 1959].

Walt Whitman Rostow, **The Stages of Economic Growth: A Non-Communist Manifesto** [New York: Cambridge University Press, second edition 1971; first edition published 1960].

Walt Whitman Rostow, **Politics and the Stages of Growth** [Cambridge: Cambridge University Press, 1971].

Walt Whitman Rostow, **The World Economy: History and Prospect** [Austin: University of Texas Press, 1978].

Walt Whitman Rostow, **Eisenhower, Kennedy and Foreign Aid** [Austin: University of Texas Press, 1985].

Walt Whitman Rostow, **Rich Countries and Poor Countries: Reflections on the Past, Lessons for the Future** [Boulder: Westview Press, 1987].

Andrew J. Rotter, **The Path to Vietnam: Origins of the American Commitment to Southeast Asia** [Ithaca: Cornell University Press, 1987].

Alain Rouquié, **The Military and the State in Latin America** [Berkeley: University of California Press, 1987; first published in French in 1982 as **L'Etat militaire en Amérique Latine**].

Leo S. Rowe, **The United States and Porto Rico: With Special Reference to the Problems Arising Out of Our Contact with the Spanish-American Civilization** [New York: Longmans Green, 1904].

Barry Rubin, **Secrets of State: The State Department and the Struggle over US Foreign Policy** [New York: Oxford University Press, 1985].

Barry Rubin, **Modern Dictators: A History of Tyranny in the Third World** [London: W. H. Allen, 1987].

Lloyd Rudolph and Suzanne Rudolph, **The Modernity of Tradition: Political Development in India** [Chicago: University of Chicago Press, 1967].

Dietrich Rueschemeyer, Evelyne Huber Stephens and John D. Stephens, **Capitalist Development and Democracy** [Chicago: University of Chicago Press, 1992].

Arthur Ruhl, **The Central Americans: Adventures and Impressions Between Mexico and Panama** [New York: Charles Scribner's Sons, 1928].

Phillip L. Russell, **El Salvador in Crisis** [Austin: Colorado River Press, 1984].

Bruce M. Russett and Elizabeth C. Hanson, **Interest and Ideology: The Foreign Policy Beliefs of American Businessmen** [San Francisco: W. H. Freeman, 1975].

Ignacy Sachs, **The Discovery of the Third World** [Cambridge: Massachusetts Institute of Technology Press, 1976, originally published in French as **La Découverte du Tiers Monde**].

Edward Said, **Orientalism** [London: Routledge and Kegan Paul, 1978].

Edward Said, **The World, the Text, and the Critic** [London: Faber and Faber, 1984; first published 1983].

Edward Said, **Beginnings: Intention and Method** [New York: Columbia University Press, 1985; first published 1975].

Edward Said, **Culture and Imperialism** [London: Chatto and Windus, 1993].

Leonardo Alberto Salazan, **Discourses on Terrorism and Nicaragua: A Case Study of Television News, Ideology and Cultural Impoverishment** [Unpublished PhD dissertation, Michigan State University, 1988].

Richard V. Salisbury, **Anti-Imperialism and International Competition in Central America 1920-1929** [Wilmington: Scholarly Resources, 1989].

John S. Saloma III, **Ominous Politics: The New Conservative Labyrinth** [New York: Hill and Wang, 1984].

Jerry W. Sanders, **Peddlers of Crisis: The Committee on the Present Danger and the Politics of Containment** [Boston: Southend Press, 1983].

Steven E. Sanderson, **The Politics of Trade in Latin American Development** [Stanford: Stanford University Press, 1992].

William Franklin Sands, **Our Jungle Diplomacy** [Chapel Hill: University of North Carolina Press, 1944].

Charles B. Saunders, Jr., **The Brookings Institution: A Fifty-Year History** [Washington: Brookings Institution, 1966].

Arthur M. Schlesinger, Jr., **A Thousand Days: John F. Kennedy in the Whitehouse** [London: Andre Deutsch, 1965].

Arthur M. Schlesinger, Jr. **The Bitter Heritage: Vietnam and American Democracy 1941-1966** [London: Sphere Books, 1967; first published 1966].

Arthur M. Schlesinger, Jr., **The Vital Center: The Politics of Freedom** [London: Andre Deutsch, 1970; first published in 1950 as **The Politics of Freedom**].

Arthur M. Schlesinger, Jr., **The Crisis of Confidence: Ideas, Power and Violence in America** [London: Andre Deutsch, 1969].

Stephen Schlesinger and Stephen Kinzer, **Bitter Fruit: The Untold Story of the American Coup in Guatemala** [New York: Anchor Press, 1983].

Hans Schmidt, **The United States Occupation of Haiti 1915-1934** [New Brunswick: Rutgers University Press, 1971].

Karl M. Schmitt and David D. Burks, **Evolution or Chaos: Dynamics of Latin American Government and Politics** [New York: Praeger, 1963].

Karl M. Schmitt, **Mexico and the United States 1821-1973: Conflict and Coexistence** [New York: Wiley, 1974].

Ronald M. Schneider, **Communism in Guatemala 1944-1954** [New York: Praeger, 1959].

Thomas J. Schoenbaum, **Waging Peace and War: Dean Rusk in the Truman, Kennedy and Johnson Years** [New York: Simon and Schuster, 1988].

Thomas D. Schoonover, **The United States in Central America, 1860-1911: Episodes in Social Imperialism and Imperial Rivalry in the World System** [Durham: Duke University Press, 1992].

Lars Schoultz, **Human Rights and United States Policy Towards Latin America** [Princeton: Princeton University Press, 1981].

Lars Schoultz, **National Security and United States Policy Towards Latin America** [Princeton: Princeton University Press, 1987].

Ellen W. Schrecker, **No Ivory Tower: McCarthyism and the Universities** [New York: Oxford University Press, 1986].

Donald E. Schulz, **The Cuban Revolution and the Soviet Union** [Unpublished PhD dissertation, The Ohio State University, 1977].

Robert D. Schulzinger, **American Diplomacy in the Twentieth Century** [New York: Oxford University Press, 1984].

Robert D. Schulzinger, **The Wise Men of Foreign Affairs: The History of the Council on Foreign Relations** [New York: Columbia University Press, 1984].

Franz Schurmann, **The Logic of World Power: An Inquiry into the Origins, Currents and Contradictions of World Politics** [New York: Pantheon, 1974].

Carl Schurz, **American Imperialism: The Convocation Address Delivered on the Occasion of the Twenty-Seventh Convocation of the University of Chicago** [Chicago: University of Chicago, 1899].

Carl Schurz, **The Policy of Imperialism: Address by Carl Schurz** [Chicago: American Anti-Imperialist League, 1899].

William L. Schurz, **This New World: The Civilization of Latin America** [New York: E. P. Dutton, 1954].

Julia R. Schwendinger and Herman Schwendinger, **The Sociologists of the Chair: A Radical Analysis of the Formative Years of North American Sociology** [New York: Basic Books, 1974].

Peter Dale Scott and Jonathan Marshall, **Cocaine Politics: Drugs, Armies and the CIA in Central America** [Berkeley: University of California Press, 1991].

Robert N. Seidel, **Progressive Pan-Americanism: Development and United States Policy Towards South America 1906-1931** [Ithaca: Cornell Latin American Studies Program Dissertation Series no. 45, 1973].

Mitchel A. Seligson, **Peasants of Costa Rica and the Development of Agrarian Capitalism** [Madison: University of Wisconsin Press, 1980].

Mitchel A. Seligson et al., **Land and Labor in Guatemala: An Assessment** [Washington: Agency for International Development and Development Associates, 1985].

Enrique Semo, **The History of Capitalism in Mexico: Its Origins 1521-1763** [Austin: University of Texas Press, 1993; first published in Spanish in 1973 as **Historia del capitalismo en México. Los** orígenes 1521-1763].

Anupam Sen, **The State, Industrialization and Class Formations in India: A Neo-Marxist Perspective on Colonialism, Underdevelopment and Development** [London: Routledge and Kegan Paul, 1982].

D. Michael Shafer, **Deadly Paradigms: The Failure of US Counterinsurgency Policy** [Princeton: Princeton University Press, 1988].

Stephen Rosskamm Shalom, **The United States and the Philippines: A Study of Neo-Colonialism** [Philadelphia: Institute for the Study of Human Issues, 1981].

Ulysses S. Grant Sharp, **Strategy for Defeat: Vietnam in Retrospect** [Novato: Presidio Press, 1978].

Edward R. F. Sheehan, **Agony in the Garden: A Stranger in Central America** [Boston: Houghton Mifflin, 1989].

Neil Sheehan, **A Bright Shining Lie: John Paul Vann and America in Vietnam** [New York: Random House, 1988].

Edward Shils, **Political Development in the New States** [London: Mouton, 1965].

Laurence H. Shoup and William Minter, **Imperial Brain Trust: The Council on Foreign Relations and United States's Foreign Policy** [New York: Monthly Review Press, 1977].

Daniel Siegel and Tom Spaulding, with Peter Kornbluh, **Outcast Among Allies: The International Costs of Reagan's War Against Nicaragua** [Washington: Institute for Policy Studies, 1985].

Paul E. Sigmund, **The Overthrow of Allende and the Politics of Chile 1964-1976** [Pittsburgh: University of Pittsburgh Press, 1977].

Paul E. Sigmund, **Multinationals in Latin America: The Politics of Nationalization** [Madison: University of Wisconsin Press, 1980].

Edward T. Silva and Sheila A. Slaughter, **Serving Power: The Making of the Academic Social Science Expert** [New York: Greenwood Press, 1984].

Kalman H. Silvert, **A Study in Government: Guatemala** [New Orleans: Tulane University Press, 1954].

Kalman H. Silvert, **The Conflict Society: Reaction and Revolution in Latin America** [New York: American Universities Field Staff, revised edition 1966; first published 1961].

Kalman H. Silvert, **Man's Power: A Biased Guide to Political Thought** [New York: Viking Press, 1970].

Kalman H. Silvert, **The Relevance of Latin American Domestic Politics to North American Foreign Policy** [New York: New York University Ibero-American Language and Area Center, 1974].

Kalman H. Silvert, **The Reason for Democracy** [New York: Viking Press, 1977].

Kalman H. Silvert, **Essays in Understanding Latin America** [Philadelphia: Institute for the Study of Human Issues, 1977].

I. Robert Sinai, **The Challenge of Modernization: The West's Impact on the Non-Western World** [New York: W. W. Norton, 1964].

Joseph M. Siracusa, **New Left Diplomatic Histories and Historians: The American Revisionists** [Port Washington: Kennikat Press, 1973].

Thomas E. Skidmore and Peter H. Smith, **Modern Latin America** [New York: Oxford University Press, 1984].

Holly Sklar, ed., **Trilateralism: The Trilateral Commission and Elite Planning for World Management** [Boston: South End Press, 1980].

Holly Sklar, **Reagan, Trilateralism and the Neoliberals: Containment and Intervention in 1980s** [Boston: Southend Press, 1986].

Holly Sklar, **Washington's War on Nicaragua** [Boston: South End Press, 1988].

Jerome Slater, **The OAS and United States Foreign Policy** [Columbus: Ohio State University Press, 1967].

Jerome Slater, **Intervention and Negotiation: The United States and the Dominican Revolution** [New York: Harper and Row, 1970].

John Sloan, **The Electoral Game in Guatemala** [Unpublished PhD dissertation, University of Texas, 1968].

Hedrick Smith, **The Power Game: How Washington Works** [London: Collins, 1988].

James Allen Smith, **The Idea Brokers: Think Tanks and the Rise of the New Policy Elite** [New York: Free Press, 1991].

Robert Freeman Smith, **The United States and Cuba: Business and Diplomacy 1917-1960** [New Haven: College and University Press, 1960].

Robert Freeman Smith, **The United States and Revolutionary Nationalism in Mexico 1916-1932** [Chicago: University of Chicago Press, 1972].

Robert Freeman Smith, **The United States and the Latin American Sphere of Influence-- Volume I: The Era of Caribbean Intervention, 1890-1930** [Malabar: Robert E. Krieger, 1983].

Robert Freeman Smith, **The United States and the Latin American Sphere of Influence-- Volume II: Era of Good Neighbors, Cold Warriors and Hairshirts, 1930-1982** [Malabar: Robert E. Krieger, 1983].

Tony Smith, **The Pattern of Imperialism: The United States, Great Britain, and the Late-industrializing World since 1815** [Cambridge: Cambridge University Press, 1987; first published 1981].

Tony Smith, **America's Mission: The United States and the Worldwide Struggle for Democracy in the Twentieth Century** [Princeton: Princeton University Press/Twentieth Century Fund, 1994].

Wayne S. Smith, **Castro's Cuba: Soviet Partner or Nonaligned?** [Washington: Woodrow Wilson International Center for Scholars, 1984].

Wayne S. Smith, **The Closest of Enemies: A Personal and Diplomatic Account of US-Cuban Relations Since 1957** [New York: W. W. Norton, 1987].

Richard C. Snyder, H. W. Bruck and Burton M. Sapin, eds., **Decision Making As An Approach to the Study of International Politics** [Princeton: Princeton University Press, 1954].

Alvin Y. So, **Social Change and Development: Modernization,**

Dependency and World-System Theories [Newbury Park: Sage, 1990].

Rose J. Spalding, **Capitalists and Revolution in Nicaragua: Opposition and Accommodation 1979-1993** [Chapel Hill: University of North Carolina Press, 1994].

John W. Spanier, **American Foreign Policy Since World War Two** [New York: Praeger, 1960].

Oswald Spengler, **The Decline of the West--Volume One: Form and Actuality** [New York: Alfred A. Knopf, 1989; first published in English in 1926; first published in German 1918].

Oswald Spengler, **The Decline of the West--Volume Two: Perspectives of World History** [New York: Alfred A. Knopf, 1989; first published in English in 1928; first published in German 1920].

Barbara Stallings, **Banker to the Third World: US Portfolio Investment in Latin America 1900-1986** [Berkeley: University of California Press, 1987].

Eugene Stanley, **The Future of Underdeveloped Countries: Political Implications of Economic Development** [New York: Praeger, 1961, for the Council on Foreign Relations].

Rodolfo Stavenhagen, **Agrarian Problems and Peasant Movements in Latin America** [Garden City: Doubleday Anchor, 1970].

L. S. Stavrianos, **Global Rift: The Third World Comes of Age** [New York: William Morrow, 1981].

Ronald Steel, **Walter Lippman and the American Century** [London: Bodley Head, 1980].

Stanley J. Stein and Barbara H. Stein, **The Colonial Heritage in Latin America: Essays on Economic Dependence in Perspective** [New York: Oxford University Press, 1970].

Peter Steinfels, **The Neoconservatives: The Men Who Are Changing America's Politics** [New York: Simon and Schuster, 1979].

Alfred Stepan, **The State and Society: Peru in Comparative Perspective** [Princeton: Princeton University Press, 1978].

John Lloyd Stephens, **Incidents of Travel in Central America, Chiapas and Yucatan** [New York: Harper and Brothers, 1841; reprinted London: Century, 1988].

John Lloyd Stephens, **Incidents of Travel in Yucatan** (2 vols.) [New York: Harper and Brothers, 1843; reprinted New York: Dover, 1963].

Steve J. Stern, **Peru's Indian Peoples and the Challenge of Spanish Conquest: Huamanga to 1640** [Madison: University of Wisconsin Press, 1982].

Bernard Sternsher, **Consensus, Conflict, and American Historians** [Bloomington: Indiana University Press, 1975].

Dick Steward, **Trade and Hemisphere: The Good Neighbor Policy and Reciprocal Trade** [Columbia: University of Missouri Press, 1975].

Dick Steward, **Money, Marines and Mission: Recent US-Latin American Policy** [New York: University Press of America, 1980].

Henry L. Stimson, **American Policy in Nicaragua** [New York: Charles Scribner's Sons, 1927; reprinted New York: Arno Press, 1970].

Henry L. Stimson, **The Far Eastern Crisis: Recollections and Observations** [New York: Harper and Brothers, 1936].

Henry L. Stimson (and McGeorge Bundy), **On Active Service in Peace and War** [New York: Harper and Brothers, 1948].

George W. Stocking, Jr., **Race, Culture, and Evolution: Essays in the History of Anthropology** [New York: Free Press, 1968].

John Stockwell, **In Search of Enemies: A CIA Story** [London: Andre Deutsch, 1978].

John Stockwell, **The Praetorian Guard: The US Role in the New World Order** [Boston: South End Press, 1991].

John G. Stoessinger, **Crusaders and Pragmatists: Movers of Modern American Foreign Policy** [New York: W. W. Norton, 1979].

Robert Stone, **A Flag for Sunrise** [New York: Alfred A. Knopf, 1977].

Samuel Z. Stone, **The Heritage of the Conquistadors: Ruling Classes in Central America from Conquest to the Sandinistas** [Lincoln: University of Nebraska Press, 1990].

Graham H. Stuart, **Latin America and the United States** [New York: Appleton-Century-Crofts, fifth revised edition 1955; first published 1922].

Graham H. Stuart and James L. Tigner, **Latin America and the United States** [Englewood Cliffs: Prentice-Hall, sixth revised edition 1975; first published 1922].

Paul Sullivan, **Unfinished Conversations: Mayas and Foreigners Between Two Wars** [New York: Alfred A. Knopf, 1989].

Harry G. Summers, Jr., **On Strategy: The Vietnam War in Context** [Novato: Presidio Press, 1981].

R. Swearingen and P. Langer **Red Flag in Japan: International Communism in Action 1919-1951** [Cambridge: Harvard University Press, 1952].

Paul M. Sweezy and Leo Huberman, **Cuba: Anatomy of a Revolution** [New York: Monthly Review Press, 1960].

Paul M. Sweezy and Leo Huberman, eds., **Whither Latin America?** [New York: Monthly Review Press, 1963].

Paul M. Sweezy and Leo Huberman, **Socialism in Cuba** [New York: Monthly Review Press, 1969].

Paul M. Sweezy, **Modern Capitalism and Other Essays** [New York: Monthly Review Press, 1971].

Paul M. Sweezy and Charles Bettelheim, **On the Transition to Socialism** [New York: Monthly Review Press, 1971].

Paul M. Sweezy and Harry Magdoff, **The Dynamics of US Capitalism: Corporate Structure, Inflation, Credit, Gold and the Dollar** [New York: Monthly Review Press, 1972].

Paul M. Sweezy and Harry Magdoff, **Revolution and Counter-Revolution in Chile** [New York: Monthly Review Press, 1974].

Tad Szulc, **Twilight of the Tyrants** [New York: Henry Holt, 1959].

Tad Szulc, **Dominican Diary** [New York: Delacorte Press, 1965].

Tad Szulc, **The Winds of Revolution: Latin America Today--And Tomorrow** [New York: Praeger, 1963, revised edition 1965].

Albert Szymanski, **The Logic of Imperialism** [New York: Praeger, 1983].

Ronald T. Takaki, **Iron Cages: Race and Culture in Nineteenth Century America** [London: Athlone Press, 1980; first published New York: Alfred A. Knopf, 1979].

Frank Tannenbaum, **The Mexican Agrarian Revolution** [New York: Alfred A. Knopf, 1928].

Frank Tannebaum, **Peace by Revolution: An Interpretation of Mexico** [New York: Alfred A. Knopf, 1933].

Frank Tannenbaum, **Whither Latin America?: An Introduction to Its Economic and Social Problems** [New York: Thomas Y. Crowell, 1934].

Frank Tannenbaum, **Slave and Citizen: The Negro in the Americas** [New York: Alfred A. Knopf, 1947].

Frank Tannenbaum, **Mexico: The Struggle for Peace and Bread** [New York: Alfred A. Knopf, 1950, fourth edition 1956].

Frank Tannenbaum, **The American Tradition in Foreign Policy** [Norman: University of Oklahoma Press, 1955].

Frank Tannenbaum, **Ten Keys to Latin America** [New York: Alfred A. Knopf, 1962].

Michael T. Taussig, **The Devil and Commodity Fetishism in South America** [Chapel Hill: University of North Carolina Press, 1988; first published 1980].

Michael T. Taussig, **Shamanism, Colonialism and the Wild Man: A Study in Terror and Healing** [Chicago: University of Chicago Press, 1987].

John G. Taylor, **From Modernization to Modes of Production: A Critique of Sociologies of Development and Underdevelopment** [London: Macmillan, 1983].

James D. Theberge and Roger W. Fontaine, **Latin America: Struggle for Progress** [Lexington: D. C. Heath, 1977].

Goran Therborn, **The Ideology of Power and the Power of Ideology** [London: Verso, 1980].

Jack Ray Thomas, **Biographical Dictionary of Latin American Historians and Historiography** [New York: Greenwood Press, 1984].

John N. Thomas, **The Institute of Pacific Relations: Asian Scholars and American Politics** [Seattle: University of Washington Press, 1974].

Lowell Thomas, **Old Gimlet Eye: The Adventures of Smedley D. Butler as Told to Lowell Thomas** [New York: Farrar and Rinehart, 1933; reprinted November 1981 by the Marine Corps Association Quantico Virginia].

Wallace Thompson, **The People of Mexico** [New York: Harper, 1921].

Wallace Thompson, **The Mexican Mind** [Boston: Little Brown, 1922].

Wallace Thompson, **Trading with Mexico** [New York: Dodd, 1922].

Wallace Thompson, **Rainbow Countries of Central America** [New York: E. P. Dutton, 1926].

Wallace Thompson, **Greater America: An Interpretation of Latin America in Relation to Anglo-Saxon America** [New York: E. P. Dutton, 1932].

James C. Thomson, Peter W. Stanley and John Curtis Perry, **Sentimental**

Imperialists: The American Experience in East Asia [New York: Harper and Row, 1981].

A. P. Thornton, **Imperialism in the Twentieth Century** [New York: Macmillan, 1977].

John Joseph Tierney, Jr., **The United States and Nicaragua, 1927-1932: Decisions for De-escalation and Withdrawal** [Unpublished PhD dissertation, University of Pennsylvania, 1969].

Michael P. Todaro, **Economic Development in the Third World** [London: Longman, fourth edition, 1989].

Guillermo Toriello, **La batalla de Guatemala** [Mexico: Cuadernos Americanos, 1955].

Guillermo Toriello, **A donde va Guatemala?** [Mexico: América Nueva, 1956].

Frank N. Trager, ed., **Marxism in Southeast Asia: A Study of Four Countries** [Stanford: Stanford University Press, 1959].

David F. Trask, Michael C. Meyer and Roger R. Trask, eds., **A Bibliography of United States-Latin American Relations Since 1810: A Selected List of Eleven Thousand Published References** [Lincoln: University of Nebraska Press, 1968].

Gregory F. Treverton, **Covert Action: The Limits of Intervention in the Postwar World** [New York: Basic Books, 1987].

Robert C. Tucker, **The Marxian Revolutionary Idea** [London: George Allen and Unwin, 1970; first published 1969].

Robert W. Tucker, **Nation or Empire?** [Baltimore: Johns Hopkins University Press, 1968].

Robert W. Tucker, **The Radical Left and American Foreign Policy** [Baltimore: Johns Hopkins University Press, 1971].

Robert W. Tucker, **The Inequality of Nations** [New York: Basic Books, 1977].

Robert W. Tucker, **The Purposes of American Power: An Essay on National Security** [New York: Praeger, 1981].

Joseph S. Tulchin, **The Aftermath of War: World War I and US Policy toward Latin America** [New York: New York University Press, 1971].

Bryan S. Turner, **Marx and the End of Orientalism** [London: George Allen and Unwin, 1978].

Bryan S. Turner, **Orientalism, Postmodernism and Globalism** [London: Routledge, 1994].

John Kenneth Turner, **Barbarous Mexico** [Austin: University of Texas Press, 1969; first published 1910].

Louis Turner, **Multinational Companies and the Third World** [New York: Hill and Wang, 1973].

Robert F. Turner, **Nicaragua Versus the United States: A Look at the Facts** [Washington: Pergamon-Brassey, A Special Report of the Institute for Foreign Policy Analysis, 1987].

Mark Tushnet, **Central America and the Law: The Constitution, Civil Liberties and the Courts** [Boston: South End Press, 1988].

Charles Tyroler, ed., **Alerting America: The Papers of the Committee on the Present Danger** [Washington: Pergamon Brassey's, 1984].

Ian Tyrrell, **The Absent Marx: Class Analysis and Liberal History in**

Twentieth Century America [New York: Greenwood Press, 1986].

Adam B. Ulam, **The Unfinished Revolution: Marxism and Communism in the Modern World** [London: Longman, revised edition 1979; first published 1960].

US Department of State, **Penetration of the Political Institutions of Guatemala by the International Communist Movement** [Washington: US Government Printing Office, 1954].

US Department of State, **Intervention of International Communism in Latin America** (Department of State Publication 5556, Inter-American Series no. 48) [Washington: US Government Printing Office, 1954].

US Department of State, **A Case History of Communist Penetration: Guatemala** (Department of State Publication 6465, Inter-American Series no. 52) [Washington: US Government Printing Office, 1954].

US Department of State, **Communist Interference in El Salvador** (Special Report no. 80, February 23, 1981) [Washington: US Government Printing Office, 1981].

US Department of State and Department of Defense, **The Challenge to Democracy in Central America** [Washington: US Government Printing Office, June 1986].

US National Bipartisan Commission on Central America (Henry Kissinger, chair), **The Report of the President's National Bipartisan Commission on Central America** [New York: Macmillan, 1984].

US National Bipartisan Commission on Central America (Henry Kissinger, chair), **Report of the National Bipartisan Commission on Central America** [Washington: US Government Printing Office, 1984].

US National Bipartisan Commission on Central America (Henry Kissinger, chair), **Appendix to the Report of the National Bipartisan Commission on Central America** [Washington: US Government Printing Office, 1984].

Jiri Valenta, **USSR, Cuba and the Crisis in Central America** [Washington: Latin American Program, Woodrow Wilson Center, 1981].

Ernest Van Den Haag and Tom J. Farer, **US Ends and Means in Central America: A Debate** [New York: Plenum Press, 1988].

Achin Vanaik, **The Painful Transition: Bourgeois Democracy in India** [London: Verso, 1990].

Mary Vanderlaan, **Revolution and Foreign Policy in Nicaragua** [Boulder: Westview Press, 1986].

Claudio Véliz, **The Centralist Tradition in Latin America** [Princeton: Princeton University Press, 1980].

Claudio Véliz, **The New World of the Gothic Fox: Culture and Economy in English and Spanish America** [Berkeley: University of California Press, 1994].

Raymond Vernon, **Sovereignty at Bay: The Multinational Spread of US Enterprises** [New York: Basic Books, 1971].

Arthur J. Vidich and Stanford M. Lyman, **American Sociology: Worldly Rejections of Religion and Their Directions** [New Haven: Yale University Press, 1985].

Carlos M. Vilas, **The Sandinista Revolution: National Liberation and**

Social Transformation in Central America [New York: Monthly Review Press, 1986].

Howard Wachtel, **The New Gnomes: Multinational Banks in the Third World** [Amsterdam: Transnational Institute, 1977].

R. Harrison Wagner, **United States Policy Towards Latin America: A Study in Domestic and International Politics** [Stanford: Stanford University Press, 1970].

Eric Wakin, **Anthropology Goes to War: Professional Ethics and Counterinsurgency in Thailand** [Madison: Center for Southeast Asian Studies/University of Wisconsin, 1992].

J. G. Walker, **Ocean to Ocean: An Account Personal and Historical of Nicaragua and its People** [Chicago: McClurg, 1902].

Thomas W. Walker, **The Christian Democratic Movement in Nicaragua** [Tuscon: University of Arizona Press, 1970].

Thomas W. Walker, **Nicaragua: Land of Sandino** [Boulder: Westview Press, 1981].

William Walker, **The War in Nicaragua** [Tucson: University of Arizona Press, 1985; first published 1860].

Henry Wallace, **The Century of the Common Man** [New York: Reynal and Hitchcock, 1943].

Immanuel Wallerstein, **Africa: The Politics of Independence** [New York: Vintage Books, 1961].

Immanuel Wallerstein, ed., **Social Change: The Colonial Situation** [New York: John Wiley, 1966].

Immanuel Wallerstein, **Africa: The Politics of Unity** [New York: Random House, 1967].

Immanuel Wallerstein, **Universities in Turmoil: The Politics of Change** [New York: Atheneum, 1969].

Immanuel Wallerstein, **The Modern World-System--I: Capitalist Agriculture and the Origins of the European World-Economy in the Sixteenth Century** [New York: Academic Press, 1974].

Immanuel Wallerstein, **The Modern World-System--II: Mercantilism and the Consolidation of the European World-Economy 1600-1750** [New York: Academic Press, 1980].

Immanuel Wallerstein, **Historical Capitalism** [London: Verso, 1983].

Immanuel Wallerstein, **The Modern World-System--III: The Second Era of Great Expansion of the Capitalist World-Economy 1730-1840s** [San Diego: Academic Press, 1989].

Knut Walter, **The Regime of Anastasio Somoza 1936-1956** [Chapel Hill: University of North Carolina Press, 1993].

Bill Warren, **Imperialism: Pioneer of Capitalism** [London: Verso, 1980].

Kay B. Warren, **The Symbolism of Subordination: Indian Identity in a Guatemalan Town** [Austin: University of Texas Press, 1978].

Frederick Stirton Weaver, **Class, State and Industrial Growth: The Historical Process of South American Industrial Growth** [Westport: Greenwood Press, 1981].

Frederick Stirton Weaver, **Inside the Volcano: A History and Political Economy of Central America** [Boulder: Westview Press, 1994].

Samuel Weber, **Institution and Interpretation** [Minneapolis: University of Minnesota Press, 1987].

Stephen Webre, **José Napoleon Duarte and the Christian Democratic Party in Salvadoran Politics 1960-1972** [Baton Rouge: Louisiana State University Press, 1979].

John Weeks, **The Economies of Central America** [New York: Holmes and Meier, 1985].

John Weeks and Andrew Zimbalist, **Panama at the Crossroads: Economic Development and Political Change in the Twentieth Century** [Berkeley: University of California Press, 1991].

Albert K. Weinberg, **Manifest Destiny: A Study of Nationalist Expansionism in American History** [Baltimore: Johns Hopkins University Press, 1935].

Al Weinrub and William Bollinger, **The AFL-CIO in Central America: A Look at the American Institute for Free Labor Development** [Oakland: Labor Network on Central America, 1989].

Fred Weinstein, **History and Theory After the Fall: An Essay on Interpretation** [Chicago: University of Chicago Press, 1990].

Sidney Weintraub, **A Marriage of Convenience: Relations Between Mexico and the United States** [New York: Oxford University Press, for the Twentieth Century Fund, 1990].

Edward Weisband, **The Ideology of American Foreign Policy: A Paradigm of Lockean Liberalism** [Beverly Hills: Sage Publications, 1973].

Bernard A. Weisberger, **Cold War Cold Peace: The United States and Russia Since 1945** [Boston: Houghton Mifflin, 1984].

Richard E. Welch. Jr., **Response to Revolution: The United States and the Cuban Revolution 1959-1961** [Chapel Hill: University of North Carolina Press, 1985].

Sumner Welles, **Naboth's Vineyard: The Dominican Republic 1844-1924** (2 vols.) [New York: Payson and Clarke, 1928].

Sumner Welles, **The Roosevelt Administration and Its Dealings with the Republics of the Western Hemisphere** [Washington: US Government Printing Office, Department of State Publication no. 692, Latin American Series no. 9, 1935].

Sumner Welles, **Pan American Cooperation** [Washington: US Government Printing Office, Department of State Publication no. 712, Latin American Series no. 10, 1935].

Jayne Werner, **Peasant Politics and Religious Sectarianism** [New Haven: Yale University Press, 1981].

Robert Wesson, **Democracy in Latin America: Promise and Problems** [New York: Praeger, 1982].

Robert C. West, **Middle America: Its Lands and Peoples** [Englewood Cliffs: Prentice-Hall, 1966].

William Westmoreland, **A Soldier Reports** [Garden City: Doubleday, 1976].

Rubin Francis Weston, **Racism in US Imperialism: The Influence of Racial Assumptions on American Foreign Policy 1893-1946** [Columbia: University of South Carolina Press, 1972].

B. K. Wheeler, **Dollar Diplomacy at Work in Nicaragua and Mexico** [Washington: US Government Printing Office, 1927].

Nathan L. Whetten, **Guatemala: The Land and the People** [New Haven: Yale University Press, 1961].

Arthur P. Whitaker, **The Spanish American Frontier 1783-1795: The Westward Movement and the Spanish Retreat in the Mississippi Valley** [Cambridge: Harvard University Press, 1927].

Arthur P. Whitaker, **The Mississippi Question 1795-1803: A Study in Trade, Politics and Diplomacy** [Gloucester: Peter Smith, 1962; first published 1932].

Arthur P. Whitaker, **The United States and the Independence of Latin America 1800-1830** [Baltimore: Johns Hopkins University Press, 1941].

Arthur Preston Whitaker, **The United States and South America: The Northern Republics** [New York: Greenwood Press, 1974; first published Cambridge: Harvard University Press, 1948].

Arthur Preston Whitaker, **The Western Hemisphere Idea: Its Rise and Decline** [Ithaca: Cornell University Press, 1965; first published 1954].

Arthur Preston Whitaker, **The United States and Argentina** [Cambridge: Harvard University Press, 1954].

Arthur Preston Whitaker, **The United States and the Southern Cone: Argentina, Chile and Uruguay** [Cambridge: Harvard University Press, 1976].

Alaster White, **El Salvador** [Boulder: Westview Press, 1973].

Hayden White, **Tropics of Discourse: Essays in Cultural Criticism** [Baltimore: Johns Hopkins University Press, 1987; first published 1978].

Richard Alan White, **The Morass: United States Intervention in Central America** [New York: Harper and Row, 1984].

Howard J. Wiarda, **Dictatorship and Development: The Methods of Control in Trujillo's Dominican Republic** [Gainesville: University of Florida Press, 1968].

Howard J. Wiarda, **The Dominican Republic: Nation in Transition** [New York: Fredrick A. Praeger, 1969].

Howard J. Wiarda, **Transcending Corporatism?: The Portuguese Corporative System and the Revolution of 1974** [Columbia: Institute of International Affairs, University of South Carolina, 1975].

Howard J. Wiarda, **Corporatism and Development: The Portuguese Experience** [Amherst: University of Massachusetts Press, 1977].

Howard J. Wiarda, **Critical Elections and Critical Coups: State, Society and the Military in the Processes of Latin American Development** [Athens: Center for International Studies, Ohio University, 1979].

Howard J. Wiarda, **Corporatism and National Development in Latin America** [Boulder: Westview Press, 1981].

Howard J. Wiarda, **Does Europe Still Stop at the Pyrenees? Or Does Latin America Begin There?: Iberia, Latin America, and the Second Enlargement of the European Community** [Washington: American Enterprise Institute, 1981].

Howard J. Wiarda, **From Corporatism to Neo-Syndicalism: The State,**

Organized Labor and the Changing Industrial Relations Systems of Southern Europe [Cambridge: Harvard University Press, 1981].

Howard J. Wiarda, ed., **Human Rights and US Human Rights Policy: Theoretical Approaches and Some Perspectives on Latin America** [Washington: American Enterprise Institute, 1982].

Howard J. Wiarda, **Trade, Aid and US Policy** [Washington: American Enterprise Institute, 1983].

Howard J. Wiarda, ed., **Rift and Revolution: The Central American Imbroglio** [Washington: American Enterprise Institute, 1984].

Howard J. Wiarda, **In Search of Policy: The United States and Latin America** [Washington: American Enterprise Institute, 1984].

Howard J. Wiarda, **Ethnocentrism in Foreign Policy: Can We Understand the Third World?** [Washington: American Enterprise Institute, 1985].

Howard J. Wiarda, **Population, Internal Unrest and US Security in Latin America** [Amherst: University of Massachusetts International Area Studies, 1986].

Howard J. Wiarda, **Latin America at the Crossroads: Debt, Development and the Future** [Boulder: Westview Press, 1987].

Howard J. Wiarda, **Finding Our Way?: Toward Maturity in US-Latin American Relations** [Washington: American Enterprise Institute, 1987].

Howard J. Wiarda and Michael J. Kryzanek, **The Dominican Republic: A Caribbean Crucible** [Boulder: Westview Press, 1987].

Howard J. Wiarda and Michael J. Kryzanek, **The Politics of External Influence in the Dominican Republic** [New York: Praeger, 1988].

Howard J. Wiarda with Ieda Siqueira Wiarda, **The Transition to Democracy in Spain and Portugal: Real or Wishful?** [New York: American University Press, 1988].

Howard J. Wiarda, **Foreign Policy Without Illusion: How Foreign Policy-Making Works and Fails to Work in the United States** [Glenview: Scott Foresman/Little Brown, 1990].

Howard J. Wiarda, **The Democratic Revolution in Latin America: History, Politics and US Policy** [New York: Holmes and Meier, for The Twentieth Century Fund, 1990].

Tom Wicker, **One of Us: Richard Nixon and the American Dream** [New York: Random House, 1990].

Timothy P. Wickham-Crowley, **Guerrillas and Revolution in Latin America: A Comparative Study of Insurgents and Regimes Since 1956** [Princeton: Princeton University Press, 1992].

Edward J. Williams and Freeman J. Wright, **Latin American Politics: A Developmental Approach** [Palo Alto: Mayfield, 1975].

Mary Wilhelmine Williams, **Anglo-American Isthmian Diplomacy 1815-1915** [Washington: American Historical Association, 1916; reprinted Gloucester: Peter Smith, 1965].

Robert G. Williams, **Export Agriculture and the Crisis in Central America** [Chapel Hill: University of North Carolina Press, 1986].

Robert G. Williams, **States and Social Evolution: Coffee and the Rise** of National Governments in Central America [Chapel Hill: University of North Carolina Press, 1994].

William Appleman Williams, **American-Russian Relations 1781-1947** [New York: Rinehart, 1952].

William Appleman Williams, **The Tragedy of American Diplomacy** [Cleveland: World, 1959].

William Appleman Williams, **The Contours of American History** [Cleveland: World, 1961].

William Appleman Williams, **The United States, Cuba and Castro: An Essay on the Dynamics of Revolution and the Dissolution of Empire** [New York: Monthly Review Press, 1962].

William Appleman Williams, **The Great Evasion: An Essay on the Contemporary Relevance of Karl Marx and on the Wisdom of Admitting the Heretic into the Dialogue about America's Future** [Chicago: Quadrangle Books, 1964].

William Appleman Williams, **The Roots of the Modern American Empire: A Study of the Growth and Shaping of Social Consciousness in a Marketplace Society** [New York: Random House, 1969].

William Appleman Williams, **The Tragedy of American Diplomacy** [New York: Dell, second revised and enlarged edition 1972; first published 1959, first revised edition 1962].

William Appleman Williams, **America Confronts a Revolutionary World 1776-1976** [New York: Morrow, 1976].

William Appleman Williams, **Americans in a Changing World: A History of the United States in the Twentieth Century** [New York: Harper and Row, 1978].

William Appleman Williams, **Empire as a Way of Life: An Essay on the Causes and Charcter of America's Present Predicament along with a Few Thoughts about an Alternative** [New York: Oxford University Press, 1980].

Garry Wills, **Reagan's America: Innocents at Home** [London: Heineman, 1988; first published 1985].

Charles Morrow Wilson, **Central America: Challenge and Opportunity** [London: George Allen and Unwin, 1942].

Charles Morrow Wilson, **Middle America** [New York: W. W. Norton, 1944].

Charles Morrow Wilson, **Empire in Green and Gold: The Story of the American Banana Trade** [New York: Henry Holt, 1947].

Charles Morrow Wilson, **Liberia: Black Africa in Microcosm** [New York: Harper and Row, 1971].

Robin Winks, **Cloak and Gown: Scholars in the Secret War 1939-1961** [New Haven: Yale University Press, 1987].

John D. Wirth, **The Politics of Brazilian Development 1930-1954** [Stanford: Stanford University Press, 1970].

David Wise and Thomas B. Ross, **The Invisible Government: The CIA and US Intelligence** [New York: Vintage, 1974; first published 1964].

Gene Wise, **American Historical Explanations: A Strategy for Grounded Inquiry** [Minneapolis: University of Minnesota Press, second revised edition, 1980; first published 1973].

Eric R. Wolf, **Sons of the Shaking Earth: The People of Mexico and Guatemala--Their Land, History and Culture** [Chicago: University of Chicago Press, 1972; first published 1959].

Eric R. Wolf, **Peasants** [Englewood Cliffs: Prentice-Hall, 1966].

Eric R. Wolf, **Peasant Wars of the Twentieth Century** [New York: Harper and Row, 1969].

Eric R. Wolf and Edward C. Hansen, **The Human Condition in Latin America** [New York: Oxford University Press, 1972].

Eric R. Wolf, **Europe and the People Without History** [Berkeley: University of California Press, 1982].

Alan Wolfe, **The Rise and Fall of the "Soviet Threat": Domestic Sources of the Cold War Consensus** [Washington: Institute for Policy Studies, 1979, second edition 1981].

Bryce Wood, **The Making of the Good Neighbour Policy** [New York: Columbia University Press, 1961].

Bryce Wood, **The United States and Latin American Wars 1932-1942** [New York: Columbia University Press, 1966].

Bryce Wood, **Aggression and History: The Case of Ecuador and Peru** [Ann Arbor: University of Michigan Press, 1978].

Bryce Wood, **The Dismantling of the Good Neighbour Policy** [Austin: University of Texas Press, 1985].

Alexander Woodside, **Vietnam and the Chinese Model: A Comparative Study of Vietnamese and Chinese Government in the First Half of the Nineteenth Century** [Cambridge: Harvard University Press, 1988; first published 1971].

Alexander Woodside, **Community and Revolution in Modern Vietnam** [Boston: Houghton Mifflin, 1976].

Ralph Lee Woodward, Jr., **Class Privilege and Economic Development: The Consulado de Comercio of Guatemala 1793-1871** [Chapel Hill: University of North Carolina Press, 1966].

Ralph Lee Woodward, Jr., **Central America: A Nation Divided** [New York: Oxford University Press, 1976].

Ralph Lee Woodward, Jr., **Nicaragua** [Santa Barbara: Clio Press, 1983].

Ralph Lee Woodward, Jr., **Central America: A Nation Divided** [New York: Oxford University Press, second revised edition 1985; first published 1976].

Peter Worsley, **The Third World** [London: Weidenfeld and Nicolson, 1978; first published 1964].

Peter Worsley, **The Three Worlds: Culture and World Development** [London: Weidenfeld and Nicolson, 1986; first published 1984].

Miles L. Wortman, **Government and Society in Central America 1680-1840** [New York: Columbia University Press, 1982].

Gary W. Wynia, **Politics and Planners: Economic Development Policy in Central America** [Madison: University of Wisconsin Press, 1972].

Daniel Yergin, **Shattered Peace: The Origins of the Cold War and the National Security State** [New York: Viking Penguin, revised and updated 1990; first published Boston: Houghton Mifflin, 1977].

Miguel Ydígoras Fuentes, **My War with Communism** [Englewood Cliffs:

Prentice-Hall, 1963].

Marilyn B. Young, **The Vietnam Wars 1945-1990** [New York: Harper Collins, 1991].

Nigel Young, **An Infantile Disorder?: The Crisis and Decline of the New Left** [London: Routledge and Kegan Paul, 1977].

Robert Young, **White Mythologies: Writing History and the West** [London: Routledge, 1990].

Maurice Zeitlin and Robert Scheer, **Cuba: Tragedy in Our Hemisphere** [New York: Grove Press, 1963].

Maurice Zeitlin, **Revolutionary Politics and the Cuban Working Class** [Princeton: Princeton University Press, 1967].

José Santos Zelaya, **La Revolución de Nicaragua y los Estados Unidos** [Madrid: Bernardo Rodriguez, 1910].

Howard Zinn, **The Politics of History** [Boston: Beacon Press, 1970].

Aristide Zolberg, **Creating Political Order: The Party States of West Africa** [Chicago: Chicago University Press, 1966].

Thomas Zoumaras, **The Path to Pan Americanism: Eisenhower's Foreign Economic Policy** [Unpublished PhD dissertation, University of Connecticut, 1987].

Articles

Janet Abu-Lughod, "On the Remaking of History: How to Reinvent the Past" in Barbara Kruger and Phil Mariani, eds., **Remaking History** [Seattle: Bay Press, 1989].

Richard N. Adams (Stokes Newbold), "Receptivity to Communist-Fomented Agitation in Rural Guatemala" **Economic Development and Cultural Change** vol. 5. no. 4. 1957.

Richard N. Adams, "Social Change in Guatemala and US Policy" in Richard N. Adams et al., eds., **Social Change in Latin America Today: The Implications for United States Policy** [New York: Harper and Brothers, for the Council on Foreign Relations, 1960].

Richard N. Adams, "The Pattern of Development in Latin America" **Annals of the American Academy of Political and Social Science** vol. 360. 1965.

Richard N. Adams, "The Development of the Guatemalan Military" **Studies in Comparative International Development** vol. 10. no. 5. 1968-69.

Richard N. Adams, "The Changing Scene of Behavioural Science Research in Latin America Today: A North American View" in Stanley R. Ross, ed., **Latin America in Transition: Problems in Training and Research** [Albany: State University of New York Press, 1970].

Richard N. Adams, "Conclusions: What Can We Know About the Harvest of Violence?" in Robert M. Carmack, ed., **Harvest of Violence: The Maya Indians and the Guatemalan Crisis** [Norman: University of Oklahoma Press, 1988].

Richard N. Adams, "Ethnic Images and Strategies in 1944" in Carol A. Smith, ed., **Guatemalan Indians and the State: 1540 to 1988** [Austin: University of Texas Press, 1990].

Richard N. Adams, "Strategies of Ethnic Survival in Central America" in Greg Urban and Joel Sherzer, eds., **Nation-States and Indians in Latin America** [Austin: University of Texas Press, 1991].

Alan Adelman, "Introduction" in Alan Adelman and Reid Reading, eds., **Confrontation in the Caribbean Basin: International Perspectives on Security, Sovereignty and Survival** [Pittsburgh: Center for Latin American Studies, University Center for International Studies, University of Pittsburgh, 1984].

Juan del Aguila, "The Politics of Confrontation: US Policy Toward Cuba" in H. Michael Erisman, ed., **The Caribbean Challenge: US Policy in a Volatile Region** [Boulder: Westview Press, 1984].

Aijaz Ahmad, "Imperialism and Progress" in Ronald H. Chilcote and Dale L. Johnson, eds., **Theories of Development: Mode of Production or Dependency** [Beverly Hills: Sage, 1983].

Hamza Alavi, "The State in Post-Colonial Societies: Pakistan and Bangladesh" **New Left Review** no. 74. 1972. reprinted in Kathleen Gough and Hari P. Sharma, eds., **Imperialism and Revolution in South Asia** [London: Monthly Review Press, 1973].

Robert J. Alexander, "The Guatemalan Revolution and Communism" **Foreign Policy Bulletin** vol. 33. April 1. 1954.

Raúl Alfonsín, "Foreword: Consolidating Democracy" in Robert A. Pastor, ed., **Democracy in the Americas: Stopping the Pendulum** [New York: Holmes and Meier, 1989].

Gilbert Allardyce, "Toward World History: American Historians and the Coming of the World History Course" **Journal of World History** vol. 1. no. 1. 1990.

Douglas Allen, "Antiwar Asian Scholars and the Vietnam/Indochina War" **Bulletin of Concerned Asian Scholars** vol. 21. nos. 2-4. 1989.

Graham T. Allison, "Conceptual Models and the Cuban Missile Crisis" in **American Political Science Review** vol. 63. no. 3. 1969. Morton Halperin and Arnold Kanter, eds., **Readings in American Foreign Policy: A Bureaucratic Perspective** [Boston: Little Brown, 1973].

Graham T. Allison, Ernest R. May and Adam Yarmolinsky, "Limits to Intervention" (1970) in Robert W. Gregg and Charles W. Kegley, eds., **After Vietnam: The Future of American Foreign Policy** [Garden City: Doubleday, 1971].

Graham T. Allison and Morton H. Halperin, "Bureaucratic Politics: A Paradigm and Some Policy Implications" in Raymond Tanter and Richard H. Ullman, eds., **Theory and Politics in International Relations** [Princeton: Princeton University Press, 1972].

Gabriel A. Almond, "A Functional Approach to Comparative Politics" in Gabriel Almond and J. S. Coleman eds., **The Politics of the Developing Areas** [Princeton: Princeton University Press, 1971; first published 1960].

Gabriel A. Almond, "Making New Nations Democratic" **Stanford Today** vol. 1. no. 10. 1964. reprinted in Howard J. Wiarda, ed., **On the Agenda: Current Issues and Conflicts in US Foreign Policy** [Glenview: Scott Foresman/Little Brown, 1990].

Gabriel A. Almond, "A Developmental Approach to Political Systems" **World Politics** vol. 17. no. 2. 1965. reprinted in Ikuo Kabashima and Lynn T. White III, eds., **Political System and Change** [Princeton: Princeton University Press, 1986].

Gabriel A. Almond, "Sphere-of-Interest Behavior: A Literature Search and Methodological Reflections" in Jan F. Triska, ed., **Dominant Powers and Subordinate States: The United States in Latin America and the Soviet Union in Eastern Europe** [Durham: Duke University Press, 1986].

Gabriel A. Almond, "The Development of Political Development" in Myron Weiner and Samuel P. Huntington, eds., **Understanding Political Development** [Boston: Little Brown, 1987].

M. S. Al'perovich, "Soviet Historiography of the Latin American Countries" **Latin American Research Review** vol. 5. no. 1. 1970.

Eric Alterman, "Washington and the Curse of the Pundit Class: The Perversion of US Foreign Policy Discourse" **World Policy Journal** vol. 5. no. 2. 1988.

Francisco A. Alvarez, "Transition Before the Transition: The Case of El Salvador" **Latin American Perspectives** vol. 15. no. 1. 1988.

Sonia E. Alvarez and Arturo Escobar, "Conclusion: Theoretical and Political Horizons of Change in Contemporary Latin American Social Movements" in Arturo Escobar and Sonia E. Alvarez, eds., **The Making of Social**

Movements in Latin America: Identity, Strategy and Democracy [Boulder: Westview Press, 1992].

Maria Helena Moreira Alves, "Something Old, Something New: Brazil's Partido dos Trabalhadores" in Barry Carr and Steve Ellner, eds., **The Latin American Left: From the Fall of Allende to Perestroika** [Boulder: Westview Press, 1993].

Samir Amin, "Democracy and National Strategy in the Periphery" **Third World Quarterly: Journal of Emerging Areas** vol. 9. no. 4. 1987.

Samir Amin, "The State and Development" in David Held, ed., **Political Theory Today** [Stanford: Stanford University Press, 1991].

Robin Andersen, "Images of War: Photojournalism, Ideology and Central America" **Latin American Perspectives** vol. 16. no. 2. 1989.

Benedict Anderson, "The Last Empires: The New World Disorder" **New Left Review** no. 193. 1992.

Charles W. Anderson, "Toward a Theory of Latin American Politics" (1964) in Howard J. Wiarda, ed., **Politics and Social Change in Latin America: Still a Distinct Tradition?** [Boulder: Westview Press, 1992].

Charles W. Anderson, "Political Factors in Latin American Economic Development" **Journal of International Affairs** vol. 20. no. 2. 1966.

Thomas D. Anderson, "Progress in the Democratic Revolution in Latin America: Country Assessments 1987" **Journal of Interamerican Studies and World Affairs** vol. 29. no. 1. 1987.

Thomas P. Anderson, "El Salvador" in Robert Wesson, ed., **Communism in Central America and the Caribbean** [Stanford: Hoover Institution Press, 1982].

Thomas P. Anderson, "Intervention in the Caribbean Basin: A Search For Stability" **Latin American Research Review** vol. 19. no. 2. 1984.

Thomas P. Anderson, "Politics and the Military in Honduras" **Current History: A World Affairs Journal** vol. 87. no. 533. 1988.

Thomas P. Anderson, "Recent Studies on Intervention and Politics in Central America" **Latin American Research Review** vol. 25. no. 3. 1990.

Sheldon Annis, "Story from a Peaceful Town: San Antonio Aguas Calientes" in Robert M. Carmack, ed., **Harvest of Violence: The Maya Indians and the Guatemalan Crisis** [Norman: University of Oklahoma Press, 1988].

Gustavo Arcia, "Assessment of Rural Development in Central America" in William Ascher and Ann Hubbard, eds., **Central American Recovery and Development: Task Force Report to the International Commission for Central American Recovery and Development** [Durham: Duke University Press, 1989].

German Arciniegas, "A New Approach: Alliance--Not Aid" in Joseph Maier and Richard W. Weatherhead, eds., **Politics of Change in Latin America** [New York: Praeger, 1964].

Arturo Arias, "Changing Indian Identity: Guatemala's Violent Transition to Modernity" in Carol A. Smith, ed., **Guatemalan Indians and the State 1540 to 1988** [Austin: University of Texas Press, 1990].

Lourdes Arizpe S., "Anthropology in Latin America: Old Boundaries, New

Contexts" in Christopher Mitchell, ed., **Changing Perspectives in Latin American Studies: Insights from Six Disciplines** [Stanford: Stanford University Press, 1988].

Robert Armstrong and Janet Shenk, "El Salvador: Why Revolution" **NACLA Report on the Americas** vol. 14. no. 2. 1980.

Robert Armstrong and Janet Shenk, "El Salvador: A Revolution Brews" **NACLA Report on the Americas** vol. 14. no. 4. 1980.

Robert C. Armstrong (with Holly Sklar), "Reagan Policy in Crisis: Will the Empire Strike Back?" **NACLA Report on the Americas** vol. 15. no. 4. 1981.

Robert Armstrong, "El Salvador: Beyond Elections" **NACLA Report on the Americas** vol. 16. no. 2. 1982.

Robert Armstrong, "By What Right?: US Foreign Policy 1945-1983" **NACLA Report on the Americas** vol. 17. no. 6. 1983.

Robert Armstrong, "El Salvador: Why Revolution?" in Stanford Central American Action Network, ed., **Revolution in Central America** [Boulder: Westview Press, 1983].

Robert Armstrong, "Are the Democrats Different?" **NACLA Report on the Americas** vol. 18. no. 5. 1984.

Robert Armstrong, "Nicaragua: Sovereignty and Non-Alignment" **NACLA Report on the Americas** vol. 19. no. 3. 1985.

Eric Arnesen, "El Salvador: Reminders of War" **Monthly Review** vol. 38. no. 5. 1986.

Cynthia J. Arnson, "The Salvadoran Military and Regime Transformation" in Wolf Grabendorff, Heinrich W. Krumwiede and Jorg Todt, eds., **Political Change in Central America: Internal and External Dimensions** [Boulder: Westview Press, 1984].

Cynthia J. Arnson, "Contadora and the US Congress" in Bruce M. Bagley, ed., **Contadora and the Diplomacy of Peace in Central America-- vol. 1: The United States, Central America and Contadora** [Boulder: Westview Press, 1987].

Cynthia J. Arnson and Johanna Mendelson Forman, "United States Policy in Central America" **Current History: A World Affairs Journal** vol. 90. no. 554. 1991.

Giovanni Arrighi, "Marxist Century, American Century: The Making and Remaking of the World Labour Movement" **New Left Review** no. 179. 1990. reprinted in Robin Blackburn, ed., **After the Fall: The Failure of Communism and the Future of Socialism** [London: Verso, 1991].

William Ascher and Ann Hubbard, "Introduction" in William Ascher and Ann Hubbard, eds., **Central American Recovery and Development: Task Force Report to the International Commission for Central American Recovery and Development** [Durham: Duke University Press, 1989].

Ed Asner, "The US War in Central America" in John M. Kirk and George W. Schuyler, eds., **Central America: Democracy, Development and Change** [New York: Praeger, 1988].

Atlantic Council's Working Group on the Caribbean Basin, "Western Interests and US Policy Options in the Caribbean Basin: The Policy Paper" in James R. Greene and Brent Scowcroft, eds., **Western Interests and US Policy**

456 Bibliography - Articles

Options in the Caribbean Basin: Report of the Atlantic
Council's Working Group on the Caribbean Basin [Boston:
Oelgeschlager, Gunn and Hain, for the Atlantic Council of the United States,
1984].

JoAnn Fagot Aviel, "'The Enemy of My Enemy': The Arab-Israeli Conflict in
Nicaragua" in Damian J. Fernandez, ed., Central America and the
Middle East: The Internationalization of the Crises [Miami:
Florida International University Press, 1990].

Andrew W. Axline, "Political Change and US Strategic Concerns in the Caribbean"
Latin American Research Review vol. 23. no. 2. 1988.

Max Azicri, "Nicaragua's Foreign Relations: The Struggle for Survival" in Jennie K.
Lincoln and Elizabeth G. Ferris, eds., The Dynamics of Latin
American Foreign Policies: Challenges for the 1980s [Boulder:
Westview Press, 1984].

Max Azicri, "Women's Development Through Revolutionary Mobilization"
International Journal of Women's Studies vol. 2. no. 1. 1981.
abridged and reprinted in Philip Brenner, William LeoGrande, Donna Rich and
Daniel Siegel, eds., The Cuba Reader: The Making of a
Revolutionary Society [New York: Grove Press, 1989].

Wilfred A. Bacchus, "Controlled Political Transition in Brazil: Abertura as a Process
for a Gradual Sharing of Political Power" in George A. Lopez and Michael
Stohl, eds., Liberalization and Redemocratization in Latin
America [New York: Greenwood Press, 1987].

Bruce Michael Bagley, "The Politics of Asymmetrical Interdependence: US-Mexican
Relations in the 1980s" in H. Michael Erisman, ed., The Caribbean
Challenge: US Policy in a Volatile Region [Boulder: Westview
Press, 1984].

Bruce Michael Bagley, "Mexico in Central America: The Limits of Regional Power"
in Wolf Grabendorff, Heinrich W. Krumwiede and Jorg Todt, eds., Political
Change in Central America: Internal and External Dimensions
[Boulder: Westview, 1984].

Bruce Michael Bagley, "Contadora: The Failure of Diplomacy" Journal of
Interamerican Studies and World Affairs vol. 28. no. 3. 1986.

Bruce Michael Bagley, "The Failure of Diplomacy" in Bruce M. Bagley, ed.,
Contadora and the Diplomacy of Peace in Central America--
vol. 1: The United States, Central America and Contadora
[Boulder: Westview Press, 1987].

Bruce Michael Bagley, "The New Hundred Years War?: US National Security and the
War on Drugs in Latin America" Journal of Interamerican Studies and
World Affairs vol. 30. no. 1. 1988.

Bruce Michael Bagley, "US Foreign Policy and the War on Drugs: Analysis of a
Policy Failure" Journal of Interamerican Studies and World Affairs
vol. 30. nos. 2-3. 1988.

Thomas A. Bailey, "Interest in a Nicaragua Canal 1903-1931" Hispanic
American Historical Review vol. 16. no. 1. 1936.

Samuel L. Baily, "The Historian's Perspective" in Samuel L. Baily and Ronald T.
Hyman, eds., Perspectives on Latin America [New York: Macmillan,
1974].

George W. Baker, Jr., "The Wilson Administration and Nicaragua 1913-1921" **The Americas: A Quarterly Review of Inter-American Cultural History** vol. 22. no. 4. 1966.

Bahman Baktiari, "Religion and Revolution in Iran and Nicaragua" in Damian J. Fernandez, ed., **Central America and the Middle East: The Internationalization of the Crises** [Miami: Florida International University Press, 1990].

Hanson W. Baldwin, "The Panama Canal: Sovereignty and Security" **American Enterprise Institute (Foreign Policy and) Defense Review** vol. 1. no. 4. 1977.

Terence Ball, "The Politics of Social Science in Postwar America" in Lary May, ed., **Recasting America: Culture and Politics in the Age of Cold War** [Chicago: University of Chicago Press, 1989].

Enrique A. Baloyra, "The Fallibility of Che" **Problems of Communism** vol. 25. no. 1. 1976.

Enrique Baloyra, Federico G. Gil and Lars Schoultz, "The Peaceful Transition to Democracy: Elections and the Restorations of Rights" **Democracy in Latin America: Prospects and Implications** Paper no. 1 [Washington: Department of State Contract 1722-020083, August 1981].

Enrique Baloyra, Federico G. Gil and Lars Schoultz, "The Deterioration and Breakdown of Reactionary Despotism in Central America" **Democracy in Latin America: Prospects and Implications** Paper no. 2 [Washington: Department of State Contract 1722-020083, August 1981].

Enrique A. Baloyra, "Reactionary Despotism in Central America: An Impediment to Democratic Transition" in Martin Diskin, ed., **Trouble in Our Backyard: Central America and the United States in the Eighties** [New York: Pantheon, 1983].

Enrique Baloyra-Herp, "Reactionary Despotism in Central America" **Journal of Latin American Studies** vol. 15. no. 2. 1983.

Enrique Baloyra, "Political Change in El Salvador" **Current History: A World Affairs Journal** vol. 83. no. 490. 1984.

Enrique A. Baloyra, "Central America on the Reagan Watch" **Journal of Interamerican Studies and World Affairs** vol. 27. no. 1. 1985.

Enrique A. Baloyra, "Dilemmas of Political Transition in El Salvador" **Journal of International Affairs** vol. 38. no. 2. 1985.

Enrique A. Baloyra, "Negotiating War in El Salvador: The Politics of Endgame" **Journal of Interamerican Studies and World Affairs** vol. 28. no. 1. 1986.

Enrique A. Baloyra, "Introduction", "Democratic Transition in Comparative Perspective" and "Conclusion: Toward a Framework for the Study of Democratic Consolidation" in Enrique A. Baloyra, ed., **Comparing New Democracies: Transition and Consolidation in Mediterranean Europe and the Southern Cone** [Boulder: Westview Press, 1987].

Enrique Baloyra-Herp, "The Persistent Conflict in El Salvador" **Current History: A World Affairs Journal** vol. 90. no. 554. 1991.

John Francis Bannon, "Alfred Barnaby Thomas" in Eugene R. Huck and Edward H. Moseley, eds., **Militarists, Merchants and Missionaries: United States Expansion in Middle America** [Tuscaloosa: University of

Alabama Press, 1970].

David Barkin, "Internationalization of Capital: An Alternative Approach" in Ronald
H. Chilcote, ed., **Dependency and Marxism: Toward a Resolution
of the Debate** [Boulder: Westview Press, 1982].

Richard J. Barnet, "The Security of Empire" in Robert W. Gregg and Charles W.
Kegley, eds., **After Vietnam: The Future of American Foreign
Policy** [Garden City: Doubleday, 1971].

Richard J. Barnet, "The Empire Strikes Back: A Pitiful, Helpless Giant Goes to
War" **The Progressive** vol. 48. no. 1. 1984.

Richard J. Barnet, "The Costs and Perils of Intervention" in Michael T. Klare and
Peter Kornbluh, eds., **Low Intensity Warfare: How the USA Fights
Wars Without Declaring Them** [New York: Pantheon, 1988; reprinted
London: Methuen, 1989].

Roland Barthes, "The Death of the Author" in Roland Barthes, **Image Music Text**
[London: Fontana/Collins, 1979].

Russell H. Bartley, "On Scholarly Dialogue: The Case of US and Soviet Latin
Americanists" **Latin American Research Review** vol. 5. no. 1. 1970.

Russell H. Bartley, "LASA-USSR Academy of Sciences Exchange: An Appraisal"
LASA Forum vol. 20. no. 3. 1989.

Russell H. Bartley, "End of an Era in Sov iet Latin American Studies" **LASA
Forum** vol. 23. no. 2. 1992.

C. Richard Bath and Dilmus D. James, "Dependency Analysis of Latin America"
Latin American Research Review vol. 11. no. 3. 1976.

P. T. Bauer, "Foreign Aid and the Third World" in Peter Duignan and Alvin
Rabushka, eds., **The United States in the 1980s** [Stanford: Stanford
University Press--Hoover Institution, 1980].

P. T. Bauer, "The Vicious Circle of Poverty" in Mitchel A. Seligson, ed., **The Gap
Between Rich and Poor: Contending Perspectives on the
Political Economy of Development** [Boulder: Westview Press, 1984].

Richard Bauer, "Progress and Pain in Latin America" **Swiss Review of World
Affairs** vol. 42. no. 1. 1992.

Christian Bay, "The Cheerful Science of Dismal Politics" in Theodore Roszak, ed.,
The Dissenting Academy [London: Chatto and Windus, 1969; first
published 1967].

Jean-François Bayart, "Finishing With the Idea of the Third World: The Concept of
the Political Trajectory" in James Manor, ed., **Rethinking Third World
Politics** [London: Longman, 1991].

Joseph O. Baylen, "Sandino: Patriot or Bandit?" **Hispanic American Historical
Review** vol. 31. no. 3. 1951.

Maurice Bazin, "Science, Technology and the People of Latin America" in Samuel
L. Baily and Ronald T. Hyman, eds., **Perspectives on Latin America**
[New York: Macmillan, 1974].

David G. Becker, "Development, Democracy and Dependency in Latin America: A
Post-Imperialist View" **Third World Quarterly: Journal of Emerging
Areas** vol. 6. no. 2. 1984.

David G. Becker, "LASA's Election Coverage: An Effort Misplaced?" **LASA
Forum** vol. 17. no. 3. 1986.

George M. Beckman, "The Role of the Foundations" **Annals of the American**

Academy of Political and Social Science vol. 356. 1964.

Roger Bell, "The Debate over American Empire in the Late Twentieth Century" **Australian Journal of International Affairs** vol. 45. no. 1. 1991.

Walden Bello and Edward S. Herman, "US Sponsored Elections in El Salvador and the Philippines" **World Policy Journal** vol. 1. no. 4. 1984.

Walden Bello, "Edging Towards the Quagmire: The United States and the Philippine Crisis" **World Policy Journal** vol. 3. no. 1. 1985-1986.

Walden Bello, "Ending the 'Special Relationship': The US and the Philippines in the Aquino Era" **World Policy Journal** vol. 5. no. 4. 1988.

Samuel Flagg Bemis, "American Foreign Policy and the Blessings of Liberty", "Woodrow Wilson and Latin America", "The Shifting Strategy of American Defense and Diplomacy" and "Fourth Front in the Caribbean" in Samuel Flagg Bemis, **American Foreign Policy and Blessings of Liberty and Other Essays** [New Haven: Yale University Press, 1962].

Reinhard Bendix, "Tradition and Modernity Reconsidered" **Comparative Studies in Society and History** vol. 9. no. 3. 1966.

Jaime Benítez, "Is the United States Losing Ground in Central and South America?" **Annals of the American Academy of Political and Social Science** vol. 500. 1988.

Jules Robert Benjamin, "The Framework of US Relations with Latin America in the Twentieth Century: An Interpretive Essay" **Diplomatic History** vol. 11. no. 2. 1987.

Medea Benjamin, "Honduras: The War Comes Home--Campesinos, Between Carrot and Stick" **NACLA Report on the Americas** vol. 22. no. 1. 1988.

Mark T. Berger, "The Limits of Power and the 'Lessons of History': North American Neo-liberalism and the US Crisis of Empire in Central America" **Australasian Journal of American Studies** vol. 9. no. 1. 1990.

Mark T. Berger, "Civilising the South: The US Rise to Hegemony in the Americas and the Roots of 'Latin American Studies' 1898-1945" **Bulletin of Latin American Research** vol. 12. no. 1. 1993.

Mark T. Berger, "Global Liberalism?: Rethinking the 'Third World' after the Cold War" **Journal of Pacific Studies** vol. 17. nos. 1-2. 1993.

Mark T. Berger, "The End of the 'Third World'?" **Third World Quarterly: Journal of Emerging Areas** vol. 15. no. 2. 1994.

Albert Bergesen, "Long Waves of Colonial Expansion and Contraction 1415-1969" in Albert Bergesen, ed., **Studies of the Modern World-System** [New York: Academic Press, 1980].

Charles W. Bergquist, "Recent United States Studies in Latin American History: Trends since 1965" **Latin American Research Review** vol. 9. no. 1. 1974.

Charles W. Bergquist, "Latin America: A Dissenting View of 'Latin American History in World Perspective'" in Georg G. Iggers and Harold T. Parker, eds., **International Handbook of Historical Studies: Contemporary Research and Theory** [New York: Greenwood Press, 1979].

Henry Bernstein, "Sociology of Development versus Sociology of Underdevelopment?" in David Lehmann, ed., **Development Theory: Four Critical Essays** [London: Frank Cass, 1979].

Ruben Berrios and Cole Blasier, "Peru and the Soviet Union (1969-1989): Distant

Partners" **Journal of Latin American Studies** vol. 23. no. 2. 1991.

Richard K. Betts and Samuel P. Huntington, "Dead Dictators and Rioting Mobs: Does the Demise of Authoritarian Rulers Lead to Political Instability?" **International Security** vol. 10. no. 3. 1985-86.

Seweryn Bialer, "Lessons of History: Soviet-American Relations in the Postwar Era" in Arnold L. Horelick, ed., **US-Soviet Relations: The Next Phase** [Ithaca: Cornell University Press, for the Rand/UCLA Center for the Study of Soviet International Behavior, 1986].

Leonard Binder, "The Natural History of Development Theory" **Comparative Studies in Society and History** vol. 28. no. 1. 1986.

William C. Binkley, "Have the Americas a Common History?: A United States View (1942)" in Lewis Hanke, ed., **Do the Americas Have a Common History?: A Critique of the Bolton Theory** [New York: Alfred A. Knopf, 1964].

Henrik Bischof, "The Socialist Countries and Central American Revolutions" in Wolf Grabendorff, Heinrich W. Krumwiede and Jorg Todt, eds., **Political Change in Central America: Internal and External Dimensions** [Boulder: Westview, 1984].

Morris J. Blachman and Ronald G. Hellman, "Costa Rica" in Morris J. Blachman, William LeoGrande and Kenneth Sharpe, eds., **Confronting Revolution: Security Through Diplomacy in Central America** [New York: Pantheon, 1986].

Morris J. Blachman, William M. LeoGrande, Douglas C. Bennett and Kenneth E. Sharpe "The Failure of the Hegemonic Strategic Vision" in Morris J. Blachman, William M. LeoGrande and Kenneth Sharpe, eds., **Confronting Revolution: Security Through Diplomacy in Central America** [New York: Pantheon, 1986].

Morris J. Blachman and Kenneth Sharpe, "El Salvador: The Policy That Failed" in Richard S. Newfarmer, ed., **From Gunboats to Diplomacy: New US Policies for Latin America** [Baltimore: Johns Hopkins University Press, 1984].

Morris J. Blachman and Kenneth E. Sharpe, "Central American Traps: Challenging the Reagan Agenda" **World Policy Journal** vol. 5. no. 1. 1987-1988.

Morris J. Blachman and Kenneth E. Sharpe, "Things Fall Apart in El Salvador: What's at Stake in the Presidential Election" **World Policy Journal** vol. 6. no. 1. 1988-89.

Morris J. Blachman and Kenneth E. Sharpe, "The War on Drugs: American Democracy Under Assault" **World Policy Journal** vol. 7. no. 1. 1989-90.

Morris J. Blachman and Kenneth E. Sharpe, "The Transitions to 'Electoral' and Democratic Politics in Central America: Asssessing the Role of Political Parties" in Louis W. Goodman, William M. LeoGrande and Johanna Mendelson Forman, eds., **Political Parties and Democracy in Central America** [Boulder: Westview Press, 1992].

George Black, "Central America: Crisis in the Backyard" **New Left Review** no. 135. 1982.

George Black, "Guatemala's Silent War" **Monthly Review** vol. 35. no. 3. 1983.

George Black, "Shadow Play: Central America's Untold Stories--Under the Gun" **NACLA Report on the Americas** vol. 19. no. 6. 1985.

George Black and Judy Butler "Target Nicaragua" **NACLA Report on the Americas** vol. 16. no. 1. 1982.

George Black (with Milton Jamail and Norma Stoltz Chinchilla), "Garrison Guatemala" **NACLA Report on the Americas** vol. 17. no. 1. 1983.

George Black (with Milton Jamail and Norma Stoltz Chinchilla), "Guatemala: The War Is Not Over" **NACLA Report on the Americas** vol. 17. no. 2. 1983.

Jan Knippers Black, "Introduction: Aproaches to the Study of Latin America" in Jan Knippers Black, ed., **Latin America: Its Problems and Its Promises** [Boulder: Westview Press, 1984].

Jan Knippers Black, "Conclusion" in Jan Knippers Black, ed., **Latin America: Its Problems and Its Promises** [Boulder: Westview Press, 1984].

Robin Blackburn, "Fin de Siècle: Socialism after the Crash" **New Left Review** no. 185. 1991; reprinted in Robin Blackburn, ed., **After the Fall: The Failure of Communism and the Future of Socialism** [London: Verso, 1991].

Calvin P. Blair, "Research in Latin America: Problems for the Policy Sciences" in Stanley R. Ross, ed., **Latin America in Transition: Problems in Training and Research** [Albany: State University of New York Press, 1970].

André Blais and Stéphane Dion, "Electoral Systems and the Consolidation of New Democracies" in Diane Ethier, ed, **Democratic Transition and Consolidation in Southern Europe, Latin America and Southeast Asia** [New York: Macmillan, 1990].

George I. Blanksten, "The Politics of Latin America" in Gabriel Almond and James S. Coleman, eds., **The Politics of Developing Areas** [Princeton: Princeton University, 1964; first published 1960].

George I. Blanksten, "Political Groups in Latin America" **American Political Science Review** vol. 53. no. 1. 1959; reprinted in John H. Kautsky, ed., **Political Change in Underdeveloped Countries: Nationalism and Communism** [New York: Wiley, 1965; first published 1962].

Cole Blasier, "Studies of Social Revolution: Origins in Mexico, Bolivia and Cuba" **Latin American Research Review** vol. 2. no. 3. 1967.

Cole Blasier, "The United States and the Revolution" in James M. Malloy and Richard S. Thorn, eds., **Beyond the Revolution: Bolivia Since 1952** [Pittsburgh: University of Pittsburgh Press, 1971].

Cole Blasier, "The Elimination of United States Influence" in Carmelo Mesa-Lago, ed., **Revolutionary Change in Cuba** [Pittsburgh: University of Pittsburgh Press, 1971].

Cole Blasier, "The United States, Germany and the Bolivian Revolutionaries 1941-1946" **Hispanic American Historical Review** vol. 52. no. 1. 1972.

Cole Blasier, "The United States and Madero" **Journal of Latin American Studies** vol. 4. no. 2. 1972.

Cole Blasier, "Security: The Extracontinental Dimension" in Kevin J. Middlebrook and Carlos Rico, eds., **The United States and Latin America in the 1980s: Contending Perspectives on a Decade of Crisis** [Pittsburgh: University of Pittsburgh Press, 1986].

Cole Blasier, "The Soviet Union" in Morris J. Blachman, William LeoGrande and

Kenneth Sharpe, eds., **Confronting Revolution: Security Through Diplomacy in Central America** [New York: Pantheon, 1986].

Cole Blasier, "The United States and Democracy in Latin America" in James M. Malloy and Mitchell A. Seligson, eds., **Authoritarians and Democrats: Regime Transition in Latin America** [Pittsburgh: University of Pittsburgh Press, 1987].

Cole Blasier, "The US/USSR Exchange in Latin American Studies" **LASA Forum** vol. 20. no. 3. 1989.

Susanne (Jonas) Bodenheimer, "The Social Democratic Ideology in Latin America: The Case of Costa Rica's *Partido Liberación Nacional* " **Caribbean Studies** vol. 10. no. 3. 1970.

Susanne (Jonas) Bodenheimer, "The Ideology of Developmentalism: American Political Science's Paradigm Surrogate for Latin American Studies" **Berkeley Journal of Sociology** vol. 15. 1970.

Susanne (Jonas) Bodenheimer, "Dependency and Imperialism: The Root of Latin American Underdevelopment" in K. T. Fann and Donald C. Hodges, eds., **Readings in US Imperialism** [Boston: Porter Sargent, 1971].

Susanne (Jonas) Bodenheimer, "Crucifixion by Adams" **Berkeley Journal of Sociology** vol. 16. 1971-72.

Demetrio Boersner, "Venezuelan Policies Toward Central America" in Wolf Grabendorff, Heinrich W. Krumwiede and Jorg Todt, eds., **Political Change in Central America: Internal and External Dimensions** [Boulder: Westview, 1984].

William Bollinger, "Villalobos on 'Popular Insurrection'" **Latin American Perspectives** vol. 16. no. 3. 1989.

Herbert E. Bolton, "The Epic of Greater America" **American Historical Review** vol. 38. no. 3. 1933; reprinted in Lewis Hanke, ed., **Do the Americas Have a Common History?** [New York: Alfred A. Knopf, 1964] and in Howard F. Cline, ed., **Latin American History: Essays on Its Study and Teaching 1898-1965** (2 vols.) [Austin: University of Texas Press, 1967].

Robert D. Bond, "Venezuelan Policy in the Caribbean Basin" in Richard E. Feinberg, ed., **Central America: International Dimensions of the Crisis** [New York: Holmes and Meier, 1982].

Blase Bonpane, "The Church and Revolutionary Struggle in Central America" **Latin American Perspectives** vol. 7. nos. 2-3. 1980.

John A. Booth and Mitchell Seligson, "Peasants as Activists: A Reevaluation of Political Participation in the Countryside" **Comparative Political Studies** vol. 12. no. 1. 1979.

John A. Booth, "A Guatemalan Nightmare: Levels of Political Violence 1966-1972" **Journal of Interamerican Studies and World Affairs** vol. 22. no. 1. 1980.

John A. Booth, "The Evolution of US Policy Toward El Salvador: The Politics of Repression" in H. Michael Erisman, ed., **The Caribbean Challenge: US Policy in a Volatile Region** [Boudler: Westview, 1984].

John A. Booth, "The Revolution in Nicaragua: Through a Frontier in History" in Donald E. Schulz and Douglas H. Graham, eds., **Revolution and Counterrevolution in Central America and the Caribbean**

[Boulder: Westview Press, 1984].

John A. Booth, "Representative Constitutional Democracy in Costa Rica: Adaptation to Crisis in the Turbulent 1980s" in Steve C. Ropp and James Morris, eds., **Central America: Crisis and Adaptation** [Albuquerque: University of New Mexico Press, 1984].

John A. Booth, "'Trickle-up' Income Redistribution and Development in Central America During the 1960s and 1970s" in Mitchel A. Seligson, ed., **The Gap Between Rich and Poor: Contending Perspectives on the Political Economy of Development** [Boulder: Westview Press, 1984].

John A. Booth, "War and the Nicaraguan Revolution" **Current History: A World Affairs Journal** vol. 85. no. 515. 1986.

John A. Booth, "Elections and Democracy in Central America: A Framework for Analysis in John A. Booth and Mitchel A. Seligson, eds., **Elections and Democracy in Central America** [Chapel Hill: University of North Carolina Press, 1989].

John A. Booth, "Costa Rica: The Roots of Democratic Stability" in Larry Diamond, Juan J. Linz and Seymour Martin Lipset, eds., **Democracy in Developing Countries--Volume Four: Latin America** [Boulder: Lynne Rienner, 1989].

John A. Booth, "Socioeconomic and Political Roots of National Revolts in Central America" **Latin American Research Review** vol. 26. no. 1. 1991.

John A. Booth and Mitchell A. Seligson, "Paths to Democracy and the Political Culture of Costa Rica, Mexico and Nicaragua" in Larry Diamond, ed., **Political Culture and Democracy in Developing Countries** [Boulder: Lynne Rienner, 1993].

Woodrow Borah, "Latin American History in World Perspective" in Charles F. Delzell, ed., **The Future of History** [Nashville: Vanderbilt University Press, 1977].

Patricia Howard Borjas, "Perspectives on the Central American Crisis: 'Reactionary Despotism' or Monopoly Capital?" **Capital and Class** no. 39. 1989.

Thomas J. Bossert, "The Promise of Theory" in Peter F. Klarén and Thomas J. Bossert, eds., **Promise of Development: Theories of Change in Latin America** [Boulder: Westview Press, 1986].

Thomas J. Bossert, "Panama" in Morris J. Blachman, William LeoGrande and Kenneth Sharpe, eds., **Confronting Revolution: Security Through Diplomacy in Central America** [New York: Pantheon, 1986].

Gordon L. Bowen, "US Foreign Policy Toward Radical Change: Covert Operations in Guatemala 1950-1954" **Latin American Perspectives** vol. 10. no. 1. 1983.

Gordon L. Bowen, "The Political Economy of State Terrorism: Barrier to Human Rights in Guatemala" in George W. Shepherd, Jr., and Ved P. Nanda, eds., **Human Rights and Third World Development** [New York: Greenwood Press, 1985].

Gordon L. Bowen, "Prospects for Liberalization by Way of Democratization in Guatemala" in George A. Lopez and Michael Stohl, eds., **Liberalization and Redemocratization in Latin America** [New York: Greenwood Press, 1987].

Donald W. Bray and Timothy F. Harding, "Cuba" in Ronald H. Chilcote and Joel C.

Edelstein, eds., **Latin America: The Struggle with Dependency and Beyond** [New York: Wiley, 1974].

Philip Brenner, "Waging Ideological War: Anti-Communism and US Foreign Policy in Central America" **The Socialist Register 1984** [London: Merlin Press, 1984].

Philip Brenner, "Change and Continuity in Cuban Foreign Policy" in Philip Brenner, William LeoGrande, Donna Rich and Daniel Siegel, eds., **The Cuba Reader: The Making of a Revolutionary Society** [New York: Grove Press, 1989].

Philip Brenner, "United States-Cuban Relations in the 1980s" in Philip Brenner, William LeoGrande, Donna Rich and Daniel Siegel, eds., **The Cuba Reader: The Making of a Revolutionary Society** [New York: Grove Press, 1989].

Robert Brenner, "The Origins of Capitalist Development: A Critique of Neo-Smithian Marxism" **New Left Review** no. 104. 1977.

Edward T. Brett and Donna W. Brett, "Facing the Challenge: The Catholic Church and Social Change in Honduras" in Ralph Lee Woodward, Jr., ed., **Central America: Historical Perspectives on the Contemporary Crisis** [New York: Greenwood Press, 1988].

Philip L. Brock and Dennis Melendez, "Currency Convertibility, the Central American Clearing House, and the Revitalization of Intraregional Trade in the Central American Common Market" in William Ascher and Ann Hubbard, eds., **Central American Recovery and Development: Task Force Report to the International Commission for Central American Recovery and Development** [Durham: Duke University Press, 1989].

Charles D. Brockett, "Malnutrition, Public Policy and Agrarian Change in Guatemala" **Journal of Interamerican Studies and World Affairs** vol. 26. no. 4. 1984.

Charles D. Brockett, "The Right to Food and United States Policy in Guatemala" **Human Rights Quarterly** vol. 6. no. 3. 1984.

David Bronheim, "Latin American Diversity and United States Foreign Policy" in Douglas A. Chalmers, ed., **Changing Latin America: New Interpretations of Its Politics and Society** [New York: Academy of Political Science, Columbia University, 1972].

David C. Brooks, "US Marines, Miskitos and the Hunt for Sandino: The Río Coco Patrol in 1928" **Journal of Latin American Studies** vol. 21. no. 1. 1989.

Philip C. Brooks, "Do the Americas Share a Common History?" (1952) in Lewis Hanke, ed., **Do the Americas Have a Common History?: A Critique of the Bolton Theory** [New York: Alfred A. Knopf, 1964].

Doug Brown, "Sandinismo and the Problem of Democratic Hegemony" **Latin American Perspectives** vol. 17. no. 3. 1990.

George W. Brown, "Have the Americas a Common History?: A Canadian View" (1942) in Lewis Hanke, ed., **Do the Americas Have a Common History?: A Critique of the Bolton Theory** [New York: Alfred A. Knopf, 1964].

Philip Marshall Brown, "American Diplomacy in Central America" **The American Political Science Review** vol. 6. 1912.

Philip Marshall Brown, "American Intervention in Central America" **Journal of Race Development** vol. 4. no. 4. 1914.

Zbigniew Brzezinski, "America's New Geostrategy" **Foreign Affairs** vol. 66. no. 4. 1988.

Raymond Leslie Buell, "Changes in Our Latin American Policy" **Annals of the American Academy of Political and Social Science** vol. 156. 1931.

Raymond Leslie Buell, "The United States and Central American Stability" **Foreign Policy Reports** vol. 7. no. 9. 1931.

Raymond Leslie Buell, "The United States and Central American Revolutions" **Foreign Policy Reports** vol. 7. no. 10. 1931.

Raymond Leslie Buell, "Union or Disunion in Central America" **Foreign Affairs** vol. 11. no. 3. 1933.

McGeorge Bundy, "The Battlefields of Power and the Searchlights of the Academy" in Edgar A. G. Johnson, ed., **Dimensions of Diplomacy** [Baltimore: Johns Hopkins University Press, 1964].

Roger Burbach, "Central America: The End of US Hegemony?" **Monthly Review** vol. 34. no. 1. 1982.

Roger Burbach, "Revolution and Reaction" and "US Policy: Crisis and Conflict" in Roger Burbach and Patricia Flynn, eds., **The Politics of Intervention: The United States in Central America** [New York: Monthly Review Press, 1984].

Roger Burbach and Marc Herold, "The US Economic Stake in Central America and the Caribbean" in Roger Burbach and Patricia Flynn, eds., **The Politics of Intervention: The United States in Central America** [New York: Monthly Review Press, 1984].

Roger Burbach, "The Conflict at Home and Abroad: US Imperialism Versus the New Revolutionary Societies" in Richard R. Fagen, Carmen Diana Deere and Jose Luis Coraggio, eds., **Transition and Development: Problems of Third World Socialism** [New York: Monthly Review Press, 1986].

Roger Burbach, "Ruptured Frontiers: The Transformation of the US-Latin American System" **The Socialist Register 1992** [London: Merlin Press, 1992].

Roger Burbach, "Roots of the Postmodern Rebellion in Chiapas" **New Left Review** no. 205. 1994.

Robert F. Burk, "Eisenhower Revisionism Revisited: Reflections on Eisenhower Scholarship" **The Historian** vol. 50. no. 2. 1988.

E. Bradford Burns, "The Modernization of Underdevelopment: El Salvador 1858-1931" **Journal of Developing Areas** vol. 18. no. 3. 1984.

E. Bradford Burns, "The Intellectual Infrastructure of Modernization in El Salvador 1870-1900" **The Americas: A Quarterly Review of Inter-American Cultural History** vol. 41. no. 1. 1985.

E. Bradford Burns, "Establishing the Patterns of Progress and Poverty in Central America" in Michael T. Martin and Terry R. Kandal, eds., **Studies of Development and Change in the Modern World** [New York: Oxford University Press, 1989].

Fernando Bustamante, "Soviet Policy Toward Latin America: Time for Renewal" **Journal of Interamerican Studies and World Affairs** vol. 32. no. 4. 1990.

Judy Butler, "Central America: No Road Back--The Wider War" **NACLA Report on the Americas** vol. 15. no. 3. 1981.

Bruce J. Calder, "Caudillos and Gavrilleros versus the United States: Guerilla Insurgency during the Dominican Intervention 1916-1924" **Hispanic American Historical Review** vol. 58. no. 4. 1978.

Julio Castellanos Cambranes, "Origins of the Crisis of the Established Order in Guatemala" in Steve C. Ropp and James A. Morris, eds., **Central America: Crisis and Adaptation** [Albuquerque: University of New Mexico Press, 1984].

Paul Cammack, "The Political Economy of Contemporary Military Regimes in Latin America: From Bureaucratic Authoritarianism to Restructuring" in Philip O'Brien and Paul Cammack, eds., **Generals in Retreat: The Crisis of Military Rule in Latin America** [Manchester: Manchester University Press, 1985].

Paul Cammack and Philip O'Brien, "Conclusion: The Retreat of the Generals" in Philip O'Brien and Paul Cammack, eds., **Generals in Retreat: The Crisis of Military Rule in Latin America** [Manchester: Manchester University Press, 1985].

Paul Cammack, "Resurgent Democracy: Threat and Promise" **New Left Review** no. 157. 1986.

Paul Cammack, "Brazil: The Long March to the New Republic" **New Left Review** no. 190. 1991.

Hugh G. Campbell, "Mexico and Central America: The Continuity of Policy" in Ralph Lee Woodward, Jr., ed., **Central America: Historical Perspectives on the Contemporary Crisis** [New York: Greenwood Press, 1988].

William L. Canak, "The Peripheral State Debate: State Capitalist and Bureaucratic-Authoritarian Regimes in Latin America" **Latin American Research Review** vol. 19. 1984.

Fernando Henrique Cardoso, "Dependency and Development in Latin America" **New Left Review** no. 74. 1972.

Fernando Henrique Cardoso, "Imperialism and Dependency in Latin America" in F. Bonilla and R. Girling, eds., **Structures of Dependency** [Stanford: Institute of Political Studies, 1973].

Fernando Henrique Cardoso, "Associated Dependent Development: Theoretical and Practical Implications" in Alfred Stepan, ed., **Authoritarian Brazil** [New Haven: Yale University Press, 1973].

Fernando Henrique Cardoso, "O Inimigo de Papel (The Paper Enemy)" **Latin American Perspectives** vol. 1. no. 1. 1974.

Fernando Henrique Cardoso, "The Consumption of Dependency Theory in the United States" **Latin American Research Review** vol. 12. no. 3. 1977.

Fernando Henrique Cardoso, "On the Characterization of Authoritarian Regimes in Latin America" in David Collier, ed., **The New Authoritarianism in Latin America** [Princeton: Princeton University Press, 1979].

Fernando Henrique Cardoso, "Towards Another Development" in Heraldo Muñoz, ed., **From Dependency to Development: Strategies to Overcome Underdevelopment and Inequality** [Boulder: Westview Press, 1981].

Manoel Cardozo, "Roscoe R. Hill" **Hispanic American Historical Review** vol. 27. no. 1. 1947.

David Carleton and Michael Stohl, "US Foreign Assistance Policy and the Redemocratization of Latin America" in George A. Lopez and Michael Stohl, eds., **Liberalization and Redemocratization in Latin America** [New York: Greenwood Press, 1987].

Robert M. Carmack, "The Story of Santa Cruz Quiché" in Robert M. Carmack, ed., **Harvest of Violence: The Maya Indians and the Guatemalan Crisis** [Norman: University of Oklahoma Press, 1988].

Robert M. Carmack, "State and Community in Nineteenth-Century Guatemala: The Momostenango Case" in Carol A. Smith, ed., **Guatemalan Indians and the State 1540 to 1988** [Austin: University of Texas Press, 1990].

Barry Carr, "Low Intensity Conflict: The El Salvador Laboratory" in Barry Carr and Elaine McKay, eds., **Low Intensity Conflict: Theory and Practice in Central America and South-East Asia** [Melbourne: La Trobe University Institute of Latin American Studies and Monash University Centre of Southeast Asian Studies, 1988].

Barry Carr, "Mexico: The Perils of Unity and the Challenge of Modernization" in Barry Carr and Steve Ellner, eds., **The Latin American Left: From the Fall of Allende to Perestroika** [Boulder: Westview Press, 1993].

Jimmy Carter, "Foreword: Human Rights and Democracy" in Robert A. Pastor, ed., **Democracy in the Americas: Stopping the Pendulum** [New York: Holmes and Meier, 1989].

Clifford B. Casey, "The Creation and Development of the Pan American Union" **Hispanic American Historical Review** vol. 13. no. 4. 1933.

George P. Castile, "The Miskito and the 'Spanish': A Historical Perspective on the Ethnogenes and the Persistence of a People" in Ralph Lee Woodward, Jr., ed., **Central America: Historical Perspectives on the Contemporary Crisis** [New York: Greenwood Press, 1988].

Marcelo J. Cavarozzi and James F. Petras, "Chile" in Ronald H. Chilcote and Joel C. Edelstein, eds., **Latin America: The Struggle with Dependency and Beyond** [New York: Wiley, 1974].

Rodolfo Cerdas, "Nicaragua: One Step Forward, Two Steps Back" in Giuseppe Di Palma and Laurence Whitehead, eds., **The Central American Impasse** [London: Croom Helm, 1986].

James Chace, "Getting Out of the Central American Maze" **The New York Review of Books** June 24, 1982.

James Chace, "The Endless War" **The New York Review of Books** December 9, 1983.

James Chace, "Deeper into the Mire" **The New York Review of Books** March 1, 1984.

James Chace, "A Quest for Invulnerability" in Sanford J. Ungar, ed., **Estrangement: America and the World** [New York: Oxford University Press, 1985].

James Chace, "A New Grand Strategy" **Foreign Policy** no. 70. 1988.

Douglas A. Chalmers, "The Demystification of Development" in Douglas A. Chalmers, ed., **Changing Latin America: New Interpretations of Its Politics and Society** [New York: The Academy of Political Science, Columbia University, 1972].

Douglas A. Chalmers, "Corporatism and Comparative Politics" in Howard J. Wiarda, ed., **New Directions in Comparative Politics** [Boulder: Westview Press, 1985].

Douglas A. Chalmers and Craig H. Robinson, "Why Power Contenders Choose Liberalization: Perspectives from South America" in Abraham F. Lowenthal, ed., **Armies and Politics in Latin America** [New York: Holmes and Meier, revised edition 1986; first published 1976].

Charles E. Chapman, "The Founding of the Review" **Hispanic American Historical Review** vol. 1. no. 1. 1918.

Charles E. Chapman, "The United States and the Dominican Republic" **Hispanic American Historical Review** vol. 7. no. 1. 1927.

Charles E. Chapman, "The Development of the Intervention in Haiti" **Hispanic American Historical Review** vol. 7. no. 3. 1927.

Charles E. Chapman, "Spanish Consulados" in A. Curtis Wilgus, ed., **Hispanic American Essays** [Freeport: Books for Libraries Press, 1970; first printed 1942].

Christopher K. Chase-Dunn, "A World-System Perspective on Dependency and Development in Latin America" **Latin American Research Review** vol. 17. no. 1. 1982.

Pamela Chasek, "Revolution Across the Sea: Libyan Foreign Policy in Central America" in Damian J. Fernandez, ed., **Central America and the Middle East: The Internationalization of the Crises** [Miami: Florida International University Press, 1990].

Partha Chatterjee, "From Balance of Power to Imperialism: Analysis of a System Change in International Politics" in Barun De, ed., **Perspectives in the Social Sciences I: Historical Dimensions** [Calcutta: Oxford University Press, 1977].

Roberto Chavez, "Urban Planning in Nicaragua: The First Five Years" **Latin American Perspectives** vol. 14. no. 2. 1987.

Bell Gale Chevigny, "Beyond the Language Barrier: Reflections on North and Latin American Intellectuals" **Socialist Review** vol. 13. no. 1. 1983.

Ronald H. Chilcote, "Dependency: A Critical Synthesis of the Literature" **Latin American Perspectives** vol. 1. no. 1. 1974.

Ronald H. Chilcote and Joel C. Edelstein, "Alternative Perspectives of Development and Underdevelopment in Latin America" in Ronald H. Chilcote and Joel C. Edelstein, eds., **Latin America: The Struggle with Dependency and Beyond** [New York: Wiley, 1974].

Ronald H. Chilcote, "A Question of Dependency" **Latin American Research Review** vol. 13. no. 2. 1978.

Ronald H. Chilcote, "Issues of Theory in Dependency and Marxism" in Ronald H. Chilcote, ed., **Dependency and Marxism: Toward a Resolution of the Debate** [Boulder: Westview Press, 1982].

Ronald H. Chilcote, "Introduction: Dependency or Mode of Production? Theoretical Issues" in Ronald H. Chilcote and Dale L. Johnson, eds., **Theories of Development: Mode of Production or Dependency** [Beverly Hills: Sage, 1983].

Ronald H. Chilcote, "Alternative Approaches to Comparative Politics" in Howard J. Wiarda, ed., **New Directions in Comparative Politics** [Boulder:

Westview Press, 1985].

Ronald H. Chilcote, "Southern European Transitions in Comparative Perspective" in Ronald H. Chilcote et al., eds., **Transitions from Dictatorship to Democracy: Comparative Studies of Spain, Portugal and Greece** [New York: Taylor and Francis, 1990].

Ronald H. Chilcote, "The Theory and Practice of Transitions: Struggle for a New Politics in Southern Europe" in Ronald H. Chilcote et al., eds., **Transitions from Dictatorship to Democracy: Comparative Studies of Spain, Portugal and Greece** [New York: Taylor and Francis, 1990].

Ronald H. Chilcote, "Post-Marxism: The Retreat from Class in Latin America" **Latin American Perspectives** vol. 17. no. 2. 1990.

Ronald H. Chilcote, "Tensions in Latin American Experience: Fundamental Themes in the Formulation of a Research Agenda for the 1990s" **Latin American Perspectives** vol. 17. no. 2. 1990.

Ronald H. Chilcote, "Left Political Ideology and Practice" in Barry Carr and Steve Ellner, eds., **The Latin American Left: From the Fall of Allende to Perestroika** [Boulder: Westview Press, 1993].

Jack Child, "Issues for US Policy in the Caribbean Basin in the 1980s: Security" in James R. Greene and Brent Scowcroft, eds., **Western Interests and US Policy Options in the Caribbean Basin: Report of the Atlantic Council's Working Group on the Caribbean Basin** [Boston: Oelgeschlager, Gunn and Hain, for the Atlantic Council of the United States, 1984].

Jack Child, "US Security and the Contadora Process: Toward a CBM Regime in Central America" in Bruce M. Bagley, ed., **Contadora and the Diplomacy of Peace in Central America--vol. 1: The United States, Central America and Contadora** [Boulder: Westview Press, 1987].

Norma Stoltz Chinchilla, "Class Struggle in Central America: Background and Overview" **Latin American Perspectives** vol. 7. nos. 2-3. 1980.

Norma Stoltz Chinchilla and James L. Dietz, "Toward a New Understanding of Development and Underdevelopment" in Ronald H. Chilcote, ed., **Dependency and Marxism: Toward a Resolution of the Debate** [Boulder: Westview Press, 1982].

Norma Stoltz Chinchilla, "Interpreting Social Change in Guatemala: Modernization, Dependency and Articulation of Modes of Production" in Ronald H. Chilcote and Dale L. Johnson, eds., **Theories of Development: Mode of Production or Dependency** [Beverly Hills: Sage, 1983].

Norma Stoltz Chinchilla and Nora Hamilton, "Prelude to Revolution: US Investment in Central America" in Roger Burbach and Patricia Flynn, eds., **The Politics of Intervention: The United States in Central America** [New York: Monthly Review Press, 1984].

Norma Stoltz Chinchilla, "Marxism, Feminism and the Struggle for Democracy in Latin America" in Arturo Escobar and Sonia E. Alvarez, eds., **The Making of Social Movements in Latin America: Identity, Strategy and Democracy** [Boulder: Westview Press, 1992].

Daniel Chirot, "Causes and Consequences of Backwardness" in Daniel Chirot, ed., **The Origins of Backwardness in Eastern Europe: Economics** and Politics from the Middle Ages Until the Early Twentieth Century [Berkeley: University of California Press, 1989].

Noam Chomsky, "The Responsibility of Intellectuals" in Theodore Roszak, ed., **The Dissenting Academy** [London: Chatto and Windus, 1969; first published, 1967].

Noam Chomsky, "Intellectuals and the State" and "Foreign Policy and the Intelligentsia" in Noam Chomsky, **Towards a New Cold War: Essays on the Current Crisis and How We Got There** [London: Sinclair Brown, 1982].

Noam Chomsky, "US Polity and Society: The Lessons of Nicaragua" in Thomas W. Walker, ed., **Reagan Versus the Sandinistas: The Undeclared War on Nicaragua** [Boulder: Westview Press, 1987].

Joseph Cirincione and Leslie Hunter, "Military Threats, Actual and Potential" in Robert S. Leiken, ed., **Central America: Anatomy of Conflict** [New York: Pergamon Press, 1984].

Renfrey Clarke, "The Soviet Union and Central America" in James R. Levy, ed., **Crisis in Central America** [Kensington: School of Spanish and Latin American Studies, University of New South Wales, 1984].

Peter Clement and W. Raymond Duncan, "The Soviet Union and Central America" in Eusebio Mujal-Leon, ed., **The USSR and Latin America: A Developing Relationship** [Boston: Unwin Hyman, 1989].

Charles Clements, "Militarization, US Aid and the Failure of Development in El Salvador" in John M. Kirk and George W. Schuyler, eds., **Central America: Democracy, Development and Change** [New York: Praeger, 1988].

J. Garry Clifford, "Bureaucratic Politics" **The Journal of American History** vol. 77. no. 1. 1990.

Howard F. Cline, "Reflections on Traditionalism in the Historiography of Hispanic America" **Hispanic American Historical Review** vol. 29. no. 2. 1949.

Howard F. Cline, "The Latin American Studies Association: A Summary Survey with Appendix" **Latin American Research Review** vol. 2. no. 1. 1966.

Howard F. Cline, "United States Historiography of Latin America" in Howard F. Cline, ed., **Latin American History: Essays on Its Study and Teaching 1898-1965** (2 vols.) [Austin: University of Texas Press, 1967].

Howard F. Cline, "The Ford Foundation Grant Program of the Conference: A Special Report" in Howard F. Cline, ed., **Latin American History: Essays on Its Study and Teaching 1898-1965** (2 vols.) [Austin: University of Texas Press, 1967].

Richard L. Clinton and R. Kenneth Godwin, "Human Rights and Development: Lessons from Latin America" in John D. Martz and Lars Schoultz, eds., **Latin America, the United States and the Inter-American System** [Boulder: Westview Press, 1980].

Judith Coburn, "Asian Scholars and Government: The Chrysanthemum on the Sword" in Edward Friedman and Mark Selden, eds., **America's Asia: Dissenting Essays on Asian-American Relations** [New York: Random House, 1971; first publshed 1969].

James D. Cochrane, "Confronting Trouble in the Backyard: Washington and Central America" **Latin American Research Review** vol. 22. no. 3. 1987.

James D. Cockcroft, "Mexico" in Ronald H. Chilcote and Joel C. Edelstein, eds., **Latin America: The Struggle With Dependency and Beyond** [New York: Wiley, 1974].

Isaac Cohen and Gert Rosenthal, "The Dimensions of Economic Policy Space in Central America" in Richard R. Fagen and Olga Pellicer, eds., **The Future of Central America: Policy Choices for the US and Mexico** [Stanford: Stanford University Press, 1983].

Joshua Cohen and Joel Rogers, "Knowledge Morality and Hope: The Social Thought of Noam Chomsky" **New Left Review** no. 187. 1991.

Forrest D. Colburn, "De Guatemala a Guatepeor" **Latin American Research Review** vol. 21. no. 3. 1986.

James S. Coleman, "The Political Systems of Developing Areas" in Gabriel Almond and J. S. Coleman, eds., **The Politics of the Developing Areas** [Princeton: Princeton University Press, 1971; first published 1960].

Kenneth M. Coleman, "The Political Mythology of the Monroe Doctrine: Reflections on the Social Psychology of Hegemony" in John D. Martz and Lars Schoultz, eds., **Latin America, the United States and the Inter-American System** [Boulder: Westview Press, 1980].

David Collier, "Overview of the Bureaucratic-Authoritarian Model" in David Collier, ed., **The New Authoritarianism in Latin America** [Princeton: Princeton University Press, 1979].

David Collier, "The Bureaucratic-Authoritarian Model: Synthesis and Priorities for Future Research" in David Collier, ed., **The New Authoritarianism in Latin America** [Princeton: Princeton University Press, 1979].

David Collier and Deborah L. Norden, "Strategic Choice Models of Political Change in Latin America" **Comparative Politics** vol. 24. no. 2. 1992.

Joseph Collins, "Sleeping with a Low-Profile Elephant: Latin America and the United States" **Latin America Review of Books** vol. 1. no. 1. 1973.

Gordon Connell-Smith, "The United States and the Caribbean: Colonial Patterns, Old and New" **Journal of Latin American Studies** vol. 4. no. 1. 1972.

Michael E. Conroy, "External Dependence, External Assistance, and Economic Aggression Against Nicaragua" **Latin American Perspectives** vol. 12. no. 2. 1985.

Michael E. Conroy, "Economic Aggression as an Instrument of Low-Intensity Warfare" in Thomas W. Walker, ed., **Reagan Versus the Sandinistas: The Undeclared War on Nicaragua** [Boulder: Westview Press, 1987].

Frederick Copper, "Africa and the World Economy" (1981) in Frederick Cooper, Allen F. Isaacman, Florencia E. Mallon, William Roseberry and Steve J. Stern, **Confronting Historical Paradigms: Peasants, Labor, and the Capitalist World System in Africa and Latin America** [Madison: University of Wisconsin Press, 1993].

Wayne A. Cornelius, "The 1984 Elections Revisited" **LASA Forum** vol. 16. no. 3. 1986.

Wayne Cornelius, "The Nicaraguan Elections of 1984: A Reassessment of Their Domestic and International Significance" in Paul Drake and Ed Silva, eds., **Elections and Democratization in Latin America 1980-1985** [San Diego: Center for Iberian and Latin American Studies, 1986].

Wayne A. Cornelius, "The United States and Latin America: 'Out of Phase' Again?"

LASA Forum vol. 17. no. 4. 1987.

Wayne A. Cornelius, "The 1984 Nicaraguan Election Observation: A Final Comment" **LASA Forum** vol. 19. no. 2. 1988.

Juan Eugenio Corradi, "Argentina" in Ronald H. Chilcote and Joel C. Edelstein, eds., **Latin America: The Struggle With Dependency and Beyond** [New York: Wiley, 1974].

Juan Eugenio Corradi, "Nicaragua: Can It Find Its Own Way?" **Dissent** vol. 31. no. 3. 1984.

José Luis Corragio and George Irvin, "Revolution and Pluralism in Nicaragua" **Millennium: Journal of International Studies** vol. 13. no. 2. 1984; reprinted as José Luis Corragio and George Irvin, "Revolution and Democracy in Nicaragua" **Latin American Perspectives** vol. 12. no. 2. 1985.

José Luis Corragio, "Economics and Politics in the Transition to Socialism: Reflections on the Nicaraguan Experience" in Richard R. Fagen, Carmen Diana Deere and Jose Luis Coraggio, eds., **Transition and Development: Problems of Third World Socialism** [New York: Monthly Review Press, 1986, PACCA/CRIES].

Julio Cotler and Richard R. Fagen, "Introduction: Political Relations Between Latin America and the United States" in Julio Cotler and Richard R. Fagen, eds., **Latin America and the United States: The Changing Political Realities** [Stanford: Stanford University Press, 1974].

Isaac Joslin Cox, "'Yankee Imperialism' and Spanish American Solidarity: A Colombian Interpretation" **Hispanic American Historical Review** vol. 4. no. 2. 1921.

Isaac Joslin Cox, "Florida, Frontier Outposts of New Spain" in A. Curtis Wilgus, ed., **Hispanic American Essays** [Freeport: Books for Libraries Press, 1970; first printed 1942].

Robert W. Cox, "Social Forces, States and World Order: Beyond International Relations Theory" **Millennium: Journal of International Studies** vol. 10. no. 2. 1981.

Robert W. Cox, "Production and Hegemony: Toward a Political Economy of World Order" in Harold K. Jacobson and Dusan Sidjanski, eds., **The Emerging International Economic Order: Dynamic Processes, Constraints and Opportunities** [Beverly Hills: Sage, 1982].

Robert W. Cox, "Gramsci, Hegemony and International Relations: An Essay in Method" **Millennium: Journal of International Studies** vol. 12. no. 2. 1983.

Robert W. Cox, "Global Perestroika" **The Socialist Register 1992** [London: Merlin Press, 1992].

Margaret E. Crahan, "International Aspects of the Role of the Catholic Church in Central America" in Richard E. Feinberg, ed., **Central America: International Dimensions of the Crisis** [New York: Holmes and Meier, 1982].

Margaret E. Crahan, "The Central American Church and Regime Transformation: Attitudes and Options" in Wolf Grabendorff, Heinrich W. Krumwiede and Jorg Todt, eds., **Political Change in Central America: Internal and External Dimensions** [Boulder: Westview Press, 1984].

Margaret E. Crahan, "Human Rights and US Foreign Policy: Realism Versus

Stereotypes" in Kevin J. Middlebrook and Carlos Rico, eds., **The United States and Latin America in the 1980s: Contending Perspectives on a Decade of Crisis** [Pittsburgh: University of Pittsburgh Press, 1986].

Margaret E. Crahan, "Bridge or Barrier?: The Catholic Church and the Central American Crisis" in Giuseppe Di Palma and Laurence Whitehead, eds., **The Central American Impasse** [London: Croom Helm, 1986].

Margaret E. Crahan, "Freedom of Worship in Revolutionary Cuba" in Philip Brenner, William LeoGrande, Donna Rich and Daniel Siegel, eds., **The Cuba Reader: The Making of a Revolutionary Society** [New York: Grove Press, 1989].

Margaret E. Crahan, "Religion and Democratization in Central America" in Louis W. Goodman, William M. LeoGrande, and Johanna Mendelson Forman, eds., **Political Parties and Democracy in Central America** [Boulder: Westview Press, 1992].

Gregory Crampton, "A Bibliography of the Historical Writings of the Students of Herbert Eugene Bolton" in Adele Ogden, ed., **Greater America: Essays in Honour of Herbert Eugene Bolton** [Berkeley: University of California Press, 1945; reprinted Freeport: Books for Libraries Press, 1968].

David Craven, "The State of Cultural Democracy in Cuba and Nicaragua During the 1980s" **Latin American Perspectives** vol. 17. no. 3. 1990.

George Washington Crichfield, "American Supremacy" (1908) in Charles Gibson, ed., **The Black Legend: Anti-Spanish Attitudes in the Old World and the New** [New York: Alfred A. Knopf, 1971].

Jackson Crowell, "The United States and a Central American Canal 1869-1877" **Hispanic American Historical Review** vol. 49. no. 1. 1969.

Arturo J. Cruz, "Nicaragua's Imperiled Revolution" **Foreign Affairs** vol. 61. no. 5. 1983.

Bruce Cumings, "The Origins and Development of the Northeast Asian Political Economy: Industrial Sectors, Product Cycles and Political Consequences" **International Organization** vol. 38. no. 1. 1984. reprinted in Frederic C. Deyo, **The Political Economy of the New Asian Industrialism** [Ithaca: Cornell University Press, 1987].

Bruce Cumings, "The Abortive Abertura: South Korea in the Light of Latin American Experience" **New Left Review** no. 173. 1989.

Lloyd N. Cutler, "The Right to Intervene" **Foreign Affairs** vol. 64. no. 2. 1985.

Victor M. Cutter, "Relations of United States Companies with Latin America" **Annals of the American Academy of Political and Social Science** vol. 132. 1927.

James M. Cypher, "The Debt Crisis as 'Opportunity': Strategies to Revive US Hegemony" **Latin American Perspectives** vol. 16. no. 1. 1989.

Robert Dash, "US Foreign Policy, National Security Doctrine and Central America" **Latin American Perspectives** vol. 16. no. 4. 1989.

Mike Davis, "The New Right's Road to Power" **New Left Review** no. 128. 1981; reprinted in Mike Davis, **Prisoners of the American Dream: Politics and Economy in the History of the US Working Class** [London: Verso, 1987; first published 1986].

Norman H. Davis, "Wanted: A Consistent Latin American Policy" **Foreign**

Affairs vol. 9. no. 4. 1931.

Shelton H. Davis, "State Violence and Agrarian Crisis in Guatemala: The Roots of the Indian-Peasant Rebellion" in Martin Diskin, ed., **Trouble in Our Backyard: Central America and the United States in the 1980s** [New York: Pantheon, 1983].

Shelton H. Davis, "Introduction: Sowing the Seeds of Violence" in Robert M. Carmack, ed., **Harvest of Violence: The Maya Indians and the Guatemalan Crisis** [Norman: University of Oklahoma Press, 1988].

Heather Dean, "Scarce Resources: The Dynamics of American Imperialism" in K. T. Fann and Donald C. Hodges, eds., **Readings in US Imperialism** [Boston: Porter Sargent, 1971].

Malcolm Deas, "The Colombian Peace Process 1982-1985 and Its Implications for Central America" in Giuseppe Di Palma and Laurence Whitehead, eds., **The Central American Impasse** [London: Croom Helm, 1986].

William Theodore De Bary, "The Association for Asian Studies: Nonpolitical but Not Unconcerned" **Journal of Asian Studies** vol. 29. no. 4. 1970.

Alexander DeConde, "Essay and Reflection: On the Nature of International History" **The International History Review** vol. 10. no. 2. 1988.

Carmen Diana Deere and Peter Marchetti, "The Worker-Peasant Alliance in the First Year of the Nicaraguan Agrarian Reform" **Latin American Perspectives** vol. 8. no. 2. 1981.

Carmen Diana Deere, "Agrarian Reform, Peasant and Rural Production, and the Organization of Production in the Transition to Socialism" in Richard R. Fagen, Carmen Diana Deere and Jose Luis Coraggio, eds., **Transition and Development: Problems of Third World Socialism** [New York: Monthly Review Press, 1986, PACCA/CRIES].

Enrique de Gandia, "Pan Americanism in History" (1942) in Lewis Hanke, ed., **Do the Americas Have a Common History?: A Critique of the Bolton Theory** [New York: Alfred A. Knopf, 1964].

Helen Delpar, "Frank Tannenbaum: The Making of a Mexicanist 1914-1933" **The Americas: A Quarterly Review of Inter-American Cultural History** vol. 45. no. 2. 1988.

Lawrence Dennis, "Revolution, Recognition and Intervention" **Foreign Affairs** vol. 9. no. 2. 1931.

Lawrence Dennis, "Nicaragua: In Again, Out Again" **Foreign Affairs** vol. 9. no. 3. 1931.

Lawrence Dennis, "What Price Good Neighbor?" **The American Mercury** vol. 45. October 1938.

David W. Dent, "Past and Present Trends in Research on Latin American Politics 1950-1980" **Latin American Research Review** vol. 21. no. 1. 1986.

Hugh De Santis, "The Imperialist Impulse and American Innocence 1865-1900" in Gerald K. Haines and J. Samuel Walker, eds., **American Foreign Relations: An Historiographical Review** [London: Pinter, 1981].

I. M. Destler, "The Elusive Consensus: Congress and Central America" in Robert S. Leiken, ed., **Central America: Anatomy of Conflict** [New York: Pergamon Press, 1984].

Frederic C. Deyo, "Introduction" in Frederic C. Deyo, ed., **The Political Economy of the New Asian Industrialism** [Ithaca: Cornell University

Press, 1987].

Larry Diamond and Juan J. Linz, "Introduction: Politics, Society and Democracy in Latin America" in Larry Diamond, Juan J. Linz and Seymour Martin Lipset, eds., **Democracy in Developing Countries--Volume Four: Latin America** [Boulder: Lynne Rienner, 1989].

Christopher Dickey, "Central America: From Quagmire to Caldron" **Foreign Affairs** vol. 62. no. 3. 1983.

Christopher Dickey, "The Saving of El Salvador" **The New York Review of Books** June 14, 1984.

Joan Didion, "In El Salvador" **The New York Review of Books** November 4, 1982.

Joan Didion, "El Salvador: Soluciones" **The New York Review of Books** November 18, 1982.

Joan Didion, "El Salvador: Illusions" **The New York Review of Books** December 2, 1982.

James L. Dietz, "Socialism and Imperialism in the Caribbean" **Latin American Perspectives** vol. 6. no. 1. 1979.

James L. Dietz, "Capitalist Development in Latin America" **Latin American Perspectives** vol. 6. no. 1. 1979.

James L. Dietz, "Destabilization and Intervention in Latin America and the Caribbean" **Latin American Perspectives** vol. 11. no. 3. 1984.

James L. Dietz, "Debt, International Corporations, and Economic Change in Latin America and the Caribbean" **Latin American Perspectives** vol. 14. no. 4. 1987.

James L. Dietz, "The Debt Cycle and Restructuring in Latin America" **Latin American Perspectives** vol. 16. no. 1. 1989.

John Dinges and Saul Landau, "An Act of Terror" in John S. Friedman, ed., **First Harvest: The Institute for Policy Studies 1963-1983** [New York: Grove Press, 1983].

Giuseppe Di Palma, "Comment: Democracy, Human Rights and the US Role in Latin America" in Kevin J. Middlebrook and Carlos Rico, eds., **The United States and Latin America in the 1980s: Contending Perspectives on a Decade of Crisis** [Pittsburgh: University of Pittsburgh Press, 1986].

Giuseppe Di Palma and Laurence Whitehead, "Introduction" in Giuseppe Di Palma and Laurence Whitehead, eds., **The Central American Impasse** [London: Croom Helm, 1986].

Giuseppe Di Palma, "The Europeans and the Central American Experience" in Giuseppe Di Palma and Laurence Whitehead, eds., **The Central American Impasse** [London: Croom Helm, 1986].

Martin Diskin, "Introduction" in Martin Diskin, ed., **Trouble in Our Backyard: Central America and the United States in the Eighties** [New York: Pantheon, 1983].

Martin Diskin and Kenneth E. Sharpe, "El Salvador" in Morris J. Blachman, William LeoGrande and Kenneth Sharpe, eds., **Confronting Revolution: Security Through Diplomacy in Central America** [New York: Pantheon, 1986].

Martin Diskin, "El Salvador: Reform Prevents Change" in William C.

Thiesenhusen, **Searching for Agrarian Reform in Latin America** [Boston: Unwin Hyman, 1989].

Martin Diskin, "Ethnic Discourse and the Challenge to Anthropology: The Nicaraguan Case" in Greg Urban and Joel Sherzer, eds., **Nation-States and Indians in Latin America** [Austin: University of Texas Press, 1991].

Marlene Dixon and Susanne Jonas, "The New Nicaragua Critics: Social Democrats with Queasy Stomachs" in Marlene Dixon and Susanne Jonas, eds., **Revolution and Intervention in Central America** [San Francisco: Synthesis Publications, 1983].

William J. Dixon, "Progress in the Provision of Basic Human Needs: Latin America 1960-1980" **The Journal of Developing Areas** vol. 21. no. 2. 1987.

H. W. Dodds, "The United States and Nicaragua" **Annals of the American Academy of Political and Social Science** vol. 132. 1927.

H. W. Dodds, "American Supervision of the Nicaraguan Election" **Foreign Affairs** vol. 7. no. 3. 1929.

Michael Dodson and Tommie Sue Montgomery, "The Churches in the Nicaraguan Revolution" in Thomas W. Walker, ed., **Nicaragua in Revolution** [New York: Praeger, 1982].

Gerardo Timossi Dolinsky, "Debt and Structural Adjustment in Central America" **Latin American Perspectives** vol. 17. no. 4. 1990.

Enrique Domínguez and Deborah Huntington, "The Salvation Brokers: Conservative Evangelicals in Central America" **NACLA Report on the Americas** vol. 18. no. 1. 1984.

Jorge I. Domínguez, "Cuba's Maturing Revolution" **Problems of Communism** vol. 25. no. 1. 1976.

Jorge I. Domínguez, "The Civic Soldier in Cuba" in Abraham F. Lowenthal, ed., **Armies and Politics in Latin America** [New York: Holmes and Meier, 1976]; also reprinted in Abraham F. Lowenthal, ed., **Armies and Politics in Latin America** [New York: Holmes and Meier, revised edition 1986; first published 1976].

Jorge I. Domínguez, "Cuba's Foreign Policy" **Foreign Affairs** vol. 57. no. 1. 1978.

Jorge I. Domínguez, "Consensus and Divergence: The State of the Literature on Inter-American Relations in the 1970s" **Latin American Research Review** vol. 13. no. 1. 1978.

Jorge I Domínguez, "Cuba: Domestic Bread and Foreign Circuses" **Washington Quarterly: A Review of Strategic and International Issues** vol. 2. no. 2. 1979.

Jorge I. Domínguez, "Literature on Inter-American Relations: Reply" **Latin American Research Review** vol. 14. no. 3. 1979.

Jorge I. Domínguez, "The President's Corner" **LASA Newsletter** vol. 12. no. 4. 1982.

Jorge I. Domínguez, "Revolutionary Politics: The New Demands for Orderliness" in Jorge I. Domínguez, ed., **Cuba: Internal and International Affairs** [Beverly Hills: Sage, 1982].

Jorge I. Domínguez, "The Nature of Professional Scholarly Responsibility" **LASA Forum** vol. 14. no. 1. 1983; reprinted as Appendix II in Jan Knippers Black, ed., **Latin America: Its Problems and Its Promises** [Boulder:

Westview Press, 1984].

Jorge I. Domínguez, "Cuba's Relations with Caribbean and Central American Countries" in Alan Adelman and Reid Reading, eds., **Confrontation in the Caribbean Basin: International Perspectives on Security, Sovereignty and Survival** [Pittsburgh: Center for Latin American Studies, University Center for International Studies, University of Pittsburgh, 1984].

Jorge I. Domínguez, "The Foreign Policies of Latin American States in the 1980s: Retreat or Reform?" in Samuel P. Huntington and Joseph S. Nye, eds., **Global Dilemmas** [Cambridge: Harvard University Press, 1985].

Jorge I. Domínguez, "Cuba in the 1980s" **Foreign Affairs** vol. 65. no. 1. 1986; abridged and reprinted as "Cuban Leadership in the 1980s" in Philip Brenner, William LeoGrande, Donna Rich and Daniel Siegel, eds., **The Cuba Reader: The Making of a Revolutionary Society** [New York: Grove Press, 1989].

Jorge I. Domínguez, "Political Change: Central America, South America, and the Caribbean" in Myron Weiner and Samuel P. Huntington, eds., **Understanding Political Development** [Boston: Little Brown, 1987].

Jorge I. Domínguez, "On Understanding the Present by Analyzing the Past in Latin America: A Review Essay" **Political Science Quarterly** vol. 107. no. 2. 1992.

Jorge I. Domínguez, "The Secrets of Castro's Staying Power" **Foreign Affairs** Spring 1993.

Elizabeth Dore and John Weeks, "Class Alliance and Class Struggle in Peru" **Latin American Perspectives** vol. 4. no. 3. 1977.

Theotonio Dos Santos, "The Structure of Dependence" in K. T. Fann and Donald C. Hodges, eds., **Readings in US Imperialism** [Boston: Porter Sargent, 1971]; reprinted in Mitchell A. Seligson, ed., **The Gap Between Rich and Poor: Contending Perspectives on the Political Economy of Development** [Boulder: Westview Press, 1984].

Theotonio Dos Santos, "Brazil: The Origins of a Crisis" in Ronald H. Chilcote and Joel C. Edelstein, eds., **Latin America: The Struggle with Dependency and Beyond** [New York: Wiley, 1974].

Theodore Draper, "Falling Dominoes" **The New York Review of Books** October 27, 1983.

Theodore Draper, "Revelations of the North Trial" **The New York Review of Books** August 17, 1989.

W. Raymond Duncan, "Jamaica" in Robert Wesson, ed., **Communism in Central America and the Caribbean** [Stanford: Hoover Institution Press, 1982].

W. Raymond Duncan, "Moscow, the Caribbean and Central America" in Robert Wesson, ed., **Communism in Central America and the Caribbean** [Stanford: Hoover Institution Press, 1982].

W. Raymond Duncan, "Cuba in the Caribbean and Central America: Limits to Influence" in H. Michael Erisman and John D. Martz, ed., **Colossus Challenged: The Struggle for Caribbean Influence** [Boulder: Westview Press, 1982].

James Dunkerley, "Central American Impasse" **Bulletin of Latin American**

Research vol. 5. no. 2. 1986.

James Dunkerley, "Reflections on the Nicaraguan Election" **New Left Review** no. 182. 1990.

James Dunkerley, "The Crisis of Bolivian Radicalism" in Barry Carr and Steve Ellner, eds., **The Latin American Left: From the Fall of Allende to Perestroika** [Boulder: Westview Press, 1993].

James Dunkerley, "Beyond Utopia: The State of the Left in Latin America" **New Left Review** no. 206. 1994.

Willim N. Dunn, "The Scholar-Diplomat Seminar on Latin American Affairs: The Promise and Illusion of the State Department Reform Movement" **Latin American Research Review** vol. 6. no. 2. 1971.

Duncan M. Earle, "Mayas Aiding Mayas: Guatemalan Refugees in Chiapas, Mexico" in Robert M. Carmack, ed., **Harvest of Violence: The Maya Indians and the Guatemalan Crisis** [Norman: University of Oklahoma Press, 1988].

Roland H. Ebel, "Political Instability in Central America" **Current History: A World Affairs Journal** vol. 81. no. 472. 1982.

Roland H. Ebel, "When Indians Take Power: Conflict and Consensus in San Juan Ostuncalco" in Robert M. Carmack, ed., **Harvest of Violence: The Maya Indians and the Guatemalan Crisis** [Norman: University of Oklahoma Press, 1988].

Marc Edelman, "Recent Literature on Costa Rica's Economic Crisis" **Latin American Research Review** vol. 18. no. 2. 1983.

Marc Edelman, "Lifelines: Nicaragua and the Socialist Countries" **NACLA Report on the Americas** vol. 19. no. 3. 1985.

Marc Edelman, "Shadow Play: Central America's Untold Stories--Back from the Brink" **NACLA Report on the Americas** vol. 19. no. 6. 1985.

Marc Edelman, "The Other Super Power: The USSR and Latin America 1917-1987" **NACLA Report on the Americas** vol. 21. no. 1. 1987.

Joel C. Edelstein, "The Evolution of Cuban Development Strategy 1959-1979" in Heraldo Muñoz, ed., **From Dependency to Development: Strategies to Overcome Underdevelopment and Inequality** [Boulder: Westview Press, 1981].

Joel C. Edelstein, "Dependency: A Special Theory Within Marxian Analysis" in Ronald H. Chilcote, ed., **Dependency and Marxism: Toward a Resolution of the Debate** [Boulder: Westview Press, 1982].

Gerald G. Eggert, "Our Man in Havana: Fitzhugh Lee" **Hispanic American Historical Review** vol. 47. no. 4. 1967.

Luigi Einaudi, "US Latin American Policy in the 1970s: New Forms of Control?" in Julio Cotler and Richard R. Fagen, eds., **Latin America and the United States: The Changing Political Realities** [Stanford: Stanford University Press, 1974].

S. N. Eisenstadt, "Culture, religions and development in North American and Latin American civilizations" **International Social Science Journal** 134. 1992.

Steve Ellner, "Introduction: The Changing Status of the Latin American Left in the Recent Past" in Barry Carr and Steve Ellner, eds., **The Latin American Left: From the Fall of Allende to Perestroika** [Boulder: Westview

Press, 1993].

David Eltis, "Europeans and the Rise and Fall of African Slavery in the Americas: An Interpretation" **American Historical Review** vol. 98. no. 5. 1993.

Thomas O. Enders, "The Central American Challenge" **American Enterprise Institute Foreign Policy and Defense Review** vol. 4. no. 2. 1982.

Robert Engler, "Social Science and Social Consciousness: The Shame of the Universities" in Theodore Roszak, ed., **The Dissenting Academy** [London: Chatto and Windus, 1969; first published 1967].

H. Michael Erisman, "Colossus Challenged: US Caribbean Policy in the 1980s" in H. Michael Erisman and John D. Martz, eds., **Colossus Challenged: The Struggle for Caribbean Influence** [Boulder: Westview Press, 1982].

H. Michael Erisman and John D. Martz, "Conclusion" in H. Michael Erisman and John D. Martz, eds., **Colossus Challenged: The Struggle for Caribbean Influence** [Boulder: Westview Press, 1982].

H. Michael Erisman, "Contemporary Challenges Confronting US Caribbean Policy" in H. Michael Erisman, ed., **The Caribbean Challenge: US Policy in a Volatile Region** [Boulder: Westview Press, 1984].

H. Michael Erisman, "Cuba and the Americas: 1972-1979" extracted from H. Michael Erisman, **Cuba's International Relations: The Anatomy of a Nationalistic Foreign Policy** [Boulder: Westview Press, 1985] and printed in Philip Brenner, William LeoGrande, Donna Rich and Daniel Siegel, eds., **The Cuba Reader: The Making of a Revolutionary Society** [New York: Grove Press, 1989].

H. Michael Erisman, "The CARICOM States and US Foreign Policy: The Danger of Centralamericanization" **Journal of Interamerican Studies and World Affairs** vol. 31. no. 3. 1989.

Arturo Escobar, "Discourse and Power in Development: Michel Foucault and the Relevance of His Work to the Third World" **Alternatives** no. 10. 1984-1985.

Arturo Escobar, "Power and Visibility: Development and the Invention and Management of the Third World" **Cultural Anthropology** vol. 3. no. 4. 1988.

Arturo Escobar, "Reflections on Development: Grassroots Approaches and Alternative Politics in the Third World" **Futures** vol. 24. no. 5. 1992.

Arturo Escobar, "Imagining a Post-Development Era? Critical Thought, Development and Social Movements" **Social Text** vol. 10. nos 2-3. 1992.

Arturo Escobar and Sonia E. Alvarez, "Introduction: Theory and Protest in Latin America Today" in Arturo Escobar and Sonia E. Alvarez, eds., **The Making of Social Movements in Latin America: Identity, Strategy and Democracy** [Boulder: Westview Press, 1992].

Arturo Escobar, "Culture, Economics and Politics in Latin American Social Movements Theory and Research" in Arturo Escobar and Sonia E. Alvarez, eds., **The Making of Social Movements in Latin America: Identity, Strategy and Democracy** [Boulder: Westview Press, 1992].

Rosario Espinal, "Development, Neoliberalism and Electoral Politics in Latin America" **Development and Change** vol. 23. no. 4. 1992.

Estudios Centroamericanos, "El Salvador 1984" **NACLA Report on the Americas** vol. 18. no. 2. 1984.

Estudios Centroamericanos, "Duarte: Prisoner of War" **NACLA Report on the Americas** vol. 20. no. 1. 1984.

Diane Ethier, "Processes of Transition and Democratic Consolidation: Theoretical Indicators" in Diane Ethier, ed, **Democratic Transition and Consolidation in Southern Europe, Latin America and Southeast Asia** [New York: Macmillan, 1990].

Ernest Evans, "Revolutionary Movements in Central America: The Development of a New Strategy" in Howard J. Wiarda and Mark Falcoff, eds., **The Communist Challenge in the Caribbean and Central America** [Washington: American Enterprise Institute, 1987].

Laurence Evans, "The Dangers of Diplomatic History" in Herbert J. Bass, ed., **The State of American History** [Chicago: Quadrangle Books, 1970].

Peter Evans, "Class, State, and Dependence in East Asia: Lessons for Latin Americanists" in Frederic C. Deyo, ed., **The Political Economy of the New Asian Industrialism** [Ithaca: Cornell University Press, 1987].

Patricia Weiss Fagen, "Latin American Refugees: Problems of Mass Migration and Mass Asylum" in Richard S. Newfarmer, ed., **From Gunboats to Diplomacy: New US Policies for Latin America** [Baltimore: Johns Hopkins University Press, 1984].

Richard R. Fagen, "Charismatic Authority and the Leadership of Fidel Castro" **Western Political Quarterly** vol. 18. no. 2. 1965.

Richard R. Fagen, "Mass Mobilization in Cuba: The Symbolism of Struggle" **Journal of International Affairs** vol. 20. no. 2. 1966.

Richard R. Fagen, "US-Cuban Relations" in David S. Smith, ed., **Prospects for Latin America** [New York: Columbia University, International Fellows Program Policy Series, 1970].

Richard R. Fagen, "The United States and Chile: Roots and Branches" **Foreign Affairs** vol. 53. no. 2. 1975.

Richard R. Fagen, "The Realities of US-Mexican Relations" **Foreign Affairs** vol. 55. no. 4. 1977.

Richard R. Fagen, "Studying Latin American Politics: Some Implications of a *Dependencia* Approach" **Latin American Research Review** vol. 12. no. 2. 1977.

Richard R. Fagen, "A Funny Thing Happened on the Way to the Market: Thoughts on Extending Dependency Ideas" **International Organization** vol. 32. no. 1. 1978.

Richard R. Fagen, "Cuba and the Soviet Union" **Wilson Quarterly** vol. 2. no. 1. 1978.

Richard R. Fagen, "Introduction" in Richard R. Fagen, ed., **Capitalism and the State in US-Latin American Relations** [Stanford: Stanford University Press, 1979].

Richard R. Fagen, "Dateline Nicaragua: The End of the Affair" **Foreign Policy** no. 36. 1979.

Richard R. Fagen, "The Politics of the United States-Mexico Relationship" in C. W. Reynolds and C. Tello, eds., **US-Mexico Relations: Economic and Social Aspects** [Stanford: Stanford University Press, 1983].

Richard R. Fagen and Olga Pellicer, "Introduction" in Richard R. Fagen and Olga Pellicer, eds., **The Future of Central America: Policy Choices for** the **US and Mexico** [Stanford: Stanford University Press, 1983].

Richard R. Fagen, "Revolution and Crisis in Nicaragua" in Martin Diskin, ed., **Trouble in Our Backyard: Central America and the United States in the 1980s** [New York: Pantheon, 1983].

Richard R. Fagen, "United States Policy in Central America" **Millennium: Journal of International Studies** vol. 13. no. 2. 1984.

Richard R. Fagen, Carmen Diana Deere and Jose Luis Coraggio, "Introduction" in Richard R. Fagen, Carmen Diana Deere and Jose Luis Coraggio, eds., **Transition and Development: Problems of Third World Socialism** [New York: Monthly Review Press, 1986, PACCA/CRIES].

Richard R. Fagen, "The Politics of Transition" in Richard R. Fagen, Carmen Diana Deere and Jose Luis Coraggio, eds., **Transition and Development: Problems of Third World Socialism** [New York: Monthly Review Press, 1986, PACCA/CRIES].

Richard R. Fagen, "Continuities in Cuban Revolutionary Politics" (1972) in Philip Brenner, William LeoGrande, Donna Rich and Daniel Siegel, eds., **The Cuba Reader: The Making of a Revolutionary Society** [New York: Grove Press, 1989].

Fernando Fajnzylber, "Democratization, Endogenous Modernization, and Integration: Strategic Choices for Latin America and Economic Relations with the United States" in Kevin J. Middlebrook and Carlos Rico, eds., **The United States and Latin America in the 1980s: Contending Perspectives on a Decade of Crisis** [Pittsburgh: University of Pittsburgh Press, 1986].

Mark Falcoff, "Latin America" in Peter Duignan and Alvin Rabushka, eds., **The United States in the 1980s** [Stanford: Stanford University Press--Hoover Institution, 1980].

Mark Falcoff, "The Timerman Case" **Commentary** vol. 72. no. 1. 1981.

Mark Falcoff, "The El Salvador White Paper and its Critics" **American Enterprise Institute Foreign Policy and Defense Review** vol. 4. no. 2. 1982.

Mark Falcoff, "Struggle for Central America" **Problems of Communism** vol. 33. no. 2. 1984.

Mark Falcoff, " The Apple of Discord: Central America in US Politics" in Howard J. Wiarda, ed., **Rift and Revolution: The Central American Imbroglio** [Washington: American Enterprise Institute, 1984].

Mark Falcoff, "Arms and Politics Revisited: Latin America as a Military and Strategic Theater" in Howard J. Wiarda, ed., **The Crisis in Latin America: Strategic, Economic and Political Dimensions** [Washington: American Enterprise Institute, 1984].

Mark Falcoff, "Regional Diplomatic Options in Central America" **American Enterprise Institute Foreign Policy and Defense Review** vol. 5. no. 1. 1984.

Mark Falcoff, "Communism in Central America and the Caribbean" in Howard J. Wiarda, Mark Falcoff, Ernest Evans, Jiri Valenta and Virginia Valenta, **The Communist Challenge in the Caribbean and Central America** [Washington: American Enterprise Institute, 1987]

Mark Falcoff, "Cuba's Strategy in Exporting Revolution" in Dennis L. Bark, ed., **The Red Orchestra: Instruments of Soviet Policy in Latin**

America and the Caribbean [Stanford: Hoover Institution Press, 1985]; reprinted in Howard J. Wiarda, Mark Falcoff, Ernest Evans, Jiri Valenta and Virginia Valenta, **The Communist Challenge in the Caribbean and Central America** [Washington: American Enterprise Institute, 1987].

Mark Falcoff, "Bishop's Cuba, Castro's Grenada: Notes Toward an Inner History" in Jiri Valenta and Herbert Ellison, eds., **Grenada and Soviet/Cuban Policy** [Boulder: Westview Press, 1986]; revised and reprinted in Howard J. Wiarda, Mark Falcoff, Ernest Evans, Jiri Valenta and Virginia Valenta, **The Communist Challenge in the Caribbean and Central America** [Washington: American Enterprise Institute, 1987].

Mark Falcoff, "Nicaraguan Harvest" **Commentary** vol. 80. no. 1. 1985 reprinted in Howard J. Wiarda, Mark Falcoff, Ernest Evans, Jiri Valenta and Virginia Valenta, **The Communist Challenge in the Caribbean and Central America** [Washington: American Enterprise Institute, 1987].

Mark Falcoff, "Somoza, Sandino and the United States" in Mark Falcoff and Robert Royal, eds., **The Continuing Crisis: US Policy in Central America and the Caribbean** [Lanham: University Press of America, 1987, published for the Ethics and Public Policy Center].

Mark Falcoff, "Making Central America Safe for Communism" **Commentary** vol. 85. no. 6. 1988.

Richard A. Falk, "What We Should Learn from Vietnam" **Foreign Policy** no. 1. 1970-1971; reprinted in Robert W. Gregg and Charles W. Kegley, eds., **After Vietnam: The Future of American Foreign Policy** [Garden City: Doubleday, 1971].

Ricardo Falla, "Struggle for Survival in the Mountains: Hunger and Other Privations Inflicted on Internal Refugees from the Central Highlands" in Robert M. Carmack, ed., **Harvest of Violence: The Maya Indians and the Guatemalan Crisis** [Norman: University of Oklahoma Press, 1988].

Tom J. Farer, "Manage the Revolution?" **Foreign Policy** no. 52. 1983.

Tom J. Farer, "At Sea in Central America: Can We Negotiate Our Way to Shore?" in Robert S. Leiken, ed., **Central America: Anatomy of Conflict** [New York: Pergamon Press, 1984].

Tom J. Farer, "Contadora: The Hidden Agenda" **Foreign Policy** no. 59. 1985.

Tom J. Farer, "A Multilateral Arrangement to Secure Democracy" in Robert A. Pastor, ed., **Democracy in the Americas: Stopping the Pendulum** [New York: Holmes and Meier, 1989].

Georges A. Fauriol, "The Dominican Republic and Haiti: The Limitations of Foreign Policies" in Richard Millet and W. Marvin Will, eds., **The Restless Caribbean: Changing Patterns of International Relations** [New York: Praeger, 1979].

Richard E., "Dependency and the Defeat of Allende" **Latin American Perspectives** vol. 1. no. 2. 1974.

Richard E. Feinberg, "Central America: No Easy Answers" **Foreign Affairs** vol. 59. no. 5. 1981.

Richard E. Feinberg, "Introduction and Overview" in Richard E. Feinberg, ed., **Central America: International Dimensions of the Crisis** [New York: Holmes and Meier, 1982].

Richard E. Feinberg, "The Recent Rapid Redefinitions of US Interests and

Diplomacy in Central America" in Richard E. Feinberg, ed., **Central America: International Dimensions of the Crisis** [New York: Holmes and Meier, 1982].

Richard E. Feinberg and Kenneth A. Oye, "After the Fall: US Policy Toward Radical Regimes" **World Policy Journal** vol. 1. no. 1. 1983.

Richard E. Feinberg and Robert A. Pastor, "Far from Hopeless: An Economic Program for Post-War Central America" in Robert S. Leiken, ed., **Central America: Anatomy of Conflict** [New York: Pergamon Press, 1984].

Richard E. Feinberg, "Costa Rica: End of the Fiesta" in Richard Newfarmer, ed., **From Gunboats to Diplomacy: New US Policies for Latin America** [Baltimore: Johns Hopkins University Press, 1985; first published 1984].

Richard E. Feinberg and Richard S. Newfarmer, "The Caribbean Basin Initiative: Bold Plan or Empty Promise?" in Richard S. Newfarmer, ed., **From Gunboats to Diplomacy: New US Policies for Latin America** [Baltimore: Johns Hopkins University Press, 1984].

Richard E. Feinberg, "Central America: Options for US Policy in the 1980s" in Wolf Grabendorff, Heinrich W. Krumwiede and Jorg Todt, eds., **Political Change in Central America: Internal and External Dimensions** [Boulder: Westview, 1984].

Richard E. Feinberg, "Comment: Debt and Trade in US-Latin American Relations" in Kevin J. Middlebrook and Carlos Rico, eds., **The United States and Latin America in the 1980s: Contending Perspectives on a Decade of Crisis** [Pittsburgh: University of Pittsburgh Press, 1986].

Richard E. Feinberg, "Third World Debt: Toward a More Balanced Adjustment" **Journal of Interamerican Studies and World Affairs** vol. 29. no. 1. 1987.

Richard E. Feinberg, "Multilateral Lending and Latin America" **The World Economy** vol. 10. no. 2. 1987.

Richard E. Feinberg, "American Power and Third World Economics" in Kenneth A. Oye, Robert J. Lieber and Donald Rothchild, eds., **Eagle Resurgent?: The Reagan Era in American Foreign Policy** [Boston: Little Brown, 1987].

Richard E. Feinberg, "Central American Debt: Genuine Case-by-Case Studies" in William Ascher and Ann Hubbard, eds., **Central American Recovery and Development: Task Force Report to the International Commission for Central American Recovery and Development** [Durham: Duke University Press, 1989].

Damian J. Fernandez, "Central America, the Middle East, and the Spiderweb Theory of Conflict" in Damian J. Fernandez, ed., **Central America and the Middle East: The Internationalization of the Crises** [Miami: Florida International University Press, 1990].

Raúl A. Fernandez and José F. Ocampo, "The Latin American Revolution: A Theory of Imperialism Not Dependence" **Latin American Perspectives** vol. 1. no. 1. 1974.

Elizabeth G. Ferris, "Interests, Influence and Inter-American Relations" **Latin American Research Review** vol. 21. no. 2. 1986.

James A. Field, Jr., "American Imperialism: The Worst Chapter in Almost Any

Book" **American Historical Review** vol. 83. no. 3. 1978.

J. Valerie Fifer, "Comment--South of Capricorn: A Review Revisited" **Bulletin of Latin American Research** vol. 12. no. 1. 1993.

Albert Fishlow, "Brazil: The Case of the Missing Relationship" in Richard S. Newfarmer, ed., **From Gunboats to Diplomacy: New US Policies for Latin America** [Baltimore: Johns Hopkins University Press, 1984].

Albert Fishlow, "The State of Latin American Economics" in Christopher Mitchell, ed., **Changing Perspectives in Latin American Studies: Insights from Six Disciplines** [Stanford: Stanford University Press, 1988].

Frances FitzGerald, "The American Millennium" in Sanford J. Ungar, ed., **Estrangement: America and the World** [New York: Oxford University Press, 1985].

Jan L. Flora, Douglas K. Benson and Cornelia B. Flora, "Central America: Cultures in Conflict" in Jan L. Flora and Edelberto Torres-Rivas, eds., **Sociology of "Developing Societies": Central America** [London: Macmillan, 1989].

Jan L. Flora and Edelberto Torres-Rivas, "Sociology of Developing Societies: Historical Bases of Insurgency in Central America" in Jan L. Flora and Edelberto Torres-Rivas, eds., **Sociology of "Developing Societies": Central America** [London: Macmillan, 1989].

Patricia Flynn, "Central America: The Roots of Revolt" in Roger Burbach and Patricia Flynn, eds., **The Politics of Intervention: The United States in Central America** [New York: Monthly Review Press, 1984].

Patricia Flynn, "The United States at War in Central America: Unable to Win, Unwilling to Lose" in Roger Burbach and Patricia Flynn, eds., **The Politics of Intervention: The United States in Central America** [New York: Monthly Review Press, 1984].

Michael W. Foley, "Agrarian Conflict Reconsidered: Popular Mobilization and Peasant Politics in Mexico and Central America" **Latin American Research Review** vol. 26. no. 1. 1991.

Roger Fontaine, "Fidel Castro: Front and Center" **Washington Quarterly: A Review of Strategic and International Issues** vol. 2. no. 2. 1979.

Roger Fontaine, Cleto DiGiovanni, Jr., and Alexander Kruger, "Castro's Specter" **Washington Quarterly: A Review of Strategic and International Issues** vol. 3. no. 4. 1980.

Aidan Foster-Carter, "From Rostow to Gunder Frank: Conflicting Paradigms in the Analysis of Underdevelopment" **World Development** vol. 4. no. 3. 1976.

Aidan Foster-Carter, "The Modes of Production Controversy" **New Left Review** no. 107. 1978.

Wilton B. Fowler, "The Way to Withdraw Is to Withdraw" **Latin American Research Review** vol. 12. no. 3. 1977.

Melvin J. Fox, "Universities and Latin American Studies" in Howard F. Cline, ed., **Latin American History: Essays on Its Study and Teaching 1898-1965** [Austin: University of Texas Press, 1967, 2 vols.].

Michael J. Francis, "United States Policy Toward Latin America During the Kissinger Years" in John D. Martz, ed., **United States Policy in Latin America: A Quarter Century of Crisis and Challenge 1961-1986** [Lincoln: University of Nebraska Press, 1988].

Andre Gunder Frank, "Dependence is Dead, Long Live Dependence and the Class Struggle: A Reply to Critics" **Latin American Perspectives** vol. 1. no. 1. 1974.

Andre Gunder Frank, "Crisis and Transformation of Dependency in the World-System" in Ronald H. Chilcote and Dale L. Johnson, eds., **Theories of Development: Mode of Production or Dependency** [Beverly Hills: Sage, 1983].

Louisa Frank, "Resistencia y revolución: el desarrollo de la lucha armada en Guatemala" in Susanne Jonas and David Tobis, eds., **Guatemala: una historia inmediata** [Mexico: Siglo veintiuno editores, 1979; first published in English in 1974].

Elizabeth Frawley, "US Policy on Haiti" in David S. Smith, ed., **Prospects for Latin America** [New York: Columbia University, International Fellows Program Policy Series, 1970].

George M. Fredrickson, "Comparative History" in Michael Kammen, ed., **The Past Before Us: Contemporary Historical Writing in the United States** [Ithaca: Cornell University Press, 1980].

Roberto Frenkel and Guillermo O'Donnell, "The 'Stabilization Programs' of the International Monetary Fund and Their Internal Impacts" in Richard R. Fagen, ed., **Capitalism and the State in US-Latin American Relations** [Stanford: Stanford University Press, 1979].

Edward Friedman, "American Power in Asia: Rationalizing the Irrational" in Marvin Surkin and Alan Wolfe, eds., **An End to Political Science: The Caucus Papers** [New York: Basic Books, 1970].

John S. Friedman, "Introduction" in John S. Friedman, ed., **First Harvest: The Institute for Policy Studies 1963-1983** [New York: Grove Press, 1983].

Hank Frundt, "To Buy the World a Coke: Implications of Trade Union Redevelopment in Guatemala" **Latin American Perspectives** vol. 14. no. 3. 1987.

Henry J. Frundt, "Guatemala in Search of Democracy" **Journal of Interamerican Studies and World Affairs** vol. 33. no. 1. 1991.

Francis Fukuyama, "US-Soviet Interaction in the Third World" in Arnold L. Horelick, ed., **US-Soviet Relations: The Next Phase** [Ithaca: Cornell University Press, for the Rand/UCLA Center for the Study of Soviet International Behavior, 1986].

Francis Fukuyama, "Soviet Strategy in the Third World" in Andrzej Korbonski and Franci Fukuyama, eds., **The Soviet Union and the Third World: The Last Three Decades** [Ithaca: Cornell University Press, for the Rand/UCLA Center for the Study of Soviet International Behavior, 1987].

Francis Fukuyama, "The End of History?" **The National Interest** vol. 16. no. 8. 1989.

J. S. Galbraith, "'The Turbulent Frontier' as a Factor in British Expansion" **Comparative Studies in Society and History** vol. 2. no. 2. 1960.

Johan Galtung, "A Structural Theory of Imperialism" **Journal of Peace Research** vol. 8. no. 2. 1971.

Lynn Garafola, "The Last Intellectuals" **New Left Review** no. 169. 1988.

José Z. Garcia, "El Salvador: Recent Elections in Historical Perspective" in John A.

Booth and Mitchel A. Seligson, eds., **Elections and Democracy in Central America** [Chapel Hill: University of North Carolina Press, 1989].

Frederick H. Gareau, "A Gramscian analysis of social science disciplines" **International Social Science Journal** no. 136. 1993.

Manuel Antonio Garreton, "Military Regimes, Democracy, and Political Transition in the Southern Cone: The Chilean Case" in George A. Lopez and Michael Stohl, eds., **Liberalization and Redemocratization in Latin America** [New York: Greenwood Press, 1987].

Manuel Antonio Garreton, "Political Democratisation in Latin America and the Crisis of Pardigms" in James Manor, ed., **Rethinking Third World Politics** [London: Longman, 1991].

Jeffrey E. Garten, "Is American Decline Inevitable?" **World Policy Journal** vol. 5. no. 1. 1987.

Charles Gati, "Another Grand Debate?: The Limitationist Critique of American Foreign Policy" **World Politics** vol. 21. no. 1. 1968.

Harry Gelman, "The Rise and Fall of Detente: Causes and Consequences" in Arnold L. Horelick, ed., **US-Soviet Relations: The Next Phase** [Ithaca: Cornell University Press, for the Rand/UCLA Center for the Study of Soviet International Behavior, 1986].

C. H. George, "The Origins of Capitalism: A Marxist Epitome and a Critique of Immanuel Wallerstein's Modern World-System" **Marxist Perspectives**, vol. 3. no. 2. 1980.

Gary Gereffi, "Paths of Industrialization: An Overview" in Gary Gereffi and Donald L. Wyman, eds., **Manufacturing Miracles: Paths of Industrialization in Latin America and East Asia** [Princeton: Princeton University Press, 1990].

Gary Gereffi, "Rethinking Development Theory: Insights from East Asia and Latin America" in A. Douglas Kincaid and Alejandro Portes, eds., **Comparative National Development: Society and Economy in the New Global Order** [Chapel Hill: University of North Carolina Press, 1994].

Gino Germani and Kalman Silvert, "Politics, Social Structure and Military Intervention in Latin America" in Abraham F. Lowenthal, ed., **Armies and Politics in Latin America** [New York: Holmes and Meier, 1976].

Carl Gershman, "The Rise and Fall of the New Foreign Policy Establishment" **Commentary** vol. 70. no. 1. 1980.

Carl Gershman, "Soviet Power in Central America and the Caribbean: The Growing Threat to American Security" **American Enterprise Institute Foreign Policy and Defense Review** vol. 5. no. 1. 1984.

Marvin Gettleman, "Against Cartesianism: Preliminary Notes on Three Generations of English-Language Political Discourse on Vietnam" **Bulletin of Concerned Asian Scholars** vol. 21. nos. 2-4. 1989. pp. 142-143.

William C. Gibbons, "Vietnam and the Breakdown of Consensus" in Richard A. Melanson and Kenneth W. Thompson, eds., **Foreign Policy and Domestic Consensus** [Lanham: University Press of America, 1985].

Charles Gibson and Benjamin Keen, "Trends of United States Studies in Latin American History" (1957) in Howard F. Cline, ed., **Latin American History: Essays on Its Study and Teaching 1898-1965** (2 vols.) [Austin: University of Texas Press, 1967].

Charles Gibson, "Latin America and the Americas" in Michael Kammen, ed., **The Past Before Us: Contemporary Historical Writing in the United States** [Ithaca: Cornell University Press, 1980].

Edward Gibson, "Nine Cases of the Breakdown of Democracy" in Robert A. Pastor, ed., **Democracy in the Americas: Stopping the Pendulum** [New York: Holmes and Meier, 1989].

Federico Gil, "Latin American Studies and Political Science: A Historical Sketch" **LASA Forum** vol. 16. no. 2. 1985.

Federico G. Gil, "The Kennedy-Johnson Years" in John D. Martz, ed., **United States Policy in Latin America: A Quarter Century of Crisis and Challenge 1961-1986** [Lincoln: University of Nebraska Press, 1988].

Dennis Gilbert, "Nicaragua" in Morris J. Blachman, William LeoGrande and Kenneth Sharpe, eds., **Confronting Revolution: Security Through Diplomacy in Central America** [New York: Pantheon, 1986].

Guy J. Gilbert, "Socialism and Dependency" **Latin American Perspectives** vol. 1. no. 1. 1974.

Stephen Gill, "American Hegemony: Its Limits and Prospects in the Reagan Era" **Millennium: Journal of International Studies** vol. 15. no. 3. 1986.

Stephen Gill, "Intellectuals and Transnational Capital" **The Socialist Register 1990** [London: Merlin Press, 1990].

Stephen Gill, "Neo-Liberalism and the Shift Towards a US-Centred Transnational Hegemony" in Henk Overbeek, ed., **Restructuring Hegemony in the Global Political Economy: The Rise of Transnational Neo-liberalism in the 1980s** [London: Routledge, 1993].

Stephen Gill, "Knowledge, Politics, and Neo-Liberal Political Economy" in Richard Stubbs and Geoffrey R. D. Underhill, eds., **Political Economy and the Changing Global Order** [London: Macmillan, 1994].

Charles Guy Gillespie, "Democratic Consolidation in the Southern Cone and Brazil: Beyond Political Disarticulation?" **Third World Quarterly: Journal of Emerging Areas** vol. 11. no. 2. 1989.

Charles Guy Gillespie and Luis Eduardo Gonzalez, "Uruguay: The Survival of Old and Autonomous Institutions" in Larry Diamond, Juan J. Linz and Seymour Martin Lipset, eds., **Democracy in Developing Countries--Volume Four: Latin America** [Boulder: Lynne Rienner, 1989].

Charles G. Gillespie, "Models of Democratic Transition in South America: Negotiated Reform Versus Democratic Rupture" in Diane Ethier, ed, **Democratic Transition and Consolidtion in Southern Europe, Latin America and Southeast Asia** [New York: Macmillan, 1990].

Richard Gillespie, "Guerrilla Warfare in the 1980s" in Barry Carr and Steve Ellner, eds., **The Latin American Left: From the Fall of Allende to Perestroika** [Boulder: Westview Press, 1993].

John P. Gillin and Kalman H. Silvert, "Ambiguities in Guatemala" **Foreign Affairs** vol. 34. no. 3. 1956.

John P. Gillin, "Some Signposts for Policy" in Richard N. Adams et al., eds., **Social Change in Latin America Today: Its Implications for United States Policy** [New York: Harper and Brothers, 1960, published for the Council on Foreign Relations].

B. K. Gills, "El Salvador in Crisis: Indigenous Conflict and Foreign Intervention" **Millennium: Journal of International Studies** vol. 13. no. 2. 1984.

Adolfo Gilly, "The Guerrilla Movement in Guatemala (I)" **Monthly Review** vol. 17. no. 1. 1965.

Adolfo Gilly, "The Guerrilla Movement in Guatemala (II)" **Monthly Review** vol. 17. no. 2. 1965.

Salvador Giner, "Economia politica y legitimación cultural en los origenes de la democracia parlamentaria: El caso de la Europa del Sur" in Julian Santamaría, ed., **Transición a la Democracia en el Sur de Europa y América Latina** [Madrid: Centro de Investigaciones Sociologicas, 1981].

Salvador Giner, "Political Economy, Legitimation, and the State in Southern Europe" in Guillermo O'Donnell, Philippe C. Schmitter and Laurence Whitehead, ed., **Transitions from Authoritarian Rule: Southern Europe** [Baltimore: Johns Hopkins University Press, 1986].

Robert H. Girling and Luin Goldring, "US Strategic Interests in Central America: The Economics and Geopolitics of Empire" in Stanford Central American Action Network, ed., **Revolution in Central America** [Boulder: Westview Press, 1983].

Michael A. Gismondi, "Transformations in the Holy: Religious Resistance and Hegemonic Struggles in the Nicaraguan Revolution" **Latin American Perspectives** vol. 13. no. 3. 1986.

John S. Gitlitz and H. A. Landsberger, "The Inter-American Political Economy: How Dependable is Dependency Theory?" in John D. Martz and Lars Schoultz, eds., **Latin America, the United States and the Inter-American System** [Boulder: Westview Press, 1980].

John Gittings, "The Great Asian Conspiracy" in Edward Friedman and Mark Selden, eds., **America's Asia: Dissenting Essays on Asian-American Relations** [New York: Random House, 1971; first publshed 1969].

Piero Gleijeses, "The Case for Power Sharing in El Salvador" **Foreign Affairs** vol. 61. no. 5. 1983.

Piero Gleijeses, "Guatemala: Crisis and Response" in Richard R. Fagen and Olga Pellicer, eds., **The Future of Central America: Policy Choices for the US and Mexico** [Stanford: Stanford University Press, 1983].

Piero Gleijeses, "Perspectives of a Regime Transformation" in Wolf Grabendorff, Heinrich W. Krumwiede and Jorg Todt, eds., **Political Change in Central America: Internal and External Dimensions** [Boulder: Westview Press, 1984].

Piero Gleijeses, "Nicaragua: Resist Romanticism" **Foreign Policy** no. 54. 1984.

Andrew Glyn, Alan Hughes, Alain Lipietz and Ajit Singh, "The Rise and Fall of the Golden Age" in Stephen A. Marglin and Juliet B. Schor, eds., **The Golden Age of Capitalism: Reinterpreting the Postwar Experience** [Oxford: Oxford University Press, 1990].

Fred Goff, "EXMIBAL: llévate otro níquel" in Susanne Jonas and David Tobis, eds., **Guatemala: una historia inmediata** [Mexico: Siglo veintiuno editores, 1979; first published in English in 1974].

Lionel Gomez, Bruce Cameron, W. Scott Thompson, J. Bryan Hehir and Olga Pellicer, "Struggle in Central America: The Current Danger" **Foreign Policy** no. 43. 1981.

Edward Gonzalez, "Cuba, the Third World, and the Soviet Union" in Andrzej Korbonski and Franci Fukuyama, eds., **The Soviet Union and the Third World: The Last Three Decades** [Ithaca: Cornell University Press, for the Rand/UCLA Center for the Study of Soviet International Behavior, 1987].

Nelly S. Gonzalez, "Latin American Doctoral Dissertations of the 1960s" **Latin American Research Review** vol. 18. no. 3. 1983.

Louis W. Goodman, "Political Parties and the Political Systems of Central America" in Louis W. Goodman, William M. LeoGrande, and Johanna Mendelson Forman, eds., **Political Parties and Democracy in Central America** [Boulder: Westview Press, 1992].

Max Gordon, "A Case History of US Subversion: Guatemala 1954" **Science and Society** vol. 35. no. 1. 1971.

Stephen C. Gorman, "Social Change and Political Revolution: The Case of Nicaragua" in Steve C. Ropp and James Morris, eds., **Central America: Crisis and Adaptation** [Albuquerque: University of New Mexico Press, 1984].

Xabier Gorostiaga, "Dilemmas of the Nicaraguan Revolution" in Richard R. Fagen and Olga Pellicer, eds., **The Future of Central America: Policy Choices for the US and Mexico** [Stanford: Stanford University Press, 1983].

Kathleen Gough, "Anthropology: World Revolution and the Science of Man" in Theodore Roszak, ed., **The Dissenting Academy** [London: Chatto and Windus, 1969; first published 1967].

Wolf Grabendorff, "Western European Perceptions of the Central American Turmoil" in Richard E. Feinberg, ed., **Central America: International Dimensions of the Crisis** [New York: Holmes and Meier, 1982].

Wolf Grabendorff, "The Central American Crisis: Is There a Role for Western Europe?" **Millennium: Journal of International Studies** vol. 13. no. 2. 1984.

Wolf Grabendorff, "The Internationalization of the Central American Crisis" in Wolf Grabendorff, Heinrich W. Krumwiede and Jorg Todt, eds., **Political Change in Central America: Internal and External Dimensions** [Boulder: Westview Press, 1984].

Wolf Grabendorff, "West European Perceptions of the Crisis in Central America" in Wolf Grabendorff, Heinrich W. Krumwiede and Jorg Todt, eds., **Political Change in Central America: Internal and External Dimensions** [Boulder: Westview Press, 1984].

Douglas H. Graham, "The Economic Dimensions of Instability and Decline in Central America and the Caribbean" in Donald E. Schulz and Douglas H. Graham eds., **Revolution and Counterrevolution in Central America and the Caribbean** [Boulder: Westview Press, 1984].

Lawrence S. Graham, "Latin America: Illusion or Reality? A Case for a New Analytic Framework for the Region" in Howard J. Wiarda, ed., **Politics and Social Change in Latin America: Still a Distinct Tradition?** [Boulder: Westview Press, 1992].

Richard Graham and Peter H. Smith, "Introduction" in Richard Graham and Peter H. Smith, eds., **New Approaches to Latin American History** [Austin: University of Texas Press, 1974].

Richard Graham, "Robinson and Gallagher in Latin America: The Meaning of Informal Imperialism" in William Roger Louis, ed., **Imperialism: The Robinson and Gallagher Controversy** [New York: Franklin Watts, 1976].

Günter Grass, "Epilogue: America's Backyard" in Martin Diskin, ed., **Trouble in Our Backyard: Central America and the United States in the 1980s** [New York: Pantheon, 1983].

David Green, "The Cold War Comes to Latin America" in Barton J. Bernstein, ed., **Politics and Policies of the Truman Administration** [Chicago: Quadrangle Books, 1970].

David Green, "Language, Values, and Policy Perspectives in Inter-American Research" **Latin American Research Review** vol. 10. no. 3. 1975.

J. Edward Greene, "The Ideological and Idiosyncratic Aspects of US-Caribbean Relations" in H. Michael Erisman, ed., **The Caribbean Challenge: US Policy in a Volatile Region** [Boulder: Westview Press, 1984].

Virginia L. Greer, "State Department Policy in Regard to the Nicaraguan Election of 1924" **Hispanic American Historical Review** vol. 34. no. 4. 1954.

Kenneth J. Grieb, "The United States and the Central American Federation" **The Americas: A Quarterly Review of Inter-American Cultural History** vol. 24. no. 2. 1967.

Kenneth J. Grieb, "Warren G. Harding and the Dominican Republic: US Withdrawal 1921-1923" **Journal of Inter-American Studies** vol. 11. no. 3. 1969.

Kenneth J. Grieb, "American Involvement in the Rise of Jorge Ubico" **Caribbean Studies** vol. 10. no. 1. 1970.

Kenneth J. Grieb, "The United States and the Rise of General Maximiliano Hernandez Martínez" **Journal of Latin American Studies** vol. 3. no. 2. 1971.

Charles C. Griffin, "Unity and Variety in American History" in Lewis Hanke, ed., **Do the Americas Have a Common History?: A Critique of the Bolton Theory** [New York: Alfred A. Knopf, 1964].

Charles C. Griffin, "Welles to Roosevelt: A Memorandum on Inter-American Relations, 1933" **Hispanic American Historical Review** vol. 34. no. 2. 1954.

Keith Griffin, "Foreign Aid after the Cold War" **Development and Change** vol. 22. no. 4. 1991.

W. J. Griffith, "The Historiography of Central America Since 1830" **Hispanic American Historical Review** vol. 40. no. 4. 1960.

Merilee Grindle, "Armed Intervention and US Latin-American Relations" **Latin American Research Review** vol. 21. no. 1. 1981.

Ernest H. Gruening, "The Issue in Haiti" **Foreign Affairs** vol. 11. no. 2. 1933.

Ernest H. Gruening, "The Withdrawal from Haiti" **Foreign Affairs** vol. 12. no. 4. 1934.

Joseph Grunwald, "Perspectives on the Latin American Economic Crisis" in Howard J. Wiarda, ed., **The Crisis in Latin America: Strategic, Economic and Political Dimensions** [Washington: American Enterprise Institute, 1984].

John G. Gunnell, "American Political Science, Liberalism and the Invention of Political Theory" **American Political Science Review** vol. 82. no. 1.

1988.

Roy Gutman, "Nicaragua: America's Diplomatic Charade" **Foreign Policy** no. 56. 1984.

Roy Gutman, "The United States, Nicaragua and Consensus Decision Making" in Bruce M. Bagley, ed., **Contadora and the Diplomacy of Peace in Central America--vol. 1: The United States, Central America and Contadora** [Boulder: Westview Press, 1987].

Roy Gutman, "Nicaraguan Turning Point: How the 1984 Vote Was Sabotaged" **LASA Forum** vol. 19. no. 2. 1988.

David T. Haberly, "Form and Function in the New World Legend" in Gustavo Pérez Firmat, ed., **Do the Americas Have a Common Literature?** [Durham: Duke University Press, 1990].

Charles W. Hackett, "Discussion of Lesley Byrd Simpson, 'Thirty Years of the *Hispanic American Historical Review*'; and Charles C. Griffin, 'Economic and Social Aspects of the Era of Spanish American Independence'" **Hispanic American Historical Review** vol. 29. no. 2. 1949.

Stephan Haggard, Frederic Deyo and Hagen Koo, "Labor in the Political Economy of East Asian Industrialization" **Bulletin of Concerned Asian Scholars** vol. 19. no. 2. 1987.

Stephan Haggard, "The Political Economy of Foreign Direct Investment in Latin America" **Latin American Research Review** vol. 24. no. 1. 1989.

Frances Hagopian, "After Regime Change: Authoritarian Legacies, Political Representation, and the Democratic Future of South America" **World Politics** vol. 45. no. 3. 1993.

Gerald K. Haines, "Roads to War: United States Foreign Policy, 1931-1941" in Gerald K. Haines and J. Samuel Walker, eds., **American Foreign Relations: An Historiographical Review** [London: Frances Pinter, 1981].

Gerald K. Haines and J. Samuel Walker, "Some Sources and Problems for Diplomatic Historians in the Next Two Decades" in Gerald K. Haines and J. Samuel Walker, eds., **American Foreign Relations: An Historiographical Review** [London: Frances Pinter, 1981].

Peter Hakim, "Clinton and Latin America: Facing an Unfinished Agenda" **Current History: A World Affairs Journal** vol. 92. no. 572. 1993.

Sandor Halebsky and Susanne Jonas, "Obstacles to the Peace Process in Central America" in John M. Kirk and George W. Schuyler, eds., **Central America: Democracy, Development and Change** [New York: Praeger, 1988].

Fred Halliday, "Triumph of the West: The Ends of the Cold War" **New Left Review** no. 180. 1990.

Fred Halliday, "International Relations: Is There a New Agenda?" **Millennium: Journal of International Studies** vol. 20. no. 1. 1991.

Fred Halliday, "An Encounter With Fukuyama" **New Left Review** no. 193. 1992.

Ernst Halperin, "Area Studies in America: The State of Latin American Studies" **Washington Quarterly: A Review of Strategic and International Issues** vol. 1. no. 2. 1978.

Morton H. Halperin and Arnold Kanter, "The Bureaucratic Perspective: A Preliminary Framework" in Morton Halperin and Arnold Kanter, eds.,

Readings in American Foreign Policy: A Bureaucratric Perspective [Boston: Little Brown, 1973].

Tulio Halperín Donghi, "*Dependency Theory* and Latin American Historiography" **Latin American Research Review** vol. 17. no. 1. 1982.

Tulio Halperín Donghi, "The State of Latin American History" in Christopher Mitchell, ed., **Changing Perspectives in Latin American Studies: Insights from Six Disciplines** [Stanford: Stanford University Press, 1988].

Clifford D. Ham, "Americanizing Nicaragua: How Yankee Marines, Financial Oversight and Baseball Are Stabilizing Central America" **The American Review of Reviews** vol. 53. 1916.

Hugh M. Hamill, Jr., "Title VI Funding: A Commentary" **LASA Forum** vol. 15. no. 3. 1984.

Thomas T. Hammond, "Moscow and Communist Takeovers" **Problems of Communism** vol. 25. no. 1. 1976.

Jim Handy, "The Guatemalan Revolution and Civil Rights: Presidential Elections and the Judicial Process Under Juan José Arévalo and Jacobo Arbenz Guzman" **Canadian Journal of Latin American and Caribbean Studies** vol. 10. 1985.

Jim Handy, "Resurgent Democracy and the Guatemalan Military" **Journal of Latin American Studies** vol. 18. no. 2. 1986.

Jim Handy, "The Most Precious Fruit of the Revolution: The Guatemalan Agrarian Reform 1952-1954" **Hispanic American Historical Review** vol. 68. no. 4. 1988.

Jim Handy, "National Policy, Agrarian Reform, and the Corporate Community During the Guatemalan Revolution, 1944-1954" **Comparative Studies in Society and History** vol. 30. no. 4. 1988.

Jim Handy, "Democracy, Military Rule and Agrarian Reform in Guatemala" in John M. Kirk and George W. Schuyler, eds., **Central America: Democracy, Development and Change** [New York: Praeger, 1988].

Jim Handy, "A Sea of Indians: Ethnic Conflict and the Guatemalan Revolution 1944-1952" **The Americas: A Quarterly Review of Inter-American Cultural History** vol. 45. no. 2. 1989.

Jim Handy, "Insurgency and Counter-insurgency in Guatemala" in Jan L. Flora and Edelberto Torres-Rivas, eds., **Sociology of "Developing Societies": Central America** [London: Macmillan, 1989].

Jim Handy, "The Corporate Community, Campesino Organizations and Agrarian Reform 1950-1954" in Carol A. Smith, ed., **Guatemalan Indians and the State 1540 to 1988** [Austin: University of Texas Press, 1990].

Jim Handy, "Anxiety and Dread: State and Community in Modern Guatemala" **Canadian Journal of History** vol. 26. no. 1. 1991.

Lewis Hanke, "Introduction" in Lewis Hanke, ed., **Do the Americas Have a Common History?: A Critique of the Bolton Theory** [New York: Alfred A. Knopf, 1964].

Lewis Hanke, "Development of Bolton's Theory" in Howard F. Cline, ed., **Latin American History: Essays on Its Study and Teaching 1898-1965** (2 vols.) [Austin: University of Texas Press, 1967].

Lewis Hanke, "The Development of Latin American Studies in the United States

1939-1945" **The Americas: A Quarterly Review of Inter-American Cultural History** vol. 4. no. 1. 1947; reprinted in Howard F. Cline, ed., **Latin American History: Essays on Its Study and Teaching 1898-1965** (2 vols.) [Austin: University of Texas Press, 1967].

Lewis Hanke, "American Historians and the World Today: Responsibilities and Opportunities" **American Historical Review** vol. 80. no. 1. 1975.

Lewis Hanke, "The Development of Latin Ameican Studies Outside the United States in Recent Years" **LASA Forum** vol. 20. no. 4. 1990.

Timothy F. Harding, "The New Imperialism in Latin America" in K. T. Fann and Donald C. Hodges, eds., **Readings in US Imperialism** [Boston: Porter Sargent, 1971].

Timothy F. Harding, "Maoism: An Alternative to Dependency Theory?" **Latin American Perspectives** vol. 1. no. 1. 1974.

Timothy F. Harding and James Petras, "Democratization and Class Struggle" **Latin American Perspectives** vol. 15. no. 3. 1988.

C. H. Haring, "South America and Our Policy in the Caribbean" **Annals of the American Academy of Political and Social Science** vol. 132. 1927.

Michael Harrington, "The Good Domino" in Marvin Gettleman et al., eds., **El Salvador: Central America in the New Cold War** [New York: Grove Press [1981].

Richard L. Harris, "The Revolutionary Process in Nicaragua" **Latin American Perspectives** vol. 12. no. 2. 1985.

Richard L. Harris, "Marxism and the Transition to Socialism in Latin America" **Latin American Perspectives** vol. 15. no. 1. 1988.

John P. Harrison, "History of the **Journal**" in **Cumulative Index Journal of Interamerican Studies and World Affairs, 1959-1989** [Miami: Institute of Interamerican Studies, 1989].

Jonathan Hartlyn, "Military Governments and the Transition to Civilian Rule: The Colombian Experience of 1957-1958" in Abraham F. Lowenthal, ed., **Armies and Politics in Latin America** [New York: Holmes and Meier, revised edition 1986; first published 1976].

Jonathan Hartlyn, "Colombia: The Politics of Violence and Accommodation" in Larry Diamond, Juan J. Linz and Seymour Martin Lipset, eds., **Democracy in Developing Countries--Volume Four: Latin America** [Boulder: Lynne Rienner, 1989].

Louis Hartz, "A Theory of the Development of the New Societies" in Louis Hartz, ed., **The Founding of New Societies: Studies in the History of the United States, Latin America, South Africa, Canada and Australia** [New York: Harcourt, Brace and World, 1964].

Louis Hartz, "United States History in a New Perspective" in Louis Hartz, ed., **The Founding of New Societies: Studies in the History of the United States, Latin America, South Africa, Canada and Australia** [New York: Harcourt, Brace and World, 1964].

Margaret Daly Hayes, "Security to the South: US Interests in Latin America" **International Security** vol. 5. no. 1. 1980.

Margaret Daly Hayes, "The Stakes in Central America and US Foreign Policy Responses" **American Enterprise Institute Foreign Policy and**

Defense Review vol. 4. no. 2. 1982.

Margaret Daly Hayes, "United States Security Interests in Central America in Global Perspective" in Richard E. Feinberg, ed., **Central America: International Dimensions of the Crisis** [New York: Holmes and Meier, 1982].

Margaret Daly Hayes, "Coping with Problems That Have No Solutions: Political Change in El Salvador and Guatemala" in Alan Adelman and Reid Reading, eds., **Confrontation in the Caribbean Basin: International Perspectives on Security, Sovereignty and Survival** [Pittsburgh: Center for Latin American Studies, University Center for International Studies, University of Pittsburgh, 1984].

Margaret Daly Hayes, "US Security Interests in Central America" **American Enterprise Institute Foreign Policy and Defense Review** vol. 5. no. 1. 1984.

Margaret Daly Hayes, "United States Policy Toward Latin America: A Prospectus" in Jack Child, ed., **Conflict in Central America: Approaches to Peace and Security** [London: C. Hurst, 1986].

Margaret Daly Hayes, "Comment: Security in the Western Hemisphere" in Kevin J. Middlebrook and Carlos Rico, eds., **The United States and Latin America in the 1980s: Contending Perspectives on a Decade of Crisis** [Pittsburgh: University of Pittsburgh Press, 1986].

Margaret Daly Hayes, "US Security Interests in Central America" in Bruce M. Bagley, ed., **Contadora and the Diplomacy of Peace in Central America--vol. 1: The United States, Central America and Contadora** [Boulder: Westview Press, 1987].

Margaret Daly Hayes, "Not What I Say But What I Do: Latin American Policy in the Reagan Administration" in John D. Martz, ed., **United States Policy in Latin America: A Quarter Century of Crisis and Challenge 1961-1986** [Lincoln: University of Nebraska Press, 1988].

Margaret Daly Hayes, "The United States and Latin America: A Lost Decade" **Foreign Affairs** vol. 68. no. 1. 1989.

Keith A. Haynes, "Mass Participation and the Transition to Socialism: A Critique of Petras and Fitzgerald" **Latin American Perspectives** vol. 15. no. 1. 1988.

Keith A. Haynes, "Authoritarianism, Democracy and Development: The Corporative Theory of Howard J. Wiarda Revisited" **Latin American Perspectives** vol. 15. no. 3. 1988.

Keith A. Haynes, "Reply to Howard J. Wiarda: Democracy, Serious Scholarship and Class Struggle" **Latin American Perspectives** vol. 16. no. 4. 1989.

David Held, "Democracy, the Nation-State and the Global System" in David Held, ed., **Political Theory Today** [Stanford: Stanford University Press, 1991].

Colin Henfrey, "Dependency, Modes of Production and the Class Analysis of Latin America" in Ronald H. Chilcote, ed., **Dependency and Marxism: Toward a Resolution of the Debate** [Boulder: Westview Press, 1982].

Edward S. Herman and James Petras, "'Resurgent Democracy': Rhetoric and Reality" **New Left Review** no. 154. 1985.

Rafael Hernandez, "Comment: The United States and Latin America: The Question of Security" in Kevin J. Middlebrook and Carlos Rico, eds., **The United**

States and Latin America in the 1980s: Contending Perspectives on a Decade of Crisis [Pittsburgh: University of Pittsburgh Press, 1986].

George C. Herring, "Vietnam, El Salvador, and the Uses of History" in Kenneth M. Coleman and George C. Herring, eds. **The Central American Crisis: Sources of Conflict and the Failure of US Policy** [Wilmington: Scholarly Resources, 1985].

George C. Herring and Kenneth M. Coleman, "Beyond Hegemony: Toward a New Central American Policy" in Kenneth M. Coleman and George C. Herring, eds. **The Central American Crisis: Sources of Conflict and the Failure of US Policy** [Wilmington: Scholarly Resources, 1985].

Gary R. Hess, "Global Expansion and Regional Balances: The Emerging Scholarship on United States Relations with India and Pakistan" **Pacific Historical Review** vol. 61. no. 2. 1987.

John D. Heyl, "'Patria Libre o Muerte!': Death Imagery and the Poetry of Revolt in Nicaragua 1900-1985" in Ralph Lee Woodward, Jr., ed., **Central America: Historical Perspectives on the Contemporary Crisis** [New York: Greenwood Press, 1988].

Richard Higgott and Richard Robison, "Introduction" in Richard Higgott and Richard Robison, eds., **Southeast Asia: Essays in the Political Economy of Structural Change** [London: Routledge and Kegan Paul, 1985].

Richard Higgott and Richard Robison with Kevin J. Hewison and Garry Rodan, "Theories of Development and Underdevelopment: Implications for the Study of Southeast Asia" in Richard Higgott and Richard Robison, eds., **Southeast Asia: Essays in the Political Economy of Structural Change** [London: Routledge and Kegan Paul, 1985].

John Higham, "Changing Paradigms: The Collapse of Consensus History" **The Journal of American History** vol. 76. no. 2. 1989.

John R. Hildebrand, "Latin American Economic Development, Land Reform and US Aid with Special Reference to Guatemala" **Journal of Inter-American Studies and World Affairs** vol. 4. no. 3. 1962.

Lawrence F. Hill, "Our Present Peril" in A. Curtis Wilgus, ed., **Hispanic American Essays** [Chapel Hill: University of North Carolina Press, 1942; reprinted Freeport: Books for Libraries Press, 1970].

Roscoe R. Hill, "Leo S. Rowe" **Hispanic American Historical Review** vol. 27. no. 2. 1947.

Roscoe R. Hill, "The Nicaraguan Canal Idea to 1913" **Hispanic American Historical Review** vol. 28. no. 2. 1948.

Roscoe R. Hill, "American Marines in Nicaragua, 1912-1925" in A. Curtis Wilgus, ed., **Hispanic American Essays** [Chapel Hill: University of North Carolina Press, 1942; reprinted Freeport: Books for Libraries Press, 1970].

Robert E. Hinshaw, "Tourist Town Amid the Violence: Panajachel" in Robert M. Carmack, ed., **Harvest of Violence: The Maya Indians and the Guatemalan Crisis** [Norman: University of Oklahoma Press, 1988].

Albert O. Hirschman, "The Turn to Authoritarianism in Latin America and the Search for Its Economic Determinants" in David Collier, ed., **The New Authoritarianism in Latin America** [Princeton: Princeton University Press, 1979].

Donald C. Hodges, "The Argentine Left Since Peron" in Barry Carr and Steve Ellner, eds., **The Latin American Left: From the Fall of Allende to Perestroika** [Boulder: Westview Press, 1993].

Paul Heath Hoeffel, "Autumn of the Oligarchs" in Donald E. Schulz and Douglas H. Graham eds., **Revolution and Counterrevolution in Central America and the Caribbean** [Boulder: Westview Press, 1984].

David Hollinger, "American Intellectual History: Issues for the 1980s" in Stanley I. Kutler and Stanley N. Katz, eds., **The Promise of American History: Progress and Prospects** [Baltimore: Johns Hopkins University Press, 1982].

K. J. Holsti, "The Horsemen of the Apocalypse: At the Gate, Detoured, or Retreating?" **International Studies Quarterly: The Journal of the International Studies Association** vol. 30. no. 4. 1986.

Ole R. Holsti and James N. Rosenau, "Consensus Lost, Consensus Regained?: Foreign Policy Beliefs of American Leaders 1976-1980" **International Studies Quarterly: The Journal of the International Studies Association** vol. 30. no. 4. 1986.

Ole R. Holsti and James N. Rosenau, "The Foreign Policy Beliefs of American Leaders: Some Further Thoughts on Theory and Method" **International Studies Quarterly: The Journal of the International Studies Association** vol. 30. no. 4. 1986.

Rex Hopper, "Research on Latin America in Sociology" in Charles Wagley, ed., **Social Science Research on Latin America** [New York: Columbia University Press, 1964].

David Horowitz, "The Alliance for Progress" **The Socialist Register 1964** [London: Merlin Press, 1964]; reprinted in Robert Rhodes, ed., **Imperialism and Under-Development: A Reader** [New York: Monthly Review Press, 1970].

David Horowitz, "Nicaragua: A Speech to My Former Comrades on the Left" **Commentary** vol. 81. no. 6. 1986.

Irving Louis Horowitz, "Masses in Latin America" in Irving Louis Horowitz, ed., **Masses in Latin America** [New York: Oxford University Press, 1970].

Irving Louis Horowitz, "The Cuba Lobby: Supplying Rope to a Mortgaged Revolution" **Washington Quarterly: A Review of Strategic and International Issues** vol. 1. no. 2. 1978.

Irving Louis Horowitz, "Latin America, Anti-Americanism and Intellectual Hubris" in Alvin Z. Rubinstein and Donald E. Smith, eds., **Anti-Americanism in the Third World: Implications for US Foreign Policy** [New York: Praeger, 1985].

Gary Nigel Howe, "Dependency Theory, Imperialism and the Production of Surplus Value on a World Scale" in Ronald H. Chilcote, ed., **Dependency and Marxism: Toward a Resolution of the Debate** [Boulder: Westview Press, 1982].

Eugene R. Huck and Edward H. Moseley, "Introduction" in Eugene R. Huck and Edward H. Moseley, eds., **Militarists, Merchants and Missionaries: United States Expansion in Middle America** [Tuscaloosa: University of Alabama Press, 1970].

Steven W. Hughes and Kenneth J. Mijeski, "Contemporary Paradigms in the Study of Inter-American Relations" in John D. Martz and Lars Schoultz, eds., **Latin America, the United States and the Inter-American System** [Boulder: Westview Press, 1980].

R. A. Humphreys, "William Spence Robertson 1872-1955" **Hispanic American Historical Review** vol. 36. no. 1. 1956.

R. A. Humphreys, "William Hickling Prescott: The Man and the Historian" in Howard F. Cline, ed., **William Hickling Prescott: A Memorial** [Durham: Duke University Press, 1959].

Michael H. Hunt, "Internationalizing US Diplomatic History: A Practical Agenda" **Diplomatic History** vol. 15. no. 2. 1991.

Jane Hunter, "The Israeli Connection: Guns and Money in Central America--Israel, The Contra's Secret Benefactor" **NACLA Report on the Americas** vol. 21. no. 2. 1987.

Jane Hunter and Sara Diamond, "The Show Goes On: The Right After Reagan" **NACLA Report on the Americas** vol. 22. no. 5. 1988.

Robert E. Hunter, "Strategy for Central America" **American Enterprise Institute Foreign Policy and Defense Review** vol. 5. no. 1. 1984.

Deborah Huntington, "Visions of the Kingdom: The Latin American Church in Conflict" **NACLA Report on the Americas** vol. 19. no. 5. 1985.

Samuel P. Huntington, "Political Development and Political Decay" **World Politics** vol. 17. no. 3. 1965; reprinted in Ikuo Kabashima and Lynn T. White III, eds., **Political System and Change** [Princeton: Princeton University Press, 1986].

Samuel P. Huntington, "Social Science and Vietnam" **Asian Survey** vol. 7. no. 8. 1967.

Samuel P. Huntington, "The Bases of Accommodation" **Foreign Affairs** vol. 46. no. 3. 1968.

Samuel P. Huntington, "American Foreign Policy: The Changing Political Universe" **Washington Quarterly: A Review of Strategic and International Issues** vol. 2. no. 4. 1979.

Samuel P. Huntington, "Human Rights and American Policy" **Commentary** vol. 72. no. 3. 1981.

Samuel P. Huntington, "Will More Countries Become Democratic?" **Political Science Quarterly** vol. 99. no. 2. 1984.

Samuel P. Huntington, "The Goals of Development" in Myron Weiner and Samuel P. Huntington, eds., **Understanding Political Development** [Boston: Little Brown, 1987].

Samuel P. Huntington, "One Soul at a Time: Political Science and Political Reform" **American Political Science Review** vol. 82. no. 1. 1988.

Samuel P. Huntington, "Coping with the Lippman Gap" **Foreign Affairs** vol. 66. no. 3. 1988.

Samuel P. Huntington, "The US--Decline or Renewal" **Foreign Affairs** vol. 67. no. 2. 1988/89.

Samuel P. Huntington, "The Modest Meaning of Democracy" in Robert A. Pastor, ed., **Democracy in the Americas: Stopping the Pendulum** [New York: Holmes and Meier, 1989].

Samuel P. Huntington, "The Clash of Civilizations?" **Foreign Affairs** vol. 72. no. 3. 1993.

Albert L. Hurtado, "Herbert E. Bolton, Racism and American History" **Pacific Historical Review** vol. 62. no. 2. 1993.

Osvaldo Hurtado, "Changing Latin American Attitudes: Prerequisite to Institutionalizing Democracy" in Robert A. Pastor, ed., **Democracy in the Americas: Stopping the Pendulum** [New York: Holmes and Meier, 1989].

C. Alan Hutchinson, "Wilfrid Hardy Callcott 1895-1969" **Hispanic American Historical Review** vol. 50. no. 2. 1970.

William G. Hyland, "The United States and the USSR: Rebuilding Relations" in Arnold L. Horelick, ed., **US-Soviet Relations: The Next Phase** [Ithaca: Cornell University Press, for the Rand/UCLA Center for the Study of Soviet International Behavior, 1986].

Ronald T. Hyman, "Studying Latin America" in Samuel L. Baily and Ronald T. Hyman, eds., **Perspectives on Latin America** [New York: Macmillan, 1974].

Richard H. Immerman, "Revisionism Revisited: The New Left Lives" **Reviews in American History** vol. 15. no. 1. 1987.

Instituto Historico Centroamericano and Universidad Centroamericana (Managua), "The United States: Redefining Central America and the World", "The Neoliberal Model in Central America: The Gospel of the New Right" , "Demilitarization: The Other Face of Democratization", "The Central American Popular Movement: A Partial Alternative", "Guatemala: The Civilian Facade Collapses", "El Salvador: UN Mediation and Civil Negotiations", "Nicaragua: Political Maturity and Economic Immaturity" and "The Popular Alternative: The Agenda and Challenges for the 90s" **Envio: The Monthly Magazine of Analysis on Nicaragua** vol. 10. no. 117. 1991.

Inter-American Dialogue (chair Sol M. Linowitz), "The Americas in 1984: A Year for Decisions" **LASA Forum** vol. 15. no. 3. 1984; excerpted from Inter-American Dialogue (chair Sol M. Linowitz), **The Americas in 1984: A Year for Decisions** (Report of the Inter-American Dialogue) [Queenstown: Aspen Institute for Humanistic Studies, 1984].

Peter Irons, "On Repressive Institutions and the American Empire" in K. T. Fann and Donald C. Hodges, eds., **Readings in US Imperialism** [Boston: Porter Sargent, 1971].

George Irvin, "New Perspectives for Modernization in Central America" **Development and Change** vol. 22. no. 1. 1991.

Allen F. Isaacman, "Peasants and Rural Social Protest in Africa" (1990) in Frederick Cooper, Allen F. Isaacman, Florencia E. Mallon, William Rosebery and Steve J. Stern, **Confronting Historical Paradigms: Peasants, Labor, and the Capitalist World System in Africa and Latin America** [Madison: University of Wisconsin Press, 1993].

Steven Jackson, Bruce Russett, Duncan Snidal and David Sylvan, "An Assessment of Empirical Research on *Dependencia*" **Latin American Research Review** vol. 14. no. 3. 1979.

Milton Jamail, "The Strongmen are Shaking" **Latin American Perspectives** vol. 7. nos. 2-3. 1980.

Milton Jamail and Margo Gutiérrez, "The Israeli Connection: Guns and Money in

Central America--A Special Relationship", "The Israeli Connection: Guns and Money in Central America--Getting Down to Business" and "The Israeli Connection: Guns and Money in Central America--Guatemala, The Paragon" **NACLA Report on the Americas** vol. 21. no. 2. 1987.

Milton Jamail and Margo Gutiérrez, "Israel's Role in Central America" in Damian J. Fernandez, ed., **Central America and the Middle East: The Internationalization of the Crises** [Miami: Florida International University Press, 1990].

Daniel James, "Mexico: America's Newest Problem?" **Washington Quarterly: A Review of Strategic and International Issues** vol. 3. no. 3. 1980.

Fredric Jameson, "Modernism and Imperialism" in Terry Eagleton, Fredric Jameson and Edward Said, **Nationalism, Colonialism and Literature** [Minneapolis: University of Minnesota Press, 1990].

J. Franklin Jameson, "A New American Historical Journal" **Hispanic American Historical Review** vol. 1. no. 1. 1918.

Rhys Jenkins, "Learning from the Gang: Are There Lessons for Latin America from East Asia" **Bulletin of Latin American Research** vol. 10. no. 1. 1991.

Rhys Jenkins, "The Political Economy of Industrialization: A Comparison of Latin American and East Asian Newly Industrializing Countries" **Development and Change** vol. 22. no. 2. 1991.

Bruce W. Jentleson, "The Reagan Administration and Coercive Diplomacy: Restraining More than Remaking Governments" **Political Science Quarterly** vol. 106. no. 1. 1991.

Carlos Johnson, "Ideologies in Theories of Imperialism and Dependency" in Ronald H. Chilcote and Dale L. Johnson, eds., **Theories of Development: Mode of Production or Dependency** [Beverly Hills: Sage, 1983].

Dale L. Johnson, "Economism and Determinism in Dependency Theory" in Ronald H. Chilcote, ed., **Dependency and Marxism: Toward a Resolution of the Debate** [Boulder: Westview Press, 1982].

Dale L. Johnson, "Class Analysis and Dependency" in Ronald H. Chilcote and Dale L. Johnson, eds., **Theories of Development: Mode of Production or Dependency** [Beverly Hills: Sage, 1983].

John J. Johnson, "One Hundred Years of Historical Writing on Modern Latin America by United States Historians" **Hispanic American Historical Review** vol. 65. no. 4. 1985.

Kenneth F. Johnson, "Scholarly Images of Latin American Political Democracy in 1975" **Latin American Research Review** vol. 11. no. 2. 1976.

Susanne Jonas, "Masterminding the Mini-Market: US Aid to the Central American Common Market" in Susanne Jonas and David Tobid, eds., **Guatemala** [New York: North American Congress on Latin America, 1974].

Susanne Jonas, "Guatemala: The Eternal Struggle" in Ronald H. Chilcote and Joel C. Edelstein, eds., **Latin America: The Struggle with Dependency and Beyond** [New York: Wiley, 1974].

Susanne Jonas, "'La democracia que sucumbió': la revolución guatemalteca de 1944-1954", "Anatomía de una intervención: la 'liberación' norteamericana en Guatemala", "'Escaparate' de la contrarrevolución", "El mejor grupo de presión en Washington" and "La neuva línea dura: estategia norteamericana de los setentas" in Susanne Jonas and David Tobis, eds., **Guatemala: una**

historia inmediata [Mexico: Siglo veintiuno editores, 1979; first published in English in 1974].

Susanne Jonas and Marlene Dixon, "Proletarianization and Class Alliances in the Americas" **Synthesis** vol. 3. no. 1. 1979.

Susanne Jonas, "The Nicaraguan Revolution and the Reemerging Cold War" in Thomas W. Walker, ed., **Nicaragua in Revolution** [New York: Praeger, 1982].

Susanne Jonas, "Central America as a Theater of US Cold War Politics" **Latin American Perspectives** vol. 9. no. 3. 1982.

Susanne Jonas, "An Overview: Fifty Years of Revolution and Intervention in Central America", "The New Cold War and the Nicaraguan Revolution: The Case of US Aid to Nicaragua" and "Contradictions of Revolution and Intervention in Central America in the Transnational Era: The Case of Guatemala" in Marlene Dixon and Susanne Jonas, eds., **Revolution and Intervention in Central America** [San Francisco: Synthesis Publications, 1983].

Susanne Jonas and Elizabeth Farnsworth, "Whose Transition? Whose Guatemala?: An Exchange" **World Policy Journal** vol. 5. no. 1. 1987-1988.

Susanne Jonas, "Contradictions of Guatemala's 'Political Opening'" **Latin American Perspectives** vol. 15. no. 3. 1988.

Susanne Jonas, "Elections and Transitions: The Guatemalan and Nicaraguan Cases" in John A. Booth and Mitchel A. Seligson, eds., **Elections and Democracy in Central America** [Chapel Hill: University of North Carolina Press, 1989].

Susanne Jonas and Nancy Stein, "The Construction of Democracy in Nicaragua" **Latin American Perspectives** vol. 17. no. 3. 1990.

Susanne Jonas. See also Susanne (Jonas) Bodenheimer

Chester Lloyd Jones, "The Development of the Caribbean" in Chester Lloyd Jones et al., **The United States and the Caribbean** [Chicago: University of Chicago Press, 1929, second edition 1934].

Chester Lloyd Jones, "Loan Controls in the Caribbean" **Hispanic American Historical Review** vol. 14. no. 2. 1934.

Chester Lloyd Jones, "Roots of the Mexican Church Conflict" **Foreign Affairs** vol. 14. no. 1. 1935.

Chester Lloyd Jones, "Indian Labor in Guatemala" in A. Curtis Wilgus, ed., **Hispanic American Essays** [Chapel Hill: University of North Carolina Press, 1942; reprinted Freeport: Books for Libraries Press, 1970].

Lynne Jones, "Murder in Guatemala" **New Left Review** no. 182. 1990.

Joseph Robert Juarez, "United States Withdrawal from Santo Domingo" **Hispanic American Historical Review** vol. 42. no. 2. 1962.

Leigh Kagan and Richard Kagan, "'Oh Say Can You See?', American Cultural Blinders On China" in Edward Friedman and Mark Selden, eds., **America's Asia: Dissenting Essays on Asian-American Relations** [New York: Random House, 1971; first publshed 1969].

David Kaimowitz, "The Role of Decentralization in the Recent Nicaraguan Agrarian Reform" in William C. Thiesenhusen, **Searching for Agrarian Reform in Latin America** [Boston: Unwin Hyman, 1989].

Mary Kaldor, "After the Cold War" **New Left Review** no. 180. 1990.

Michael Kammen, "The Historian's Vocation and the State of the Discipline in the

United States" in Michael Kammen, ed., **The Past Before Us: Contemporary Historical Writing in the United States** [Ithaca: Cornell University Press, 1980].

Antoni Kapcia, "What Went Wrong? The Sandinista Revolution" **Bulletin of Latin American Research** vol. 13. no. 3. 1994.

Terry Lynn Karl, "The Prospects for Democratization in El Salvador" **World Policy Journal** vol. 2. no. 2. 1985.

Terry Lynn Karl, "Democracy by Design: The Christian Democratic Party in El Salvador" in Giuseppe Di Palma and Laurence Whitehead, eds., **The Central American Impasse** [London: Croom Helm, 1986].

Terry Lynn Karl, "Mexico, Venezuela, and the Contadora Initiative" in Morris J. Blachman, William LeoGrande and Kenneth Sharpe, eds., **Confronting Revolution: Security Through Diplomacy in Central America** [New York: Pantheon, 1986].

Terry Lynn Karl and Richard R. Fagen, "The Logic of Hegemony: The United States as a Superpower in Central America" in Jan F. Triska, ed., **Dominant Powers and Subordinate States: The United States in Latin America and the Soviet Union in Eastern Europe** [Durham: Duke University Press, 1986].

Terry Lynn Karl, "El Salvador: Negotiations or Total War--Interview With Salvador Samayoa" **World Policy Journal** vol. 6. no. 2. 1989.

Terry Lynn Karl, "The Christian Democratic Party and the Prospects for Democratization in El Salvador" in Jan L. Flora and Edelberto Torres-Rivas, eds., **Sociology of "Developing Societies": Central America** [London: Macmillan, 1989].

Terry Lynn Karl, "Dilemmas of Democratization in Latin America" **Comparative Politics** vol. 23. no. 1. 1990.

Joshua Karliner, "Central America's Other War: The Environment Under Siege" **World Policy Journal** vol. 6. no. 4. 1988.

Michael T. Katzman, "The Brazilian Frontier in Comparative Perspective" **Comparative Studies in Society and History** vol. 17. 1975.

Ira Katznelson and Kenneth Prewitt, "Constitutionalism, Class and the Limits of Choice in US Foreign Policy" in Richard R. Fagen, ed., **Capitalism and the State in US-Latin American Relations** [Stanford: Stanford University Press, 1979].

Robert R. Kaufman, "Industrial Change and Authoritarian Rule in Latin America: A Concrete Review of the Bureaucratic-Authoritarian Model" in David Collier, ed., **The New Authoritarianism in Latin America** [Princeton: Princeton University Press, 1979].

Robert R. Kaufman, "Liberalization and Democratization in South America: Perspectives from the 1970s" in Guillermo O'Donnell, Philippe C. Schmitter and Laurence Whitehead, ed., **Transitions from Authoritarian Rule: Comparative Perspectives** [Baltimore: Johns Hopkins University Press, 1986].

Robert R. Kaufman, "How Societies Change Developmental Models or Keep Them: Reflections on the Latin American Experience in the 1930s and the Postwar World" in Gary Gereffi and Donald L. Wyman, eds., **Manufacturing Miracles: Paths of Industrialization in Latin America and East**

Asia [Princeton: Princeton University Press, 1990].

Cristobal Kay, "Reflections on the Latin American Contribution to Development Theory" **Development and Change** vol. 22. no. 1. 1991.

Harvey J. Kaye, "The Use and Abuse of the Past: The New Right and the Crisis of History" **The Socialist Register 1987** [London: Merlin Press, 1987].

Benjamin Keen, "Main Currents in United States Writings on Colonial Spanish America 1884-1984" **Hispanic American Historical Review** vol. 65. no. 4. 1985.

Charles W. Kegley, Jr., "Assumptions and Dilemmas in the Study of Americans' Foreign Policy Beliefs: A Caveat" **International Studies Quarterly: The Journal of the International Studies Association** vol. 30. no. 4. 1986.

Penn Kemble and Arturo J. Cruz, Jr., "How the Nicaraguan Resistance Can Win" **Commentary** vol. 82. no. 6. 1986.

Frank J. Kendrick, "The Nonmilitary Neutrality of Costa Rica" in Ralph Lee Woodward, Jr., ed., **Central America: Historical Perspectives on the Contemporary Crisis** [New York: Greenwood Press, 1988].

Henry C. Kenski, "Teaching Latin American Politics at American Universities: A Survey" **Latin American Research Review** vol. 10. no. 1. 1975.

Eldon Kenworthy, "The US and Latin America: Empire vs. Social Change" **Democracy** vol. 1. no. 3. 1981.

Eldon Kenworthy, "Reagan Rediscovers Monroe" **Democracy** vol. 2. no. 3. 1982.

Eldon Kenworthy, "Why the United States is in Central America" **Bulletin of the Atomic Scientists** vol. 39. no. 8. 1983.

Eldon Kenworthy, "Central America: Beyond the Credibility Trap" **World Policy Journal** vol. 1. no. 1. 1983.

Eldon Kenworthy, "Grenada as Theater" **World Policy Journal** vol. 1. no. 3. 1984.

Eldon Kenworthy, "Central America: Beyond the Credibility Trap" **World Policy Journal** vol. 1. no. 1. 1983; updated and reprinted in Kenneth M. Coleman and George C. Herring, eds., **The Central American Crisis: Sources of Conflict and the Failure of US Policy** [Wilmington: Scholarly Resources, 1985].

Eldon Kenworthy, "Central America's Lost Decade" in Jan Knippers Black, ed., **Latin America, Its Problems and Its Promise: A Multidisciplinary Introduction** [Boulder: Westview Press, second edition 1991].

Dermot Keogh, "The Myth of the Liberal Coup: The United States and the 15 October 1979 Coup in El Salvador" **Millennium: Journal of International Studies** vol. 13. no. 2. 1984.

James F. King and Samuel Everett, "Latin American History Textbooks" in Howard F. Cline, ed., **Latin American History: Essays on Its Study and Teaching 1898-1965** (2 vols.) [Austin: University of Texas Press, 1967].

John M. Kirk and George W. Schuyler, "Introduction" in John M. Kirk and George W. Schuyler, eds., **Central America: Democracy, Development and Change** [New York: Praeger, 1988].

Jeane J. Kirkpatrick, "Dictatorship and Double Standards" **Commentary** vol. 68. no. 5. 1979; reprinted in Jeane J. Kirkpatrick, **Dictatorship and Double**

Standards: Rationalism and Reason in Politics [Washington: American Enterprise Institute, 1982].

Jeane J. Kirkpatrick, "US Security and Latin America" **Commentary** vol. 71. no. 1. 1981; reprinted in Jeane J. Kirkpatrick, **Dictatorship and Double Standards: Rationalism and Reason in Politics** [Washington: American Enterprise Institute, 1982], also revised and reprinted in Howard J. Wiarda, ed., **Rift and Revolution: The Central American Imbroglio** [Washington: American Enterprise Institute, 1984].

Jeane J. Kirkpatrick, "The Reagan Phenomenon and the Liberal Tradition", "Ideas and Institutions", "Human Rights in El Salvador", "Human Rights in Nicaragua", "Managing Freedom", "Nicaragua and Her Neighbours", "Sandino Betrayed I" and "Sandino Betrayed II" in Jeane J. Kirkpatrick, **The Reagan Phenomenon--And Other Speeches on Foreign Policy** [Washington: American Enterprise Institute, 1983].

Jeane J. Kirkpatrick, "The Modernizing Imperative" **Foreign Affairs** vol. 72. no. 4. 1993.

Michael T. Klare and Cynthia Arnson, "Exporting Repression: US Support for Authoritarianism in Latin America" in Richard R. Fagen, ed., **Capitalism and the State in US-Latin American Relations** [Stanford: Stanford University Press, 1979].

Michael T. Klare, "Deadly Convergence: The Perils of the Arms Trade" **World Policy Journal** vol. 6. no. 1. 1988-89.

Michael T. Klare and Peter Kornbluh, "The New Interventionism: Low-Intensity Warfare in the 1980s and Beyond" in Michael T. Klare and Peter Kornbluh, eds., **Low Intensity Warfare: How the USA Fights Wars Without Declaring Them** [New York: Pantheon, 1988; reprinted London: Methuen, 1989].

Michael T. Klare, "The Interventionist Impulse: US Military Doctrine for Low-Intensity Warfare" in Michael T. Klare and Peter Kornbluh, eds., **Low Intensity Warfare: How the USA Fights Wars Without Declaring Them** [New York: Pantheon, 1988; reprinted London: Methuen, 1989].

Michael T. Klare, "Subterranean Alliances: America's Global Proxy Network" **Journal of International Affairs** vol. 43. no. 1. 1989.

Peter F. Klarén, "Lost Promise: Explaining Latin American Underdevelopment" in Peter F. Klarén and Thomas J. Bossert, eds., **Promise of Development: Theories of Change in Latin America** [Boulder: Westview Press, 1986].

Ignacio Klich, "Israel, the PLO and Nicaragua: The Kernel and the Shell" in Damian J. Fernandez, ed., **Central America and the Middle East: The Internationalization of the Crises** [Miami: Florida International University Press, 1990].

Merle Kling, "Towards a Theory of Power and Political Instability in Latin America" **Western Political Quarterly** vol. 9. no. 1. 1956; reprinted in John H. Kautsky, ed., **Political Change in Underdeveloped Countries: Nationalism and Communism** [New York: Wiley, fourth edition 1965; first published 1962].

Merle Kling, "The State of Research on Latin America: Political Science" in Charles

Wagley, ed., **Social Science Research on Latin America** [New York: Columbia University Press, 1964].

J. Jorge Klor de Alva, "The Postcolonization of the (Latin) American Experience: A Reconsideration of 'Colonialism', 'Postcolonialism' and 'Mestizaje'" in Gyan Prakash, ed., **After Colonialism: Imperial Histories and Postcolonial Displacements** [Princeton: Princeton University Press, 1995].

Alan Knight, "Social Revolution: A Latin American Perspective" **Bulletin of Latin American Research** vol. 9. no. 2. 1990.

Alan Knight, "Revisionism and Revolution: Mexico Compared to England and France" **Past and Present** no. 134. 1992.

Peter Kornbluh and Joy Hackel, "Low-Intensity Conflict: A Debate--Is It Live, or Is It Memorex?" **NACLA Report on the Americas** vol. 20. no. 3. 1984.

Peter Kornbluh, "The Covert War" in Thomas W. Walker, ed., **Reagan Versus the Sandinistas: The Undeclared War on Nicaragua** [Boulder: Westview Press, 1987].

Peter Kornbluh, "The Iran-Contra Scandal: A Postmortem" **World Policy Journal** vol. 5. no. 1. 1987-1988.

Peter Kornbluh, "Nicaragua: US Proinsurgency Warfare Against the Sandinistas" in Michael T. Klare and Peter Kornbluh, eds., **Low Intensity Warfare: How the USA Fights Wars Without Declaring Them** [New York: Pantheon, 1988; reprinted London: Methuen, 1989].

Francisco Villagran Kramer, "The Background to the Current Political Crisis in Central America" in Richard E. Feinberg, ed., **Central America: International Dimensions of the Crisis** [New York: Holmes and Meier, 1982].

Micahel L. Krenn, "Lions in the Woods: The United States Confronts Economic Nationalism in Latin America 1917-1929" in **Radical History Review** no. 33. 1985.

Ekkehart Krippendorf, "The Dominance of American Approaches in International Relations" **Millennium: Journal of International Studies** vol. 16. no. 2. 1987.

Clifton B. Kroeber, "The Tradition of Latin American History in the United States: A Preliminary View" [1953] in Howard F. Cline, ed., **Latin American History: Essays on Its Study and Teaching 1898-1965** (2 vols.) [Austin: University of Texas Press, 1967].

Heinrich W. Krumwiede, "Regimes and Revolution in Central America" in Wolf Grabendorff, Heinrich W. Krumwiede and Jorg Todt, eds., **Political Change in Central America: Internal and External Dimensions** [Boulder: Westview Press, 1984].

Heinrich W. Krumwiede, "Sandinist Democracy: Problems of Institutionalization" in Wolf Grabendorff, Heinrich W. Krumwiede and Jorg Todt, eds., **Political Change in Central America: Internal and External Dimensions** [Boulder: Westview Press, 1984].

Michael J. Kryzanek, "The Dominican Intervention Revisited: An Attitudinal and Operational Analysis" in John D. Martz, ed., **United States Policy in Latin America: A Quarter Century of Crisis and Challenge 1961-1986** [Lincoln: University of Nebraska Press, 1988].

Pedro Pablo Kuczynski, "Is Latin American Development Dead?: A View From the Mid-1980s" **LASA Forum** vol. 17. no. 4. 1987.

James R. Kurth, "Industrial Change and Political Change: A European Perspective" in David Collier, ed., **The New Authoritarianism in Latin America** [Princeton: Princeton University Press, 1979].

James R. Kurth, "The United States and Central America: Hegemony in Historical and Comparative Perspective" in Richard Feinberg, ed., **Central America: International Dimensions of the Crisis** [New York: Holmes and Meier, 1982].

James R. Kurth, "The New Realism in US-Latin American Relations: Principles for a New US Foreign Policy" in Richard S. Newfarmer, ed., **From Gunboats to Diplomacy: New US Policies for Latin America** [Baltimore: Johns Hopkins University Press, 1984].

James R. Kurth, "The United States, Latin America, and the World: The Changing International Context of US-Latin American Relations" in Kevin J. Middlebrook and Carlos Rico, eds., **The United States and Latin America in the 1980s: Contending Perspectives on a Decade of Crisis** [Pittsburgh: University of Pittsburgh Press, 1986].

James R. Kurth, "Economic Change and State Development" in Jan F. Triska, ed., **Dominant Powers and Subordinate States: The United States in Latin America and the Soviet Union in Eastern Europe** [Durham: Duke University Press, 1986].

Richard Allen LaBarge, "Impact of the United Fruit Company on the Economic Development of Guatemala 1946-1954" in Richard Allen LaBarge et al., **Studies in Middle American Economics** [New Orleans: Middle American Research Institute, Tulane University, 1968, publication no. 29.; first published 1960].

Ernesto Laclau, "Feudalism and Capitalism in Latin America" **New Left Review** no. 67. 1971; reprinted in Ernesto Laclau, **Politics and Ideology in Marxist Theory** [London: Verso 1979; first published 1977].

Walter LaFeber, "The Last War, The Next War and the New Revisionists" **Democracy** vol. 1 no. 1. 1981; reprinted in Marvin E. Gettleman, et al., eds., **El Salvador: Central America in the New Cold War** [New York: Grove Press, 1981].

Walter LaFeber, "Latin American Policy" in Robert A. Divine, ed., **Exploring the Johnson Years** [Austin: University of Texas Press, 1981].

Walter LaFeber, "Inevitable Revolutions" **The Atlantic Monthly** vol. 249. no. 6. 1982.

Walter LaFeber, "An Overview of Central America" **Bulletin of the Atomic Scientists** vol. 39. no. 8. 1983.

Walter LaFeber, "The Reagan Administration and Revolution in Central America" **Political Science Quarterly** vol. 99. no. 1. 1984.

Walter LaFeber, "The Burdens of the Past" in Robert S. Leiken, ed., **Central America: Anatomy of Conflict** [New York: Pergamon Press, 1984].

Walter LaFeber, "The Reagan Policy in Historical Perspective" in Kenneth M. Coleman and George C. Herring, eds., **The Central American Crisis: Sources of Conflict and the Failure of US Policy** [Wilmington: Scholarly Resources, 1985].

Walter LaFeber, "The Evolution of the Monroe Doctrine from Monroe to Reagan" in Lloyd C. Gardner, ed., **Redefining the Past: Essays in Diplomatic History in Honor of William Appleman Williams** [Corvallis: Oregon State University Press, 1986].

Walter LaFeber, "Four Themes and an Irony" in John M. Kirk and George W. Schuyler, eds., **Central America: Democracy, Development and Change** [New York: Praeger, 1988].

Gustavo Lagos and Alberto Van Klaveren, "Inter-American Relations in Global Perspective" in John D. Martz and Lars Schoultz, eds., **Latin America, the United States and the Inter-American System** [Boulder: Westview Press, 1980].

Bolivar Lamounier, "Brazil: Inequality Against Democracy" in Larry Diamond, Juan J. Linz and Seymour Martin Lipset, eds., **Democracy in Developing Countries--Volume Four: Latin America** [Boulder: Lynne Rienner, 1989].

Saul Landau, "Asking the Right Questions About Cuba" in Philip Brenner, William LeoGrande, Donna Rich and Daniel Siegel, eds., **The Cuba Reader: The Making of a Revolutionary Society** [New York: Grove Press, 1989].

David Landes and Patricia Flynn, "Dollars for Dictators: US Aid in Central America and the Caribbean" in Roger Burbach and Patricia Flynn, eds., **The Politics of Intervention: The United States in Central America** [New York: Monthly Review Press, 1984].

William L. Langer, "A Critique of Imperialism" **Foreign Affairs** vol. 14. no. 1. 1935.

Lester D. Langley, "Military Commitments in Latin America 1960-1968" **Current History: A World Affairs Journal** vol. 56. no. 334. 1969.

Lester D. Langley, "The Diplomatic Historians: Bailey and Bemis" **The History Teacher** vol. 6. no. 1. 1972.

Lester D. Langley, "Fire Down Below: A Review Essay on the Central American Crisis" **Diplomatic History** vol. 9. no. 2. 1985.

Lester D. Langley, "The United States and Latin America in the Eisenhower Era" **Diplomatic History** vol. 14. no. 2. 1990.

Brooke Larson, "Rural Rhythms of Class Conflict in Eighteenth Century Cochabamba" **Hispanic American Historical Review** vol. 60. 1980.

Christopher Lasch, "Consensus: An Academic Question?" **The Journal of American History** vol. 76. no. 2. 1989.

Latin American Studies Association (LASA), "Suggested Guidelines for the Relations Between US Scholars and Universities and Latin American Scholars and Universities Under Repressive Regimes" reprinted as Appendix I in Jan Knippers Black, ed., **Latin America: Its Problems and Its Promises** [Boulder: Westview Press, 1984].

Latin American Studies Association (LASA), "Nicaragua Report Stirs Controversy" **LASA Forum** vol. 16. no. 1. 1985.

Latin American Studies Association (LASA), "International Commission of the Latin American Studies Association to Observe the February 25 1990 Nicaraguan Election: Interim Report December 15 1989" **LASA Forum** vol. 20. no. 4. 1990.

Latin American Studies Association (LASA), "US Government Officials Respond to

LASA Statement on Murder of Jesuit Priests" **LASA Forum** vol. 21. no. 1. 1990.

Margaret E. Leahy, "The Harrassment of Nicaraguanists and Fellow Travelers" in Thomas W. Walker, ed., **Reagan Versus the Sandinistas: The Undeclared War on Nicaragua** [Boulder: Westview Press, 1987].

Michael A. Ledeen and William H. Lewis, "Carter and the Fall of the Shah: The Inside Story" **Washington Quarterly: A Review of Strategic and International Issues** vol. 3. no. 2. 1980.

Robert S. Leiken, "Eastern Winds in Latin America" **Foreign Policy** no. 42. 1981.

Robert S. Leiken, "Can the Cycle Be Broken?" in Robert S. Leiken, ed., **Central America: Anatomy of Conflict** [New York: Pergamon Press, 1984].

Robert S. Leiken, "The Salvadoran Left" in Robert S. Leiken, ed., **Central America: Anatomy of Conflict** [New York: Pergamon Press, 1984].

William M. LeoGrande, "The Revolution in Nicaragua: Another Cuba?" **Foreign Affairs** vol. 58. no. 1. 1979.

William M. LeoGrande, "Party Development in Revolutionary Cuba" **Journal of Interamerican Studies and World Affairs** vol. 21. no. 4. 1979; abridged and reprinted in Philip Brenner, William LeoGrande, Donna Rich and Daniel Siegel, eds., **The Cuba Reader: The Making of a Revolutionary Society** [New York: Grove Press, 1989].

William M. LeoGrande, "The Evolution of Nonalignment" **Problems of Communism** vol. 29. no. 1. 1980.

William M. LeoGrande, "Cuban-Soviet Relations and Cuban Policy in Africa" **Cuban Studies** vol. 10. no. 1. 1980.

William M. LeoGrande and Carole Ann Robbins, "Oligarchs and Officers: The Crisis in El Salvador" **Foreign Affairs** vol. 58. no. 5. 1980.

William M. LeoGrande, "Cuba's Policy in Africa" extracted from William M. LeoGrande, **Cuba's Policy in Africa 1959-1980** [Berkeley: University of California Press, 1980] and reprinted in Philip Brenner, William LeoGrande, Donna Rich and Daniel Siegel, eds., **The Cuba Reader: The Making of a Revolutionary Society** [New York: Grove Press, 1989].

William M. LeoGrande, "Mass Political Participation in Socialist Cuba" in John A. Booth and Mitchell A. Seligson, eds., **Political Participation in Latin America: Citizen and State** [New York: Holmes and Meier, 1981]; abridged and reprinted in Philip Brenner, William LeoGrande, Donna Rich and Daniel Siegel, eds., **The Cuba Reader: The Making of a Revolutionary Society** [New York: Grove Press, 1989].

William M. LeoGrande, "A Splendid Little War: Drawing the Line in El Salvador" **International Security** vol. 6. no. 1. 1981; reprinted in Marvin E. Gettleman, Patrick Lacefield, Louis Menashe, David Mermelstein and Ronald Radosh, eds., **El Salvador: Central America in the New Cold War** [New York: Grove Press, 1981].

William M. LeoGrande, "Cuba Policy Recycled" **Foreign Policy** no. 46. 1982.

William M. LeoGrande, "The United States and the Nicaraguan Revolution" in Thomas W. Walker, ed., **Nicaragua in Revolution** [New York: Praeger, 1982].

William M. LeoGrande, "US Policy Options in Central America" Richard R. Fagen and Olga Pellicer, eds., **The Future of Central America: Policy Choices for the US and Mexico** [Stanford: Stanford University Press, 1983].

William M. LeoGrande, "Through the Looking Glass: The Kissinger Report on Central America" **World Policy Journal** vol. 1. no. 2. 1984.

William M. LeoGrande, "Cuba: Going to the Source" in Richard S. Newfarmer, ed., **From Gunboats to Diplomacy: New US Policies for Latin America** [Baltimore: Johns Hopkins University Press, 1984]. (This article was originally published as "Cuba Policy Recycled" **Foreign Policy** no. 46. 1982.)

William M. LeoGrande, "Cuba" in Morris J. Blachman, William M. LeoGrande and Kenneth Sharpe, eds., **Confronting Revolution: Security Through Diplomacy in Central America** [New York: Pantheon, 1986].

William M. LeoGrande, Douglas C. Bennett, Morris J. Blachman and Kenneth E. Sharpe "Grappling with Central America: From Carter to Reagan" in Morris J. Blachman, William M. LeoGrande and Kenneth Sharpe, eds., **Confronting Revolution: Security Through Diplomacy in Central America** [New York: Pantheon, 1986].

William M. LeoGrande, "The Contras and Congress" in Thomas W. Walker, ed., **Reagan Versus the Sandinistas: The Undeclared War on Nicaragua** [Boulder: Westview Press, 1987].

William M. LeoGrande, "Roll-back or Containment?: The United States, Nicaragua and the Search for Peace in Central America" **International Security** vol. 11. no. 2. 1986; reprinted in Bruce M. Bagley, ed., **Contadora and the Diplomacy of Peace in Central America--vol. 1: The United States, Central America and Contadora.** [Boulder: Westview Press, 1987].

William M. LeoGrande, "Central America: Counterinsurgency Revisited" **NACLA Report on the Americas** vol. 21. no. 1. 1987.

William M. LeoGrande, "El Salvador after Duarte--Interview with Rubén Zamora" **World Policy Journal** vol. 5. no. 4. 1988.

William M. LeoGrande, "Regime Illegitmacy and Revolutionary Movements: Central America" in Barry M. Schutz and Robert O. Slater, eds., **Revolution and Political Change in the Third World** [Boulder: Lynne Rienner, 1990].

William M. LeoGrande, "After the Battle of San Salvador: Breaking the Deadlock" **World Policy Journal** vol. 7. no. 2. 1990.

William M. LeoGrande, "From Reagan to Bush: The Transition in US Policy Towards Central America" **Journal of Latin American Studies** vol. 22. no. 3. 1990.

William M. LeoGrande, "Political Parties and Postrevolutionary Politics in Nicaragua" in Louis W. Goodman, William M. LeoGrande, and Johanna Mendelson Forman, eds., **Political Parties and Democracy in Central America** [Boulder: Westview Press, 1992].

Thomas M. Leonard, "The United States and Central America 1955-1960" **The Valley Forge Journal: A Record of Patriotism and American Culture** vol. 3. no. 1. 1986.

Thomas M. Leonard, "'Keeping the Europeans Out': The United States and Central

America Since 1823" in Ralph Lee Woodward Jr., ed., **Central America: Historical Perspectives on the Contemporary Crisis** [New York: Greenwood Press, 1988].

Thomas M. Leonard, "Search for Security: The United States and Central America in the Twentieth Century" **The Americas: A Quarterly Review of Inter-American Cultural History** vol. 47. no. 4. 1991.

Richard W. Leopold, "The History of United States Foreign Policy: Past, Present and Future" in Charles F. Delzell, ed., **The Future of History** [Nashville: Vanderbilt University Press, 1977].

Richard W. Leopold, "Historians and American Foreign Policy: An Encyclopedic Endeavor" **Pacific Historical Review** vol. 50. no. 3. 1981.

Penny Lernoux, "Revolution and Counterrevolution in the Central American Church" in Donald E. Schulz and Douglas H. Graham, eds., **Revolution and Counterrevolution in Central America and the Caribbean** [Boulder: Westview, 1984].

Barry B. Levine, "A Return to Innocence?: The Social Construction of the Geopolitical Climate of the Post-Invasion Caribbean" **Journal of Interamerican Studies and World Affairs** vol. 31. no. 3. 1989.

Daniel H. Levine, "Venezuela: The Nature, Sources, and Future Prospects of Democracy" in Larry Diamond, Juan J. Linz and Seymour Martin Lipset, eds., **Democracy in Developing Countries--Volume Four: Latin America** [Boulder: Lynne Rienner, 1989].

Daniel H. Levine, "Constructing Culture and Power" in Daniel H. Levine, ed., **Constructing Culture and Power in Latin America** [Ann Arbor: University of Michigan Press, 1993].

Jerome I. Levinson, "After the Alliance for Progress: Implications for Inter-American Relations" in Douglas A. Chalmers, ed., **Changing Latin America: New Interpretations of Its Politics and Society** [New York: Academcy of Political Science, Columbia University, 1972].

Daniel C. Levy, "LASA's Election Coverage: Reflections and Suggestions" **LASA Forum** vol. 16. no. 4. 1986.

Daniel C. Levy, "Mexico: Sustained Civilian Rule Without Democracy" in Larry Diamond, Juan J. Linz and Seymour Martin Lipset, eds., **Democracy in Developing Countries--Volume Four: Latin America** [Boulder: Lynne Rienner, 1989].

James R. Levy, "Background to the Crisis in Central America" **World Review** vol. 21. no. 4. 1982.

James R. Levy, "Towards an Understanding of US Policy in Central America" in James R. Levy, ed., **Crisis in Central America** [Kensington: School of Spanish and Latin American Studies, University of New South Wales, 1984].

James R. Levy, "Nicaragua: The Revolution Pending" **Third World Update** vol. 1. no. 1. 1986.

Jim Levy and Peter Ross, "A Common History?: Two Latin Americanists View the Writing of US History in Hemispheric Perspective" **Australasian Journal of American Studies** vol. 12. no. 1. 1993.

David Levering Lewis, "Radical History: Toward Inclusiveness" **The Journal of American History** vol. 76. no. 2. 1989.

Colin Leys, "Samuel Huntington and the End of Classical Modernization Theory" in

Hamza Alavi and Teodor Shanin, eds., **Introduction to the Sociology of Developing Societies** [London: Macmillan Press, 1982, reprinted 1983].

Ronald T. Libby, "Listen to the Bishops" **Foreign Policy** no. 52. 1983.

Edwin Lieuwen, "Bryce Wood (1909-1986)" **Hispanic American Historical Review** vol. 67. no. 1. 1987.

Edwin Lieuwen, "The Changing Role of the Military in Latin America" in Howard F. Cline, ed., **Latin American History: Essays on Its Study and Teaching 1898-1965** (2 vols.) [Austin: University of Texas Press, 1967].

Marc Lindenberg, "Central America: Crisis and Economic Strategy 1930-1985, Lessons from History" **The Journal of Developing Areas** vol. 22. no. 2. 1988.

Marc Lindenberg, "World Economic Cycles and Central American Political Instability" **World Politics** vol. 42. no. 3. 1990.

Sol M. Linowitz, "Latin America: The President's Agenda" **Foreign Affairs** vol. 67. no. 2. 1988/1989.

Juan Linz and Alfred Stepan, "Political Crafting of Democratic Consolidation or Destruction: European and South American Comparisons" in Robert A. Pastor, ed., **Democracy in the Americas: Stopping the Pendulum** [New York: Holmes and Meier, 1989].

Leslie M. Lipson, "Vietnam, Western Europe, Latin America: Where Do Our Vital Interests Lie?" in Paul Seabury and Aaron Wildavsky, eds., **US Foreign Policy: Perspectives and Proposals for the 1970s** [New York: McGraw-Hill, 1969]; reprinted in Robert W. Gregg and Charles W. Kegley, eds., **After Vietnam: The Future of American Foreign Policy** [Garden City: Doubleday, 1971].

Eduardo Lizano, "Prospects for Regional Economic Integration" in William Ascher and Ann Hubbard, eds., **Central American Recovery and Development: Task Force Report to the International Commission for Central American Recovery and Development** [Durham: Duke University Press, 1989].

Francis L. Loewenheim, "A Legacy of Hope and a Legacy of Doubt: Reflections on the Role of History and Historians in American Foreign Policy Since the Eighteenth Century" in Francis L. Loewenheim, ed., **The Historian and the Diplomat: The Role of History and Historians in American Foreign Policy** [New York: Harper and Row, 1967].

George A. Lopez and Michael Stohl, "Introduction" and "Liberalization and Redemocratization in Latin America: The Search for Models and Meanings" in George A. Lopez and Michael Stohl, eds., **Liberalization and Redemocratization in Latin America** [New York: Greenwood Press, 1987].

Joseph L. Love, "Raúl Prebisch and the Origins of the Doctrine of Unequal Exchange" **Latin American Research Review** vol. 15. no. 3. 1980.

Joseph L. Love, "The Origins of Dependency Analysis" **Journal of Latin American Studies** vol. 22. no. 1. 1990.

W. George Lovell, "Resisting Conquest: Development and the Guatemalan Indian" in John M. Kirk and George W. Schuyler, eds., **Central America: Democracy, Development and Change** [New York: Praeger, 1988].

W. George Lovell, "Surviving Conquest: The Maya of Guatemala in Historical Perspective" **Latin American Research Review** vol. 23. no. 2. 1988.

Brian Loveman, "The Political Left in Chile 1973-1990" in Barry Carr and Steve Ellner, eds., **The Latin American Left: From the Fall of Allende to Perestroika** [Boulder: Westview Press, 1993].

Abraham F. Lowenthal, "The Dominican Republic: The Politics of Chaos" in A. Van Lazar and Robert R. Kaufman, eds., **Reform and Revolution: Readings in Latin American Politics** [Boston: Allyn and Bacon, 1969].

Abraham F. Lowenthal, "The United States and the Dominican Republic to 1965: Background to Intervention" **Caribbean Studies** vol. 10. no. 2. 1970.

Abraham F. Lowenthal, "The Political Role of the Dominican Armed Forces: A Note on the 1963 Overthrow of Juan Bosch and on the 1965 Dominican Revolution" **Journal of Interamerican Studies and World Affairs** vol. 15. no. 3. 1973; reprinted in Abraham F. Lowenthal, ed., **Armies and Politics in Latin America** [New York: Holmes and Meier, 1976], also reprinted in Abraham F. Lowenthal, ed., **Armies and Politics in Latin America** [New York: Holmes and Meier, revised edition 1986; first published 1976].

Abraham F. Lowenthal, "United States Policy Towards Latin America: 'Liberal', 'Radical' and 'Bureaucratic' Perspectives" **Latin American Research Review** vol. 8. no. 3. 1973; revised and reprinted as Abraham F. Lowenthal, "'Liberal', 'Radical' and 'Bureaucratic' Perspectives on US Latin American Policy: The Alliance for Progress in Retrospect" in Julio Cotler and Richard R. Fagen, eds., **Latin America and the United States: The Changing Political Realities** [Stanford: Stanford University Press, 1974].

Abraham F. Lowenthal, "Peru's Ambiguous Revolution" **Foreign Affairs** vol. 52. no. 4. 1974.

Abraham F. Lowenthal, "Armies and Politics in Latin America" **World Politics** vol. 27. no. 1. 1974; reprinted in Abraham F. Lowenthal, ed., **Armies and Politics in Latin America** [New York: Holmes and Meier, 1976], also reprinted in Abraham F. Lowenthal, ed., **Armies and Politics in Latin America** [New York: Holmes and Meier, revised edition 1986; first published 1976].

Abraham F. Lowenthal, "The United States and Latin America: Ending the Hegemonic Presumption" **Foreign Affairs** vol. 55. no. 1. 1976.

Abraham F. Lowenthal, "Cuba's African Adventure" **International Security** vol. 2. no. 1. 1977.

Abraham F. Lowenthal and Milton Charlton, "The United States and Panama: Confrontation or Cooperation?" **American Enterprise Institute (Foreign Policy and) Defense Review** vol. 1. no. 4. 1977.

Abraham F. Lowenthal, "Latin America: A Not So Special Relationship" **Foreign Policy** no. 32. 1978.

Abraham F. Lowenthal, "Changing Patterns in Inter-American Relations" **Washington Quarterly: A Review of Strategic and International Issues** vol. 4. no. 1. 1981.

Abraham F. Lowenthal, "Ronald Reagan and Latin America: Coping With

Hegemony in Decline" in Kenneth A. Oye, Robert J. Lieber and Donald S. Rothchild, eds., **Eagle Defiant?: United States Foreign Policy in the 1980s** [Boston: Little Brown, 1983].

Abraham F. Lowenthal, "The Peruvian Experiment Reconsidered" in Cynthia McClintock and Abraham F. Lowenthal, eds., **The Peruvian Experiment Reconsidered** [Princeton: Princeton University Press, 1983].

Abraham F. Lowenthal, "Research in Latin America and the Caribbean on International Relations and Foreign Policy: Some Impressions" **Latin American Research Review** vol. 18. no. 1. 1983.

Abraham F. Lowenthal, "Changing the Agenda" **Foreign Policy** no. 52. 1983.

Abraham F. Lowenthal, "The Insular Caribbean as a Crucial Test for US Policy" in H. Michael Erisman, ed., **The Caribbean Challenge: US Policy in a Volatile Region** [Boulder: Westview Press, 1984].

Abraham F. Lowenthal, "The United States and Central America: Reflections on the Kissinger Commission Report" in Kenneth M. Coleman and George C. Herring, eds. **The Central American Crisis: Sources of Conflict and the Failure of US Policy** [Wilmington: Scholarly Resources, 1985].

Abraham F. Lowenthal, "Rethinking US Interests in the Western Hemisphere" **Journal of Interamerican Studies and World Affairs** vol. 29. no. 1. 1987.

Abraham F. Lowenthal, "The United States and South America" **Current History: A World Affairs Journal** vol. 87. no. 525. 1988.

Abraham F. Lowenthal, "The United States, Central America and the Caribbean" in John D. Martz, ed., **United States Policy in Latin America: A Quarter Century of Crisis and Challenge 1961-1986** [Lincoln: University of Nebraska Press, 1988].

Abraham F. Lowenthal, "Rediscovering Latin America" **Foreign Affairs** vol. 69. no. 4. 1990.

Abraham F. Lowenthal, "Latin America: Ready for Partnership?" **Foreign Affairs** vol. 72. no. 1. 1993.

Ilja A. Luciak, "Democracy in the Nicaraguan Countryside: A Comparative Analysis of Sandinista Grassroots Movements" **Latin American Perspectives** vol. 17. no. 3. 1990.

William H. Luers, "US Interests in Central America" **American Enterprise Institute Foreign Policy and Defense Review** vol. 5. no. 1. 1984.

William H. Luers, "The Soviets and Latin America: A Three-Decade US Policy Triangle" **Washington Quarterly: A Review of Strategic and International Studies** vol. 7. no. 1. 1984.

Christopher H. Lutz and W. George Lovell, "Core and Periphery in Colonial Guatemala" in Carol A. Smith, ed., **Guatemalan Indians and the State 1540 to 1988** [Austin: University of Texas Press, 1990].

Alan H. Luxenberg, "Did Eisenhower Push Castro into the Arms of the Soviets?" **Journal of Interamerican Studies and World Affairs** vol. 30. no. 1. 1988.

Charles S. Maier, "Marking Time: The Historiography of International Relations" in Michael Kammen ed., **The Past Before Us: Contemporary Historical Writing in the United States** [Ithaca: Cornell University

Press, 1980].
Joseph Maier, "The Problem of Color in Foreign Relations" in Joseph Maier and Richard W. Weatherhead, eds., **Politics of Change in Latin America** [New York: Praeger, 1964].
Joseph Maier and Richard W. Weatherhead, "Introduction" in Joseph Maier and Richard W. Weatherhead, eds., **The Future of Democracy in Latin America: Essays by Frank Tannenbaum** [New York: Alfred A. Knopf, 1974].
Joseph Maier and Richard W. Weatherhead, "Frank Tannenbaum 1893-1969" in Joseph Maier and Richard W. Weatherhead, eds., **The Future of Democracy in Latin America: Essays by Frank Tannenbaum** [New York: Alfred A. Knopf, 1974].
Luis Maira, "The US Debate on the Central American Crisis" in Richard R. Fagen and Olga Pellicer, eds., **The Future of Central America: Policy Choices for the US and Mexico** [Stanford: Stanford University Press, 1983].
Luis Maira, "Reagan and Central America: Strategy Through a Fractured Lens" in Martin Diskin, ed., **Trouble in Our Backyard: Central America and the United States in the 1980s** [New York: Pantheon, 1983].
Luis Maira, "Authoritarianism in Central America: A Comparative Perspective" in Giuseppe Di Palma and Laurence Whitehead, eds., **The Central American Impasse** [London: Croom Helm, 1986].
Florencia E. Mallon, "Dialogues Among the Fragments: Retrospect and Prospect" in Frederick Cooper, Allen F. Isaacman, Florencia E. Mallon, William Roseberry and Steve J. Stern, **Confronting Historical Paradigms: Peasants, Labor, and the Capitalist World System in Africa and Latin America** [Madison: University of Wisconsin Press, 1993].
Florencia E. Mallon, "The Promise and Dilemma of Subaltern Studies: Perspectives from Latin American History" **American Historical Review** vol. 99. no. 5. 1994.
Richard D. Mallon, "The Influence of Raúl Prebisch on Argentine Economic Policy-Making 1950-1962: A Comment" **Latin American Research Review** vol. 23. no. 2. 1988.
Beatriz Manz, "The Transformation of La Esperanza, an Ixcan Village" in Robert M. Carmack, ed., **Harvest of Violence: The Maya Indians and the Guatemalan Crisis** [Norman: University of Oklahoma Press, 1988].
Peter E. Marchetti, "War, Popular Participation and Transition to Socialism: The Case of Nicaragua" in Richard R. Fagen, Carmen Diana Deere and Jose Luis Coraggio, eds., **Transition and Development: Problems of Third World Socialism** [New York: Monthly Review Press, 1986, PACCA/CRIES].
Frederick W. Marks III, "The CIA and Castillo Armas in Guatemala, 1954: New Clues to an Old Puzzle" **Diplomatic History** vol. 14. no. 1. 1990.
Michael T. Martin, "The Current Economic Crisis and the Caribbean/Central American Periphery: US International Economic Policy During the Republican Administration of 1981 to 1984" in Michael T. Martin and Terry R. Kandal, eds., **Studies of Development and Change in the Modern World** [New York: Oxford University Press, 1989].

Michael T. Martin, "On Culture Politics and the State in Nicaragua: An Interview with Padre Ernesto Cardenal, Minister of Culture" **Latin American Perspectives** vol. 16. no. 2. 1989.

Mario Solorzano Martínez, "Guatemala: Between Authoritarianism and Democracy" in Giuseppe Di Palma and Laurence Whitehead, eds., **The Central American Impasse** [London: Croom Helm, 1986].

John D. Martz, "Political Science and Latin American Studies: A Discipline in Search of a Region" **Latin American Research Review** vol. 6. no. 1. 1971.

John D. Martz, "Ecuador: Authoritarianism, Personalism and Dependency" in Howard J. Wiarda and Harvey F. Kline, eds., **Latin American Politics and Development** [Boston: Houghton, Mifflin, 1979].

John D. Martz, "Democracy and the Imposition of Values: Definitions and Diplomacy" in John D. Martz and Lars Schoultz, eds., **Latin America, the United States and the Inter-American System** [Boulder: Westview Press, 1980].

John D. Martz, "The Quest for Popular Democracy in Ecuador" **Current History: A World Affairs Journal** vol. 78. no. 454. 1980.

John D. Martz, "Ideology and Oil: Venezuela in the Circum-Caribbean" in H. Michael Erisman and John D. Martz, ed., **Colossus Challenged: The Struggle for Caribbean Influence** [Boulder: Westview Press, 1982].

John D. Martz and David J. Myers, "Understanding Latin American Politics: Analytic Models and Intellectual Traditions" (1983) in Howard J. Wiarda, ed., **Politics and Social Change in Latin America: Still a Distinct Tradition?** [Boulder: Westview Press, 1992].

John D. Martz, "Latin America and the Caribbean" in Robert Wesson, ed., **Democracy: A Worldwide Survey** [New York: Praeger, 1987].

John D. Martz, "Introduction" in John D. Martz, ed., **United States Policy in Latin America: A Quarter Century of Crisis and Challenge 1961-1986** [Lincoln: University of Nebraska Press, 1988].

John D. Martz, "Images, Intervention and the Cause of Democracy" in John D. Martz, ed., **United States Policy in Latin America: A Quarter Century of Crisis and Challenge 1961-1986** [Lincoln: University of Nebraska Press, 1988].

John D. Martz, "National Security and Politics: The Colombian-Venezuelan Border" **Journal of Interamerican Studies and World Affairs** vol. 30. no. 4. 1988/89.

John D. Martz, "Political Science and Latin American Studies: Patterns and Asymmetries of Research and Publication" **Latin American Research Review** vol. 25. no. 1. 1990.

John D. Martz, "Colombia at the Crossroads" **Current History: A World Affairs Journal** vol. 90. no. 553. 1991.

Herbert L. Matthews, "Diplomatic Relations" in Herbert L. Matthews, ed., **The United States and Latin America** [New York: Columbia University-American Assembly, 1959].

Robert Matthews, "The Limits of Friendship: Nicaragua and the West" **NACLA Report on the Americas** vol. 19. no. 3. 1985.

Robert Matthews, "Sowing Dragon's Teeth: The US War Against Nicaragua"

NACLA Report on the Americas vol. 20. no. 4. 1986.

Philip Mauceri, "Nine Cases of Transitions and Consolidations" in Robert A. Pastor, ed., **Democracy in the Americas: Stopping the Pendulum** [New York: Holmes and Meier, 1989].

Ernest R. May, "The Decline of Diplomatic History" in George A. Billias and Gerald N. Grobs, eds., **American History: Retrospect and Prospect** [New York: Free Press, 1971].

Ernest R. May, "The 'Bureaucratic-Politics' Approach: US-Argentine Relations 1942-1947" in Julio Cotler and Richard R. Fagen, eds., **Latin America and the United States: The Changing Political Realities** [Stanford: Stanford University Press, 1974].

Charles William Maynes, "America's Third World Hangups" **Foreign Policy** no. 71. 1988.

Ali A. Mazrui, "From Social Darwinism to Current Theories of Modernization: A Tradition of Analysis" **World Politics** vol. 21. no. 1. 1968.

Richard L. McCall, "From Monroe to Reagan: An Overview of US-Latin American Relations" in Richard Newfarmer, ed., **From Gunboats to Diplomacy: New US Policies for Latin America** [Baltimore: Johns Hopkins University Press, 1985; first printed 1984].

Richard L. McCall, "The Alliance for Progress: An Appraisal" in William Ascher and Ann Hubbard, eds., **Central American Recovery and Development: Task Force Report to the International Commission for Central American Recovery and Development** [Durham: Duke University Press, 1989].

Cynthia McClintock, "Peru: Precarious Regimes, Authoritarian and Democratic" in Larry Diamond, Juan J. Linz and Seymour Martin Lipset, eds., **Democracy in Developing Countries--Volume Four: Latin America** [Boulder: Lynne Rienner, 1989].

Cynthia McClintock, "The Prospects for Democratic Consolidation in a 'Least Likely' Case: Peru" **Comparative Politics** vol. 21. no. 2. 1989.

Michael McClintock, "US Military Assistance to El Salvador: From Indirect to Direct Intervention" **Race and Class** vol. 26. no. 3. 1985.

Thomas J. McCormick, "The State of American Diplomatic History" in Herbert J. Bass, ed., **The State of American History** [Chicago: Quadrangle Books, 1970].

Thomas J. McCormick, "Drift or Mastery? A Corporatist Synthesis for American Diplomatic History" in Stanley I. Kutler and Stanley N. Katz, ed., **The Promise of American History: Progress and Prospects** [Baltimore: Johns Hopkins University Press, 1982].

Thomas J. McCormick, "Every System Needs a Center Sometimes: An Essay on Hegemony and Modern American Foreign Policy" in Lloyd C. Gardner, ed., **Redefining the Past: Essays in Diplomatic History in Honor of William Appleman Williams** [Corvallis: Oregon State University Press, 1986].

Alfred W. McCoy, "Philippine American Relations: A Problem of Perception" **The Australasian Journal of America Studies** vol. 6. no. 2. 1987.

Jennifer L. McCoy, "Nicaragua in Transition" **Current History: A World Affairs Journal** vol. 90. no. 554. 1991.

David McCreery, "State Power, Indigenous Communities and Land in the Nineteenth-Century Guatemala, 1820-1920" in Carol A. Smith, ed., **Guatemalan Indians and the State 1540 to 1988** [Austin: University of Texas Press, 1990].

Ronald H. McDonald, "Redemocratization in Uruguay" in George A. Lopez and Michael Stohl, eds., **Liberalization and Redemocratization in Latin America** [New York: Greenwood Press, 1987].

William J. McDonough, "US Foreign Assistance Strategy for Latin America" in David S. Smith, ed., **Prospects for Latin America** [New York: Columbia University, International Fellows Program Policy Series, 1970].

Robert J. McMahon, "United States Relations with Asia in the Twentieth Century: Retrospect and Prospect" in Gerald K. Haines and J. Samuel Walker, eds., **American Foreign Relations: An Historiographical Review** [London: Pinter, 1981].

Robert J. McMahon, "Interpreting America's Failures in the Third World" **Diplomatic History** vol. 15. no. 1. 1991.

J. Lloyd Mecham, "Federal Intervention in Mexico" in A. Curtis Wilgus, ed., **Hispanic American Essays** [Chapel Hill: University of North Carolina Press, 1942; reprinted Freeport: Books for Libraries Press, 1970].

J. Lloyd Mecham, "Latin American Constitutions: Nominal or Real" in Harvey Kebschull, ed., **Politics in Transitional Societies** [New York: Appleton-Century-Crofts, 1973].

Richard A. Melanson, "The Grenada Intervention: Prelude to a New Consensus?" in Richard A. Melanson and Kenneth W. Thompson, eds., **Foreign Policy and Domestic Consensus** [New York: University Press of America, 1985].

Constantine C. Menges, "Public Policy and Organized Business in Chile: A Preliminary Analysis" **Journal of International Affairs** vol. 20. no. 2. 1966.

Constantine C. Menges, "Central America and its Enemies" **Commentary** vol. 72. no. 2. 1981.

Contantine C. Menges, "The United States and Latin America in the 1980s" in Prosser Gifford, ed., **The National Interest of the United States in Foreign Policy: Seven Discussions at the Wilson Center, December 1980-February 1981** [Washington: University Press of America, 1981].

Gilbert Merkx, "The Washington Policy Process: Implications for Latin American Studies" **LASA Newsletter** vol. 12. no. 4. 1982.

Gilbert Merkx, "Research Manpower Needs for Latin America and the Caribbean: An Assessment" **LASA Forum** vol. 15. no. 3. 1984.

Gilbert Merkx, "Title VI Accomplishments, Problems and New Directions" **LASA Forum** vol. 21. no. 2. 1990.

Gilbert Merkx and Deborah Jakubs, "Task Force on Scholarly Resources Report: Crisis in Foreign Periodicals Acquistions" **LASA Forum** vol. 21. no. 4. 1991.

Charles A. Meyer, "US Military Assistance Policy Toward Latin America" **Department of State Bulletin** no. 61. August 4. 1969; reprinted in Helen Delpar, ed., **The Borzoi Reader in Latin American History--**

volume 2: The Nineteenth and Twentieth Centuries [New York: Alfred A. Knopf, 1972].

Lorenzo Meyer, "Democracy from Three Latin American Perspectives" in Robert A. Pastor, ed., **Democracy in the Americas: Stopping the Pendulum** [New York: Holmes and Meier, 1989].

Michael C. Meyer, "Edwin Lieuwen (1923-1986)" **Hispanic American Historical Review** vol. 69. no. 1. 1989.

Victor Meza, "Honduras: The War Comes Home--The Military, Willing to Deal" **NACLA Report on the Americas** vol. 22. no. 1. 1988.

Kevin J. Middlebrook and Carlos Rico, "The United States and Latin America in the 1980s: Change, Complexity and Contending Perspectives" in Kevin J. Middlebrook and Carlos Rico, eds., **The United States and Latin America in the 1980s: Contending Perspectives on a Decade of Crisis** [Pittsburgh: University of Pittsburgh Press, 1986].

Sara Miles, "The Real War: Low-Intensity Conflict in Central America" **NACLA Report on the Americas** vol. 20. no. 2. 1986.

Sara Miles and Bob Ostertag, "D'Aubisson's New ARENA" **NACLA Report on the Americas** vol. 23. no. 2. 1989.

Sara Miles and Bob Ostertag, "FMLN New Thinking" **NACLA Report on the Americas** vol. 23. no. 3. 1989.

Sara Miles and Bob Ostertag, "El Salvador: The Offensive in Perspective" **NACLA Report on the Americas** vol. 23. no. 6. 1990.

Hubert J. Miller, "Catholic Leaders and Spiritual Socialism during the Arévalo Administration in Guatemala 1945-1951" in Ralph Lee Woodward, Jr., ed., **Central America: Historical Perspectives on the Contemporary Crisis** [New York: Greenwood Press, 1988].

Richard L. Millett, "Central American Paralysis" **Foreign Policy** no. 39. 1980.

Richard L. Millett, "The Politics of Violence: Guatemala and El Salvador" **Current History: A World Affairs Journal** vol. 80. no. 463. 1981.

Richard L. Millett, "The United States and Latin America" **Current History: A World Affairs Journal** vol. 83. no. 490. 1984.

Richard L. Millett, "From Somoza to the Sandinistas: The Roots of Revolution in Nicaragua" in Wolf Grabendorff, Heinrich W. Krumwiede and Jorg Todt, eds., **Political Change in Central America: Internal and External Dimensions** [Boulder: Westview Press, 1984].

Richard L. Millett, "Historical Setting" in James A. Rudolph, ed., **Honduras: A Country Study** [Washington: Foreign Area Studies, American University and the US Department of the Army, 1984].

Richard L. Millett, "The Central American Region" in Jan Knippers Black, ed., **Latin America: Its Problems and Its Promise** [Boulder: Westview Press, 1984].

Richard L. Millett, "Praetorians or Patriots? The Central American Military" in Robert S. Leiken, ed., **Central America: Anatomy of Conflict** [New York: Pergamon Press, 1984]; revised, updated and reprinted as Richard L. Millett, "The Central American Militaries" in Abraham F. Lowenthal, ed., **Armies and Politics in Latin America** [New York: Holmes and Meier, revised edition 1986; first published 1976].

Richard L. Millett, "Honduras: An Emerging Dilemma" in Richard S. Newfarmer, ed., **From Gunboats to Diplomacy: New US Policies for Latin America** [Baltimore: Johns Hopkins University Press, 1984].

Richard L. Millett, "The United States and Central American: A Policy Adrift" **Current History: A World Affairs Journal** vol. 87. no. 533. 1988.

Richard L. Millett, "An Unclear Menace: US Perceptions of Soviet Strategy in Latin America" in Eusebio Mujal-Leon, ed., **The USSR and Latin America: A Developing Relationship** [Boston: Unwin Hyman, 1989].

Richard L. Millett, "Limited Hopes and Fears in Guatemala" **Current History: A World Affairs Journal** vol. 90. no. 554. 1991.

Richard L. Millett, "Central America: Background to the Crisis" in Jan Knippers Black, ed., **Latin America, Its Problems and Its Promise: A Multidisciplinary Introduction** [Boulder: Westview Press, second edition 1991].

Richard L. Millett, "Politicized Warriors: The Military and Central American Politics" in Louis W. Goodman, William M. LeoGrande, and Johanna Mendelson Forman, eds., **Political Parties and Democracy in Central America** [Boulder: Westview Press, 1992].

Christopher Mitchell, "Dominance and Fragmentation in US Latin American Policy" in Julio Cotler and Richard R. Fagen, eds., **Latin America and the United States: The Changing Political Realities** [Stanford: Stanford University Press, 1974].

Christopher Mitchell, "Introduction" in Christopher Mitchell, ed., **Changing Perspectives in Latin American Studies: Insights from Six Disciplines** [Stanford: Stanford University Press, 1988].

Michael Moffitt, "Shocks, Deadlocks, and Scorched Earth: Reaganomics and the Decline of US Hegemony" in Michael T. Martin and Terry R. Kandal, eds., **Studies of Development and Change in the Modern World** [New York: Oxford University Press, 1989].

Tommie Sue Montgomery, "Liberation and Revolution: Christianity as a Subversive Activity in Central America" in Martin Diskin, ed., **Trouble in Our Backyard: Central America and the United States in the 1980s** [New York: Pantheon, 1983].

Tommie Sue Montgomery, "El Salvador: The Roots of Revolution" in Steve C. Ropp and James Morris, eds., **Central America: Crisis and Adaptation** [Albuquerque: University of New Mexico Press, 1984].

Tommie Sue Montgomery, "Armed Struggle and Popular Resistance in El Salvador: The Struggle for Peace" in Barry Carr and Steve Ellner, eds., **The Latin American Left: From the Fall of Allende to Perestroika** [Boulder: Westview Press, 1993].

Parker Thomas Moon, "'Self Defense' and 'Unselfish Service' in the Caribbean" in Chester Lloyd Jones et al., **The United States and the Caribbean** [Chicago: University of Chicago Press, 1929, second edition 1934].

Marilyn B. Moors, "Indian Labor and the Guatemalan Crisis: Evidence from History and Anthropology" in Ralph Lee Woodward Jr., ed., **Central America: Historical Perspectives on the Contemporary Crisis** [New York: Greenwood Press, 1988].

Theodore Moran, "The Cost of Alternative US Policies Toward El Salvador 1984-1989" in Robert S. Leiken, ed., **Central America: Anatomy of**

Conflict [New York: Pergamon Press, 1984].

Dario Moreno, "Peace and the Nicaraguan Revoluton" **Current History: A World Affairs Journal** vol. 87. no. 533. 1988.

Dario Moreno, "Thunder on the Left: Radical Critiques of US Central American Policy" **Latin American Research Review** vol. 26. no. 3. 1991.

Morris H. Morley, "The US Imperial State in Cuba 1952-1958: Policymaking and Capitalist Interests" **Journal of Latin American Studies** vol. 14. no. 1. 1982.

Morris H. Morley, "Violence and Terror in American Foreign Policy in the 1980s: A Framework for Analysing Low Intensity Conflict" in Barry Carr and Elaine McKay, eds., **Low Intensity Conflict: Theory and Practice in Central America and South-East Asia** [Melbourne: La Trobe University Institute of Latin American Studies and Monash University Centre of Southeast Asian Studies, 1988].

Magnus Morner, "The Study of Latin American History Today" **Latin American Research Review** vol. 8. no. 2. 1973.

J. P. Morray, "The United States and Latin America" in James Petras and Maurice Zeitlin, eds., **Latin America: Reform and Revolution?: A Reader** [Greenwich: Fawcett Publications, 1968]; reprinted in Gustav Ranis, ed., **The United States and the Developing Economies** [New York: W. W. Norton, revised edition 1973].

James A. Morris and Steve C. Ropp, "Corporatism and Dependent Development: A Honduran Case Study" **Latin American Research Review** vol. 12. no. 2. 1977.

James A. Morris, "Honduras: The Burden of Survival in Central America" in Steve C. Ropp and James A. Morris, eds., **Central America: Crisis and Adaptation** [Albuquerque: University of New Mexico Press, 1984].

Rising Lake Morrow, "A Conflict Between the Commercial Interests of the United States and Its Foreign Policy" **Hispanic American Historical Review** vol. 10. no. 1. 1930.

Richard M. Morse, "The Heritage of Latin America" in Louis Hartz, ed., **The Founding of New Societies: Studies in the History of the United States, Latin America, South Africa, Canada and Australia** [New York: Harcourt, Brace and World, 1964].

Richard M. Morse, "The Strange Career of 'Latin-American Studies'" **Annals of the American Academy of Political and Social Science** vol. 356. 1964.

Richard M. Morse, "Toward a Theory of Spanish American Government" **Journal of the History of Ideas** vol. 15. 1964; reprinted in Howard J. Wiarda, ed., **Politics and Social Change in Latin America: Still a Distinct Tradition?** [Boulder: Westview Press, 1992].

Richard M. Morse, "Language as a Key to Latin American Historiography" in Howard F. Cline, ed., **Latin American History: Essays on Its Study and Teaching 1898-1965** (2 vols.) [Austin: University of Texas Press, 1967].

Richard M. Morse, "The Care and Grooming of Latin American Historians: Or Stop the Computer I Want to Get Off" in Stanley R. Ross, ed., **Latin America in Transition: Problems in Training and Research** [Albany: State

University of New York Press, 1970].

Richard M. Morse, "Claims of Political Tradition" in Richard M. Morse, **New World Soundings: Culture and Ideology in the Americas** [Baltimore: Johns Hopkins University Press, 1989]; reprinted in Howard J. Wiarda, ed., **Politics and Social Change in Latin America: Still a Distinct Tradition?** [Boulder: Westview Press, 1992].

Rex Mortimer, "Futurology and the Third World: Beyond the Limits of Liberalism" in Rex Mortimer, **Stubborn Survivors: Dissenting Essays on Peasants and Third World Development** (edited by H. Feith and R. Tiffen) [Melbourne: Centre of Southeast Asian Studies, 1984].

Rex Mortimer, "Wallerstein, Dependency, Passion and Vision: The Search for Class in the Capitalist Periphery" in Rex Mortimer, **Stubborn Survivors: Dissenting Essays on Peasants and Third World Development** (edited by H. Feith and R. Tiffen) [Melbourne: Centre of Southeast Asian Studies, 1984].

Louis Morton, "The Cold War and American Scholarship" in Francis L. Loewenheim, ed., **The Historian and the Diplomat: The Role of History and Historians in American Foreign Policy** [New York: Harper and Row, 1967].

Bernard Moses, "The Neglected Half of American History" in Lewis Hanke, ed., **Do the Americas Have a Common History?: A Critique of the Bolton Theory** [New York: Alfred A. Knopf, 1964].

Sanford A. Mosk, "Latin America versus the United States" in Lewis Hanke, ed., **Do the Americas Have a Common History?: A Critique of the Bolton Theory** [New York: Alfred A. Knopf, 1964].

Ambler H. Moss, Jr., "The Panama Treaties: How an Era Ended" **Latin American Research Review** vol. 21. no. 3. 1986.

George Mosse, "New Left Intellectuals/New Left Politics" in Paul Buhle, ed. **History and the New Left: Madison, Wisconsin 1950-1970** [Philadelphia: Temple University Press, 1990].

David P. Mozingo, "Containment in Asia Reconsidered" **World Politics** vol. 19. no. 3. 1967; reprinted in Burton M. Sapin, ed., **Contemporary American Foreign and Military Policy** [Glenview: Scott Foresman, 1970].

John Mueller, "The Cold War Consensus: From Fearful Hostility to Wary Contempt" in Richard A. Melanson and Kenneth W. Thompson, eds., **Foreign Policy and Domestic Consensus** [New York: University Press of America, 1985].

Eusebio Mujal-Leon, "Introduction" in Eusebio Mujal-Leon, ed., **The USSR and Latin America: A Developing Relationship** [Boston: Unwin Hyman, 1989].

Eusebio Mujal-Leon, "Conclusion" in Eusebio Mujal-Leon, ed., **The USSR and Latin America: A Developing Relationship** [Boston: Unwin Hyman, 1989].

Gerardo L. Munck, "Between Theory and History and Beyond Traditional Area Studies: A New Comparative Perspective on Latin America" **Comparative Politics** vol. 25. no. 4. 1993.

Ronaldo Munck, "Imperialism and Dependency: Recent Debates and Old Dead-Ends" **Latin American Perspectives** vol. 8. nos. 3-4. 1981; reprinted in Ronald

H. Chilcote, ed., **Dependency and Marxism: Toward a Resolution of the Debate** [Boulder: Westview Press, 1982].

Ronaldo Munck, "Farewell to Socialism?: A Comment on Recent Debates" **Latin American Perspectives** vol. 17. no. 2. 1990.

Heraldo Muñoz, "Introduction: The Various Roads to Development" in Heraldo Muñoz, ed., **From Dependency to Development: Strategies to Overcome Underdevelopment and Inequality** [Boulder: Westview Press, 1981].

Heraldo Muñoz, "The Strategic Dependency of the Centers and the Economic Importance of the Latin American Periphery" in Heraldo Muñoz, ed., **From Dependency to Development: Strategies to Overcome Underdevelopment and Inequality** [Boulder: Westview Press, 1981].

Heraldo Muñoz, "Beyond the Malvinas Crisis: Perspectives on Inter-American Relations" **Latin American Research Review** vol. 19. no. 1. 1984.

Dana G. Munro, "The Establishment of Peace in Nicaragua" **Hispanic American Historical Review** vol. 11. no. 4. 1933.

Dana G. Munro, "Relations Between Central America and the United States" **International Conciliation** no. 296. 1934.

Dana G. Munro, "The Mexico City Conference and the Inter-American System" **US Department of State Bulletin** vol. 12. no. 301. 1945.

Dana G. Munro, "Dollar Diplomacy in Nicaragua 1909-1913" **Hispanic American Historical Review** vol. 38. no. 2. 1958.

Dana G. Munro, "The American Withdrawal From Haiti 1929-1934" **Hispanic American Historical Review** vol. 49 no. 1. 1969.

Alun Munslow, "Andrew Carnegie and the Discourse of Cultural Hegemony" **Journal of American Studies** vol. 22. no. 2. 1988.

Joshua Muravchik, "Reading the Barometer: Sea Change in the Senate" **Washington Quarterly: A Review of Strategic and International Issues** vol. 3. no. 4. 1980.

Joshua Muravchik, "The Nicaragua Debate" **Foreign Affairs** vol. 65. no. 2. 1986/87.

Joshua Muravchik, "The Slow Road to Communism" in Mark Falcoff and Robert Royal, eds., **The Continuing Crisis: US Policy in Central America and the Caribbean--Thirty Essays by Statesmen, Scholars, Religious Leaders and Journalists** [Washington: Ethics and Public Policy Center and Lanham: University Press of America, 1987].

Allan Nairn, "Endgame: US Military Strategy in Central America" **NACLA Report on the Americas** vol. 18. no. 3. 1984.

Allan Nairn, "Low-Intensity Conflict: A Debate--One Hit, Two Misses" **NACLA Report on the Americas** vol. 20. no. 3. 1984.

Robert A. Naylor, "Research Opportunities: Mexico and Central America" in Howard F. Cline, ed., **Latin American History: Essays on Its Study and Teaching 1898-1965** (2 vols.) [Austin: University of Texas Press, 1967].

Martin C. Needler, "Political Development and Military Intervention in Latin America" **American Political Science Review** vol. 60. no. 3. 1966.

Martin C. Needler, "Political Development and Socioeconomic Development: The Case of Latin America" **American Political Science Review** vol. 62. no. 3. 1968.

Martin C. Needler and Thomas W. Walker, "The Current Status of Latin American Studies Programs" **Latin American Research Review** vol. 6. no. 1. 1971.

Martin C. Needler, "Toward a Reappraisal of United States Foreign Policy in Latin America After Vietnam" in Robert W. Gregg and Charles W. Kegley, eds., **After Vietnam: The Future of American Foreign Policy** [Garden City: Doubleday, 1971].

Martin C. Needler, "The Influence of American Institutions in Latin America" **Annals of the American Academy of Political and Social Science** vol. 428. 1976.

Jorge Nef, "Canada and Latin America: Solitudes in Search of a Paradigm" in Jorge Nef, ed., **Canada and the Latin American Challenge** [Guelph: O.C.P.L.A.C.S., 1978].

Jorge Nef, "Pentagonism, Trilateralism and Military Withdrawal in Latin America" in David H. Pollock and A. R. M. Ritter, eds., **Latin American Prospects for the '80s: What Kinds of Development? Deformation, Reformation or Transformation?** [Ottawa: Norman Patterson School of International Affairs, Carleton University, 1981].

Jorge Nef, "Latin American and Caribbean Studies in Canada: A Developmental Perspective" **Canadian Journal of Development Studies** vol. 3. no. 1. 1982.

Jorge Nef, "The Trend Toward Democratization and Redemocratization in Latin America: Shadow and Substance" **Latin American Research Review** vol. 23. no. 3. 1988.

Jorge Nef, "'Normalization', Popular Struggles and the Receiver State" in Jan Knippers Black, ed., **Latin America, Its Problems and Its Promise: A Multidisciplinary Introduction** [Boulder: Westview Press, second edition, 1991].

Jorge Nef, "The Political Economy of Inter-American Relations: A Structural and Historical Overview" in Richard Stubbs and Geoffrey R. D. Underhill, eds., **Political Economy and the Changing Global Order** [London: Macmillan, 1994].

Richard S. Newfarmer, "Introduction: Issues in the Americas" in Richard S. Newfarmer, ed., **From Gunboats to Diplomacy: New US Policies for Latin America** [Baltimore: Johns Hopkins University Press, 1984].

Richard S. Newfarmer, "US Economic Policy Toward Latin America: The Deepening Problem" in Richard S. Newfarmer, ed., **From Gunboats to Diplomacy: New US Policies for Latin America** [Baltimore: Johns Hopkins University Press, 1984].

Richard S. Newfarmer and Richard E. Feinberg, "The Caribbean Basin Initiative: Bold Plan or Empty Promise?" in Richard S. Newfarmer, ed., **From Gunboats to Diplomacy: New US Policies for Latin America** [Baltimore: Johns Hopkins University Press, 1984].

Richard S. Newfarmer, "The Economics of Strife" in Morris J. Blachman, William LeoGrande and Kenneth Sharpe, eds., **Confronting Revolution: Security Through Diplomacy in Central America** [New York: Pantheon, 1986].

Ann-Sofie Nilsson, "Swedish Social Democracy in Central America: The Politics of

Small State Solidarity" **Journal of Interamerican Studies and World Affairs** vol. 33. no. 3. 1991.

Frank Ninkovich, "The Rockefeller Foundation, China, and Cultural Change" **Journal of American History** vol. 70. no. 4. 1984.

Frank Ninkovich, "Interests and Discourse in Diplomatic History" **Diplomatic History** vol. 13. no. 2. 1989.

Richard Nixon, "American Foreign Policy: The Bush Agenda" **Foreign Affairs** vol. 68. no. 1. 1989.

David W. Noble, "William Appleman Williams and the Crisis of Public History" in Lloyd C. Gardner, ed., **Redefining the Past: Essays in Diplomatic History in Honor of William Appleman Williams** [Corvallis: Oregon State University Press, 1986].

David W. Noble, "The Reconstruction of Progress: Charles Beard, Richard Hofstadter, and Postwar Historical Thought" in Lary May, ed., **Recasting America: Culture and Politics in the Age of the Cold War** [Chicago: University of Chicago Press, 1989].

J. F. Normans, "Changes in Latin American Attitudes" **Foreign Affairs** vol. 11. no. 1. 1932.

Lüsa L. North, "Democratization in El Salvador: Illusion or Reality?" in John M. Kirk and George W. Schuyler, eds., **Central America: Democracy, Development and Change** [New York: Praeger, 1988].

Chris Norton, "Shadow Play: Central America's Untold Stories--Build and Destroy" **NACLA Report on the Americas** vol. 19. no. 6. 1985.

Henry K. Norton, "The United States in the Caribbean" in Chester Lloyd Jones et al., **The United States and the Caribbean** [Chicago: University of Chicago Press, 1929, second edition 1934].

Michael Novak, "El Salvador: Rule by Ballot" **Orbis: A Journal of World Affairs** vol. 26. no. 2. 1982.

Richard A. Nuccio, "Reagan and Congress: Consensus and Conflict in Central American Policy" in Bruce M. Bagley, ed., **Contadora and the Diplomacy of Peace in Central America--vol. 1: The United States, Central America and Contadora** [Boulder: Westview Press, 1987].

Orlando Nuñez Soto, "The Third Social Force in National Liberation Movements" **Latin American Perspectives** vol. 8. no. 2. 1981.

Orlando Nuñez Soto, "Ideology and Revolutionary Politics in Transitional Societies" in Richard R. Fagen, Carmen Diana Deere and Jose Luis Coraggio, eds., **Transition and Development: Problems of Third World Socialism** [New York: Monthly Review Press, 1986, PACCA/CRIES].

Joseph S. Nye, Jr., "The Domestic Environment of US Policymaking" in Arnold L. Horelick, ed., **US-Soviet Relations: The Next Phase** [Ithaca: Cornell University Press, for the Rand/UCLA Center for the Study of Soviet International Behavior, 1986].

Donal Cruise O'Brien, "Modernization, Order, and the Erosion of a Democratic Ideal: American Political Science 1960-1970" in David Lehmann, ed., **Development Theory: Four Critical Essays** [London: Frank Cass, 1979].

Philip O'Brien, "Authoritarianism and the New Orthodoxy: The Political Economy of the Chilean Regime 1973-1982" in Philip O'Brien and Paul Cammack, eds., **Generals in Retreat: The Crisis of Military Rule in Latin America** [Manchester: Manchester University Press, 1985].

Guillermo A. O'Donnell, "Modernization and Military Coups: Theory, Comparisons and the Argentine Case" in Abraham F. Lowenthal, ed., **Armies and Politics in Latin America** [New York: Holmes and Meier, 1976]; also reprinted in Abraham F. Lowenthal, ed., **Armies and Politics in Latin America** [New York: Holmes and Meier, revised edition 1986; first published 1976].

Guillermo A. O'Donnell, "Corporatism and the Question of the State" in James M. Malloy, ed., **Authoritarianism and Corporatism in Latin America** [Pittsburgh: University of Pittsburgh Press, 1977].

Guillermo A. O'Donnell, "Reflections on the Patterns of Change in the Bureaucratic-Authoritarian State" **Latin American Research Review** vol. 13. no. 1. 1978.

Guillermo O'Donnell, "State and Alliances in Argentina" **Journal of Development Studies** vol. 15. no. 1. 1978.

Guillermo O'Donnell, "Tensions in the Bureaucratic-Authoritarian State and the Question of Democracy" in David Collier, ed., **The New Authoritarianism in Latin America** [Princeton: Princeton University Press, 1979]; reprinted in Peter F. Klarén and Thomas J. Bossert, eds., **Promise of Development: Theories of Change in Latin America** [Boulder: Westview Press, 1986].

Guillermo O'Donnell, "The United States, Latin America, Democracy: Variations on a Very Old Theme" in Kevin J. Middlebrook and Carlos Rico, eds., **The United States and Latin America in the 1980s: Contending Perspectives on a Decade of Crisis** [Pittsburgh: University of Pittsburgh Press, 1986].

Guillermo O'Donnell, "Introduction to the Latin American Cases" in Guillermo O'Donnell, Philippe C. Schmitter and Laurence Whitehead, ed., **Transitions from Authoritarian Rule: Latin America** [Baltimore: Johns Hopkins University Press, 1986].

Guillermo O'Donnell, "Transitions to Democracy: Some Navigation Instruments" in Robert A. Pastor, ed., **Democracy in the Americas: Stopping the Pendulum** [New York: Holmes and Meier, 1989].

Adele Ogden, "A Bibliography of the Writings of Herbert Eugene Bolton" in Adele Ogden, ed., **Greater America: Essays in Honour of Herbert Eugene Bolton** [Berkeley: University of California Press, 1945; reprinted Freeport: Books for Libraries Press, 1968].

J. C. M. Ogelsby, "Latin American Studies in Canada" **Latin American Research Review** vol. 2. no. 1. 1966.

Carl Oglesby, "Vietnamese Crucible: An Essay on the Meaning of the Cold War" in Carl Oglesby and Richard Shaull, eds., **Containment and Change** [London: Macmillan, 1970; first published 1967].

Edmundo O'Gorman, "Do the Americas Have a Common History? (1941)" in Lewis Hanke, ed., **Do the Americas Have a Common History?: A Critique of the Bolton Theory** [New York: Alfred A. Knopf, 1964].

Mario Ojeda, "Mexican Policy Toward Central America in the Context of US-

Mexican Relations" in Richard R. Fagen and Olga Pellicer, eds., **The Future of Central America: Policy Choices for the US and Mexico** [Stanford: Stanford University Press, 1983].

Trish O'Kane, "Nicaragua: Haunted by the Past--The New Old Order" **NACLA Report on the Americas** vol. 24. no. 1. 1990.

Mancur Olson, "Dictatorship, Democracy and Development" **American Political Science Review** vol. 87. no. 3. 1993.

Marvin Ortega, "Workers' Participation in the Management of Agro-Enterprises of the APP" **Latin American Perspectives** vol. 12 no. 2. 1985.

Laura Nuzzi O'Shaughnessy, "Redemocratization in Mexico: The Unique Challenge" in George A. Lopez and Michael Stohl, eds., **Liberalization and Redemocratization in Latin America** [New York: Greenwood Press, 1987].

J. Gregory Oswald, "Contemporary Soviet Research on Latin America" **Latin American Research Review** vol. 1. no. 2. 1966.

Stuart Ozer, "Back from the Future: Notes on the Central American Movement" **Socialist Review** vol. 16. no. 2. 1986.

Robert A. Packenham, "Capitalist Dependency and Socialist Dependency: The Case of Cuba" in Jan F. Triska, ed., **Dominant Powers and Subordinate States: The United States in Latin America and the Soviet Union in Eastern Europe** [Durham: Duke University Press, 1986].

Alfonso Bauer Paiz, "The 'Third Government of the Revolution' and Imperialism in Guatemala" **Science and Society** vol. 34. no. 2. Summer 1970.

David Scott Palmer, "Military Governments and US Policy: General Concerns and Central American Cases" **American Enterprise Institute Foreign Policy and Defense Review** vol. 4. no. 2. 1982.

Dick Parker, "Trade Union Struggle and the Left in Latin America 1973-1990" in Barry Carr and Steve Ellner, eds., **The Latin American Left: From the Fall of Allende to Perestroika** [Boulder: Westview Press, 1993].

James J. Parsons, "The Contribution of Geography to Latin American Studies" in Charles Wagley, ed., **Social Science Research on Latin America** [New York: Columbia University Press, 1964].

Robert A. Pastor, "Our Real Interests in Central America" **The Atlantic Monthly** vol. 250. no. 1. 1982.

Robert A. Pastor, "The Target and the Source: El Salvador and Nicaragua" **Washington Quarterly: A Review of Strategic and International Issues** vol. 5. no. 3. 1982.

Robert A. Pastor, "Sinking in the Caribbean Basin" **Foreign Affairs** vol. 60. no. 5. 1982.

Robert A. Pastor, "Cuba and the Soviet Union: Does Cuba Act Alone?" in Barry B. Levine, ed., **The New Cuban Presence in the Caribbean** [Boulder: Westview Press, 1983]; abridged and reprinted in Philip Brenner, William LeoGrande, Donna Rich and Daniel Siegel, eds., **The Cuba Reader: The Making of a Revolutionary Society** [New York: Grove Press, 1989].

Robert A. Pastor, "A Question of US National Interests in Central America" in Wolf Grabendorff, Heinrich W. Krumwiede and Jorg Todt, eds., **Political Change in Central America: Internal and External Dimensions** [Boulder: Westview Press, 1984].

Robert A. Pastor, "Continuity and Change in US Foreign Policy: Carter and Reagan on El Salvador" **Journal of Policy Analysis and Management** vol. 3. no. 2. 1984.

Robert A. Pastor, "Explaining US Policy Toward the Caribbean Basin" **World Politics** vol. 38. no. 3. 1986.

Robert A. Pastor, "The Reagan Administration and Latin America: Eagle Insurgent" in Kenneth A. Oye, Robert J. Lieber and Donald Rothchild, eds., **Eagle Resurgent?: The Reagan Era in American Foreign Policy** [Boston: Little Brown, 1987].

Robert A. Pastor, "The Carter Administration and Latin America: A Test of Principle" in John D. Martz, ed., **United States Policy in Latin America: A Quarter Century of Crisis and Challenge 1961-1986** [Lincoln: University of Nebraska Press, 1988].

Robert A. Pastor, "Securing a Democratic Hemispheric" **Foreign Policy** no. 73. 1988-1989.

Robert A. Pastor, "Forging a Hemispheric Bargain: The Bush Opportunity" **Journal of International Affairs** vol. 43. no. 1. 1989.

Robert A. Pastor, "Introduction: The Swing of the Pendulum" in Robert A. Pastor, ed., **Democracy in the Americas: Stopping the Pendulum** [New York: Holmes and Meier, 1989].

Robert A. Pastor, "How to Reinforce Democracy in the Americas: Seven Proposals" in Robert A. Pastor, ed., **Democracy in the Americas: Stopping the Pendulum** [New York: Holmes and Meier, 1989].

Robert A. Pastor, "Nicaragua's Choice: The Making of a Free Election" **Journal of Democracy** vol. 1. no. 3. 1990.

Robert A. Pastor, "The Bush Administration and Latin America: The Pragmatic Style and the Regionalist Option" **Journal of Interamerican Studies and World Affairs** vol. 33. no. 3. 1991.

Thomas G. Paterson, "Historical Memory and Illusive Victories: Vietnam and Central America" **Diplomatic History** vol. 12. no. 1. 1988.

Richard Pattee, "A Revisionist Approach to Hispanic American Studies" in Howard F. Cline, ed., **Latin American History: Essays on Its Study and Teaching 1898-1965** (2 vols.) [Austin: University of Texas Press, 1967].

Jerry E. Patterson, "Hiram Bingham 1875-1956" **Hispanic American Historical Review** vol. 37. no. 1. 1957.

Benjamin D. Paul and William J. Demarest, "The Operation of a Death Squad in San Pedro la Laguna" in Robert M. Carmack, ed., **Harvest of Violence: The Maya Indians and the Guatemalan Crisis** [Norman: University of Oklahoma Press, 1988].

Walter A. Payne, "The Guatemalan Revolution 1944-1954: An Interpretation" **The Pacific Historian** vol. 17. no. 1. 1973.

Michael N. Pearson, "Introduction" in Michael N. Pearson and Blair B. Kling, eds., **The Age of Partnership: Europeans in Asia before Dominion** [Honolulu: University of Hawaii Press, 1979].

Neale J. Pearson, "Some Central American Perceptions and Positions in the Face of Big and Middle Power Politics in the Caribbean" in H. Michael Erisman and John D. Martz, ed., **Colossus Challenged: The Struggle for Caribbean Influence** [Boulder: Westview Press, 1982].

James Peck, "The Roots of Rhetoric: The Professional Ideology of America's China Watchers" in Edward Friedman and Mark Selden, eds., **America's Asia: Dissenting Essays on Asian-American Relations** [New York: Random House, 1971; first publshed 1969].

John A. Peeler, "Democracy and Elections in Central America: Autumn of the Oligarchs?" in John A. Booth and Mitchell A. Seligson, eds., **Elections and Democracy in Central America** [Chapel Hill: University of North Carolina Press, 1989].

Olga Pellicer, "Mexico in Central America: The Difficult Exercise of Regional Power" in Richard R. Fagen and Olga Pellicer, eds., **The Future of Central America: Policy Choices for the US and Mexico** [Stanford: Stanford University Press, 1983].

Gabriel Aguilera Peralta, "Terror and Violence as Weapons of Counter-Insurgency in Guatemala" **Latin American Perspectives** vol. 7. nos. 2-3. 1980.

Gustavo Pérez Firmat, "Introduction: Cheek to Cheek" in Gustavo Pérez Firmat, ed., **Do the Americas Have a Common Literature?** [Durham: Duke University Press, 1990].

Gustavo Pérez Firmat, "The Strut of the Centipede: José Lezama Lima and New World Exceptionalism" in Gustavo Pérez Firmat, ed., **Do the Americas Have a Common Literature?** [Durham: Duke University Press, 1990].

Louis A. Pérez, Jr., "Supervision of a Protectorate: The United States and the Cuban Army 1898-1908" **Hispanic American Historical Review** vol. 52. no. 2. 1972.

Louis A. Pérez, Jr., "Scholarship and the State: Notes on 'A History of the Cuban Republic'" **Hispanic American Historical Review** vol. 54. no. 4. 1974.

Louis A. Pérez, Jr., "Intervention, Hegemony, and Dependency: The United States in the Circum-Caribbean 1898-1980" **Pacific Historical Review** vol. 51. no. 2. 1982.

Louis A. Pérez, Jr., "Toward Dependency and Revolution: The Political Economy of Cuba Between Wars 1878-1895" **Latin American Research Review** vol. 18. no. 1. 1983.

Louis A. Pérez, Jr., "Armies of the Caribbean: Historical Perspectives, Historiographical Trends" **Latin American Perspectives** vol. 14. no. 4. 1987.

Bradford Perkins, "The Tragedy of American Diplomacy: Twenty-Five Years After" **Reviews in American History** vol. 12. no. 1. 1984; reprinted in Lloyd C. Gardner, ed., **Redefining the Past: Essays in Diplomatic History in Honor of William Appleman Williams** [Corvallis: Oregon State University Press, 1986].

Dexter Perkins, "Bringing the Monroe Doctrine up to Date" **Foreign Affairs** vol. 20. no. 2. 1942.

Betty Petras and James Petras, "Ballots into Bullets: Epitaph for a Peaceful Revolution" **Ramparts** vol. 12. no. 4. 1973; reprinted in Ronald H. Chilcote and Joel C. Edelstein, eds., **Latin America: The Struggle with Dependency and Beyond** [New York: Wiley, 1974].

James Petras, "United States Business and American Foreign Policy in Latin America" **New Politics** vol. 4. no. 4. 1967.

James Petras, "Patterns of Intervention: US Foreign Policy and Business in Latin America" in Marvin Surkin and Alan Wolfe, eds., **An End to Political Science: The Caucus Papers** [New York: Basic Books, 1970].

James Petras, "The United States and the New Equilibrium in Latin America", "US Business and Foreign Policy in Latin America", "Latin American Studies in the US: A Critical Assessment", "US Policy Toward Agrarian Reform" and "Pentagonism: A Substitute for Imperialism" in James Petras, **Politics and Social Structure in Latin America** [New York: Monthly Review Press, 1970].

James Petras, "Socialism in One Island!: A Decade of Cuban Revolutionary Government" **Politics and Society** vol. 1. no. 2. 1971.

James Petras, " Political and Social Change in Chile" and "Chile: Nationalization, Socioeconomic Change and Popular Participation" in James Petras, ed., **Latin America: From Dependence to Revolution** [New York: Wiley, 1973].

James Petras and Thomas Cook, "Dependency and the Industrial Bourgeoisie: Attitudes of Argentine Executives Toward Foreign Economic Investments and US Policy" and "Politics in a Nondemocratic State: The Argentine Industrial Elite" in James Petras, ed., **Latin America: From Dependence to Revolution** [New York: Wiley, 1973].

James Petras, H. Michael Erisman and Charles Mills, "The Monroe Doctrine and US Hegemony in Latin America" in James Petras, ed., **Latin America: From Dependence to Revolution** [New York: Wiley, 1973].

James Petras and Robert LaPorte, Jr., "US Response to Economic Nationalism in Chile" in James Petras, ed., **Latin America: From Dependence to Revolution** [New York: Wiley, 1973].

James Petras and Kent Trachte, "Liberal, Structural and Radical Approaches to Political Economy: An Assessment and an Alternative" in James Petras, ed., **Critical Perspectives on Imperialism and Social Class in the Third World** [New York: Monthly Review Press, 1978].

James Petras and Morris H. Morley, "The Venezuelan Development 'Model' and US Policy" in James Petras, ed., **Critical Perspectives on Imperialism and Social Class in the Third World** [New York: Monthly Review Press, 1978].

James F. Petras and Morris H. Morley, "The US Imperial State" **Review** (Fernand Braudel Center for the Study of Economies, Historical Systems and Civilizations) vol. 4. no. 2. 1980.

James Petras, "Nicaragua: The Transition to a New Society" **Latin American Perspectives** vol. 8. no. 2. 1981.

James Petras, "Dependency and World System Theory: A Critique and New Directions" **Latin American Perspectives** vol. 8. nos. 3-4. 1981; reprinted in Ronald H. Chilcote, ed., **Dependency and Marxism: Toward a Resolution of the Debate** [Boulder: Westview Press, 1982].

James F. Petras and Morris H. Morley, "Supporting Repression: US Policy and the Demise of Human Rights in El Salvador 1979-1981" **The Socialist Register 1981** [London: Merlin Press, 1981].

James F. Petras and Morris H. Morley, "Imperialism and Intervention in Third World: US Foreign Policy and Central America" **The Socialist Register**

1983 [London: Merlin Press, 1983].

James F. Petras and Morris H. Morley, "Economic Expansion, Political Crisis and US Policy in Central America" in Marlene Dixon and Susanne Jonas, eds., **Revolution and Intervention in Central America** [San Francisco: Synthesis Publications, revised edition, 1983].

James F. Petras and Morris H. Morley, "Anti-Communism in Guatemala: Washington's Alliance with Generals and Death Squads" **The Socialist Register 1984** [London: Merlin Press, 1984].

James Petras and Frank T. Fitzgerald, "Authoritarianism and Democracy in the Transition to Socialism" **Latin American Perspectives** vol. 15. no. 1. 1988.

James Petras and Frank T. Fitzgerald, "Confusion About the Transition to Socialism: A Rejoinder to Haynes" **Latin American Perspectives** vol. 15. no. 1. 1988.

James Petras and Fernando Ignacio Leiva, "Chile: The Authoritarian Transition to Electoral Politics: A Critique" **Latin American Perspectives** vol. 15. no. 3. 1988.

James F. Petras and Morris H. Morley, "Central America: Dependent-Welfare, Authoritarian and Revolutionary Conceptions of Development" in John M. Kirk and George W. Schuyler, eds., **Central America: Democracy, Development and Change** [New York: Praeger, 1988].

James F. Petras, "New Social Movements in Central America: Perspectives on Democratic Social Transformations" in John M. Kirk and George W. Schuyler, eds., **Central America: Democracy, Development and Change** [New York: Praeger, 1988].

James F. Petras, "State, Regime and the Democratization Muddle" **LASA Forum** vol. 18. no. 4. 1988.

James F. Petras, "State, Regime and the Democratization Muddle" **Journal of Contemporary Asia** vol. 19. no. 1. 1989.

James F. Petras, "Class and Political-Economic Development in the Mediterranean: An Overview" in Michael T. Martin and Terry R. Kandal, eds., **Studies of Development and Change in the Modern World** [New York: Oxford University Press, 1989].

James Petras, "The Metamorphosis of Latin America's Intellectuals" **Latin American Perspectives** vol. 17. no. 2. 1990.

James Petras and Steve Vieux, "Twentieth-Century Neoliberals: Inheritors of the Exploits of Columbus" **Latin American Perspectives** vol. 19. no. 3. 1992.

James Petras, "Cultural Imperialism in the Late Twentieth Century" **Journal of Contemporary Asia** vol. 23. no. 2. 1993.

James Petras and Steve Vieux, "The Decline of Revolutionary Politics: Capitalist Detour and The Return of Socialism" **Journal of Contemporary Asia** vol. 24. no. 1. 1994.

Jan Nederveen Pieterse, "Dilemmas of Development Discourse: The Crisis of Developmentalism and the Comparative Method" **Development and Change** vol. 22. 1991.

Jan Nederveen Pieterse, "Fukuyama and Liberal Democracy: the Ends of History" **Economy and Society** vol. 22. no. 2. 1993.

Fredrick B. Pike, "Guatemala, the United States and Communism in the Americas" **Review of Politics** vol. 17. no. 2. 1955.

Fredrick B. Pike, "The Catholic Church and Modernization in Peru and Chile" **Journal of International Affairs** vol. 20. no. 2. 1966.

Fredrick B. Pike, "Corporatism and Latin American-United States Relations" in Fredrick B. Pike and Thomas Stritch, eds., **The New Corporatism: Social-Political Structures in the Iberian World** [Notre Dame: University of Notre Dame Press, 1974].

David Pion-Berlin, "Military Breakdown and Redemocratization in Argentina" in George A. Lopez and Michael Stohl, eds., **Liberalization and Redemocratization in Latin America** [New York: Greenwood Press, 1987].

David Pion-Berlin, "Military Autonomy and Emerging Democracies in South America" **Comparative Politics** vol. 25. no. 1. 1992.

John N. Plank, "The Caribbean: Intervention, When and How" **Foreign Affairs** vol. 44. no. 1. 1965.

Norman Podhoretz, "The Culture of Appeasement" **Harper's** vol. 255. no. 1529. 1977.

Deborah Poole and Gerardo Renique, "The New Chroniclers of Peru: US Scholars and Their 'Shining Path' of Peasant Rebellion" **Bulletin of Latin American Research** vol. 10. no. 2. 1991.

Roger B. Porter, "The Enterprise for the Americas Initiative: A New Approach to Economic Growth" **Journal of Interamerican Studies and World Affairs** vol. 32. no. 4. 1990.

Roger B. Porter, "Fortress Fears Unfounded" **Far Eastern Economic Review** vol. 154. no. 47. 1991.

Alejandro Portes, "Latin American Sociology in the Mid-1980s: Learning from Hard Experience" in Christopher Mitchell, ed., **Changing Perspectives in Latin American Studies: Insights from Six Disciplines** [Stanford: Stanford University Press, 1988].

Mario Posas, "Honduras at the Crossroads" **Latin American Perspectives** vol. 7. nos. 2-3. 1980.

Gyan Prakash, "Writing Post-Orientalist Histories of the Third World: Perspectives from Indian Historiography" **Comparative Studies in Society and History** vol. 32. no. 2. 1990.

Gary Prevost, "Cuba and Nicaragua: A Special Relationship?" **Latin American Perspectives** vol. 17. no. 3. 1990.

Adam Przeworski, "Some Problems in the Study of the Transition to Democracy" in Guillermo O'Donnell, Philippe C. Schmitter and Laurence Whitehead, ed., **Transitions from Authoritarian Rule: Comparative Perspectives** [Baltimore: Johns Hopkins University Press, 1986].

John F. H. Purcell, "The Perceptions and Interests of United States Business in Relation to the Political Crisis in Central America" in Richard E. Feinberg, ed., **Central America: International Dimensions of the Crisis** [New York: Holmes and Meier, 1982].

Susan Kaufman Purcell, "War and Debt in South America" **Foreign Affairs** vol. 61. no. 3. 1982.

Susan Kaufman Purcell, "Carter, Reagan and Central America" **Orbis: A Journal** of **World Affairs** vol. 26. no. 2. 1982.

Susan Kaufman Purcell, "Demystifying Contadora" **Foreign Affairs** vol. 64. no. 1. 1985; reprinted in Bruce M. Bagley, ed., **Contadora and the Diplomacy of Peace in Central America--vol. 1: The United States, Central America and Contadora** [Boulder: Westview Press, 1987].

Susan Purcell, "The Choice in Central America" **Foreign Affairs** vol. 66. no. 1. 1987.

Robert D. Putnam, "Toward Explaining Military Intervention in Latin American Politics" **World Politics** vol. 20. no. 1. 1967; reprinted in Ikuo Kabashima and Lynn T. White III, eds., **Political System and Change** [Princeton: Princeton University Press, 1986].

Anibal Quijano, "Imperialism, Social Classes and the State in Peru 1890-1930" in Ronald H. Chilcote and Dale L. Johnson, eds., **Theories of Development: Mode of Production or Dependency** [Beverly Hills: Sage, 1983].

Anibal Quijano and Immanuel Wallerstein, "Americanity as a Concept, or the Americas in the Modern World-System" **International Social Science Journal** 134. 1992.

Stephen G. Rabe, "The Elusive Conference: United States Economic Relations with Latin America 1945-1952" **Diplomatic History** vol. 2. no. 3. 1978.

Stephen G. Rabe, "Historic Patterns of Intervention: US Relations with Latin America" **Latin American Research Review** vol. 23. no. 2. 1988.

Stephen G. Rabe, "Marching Ahead (Slowly): The Historiography of Inter-American Relations" **Diplomatic History** vol. 13. no. 3. 1989.

Stephen G. Rabe, "The Clues Didn't Check Out: Commentary on 'The CIA and Castillo Armas'" **Diplomatic History** vol. 14. no. 1. 1990.

Charles Ragin and Daniel Chirot, "The World System of Immanuel Wallerstein: Sociology and Politics as History" in Theda Skocpol, ed., **Vision and Method in Historical Sociology** [Cambridge: Cambridge University Press, 1984].

Margaret Randall, "Threatened with Deportation" **Latin American Perspectives** vol. 14. nos. 4. 1987.

Margaret Randall, "When the Imagination of the Writer is Confronted by the Imagination of the State" **Latin American Perspectives** vol. 16. no. 2. 1989.

Carlos Rangel, "Mexico and Other Dominoes" **Commentary** vol. 71. no. 6. 1981.

Peter Ranis, "Trends in Research on Latin American Politics: 1961-1967" **Latin American Research Review** vol. 3. no. 3. 1968.

David Ray, "The Dependency Model of Latin American Underdevelopment: Three Basic Fallacies" **Journal of Interamerican Studies and World Affairs** vol. 15. no. 1. 1973.

James Lee Ray, "US-Central American Relations: Dilemmas, Prophets and Solutions" **Latin American Research Review** vol. 21. no. 1. 1986.

Henry Raymont, "'Mainstreaming' the New World" **Washington Quarterly: A Review of Strategic and International Issues** vol. 3. no. 4. 1980.

Reid Reading, "Conclusion" in Alan Adelman and Reid Reading, eds., **Confrontation in the Caribbean Basin: International**

Perspectives on Security, Sovereignty and Survival [Pittsburgh: Center for Latin American Studies, University Center for International Studies, University of Pittsburgh, 1984].

Reid Reading, "On the Panama Invasion" **LASA Forum** vol. 21. no. 1. 1990.

Andrew Reding, "Costa Rica: Democratic Model in Jeopardy" **World Policy Journal** vol. 3. no. 2. 1986.

Andrew Reding, "Mexico at the Crossroads: The 1988 Election and Beyond" **World Policy Journal** vol. 5. no. 4. 1988.

Andrew Reding, "Mexico Under Salinas: A Facade of Reform" **World Policy Journal** vol. 6. no. 4. 1989.

Nola Reinhardt, "Contrast and Congruence in the Agrarian Reforms of El Salvador and Nicaragua" in William C. Thiesenhusen, **Searching for Agrarian Reform in Latin America** [Boston: Unwin Hyman, 1989].

Karen L. Remmer and Gilbert W. Merkx, "Bureaucratic-Authoritarianism Revisited" **Latin American Research Review** vol. 17. no. 2. 1982.

Karen L. Remmer, "Neopatrimonialism: The Politics of Military Rule in Chile 1973-1987" **Comparative Politics** vol. 21. no. 2. 1989.

Karen L. Remmer, "Democracy and Economic Crisis: The Latin American Experience" **World Politics** vol. 42. no. 3. 1990.

Karen L. Remmer, "New Wine or Old Bottlenecks?: The Study of Latin American Democracy" **Comparative Politics** vol. 23. no. 4. 1991.

Karen L. Remmer, "The Political Economy of Elections in Latin America 1980-1991" **American Political Science Review** vol. 87. no. 2. 1993.

Julio Adolfo Rey, "Revolution and Liberation: A Review of Recent Literature on the Guatemalan Situation" **Hispanic American Historical Review** vol. 38. no. 2. 1958.

Pierre-Philippe Rey, "Reflections on the Pertinence of a Theory of the History of Exchange" **Economy and Society** vol. 2. no. 2. 1973.

Pierre-Philippe Rey, "The Lineage Mode of Production" **Critique of Anthropology** no. 3. 1975.

Robert I. Rhodes, "The Disguised Conservatism of Evolutionary Development Theory" **Science and Society** vol. 32. no. 4. 1968.

Ernesto Richter, "Social Classes, Accumulation, and the Crisis of 'Overpopulation' in El Salvador" **Latin American Perspectives** vol. 7. nos. 2-3. 1980.

Alan Riding, "The Central American Quagmire" **Foreign Affairs** vol. 61. no. 3. 1982.

Barry Rigby, "The Origins of American Expansion in Hawaii and Samoa 1865-1900" **The International History Review** vol. 10. no. 2. 1988.

J. Fred Rippy, "Justo Rufino Barrios and the Nicaraguan Canal" **Hispanic American Historical Review** vol. 20. no. 2. 1940.

J. Fred Rippy, "Relations of the US and Guatemala during the Epoch of Justo Rufino Barrios" **Hispanic American Historical Review** vol. 22. no. 4. 1942.

J. Fred Rippy "Justo Rufino Barrios" in A. Curtis Wilgus, ed., **Hispanic American Essays** [Chapel Hill: University of North Carolina Press, 1942; reprinted Freeport: Books for Libraries Press, 1970].

J. Fred Rippy, "Notes on the Early Telephone Companies of Latin America" **Hispanic American Historical Review** vol. 26. no. 1. 1946.

J. Fred Rippy, "The British Investment 'Boom' of the 1880s in Latin America" **Hispanic American Historical Review** vol. 29. no. 2. 1949.

J. Fred Rippy, "Notes on Early British Gas Companies in Latin America" **Hispanic American Historical Review** vol. 30. no. 1. 1950.

J. Fred Rippy, "Public Policy and the Foreign Investor in Latin America" **Inter-American Economic Affairs** vol. 4. no. 4. 1951.

J. Fred Rippy, "British Investments in Latin America: A Decade of Rapid Reduction, 1940-1950" **Hispanic American Historical Review** vol. 32. no. 2. 1952.

J. Fred Rippy, "British Investments in Latin America at Their Peak" **Hispanic American Historical Review** vol. 34. no. 1. 1954.

J. Fred Rippy, "British Investments in Latin-American Electrical Utilities" **Hispanic American Historical Review** vol. 34. no. 2. 1954.

J. Fred Rippy, "US Aid to Latin America" **Journal of Interamerican Studies** vol. 1. no. 1. 1959.

Donald Castillo Rivas, "Reasons for the Success of the Nicaraguan Revolution" in Wolf Grabendorff, Heinrich W. Krumwiede and Jorg Todt, eds., **Political Change in Central America: Internal and External Dimensions** [Boulder: Westview Press, 1984].

Carla A. Robbins, "The 'Cuban Threat' in Central America" in Wolf Grabendorff, Heinrich W. Krumwiede and Jorg Todt, eds., **Political Change in Central America: Internal and External Dimensions** [Boulder: Westview, 1984].

Bryan Roberts, "The Social Structure of Guatemala: The Internal Dynamics of US Influence" in Emanuel deKadt, ed., **Patterns of Foreign Influence in the Caribbean** [London: Oxford University Press, 1971].

Cedric Robinson, "Indiana Jones, the Third World and American Foreign Policy: A Review Article" **Race and Class** vol. 26. no. 2. 1984.

Linda Robinson, "Peace in Central America?" **Foreign Affairs** vol. 66. no. 3. 1988.

Ronald Robinson and John Gallagher, "The Imperialism of Free Trade" **Economic History Review** vol. 6. no. 1. second series 1953.

Ronald Robinson, "The Non-European Foundations of European Imperialism: Sketch for a Theory of Collaboration" in Roger Owen and Bob Sutcliffe, eds., **Studies in the Theory of Imperialism** [London: Longman, 1972].

William I. Robinson and Kent Norsworthy, "Elections and US Intervention in Nicaragua" **Latin American Perspectives** vol. 12. no. 2. 1985.

William I. Robinson and Kent Norsworthy, "A Critique of the 'Antidemocratic Tendency' Argument: The Case of Mass Organizations and Popular Participation in Nicaragua" **Latin American Perspectives** vol. 15. no. 1. 1988.

William I. Robinson, "Nicaragua: The Making of a 'Democratic' Opposition" **NACLA-Report on the Americas** vol. 23. no. 5. 1990.

William I. Robinson, "The Sao Paulo Forum: Is There a New Latin American Left?" **Monthly Review** vol. 44. no. 7. 1992.

Richard Robison, Kevin Hewison and Garry Rodan, "Political Power in Industrialising Capitalist Societies: Theoretical Approaches" in Kevin Hewison, Richard Robison and Garry Rodan, eds., **Southeast Asia in the**

1990s: Authoritarianism, Democracy and Capitalism [Sydney: Allen and Unwin, 1993].

Riordan Roett, "The Debt Crisis: Economics and Politics" in John D. Martz, ed., **United States Policy in Latin America: A Quarter Century of Crisis and Challenge 1961-1986** [Lincoln: University of Nebraska Press, 1988].

Anibal Romero, "The Kissinger Report and the Restoration of US Hegemony" **Millennium: Journal of International Studies** vol. 13. no. 2. 1984.

C. Neale Ronning, "Introduction" in C. Neale Ronning, ed., **Intervention in Latin America** [New York: Alfred A. Knopf, 1967].

Theodore Roosevelt, "Puerto Rico: Our Link with Latin America" **Foreign Affairs** vol. 12. no. 2. 1934.

Steve C. Ropp and James A. Morris, "Introduction", "The Setting" and "Conclusions" in Steve C. Ropp and James A. Morris, eds., **Central America: Crisis and Adaptation** [Albuquerque: University of New Mexico Press, 1984].

Steve C. Ropp, "Leadership and Political Transformation in Panama: Two Levels of Regime Crisis" in Steve C. Ropp and James A. Morris, eds., **Central America: Crisis and Adaptation** [Albuquerque: University of New Mexico Press, 1984].

Steve C. Ropp, "Negotiating the 1978 Panama Canal Treaties: Contending Theoretical Perspectives" in John D. Martz, ed., **United States Policy in Latin America: A Quarter Century of Crisis and Challenge 1961-1986** [Lincoln: University of Nebraska Press, 1988].

Steve C. Ropp, "Panama and the Canal" in Jan Knippers Black, ed., **Latin America, Its Problems and Its Promise: A Multidisciplinary Introduction** [Boulder: Westview Press, second edition 1991].

Jerel A. Rosati, "Developing a Systematic Decision-Making Framework: Bureaucratic Politics in Perspective" **World Politics** vol. 33. no. 2. 1981.

Susan D. Rose and Steve Brouwer, "The Export of Fundamentalist Americanism: US Evangelical Education in Guatemala" **Latin American Perspectives** vol. 17. no. 4. 1990.

William Roseberry, "Americanization in the Americas" and "Anthropology, History and Modes of Production" in William Roseberry, **Anthropologies and Histories: Essays in Culture, History, and Political Economy** [New Brunswick: Rutgers University Press, 1989].

William Roseberry, "Beyond the Agrarian Question in Latin America" in Frederick Cooper, Allen F. Isaacman, Florencia E. Mallon, William Roseberry and Steve J. Stern, **Confronting Historical Paradigms: Peasants, Labor, and the Capitalist World System in Africa and Latin America** [Madison: University of Wisconsin Press, 1993].

James N. Rosenau, "National (and Factional) Adaptation in Central America: Option for the 1980s" in Richard E. Feinberg, ed., **Central America: International Dimensions of the Crisis** [New York: Holmes and Meier, 1982].

Mark B. Rosenberg, "Political Obstacles to Democracy in Central America" in James M. Malloy and Mitchell A. Seligson, eds., **Authoritarians and Democrats: Regime Transition in Latin America** [Pittsburgh:

University of Pittsburgh Press, 1987].

Mark B. Rosenberg, "Narcos and Politicos: The Politics of Drug Trafficking in Honduras" **Journal of Interamerican Studies and World Affairs** vol. 30. nos. 2-3. 1988.

Mark B. Rosenberg, "Can Democracy Survive the Democrats? From Transition to Consolidation in Honduras" in John A. Booth and Mitchel A. Seligson, eds., **Elections and Democracy in Central America** [Chapel Hill: University of North Carolina Press, 1989].

Mark B. Rosenberg, "Honduras" in Abraham F. Lowenthal, ed., **Latin America and Caribbean Contemporary Record 1986-1987** (volume 6) [New York: Holmes and Meier, 1989].

Michael Rosenfeld, "How Kinzer Changed with the **Times**" **In These Times** vol. 15. no. 26. 1991.

Dorothy Ross, "On the Misunderstanding of Ranke and the Origins of the Historical Profession in America" in Georg G. Iggers and James M. Powell, eds., **Leopold von Ranke and the Shaping of the Historical Discipline** [Syracuse: Syracuse University Press, 1990].

Peter Ross, "Nicaragua's Revolution: Contradictions and Ambiguities" **World Review** vol. 21. no. 4. 1982.

Peter Ross, "Theory and Practice of Revolution: What Works in Central America" in James R. Levy, ed., **Crisis in Central America** [Kensington: School of Spanish and Latin American Studies, University of New South Wales, 1984].

Peter Ross, "Cultural Policy in a Transitional Society: Nicaragua 1979-1989" **Third World Quarterly: Journal of Emerging Areas** vol. 12. no. 2. 1990.

Stanley R. Ross, "Introduction" in Stanley R. Ross, ed., **Latin America in Transition: Problems in Training and Research** [Albany: State University of New York Press, 1970].

Theodore Roszak, "On Academic Delinquency" in Theodore Roszak, ed., **The Dissenting Academy** [London: Chatto and Windus, 1969; first published 1968].

Morris Rothenberg, "Since Reagan: The Soviets and Latin America" **Washington Quarterly** vol. 5. no. 2. 1982.

Morris Rothenberg, "Latin America in Soviet Eyes" **Problems of Communism** vol. 32. no. 5. September-October 1983.

Morris Rothenberg, "The Soviets and Central America" in Robert S. Leiken, ed., **Central America: Anatomy of Conflict** [New York: Pergamon Press, 1984].

Ian Roxborough, "Neo-liberalism in Latin America: Limits and Alternatives" **Third World Quarterly: Journal of Emerging Areas** vol. 13. no. 3. 1992.

Cheryl A. Rubenberg, "US Policy Towards Nicaragua and Iran and the Iran-Contra Affair: Reflections on the Continuity of American Foreign Policy" **Third World Quarterly: Journal of Emerging Areas** vol. 10. no. 4. 1988.

Cheryl A. Rubenberg, "The United States, Israel and Guatemala: Interests and Conflicts" in Damian J. Fernandez, ed., **Central America and the Middle East: The Internationalization of the Crises** [Miami: Florida International University Press, 1990].

Barry Rubin, "Reagan Administration Policymaking and Central America" in Robert S. Leiken, ed., **Central America: Anatomy of Conflict** [New York:

Pergamon Press, 1984].

Alvin Z. Rubinstein and Donald E. Smith, "Anti-Americanism: Anatomy of a Phenomenon" in Alvin Z. Rubinstein and Donald E. Smith, eds., **Anti-Americanism in the Third World: Implications for US Foreign Policy** [New York: Praeger, 1985].

Roy R. Rubottom, "The Goals of United States Policy in Latin America" **Annals of the American Academy of Political and Social Science** vol. 342. 1962.

Roy R. Rubottom, "An Assessment of Current American Influence in Latin America" **Annals of the American Academy of Political and Social Science** vol. 366. 1966.

David F. Ruccio, "State, Class and Transition in Nicaragua" **Latin American Perspectives** vol. 15. no. 2. 1988.

David F. Ruccio and Lawrence H. Simon, "Perspectives on Underdevelopment: Frank, the Modes of Production School, and Amin" in Charles K. Wilber and Kenneth P. Jameson, **The Political Economy of Development and Underdevelopment** [New York: McGraw Hill, fifth edition 1992].

Susan Hoeber Rudolph, "Beyond Modernity and Tradition: Theoretical and Ideological Aspects of Comparative Social Sciences" in R. J. Moore, ed., **Tradition and Politics in South Asia** [New Delhi: Vikas, 1979].

J. Mark Ruhl, "Agrarian Structure and Political Stability in Honduras" **Journal of Interamerican Studies and World Affairs** vol. 26. no. 1. 1984.

J. Mark Ruhl, "Understanding Central American Politics" **Latin American Research Review** vol. 19. no. 3. 1984.

Michael Rustin, "No Exit from Capitalism" **New Left Review** no. 193. 1992.

Dankwart A. Rustow, "Transitions to Democracy: Toward a Dynamic Model" **Comparative Politics** vol. 2. no. 3. 1970.

Dankwart A. Rustow, "Democracy: A Global Revolution?" **Foreign Affairs** vol. 69. no. 4. 1990.

Helen Icken Safa, "Latin America from the Anthropologist's Viewpoint: Continuity and Change" in Samuel L. Baily and Ronald T. Hyman, eds., **Perspectives on Latin America** [New York: Macmillan, 1974].

Edward W. Said, "Yeats and Decolonization" in Barbara Kruger and Phil Mariani, eds., **Remaking History** [Seattle: Bay Press, 1989]; reprinted in Terry Eagleton, Fredric Jameson and Edward Said, **Nationalism, Colonialism and Literature** [Minneapolis: University of Minnesota Press, 1990].

Edward W. Said, "Narrative, Geography and Interpretation" **New Left Review** no. 180. 1990.

José David Saldívar, "The Dialectics of Our America" in Gustavo Pérez Firmat, ed., **Do the Americas Have a Common Literature?** [Durham: Duke University Press, 1990].

Richard V. Salisbury, "Domestic Politics and Foreign Policy: Costa Rica's Stand on Recognition" **Hispanic American Historican Review** vol. 54. no. 3. 1974.

Richard V. Salisbury, "Costa Rica and the 1920-1921 Union Movement: A Reassessment" **Journal of Interamerican Studies and World Affairs** vol. 19. no. 3. 1977.

Richard V. Salisbury, "United States Intervention in Nicaragua: The Costa Rican

Role" **Prologue: The Journal of the National Archives** vol. 9. no. 4. 1977.

Richard V. Salisbury, "The Anti-Imperialist Career of Alejandro Alvarado Quiros" **Hispanic American Historical Review** vol. 57. no. 4. 1977.

Richard V. Salisbury, "Jorge Volio and Isthmian Revolutionary Politics" **Red River Valley Historical Journal of World History** vol. 4. no. 4. 1980.

Richard V. Salisbury, "Good Neighbours: The United States and Latin America in the Twentieth Century" in Gerald K. Haines and J. Samuel Walker, eds., **American Foreign Relations: An Historiographical Review** [London: Pinter, 1981].

Richard V. Salisbury, "The Middle American Exile of Víctor Raúl Haya de la Torre" **The Americas: A Quarterly Review of Inter-American Cultural History** vol. 40. no. 1. 1983.

Richard V. Salisbury, "Mexico, the United States, and the 1926-1927 Nicaraguan Crisis" **Hispanic American Historical Review** vol. 66. no. 2. 1986.

Richard V. Salisbury, "Recent Writing on Nicaragua" **Hispanic American Historical Review** vol. 71. no. 3. 1991.

Richard V. Salisbury, "Revolution and Recognition: A British Perspective on Isthmian Affairs During the 1920s" **The Americas: A Quarterly Review of Inter-American Cultural History** vol. 48. no. 3. 1992.

Nestor D. Sanchez, "The Communist Threat" **Foreign Policy** no. 52. 1983.

Jerry W. Sanders, "Forty Years of *Pax Americana*: What Comes Next?: Security and Choice" **World Policy Journal** vol. 1. no. 4. 1984.

Jerry W. Sanders, "Para-Institutional Elites and Foreign Policy Consensus" in Richard A. Melanson and Kenneth W. Thompson eds., **Foreign Policy and Domestic Consensus** [New York: University Press of America, 1985].

Pedro A. Sanjuan, "Why We Don't Have a Latin America Policy" **Washington Quarterly: A Review of Strategic and International Issues** vol. 3. no. 4. 1980.

Pedro A. Sanjuan, "To See Ourselves as Others See Us: Some Latin American Perspectives on US Policy" **Washington Quarterly: A Review of Strategic and International Issues** vol. 2. no. 2. 1979.

John Saxe-Fernandez, "The Central American Defense Council and *Pax Americana*" in Irving Louis Horowitz, Josue de Castro and John Gerassi, eds., **Latin American Radicalism: A Documentary Report on Left and Nationalist Movements** [New York: Random House, 1969].

Robert A. Scalpino, "Asia" in Peter Duignan and Alvin Rabushka, eds., **The United States in the 1980s** [Stanford: Stanford University Press--Hoover Institution, 1980].

Hector E. Schamis, "Reconceptualizing Latin American Authoritarianism in the 1970s: From Bureaucratic-Authoritarianism to Neoconservatism" **Comparative Politics** vol. 23. no. 2. 1991.

L. Ronald Scheman, "Rhetoric and Reality: The Inter-American System's Second Century" **Journal of Interamerican Studies and World Affairs** vol. 29. no. 3. 1987.

L. Ronald Scheman and Norman A. Bailey, "Putting Latin American Debt to Work:

A Positive Role for the US" **Journal of Interamerican Studies and World Affairs** vol. 31. no. 4. 1989.

Arthur M. Schlesinger, Jr., "The Theory of America: Experiment or Destiny" "The Cycles of American Politics", "Foreign Policy and the American Character", "America and Empire" and "Why the Cold War" in Arthur M. Schlesinger, Jr., **The Cycles of American History** [Boston: Houghton Mifflin, 1986].

Philippe C. Schmitter, "Paths to Political Development in Latin America" in Douglas A. Chalmers, ed., **Changing Latin America: New Interpretations of Its Politics and Society** [New York: Academy of Political Science, 1972].

Philippe C. Schmitter, "Still the Century of Corporatism?" in Philippe C. Schmitter and Gerhard Lehmbruch, eds., **Trends Toward Corporatist Intermediation** [Beverly Hills: Sage, 1979].

Philippe C. Schmitter, "An Introduction to Southern European Transitions from Authoritarian Rule: Italy, Greece, Portugal, Spain, and Turkey" in Guillermo O'Donnell, Philippe C. Schmitter and Laurence Whitehead, ed., **Transitions from Authoritarian Rule: Southern Europe** [Baltimore: Johns Hopkins University Press, 1986].

Ronald M. Schneider, "Guatemala: An Aborted Communist Takeover" in Thomas T. Hammond, ed., **The Anatomy of Communist Takeovers** [New Haven: Yale University Press, 1975].

Thomas D. Schoonover, "Central American Commerce and Maritime Activity in the 19th Century: A Quantitative Approach" **Latin American Research Review** vol. 13. no. 2. 1978.

Thomas D. Schoonover, "Misconstrued Mission: Expansionism and Black Colonization in Mexico and Central America during the Civil War" **Pacific Historical Review** vol. 49. no. 4. 1980.

Thomas D. Schoonover, "Imperialism in Middle America: United States, Britain, Germany and France Compete for Transit Rights and Trade 1820s-1920s" in Rhodri Jeffreys-Jones, ed., **Eagle Against Empire: American Opposition to European Imperialism 1914-1982** [Aix-en-Provence, France: Publications Université de Provence for the European Association for American Studies, 1983].

Thomas D. Schoonover, "Prussia and the Protection of German Transit Through Middle America and Commerce with the Pacific Basin 1848-1851" **Jahrbuch für Geschichte von Staat, Wirtschaft und Gesellschaft Lateinamerikas** vol. 22. 1985.

Thomas D. Schoonover, "Metropole Rivalry in Central America 1820-1929: An Overview" in Ralph Lee Woodward, Jr., ed., **Central America: Historical Perspectives on the Contemporary Crisis** [New York: Greenwood Press, 1988].

Thomas D. Schoonover, "A United States Dilemma: Economic Opportunity and Anti-Americanism in El Salvador 1901-1911" **Pacific Historical Review** vol. 58. no. 4. 1989.

Lars Schoultz, "US Diplomacy and Human Rights in Latin America" in John D. Martz and Lars Schoultz, eds., **Latin America, the United States and the Inter-American System** [Boulder: Westview Press, 1980].

Lars Schoultz, "Guatemala: Social Change and Political Conflict" in Martin Diskin, ed., **Trouble in Our Backyard: Central America and the United States in the Eighties** [New York: Pantheon, 1983].

Lars Schoultz, "Nicaragua: The United States Confronts a Revolution" in Richard S. Newfarmer, ed., **From Gunboats to Diplomacy: New US Policies for Latin America** [Baltimore: Johns Hopkins University Press, 1984].

Lars Schoultz, "The Responsiveness of Policy and Institutional Reform to Aid Conditionality" in William Ascher and Ann Hubbard, eds., **Central American Recovery and Development: Task Force Report to the International Commission for Central American Recovery and Development** [Durham: Duke University Press, 1989].

Robert D. Schulzinger, "Patterns in the Mess: The United States and Nicaragua" **Diplomatic History** vol. 13. no. 2. 1989.

Barry M. Schutz and Robert O. Slater, "A Framework for Analysis" in Barry M. Schutz and Robert O. Slater, eds., **Revolution and Political Change in the Third World** [Boulder: Lynne Rienner, 1990].

Barry M. Schutz and Robert O. Slater, "Patterns of Legitimacy and Future Revolutions in the Third World" in Barry M. Schutz and Robert O. Slater, eds., **Revolution and Political Change in the Third World** [Boulder: Lynne Rienner, 1990].

George W. Schuyler, "Perspectives on Canada and Latin America: Changing Context...Changing Policy?" **Journal of Interamerican Studies and World Affairs** vol. 33. no. 1. 1991.

Klaus Schwabe, "The Global Role of the United States and its Imperial Consequences, 1898-1973" in Wolfgang J. Mommsen and Jürgen Osterhammel, eds., **Imperialism and After: Continuities and Discontinuities** [London: Allen and Unwin, 1986].

Hugh Schwartz, "Raúl Prebisch and Argentine Economic Policy-Making, 1950-1962: A Comment" **Latin American Research Review** vol. 23. no. 2. 1988.

Robert E. Scott, "The Government Bureaucrats and Political Change in Latin America" **Journal of International Affairs** vol. 20. no. 2. 1966.

Paul Seabury, "The Revolt Against Obligation" in Paul Seabury and Aaron Wildavsky, eds., **US Foreign Policy: Perspectives and Proposals for the 1970s** [New York: McGraw-Hill, 1969].

Ron Seckinger, "The Central American Militaries: A Survey of the Literature" **Latin American Research Review** vol. 16. no. 2. 1981.

Patricia Seed, "Colonial and Postcolonial Discourse" **Latin American Research Review** vol. 26. no. 3. 1991.

Mitchell A. Seligson and John A. Booth, "Political Participation in Latin America: An Agenda for Research" **Latin American Research Review** vol. 11. no. 3. 1976.

Mitchell A. Seligson, "The Dual Gaps: An Overview of Theory and Research" and Seligson, "Inequality in a Global Perspective: Directions for Further Research" in Mitchell A. Seligson, ed., **The Gap Between Rich and Poor: Contending Perspectives on the Political Economy of Development** [Boulder: Westview Press, 1984].

Mitchell A. Seligson, "Democratization in Latin America: The Current Cycle" and "Development, Democratization and Decay: Central America at the

Crossroads" in James M. Malloy and Mitchell A. Seligson, eds., **Authoritarians and Democrats: Regime Transition in Latin America** [Pittsburgh: University of Pittsburgh Press, 1987].

Mitchell A. Seligson and E. Muller, "Democratic Stability and Economic Crisis: Costa Rica 1979-1983" **International Studies Quarterly** vol. 31. no. 3. 1987.

Mitchell A. Seligson, "Introduction--From Uncertainty to Uncertainty: The Institutionalization of Elections in Central America" in John A. Booth and Mitchell A. Seligson, eds., **Elections and Democracy in Central America** [Chapel Hill: University of North Carolina Press, 1989].

Mitchell A. Seligson and Miguel Gomez, "Ordinary Elections and Extraordinary Times: The Political Economy of Voting in Costa Rica" in John A. Booth and Mitchel A. Seligson, eds., **Elections and Democracy in Central America** [Chapel Hill: University of North Carolina Press, 1989].

Nina M. Serafino, "Dateline Managua: Defining Democracy" **Foreign Policy** no. 70. 1988.

Samuel Shapiro, "A Common History of the Americas?" in Samuel Shapiro, ed., **Cultural Factors in Inter-American Relations** [Notre Dame: University of Notre Dame Press, 1968].

Howard Sharckman, "La vietnamización de Guatemala: los programas de contra-insurgencia norteamericanos" in Susanne Jonas and David Tobis, eds., **Guatemala: una historia inmediata** [Mexico: Siglo veintiuno editores, 1979; first published in English in 1974].

Kenneth E. Sharpe, "El Salvador Revisited : Why Duarte is in Trouble" **World Policy Journal** vol. 1. no. 1. 1983.

Kenneth E. Sharpe and Martin Diskin, "Facing Facts in El Salvador" **World Policy Journal** vol. 1. no. 3. 1984.

Kenneth E. Sharpe, William M. LeoGrande, Douglas C. Bennett and Morris J. Blachman "Security Through Diplomacy: A Policy of Principled Realism" in Morris J. Blachman, William M. LeoGrande and Kenneth Sharpe, eds., **Confronting Revolution: Security Through Diplomacy in Central America** [New York: Pantheon, 1986].

Kenneth E. Sharpe, "The Drug War: Going After Supply--A Commentary" **Journal of Interamerican Studies and World Affairs** vol. 30. nos. 2-3. 1988.

Janet Shenk, "Central America: No Road Back--El Salvador" **NACLA Report on the Americas** vol. 15. no. 3. 1981.

Janet Shenk, "El Salvador: The New and the Old War" **NACLA Report on the Americas** vol. 19. no. 3. 1985.

Philip L. Shepherd, "Troubled 'Allies' and Fragile Peace: The Tragic Course and Consequences of US Policy in Honduras" **World Policy Journal** vol. 2. no. 1. 1984.

Philip L. Shepherd, "Honduras" in Morris J. Blachman, William LeoGrande and Kenneth Sharpe, eds., **Confronting Revolution: Security Through Diplomacy in Central America** [New York: Pantheon, 1986].

Philip L. Shepherd, "Honduras: The War Comes Home--The Case of the Invisible Aid" **NACLA Report on the Americas** vol. 22. no. 1. 1988.

William R. Shepherd, "The Reconciliation of Fact with Sentiment in Our Dealings with Latin America" **Annals of the American Academy of Political**

and Social Science vol. 132. 1927.

William R. Shepherd, "The Contribution of the Romance Nations to the History of the Americas (1910)" in Lewis Hanke, ed., **Do the Americas Have a Common History?: A Critique of the Bolton Theory** [New York: Alfred A. Knopf, 1964].

Matthew Soberg Shugart, "Thinking about the Next Revolution: Lessons from US Policy in Nicaragua" **Journal of Interamerican Studies and World Affairs** vol. 29. no. 1. 1987.

Daniel Siegel and Joy Hackel, "El Salvador: Counterinsurgency Revisited" in Michael T. Klare and Peter Kornbluh, eds., **Low Intensity Warfare: How the USA Fights Wars Without Declaring Them** [New York: Pantheon, 1988; reprinted London: Methuen, 1989].

Paul E. Sigmund, "Introduction" in Paul E. Sigmund, ed., **The Ideologies of the Developing Nations** [New York: Praeger, 1963].

Paul E. Sigmund, "Introduction" in Paul E. Sigmund, ed., **The Ideologies of the Developing Nations** [New York: Praeger, revised and enlarged edition 1968].

Paul E. Sigmund, "Christian Democracy in Chile" **Journal of International Affairs** vol. 20. no. 2. 1966.

Paul E. Sigmund, "Latin America: Change or Continuity?" **Foreign Affairs** vol. 60. no. 3. 1982.

Paul E. Sigmund, "Reagan's Two-Track Policy in Central America" **New Leader** vol. 46. no. 15. 1983.

Paul E. Sigmund, "US Latin American Relations from Carter to Reagan: Change or Continuity" in Jennie K. Lincoln and Elizabeth G. Ferris, eds., **The Dynamics of Latin American Foreign Policies: Challenge for the 1980s** [Boulder: Westview Press, 1984].

Paul E. Sigmund, "Crisis Management: Chile and Marxism" in John D. Martz, ed., **United States Policy in Latin America: A Quarter Century of Crisis and Challenge 1961-1986** [Lincoln: University of Nebraska Press, 1988].

Paul E. Sigmund, "Christian Democracy, Liberation Theology, and Political Culture in Latin America" in Larry Diamond, ed., **Political Culture and Democracy in Developing Countries** [Boulder: Lynne Rienner, 1993].

Kathryn Sikkink, "The Influence of Raúl Prebisch on Economic Policy-Making in Argentina, 1950-1962" **Latin American Research Review** vol. 23. no. 2. 1988.

Kalman H. Silvert, "Political Change in Latin America" in Herbert L. Matthews, ed., **The United States and Latin America** [New York: Columbia University--Sixteenth American Assembly 1959].

Kalman H. Silvert, "The Strategy of the Study of Nationalism" and "The Cost of Anti-Nationalism: Argentina" in Kalman H. Silvert, ed., **Expectant Peoples: Nationalism and Development** [New York: Vintage Books, 1967; first published 1963].

Kalman H. Silvert, "Leadership Formation and Modernization in Latin America" **Journal of International Affairs** vol. 20. no. 2. 1966.

Kalman H. Silvert, "An Essay on Interdisciplinary and International Collaboration in Social Science Research in Latin America" in Stanley R. Ross, ed., **Latin**

America in Transition: Problems in Training and Research [Albany: State University of New York Press, 1970].

Marlise Simons, "Guatemala: The Coming Danger" **Foreign Policy** no. 43. 1981.

Harold D. Sims, "Revolutionary Nicaragua: Dilemmas Confronting Sandinistas and North Americans" in Alan Adelman and Reid Reading, eds., **Confrontation in the Caribbean Basin: International Perspectives on Security, Sovereignty and Survival** [Pittsburgh: Center for Latin American Studies, University Center for International Studies, University of Pittsburgh, 1984].

Max Singer, "Can El Salvador Be Saved?" **Commentary** vol. 72. no. 6. 1981.

Max Singer, "The Record in Latin America" **Commentary** vol. 74. no. 6. 1982.

Max Singer, "Losing Central America" **Commentary** vol. 82. no. 1. 1986.

Milton Singer, "The Social Sciences in Non-Western Studies" **Annals of the American Academy of Political and Social Science** vol. 356. 1964.

Lesley Byrd Simpson, "Thirty Years of the *Hispanic American Historical Review*" **Hispanic American Historical Review** vol. 29. no. 2. 1949.

Thomas E. Skidmore, "The Political Economy of Policy Making in Authoritarian Brazil 1967-1970" in Philip O'Brien and Paul Cammack, eds., **Generals in Retreat: The Crisis of Military Rule in Latin America** [Manchester: Manchester University Press, 1985].

Thomas E. Skidmore, "The Future of Democracy: An Analytical Summary" in Robert A. Pastor, ed., **Democracy in the Americas: Stopping the Pendulum** [New York: Holmes and Meier, 1989].

Thomas E. Skidmore, "Brazil's Slow Road to Democratization: 1974-1985" in Alfred Stepan, ed., **Democratizing Brazil: Problems of Transition and Consolidation** [New York: Oxford University Press, 1989].

Holly Sklar, "Born-Again War: The Low-Intensity Mystique" **NACLA Report on the Americas** vol. 21. no. 2. 1987.

Richard L. Sklar, "Developmental Democracy" **Comparative Studies in Society and History** vol. 29. no. 4. 1987.

Theda Skocpol, "Wallerstein's World Capitalist System: A Theoretical and Historical Critique" **American Journal of Sociology** vol. 82. no. 5. 1977.

Jerome Slater, "Is United States Foreign Policy 'Imperialist' or 'Imperial'?" **Political Science Quarterly** vol. 91. no. 1. 1976.

Jerome Slater, "United States Policy in Latin America" in Jan Knippers Black, ed., **Latin America: Its Problems and Its Promise** [Boulder: Westview Press, 1984].

John W. Sloan, "Electoral Fraud and Social Change: The Guatemalan Example" **Science and Society** vol. 34. no. 1. 1970.

John W. Sloan, "Challenges to US Influence in Latin America" **Latin American Research Review** vol. 19. no. 1. 1984.

Carol A. Smith, "Does a Commodity Economy Enrich the Few While Ruining the Masses?: Differentiation Among Petty Commodity Producers in Guatemala" **Journal of Peasant Studies** vol. 11. no. 3. 1984.

Carol A. Smith, "Local History in Global Context: Social and Economic Transitions in Western Guatemala" **Comparative Studies in Society**

and History vol. 26. no. 2. 1984. reprinted in in Daniel H. Levine, ed., **Constructing Culture and Power in Latin America** [Ann Arbor: University of Michigan Press, 1993].

Carol A. Smith, "Destruction of the Material Bases for Indian Culture: Economic Changes in Totonicapan" in Robert M. Carmack, ed., **Harvest of Violence: The Maya Indians and the Guatemalan Crisis** [Norman: University of Oklahoma Press, 1988].

Carol A. Smith, "The Militarization of Civil Society in Guatemala: Economic Reorganization as a Continuation of War" **Latin American Perspectives** vol. 17. no. 4. 1990.

Carol A. Smith, "Introduction: Social Relations in Guatemala over Time and Space", "Origins of the National Question in Guatemala: A Hypothesis", "Class Position and Class Consciousness in an Indian Community: Totonicapan in the 1970s" and "Conclusion: History and Revolution in Guatemala" in Carol A. Smith, ed., **Guatemalan Indians and the State 1540 to 1988** [Austin: University of Texas Press, 1990].

Clint E. Smith, "The Discussions at Guanajuato: An Afterword" in Richard R. Fagen and Olga Pellicer, eds., **The Future of Central America: Policy Choices for the US and Mexico** [Stanford: Stanford University Press, 1983].

Gaddis Smith, "The Two Worlds of Samuel Flagg Bemis" **Diplomatic History** vol. 9. no. 4. 1985.

Hazel Smith, "Agenda Setting: The Intellectual Corollary of the Reagan Doctrine" **Latin American Research Review** vol. 26. no. 1. 1991.

Peter H. Smith, "Academia and Politics: The Role of US Universities" in David S. Smith, ed., **Prospects for Latin America** [New York: Columbia University, International Fellows Program Policy Series, 1970].

Peter H. Smith, "History" in Robert S. Byars and Joseph L. Love, eds., **Quantitative Social Science Research on Latin America** [Urbana: University of Illinois Press, 1973].

Peter H. Smith, "Political Legitimacy in Spanish America" in Richard Graham and Peter H. Smith, eds., **New Approaches to Latin American History** [Austin: University of Texas Press, 1974].

Peter H. Smith, "The Intellectual Integrity of Latin American Studies" **LASA Newsletter** vol. 12. no. 4. 1982.

Peter H. Smith, "Mexico: The Continuing Quest for a Policy" in Richard S. Newfarmer, ed., **From Gunboats to Diplomacy: New US Policies for Latin America** [Baltimore: Johns Hopkins University Press, 1984].

Peter H. Smith, "The Origins of the Crisis" in Morris J. Blachman, William LeoGrande and Kenneth Sharpe, eds., **Confronting Revolution: Security Through Diplomacy in Central America** [New York: Pantheon, 1986].

Peter H. Smith, "Crisis and Democracy in Latin America" **World Politics** vol. 43. no. 4. 1991.

Peter H. Smith, "On Democracy and Democratization" in Howard J. Wiarda, ed., **Politics and Social Change in Latin America: Still a Distinct Tradition?** [Boulder: Westview Press, 1992].

Robert Freeman Smith, "American Foreign Relations 1920-1942" in Barton J.

Bernstein, ed., **Towards a New Past: Dissenting Essays in American History** [New York: Random House, 1968].

Robert Freeman Smith, "A Note on the Bryan-Chamorro Treaty and German Interests in a Nicaraguan Canal 1914" **Caribbean Studies** vol. 9. no. 1. 1969.

Robert Freeman Smith, "The Morrow Mission and the International Committee of Bankers on Mexico: The Interaction of Finance Diplomacy and the New Mexican Elite" **Journal of Latin American Studies** vol. 1. no. 2. 1969.

Robert Freeman Smith, "The Good Neighbour Policy: The Liberal Paradox in US Relations with Latin America" in Leonard Liggio and James J. Martin, eds., **Watershed of Empire: Essays on New Deal Foreign Policy** [Colorado Springs: Ralph Myles, 1976].

Robert Freeman Smith, "The American Revolution and Latin America: An Essay in Imagery, Perceptions and Ideological Influence" **Journal of Inter-American Studies and World Affairs** vol. 20. no. 4. 1978.

Steve Smith, "The Development of International Relations as a Social Science" **Millennium: Journal of International Studies** vol. 16. no. 2. 1987.

T. Lynn Smith, "The Development of Sociological Studies of Latin America in the US" in T. Lynn Smith, **Studies of Latin American Societies** [New York: Doubleday, 1970].

Tony Smith, "The Underdevelopment of Development Literature: The Case of Dependency Theory" **World Politics** vol. 31. no. 2. 1979; reprinted in Atul Kohli, ed., **The State and Development in the Third World** [Princeton: Princeton University Press, 1986].

Tony Smith, "Requiem or New Agenda for Third World Studies?" **World Politics** vol. 37. no. 4. 1985; reprinted in Ikuo Kabashima and Lynn T. White III, eds., **Political System and Change** [Princeton: Princeton University Press, 1986].

Tony Smith, "The Dependency Approach" in Howard J. Wiarda, ed., **New Directions in Comparative Politics** [Boulder: Westview Press, 1985].

Tony Smith, "American Imperialism is Anti-Communism" in Wolfgang J. Mommsen and Jürgen Osterhammel, eds., **Imperialism and After: Continuities and Discontinuities** [London: Allen and Unwin, 1986].

Wayne S. Smith, US Central American Policy: The Worst-Alternative Syndrome" **SAIS Review** Summer-Fall 1983.

Wayne S. Smith, "Bringing Diplomacy Back In: A Critique of US Policy in Central America" in Bruce M. Bagley, ed., **Contadora and the Diplomacy of Peace in Central America--vol. 1: The United States, Central America and Contadora** [Boulder: Westview Press, 1987].

Wayne S. Smith, "Lies About Nicaragua" **Foreign Policy** no. 67. 1987.

Wayne S. Smith, "Castro, Latin America and the United States" in John D. Martz, ed., **United States Policy in Latin America: A Quarter Century of Crisis and Challenge 1961-1986** [Lincoln: University of Nebraska Press, 1988].

Wayne S. Smith, "The Reagan Administration and its Attempts to Thwart Change" in John M. Kirk and George W. Schuyler, eds., **Central America: Democracy, Development and Change** [New York: Praeger, 1988].

Wayne S. Smith, "Castro's Cuba: Soviet Partner or Nonaligned?" extracted from Wayne S. Smith, **Castro's Cuba: Soviet Partner or Nonaligned?** [Washington: Woodrow Wilson International Center for Scholars, 1984]; and reprinted in Philip Brenner, William LeoGrande, Donna Rich and Daniel Siegel, eds., **The Cuba Reader: The Making of a Revolutionary Society** [New York: Grove Press, 1989].

Wayne S. Smith, "The United States and South America: Beyond the Monroe Doctrine" **Current History: A World Affairs Journal** vol. 90. no. 553. 1991.

Wayne S. Smith, "The Soviet Union and Cuba in Central America: Guardians Against Democracy?" in Louis W. Goodman, William M. LeoGrande, and Johanna Mendelson Forman, eds., **Political Parties and Democracy in Central America** [Boulder: Westview Press, 1992].

William C. Smith, "Reflections on the Political Economy of Authoritarian Rule and Capitalist Reorganization in Contemporary Argentina" in Philip O'Brien and Paul Cammack, eds., **Generals in Retreat: The Crisis of Military Rule in Latin America** [Manchester: Manchester University Press, 1985].

Frank Smyth, "Consensus or Crisis?: Without Duarte in El Salvador" **Journal of Interamerican Studies and World Affairs** vol. 30. no. 4. 1988/1989.

D. Neil Snarr and E. Leonard Brown, "An Analysis of PhD Dissertations on Central America: 1960-1974" **Latin American Research Review** vol. 12. no. 2. 1977.

Richard Snyder, "Explaining Transitions from Neopatrimonial Dictatorships" **Comparative Politics** vol. 24. no. 4. 1992.

Glaucio Ary Dillon Soares, "Latin American Studies in the United States: A Critique and a Proposal" **Latin American Research Review** vol. 11. no. 2. 1976.

Hobart A. Spalding, Jr., "US and Latin America: The Dynamics of Imperialist Control" **Latin American Perspectives** vol. 3. no. 1. 1976.

Jack Spence and George Vickers, "The Chamorro Government After 200 Days" **LASA Forum** vol. 21. no. 4. 1991.

Richard Stahler-Sholk, "Building Democracy in Nicaragua" in George A. Lopez and Michael Stohl, eds., **Liberalization and Redemocratization in Latin America** [New York: Greenwood Press, 1987].

Barbara Stallings, "Peru and the US Banks: Privatization of Financial Relations" in Richard R. Fagen, ed., **Capitalism and the State in US-Latin American Relations** [Stanford: Stanford University Press, 1979].

Barbara Stallings, "External Finance and the Transition to Socialism in Small Peripheral Societies" in Richard R. Fagen, Carmen Diana Deere and Jose Luis Coraggio, eds., **Transition and Development: Problems of Third World Socialism** [New York: Monthly Review Press, 1986, PACCA/CRIES].

Barbara Stallings, "The Role of Foreign Capital in Economic Development" in Gary Gereffi and Donald L. Wyman, eds., **Manufacturing Miracles: Paths of Industrialization in Latin America and East Asia** [Princeton: Princeton University Press, 1990].

Charles L. Stansifer, "Application of the Tobar Doctrine to Central America" **The Americas: A Quarterly Review of Inter-American Cultural**

History vol. 23. no. 3. 1967.

Charles L. Stansifer, "E. George Squier and the Honduras Interoceanic Railroad Project" **Hispanic American Historical Review** vol. 46. no. 1. 1967.

Charles L. Stansifer, "A New Look at Nicaragua's 'Liberal' Dictator" **Revista Interamericana** vol. 7. no. 3. 1977.

Jeffrey Stark, "Against the Grain" **Journal of Interamerican Studies and World Affairs** vol. 30. no. 4. 1988/89.

Jeffrey Stark, "Going for Baroque?: Ways of Thinking About Democracy in Latin America" **Journal of Interamerican Studies and World Affairs** vol. 33. no. 1. 1991.

Orin Starn, "Rethinking the Politics of Anthropology: The Case of the Andes" **Current Anthropology** vol. 35. no. 1. 1994.

Rodolfo Stavenhagen, "Classes, Colonialism and Acculturation: A System of Inter-Ethnic Relations in Mesoamerica" **Studies in Comparative International Development** vol. 1. no. 6. 1965; reprinted in Irving Louis Horowitz, ed., **Masses in Latin America** [New York: Oxford University Press, 1970].

Rodolfo Stavenhagen, "Seven Erroneous Theses About Latin America" **New University Thought** vol. 4. no. 4. 1966-1967; reprinted in Irving Louis Horowitz, Josué de Castro and John Gerassi, eds., **Latin American Radicalism: A Documentary Report on Left and Nationalist Movements** [New York: Vintage Books, 1969].

Rodolfo Stavenhagen, "Decolonializing Applied Social Sciences" **Human Organization** vol. 30. no. 4. 1971; reprinted in Rodolfo Stavenhagen, **Between Underdevelopment and Revolution: A Latin American Perspective** [New Delhi: Abhinav Publications, 1981].

Rodolfo Stavenhagen, "The Future of Latin America: Between Underdevelopment and Revolution" **Latin American Perspectives** vol. 1. no. 1. 1974. condensed, revised and reprinted in Heraldo Muñoz, ed., **From Dependency to Development: Strategies to Overcome Underdevelopment and Inequality** [Boulder: Westview Press, 1981].

Ronald Steel, "The Kennedys and the Missile Crisis" in Morton Halperin and Arnold Kanter, eds., **Readings in American Foreign Policy: A Bureaucratic Perspective** [Boston: Little Brown, 1973].

Stanley J. Stein, "The Task Ahead for Latin American Historians" **Hispanic American Historical Review** vol. 41. no. 3. 1961; reprinted in Howard F. Cline, ed., **Latin American History: Essays on Its Study and Teaching 1898-1965** (2 vols.) [Austin: University of Texas Press, 1967].

Stanley J. Stein, "Latin American Historiography: Status and Research Opportunities" in Charles Wagley, ed., **Social Science Research on Latin America** [New York: Columbia University Press, 1964]; reprinted in Howard F. Cline, ed., **Latin American History: Essays on Its Study and Teaching 1898-1965** (2 vols.) [Austin: University of Texas Press, 1967].

Ryszard Stemplowski, "Latin America, The US and Diplomacy: New Books, Old Problems" **Latin American Research Review** vol. 15. no. 1. 1980.

Alfred Stepan, "Political Development Theory: The Latin American Experience" **Journal of International Affairs** vol. 20. no. 2. 1966.

Alfred Stepan, "State Power and the Strength of Civil Society in the Southern Cone of Latin America" in Peter B. Evans, Dietrich Rueschemeyer and Theda Skocpol, eds., **Bringing the State Back In** [Cambridge: Cambridge University Press, 1985].

Alfred Stepan, "Paths Toward Redemocratization: Theoretical and Comparative Considerations" in Guillermo O'Donnell, Philippe C. Schmitter and Laurence Whitehead, ed., **Transitions from Authoritarian Rule: Comparative Perspectives** [Baltimore: Johns Hopkins University Press, 1986].

Alfred Stepan, "Introduction" in Alfred Stepan, ed., **Democratizing Brazil: Problems of Transition and Consolidation** [New York: Oxford University Press, 1989].

Steve J. Stern, "The Rise and Fall of Indian-White Alliances: A Regional View of 'Conquest' History" **Hispanic American Historical Review** vol. 61. August. 1981.

Steve J. Stern, "The Struggle for Solidarity: Class, Culture and Community in Highland Indian America" **Radical History Review** no. 27. 1983.

Steve J. Stern, "New Approaches to the Study of Peasant Rebellion and Consciousness: Implications of the Andean Experience" in Steve J. Stern, ed., **Resistance, Rebellion and Consciousness in the Andean Peasant World, 18th to 20th Centuries** [Madison: University of Wisconsin Press, 1987].

Steve J. Stern, "Feudalism, Capitalism and the World-System in the Perspective of Latin America and the Caribbean" **American Historical Review** vol. 93. no. 4. 1988; reprinted in Frederick Cooper, Allen F. Isaacman, Florencia E. Mallon, William Roseberry and Steve J. Stern, **Confronting Historical Paradigms: Peasants, Labor, and the Capitalist World System in Africa and Latin America** [Madison: University of Wisconsin Press, 1993].

Steve J. Stern, "Reply: 'Ever More Solitary'" **American Historical Review** vol. 93. no. 4. 1988.

Steve J. Stern, "Africa, Latin America, and the Splintering of Historical Knowledge: From Fragmentation to Reverberation" in Frederick Cooper, Allen F. Isaacman, Florencia E. Mallon, William Rosebery and Steve J. Stern, **Confronting Historical Paradigms: Peasants, Labor, and the Capitalist World System in Africa and Latin America** [Madison: University of Wisconsin Press, 1993].

Marvin Sternberg, "Dependency, Imperialism and the Relations of Production" **Latin American Perspectives** vol. 1. no. 1. 1974.

Alan L. Sternberger, "US Security and Central America: Why Be So Concerned?" in Bruce M. Bagley, ed., **Contadora and the Diplomacy of Peace in Central America--vol. 1: The United States, Central America and Contadora** [Boulder: Westview Press, 1987].

Alan J. Stoga, "The Crisis in Central America: Economic Problems, Prospects and Proposals" **American Enterprise Institute Foreign Policy and Defense Review** vol. 5. no. 1. 1984.

Alan J. Stoga, "Four Years Later: President Reagan's National Bipartisan Commission on Central America" in William Ascher and Ann Hubbard, eds., **Central American Recovery and Development: Task Force**

Report to the International Commission for Central American Recovery and Development [Durham: Duke University Press, 1989].

David Stoll, "Evangelical Guerrillas and the Army: The Ixil Triangle Under Ríos Montt" in Robert M. Carmack, ed., **Harvest of Violence: The Maya Indians and the Guatemalan Crisis** [Norman: University of Oklahoma Press, 1988].

Norma Stoltz, "La minoría que es una mayoría: los indios de Guatemala" in Susanne Jonas and David Tobis, eds., **Guatemala: una historia inmediata** [Mexico: Siglo veintiuno editores, 1979; first published in English in 1974].

Susan C. Stonich, "The Promotion of Non-traditional Agricultural Exports in Honduras: Issues of Equity, Environment and Natural Resource Management" **Development and Change** vol. 22. no. 4. 1991.

John Strasma, "Unfinished Business: Consolidating Land Reform in El Salvador" in William C. Thiesenhusen, **Searching for Agrarian Reform in Latin America** [Boston: Unwin Hyman, 1989].

James H. Street, "Economic Issues in a Growing Latin America" in Samuel L. Baily and Ronald T. Hyman, eds., **Perspectives on Latin America** [New York: Macmillan, 1974].

Arnold Strickson, "Anthropology in Latin America" in Charles Wagley, ed., **Social Science Research on Latin America** [New York: Columbia University Press, 1964].

Randy Stringer, "Honduras: Toward Conflict and Agrarian Reform" in William C. Thiesenhusen, **Searching for Agrarian Reform in Latin America** [Boston: Unwin Hyman, 1989].

Osvaldo Sunkel, "Development Styles and the Environment: An Interpretation of the Latin American Case" in Heraldo Muñoz, ed., **From Dependency to Development: Strategies to Overcome Underdevelopment and Inequality** [Boulder: Westview Press, 1981].

Marvin Surkin and Alan Wolfe, "Introduction: An End to Political Science" in Marvin Surkin and Alan Wolfe, eds., **An End to Political Science: The Caucus Papers** [New York: Basic Books, 1970].

Lewis Tambs and Frank Aker, "Shattering the Vietnam Syndrome: A Scenario for Success in El Salvador" **Conflict Quarterly** vol. 4. no. 1. 1983.

Frank Tannenbaum, "Towards an Appreciation of Latin America" in Herbert L. Matthews, ed., **The United States and Latin America** [New York: Columbia University--Sixteenth American Assembly 1959].

Frank Tannenbaum, "An American Commonwealth of Nations" in Joseph Maier and Richard W. Weatherhead, eds., **The Future of Democracy in Latin America: Essays by Frank Tannenbaum** [New York: Alfred A. Knopf, 1974].

Frank Tannenbaum, "The Future of Democracy in Latin America (I)" and "The Future of Democracy in Latin America (II)" in Joseph Maier and Richard W. Weatherhead, eds., **The Future of Democracy in Latin America: Essays by Frank Tannenbaum** [New York: Alfred A. Knopf, 1974].

Frank Tannenbaum, "Latin America as a Field of Study for the Social Scientist" in Joseph Maier and Richard W. Weatherhead, eds., **The Future of Democracy in Latin America: Essays by Frank Tannenbaum** [New York: Alfred A. Knopf, 1974].

Frank Tannenbaum, "The Continuing Ferment in Latin America" in Joseph Maier and Richard W. Weatherhead, eds., **The Future of Democracy in Latin America: Essays by Frank Tannenbaum** [New York: Alfred A. Knopf, 1974].

George E. Taylor, "The Leadership of the Universities" **Annals of the American Academy of Political and Social Science** vol. 356. 1964.

Philip B. Taylor, Jr., "The Guatemalan Affair: A Critique of United States Foreign Policy" **American Political Science Review** vol. 50. no. 3. 1956.

William B. Taylor, "Between Global Process and Local Knowledge: An Inquiry into Early Latin American Social History 1500-1900" in Olivier Zunz, ed., **Reliving the Past: The Worlds of Social History** [Chapel Hill: University of North Carolina Press, 1985].

Sanford G. Thatcher, "Latin American Studies and the Crisis in Scholarly Communication" **LASA Forum** vol. 23. no. 4. 1993.

Goran Therborn, "The Travail of Latin American Democracy" **New Left Review** nos. 113-114. 1979.

William C. Thiesenhusen, "Introduction: Searching for Agrarian Reform in Latin America" in William C. Thiesenhusen, **Searching for Agrarian Reform in Latin America** [Boston: Unwin Hyman, 1989].

William C. Thiesenhusen, "Conclusions: Searching for Agrarian Reform in Latin America" in William C. Thiesenhusen, **Searching for Agrarian Reform in Latin America** [Boston: Unwin Hyman, 1989].

Carol B. Thompson, "War by Another Name: Destabilization in Nicaragua and Mozambique" **Race and Class** vol. 29. no. 4. 1988.

J. A. Thompson, "William Appleman Williams and the 'American Empire'" **American Studies** vol. 7. no. 1. 1973.

Kenneth W. Thompson, "American Education and the Developing Areas" **Annals of the American Academy of Political and Social Science** vol. 366. 1966.

Leonard Thompson and Howard Lamar, "Comparative Frontier History" in Howard Lamar and Leonard Thompson, eds., **The Frontier in History: North America and Southern Africa Compared** [New Haven: Yale University Press, 1981].

Wallace Thompson, "The Doctrine of the 'Special Interest' of the United States in the Region of the Caribbean Area" **Annals of the American Academy of Political and Social Science** vol. 132. 1927.

Lori Ann Thrupp, "Pesticides and Policies: Approaches to Pest Control Dilemmas in Nicaragua and Costa Rica" **Latin American Perspectives** vol. 15. no. 4. 1988.

Walter C. Thurston, "Relations with Our Latin American Neighbors" **Annals of the American Academy of Political and Social Science** vol. 156. 1931.

Dean C. Tipps, "Modernization Theory and the Comparative Study of Societies: A Critical Perspective" **Comparative Studies in Society and History** vol. 15. no. 2. 1973; reprinted in Cyril E. Black. ed., **Comparative Modernization: A Reader** [New York: Free Press, 1976].

David Tobis, "Foreign Aid: The Case of Guatemala" in K. T. Fann and Donald C. Hodges, eds., **Readings in US Imperialism** [Boston: Porter Sargent,

1971].

David Tobis, "Las corporaciones norteamericanas más importantes de Guatemala" in Susanne Jonas and David Tobis, eds., **Guatemala: una historia inmediata** [Mexico: Siglo veintiuno editores, 1979; first published in English in 1974].

Edelberto Torres-Rivas, "Guatemala: Crisis and Political Violence" **NACLA Report on the Americas** vol. 14. no. 1. 1980.

Edelberto Torres-Rivas, "The Central American Model of Growth: Crisis for Whom?" **Latin American Perspectives** vol. 7. nos. 2-3. 1980.

Edelberto Torres-Rivas, "Central America Today: A Study in Regional Dependency" in Martin Diskin, ed., **Trouble in Our Backyard: Central America and the United States in the 1980s** [New York: Pantheon, 1983].

Edelberto Torres-Rivas, "Problems of Democracy and Counterrevolution in Guatemala" in Wolf Grabendorff, Heinrich W. Krumwiede and Jorg Todt, eds., **Political Change in Central America: Internal and External Dimensions** [Boulder: Westview, 1984].

Edelberto Torres-Rivas, "Comment: Constraints on Policies Regarding Human Rights and Democracy" in Kevin J. Middlebrook and Carlos Rico, eds., **The United States and Latin America in the 1980s: Contending Perspectives on a Decade of Crisis** [Pittsburgh: University of Pittsburgh Press, 1986].

Edelberto Torres-Rivas, "Authoritarian Transition to Democracy in Central America" in Jan L. Flora and Edelberto Torres-Rivas, eds., **Sociology of "Developing Societies": Central America** [London: Macmillan, 1989].

David F. Trask, "Gunboats in the Caribbean Danger Zone" **Latin American Research Review** vol. 13 no. 3. 1978.

Roger R. Trask, "Inter-American Relations" in Robert Esquenazi-Mayo and Michael C. Meyer, eds., **Latin American Scholarship Since World War II: Trends in History, Political Science, Literature, Geography and Economics** [Lincoln: University of Nebraska Press, 1971].

Roger R. Trask, "The Impact of the Cold War on US-Latin American Relations, 1945-1949" **Diplomatic History** vol. 1. no. 3. 1977.

Roger R. Trask, "George F. Kennan's Report on Latin America (1950)" **Diplomatic History** vol. 2. no. 3. 1978.

Gregory F. Treverton, "US Strategy in Central America" **Survival** vol. 28. no. 2. 1986.

Gregory F. Treverton, "Interstate Conflict in Latin America" in Kevin J. Middlebrook and Carlos Rico, eds., **The United States and Latin America in the 1980s: Contending Perspectives on a Decade of Crisis** [Pittsburgh: University of Pittsburgh Press, 1986].

Jan F. Triska, "Introduction" in Jan F. Triska, ed., **Dominant Powers and Subordinate States: The United States in Latin America and the Soviet Union in Eastern Europe** [Durham: Duke University Press, 1986].

Jan F. Triska, "Summary and Conclusion" in Jan F. Triska, ed., **Dominant Powers and Subordinate States: The United States in Latin America and the Soviet Union in Eastern Europe** [Durham: Duke

University Press, 1986].

Robert H. Trudeau, "Guatemala: The Long Term Costs of Short-Term Stability" in Richard Newfarmer, ed., **From Gunboats to Diplomacy: New US Policies for Latin America** [Baltimore: Johns Hopkins University Press, 1984].

Robert Trudeau and Lars Schoultz, "Guatemala" in Morris J. Blachman, William LeoGrande and Kenneth Sharpe, eds., **Confronting Revolution: Security Through Diplomacy in Central America** [New York: Pantheon, 1986].

Robert W. Tucker, "Reagan's Foreign Policy" **Foreign Affairs** vol. 68. no. 1. 1989.

Stuart K. Tucker, "Trade Unshackled: Assessing the Value of the Caribbean Basin Initiative" in William Ascher and Ann Hubbard, eds., **Central American Recovery and Development: Task Force Report to the International Commission for Central American Recovery and Development** [Durham: Duke University Press, 1989].

Joseph S. Tulchin, "Inhibitions Affecting the Formulation and Execution of the Latin American Policy of the United States" **Ventures** vol. 6. no. 4. 1967.

Joseph S. Tulchin, "The United States and Latin America in the 1960s" **Journal of Interamerican Studies and World Affairs** vol. 30. no. 1. 1988.

Frederick C. Turner, "Attitudes and Strategies in Latin American Politics" in Samuel L. Baily and Ronald T. Hyman, eds., **Perspectives on Latin America** [New York: Macmillan, 1974].

Ian Tyrrell, "American Exceptionalism in an Age of International History" **The American Historical Review** vol. 96. no. 4. 1991.

Richard H. Ullman, "At War with Nicaragua" **Foreign Affairs** vol. 62. no. 1. 1983.

Richard H. Ullman, "Paths to Reconciliation: The United States in the International System of the Late 1980s" in Sanford J. Ungar, ed., **Estrangement: America and the World** [New York: Oxford University Press, 1985].

Sanford J. Ungar, "The Roots of Estrangement: An Introduction" in Sanford J. Ungar, ed., **Estrangement: America and the World** [New York: Oxford University Press, 1985].

Universidad de El Salvador, Department of Social Sciences, "An Analysis of the Correlation of Forces in El Salvador" **Latin American Perspectives** vol. 14. no. 4. 1987.

Greg Urban and Joel Sherzer, "Introduction: Indians, Nation-States and Culture" in Greg Urban and Joel Sherzer, eds., **Nation-States and Indians in Latin America** [Austin: University of Texas Press, 1991].

Greg Urban, "The Semiotics of State-Indian Linguistic Relationships: Peru, Paraguay, and Brazil" in Greg Urban and Joel Sherzer, eds., **Nation-States and Indians in Latin America** [Austin: University of Texas Press, 1991].

Victor L. Urquidi, "Some Misunderstandings on the Alliance for Progress" in Joseph Maier and Richard W. Weatherhead, eds., **Politics of Change in Latin America** [New York: Frederick A. Praeger, 1964].

Viron P. Vaky, "Reagan's Central American Policy: An Isthmus Restored" in Robert S. Leiken, ed., **Central America: Anatomy of Conflict** [New York:

Pergamon Press, 1984].

Viron P. Vaky, "Positive Containment in Nicaragua" **Foreign Policy** no. 68. 1987.

Jiri Valenta, "Soviet and Cuban Responses to New Opportunities in Central America" in Richard E. Feinberg, ed., **Central America: International Dimensions of the Crisis** [New York: Holmes and Meier, 1982].

Jiri Valenta, "Soviet Policy and the Crisis in Central America" in H. Michael Erisman and John D. Martz, ed., **Colossus Challenged: The Struggle for Caribbean Influence** [Boulder: Westview Press, 1982].

Jiri Valenta and Virginia Valenta, "Soviet Strategy in the Caribbean Basin" in Alan Adelman and Reid Reading, eds., **Confrontation in the Caribbean Basin: International Perspectives on Security, Sovereignty and Survival** [Pittsburgh: Center for Latin American Studies, University Center for International Studies, University of Pittsburgh, 1984].

Jiri Valenta, "Nicaragua: Soviet Pawn or Non-Aligned Country?" **Journal of Interamerican and World Affairs** vol. 27. no. 3. 1985.

Jiri Valenta, "Military Interventions: Doctrines, Motives, Goals and Outcomes" in Jan F. Triska, ed., **Dominant Powers and Subordinate States: The United States in Latin America and the Soviet Union in Eastern Europe** [Durham: Duke University Press, 1986].

Arturo Valenzuela and Robert R. Kaufman, "Chile: From Democracy to Authoritarianism" in Richard S. Newfarmer, ed., **From Gunboats to Diplomacy: New US Policies for Latin America** [Baltimore: Johns Hopkins University Press, 1984].

Arturo Valenzuela, "Political Science and the Study of Latin America" in Christopher Mitchell, ed., **Changing Perspectives in Latin American Studies: Insights from Six Disciplines** [Stanford: Stanford University Press, 1988].

Arturo Valenzuela, "Chile: Origins, Consolidation and Breakdown of a Democratic Regime" in Larry Diamond, Juan J. Linz and Seymour Martin Lipset, eds., **Democracy in Developing Countries--Volume Four: Latin America** [Boulder: Lynne Rienner, 1989].

J. Samuel Valenzuela and Arturo Valenzuela, "Modernization and Dependency: Alternative Perspectives in the Study of Latin American Underdevelopment" **Comparative Politics** vol. 10. no. 4. 1978; reprinted in Heraldo Muñoz, ed., **From Dependency to Development: Strategies to Overcome Underdevelopment and Inequality** [Boulder: Westview Press, 1981]. (Also reprinted in Mitchell A. Seligson, ed., **The Gap Between Rich and Poor: Contending Perspectives on the Political Economy of Development** [Boulder: Westview Press, 1984].)

Mary Vanderlaan, "The Dual Strategy Myth in Central American Policy" **Journal of Interamerican and World Affairs** vol. 26. no. 2. 1984.

John Van Oudenaren, "Containment: Obsolete and Enduring Features" in Arnold L. Horelick, ed., **US-Soviet Relations: The Next Phase** [Ithaca: Cornell University Press, for the Rand/UCLA Center for the Study of Soviet International Behavior, 1986].

Augusto Varas, "Ideology and Politics in Latin America-USSR Relations" **Problems of Communism** vol. 33. no. 1. 1984.

Paul A. Varg, "The US as a World Power 1900-1917: Myth or Reality?" in Gerald N. Grob and George A. Billias, eds., **Interpretations of American History: Patterns and Perspectives--volume 2: Since 1865** [New York: Free Press, third edition, 1978; first published 1967].

Adalbert Krieger Vasena, "Comments on the Influence of Raúl Prebisch on Economic Policy-Making in Argentina, 1950-1962" **Latin American Research Review** vol. 23. no. 2. 1988

José Luís Vega-Carballo, "Parties, Political Development and Social Conflict in Honduras and Costa Rica: A Comparative Analysis" in Jan L. Flora and Edelberto Torres-Rivas, eds., **Sociology of "Developing Societies": Central America** [London: Macmillan, 1989].

Claudio Véliz, "Introduction" in Claudio Véliz, ed., **The Politics of Conformity in Latin America** [New York: Oxford University Press, 1967, reprinted 1970].

Claudio Véliz, "Centralism and Nationalism in Latin America" (1968) in Howard J. Wiarda, ed., **Politics and Social Change in Latin America: Still a Distinct Tradition?** [Boulder: Westview Press, 1992].

Henry Veltmeyer, "Surplus Labor and Class Formation on the Latin American Periphery" in Ronald H. Chilcote and Dale L. Johnson, eds., **Theories of Development: Mode of Production or Dependency** [Beverly Hills: Sage, 1983].

Sidney Verba, "Comparative Politics: Where Have We Been, Where Are We Going?" in Howard J. Wiarda, ed., **New Directions in Comparative Politics** [Boulder: Westview Press, 1985].

George R. Vickers, "Nicaragua: Haunted by the Past--A Spider's Web" **NACLA Report on the Americas** vol. 24. no. 1. 1990.

Carlos M. Vilas, "Popular Insurgency and Social Revolution in Central America" **Latin American Perspectives** vol. 15. no. 1. 1988.

Carlos M. Vilas, "The Impact of Revolutionary Transition on the Popular Classes: The Working Class in the Sandinista Revolution" in Jan L. Flora and Edelberto Torres-Rivas, eds., **Sociology of "Developing Societies": Central America** [London: Macmillan, 1989].

Carolos M. Vilas, "Nicaragua: Haunted By the Past--What Went Wrong" **NACLA Report on the Americas** vol. 24. no. 1. 1990.

Joaquín Villalobos, "Popular Insurrection: Desire or Reality?" **Latin American Perspectives** vol. 16. no. 3. 1989.

Steven Volk, "The International Competitiveness of the US Economy: A Study of Steel and Electronics" in Richard R. Fagen, ed., **Capitalism and the State in US-Latin American Relations** [Stanford: Stanford University Press, 1979].

Steven Volk, "Honduras: On the Border of War" **NACLA Report on the Americas** vol. 15. no. 6. 1981; reprinted in Martin Diskin, ed., **Trouble in Our Backyard: Central America and the United States in the 1980s** [New York: Pantheon, 1983].

Steven Volk, "History Through the Looking Glass" **NACLA Report on the Americas** vol. 20. no. 5. 1986.

Victor Vol'skii, "The Study of Latin America in the USSR" **Latin American Research Review** vol. 3. no. 1. 1967.

Pedro Vuskovic, "Economic Factors in the Evolution of Central American Societies" in Richard R. Fagen and Olga Pellicer, eds., **The Future of Central America: Policy Choices for the US and Mexico** [Stanford: Stanford University Press, 1983].

Charles Wagley, "Introduction" in Charles Wagley, ed., **Social Science Research on Latin America** [New York: Columbia University Press, 1964].

Charles Wagley, "Research Opportunities and Problems in Latin America in 1968" in Stanley R. Ross, ed., **Latin America in Transition: Problems in Training and Research** [Albany New York: State University of New York Press, 1970].

Charles Wagley, "A Framework for Latin American Culture" in Howard J. Wiarda, ed., **Politics and Social Change in Latin America: Still a Distinct Tradition?** [Boulder: Westview Press, 1992].

Carolos H. Waisman, "Argentina: Autarkic Industrialization and Illegitimacy" in Larry Diamond, Juan J. Linz and Seymour Martin Lipset, eds., **Democracy in Developing Countries--Volume Four: Latin America** [Boulder: Lynne Rienner, 1989].

Thomas W. Walker, "Introduction" and "Images of the Nicaraguan Revolution" in Thomas W. Walker, ed., **Nicaragua in Revolution** [New York: Praeger, 1982].

Thomas W. Walker, "Introduction: Revolution in General, Nicaragua to 1984" in Thomas W. Walker, ed., **Nicaragua: The First Five Years** [New York: Praeger, 1985].

Thomas W. Walker, "Nicaraguan-US Friction: The First Four Years, 1979-1983" in Kenneth M. Coleman and George C. Herring, eds., **The Central American Crisis: Sources of Conflict and the Failure of US Policy** [Wilmington: Scholarly Resources, 1985].

Thomas W. Walker, "Introduction" in Thomas W. Walker, ed., **Reagan Versus the Sandinistas: The Undeclared War on Nicaragua** [Boulder: Westview Press, 1987].

Thomas W. Walker, "Research Seminar in Nicaragua" **LASA Forum** vol. 21. no. 3. 1990.

Immanuel Wallerstein, "The Rise and Future Demise of the World Capitalist System: Concepts for Comparative Analysis", "Old Problems and New Syntheses: The Relation of Revolutionary Ideas and Practices", "Dependence in an Interdependent World: The Limited Possibilities of Transformation within the Capitalist World-Economy", "A World-System Perspective on the Social Sciences" and "The Rural Economy in Modern World Society" in Immanuel Wallerstein, **The Capitalist World Economy: Essays by Immanuel Wallerstein** [London: Cambridge University Press, 1980; first published 1979].

Immanuel Wallerstein, "Dependence in an Interdependent World: The Limited Possibilities of Transformation Within the Capitalist World Economy" in Heraldo Muñoz, ed., **From Dependency to Development: Strategies to Overcome Underdevelopment and Inequality** [Boulder: Westview Press, 1981].

Immanuel Wallerstein, "The Present State of the Debate on World Inequality" in

Mitchell A. Seligson, ed., **The Gap Between Rich and Poor: Contending Perspectives on the Political Economy of Development** [Boulder: Westview Press, 1984].

Immanuel Wallerstein, "Comments on Stern's Critical Tests" **American Historical Review** vol. 93. no. 4. 1988.

Immanuel Wallerstein, "The Collapse of Liberalism" **The Socialist Register 1992** [London: Merlin Press, 1992].

Immanuel Wallerstein, "The Agonies of Liberalism: What Hope Progress?" **New Left Review** no. 204 1994.

John Walton, "Small Gains for Big Theories: Recent Work on Development" **Latin American Research Review** vol. 22 no. 2. 1987.

Robert E. Ward, "International Studies and the National Interest: Too Little But Not Too Late" **Washington Quarterly: A Review of Strategic and International Issues** vol. 3. no. 3. 1980.

Harris Gaylord Warren, "Isaac Joslin Cox 1873-1956" **Hispanic American Historical Review** vol. 37. no. 1. 1957.

Robert Wasserstrom, "Revolution in Guatemala: Peasants and Politics Under the Arbenz Government" **Comparative Studies in Society and History** vol. 17. no. 4. 1975.

John M. Watanabe, "Enduring Yet Ineffable Community in the Western Periphery of Guatemala" in Carol A. Smith, ed., **Guatemalan Indians and the State 1540 to 1988** [Austin: University of Texas Press, 1990].

James E. Watson, "Bernard Moses: Pioneer in Latin American Scholarship" **Hispanic American Historical Review** vol. 42. no. 2. 1962.

Frederick S. Weaver, "Capitalist Development, Empire, and Latin American Underdevelopment: An Interpretive Essay on Historical Change" **Latin American Perspectives** vol. 3. no. 4. 1976.

David J. Weber, "Turner, the Boltonians and the Borderlands" **American Historical Review** vol. 91. no. 1. 1986.

Stephen Webre, "Central America and the United States in the 1980s: Recent Descriptions and Prescriptions" **Latin American Research Review** vol. 21. no. 3. 1986.

John Weeks, "Backwardness, Foreign Capital and Accumulation in the Manufacturing Sector of Peru 1954-1975" **Latin American Perspectives** vol. 4. no. 3. 1977.

John Weeks and Elizabeth Dore, "International Exchange and the Causes of Backwardness" **Latin American Perspectives** vol. 6. no. 2. 1979.

John Weeks, "The Differences Between Materialist Theory and Dependency Theory and Why They Matter" in Ronald H. Chilcote, ed., **Dependency and Marxism: Toward a Resolution of the Debate** [Boulder: Westview Press, 1982].

John Weeks, "The Industrial Sector" in Thomas W. Walker, ed., **Nicaragua: The First Five Years** [New York: Praeger, 1985].

John Weeks, "An Interpretation of the Central American Crisis" **Latin American Research Review** vol. 21. no. 3. 1986.

John Weeks, "Land, Labour and Despotism in Central America" in Giuseppe Di Palma and Laurence Whitehead, eds., **The Central American Impasse** [London: Croom Helm, 1986].

John Weeks, "The Mixed Economy in Nicaragua: The Economic Battlefield" in Rose J. Spalding, ed., **The Political Economy of Revolutionary Nicaragua** [Boston: Allen and Unwin, 1987].

John Weeks, "Panama: Reagan's Last Stand--Of Puppets and Heroes" **NACLA Report on the Americas** vol. 22. no. 4. 1988.

Sidney Weintraub, "Options for US Policy in the Caribbean Basin in the 1980s" in James R. Greene and Brent Scowcroft, eds., **Western Interests and US Policy Options in the Caribbean Basin: Report of the Atlantic Council's Working Group on the Caribbean Basin** [Boston: Oelgeschlager, Gunn and Hain, for the Atlantic Council of the United States, 1984].

Sidney Weintraub, "The New US Initiative Toward Latin America" **Journal of Interamerican Studies and World Affairs** vol. 33. no. 1. 1991.

George T. Weitzel, "The United States and Central America--Policy of Caly and Knox" **Annals of the American Academy of Political and Social Science** vol. 132. 1927.

Robert Wesson, "Historical Overview and Comparative Analysis" in Jan F. Triska, ed., **Dominant Powers and Subordinate States: The United States in Latin America and the Soviet Union in Eastern Europe** [Durham: Duke University Press, 1986].

W. Gordon West, "Developing Democratic Education in Central America Means Revolution: The Nicaraguan Case" in John M. Kirk and George W. Schuyler, eds., **Central America: Democracy, Development and Change** [New York: Praeger, 1988].

Philip E. Wheaton, "US Strategies in Central America" in Marlene Dixon and Susanne Jonas, eds., **Revolution and Intervention in Central America** [San Francisco: Synthesis Publications, revised edition, 1983].

David E. Whisnant, "Sandinista Cultural Policy: Notes Toward an Analysis in Historical Context" in Ralph Lee Woodward Jr., ed., **Central America: Historical Perspectives on the Contemporary Crisis** [New York: Greenwood Press, 1988].

Arthur Preston Whitaker, "From Dollar Diplomacy to the Good Neighbor Policy" **Inter-American Economic Affairs** vol. 4. no. 4. 1951.

Arthur Preston Whitaker, "Our Reaction to Communist Infiltration in Latin America" **Annals of the American Academy of Political and Social Science** vol. 330. 1960.

Arthur Preston Whitaker, "The Americas in the Atlantic Triangle" and "Developments of the Past Decade in the Writing of Latin American History" in Howard F. Cline, ed., **Latin American History: Essays on Its Study and Teaching 1898-1965** (2 vols.) [Austin: University of Texas Press, 1967].

Donald W. White, "History and American Internationalism: The Formulation From the Past After World War II" **Pacific Historical Review** vol. 58. no. 2. 1989.

Laurence Whitehead, "Explaining Washington's Central American Policies" **Journal of Latin American Studies** vol. 15. no. 2. 1983.

Laurence Whitehead, "The International Aspects of the Central American Crisis" **Millennium: Journal of International Studies** vol. 13. no. 2. 1984.

Laurence Whitehead, "International Aspects of Democratization" in Guillermo O'Donnell, Philippe C. Schmitter and Laurence Whitehead, ed., **Transitions from Authoritarian Rule: Comparative Perspectives** [Baltimore: Johns Hopkins University Press, 1986].

Laurence Whitehead, "Debt, Diversification and Dependency: Latin America's International Political Relations" in Kevin J. Middlebrook and Carlos Rico, eds., **The United States and Latin America in the 1980s: Contending Perspectives on a Decade of Crisis** [Pittsburgh: University of Pittsburgh Press, 1986].

Laurence Whitehead, "The Prospects for a Political Settlement: Most Options Have Been Foreclosed" in Giuseppe Di Palma and Laurence Whitehead, eds., **The Central American Impasse** [London: Croom Helm, 1986].

Laurence Whitehead, "The Consolidation of Fragile Democracies: A Discussion with Illustrations" in Robert A. Pastor, ed., **Democracy in the Americas: Stopping the Pendulum** [New York: Holmes and Meier, 1989].

Howard J. Wiarda, "Toward a Framework for the Study of Political Change in the Iberic-Latin Tradition: The Corporative Model" **World Politics** vol. 25. no. 1. 1973.

Howard J. Wiarda, "Corporatism and Development in the Iberic-Latin World: Persistent Strains and New Variations" **Review of Politics** vol. 36. no. 1. 1974.

Howard J. Wiarda, "The Ethnocentrism of the Social Sciences: Implications for Research and Policy" **Review of Politics** vol. 43. no. 2. 1981.

Howard J. Wiarda, "The Central American Crisis: A Framework for Understanding" **American Enterprise Institute Foreign Policy and Defense Review** vol. 4. no. 2. 1982.

Howard J. Wiarda, "Social Change, Political Development and the Latin American Tradition" in Howard J. Wiarda, ed., **Politics and Social Change in Latin America: The Distinct Tradition** [Amherst: University of Massachusetts Press, second revised edition 1982; first published 1974]; reprinted in Peter F. Klarén and Thomas J. Bossert, eds., **Promise of Development: Theories of Change in Latin America** [Boulder: Westview Press, 1986].

Howard J. Wiarda, "Law and Political Development in Latin America: Toward a Framework for Analysis" and "Toward a Model of Social Change and Political Development in Latin America: Summary, Implications, Frontiers" in Howard J. Wiarda, ed., **Politics and Social Change in Latin America: The Distinct Tradition** [Amherst: University of Massachusetts Press, second revised edition 1982; first published 1974].

Howard J. Wiarda, "Toward a Nonethnocentric Theory of Development: Alternative Conceptions from the Third World" **The Journal of Developing Areas** vol. 17. no. 4. 1983; reprinted in Howard J. Wiarda, ed., **New Directions in Comparative Politics** [Boulder: Westview Press, 1985].

Howard J. Wiarda, "The United States and Latin America: Change and Continuity" in Alan Adelman and Reid Reading, eds., **Confrontation in the Caribbean Basin: International Perspectives on Security, Sovereignty and Survival** [Pittsburgh: Center for Latin American Studies, University Center for International Studies, University of Pittsburgh, 1984].

Howard J. Wiarda, "At the Root of the Problem: Conceptual Failures in US-Central American Relations" in Robert S. Leiken, ed., **Central America: Anatomy of Conflict** [New York: Pergamon Press, 1984].

Howard J. Wiarda, "Conceptual and Political Dimensions of the Crisis in US-Latin American Relations: Toward a New Policy Formulation" in Howard J. Wiarda, ed., **The Crisis in Latin America: Strategic, Economic and Political Dimensions** [Washington: American Enterprise Institute, 1984].

Howard J. Wiarda, "The Kissinger Commission Report: Background and Political Dimensions" **American Enterprise Institute Foreign Policy and Defense Review** vol. 5. no. 1. 1984.

Howard J. Wiarda, "US Policy in Central America: Toward a New Relationship" in Henry Kissinger (Chair US National Bipartisan Commission on Central America), **Appendix to the Report of the National Bipartisan Commission on Central America** [Washington D.C.: US Government Printing Office, 1984]; reprinted in Howard J. Wiarda, **In Search of Policy: The United States and Latin America** [Washington: American Enterprise Institute, 1984].

Howard J. Wiarda, "Political Developments in Central America: Options and Possibilities" statement prepared for the National Bipartisan Commission on Central America, US Department of State, Washington, November 9, 1983; reprinted in **American Enterprise Institute Foreign Policy and Defense Review** vol. 5. no. 1. 1984.

Howard J. Wiarda, "Changing Realities and US Policy in the Caribbean Basin: An Overview" in James R. Greene and Brent Scowcroft, eds., **Western Interests and US Policy Options in the Caribbean Basin: Report of the Atlantic Council's Working Group on the Caribbean Basin** [Boston: Oelgeschlager, Gunn and Hain, for the Atlantic Council of the United States, 1984].

Howard J. Wiarda, "Comparative Politics Past and Present" and "Future Directions in Comparative Politics" in Howard J. Wiarda, ed., **New Directions in Comparative Politics** [Boulder: Westview Press, 1985].

Howard J. Wiarda, "Iberia and Latin America: Reforging the Historic Linkages?", "Interpreting Iberian-Latin American Inter-relations: Paradigm Consensus and Conflict" and "Conclusion: The Relations of Iberia and Latin America--And Some Implications for the United States" in Howard J. Wiarda, ed., **The Iberian-Latin American Connection: Implications for US Foreign Policy** [Washington: American Enterprise Institute/Boulder: Westview Press, 1986].

Howard J. Wiarda, "Can Democracy Be Exported?: The Quest for Democracy in US-Latin American Policy" in Kevin J. Middlebrook and Carlos Rico, eds., **The United States and Latin America in the 1980s: Contending Perspectives on a Decade of Crisis** [Pittsburgh: University of Pittsburgh Press, 1986].

Howard J. Wiarda, "Introduction", "The Impact of Grenada in Central America" and "Soviet Policy in the Caribbean and Central America in Howard J. Wiarda and Mark Falcoff, eds., **The Communist Challenge in the Caribbean and Central America** [Washington: American Enterprise Institute, 1987].

Howard J. Wiarda, "Mexico: The Unravelling of a Corporatist Regime?" **Journal** of Interamerican Studies and World Affairs vol. 30. no. 4. 1988/1989.

Howard J. Wiarda and Iéda Siqueira Wiarda, The United States and South America: The Challenge of Fragile Democracy" **Current History: A World Affairs Journal** vol. 88. no. 536. 1989.

Howard J. Wiarda, "The Dominican Republic: Mirror Legacies of Democracy and Authoritarianism" in Larry Diamond, Juan J. Linz and Seymour Martin Lipset, eds., **Democracy in Developing Countries--Volume Four: Latin America** [Boulder: Lynne Rienner, 1989].

Howard J. Wiarda, "Response to Keith A. Haynes's 'Authoritarianism, Democracy and Development: The Corporative Theories of Howard J. Wiarda Revisited" **Latin American Perspectives** vol. 16. no. 4. 1989.

Howard J. Wiarda, "The United States and Latin America: Historic Continuities, New Directions", "The United States and Latin America: Toward the 1990s", "The United States, Latin America, and the International Debt: Toward a Resolution?" and "Unresolved Issues of Human Rights" in Howard J. Wiarda, ed., **On the Agenda: Current Issues and Conflicts in US Foreign Policy** [Glenview: Scott Foresman/Little Brown, 1990].

Howard J. Wiarda, "Introduction: Social Change, Political Development and the Latin American Tradition" and "Conclusion: Toward a Model of Social Change and Political Development in Latin America--Summary, Implications, Frontiers" in Howard J. Wiarda, ed., **Politics and Social Change in Latin America: Still a Distinct Tradition?** [Boulder: Westview Press, 1992].

Timothy P. Wickham-Crowley, "An Epitaph for Latin American Revolutionaries" **Third World Quarterly: Journal of Emerging Areas** vol. 15. no. 3. 1994.

Jonathan M. Wiener, "Radical Historians and the Crisis in American History 1959-1980" **The Journal of American History** vol. 76. no. 2. 1989.

Alexander Wilde and Bonnie Tenneriello, "Panama: The Aftermath" **LASA Forum** vol. 21. no. 1. 1990.

A. Curtis Wilgus, "The Published Writings of James Alexander Robertson" and "The Life of James Alexander Robertson" in A. Curtis Wilgus, ed., **Hispanic American Essays** [Freeport: Books for Libraries Press, 1970; first printed 1942].

A. Curtis Wilgus, "The Chemistry of Political Change in Latin America" **Annals of the American Academy of Political and Social Science** vol. 342. 1962.

Edward J. Williams, "Mexico's Central American Policy: Revolutionary and Prudential Dimensions" in H. Michael Erisman and John D. Martz, ed., **Colossus Challenged: The Struggle for Caribbean Influence** [Boulder: Westview Press, 1982].

Philip J. Williams, "Elections and Democratization in Nicaragua: The 1990 Elections in Perspective" **Journal of Interamerican Studies and World Affairs** vol. 32. no. 4. 1990.

Whiting Williams, "Geographic Determinism in Nicaragua" **Annals of the American Academy of Political and Social Science** vol. 132. 1927.

William Appleman Williams, "Brooks Adams and American Expansion" **New England Quarterly** vol. 25. no. 1. 1952.
William Appleman Williams, "The Frontier Thesis and American Foreign Policy" **Pacific Historical Review** vol. 24. no. 4. 1955.
William Appleman Williams, "The Vicious Circle of Imperialism" in K. T. Fann and Donald C. Hodges, eds., **Readings in US Imperialism** [Boston: Porter Sargent, 1971].
Patricia A. Wilson, "Regionalization and Decentralization in Nicaragua" **Latin American Perspectives** vol. 14. no. 2. 1987.
Marshall Windmiller, "International Relations: The New American Mandarins" in Theodore Roszak, ed., **The Dissenting Academy** [London: Chatto and Windus, 1969; first published 1967].
Anthony Winson, "Class Structure and Agrarian Transformation in Central America" **Latin American Perspectives** vol. 5. no. 4. 1978.
M. M. Wise, "Development of Bibliographical Activity During the Past Five Years: A Tentative Survey" **Handbook of Latin American Studies: 1939** [Cambridge: Harvard University Press, 1940].
Eugene R. Wittkopf, "On the Foreign Policy Beliefs of the American People: A Critique and Some Evidence" **International Studies Quarterly: The Journal of the International Studies Association** vol. 30. no. 4. 1986.
Daniel H. Wolf, "ARENA in the Arena" **LASA Forum** vol. 23. no. 1. 1992.
Eric R. Wolf, "Introduction" in Norman Miller and Roderick Aya, eds., **National Liberation: Revolution in the Third World** [New York: Free Press, 1971].
Eric R. Wolf, "Peasant Rebellion and Revolution" in Norman Miller and Roderick Aya, eds., **National Liberation: Revolution in the Third World** [New York: Free Press, 1971].
Alan Wolfe, "The Professional Mystique" in Marvin Surkin and Alan Wolfe, eds., **An End to Political Science: The Caucus Papers** [New York: Basic Books, 1970].
Alan Wolfe and Jerry Sanders, "Resurgent Cold War Ideology: The Case of the Committee on the Present Danger" in Richard R. Fagen, ed., **Capitalism and the State in US-Latin American Relations** [Stanford: Stanford University Press, 1979].
Alan Wolfe, "The Ideology of US Conservatism: Sociology, Liberalism and the Radical Right" **New Left Review** no. 128. 1981.
Alan Wolfe, "The Irony of Anti-Communism: Ideology and Interest in Post-War American Foreign Policy" **The Socialist Register 1984** [London: Merlin Press, 1984].
Bryce Wood, "The Department of State and the Non-national Interest: The Cases of Argentine Meat and Paraguayan Tea" **Inter-American Economic Affairs** vol. 15. no. 2. 1961.
Bryce Wood, "External Restraints on the Good Neighbor Policy" **Inter-American Economic Affairs** vol. 16. no. 2. 1962.
Bryce Wood, "Self-Plagiarism and Foreign Policy" **Latin American Research Review** vol. 3. no. 3. 1968.
Bryce Wood, "How Wars End in Latin America" **Annals of the American**

Academy of Poliical and Social Science vol. 392. 1970.

Bryce Wood, "Scholarly Exchanges Between Latin America and the United States" in Douglas A. Chalmers, ed., **Changing Latin America: New Interpretations of Its Politics and Society** [New York: Academy of Political Science, Columbia University, 1972].

Bryce Wood and Michael Potashnik, "Government Funding for Research in Latin America 1970-71" **Latin American Research Review** vol. 8. no. 1. 1973.

Bryce Wood, "Literature on Inter-American Relations: Comment" **Latin American Research Review** vol. 14. no. 3. 1979.

Bryce Wood, The End of the Good Neighbor Policy: Changing Patterns of US Influence" **Caribbean Review** vol. 11. no. 2. 1982.

Ralph Lee Woodward, Jr., "Octubre: Communist Appeal to the Urban Labor Force of Guatemala 1950-1953" **Journal of Interamerican Studies** vol. 4. no. 3. 1962.

Ralph Lee Woodward, Jr., "The Guatemalan Merchants and National Defense: 1810" **Hispanic American Historical Review** vol. 45. no. 3. 1965.

Ralph Lee Woodward, Jr., "Economic and Social Origins of the Guatemalan Political Parties 1773-1823" **Hispanic American Historical Review** vol. 45. no. 4. 1965.

Ralph Lee Woodward, Jr., "The Merchants and Economic Development in the Americas 1750-1850: A Preliminary Study" **Journal of Interamerican Studies** vol. 10. no. 1. 1968.

Ralph Lee Woodward, Jr., "The Rise and Decline of Liberalism in Central America: Historical Perspectives on the Contemporary Crisis" **Journal of Interamerican Studies and World Affairs** vol. 26. no. 3. 1984.

Ralph Lee Woodward, Jr., "The Historiography of Modern Central America Since 1960" **Hispanic American Historical Review** vol. 67. no. 3. 1987.

Ralph Lee Woodward, Jr., "Introduction: Central America and Historical Perspective" in Ralph Lee Woodward Jr., ed., **Central America: Historical Perspectives on the Contemporary Crisis** [New York: Greenwood Press, 1988].

Ralph Lee Woodward, Jr., "Changes in the Nineteenth-Century Guatemalan State and Its Indian Policies" in Carol A. Smith, ed., **Guatemalan Indians and the State 1540 to 1988** [Austin: University of Texas Press, 1990].

Peter Worsley, "One World or Three?: A Critique of the World-System Theory of Immanuel Wallerstein" **The Socialist Register 1980** [London: Merlin Press, 1980].

Sandra Woy-Hazelton and William A. Hazelton, "Sustaining Democracy in Peru: Dealing with Parliamentary and Revolutionary Changes" in George A. Lopez and Michael Stohl, eds., **Liberalization and Redemocratization in Latin America** [New York: Greenwood Press, 1987].

Bruce E. Wright, "Pluralism and Vanguardism in the Nicaraguan Revolution" **Latin American Perspectives** vol. 17. no. 3. 1990.

Theodore P. Wright, Jr., "Free Elections in the Latin American Policy of the United States" **Political Science Quarterly** vol. 74. no. 1. 1959.

Theodore P. Wright, Jr., "Honduras: A Case Study of United States Support of Free Elections in Central America" **Hispanic American Historical Review** vol. 40. no. 2. 1960.

Lawrence A. Yates, "The United States and Rural Insurgency in Guatemala 1960-1970: An Inter-American 'Success Story'?" in Ralph Lee Woodward, Jr., ed., **Central America: Historical Perspectives on the Contemporary Crisis** [New York: Greenwood Press, 1988].

Marvin R. Zahniser and W. Michael Weiss, "A Diplomatic Pearl Harbor?: Richard Nixon's Goodwill Mission to Latin America in 1958" **Diplomatic History** vol. 13. no. 2. 1989.

Michael Zalkin, "Nicaragua: The Peasantry, Grain Policy and the State" **Latin American Perspectives** vol. 15. no. 4. 1988.

Lois Parkinson Zamora, "The Usable Past: The Idea of History in Modern US and Latin American Fiction" in Gustavo Pérez Firmat, ed., **Do the Americas Have a Common Literature?** [Durham: Duke University Press, 1990].

Leon Zamosc, "Class Conflict in an Export Economy: The Social Roots of the Salvadoran Insurrection of 1932" in Jan L. Flora and Edelberto Torres-Rivas, eds., **Sociology of "Developing Societies": Central America** [London: Macmillan, 1989].

Maurice Zeitlin, "The Social Determinants of Political Democracy in Chile" in James F. Petras and Maurice Zeitlin, eds., **Latin America: Reform or Revolution?** [New York: Fawcett, 1968].

Robert Zevin, "An Interpretation of American Imperialism" **The Journal of Economic History** vol. 32. no. 1. 1972.

Adolfo Aguilar Zinser, "Mexico and the Guatemalan Crisis" in Richard R. Fagen and Olga Pellicer, eds., **The Future of Central America: Policy Choices for the US and Mexico** [Stanford: Stanford University Press, 1983].

Thomas Zoumaras, "Eisenhower's Foreign Economic Policy: The Case of Latin America" in Richard A. Melanson and David Mayers, eds., **Reevaluating Eisenhower: American Foreign Policy in the 1950s** [Urbana: University of Illinois Press, 1987].

Voytek Zubek, "Soviet 'New-thinking' and the Central American Crisis" **Journal of Interamerican Studies and World Affairs** vol. 29. no. 3. 1987.

René Herrera Zuniga and Mario Ojeda, "Mexican Foreign Policy and Central America" in Richard E. Feinberg, ed., **Central America: International Dimensions of the Crisis** [New York: Holmes and Meier, 1982].

Clarence Zuvekas, "Political Democracy and Economic Growth in Latin America 1980-1985" **LASA Forum** vol. 17. no. 3. 1986.

INDEX

57

wo
s
Ya
2
Zei
Zir